Routledge Handbook
of Asian Theatre

Routledge Handbook of Asian Theatre is an advanced-level reference guide which surveys the rich and diverse traditions of classical and contemporary performing arts in Asia, showcasing significant scholarship in recent years. An international team of over fifty contributors provide authoritative overviews on a variety of topics across Asia, including dance, music, puppetry, makeup and costume, architecture, colonialism, modernity, gender, musicals and intercultural Shakespeare.

This volume is divided into four sections covering:

- representative theatrical traditions in Asia;
- cross-regional aspects of traditional and folk theatres;
- modern and contemporary theatres in Asian countries; and
- modernity, gender performance, intercultural and musical theatre in Asia.

Offering a cutting-edge overview of Asian theatre and performance, the *Handbook* is an invaluable resource for academics, researchers and students studying this ever-evolving field.

Siyuan Liu is a former President of the Association for Asian Performance and an Assistant Professor of Theatre at the University of British Columbia, Canada.

Routledge Handbook of Asian Theatre

Edited by Siyuan Liu

Routledge
Taylor & Francis Group

LONDON AND NEW YORK

First published 2016
by Routledge
2 Park Square, Milton Park, Abingdon, Oxon OX14 4RN

and by Routledge
711 Third Avenue, New York, NY 10017

First issued in paperback 2017

Routledge is an imprint of the Taylor & Francis Group, an informa business

British Library Cataloguing in Publication Data
A catalogue record for this book is available from the British Library

Library of Congress Cataloging in Publication Data
Routledge handbook of Asian theatre/edited by Siyuan Liu.
   pages cm
   Includes bibliographical references and index.
   1. Theater – Asia – History. I. Liu, Siyuan, 1964 November 7 – editor.
PN2860.R68 2016
792.095 – dc23
2015032715

Typeset in Bembo and Stone Sans
by Florence Production Ltd, Stoodleigh, Devon, UK

ISBN 13: 978-1-138-09931-9 (pbk)
ISBN 13: 978-0-415-82155-1 (hbk)

Dedicated to James R. Brandon, 1927–2015

Contents

Contents

Contents

Illustrations

Tables

Figures

Editorial board

Kathy Foley, Farley Richmond, Carol Fisher Sorgenfrei

Notes on contributors

Syed Jamil Ahmed is a theatre practitioner and professor at the Department of Theatre and Performance Studies, University of Dhaka, Bangladesh. His research interest is in South Asian theatre, applied theatre, folklore and cultural studies. His book-length publications include *Reading Against the Orientalist Grain: Performance and Politics Entwined with a Buddhist Strain* (2008) and *Applied Theatricks: Essays in Refusal* (2013).

Ty Bamla is an actor, choreographer and director based in Los Angeles and New York City. He graduated with an MFA in Theatre from Naropa University at Boulder, Colorado. Taik is the artistic director of the Blacksheep Collective and his work is in the permanent collections of the Library of Congress, Washington, DC under the Asian-American Archive (https://ye-taik.squarespace.com/about-ba/).

Monica Bethe is Director of Medieval Japanese Studies Institute in Kyoto, a Noh and textile researcher and a university professor. Textile publications cover Japanese kosode (Japan Society, Los Angeles County Museum), Noh costumes (Rhode Island School of Design, Chicago Art Institute and Los Angeles County Museum) and Japanese priests' robes (Kyoto National Museum).

Michael Bodden is Professor of Indonesian/Malay and Southeast Asian Studies at the University of Victoria, Canada. He is the author of *Resistance on the National Stage: Theater and politics in Late New Order Indonesia* (2010). He also edited the *Lontar Anthology of Modern Indonesian Drama, Volume 2: Building A National Theater* (2010) and translated several plays included therein.

Alexandra Bonds is Professor Emerita of Costume Design at the University of Oregon. An internationally recognized costume designer, she is the author *of Beijing Opera Costumes: The Visual Communication of Character and Culture.* Her book is the most extensive study of *jingju* costumes in English, covering both theory and practice.

Shelby Kar-yan Chan is Associate Professor at the School of Translation of Hang Seng Management College in Hong Kong. She obtained her doctorate from the School of Oriental and African Studies, University of London. Her monograph *Identity and Theatre Translation in Hong Kong* was published in 2015. She is also interested in cinematic adaptation and interpreting.

Khuon Chanreaksmey has been with the Cambodian arts NGO Phare Ponleu Selpak Association for 11 years and now serves as the deputy director of its performing arts school.

Fan-Ting Cheng is an Assistant Professor of Graduate Institute of Taiwan Literature at National Taiwan University. She works on contemporary performances related to queer issue, national identification, and social protest. Her recent publications include 'Local Theater and Dreg Aesthetic: The Taiwanese Queerness of Trainer Ensemble's *Belle Reprieve*' and 'Protesting Self-Reflexive Theatricality: The Cyclops Troup's *The Rose Colored Country*' in the Journal of Theater Studies.

Katherine Hui-ling Chou is Professor of English at National Central University in Taiwan, project director of NCU's Performance Center and coordinator of ETI, and playwright/director of Creative Society Theatre Troupe. Her recent research focus is performing arts in creative industry, and cultural economy. She is the author of *Performing China: Actresses, Visual Politics and Performance Culture, 1910s–1945* (2004).

Matthew Isaac Cohen is Professor of International Theatre at Royal Holloway, University of London. Born in the United States and trained in Indonesia in puppetry arts, his books include *The Komedie Stamboel: Popular Theater in Colonial Indonesia, 1891–1903* (2006) and *Performing Otherness: Java and Bali on International Stages, 1905–1952* (2010).

Margaret Coldiron is Deputy Head of BA in World Performance at East 15 Acting School, University of Essex. A specialist in Asian performance and masks, she is the author of *Trance and Transformation of the Actor in Japanese Noh and Balinese Masked Dance Drama* (2004). Current research includes work on performance pedagogy and Balinese *Gambuh* court dance-drama.

Jan Creutzenberg is a doctoral candidate at Freie Universität Berlin. He conducts field research in Seoul on contemporary perfomances of the traditional singing-storytelling art pansori and has published on modern theatre in Korea particularly on intercultural interpretations of Shakespeare and Brecht in pansori and modern theatre in Korea. His blog seoulstages. wordpress.com presents his thoughts on theatre, music and art in Korea.

Carol C. Davis is Associate Professor of Theatre at Franklin & Marshall College and Founding Artistic Director of Nepal Health Project, which treks plays to Nepali villages, teaches in Kathmandu orphanages and sponsors girls' education. Carol holds a PhD from University of California, Berkeley, and has published in *Asian Theatre Journal* and in *Mapping South Asia Through Theatre* (2014).

Kanchuka Dharmasiri is a theatre director and translator. She is currently teaching postcolonial and Sri Lankan theatre, performance theory and alternative theatre in the Fine Arts Department at the University of Peradeniya, Sri Lanka. She completed her PhD in Comparative Literature at the University of Massachusetts Amherst. Dharmasiri's interdisciplinary research interests include postcolonial studies, translation studies and early Buddhist women's writing.

Aparna Dharwadker is Professor of English and Interdisciplinary Theatre Studies at the University of Wisconsin–Madison, and author of *Theatres of Independence: Drama, Theory, and Urban Performance in India Since 1947* (2005), which won the 2006 Joe A. Callaway Prize. Her recent projects include an edited collection of primary sources in modern Indian theatre theory, and a study of modernist theatre in India.

Xing Fan is Assistant Professor in Asian Theatre and Performance Studies at the Centre for Drama, Theatre, and Performance Studies at the University of Toronto. Her research interests include theatre and politics in the People's Republic of China, Chinese dramatic literature, performance and aesthetics in Asian theatre and intercultural collaborations.

Kati Fitzgerald is a PhD student in the Ohio State University Department of Comparative Studies. She is a graduate of Barnard College's Department of Theatre and Tibet University's Foreign Student's Department. She has worked with the Nepal Tibetan Lhamo Association in Jorpati, Nepal and students majoring in Tibetan opera at Tibet University in Lhasa, Tibet.

Kathy Foley, Professor at the University of California Santa Cruz, is editor of *Asian Theatre Journal*.

Gilbert C. F. Fong is Provost and Dean of School of Translation of Hang Seng Management College in Hong Kong. He has written profusely on Chinese literature, translation, subtitling and Hong Kong drama. He has also translated many plays by the Nobel laureate Gao Xingjian. He also served as the editor of *Hong Kong Drama Review* and published *History of Hong Kong Drama* with Tian Benxiang.

John K. Gillespie is President of Gillespie Global Group, a cross-cultural business consultancy in New York City. He also translates contemporary Japanese plays and writes extensively on modern Japanese theatre and culture, including, with Robert T. Rolf, *Alternative Japanese Drama: Ten Plays* (University of Hawai'i Press, 1992).

Ronald Gilliam is a doctoral candidate in Asian theatre at the University of Hawai'i at Mānoa and an educational affiliate of the East-West Center. In addition to his scholarship on Uyghur performing arts, he is the performance studies field editor for Dissertation Reviews and a professional stage director in Honolulu.

Caleb Goh was a musical theatre lecturer at Lasalle, Singapore and also served as the artist-in-residence at NUS, Singapore. Previously he was the glee club director and musical theatre, dance and drama teacher at LJCDS, California. Goh just completed his PhD in Musical Theatre at WAAPA, Australia, and is currently doing reseach and workshops dealing with musical theatre education in Asia and Asian representation in musicals.

Jennifer Goodlander is Assistant Professor at Indiana University, and has presented and published her research on Southeast Asian performance, especially puppetry, focusing on intersections of gender, tradition, material culture and national identity. Her book *Women in the Shadows: Gender, Puppets, and the Power of Tradition in Bali* will be available in 2016.

Alexa Huang is Professor of English, Theatre and Dance, East Asian Languages and Literatures and International Affairs at George Washington University where she has co-founded and co-directs the Digital Humanities Institute and directs the Dean's Scholars in Shakespeare Program and the graduate program in English. She holds the Fulbright Distinguished Chair at Queen Mary University of London, 2014–2015.

Julie A. Iezzi, professor of Asian Theatre at the University of Hawaii, specializes in traditional Japanese performance genres. A long-time student of tokiwazu narrative singing and kyogen, she has published English language performance translations of kyogen and kabuki plays, many of which she first directed at the University of Hawaii.

Maki Isaka teaches Japanese theatre and literature and gender studies at the University of Minnesota. Author of *Secrecy in Japanese Arts* (2005), *Onnagata: A Labyrinth of Gendering in Kabuki Theater* (2016) and articles on shingeki, etc., Isaka currently works on discourse on arts as a realm of philosophy and women's gidayu music and its fandom in modern Japan.

Ayako Kano is Associate Professor in the Department of East Asian Languages and Civilizations at the University of Pennsylvania, where she teaches courses in Japanese theatre, modern literature, film, and gender studies. She is the author of *Acting Like a Woman in Modern Japan: Theater, Gender, and Nationalism* (Palgrave 2001).

Jay Keister is Associate Professor of Ethnomusicology at the University of Colorado, Boulder. He is the author of *Shaped By Japanese Music: Kikuoka Hiroaki and Nagauta Shamisen in Tokyo* and has published articles on Japanese music in the journals *Ethnomusicology, Asian Music, The World of Music* and *Asian Theatre Journal*.

Andrew Killick is Reader in Ethnomusicology at the University of Sheffield. He is the author of *In Search of Korean Traditional Opera: Discourses of Ch'anggŭk* (University of Hawai'i Press, 2010) and an associate editor and substantial contributor to the East Asia volume of the *Garland Encyclopedia of World Music* (Garland, 2002).

Yun-Cheol Kim is President of International Association of Theatre Critics; Professor at the School of Drama, Korean National University of the Arts; editor-in-chief of *Critical Stages*, IATC Webjournal. Two-time winner of the 'Critic of the Year Award', he has published ten books so far, two of which are anthologies of theatre reviews.

Colleen Lanki is a theatre practitioner and artistic director of TomoeArts, a company specializing in interdisciplinary performance and Japanese classical dance-based work. She has trained extensively in Japanese dance, holding the professional name Fujima Sayū, and is a founding member of Theatre Nohgaku. Current research includes contemporary Japanese women playwrights, gender and Japanese dance, and the use of *ma* (space-time) in performance.

Sissi Liu is a doctoral candidate in Theatre at the Graduate Center of the City University of New York. She is currently writing her dissertation entitled *Wukongism, or Monkey King Consciousness: Kung fu, Jazz, and the performing of Asia/America*. She has lectured at Baruch College and City College of New York. She is a trained classical pianist and composer.

Siyuan Liu is an assistant professor of theatre at the University of British Columbia. He is the author of *Performing Hybridity in Colonial-Modern China* (2013), co-author of *Modern Asian Theatre and Performance 1900–2000* (2014), and co-editor of *The Methuen Drama Anthology of Modern Asian Plays* (2014). He was President of the Association for Asian Performance (2011–2015).

Colin Mackerras was a Professor Emeritus at Griffith University, Australia from 1974 to 2004. He has written widely on Chinese theatre, ethnic minorities and Western images of China. Among his numerous books and articles on Chinese theatre, the most prominent are *The Rise of the Peking Opera* (1972) and *Chinese Drama: a historical survey* (1990).

Arya Madhavan is a Senior Lecturer in Drama at the Lincoln School of Performing Arts, University of Lincoln, UK. Arya is a *kudiyattam* performer, specializing in the research of Indian aesthetics and performance theory. Since 2012, she has also been developing a new area of study, exploring the contributions of women in Asian performance.

Pawit Mahasarinand has taught at Chulalongkorn University since 1992, and written dance and theatre reviews for the English-language daily newspaper *The Nation* since 2001. The first president of the International Association of Theatre Critics (IATC)–Thailand centre, he is a critic-in-residence at Festival/Tokyo 2011 and Asia-Pacific Dance Festival 2015 in Hawaii.

David Mason is Chair of Theatre and Director of Asian Studies at Rhodes College in Memphis, Tennessee. He is the author of *Theatre and Religion on Krishna's Stage* (2009) and *Brigham Young: Sovereign in America* (Routledge, 2014). He is a board member of the Association for Asian Performance.

Lauren Meeker is Associate Professor of Anthropology at SUNY at New Paltz. Her research focuses on cultural politics, representation and performance in Vietnam. She has published articles about *quanhọ* folk song and *chèo* theatre and a book, *Sounding Out Heritage: Cultural Politics and the Social Practice of Quan họ Folk Song in Northern Vietnam* (2013).

Trinh Nguyen is an educator, activist and independent researcher. She holds a PhD in Asian Theatre History at the University of Hawai'i at Mānoa and is a recipient of many academic awards and fellowships. Some of her academic interests include colonial and contemporary theatre in Asia and the Pacific; performances in an age of globalization; and oral history in the context of theatre and performances.

Shormishtha Panja is Professor of English and Joint Director, Institute of Lifelong Learning, University of Delhi. Her books include *Shakespeare and the Art of Lying* (ed.), *Shakespeare and Class* (co-ed.), *Word Image Text: Studies in Literary and Visual Culture* (co-ed.) and *Signifying the Self: Women and Literature* (co-ed.). She has published articles on Renaissance studies in the international journals and collections.

Kirstin Pauka is Professor of Asian Theatre at the University of Hawaii, specializing in theatre of Southeast Asia. She has published widely on Indonesian Randai theatre and related topics and has directed several Southeast Asian theatre productions at the UHM Kennedy Theatre, including the US premieres of three Randai productions.

Diego Pellecchia is a noh theatre scholar and practitioner. He holds a PhD in Drama & Theatre from Royal Holloway, University of London. He has published widely on noh theatre and on its reception abroad, and is currently a visiting researcher at Ritsumeikan University, Kyoto.

Farley Richmond is Professor of the Department of Theatre and Film Studies, University of Georgia/Athens. He continues to work on the website kutiyattam.wikispaces.com. He also directs for Epic Actors Workshop and for the Indian Cultural Society of New Jersey. Recent productions include *Hayavadana* and *Tartuffe*.

Ashley Robertson is a PhD candidate at the University of Melbourne, Asia Institute. Her research has focused on female puppeteers in Java (2012–present), the form and function of Indonesian shadow theatre (2009) and the display and interpretation of Indonesian ritual objects within museums (2011).

CedarBough T. Saeji is a scholar with a PhD in Culture and Performance, working at the intersection of heritage and the Korean performing arts. Previous work has been published in *Journal of Korean Studies*, *Asian Theatre Journal* and *Acta Koreana*, among others.

Jonah Salz is Professor of Comparative Theatre, Ryukoku University, Kyoto. Research interests include intercultural theatre, Beckett plays, and translation. He has co-translated kyogen and contemporary theatre. He co-directs the Noho Theatre Group (1981–) with kyogen master Shigeyama Akira and was program director for Traditional Theatre Training (1984–2014). He is chief editor of *A History of Japanese Theatre* (Cambridge, 2016).

I Nyoman Sedana, PhD University of Georgia, performer and Professor of Indonesian Arts Institute, currently holds an ICCR Senior Fellowship to research on Indian puppet theatre. Author of 'Theater in a Time of Terrorism' & co-author of *Balinese Performance*. Sedana taught at Ohio University, Essex University and Butler University, He holds an IIAS Fellowship, and has awards from the Asia Research Institute and ASF-Bangkok.

Anita Singh is Professor in the Department of English at Banaras Hindu University, Varanasi, India. Her areas of interest are Gender Studies and Performance Studies. Her recent book is *Gender, Space and Resistance: Women and Theatre in India*. She was at the University of Virginia, USA as a Fulbright Visiting Scholar (2013).

Carol Fisher Sorgenfrei is Professor Emerita of Theatre at UCLA. She is an authority on postwar Japanese and cross-cultural performance, a translator, director, and award-winning playwright. Her books include *Unspeakable Acts: The Avant-Garde Theatre of Terayama Shūji and Postwar Japan* and the co-authored *Theatre Histories: An Introduction*. She is Associate Editor of *Asian Theatre Journal*.

Suematsu Michiko is a Professor of English at Gunma University, Japan. She is the author of 'Import/export: Japanizing Shakespeare' in *Shakespeare in Asia: Contemporary Performance* (2010) and Co-Director of A|S|I|A (Asian Shakespeare Intercultural Archive), a web archive of Asian Shakespeare productions (http://a-s-i-a-web.org).

Ashley Thorpe is Senior Lecturer in the Department of Drama & Theatre, Royal Holloway, University of London. He has published articles about jingju in international contexts in a number of journals, and is the author of the monographs *Mirrors of Empire: Chinese Opera on the London Stage, 1759–2008* (Palgrave, 2016) and *The Role of the Chou ('Clown') in Traditional Chinese Drama: Comedy, Criticism and Cosmology on the Chinese Stage* (Edwin Mellen Press, 2007).

Min Tian has taught as associate professor at China Central Academy of Drama and currently works at the University of Iowa. He is the author of *The Poetics of Difference and Displacement: Twentieth-Century Chinese–Western Intercultural Theatre* (2008) and *Mei Lanfang and the Twentieth-Century International Stage: Chinese Theatre Placed and Displaced* (2012).

Celia Tuchman-Rosta is a PhD candidate in the Department of Anthropology at the University of California, Riverside and an Adjunct Lecturer at York College (CUNY). Her research explores dance, globalization, labour and the body in Cambodia. Her work is supported by the Center for Khmer Studies, Fulbright IIE, and a Chancellor's Distinguished Fellowship Award (UCR).

Makiko Yamanashi is Lecturer at Waseda University and a research fellow affiliated with Hosei University. Her current work engages with urban studies in relation to theatre as an intercultural phenomenon. Recent publications include *A History of the Takarazuka Revue Since 1914: Modernity, Girls' Culture, Japan Pop* (Global Oriental/Brill, 2012).

Yong Li Lan is director of the Asian Shakespeare Intercultural Archive (A|S|I|A), an online archive of East/Southeast Asian Shakespeare performance containing videos, scripts and data in English, Chinese, Japanese and Korean (www.a-s-i-a-web.org). Her research focuses on Shakespeare and intercultural performativity in the theatre, cinema and internet.

Ji Hyon (Kayla) Yuh is a PhD candidate in Theatre at CUNY Graduate Center. Her dissertation examines the global circulation of race through musical theatre productions in South Korea and East Asia. She is also a contributing author of the forthcoming anthology, *Handbook of Musical Theatre Producers* (edited by Laura MacDonald).

Acknowledgements

This book resulted from the joint efforts from scholars and artists in the field of Asian theatre studies from Asia, Europe and North America. I am deeply grateful to everyone who contributed to the project in one form or another.

I would like to thank the late James Brandon and Samuel Leiter for kindly sharing their invaluable experience and insights in editing *The Cambridge Guide to Asian Theatre* and *Encyclopedia of Asian Theatre*. Three other senior scholars kindly provided advice and comments as members of the editorial board in addition to contributing articles: Farley Richmond, Carol Fisher Sorgenfrei and especially Kathy Foley who, as editor of *Asian Theatre Journal*, generously lent her vast knowledge of current scholarship. I am grateful to Jonah Salz, editor of *A History of Japanese Theatre*, for his valuable advice on content and editing. Several other scholars kindly provided comments to one or more articles: Matthew Cohen, Jan Creuzenberg, John Gillespie, Jennifer Goodlander, Colin Mackerras, Claudia Orenstein and Elizabeth Wichmann-Walczak. I am deeply indebted to all board members, commenters and contributors. In addition, I would also like to thank the Asian artists, theatre companies and museums for their kind permission to reprint their production photos.

I am most grateful to my editors at Routledge: Leanne Hinves for entrusting me with this project, and Helena Hurd and Lucy McClune for their advice and support throughout the process. I am indebted to Megan Symons and Annette Abel for their advice and assistance during the editing and production process. Finally, I want to thank Rui Zhang for his kind assistance in preparing the manuscript and during the production process.

Introduction

Understanding Asian theatre

Siyuan Liu

The systematic study of Asian theatre in the west started after the Second World War, in part as a result of increased postwar Euro-American presence in Asia. For example, Earl Ernst, who started the first Asian theatre programme in the United States (University of Hawai'i), and Faubion Bowers, who wrote the first survey of Asian theatre in English (*Theatre in the East: A Survey of Asian Dance and Drama*, 1956), were members of the American occupation authority's theatre censorship committee in Japan (Brandon 2006, 2011; Leiter 2011). Similarly, A. C. Scott, who started the Asian theatre programme at the University of Wisconsin and wrote *The Theatre in Asia* (1972), worked after the war for the British Council for Cultural Relations in China and, after 1949, Hong Kong (Liu 2011). As significant early attempts at surveying Asian theatre, *Theatre in the East* and *The Theatre in Asia* also revealed the substantial challenge of understanding and presenting the impossibly rich performance traditions and contemporary practices of the continent, especially as a one-person endeavour, which prompted James R. Brandon to declare in 1976 that 'we do not yet have a comprehensive, even-handed Asian theatre history text . . . nor an introduction' (425). Since then, however, two edited volumes involving field-wide scholars have been published, namely Brandon's *Cambridge Guide to Asian Theatre* (1993) and Samuel L. Leiter's *Encyclopedia of Asian Theatre* (2007).

A number of parameters and themes have emerged from these four volumes that affect future books on Asian theatre, including this one. The first such parameter is the geographical scope of Asian theatre. As a first attempt, *Theatre in the East* includes South, East and Southeast Asia: 'In terms of theatre, Asia defines itself clearly as that area which starts with India and extends eastward as far as Indonesia and the Philippine Islands, and northward through China and Japan as far as Siberia' (Bowers 1956: vi). Excluded from this list is the Middle East:

> As far as dance and drama are concerned, those countries are not, however, what I feel to be characteristically Asian. That area has in common the Mohammedan religion, which on the whole condemns theatre, and must of necessity be omitted from our attention, partly because of the virtual absence of dance and drama there, partly because of the 'un-Asian' atmosphere of what little has survived.

> (Ibid)

Both Brandon and Leiter followed Bowers' precedent – with the addition of an eight-page chapter on Oceania in Brandon – while Scott included the Middle East and excluded Southeast Asia, choices that Leiter and Brandon deemed 'questionable' and 'highly idiosyncratic' (Leiter 1974: 272; Brandon 1976: 425).

Indeed, this geographical definition has become settled practice in Asian theatre studies as evident in the membership expertise of the Association for Asian Performance (AAP), the content of its publication *Asian Theatre Journal (ATJ)* and the presentations at the annual AAP conference. At the same time, new scholarship on Arabic performance has emerged in the past decade. One such effort is the 2005 *TDR* special issue on the Iranian devotional drama *Ta'ziyeh*, which starts with an introduction by the journal's contributing editor John Bell criticizing 'the West's problem with Middle Eastern and Arabic performance traditions' (Bell 2005: 5). On the modern and contemporary theatre front, *ATJ* published an article on modern Iranian theatre (Sohi and Ghorbaninejad 2012) and AAP has, for several years, sponsored a panel on modern Arabic and Arab-American theatre at the annual Association for Theatre in Higher Education (ATHE) conference. These developments seem to point to a promising if still somewhat uneasy relationship between Asian theatre studies and the scholarship of theatre in the Middle East. Still another consideration affecting the present volume is the scope of Asian studies as an academic field and the Routledge Asian Handbook series, both of which exclude the Middle East. Consequently, this book is confined to traditional and modern theatres in South, East and Southeast Asia.

Another issue concerns the structure of the volumes, which falls into two camps. The first format is to devote a chapter to each country (or region), arranged either geographically or alphabetically. *The Theatre of the East*'s fourteen chapters start from South Asia (India and Ceylon [Sri Lanka]), followed by Southeast Asia (Burma, Thailand, Cambodia, Laos, Indonesia, Philippines), and ending in East Asia (China, Vietnam, Hong Kong, Okinawa, and Japan). Bowers' ordering is based on the belief that 'India was the source of most theatre in Asia and still remains the immediate origin of some of its most highly evolved and important arts' (Bowers 1956: 3). Scott's *The Theatre in Asia* starts with an introductory chapter, followed by four chapters on India, The Islamic World, China and Japan. By contrast, Brandon's *The Cambridge Guide to Asian Theatre* arranges its chapters of nineteen Asian countries/regions plus Oceania alphabetically, from Bangladesh to Vietnam. Each chapter discusses a country/region's history and conventions of traditional and modern theatre plus important genres, conventions and artists for countries where 'information is abundant and the theatre complex' (Brandon 1993: vii). The other structural approach is the A–Z entries used in Leiter's *Encyclopedia of Asian Theatre*. It lists alphabetical entries on general country/region histories, artist biographies, theatrical genres and forms, and about thirty general topics on acting/directing, technical theatre, theatre organization and other issues such as censorship, western influence, and women in Asian theatre. Each of these general-topic entries includes a varying number of countries.

While indebted to these approaches, *Routledge Handbook of Asian Theatre* offers a third way of structuring – and understanding – Asian theatre. Designed to partially fulfil the Routledge Asian Handbook series' mandate of thematically arranged chapters, it adopts a hybrid structure that seeks to balance country coverage with thematic discussion and cross-region comparison, give equal weight to spectacular traditional forms and vibrant modern and contemporary practices, and showcase recent scholarship. Consequently, this book's twenty-four chapters are arranged into four parts, two of which (one and three) are devoted to countries/regions in traditional and modern theatres respectively and the other two offering thematic analyses with a rough although often blurred traditional/modern divide. Specifically, Part I focuses on the theatrical traditions of India, China, Japan and Indonesia, widely considered the most representative sites of classical and folk theatre in Asia. They are followed by the six chapters in Part II that examine dance, music, masks, puppets, costume and makeup, and space/ architecture in traditional Asian theatre, using examples from these four and other performance cultures such as other Southeast Asian countries, Tibet, Uighur and Korea. Part III focuses on modern and contemporary theatre and performance in virtually all countries/regions in South, East and Southeast Asia, with some chapters including multiple countries or regions. Finally, Part IV examines critical topics of Asian theatre in modern and contemporary times that have attracted significant scholarship in recent years.

This geographically and thematically hybrid structure highlights several active areas of current scholarship, starting from the interrelatedness between traditional and modern theatres since the onset of colonialism and modernity. On the one hand, traditional Asian performance, with its dazzling display of total theatre, has continued to attract the majority of attention outside Asia, at times eclipsing modern theatre in the vision of general theatrical practitioners, scholars and teachers in the west. Consequently, while the book devotes significant portions to traditional performance, its dedicated sections on modern and contemporary Asian performance are designed to attract attention to this significant and vibrant component of the Asian theatrical fabric. It also reflects the substantial scholarship in recent decades.[1]

On the other hand, current scholarship has also contested previous tendencies to dichotomize traditional and modern Asian theatres in the modern era and has instead focused on the fluid hybridity between them. As attested by a number of recent studies (Mee 2008; Tian 2008; Brandon 2009; Diamond 2012; Liu 2013), the division between traditional and modern theatre has been blurry at best throughout the twentieth century and well into the new millennium. To start with, the so-called traditional theatres have continued their evolution after the onset of modernity, partially in response to colonialism (Cohen 2010), nationalism (Goldstein 2007; Brandon 2009) and globalization (Diamond 2012). We know now, for example, that kabuki was an active participant of Japan's imperial war efforts and only stopped mass production of new plays after the Second World War as a deliberate effort to evade the American occupational authority's demand for democratic kabuki (Brandon 2006, 2009, 2014). Today, much of the traditional theatre in Asia has continued to respond to the challenges of the new century, as exemplified by Balinese artists' response to a 2002 terrorist bombing by staging a new *wayang kulit* puppet play in an effort to renew natural harmony (Sedana 2005).

Moreover, recent studies have challenged previous tendencies to denigrate attempts by modern theatre artists at literary and performative hybridities as crowd-pleasing ploys that were artistically inferior to those adhering to the western original (Liu 2013). Consequently, the recent *Modern Asian Theatre and Performance 1900–2000* regards the history of modern theatre in much of Asia as encompassing four periods: (1) initial 'intercultural adaptation, appropriation and hybridization'; (2) 'modernist orthodoxy' of speech-only illusionist realism; (3) 'emergence of nationalistic culture and identity from the sixties to the eighties'; and (4) 'contemporary pluralism and theatrical globalism' (Wetmore et al. 2014: 12–13). In other words, despite the fact that spoken theatre is often known in Asian countries as 'spoken drama' or 'new drama', its fate has been intertwined with traditional performance from its beginning, despite futile attempts to rid itself of indigenous influence in mid-century (Rolf and Gillespie 1992; Oh 1999; Poulton 2001, 2010; Cohen 2006; Mee 2008; Liu 2013). Two chapters in Part IV examine this interrelatedness between traditional and modern theatres from different angles: Chapter 18 (The beginning of spoken theatre in Asia: colonialism and colonial modernity) and Chapter 21 (Modern Asian theatre and indigenous performance). In addition, many country/region chapters in Part III also offer insights on the traditional/modern dynamic.

Two related chapters in Part IV consider the fate of traditional and folk performance in the modern era (Chapter 22) and Shakespearean productions in Asia as the representative of intercultural theatre (Chapter 23). The latter has been a particularly fascinating area of research in recent years, having inspired databases with full-length videos (A|S|I|A; MIT) and numerous studies (Sasayama *et al.* 1998; Minami *et al.* 2001; Li 2003; Trivedi and Bartholomeusz 2005; Kishi and Bradshaw 2006; Huang 2009; Kennedy and Yong 2010; Trivedi and Minami 2010).

Another area of recent scholarship related to the disruptive power of modernity is gender performance and the rise of actresses in the twentieth century in both traditional and modern theatre. While female (and at times male) impersonation in many Asian cultures has long drawn critical attention, the fate of actresses who (re)emerged in the past century, together with their complex relations with the theatrical establishment (including female impersonators) and the society at large, has been the focus of a number of studies in recent years (Kano 2001; Edelson 2009; Goodlander 2010; Singh and Mukherjee 2013; Madhavan 2015). Chapters 19 and 20 examine this issue from the perspectives of traditional and modern theatres.

Finally, the *Handbook*'s last chapter is devoted to American-style musicals in Asia, a fast-growing genre with palpable appeal, especially to the young generation (including emerging scholars), as well as the capacity for probing deconstructions of cultural identity and nationalist myths.

Conventions used in this book

Chapter, sections, authors: The chapters, many with multiple regional sections, are by experts of individual countries/regions. The chapters and sections generally follow the geographical order from west to east and from north to south, roughly in line with Bowers' schema with the exception of placing East Asia ahead of Southeast Asia so as to reflect certain performative influence by the former on the latter. For multi-author chapters, the author names are listed twice: first after the chapter title in the order of the sections, and then after the title of each section.

Diacritics: Diacritics are little signs seen on the top (and occasionally bottom) of characters to indicate tones or elongation. Following the recent trend of academic publishing (Leiter 2007) and some national Romanization standards (e.g. Revised Romanization of Korean), this *Handbook* uses diacritics only for Japanese words.

Names: Many Asian countries list the family name first, followed by the given name, while others use the western convention. This book follows the custom of the native languages. In references following each chapter, there is no comma after the family name if it naturally appears first.

Translation: Unless otherwise noted, all translations are by the authors of the specific chapter or section.

Native terms: A native term is in italic when it first appears in a single-authored chapter or a section of a multi-authored chapter, after which it no longer appears in italic.

Note

1 Some bibliographies can be found in Wetmore (2006), Liu and Wetmore (2009) and Wetmore *et al.* (2014).

Bibliography

Asian Shakespeare Intercultural Archive (A|S|I|A), available at http://a-s-i-a-web.org.
Bell, John (2005) 'Islamic Performance and the Problem of Drama', *TDR*, 49 (4): 5–10.
Bowers, Faubion (1956) *Theatre in the East: A Survey of Asian Dance and Drama*, New York: Nelson.

Brandon, James R. (1976) 'Asian Theatre: A Review of Current Scholarship', *Educational Theatre Journal*, 28 (3): 423–9.

—— (ed.) (1993) *The Cambridge Guide to Asian Theatre*. New York: Cambridge University Press.

—— (2006) 'Myth and Reality: A Story of Kabuki during American Censorship, 1945–1949', *Asian Theatre Journal*, 23 (1): 1–110.

—— (2009) *Kabuki's Forgotten War: 1931–1945*, Honolulu: University of Hawai'i Press.

—— (2011) 'Earle S. Ernst', *Asian Theatre Journal*, 28 (2): 332–40.

—— (2014) '"Democratic Kabuki" for a "Democratic Japan": 1945–1946', *Asian Theatre Journal*, 31 (1): 103–25.

Chelkowski, Peter J. (guest ed.) (2005) Special Issue on Ta'ziyeh, *TDR*, 49 (4).

Cohen, Matthew Isaac (2006) *The Komedie Stamboel: Popular Theater in Colonial Indonesia, 1891–1903*, Athens: Ohio University Press.

—— (2010) *Performing Otherness: Java and Bali on International Stages, 1905–1952*, New York: Palgrave Macmillan.

Diamond, Catherine (2012) *Communities of Imagination: Contemporary Southeast Asian Theatres*, Honolulu: University of Hawai'i Press.

Edelson, Loren (2009) *Danjūrō's Girls: Women on the Kabuki Stage*, New York: Palgrave Macmillan.

Goldstein, Joshua (2007) *Drama Kings: Players and Publics in the Re-creation of Peking Opera, 1870–1937*, Berkeley: University of California Press.

Goodlander, Jennifer L. (2010) *Body of Tradition: Becoming a Woman Dalang in Bali*, Ohio University.

Huang, Alexa (2009) *Chinese Shakespeares: Two Centuries of Cultural Exchange*, New York: Columbia University Press.

Kano, Ayako (2001) *Acting Like a Woman in Modern Japan: Theater, Gender, and Nationalism*, New York: Palgrave.

Kennedy, Dennis, and Yong Li Lan (2010) *Shakespeare in Asia: Contemporary Performance*, Cambridge: Cambridge University Press.

Kishi, Tetsuo, and Graham Bradshaw (2006) *Shakespeare in Japan*, New York: Continuum.

Leiter, Samuel L. (1974) 'Book Review of *The Theatre in Asia*', *Educational Theatre Journal*, 26 (2): 272–3.

—— (2007) *Encyclopedia of Asian Theatre*, Westport, CT: Greenwood Press.

—— (2011) 'Faubion Bowers', *Asian Theatre Journal*, 28 (2): 314–21.

Li Ruru (2003) *Shashibiya: Staging Shakespeare in China*, Hong Kong: Hong Kong University Press.

Liu, Siyuan (2011) 'A. C. Scott', *Asian Theatre Journal*, 28 (2): 416–26.

—— (2013) *Performing Hybridity in Colonial-Modern China*, New York: Palgrave Macmillan.

Liu, Siyuan, and Kevin J. Wetmore, Jr. (2009) 'Modern Chinese Drama in English: A Selective Bibliography', *Asian Theatre Journal*, 26 (2): 321–50.

Madhavan, Arya (guest ed.) (2015) 'Special Issue Section: Women in Asian Theatre', *Asian Theatre Journal*, 32 (2): 345–571.

Mee, Erin B. (2008) *Theatre of Roots: Redirecting the Modern Indian Stage*, New York: Seagull.

Minami, Ryuta, Ian Carruthers, and John Gillies (eds) (2001) *Performing Shakespeare in Japan*, New York: Cambridge University Press.

MIT Global Shakespeares, available at http://globalshakespeares.mit.edu/.

Oh, T'ae-Sok (1999) *The Metacultural Theater of Oh T'ae-Sok, Five Plays from the Korean Avant-Garde*, Ah-Jeong Kim and R. B. Graves (trans), Honolulu: University of Hawai'i Press.

Poulton, M. Cody (2001) *Spirits of Another Sort: The Plays of Izumi Kyōka*, Ann Arbor, MI: Center for Japanese Studies, The University of Michigan.

—— (2010) *A Beggar's Art: Scripting Modernity in Japanese Drama, 1900–1930*, Honolulu: University of Hawai'i Press.

Rolf, Robert T., and John Gillespie (eds) (1992) *Alternative Japanese Drama*, Honolulu: University of Hawai'i Press.

Salz, Jonah (ed.) (2016) *A History of Japanese Theatre*, New York: Cambridge University Press.

Sasayama, Takashi, J. R. Mulryne, and Margaret Shewring (eds) (1998) *Shakespeare and the Japanese Stage*, Cambridge: Cambridge University Press.

Scott, A. C. (1972) *The Theatre in Asia*, London: Weidenfeld & Nicolson.

Sedana, I. Nyoman (2005) 'Theatre in a Time of Terrorism: Renewing Natural Harmony after the Bali Bombing via *Wayang Kontemporer*', *Asian Theatre Journal*, 22 (1): 73–86.

Singh, Anita, and Tarun Tapas Mukherjee (eds) (2013) *Gender, Space and Resistance: Women and Theatre in India*, New Delhi: D.K. Printworld.

Sohi, Behzad Ghaderi, and Masoud Ghorbaninejad (2012) 'Ali Nassirian and a Modern Iranian "National" Theatre', *Asian Theatre Journal*, 29 (2): 495–527.

Tian, Min (2008) *The Poetics of Difference and Displacement: Twentieth-Century Chinese–Western Intercultural Theatre*, Hong Kong: Hong Kong University Press.

Trivedi, Poonam, and Dennis Bartholomeusz (2005) *India's Shakespeare: Translation, Interpretation, and Performance*, Newark: University of Delaware Press.

Trivedi, Poonam, and Ryuta Minami (2010) *Re-Playing Shakespeare in Asia*, New York: Routledge.

Wetmore, Kevin J., Jr. (2006) 'Modern Japanese Drama in English', *Asian Theatre Journal*, 23 (1): 179–205.

Wetmore, Kevin J., Jr., Siyuan Liu, and Erin B. Mee (2014) *Modern Asian Theatre and Performance 1900–2000*, New York: Bloomsbury Methuen Drama.

Part I
Traditional theatre in Asia

Traditional Indian theatre

Farley Richmond

Introduction

Given the age of the sophisticated civilization that inhabited the Indian subcontinent along the Indus river valley in what is now the modern state of Pakistan about 4000 BCE, it might be reasoned that theatre and drama would have developed far earlier than it did on the Indian subcontinent. Yet a glimmer of what is thought of today as theatre performance and the birth and growth of a substantial body of dramatic literature appears to have emerged perhaps no earlier than 500 BCE. And the first fragments of plays to be discovered date from no earlier than the first century CE.

We begin our search for traditional Indian theatre by examining surviving primary sources: the *Natyasastra* (The Science of Dramaturgy), considered the earliest text of dramaturgy, and the surviving plays written in Sanskrit, Prakrit and a variety of regional dialects. Unlike the physical remains of architecture, sculpture, vase painting, tiled walls and mosaic floors that further our understanding of the character and life of the ancient Greek and Roman theatre, we must rely on written material alone to paint a picture of the earliest phases of traditional theatre in India.

Natyasastra

Because the *Natyasastra* is such a rich and complex text it is not possible to do justice to it in this short space. The title is composed of two separate Sanskrit words: *natya* (drama) and *sastra* (variously understood as rule, science or scripture). It has long been considered an encyclopaedia of information concerning Sanskrit drama and theatre in ancient India, and has exerted a profound influence over the development of later genres of performance in India. Without it we would know considerably less about ancient Indian theatre and drama than we currently do.

The authorship of the work has been attributed to Bharata, a brahmin sage. Virtually nothing is known about the man except what is contained in the text. Given the unevenness of the writing style and other inconsistencies, some critics reason that the work is really a compilation of several works assembled over time by different authors. Scholars have variously dated it between 500 BCE and the eighth century CE.

The *Natyasastra* contains thirty-six chapters, which are briefly described below. Like most important Sanskrit texts, the *Natyasastra* begins with an invocation of respect to the gods. The first chapter concerns the origin of drama and theatre. According to Bharata, Brahma, the creator god, conceived this art by combining elements from the four *Vedas*, books of hymns sacred to the Hindus. Recitation was inspired by the *Ṛg* Veda – the oldest books of hymns, song from the *Sama* Veda, acting from the *Yajur* Veda and aesthetics from the *Atharva* Veda. Brahma then charged Bharata and his sons to learn the art, assisted in acting and dancing by divine nymphs and musicians who accompanied the performers.

Chapter 2 concerns the shape and construction of theatre buildings to house the art. Visvakarma, the heavenly architect, is said to have designed the original structure as a means of protecting the actors from malevolent forces that attempted to disrupt the first performance. Chapter 3 prescribes procedures by which a suitable spot is to be chosen for constructing such an edifice and what parts of the stage and the theatre building are to be protected by which gods. Regrettably, no theatre structures or their remnants have survived from ancient India.

Chapter 4 deals with the characteristics of the *tandava* dance associated with Lord Shiva, one of three principal deities. Chapter 5 lists preliminary rituals that are appropriate to be performed at the beginning of all performances.

Among the more important chapters of the work, chapters six and seven relate details about the sentiments and emotions to be depicted in a performance. The theory and aesthetics described are original to India and unique in world theatre. Chapter 6 focuses on *rasa* (sentiment) that a spectator is expected to experience when seeing and hearing a performance. Eight basic human sentiments are identified: erotic, comic, pathetic, furious, heroic, terrible, odious and marvellous. Although every performance contains permutations and combinations of all the sentiments, only one is expected to dominate a performance. Chapter 7 identifies eight *bhavas* (emotions) that correspond to the eight rasas. They are love, mirth, anger, sorrow, energy, terror, disgust and astonishment. It is these that the actors depict on stage and that generate the experience of rasa in the spectators.

Next are extensive discussions of *abhinaya* (acting) in chapters 8–14, focusing on physical movements of the head, eyes and hands, physical movements on stage, and a number of related matters known as *angika* abhinaya.

At the end of Chapter 14 Bharata draws an interesting distinction between plays of two different 'natures' (*dharma*). He says that there are *lokadharmi* (realistic) plays 'in which men and women, in their own nature, without any change, without any gestures behave naturally'. These stand in sharp contrast to *natyadharmi* (dramatic) plays 'in which speech is artificial and exaggerated, actions unusually emotional, and gestures graceful' (Rangacharya 1986: 76–7). The *Natyasastra* mainly deals with aspects of natyadharmi.

Chapters 15–19 concern *vacika abhinaya* (acting with the voice and speech).

Chapter 20 focuses on the nature of ten types of play and Chapter 21 concerns the plots of the play. (The material in these two chapters is discussed at greater length with regard to the surviving Sanskrit plays.)

Chapter 22 is concerned with *vrtti-s*. The subjects of this short chapter are considered confusing and unnecessary by Rangacharya in his translation of the *Natyasastra* (Rangacharya 1986: 117).

Chapter 23 focuses on *aharya abhinaya* (that is, the projection of a character through costume, makeup and stage properties). Chapter 24 contains miscellaneous information about a number of general topics related to performance.

Chapter 25 concerns the art of the courtesan. Chapter 26 discusses additional miscellaneous matters dealing with acting.

In Chapter 27 we are introduced to the means by which spectators are expected to judge a performance.

Chapters 28–33 concern themselves with musical instruments, such as the lute and flute, various types of rhythm and songs that are appropriate for the stage. Percussion instruments are discussed in the final chapter of this section.

Chapter 34 identifies the various character types found in the plays. Chapter 35 articulates the types of role needed to make up a theatre company.

And the final chapter of the work relates the story of why and how natya eventually came to earth and who sought to protect and preserve it.

The benediction at the end of the works says much about the importance of drama and theatre in ancient India:

> This sastra is entertaining; it purifies; it is holy; it destroys sin. Those who read it and those who listen to it, those who produce plays in accordance with it, and those who attentively watch the performance, all those derive the same merit as may be derived by those who study the Vedas, those who perform sacrifices, and those who perform acts of charity and religion. This is the greatest gift of all the gifts, viz. the giving of an opportunity to watch a performance. The production of a play is pleasing to the gods as no other form of worship with sandal paste or flowers is.
>
> (Rangacharya 1986: 226)

Sanskrit plays

The second major primary source for gaining an understanding of ancient Sanskrit drama and theatre is the surviving plays. The manner in which Sanskrit plays were to be composed is laid down in chapters twenty and twenty-one of the *Natyasastra*. The requirements are reiterated and made clear in Danamjaya's *Dasarupa* (literally ten beautiful forms), a dramaturgical text written in the tenth century CE. Unlike the *Natyasastra*, this short work provides brief examples from existing plays composed by different playwrights. From both works we are told that there are ten kinds of play. They are: *nataka, prakarana, samavakara, ihamrga, dima, vyayoga, anka, prahasana, bhana* and *vithi*.

Owing to the number of surviving natakas written over the centuries by India's best-known Sanskrit playwrights, this is clearly the most important dramatic form. According to the *Dasarupa*, 'Dramas are classified according to Subject matter, Hero, and Sentiment' (Dhanamjaya 1962: 6). Natakas should have a well-known story, a hero who is of an exalted nature, such as a king or royal sage, and should contain various rasas of which either *srngara* (love) or *vira* (heroic) may be the dominant one. It must have between five and seven acts. Among the surviving examples of natakas are Bhasa's *Svapnavasavadatta* (The Vision of Vasavadatta), Kalidasa's *Abhijnanasakuntala* (Shakuntala), Bhavabhuti's *Uttararamacarita* (The Latter History of Rama) and Harsa's *Nagananda* (Joy of the Serpents).

By contrast, a play written as a prakarana should have a story that is the original idea of the author, a hero who is a member of the brahmin caste, a minister or a merchant, and deal with characters who are from many different walks of life, including slaves, gallants and courtesans. Prakaranas should have no fewer than five and no more than ten acts and should also contain various rasas. *Mrcchakatika* (The Little Clay Cart) is the best known and one of only two surviving examples of this kind of drama. Srngara is the main rasa of a prakarana.

The third kind of drama is samavakara. It is to have only three acts. The story is to deal with gods and *asuras* (demons); the hero is to be well known. The dominant rasa is heroism (vira). In Chapter 1 of the *Natyasastra*, Bharata describes *Samudra Mathanam* (Churning of the Ocean), the first play to be performed, which celebrated the defeat of the demons by the gods. The work is a samavakara.

Like the samavakara, the other types of drama mentioned by the *Natyasastra* are far less significant and there are relatively few surviving examples.

With reference to the plot of a play, the *Dasarupa* says, 'The denouement (*karya*) [of the action consists of one of] the three objects of human existence (*trivarga*)' (Dhanamjaya 1962: 8). The three are *dharma* (virtue), *artha* (wealth) and *kama* (pleasure). We learn that the outcome of the action begins early in the play with a *bija* (germ) in which *bindu* (expansion) takes place, similar to what happens when a drop of oil floats on water. The expansion results in the development of *pataka* (episodes) and *prakari* (episodical incidents) that finally result in the denouement. These are regarded as the five elements of a plot.

The *Dasarupa*, like the *Natyasastra* before it, lists five stages of dramatic action: beginning, effort, prospect of success, certainty of success and attainment of the result. Parallel to these are five *sandhis* (junctures). They are opening, progression, development, pause and conclusion. There are additional subdivisions of these aspects of a plot that are complicated and unnecessary to consider here.

Moving next to the heroes, heroines and other categories of character appropriate for a play, we quickly understand that ancient Indian drama developed a number of character types appropriate for use in various kinds of plays and that the language of these types was to follow specific rules. For example, 'Sanskrit is to be spoken by men that are not of low rank, by devotees, and, in some cases, by female ascetics, the chief queen, by daughters of ministers, and by courtesans' and 'Prakrit is generally [to be the language] of women and Sauraseni [a regional dialect] in the case of male characters of low rank' (Dhanamjaya 1962: 75). Other regional languages are mentioned as appropriate for different types of character. The text even goes so far as to identify specific forms of address by a character of a particular rank to those of another rank and type.

Fragments of the earliest plays to have survived from ancient India date from between 78 CE and 144 CE. Asvaghosa is presumed to be the author of at least one of these fragments, *Sariputraprakarana* (The Story of Sariputra). Asvaghosa was probably a member of the court of Kaniska, a powerful king who ruled a vast swathe of land from Turfan to Pataliputra in the Gangetic plain. The king patronized Buddhism and the fragments of the plays concern Buddhist teaching. From the fragments it is clear that this playwright abided by the rules laid down in the *Natyasastra*.

Among the more significant playwrights of ancient India is Bhasa, of whom little is known, including exactly when and where he lived and worked. In 1912 thirteen plays attributed to Bhasa were published. Although the authorship of some of the works has been contested, the subject matter of the plays is drawn from a wide variety of sources, such as the two great epics *Ramayana* and *Mahabharata*, the Puranas, semihistorical tales, and from his own imagination. It is also clear that the author experimented with different kinds of dramatic composition, including natakas, prakaranas, samvakaras and vyayogas. It is significant that parts of some of his plays are still being performed by performers in Kerala state, south India. Even the opening verse of his play *Balacarita* is required to be learnt and performed by fledgling actors as part of their initiation into *kutiyattam*.

In the prologue to *The Little Clay Cart*, the stage manager ascribes the play to King Sudraka. However, there is no historical evidence that there was ever such a ruler. We do know that the play is clearly an expansion and elaboration of Bhasa's unfinished play *Carudattam*, named after the hero of the piece, suggesting that the author of *The Little Clay Cart* borrowed Bhasa's original work and made it uniquely his own. The plot is elaborate and in ten acts introduces us to a host of fascinating characters: a brahmin who is down on his luck, his faithful friend the *vidusaka* (clown), a beautiful and generous courtesan, her grief-stricken mother and a faithful and supportive maid servant, a boastful, spiteful courtier, good-hearted and trustworthy servants, a masseur turned Buddhist monk, gamblers, assorted bullock cart drivers, executioners, officers of the court and a reluctant judge. Because of its vivid picture of life in an ancient Indian city and its interesting plot, the work is an acknowledged masterpiece of dramatic literature that is still performed throughout the world.

Kalidasa is regarded as the best and certainly the most famous playwright of ancient India. Precisely when he lived and where he worked is still debatable. Some scholars identify him as one of nine 'jewels' at the court of King Chandragupta II in the mid-fifth century CE. His acknowledged masterpiece is *Abhijnanasakuntala* (Sakuntala). Kalidasa's genius is demonstrated in his vivid depiction of love in union and love in separation through a finely composed plot that is full of excellent poetry. Besides this masterpiece Kalidasa wrote two other fine natakas, *Malavikagnimitra* and *Vikramaurvasiya*, both titled after their central characters, as well as several excellent poems of which *Meghadutam* (The Cloud Messenger) may be the most beautiful.

Other significant playwrights from ancient India are Bhavabhuti who wrote *Uttararamacarita* (The Latter History of Rama), Harsa whose *Nagananda* was also in the repertory of the artists of kutiyattam for centuries, and Visakadatta whose *Mudraraksasa* (The Minister's Seal) is one of the few plays that centres on a political theme. King Mahendra Vikrama Varman and his plays will be dealt with below.

Although Sanskrit plays are still being written today, ancient Sanskrit drama and theatre was virtually dead by the tenth century owing to a number of contributing factors, not the least of which was a slavish tendency to follow the rules laid down in the *Natyasastra*. It was created, matured, grew and eventually declined over a period of a thousand years.

Not long after the classical period when Sanskrit drama and theatre began its steady decline, a wealth of performance genres began to spring into life among many cultural and linguistic groups on the subcontinent. So many of these living examples exist that only a few may be discussed below.

We begin with kutiyattam of Kerala state, which exhibits strong links to the Sanskrit drama and theatre of the past and yet exhibits characteristics that connect it to other regional genres of performance. This is followed by an examination of the *bhavai* of Gujarat, a state in western India. Bhavai is among the oldest of the surviving forms and serves in sharp contrast to the classical model of performance described in the *Natyasastra*. Bhavai is secular and closely connected to village life and culture. Then we turn to the *ankiya nat* of Assam state located in northeastern India. Ankiya nat is an excellent example of the many different religious genres of performance that spread across all of India during the medieval period. Next we focus on *yakshagana*, a popular genre of performance in the state of Karnataka in south India. Yakshagana places particular emphasis on the combination of lively dance and improvised acting techniques. It developed various subcategories of expression in a relatively small geographical area. Like many rural genres, yakshagana has begun to respond to the pressures of making adjustments to modernization. Finally, we look further south and a little later on in time to kathakali of Kerala. Kathakali may well be the best-known genre of performance in India and the western world. It demonstrates how elements of the ancient Sanskritic tradition have been successfully wedded to regional performance practices, producing a lively, colourful and unique form of expression.

Kutiyattam

The traditions of performing Sanskrit plays based on techniques articulated in the *Natyasastra* might well have declined and disappeared altogether had it not been for the kutiyattam, a regional genre of performance that has survived in Kerala state, south India.

Kutiyattam means combined acting and may well have been in existence as early as the first century CE. Kutiyattam's origin and early development is still cloudy and continues to be subject of scholarly speculation. A tantalizing reference to an artist that might have performed this unique traditional genre of performance is found in the *Silappatikaram*, a Tamil epic that dates from the Sangam age (approximately 600 BCE to 200 CE). The art is thought to have been reformed during in the tenth century CE under the direction of King Kulasekhara Varman (Bhaskara Ravi Varma I) who composed two plays still in the repertory of the kutiyattam. They are *Subhadradhananjaya* (The Wedding of Subhadra and Dhananjaya) and *Tapatisamvaranam* (The Sun God's Daughter and King Samvarana).

What is clear is that the art is now very much a part of Kerala. It was nurtured at the court of local rulers as well as within the confines of the Hindu temples of Kerala. By the late twentieth century kutiyattam had joined the ranks of 'classical' Indian performing arts owing to changing social and cultural traditions. The designation awarded to kutiyattam in 2001 as a Masterpiece of the Oral and Intangible Heritage of Humanity by UNESCO indicates the importance that the art enjoys within India and the international community.

The relatively few performers who still practise the art today come from a number of different castes, although originally the artists were *ambalivasis* (temple servants) who were the only ones permitted to perform within the confines of a number of important temple complexes, including those at Guruvayur, Trichur, Irinjalakuda, Kidangur, Thrippunithura and Haripad. Male actors who belong to the older tradition of artists belong to the *cakyar* caste. According to recent scholarship, different cakyar families preserve the exclusive right to perform in certain temples.

The female artists of this older tradition belong to the *nangyar* caste. They perform most of the female roles, play small bell metal cymbals, sing songs, recite verses and dialogue when called for in a performance, and perform a special genre of performance called *nangyar kuttu*. It should be noted that kutiyattam is one of the few genres of rural theatre in which women were allowed to participate.

Those of the *nambyar* caste are male drummers who, by tradition, are permitted to play the *mizhavu* (a large pot-shaped copper drum struck by hand) used to accompany the performers. Indeed, without the rhythms and subtle accents of the mizhavu the gestures and special patterns of movement and dance of kutiyattam could not be performed. And from time to time artists from other castes of temple servants assist the musicians, playing other types of drum and wind instruments.

Not until the mid-twentieth century was kutiyattam first seen outside the confines of the Kerala temples that were (as many of them still are) off limits to non-Hindus. Eventually training was offered to students from many different castes, as well as curious foreigners from a variety of different countries who had heard about and seen the art and were captivated by it.

Kutiyattam is not an art that is easily understood and appreciated on first viewing. To begin with, it is performed by characters who chant their parts slowly in Sanskrit and Prakrit, a virtually dead language, as well as an older form of Malayalam, the regional language of Kerala. Then, too, the artists use a symbolic gesture language that appears to be – but in fact is not – similar to gesture languages used in other genres of performance and dance in Kerala, such as in *krsnanattam*, kathakali and *mohiniyattam* (Figure 1.1). To untutored spectators, a performance moves relatively slowly and systematically, seeming to linger over obscure points. And finally it might surprise an unsuspecting spectator to learn that usually only one act of a play is performed

Figure 1.1 Jatayu the bird-like demi-god in a kutiyattam performance from a play based on the *Ramayana*.

(Photo by Farley Richmond)

and that too over a period of at least five days. And some acts require as many as forty-one days to complete!

It is not clear how the *Natyasastra* might have been used by theatre artists to mount a Sanskrit play in ancient India. However, performance practices in kutiyattam suggest a regional alternative to performing Sanskrit plays. Among a number of documents providing the manner in which the act is to be performed, the cakyar families definitely require one and often two staging manuals concerning the act of any given play. These are manuals concerning the manner in which the act is to be executed. They are preserved on palm leaf and, until late in the twentieth century, they were lovingly preserved and protected by the eldest member of the different cakyar families. The works are written in simply Malayalam and although they are anonymous and undated, they may have been composed by Tolan, a brahmin minister to Kulasekhara.

The first of these manuals is known as an *attaprakara*, which normally explains in detail what an actor should do to interpret and enact the verses and prose sequences of each of the characters of a particular act. The second type of manual is known as a *kramadipika*. It provides details such as the makeup and costuming required, the manner of entrances, the properties needed and ritual procedures to be followed. Both manuals are coded to be understood by a theatre artist and not by a layperson. We are fortunate to have translations of a number of these important works accompanying various plays.[1]

At first glance the repertory of kutiyattam may seem to be limited, but considering the number of days required for performing many of the plays, this is a considerable range of characters and performance challenges. For example, Act Three of Bhasa's Pratijnayaugandharayanam (The Minister's Vow), called Mantrankam by the artists, requires forty-one days to complete because of the verbal elaboration of the clown, and Act Six of Ascharyacudamani (The Wondrous Crest-Jewel), known as Anguliyankam by the artists, may take as many as twenty-one days to complete from start to finish. The remarkable thing about this latter act is that it is performed entirely by one character who enacts and makes comments on the entire *Ramayana* epic, as well as the origin of the monkey race.

Bhavai

Bhavai (literally 'emotion') is a genre of performance that developed and grew principally in western India, especially in the villages of northern Gujarat state. It is also known to have been performed in the rural areas of the states of Madhya Pradesh and Rajasthan. But north Gujarat is said to be the ancestral home of bhavai and it was here that the arts of dancers, actors and singers flourished.

The father of bhavai is thought to be Asaita Thakar who lived in the town of Sidhapur in the mid-fourteenth century during the reign of the Tughlaq dynasty. The Tughlaqs ruled over a large portion of north and central India from 1320 to 1413 and were known for the harsh treatment of their subjects.

There is a myth about Asaita among present-day performers as to why and how he became the progenitor of bhavai. The story goes that Asaita Thakar was born a brahmin and served as the family priest of Patel Hema, headman of the village of Unza. According to the story, Patel Hema's daughter was abducted by a Muslim captain. Asaita sought the release of the girl by entertaining the captain with songs and dances and claiming that she was his daughter. The suspicious captain agreed to her release on the condition that Asaita dine with the girl. Since she was from a lower caste, he knew that it was forbidden for brahmins to dine with lower-caste Hindus. But to his surprise Asaita shared a meal with the girl, whereupon the captain released her. Patel Hema was overjoyed by the safe return of his daughter but the local brahmin community was anything but pleased. Asaita was promptly excommunicated. This meant that he could no longer practise his hereditary occupation as a priest. Asaita accepted his fate and took up the low-caste profession of singing and dancing for a living. With the help of his sons he assembled the first company of strolling players in Gujarat, the *bhavaiyas* (those who arouse sentiments in spectators through their performance). In gratitude for the safe return of his daughter, Patel Hema bestowed a small plot of land and financial support for Asaita, thereby initiating a pattern of village patronage of bhavaiyas that persists to the present day.

Bhavai is traditionally performed in connection with Hindu religious festivals. Among the festivals, the birthday of Krishna is the favourite and the performers observe it with as much pomp and glory as their scanty means allows. The contents of most of the *vesas* (literally costume or dress but in this case the term means short plays) centre on the vices and virtues of members of various communities in village society. The brahmin, the tailor, the potter, the scavenger, the money-lender, all are satirized in bhavai. There are some vesas that deal with Hindu mythology, namely the *Ramayana*, and others which provide vignettes of famous historical personages of the area, but even these plays have an abundance of satire and an inevitable didactic message.

An evening of bhavai is normally composed of a chain of short plays and skits. Asaita is said to have composed 360 vesas, of which only forty or so survive. Each vesa is introduced by an *avanu* (song). The stories of the vesas are simple. The dramatic action is punctuated with a number of elements such as music, dance, narration, tricks, and relevant and irrelevant jokes sometimes bordering on the obscene. Since there is no scenery needed for each vesa, the changes of incident are indicated either by some physical action or orally. Typically, the vesas require a small cast of characters. The language of these small playlets is a mix of Gujarati, Hindi-Urdu and Marwadi.

Hasya (humour) is the dominant rasa in bhavai, although the other rasas described in the *Natyasastra* find a place in bhavai. The predominance of hasya, however, sets bhavai apart from many other genres of performance in India.

Bhavai is played out of doors either in front of a temple or in a village square. The spectators are drawn to the playing area after their evening meal by dances and songs meant to entertain and entice them to the show. About 10 p.m. the preliminaries begin.

The *naik* (company manager) draws a large circle on the bare ground with castor oil to define the playing area. This act is meant to drive away evil spirits and to sanctify the acting area. Then he applies kumkum (a powder used for social and religious markings) to a torch traditionally held by the village barber (Figure 1.2). The light of the torch is believed to symbolize the presence of Ambamata, the mother goddess of the Gujaratis and one of the various manifestations of *shakti* (the female force in the universe). The torch is continuously fed and kept burning throughout the long hours of the night until the performance is concluded. The naik sprinkles flowers and kumkum in the playing area, on the musical instruments and also on the spectators who fringe the circle. Before he leaves the performance arena he invokes Ambaji and Bahucharan (another manifestation of shakti and the patron saint of the performers).

The preliminaries continue with a musical concert. An instrument unique to bhavai is the *bhungal* (a four-foot-long copper pipe). Two of these instruments are required for a performance. Their shrill and forceful cry provides a lively cadence during the dance sequences and serves to announce the arrival of important characters in the acting area. Among the other instruments is a *dholak* (a two-headed drum) or a *tabla* (a pair of drums) popularly used in classical north Indian music concerts. Small bell metal cymbals provide a steady accompaniment to the rhythmic sections of the music. The *harmonium* (a keyboard instrument powered by hand-pump bellows) facilitates the choral songs. On occasion, various other musical instruments are used to achieve special effects.

Figure 1.2 The village barber in Bhavai holding a torch in the acting arena.
(Photo by Farley Richmond)

On a cue from the musicians the first vesa of the evening begins. A performer dressed to represent Ganapati, the elephant-headed god of beginnings and success, enters holding a brass plate before his face. Painted on the flat surface of the bottom of the plate are two holy signs, the swastika and the *trisula* (trident), both of which symbolize Shiva and Shakti. As he dances the musicians sing his praise. After his exit, the second vesa begins when another actor enters the arena dressed to represent the goddess Kali, the bloodthirsty destroyer of evil. The naik questions her as to her name and business but gets nothing more than a few monosyllables for a reply as Kali dances in a frenzy to loud songs of praise. At the end of her dance all the musicians implore her to remove all impediments that might hinder their performance, which she symbolically does by forming a circle over their heads and cracking her knuckles on her temples.

To conclude the preliminary rituals, the third vesa begins when an actor dressed as a brahmin priest comes from the dressing room through the noisy crowd of spectators that circle the arena. He provides the first bit of fun of the evening. When questioned by the naik as to his name and business, he replies in a ridiculous manner using all kinds of obscene remarks, to the delight of the spectators. His costume is a caricature of that of a brahmin. Sometimes an actor portraying the role wears small clay pots on his stomach and on his hips, which are concealed under the folds of his dress. His appearance is grotesque and provokes roars of laughter. When he dances, his movements are the very antithesis of grace. After his antics have been completed the preliminaries come to an end and are followed by a variety of other vesas chosen for the evening.

The play about Zanda Zulan stands as one of the finest examples of the bhavai vesas. The play liberally mingles hasya rasa and *srngara* (love) rasa and strangely incorporates an element of *karuna* (pathos) rasa by the unexpected twist at the end of the play.

The play more closely resembles western dramas because it has a plot, however slim, and several characters who bring about a conflict in the dramatic action. Below the surface, the play has a deep philosophical significance. The main character Tejo Vanio represents material wealth. Teji, his wife, is the embodiment of Lakshmi, goddess of wealth. She also represents *jivatma* (the lesser soul) who longs for union with *paramatma* (the greater soul), personified by Zanda Zulan, the Muslim officer with whom she is in love. The struggle between these forces is a rural interpretation of some of the finest thoughts of Hindu philosophy. The conflict that results is reminiscent of the struggle of the brahmin women who chose to follow and worship Lord Krishna at the expense of arousing the scorn of their husbands.

On another level *Zanda Zulan* deals with a social question that is particularly timely among urbanites today: the relationship between Hindus and Muslims. Gujarat borders on Pakistan and has been the scene of numerous Hindu–Muslim conflictions since partition of the two countries in the 1940s. Fortunately, one may still see performances of *Zanda Zulan* in remote villages in the interior of Gujarat.

Ankiya nat

Ankiya nat (literally 'one-act drama') is a genre of performance that was created to proselytize vaisnavism (worship of the god Vishnu manifested in the form of Krishna). It is to be found in the state of Assam in northeastern India. The man who is attributed with creating this genre is Sankaradeva, who lived from 1449 to 1568. Sankaradeva was a poet-saint who, like many other vaisnava philosophers, travelled widely in India spreading a message of *bhakti* (love) for and devotion to Krishna among the common people. Much is known and has been written about this extraordinary man.

Sankaradeva began to write plays at an unusually advanced age, when he was between the ages of 67 and 94. He continued to do so until his death at the age of 119. Performances of ankiya nat are usually given at night during the winter months from mid-January to mid-April on special festival occasions (Figure 1.3). Plays were also performed on full-moon nights during the planting season and at harvest time, essentially when the villagers are free from agricultural duties. Shows were occasionally held at the royal palaces of the local rulers in celebration of some special occasion, such as the visit of a royal guest.

A typical performance is staged in the *namghar* (prayer hall), which also serves as a court room or a public meeting hall because it is usually the most spacious building in any village. Normally the prayer hall is a two-roofed, thatched structure, rectangular in shape and about fifty feet long. The axis of the building normally runs from east to west. At the eastern end is the *manikut* (house of jewels) where the most valuable articles of religious significance are kept. Among the prize objects in the manikut is a copy of the *Bhagavata Purana*, a work that relates stories from the life of Lord Krishna. Unlike the sanctum sanctorum of Hindi temples elsewhere in India, the Assamese *vaisnavas* do not worship idols but turn their devotion towards this sacred text.

The musicians and actors traditionally face the manikut when they perform. The positioning of the players in relation to the manikut suggests that the play is given for the benefit of the deity, who is an honoured spectator.

Prior to the performance of an ankiya nat, a rectangular passageway formed by the rows of permanent pillars supporting the central roof of the prayer hall is marked off to keep overzealous devotees from interfering with the movement of the musicians and performers. The entrance to the prayer hall, opposite the manikut, is used as the main entrance for the musicians, stage manager and actors. The long narrow passageway between the entrance and the manikut serves

Figure 1.3 An ankiya nat scene with the stage manager in white cueing actors and surrounded by the audience.

(Photo by Farley Richmond)

as a neutral playing space, similar to the platea of medieval European performances. The spectators sit on the ground or on mats along either side of the pathway facing each other, permitting the actors to perform in their midst. The arrangement helps to promote the feeling of intimacy between actors and spectators.

The closeness of the actors and spectators is also emphasized by the use of additional playing spaces behind the spectators at the extreme corners of the prayer hall. These special acting areas symbolize various locales – a forest, a shrine, a throne room, or whatever is associated with the character that occupies it. Again, this practice has a European parallel in the medieval 'houses' or 'mansions'. Often the actors shout their dialogue back and forth above the heads of the spectators from the passageway to a symbolic locale. This is especially exciting when a moment of physical conflict erupts in the dramatic action, such as the conflict with Kali, the snake god whom Krishna overcomes in battle, or between Krishna and Sisupala, the demonic suitor for the hand of Krishna's intended bride, Rukmini. One of the most exciting moments to be seen in the ankiya nat is the battle scene between Rama and the demon brothers of Ravana, king of Lanka. In Bardowa-sattra, the birthplace of Sankaradeva, the fierce-looking, gigantic effigies of the demons are brought into the darkened hall by torchlight where they cast foreboding shadows on the walls and ceiling of the narrow enclosure.

The traditional Assamese costumes of the heroes, kings and warriors are thought to have been discarded in the late nineteenth century in favour of apparel worn by the *jatra* players of neighbouring Bengal, a region that had strong cultural and political influence over Assam at that time. In recent years the female characters have also discarded older garments in favour of the typical Assamese two-piece sari. The only participant in ankiya nat who seems to have maintained a costume thought to have been worn at the time of the form's creation is the stage manager, who wears a full ankle-length white skirt resembling that of the *kathak* dancers of north India, a thin, white, long-sleeved shirt buttoned below the armpit, a richly embroidered waistband and collar studded with pearl-like beads, and a turban resembling that of the Moghul emperors or the male kathak dancers.

Many of the plays require the actors to impersonate monkeys, bears, horses, elephants and serpents. To aid the imagination of the spectators, the actors use special effigies constructed from bamboo frames covered with cloth or papier-mâché painted in a stylized fashion to symbolize the personality and temperament of the particular characters for which they are created. Other items with symbolic meaning are the face masks, such as that of the ten-headed demon king Ravana, his giant supporters Subahu and Marica, the four-headed god of creation Brahma, and Garuda and Jatayu, mythical bird-like creatures with beaks and wings. Sometimes even the clowns of the demon kings wear masks constructed of clay, wood or bamboo, and cloth that have distorted facial features.

The auspiciousness of the performance is nowhere more apparent to the spectators than during the preliminary rituals that precede the dramas. The exact number and type of these rituals varies from village to village depending on the traditions that have been passed down from generation to generation. The preliminaries practised in Sankaradeva's own time are uncertain, in part because he gave them no set form. Traditional performances of ankiya nat are all-night affairs, beginning after the evening meal and continuing from approximately nine at night until daybreak. However, performances may be shortened without any forewarning, even when the show is in progress.

An *agni gad* (special archway of lights) is raised just inside the entrance to the prayer hall. Such an arch is constructed of two bamboo logs held upright and joined at the top by a horizontal log of bamboo. Small torches are lit and placed in holes drilled at the top of the bamboo arch. The shape of the arch differs from place to place. The arch may symbolize the bridge between the physical and the spiritual world or merely the point of transition between the everyday world and that of the play.

Once the arch is firmly in place, a white curtain is stretched in front of it as the musicians make their entrance. They begin to play after a short song poem is sung. The curtain is removed and the congregation shouts 'Jaya hari bola! Jaya rama bola!' (Say Victory to Hari (Krishna)! Say Victory to Rama!). Then a long series of elaborate rhythmic passages begin in which the drummers make their way in a line between the archway of lights and the manikut.

At the conclusion of the musical performance the stage manager makes his dramatic entrance accompanied by exploding fireworks. As the white curtain stretched before the arch of lights is quickly removed, he is discovered bowing in the direction of the manikut, his head, hands, elbows and knees reverently touching the earth in supplication. To a slow hypnotic rhythm from the drums he begins to rise, swaying from side to side as though in a deep trance, until finally he stands erect. As the tempo increases he dances in a sweeping clockwise circle around the playing area. Again and again he reverently touches the playing area, bowing in the direction of the manikut to show his respect for Krishna. Upon completion of his dance he recites the first Sanskrit verse of the benediction of the drama.

In ankiya nat the *sutradhara* plays the role of the main dancer. After the recitation of the opening verse that begins the play, he interprets the story in Assamese and interprets the Sanskrit verses through his dance. This is done throughout the play. There are ordinarily three dances of major importance in this genre: the dance of the sutradhara, the dance of Krishna and the dance of the milkmaid companions of Krishna.

The entire performance is under the watchful eye of the stage manager who is sometimes helped by an assistant. The role of the stage manager in ankiya nat is like that of a guru to his pupils. He remains on stage throughout, from the beginning of the preliminaries to the final invocation in praise of Krishna, which he traditionally delivers. Besides participating in the preliminary rituals, he has the important task of announcing all the characters before their entrances and calling attention to their exits. He often prefaces the speeches and songs of Rama and Krishna with 'Rama bola' (Rama says) or 'Krishna bola' (Krishna says), as if to imply to the spectators that they are to pay attention and listen. When he thinks it necessary, he halts the action to deliver a discourse on the ethical and spiritual meaning of the plot. At times he describes the proceedings or bridges gaps in the dramatic action with improvised narration. He pays close attention to the actors' execution of precise details of the performance as the playwright conceived and arranged it. He is not hesitant to prompt an actor who has forgotten a line or to chide him for misspeaking his dialogue. If he thinks it necessary, he quotes the stage directions from the text as though to order the actors to follow them to the letter. His active participation in the process of the production, in which no part is specifically written for him, reminds one of the French director pictured by Jean Fauquet in *The Painting of the Martyrdom of St. Apollonia* (c. 1460) guiding his amateur actors throughout performance with his baton and text in hand.

Yakshagana

Yakshagana (song of the heavenly Yaskhas) is a genre of dance-drama found mainly in Karnataka state, south India. It probably came into existence before 1500 during the rule of the Vijayanagara kings (1336–1565). The earliest known yakshagana play is dated 1564.

There are several kinds of yakshagana. Yaksagana badagatittu bayalata (*badagatittu* means northern style and *bayalata* means field performance) is found mainly in south Kanara, a district of Karnataka. Yakshagana nataka sabha mandali (or simply tent ata) is a commercial offshoot of the earlier genre and has recently become very popular. Tulu yakshagana is also becoming popular and is performed in the Tulu language. Yaksagana tenkutittu (southern style) is a popular genre of the art located around the city of Mangalore and even into northern sections of Kerala state. There have been and still are other examples of yakshagana to be seen in the state of Andhra Pradesh. What follows below mainly concerns the older style of yaksagana badagatittu bayalata.

The *bhagavata* (leader of the company) is the chief singer. His duties include singing the entire programme of plays chosen to be performed and, except when he is relieved by an assistant vocalist, he must perform for an entire night. He introduces each character. He sings the *prasanga* (a play principally written in verse) and keeps time with the small bell metal cymbals used to control the rhythm and pace of the performance. He is regarded as the 'first' actor. Below him in rank are the secondary actors who play the important roles of male characters such as heroes and kings.

The bhagavata also speaks short prose passages found in the prasangas. In a live perform-ance the long sections of prose dialogue between the bhagavata and the actors and between and among the actors are improvisations created by the actors. Since these sections were not composed by the creator of the prasangas they are not published in existing palm leaf and paper manuscripts that have come down to us from the past.

The dramatic repertory of this genre of performance is composed of stories drawn from Kannada versions of the Hindu epic literature, principally from the *Mahabharata* and the *Ramayana*, as well as episodes found in the Puranas that deal with the life of Krishna. To a lesser extent some of the plays deal with other mythologies available in the Kannada language. Some five hundred prasangas are said to have been composed since yakshagana began, but only forty or fifty are currently produced today. Owing to the fact that most of the written song texts or plays concern marriages and battles, the three main rasas of the works are the heroic, the furious and the erotic. However, the remaining rasas mentioned in the *Natyasastra* find a limited place in most of the dramas. It should be noted that the comic rasa plays a lively part, sometimes a large part, in many yakshagana performances, but comedy is mainly confined to the improvised dialogue between the actors and between the actors and the bhagavata.

Music is integral to yakshagana. It is an essential accompaniment to the ritual beginnings of the show. It accompanies the songs and poems that the bhagavata uses to tell the story. It provides the rhythmic accompaniment to support the pace and mood of the dances. The various melodic scales (ragas) that are required for particular songs and dances, the *sruti* (base note) of the particular raga scale, and the tala of the music are all dictated by the author of the prasanga. The yakshagana music generally abides by the classical south Indian musical scales and not those found in north Indian music. Four instruments make up a yakshagana orchestra: a pair of small bell metal cymbals, a *maddale* (a small two-headed drum played in the lap of the musician), a *chande* (barrel drum struck at one end with sticks), and either a harmonium or an electrical sruti box that establishes the base note underlying each raga. When struck, the chande produces a particularly penetrating, powerful and high-pitched sound that is capable of travelling great distances. It is normally used for entrances and dances of male characters and for battle scenes. The maddale has a subdued tone and serves to signal the entrance of female characters and their dances.

The acting area for performance is known as the *rangasthala*. It is the responsibility of the local patron of the show to identify a suitable performance space, such as a paddy field or open space where there is plenty of room for spectators to sit on mats on the ground arranged three-quarters around the rangasthala during the long hours of the night. The space is normally a 10-foot by 15-foot rectangle. Rocks, small stones and debris are removed before the space is demarcated by a tall frame of bamboo poles buried deep in the dry earth and linked by rope from which mango leaves, flowers, coconuts, plantains and coloured paper festively serve as the only decoration of the space. At one end of the long sides of the rectangle is placed a wooden table on which the bhagavata and maddale player sit cross-legged and between which the harmonium or sruti box is placed. The chande player sits on a chair several yards to the right of the table, facing the centre of the performance area where he can clearly see the dancers and actors, as well as his fellow musicians. The space is lit by traditional shovel-shaped oil lamps, bare electric light bulbs connected to electrical wires strung from a nearby house or Colman lanterns.

The actor/dancers normally enter the performance space to the stage-left side of the table where the bhagavata is sitting. They normally exit to the right side of the table where the maddale performer sits. The only stage furniture that is used during a show is a *ratha* (an unpainted wooden stool with four wheels). Whenever needed it may be rolled into place to symbolize a throne, a chariot, a mountain or virtually anything needed for the scene.

The local patron is also responsible for seeing to the construction of a dressing room situated relatively close to the rangasthala. It is here that the actors prepare for the show by putting on their elaborate makeup and costumes, where they offer prayers to the deities who preside over the space and the show, where local children may peep in to watch the proceedings and where actors greet their guests and friends, and where tea and coffee are regularly served throughout the entire length of the show. The actors place their trunks in this space according to their status and follow a decorum established by the traditions of the company.

Like other genres of performance in rural India, the yaksagana season coincides with the non-agricultural period, which extends from November to the onset of the monsoon in late May or early June. The troupes usually arrive in the village before noon, are ceremonially welcomed by the patron, and take their midday meal. Then the members sleep or relax before the time for their early evening meal, after which they set about putting on their makeup, ornaments and costumes. The play begins with a lengthy prologue of rituals and dances designed to attract audiences to the playing area. Typically a show is made up of several prasangas chosen by the patron from among some twenty or thirty in the repertory. Sometimes the decision about which prasangas are to be performed is not made until the very day of the show, even as late as a few hours before the performance is to commence, just in time for the actors to don the appropriate makeup and costumes of the characters they are to portray.

The bhagavata and the other musicians make their way to the rangastala followed by the clown and the kodangis (his monkey assistants). A song is sung in praise of Ganesa, the elephant-headed god of good fortune, and deities of the local temples. Afterwards two young dancers named Balarama and Gopala dance. This is followed by an introduction of the clown and his kodangi tribe. Next the mask of Ganesa is presented behind a curtain held by assistants. Songs of praise are sung in honour of the god. After this ritual segment is completed, the bhagavata and the clown converse. Eventually, there is a dance of the *strivesa* (male performers dressed in female costumes) featuring many complicated rhythmic patterns and movements. Finally the first prasanga of the evening begins. It starts with a dance presentation of the chief male characters. Eventually, the chief of these characters converses with the bhagavata and the prasanga is fully under way (Figure 1.4).

There are some eleven different character types in yakshagana that are known by their costumes and makeup, among them warriors and kings, religious leaders, seers or sages, forest people, certain deities, demons and demonesses, non-threatening demons, queens, princesses and their servants or female deities, warlike women, clowns, and mythological animals, such as Hanuman the monkey chief of the *Ramayana*, Garuda the bird who serves as Lord Vishnu's vehicle, and Nandi, the bull who serves as the vehicle of Lord Shiva.

With changing social and economic conditions in Karnataka in the 1950s, some troupe leaders began to seek a means to commercialize yakshagana. Instead of relying on rich patrons and landlords to sponsor shows, they sought to control the genre by putting it in tents and selling

Figure 1.4 A heroic character dancing in yakshagana.
(Photo by Farley Richmond)

tickets to each show. This allowed them to create separate sections and classes of seats depending on their location in the tent. Instead of the traditional three-quarter-round juxtaposition of the actors and audience, the tents allowed them to create a proscenium arrangement with the audience on one side and the performers playing on a raised platform on the other. One of the results of this effort was that the individual ticket holder began to exercise some degree of influence over the choice of prasangas, as well as the manner in which they were presented. New prasangas with different themes began to be composed that were designed to appeal to the tastes of this new breed of audience. Electrical lighting instruments with dimming devices were employed to light the raised platform stage. This led to use of different makeup products that worked better under electrical lighting. Microphones could now be used to amplify and control the balance between the singer and the drummers as well as between the actors and the audience. Eventually the shows were handed over to contractors who, for a set fee, agreed to take care of setting up and striking the tent and chairs, advertising the show and selling tickets (Bapat 2006: 156–62).

Kathakali

Kathakali (literally story play) is a popular genre of dance-drama that originated and developed in the state of Kerala in southwestern India beginning in the mid-seventeenth and early eighteenth centuries. It was born out of a genre of performance called *ramanattam* that was originated by the Raja of Kottarakara. At this early stage of its evolution kathakali drew inspiration and ideas from a wide range of Kerala performing arts: krsnanattam (a religiously inspired genre of performance), kutiyattam, *kalarippayatt* (the martial art of Kerala) and *mudiettu* and *theyyam* (both ritual genres of performance). With the composition of four plays by the Raja of Kottayam during the first half of the eighteenth century, kathakali was well on its way to becoming the leading popular genre of performance among the people of Kerala.

Early in its history kathakali also developed three different styles of performance named after the men who originated them. Each of the styles is associated with a different region of the state.

The *attakathas* (scripted play texts) written for kathakali are composed in a Sanskritized Malayalam known as *manipravalam*. The stories they depict are drawn from the great Hindu epics, the *Ramayana*, *Mahabharata* and the *Bhagavata Purana*. Upper-caste patrons wrote about five hundred attakathas over the centuries but today acts and scenes from only about forty or fifty are performed. It is not possible to understand kathakali simply by reading a translation of an attakatha, however. Associated with the literary text is a performance text crafted by the choreography added to it by the dancers and the musical accompaniment in song and chants that breathes life into the words. The performance text has rarely appeared in print along with the literary text.

The literary text is divided into verses and dialogue. The verses are usually narrative descriptions of the scene of the action and the mood of the characters. Two singers take turns singing the verses in the melody and rhythm specified by the writer of the attakatha. They sing without rhythmic accompaniment. For example, in the first scene of the first of four plays of *Nalacharitham* by Unnayi Warrier, Sloka 2 is set in *Mukhari* Raga and *Atantha* Tala. It reads: 'Thus when King Nala ruled the land the great sage Narada, son of Brahma, as an earnest of his good will paid him a visit one day' (Warrier 1977: 68). In an attempt to indicate the physical action on stage, another translator of the same scene adds:

After the sloka, when the curtain is lowered, Nala appears, seated on a throne. Gesticulating, as though seeing something in the sky, 'What could be the brilliance in the sky?' (Taking a closer look) 'Whose form could that be seen in the middle?' (Taking a still closer look) 'It is Sage Narada. He seems to be coming to meet me.' Showing so much with a rhythmical sequence of kitatimtam, with feelings of reverence, respect and joy, [At this point, the dancer playing Narada has obviously entered the stage] Nala gets up, offers a seat to Narada, pays obeisance to him with a leaping dance step during the second kitatimtam and starts enacting the pada, beginning with 'Lord Narada'). [The singers begin to sing the dialogue of the pada and charanam which the playwright has composed and which the dancer executes by stylized gestures, facial expressions and eye movements and punctuates with stylized passages of dance, known as *kalasam*. The dialogue is as follows:] Lord Narada, I bow to you. My sins have perished, this house is sanctified. Son of the lotus-born lord, where is your arrival from? Is it from the abode of Hari, or from the palace of devas? My mind reveals when I behold your form like a water lily at the sight of the full moon. What shall I do now, at your command?

(Uṇṇāyivāriyar 2001: 2–3)

The vocalists sing in a vocal style known as *sopana*. Throughout the show they narrate the dramatic action and assume the dialogue of all the characters. The dancers perform the stylized gestures (literally the language of the text in gesture), facial expressions (the emotions or bhava associated with the character at any given moment), and subtle eye movements needed to convey the thoughts and feelings suggested by the words. The percussion instruments provide a wide variety of different rhythmic patterns associated with the movement patterns of the characters. Given this separation of duties this might mistakenly suggest that the performances are fragmented affairs. In fact, all the elements are blended together into a perfect whole that leads to a unity of expression. In addition, costumes and makeup signify different character types, making it easy for the audience to identify just exactly who each actor is playing: heroic males (*pacca* characters with green faces); demons (*katti* characters with a knife-like black slash from cheek to cheek on a field of green makeup and with pith knobs fixed to their nose and forehead); hot-headed characters (*chuvanna tadi* characters with red beards); strong and valiant characters such as Hanuman – the monkey devotee of Lord Rama (*vella tadi* characters with white beards) – and forest characters (*karutta tadi* characters with black beards), heroic female characters (*minukku* or women of high rank with 'shining faces'), and brahmin priests or deities (minukku male characters with 'shining faces'); and a wide variety of characters with special costumes and makeup patterns unique to that character (Figure 1.5).

By tradition, all performers of kathakali are male. Originally the actors who studied kathakali came from the nair community. The duty of the nairs was originally to serve as soldiers to the local rajas. Today, performers come from many castes and even from the Muslim and Christian communities. There is even a company of women who perform the art.

If a performance is held out of doors near a temple compound where many people may witness the show, tea stalls and cigarette and toy venders set up shop on the periphery of the audience area and do a lively business throughout the night.

Traditionally the preliminaries before a kathakali performance follow a set pattern. At sunset a ceremonial performance of drums, gong and cymbals, lasting about half an hour, takes place near the performance area. This is obviously designed to attract spectators to the area to watch a show. It also serves to provide the musicians with a chance to perform various complicated rhythmic patterns, beginning with those that are slow and continuing through the fastest and more complex ones that might be used later in the performance. Next comes the ceremonial lighting of a large oil lamp, nearly shoulder high, that sits downstage centre on the performance area. This act is accompanied by a brief performance of drumming on the maddalam drum.

Figure 1.5 A kathakali hero character praying before a performance.
(Photo by Farley Richmond)

In a traditional performance the next thing that takes place is that two attendants hold the large colourful rectangular curtain upstage of the oil lamp. Sometimes two beginning students are assigned to perform complicated dance patterns that test their skill. This section is generally very popular with the spectators. Eventually the preliminaries are completed with the singing of the opening verse of the play to be performed that evening. With the removal of the curtain a conch shell is sounded, introducing the first *purapad* (going forth) dance of the evening by the chief character of the attakatha.

Note

1 Notable examples of staging manual accompanied by performance execution are as follows: G. Venu's *Production of a Play in Kutiyattam* containing translations of Act One of Bhasa's *Abhisekanataka* and both a kramadipika and a attaprakaram explaining how the work is to be performed; *The Wondrous Crest-Jewel in Performance*, edited by Clifford Reis Jones, containing the Sanskrit text, edited by

V. Raghavan in *devanagari*, of Saktibhadra's play and the translation of a stage manual for each of the play's seven acts; Act One of Kulasekharavarman's *Subhadradhananjaya* with staging manual integrated with the English and devanagari Sanskrit text found in K. G. Paulose's *Kutiyattam Theatre: The Earliest Living Tradition*; and Act Five of *Ascharyachudamani* (The Wondrous Crest Jewel) integrated with the staging manual for all fifteen days of the play in Sudha Gopalakrishnan's *Kutiyattam: The Heritage Theatre of India*.

At one time or another all thirteen plays by Bhasa have been performed in kutiyattam. Today, all but the last act of Abhishekanataka is performed. Only Act Two of *Pratijnayaugandharayanam* (The Minister's Vow), Act Five and part of Act One of *Svapnavasavadatham* (The Dream of Vasavadatta), Sutradharan Purappad (entry of the stage manager), the Nirvahanam (expansion of a story from the point of view of a particular character) and the act titled Kaliyankam of *Balacharitam* (The Tale of Childhood), the *Dutaghatotkacham* (Ghatotkacha as Envoy), *Dutavakyam* (The Envoy's Message) and *Karnabharam* (Karna's Burden) are still in the repertory. Act One of Harsha's Naganandam (The Joy of Serpents), all seven acts of Saktibhadra's *Ascharyachudamani*, and Acts One, Two and the *purappad* (introductory segment) of Act Five of Kulasekharavarman's Subhadradhananjayam are being performed. Act One of Kulasekharavarman's *Tapatisamvaranam*, the one-act *Mattavilasam* (The Farce of Drunken Sport) by Mahendravikrama, Bodhayanan's *Bhagavadajjukiyam* (The Hermit and the Harlot) and Neelakantan's *Kalyanasaugandhikam* (The Flower of Good Fortune) are still part in the repertory. Each of the acts of the different plays bears a separate title, except for the one-act plays that continue to be known by their original title (Venugopalan 2007: 62–3).

Bibliography

Ashton, Martha Bush, and Bruce Christie (1977) *Yaksagana: A Dance Drama of India*, New Delhi: Abhinav.

Bapat, Guru Rao (2006) 'Modernising Tradition: The Commercialisation of Yakshagana in Karnataka', in Simon Charsley and Laxmi Narayan Kadekar (eds) *Performers and Their Arts: Folk, Popular and Classical Genres in a Changing India*, London: Routledge.

Barua, Hem (1965) *Assamese Literature*, New Delhi: National Book Trust.

Bharata (1967) *Natyasastra*, Manmohan Ghosh (trans and ed.) 2nd rev. edn Volume 1, Calcutta: Manisha Granthalaya.

Bolland, David (1996) *A Guide to Kathakali: With the Stories of 35 Plays*, New Delhi: Sterling.

Desai, Sudha R. (1972) *Bhavai: A Medieval Form of Ancient Indian Dramatic Art (Natya) as Prevalent in Gujarat*, Ahmedabad: Gujarat University.

Dhanamjaya (1962) *The Dasarupa: A Treatise on Hindu Dramaturgy*, George C. O. Haas (trans), Delhi: Motilal Banarsidass.

Gopalakrishnan, Sudha (2011) *Kutiyattam: The Heritage Theatre of India*, New Delhi: Niyogi Books.

Karanth, K. Shivarama (1975) *Yaksagana*, Mysore: The Institute of Kannada Studies.

Koizumi, Fumio, *et al.* (1983) *Dance and Music in South Asian Drama: Chhau, Mahakali pyakhan and Yakshagana: Report of Asian Traditional Performing Arts 1981*, Tokyo: The Japan Foundation.

Nair, D. Appukuttan and K. Ayyappa Paniker (eds) (1993) *Kathakali: The Art of the Non-worldly*, Bombay: Marg Publications.

Neog, Maheswar (1965) *Sankaradeva and His Times: Early History of the Vaisnava Faith and Movement in Assam*, Gauhati: Department of Publication.

Panchal, Gaverdhan (1983) *Bhavai and its Typical Aharya: Costume Makeup and Props in Bhavai, the Traditional Dramatic Form of Gujarat*, Ahmedabad: Darpana Academy of the Performing Arts.

Paulose, K. G. (2006) *Kutiyattam Theatre: The Earliest Living Tradition*, Kottayam: DC Books.

Rajagopalan, L. S., and V. Subramanya Iyer (1975) 'Aids to the Appreciation of Kathakali', *Journal of South Asian Literature*, X, 2, 3, 4: 205–10.

Rangacharya, Adya (trans and ed.) (1986) *Natyasastra: English Translation with Critical Notes*, Bangalore: IBH Prakashana.

—— (1998) *Introduction to Bharata's Natyasastra*, New Delhi: Munshiram Manoharlal.

Richmond, Farley (1974) 'The Vaisnava Drama of Assam', *Educational Theatre Journal*, May: 145–63.

—— (2002) *Kutiyattam: Sanskrit Theater of India*, CD-ROM, Ann Arbor: The University of Michigan Press.

Richmond, Farley P., Darius L. Swann, and Phillip B. Zarrilli (eds) (1990) *Indian Theatre: Traditions of Performance*, Hawai'i: University of Hawai'i Press.

Saktibhadra, Clifford Reis Jones, and V. Raghavan (1984) *The Wondrous Crest-Jewel in Performance: Text and Translation of the Ascaryacudamani of Saktibhadra with the Production Manual from the Tradition of Kutiyattam Sanskrit Drama*, Delhi: American Institute of Indian Studies and Oxford University Press.

Schwartz, Susan L. (2004) *Rasa: Performing the Divine in India*, New York: Columbia University Press.

Sowle, John Steven (1982) 'The Traditions, Training, and Performance of Kutiyattam: Sanskrit Drama in South India', unpublished PhD thesis, University of California/Berkeley.

Thakar, Asaita (1971) *Vanio and Zanda Zulan*, Farley Richmond and Tevia Abrams (adapt.) Harish Trivedi (trans), Calcutta: Writers Workshop.

Uṇṇāyivāriyar (trans. by Sudha Gopalakrishnan) (2001) *Unnayi Varier's Nalacaritam: With Performance Manual Based on Kalamandalam Krishnan Nair's Stage Version*, Bangalore: Sahitya Akademi Centre for Translation.

Unni, N. P. (trans and ed.) (1998) *Natyasastra: Text with Introduction, English Translation and Indices in Four Volumes*, Delhi: Nag.

Venu, G. (1989) *Production of a Play in Kutiyattam: Text and Translation of the First Act of Abhiseka Nataka of Bhasa with the Kramadipika (Production Manual) and the Attaprakaram (Acting Manual) from the Sanskrit Drama Tradition of Kerala*, Irinjalakuda: Natanakairali.

Venugopalan, P. (2007) *Kutiyattam Register*, Thiruvananthapuram: Margi.

Warrier, Unnayi (1977) *Nalacharitham*, V. Subramania Iyer (trans), Trichur: Kerala Sahitya Akademi.

Wells, Henry W. (ed.) (1964) *Six Sanskrit Plays*, Bombay: Asia Publishing House.

Zarrilli, Phillip (1984) *The Kathakali Complex: Actor, Performance, Structure*, New Delhi: Abhinav.

2
Traditional Chinese theatre

Colin Mackerras

Introduction

China's theatre tradition is among the oldest and most varied in the world. Despite the proscriptions of authorities, it has been tightly interwoven with society and enjoyed by people of all classes. This chapter restricts itself to the Han people, who (according to the 2010 census) were 91.51 per cent of a total of nearly 1.4 billion people, with some particularly important minority traditions covered separately.

Definition

Traditional Chinese theatre is termed *xiqu* in Chinese. Major features of xiqu items are a plot and live actors impersonating particular personalities, with interrelationships between or among the play's characters. The bulk of the dialogue in xiqu is undertaken either through singing or a conventionalized chanting, but comic characters often speak to the audience and a few items depend mostly on mime, being almost completely soundless.

Because singing was so important for dialogue, the term xiqu is often translated as 'opera.' There is, of course, logic in the translation and it is used in particular contexts below, but as a general term it gives a somewhat false impression, because the style of singing, the spectacle and the staging in Chinese xiqu are so different from western opera. Despite a rich history in China, certain types of performing arts are noted here only if they are part of xiqu, such as dance or acrobatics.

A chronological survey

Ritual performances, possibly with actors and dancers wearing costumes and makeup, existed from the earliest times. The courts of the pre-imperial period (that is, before the third century BCE) included some known to employ jesters able to impersonate dignitaries. During the Han dynasty (206 BCE–220 CE), there was a kind of entertainment called 'hundred games circus' (*baixi*). Among its numerous performance forms were dances with simple stories and actors impersonating people or animals.

Emperor Xuanzong (reigned 712–56), also called Minghuang, among the most prominent of rulers of the Tang dynasty (618–907), established a music school in a pear garden north of the main walled city of his capital Chang'an (present-day Xi'an). It achieved enough fame that to this day actors are sometimes called 'children of the Pear Garden', even though it appears that his actual aim was more to teach Buddhist music than anything we might consider theatrical. The Tang dynasty spawned another antecedent to drama, called 'adjutant plays' (*canjunxi*). These were comic skits with very simple stories, dialogue, song, acting and the beginnings of role types that were to become extremely important in later Chinese theatre.

Song to Yuan dynasty: the rise of full-fledged drama

The Song dynasty (960–1279) saw the growth of a commercialized urban culture and a highly sophisticated array of literature and arts, including landscape painting. However, in 1126 the Jurched people seized the Song capital and established a dynasty in the north called the Jin. The Song survived only in the south, meaning that China was divided. The Mongols, who arose to be the greatest power of the Eurasian continent in the thirteenth century, then conquered the Jin in 1234 and in 1279 reunited China under their own rule, their Yuan dynasty lasting until 1368.

The adjutant plays survived into the Song period, their role types and stories becoming more varied and complex, though skits and farces continued to predominate. More important, however, was the emergence of a form of theatre termed *nanxi* ('southern drama'). The origins were in southeast China (Wenzhou in Zhejiang Province) in the years just before the Jurched conquered the north, and the genre developed greatly in the following centuries.

There were over 100 of these southern dramas, but the complete texts of only very few survive, plus fragments of some others. The authors' names are unknown, but they may have been amateur literary men who formed themselves into writing clubs. The *nanxi* had complex stories, with clear interrelationships among the characters, dialogue being through singing and stylized chanting, but musical accompaniment confined to percussion instruments. There were seven role types, the basis of almost all later Chinese theatrical genres. The dramatists adopted pre-existing tunes for the words they wrote, rather than setting words to music. This method was called 'joined song system' (*lianquti*), and remained predominant in south China for many centuries.

During the Yuan dynasty, another form of drama developed, this time in north China. It was called the *zaju*, or 'variety drama'. From a literary point of view, many specialists regard these zaju and the century or so following 1260 as the 'golden age' of Chinese drama, one saying specifically that the 171 or so extant items 'are the earliest surviving and most brilliant body of Chinese dramatic literature' (Shih 1976: ix). In the course of time the variety drama spread to the south, replacing the 'southern drama' in audience affection.

The variety dramas were similar to the nanxi in following the lianquti method. However, the structure of these dramas was much stricter than the nanxi. The number of acts was more or less fixed at four, sometimes with a prologue and/or interlude (termed *xiezi* or 'wedge') added. Only one character, either the main male or the main female, could sing in each act and it was there that the emotional expression was at its highest point.

Though the status of the dramatist was not high, we can attribute specific authors to the main zaju items and even know something of their lives. The most famous and prolific is Guan Hanqing whose career, centred in Beijing, spanned the second half of the thirteenth century. Over sixty dramas are attributed to him, the most famous being *Dou E yuan* (Injustice to Dou E). Fifteen items survive in full and three in part. His younger contemporary Wang Shifu was the author of the much longer *Xixiang ji* (The Story of the West Wing), which one specialist typically describes as 'the most famous Chinese play through the ages' (Dolby 1976: 48).

The same authority has written of the Yuan drama overall: 'For the first time in China we can unquestionably see that combination of acting, costume, stagecraft, and the complex inter-relation of characters in a detailed story that makes real drama' (Dolby in Mackerras 1983: 57). What is striking is how this genre, designed for performance, entered the canon of Chinese written literature. Despite 'the near-obsolescence of early operatic music' by the seventeenth century (Sieber 2003: xv), many of the texts survived. They were adapted and readapted for later genres of theatre, and it is a process that continues to this day.

The rise and flowering of the regional theatre in the Ming and Qing

With the overthrow of the Mongols, China was again controlled by the Han people, in the spectacular and culturally sophisticated Ming dynasty (1368–1644). In the seventeenth century, the Manchus from northeast China were able to take over the whole country and establish the Qing (1644–1911) dynasty. They expanded China's territory considerably, their political power and culture reaching an apogee in the eighteenth century under the Qianlong Emperor (reigned 1735–95).

During this period the xiqu developed into over 300 different styles of regional theatre. Most of them began as small-scale folk theatre in the countryside, but quite a few developed into larger-scale urban genres that became well known throughout China. They differ in their dialect, music, instrumentation and in other ways, but the stories tend to be very similar, and there is some consistency also in their acting styles and costuming. They proliferated into different regions in various ways, among the most important being the absorption of elements of the art of one area into that of another through the agency of wandering acting troupes. Apart from the *kunqu*, to be considered later, most of the regional styles, and certainly all the small-scale ones, were mass theatre, despised by the elite.

Although the 'southern drama' declined greatly during the Yuan, it was reinvented in changed form during the Ming, certainly by the sixteenth century and probably earlier. A group of styles beginning in Yiyang, Jiangxi Province, resembled the southern drama in many ways, including in being accompanied only by percussion instruments. These styles became very widespread in the south and even spread to Beijing in the north.

Meanwhile, in the sixteenth century we find in north China a new array of theatre styles collectively known as *bangzi qiang* (usually translated 'clapper operas'). Actually, the *bangzi* is a hardwood percussion instrument, struck with a stick. It is not really 'clapped'. Yet the translation has become widespread enough to be accepted and the use of the instrument to mark accented beats is universal in clapper opera styles. Another extremely important characteristic of the clapper opera was that it followed the musical system known as *banqiangti* (literally 'accented-beat tune system'). This was the opposite of the lianquti familiar in the south and in the Yuan zaju. Whereas the lianquti used pre-existing tunes and rhythm for newly written lyrics, the banqiangti did the opposite; in other words, tunes were specially written for pre-existing words. This made it possible to change the rhythm and metre frequently within the same act, enabling a wider range of emotional expression.

Kunqu

The most famous of forms evolving during the Ming is the kunqu, individual items usually known in their own time as *chuanqi* or 'marvel tales'. This originated in the sixteenth century in Kunshan, very near Shanghai, mainly through the work of Wei Liangfu and his approximate contemporary Liang Chenyu (1520–94), who fashioned earlier southern dramas and the folk music of their region into a new, integrated form of drama. It follows the lianquti system, and the music is soft and gentle, with the orchestration dominated by the side-blown flute (*dizi*), while the rhythm is mainly in four-four time. Unlike any of the other genres of the post-Yuan era, it was an elite theatre that spawned a significant written literature.

The greatest and most famous dramatist of the Ming dynasty was Tang Xianzu (1550–1616), from Jiangxi Province. Because of his distinction and because he was contemporary with his English counterpart (he died in the same year), Tang Xianzu is often described as 'China's Shakespeare'. His surviving works are mostly based on dreams, the most important being the love story *Mudan ting* (Peony Pavilion), completed in 1598 (Figure 2.1). Tang was caught up in an early controversy in the history of kunqu. One school believed drama should be based

Figure 2.1 A scene from *Peony Pavilion*.

(Photo by Colin Mackerras)

on reason (*li*), restraint and the promotion of public morality. Tang represented the opposing school, which thought the basis of drama should be feeling (*qing*), with the focus on human passion and spontaneity.

A good representative of Qing dramatists was Hong Sheng (1645–1704), from Zhejiang, best known for his drama *Changsheng dian* (The Palace of Eternal Youth), which was completed in 1688. The only one of Hong's eleven dramas to survive, it deals with the Tang Emperor Xuanzong, mentioned above, and his love for his favourite concubine Yang Guifei. Unfortunately, Hong was banished from Beijing and the item banned in 1689 due to its performance within two months of an empress's death, thus breaking an official taboo. Despite this, it has remained among the most popular of Chinese dramas.

A contemporary of Hong Sheng's was Kong Shangren (1648–1718), who was a descendant of Confucius. He is best known for his *Taohua shan* (Peach Blossom Fan) of 1699, a long item that tells a love story against the background of the defeat of the Ming by the Manchus. It is unusual in that it dramatizes events within living memory and Kong even seems to mourn the defeated Ming, for all its corruption, even though he tries to be fair to the Manchus, who were after all in power when he wrote. Though the Kangxi Emperor (reigned 1661–1722) was initially very favourable to Kong, after the play's composition he cooled towards the dramatist, who was dismissed in 1700.

In sharp contrast to the Yuan zaju, operas in the kunqu style usually had many acts. *Peony Pavilion*, for instance, is immensely long, having fifty-five scenes in its full form. There are records of plays lasting three days and three nights. So it became customary for individual scenes or groups of scenes to be played separately from the full drama. This had become nearly universal practice by the end of the Ming.

Kunqu probably reached its apogee with Tang Xianzu and declined thereafter. Although there were some good items produced during the Qing, the genre never regained the inventiveness that had earlier characterized it. The Taiping Rebellion, which ravaged China and especially the south from 1850 to 1866, produced a devastating effect on this elite theatre and kunqu was approaching extinction by the time the Qing fell.

The Yuan drama 'favored female players and female cross-dressing' (Li 2003: 40). Mixed-gender troupes were common. There is evidence even of troupes functioning as family businesses, with the wife and daughters-in-law of the troupe leader involved in acting or other functions. Also, the material on actresses in the Yuan praises them both for their skills on the stage and attractiveness as courtesans.

However, from the Ming dynasty on, single-gender troupes were the norm, with all-male troupes much commoner than all-female. Confucian ideology demanded the public separation of the sexes and was very restrictive of any behaviour that authorities thought could lead to sexual immorality. Although the practice of foot-binding for women predated the Ming, it appears to have taken stricter hold at that time, making it very difficult for women to go on the stage as performers. Mixed troupes became rare, with most actresses being prostitutes, the exceptions being girls in private mansions trained in theatre.

The Pihuang system

In the eighteenth century, as kunqu declined, the growth of the regional theatre gathered momentum. For the popular theatre the main development was the combination of two styles, *erhuang* and *xipi*, collectively termed *pihuang*. Erhuang, of southern derivation, came dominantly to express grief, remembrance and lyricism, while xipi, which came from the north, was reserved more to show joy or vehemence. Belonging to the 'accented-beat tune system', a major feature

Figure 2.2 A scene from jingju *Da bao guo* (Defending the State), showing the royal palace.
(Photo by Alexandra Bonds)

of pihuang dramas was that musical accompaniment was dominated by a two-string fiddle called *huqin*, with a clapper termed *ban* beating out the rhythm.

Dramas belonging to a pihuang genre came to be found all over China. In the south the most famous genre was the Cantonese opera (*yueju*), which by the 1730s was known in a popular form probably fairly similar to the items still performed in Guangdong, Guangxi and Hong Kong. There were also major pihuang genres in Hubei, Hunan, Yunnan and other southern provinces.

Meanwhile in north China, the most important of the pihuang genres, namely the *jingju*, often translated as Peking Opera, established itself in the capital towards the end of the eighteenth century, the nineteenth seeing major development there. Rather than great dramatists, its main creators were troupes and actors. Among the former, the Four Great Anhui Troupes (*Sida huiban*) were pre-eminent. The actor of mature male roles Cheng Changgeng is sometimes called 'the father of Peking Opera' for his leadership in integrating and developing the various musical and acting components that have come to make up the Peking Opera. Jingju became strong and popular enough that in the twentieth century it was on occasion even termed *guoju* or national theatre, since some xiqu enthusiasts regarded it as equivalent to a form of theatre that could represent not only Beijing, but all China (Figure 2.2).

The beginnings of reform: late Qing and the Republic

Intensified Chinese reaction to increasing western influence, even dominance, in the late decades of the nineteenth century contributed to a revolutionary process in China. Specific events included the Boxer Uprising of 1900 and the 1911 Revolution that saw the fall of the Qing monarchy. The date of student demonstrations in Beijing on 4 May 1919 has given its name to a thrust towards modernization called the May Fourth Movement. From the point of view of this chapter, it is most important for its cultural component and its effects on impulses often called the New Culture Movement.

For theatre, this period was most significant for the 1907 birth of the new form called *huaju* (spoken drama), and for China's first proscenium-arch theatre in 1908, both considered in more detail elsewhere. The idea of using drama as a propaganda weapon for reform and against the monarchy started to take root. In Beijing, the destruction of the main theatres resulting from the Boxer Uprising necessitated a new system of presenting jingju to the public, which wanted new styles, content and even modes of presentation.

The great star Tan Xinpei (1847–1917), who was actually a student of Cheng Chenggang's, was the leading actor of the time. In many ways highly traditionalist, he took no interest in the revolution and performed for high officials and even royalty, being the favourite actor of the Empress Dowager Cixi (1835–1908). On the other hand, he founded his own school of acting and, most important of all, was the star of China's first-ever motion picture, *Dingjun shan* (Mt Dingjun), made in 1905 from the jingju of the same name. Mei Lanfang (1894–1961), considered in much more detail elsewhere, had already begun his highly reformist xiqu career by 1919.

He and three other male dan dominate the history of jingju during the Republican period. These were Cheng Yanqiu (1904–58), Shang Xiaoyun (1900–76) and Xun Huisheng (1900–68), and with Mei Lanfang they are known as the 'four great famous male dan' (*sida mingdan*). Their careers and contribution to the reform of theatre in China are considered elsewhere.

Outside Beijing, the Cantonese opera (yueju) developed during these decades in ways rather special for the traditional Chinese theatre. Through its popularity in the commercialized British colony of Hong Kong, it adopted western influence, such as the addition of instruments like the saxophone, guitar and violin. Above all other forms of xiqu it spread overseas to Southeast Asia, North America and elsewhere, because the areas of its greatest popularity in China itself were also the main source of the Chinese diaspora at the time.

New xiqu styles continued to evolve. The most famous was the Shaoxing Opera (*yueju* in Chinese, but with a different first character from the homophone that means Cantonese opera). Arising from a small-scale folk form, accompanied only by a clapper, in Zhejiang Province's Shaoxing area in the late Qing, it was introduced into Shanghai in 1916 and there added stringed and other musical instruments to the accompaniment and more complexities to the makeup and performance. The feature for which it became most famous, namely all-female troupes, followed later, but the introduction into Shanghai signalled the transition to urban theatre.

Other than those involved in theatre reform (see Chinese section in Chapter 22), the most important new genre of xiqu in the twentieth century was the 'newly written historical drama' (*xinbian lishi ju*). Using themes from the imperial past and music in the style of the xiqu, known script-writers and composers designed these dramas to fill an afternoon or evening. Not episodic like the traditional items, newly written historical dramas followed the modern form of rising to a climax with a *denoument*. Newly written items can belong to any of the regional styles.

The People's Republic of China

Although originating in the Republican period, the 'newly written historical dramas' reached their height under the People's Republic after 1949. Early items were deliberately highly politicized to take account of the Chinese Communist Party (CCP) line. A very good example is the jingju *Yangmen nüjiang* (Women Generals of the Yang Family), a 1960 work set in the eleventh century and showing women contributing patriotically to the nation, even as military leaders. During the Cultural Revolution (1966–76), the form was banned and replaced by Jiang

Qing's model dramas (*yangbanxi*), which are considered in more detail separately. In the 1980s, however, they revived strongly, with many very good items produced. An author notable for his work in the *chuanju* (Sichuan opera) is Wei Minglun (b. 1940), whose newly written historical drama *Bashan xiucai* (The Scholar of Bashan, 1983) brought him national fame.

The CCP has normally patronized traditional theatre enthusiastically, setting up troupes belonging to the regional styles. However, during the Cultural Revolution, all traditional themes were banned, causing an interruption in the popular memory. When the tradition was revived in the late 1970s, young people found the old dramas unfamiliar, tedious and lacking in action. Tastes are also changing rapidly as China modernizes, making people more interested in the present and in western patterns than in history, even that of quite recent times. The result has been a great decline in the popularity of traditional theatre among young people, with troupes finding it very difficult to make ends meet.

The twenty-first century has seen a few attempts to revive traditional Chinese operas. UNESCO has supported kunqu, jingju and Cantonese opera, while relevant professional troupes have done their best to introduce these traditional arts to students, especially those at university. Meanwhile, traditional theatre items have become a part of the tourist experience, which lends an important commercial incentive to the survival of this spectacular art.

Ideology of theatre: purpose, censorship

Though theatre originates in ritual and to some extent retains its role in religious ceremonies, the weight of opinion among thinkers in imperial China was to welcome theatre 'as an important participant in and contributor to a well-ordered society' (Fei 1999: x). Some societies have regarded the whole notion of artificially representing a make-believe world as inappropriate or even immoral. However, the Chinese love to watch representations of life as a form of entertainment or relaxation. They regard theatre as a way to be amused and to dream of good things, such as love and prosperity; they can be taken out of their daily humdrum existence though watching stage performances.

A way to spread a message

There have also been other purposes in theatre, such as promoting good morals among the people. Some Confucianists and dramatists specifically regarded theatre as a way of instilling Confucian moral virtues into audiences. Early-Ming laws specifically promoted values such as filial piety, obedience to the state and women's chastity. The Qing emperors went even further than the Ming in their advocacy of Confucian moral values, including through theatre, perhaps because as Manchus they wanted to show loyalty to what had originally been, and remained in essence, a Han ethical system.

A related purpose was to teach people about their own history. Since Chinese plays are set in China, and a great many take episodes from history, they can promote a particular view of the events they are representing on stage. Over the centuries certain characters have established their reputations as benign, heroic, tyrannical or evil. For ordinary people, who were usually illiterate, the theatre was an excellent way of learning about their own history, appreciating its importance, and imbibing the values that theatrical representations of historical figures inevitably impart.

The idea of using drama to promote one's own regime is not new to the modern era. Early in the Qing dynasty, the Manchu emperors organized troupes of entertainers to perform in the Beijing area to try to persuade ordinary people of the advantages of their rule. The Qianlong Emperor, one of whose main characteristics was that he 'loved theatre, music, and grand celebrations' (Elliott 2009: 167), wanted to use the theatre to glorify his empire, and especially his own achievements, to his own people and to foreign delegations.

In 1902 the great reformist thinker Liang Qichao (1873–1929) proposed that reviving the nation necessitated reform of drama and the novel. His reason was that these art forms wielded immense influence over the minds, hearts and character of ordinary people. Liang's argument was an early attempt to politicize drama in a way that has the feeling of the modern era, and it was to become central to the twentieth century.

The specifically religious purpose of drama is probably weaker in China than in several other civilizations. Yet it is worth mentioning that temples were traditionally the sites of theatrical performance, many having inbuilt stages. The content was sometimes religious, such as plays that featured the way the virtuous Mulian saved his mother from hell, but it was no problem to perform entirely secular operas in temples or on temple stages.

Probably no group has done more to use theatre to push a political line than the CCP. They did this extensively for patriotic purposes during the War Against Japan (1937–45) and again during the People's Republic. This phenomenon reached its height during the Cultural Revolution, which saw the official adoption of a theory based on class struggle that advocated theatre directly propagating CCP ideology (see more detail in Chapter 22).

Censorship

Despite a generally non-condemnatory attitude towards theatrical performances, Chinese history shows no lack of attempts on the part of authorities to censor the theatre. Rural popular folk shows were often rather raunchy and authorities often left them alone, preferring to turn a blind eye rather than meddling, given how common and popular these performances were. However, if any member of the official classes attended he was likely to make sure that there was no going outside the bounds of propriety. Also, urban performances were somewhat easier to censor than rural, simply because official control was tighter in the cities than in the countryside. The Sichuanese actor Wei Changsheng (1744–1802), whose entry into Beijing in 1779 created such an impact, was actually forced to leave the capital because authorities regarded his acting as infringing the rules of sexual propriety.

During both the Ming and Qing, edicts were issued against the novel *Shuihu zhuan* (Water Margin) and dramas based on it because they were about rebels against authority. Qianlong began a literary inquisition of books in 1772 and in the late 1770s set up a commission that, despite his love of theatre, extended it to drama. His edict of December 1780 stated: 'It has now occurred to me that the scripts of drama are not necessarily without seditious passages. For example, stories based on events during the late Ming and the early Qing must have borne some reference to the current dynasty' (cited in Ye 2012: 183). Though he noted the Suzhou and Yangzhou area of Jiangsu Province as an area where such dramas would be concentrated – one thinks of *Peach Blossom Fan* as a famous example of what he had in mind – the inquisition was to be national. It involved banning particular dramas and expurgating seditious and offensive passages from others.

Censorship continued and to some extent worsened during the twentieth century. The People's Republic's Ministry of Culture banned items it believed unpatriotic, lewd, or in other ways 'unhealthy'. During the Cultural Revolution censorship was probably worse than at any other time in Chinese theatre history. Not only were traditional items banned, but only a small number of models were allowed performance. Although censorship eased enormously during the reform period since the late 1970s, it continues to affect 'newly written historical dramas', with authors careful not to overstep a line that is occasionally quite unclear.

The content of traditional Chinese theatre

The main distinction in the content of traditional Chinese theatre is that between *wen* (civil) and *wu* (military), not between tragedy and comedy. 'Civil' items are about domestic matters, family life, marriage and love affairs. 'Military' items are about battles and wars, and include a great deal of fighting, represented by actions such as complex gymnastics and skilful catching of spears. Women are much better represented in the civil items, but there are several famous female military heroes.

With the exception of plays on strongly Buddhist themes, virtually all pre-twentieth-century operas were set in China in the remote or fairly distant past. A great many deal with historical figures and there is some connection with reality. Among many examples, I cite only two. In *Peach Blossom Fan*, events in many of the scenes are specifically dated (1643 to 1645). The love affair between the Tang Emperor Xuanzong and his concubine Yang Guifei that is the focus of Hong Shen's *The Palace of Eternal Youth* actually took place.

In general, the Chinese prefer a happy ending. Light folk plays may emphasize problems in relations between men and women, but overall they are light-hearted and comic, and end happily. Of course, there are items with sad endings, but tragedy in the sense of the hero struggling unsuccessfully with a fatal flaw is not a feature of the Chinese tradition. Bad or negative characters will likely get their just deserts in the end in the form of punishment.

Storytelling is a very ancient art in China. It is the basis of many dramas and novels, the latter themselves being a major source for regional operas and the sophisticated genres such as jingju. An interesting point to follow from this is that the novels and the plays based on them tend to be episodic. Each chapter can be made into a short play, lasting less than an hour. The characterization of each figure is stark and simple, lacking complexity, and does not develop much. What tends to be lacking in the stories of Chinese traditional dramas is the tightly structured story rising to a climax and ending with a denouement.

Many early 'southern operas' of the Song were love stories or involved issues relating to marriage. The oldest extant drama script in Chinese literature is *Zhang Xie zhuangyuan* (Top Graduate Zhang Xie), perhaps from the early thirteenth century. It tells of a scholar with a poor wife; he comes top in the official examinations and is offered the prime minister's daughter in marriage. He accepts her, disowning his previous wife. However, his new wife dies of grief, the previous wife comes to court and exposes her husband's inhumane treatment of her, but this does not prevent reconciliation between them and a happy ending. The theme of the man who deserts his wife for one of a higher social status after doing well in the examinations is a typical one in traditional Chinese theatre. There are of course variants on the theme, with the wronged wife sometimes seeing her husband taken to law and punished.

The Yuan zaju are various in their content. Love interest, featuring virtuous women, courtesans or even nuns, is a very common theme. Wang Shifu's *The Story of the West Wing* is a typical love story with an ultimately happy ending, although with many vicissitudes along the way. Guan Hanqing's *Injustice to Dou E* is an example of a noble and self-sacrificing woman who, to save her mother-in-law from torture, confesses to a crime she never committed, is executed and then posthumously cleared through the occurrence of unnatural phenomena, including a midsummer snow-fall. Although the heroine dies unfairly, heaven can restore the balance of justice.

Part of the story is a court case. Courtroom dramas are common in Yuan zaju and in later theatre. An especially popular figure is Judge Bao. Actually, Bao Zheng (999–1062) was a real historical figure, and became lionized in Yuan and other dramas and in tradition as an icon of justice. He is presented as benevolent as well as just, and as detective as well as judge, always able to solve the cases he confronts.

Many Yuan dramas are about high politics and warfare, featuring items definitely belonging in the 'military' category. The warrior-heroes of the Three Kingdoms period of the third century are the protagonists of many Yuan dramas, as well as later plays. They became the source of the novel *Sanguo yanyi* (The Romance of the Three Kingdoms), which was itself to be a major source of plays of all genres.

Kunqu, like preceding genres originating in the south, tend to feature 'civil' drama over 'military'. Tang Xianzu's 1598 drama *Peony Pavilion* was mentioned above as an outstanding example of Ming dynasty drama. It illustrates very well the theme of love and the happy ending. Its main proponent is Du Liniang, the daughter of a stern Confucian bureaucrat. She falls in love in a dream, dies of love, but comes back to life through the courage and devotion of her lover; in the end he tops the official examinations and they marry.

In *The Palace of Eternal Youth* the Emperor Xuanzong's beloved Yang Guifei is blamed for the outbreak of a major rebellion in 755. When they flee towards Sichuan, the troops demand her death, and the emperor commands her to commit suicide. Although the ending is happy, with the lovers reunited in the moon, this drama is one of the items that have tended strongly to put a Confucian interpretation on these unhappy events, colouring Chinese views of them throughout the ages.

On the other hand, the love affair in Kong Shangren's *Peach Blossom Fan* ends sadly: after many vicissitudes the lovers are finally reunited, only to be told that the circumstances of the world in the early Qing dictate that they should separate, which they obediently do. This ending perhaps reflects Kong's support for the 'reason (*li*)' school of thought in theatre, as against that expressing 'feeling (*qing*)', as discussed above.

Kunqu dramas are very long, and though the great majority of scenes are 'civil', there are a few 'military' ones. The converse is true of pihuang and clapper operas, which tended much more to the 'military' than did the kunqu and other southern dramas. In addition, they broke down the long novels and earlier dramas into much shorter episodes that could be presented individually to audiences, most of whom were illiterate. Characterization is stark, and excitement is more evident than tenderness.

The records suggest that items performed in Beijing in the late eighteenth century had mainly female protagonists, belonging to the 'civil' category. However, during the nineteenth century, the Four Great Anhui Companies and stars such as Cheng Changgeng changed the emphasis strongly towards heroic drama and items in which war dominated. Though the content of the developed jingju included stories from earlier kunqu dramas, its most important source was novels, among which the main one was *The Romance of the Three Kingdoms*. The main interest is not love but loyalty versus treachery, courage versus cowardice, strategy versus deception, and overcoming tyranny. According to one specialist (Guo 2006: 135–67), Judge Bao dramas had come to represent a thirst for increased equality before the law (Figure 2.3). By the nature of its themes, jingju became much more male-centred, with the 'military' dramas predominating.

In the twentieth and twenty-first centuries, the content of traditional Chinese theatre has shown some continuity but much change. Almost all items, including those newly written, continue to be set in China in a past age. However, although purely aesthetic items exist, theatre is incomparably more likely to promote a conscious social or political theme than it used to do.

Mei Lanfang exemplifies both patterns. *Guifei zuijiu* (The Drunken Beauty), which is about the misery of Yang Guifei when stood down for a banquet by Emperor Tang Minghuang, shows brilliant choreography in feigning drunkenness, while *Niehai bolan* (Waves in a Sea of Sin) is much more direct in denouncing the evils of prostitution and the low status of women and pushing for reform.

Figure 2.3 Judge Bao from jingju *Da longpao* (The Beating of the Dragon Robe).
(Photo by Alexandra Bonds)

In the People's Republic, many items revised traditional items and stories to give them a more politically correct slant. A good example is the jingju and love story *Baishe zhuan* (The White Snake) about a snake who turns into a beautiful woman and marries a scholar. The monk who tries to destroy their happiness is portrayed as evil, while the snake is characterized as loving and virtuous.

Quite new themes are also very common, especially those written in the 1980s and since, but still tend strongly to illustrate a political or social theme. One extraordinary example is *Pan Jinlian*, a Sichuan opera by Wei Minglun, about the woman Pan Jinlian who kills her husband. The item takes the form of a law case with people from around the world giving their testimony on Pan's actions. It was highly controversial in placing the blame not so much on Pan herself but on the patriarchal system that oppressed women.

Several other items extolled famous Chinese of the past in political ways. A good illustration is Guo Qihong's *Sima Qian*, about the famous historian of that name of the first and second centuries BCE who compiled the first of China's standard histories, the *Shiji* (Records of the Historian). This item, a jingju, shows how Sima Qian suffered castration for supporting the cause of a defeated general, but overcame all difficulties to write what many consider the greatest of all Chinese traditional histories. Another excellent newly written item is *Cao Cao yu Yang Xiu* (Cao Cao and Yang Xiu), a Shanghai work dating from 1988, which dealt with an incident in the life of the tyrant Cao Cao (155–220) and represented the relations of political masters with intellectuals. This item became politically sensitive, because many saw a representation of Mao Zedong in the characterization of Cao Cao.

Performance

We turn next to some of the main conventions of the Chinese theatre, which are similar to the genres in showing great diversity, richness and inventiveness. They indicate a synthetic approach to theatre, combining song, musical accompaniment, dance, gesture and mime, with strong emphasis on makeup and costume. The important aspects of music and costume are separately considered and omitted here.

The stage on which the performance takes place is square and faces the audience on three sides. It is fairly bare, with a carpet and usually a table and two chairs of traditional style. There is a curtain at the back, but not at the front. Actors enter on stage right and exit on the left. However, the modern 'newly arranged historical dramas' of the People's Republic depart radically from traditional patterns, with complex scenery typically projected on the stage, properties often extensive, and a curtain at the front.

Role types

The use of role types in China dates back to the Tang dynasty. Both the nanxi and the Yuan zaju had role types that are different but essentially similar to all later genres of Chinese theatre. There are developments and changes in the Ming dynasty kunqu and in the various regional forms.

In jingju there are four main role types. These are male (*sheng*), female (*dan*), painted face (*jing*) and clown (*chou*). These categories indicate type of voice as well as acting techniques and the character of the person represented. Sheng are close to life, but jing are larger than life.

Each of the four role types is divided into subcategories, and these can be immensely complex. *Laosheng* (literally 'old male characters') are mature men, such as statesmen, *wusheng* ('military male characters') are the male warriors, while *xiaosheng* (young men), who sing falsetto, are figures such as scholar lovers. Among women, the *qingyi* (literally 'black clothing') are the demure and dignified women, *huadan* (flower *dan*) are more light-hearted and often flirts, *laodan* are the matriarchs, while *wudan* are the female warriors. On the whole, masks are quite rare in Chinese theatre, with the tradition requiring patterns and colour in the painting of the face of jing to represent character. There is often a judgement implied, with sheng and dan usually positive characters and bad or evil ones generally confined to the jing or chou categories (Figure 2.4).

Because from the Ming dynasty onwards public acting troupes were either overwhelmingly male or female, almost all the former, the boy or man who performed female roles became a major phenomenon in the traditional Chinese theatre. By no means exclusive to China, it is found in many parts of the world, usually associated with social taboos against the appearance of women on the stage. In China, these male female impersonators were called *nandan* (literally 'male dan') and became an important part of the history of acting in China. One of the most important actors in China's theatrical history was Wei Changsheng whose first appearance in Beijing in 1779 made the city the most important in China's theatre for the first time in centuries and marked an early stage in jingju's development. Even more important was Mei Lanfang, the most distinguished and famous actor in all China's theatre history. Under the People's Republic, the training of nandan has been discouraged, because authorities believe women should play female roles. A few nandan still perform, but the number has become vanishingly small.

Comic figures are generally clowns (chou) but the converse does not hold, since not all chou are comic. It is lack of dignity that characterizes them. They talk directly to the audience. Most clown characters are male, but a few are female. In the early mentions of the chou in the Song dynasty 'southern drama', the chou was characterized by a face daubed with black powder. However, in many recent styles the clown is immediately recognizable through the white patch on and around the nose.

For audiences used to divisions such as soprano, tenor, baritone, contralto and bass, these Chinese role types are very striking. Of course the *dan* sings falsetto, whether the artist is a man or a woman, but there is no real equivalent to categories such as tenor or bass. Indeed, one feature of Chinese musical theatre is *the lack* of the really deep voice.

The social context

It is obvious from the use of performances in rituals in ancient China that theatre has, from earliest times, been tightly interwoven with society. In the spring, a drama could mark making entreaties to the gods for a good harvest and in the autumn was a good way of giving thanks. Festivals were occasions for theatre performances, which could express joy or whatever emotions the particular festival required. This interrelationship between theatre and society applied to all levels of society, from imperial courts to commoners.

Beginning at the top of society we find that, though emperors and the aristocracy might be quite censorious about the theatre of the common people, they were frequently enthusiasts themselves. The court of the Mongol Yuan dynasty patronized drama as well as the composition of zaju. In 1390, the Ming emperor Zhu Yuanzhang (the Hongwu Emperor, reigned 1368–98) set up a eunuch agency to organize court theatre. It played both the Yuan zaju and southern drama, and, from the sixteenth century on, kunqu as well.

Court theatre reached its height during the Qing. Kangxi set up a special agency, initially for his personal entertainment, but it was greatly expanded under Qianlong. The actors were eunuchs of the court, but until 1827, some were brought from the south to perform and teach. In 1860, the Xianfeng Emperor had actors brought from the city of Beijing in celebration of

Figure 2.4 The character Liu Jinding from *Zhulin ji* (The Ruse of the Bamboo Forest), a jingju wudan (female warrior).

(Photo by Alexandra Bonds)

his thirtieth birthday, but only temporarily. However, when in 1884 the Empress Dowager Cixi brought actors to court as part of her own fiftieth birthday celebrations, they were at the head of a stream that persisted until virtually the end of the dynasty. Her favourite actor was Tan Xinpei, who frequently performed at court.

The great majority of court performances in the early days were kunqu. The actors that came to court in honour of Xianfeng's thirtieth birthday were jingju artists, as were those the Empress Dowager introduced from 1884 on. However, it was quite unprecedented for the court to favour an entertainment associated with the common people of the city. What this implies is that the patronage of the late Qing court contributed to the rise of the Peking Opera, which means that the court could take some credit for this development, which was so important for Chinese theatre.

Although the Qing emperors had drama performed at court for their personal entertainment, they also used it for ritual purposes, especially Qianlong. Among the various types of ritual that could occasion drama performances were the 'auspicious rites' (jili), the 'martial rites' (junli) and 'protocol rites' (binli). One writer (Ye 2012: 2) states that 'Qianlong provided a complete set of ritual dramas, in fact a complete set of palace rituals, for succeeding emperors to follow'. Another type of occasion that could be honoured by a drama performance was the visit of a foreign dignitary. A well-known specific example was the 1793 embassy of the British Lord George Macartney (1737–1806). Though he did not like them much, he and his embassy were treated to some spectacular drama performances, including in the emperor's summer residence in Jehol.

Moving down the social ladder, we find that theatre performances also took place in the mansions of the rich. During the Ming and Qing dynasties, many members of the educated or social elite had specially trained private troupes and would put on performances for personal enjoyment or to entertain friends. A man from an elite class who invited friends to dinner might seat them on three sides of a square space within which actors could perform. It was normally kunqu that received favour at such private performances. However, in nineteenth-century Beijing the elite often preferred jingju and could hire special small theatres where there were provisions for tea and food appropriate to a party.

In the major teahouse theatres of Qing dynasty Beijing, the audience was stratified into rich and poor, but there were at least some from the educated elite. Both in Beijing and in other parts of the country, the common people usually got their theatrical entertainment through open-air temple or market-square performances. These featured regional theatre styles that were definitely popular theatre, and despised by the educated elite. If educated men attended such performances along with the people, as occasionally happened, they could expect criticism from their social equals.

Another area exemplifying social restrictiveness was that women were barred from public performances. Numerous government edicts warned that for men and women to mix together at theatre performances was a prescription for moral disaster and sexual licence. These prohibitions appear to have been less rigidly enforced in the south than the north, but applied everywhere.

The twentieth century saw the breaking down of the rules preventing the elite from watching performances together with the common people and against audiences with both women and men. Private performances in mansions sank in number along with the decline of the kunqu. The May Fourth Movement accelerated the social change that allowed women access to theatre, but the process had begun before then. In Beijing, females at first sat in separate parts of the theatre, but from 1924 together with males.

The actor

All through Chinese history, the performing profession was a disreputable one holding a low social status. Confucius is said to have demanded capital punishment for a group of jesters, singers and dwarfs on the grounds that they were commoners who beguiled their lords. Still, there were variations according to period in the extent to which actors were held in contempt by society.

A comparatively good period for actors was the Yuan dynasty, when performing families attracted some admiration. The situation worsened when the Ming dynasty came to power and puritanical Confucianism tightened its grip over society and family life. Actors were accused of beguiling decent people by presenting unreal images and of sexual immorality through association with prostitution, either male or female. Another reason for their low social image was that wandering troupes were quite common, especially at times when festivals required the services of actors in the countryside, and people of no fixed address could not count on any legal protection or social respect.

However, the nineteenth century saw the rise of major theatre families in Beijing, with sons inheriting their father's skills. Some of the most important stars of the time came from these theatre families. The nineteenth century was the age when stars like Cheng Changgeng graced the Beijing stage. This could only exercise a benign effect on the status of the actor in general. The reforms of the late Qing and succeeding period also helped to give the actor a small modicum of respect, especially in the cities.

In the twentieth and twenty-first centuries, though contempt for the performing profession is not quite dead, the social status of actors has risen greatly. Stars like Mei Lanfang greatly intensified the process already begun with Cheng Changgeng. The People's Republic made a point of patronizing actors and actresses, making their profession one important to national politics and society. Mei Lanfang and Cheng Yanqiu were even chosen as members of the National People's Congress.

Entry into the acting profession; training

Ways of entry to the kunqu acting profession have varied with time. In imperial times, court eunuchs were designated for training in the official theatre bureau. Private householders could hire teachers to train their house-slaves or do so themselves. A major factor in the growth of jingju in the nineteenth century was a kind of slave system that saw the purchase of boys from their fathers on contract in several southern provinces to be taken north to Beijing and trained as actors. It is important to note that, however cruel the contract system, the boys never suffered castration, a practice restricted among actors to those at court.

Jingju troupes had training schools attached to them, the function of which was to provide future actors and teach the boys from the south, with the masters teaching individual disciples the complex singing, musical and acting arts. The early twentieth century saw the establishment of several private training schools for actors, the most important being the Xiliancheng in 1904, renamed Fuliancheng in 1912. Discipline was very rigid and included severe beatings among punishments. However, the general life conditions were probably somewhat better in the training schools of the twentieth century than in the previous system. The main method of training remained imitation of the teacher and learning his instructions by heart.

Under the People's Republic a formal system of training schools for traditional theatre actors has been established. Although schools of this kind were not unprecedented, it was the first time that a consolidated system existed for the training of actors and artists. These schools maintain strict standards of performance, but also ensure general knowledge so that actors are no longer illiterate. Entry is open both to boys and girls, and competition is keen.

Summary and conclusion

From the above, the following appear to be the main characteristics of Chinese traditional theatre.

The classifications normal for traditional Chinese theatre are quite different from those of western opera. For instance, content is divided into *wen* (civil) and *wu* (military), not tragedy and comedy, with 'civil' items putting the focus on love, marriage and domestic affairs, and the 'military' ones on war and heroism. The stories come from old novels, dramas and long poems.

The types of character are divided into *sheng* (male), *dan* (female), *jing* (painted face) and *chou* (clown), not tenor, soprano, baritone and bass. Each of these is subdivided into various categories. Gestures, actions, makeup and costumes are complex. They follow the conventions of the particular type of character and stress the aesthetic, making no attempt to be realistic.

The oldest form for which there is a substantial surviving corpus of works is the zaju (variety drama) of the period running from about 1260 to 1360. There is no surviving music for this form, but it has definitely entered the Chinese literary canon. Another type of theatre to become recognized in the literary canon is kunqu, a highly elite genre dating from the sixteenth century. Both variety drama and kunqu have spawned some very famous dramatists, the best known for the former being Guan Hanqing (flourished second half of the thirteenth century) and for the latter Tang Xianzu. Among specific items, the most famous variety drama is probably Wang Shifu's *The Story of the West Wing*, which dates probably from around the turn of the fourteenth century; among kunqu, *Peony Pavilion* by Tang Xianzu is pre-eminent.

The types of popular (non-elite) traditional Chinese theatre are numerous and tend strongly to the locally based. Among these the most important and famous is the jingju, which evolved from the late eighteenth and through the nineteenth century. One feature of these regional operas is that they are rather low in social status. They are known not through their dramatists or musical composers but through the famous actors who performed them and the troupes to which they belonged. Before the modern era, probably the most famous of Chinese actors was Cheng Changgeng, a performer of old male roles, who is sometimes called 'the father of the Peking Opera' for his work in developing the acting styles and in moulding the various theatrical arts into an integrated whole. In the modern era the most distinguished of all jingju actors, and the most famous domestically and internationally of all Chinese performers of any period, was Mei Lanfang, a performer of female impersonator roles.

Chinese ideologies were quite open to drama, raising no objection to people enjoying themselves at theatrical performances. On the other hand, various regimes attempted to use the theatre for political or moral purposes. Some tried to promote their own rule through the theatre. In particular, censorship has been very common throughout the ages. Authorities often kept an eye out for performances they believed subversive politically or offensive from a moral point of view.

This emphasizes the tight connection between society and theatre. Authorities believed that performances could influence the people's views and behaviour. The popular theatre was also a regular companion for festivals and festivities, and for thanksgiving to the gods. It played a significant role in the lives of the people and was the main way they learnt about their own history.

Actors were on the whole a very low group within society. Yet many were also real artists and made major contribution to Chinese culture. Among actors a distinctive group was the males who mastered the art of playing the roles of women. Although this cross–gender performance became associated with homosexuality and was a factor making for the low status of the acting profession within society, it also gave rise to a highly aesthetic art that not only became one of the most famous aspects of the Chinese theatre but also spawned the greatest and most famous of all Chinese actors of any period: Mei Lanfang.

And finally Chinese traditional theatre is noted for the degree to which it integrates the arts. The good actor needs not only to be able to sing and act properly, but to look the part and to have good command over other arts such as costuming, makeup and gesture. This integration is not necessarily a given in the history of opera. For instance, in the operas of Richard Wagner (1813–83), the demands on the singers are such that during some eras artists have not necessarily looked fully suitable for the role they are singing. At the end of *Götterdämmerung* (The Twilight of the Gods), the last of his great cycle *Der Ring des Niebelungen* (The Ring of the Niebelung), the lead soprano Brünnhilde sings music of extreme beauty, grandeur and depth. But some Brünnhildes able to meet the musical demands have been too overweight or not beautiful enough to look ideal for the part. Although acceptable in Wagner, this would not be possible in the Chinese traditional theatre.

Bibliography

Brandon, James R. (ed.) (1993) *The Cambridge Guide to Asian Theatre*, Cambridge: Cambridge University Press.

Dolby, William (1976) *A History of Chinese Drama*, London: Paul Elek.

Elliott, Mark (2009) *Emperor Qianlong, Son of Heaven, Man of the world*, New York: Longman.

Fei, Faye Chunfang (ed. and trans) (1999) *Chinese Theories of Theater and Performance from Confucius to the Present*, Ann Arbor: The University of Michigan Press.

Guo Jingrui (2006) *The Features and Significance of Jingju (Beijing Opera) Plays (1790–1911)*, Hong Kong: Tin Ma.

Hsu Tao-Ching (1985) *The Chinese Conception of the Theatre*, Seattle: University of Washington Press.

Leiter, Samuel L. (ed.) (2007) *Encyclopedia of Asian Theatre*, 2 vols, Westport, CT: Greenwood.

Li Ruru (2010) *The Soul of Beijing Opera: Theatrical Creativity and Continuity in the Changing World*, Hong Kong: Hong Kong University Press.

Li, Siu Leung (2003) *Cross-Dressing in Chinese Opera*, Hong Kong: Hong Kong University Press.

Mackerras, Colin (1972) *The Rise of the Peking Opera, 1770–1870, Social Aspects of the Theatre in Manchu China*, Oxford: Clarendon Press.

—— (1975) *The Chinese Theatre in Modern Times from 1840 to the Present Day*, London: Thames & Hudson.

—— (ed.) (1983) *Chinese Theater from its Origins to the Present Day*, Honolulu: University of Hawai'i Press.

—— (1990) *Chinese Drama: A Historical Survey*, Beijing: New World Press.

Scott, A. C. (1957) *The Classical Theatre of China*, London: George Allen & Unwin.

—— (1982) *Actors Are Madmen, Notes of a Theatregoer in China*, Madison: The University of Wisconsin Press.

Shen, Guangren Grant (2005) *Elite Theatre in Ming China, 1368–1644*, London: Routledge.

Shih, Chung-wen (1976) *The Golden Age of Chinese Drama: Yüan Tsa-chü*, Princeton, NJ: Princeton University Press.

Sieber, Patricia (2003) *Theaters of Desire: Authors, Readers, and the Reproduction of Early Chinese Song-Drama 1300–2000*. New York: Palgrave Macmillan.

Stock, Jonathan P. J. (2003) *Huju: Traditional Opera in Modern Shanghai*, Oxford: Oxford University Press.

Swatek, Catherine C. (2002) *Peony Pavilion Onstage: Four Centuries in the Career of a Chinese Drama*, Ann Arbor: Center for Chinese Studies, The University of Michigan.

Thorpe, Ashley (2007) *The Role of the Chou ('Clown') in Traditional Chinese Drama: Comedy, Criticism and Cosmology on the Chinese Stage*, Lewiston, NY: The Edwin Mellen Press.

Tian, Min (ed.) (2010) *China's Greatest Operatic Male Actor of Female Roles, Documenting the Life and Art of Mei Lanfang, 1894–1961*, Lewiston, NY: The Edwin Mellen Press.

—— (2010) *Mei Lanfang and the Twentieth-Century International Stage: Chinese Theatre Placed and Displaced*, New York: Palgrave Macmillan.

Wichmann, Elizabeth (1991) *Listening to Theatre: the Aural Dimension of Beijing Opera.* Honolulu: University of Hawai'i Press.

Wu Zuguang, Huang Zuolin, and Mei Shaowu (1981, 2008) *Peking Opera and Mei Lanfang, a Guide to China's Traditional Theatre and the Art of Its Great Master,* Beijing: New World Press.

Ye, Tan (2008) *Historical Dictionary of Chinese Theater,* Lanham, MD: Scarecrow Press.

Ye, Xiaoqing (2012) *Ascendant Peace in the Four Seas, Drama and the Qing Imperial Court,* Hong Kong: The Chinese University Press.

3

Traditional Japanese theatre

Jonah Salz

Japanese traditional theatre is buttressed by four pillars of classical genres: *noh*, *kyogen*, *bunraku* and *kabuki*. Sharing an unbroken history of over six centuries, they were largely codified by the eighteenth century. They coexist today at specialist stages at family, commercial and national theatres, and also at civic halls and multi-purpose theatres throughout the country and abroad. While shifting tastes have threatened them in the modern era, a knowledgeable and passionate fan base, including many amateur students, assures that these traditional genres will continue to fascinate domestic and foreign spectators and practitioners.

Early imported and native rituals and entertainment

Performers trace their art's origins to Amaterasu, the Sun Goddess, who shut herself in a cave. As told in Japan's oldest records, the eighth-century *Kojiki* and *Nihongi*, she was resentful that her brother's insults had gone unpunished. Myriad anxious gods gathered on a riverbed to deliberate. Then on an upturned barrel, in front of a tree bedecked in jewels and cloth, the goddess Ame-no-Uzume performed a dynamic and obscene dance. The gods erupted in laughter, and when the Sun Goddess peeked out, she was forcibly removed, the cave shut, and light returned to the world. Although suspect as history, the myth reveals the role of shamanism in early performing arts, gateways welcoming benevolent gods into the community.

Although noh and kyogen were the first Japanese text-based theatre forms, developed in the fourteenth century, earlier imported dance-theatre genres influenced their movement, instrumentation, rhythms and aesthetic principles.

Despite Japan's relative isolation, the Silk Road brought a continuous flow of information and goods. Beginning in the sixth century, Buddhist philosophy, Chinese ideographs, and poetry were introduced to Japan. In 612, the Korean performer Mimashi brought *gigaku*, elegant entertainment, to the imperial court. It consisted of a procession of Buddhas and dramatic enactments of legends and comic skits on Buddhist sins, featuring mythical kings, demons and animals. Yet it disappeared in the twelfth century, its only remnants 200 large, exquisitely carved, masks with powerful contorted expressions. *Gagaku*, elegant music that included dance theatre (*bugaku*), arrived via China and Korea and a school established in 701 in Nara. Over 200 court-appointed performers enacted dance-plays about legendary battles of Indian kings and beasts, and other dramatic scenes, drawing upon music and dance from China and Korea, and later those of southern India and Vietnam. By the twelfth century gagaku had become thoroughly Japanese, yet ceased active development by the seventeenth century with the decline of imperial control and rise of samurai power. Lacking dialogue or dramatic elements, bugaku dances are still performed as stately solos or group dances of serene geometries on raised platforms within Tokyo's imperial palace and a few temples.

These genres flourished alongside native performance in court, cities and villages. Theatrical entertainments were a vital activity for the medieval world: expressions of ritual devotion, community solidarity, social criticism and aesthetic entertainment. Seasonal, shamanistic ritual performances for the gods were given at annual court ceremonies (*mikagura*). Shrines and temples sponsored *sato kagura* dance and ritual performances in towns and villages throughout the Middle Ages to delight the Shinto gods, attract believers or proselytize Buddhist teachings. Recounting legendary miracles and saints' lives, they also included secular comic tales and romantic adventures, and fantastically acrobatic lion dances. Dramatic narratives (*katari*), first of religious miracles or origin stories (*kōshaku*) to the beat of drum or fan, then of martial bravery to biwa lute accompaniment (*Heikebushi*), were performed at court, temples and tours. *Shirabyōshi* female dancers dressed as men performed lively, rhythmic dances to popular songs, drum and flute. Many early entertainers came from the outcaste ghetto, where inter-genre mingling occurred. The continued popularity of singers and dancers, both female and male, in the capitals of Nara and then Kyoto, and on local tours – itinerant entertainers were near-synonymous with prostitution – created a highly skilled professional class of performers. They sought patronage from high and low, some even gaining great status as emperors' concubines.

Whether ritually efficacious or secularly entertaining, these early performances demonstrate dramaturgic and mise-en-scène continuities that can be found in later genres:

1 Spectators are separated from performers playing on a square, raised stage, the pathway to it symbolizing a journey or visitation from the Other world.
2 An open space without curtains or walls, the stage features spatial hierarchies distinguishing role types.
3 Rites follow a symbolic structure of welcoming the Other (stranger, god or demon), entertaining them with song and dance, before sending them off.
4 Performances are gender-specific, with masks or headgear employed for cross-dressing, and include dramatic onstage transformations.
5 Masks or neutral faces force expression to the entire body.
6 Dances with hand-held objects (fans, spears, umbrellas) are presented frontally, featuring circles and stamps.
7 Language interweaves archaic and colloquial dialogue, court poetry and popular song.
8 Music and song support and accent dramatic action.
9 Vocal and gestural patterns (*kata*) are prescribed, repeated with variations in new contexts, transposed whole to new works or subsequent genres.
10 Multiple variations on similar plots are performed, sometimes on the same programme, with the serious drama followed by a parody or slapstick version.
11 Strict codes are observed by genre, but plots and stage conventions of older or contemporary genres are promiscuously adapted.
12 Playfulness with words, scatological and obscene gestures, and amusing stories garner laughter and joy beloved by the gods.
13 Short scenes are assembled into a varied programme, with an accelerating pace.

Noh: masked, lyric dance-drama

Noh is lyric, masked dance theatre performed continuously for over half a millennium, in turn as popular entertainment, martial ceremony and elite pastime. Texts date back over 650 years; some masks are even older; its current repertoire of approximately 250 plays and its performance structure and style were established over 300 years ago. Kyogen is its comic cousin, employing stylized pantomime and rhythmic banter to ridicule the foibles of quotidian life in medieval Japan. Coupled on programmes exclusively since the fifteenth century, noh-kyogen has been consolidated and preserved within designated artistic families. Nōgaku (noh and kyogen), perhaps the world's oldest extant theatre form, was designated in UNESCO's first selection as Intangible World Cultural Treasures in 2001. Noh's minimalist ghost-plays, accompanied by kyogen slapstick and satiric interludes, have fascinated vanguard western poets, playwrights and directors for over a century.

From riverbank beggar to palace artist

Noh's origins are obscure, a synthesis of religious rites and popular entertainments. The Chinese *sangaku* variety entertainments imported in the eighth century eventually became native *sarugaku*; *sarugaku noh* was one segment of a quasi-circus spectacle that included juggling, acrobatics and dances. It was performed at temporary stages set up in shrines and temples, but also on invitation to noble homes. Even older than noh was the ancient *Shikisamban* ritual, performed by specialist troupes. The dignified old man blesses the harvest, followed by the joyful, stamping dance by Sambasō old man, preparing the ground and planting seedlings. *Furyū* were dialogue-based skits describing the origins of temples, accompanied by noisy percussion, with gaudy costumes and properties. *Dengaku* were originally rustic performances played alongside rice-planting ceremonies, obscenely comic skits, song and dance, welcoming the harvest. Sangaku, sarugaku and dengaku were interchangeable terms for the same dance and drama entertainments from the eleventh to fourteenth centuries. They became popular in the capital of Kyoto, where they shared both repertoire and festival stages.

Eventually, noh synthesized these syncretic contemporary song and dance genres into a clear dramatic structure, then raised the sketches beyond the level of mere festival entertainment. Kan'nami (1333–1384) is credited with introducing into noh the *kusemai*, popular dances to rhythmic drum music. He combined *shushi* exorcism rituals by *yamabushi* (mountain priests), *koutabushi* short popular songs, and *soko*, songs popular among military clans and Kyoto populace, as well as Tendai Buddhist chant. Playwrights culled themes from legends and literature, concentrated into dramatic episodes, enhanced through poetry and dance.

At a performance in Kyoto in 1374, Kan'nami's eleven-year old son Zeami Motokiyo (1363?–1443?) met the 15-year-old shōgun Ashikaga Yoshimitsu (1358–1408), who immediately recognized his beauty and talent. Scandalously, the 'riverbank beggar' actor Zeami was brought into the court, studying Chinese poetry and Japanese waka, history and Zen Buddhist philosophy. Zeami wrote and performed refined plays based on concentrated dramatic situations re-enacted by warriors and beautiful women, or their spirits. Although dengaku noh performers and his father Kan'ami had gained success through naturalistic *monomane* (imitation), and other playwrights through dramatic dialogue and plot twists, Zeami insisted that *yūgen*, mysterious grace or profound elegance, be achieved through a measured approach to a play's structure. Rather than spectacle or realism, Zeami made external manifestation of an inner turmoil or single theme noh's highest goal. Zeami also invented and refined the two-act play, where an ambiguous character in the first act reveals herself in the second as a ghost or spirit, re-enacting a prior, traumatic event to bring closure.

Zeami was an astounding actor and gifted playwright – fifty of his plays survive, sixteen in manuscript form – securing support from the shōgun for his company and establishing it as pre-eminent among rivals. However, he is best known today for his twenty-odd 'notes on performance.' These secret treatises share advice born of long experience, intended for transmission to one chief disciple in his Kanze troupe.

Zeami displays both an actor's understanding of technical skills and directorial appreciation for how spectators will be affected. Particularly important is Zeami's notion of *hana*, flower, the charming charisma naturally apparent in young boys which, if nurtured properly, may continue blossoming at any age. He wrote that the full range of characters in hundreds of plays could be enacted through the proper mixture of three role types: the female, the warrior and the old man. Although this may appear too rigorous a template for successful performance, Zeami emphasized the necessity of adapting to particular audiences – samurai, aristocrats or rustics – and situations – festivals, rainy days, long programmes and latecomers. Zeami's notes demonstrated sensitivity to all aspects of performance – music, costumes, song and dance – and evolving sense of aesthetic excellence. His treatises, when disseminated in bowdlerized versions in the eighteenth century and then 'discovered' in the early twentieth century, became professional bibles and scholarly textbooks.

Professional players

At first, noh actors belonged to troupes, affiliated with temples, supplementing their income with 'subscription' (*kanjin*) performances to raise money to restore a temple or build a bridge. They grew in popularity among commoners in the regions but also among the court aristocracy and military rulers in the ancient Nara and new Kyoto capital. Noh struggled among these various patrons during the long civil wars of the fifteenth and sixteenth centuries. With the triumph of Hideyoshi Toyotomi (1536–98), which was consolidated by Tokugawa Ieyasu (1543–1616), and the shift of power to Edo (Tokyo) during the long Tokugawa period (1603–1867), previously fluid distinctions of class and affiliation were made permanent. Noh players were placed into designated troupes. Stylistic school family heads all served the shōgun, while regional daimyo eager to show their political affiliation and cultural savvy, studied under and supported their own troupes. Those unamalgamated into the designated schools became freelancers, lumped with other '*tesarugaku*' semi-professional performers filling out a chorus or playing minor roles at regional temples and shrines, and at Kyoto's Imperial Court.

Originally jacks-of-all-trades, noh actors began to specialize within troupes. There are approximately a thousand performers today. *Shite* specialize in acting the main role and secondary characters, but also sing in the chorus and assist with costuming and stage properties. Subsidiary performers include the *waki* (accompanying characters), *hayashi* musicians (flute, shoulder-drum, hip-drum and *taiko* stick-drum) and kyogen actors, who offer narrative interludes between acts and full comedies between plays. Roles are learnt in family-like groups affiliated with stylistic schools. Female professionals were recognized as professionals in the 1920s, and now represent 10–15 per cent of the professional ranks.

Song and dance

Zeami wrote that noh was based not on acting, but on song and dance. 'Song' may be conceived broadly as a range of voices. Actors speak in a distinctive singsong, while chorus members chant melodically or rhythmically. The verse weaves poetry with prose, references to actual and legendary places, and the changing seasons of nature. It includes esoteric Buddhist scripture, contemporary medieval popular tunes, and fragments from other works of literature. The chorus may sing objectively or in the first person, standing in for the shite, allowing the dancer to concentrate fully on the subtle timing and careful angles of masked physical expression. The two or three drummers create the atmosphere, supporting the singing and dancing with a complex, dynamic rhythm accompanied by loud energetic cries. The flute enters sporadically with mysterious or frenzied melodies. Many connoisseur audiences today close their eyes to appreciate the play as concert, or follow along in annotated libretti.

Plays normally culminate with a long dance, accompanied by chorus and/or pure instrumental music. Within the wooden frame of pillars and roof, the shite is the stage-centre focus of spectators' attention. He emanates dynamic presence within a gorgeous costume and luminous, ephemeral mask. The patterned movements can be both imitative and abstract, expressed hypnotically while sliding along the smooth cypress stage, punctuated in samurai or god plays with sudden whirls of sleeves, circling, zigzags or stamps. The mask, framed by wig and headband, is carefully fitted for the actor to manipulate light and shadow through subtle tilts and turns, revealed beneath a hat, kimono sleeve or opened fan.

Gods, ghosts and madwomen

Noh is minimalist theatre. A single lead actor on a bare stage enacts highly concentrated themes, often undramatic from a western perspective. Self-introductions, narrative interludes and choral commentary provide relevant information so that spectators can imagine the locale, time and core theme. Seasonal settings change through choral description, and great distances are traversed with a few steps.

In a typical play, a wandering priest happens across an unusual site, an ancient temple or natural wonder, then sits to rest. A mysterious stranger appears, engaging him in enigmatic banter, then disappears. A local person approaches and, prodded by the priest, relates an episode that had once occurred at this site, or a similar one in China long ago. The mysterious character reappears, revealed now as a ghost, demon or god. The priest prays to calm the angry demon or grieving ghost, or to receive the god's blessing. The audience, represented by the kneeling priest, thus witnesses a traumatic re-enactment by a vengeful ghost or is blessed by the god's felicitous performance.

Thousands of plays were written over the centuries. However, in the early seventeenth century, troupes were required to submit lists of actors, plays, properties and costumes. Through rivalry, rationalization and self-censorship of anything overtly political or sexual, the standard repertoire was winnowed to its present 250 plays. Although these fall within five categories comprising a typical full programme in the Edo period, many plays were given arbitrary or multiple designations. Plots vary greatly, from simple yet evocative dance-poems to tales of cruel, unrequited love, separation of parents and children, fierce battles lost and won, and sacrifice for the emperor. The five categories, performed in a prescribed order, following Shikisamban, were god, warrior, woman, miscellaneous and demon plays.

God plays are believed to be oldest. They are simple manifestations to a wandering priest of a god or spirit of a particular geographic area, a temple or shrine, or eponymous site. *Kamo*, in which the founding myth of the Kamigamo Shrine is re-enacted, is exemplary. Warrior plays feature samurai who have sacrificed themselves in battle or, rarely, been victorious. The waki is often a comforting priest, unsure whether he is dreaming, praying to ease the suffering of the limbo-lost soul, as in *Yashima*, based on *The Tales of the Heike*. Women plays feature spirits of flowers and plants or beautiful women, expressed in elegant costumes, allusive poetry and gentle dance evoking a mood of otherworldly beauty, such as Yugaō, one of Genji's lovers from *The Tale of Genji*.

Miscellaneous is a catch-all category, plays about living persons, rather than spirits, ghosts, gods or demons. They portray the tragic loss of sons by mothers, husbands by wives, unrequited love and unquenchable jealousy. A sub-category of 'madwoman' plays features lovers and mothers driven insane by grief, such as *Sumidagawa* (The Sumida River), in which a mother discovers that her long-lost son has died when taken by slave-traders; in the second half she holds a prayer service for his eternal soul. In other variations, the cruel medieval amusement of a madwoman dance – a play within the play – may then lead to her recognition by her lost loved one. The flashy fifth-category demon plays portray disguised gods and demons who reveal themselves in the second act, and then are killed by valiant samurai or quelled by prayers of Buddhist monks or yamabushi. Gold or darker masks, grimacing and with bulging eyes, are framed by long red or white wigs, and bright costumes, such as *Nue* (Night-bird). These plays are relatively short, employing quick stamps, leaps, turns, and sword or halberd battles. With the loud, pulsing rhythms of the *taiko* stick-drum, they serve to wake spectators for the grand finale.

Some of the last plays to enter the repertoire stretched the confines of the simple protagonist/ listener of the shite/waki relationship. *Ataka, Benkei on a Boat, the Earth Spider* and *Dōjōji* portray complex psychological states and structures. However, when commoners were barred from viewing noh and kyogen, kabuki took over as the people's entertainment, and noh ceased further new play development. Instead, variants by particular schools or performers expanded the repertoire. These *kogaki* might vary the colour of a wig or employ a distinctive ending.

The lead actor could interpret the play within the limited scope of recognized kogaki variants, but also with his choice of masks, costume combinations, and fans.

Mise-en-scène maximalism

Noh has often been described as minimalist, but might better be considered 'maximalist': a few carefully chosen large set pieces and small properties convey an immense potency on the bare, open stage. Noh performances make potent use of a few carefully considered elements: the stage, costumes, masks and properties.

Noh was originally performed at shrine or temple stages, elaborations of earlier raised stages for bugaku, kagura and dengaku. A temporary, purpose-built theatre for 'subscription' performances became the basis for permanent stages, built with near-identical dimensions from the late sixteenth century. A five-colour striped curtain separates the backstage 'mirror room' from the *hashigakari* bridgeway leading to the rear of the 6 m^2 stage. Three pine trees of increasing height separate the bridgeway space, providing the perspectival illusion of distance. The large painted pine tree on the back wall and pillars in each corner of the main stage frame the masked actor, and provide vital sightline coordinates.

Space is segmented by role: the main actor plays on the bridgeway and smooth cypress boards of the main stage, with separate porch-like areas at the back for musicians and stage left for the chorus. The vestigial pebble-garden disconnecting the stage from the spectator area separates the onstage sacred deities and dangerous demon spirits from their human audience. They also reflect sound and light to the stage centre. The bare stage is simply decorated with temporary set pieces. A platform, one by two yards long, covered in cloth of different hues, can become a bridge, throne or ritual altar. A standing bamboo frame, covered in cloth, becomes a humble mountain hut, well or burial mound; on its side, the box becomes a carriage or boat.

Actors choose costumes as one means of interpreting their roles. These robes, under-kimono, headbands and obi sashes are the zenith of Edo-period dyeing, weaving and stencilling techniques. A single garment can be folded, tucked, sewn or released on stage into a myriad of expressive shapes and styles.

Dressing culminates with the mask. Made from cypress or other softwoods according to templates passed down among carvers, they are smaller than the human face. The sixty types include ferocious gods, angry demons and forlorn warriors, pure maidens and samurai, anguished mothers and wives, hollow-cheeked mountain hags and wise grandmothers. There is great variation within a single type, and a particular role may be portrayed using numerous types. This permits the well-stocked actor many interpretive choices. Once the mask angle most conducive to conveying a variety of emotions is found in the dressing area, it is maintained onstage by the actor's gliding walk. A single mask can suggest a wealth of shifting expression, according to slight angle variations of tilts – lowering (clouding = sadness), raising (shining = happiness) or sharp diagonal turns (cutting = intense anger or shock).

Large, gorgeously painted fans with designs related to the play's themes are noh's essential property. Closed, they extend the hand, become a pointer, a thrusting sword or a blind man's staff. Opened, they scoop water, describe a sweeping vista, transform in an instant to a shield or the crescent moon. More abstract movement may convey the shudders of the heart. The fan may cover the face in shyness or shame, be dropped in anguish, thrown down in anger or spread wide as the wings of an angel. Most often it serves as an ornamental extension of graceful turns, circles and zigzags, or as punctuation to a stamp (Figure 3.1).

Figure 3.1 Matsui Akira in noh *Jinen Koji* (Jinen the Lay Monk).
(Courtesy of Matsui Akira)

Performances today

Noh performance is a cultural vessel that has carried many treasures intact to the present day. Noh texts are marvels of compressed poetic imagery; fans and kimonos are supreme masterworks of design, medieval elegance and dramatic effect; masks are museum-quality art objects, expressing heroism, beauty, wisdom and sorrow, carved by master craftspersons following time-honoured techniques. The carefully fashioned and preserved art has managed to ride the waves of urban Japanese modernity and continues to produce inspired professionals, dedicated students and eager fans, a tribute to the delicate but sturdy craft's adaptation to its changing environment for over half a millennium.

Kyogen: stylized comedy

Contrary to common belief and intuition, noh and kyogen did not develop together before splitting into serious versus comic specialist genres. Rather, kyogen preceded noh as comic skits and dances derived from sangaku variety skits from the mainland. The popular entertainment merged with native forms in sarugaku, a travelling entertainment that included diverse acts of magic, juggling, acrobatics, storytelling, dance to drum and flute, and comic skits. Refined through repeated performances in diverse venues for both popular and aristocratic audiences, kyogen developed stylized conventions similar to the noh with which it shared the stage. Contemporary aristocratic diaries and Zeami's criticisms attest that kyogen players continued to test the boundaries of taste and propriety in their slapstick, ribaldry and satire for at least a century after becoming part of a noh programme.

Guild-like family-based kyogen acting troupes joined as specialists within noh troupes, employed by daimyo throughout the land. Kyogen actors were responsible for the Senzai mask-bearer and Sambasō old man portions of the ritual opening piece *Okina*, for staging short comedies in between the serious noh dance-plays, and for serving as narrator or dramatic foils as *ai* (interlude) players within the noh itself. With their clear, relaxed language, simple costumes and need for few properties beyond the all-purpose fan or occasional stool, the kyogen narrator became an indispensable gap-filler between acts of noh plays, enabling the shite's transformation via increasingly elaborate costume changes.

Tricksters and shysters

Kyogen plays were anonymous, continuously revised for four centuries; the first book of summaries dates from 1578, a full two centuries after similarly titled plays were performed. Not until 1642 did Okura Tora'akira (1597–1662), the thirteenth headmaster of the Okura school, first write down 180 texts with dialogue, songs and stage directions. The current repertoire of 250 plays is now standardized, but distinct versions are still maintained by regional families, even within the same stylistic school, demonstrating that kyogen actors continued to improvise, adapt popular songs and poetry, and maintain local colour and colloquial language into the eighteenth century.

In addition to the kyogen comedies, kyogen actors in a troupe were responsible for *ai-kyogen*, narrative interludes at the beginning or middle of a noh play itself. Playing a local priest or villager, the *ai* retells some ancient lore about the site, or acts as go-between servant or innkeeper to the more formal movements of the masked noh actors. Kyogen actors display formidable memories to recall these long ai-kyogen *katari* for the noh in all five stylistic schools, and dialogue for all roles in the repertory. They employ a singsong intonation, formulaic expressions for self-introduction, calling a servant or scolding chases, and limit the number of alternative songs and dances that can be used in any number of plays.

Language is straightforward, enunciated clearly, enhanced by exaggerated mimetic gestures accompanied by onomatopoeia: *sarasara* opening a door, *zukazuka* sawing wood, *dobudobu* pouring liquid. Masks are employed only for animals, gods and demons, and ugly women, but can also be worn for disguise. Costumes are the Edo-period commoners' everyday clothing, with

Figure 3.2 Shigeyama Sennojō as a farmer pretending to commit suicide by scythe only to be stopped by his repentant wife, in kyogen *Kamabara* (Suicide by Sickle).

(Courtesy of Osamu Muranaka)

checks and bold colours of persimmon and green, or vests decorated with patterns of vegetables, flowers and the moon. The characters are all living persons embroiled in the fun and foibles of farm and town life; there are no ghosts. Mountain wizards and demons, so frightening in noh, prove to have soft hearts or human weaknesses in kyogen.

Kyogen plays span a wide spectrum of comedy types, including festive joy, comedy of situations, satire and slapstick. Auspicious plays feature devotion rewarded by a benevolent god. Clever servants outwit arrogant masters through disguises or tricks. City slickers fleece country bumpkins with outrageous lies, which they then must conceal with increasingly antic explanations. Few escape their comeuppance: lazy husbands are browbeaten by wives, naïve priests fooled by acolytes, blind men teased by the sighted, and arrogant daimyo shamed by their servants.

The most common comic mode in kyogen is escalating panic at the inevitable consequences for wrongful actions (Figure 3.2). Most of the 250 plays in the extant repertoire feature two to four characters in pieces lasting twenty to forty minutes. A Mountain Priest in *Fukuro* (Owls) seeking to exorcise a forester when an infestation of owls manages to afflict his brother and himself. In *Mikazuki* (Winnowing), a husband divorces his wife when she tries to stop him from spending all his time at poetry parties, but reverses his decision when in parting she shows herself capable of poetry-making. *Kintozaemon* is a thief intending to rob a young woman but has the tables turned, losing his halberd and robe. Two arrogant provincial chiefs in *Futari Daimyo* (Two Lords) force a commoner to carry their swords; he rebels, terrorizing them into making fools of themselves playing childhood games.

Over a third of the plays feature Tarō Kaja, the wily servant. Possessed of an astounding appetite for delicious food, singing and dancing, and drinking sake, he is lazy, avaricious, clever and capricious. He manages to quench his desires (if only temporarily) but evades punishment through his quick wit and imaginative storytelling. The straight man to this trickster is his master, sometimes a daimyo, invariably portrayed as ignorant, arrogant and bad-tempered. They receive just comeuppance from a fed-up servant or passerby, who may force them to perform childish games – which they then end up enjoying immensely.

Rare, large-cast kyogen include many that began as *ai-kyogen* but expanded beyond the bounds of interludes to noh plays. These include parodies of noh plays, with masked characters and full orchestra, but featuring lesser spirits such as an octopus or monkey. A few longer plays show a maturity of dramaturgy more tragicomedy than farce. In *Buaku* (Buaku the Bold), a brother servant is ordered to kill his friend and colleague for his alleged misdeeds; in *Tsurigitsune* (Fox-Hunting), an old fox disguised as a priest warns the hunter of the Buddhist of hell awaiting his sins. These deft, psychologically complex plots concerning filial piety, featuring disguise, multiple locales and ironic twists, are prologue to themes taken up by subsequent genres.

Bunraku: a literary puppet theatre for adults

Bunraku theatre, or *ningyō jōruri*, is comprised of metre-high puppets controlled by three operators, the dialogue and descriptive passages chanted and sung by a narrator, accompanied by plangent *gidayu* shamisen. The independent arts merged in the late sixteenth century to become popular entertainment for adults, rivalling kabuki for over a century. Technical innovations such as articulated facial features and hands, and wind-up mechanisms, added to the doll's fascination. Talented playwrights were attracted to the new art's fealty to the playscripts, writing increasingly complex dramatic texts. Eventually the human performers of kabuki, borrowing heavily from bunraku texts and dramaturgy, outstripped it as popular art in the Edo period. Bunraku, designated a UNESCO Intangible Cultural Heritage in 2003, is maintained by a single professional troupe based at the National Bunraku Theatre in Osaka.

From barnstormers to headliners

Street-corner performers of religious tales appeared at the Ebisu Shrine in Nishinomiya, in central Japan, from the fifteenth century. Slinging a box around his neck, a puppeteer acted all parts while manipulating dolls on sticks poking up onto a miniature noh stage. When the shamisen arrived via the Ryukyu Islands (present-day Okinawa) in the late sixteenth century, the combination of sharp percussion and mournful strings proved ideal partners to the articulated doll movements and sentimental stories.

Japan had a long history of solo narrative, accompanied by drums or biwa, or the beating of a fan. Raconteurs from the twelfth century related the great battles and love episodes from war tales such as *The Tale of the Heike* and *The Tale of the Soga Brothers*. *The Tale of Princess Jōruri*, a twelve-act melodrama, became popular in the fifteenth century, an adventure depicting the legendary hero Yoshitsune's romance with the fictional Princess Jōruri. By the end of the sixteenth century, the adventure tale had not only spawned a host of similar melodramas, but the term 'Jōruri' had become synonymous with the art of chanted storytelling. By the early seventeenth century, Jōruri chanters were accompanying puppets of the Ebisu puppetry tradition in newly written plays, and adapting the noh-kyogen repertoire. A single puppeteer held the doll above a short screen. The combination of nuanced narration, delicate doll movements and sonorous shamisen combined to create an art that stimulated the imagination and tugged the heart. Eventually, the demands of supporting the heavier, larger puppets forced operators to step out into full view, alongside storyteller and shamisen.

Twisting plots by chanter specialists

Scripts of high dramatic and literary quality were slow to develop. Early plots were mere excuses for sword-fights or miracle plays, or adaptations of noh and kyogen. Chanters had served also as the main puppet theatre playwrights until Chikamatsu Monzaemon (1653–1725) collaborated with chanter Uji Kaganojō (1635–1711), permitting specialization that extended the range and complexity of the art.

A double suicide provided the creative impetus for another vital change in play content. In 1703 a clerk and prostitute, feeling that society could not permit their continued dalliance, committed love suicide. *Love Suicides at Sonezaki*, a puppet version of their fatal romance, was dashed off a month later. The 'living newspaper' transformed their sordid tale into a romantic tragedy, while offering a titillating peek at the elegant and gay teahouses of the licensed quarter. The play was a hit, spawning copycat suicides, as well as many competing versions in an emerging genre.

Bunraku topics expanded instantly to include *sewamono*, the trials and tribulations of the everyday life of commoners. They joined the Princess Jōruri-type romantic adventures *jidaimono*, five-act histories concerning legendary military battles or succession disputes among aristocrats or samurai families. *Sewamono* were usually two-act plays concerning the everyday tribulations and tragedies of commoners. Programmes were leavened by comic plays or scenes adapted from the kyogen repertoire, and dance scenes of virtuoso teamwork in imitation of kabuki dance-plays. The chanted text, opened like a sacred text on a candle-lit tasselled stand in front of the gidayu chanter, was as carefully artificial and charming as the dolls themselves. Chikamatsu, who wrote over a hundred plays for kabuki and bunraku, employed strings of related imagery, puns, internal rhymes, and repetition. He painted a dramatic soundscape, carefully distinguishing among different voices and relationships through varying hierarchical forms of politeness. The bunraku texts, published immediately in illustrated editions, could be enjoyed for such lyric stage language crammed with rhymes and references.

Figure 3.3 A princess is tortured by the villain and comic henchman in bunraku *Hibari Yama* (The Skylark Mountain, 1740).

(Photo by Francis Haar. Courtesy of Tom Haar.)

Technical and literary innovation went hand in glove. The dolls featured movable eyes, lips and fingers, and so required three manipulators for major roles, although a single manipulator was sufficient for maids, policemen and other smaller dolls. Playwrights played to puppet strengths, convincingly enacting gory tortures and sword-fights, flying animals and gods, decapitations and demon transformations, and miracles and romantic scenes. What might have been unbearable or unbelievable with actual humans on the kabuki stage became riveting in bunraku, where every action by the dolls was as real and beautiful as another. As dolls grew more articulated and able to express emotions physically, plays featured greater portions of dialogue spoken by characters. Ironically, Chikamatsu's texts' detailed narration, which had spurred the doll theatre's popularity, fell out of favour. The trio of Namiki Senryu, Miyoshi Shoraku and Takeda Izumo wrote as a team the three great plays of the bunraku repertoire – *Sugawara Denju Te-narai Kagami* (The Secret of Sugawara's Calligraphy), *Yoshitsune Senbon-zakura* (Yoshitsune and the Thousand Cherry Trees) and *Kanadehon Chushingura* (The Treasury of Loyal Retainers), helping bunraku to achieve its golden age in the mid-eighteenth century (Figure 3.3).

Triangular tensions

Bunraku derived its appeal from the balance of superb artists in three specialties: chant, shamisen and puppetry. Bunraku narration is called gidayu, a once-independent form that continues as a concert genre. A single chanter might portray all roles in a single act, or the characters might be divided among chanters, especially for longer acts. The storyteller alternates freely among four different styles: *kotoba*, spoken dialogue; *ji*, a rhythmic chant, synchronized with the shamisen; *fūshi*, melodic singing; and *iro*, a speech–song hybrid. In addition to dialogue, texts provide a descriptive function quite apart from giving voice to individual characters. Juggling the character roles and vocal styles for an entire scene is challenging. The chanter often wipes sweat from his brow or sips hot tea, acknowledging the strain of his over-the-top performance.

Kaganojō is said to have invented a particularly magniloquent chant, bombastic and romantic in turns, straining the voice to the utmost registers to convey the emotional subtexts in a dynamic, rhythmic manner. Early plays about martial derring-do were popular among samurai and even summoned for performances at the imperial palace. Takemoto Gidayū I (1651–1714) combined numerous prior styles to create his own eponymous chanting style, sonorous and carefully enunciated. He left scripts with performance notes, acknowledging bunraku's debt to noh's five-act structure and jo-ha-kyū pace. Another late master, Uemura Bunrakuken (1751–1810), gave the genre its current name, managing a theatre in Osaka for three generations.

The chanter has relied on the shamisen, which became Japan's most popular instrument, used to accompany love ballads, long narratives and lyric poetry. The large shamisen with outsized plectrum employed in jōruri provides plaintive, sharp and percussive accents, employing rapid fingering, plucked plectrum pizzicato or glissandos slides. Scenes usually begin with a mood-making solo shamisen prelude, with specific patterns indicating 'resignation', 'sadness' or 'anger'. In dance-plays, a lively group shamisen with the chorus sing popular ballads, or lyric song on a *michiyuki* 'travel song'. Besides these few opportunities to display such virtuosity, the shamisen normally takes a collaborative role, often partnering for life with the same chanter as a 'married couple'.

Puppet heads are carved and painted from cypress or paulownia wood to high artistic standards according to approximately seventy types, thirty speciality roles and forty more general types. Their fixed expressions are determined by shading and variant wigs and costumes. Wigs, as in the contemporary Japan hairstyles, indicated age, class and occupation. Faces are unchanging, so demand consistent personalities throughout a scene; different heads of the same type may be used in different scenes. Movable eyebrows, eyes and mouths are expressive when used sparingly. The torso is a padded wooden frame, costumed by the operator for each performance. Beauties are portrayed placing heads on torsos in the ideal 1:8 proportions. Shoulders, legs and hands are charged with the burden of expressing detailed emotions – there are over forty hand-styles, on a continuum from movable wrists to articulated fingers, used mainly by martial males.

Controlling this machinery to facilitate such stylized realism requires three highly skilled technicians. Bunraku performers are said to train for a decade as leg manipulators, another decade on the left arm, and finally a decade on the head and right arm before being considered true masters. The leg manipulator stands in the trough running the length of the stage, maintaining the illusion that the doll is standing on solid ground. Alternating the male legs to simulate walking, sitting or standing, he also strikes a pose, runs or stamps, making the appropriate accompanying sounds with his own feet. Female characters do not have legs, so the leg operator pushes out against her kimono hem, or makes fists simulating her knees while sitting. The left arm manipulator stands slightly apart from the other two, controlling a half-metre-long rod inserted at the puppet's elbow. His right hand manipulates toggles to articulate the hand, while his left is free to bring on properties, straighten a costume-piece or assist the main operator in a particularly difficult pose.

The main operator controls the movements of the doll while at the same time signalling to others; accompanying operators learn to react to his subtle physical cues or occasional grunts.

His left hand enters the puppet from behind through a hole in the kimono, gripping the toggle and supporting the heavy doll. Pulleys and springs articulate the eyebrows, eyes and mouth. His right hand inside the puppet's kimono sleeve holds the rod controlling the right wrist and fingers. Practised in dance and music, he manipulates the doll with subtle timing, sometimes rushing to or falling behind the narration, building suspense through these gaps, riding surges of resentment or ecstasy.

All three operators work in silent triangular tension, breathing together and responding to the physical cues and occasional grunts of the lead operator. When operators work as a team, they seem to provide a soul to the wood-and-cloth doll. Quotidian situations are enchanting, subtle turns and sleeve movements betray great wells of emotion, and their articulated bodies create a calculatedly beautiful living picture. And nothing is stiller than the bodies of a couple after suicide, literally 'unmanned' and lifeless when the puppets' black-clad operators have slipped away.

Movement is categorized as *furi*, mimetic gestures of everyday life, and *kata*, a sequence of movements that convey the emotion and action through conventional patterns. In furi, a young girl might sweep the floor, sew a hem or light a lantern with delicate movements imitating in stylized manner everyday actions. Whole patterns of effective movement have evolved into kata, fixed conventions: an anguished young woman tremblingly bites her handkerchief or sleeve; a fixed pose, a common framing and highlighting device in kabuki, is employed also by dolls, arms and legs akimbo in a fierce frontal pose. However, the courtesan's pose, facing away from the audience, displaying the kimono's beauty of colour and line divorced from both character or story, is an aesthetically abstract kata, accomplished easily in kabuki but a tour de force when created by the three contorted doll operators.

Bunraku today

Bunraku was eventually eclipsed as popular theatre by kabuki, which stole plots, movement, staging and even 'acting' techniques from the doll theatre. Bunraku, struggling with the economies of smaller theatres (puppets are one-half to two-thirds human size) in plays demanding large staff – triple-casting in effect for each main character – was reduced to a few theatres with little innovation since the eighteenth century. With the establishment of the Bunraku Kyokai (Association) in 1963 and government support, a single professional troupe emerged, alternating performances at the National Theatre in Tokyo (1966), the National Bunraku Theatre in Osaka (1984) and regional tours. Local variants by amateurs continue as folk traditions.

Kabuki: passion and spectacle

For nearly four centuries, kabuki has been the Broadway and Hollywood of Japanese theatre: commercial entertainment and stimulus to a large industry of ancillary arts and businesses. Driven by stars, kabuki is eclectic in its borrowings from other genres, adapting both legendary and contemporary events, all refashioned to its own potent brand. Psychologically rich portraits of men and women torn by contradictory obligations are depicted with swift and subtle dialogue, fluid and emotionally expressive dance, and dynamic *tableaux vivants*. Virtuoso shamisen players and singers specialize in a veritable encyclopaedia of historic styles, supplying almost constant aural accompaniment, punctuated by sharp accents of resonant gongs, drums small and large, and clacks of wooden sticks.

Since the Edo period, when noh and kyogen became the exclusive preserve of the samurai and nobility, commoners embraced kabuki's star-studded spectacle as their own, a source for news and fashion, and distorted mirror of flattering self-images. Kabuki was popular culture by and for aspiring classes: gorgeous and gigantic, elegant yet erotic, larger than life but eminently sympathetic.

From skit to popular dramatic entertainment

Kabuki's art emerged from almost continuous struggles among rival troupes and acting styles, in early commercial competition with bunraku, and near-constant resistance to shōgunate rules and restrictions. As with many performing arts in Japan, kabuki began as a provincial fad that caught on in the capital, then filtered once more to the provinces. A dancer at the Izumo Shrine of Shimane Prefecture in western Japan led a dance troupe in a type of *furyū*, a gaudily costumed group dance. Okuni's fame preceded her to Kyoto, where she incorporated *nembutsu odori*, a Buddhist group song and dance. She was joined by kyogen actors, unable or unwilling to join the designated noh troupes, and performed *yayoko odori*, a girls' dance to short *kouta* popular songs, as dramatic counterpoint and interlude for group dances in a variety of styles. Okuni's all-female, mixed-gender and other all-male troupes emerged in this new style of dance performance, termed 'kabuku', for its 'outlaw' or 'eccentric' depictions of eponymous common city types. It later came to be written as 'kabuki' – 'song, dance and acting skill'.

Early kabuki performances were comic and erotic skits concerned with bargaining for prostitutes, featuring cross-dressing and lively dances. A typical storyline featured a dashing young man (played by a woman) entering a brothel. He bargains for the alluring prostitutes (some played by young men), and then is entertained by a lively group dance *odori*. Contemporary prints show a swaggering Okuni, in male robes and headgear, slinging a sword. Another play parodies noh dramaturgy: a priest summons the ghost of legendary playboy Nagoya Sanza, who enters through the audience to be entertained and comforted onstage by teahouse prostitutes. Such gender-bending, and the insider views such skits afforded of the licensed quarters, were performed in Kyoto's capital at fenced-off areas of Kyoto's Kamogawa dry riverbed, a flatland both untaxed and unregulated, and proved a hit there and everywhere they appeared throughout the land.

Okuni's troupe's success gave rise to many imitators, a platform for young women and men to show off their wares. Yet the jostling crowds and private party patrons included masterless samurai (*rōnin*) and merchants, squandering their inheritances and forgetting their familial obligations, fighting over admired dancers, both male and female, and imitating the flamboyant stage fashions and language. Such disruptions of public decorum and mingling of distinct classes were dangerous precedent for the emerging class system and Confucian values undergirding the nascent Tokugawa shōgunate (1603–1867). In 1629 females were banned from the stage.

Yet townspersons' passion for kabuki, once kindled, could not be so easily extinguished. Teenage boys with long forelocks, who were already achieving success with rival mixed and all-male kabuki performances, quickly took advantage of their monopoly. When boy dancer-prostitutes proved similarly disruptive, actors were ordered to shave the sexy forelock and heads. As shorn teenagers or adults took over kabuki, they learnt to make up for their lack of youthful appeal with artistic technique. The *onnagata*, or female-role specialist, emerged. Replacing his wavy hair with a cloth cap, purple handkerchief, or wig, the onnagata stood upstage, appearing smaller behind male characters. With feet turned in, muscular arms hidden in sleeves, his sinuous shape supporting a supple neck expressed an alluringly synthetic femininity.

The simple skits framing sexy dances were elaborated by the 1680s into two-act plays, with curtains and simple properties and sets. The range of male roles expanded from the swaggering rakes of early skits to include the bravado *aragoto* (rough style) heroes popularized in Edo by the Danjurō line, and romantic but bumbling playboy *wagoto* (gentle) roles, first popularized in the Kansai era by Sakata Tōjurō (1647–1709). There were many additional subdivisions, such as clown and villain roles. The specialist in female roles developed further under Yoshizawa Ayame (1673–1729), from mere alluring courtesans' burlesque into an elegant and internalized ideal of femininity, created by actors who lived offstage in the public eye as women. Onnagata role types expanded to include many ages and characters, including strong-willed princesses and shy commoner daughters, loyal wives and villainous grannies. Segawa Kikunojo I (1693–1749) and II (1741–1773) took advantage of the glamorous appeal of the onnagata for male spectators to promote makeup, hair ornaments and kimonos as authorized fashion trend-setters.

Necessity breeds invention

Yet as kabuki rose ever higher as popular entertainment, the shōgunate treated it, along with gambling and prostitution, as a necessary evil demanding strict oversight. Regulations were made on theatre numbers, size, capacity, decoration and architecture. Sumptuary laws restricted actors onstage and in real life, regulating dress and living quarters. Yet frequent reiterations of edicts show that laws were enforced haphazardly and with great regional variation.

Attempts to separate the classes had similarly unintended consequences, as kabuki culture seeped or overflowed easily beyond any government barriers erected to prevent it. The outcast actors of Edo were separated in living and performing into sequestered quarters abutting the prostitutes' areas frequented by merchants and samurai in disguise. Kabuki was officially reviled as morally degenerate and trivial fiction. Yet when samurai were banned from attending kabuki, kabuki actors left their ghettoes secretly to entertain them at parties. Eventually samurai wives or surrogate 'maids' were sent to the kabuki theatre to observe and imitate dances on their return. Learning kabuki dances became a popular hobby that trickled down to the *arriviste* merchant class, taught by the early eighteenth century by professional choreographer-teachers.

Theatre managers grew adept at finding ways around every new regulation. Teahouses abutting theatres were matchmaking salons that served food and drink, connected by secret passages to expensive *sajiki* boxed seats, making assignations between patrons with performers easy, and difficult to thwart. If actors were banished from Edo, they developed followings in Kyoto, Osaka or other lesser theatres in other urban areas. Some regulations backfired: denied brocade and silk for costuming, actors used lighter cotton prints, permitting easier yet fantastic costume changes. Given the irrepressible popularity and consequent commercial stimulus, kabuki managers and actors continuously discovered creative solutions that made kabuki ever more gorgeous, regionally known and star-driven, cultivating a reputation for anti-authoritarian verve.

Plots and players

The extant kabuki repertoire of 300 plays (some full-length, others a single act from longer works) are a palimpsest of texts, rewritten to suit different needs of actors and audiences, as well as accommodation to shōgunal codes. Unlike other classical genres (excepting *rakugo* storytelling), its regular repertory features new plays added over three centuries, expressing romance and spectacle to the changing regulatory and technological limits.

Kabuki was primarily dance-centred for its first century. Texts were of secondary importance to their interpretation by charismatic actors. New plays were cobbled together from existing ones, popular scenes excised from longer, now forgotten, plays, popular characters reappearing in prequels and sequels. Plays written by house playwrights for company stars would be 'improved' upon through inspired improvisations. Entire 'worlds' – familiar episodes of historical or fictional characters in set time periods – once established, might then be made to collide with wholly distinct worlds. Actors were hired for annual contracts, further developing their fan base by honing particularly well-received roles. Popular play themes and acting styles varied greatly in the major cities, epitomized by the Edo outlaw, Osaka dandy and Kyoto beauty. Accommodation to the varied political and economic cultures of samurai and new urbanites of Edo, commercial Osaka and imperial Kyoto forged kabuki into a national pastime with regional variants.

Restrictions on content had pushed kabuki away from contemporary realism or political satire. Denied overt patronage by the cultural elite who might have raised their texts to poetry or great literature, and forbidden to criticize the status quo, kabuki produced moving melodramas and frivolous spectacles, convoluted adventures and stunning revelations. Since contemporary plays involving samurai could not be staged, these were reset in earlier periods, with geographic references appropriately transposed. These stylized codes and conventions, along with males impersonating women and stylized speech and gesture, could be appreciated for their subtly nuanced hyper-reality. Kabuki became an expensive pastime, with female spectators providing the majority of income in the eighteenth century. Although depictions of teahouse luxury and lubricious scenes between potential customers and high-ranging courtesans were also banned, as real-life courtesans and nouveau-riche matrons followed the stage fashions, the gap between reality and fiction narrowed.

Kabuki's maturing dramaturgy borrowed from noh, kyogen and especially the puppet theatre. Bunraku had proved popular from the mid-1600s with literate, multi-act plays, including adaptations of noh plays, and oral epics such as *Tale of Heike* and *The Tale of the Soga Brothers*. Kabuki managers borrowed texts and spectacle from the doll theatre, including chanted narrative that freed actors from most dialogue for full-throttle presentational performances. Chikamatsu returned to write for kabuki, and bunraku plays became kabuki staples by the mid-eighteenth century. Plays were written by teams, careless of the unevenness of one scene from another. Ultimately actors, always the most important element, would improvise and create a character trajectory to bring coherence to a role. Playwrights attached to particular troupes wrote to the strengths (and weaknesses) of the headliners and minor performers, so pure kabuki plays, often convoluted romantic adventures, continued to coexist with more dialogue-heavy plays. And thrilling displays of daredevil spectacle alternated with slice-of-life observation of samurai or contemporary commoner culture.

If performance was outlandish, the morality of the plots was generally conservative, displaying Confucian ideals of loyalty to elders and the group: vassal to lord, apprentice to master, disciple to teacher, wife to husband, and child to parent. Dramatic action often resulted from how characters resolved conflicts between their social obligations and personal feelings. For the heroes and heroines, suicide was the ultimate self-sacrifice, proof of honour, atonement for a repented sin or repayment of a debt. Villains would eventually be punished, as rōnin, orphaned children, or ghosts avenged perceived wrongs. Kabuki in the nineteenth century turned to grittier realism in the *kizewamono*, 'raw' depictions of the lowest strata of urban society – thieves, usurers, gangsters – and shocking depictions of the gory, grotesque and supernatural. Kabuki's decadent period is exemplified by the nihilistic anti-heroes of Tsuruya Namboku (1755–1829) and more romantic and lyric portrayals of the lower classes by Kawatake Mokuami (1816–1893) (Figure 3.4).

Rough and gentle men, alluring women

Kabuki productions are depicted with shades of the brilliant hues of its primary colours, the bravura acting of the aragoto males, romantic confusion of the wagoto hero and erotic mincings of the onnagata.

Figure 3.4 Kabuki *Meiboku Sendai Hagi* (The Disputed Succession, 1785) in which a child is sacrificed as a substitute to save his lord's son.

(Photo by Francis Haar. Courtesy of Tom Haar.)

The three styles, developed through highly codified movement and vocal patterns developed over centuries, traditionally are played exclusively by specialists. Only a few great actors have shown their versatility be playing multiple styles, sometimes within a single day's programme, or even a single dance in *hengemono* transformation pieces. Kabuki acting styles are hereditary. Names and roles are passed down among great acting families such as Ichikawa, Bandō, Matsumoto, Onoe and Nakamura through adoption of successors, often with elaborate name-taking ceremonies.

Aragoto (wild warrior) is the grandiloquent style most commonly associated with kabuki. Heroes' and villains' faces are drawn with 'power veins', garish warpaint of blue, red and brown stripes above a white or shaded base. Aragoto actors wear exaggeratedly large kimonos and wigs, and sling over-long swords, as they swagger on high wooden clogs. Early plays borrowed from the popular Kinpira-style puppetry, featuring bombastic narratives illustrated by leaping and acrobatic fighting. Ichikawa Danjūrō I (1660–1704) perfected the style, derived from his devotion to the god Fudō Myōō of Shingon Buddhism, featuring cross-eyed glare, dynamic but contorted poses and demon-quelling stamps. Whether hero, villain or clown, aragoto characters erupt in a rumbling, roaring war of words, or effortless displays of swordplay. A serenely confident hero brushes aside a seemingly endless group of attackers, slashing and stacking them into a human pyramid like logs. The swashbuckling is punctuated by mime poses to wooden clacks, and shouts of encouragement from the stalls: 'We've been waiting for you!'; 'Number One in Japan!'

Wagoto-style romantic heroes are handsome yet faintly effeminate, bullied and bumbling, portrayed relatively realistically. Their emotional transparency, endearing honesty, and sensitivity win them friends and lovers, but they are often betrayed or abandoned, provoking uncontrollable piques of jealousy and sometimes violence.

Maruhon are plays adapted whole from the bunraku puppet repertoire, featuring movements strictly following the gidayu narrative accompaniment. *Shosagoto*, pure dance scenes, often including extravagant costume changes, are interspersed with serious dramatic scenes or plays on a programme. Shosagoto give full range to the erotic beauty of the onnagata, potent dynamism of young men, and anguish of star-crossed couples' romantic entanglements in michiyuki travel scenes.

Some say that *all* kabuki is dance. Seemingly insignificant, practical stage business – lighting a lamp, drinking sake – is performed with the economic, rhythmic, graceful choreography of dance. Movement follows traditionally transmitted kata patterns to music, song or precisely inflected dialogue. Yet there are no pure dance specialists; all actors can, in theory, dance. Dance in kabuki absorbed every manner of preceding popular genre: ritual shrine maiden kagura, lively folk dance, elegant dance from noh and kyogen, courtesans' erotic displays, as well as original comic and heroic choreographic portraits of firemen, craftsmen and Edo street-scenes. A tour de force, *hengemono* (transformation pieces) were dance-plays comprised of independent scenes requiring elaborate onstage costume changes. Independent segments lifted from these plays became a staple for teaching amateurs.

Dance is broadly classified as *mai*, gliding, circular, solemn and elegant, including noh, but also shrine and court dances to drum and flute, and *odori*, dynamic, rhythmic dance employing both arm and leg movements, with feet frequently leaving the ground in stamps and jumps. These dances are performed to harvest and drinking songs, popular ballads with erotic double-entendre, and katari narratives. Gestures illustrating a song's lyrics or abstract design elements are known as *furi*; *ningyōburi* imitate puppet movements. Handling properties is occasionally employed as important stage business, indices of inner character, and presages plot twists. The fan, handkerchief, umbrella, pipe, lantern and pike are used decoratively, adding to the visual splendour of the stage picture.

Scenic spectacle

Kabuki developed as colourful, exuberant performance taking full advantage of elaborate stage machinery. As shrewd self-marketers, kabuki actor-managers were quick to ride successive waves of technological innovation and shifting audience tastes to create ever more spectacular stage tricks. The *hanamichi* ramp running through the theatre included traps (as did the stage) for surprise entrances and highlighted exits. Acrobatics, 'flying' and stage mechanic gimmickry allowing quick changes of costume and set are hallmarks of *keren* spectacle. The large revolving stage first used in 1758, elevator-lifted stage sections, and scenery boards that could be flipped down instantly, allowed scenes to shift from snowy exterior to cosy interior without pause. An example of kabuki's theatrical versatility: rushing rivers or stormy seas could be created with cloth whipped up by stage assistants, shown by actors 'swimming' in slow motion, or in a pool with actual water built on stage. Spectacular moments could be drawn out indefinitely with kabuki's elastic time conventions; punctuated by wooden clacks, actors froze in dynamic poses at climactic moments in stunning *tableaux vivants*. These echoed images of their namesakes, transmitted by popular, mass-produced souvenir woodblock prints.

If star actors were the great engines of kabuki showmanship, the *kuroko* (or *kōken*) was the indispensable engineer. The man-in-black stage assistant, whether black-hooded and scampering, or dignified in black kimono with *kamishimo* vest, enabled actors to concentrate on their full-frontal display. The assistant provided indispensable support by placing and retrieving properties with just-in-time exactitude, smoothing, displaying or removing costumes for stunning effect, surreptitiously applying makeup, serving tea and prompting lines.

Enduring popularity as commercial theatre

Kabuki was a vital site for community worship of idolized stars, and the common coin for expressing personal ambition throughout the Edo period. By the late 1700s, grand kabuki was so expensive that none but the wealthiest merchants, and their wives, could afford good seats regularly, yet varied price-points permitted fanatic followings from all classes. Those who could not attend these could still see lesser actors in smaller urban theatres set up for temporary runs at shrines and temples, or on regional tours. They could collect illustrated tales and woodblock prints, and watch fairground performers impersonate famous actors in favourite roles. They could study the singing and dance with a mushrooming group of licensed guild professionals.

Such connoisseurship and idolatry were fed by and further fired up the burgeoning publishing industry. Plays from bunraku were published immediately, with copious illustrations. Woodblock prints, showing famous players in their greatest roles, were available in all sizes and ranges of quality, heroic portraits to idiosyncratic caricatures. *Hyōbanki* critical handbooks resembled the fanzines or sports magazines of today, combining news, gossip, criticism and images to feed the seemingly insatiable appetites of fanatic followers. Emulating guidebook rankings of prostitutes, hyōbanki listed actors hired by the great theatres for a given season ranked according to beauty, acting abilities and especially effective roles. Aficionados and fashion mavens helped secure kabuki's place on the forefront of Edo culture.

Kabuki today

Produced by the Shochiku Corporation and National Theatre, programmes today normally comprise highlight scenes from different plays. Designed to show off the qualities of the actors in trademark roles, they can also feature a single, multi-act play. Monthly runs are given regularly at theatres in Tokyo, Nagoya, Kyoto, Osaka and Fukuoka, with regional tours in between. Kabuki can still sell-out $150 top-tier seats for 25-day runs, proving that, in a remarkable four centuries of continuous adaptation, kabuki today remains popular, commercial entertainment.

One reason for its success might be that there is something for everyone. Kabuki is a supremely hybrid art, assimilating popular music, plots from noh, kyogen and bunraku, and acting techniques from courtesans, kyogen actors and puppets. Rather than fusing them into a seamless whole, they are offered unapologetically as a hodge-podge of contrasting parts, challenging audiences' understanding and imagination, but providing endless variety. This eclectic aesthetic and bricolage approach permitted kabuki to some extent to go with the flow in the modern era.

By the time American warships forcibly opened Japan to foreign trade in 1853, and the shōgunate fell in 1867 to begin the Meiji Restoration, Japanese traditional theatre, arguably except kabuki, had largely become classical. Repertoire was fixed by acting conventions, family styles codified, documented by published illustrations and books. However, the sudden absence of samurai patronage and oversight, release from regulations on theatre architecture and content, and gradual import of western theatre dramaturgy and technologies created much creative turmoil. These changes will be examined in Chapter 22 on traditional theatre in modern Asia.

4

Traditional Indonesian theatre

I Nyoman Sedana and Kathy Foley

It is impossible to speak in a short time about how traditional yet contemporary theatre is operating in all the 6,000 inhabited islands of the Indonesian archipelago with enormous cultural/ethnic (Austronesian, Chinese, Papuan, Indo [European-Malay]) and religious diversity (animist, Hindu, Buddhist, Muslim, Christian). Categories may overlap and create mixtures of different ethnic and religious influences. This chapter will often focus on examples from Bali where the first author is a practitioner. Some Balinese traits reflect wider national patterns, but others are specific due to local religious needs and a robust tourist industry in which performance is emphasized. Selected aspects (e.g. training in secondary and tertiary arts education institutions; heritage art practice in culture formation; impacts of urbanization, globalization and new media) are shared with other regions of the nation.

Indonesian performance is rather sporadically reflected in western theatre scholarship, and anthropologists, ethnomusicologist/dance ethnologists and emergent cultural studies scholars have perhaps given more attention to the area than theatre scholars until recently. The tendencies of the traditional arts to be improvised rather than written texts and language limitations (i.e. few indigenous scholars are writing in European languages and international scholars often have curtailed understanding of local languages used in performance) have led to more writing around music, movement or social/ritual aspects of theatre than works that look at theatre roundly as a holistic performance including music–dance–text.[1] Relatively few international scholars have had the tools of musical, movement, language and cultural skills to deal with the unified entity that performance often is in Indonesia.

Theatre has long been and continues to be an important element of life cycle and community celebrations. It is a public site where artists and viewers expand their aesthetic imagination, critique life and formulate their spiritual norms. Ritual and secular genres are shared in private house compounds, village halls, cultural centres, temples (in Bali), arts schools, government venues and large public spaces.

Broadly speaking, Indonesian traditional theatre divides into three groups: (1) dance genres – which range from archaic rituals to martial displays to pure social dances; (2) *wayang* (puppet theatre) and masking – considered the oldest fully formed theatres in areas influenced by Javanese; and (3) various dance-drama theatres that may have first emulated puppet models but have increasingly diverged, especially since the nineteenth century as popular urban folk theatres have emerged. These last two groups (puppet and actor theatre) have normally been defined by the narrative source (i.e. local legends, Indian epics, historical chronicles) and song/musical accompaniment, which varies by area but often uses percussive instruments as a base.

For the first group, dance, it may be non-narrative, but it supplies features that feed into narrative dance. For example, ritual trance dances such as Balinese *sanghyang dedari* (where prepubescent girls are used in healing) may form the backdrop of the three-girl *legong keraton* (palace female dance which has a rather abstract story), and that, in turn, can develop into a more robust dramatic form when presented as a thesis project by an arts college student who may explore the form with more characters and a different story. On Java we see similar progression from trance dances such as *sintren* (village female trance dance) to the abstract *srimpi* and *bedhaya* (court female dances with ceremonial implications) to more elaborate choreographies with stories such as *Arjuna's Meditation* choreographed by Yogyakarta dance master Rama Sasminta Mardawa in the 1970s – there the dancers become seductive goddesses trying to test the hero's meditative strength.

Martial-arts-inflected dances such as the Balinese *baris* may give parameters of male dance in other performances, while the pan-Indonesian *silat* becomes important in many folk theatres (Sumatran *randai*, Jakarta area *lenong*, Sundanese *sandiwara*, Javanese *ketoprak*, to give just some examples), which mostly developed between around 1890 and 1930 and are less linked to puppet theatre models. Female folk forms that derive from sexy courtesan social dances such as Balinese *joged*, Javanese *tayuban*, Sumatran *mak yong* or the Sundanese *ketuk tilu/jaipongan* likewise can be the opening or part of theatre performances. Since the 1980s, neo-traditional dances have been creatively devised and modified from earlier sacred or ceremonial or social forms and are often used for opening government gatherings, celebrating the end of the fasting month, or other entertainments, and such genres are routinely presented for tourists, especially in areas such as Bali and Java which have a regular demand for cultural shows for national or international visitors.

On these two islands of Java and Bali, highly stylized dance-acting, speech diction, recitative and narrative repertoire predominate in traditional dance-drama forms – and genres are influenced by the models of the puppet theatre. In areas with no tradition of puppet theatre, the style of dancing is more naturalistic, without these set conventions of character type based on wayang or mask dance (*topeng*) characters. Instead, they just use the social and martial dance styles added to elements (painted scenery, proscenium) derived from practices of early twentieth-century touring theatre goups from Malaysia, Singapore and the coastal cities of Java's north coast (see, for example, Cohen 2006).

In colonial Indonesia, dance-dramas used struggle – of a local hero against an overseas intruder (normally an ogre king) – and protest – of the 'little guy'/clown against injustice of the powerful elite – as ongoing themes. Local myths might be celebrated too. For example, in Sumbawa, a legend tells of the Komodo dragon who is the prince's sibling, helping viewers to understand the need to foster nature as our brother/sister. Contemporary performances tap such legends to communicate environmental messages in an age of eco-consciousness.

The prime theatre tradition, and arguably a source of traditional dance-drama practices on Bali and Java, is wayang puppetry, which primarily popularized the Indian *Mahabharata* stories albeit in indigenous versions. The term wayang traditionally has many variants, but the most important are: (1) *wayang kulit* (leather shadow puppet), (2) *wayang golek* (wooden rod puppet) and (3) *wayang wong* ('human puppet', i.e. dance-drama taking repertoire, music, diction, costumes, movements and acting from puppet style). For over a millennium before UNESCO declared wayang a masterpiece of the intangible heritage of humanity (2003), wayang was a deeply important psycho-social ritual-cultural practice, linked to shamanic roots, magnified via

Hindu–Buddhist ritual practices (which remain central in Bali) and, with some changes due to Islamic mystical thinking, in Java and other areas. In the contemporary period, artists explore how digital effects, rap music, Middle Eastern musical instruments and so on can fit into new hybrids of wayang.

Puppetry is often relegated to children in the west, but in Indonesia it is the culturally high genre and an 'encyclopaedia' of spiritual norms (*Shivam*), philosophical insights (*Satyan*) and high aesthetics (*Sundaram*). Even the objects merit careful attention – people never step on/over the wayang puppet or sit on top of the chest in which the puppets are stored in Java or Bali (though such beliefs may be weaker among puppeteers in outer islands such as Kalimantan or Sumatra). However, wayang, while often still related to traditional rituals/rites of passage, has seen innovation and secularization, especially since the 1970s.

Historically, performance is important in social-ritual frames. It was integral to village rituals and highlighted in court ceremonials, which often provided significant patronage for the arts and included participation by aristocrats as both performers and honoured audience. This persisted in the colonial period and court traces continue to the present. When court subsidies failed with the advent of the nation-state in the period after the Second World War, other support sometimes filled the gap – temples in places such as Bali, plantation or factory events (sponsored by the owners) on Java, or with emerging middle-class households sponsoring family rituals such as circumcisions/weddings. In the twentieth century some areas geared cultural perform-ances to tourists, balancing differentials such as ritual, economic and entertainment impacts.

For tourist performances, a five- or eight-hour wayang might be reduced to 2 hours or even 45 minutes; lengthy narration and story complexity might be reduced to a love scene, some low humour and a battle. Voluptuous singers or dancers might be prioritized over vocal/musical quality, and English sometimes substituted for the local language in performances in tourist areas or for touring overseas, as with the Bali Kamajaya Arts Company.

While there has been some movement in recent years, via the arts training schools, towards the use of scripted texts with clear, repeatable cues for particular music, this is not the norm in tradition-based theatres such as wayang. The improvised lines of the *dalang* (master puppeteer) or actor-dancer supersede any set script. Even in intercultural experiments, the performances gave full authority to actors on stage instead of to a playwright's words on the page, as was the case in co-author I Nyoman Sedana's *Bali Dream* (*A Midsummer Night's Dream*, 2012) at Butler University in Indianapolis or *Bali Tempest* (2014) at East 15th Acting School, Essex University, UK (Figure 4.1). Other artists who have worked in similar intercultural formats include Balinese choreographers I Wayan Dibia and I Made Bandem, Javanese master artist Dalang Sumarsam and choreographer Sardono Kusumo, and Sundanese choreographers Irawati Durban and Endo Suanda.

Through transmigration, many classical theatres have moved – especially from Java – to other islands, such as Sulawesi, Sumatera and Kalimantan. Similarly, Indonesian performing arts from various islands are taught theoretically and practically in all Indonesian art institutes at the secondary and tertiary levels. These schools, administered by the Indonesian Ministry of National Education and Culture, allow thousands of students to study up to doctoral level in dance, music, folk theatres and wayang. Thousands of school and college artist-students from such institutions compete in national arts festivals held annually and biannually.

Bali

In the *wayang parwa* (literally 'chapter' [of the *Mahabharata*]) shadow puppet shows, the prologue in old Javanese (Kawi) always begins:

Figure 4.1 Last scene of *Bali Dream.*
(Courtesy of I. Nyoman Sedana)

May there be no hindrances or obstacles; once upon a time who knows how long ago, there was holy emptiness; great emptiness appeared like a screen with lightning penetrating the entire cosmos. Then down like a torrent came the earth, water, wind, fire, space, star, planet, sun, and moon; the sacred shadow figures suddenly appeared at the behest of God the most High – God the Teacher. Then, Holy Mighty Voice of Poetry appeared and divided the stories into chapters and all was set down in eighteen parwas by the holyman Kresna Dwipayana.[2]

Arts, culture and religion are integrated in Bali and *bayu* (energy), *sabda* (voice/sound) and *idep* (thought) integrate *satyam* (truth), *shivam* (purity) and *sundaram* (beauty). Art is needed in spiritual, social, cultural, economic and political life, and, even if a performance is commissioned by a political party, ethics and beauty must still inhere therein.

Lontar palm-leaf holy scriptures such as *Siwagama*, *Purwagama*, *Cudamani* and others, and dramatic reservoirs such as *kakawin* (old Javanese narrative poems), *kidung* (middle Javanese poems), Indian epics and local legends are still favoured in performance over modern history and literature. Wayang theatre demonstrates that life is just a temporal shadow of the unfathomable reality: we live in a world under the control of the demon Kala (time). In this world of illusions the wayang's shadows help us to see the ultimate truth.

This Balinese sacred wayang is still performed by noted dalang such as Dalang I Wayan Wija and Dalang Cenk Blong (I Wayan Nardayana) to purify and release people or spirits who might be entangled in the web of negative/demonic forces. This purificatory function is analogous to performance/ceremonies for souls during the Chinese Hungry Ghost Festival where the

Mu Lian jiu mu (Mulain Redeems his Mother) puppet story shows a hero who releases spirits of his dead mother or the comparable *Mokuren* story linked to Obon when spirits visit in Japan.

Recently the regent/mayor of Badung, Bali sponsored a ritual *wayang sapuleger* ('releasing misfortune') purification for 2,000 people. Ironically, while such wayang-based mass purifications spread, puppeteers complained about their reduced opportunities as colossal ceremonies replaced the older, more local/personal hiring of a show. Likewise, people turn to performance in times of difficulty; when Islamic terrorists hit a tourist nightspot with the Bali bomb in 2002, one local response was ritual purification to renew natural harmony. Dalang I Made Sidja and his son I Made Sidia took an old story from the *Siwagama* scripture, in which the gods Brahma, Wisnu (Vishnu) and Siwa (Shiva) descend into the world as performers of wayang, *topeng* (mask dance), *barong* (lion-like protective figure/body puppet) and so on, to pacify and remind lower spirits of their origins in the divine and to encourage spirits to help human beings instead of inciting misguided men to join terrorist organizations (Figure 4.2). In addition to traditional shadows, digital projections were displayed on the extra-long shadow screen to create colourful scenery, and rather than the solo puppeteer of traditional wayang, multiple puppeteers sitting on skateboards sped across behind the screen holding animal and human figures fleeing the flames of bombs and karma gone awry. The tradition of curing through art and the appeal of

Figure 4.2 Dalang Sidia and his students performed *Wayang Dasanama Kerta* (Wayang of the Ten Sacred Things) riding on skateboards and using projections at the Institute of the Arts, Denpasar, Bali in 2003 to 'cure' the post-traumatic stress caused by the Bali terrorist bombing on Kuta Beach.

(Photo by Kathy Foley)

new technologies were conjoined in this show, which was funded in part by a non–governmental organization (NGO) to cure Balinese post-traumatic stress as tourists vanished overnight and the economy went into a nosedive.

Balinese theatrical form is derived from the traditional concepts of *Sang Hyang Tunggal* (the holy oneness/unity/divine), *rwa bhineda* (the two opposite forces in dynamic balance), *tri angga* (the three concentric components of *desa–kala–patra*, meaning place–time–circumstance) and mandala as the cosmic centre.[3] To begin *kawi dalang* (creativity of the puppet master), the dalang has to recall the names of gods and activate their attributes to reflect certain aesthetic elements. For example, in selecting a play the dalang has to activate three attributes of God Rudra at the southwest: (1) the patron's expectation, (2) the performance context and (3) the dalang's intention.

Wayang kulit is the oldest extant leather puppet theatre on Bali, as it is on Java. The most popular shadow puppet show on Bali enacts stories from the *Mahabharata* and is called *wayang kulit parwa*; the dalang is accompanied by two or four musicians who each play the metallophone *gender wayang*, bronze keyed instruments with two mallets. A second form is *wayang kulit ramayana* (which tells the story of Rama) in which the puppeteer is accompanied by fifteen musicians (who play the four *gender wayang*, a pair of medium *kendang* drums, and other percussion instruments). Other forms of wayang are denoted by the narrative reservoir: *wayang tantri* which tells animal stories, *wayang babad* which relates historical chronicles; *wayang calonarang* which tells of the eponymous widow/witch; *wayang cupak* which shows how a greedy brother besets his good-hearted sibling, and so on. In each show, the dalang executes multiple roles – art director, narrator, singer, puppet manipulator, shadow master, storyteller, and even priest, since a purification ceremony may be added (if requested) at the end of the show.

Beyond the popular traditional presentations discussed above, at least fifty creative experiments in new wayang have been developed as final projects by students completing an academic degree at the Indonesian Arts Institute in Denpasar (Institute Seni Indonesia, ISI). Different types of puppet, aesthetic approach, performance technique (including ventriloquism), story sources or music are usually part of the offering and recent presentations have included *wayang golek agung* (large rod puppets) and *wayang papan* (flat panel puppets taller than human size).

While interest in traditional *wayang* is declining, innovative artists gain viewers. Dalang Nardayana with *wayang chenk blonk* uses an enlarged orchestra and multiple female singers, and has introduced new comic characters such as the eponymous Chenk and Blonk. These innovations and his creativity in storytelling allow Nardayana to flourish and grow rich. His shows or those of Dalang Joblar (I Ketut Muada) are still often commissioned by the government, businesses or political parties to communicate messages to the public. Joblar's performances, which include electric keyboard music, achieved great popularity around the time of the 1997 Asian financial crisis – Joblar comes from the first letters of 'Jeritan Orang Berani Lantaran Anjloknya Rupiah' (Screams of the Brave due to the Fall of the Rupiah [the Indonesian currency]).

Dance theatre

Gambuh is the oldest extant dance-drama in Bali enacting story of Panji (also known as the Malat cycle), which is about an early prince of East Java and can be traced back to Java–Bali historical connections during the pre-fourteen-century Majapahit era. Two popular dance-dramas of the Majapahit kingdom of Java – *raket* and *tekes* – supposedly were adopted and combined by the Balinese with the fall of the Madjapahit kingdom in the fifteenth century as Hindu-Buddhist aristocrats left Java rather than accept Islam. Thereafter gambuh was performed for palace celebrations. After near-extinction in the late twentieth century, the revitalization of gambuh was helped by a Ford Foundation grant, coordinated by the Italian-Balinese dancer Maria Cristina Formaggia. One of the activities was scheduling gambuh for tourist shows every first and fifteenth day of the month in the village hall, outside the village temple of Batuan, Gianyar. Now gambuh is performed for the grandest temple ceremonies, lasting for up to 42 days, or for large home dedication ceremonies, lasting up to 11 days.

Topeng mask theatre is presented by one to five dancers in Bali, enacting a story from *babad* (royal genealogical chronicles) and applying historical incidents creatively to address current social and political issues. Contemporary masters such as I Ketut Kodi excel in creative plot interpretations that make history speak to the problems of the present. However, although performers continue to use these stories to teach social and religious ideas, current audiences demand a greater percentage of time spent on humour and pure entertainment than was the case 50 years ago. Although topeng is normally an all-male genre, by the late 1990s, thanks to the efforts of women artists such as Desak Suarti Laksmi, an all-female group, Topeng Shakti, was initiated and even went on a European tour before it disbanded.

Wayang wong is related to puppet models but uses actors (usually masked) to emulate what puppets would do in a shadow show. There are two types of Balinese wayang wong. In wayang wong *ramayana* dancers present the story of Rama and his spouse Sita; in this form all characters wear masks. Wayang wong *parwa* or simply *parwa* shares *Mahabharata* stories, but in this form some refined characters such as the two Padawa heroes, Arjuna and Nakula, and their wife, Draupadi, are unmasked.

Barong is the lion-like mask and two-man body puppet and a dance-drama enacting local mythology, and is often integrated with the *kris* or dagger dance. The barong mask is religiously enshrined in the temple and serves as a protector of the village. This mythical animal character may relate to lion dance figures found throughout South, Southeast and East Asia (though parade figures are not just lions, but also pigs, tigers and the mythical 'banaspati raja' [king of the forest]). Related masked characters may include the widow/witch (*rangda*), her demonic followers, monkeys and so on. Barong is regularly performed in processions or in narrative forms on ceremonial days in the temples where such masks are enshrined, but secular performances are also given at arts festivals or for tourists, with little or no attention to auspicious days or spaces.

Calonarang is a genre in which the barong appears. At present this genre, which is thought to have developed in the nineteenth century, is usually performed in death/chthonic temples; these are situated near graveyards, places associated with sickness, magic and malevolent forces. In some ways the performance, while religiously robust, fills a bit of the same need that teen horror films may in the west – magic, marriage plans gone awry, monstrous forces stalking the land, sickness and death are common themes. Young unmarried males usually make up the bulk of the chorus – in trance they may try to stab themselves, while the barong and the nearby priest with his holy water provide protection. Some paid actors specialize in clown characters and/or the corpse, and these performers are invariably invited to play in various villages – humour to lighten midnight near the graveyard and the ability to withstand the magical onslaughts are handled by professionals. The most frequent narrative is about King Erlangga's refusal to marry Ratna Mengali, daughter of a widow-witch (Rangda) of East Java – she brings disaster and death through magical powers. There are also stories (e.g. *Balian Batur, Wayan Buyar* and *Basur*) dealing with other witch or warlock-type figures who must be stopped. The crisis of the Bali bomb of 2002 brought on a spate of performances of this genre; magically charged performances fit difficult times.

Kecak or *cak* was originally the chorus that accompanied trance-dance ceremonies related to old shamanistic behaviours. In the 1930s, hundreds of male chorus members in Bedulu village dressed in the protective black-and-white (*poleng*) sarong to sit bare-chested around a branched torch that illuminated the black night with its flickering flames. This was a secular redesign in which a western musician-painter, Walter Spies, participated to create entertainment for the increasing tourist market. Spies and local artists devised a new dance-drama enacting the *Ramayana* story. The magical beauty of the kecak dance-drama – in which the actor-dancers move to the exciting and sometimes eerie sounds of vocal chanters as they raise their hands high or make other gestures, while vocalizing interlocking rhythms of 'cak, cak, cak' and so on – made this new *kecak* seem an exquisitely ancient (albeit new) musical dance-drama. Vocals have patterns related to the structured interlocks of *gamelan* instruments. The conductor leads the dynamic structure; the narrator improvises the drama in the spoken and sung lines; and each actor-dancer enacts his specific dramatic character. The genre received the nickname 'monkey dance' on account of the chorus, who sometimes play the monkey army in battle scenes – and these monkeys were an easy element for tourists to grasp. They help Prince Rama, the hero, to rescue his wife Sita who has been kidnapped by demonic King Rahwana. Since the 1960s major choreographers such as Sardono Kusumo from Java and I Wayan Dibia from Bali have developed new stories/ choreographies for local festivals and Indonesian audiences using this hybrid genre.

Performed by a dozen actor-dancers telling Panji/Malat stories, *arja* is essentially Balinese opera, in which the narration, dialogue and characterization are communicated through improvised sung poetry (but with an occasional translation and comic interludes in vernacular language added by servant characters). The challenge lies in the rigid prosody governing the *tembang* (sung poetry). Contemporary youth, while still practising the form, have difficulty in achieving mastery comparable to famous artists such as I Made Kredek and his daughter Ni Nyoman Candri, still a well-known performer of the *condong* (maid) character.[4] Innovations in arja have led to other new forms, such as *wayang arja* created in 1975 by dalang and topeng master I Made Sidja – it uses puppetry by a solo dalang rather than individual actors to present arja sung stories. Artists such as I Wayan Dibia have in recent years created new arja telling the stories of Oedipus, Romeo and Juliet, and modern Indonesia.

Secondary and tertiary education has, as previously noted, become a site where many innovations within tradition occur. In Bali as in other colleges of performing arts in Indonesia,[5] students normally study arts in the classroom setting, but they may simultaneously study with village artists to gain deeper understanding of the older traditions; some of the students are, of course, the offspring of major village performers. The students participate in large dance-drama events at festivals where arts schools gather together; for events such as the Bali Arts Festival, which takes place each June–July; or participate in international tours in which teachers from these academies play the major roles.

Conservative Balinese scholars, who were worried about the presentation of sacred Balinese arts in international touring shows and tourist venues, assembled in 1971 and went on to debate and demarcate some performances as *wali* (sacred and not to be performed in non-religious contexts), *bali* (semi-sacred and performed in semi-religious context) and *balibalihan* (secular). But this distinction between sacred and entertainment in Balinese performance is not fixed; rather, it fluctuates according to time, place and circumstances. What makes art sacred or profane requires more than outside dictums of government or religious officials: the internal spirit with which the dancer, puppeteer, musician and/or actor approach the art is the key.

Although the guru/elder may be a conservative artist/scholar attempting to maintain the authenticity of the past, the artist/child, trained through imitation, repetition and emulation, will explore her dream of expanding from heritage roots to be an innovative artist who departs from tradition. In time, such innovations are welcomed back into the tradition at the local temple festival. Art that sustains itself in the heart of tension between tradition and innovation is worth seeing for its aesthetic, educational, cultural and spiritual values.

Performance in Balinese culture begins from the idea of offering and devotion (*ngayah*). The passion with which villages train their children to dance and with which they themselves make and enjoy music begins and ends in the idea of dance, music, sung poetry, beautiful puppets, finely made masks, decorative offerings, brilliant dancers and raucous comedians as essential to ceremonies that honour the gods and the ancestors, in order to bind together/protect the community. Wayang and other arts performed by highly trained specialists can be essential to the completion of some ceremonies, and are also utilized to invite others to gather and participate. Noted artists will be invited to work with local village groups to develop new pieces of music or dance for an upcoming temple festival. Dances that the 1971 Listibya (Majelis Pertimbangan dan Pembinaan Kebudayaan, The Council to Develop and Protect the Cultural Arts) arts council declared *balih-balihan* (purely entertainment), which made their first appearance on a secular stage at the Bali Arts Festival, may later be included as part of temple festivals presented in the spirit of ngayah. Thus performing in Bali begins in the temple and returns to it.

The arts beyond Bali

Bali has particular idiosyncrasies, but the Hindu-Buddhist traditions we see there are just a continuation of a longer heritage of the archipelago, which includes arts practice as part of personal and community rituals – a theme that unites all regions. In Islamic areas, of course, the activities will reflect modifications that came with that heritage, while Christian communities modify differently, and have, for example, developed forms of wayang to deliver Bible stories (*wayang wahyu*). In many areas there were traditionally trained artists who were based in village traditions and were needed for ceremonies; in other cases, artists were connected to aristocratic ceremonial and social entertainments. With independence some new patterns emerged. The arts as explicit tool of government-defined propaganda was a lesson well learnt by Indonesians who worked in the arts during the Japanese occupation in the Second World War when the propaganda bureau strictly oversaw messaging. Thereafter, both Sukarno's (socialist/eastern bloc leaning) and Suharto's (capitalist/western bloc leaning) governments used the arts in cultural diplomacy and local representation (in the run-up to elections, introducing government programmes and so on), and developed methods of censorship through registration and other measures. Artists were often the victims of killings or imprisonment between 1965 and 1967 if they had in any way been associated with the PKI (Partai Komunis Indonesia) when the Sukarno government fell. This, of course, led to subsequent caution in political issues, especially in launching critiques of the government in the following years.

In the Suharto era (1965–98), regional 'Highpoints of Culture' (Puncak Kebudayan), as chartered in paragraph 32 of the Undang Undangan Darar 1945 (National Constitution), were emphasized. While including representation from various ethnic groups, Suharto's New Order valorized the wayang, dance and dramatic traditions of Central Java. With the fall of Suharto in the late 1990s, economic resources were returned to the various regions, and perhaps since that time a more level playing field has been possible, as each region of Indonesia seems to line up for its 'turn' to have their performing art declared an intangible cultural heritage by UNESCO since 7 November 2003. Wayang was, of course, the first Indonesian art declared as a masterpiece and this included wayang from all areas; however, due to Java's large population as well as its historical, political and civic centrality, the bulk of support for maintaining the tradition has gone to *wayang kulit purwa*, the prime Javanese puppet form.

Javanese traditional theatre

Although some countries on the Arab peninsula may consider theatre 'un-Islamic', Indonesia as the nation with the largest Muslim population in the world has long held performance central. Some villages in Java continue to use wayang kulit for village purifications (*bersih desa*, literally 'cleansing the village'), personal purifications (*ruwatan*, literally 'making safe'), life-cycle celebrations (weddings and circumcisions) and so on.

Wayang

Wayang kulit purwa, *s*hadow puppet theatre telling stories of characters from the *Mahabharata* and *Ramayana*, is performed with flat leather puppets, the shadows of which are cast on a white screen by the puppeteer (Figure 4.3). Stories are most often 'branch' episodes, which are not found in Indian versions of the epics, but tell newly invented stories that use the Hindu epic characters as their heroes and villains. The audience will watch the puppets, manipulated by the single puppeteer, usually from the puppeteer's side of the screen. At least one, or as many as nine, women singer(s) (*sinden*) embellish the show with vocals. The sinden and dalang sing to the gamelan orchestra, which uses both the minor-key sounding *pelog* and the pentatonic *slendro* tunings. In recent decades *campusari* ('mixed entertainments/pleasures') performance has often added comics who interact with puppets or singers, music which may now incorporate a keyboard and drumset, and other changes. As previously noted, in 2003 UNESCO declared wayang a masterpiece of the intangible heritage of humanity. At that time, the puppetry organization PEPADI (Persatuan Padalangan Indonesia, Indonesian Union of Dalangs) developed plans for safeguarding and developing wayang. The form is frequently sent on international tours and the work of Dalang Purbo Asmoro has become well known in the international community because Kristie Emerson, an American who lives in Java, has provided digital simultaneous translations that allow Dalang Purbo frequently to stream performances worldwide, making international audiences part of a Java-centred global wayang community. Meanwhile, many younger dalang, who often come from traditional puppetry families, have appeared, hoping someday to match the esteem given to puppetmasters such as Dalang Narto Sabdo (the top performer of the 1950s–1970s), or more recent superstars such as Dalang Anom Suroto, Ki Mateb Sudasono or Dalang Enthus Susmono (whose popularity has now led him to be an elected regent/governor).

Today's hopeful artists usually train in puppetry programmes at the tertiary academies of the arts in Yogyakarta or Surakarta. Many begin their new wayang styles while still students. Dalang Slamet Gundono (1966–2014) was famed for his *wayang suket* (grass wayang). His gamelan included a mixture of traditional and western instruments. He abandoned the screen and, holding the figures woven from stalks in his hands, would share the story – now acting a role, now calling a dancer out to present one of the characters. In his avant-garde wayang, which called for social justice and ecological attention, he represented the views of youthful Javanese. Yogyakarta's Wayang Hip Hop's website advertises that the group combines 'Javanese traditions and hip-hop beats' (see http://wayanghiphop.com). The dalang, Ki Catur 'Benyek' Kuncoro, manipulates puppets that may discuss the drug habit of one of the clowns. Rap songs are punctuated by the appearances of actors costumed half in traditional *wayang wong* dance-drama costumes and half in contemporary grunge. Traditional stories may be radically revised or a hero like Gatotkoca may talk back to his heroic parent (such as the *Mahabharata* hero Bhima) in a way that would not be accepted in traditional performance, where this would be considered 'against wayang ethics'. But such questioning seems to provide a megaphone for issues of urban youth and wins young viewers to an art that they know, but might not otherwise watch (Varela 2014).

Figure 4.3 Javanese Wayang Kulit Purwa leather shadow puppet the demon King
Nirwatakawaca meets his minister and a bowing demoness in the
story *Arjuna's Meditation.*

(Courtesy of ShadowLight Productions)

Wayang wong (also *wayang orang*) literally means 'human' wayang and is a Javanese court classical theatre based on puppet theatre practice that features stylized dance–acting, elaborate costumes, improvised speech, and singing to enact the *Ramayana*- or *Mahabarata*-based stories. Large-scale palace performances that might involve a hundred dancers continued in central Javanese palaces until the late 1930s. Public theatres for wayang wong were also started in entertainment parks during the colonial era and some of these spaces may limp along even to the present day, such as Taman Sriwidari in Solo, where artists have been partially subsidized by the government. However, audiences are sparse and the threat of closure always looms.

Tourist shows are mounted in Yogyakarta, but, rather than a multi-day or 6-hour performance, these shows are just snippets of dance with a short scene or two. A large performance that has aspects of wayang wong but has abandoned the language has become a new form called *sendratari* (dance-drama); a major sendratari version of the *Ramayana* story is presented at Prambanan temple near Yogyakatrta and has been running almost uninterrupted since the 1960s. However, flashy spectacle and bored performers, rather than a fine aesthetic of high-quality dance, characterize this show for tourist audiences.

New sendratari choreographies based on tradition are offered by major artists such as Sardono Kusomo of Solo/Jakarta, and he may borrow from court theatre traditions such as wayang wong or the female court dance discussed below. Performances play in major cities and sometimes tour internationally with government sponsorship.

The many travelling groups that performed in markets or temporary theatres with walls of plaited bamboo in times past are gone, but for major provincial or national festivals a college of the performing arts or a local school of Javanese dance may present neo-traditional wayang wong, usually supported by government funding. The wayang festival (Pekan Wayang), which is normally mounted by PEPADI every 5 years, always includes wayang wong. Sometimes these festivals featured works of innovative artists, for example Ki Sukasman, whose finely carved figures, multicoloured lighting effects, multiple puppeteers and dancers who cast their own shadows alongside the puppets made for intricate performances in the 1980s and 1990s. Since Sukasman's death his students and collaborators have carried on.

Srimpi *and bedhaya court dance*

Some dances were reserved for aristocratic ceremonial events such as *srimpi*, which required four or five females and *behaya* with seven or nine dancers. Choreographies were heirloom treasures that belonged to a royal lineage, and, when a noble family fought, peace agreements might include which member of the family got which choreography. The sacred, smooth *bedhaya ketawang* of Surakarta is presented by palace women who are, even today, conceptualized as (or, in times past, were) consorts of the ruling king. Mystical lore and tantric concepts surround this dance and, to the present day, female court choreographies are seen as repositories of mystical power. Though dancers today may study the steps at the arts academy in Surakarta, some female dancers avoid this study, since they say they would, just by doing the dance, become implicated in the royal household. Dancers may also worry about having their period when a rehearsal or performance is scheduled: they are banned from dancing during menses. Meanwhile, modern performances that reflect court female dance are mounted by dancers such as Didik Nini Towok, a male choreographer who specializes in female dance. His intercultural *Bedhaya Hagoromo* combined Yogyakarta-style female court dance with Japanese *noh* and was presented in Indonesia and Japan.

Urban popular theatres

Kethoprak is a traditional theatre in Central Java, enacting stories from chronicles or other sources through sung and spoken lines with limited dance and martial arts movements. The costume is stylized. This form has suffered attrition of audiences, but may still be mounted for Independence Day and other events (Hatley 2008). *Ludruk* is the popular theatre of East Java, enacting stories and characters derived from local myths and chronicles or domestic melodramas. *Ngremo* dance of East Java is traditionally performed by a female impersonator; song and clowning are part of the show. Improvised theatres such as *ketoprak* and *ludruk* can still be found, but they are rarer than wayang or female court dance and are less likely to be highlighted in the curricula of the colleges and high schools of the arts.

Sundanese traditional theatre

Another form of puppetry is *wayang golek*, the Indonesian three-dimensional rod puppets, carved from wood and elaborately painted and costumed (Figure 4.4). This genre is still found in Central Java, but is the central traditional theatre among the Sundanese of West Java. The origin of *wayang golek* century is often credited to Sunan Kudus (d. 1550?), one of the nine Islamic saints (*Wali Songo*) who converted the island to Islam. Each three-dimensional doll figure is controlled by a central rod, which goes through its body and holds its head, and two rods attached to the hands. Dalangs of this genre emigrated from the north coast where wayang golek is used to tell history tales of Panji – a prince of East Java – as an idealized handsome hero and tales of Amir Hamzah – the uncle of Mohammed – in a genre known as *wayang golek cepak*. However, in Sunda these puppets present stories based on the *Mahabharata* and *Ramayana* (known as *wayang golek purwa*). Most stories are newly invented tales about known characters, such as the *Mahabharata* hero, Arjuna. This demands dramaturgical ability from the dalang in creating meaningful plots. The female singers are sometimes more popular than the puppeteers: this was especially true of the

Figure 4.4 Dalang Abah Sunarya performs a 1978 exorcism using Sundanese wayang golek purwa.

(Photo by Kathy Foley)

1960s when Upit Sarimanah and Titim Fatimah were the superstar singers. Beginning in the 1970s, Dalang Asep Sunandar (1955–2014) and his brother Ade Kosaih Sunarya emerged as major star dalangs. Asep's masterful manipulation and quick humour brought crowds of thousands. At present, Dalang Asep's sons, nephews and students are trying to fill the gap left by this master artist whose innovations in music allowed two different tunings to be played on the same set of instruments. He showed creativity in introducing slow-motion fight scenes inspired by kung fu films from Hong Kong, devising elaborate chase scenes and inserting raucous comedy.

Topeng (mask dance) in West Java comes in a number of forms. In times past, *topeng Cirebon* from the coastal city of Cirebon was called the 'small mask dance' since only five major mask types were presented by one dancer, who interacted with a clown (*badut*). By contrast, the 'large mask dance' was a multi-person dance-drama similar to Javanese wayang wong but using masks as the dancers presented *Mahabharata, Ramayana, Panji* or other stories. Dancers mimed the movement while a dalang spoke lines for the characters from where he sat in the gamelan. Both of these mask genres moved from the coast of West Java into the Sundanese highlands and were popular until the 1960s, but today, while the small mask dance remains, the large wayang wong performances with masks are seldom presented.

Other mask dances related to these two Cirebon area forms once flourished throughout West Java, with names such as *topeng banyet* and *topeng betawi*. These forms might start with a few mask dances by the female star dancer, but then devolve into melodramatic scenes in which the dancer becomes the heroine, the troupe head might play the clown, and some young man proficient in martial dance would present the hero. While the Department of Culture or the arts academies may sometimes present the few troupes that survive, the female dancer is now usually advanced in years and the clown a grey-haired man. Music from such performances, called *ketuk tilu*, is traditionally derived from the repertoire of *ronggeng*, courtesan singer-dancers.

Ronggeng genres highlighted melodramatic stories that were improvised. They related back in some ways to trance-dance games such as *sintren*, found along the north coast where the entranced dancer changes costume and is 'possessed' by the spirit of a heavenly goddess. However, today most of these older forms have been overshadowed by the newer version of ketuk tilu – *jaipongan* was innovated in the 1970s by graduates of the performing arts schools.

By the 1980s jaipongan, under the leadership of choreographer Gugum Gumbira, female dancer and film star Tatih Saleh and Dalang Nandang Barmaya, became the iconic dance of Sunda and swept across the nation before earning popularity in the Middle East, Europe and beyond. First called 'developed ketuk tilu', it borrowed features from traditional folk social dance, martial arts, disco and cha-cha-cha, among others. Elaborate choreographies where music and movement were preset, rather than improvised in the moment (as in ronggeng forms), were developed, and stage performances prevailed, with sexy women in traditional dress who danced flirtatiously with male partners who used martial arts moves. Despite the cries of impropriety when middle-class women took up the dance, the movement fitted the relatively liberal times of the 1970s and 1980s. As women have increasingly participated in the Muslim revival and adopted the veil, some have turned away from the dance. Politicos, dancers and audiences have argued back and forth whether jaipongan is too erotic or just good, clean, aerobic fun. All theatre forms in West Java have been affected by the musical style of this art.

There are a variety of urban theatre forms that emerged in the early twentieth century and which are sometimes presented. Lenong is a Jakarta theatre that used martial arts dance, raucous humour attacking pompous government officials, and melodramatic stories. While it still is revived for arts festivals, ongoing troupes are rare. Sandiwara, which flourished as a popular theatre until the 1960s, is also seldom seen. *Lengser*, another such theatre of the Bandung area, is similarly gone. TV, film and digital media have absorbed the time and attention that urban lower-class viewers and villagers gave to these genres. Meanwhile, modern spoken theatre attracts educated youth who hope for careers in cinema or television performance.

The arts academy in Bandung has been a base for many noted artists. Enoh Atmadibarata developed major wayang wong/orang on Sundanese themes in the 1960s, such as *Lutung Kasarung* (Outcast Monkey). Operatic performances, called *gending karesman*, are another innovation of the academy. Choreographer Irawati Durban Arjo, who taught at the academy and her own studio Pusbitari, has carried on the legacy of Tjetjeh Somantri, a major choreographer of the years after independence. She and others have frequently collaborated with the University of California, Santa Cruz in creating works.

Sumatra

Traditional theatre from Sumatra is typically presented in the form of group dances rather than solos. Recently, choreographers who develop their work in the cities have integrated aesthetic elements from different ethnic groups in hybrid artistic approaches (Sedyawati et al. 1991: 15). However, since Sumatra has long experienced transmigrations from Bali and Java, arts including wayang kulit and dance of those islands are found in places where people have settled, including Lampung, South Sumatra. Among the more indigenous Sumatran genres are *mak yong* and randai; additionally there are many dances such as *saman, rantak, piring, indang badindin*, and others (Erlinda 2010: 22). Only a few forms will be discussed here.

Mak yong is the traditional folk theatre of Riau and is related to the theatre of the same name found in Malaysia. The performance is believed to have come from Malaysia about a hundred years ago. Performance was traditionally held in the rice field after the harvest and the genre relates to wider traditions of ronggeng-style dance. It was supported by the palace and flourished until the 1950s. Musicians accompanied masked dancers in the simple play. The major characters, both male and female, were enacted by women. Other characters were typically clowns, gods, ghosts, court officers and animals. Following the show, audience members would mount the stage for joget social dance with the mak yong dancer-courtesans. Links to prostitution led to the form's demise, but at present some attempt to revive mak yong by consulting with former dancers has occurred. A performance of Riau mak yong was included in a presentation at a pan-Southeast Asian festival of mak yong in 2011, but Kelantanese dance scholar Zulkifli Mohammed (2012) felt that the performance was more a *kreasi baru* (new creation) than a replication of the old form.

Randai is a dance-drama of the Minangkabau people of West Sumatra that developed in the twentieth century. It features songs and martial arts (*silat/silek*) which have been developed into *galombang* dance, combining fight sequences into aesthetically complex choreographies and drama. Although previously all-male, today's randai is presented by performers of both sexes, who sing, recite, narrate and act out the story while moving or sitting in a circle. The art was developed for training young males when they moved into the village young men's house around the age of 7. Martial arts training and *sijobang* (story narration) were part of the life of these young men. Randai grew from these two roots. The manipulation of slapping baggy martial arts pants stretched taut with the hands while dancing creates exciting percussion as the costume itself becomes a drum. Pauka (1998) notes that in Sumatra women have emerged as leaders of groups in this generation. In recent years, Minagkebau masters have collaborated on international productions at the University of Hawaii and, in Australia, Indonesian–Australian Idija Mahjoeddin has created fusion productions such as *The Butterfly Seer*, with a mixed Indonesian–Australian and Euro-Australian cast and musicians. The genre is taught at the tertiary arts academy (ISBI) in Padang Panjang and they present randai around Indonesia or internationally.

In addition, there are numerous dances of Sumatra, some of which continue to be performed at festivals and government events, and tour abroad for cultural diplomacy. *Saman* is the group dance traditionally presented for formal occasions or ritual ceremonies by the Gayo in the province of Aceh, North Sumatra. Using only vocal accompaniment, the performers, consisting of about a dozen young men (or more recently sometimes women) wearing traditional dress, kneel in a row as they move their upper bodies and hands, slapping their chests, clapping hands or hitting their thighs to create joint percussion, as they recite Islamic chants. The group is led by the 'syekh' who cues changes in a high-pitched voice. In 2011 the form was declared a UNESCO Intangible Cultural Heritage of Humanity genre and plans for safeguarding the form have been developed. Sometimes, lyrics in Gayo language deal with education, religion, morality, heroism/ patriotism and equality. Some conservative voices decry the advent of all-female saman groups, saying that women's performance is 'not real saman'.

Indang badindin dance is believed to be related to the fourteenth-century preaching of Islam in West Sumatra. Dancers move through elaborate synchronized gestures of the torso and arms while kneeling in a row. While the percussion aspect is gone, there are parallels to saman. The lyrics tell of the Prophet Muhammad and glorify the greatness of Allah. It is presented in a group and performers sometimes play small *rebanas* (frame drums); this dance is oral literature, helping to deliver religious messages for the Minangkabau community, especially in the region of Padang Pariama.

Rantak kudo (horse kick) dance is a ritual form of the Minangkabau and Kerinci areas traditionally used to request prosperity for farmers. In the Kerinci region, rantak was performed for several days without cease in thanks for a successful harvest. During drought it could be performed as incense was burnt, to help performers achieve a trance-like state and pray for rain. The musical ensemble may vary by region; *pantun*'s four-line rhymed poetry is sung; and martial arts movements prevail.

Thomas (2013) reports that *sakura*, a little-known ancient genre of masked theatre found in the Indonesian province of Lampung in southern Sumatra, has received a recent makeover as modern entertainment that references tradition by the Balinese-born artist I Nyoman Mulyawan, who has showcased his series of 'new dance creations' in the style of the coastal Saibatin people. Thomas's research reminds us of the widespread links in the archipelago between mask performance and ritual and shows that in Sumatra, as in other areas, young artists are finding ways to make the tradition anew.

In the pre-Islamic era, *piring* (plate) dance was a ritual thanksgiving dance for a good harvest. Originally, it is thought, offerings were on the plates while performers danced and music played. After Islamization the dance became a public entertainment. Plates are swung on the hands, with inertia keeping them in place even when turned upside down. At the end of the dance, plates are smashed and the dancer continues to dance on the shards.

In addition, there are many other dances that are taught at the high school of performing arts (SMKN 7, Sekolah Menengah Karawitan Negara 7) in Padang Panjang (Erlinda 2010: 148) and of course at the college of performing arts (ISBI) in the same city. A number of the regional dances were re-choreographed and modernized by outstanding dance masters such as Sofyan Naan, Adam Huriah (1936–71) and, especially, Gusmiati Suid (1942–2001), who in the late twentieth century brought neo-traditional martial arts dance to international acclaim. Dances of these artists are taught in the schools.

For example, Gusmiati Suid won the prestigious Bessie award in 1991 for creations she toured to New York as part of the 1989–90 Festival of Indonesia. Her works were performed by her Jakarta-based troupe, Gumarang Sakti. Her choreographies were based on traditional Minang martial style, but with greater choreographic complexity. Dance abstraction moved beyond the martial to the mystical even as she took on issues such as government corruption or the loss of Minang traditional values. *Asa di Ujung Tanduk* (Hope on the Tip of A Buffalo's Horn, 1997), *Api dalam Sekam* (Fire in the Chaff, 1998) and *Menggantang Asap* (Catching the Smoke, 2000) are a trio of late works that responded to the tense years leading to the fall of Suharto's New Order government. Gusimati's son, Boi G. Sakti (b. 1966), who graduated from IKJ (Institut Kesenian Jakarta, Jakarta Institute of the Arts), currently leads the company, carrying forward her innovations in traditional Minangkabau dance theatre practice, touring internationally and nationally.

Kalimantan

Most traditional theatres in Kalimantan (Borneo) derive from the ritual celebrations of the aboriginal Dayak and rituals of Hindu-Kaharingan traditional religion, which honoured the ancestors and used images of the hornbill to represent the divine. With modernization, urbanization and erosion of indigenous traditions in the face of world religions, the social need for performance weakens, yet aspects continue to be fostered as intangible heritage. Traditionally, *karungut* oral narrators recited rhyme in pantun-style poetry's quatrains accompanied by a string instrument called *kecapi*, gongs, and eventually have added organ and other western instruments. Narrative and dance forms are still presented in regional festivals, for religious dance processions, as part of competitions for newly choreographed dance at the regional or national level, or in performing arts festivals in places such as Jakarta and Bali. Theatre evolved from forms such as *mandau* battle dance, which symbolizes the bravery and strength of the Dayak man. With a weapon (*mantau*) in the right hand and a shield (*talawang*) balanced on the right arm, each dancer moves to the tune of *gandang* and *garantung* percussive music to *karungut* lyrics, which are meant to inspire the warrior.

Wayang kulit banjar is a variant of shadow puppetry, which is thought to have been imported from Java in centuries past. It is little performed at present, but the efforts to preserve it have accelerated with UNESCO funding to PEPADI in the wake of the designation of wayang as a world heritage form. Under the National Ministry of Religion, Yuddha Triguna, Director General of Hinduism and Buddhism, commissioned a research team – the co-author I. Nyoman Sedana is one of the deputies – to design continued supporting strategies for fostering the Indonesian Hindu religious arts in several regions of Kalimantan, Sumatra, Java, Sulawesi and Lombok.

Mamanda is another endangered theatre form found in south and east Kalimantan, invariably featuring dramatic characters such as king, queen, princess, prime minister, army commander, courtiers and court assistants, with servants to provide comic intermezzi. Shows often incorporate overseas kings who attack the kingdom, robbers and ghosts. The term mamanda derives from how the main characters are addressed as 'pamananda' or 'mamanda', a term of respect meaning 'uncle'. The dialogue is improvised in performance based on the plot outline and the genre first arose in response to the popular touring theatres of the late nineteenth and early twentieth centuries, such as the Malay *bagsawan* or Indonesian sandiwara. Themes remain relatively conservative, reflecting struggles of aristocratic characters – a society of kings and courtiers that no longer exists in reality.

Sulawesi

The relevance and context of traditional theatre in Sulawesi is mostly related to the livelihood of the people, who depend on their rice fields and the infinite intangible power that controls crops and prosperity. Though there were minor kingdoms in the regions, artistic expression throughout history did not develop into a highly formalized court culture as in Java or Bali. Sulawesi's spiritual norms, ritual practices and artistic expressions were primarily concerned with interactions with nature and the spiritual world and aimed at maintaining well-being. While there are Balinese and Javanese genres that have come with transmigrations, only indigenous forms will be mentioned here.

Dance is important, as in other areas of Indonesia. *Maengket* is a folk dance from Minahasa, north Sulawesi, performed by a group of men or women in white or now bright clothing, accompanied by musical instruments of *tambur* and *tifa* (drums) and *kulintang* (gongs), along with song in the Minahasa vernacular. Initially maengket was not a single dance, but a suite, which consisted of *sumempung*, to worship and invite the divine, and then *mangalei* to receive the spirit. A traditional show is initiated by a lead dancer who waves a handkerchief to invite the goddess of earth to enter the dancers, who experience trance. To avoid evil spirits entering the dancers' bodies instead of the goddess, an older man holds a spear, a symbol of the sun god, to protect the performers. In times past, as part of local animism, people would stick many such spears around the perimeter of the house yard to provide protection. Maengket is derived from the word '*engket*', which means lifting the foot and stepping. The dance has become increasingly separated from its earlier ritual agricultural function and is now usually performed to welcome honoured guests, to present on overseas cultural missions and to share as a tourist attraction.

Pakarena (from 'playing') is a traditional dance from Gowa and the island of Selayar, South Sulawesi. This dance is performed with a fan by four or sometimes up to seven women who are dressed in beautiful local clothing and the elaborate jewellery of South Sulawesi. The dance is accompanied by two *gandrang* (also *gendang*, drum); *kanong-kanong* (gong); *kancing* (gongs and metallophone instruments); and a pair of *puik-puik* flutes.

There are different stories related to the origin of pakarena: a version known as *pakarena gantarang* is derived from the kingdom of Gantarang Lalang Bata in the Selayar islands and the dance was performed during Pangali Patta Raja's coronation in the seventeenth century. Others say pakarena is related to the descent of the goddess, who taught people through symbolic movement. Another story says that before the separation of earth and sky, the god of sky taught people how to hunt and plant rice through these movements. When imitated and repeated, the gestures give thanks to the divine during ritual ceremony.

Traditionally, pakarena's soft, artistic gestures were a 2-hour choreography divided into twelve segments. The segments are endowed with meaning: sitting signifies the start and the end of the dance; turning in a clockwise direction signifies the life process; moving up and down signifies life dynamics. The eyes should not be opened very wide; feet should not be lifted too high; and a serene trance-like demeanour is required of the female dancers, who are not allowed to laugh at or acknowledge the humour of the musicians. In recent years, pakarena dance has been a part of the performance work of Teater Kala (Time Theatre), led by actress Shinta Febriani, who did a series of works dealing with women's issues.

Bodden (2013) reports that, from the 1980s to the 1990s, a number of modern theatre companies doing avant-garde performances exploring issues of government corruption, gender and local identity had incorporated aspects of traditional arts in a way similar to 'roots' exploration by young artists in other areas such as Java and Bali. Jamaluddin Latief and Meggy Waworuntu did a new version of a simple bird dance called *kondo buleng* in 1986. By having this bird appear to a king, who allows ecological rapaciousness and corruption in his underlings, the play combined this traditional dance and comic scenes to attack Suharto's New Order misgovernment (Bodden 2013). *Il La Galigo* is the traditional epic of *bissu* (transgender priests) who use pakarena dance. More recently, Firman Jamil has used philosophical ideas drawn from this traditional Bugis literary epic for *La Galigo*, his experimental installation and happening. And Robert Wilson did another version of the same epic in 2004 with a group of performers from the whole of Indonesia, including a number from Sulawesi in a production which was performed at international festivals over the following years. Other groups have explored tradition as well. Teater Kita (Our Theatre), a group led by Asia Ramli Prapana, has created its 'ritual theatre', such as the 1999 production *Inang Samudera 999, HU – Untukmu* (Mother Ocean 999, HU – For You), in which offerings were made ritually to the sea.

West Papua and Papua

The performance traditions of the Melanesian areas are distinctly different from Austronesian areas where Malay peoples predominate. Ritual performance and social performance (often combined in one event) rather than representational theatre are emphasized. With the advent of Christian missionization, practices that were thought to be linked to animist or ancestor rites were frowned upon and accused of creating social disturbances via the all-night participatory performance pattern. However, the need for dances for Indonesian government ceremonial purposes and tourist presentations has had some counterbalancing effect. Among various folk dances in Biak, *yospan* – a portmanteau word for two older dances *yosim* and *pancar* – is a folk social dance from Biak-Numfor and Yapen-Waropen that combines elements of various traditional dances for village rites and festivals; it was a new creation in the 1960s. Movements, song and instruments mix older elements and new ones. For example, the indigenous *tifa* drum is mixed with guitar, ukulele and an indigenous bass-like instrument beaten with a stick; bright costumes, headdresses and body painting are made; and movements are borrowed from many other dances (*gale-gale, pacul tiga, seka, sajojo, balada, cendrawasih* [bird of paradise], *poco-poco* [an Indonesian line dance] and *pancar* [smoke]).

Pancar movements were inspired by the aerial acrobatics of the jets that Indonesia and the Dutch used to fight each other as Indonesia struggled to extend itself to West Papua in the 1960s. The elaborate jet manoeuvres, which left smoke trails – referred to locally as pancar – curlicued in the sky, inspired new dance movements. Performances can be done by a small or large group and sometimes last all night. In this social dance, any viewer can join in, and the costumed groups also welcome tourists. The dance may open official events.

Though no longer as popular as in times past, *musyoh* is a welcome dance from East Papua, which was originally a ritual to appease the spirits of dead people who died in accidents. *Suanggi* dance from West and Central Papua depicts a husband and dead wife who have been victims of black magic and is accompanied by musical instruments such as *pikon* (jaw harp), *atowo* (goblet drum) and *fu* (conch), playing to folk singing. Many other dances still exist, although areas that have been missionized have seen movement against performances that are supposedly at odds with Christian beliefs. By contrast, the need to present at national dance festivals has led to the creation of new dance works elaborated from tradition. For example, Yapen regency developed a presentation depicting a tribal war between the Menawai and Ambai tribes that led to a peace ceremony as chief Ondoafi promised safety for the groups, which came from a common ancestor; this narrative/dance-drama was presented for the National Arts Festival of the Archipelago in 2011.

Traditional dances are, of course, used variously. In 1978 Arnold Ap, who was Curator of the Bird of Paradise University Museum, founded a musical group called Mambesak which used mixes of traditional and modern music to sing songs of freedom; he was later executed in government custody in 1983 for his work for Papuan independence (Kirksey 2014).

In 2000 Megawati Sukarnoputri, then president of the country, was greeted by Papuans running around her helicopter counter-clockwise wearing grass skirts and penis sheaths doing the *waita* 'war' dance while protesters held up signs calling for Papuan self-determination; she quickly took off again (Kirksey 2014). The *Jakarta Post* in December 2014 reported on the deaths of five of the protesters who gathered for a *waita* dance to protest an incident where local youth gathering for a Christmas celebration were beaten near Ipakiye village (Jayapurat 2014). War dances still seem to be part of contemporary political struggle.

West Nusa Tenggara

Rudat dance of the Sasak of Lombok derived from an older popular theatre form called *komidi rudat* which presented stories based on *1001 Nights*. It was selected for government upgrading into a representative art in the 1980s and the dance, featuring males in costumes meant to evoke the Middle East, thereafter was often included in hotel shows for tourists, government displays and celebratory events. Decontextualized from drama, shortened and given flashier costumes, contemporary rudat features martial-arts-style dance by a team of males wearing Islamic-style hats and military uniforms. It is led by a commander, who holds a sword. Songs are in Indonesian or Arabic to a mandolin-style instrument, tambourine and drum. This dance is used to welcome official guests of the local government. The theatre form is traced to the fifteen century, but in the past two decades rudat has perhaps been most often presented along the road to accompany the bridegroom going to the bride's house for their wedding. Rudat is also claimed to be a dance and song style containing the dictums of Muslims to the tune of rebana's frame drum music.

Wayang sasak is said to date from the sixteenth or seventeenth century from Java. Sometimes it is associated with a Muslim culture bringer, Pangeran Sangupati, who was associated with the Wali Songo or nine Islamic saints of Java. In other words, this form entered the island with Islam. The repertoire focuses on stories about Amir Hamzah, an uncle of the Prophet Muhammed. Though wayang sasak was once thought of as an instrument for teaching Islam, increasingly in the past 30 years the form has been attacked as 'un-Islamic', leading to significant decline in the number of performers despite assistance from the government arts department. While Dalang Lalu Nasib has been rather successful as a dalang of this generation by increasing the entertainment factors, including use of figures with anatomically correct genitalia, some have decried his work as *wayang pop* or *wayang porno* (see Harnish 2003).

The local Sasak people celebrate the Bau Nyale (Catch Sea Worms) Festival. In the Suharto period, there was an attempt to develop a drama with the hope of attracting more tourism to this annual event. Unmarried adolescents sing to each other on nights when fluorescent sea worms appear on the coast. A team from government offices led by theatre specialist/director Max Arifin and dance specialists Bu Endah, Pak Hamid and Luh Ekasari created a dance-drama that told the story of Mandalika, a local princess who avoided a marriage choice by flinging herself into the sea and turning into a sea worm (Harnish 2003: 73).

East Nusa Tenggara

Theatre incorporating popular songs and dances focused on a myth from the island of Komodo, East Nusa Tenggara, and was performed in Jakarta by the Indonesian Institute of Musik Daya (IMDI) in July 2014. In the same venue Kinarya GSP (a company led by impresario Guruh Soekarnoputra, son of the first president of Indonesia) presesented *paci* dance-drama with the participation of Doris, a Flores master musician. Paci is done as an offering for plentiful crops.

Female dancers wore the distinctive *bali belo* crowns and male dancers had buffalo horn headdresses, symbolizing their warrior status. The presentation was a modern depiction, expressing gratitude for the plentiful rice crop in Manggarai. The legend tells the story of three kings fighting to marry the same beautiful woman, named Manggarai. To prevent bloodshed, the woman told people to take her skin and make a drum. People say this drum is still extant.

Presentations of folk tales and legends of the islands such as those from East Nusa Tenggara are part of efforts by IMDI to acquaint the wider Indonesian public with dance traditions and stories of the whole archipelago. Another Sumbawa legend, mentioned earlier and presented in dance-drama, tells of a Komodo dragon and prince who were born together from the egg of a princess. As her human child starts to hunt, the princess teaches this son that the dragon is his brother. In today's world, dramas like these continue to be performed to plumb traditional thought, maintain linkage to ancestral culture and assert regional identity in the national and international frame.

Conclusion

This chapter has only sketched a broad outline of selected genres of traditional theatre that are of significance in Indonesia of the past and present. What should be clear is that even in an age of global media that sends floods of films and images from around the world, the significance of local intangible cultural heritage remains strong for Indonesians. Where traditional religious culture holds firm, as in Bali, the arts remain central; in places where traditional Islam is not being replaced by a modern Sunni rethinking, the arts remain firm as links to Islamic saints, ancestors and community – and everywhere the arts are used to represent the local and national heritage. Where fundamentalisms arise – be it Christian missionization or Wahabi Islam – the performing arts and the rituals that once required a particular form may grow muted. Images of wayang heroes may be smashed or wayang performances attacked by zealots in particular instances, but significant counterbalances exist. The long tradition and deep pride in cultural traditions and respect for ancestors who communicated cultural values via arts combine with nationalism and regionalism. Each province and city needs to have a welcome dance/song/ musical ensemble. For tourism at home or touring to represent the local in national gatherings or international capitals, impressive displays of local dance or dance-drama or music are required. The nationally funded schools of performing arts at the secondary and tertiary levels are seen as repositories of major choreographies or performance arts that need to be supported and the faculty and students can be called upon to represent the nation or the region. It is out of these same sites that many of the experimental new arts come as students who are trained in the past (often themselves coming from the families of village artists) are readied and challenged to invent arts of the future. Many of those young artists build their new works on the firm foundation of the past, reinventing tradition in ways that feel right for them.

Notes

1 Among others, international scholars on Bali include Christian Hooykaas, Walter Spies and Beryl De Zoete, Colin McPhee, Heidi Hinzler, Urs Ramseyer, Mary Sabina Zurbuchen, Fredrik deBoer, Rucina Ballinger, Leon Rubin, Michael Tenzer, Margaret Coldiron, and Camincita Palermo; on Java they include Claire Holt, Theodore Robson, James R. Brandon, Kathy Foley, Ward Keeler, Clara Brakel-Papenhuyzen, Barbara Hatley Felicia Hughes-Freeland, Andrew Weintraub, Henry Spiller, R. Anderson Sutton and Matthew Cohen. Regarding Sumatra, there are works by Kirsten Pauka. Indonesian indigenous scholars have begun to follow and expand this scholarship since the 1970s, including, among others, Sumarsam, I Made Bandem, Soedarsono, I Wayan Dibia and I Nyoman Sedana.

2 Hermit Abiasa, author of the *Mahabharata*.

3 Numbers are important to Indonesian thought. The holistic concept of oneness is behind thinking about theatre and the cosmos; it is exemplified by the *kayon* (tree of life) in puppetry. The two-opposite-dynamic balance manifests in numerous theatre elements: protagonist–antagonist, male–female characters, musical timbre where interlocking parts are played by pairs of instruments, strong–soft movement styles, good–evil temperament. The three concentric harmonic components typically manifest into the structural head–body–feet of the musical compositions; *tri hita karana* (the three balancing harmonies of human–God–nature); *tri mandala* (the realms of the middle, upper and lower worlds), or the triadic interplay of form–story–characters. Another dominant concept, the cosmic harmonic circle, may manifest variously in four, five, nine or eleven masks/puppets/flower types/objects to renew the natural balance or to purify someone from ritual or social impurity. The *kayon* or tree puppet that opens and closes the show in wayang represents natural balance and harmony of the cosmos in synchronicity with the divine plan.

4 In addition to the seven theatrical forms introduced briefly above, Bali actually has hundreds of theatrical expressions: from the proto-theatrical practices in the forms of *pesantian* ritual chorus and readings, to the sacred trance dances, to the ceremonial dramatic theatres and hundreds of secular art forms, to the neo-classical and post-traditional theatres. Several versions of *joged* social dances, *janger* flirtatious youth group dances, several types of *ngelawang* barong street shows, hundreds of titles of *sendratari* dance-drama, *sandya gita* musical theatres, sung arja opera and *prembon* dance-drama, realistic-acting-based *drama gong* and *bondes* masked comedy are still seen in the annual Bali Arts Festival. In addition, Bali has more than thirty gamelan traditional music ensembles and several hybrid music forms to accompany the theatre performances, or to present concerts of instrumental music in sacred, ceremonial or secular contexts.

5 The state schools of the arts have gone through many name changes over the years as they have added the equivalent of MA, then PhD and other programmes. They are usually designated by acronyms derived from a current name, thus the institutions known as ASTI or ASKI became STSI, then ISI and, reportedly, they are now changing the name to ISBI (Institut Seni Budaya Indonesia, Institute of Art and Culture of Indonesia). Though the names are many, they all refer to the same institutions funded by the national government to train artists.

Bibliography

Bandem, I Made, and Fredirik deBoer (1995) *Balinese Dance in Transition: Kaja and Kelod*, Kuala Lumpur: Oxford University Press.

Bodden, Michael (2013) 'Regional Identity and National Theatre in South Sulawesi', *Journal of Southeast Asian Studies*, 44 (1): 24–48.

Brakel-Papenhusen, Clara (1992) *The Bedhaya Court Dances of Central Java*, Leiden: Brill.

Brandon, James R. (ed.) (1993) *The Cambridge Guide to Asian Theatre*, Cambridge: Cambridge University Press.

Brandon, James R. (1967) *Theatre in Southeast Asia*, Cambridge MA: Harvard University Press.

Catra, I Nyoman (1996) 'Topeng: Mask Dance Drama as a Reflection of Balinese Culture; a Case Study of Topeng/Prembon', unpublished MA thesis, Emerson College.

Cohen, Matthew (2006) *The Komedie Stamboel: Popular Theater in Colonial Indonesia, 1891–1903*, Athens: Ohio University Press.

Coldiron, Margaret (2004) *Trance and Transformation of the Actor in Japanese Noh and Balinese Masked dance-Drama*, Lewiston, NY: Edwin Mellen Press.

De Zoete, Beryl (1939) *Dance and Drama in Bali*, New York: Harper and Brothers.

Dibia, I Wayan (1992) '*Arja*: A Sung Dance-Drama of Bali: A Study of Change and Transformation', unpublished dissertation, University of California, Los Angeles.

Dibia, I Wayan (2000) *Kecak the Vocal Chant of Bali*, Denpasar: Hartono Art Books Studio.

Dibia, I Wayan and Rucina Ballinger (2004) *Balinese Dance, Drama and Music*, Singapore: Periplus.

Emigh, John (1996) *Masked Performance: The Play of Self and Other in Ritual and Theater*, Philadelphia: University of Pennsylvania Press.

Erlinda (2010) 'Diskursus Estetika Tari Minangkabau di Kota Padang Sumatera Barat dalam Era Globalisasi' (Discourse on the Aesthetics of Minangkabau Dance in Padang, West Sumatra in an Era of Globalization), unpublished dissertation, Denpasar: University of Udayana.

Foley, Kathy (1993) 'Indonesia', in James R. Brandon (ed.) *Cambridge Guide to Asian Theatre*, Cambridge: Cambridge University Press.

—— (1980) 'The Sudanese *Wayang Golek*: The Rod Puppet Theatre of West Java', unpublished dissertation, University of Hawai'i.

Harnish, David (2003) 'Worlds of Wayang Sasak: Music, Performance, and Negotiations of Religion and Modernity', *Asian Music*, 34 (2), 91–120.

—— (2007) '"Digging" and "Upgrading": Government Efforts to "Develop" Music and Dance in Lombok, Indonesia', *Asian Music*, 38 (1), 61–87.

Hatley, Barbara (2008) *Javanese Performances on the Indonesian Stage: Contesting Culture, Embracing Change*. Hawai'i: Asian Studies of Australia, University of Hawai'i.

Hinzler, H. I. R (1981) *Bima Swarga in Balinese Wayang*, The Hague: Martinus Nijhof.

Hobart, Angela (1987) *Dancing Shadows of Bali*, London: Routledge & Kegan Paul.

Holt, Claire (1967) *Art in Indonesia: Continuities and Change*, Ithaca; Cornell University Press.

Hooykas, Christian (1973) *Kama and Kala Materials for the Study of Shadow Theatre in Bali*, Amsterdam: North Holland Pub. Co.

Hughes-Freeland, Felicia (2008) *Embodied Communities: Dance Traditions and Change in Java*. New York, Oxford: Berghahn Books.

Jayapurat, Nethy Dharma Somba (2014) 'Five Papuans Shot Dead for Dancing and Protesting', *Jakarta Post*, 9 December, www.thejakartapost.com/news/2014/12/09/five-papuans-shot-dead-dancing-and-protesting.html, accessed 6 March 2015.

Kirksey, Eben (2014) 'Playing Up The Primitive', *New Internationalist*, 9 December 2002, http://newint.org/features/2002/04/05/playing/, accessed 6 March 2015.

Keeler, Ward (1987) *Javanese Shadow Plays, Javanese Selves*, Princeton: Princeton University Press.

McPhee, Colin (1966) *Music in Bali*. New Haven: Yale University Press.

Mulyono, Sri (1989) *Wayang, Asal Usul Filsafat dan Masa Depannya* (The Origin, Philosophy and Future of Wayang) 2nd ed.n, Jakarta: CV Haji Masagung.

Murgiyanto, Sal. 'Gusmiati Suid & Gumarang Sakti: Moving Forward with Tradition', Pew Center for Arts & Heritage, www.pcah.us/media/files/548c088f287ffe4206a1f2f5e66a0b8f.pdf, accessed 6 March, 2015.

Palermo, Carmencita (2005) 'Crossing Male Boundaries', *Inside Indonesia*, 83, www.insideindonesia.org/crossing-male-boundaries, accessed 7 March 2015.

Parani, Yulianti L. (1985) 'Seni Tari Melayu Fungsi dalam Kebudayaan Melayu' (Malay Dance's Function in Malay Culture), *Kumpulan Seminar Masyarakat Melayu dan Kebudayaan* (Proceedings of the Seminar on Malay Peoples and Culture), Tanjung Pinang: Department Pendidikan dan Kebudayaan.

Pauka, Kirstin (1998) 'The Daughters Take Over? Female Performers in Randai', *TDR*, 42 (1): 113–21.

Ramseyer, Urs (1986) *The Art and Culture of Bali*. Singapore, Oxford, New York: Oxford University Press.

Robson, Stuart Owen (1971) *Wangbang Wideya*, The Hague: M. Nijhoff.

Rubin, Leon and I. Nyoman Sedana (2007) *Performance in Bali*. London: Routledge.

Sedana, I. Nyoman (2005) 'Theatre in a Time of Terrorism: Renewing Natural Harmony after the Bali Bombing via *Wayang Kontemporer*', *Asian Theatre Journal*, 22 (1): 73–86.

Sedyawati, Edi (1981) *Pertumbuhan Seni Pertunjukan Indonesia* (Development of Performing Arts of Indonesia) Jakarta: Sinar Harapan.

Sedyawati, Edi, *et al.* (1991) 'Tari Sebagai Media Budaya Suatu Penilaian Perkembangan di Minangkabau' (Dance as a Cultural Media a Mode of Minagkabau Development) Laporan Penelitian (Research Report) Jakarta: IKJ.

Seni Tradisional, Wikipedia untuk Indonesia, Ensiklopedia Bebas, http://id.wikipedia.org/wiki/Seni_Tradisional, Depok, Jakarta: Media Wiki, accessed 4 November 2014.

Soedarsono (2003) *Seni Pertunjukan dari Perspektif Politik, Sosial, dan Ekonomi* (Performing Arts from Political, Social, and Economic Perspectives), Yogyakarta: Gadjah Mada University Press.

Spies, Walter and Beryl de Zoete (2002) *Dance and Drama in Bali*, Singapore: Periplus [London: Faber and Faber, 1938].

Spiller, Henry (2010) *Erotic Triangles: Sundanese Dance and Masculinity in West Java*. Chicago; University of Chicago.

Sudarsono (1984) *Wayang Wong: the State Ritual Dance Drama in the Court of Yogyakarta*, Yogyakarta, Indonesia: Gadjah Mada University Press.

Sumardjo Jakob, *et al.* (2001) *Seni Pertunjukan Di Indonedia Suatu Pendekatan Sejarah* (Performing Arts in Indonesia, An Approach to the History), Bandung: STSI Press Bandung

Sumarsan (1995) *Gamelan: Cultural Interaction and Musical development in Central Java*, Chicago: University of Chicago.

Sutton, R Anderson Sutton (2001) *Calling Back the Spirit: Dance and Cultural Politics in Lowland South Sulawesi*, New York: Oxford University Press.

Tenzer, Michael (1991) *Balinese Music*, Singapore: Periplus.

Thomas, Karen Kartomi (2013) 'Enchanting the Audience: Dramatic Devices of *Sakura* Mask Theatre in West Lampung, Sumatra', *Asian Theatre Journal*, 30 (2): 390–414.

Varela, Miguel Escobar (2014) 'Wayang Hip Hop: Java's Oldest Performance Tradition Meets Global Youth Culture,' *Asian Theatre Journal*, 31 (2): 481–504.

Wayang Hip Hop Website, http://wayanghiphop.com, accessed 3 March 2014.

Zulkifli (1993) 'Randai Sebagai Teater Rakyat Minangkabau di Sumatera Barat: Dalam Dimensi Sosial Budaya' (Randai as a Folek Theatre of the Minagkabau of West Sumatera: In the Socio-cultural Dimensions), thesis, Yogyakarta: Universitas Gadjah Mada. Program Pasca Sarjana.

Zulkifli Mohamed (2012) 'The Mak Yong Spiritual Dance Heritage Conference, Performances and Workshops', *Asian Theatre Journal*, 27 (2): 445–60.

Zurbuchen, Mary (1987) *The Language of Balinese Shadow Theatre*, Princeton: Princeton University Press.

Part II
Dimensions of traditional Asian theatre

5

Dance in traditional Asian theatre

Arya Madhavan, Xing Fan, Kati Fitzgerald,
Ronald Gilliam, Colleen Lanki, CedarBough T. Saeji,
Kathy Foley and Celia Tuchman-Rosta

This is the first of six chapters in Part II, each examining a specific area of traditional Asian theatre: dance, music, masks, puppets, costume and makeup, and space/architecture.

Dance has always been an important and inseparable part of traditional and folk performance in Asia. As independent showstoppers or, more generally, stylized physical movement, it provides part of the total theatrical experience, together with speech, singing and musical accompaniment, as exemplified in Indian *kutiyattam*, Chinese *jingju*, Japanese *noh* and *kabuki*. Dance can also be the major venue of storytelling in the many forms of 'dance-dramas', such as Indian *kathakali*, Korean mask dance-dramas and various Southeast Asian genres re-enacting the *Mahabharata* and *Ramayana* epics. Furthermore, dance features significantly in ritual performances, as in the case of Tibetan *'cham*, or folk gatherings with dramatic features, such as Uyghur *meshrep*. This chapter surveys dance forms, theories and techniques in traditional, folk and ritual performance in India, China, Tibet, Uyghur, Japan, Korea and Southeast Asia (with a special case study of Cambodia).

I. India, by Arya Madhavan

Complexity, plurality, corporeality. When one thinks about dances of India, one thinks about these three interconnected defining features. Dances of India (this chapter consciously avoids using 'Indian dance', since there is no such thing as the 'Indian dance') are technically complex, combining the movements of limbs, footwork, kinetic eye movements, facial expressions and *mudra* (hand gestures). Principles defining dance and dramatic forms of India are uniquely inter-blended, making it hard to isolate one from the other. Drama, according to *Natyasastra* (dated between 200 BCE and 200 CE), the dramatic treatise written by Bharata, combines all arts and crafts and various actions (Vatsyayan 1974: 5). Action – in other words, physicality – is placed at the core of Indian dramatic practice. Theatre, for Bharata, is neither verbal nor corporeal, but a unique concoction, a symbiotic liveliness, blending all knowledge, arts and actions. Dance, or physical movement, is therefore a major ingredient of Indian theatre. As the leading classical dance scholar Kapila Vatsyayan asserts, 'the dance was very much a part of drama. . . . The *Natyasastra*, thus, is neither a treatise on drama alone . . . nor a treatise on dance alone as is erroneously believed by many devotees of dance. . . . While dance does emerge as an independent art . . . it nevertheless continues to be a very important part of the many-branched tree of drama' (1974: 6). Therefore, the dramatic forms such as *kathakali* or *kutiyattam* (Figure 5.1) incorporate physical movements, including elements of dance, whereas dance forms such as *mohiniyattam* (a dance form from the south Indian state of Kerala) and *bharatanatyam* (from Tamil Nadu, another south Indian state) fuses dramatic, facial and ocular expression (*abhinaya*) in their kinetic architecture. The focus is mainly on the corporeality of the expression; the body and its non-verbal exploration of meaning are equally significant, both to an actor and to a dancer. This chapter aims to provide a brief overview of the dances of India and their relation to theatre as well as explaining some aspects of their theoretical foundations.

Literary and archaeological evidence traces the earliest existence of the dances of India to the Indus valley civilization, dated between 3300 BCE and 1700 BCE. The Indus valley bronze figure 'of a dancing girl and other testimonies such as seals that clearly indicate postures associated with dance' (Dutt 2008: 427) bear proof for the beginnings of dance traditions in ancient India. Sanskrit texts such as *Veda* (dated back to 1500 BCE) as well as epics such as *Ramayana* and *Mahabharata* consist of several dance-specific metaphors (Dutt 2008; Vatsyayan 1974). Vatsyayan also notes that the heroes in Indian epics such as Rama and Arjuna were taught dance and God Krishna, of course, was considered the 'Supreme Dancer' (1974: 2), thus linking dance to the philosophical concept of *lila*, playfulness.[1] Besides, dance postures (*karana*) can be found inscribed

Figure 5.1 A 2010 performance of kutiyattam *Bhagavadajjukam* (The Hermit and the Courtesan), with Margi Sathi (sitting in front of the curtain), Kalamandalam Krishnakumar (behind the curtain) and Kalamandalam Sivan Namboothiri (in yellow costume).

(Courtesy of Devika Wasson)

in the temple sculptures across India, such as in the Chidambaram and Thanjavur temples in the south Indian state of Tamil Nadu, as well as the Jagannatha temple and Sun temple in the eastern state of Orissa.

According to the Indian National Academy of Music, Dance and Drama, there are eight Indian classical dance forms: *bharatanatyam* (from Tamil Nadu), *mohiniyattam* (Kerala), *kathakali* (Kerala), *kuchipudi* (Andhra Pradesh), *odissi* (Orissa), *Manipuri* (Manipur), *kathak* (north India) and *sattriya* (Assam). Although the performance techniques of the classical dances claim an ancient origin, some of them, such as bharatanatyam, mohiniyattam and odissi, were revived to their current forms of organized repertoire during the 1930s, 1940s and 1950s, respectively. Bharatanatyam, a relatively 'new' classical dance, revived in the 1930s under the leadership of Rukmini Devi Arundale,[2] from *sadir* or *dasi attam*, as it was once called, claims that it has existed for some 2,000 years.[3] Although the codification of its stage performance into well-structured repertoire[4] came in the first half of the nineteenth century (Dutt 2008: 459), the systematic structuring of its training pattern took place under the initiative of Arundale.

India is also the home of numerous tribal and folk dances. In Kerala alone, there are over 200 known folk and tribal dances (or dance theatres), but there are several more that still remain undocumented. Folk dances are associated with religious ceremonies, rituals, birth, death or marriage. Folk performances such as *mudiyettu*[5] from Kerala is a prototype of kathakali and striking similarities between these two forms are visible with regard to the use of the half-curtain (*tirasheela*), costumes, makeup, music and movements, particularly the footwork.

Dance theory

Any theoretical discussion on the dances of India will invariably start from the *Natyasastra*. Dance and drama, as far as the *Natyasastra* is concerned, are not strictly compartmentalized as they are in the west, and 'cannot be understood in isolation' (Vatsyayan 1974: 5). *Natya*, the dramatic performance, consists of various elements such as drama, dance, music and percussion, and dance is placed at the centre of bodily action in the *Natyasastra*. According to the *Natyasastra*, highly skilful women were assigned by the god of creation, Brahma, for the purpose of 'embellishing' the dramatic practice through their dance (Pisharodi 1987: 88–9).[6] Shiva, the mythical god of performance, choreographed several dance postures (karana) and sequential movements (*angahara*) suitable for a dramatic performance. Essentially, dance and drama are conceived by the *Natyasastra* as two sides of the same coin, and the mythical stories further emphasize the interdependency of dance and drama in a dramatic performance.

Texts such as *Dasarupaka*, a tenth-century treatise on drama written by Dhananjaya, and *Abhinaya Darpana* (varyingly dated by scholars between the second and the fifth centuries CE) by Nandikeswara, identify three major concepts in relation to dance: *nritta*, *nritya* and natya (Dutt 2008: 431). Nritta denotes pure dance, where the emphasis is completely placed on the rhythmic movement (*tala*) of the body to the accompanying music. *Dasarupaka* famously states that dance is dependent on rhythm and one's absorption in the act (the verse, *Nrittam talalayasrayam*, meaning the same, is known to the dancers of India from a very young age). The systematic pattern of meaningless rhythmic syllables guides the dancer through the patterns of movements. Such rhythmic syllables are termed *jati* (which will be used in this chapter), *vayttari* or *bol*. Forming the basic vocabulary for the rhythmic pattern of any performance, jati is employed to carve the time during a dance performance. Jati also serves the purpose of a significant pedagogical tool during dance training. Recited by the teacher, jati guides the students through the complex patterns of rhythm and foot movements during performance. These verbal notations form the basis of nritta in Indian dances.

Then comes nritya, which is the interpretative dance. The dancers will combine dance movements with facial and physical expressions using mudra, eye movements and physical postures. *Varnam*, a dance number in bharatanatyam that combines both dance movements and facial acting, is a typical example of nritya. Natya, literally the drama, is a dance number giving particular importance to abhinaya, or acting. Non-verbal exploration of the sung verses will be rendered by the dancer through combining facial expressions, *rasa* and mudra.

Although the dances in India differ considerably in style and technique, there are three common distinguishable features in them. These are the most important features that define the dances of India as a clearly delineable genre. The first one is the use of mudra – the systematically codified set of hand gestures – which forms its basic category for non-verbal acting. The second is the use of facial expression, including the complex patterns of eye movements and neck flexion. The third is the inherently complex orbits of rhythm that form the all-encompassing structural element of the patterns of movements in a dance performance. These three features further emphasize the symbiotic nature of dance and drama since they are the fundamental semiotic tools also employed by dramatic forms such as kutiyattam in its meaning-making process.

Dances, and indeed, dramatic forms, use a variety of mudras to 'speak'. Even though *Natyasastra* provides detailed functions and applications of sixty-six mudras, various dance forms choose to use mudra patterns based on Sanskrit texts of their choice. If bharatanatyam uses the mudras in *Abhinaya Darpana*, kutiyattam, kathakali and mohiniyattam use the mudra structure in *Hasta Lakshana Deepika*, a treatise by an unknown author. Mohiniyattam, although a dance form, maintains close affinity to the acting and movement patterns of kathakali (e.g. the movement pattern of kathakali's *sari* dance, set for the entry and introduction of heroines such as Damayanthi, is also adopted by mohiniyattam), particularly its mudra pattern. However, any student of dance will be taught the short verse from *Abhinaya Darpana*, which explains 'wherever the hand moves, there the glances follow; where the glances go, the mind follows; where the mind goes, the mood follows; where the mood goes, there is the flavour (rasa)' (Coomaraswamy and Duggirala 1917: 17).[7] Clearly, mudra is the starting point to the rasa experience. Sreenath Nair, in his essay titled 'Mudra: Choreography in Hands' (2013), states that '[m]udra is a kinetic event. . . . By arranging patterns of dancing fingers in the hands, mudra notates the visibility and emergence of the body as a process of the dancer's expression of meaning, emotion and rhythmic experience in performance.' Mudras could address a wide range of linguistic vocabulary through their use, in combination (combining two separate mudra, one in each hand) or in isolation (using the same mudra in both hands). Mudra obtains meaning, when used in combination with the facial expressions and eye movements during the acting sequence. The use of hand gestures, which form the basis of non-verbal delivery of meaning, is one of the key features of the dances of India.

Manipulation of rhythm through the complex patterns of footwork is another key feature of the dances of India. Effectively, what the rhythmic pattern in dances does is to divide silence and sound 'into organised and repeatable unit' (Martin 2004: 82); what a dancer does, in effect, is to produce a garland of silence and sound through the placing of heels, tapping of the toes, stomping and jumping in a dance performance. Rhythm sets the body in motion – every flicker of the eyelids, every shaking of the fingers and every movement of the neck is set to a specific rhythm. There are two terms which are significant to mention here – *kala*, tempo, and *tala*, rhythm. One cannot be considered in isolation of the other. When students learn to manipulate tala in performance, they are taught to manipulate kala too. Therefore, the students are instructed to move their feet in varying kala of the same tala. These movements are set to specific jati and the chanting of jati syllables controls kala and tala. Rhythm codifies the bodily movements in performance: in kathakali training, for instance, jati for the initial set of leg movements (*kalsadhakam*) is *dhi ta ta ta*. The feet position is peculiar and the students stand on the outer edge of their feet throughout this footwork exercise. The pattern of footwork itself is very complex. Always starting with the right foot, first are two in-steps (*dhi ta*) in this rhythmic pattern, followed by two out-steps (*ta ta*). Students start at a slow pace, kala, which is progressively increased to second and third speed. The aim of this exercise is to provide unwavering grasp on tala to a student as well as the muscular stamina for their legs and body as a whole. Similar exercises are devised in all traditional performance forms of India, including the independent dance forms such as bharatanatyam. The bharatanatyam training method devised nine codified rhythmic groups, each consisting of a set of *adavu* (movement patterns), that form the basic units of choreography. Rhythm is the category that codifies the set of movements in most dances of India. Rhythm also contributes to sustaining the audience's (and the dancer's) attention to the performance event. Rhythm permeates throughout the performance, through the bodily movements of the dancers, the percussion and the music. Kala manipulation of the performance's rhythmic orbits encapsulates the kinetic experience emanating from the perform-ance. This is the most significant feature of the dances of India.

The lines dividing drama and dance in Indian performance traditions are remarkably thin and do not sit comfortably within the strict, western compartmentalization between dance, drama, musical theatre and physical theatre. Indian theatre is an overarching performance genre, combining all of the above elements in its performance. Dance is a key ingredient in that theatrical practice, linking body to musicality, emotionality and fluidity.

II. China, by Xing Fan

In traditional Chinese theatre, dance (*wu*) is an umbrella term that includes dance-acting (*zuo*) and combat (*da*). In complementing singing (*ge*), which includes songs (*chang*) and musical speeches (*nian*) that focus on vocal and aural dimensions, dance embraces the physical and visual aspects of acting. Some sections of dance and stage combat are performed with only musical accom-paniment; in other cases, actors perform dance-acting and/or combat while delivering speeches or arias. Overall, it is by means of a combination of songs, speeches, dance-acting and combat that performers of traditional Chinese theatre tell stories and portray characters. Although the level of sophistication may vary in the dance of the more than three hundred indigenous theatrical forms in China, combat is widely used in most forms, and dance-acting is fundamental for each form.

The foundation of dance is an assemblage of movement conventions. With gestures, postures and sequences that are refined from those of daily actions, these conventions contain the vocabulary with which a precise body language is established and communicated. Dance-acting is based on conventions prescribing the movement of hands, eyes, body and steps, as well as those that govern the use of costume pieces such as beards, feathers and water-sleeves. Combat includes conventions of hand-to-hand fighting, the usage of weapons such as swords and spears, and acrobatic leaping and jumping (Figure 5.2). According to training practice, acting techniques in dance may be divided into three categories: basic techniques commonly used by all characters, techniques applied differently to specific role types, and techniques with particular uses and/or with stage properties or costume pieces. Through professional training, traditional Chinese theatre performers acquire expertise in performing movement conventions and the principles of sequencing these conventions in performance; they are then able to further rearrange these conventions when developing a character. The ideal achievement in traditional Chinese theatre character portrayal is the precise presentation of a dramatic character using the

Figure 5.2 Combat using swords in jingju *Sancha kou* (Crossroads Inn).
(Photo by Alexandra Bonds)

most effective conventions while allowing for the maximum demonstration of the actor's most distinctive performance techniques.

Dozens of techniques of the legs and the *yao* (the area between the rib cage and the top of the pelvis) are commonly used for all characters, hence are the most basic. Requiring flexibility and control, each technique may appear as an individual unit in performance, or serve as the foundation of more elaborate ones. For example, the basic movement convention *woyu* (literally 'crouching fish') requires combined use of the legs and the yao. It can be performed on either side of the body. For a woyu on the right side, a performer begins by standing with weight primarily on the left foot and partly on the front part of the right sole, which touches the ground diagonally behind – but not too far from – the left foot. He/she then slowly lowers the body to the floor, knees bent, with the left knee on top of the right one, with feet splayed out to the sides in a modified cross-legged tailor-fashion posture; the torso stays straight up. With the right leg and posterior touching the ground, the body turns counter-clockwise until the back, or the right side of the back, touches the ground and eyes look up to the sky. After holding the posture for a short while, the torso slowly returns to the upright position, and the performer stands up and returns to the original standing pose. When performed with empty hands, the left hand goes to the back of the left side of the yao while the body turns, and the right hand goes to hold the head; if weapons and stage properties are used, performers may adjust the positions of hands (Wan 2005: 135; Yu 1994: 101).

In conjunction with leg and yao positioning and movement, characters of different role types use assorted techniques – or different movement sizes of similar techniques – involving the eyes, stance and steps, and hands and arms, each technique grouping containing dozens of variations. One basic eye technique, *tishen* (literally 'holding the attention'), also called *dingshen* (literally 'focusing the attention') or *lingshen* (literally 'leading the attention'), is performed by focusing the eyes on one object without blinking and holding the gaze for a short while. Performers do not necessarily need to really see anything; the goal is to make the audience believe they do. *Yuanchang* (literally 'round circles') is one of the basic step techniques. Starting with relatively slow steps and then accelerating, the feet move forward alternately, with the weight transferred to the heel, sole and then toes, respectively. The knees bend slightly. The length of steps should be even and the pace needs to be steady. Techniques concerning the hands and arms include gestures involving the palms, fists, fingers and arms. For example, young and middle-aged female characters have about ten basic finger gestures, one of which is *lanhua zhi* (literally 'orchid-fingers'): with the index finger pointing out, the thumb gets close to the palm and the other three fingers curve towards the palm until the tip of the middle figure lightly presses on the tip of the thumb. *Yunshou* (literally 'cloud hands'), on a more elaborate level, consists of interlocking circular movements of the hands and arms with accompanying movements of the neck, eyes, shoulders and torso, all motivated from the yao, and involving shifts of weight between the feet.

In dance, movement design and body language are closely associated with a character's role type. Each type is indicative of a specific age, social status and level of dignity, and has associated with it corresponding practices of acting and costuming. Specific categories may vary in particular theatrical forms, but generally characters are grouped into four major role types: *sheng* (dignified male), *dan* (female), *jing* (larger-than-life male) and *chou* (comic earthy male), with each type containing multiple subcategories. Individual role-subcategories require a specific dimension or size of movement and, in general, those for female characters are smaller in size than those for male characters. For instance, the movement arrangement of yunshou is basically the same across all role-subcategories, but each performer conforms to the specific movement size of his/her role type specialization. In traditional *jingju* (Beijing opera) performance, for a jing role, the highest level of the right hand during the movement sequence should be higher than the performer's head. For a *laosheng* (older dignified male) role, the right hand should rise only to the level of the performer's eyebrows. For a *wusheng* (martial dignified male) role, it should be at the level of the performer's forehead. But the highest level of the right hand for a dan role should not be above the performer's nose (Zou 1985: 8, 30–1).

In addition, some techniques are specifically applied to particular usages with individual stage properties and costume pieces. *Tanzi gong* (literally 'techniques on carpets') and *bazi gong* (literally 'techniques with weapons') are especially important for characters with martial skills. Tanzi gong includes techniques involving elementary flips, single flips, multiple flips, rolling and twisting, one-on-one fighting, leaping with a spring board, and other assorted techniques (Lu and Wang 2005). Bazi gong contains more than one hundred movement sequences used for combat scenes with stage properties such as swords and spears; performers can be alone or in pairs, or as an individual fighting against multiple opponents (Lü 2006: 62–75).

Techniques with costume pieces can externalize a character's emotional changes, psychological states and spiritual status. For young and middle-aged female characters, *shuixiu gong* (literally 'techniques of water-sleeves') is performed via skilful manoeuvring of the silk pieces, normally 2 to 3 feet in length, that extend from each sleeve. In *jiju*, popular in northeastern China, the water-sleeves can be as long as 10 feet. Controlling the moving shapes and flowing patterns of the water-sleeves, shuixiu gong requires coordinated movements of the shoulders, arms, elbows, wrists and fingers. *Lingzi gong* (literally 'techniques of feathers') is the most frequently used by *xiaosheng* (young dignified male) roles; the single or double feathers, normally 5 to 8 feet in length and attached to the hat, are often used for valiant warriors. In performance, the techniques of holding and dancing with feathers are associated with a character's spiritual status and emotional situation. *Puju* and *jinju*, forms originating in the Shanxi Province, are famous for special techniques of manoeuvring feathers to form patterns of movement, controlled by the head and the neck. Other techniques with costume pieces include *shuaifa gong* (literally 'techniques of hair'), *rankou gong* (literally 'techniques of beards'), *shanzi gong* (literally 'techniques of fans') and *shoujuan gong* (literally 'techniques of handkerchiefs').

The highest aesthetic goal of traditional Chinese theatre is *mei* (beauty; to be beautiful). In dance, two aesthetic features are significant: roundness and coordination. Taking jingju as an example, Ouyang Yuqian maintains, 'We can say that not a single dance movement in jingju is not round. . . and it is an art of drawing circles' (quoted in Wang Shiying 2003: 18). Elizabeth Wichmann further describes roundness in acting as follows:

> Roundness applies to posture and movement, both of various parts of the body in isolation and of the entire body in or through space. Straights lines and angles are to be avoided; positive aesthetic value is perceived in the presentation of a three-dimensional network of circles, arcs, and curved lines.
>
> (Wichmann 1991: 4)

The roundness in dance-acting and combat requires superb coordination among all parts of the body. A beautifully executed movement convention involves the smooth synchronization of hands, eyes, body and steps, carefully controlled with breathing, awareness of the appropriate rhythms and the correct use of strength. The yao is considered the key for this coordination, in that it initiates, leads and controls the movement of limbs and torso. Regarding the pursuit of beautiful dance, the Qian (Jinfu) School of jingju performance subscribes to the following theory:

[On a scale of one to ten with ten being the best,] to grasp the form is three, to understand the coordination among body parts is six, to associate it with the internal feelings is eight, and to be able to execute it naturally whenever necessary is ten.

(Zou 1985: 10)

III. Tibet, by Kati Fitzgerald

The Tibet Autonomous Region (TAR) represents a land area of more than a million square kilometres and a population of nearly three million people. Parts of northern Nepal, Sikkim, Bhutan, Assam, Baltistan, northeastern India and the Chinese administrative units of Xinjiang, Qinghai and Sichuan also contain Tibetan-speaking communities, although each region has its own distinct cultural characteristics. Worldwide, it is estimated that there are approximately six million ethnic Tibetans. Below and in the following sections are examples of some of Tibet's vast array of musical and performance traditions.

'Cham is a form of monastic performance now open to public spectators. The performance lengths vary and events occur on important festivals of the Buddhist calendar. Performers are all male and important roles are played by monks and high members of the clergy. 'Cham performances are held primarily outdoors in the courtyard of certain monasteries. The performances are sometimes backdropped by a large *thang ka* (painting of a deity or religious figure on silk) of important figures of Buddhist traditions in Tibet. The performance is accompanied by an orchestra of trumpets (*dung chen* or *dung ring*), oboes (*rgya gling*), conch shells (*dung dkar*), drums (*rnga chen*) and cymbals (*rol mo, bsil bsnyen* and *sbub 'chal*) (De Nebesky-Wojkowitz 1976: 69). Dance steps are extremely precise and each performer's movement embodies the qualities of the particular deity they play. Movements of the performers draw a mandala (*dkyil 'khor*) in the performance space, with the *'cham dpon* ('cham master) at the centre. 'Cham performances have become didactic in nature, but continue to function as sacred ritual in which performers take on the qualities of the deities and root out evil forces (Figure 5.3).

Gar is most commonly known as the secular court performance of the Dalai Lama, but the term also refers to certain tantric monastic rituals that are not publicly performed (aka *mchod gar*). We know little about tantric gar performances, as they are guarded well by the masters who teach them. Gar, in its secular iteration, is performed by young, male dancers known as *gar phrug pa*. The ensemble of dancers and musicians, *gar pa*, was previously maintained by the court of the Dalai Lama. The gar pa use mainly kettle-drums (*brda ma* or *lda ma*) and oboes (*bsu rna* or *sur na*). The dancing technique is masculine and angular in execution. Props, such as axes or swords, add to the militaristic nature of the dance. There are various theories surrounding the origination of gar, but there is compelling evidence that the performance form came to Tibet through Baltistan and Ladakh (Jamyang Norbu and Tashi Dhondup 1986: 132). Gar performances are not nearly as common as other dance performances in and outside Tibet, as the art form seems to have disappeared with the flight of the Dalai Lama to India in 1959, but was revived in the exile community, as well as in Lhasa in the 1980s.

Nang ma songs were traditionally performed during picnics, festivals or official functions. Nang ma is performed using four instruments: *sgra snyan* (Tibetan lute), *pi wang* (a two-stringed fiddle), *rgyud mang* (hammered dulcimer) and *gling bu* (flute) or *'phred gling* (transverse flute). Nang ma, similar to the Tibetan musical genre *stod gzhas*, generally begin in a slow, instrumental style (*dal gzhas* or *'jog gzhas*), and include a section of dancing, singing and playing simultaneously (*rgyang gzhas*) as well as a faster step dance (*mgyogs gzhas* or *'khrug gzhas*). Nang ma was banned in Tibet in the 1960s and 1970s owing to its association with the Tibetan aristocracy (Tashi Tsering 2012). Like gar, a revival occurred in the 1980s and, starting in the late 1990s, Lhasa

Figure 5.3 'Cham performance with trumpets.

(Photo by Colin Mackerras)

saw a resurgence of popularity in nang ma bars (simply called nang ma). Nang ma in modern-day Tibet are cabaret-style bars in which audience members sit at tables below a stage. Traditional songs and dances are interspersed with modern Tibetan, Chinese, Hindi and English songs. Songs are sung by local singing sensations and audience members gather on the stage for group dances throughout the night.

Lha mo is a form of opera performed within both the Tibet Autonomous Region and the exile communities of Nepal, India and even the United States and Europe. This theatrical form includes elaborate costumes, a small orchestra of percussion instruments, high-register vocal pieces, and repetitive, yet highly complex dance steps. Lha mo is performed throughout Tibet, the most prominent performances occurring during the Shoton Festival (*zho ston dus chen*) both in the TAR and in exile. The canon consists of eight or nine opera librettos, which tell historical, mythical and religious tales. Dancing technique is divided between male and female characters, with many character-specific movement styles. The male and female chorus members dance in unison, but male movements are more exaggerated and extraverted than the female gestures. Lha mo is perhaps most famous, especially among Tibetan children, for the gravity-defying barrel turns of the hunters (colloquially *'phag chen*) and the yak dances performed by two dancers in thick, black yak costumes.

'Cham, gar, nang ma and lha mo represent only a fraction of the Tibetan performance styles that incorporate dance currently performed in the TAR and around the world. The forms, although they have distinct characteristics, are constantly evolving through the emergence of new generations of performers and the ingenious innovations of the masters.

IV. Uyghur, by Ronald Gilliam

The Uyghurs, native to the Altay Mountains in Central Asia, today constitute the largest ethnic group inhabiting Xinjiang Uygur Autonomous Region in northwestern China.[8] Throughout their 4,000-year history, the Uyghurs have played an important role in cultural exchange along the Silk Road, developing an advanced society that differs culturally and linguistically from their East Asian neighbours while sharing similarities with such other Turkic-speaking Central Asian ethnicities as the Kazakhs and Uzbeks. The Uyghur people are proud of their heritage and especially of their contributions in medicine, linguistics, literature, printing, architecture, and the visual and performing arts.

The development of Uyghur performing art forms can be understood in part as a response to the harsh environment of Central Asia, the dry, rugged mountainous landscapes where the ancient Uyghurs gathered around oases. The severe climate fostered deep connections between the Uyghurs and their surroundings as they struggled for survival, and the challenges to raising both crops and livestock on the steppe encouraged a profound reverence for the cycles of life. Traditional Uyghur dance and music are both ceremonial and emotionally expressive and emphasize the Uyghurs' tangible connections to the raw elements of their homeland: sandy soil, water, fire and air.

Evidence suggests that the earliest performing arts of the ancient Uyghurs mainly focused around harvest celebrations whose chief purpose was to provide entertainment and recreation for the oasis dwellers. Other performances occurred at auspicious social and religious occasions, especially weddings, including music, dancing and feats of human skill such as balancing objects, gymnastics and sleight of hand. All of these performance practices became deeply ingrained in Uyghur culture, and the essentially communal aspect of Uyghur performing arts persists today.

Uyghurs began converting to Islam in the tenth century CE, and the majority had converted by the end of the seventeenth century. Islamic prohibitions against the performing arts – partly rooted in attempts to sever links to Buddhism and shamanism throughout Central Asia – influenced Uyghur folk entertainments by lending an overtly religious and ritual cast to performance practices that had previously been primarily social in nature. The adoption of Islam also entailed many innovations, including singing in Arabic and Persian at sacred occasions such as weddings.

Localized versions of the folk entertainment gathering called *meshrep*, in which both dance and music play prominent roles, likewise developed under influences from outside cultures, and the elaboration of local meshrep types expanded and refined traditional Uyghur dance styles. External cultural borrowing in Uyghur performing arts continues today as Uyghurs absorb foreign elements, especially those derived from Chinese popular and official folk culture, while striving to ensure that their performance traditions remain quintessentially Uyghur.

Meshrep (gathering) are celebratory communal Uyghur gatherings incorporating several traditional performing arts forms. Meshrep vary in character across the Uyghur homeland and may be held on a variety of occasions, yet most gatherings share similar activities that characterize the genre and an underlying purpose of cultural education of the community through entertainment. The Uyghur people have over many centuries come to value the meshrep as a pre-eminent means of communal bonding; indeed, the meshrep is an event in which Uyghur society itself is created, performed and maintained.

Most of the Uyghur performing arts trace their roots to the meshrep. In a single meshrep event, all the traditional Uyghur performance forms may be displayed, including instrumental and vocal music, dance, poetry, drama, artisanal crafts and feats of dexterity. Most meshrep include feasting, music, dancing and short dramatic skits; spoken word performances, joke telling and various games may also be included. These games constitute a form of social policing by the community by creating moments of public shaming in a comedic manner. The majority of such performances involve improvised micro-dramas that display exaggerated consequences of behaving contrary to cultural norms. For example, an audience member may be required to join actors to participate in a mock courtroom drama during which he is put on trial for not respecting his elders, drinking alcohol or violating some other cultural taboo. Irony, mockery and inversion of social norms become powerful tools of social education in these skits.

Like the muqam, the traditional Uyghur music always included in such gatherings, the meshrep developed in an agrarian society in which people desired entertainment after long days tending to their crops and livestock. The ancient meshrep are thought to have blended playful elements with religious ritual and social education. The earliest evidence of Uyghur meshrep possibly occurs within depictions of totemic dances performed as a form of ritualized prayer to shamanistic gods. Cave paintings in Ghulja, Turpan and other archaeological sites across Xinjiang clearly display such dances, suggesting how ancient Uyghur dances celebrated such communal activities as hunting, the harvest, war and village gatherings. Today's folk dances, including the range of dance styles performed in contemporary meshrep, are all thought by Uyghurs to have originated in these ancient antecedents.

Within a framework of entertainment and celebration, core community values are instilled in Uyghur meshrep relating to a wide variety of cultural customs and traditions, including religion, law, manners, morals, language, literature, music, dance, sports, textiles, handicrafts, food, animal husbandry and agriculture. Most traditional meshrep also incorporate historical references to ancient Uyghur philosophical ideas of aesthetic beauty and emphasize the value of artistic skill. The educational aspect of meshrep is always deeply integral to their purpose.

Because all meshrep involve local communities and are organized around specific events, varying in their use of space, locale and content, further generalizations about the genre as a whole are problematic. For example, a Xotan wedding meshrep, a Qumul New Year (noruz) meshrep and a Kelpin melon-harvest meshrep each has its own unique regional characteristics. In addition, meshrep are performed in a range of locales, from community squares and parks to small private homes. Typically, the venue is not as important as the context of the performance, and the location is determined by the event's overall intent.

All meshrep share the feature of active audience participation; the entire community simultaneously performs the roles of audience and performers. An atmosphere of social equality is created as the boundaries between the roles of audience and performer are blurred, a levelling effect reinforced by the equal participation of Uyghurs of all social classes.

Improvisation is an important aspect of all meshrep performances within a roughly similar structure, occurring mostly during the musical components, group dances and comedic micro-dramas. An improvisatory genre of special importance is the *qoshaq* (spontaneous folk songs/poems), which are often recited extempore by audience members, displaying the speaker's ability to use the Uyghur language to express their personal views on human relationships, their engagement with local culture, and other emotions relating to community matters (Figure 5.4).

Most sources on meshrep state that the genre's decline began as China rapidly developed in the 1980s, yet other events are also possible catalysts in its deterioration. During the Cultural Revolution, the Chinese central government officially banned almost all performances other than the government-approved revolutionary model plays (*geming yangbanxi*) from 1966 to 1976; in the Uyghur areas, public meshrep performances were thus outlawed or at least discouraged. Later, in the aftermath of the 1997 Ghulja riots, meshrep were temporarily prohibited across Xinjiang. Eventually meshrep returned to Uyghur public life in the form of both

Figure 5.4 **A family homecoming meshrep featuring dancers and musicians from the Dolan Cultural Center as well as local community members.**

(Taken in Yantaq Village, Xinjiang on 6 June 2012 by the author.)

community-based performances that mirrored traditional structures and professional performances that shared traditional aesthetics, but in which social education no longer provided a main impetus.

The creation of professional televised meshrep performances in 2003 constituted perhaps the first widespread commercialization of the genre. Since these performances were not created, maintained or funded by local Uyghur communities, the emphasis inevitably shifted from the communal to the commercial. Various businessmen, for-profit corporations, charities and cultural associations instead funded the 2003 televised meshrep performances. Muhemmet Zunun (2011) has criticized these performances as attempting to create a meshrep 'brand' rather than realizing the potential of mass media as a means of wide-reaching cultural education (168). Zunun contends that these televised meshrep merely provided a professional stage for choreographed dance and music and that they specifically targeted younger Uyghur consumers. In televised meshrep performances, the gatherings' tradition of communal involvement is eliminated, as the audience cannot participate.

In contemporary Uyghur society, meshrep continue to function as a social institution and more recently as a source of national pride. Professionalized meshrep performances featuring dances choreographed by Küresh Rejep gained national attention by winning numerous Chinese national dance competitions, and in 2010 UNESCO added the Uyghur meshrep to its list of Intangible Cultural Heritage in Urgent Need of Safeguarding. Despite criticism of their purpose, effects and meaning, professionalized meshrep performances today exist side by side with local, more traditionally structured events; both can be seen as attempts to revitalize and safeguard the meshrep for future generations of Uyghurs.

V. Japan, by Colleen Lanki

In traditional Japanese theatre, dance is not considered a separate discipline, but an intrinsic part of each form. Actors are also dancers, and dance is the basis of each movement or gesture. Dance found in traditional Japanese theatre can be divided into three categories: *mai*, *odori* and *furi*. Each of these words is literally translated as 'dance' but they describe quite different kinds of movement. Mai is generally slow and circular, with the steps remaining low to the ground, while odori is more lively and active, using frequent jumping movements. Furi is used for mimetic and gestural dance patterns. Plays may have fully danced sections, danced phrases connected to dialogue and/or danced poses or movements integrated into a scene.

All traditional Japanese dance shares certain physical characteristics. The basis of all movement is *koshi*, often translated as 'hips' but more correctly referring to the use of the entire hip girdle and lower back. *'Koshi wo ireru'* – literally 'put in your koshi' – appears to mean lowering the hips by bending the knees, but it is really a more involved practice of grounding the body to the earth through a point just below the navel, while maintaining an upwards energy from the top of the spine and crown of the head. As Japanese classical dancer Fujima Yūko says, 'The muscles of the body are always pulled between heaven and earth' (Fujima 1992: 10). All dances in traditional Japanese theatre require a straight spine, which may twist around a vertical axis,

Figure 5.5 Fujima Yūko dancing the *jiuta-mai* (dance of the Kansai area geisha) 'Yukari no Tsuki', a female form piece. National Theatre, Tokyo, 17 January 2003.

(Photo by Fujiwara Atsuko)

but never bends or contracts. Another overall characteristic is the incorporation of various fans, props and costume elements that can be used in a transformative or narrative way; depending on the needs of the story, a folding fan can become a pine bough or warrior's shield, while kimono sleeves can be used as angel wings or a strip of writing paper (Figure 5.5).

Dance in noh and kyogen

In noh, '[d]ance is not a sub-category of acting; acting is an aspect of dance' (Bethe and Brazell 1982: 3). Dances are largely done by the *shite* (main character), although they can involve the *tsure* (lead character's companion) and occasionally the *waki* (secondary character/listener). The first part of a noh play is often physically still, with characters being introduced and ideas or

Figure 5.6 Matsui Akira as the *shite* in the noh play *Sumidagawa* performing a *shiori*, a mimetic hand gesture indicating crying.

(Courtesy of Rick Emmert)

images evolving through the chanted text with a few connected dance movements. Physical action increases throughout a play, and often includes an instrumental dance section in the second half. The choice of dance is determined by the qualities of the main character; for example, a play where the main character is a warrior may include *otoko-mai* (male dance), while one in which the main character is a deity could include *kami-mai* (god dance). The end of a noh performance generally includes quicker and more complex dance patterns and gestures. The increase of physical movement within a noh play is consistent with the overall *jo-ha-kyū* (slow-breaking-fast) structure of every level of noh.

Noh uses the slow, circular movement of *mai*, with a limited number of repeated floor patterns in arcs, diagonals and straight lines. The core movement in noh is *suriashi* (sliding step), a walk in which the whole foot glides along the floor, then lifts from the toes as the step is completed; the body does not rock from side to side or move up and down while travelling through space. Proper suriashi is achieved only with a strong use of koshi. Stamping is another important aspect of noh dance, the sound of the foot adding to the rhythmic quality of the music.

Many dance movements in noh are highly stylized mimesis, while others are abstract and take on the emotions of the text being chanted. Mimetic gestures include striking or slashing with a fan to show action in battle, or raising one or both hands slowly to the face to indicate crying. Abstract movements include *shikake* (slow drawing forward of hands and feet), *hiraki* (an accompanying movement backwards while opening the arms) or *sayū* (a left–right zigzag pattern), which add mood or story elements depending on their rhythm, placement or gestural qualities (Figure 5.6). Dance movements can also give character information or be specific to a particular mask. Quick movements of the head from side to side indicate agitation or madness, and may tell the audience that the character is not what he or she appears to be; female demons have specific movements in which they use the horns on their masks to threaten their adversaries.

In kyogen, clever, comic dialogue is paramount, but dance is the basis of the gestures and physical comedy. Like noh, kyogen uses suriashi and a combination of mimetic and abstract movements, but in kyogen the emphasis is on the mimetic. Many kyogen include *komai*, small comic dances and songs which enhance the sense of fun or absurdity of a play. Like kyogen plays themselves, komai deal with familiar, everyday themes such as hopping rabbits, pretty girls hanging laundry, or the pleasures of drinking sake. Dance in kyogen is meant to support the character, enhance the story and make the audience laugh.

Dance in kabuki

Kabuki has been intimately connected to dance from its origins in 1603 when Okuni named her special combination of theatre and dance *kabuki odori* (kabuki dance). When women were banned from the professional stage in 1652 and men took over playing women's roles, dance became important as a way to emphasize the art of *onnagata* (literally 'female form'). Some kabuki actors became dance specialists, choreographing themselves in increasingly elaborate and virtuosic dances or dance-plays. By the eighteenth century the role of choreographer had emerged, working in kabuki theatres while also creating repertoire to be performed in concert settings by both female and male dancers. Currently *nihon buyō* (Japanese classical dance) has become an overall term encompassing many genres, including *kabuki odori* (kabuki dance), *jiuta-mai* (dances of the Kansai area geisha) and *shin buyō* (new dances). Some schools or traditions of Japanese dance are still headed by kabuki actors.

Dance in kabuki is designed to tell a story, as well as to showcase an actor's talent. It is choreographed predominantly to the lyrics; movements echo or elaborate the meaning of the words. Dance movements performed to purely instrumental *shamisen* (a three-stringed banjo-like instrument) sections tend to be elaborate and rhythmic, incorporating the use of props or costumes. Dance props such as the *tenugui* (a long towel or strip of silk) or specialized use of kimono sleeves can illustrate the story or extend and beautify movements. The *sensu* (folding dance fan) is the most important dance prop for any actor. A fan can be transformed into any object through mimetic gestures such as the pouring of sake or the rising of the sun, express emotion with rhythm or movement quality, and demonstrate virtuosity through tosses, flips and twirls.

The stances, gaits, limb positions and gestural qualities of dance in kabuki are signifiers of a character's gender, status, age and personality. A female character is portrayed with toes turned in and knees held together, and by arm gestures made with elbows pointing downwards and the hands lightly cupped. Another onnagata signifier is a movement where one shoulder lowers slightly and the chin drops towards it. Male form has more variation, with many layers of masculinity coded into the movements, but in general, male characters have legs rotated outward, arms moving with elbows up or back, and there is no softness in the shoulders. The stronger or more 'rough' a male character is, the wider the stance and more expansive the gestures. There are many fine details to the movements determined by the specifics of each character (Figure 5.7).

There are three levels of dance integration in kabuki: fully danced plays, danced sections within plays, and danced gestural phrases. *Shosagoto* (dance-plays), such as *Sagimusume* (The Heron Maiden) or *Tsumoru koi yuki no sekinoto* (The Barrier Gate), are virtuosic pieces, featuring one or two main roles. They have limited or no spoken dialogue, with text mostly sung by the

Figure 5.7 Fujima Shōgo as Sekibei in *The Barrier Gate*.
(Photo by Ogawa Tomoko)

music ensemble. Danced sections within plays appear in many forms, such as movement scenes to the accompaniment of Gidayu narrative chant and shamisen, or entrances and exits on the *hanamichi* (walkway through the audience). Another common danced section in a play is the *tachimawari* – stylized, choreographed fight scenes full of group poses and acrobatics. Danced gestural phrases can be anything from the stylized smoking of a pipe, the use of a fan during a very rhythmic monologue, or the action of a *mie* or *kimari*, danced poses that punctuate scenes. Many of these shorter danced sections and individual gestures are considered to be acting *kata* (forms), showing that dance and acting are inseparable. Dance is the physical life of kabuki.

Dance in ningyō jōruri/bunraku

Throughout their histories, bunraku and kabuki competed for audience, and practitioners stole from each other in order to create interest and novelty. Choreographies and movement styles were part of this borrowing, often making the puppets look more human, and the humans more puppet-like. Dance plays that were created for live actors in kabuki have been adapted for the bunraku, while many sections of plays originally danced by puppets were set on the human body in kabuki. Kabuki actors use several levels of puppet imitation in their movements, including the technique of *ningyōburi*, where an actor moves while manipulated by a second actor (Brandon 1978: 76). The borrowing of content and style between kabuki and bunraku enriched kabuki dance as a whole, giving choreographers and performers new physical vocabularies and challenges.

In noh, kyogen, kabuki and bunraku, a performer is taught through physical transmission of form and style by one-on-one training with a teacher. This kind of instruction preserves the forms and traditions of the dance through generations, and emphasizes the complete integration of movement, voice and character. Japanese traditional theatre performances are not combinations of separate disciplines, but total theatre traditions with dance woven into all aspects of their creation and presentation.

VI. Korea, by CedarBough T. Saeji

Traditional Korean dance can be loosely divided into ritual, court, folk and professional folk dances. Ritual dances include Buddhist dances such as *barachum* (cymbal dance), *nabichum* (butterfly dance) and *beopgochum* (large barrel drum dance); Confucian dances such as *ilmu* (Confucian ritual dance); and shamanic dance. Many of the court dances, such as *cheoyongmu* (Dance of Cheoyong) and *geommu* (Sword Dance), have an extensive historical record, with documents describing the dances and paintings of the choreography. Records concerning folk dances, however, are almost non-existent and consist mostly of passing descriptions of dances interspersed with the writings of government officials in diaries, letters and reports. Folk dances are divided into folk and professional folk dances. Folk dances incorporated into Korean mask dance-dramas, *pungmul* drumming music, or as part of the women's song/dance/game *ganggangsullae*, are performed by large groups and the dance motions are relatively simple. The folk professional dances are much more complex and include *salpuri* (shaman's dance), *seungmu* (monk's dance) and *taepyeongmu* (great peace dance).

Key words used explicitly in discussions of Korean dance include *heung* (enthusiasm and liveliness), *meot* (inner style and grace), *han* (suffering and bitterness) and *sinmyeong* (communal cathartic release through sharing in the performance). The terms are not all used to describe the same performance: han is usually used to talk about dances such as *salpuri* inspired by shamanic mourning ritual movements, while sinmyeong is most often evoked in the case of outdoor group performance of folk dances that may evolve into audience participation, such as in *pungmul*. In premodern Korea, improvisation was a key part of Korean dance, but the codification of dances within Korea's system to protect intangible cultural heritage has pushed registered dances to adhere to a consistent choreography. The problem for the dancers then becomes how to communicate heung, meot, han or sinmyeong within a framework that only the highest-ranked dancers ever challenge.

Korean traditional dance features a distinctive use of the knees and the shoulders – knees bend and straighten, the shoulders are loose, often rising and falling, and motions of the arm and hand are not isolated from the shoulder or each other. Dance steps are often heel-toe, until the speed of a dance accelerates, and dancers often employ a duck-footed stance (heels together, toes pointed out at a 45-degree angle). Flow from one motion to another is emphasized, although many folk dances play with the rhythm in the dance by pausing and resuming movement with dramatic flair. Unlike western dance forms, Korean dance eschews extensions and grand poses, and with the exception of some humorous motions in mask dance-dramas originally danced by men acting the part of women, dance motions never work to sexualize the dancer or draw attention to sexualized parts of the body. Dance aesthetics are understated: the highlight of a dance could be a single fleeting close-mouthed smile, and allure could be portrayed by lifting a voluminous skirt until the audience can see flashes of the quick, delicate steps of sock-clad feet.

Ritual dances are part of larger rites performed in Buddhism, Confucianism and shamanism. Although the Buddhist dances are, occasionally, presented on a proscenium stage as distinct art forms, ilmu and *mumu* (Shamanic ritual dance) are rarely seen outside of a re-enacted rite or, in the case of shamanism, an actual ceremony. One reason may be that these dances are less complex and stripped of ritual significance; they are not visually compelling after the first few minutes. Ilmu, for example, is a ritual dance introduced to Korea during the reign of King Yejong (1105–22). This dance is formal and ceremonial, with lines of eight identically costumed dancers in up to eight rows holding props such as a flute and dragon-headed stick. The dancers perform simple, deliberate motions of raising and extending their hands and arms without varying their expression. The dance is performed yearly as part of the ancestral rite for the Joseon royal family. Although the dance motions cannot capture audience attention for long, when watching it accompanied by the ritual music, and the entire pageantry of the Confucian ritual Jongmyo *jerye*, it becomes a grand sight worth a trip to Seoul.

Korean court culture was heavily influenced by Chinese culture, and various dances entered Korea due to the intergovernmental relationship. However, in the decades after the 1644 dynastic change in China, the Koreans – antipathetic to the new Manchu-ruled Qing court – revised court arts, removing Chinese-style formalities and using *hyanggak*, Korean court music, instead of *dangak*, a court music imported from China, to accompany the dancers. Among the registered court dances is cheoyongmu, a dance performed by five masked dancers representing the five directions (including the centre). The dance is named after the legend of prince Cheoyong, who became a protective figure, and the dance is said to repel evil spirits, while the movements sketch Taoist theories of yin–yang and the five directions.

Korean folk dances are lively and full of energy. Folk dances include those performed while singing, such as *ganggangsullae*, those that are part of Korean mask dance-dramas (see Korean section in Chapter 7), and dance while drumming as in the various types of pungmul (Figure 5.8).

The technically challenging solo dances salpuri, seungmu and taepyeongmu are considered to be professionalized folk dances: even though these dances emerged from folk culture, they require dance training to perform. All three of these dances survived the Japanese occupation,

Figure 5.8 A scene from the mask dance-drama *Yangju byeolsandae*.
(Photo by CedarBough T. Saeji)

partially because of the successful interpretations choreographed by Han Seongjun in the 1930s based on Han's research on dance history and exposure to all aspects of traditional performing arts. Han's seungmu, and another major variant by Yi Maebang, are popular and frequently performed. Seungmu, or the monk's dance, once performed by *gisaeng* (the Korean equivalent of the Japanese *geisha*), features a dancer in Buddhist ritual clothing with long sleeve extensions or *hansam*. At the climax of the dance the performer beats a large barrel drum in the ritual style of *beopgochum*, a Buddhist ritual drum dance that is still performed in Korean Buddhist temples.

Over the past few decades a variety of exciting new dances in a traditional style have also emerged. Three of these are *jangguchum*, *buchaechum* and *hwagwanmu*. Jangguchum is the staging of the solo of a talented *janggu* or hourglass drum player previously performed within the context of pungmul but with a focus on dance elements, even to the extent of having an offstage drummer providing the anchoring beat. The large group dance with fans known as *buchaechum* is a crowd favourite, but it was first performed less than fifty years ago. *Hwagwanmu* is a dance originally created by colonial-era dancer Choi Seunghui to bring court dance to the stage, but only the costumes adhere to the court theme; the motions lack the dignity and depth of those that were previously performed for the royalty.

VII. Southeast Asia, by Kathy Foley

This section will briefly discuss dance in Southeast Asia noting commonalities and categories, and then touch on specifics of areas: the Christian-influenced Philippines; Muslim-dominated Indonesia and Malaysia; the Buddhist-majority Khmer–Thai–Lao–Burmese region; and the largely Sinitic Vietnam and Singapore.

Commonalities: Dance in most areas of Southeast Asia is executed within musical phrases that may have units of eight as a basic time cycle. The movements of dancers are in a number of areas accompanied by the drum, and drum syllables are sometimes used while learning/ teaching, especially in the Indo-Malay area. Dance often has the torso in a set stance for the character portrayed. Movements of the periphery (arm–hand, leg–foot, head) seem dominant and fingers often bend back from rotating wrists. The weight of the body is generally earthward and bending at the knees, and contrasts ballet's use of elevations, extensions of limbs, or jumps. Indigenous movement is sometimes linked to puppetry; for example, Burmese dancers squat and bounce rotating their arms, recalling the *yokthe* marionettes of the region. Javanese dancers 'float' while flattening their profile, emulating the two-dimensional *wayang kulit* shadow theatre, while the Sundanese of West Java cultivate the sharp three-dimensional movement of their wooden doll puppets.

Social dance and court dance can be divided by gender characteristics into 'male' or 'female', with women's roles using a more confined kinesphere. Yet in theatre dance the character type – usually one of four basic types (refined male, female, warrior/monkey, ogre) – dictates movement and the gender of the dancer may not match the character. While some of the stylized gestures may have meanings as in the sixty-eight signs of Thai *ma bot yae* 'dance alphabet', most gestures are ornamental or mimetic, unlike the elaborated gesture language (*hasta/mudra*) of south India.

Dance in Southeast Asia can be divided into four groups: (1) ritual dance; (2) functional dance (i.e. martial art and social dance – often incorporated in popular/folk theatre; (3) classical dramatic dance; and (4) dance influenced by global models from foxtrot to ballet to breakdance.

Ritual dances may be linked with local shamanic heritage, curing, ancestral/death rites and harvest rituals. Some performances have significant mimetic aspects. Trance performances are still common in some areas such as Bali, Kalimantan/Borneo and northern Malaysia/southern Thailand. One can find both soft and somatic movements which give a floating impression, often seen in female trance genres as in Malay *main peteri* ('playing the princess'), a healing trance genre with a female clientele. This contrasts with the more jerky movements in male trance forms, as in *dabus* of West Java where males dance with aggressive moves, making them 'invulnerable' to knives. Islamic religious dances that seek to attain union with the divine, such as *dikir/zikir* dance-chant, include genres such as Aceh's *saman* where men slap their chests, bow in syncopated waves and execute elaborate group figures. Popular theatres (Thai *likay*, Khmer *yike*) evolved from this source. Hindu Balinese dances, such as the soft *gabor*, a stately women's group dance, and the martial male *baris* highlighted by dynamic drumming, have functions of warship in temple celebrations. Buddhists in Burma perform semi-shamanic *nat* dances and Thai shrines can have refined female dancers to honour the spirits.

Functional dances include martial arts dances, which are taught and performed in part via set choreographies performed to music. The more improvisational fighting is often done with musical accompaniment. In Indonesia and Malaysia *pencak silat* martial arts are taught via dance. Thai boxing (*muay thai*) starts with *ram wai kru* (dance honouring teachers) and has postures that may remind us of dance. Theatre and classical dances incorporate, but also aestheticize, martial arts positions. Stable standing positions, especially for warriors or demons, may have come from martial training. Theatre's battle/weapon scenes are heavily influenced by martial arts dances. Circus acrobatics also figure in some dances, such as Thai/Malay *nora*.

Female social dance of the Indo-Malay world is often associated with *ronggeng* (courtesan singer-dancers). Some ronggeng dances use martial arts as a base, but others use pure dance which sometimes might be an opening to a play in which the ronggeng acts/jokes, before couples dance with male audience members who tip: males use martial arts movements while the females use small steps with gracefully circling wrists. These ronggeng performers (sometimes transvestite males) were common in many areas. Performers in times past were considered sexually available, so village versions were considered low class, but palaces of the Indo-Malay world had elite versions. The entertainment of watching sensuously moving females/transvestites and dynamic (or comic) males stimulated romantic imaginings and provided sexually charged encounters in often restricted societies.

Classical dances were, in periods when Hinduism and Buddhism prevailed, often associated with temple complexes such as those at Angkor where hundreds of dancers might be dedicated. Temple carvings are thought to capture dances of forgotten eras. From the sixteenth to the twentieth century, classical dances were localized in rulers' or aristocrats' courts, with dance as a symbolic representation of power; display helped create and sustain rule. Southeast Asian Islam was supportive of dance activities and is routinely credited to the *wali* (saints-rulers who converted the area to Islam). The fifteenth-century Sunan Kalijaga is cited as the inventor of *topeng* (mask dance), *barongan* (danced body puppets of animals) and *wayang* (puppetry and dance-drama). Kalijaga is even said to have been the first ronggeng as a transvestite performer. Javanese dancers of topeng and wayang from traditional families considered themselves artistic and lineal descendants of these saints.

The classical court dances were generally differentiated by gender. Women dancers often were considered part of the extended family of the ruler or powerful male and these women might perform semi-ritual choreographies such as the *bedhaya* of Java to celebrate the king's coronation or the *buong song* of the Khmer to bring rain. In some palaces women were organized into all-female theatre troupes. In such groups, dancers specialized in a role type, with the most beautiful and petite being cast in the lead female roles and taller, stronger females dancing demons. In such groups, male performers were traditionally banned or restricted to clown roles.

Meanwhile, male presentations were more often mask genres; lovely females playing refined roles were less likely to wear masks. Greater emphasis on battle scenes and martial dance might mark male dance-dramas, while female troupes were often thought to excel in graceful moves or scenes of pathos and melodrama. In male genres the ruler or his siblings might play the major roles. Traditionally, the elite oversaw dance and good dancers were prized.

In the past century we have seen a proliferation of dance techniques from all over the globe. Charleston or tango became 'extra turns' – entertainment interludes between acts – of popular theatres such as Malay *bangsawan* or the Filipino *bodavil* in the 1930s. Versions of *butō* proliferated in the 1980s. 'Sexy dancing' of *dangdut* (popular music with an Indian rhythm) by Indonesia's Inul Daratista (1979–) with her drill (*ngebor*) of undulating hips led to outcries from Islamic religious conservatives who pushed through 'anti-pornography' legislation in 2008 to still the provocative bodies of female performer-dancers. Ballet thrives in areas such as the Philippines, adopting local themes. Jazz dance and K[orean]-pop flood stages and appear in the media. From modern melds of traditional dance with innovative subject matter staged in art gallery settings, to musical comedy flash or tourist displays, Southeast Asia is dancing.

Philippines

The Christianized areas have European dance influence, but animist dances using gongs and group choreographies persisted until the twentieth century in remote and highland areas. Dancing female shamans were noted in early literature. Muslim social and court dances persisted in the southern Islamic areas. European social dance was highly developed during the Spanish period. Theatrical versions of all these genres were developed in the American colonial period through the efforts of educators such as Francisca Reyes Aquino (1899–1984) who established urban re-interpretations, later adopted by the national folk dance company Bayanihan, founded in 1957. Bayanihan's choreographies might later be taught in communities from which dances had originally come and have accompanied the Filipino diaspora globally. Filipinos have excelled at repurposing all western dance forms from modern dance to ballet (Ballet Philippines and Philippines Ballet Theatre). Agnes Locsin (1957–) is the most successful at fusing ballet and modern with traditional dance in works described locally as 'neo-ethnic'. Her *La Revolution Filipina* is about the 1890s anti-colonialist Apolinario Mabini. Myra Beltran (1960–) is another major contemporary choreographer with a ballet background.

Indonesia and Malaysia

Indonesia is rich in dance. Trance or ritual dances remain important among the Toradja of Sulawesi and Iban of Kalimantan whose graceful female dancers emulate the hornbill (a bird linked to ancestors). In Sumatran *sakura* mask dancers representing forest spirits parade in raucous style. Horse trance performances of Java involve people acting like horses or walking on coals. Many Indonesian lion-like figures (*barongan*, *reog ponorogo*, etc.) dance and perhaps the most famous is the *barong* of Bali's *calonarang* dance-drama.

Social dances reappear in theatre. Ronggeng dances are historically widespread. Females might dance in simple steps to a *ketuk tilu* (literally 'three gong') orchestra while men danced in the martial arts style of *pencak silat*. *Pencak* is, for example, basic to Minangkabau *randai* of Sumatra, a dance theatre done in a circular arrangement. *Ketuk tilu* and *pencak* were modernized and developed into the *jaipongan* dance craze spearheaded by Gugum Gumbira (1945–) in the last quarter of the twentieth century.

Figure 5.9 Bulantrisna Jelantik wears the costume of *legong*, the Balinese female court dance genre.

(Courtesy of Bulantrisna Jelantik)

Classical palace female dances include *bedhaya* and *srimpi* of the Central Javanese courts, *legong* of Balinese palaces (Figure 5.9) and so on. Mask dance (*topeng*) is important in Bali, Madura, Java and Sunda, and even in Kutai, Kalimantan (Figure 5.10). Dance-dramas such as *wayang wong* are mostly found among Balinese, Sundanese and Javanese. Dance was traditionally improvised by dancer-actors according to the type (usually refined, semi-refined, strong and demonic). Modern choreographers – such as the Sundanese masters Tjetje Somantri (1891–1963) and Irawati Durban (1943–); Javanese artists Sasminta Mardawa (1929–96), Bagong Kussidiarjo (1928–2004) and Sardono Kusumo (1945–); Balinese I Made Bandem (1945–) and I Wayan Dibia (1948–); or Sumatran Gusmiati Suid (1942–2001) and Boy G. Suid (1966–) – combine aspects of traditional dance, elements from other areas of Indonesia and Southeast Asia, or western dance in their innovations.

Malaysia's dance culture shares characteristics with Indonesia. A sample ritual genre is the previously mentioned *main peteri*. Functional dances include ronggeng dance, called *joget*, popular in the early twentieth century, and Malaysian forms of martial arts or *silat*. *Zapin* dance has Middle Eastern roots. *Dikir barat* includes solo narrative improvisation and group movement similar to Indonesia's *saman*. Classical female dances (such as *asiq*, *joget gamelan*, *inai* etc.) were found in Malay courts. The all-female dance-drama *mak yong* was performed in the Kelantan palace in the early twentieth century and became a UNESCO Intangible Cultural Heritage form in 2005, with Katijah Awang (1941–2005) the most noted recent exponent. Palace genres are preserved in classes at ASWARA, the national academy of the arts in Kula Lumpur, where modern dance choreographer Joseph Gonzales (1960–) leads the programme. Vibrant Indian and Chinese dance communities are also found. Kuala Lumpur's Temple of Fine Arts dance programme was founded by Gopal (d. 1990) and Radha Shetty and V. K. and Vatsala Srivadas, and remains a site of all Malaysian dance styles. Ramli Ibrahim (1953–), a student of Guru Debra Prasad Das, creates innovative odissi influenced by contemporary ballet. Low Kee Sein (1937–2010) was a force in Chinese dance education, as is Vincent Tan Lian Ho (1960–), a current master. Chinese lion dance flourishes, with elaborate competitions testing acrobatic skills on high poles. Global genres are part of the Malaysian scene: Lee Lee Lan founded the Federal Academy of Ballet in 1967 and contemporary dance notables include Marion D'Cruz (1953–) in modern dance, Lee Swee Keong (1967–) in *butō* and Lex Lakshman Balakrishnan in contemporary *bharatanatayam* and musical comedy.

Thai–Khmer–Lao–Burmese dance

Ritual dance continues to be a part of Thai performance and *wai kru* ('honouring the teacher') commemorates gurus. Functional dances include ronggeng and pencak in the Malay south; in the central region and north we find graceful social dances (*fawn*) and *muay boran* (martial arts), including *krabi krabong* (sword and baton) dance, a source theatre fight dance. Southern *nora/lakhon chatri* traditionally included extensive dance with acrobatic techniques. The *mohlam* of the Lao of the north included improvised male–female singing accompanied by dance interludes. The classical dance of central Thailand is the most theatrically extended. Major role types are prince (*phra*), princess (*nang*), monkey (*ling*) and demon (*yak*). Traditionally, dance was overseen by the elite, with the female dance (*lakon nai*) done by court ladies and the mask dance (*khon*) by the male aristocrats. Outside the palace, troupes of male performers did a more rustic mask dance (*lakon nok*). Today, classical theatre (*natasin*) is overseen by the *Krom Silpkorn* (Department of Fine Arts), with training at Witthayalai Natasin (College of Dance) in Bangkok and other sites. Noted performer-choreographers of the twentieth century include Seri Wangnaitham (1937–2007) and Surpone Virlurak in *khon*. Pichet Klunchun's (1971–)

Figure 5.10 In Cirebon-style *topeng babakan* of West Java, a solo dancer goes through a
sequence of various character types from refined female to strong male.

(Courtesy of dancer Ben Archangel)

modernized khon has been controversial. Manop Meejamrat, Patravadi Theatre's choreographer since 1992, innovates on his contemporary dance base. Sonoko Prow of Kandha Arts 'n Theatre does butō. Thongchai Hannarong combines western and Thai dance. Jitee Chompee works in ballet and modern dance.

Laos, like northeast Thailand, has *fawn* and *mohlam* performance. Traditional court dance shared many aspects with that of Thailand and revival of the mask dance for tourists has been attempted in recent years. Meanwhile in Cambodia, *Lokhon Preah Reach Trop* (Royal Cambodian Ballet) has and continues a ritual aspect, honouring the king. Khun Than was the head of the all-female troupe and a royal consort during the time of King Ang Dong (1796–1860) and his son Norodom (1860–1904). Queen Kossomak (1904–1975) and her granddaughter, Princess Buppha Devi (1943–), have had a profound effect in modernizing the dance. Kossamak made the image of the *apsara*, with costumes emulating the friezes of Angkor Wat, famous worldwide, and integrated male dancers in the monkey role. Buppha Devi continues innovations with Chhieng Proeung, head of the school of fine arts, as collaborator: productions including *Legend of Apsara Mera* (2010), which used males for the first time in giant (*yak*) roles. Sophiline Shapiro (1967–) is an innovative classical chorographer whose *Samritechak* (2000) melded *Othello* and the Cambodian Holocaust. Phon Sopheap (1981–) has developed the monkey role into a contemporary dance exploration and Chey Chankethya (1985–) mixes tradition and new movement.

Burma includes ritual dance such as the inspired dance of the shamanic *nat pwe apodaw* (shamaness). Court dance existed in patterns similar to the Thai, with *anyein pwe* the female palace dance and a mask dance on the *Ramayana* theme borrowed from the Thai.

Singapore and Vietnam

Singapore today puts emphasis on the modern and boasts Chinese, Malay, Indian and western-influenced traditions. A major figure in Chinese dance was Lee Shu Fen (1925–2012) from Taiwan who trained many of today's figures. Malay dance parallels that in Malaysia. An important Indian dance institution is Bhaskar Arts Academy, led by Santha Bhaskar (1939–) who created multicultural works such as *Butterfly Lovers* (1959) and *Manhora* (1996). The professional ballet company Singapore Dance Theatre founded (1988) by Goh Soo Khim and Anthony Then – currently led by Janek Schergen – presents choreography of Singapore's internationally known Goh Choo San (1948–1987). In contemporary dance, China-born and U.S.-trained Angela Liong (1951–) of Arts Fission has created programmes at Nanyang Academy of Fine Arts and La Salle-SIA College of the Arts, responding to social and ecological issues, as in *Mahabharata: A Grain of Rice* (1994). ECNAD (dance spelt backwards), founded by Tan How Choon and Lim Chin Huat in 1996, does site-specific, new work.

Ritual dance in Vietnam may include aspects of shamanic sword and other trance modes. Lion dance is widely practised for Tet (New Year). Classical *nhã nhạc*, court dance/music of Hue, was declared a UNESCO Intangible Cultural Heritage of Humanity (2005); preservation efforts are under way. Ballet and contemporary dance thrive. Vietnamese-born French citizen Ea Sola has collaborated with peasant dancers, aged 50–76, to create *Drought and Rain* (*Sécheresse et pluie*, 1995) and did a new version with the Hanoi Ballet artists (2005). Tran Ly Ly is Vietnam's most active choreographer for contemporary ballet and teaches at Vietnam National Institute of Dance.

This section has named only a few of the ideas, forms and artists that enliven Southeast Asian dance.

VIII. Cambodia, by Celia Tuchman-Rosta

Musty costumes were in piles on the palace grounds unused and abandoned. Many of the valuable gold crowns and jewels worn by the dancers of the past had disappeared.[9] In 1979, the streets of Phnom Penh, Cambodia's capital city, were beginning to fill up again as people returned after 3 years and 10 months of forced agricultural labour imposed by the extreme policies of the Democratic Republic of Kampuchea (Khmer Rouge) during which an estimated 80–90 percent of all artists in the country died (Sam 1994: 42). As soon as the Vietnamese military pushed the Khmer Rouge to the outskirts of the country, dance and theatre troupes sprang up around Cambodia trying to quickly recover traditions that were nearly lost (Phim and Thompson 1999: 42–3).

Dance, music and theatre are inseparable in many of Cambodia's performing art forms (Phim and Thompson 1999: 11). According to the Ministry of Culture and Fine Arts, there are more than twenty *lakhon* (genres of theatre) and three distinct *robam* (genres of dance). This section will briefly outline the characteristics of just a few performance traditions that have been revived: *robam boran* (classical dance), *lakhon khol* (all-male masked dance-drama), *robam prapreiney* (folk dance) and *lakhon yike*, a form of opera.

Dance and theatre have a long history in Cambodia. In the Ancient Khmer Civilization (ninth–fifteenth centuries), the kings built massive religious edifices to show their devotion to the gods (Cravath 2008: 41). The walls of these edifices are chiselled with thousands of bas-reliefs and etchings of devatas and apsaras (celestial dancers). The hyper-extended fingers and wrists of the dancers sculpted into the walls of Angkor indicate similarities between ancient dance movement and the robam boran tradition today (Miettinen 2008: 107). Historically, the dance practice was a ritual tradition. The dances maintain balance and harmony in the natural world (Cravath 2008: 416).

Once taught and performed in the palace, robam boran is now one of several performance genres taught at the government's performing arts schools. Upon entering the dance school, students are divided into four basic roles, *neang* (female), *nirong* (male), *yak* (giant or ogre) or *swa* (monkey) – the only role performed by men. Students learn the *kbach baht*, a role-specific series of gestures that form the building blocks of all dances (Phim and Thompson 1999: 46). Every day, students bring fruits and incense to offer their teachers and the spirits of the dance in what is known as a *sampeah kru* through which they pay respects (Cravath 2008: 427). After years of training, the dancers are sewn into colourful and sequined performance costumes made of silk and become the royalty and divinity of Cambodian myth and legend. In one dance-drama, they become the goddess of water, Moni Mekhala, who battles with the ogre, Ream Eyso, resulting in the creation of lightning and rain (ibid.: 230). In another, they become the giants, monkey, princes and princesses of the *Reamker*, the Cambodian version of the *Ramayana* epic (Figure 5.11).

In recent years, there have been three main branches in the growth of robam boran. First, some older dance masters under the guidance of HRH Princess Norodom Bopha Devi, the former Minister of Culture and Fine Arts, have been working to re-create and expand dances that were created in the 1960s and create new works based on the existing repertoire such as *The Legend of Apsara Mera* (2013). Second, the artist Sophiline Cheam Shapiro, trained in robam boran in the 1980s, has created new choreography that expands on traditional movement vocabulary and themes. Her works include *Seasons of Migration* (2004), which examines the stages of transitioning to life in a new place, and *Stained* (2011), which tells parts of the story of the *Ramayana* from the female perspective (Shapiro 2011).[10] Finally, some young artists are experimenting with contemporary dance, using their training in robam boran as inspiration. This is

Figure 5.11 Robam boran students from the Siem Reap School of Art performing an excerpt
from the *Reamker* (2012). Characters pictured include Neang Seda, Preah Ream
and Ream's younger brother. They are sleeping in the forest before the giant,
Ravana, abducts Neang Seda.

(Photo by Celia Tuchman-Rosta)

evidenced by Chey Chankethya's *My Mother and I* (2013), a performance I attended that explored
the artist's connection to her family and teachers.

Lakhon khol, the all-male masked drama, is like a cousin to robam boran. According to the
Cambodian theatre scholar Pich Tum Kravel (2001: 6–7), lakhon khol originated in the
Angkorean period (1218–43) during a time of political turmoil. Dance imagery on Angkorean
temples showing mythological stories being acted out by males may point to this early origin
of lakhon khol as an outdoor spectacle (Miettinen 2008: 155, 158). The *Reamker* is currently
the only source material for lakhon khol (Phim and Thompson 1999: 54). In contrast to robam
boran, the dance sequences of lakhon khol focus on the battles and war scenes of the Hindu
epic (Diamond 2012: 132). While the gestures are reminiscent of robam boran, the performers
do not move with the fluidity of the female classical dancers. Svay Andet, a village located
across the river from Phnom Penh, is particularly noted for its lakhon khol troupe, a troupe
made up of local farmers that traditionally performed ceremonial dances (Lobban 1994: 49). In
the village, lakhon khol was performed to honour the *neak ta* (local spirits that control water,
prosperity and health) in order to guarantee success in the coming year (Cravath 2008: 434).
Lakhon khol is also a part of the course work at the Royal University of Fine Arts where dancers
perform short excerpts of the *Reamker* for the stage (Figure 5.12).[11]

Figure 5.12 A lakhon khol piece choreographed by a fourth-year bachelor's student at the Royal University of Fine Arts for his final exam (2012). In this photo, Hanuman (in white), the king of the monkeys, and his warrior generals are flying Preah Ream to battle.

(Photo by Celia Tuchman-Rosta)

Recently, faculty members of the Royal University of Fine Arts and young emerging artists have been choreographing new excerpts from the *Reamker* in the lakhon khol genre. These include longer works such as *Weyreap's Battle* choreographed in 2003 by Pok Sarann and Cheng Phon, which tells the story of Hanuman's rescue of Preah Ream (Diamond 2012: 133). They also include more experimental works such as the workshop *Revitalizing Monkeys and Giants* (2006), which resulted from a workshop guided by the Thai choreographer Pichet Klunchun and designed to relate lakhon khol to the present day (Damrhung 2010: 70). Participants included Kiev Sovannarith and Phon Sopheap. Phon has continued to experiment with the monkey role in more contemporary works I attended, including *Source Primate* (2013) choreographed by Emanuele Phuon.

While both lakhon khol and robam boran are historically connected with the court, folk dance has always been connected with everyday Cambodians. The genre can be divided into two categories, ceremonial and theatrical folk dance. Ceremonial folk dances are performed as part of ritual celebrations in villages today. Theatrical folk dances are interpretations of these dances and pieces created to mimic the villagers' daily life by professional performers in Phnom Penh (Phim and Thompson 1999: 65). One ceremonial folk dance, *Trot,* is still performed in many areas in northeastern Cambodia (particularly in Siem Reap and Battambang) during the

Cambodian New Year. Players tap the *kancha* (a long bamboo pole with hollowed-out seeds filled with metal at the top) on the ground to create the rhythm as they sing the narrative. A buck, played by a young slender man, trots to the forefront taunting two hunters and then runs to hide behind other performers. The buck is eventually killed and taken home by the fumbling hunters. Next, the spectators throw money to the dance troupe and six female dancers scoop the money into their baskets.[12] Some feel that this ritual dance began as a rite to bring rains and increase the productivity of the land (Cravath 2008: 416). The theatrical dances' movements are similar to the movements of the classical genre: they are grounded and the dancers move with bent knees, arched backs and hyper-extended fingers (Phim and Thompson 1999: 75). Folk dance is versatile and new choreography by the dance faculty and students is fairly frequent. New works address cultural practices throughout the country. For example, *Robam Krama* (Scarf Dance), a dance about how a common scarf is used, was choreographed by an undergraduate student in 2001 and later perfected by several teachers (MCFA and UNESCO 2004: 37). In 2011, I observed the creation of a new beer dance by teachers Soeur Vuthy and Nop Thyda to celebrate the opening of a distillery in Cambodia.

Lakhon Yike is a popular theatre form that incorporates dance, music and drama. It is set apart from the performance traditions discussed thus far by the use of the *skor yike* (a large framed drum) (Diamond 2003: 155). Yike performances begin with a *hamron* dance. The dance is performed to honour the ancestors and spirits of performance (Diamond 2012: 134). In this regard it is similar to the sampheah kru of the classical dance form, but the hamron dance is performed as an integral part of each performance. The hamron dance borrows gestures from classical dance, including the hyper-flexible hand positions and the curved toes (Cravath 2008: 175). According to Catherine Diamond (2003: 157–8), although yike does not look like a dance-drama outside of the opening hamron, stage crossings and gesture sequences require such precise movements and rhythmic timing that these choreographed phrases are incredibly difficult for young students to learn. Yike stories often derive from mythology, although today some yike performances address contemporary issues.

Whether singing and moving across the stage to the rhythm of the skor yike, enacting war through acrobatic movements or gathering money to the beat of the kanchas, yike, lakhon khol and folk dance as they are performed in Cambodia today all use the basic gestures of robam boran. Cambodian dance, music and theatre are truly intertwined, and after years of instability and war in the country, they have become a symbol of national identity and resilience.

Notes

1 *Lila*, literally the playfulness, is a key Indian philosophical concept permeated into all genres of arts, aesthetics and literature. *Lila* represents the ever-changing, fluid nature of existence of the world.

2 Rukmini Devi Arundale was a theosophist and a dancer who led the movement to revive bharatanatyam from *sadir*. She established the Kalakhetra, a leading dance institution based at Chennai, Tamil Nadu in 1936 to popularize bharatanatyam.

3 References to the dancer, *natya-ganikai*, is referred to the second century CE Tamil epic, *Chilappathikaram*. References to *devadasi*, the temple dancer, can easily be traced from temple sculptures and literary evidences from the fourth century CE onwards. *Devadasi*, literally the servant of the god, later became the servants of the reigning kings. Soon, the institution became synonymous with prostitution and the revival from its problematic past saved the existence of the dance form today (Dutt 2008: 458–9).

4 A typical bharatanatyam performance lasting for about two hours (not a strict rule, but this is the typical length) will consist of six individual items with short breaks in between. These are *alarippu* (the invocation), *jatiswaram* (a pure dance sequence), *sabdam* (a combination of dancing and limited facial acting), *vamam* (a combination of acting and dance), *padam* (an acting sequence) and *tillana* (another pure dance item).

5 *Mudiyettu* performances are staged at the temples in northern Kerala where the mother goddess Kali is worshipped. It tells the story of the slaying of the demon Darika by Kali. The performance lasts for an entire night, starting in the early hours of the evening. The entire village will witness the performance with ultimate devotion and the performance finishes in the early hours of the morning, with the killing of the demon.

6 According to the *Natyasastra* there are four functions for *natya*, such as: *bharati* – words, *sattvati* – subtle acting, *arabhati* – martial movement and *kaisiki* – dance.

7 yato hasta tato drishti, yato drishti tato mana, yato manah tato bhavah, yato bhava tato rasa.

8 For the purpose of this publication, the Uyghur Latin Yéziqi script is used rather than the more commonly used Uyghur Ereb Yéziqi (Arabic). Uyghur publications listed in both the text and bibliography utilize the standards set by the Uyghur Kompyutér Ilimi Jem'iyiti Fontliri (Uyghur Computer Language Organization) for Latin-based Uyghur language. Variations from this standard occur when referencing a past publication that used a different standardization and/or if an alternate spelling exists in established scholarship across multiple disciplines. The official governmental spelling of the Xinjiang Uygur Autonomous Region is used throughout this publication rather than the Uyghur Latin Yéziq spelling of the area.

9 Paul Cravath (2008: 177) discusses the possible looting of the classical dancers' jewellery and costumes by the Khmer Rouge. It is unclear if they were stolen by Khmer Rouge soldiers, but most have disappeared.

10 I observed the early choreographic process of *Stained* in November 2011.

11 Phim and Thompson (1999: 62–4) note the distinction between ceremonial and professional performances of lakhon khol, including one-hour stage performances instead of week-long events, and dance sequences choreographed just for the stage.

12 This account of the ritual is based on personal field research in Siem Reap's provincial centre, April 2012. Phim and Thompson (1999: 66–7) describe the ritual slightly differently and describe the kancha.

Bibliography

Bellér-Hann, Ildiko (2008) *Community Matters in Xinjiang: 1880–1949: Towards a Historical Anthropology of the Uyghur*, Leiden: Brill.

Bethe, Monica, and Brazell, Karen (1982) *Dance in the Nō Theatre, Volume 1: Dance Analysis*. Cornell East Asia Papers Number 29, Ithaca, New York: Cornell University.

Brandon, James. R. (1978) 'Form in Kabuki Acting', in Brandon, James R., William P. Malm, and Donald H. Shively (eds) *Studies in Kabuki: Its Acting, Music and Historical Context*, Honolulu: University of Hawai'i Press.

Cho Dong-il (2006) *Talchumui Wonri Sinmyeongpuli* (Talchum's Origin in Expression of Sinmyeong), Seoul: Jishiksaneopsa.

Cho, Oh Kon (1988) *Traditional Korean Theatre*, Fremont, CA: Asian Humanities Press.

Coomaraswamy, Anando, and Gopala Krisrnayya Duggirala (1917) *The Mirror of Gesture: Being the Abhinaya Darpan of Mandikesvara*, Cambridge: Cambridge University Press.

Cravath, Paul (2007) *Earth in Flower: the Divine Mystery of the Cambodian Dance Drama*, Holmes Beach: DatAsia.

Damrhung, Pornat (2010) 'Cambodians Dancing Beyond Borders: Three Contemporary Examples', in Stephanie Burridge and Fred Frumberg (eds) *Beyond the Apsara: Celebrating Dance in Cambodia*, 61–85, London: Taylor & Francis.

Dawamat, Tümür (ed.) (2009) *Jonggo Uyghur Meshrepliri* (Uyghur Meshrep of China), Ürümchi: Shinjang helq neshriyati.

De Nebesky-Wojkowitz, René (1976) *Tibetan Religious Dances: Tibetan Text and Annotated Translation of the 'Chams Yig'*, Delhi: Pilgrims Book.

Diamond, Catherine (2003) 'Emptying the Sea by the Bucketful: The Dilemma in Cambodian Theatre', *Asian Theatre Journal*, 20 (2): 147–78.

—— (2012) *Communities of Imagination: Contemporary Southeast Asian Theaters*, Honolulu: University of Hawai'i Press.

Dutt, Amita (2008) 'Some Indian Dance Forms: *Kathaka, Bharata Natyam, Kuchipudi*', in Kapila Vatsyayan and D.P. Chattopadhyaya (eds) *Aesthetic Theories and Forms in Indian Tradition*, New Delhi: Centre for Studies in Civilization, 427–89.

Erkin, Adila (2009) 'Locally Modern, Globally Uyghur: Geography, Identity and Consumer Culture in Contemporary Xinjiang', *Central Asian Survey* 28 (4): 417–28.

Ezizi, Seypidin (1983) *Amannisaxan: Tarixi Drama* (Amannisaxan: A Historical Drama), Beyjing: Milleter neshriyati.

Fujima Yūko (1992) *Konnichiwa Kabuki Dance*, Mark Oshima and Hiroshi Tanaka (trans), Tokyo: Japan Cross Culture Association.

Jamyang Norbu and Tashi Dhondup (1986) 'A Preliminary Study of Gar, the Court Dance and Music of Tibet', in Jamyang Norbu (ed) *Zlos-gar: Performing Traditions of Tibet*, Dharamsala, HP, India: Library of Tibetan Works & Archives, 132–42.

Jeon, Kyungwook (2005) *Korean Mask Dance Dramas: Their History and Structural Principles*, Seoul: Youlhwadang.

—— (2008) *Traditional Performing Arts of Korea*, Seoul: Korea Foundation.

Lee, Byoung-ok (Yi Byeong-ok) (2008) *Korean Folk Dance*, Seoul: Korea Foundation.

Lobban, William (1994) 'The Revival of Masked Theater, *Lkhon Khol*, in Cambodia', in May M. Ebihara, Carol Mortland, and Judy Ledgerwood (eds) *Cambodian Culture since 1975: Homeland and Exile*, 39–47, Ithaca, NY: Cornell University Press.

Lu Jianrong, and Wang Peifu (2005) *Zhongguo xiqu tanzi gong jiaocheng* (Textbook on Techniques on Carpets in Chinese Indigenous Theatre), Beijing: Zhongguo xiju chubanshe.

Lü Suosen (2006) *Zhongguo xiqu wuda gailun* (General Introduction to Combat in Chinese Indigenous Theatre), Beijing: Zhongguo xiju chubanshe.

Mackerras, Colin (1985) 'Traditional Uygur Performing Arts', *Asian Music*, 16: 29–58.

Martin, John (2004) *The Intercultural Performance Handbook*, London: Routledge.

MCFA and UNESCO (2004) *Inventory of Intangible Cultural Heritage of Cambodia*, Phnom Penh: JSRC Printing House.

Miettinen, Jukka (2008) *Dance Images in Temples of Mainland Southeast Asia*, Helsinki: Yliopistopaino.

Millward, James A. (2007) *Eurasian Crossroads: A History of Xinjiang*, New York: Columbia.

Nair, Sreenath (2013) 'Mudra: Choreography in Hands', *Body Science Technology Journal*, winter, http://people.brunel.ac.uk/bst/vol1102/sreenathnair/home.html, accessed 3 July 2014.

Phim, Toni Shapiro, and Ashley Thompson (1999) *Dance in Cambodia*, New York: Oxford University Press.

Pisharodi, K. P. Narayana (trans) (1987) *Bharatamuniyude Natyasastram*, K. Vijayan (ed.), Trichur: Kerala Sahitya Academy.

Rejep, Küresh (2007) *Hazirqi Zaman Uyghur Ussulchiliqi* (Modern Uyghur Dance), Ürümchi: Shinjang xelq neshriyati.

sa gong dbangs 'dus (2003) *bod mi'i yul srol goms gshis* (Customs of the Tibetan People), Beijing: mi rigs dpe skrun khang (Nationalities Publishing House).

Saeji, CedarBough T. (2012) 'The Bawdy, Brawling, Boisterous World of Korean Mask Dance Dramas', *Cross-Currents: East Asian History and Culture Review* no. 4: 146–68.

Sam, Sam Ang (1994) 'Khmer Traditional Music Today', in May M. Ebihara, Carol Mortland, and Judy Ledgerwood (eds), 48–56, *Cambodian Culture since 1975: Homeland and Exile*, Ithaca, NY: Cornell University Press.

Seo Yeonho (2002) *Han'guk Gamyeongeuk Yeongu* (Research on Korean Mask Dance Drama), Seoul: Wolin.

Shapiro, Sophiline Cheam (2011) Interview with the Author, 27 September.

Tashi Tsering (2012) Interviewed by Kati Fitzgerald, Woodside, New York, 6 March.

Tum Kravel, Pich (2001?) *Lkhon khol* (Khmer Mask Theater), Phnom Penh: Toyota Foundation.

UNESCO (2010) UNESCO Culture Sector – Intangible Heritage – 2003 Convention: Meshrep, available at: www.unesco.org/culture/ich/en/USL/00304, accessed 18 June 2014.

Van Zile, Judy (2001) *Perspectives on Korean Dance*, Middletown, CT: Wesleyan University Press.

Vatsyayan, Kapila (1974) *Indian Classical Dance*, New Delhi: Ministry of Information and Broadcasting, Government of India.

—— (1980) *Traditional Indian Theatre: Multiple Streams*, New Delhi: National Book Trust.

Wan Fengshu (2005) *Xiqu shenduan biaoyan xunlian fa* (Training Strategies for Body Movements in Indigenous Theatre), Beijing: Zhongguo xiju chubanshe.

Wang Shiying (2003) *Xiqu danhang shenduan gong* (Movement Vocabulary and Techniques of Female Characters in Chinese Indigenous Theatre), Beijing: Zhongguo xiju chubanshe.

Wichmann, Elizabeth (1991) *Listening to Theatre: The Aural Dimension of Beijing Opera*, Honolulu: University of Hawai'i Press.

Bibliography

Yi Duhyon (Yi Duhyeon) (1964 [1981]) *Han'gukui Talchum* (Korean Mask Dance Dramas), Seoul: Iljisa.

Yu Handong (1994) *Zhongguo xiqu biaoyan yishu cidian* (Dictionary of the Performing Art of Chinese Indigenous Theatre), Wuhan: Hubei cishu chubanshe.

Zou Huilan (1985) *Shenduanpu koujue lun* (On the Movement Vocabulary Formula), Lanzhou: Gansu renmin chubanshe.

Zunun, Muhemmet (2009) *Meshrep*, Béyjing: Milletler neshriyati.

—— (2011) 'Meshrep Filimliri Toghrisida' (On Meshrep Films), in *Yingi Esirge Qedem Qoyghan Uyghur Medeniyet – Seniti* (Uyghur Culture in the New Century), Ürümchi: Shinjang uniwérsitéti neshriyati.

6

Music in traditional Asian theatre

*Arya Madhavan, Ashley Thorpe, Kati Fitzgerald,
Ronald Gilliam, Jay Keister, Andrew Killick
and Kirstin Pauka*

Like dance, music is at the core of the Asian theatrical experience where it not only provides instrumental and percussive accompaniment to recitation, singing and dance, but also underscores the precise movement patterns and emotional essence of scenes. In other words, musicality is essential to the aesthetic quality of Asian performance, from well-known theatrical genres to ritual and folk recitations and dances. This chapter discusses some of the representative musical systems in Asia, including that of the Kerala region of India (home of *kutiyattam* and *kathakali*), the *banqiangti* and *lianquti* systems of traditional Chinese theatre, the accompaniment of Japanese *noh* and *kyogen*, *bunraku* and *kabuki*, the Southeast Asian *gamelan* ensembles, and the role of music in ritual, dance, and storytelling practices in Tibet, Uyghur and Korea.

I. India, by Arya Madhavan

Music (*gita*), percussion (*vadya*) and their complex rhythmic patterns (*tala*) breathe life into Indian performances. It is impossible to undertake a discussion on the use of music in Indian performances without first discussing the kinetic movement patterns, the emotional underscore of the scene or the gender identity of the character. Manmohan Ghosh, in the introduction to his translation of *Natyasastra*, mentions that 'according to Indian conception, dance (*nrtta, nrtya*) owing its origin to rhythm like its vocal and instrumental counterparts, was a kind of music, the vehicle of rhythm in this case being the human body with its different limbs' (Bharata 1961: 5). Rhythmic precision is extremely significant to a dancer, singer and percussionist, and their trained proficiency in the highly complex patterns of rhythm measures the quality of their performance practice. *Tauryatrikam*, a single term denoting the collective of music, dance and percussion instruments, further justifies the interdependency and inseparability of music and theatrical spectacles in Indian performance traditions.

Natyasastra details precise instructions on the use of music in performance and classifies four distinct kinds of musical instrument, including the stringed, covered, solid and hollow (ibid.: 52). Interestingly, for *Natyasastra*, the human throat, used for the vocal delivery of music, is also an instrument (*sareera veena*), a sub-category of the stringed instrument. Bharata defines a musical category called *gandharva*, which is characterized by the presence of 'notes (*swara*), tala (time measure) and verbal themes (*pada*)' (ibid.: 55), its sources being the human throat, *veena* (a stringed instrument) and flute. What follows next in *Natyasastra* is a meticulously detailed illustration of the use of each of these elements. Bharata devotes five long chapters to music, rhythm and the ways it is used in performance. In addition to *Natyasastra*, there are numerous texts in Sanskrit as well as various local languages that analyse the theory and practice of Indian music, some in relation to bodily performances.

Classical music traditions of India, such as the one referred to in *Natyasastra*, has two key derivations, namely the Carnatic and Hindustani styles. In simple terms, the former is sung in southern India and the latter in northern India. The music used for dance forms such as *kathak* follows the Hindustani genre, whereas the *bharatanatyam* or *yakshagana* music follows the Carnatic style. In addition to this dichotomy, there are numerous subgenres of music used for local performances, such as the *sopana* style of music from the southwestern region of Kerala, which maintains a distinct style of rendering. Sopana music is a 'minimally ornamented, slow melodic style. . . employed in compositions sung on the steps (sopana), leading up to a deity' in a temple (Catlin 2000: 230). Swathi Tirunal (1813–1846), a south Indian king and a patron of music, is credited with blending the Carnatic style of music with the sopana music. Therefore, some of the sopana melodic modes (*raga*[1]) are stylistically similar to Carnatic and the vocal music for *kathakali* and *mohiniyattam* is rendered primarily in sopana style.

In the interest of focus, the following part of this chapter mainly examines the musical style of Kerala performances. Kathakali music is created by a combination of five musical instruments, all used exclusively in Kerala, as well as two male vocalists. The vocalists sing the entire text, relating to both male and female characters, throughout the performance and the actors enact the text through gestures, body movements and facial expressions. The lead singer, called the *ponnani*, sings the text first, repeated by the second singer, *shinkiti*, who also repeats the tempo and pace set by the ponnani. A mutually supportive coordination between ponnani and shinkiti is an integral constituent for any successful kathakali performance. One of the most celebrated music combinations in recent history was between the late Kalamandalam Sankaran Embranthiri (1944–2007) and Venmani Haridas (1946–2005), who drastically reshaped the topography of kathakali music. Similarly, the partnership of Kalamandalam Appukutty Pothuval (1924–2008) and Kalamandalam Krishnankutty Pothuval (1924–92) is known for its 'rhythmic euphoria' (*melakkozhuppu*), which captivated the audience. Both the percussionists and the singers are positioned on the stage in full view of the audience, who come to listen to the music as much as to watch the actors. The singers stand at upstage left while the percussionists are positioned at the upstage right, behind the actors. It is the musicians who enter the stage first and remain on the stage throughout the performance.

Rhythmic accompaniment to kathakali is provided by two kinds of drum, the cylindrical drum called *chenda*, which is beaten with a pair of sticks, and *maddalam*, beaten with hands. *Idakka*, a third drum, is exclusively used for female characters. Additionally, a brass gong called *chengila*, beaten with a wooden stick, and a pair of heavy cymbals, *ilathalam*, are used by the vocalists to keep the basic rhythm. Kathakali singing, drumming, acting and backstage roles are traditionally undertaken by men, but women are increasingly taking up the role of singing, at least for all-female performances.

Kerala is also home to a rich repository of folk music, often called the *pattu* tradition. Literally translated as song, pattu ranges from the music rendered for ritualistic trance dance performances such as *kalam* pattu – a performance in which elaborately drawn three-dimensional floor drawings of a god or a goddess is rubbed by a male or female performer through their trance dance.[2] Similarly, *pulluvan* pattu is a devotional song rendered with the accompaniment of a string instrument called pulluvan veena and a pot made of earth with a string attached to it, called pulluvan *kudam*. The musical style followed by the folk performances of Kerala adopts a stylistic trajectory dissimilar to any of the musical genres mentioned above, including sopana music, as their rhythmic patterns as well as the means they use to remember the rhythmic structures are often more complex than the Carnatic genre.

The importance of tala in another Kerala theatrical form, *kutiyattam*, is equated with the Hindu god Siva and his wife Parvathi: 'Just as Siva and Sakti are the source and basis of the universe, tala is also the basis of this universe' (Nambiar 1995: 104). Rhythm in kutiyattam is inherently connected to the emotional mode of a scene or character. Musical instruments used for kutiyattam are *mizhavu*, a pot drum exclusively used for kutiyattam; *edakka*, a cylindrical drum which is beaten with a stick; a pair of cymbals (*talakuttam*); and *thimila*, another cylindrical drum suspended from the left shoulder of the drummer and beaten with the hand. Thimila was recently introduced to kutiyattam by the Margi school in the 1990s. Rhythmic accompaniment magnifies the visual impact of an image or the expression of an emotion that the actor creates non-verbally, such as a mountain or the intensity of passion that a character feels.[3] Therefore, a slow-paced *ekatala*, the four-beat rhythmic cycle, follows the soft and subtle emotions of a character and the vigorous *triputatala* in 7 beats accentuates sexual passion. Nine main patterns of tala cycles are currently taught to a mizhavu student, although there are several special tala, such as the *malla* tala employed for the kinetic movements of a wrestler. Narayanan Nambiar, the most senior guru of mizhavu, claims that '[although] many others are said to have been used, . . . the mode of drumming these is unknown' (1995: 105). Malla tala rhythmic beats follow a unique ascending and descending pattern as follows:

1
1–2
1–2–3
1–2–3–4
1–2–3–4
1–2–3
1–2
1

Each of these numbers denotes a hand-beat and the way the pattern is remembered is through the chanting of a senseless poem that integrates these beats.[4] The actor's movements and rhythm are set to the basic beats of malla tala and it is extremely challenging for a performer and drummer to co-ordinate such highly complex patterns of rhythm.

The music used for kutiyattam is yet another musical strand, maintaining close affinity to the *Veda* chanting style of Kerala known as *otthu chollal*.[5] The vocal chanting of kutiyattam is called *swarikkal* or *swarathil cholluka*. If the classical music tradition of Kerala follows the seven-note system, swarikkal recitation uses only three notes, bearing no resemblance to either of the two Indian classical music genres, sopana music or pattu traditions. All vocal rendering in kutiyattam, whether it is in the form of dialogues or intermittent poems, is undertaken in *swara* (the equivalent of *raga* in classical music). Swaras are melodic modes used in kutiyattam. Twenty swaras are taught to a student and each one of them has a specific purpose. Some swaras are designed for the exclusive use of certain characters (e.g. swara *muralindala* for the sole use of expressing Rama's sexual passion), but there are swaras such as *tarkkan* (for anger) used to define the emotional state of a character. Still another category is used for describing nature; an example from the category is swara *anthari* (Rajagopalan 1995: 113–5). Unlike kathakali and Indian dance forms, all actors in kutiyattam must learn swara because swara chanting takes place intermittently during acting. The actors chant their dialogues and poems in swara, which will be followed by the corporeal expression of its meaning. Often, the non-verbal enactment of poems or dialogues could take several hours of performance to complete.

The layout of a kutiyattam stage is square shaped, with the percussionists and their instruments behind the actor, an actress who plays a pair of cymbals sitting on a white cloth on the floor to the right of the actor, and a bronze lamp placed at downstage centre. Even the actors marvel at the skills of a mizhavu percussionist who drums for every subtle facial expression or hand gesture of the actors with surprising dexterity, while not being able to see their face.

It is a highly challenging task to discuss some of the basic aspects of Indian music in relation to theatre because of their sheer complexity, breadth and variety. To summarize, rhythmicity, emotionality and melodic modes define the relationship between music and bodily performances in India.

II. China, by Ashley Thorpe

Music gives coherence and synchronicity to the four skills that underpin the xiqu actor's performance: *chang* (singing), *nian* (recitation), *zuo* (dance-acting) and *da* (combat). While singing and recitation are aural skills, rhythm and musicality are also integral to dance-acting and combat: the actor's instruction in the choreography of a play also includes the memorizing of relevant percussive patterns as mnemonics. Not only does this ensure that the actor's movement and percussion match, but it also gives the movements a rhythmic quality that is aesthetically significant (Yao, 1990: 39–40).

In xiqu, there are two general types of musical system. *Banqiangti*, or 'beat-tune form', is constructed around the interplay between musical modes (*diaoshi*) and metrical types (*banshi*). The composition of arias, often undertaken by actors in collaboration with one or two musicians, involves combining musical modes and metrical types to depict the circumstances of a specific character, and to create the appropriate dramatic atmosphere. In banqiangti, lyrics are usually structured as rhyming couplets in lines of seven or ten characters. Each line is subdivided into three *dou* (semantic and musical units) of characters. For instance, in lines of seven characters, the first dou has two characters, the second has two, and the third has three. In lines of ten characters, the first dou has three characters, the second has three, and the third has four (or two plus two). Variations in the length of lyrics are made possible through the use of padding characters (*chenzi*) within the dou of a line, or even padding lines (*chenju*) between the first and second line of a couplet. The musical system of banqiangti includes sub-types such as *pihuang* (*xipi* and *erhuang*), which structures jingju and is discussed below, and *bangziqiang* (bangzi melodies), found in xiqu genres across northern China.

The other kind of musical system in xiqu is *lianquti*, or 'joined song form'. This system consists of a large number of basic fixed-tunes (*qupai*), each of which has its own distinct set of characteristics: tune, a prescribed number of Chinese characters in a lyric line, and sentence structure (including a specific relationship between the linguistic tones of the lyrics and the tune itself). Tempo, metrical structure and the use of melisma are used to individualize fixed-tunes for dramatic effect. Due to the emphasis on the writing of lyrics to fit the demands of a specific tune, lianquti verses tend to be composed by playwrights, who choose a fixed-tune that best expresses the dramatic sentiment of the narrative, and then composes lyrics to set to it. Lyrics may be in rhyming couplets, but they may also consist of irregular-length lines with rhyming structures running across a sung passage. Although considered 'fixed', in the writing of contemporary plays fixed-tunes often serve as a template for the creation of new variations that are discrete from their source.

The system of lianquti includes sub-types such as *yiyangqiang* (yiyang tunes) found in chuanju (Sichuan opera), and *kunshanqiang* (kunshan tunes) found in kunju opera.

Traditionally, music was written using the *gongche* notation; it dates from at least the North Song dynasty (960–1127), and is named after two pitches from the Chinese scale (*gong* and *che*). In gongche, Chinese characters are used to represent the relative pitches that constitute the pentatonic scale, with the addition of characters or symbols to indicate metre (especially strong and weak beats). In the early twentieth century a cipher notation system (*jianpu*) was introduced, in which the number 1 refers to the western solmization of 'Do', 2 to 'Re', 3 to 'Mi', and so on. This system is now the most widely used in China for indigenous music. Nevertheless, whichever style of score is used, percussion is still denoted using characters rather than numeric or western staff notation (Lu 1991: 19).

In general, seven relative pitches form the basic scale of xiqu music, with five emphasized in a pentatonic scale, and the other two notes used for expression. In jingju, the primary tones in the scale are the standard pentatonic tones of *gong, shang, jiao, zhi* and *yu*, equivalent to Do, Re, Mi, So, La in western solmization, or 1, 2, 3, 5, 6 in cipher notation, with 'the tones 4, *fa*, and 7, *ti*' (the former between a natural and a sharp 'fa', and the latter between a flat and a natural 'ti') used 'as coloration tones' and for modulation (Wichmann 1991: 83).

Scales are not the same for all xiqu genres. In yuet kahk (yueju in Mandarin, Cantonese opera), the tones are still derived from the gongche system but are called (Cantonese in brackets) *ho, shi (si), yi, shang (saang), che, gong (gung)*, and *fan (faan)*, So, La, Ti, Do, Re, Mi, Fa in western solmization, or 5, 6, 7, 1, 2, 3, 4 in cipher notation (Shanghai *et al.* 1981: 120–21). In principle, pitch in xiqu is relative: actors alter the key of the music to suit their voices and attain the most pleasing sound. In contemporary yuet kahk practice, however, there is a rough approximation of western tones, described by Bell Yung as 'flexible absolute pitch' (Yung 1989: 15). Yung suggests that most *ho* (So, 5) pitches do not deviate far from a G in the western octave, though *fan*, Fa, or 4, remains pitched halfway between what might roughly equate to an F and an F sharp (depending on the overall tuning), and *ti*, Ti, or 7, is pitched in between what might roughly equate to a B and a B flat (Yung 1989: 15).

From the above, it can be seen that the music of xiqu shares some commonality, but there are also clear differences. In performance, this differentiation is also apparent in the actor's vocal technique, and in speech and recitation in dialect. While instruments are common across orchestras, they are often deployed quite differently. Thus, once regionally specific instruments, and even tunes, are incorporated, different textures of sound are created that become uniquely associated with the form, and a xiqu genre speaks to the music of its locality. The following focuses on the compositional structures that underpin two of the most famous xiqu genres, jingju and yuet kahk, to highlight compositional similarities and differences between xiqu forms.

The music of Jingju

One of the distinguishing features of any xiqu is its orchestra. The basic jingju orchestra consists of eight instruments: *jinghu* (a higher-pitch spike fiddle distinctive to jingju – the lead melodic instrument – so much so that the actor-singer and jinghu player traditionally composed together), *erhu* (a lower-pitch spike fiddle), *yueqin* (literally 'moon stringed instrument' – a fretted instrument with four strings), *guban* (drum and clappers, the lead percussion instrument, played by the conductor), *daluo* (large gong), *naobo* (cymbals) and *xiaoluo* (small gong). The conductor uses the *danpigu* (single-skin drum) alone when conducting the percussion orchestra, synchronizing it with the actor's speech and/or movement; the two-piece clapper (*ban*), held in the left hand, is added for accompanying song, to mark accented beats and direct the relationship between melodic and percussion sections of the orchestra. It is, therefore, the business of the conductor (*sigu*) to understand the play from a number of perspectives, not the least the stylistic choices made by actors, and improvisation from role types such as the clown (Thorpe 2007: 181–2).

Other instruments commonly found in the orchestra include the *ruan* (similar to the *yueqin*), *sanxian* (three-stringed 'banjo'), *pipa* (lute), *xiao* and *dizi* (transverse flutes), *suona* (a reed instrument with a flared movable metal bell), *guan* (similar to the *suona*, but with an immovable bell), and *sheng* (reed-pipe), as well as supplementary drums, cymbals and gongs. Additional spike fiddles (*huqin*) also feature if required, including the *zhonghu* (medium *hu*, pitched a fourth lower than the *erhu*), *dahu* (large *hu*, pitched an octave lower) and *dihu* (bass *hu*, pitched two octaves lower).

A distinctive feature of jingju music is the pre-eminence of pihuang, which is shorthand for the two musical modes of xipi and erhuang. In creating a new work, an actor or playwright would first choose the appropriate mode for each section of the opera. Choosing from only two modes may appear limiting, but no more so than the use of major and minor keys in western music. Xipi is typically used to accompany lively, vigorous and dramatically resolute scenes, whereas erhuang is used to suggest darkness, anguish and sorrow. Thus, pihuang enables a great deal of expression and flexibility, altering rhythm, song structure, keys and cadences. A character might move across different musical modes during the course of a play, enabling the emotional arc of a character's narrative journey to be fully expressed. Some general characteristics of these two modes are described in Table 6.1.

Xipi and erhuang also appear as inverse (*fan*) secondary modes, which are pitched a fourth lower and have a decelerating effect on all metres, allowing for more nuanced singing. Xipi also includes *nanbangzi*, which is used only by young female and young male roles in 'female' passages that express 'femininity' (young males are deemed not yet to have attained masculine maturity), and is an adaptation of tunes from the regional clapper operas of northern China. Erhuang has two further secondary modes: *sipingdiao* is used by all role types except the *hualian*

Table 6.1 Some general characteristics of jingju's modes, *xipi* and *erhuang*.

Mode	Xipi	Erhuang
Dramatic tone	Sprightly, bright, joyous, resolute.	Dark, profound, sorrowful.
Tonal centre	1 (equivalent to Western Do)	2 (equivalent to Western Re)
Melodic construction	Moves across a relatively wide pitch range with disjunctive soars and drops.	Smoothly moves across a narrower pitch range.
Modal rhythms	The first character of a lyric line in a couplet begins on an unaccented beat, while the last begins on an accented beat.	Both the first and last character in a lyric line begin on an accented beat.
Melodic lines for couplets	Equal melodic length: the first and second *dou* have the same melodic length, but the third is different.	Different melodic length: the opening line is twice as long as the closing line.
Discernible trend in melodic shaping	1 2 3 and 3 2 1 (Do, Re, Mi and Mi, Re, Do)	2 3 2 and 1 2 1 (Re, Mi, Re and Do, Re, Do)

(Source: Wichmann, 1991: 71–130)

(or *jing*, painted face) to express a wide range of emotional states, and has a flexible structure that enables padding characters to be inserted into the lines, while *gaobozi* uses special instruments (the slightly larger *bohu* spike fiddle, a small *suona* and special clappers from *bangzi* clapper opera) and is sung primarily by male role types to express intense indignation (such as in the play *Xu Ce paocheng* [Xu Ce Runs on the City Walls]).

Because pihuang belongs to the banqiangti, or 'beat-tune form' of musical structure, metrical types are a significant compositional aspect of jingju music. Once modes have been arranged, an actor or playwright would then choose the metrical type most appropriate to each passage of text. The metrical types used in jingju are listed in Table 6.2, though not all modes use all metrical types (e.g. nanbangzi appears only in primary metre, lead-in metre and shaking metre). The first seven are metred metrical types (with accented and unaccented beats), and the final three are free metrical types. In both cases, the entries have been arranged to descend from the slowest to the fastest tempo. All of the metrical types listed are used in both xipi and erhuang modes, but they are generally performed with a faster tempo in the xipi mode.

Finally, with the modes and metrical types in place, an actor or playwright would set the text to a melody. Jingju music has 'male' melodic-passages (sung by old female, many male and all painted face and clown role types) and 'female' melodic-passages (sung by most female, as well as young male, role types). 'Female' melodic-passages have a higher relative pitch than the 'male' ones: 'female' melodic-passages are pitched a fifth higher than the 'male' in xipi, whereas in erhuang they are ideally a full octave higher. This differentiation in pitch affects the intervallic relationships between 'male' and 'female' melodic-passages as they appear in xipi and erhuang. In erhuang, there is broader similarity in the intervals between notes in the 'male' and 'female' melodic-passages, partly arising from the fact that they are set one octave apart. In xipi, melodic-passages are pitched a fifth apart, and there is greater melodic discrepancy between the two.

Table 6.2 Metrical types in jingju music.

Metrical type	Translation	Structure in jingju terminology [ban = beat; yan (literally 'eye') = unaccented beat]	Western equivalent [X = accented beat, \ = unaccented beat]
Manban	Slow metre	One *ban* with three *yan*	4/4 [X \ \ \ ]
Kuaisanyan	Fast three-eye metre	One *ban* with three *yan*	4/4 [X \ \ \ ]
Yuanban	Primary metre	One *ban* with one *yan*	2/4 [X \ ]
Erliuban	Two-six	Generally one *ban* with one *yan*	2/4 [X \ ] metre
Kuai Erliu	Fast two-six metre	Four *ban* with no *yan*	1/4 [X]
Liushuiban	Flowing-water metre	Four *ban* with no *yan*	1/4 [X]
Kuaiban	Fast metre	Four *ban* with no *yan*	1/4 [X]
Daoban	Lead-in metre	Dispersed metre	Free metre
Sanban	Dispersed metre	Dispersed metre	Free metre
Yaoban	Shaking metre	Urgent beating with dispersed singing	Free metre singing with 1/4 percussion underneath it

(Source: Wichmann, 1991: 59–70).

The music of yuet kahk

Some of the instruments found in jingju are also used in yuet kahk, but there are important differences in emphasis. Whereas the *jinghu* is the principal instrument in jingju, in yuet kahk it is the *erhu*. The core yuet kahk orchestra also includes *yangqin* (struck zither), *sanxian* and *dizi*. A full orchestra contains the various spike fiddles described above, as well as *pipa*, *yueqin*, *xiao* and *guan*. In distinction, however, the orchestra also includes the *qinqin* (a plucked lute popular in southern China), providing a regional flavour to the instrumentation. The percussion section also differs considerably; the central instrument is a large woodblock (*bangzi* or *bongji*), accompanied by a medium and small woodblock. Conceived of as one instrument, these blocks are struck with bamboo sticks and, like the *guban* in jingju, are used to control tempo. A total of eight gongs are used, three of which are identical to those used in jingju.[6] Two large drums also feature: the *zhangu* (*jingo*, 'war drum') and *dagu* (*daaigu*, 'big drum'), both of which are suspended vertically on wooden frames. Percussionists also play two different kinds of *suona*, large (*daideik*) and small (*saideik*), almost always accompanied by percussion patterns, hence its classification as part of the percussion section.

The majority of yuet kahk vocal music is in lianquti or 'joined song form'. Fixed-tunes in yuet kahk are derived from numerous sources: 'little tunes' (*xiaoqu*, or *siukuk*) derived from the Guangdong area; tunes called *paizi*, or *paaiji*, largely derived from kunju; Cantonese instrumental music; and new tunes written specifically for yuet kahk. Since the early twentieth century, narrative songs (*quyi* or *kuk'ngai*) with fixed-tunes have also been included, and popular western tunes were incorporated into the repertoire during the 1930s and 1940s (Yung, 1989: 129). As the term 'fixed-tunes' implies, fixed-tunes are deployed with noticeably less melodic variation than the aria types described above. As a result, well-versed audiences can discern and appreciate the ways in which a playwright has set lyrics to, or how an actor improvises around, a fixed-tune (Chan 1991: 195–8). A further significant structural component of yuet kahk music is *sin* (*xian*, scale/key/mode); the arrangement of notes to produce scales, keys and modes. This enables the music of yuet kahk to modulate between keys, heightening the emotional impact of the music.

Table 6.3 The elements that construct aria types in yuet kahk.

Types of scale/mode/ key	Number of syllables in a line	Tune families	Tempos with Western equivalents [X = accented beat, \ = unaccented beat]
Jingsin (regular *sin*)	*Sapji* (ten syllables in a line)	*Bongji* (which has a brighter feel)	*Maanbaan* (slow metre) 4/4 [X \ \ \ ]
Faansin (reverse *sin*)	*Chatji* (seven syllables in a line)	*Yiwong* (which has a more sombre feel)	*Jungbaan* (medium metre) 2/4 [X \ ]
Yifaansin (which draws its name from the two pitches *yi* and *faan* in the heptatonic scale)			*Faaijungbaan* (fast-medium metre) 1/4 [X] *Faaibaan* (fast metre) 1/4 [X]
			Saanbaan (non-metrical metre)

(Source: Yung, 1989:67–81)

Some vocal music in yuet kahk also appears in the banqiangti or 'beat-tune form'. It draws upon *bongwong* (*banghuang* in Mandarin), which is shorthand for two principal families of melody, *bongji* (bangzi) and *yiwong* (erhuang). These two families are thought to have developed in parallel from the same ancestry as jingju's xipi and erhuang (Gong 2004: 9–10; Yung 1989: 68).[7] Arias in bongwong are based upon fixed-tunes of which there are principally two: one tune called bongji, and another called yiwong (Yung 2010: 14). However, by combining different scales/keys/modes, the number of syllables in a line, and tempo (see Table 6.3), there results a high degree of variation. The names of tune variations often refer to the specific components that structure them, for example 'jingsin sapji bongji jungbaan' (regular mode, ten syllables, bongji tune family, medium tempo) and 'jingsin sapji yiwong maanbaan' (regular mode, ten syllables, yiwong tune family, slow tempo). Key types are not referred to in full: 'sapji bongji jungbaan' is simply known as 'jungbaan', but is extended to acknowledge variation as required (for example, jungbaan becomes chatji jungbaan if seven syllables are used in a lyric line rather than ten).

From the above overview, it is possible to conclude that both jingju and yuet kahk (and, by extension, xiqu genres in general) draw upon a diverse range of musical structures to tell stories, communicate character psychologies and elicit emotion creatively and dynamically. The more an audience is familiar with the musical characteristics of the form, the greater their appreciation of the artistry of the actors, musicians and playwright–composers. While cerebral pleasure might be discerned from an appreciation of the compositional choices made by artists, fundamentally the aim of xiqu music is to act viscerally on the senses, to increase and decrease tempo for the purposes of dramaturgy, to heighten feelings of tension, excitement, joy, sorrow or despair. Both jingju and yuet kahk utilize structure creatively to produce a rich range of variations, and, depending on the musical structure being used, offer the actor or playwright a great deal of creative authority in the making of performance.

III. Tibet, by Kati Fitzgerald

Chant, instrumentation and ritual dance play important roles in the monastic liturgy of Tibetan Buddhism. There are four major schools of Tibetan Buddhism: Nyingma (*rnying ma*), Kagyu (*bka' brgyud*), Sakya (*sa skya*) and Gelug (*dge lugs*). Bön, which can be viewed as a sect of Tibetan Buddhism or as a disparate religion, is also practised in Tibet and incorporates the use of ritual music. Rhythmic and stylistic variations exist between the ritual use of music in Bön and Buddhist monasteries, as well as between the sects, subsects and various monasteries of those sects. Despite the variants, liturgical texts are performed through intonation (*skad*) and chant (*dbyangs* or *gyer*). The chant masters of the monastery (*dbu mdzad*) utilize notated texts, but rely primarily on the oral transmission of the chant melodies and instrumentations from their predecessors. Some specifically gifted chant directors also receive direct transmissions in the form of meditative vision.

Liturgical music is accompanied by percussion instruments: drums (*mchod rnga, lag rnga, da ma ru*), bells (*gshang, dril bu*), gongs (*mkhar rnga*) and cymbals (*sil snyan, shub chal*), and wind instruments: conches (*dung dkar*), short trumpets (*rkang gling*) and long trumpets (*dung chen*) (Helffer 1986: 70). The combination of sacred chant and accompaniment serves as a memory aid for practising monks and nuns, as well as a form of *mchod pa*, or offering to the deities. Although string instruments are not considered part of the religious vernacular, Peter Crossley-Holland brings to attention the Great King of the East (Sanskrit *Dhritarashtra*; Tibetan *yul 'khor srung*), a protective deity and leader of the *Gandharvas* (Tibetan *dri za*). Interestingly, this deity is depicted holding a Tibetan lute (*sgra snyan*). Goddess Saraswati (Tibetan *dbyangs can ma*) is also often depicted with a lute (Crossley-Holland 1982: 70).

Outside of the monastic tradition, yogis and siddhas of Tibetan Buddhism are also known for their contributions to poetry and music. *Mi la ras pa* (1052–1135, credited with composing the *mgur 'bum*) and the 6th Dalai Lama *tshangs dbyangs rgya mtso* (1681–1706, who wrote love songs or *mgul glu* or *mgur glu*) are two examples of religious figures who used poetry and song to express their own experience and disseminate their ideas.

Gling rje ge sar rgyal po'i sgrung (The Epic of King Gesar) is an oral storytelling tradition, which consists of hundreds of hours of anecdotes from the life of King Gesar. The epic is told and sung by a solo storyteller (*sgrung mkhan*) who uses exaggerated speech and character tropes to tell the heroic tales. The sgrung mkhan exhibits extraordinary powers of memorization and some receive transmissions of the epic through dream or meditation. The melody of the songs may be passed down from bard to bard, but is also divinely inspired and depends on the creativity of the individual performer.

Tibetan folk songs (*glu* or *gzhas*, more recently *dmangs glu* or *dmangs gzhas*) vary by region and centre around vocal melodies and lyrics. Both the Tibetan words *glu* and *gzhas* convey the meaning 'song' in English. The distinction between the two words may be regional (glu more often referring to songs from Amdo and Kham, while gzhas refers more frequently to the music of Central Tibet, although this binary does not hold entirely true). The distinction may also be based on the accompanying dances (glu are not generally danced to, while gzhas can have accompanying movement, but again this distinction is not entirely accurate). Folk encompasses a wide range of musical traditions including regional songs (named after the region in which they originated), songs about the environment or landscape (*gnas gzhas*), nomadic songs (*'brog glu*), archery songs (*mda' gzhas*), love songs (*la glu* or *la gzhas*), drinking songs (*chang gzhas*), wedding songs (*bag glu*), astrology or divination songs (*mo gzhas* or *mgur mo*), children's songs (*byis pa'i glu gzhas*) and work songs (*las gzhas*), which encompass a large number of agricultural and labour songs, including bricklaying songs (*ar gzhas*). Comedic songs (*kha mtshar*), songs of friendship (*glu chu*) and songs of praise (*bstod glu*) are performed in Amdo. The above list is only a fraction of the repertoire sung in Cultural Tibet.

Most folk music can be played without accompanying dance steps, but choreography exists for specific genres, specifically *bro* and *sgor gzhas*. The form of dance sometimes mimics the activities described in the lyrics themselves, as in work and drinking songs. Folk music is sometimes accompanied by an informal circle dance (*sgor gzhas*), which can form spontaneously among participants of festivals and celebrations. Folk music, though mainly vocal, can be accompanied by the lute (*sgra snyan*), flute (*gling bu*) and fiddle (*pi wang*), depending on the genre and region.

Contemporary pop music, which is one of the main staples of Tibetan musical performance still thriving in the nangmas (nightclubs) and through copied VCDs (video CDs, a popular format in Asia that preceded DVDs), is influenced by many factors, including traditional folk music, western rock music and Bollywood. Pop musicians even sometimes sample traditional monastic chant and *lha mo rnam thar* (Tibetan opera responsorial arias). Songs are sung about the environment, family, love, and especially of Buddhism and nostalgia for the homeland. Inside Tibet, popular singers include Yadong, from Derge; Kunga (*kun dga'*), Yadong's nephew, also born in Derge, owns a nangma bar in Lhasa and performs widely in China; and Sherten, from Amdo. In exile, because of the strong influence of the Tibetan Institute of Performing Arts (TIPA), many artists received a traditional training in the folk arts before producing their own work. Artists include Tashi Dhondup Sharzur (known as Techung), who co-founded the San Francisco-based performing arts group Chaksam-pa; Lhasa singer Dadon, whose life story is retold in the film *Windhorse* (Diehl 2002: 185–6); Lhasa-born Yungchen Lhamo; and most recently, a rapper named Karma MC (aka *sha bak lep*), who has amazed audiences with his entirely Tibetan language raps about being respectful and learning Tibetan. While pop music performances have largely superseded traditional performance in the sense of music as entertainment and leisure, contemporary artists use unique and creative methods of integrating traditional instruments, melodies, rhythms and lyrics into their performances.

IV. Uyghur, by Ronald Gilliam

At the height of the Silk Road trade era (approximately between the twelfth and fourteenth centuries), exchanges between the Uyghurs and other cultural groups proliferated.[8] Visiting travellers and tradesmen shared their dance, music and other performance practices, and the Uyghurs absorbed many foreign traditions. From this cultural exchange various localized traditions of Uyghur dance and music developed. Most important was the transformation of traditional Uyghur music through the influence of the *muqam* system of modal scales and melody types derived from Arabic music. The predominant Uyghur musical style in a sense matured from the twelfth to fifteenth centuries under the influence of other Islamic cultures, becoming more elaborate and sophisticated. Despite prohibitions against performance generally, the muqam were permitted throughout Uyghur society as a sanctioned art form of primarily vocal music. (For background information on Uyghur culture generally and on the relationship between Uyghur dance and musical tradition, see the 'Uyghur Meshrep', pp. 107–109)

The term muqam is likely derived from the Arabic word *megam*, first found in tenth-century Arabic literature, where it refers to dramatic rhyming poems that could be sung. Their arrival in Central Asia can be attributed to the Silk Road, through which, from the eleventh to the fourteenth centuries, numerous cultures shared their popular entertainment traditions. The trade routes introduced disparate cultures, languages and musics to the Uyghurs, who absorbed many foreign cultural traditions into their own. In this period, the melodies to which the megam were sung gradually developed into a system of modal scales and melodic formulae called muqam that supported partly improvisatory musical traditions, which, in the Uyghur homeland, retained older local features characteristic of the various oases around which the Uyghurs gathered. Most muqam lyrics derive from Sufi poetry by Central Asian poets based on religious themes and/or romantic folk legends. Over time, the Uyghurs began to include muqam in their religious ceremonies, modifying both melodies and lyrics to reflect local cultures. The hybrid creation of the Uyghur muqam is therefore an organic product of Central Asian oasis culture.

Prior to the development of the muqam, the Uyghurs had enjoyed a variety of local forms of folkloric musical entertainment, none apparently as systematically structured as the muqam. Professionalization and the systematic categorization of Uyghur musical genres only arrived later, with a conscious impulse to create a canon of indigenous musical forms.

The first major attempt at categorization is believed by most Uyghurs to have occurred during the Yarkent Khanate (1514–1677), led by Sultan Saiyid Khan (1490–1530), who ruled an area south of the Tarim basin. Saiyid and his son, Abduréshid Khan (1509–70), sought to develop an Uyghur empire expanding outward from the Tengritagh region, which was both culturally and economically rich. Both men were considered accomplished poets and musicians and were determined to develop Uyghur culture by advocating the first large-scale collection of Uyghur muqam.

Amannisa Khan (1526–60), the wife of Abduréshid, assisted by a colleague named Yüsüp Qadirxan, led numerous scholars, poets and musicians in this effort. Amannisa spent most of her life collecting and organizing the muqam melodies, until her death in childbirth at 34, in the process, many believe, of notating many of the muqam for the first time. Her collection was periodically reorganized by numerous musicians until 1879, when three prominent Uyghur musicians, the Helim-Selim brothers and the Yarkend musician Sitiwaldi, completed the collection, giving credit to Amannisa as its original organizer (Ju 2007: 187–90). However, the historical narrative establishing Amannisa as the first to conduct widespread muqam research only became popular after Seypidin Ezizi, the first chairman of the Xinjiang Uygur Autonomous Region in the People's Republic of China, wrote a play, *Amannisaxan*, in 1983, about her life. Ezizi's writing was based on a brief account of Amannisa written by Mulla Ismatulla Möjizi in the mid-nineteenth century in the book *Tavārikh-i mūsīqiyyūn* (History of Musicians), yet Ezizi's new dramatic narrative, including a later film based on his version of Amannisa's story, quickly became accepted as historical truth (Anderson 2012: 71–3; Harris 2008: 46; Light 2008: 170–8).

The early to mid-twentieth century witnessed the emergence of a strong collective Uyghur identity, which fuelled scholarly and artistic discussion about the official muqam melodies. Later research – aimed to both legitimize and revise the genre – was rooted in political developments, as socialist attitudes to indigenous minority cultural policy in Soviet Union and China influenced the Uyghurs. In 1934, the creation of the Uyghur Sanayinepise (Uyghur Art Associations) formally established a professional training system for all Uyghur performing arts – part of a pattern in which folk performance traditions were systematized on Soviet models. The Sanayinepise used raw materials from the collected muqam to mount the first professional stage performances of Uyghur dramas, music and dances. The first drama to include the Uyghur muqam was *Ghérip-Senem*, a 1937 play based on a popular folk legend about the lovers Ghérip and Senem. Uyghur dramas flourished in this new form, which combined elements from the muqam, dance and spoken word traditions into one professionalized genre. *Padichi Qiz* (Shepherd Girl), *Qanliq Tagh* (Bloody Mountain), *Rabiye-Seydin*, *Parhad-Shérin* and *Tahir-Zöhre* were some of the other earliest professionally staged dramas that included music from the muqam.

The canonization of twelve distinct suites of Uyghur muqam began in the early twentieth century. Various political developments often intersected with the artistic or scholarly rationales for canonizing the genre. In her research on the Uyghur Twelve Muqam, Rachael Harris (2008) points to a 1920s publication by Jusupjan Ghapparov calling for the formation of nationalistic music for Uyghurs (31). She postulates that this article greatly influenced Uyghur music, especially in the Ili region, where the government established the first professional muqam group, led by Rozi Tembur, in 1931. The brief formation of the East Turkistan Republic in the Ili region from 1944 to 1949 supported the work of Tembur and others as muqam tunes became a source for nationalistic pride. After the founding of the People's Republic of China in 1949, the Uyghur Twelve Muqam continued to be a source of nationalist sentiment under the socialist rule of the newly established nation.

In the 1950s, the Uyghur musicians Turdi Axun, Qasim Axun, Hoshur Axun and Rozi Tembur, and various cultural and political leaders including Wang Zhen (a Commander of the Xinjiang Military District People's Liberation Army and later the vice president of the People's Republic of China) and Seypidin Ezizi, pursued the project of canonizing the Uyghur Twelve Muqam with support from the Chinese central government. The initial Ili group moved to the newly established capital in Ürümchi and broadened the repertory by including a previously little-known group of muqam melodies, the *chong neghme* (great music), performed by Turdi Axun. In 1960 the group published the first Uyghur Twelve Muqam lyric book with assistance from the Chinese musicologist Wan Tongshu. The choice to use Turdi Axun's version (considered the Kashgar-Yarkend variant) of the Uyghur Twelve Muqam rather than the Ili variant collected under Rozi Tambur established the Kashgar-Yarkend variant as the standard suite of Uyghur Twelve Muqam. Other localized versions of the muqam (including muqam from Dolan, Qumul, Ili etc.) now came to be viewed as folk variations.

In the 1980s, as China returned to promoting traditional arts in the wake of the Cultural Revolution (1966–76), the government encouraged scholars to continue their research into the Uyghur Twelve Muqam. In 1993, the Xinjiang People's Publishing House published a Uyghur Twelve Muqam lyric book in Uyghur and Chinese. In 1997 the same lyric book was republished in the *China Encyclopedia*, thus establishing the Uyghur Twelve Muqam as a national heritage. On 25 November 2005, the Twelve Uyghur Muqam became a UNESCO Intangible Cultural Heritage of Humanity (Figure 6.1).

The Uyghur Twelve Muqam based on Turdi Axun's version are as follows: Rak, Chebbiyat, Sigah, Chehargah, Penjigah, Özhal, Ejem, Oshshaq, Bayat, Nawa, Mushawirek and Iraq. A performance of each of the Twelve Uyghur Muqam begins with the *chong neghme* (an exposition of the mode in free rhythm, followed by several rhythmical pieces of vocal and instrumental music of increasing speed), followed by *dastan* (narrative songs) and concluding with a *meshrep* (gathering), during which the sung lyrics relate romantic stories and the audience is invited to dance. It is important to note that the number twelve is in a sense contrived, as some of the suites are incomplete. The Muqam Research Committee, headquartered at the Xinjiang Song and Dance Troupe, is responsible for filling the missing sections and conducting further research on the Uyghur Twelve Muqam.

Despite the conflicted history of their official systematization, the muqam continue to play an integral role in Uyghur life. Muqam tunes are often used in popular culture, from television advertising to Uyghur pop music. In addition, training in the muqam has been formalized in art schools across the Xinjiang region, where it remains a central element of the curriculum.

Figure 6.1 Dolan muqam musicians. Left to right, Exet Toxti and the late Abdujélil Ruzi.
(Taken in Yantaq Village, Xinjiang on 6 June 2012 by the author)

V. Japan, by Jay Keister

Music is functionally integrated into most genres of Japanese traditional theatre, yet maintains a relationship to drama and dance that is aesthetically separate and distinct. Among its most important functions, music adds a sonic dimension to drama and dance that provides vital information to an initiated audience about characters and contexts as well as marking structural divisions of a performance. Beyond its functional role, music in Japanese theatre also becomes a central focus of appreciation and has spawned genres of pure concert music. The functional and aesthetic aspects of theatre music are evident onstage in major genres such as *noh*, *kabuki* and *bunraku*, in which most musicians are visible to the audience performing in a mannered style that can either blend into the background or become the focus of attention, especially when performed by noted musicians. Theatre musicians, like actors and dancers, are highly trained specialists who belong to exclusive artistic guilds that govern performance style and control access to performances.

Just as theatrical genres have absorbed many different styles and instruments in the course of their historical development, theatre music is similarly diverse and eclectic, yet compartmentalized, with distinctions between styles being clearly marked. Instead of fixed compositions, music for specific plays tends to consist of assemblages of standardized component parts such as named musical patterns and short songs. This diversity is most evident in a genre such as kabuki in which several different ensembles may be arranged in separate spaces on stage within a single play, each with their own distinct instruments, repertoire and performance style. In spite of the aesthetic separation and compartmentalization that occurs in practice, music is nevertheless inseparable from any performance of traditional Japanese theatre in which it operates as an essential component of the total theatrical work.

Nōgaku: *music of noh and* kyogen

Noh drama features sung text (*utai*) and instrumental music (*hayashi*) that is fully integrated into performance, creating the mood and atmosphere that gives noh its dramatic power. Although a distinction is made between spoken text (*kotoba*) and sung text (utai), kotoba has developed historically into such a stylized form of heightened speech that both forms of declamation are referred to as utai. The overall vocal quality of utai is chant-like, with a tense voice employing a wide vibrato on vocal lines that often ascend in pitch. Melodic utai is divided into two categories: *yowagin* ('weak' style), which employs a range of about an octave and tends to be used for expression of emotional texts; and *tsuyogin* ('strong' style), which uses a narrower range of a minor third and tends to be used for auspicious texts or battle scenes.

In the performance of a play, the main actors (*shite* and *waki*) vocalize both spoken text and sung text, with the words of the shite muffled by a mask that covers the mouth. In early noh of the fourteenth century, most of the vocalization was intended for the principal actors. As noh developed, the role of the supporting chorus (*jiutai*) grew in importance – partly due to the rise in popularity of amateur utai singing – and today most of the sung text is performed in unison by this chorus of usually eight singers. Typically the principal characters speak and chant at the beginning of a section (*dan*) followed by the chorus taking over the chant, freeing the actors to move about the stage in silence. The chorus may sing in the first person expressing the actor's perspective or in the third person as a narrator, but the chorus does not have a character identity of its own. Another vocal dimension is added by the hayashi musicians, some of whom add vocal calls (*kakegoe*) that regulate rhythm and make up a distinctive part of the vocalization of noh plays.

The standard hayashi ensemble consists of four musicians playing four different instruments: *nōkan* (seven-hole transverse flute), *kotsuzumi* (small hourglass drum played at the shoulder), *ōtsuzumi* (larger hourglass drum played at the hip) and *shimedaiko* (stick-struck barrel-shaped drum). As a whole these instruments form a rhythmic foundation for noh performances that are structured by standardized rhythmic patterns. The kotsuzumi and ōtsuzumi drums articulate various points of these mostly 8-beat patterns with drum strokes that vary in volume and timbre. Although the nōkan flute is a pitched instrument, its pitches are not fixed and do not match the utai chanting, producing an ambiguous sound that is completely independent of the chant. However, the flute does synchronize its patterns rhythmically with the shimedaiko drum, particularly noticeable in the accompaniment for the dance sections (*maigoto*) that provide a musical climax to many noh plays.

Gidayū-bushi: *music of bunraku*

While the narratives that constitute bunraku puppet plays are highly revered as literary texts, they are designed to be narrated by trained vocalists who bring the puppets and their stories to life along with accompaniment on the *shamisen*, a three-string, skin-covered plucked lute. This narrative genre is known as gidayū-bushi, named after its founder, vocalist Takemoto Gidayū (1651–1714). Nearly all of the sound in a bunraku play is produced by a single vocalist (*tayū*) and a single shamisen player situated on a dais off to the side of the stage, which revolves to allow rapid replacement of musicians during performance. While additional music is provided by instrumentalists hidden in an offstage room (similar to offstage music in kabuki), the sounds produced by the narrator and shamisen player are so striking that audience members commonly shift their attention back and forth between the onstage action and the gidayū musicians who are also visible to the audience.

To support the powerful voice required to express all the onstage action, including the voices of all the characters and narration, vocalists derive extra support to the diaphragm by using a specially designed sandbag tucked into the sash. The largest and loudest type of shamisen is used to accompany the vocal parts and help depict various dramatic passages and the emotional states of the characters. A distinction is made between spoken non-melodic text (*kotoba*) and sung melodic text (*ji*), with an intermediate, half-spoken/half-sung style of delivery (*iro*). Any of these three types of delivery may be used for either character dialogue or narration and vocalists shift rapidly between these three types, often within a single line of text. Shamisen accompaniment is made up of a variety of fixed melodic patterns and solo melodies (*meriyasu*) that provide melodic support to the vocalist/narrator as well as accompany movements of the puppets and help express their emotional states.

Music of kabuki

The music of kabuki reflects the diversity of the different kinds of drama and dance that the theatre has absorbed throughout its history. The earliest kabuki performances in the early seventeenth century adopted the instruments of the hayashi ensemble from noh and by mid-century the shamisen began to be used, eventually becoming the most prominent instrument in kabuki. Ensembles are divided into two broad categories: offstage and onstage.

The offstage ensemble (*geza*), which performs unseen in a room at stage right, provides sound effects and background music using shamisen, voice, flute and a variety of percussion instruments. For experienced audience members, geza music can indicate the status of characters, specific locations, weather conditions and a variety of moods through specific rhythmic patterns and songs. Functioning mainly as support for onstage action, *geza* music is performed in relatively short fragments that may be repeated or extended as needed and as such is not typically performed independent of kabuki.

Onstage ensembles are prominently featured in kabuki dance scenes (*shosagoto*) that feature music and sung poetry as the central sonic element. There are several kinds of onstage ensemble, all of which feature sung texts accompanied by shamisen but may also be accompanied by the hayashi ensemble from noh. Shamisen genres are classified as belonging to either narrative style (*katarimono*) or lyric style (*utamono*), but a great deal of musical interchange has occurred historically and many stylistic and structural features are shared across genres. Nevertheless, each of these ensembles exists as a distinct genre and is easily identified by its position onstage.

The main narrative styles still used in kabuki today are rooted in medieval *jōruri* musical narratives that were imported into kabuki. *Tokiwazu-bushi* and *kiyomoto-bushi* are the two closely related narrative styles which are most commonly used today, as is gidayū-bushi from bunraku theatre. Other narrative styles are occasionally used, such as *kato-bushi*, which survives only in the classic play *Sukeroku*. Lyric style music consists of *nagauta* ('long song'), a genre that developed exclusively for kabuki theatre and has built up the largest repertoire of kabuki music, used in roughly half of all kabuki dance pieces. Although originating as suites of short songs, nagauta adopted elements of jōruri narrative and absorbed a number of smaller genres which are now defunct. The wide variety of nagauta music includes extensive use of the onstage hayashi ensemble, virtuosic shamisen instrumental passages, which act as interludes between scenes, and the offstage geza music, which is also classified as nagauta.

As accompaniment to shamisen music, when the hayashi ensemble that is visible onstage is expanded for kabuki, additional kotsuzumi and shimedaiko players are commonly added, and the player of the nōkan flute doubles on the *shinobue* flute. Hayashi music in kabuki is also functionally integrated yet aesthetically separate, in that the musical patterns imported from noh operate somewhat independently from the shamisen music. This is especially noticeable in the tonal clash between the ambiguous pitch of the nōkan flute and the fixed pitch of the shamisen/vocal melody. However, hayashi rhythmic patterns created specifically for kabuki (*chirikara*) are synchronized with shamisen music; in addition, the hayashi flute player's use of the shinobue flute tonally matches the melodies of the shamisen and voice.

Music in the folk performing arts

Music also plays an important role in the folk performing arts (*minzoku geinō*), of which there are many performance types in many diverse settings throughout Japan. Musical accompaniment for the folk dances and stage plays of *kagura*, *furyū*, *nōmai* and other folk genres varies from region to region, with transverse flutes (shinobue), taiko drums of various sizes and hand-held gongs or cymbals the most commonly used instruments. Unlike classical theatre genres in which musicians are highly trained specialists, folk performing traditions are kept alive mostly by local amateurs, but skilled semi-professionals are sometimes used in the absence of community musicians.

VI. Korea, by Andrew Killick

Although Korea had no theatres before the twentieth century, Koreans of all social classes had access to performing arts and ritual practices that were theatrical in the sense of presenting narrative through impersonation. These invariably involved music, and indeed their aesthetic emphasis seems often to have been more on music, words and movement (including dance) than on the elaboration of specifically theatrical conventions. Thus, in Korea's case it may be less appropriate to speak of 'music in theatre' than of theatre in music, and also in ritual, dance and storytelling practices that involve music. Beyond that, it is difficult to generalize about the relationship between musical and theatrical elements, which tends to be different in each genre.

Probably the oldest form of theatrical performance still to be seen in Korea is that of the ritual specialists known as *mudang*, usually glossed in English as 'shaman'. Some Korean shamans believe themselves to be 'possessed' by the various spirits whose personae they take on in the course of a ceremony, and although this is not exactly 'acting', the impersonation represents an element of 'theatre in ritual'. Other Korean shamans explicitly describe themselves as 'playing a part, like an actor', and perform ceremonies that include 'episodes of pantomimic theatre' for entertainment as well as 'psychodrama' for healing psychological ills (Mills 2007: 2, 6, 32n39). In either case, the shaman both sings and dances, and accompanying music is essential. Typical instruments are drums and gongs, the *piri* oboe and the *haegeum* fiddle, and the music is rhythmically and melodically similar to the secular folk music of its region. Common features of Korean folk music include the prevalence of rhythms based on units of 3 beats (as opposed to 2 in most Chinese and Japanese music) and a preference for rough-edged vocal and instrumental timbres. Shamanistic practices probably lie at the root of most other forms of traditional theatrical performance in Korea, including their musical resources.

In rural areas, percussion bands known as *pungmulpae* historically provided a multifunctional music used in situations of ritual, work and entertainment (Hesselink 2006). Carrying their instruments while playing, the band would move around a succession of performance sites, often accompanied by *japsaek*, literally a 'motley crew' of actors costumed to represent stock characters such as the hunter, monk, shaman, maiden and aristocrat. The japsaek would dance and interact humorously with onlookers while the band played, and when it rested, they would improvise comic skits around familiar situations involving these characters and sometimes incorporating songs and dances. If pungmul is primarily a musical genre, this is a case of 'theatre in music'.

The japsaek might also include masked clowns or dancers, and many of the character types they impersonate recur in the masked dance-dramas known as *talchum* (Cho 1988; Choe *et al.* 2004: 1–81). Performed in outdoor spaces, these usually comprise a series of episodes loosely linked by theme rather than narrative continuity. It would be as accurate to describe talchum as a form of dance with theatrical elements, or 'theatre in dance', as the reverse. The dancing in talchum, characterized by exaggerated and athletic movements with many leaps and flourishes, requires accompanying music, and when not dancing the actors both speak and sing. The accompaniment is extemporized by a flexible ensemble of instruments similar to the ones used in shamanistic ceremonies, including a few wind and bowed string instruments as well as the drums and gongs of the pungmul band, and the music is in the generic folk style of its region.

Similar themes and resources are found in the puppet plays known by the name of one of their characters, *kkokdugaksi* (Madam Kkokdu), and indeed, puppet plays are sometimes given at the end of a talchum programme (Cho 1979; Choe *et al.* 2004: 83–120). The puppeteers stand hidden behind a screen, each manipulating a single stick puppet and speaking or singing its part in the dialogue, while one of the musicians seated in front of the screen engages in commentary and dialogue with the puppets. The musical accompaniment is essentially a reduced-scale version of the pungmul band, and the music is largely improvised from melodic and rhythmic materials shared with talchum and the folk culture generally. The dances and other movements of the puppets are often precisely coordinated with the instrumental sounds, and in addition, the band provides overtures to each scene, changes of tempo and mood, and respite between bursts of action.

The narrative chants of shamans, as well as the melodic and rhythmic materials of shamanistic music, are also believed to lie behind the origins of the musical storytelling form *pansori* (Um 2014). Though performed by a single vocalist, pansori contains elements of theatre in the singer's intermittent adoption of the roles of specific characters, the practice of addressing the drummer as if he were another character in the scene, and the use of gesture and movement. In that sense, pansori makes use of 'theatre in storytelling'. It also makes rich use of music, with sung passages often in the first person alternating with passages of third-person narration in stylized speech. The music, as well as the words, has been affected by the expansion of pansori's audience during the nineteenth century, from the commoners of the southwestern provinces to all regions and levels of Korean society. As elite patronage led to an accretion of Confucian moral themes and erudite poetic expressions in the texts, contact with other regions and social classes also enabled pansori to absorb new melodic modes which could be used in appropriate narrative contexts. For instance, the *gyeongdeureum* mode was adopted from the folk music of Gyeonggi Province around Seoul, and came to be used for the voices of characters from that area, while the *ujo* mode came from the music of the court and aristocracy, and was used for characters of high status and for scenes of pomp and grandeur (Lee 1978). In this way, pansori developed a versatile musical style capable of creating an appropriate mood for each scene, often with a stress on the darker emotions projected by a distinctive husky vocal tone.

In the early twentieth century, pansori was performed in Korea's first theatres by multiple singers in dialogue fashion, and came to provide the musical resources and often the plots and

Figure 6.2 A love scene from the 2005 production *Chunhyang* by the National Changgeuk Company of Korea.

(Photograph by Andrew Killick)

texts for more fully theatrical art forms: *changgeuk* (opera with pansori-style singing) and later its all-female equivalent *yeoseong gukgeuk* (Killick 2010). This was more like a case of 'music in theatre', with the music forming one component of the performance along with acting, dancing, costumes and scenery, although, as with western opera, audiences were still often more interested in hearing their favourite singers than in the total effect of the drama. Changgeuk and yeoseong gukgeuk used other kinds of Korean music as well, and thus contributed to the construction of *gugak* ('national music') as a unified category embracing what had previously been a heterogeneous collection of genres belonging to different sectors of Korean society. Later, they also absorbed western musical elements such as chordal harmony and synthesizers, to the point where their standing among 'traditional' performing arts, never very secure to begin with, became marginal at best (Figure 6.2).

VII. Southeast Asia, by Kirstin Pauka

Gamelan is the general term describing a large variety of bronze percussion or gong-chime ensembles found mainly in Indonesia (Java, Bali, Sunda) and to some extent in Malaysia. Gamelan, also performed as stand-alone concert music, provides musical accompaniment for a wide range of theatrical performances, including *wayang kulit*, dance-dramas and ritual theatre, as well as contemporary genres such as *sendratari* or *drama gong*. In Bali alone there are more than thirty different distinct types of gamelan ensembles, ranging from small two-instrument sets (*gender wayang*) to the large contemporary *gamelan gong kebyar* orchestra with up to twenty-six instruments. Some ensembles feature unique additional instruments such as the four-foot-long *suling* flutes, accompanying *gambuh* theatre. Gamelan instruments are tuned to each other within each set, not to a standard scale; they follow two basic types of tuning (*slendro* and *pelog*), with different subsets in Java and in Bali. The instruments are classified into different categories: metallophones, xylophones, hanging gongs, drums (*kendang*) and flutes (*suling*). Some ensembles also include bowed (*rebab*) or plucked string instruments (zither). Vocalists (*pesinden* or *penggerong*) are often included, especially in Java and Sunda.

The musical structure of gamelan music is colotomic, based on gong phrases, in which the largest gong is struck on the last note of an 8-, 16-, 32-beat or longer phrase and smaller gongs punctuate subdivisions in the each cycle. Within this cyclical structure, different combinations of melodic instruments play either basic or elaborative melodies. Various drums provide the rhythmic framework, and add accents and cues. The drummer functions as conductor of the gamelan and uses particular patterns to cue the other musicians for changes in tempo, volume, or beginnings and endings of phrases within each musical composition. In the context of theatrical performances the drummer is responsible for following the movements of dancers, actors or puppets on stage, or responding to cues from the puppeteer (dalang). Drum syllables and gong phrases also function as reference points in the communication between dancers and musicians. Balinese gamelan differs from Javanese in several important aspects. The metal instruments and drums are tuned in pairs, with one slightly higher than the other, which when played together produce an aural texture often described as 'shimmering'. Most melodies are played with interlocking patterns (*kotekan*). Overall, Balinese gamelan is characterized as faster paced, more vibrant, and with a wider dynamic range than Javanese gamelan.

Besides gamelan, a variety of other types of bronze percussion ensemble provide musical accompaniment for theatrical performances, such as the *talempong* in West Sumatran *randai* theatre, and the gong and drum ensemble in Malay *mak yong*. Purely vocal music is also prominent, for example as choral arrangements in Balinese *sangyang dedari* and *kecak*, or by a single vocalist, for instance when a dalang sings mood songs (*suluk*) within wayang kulit. The function of music within theatre performances is manifold and particular to each genre. Some shared elements are specific opening, transitional and closing numbers, and special tunes for particular characters (clowns, refined warriors, princesses) or for specific situations (character entrances, fighting scenes, court scenes, moments of upheaval). In ritual performances, specific tunes facilitate inducing and sustaining trance states (*barong*, *sangyang*) or indicate the conclusion of a ritual (*ruwatan*). Of special note here is the function of the rebab as used in ritual *main putri* (Malaysia) to induce trance. Special rebab tunes guide the lead performer into trance in rituals intended for diagnostic or healing purposes.

The primary ensembles to accompany dance-drama, theatre and puppetry in Cambodia and Thailand are called *pinn peat* and *piphat* respectively. They share several core features in instrumentation and functionality, although the individual compositions vary greatly in terms of tuning, modes and arrangements between the two countries and between various genres.

The minimum instrumentation for this type of ensemble in Cambodia consists of a double-reed oboe (*sralai*), a wooden xylophone (*roneat*), a circle of bossed gongs (*korng vung thomm*), a pair of large barrel drums (*skor thomm*) and a set of small cymbals (*chhing*). Additional instruments found in larger sets are another xylophone, metallophones, another gong cycle and more drums. The smaller ensembles are predominately used for folk theatre forms such as *yike* and *sbek tauch*, while larger ensembles accompany court dance-drama, masked theatre and large-scale puppetry (*sbek thom*). The Thai *piphat* ensemble has a similar minimum instrumentation: oboe (*pi nai*), xylophone (*ranat ek*), gong circle (*khawng wong yai*), set of barrel drums (*klawng that*), a two-headed drum (*taphon*) and a set of small cymbals (*ching*) as beat keepers. Larger versions of this ensemble include up to thirteen instruments, which accompany *lakon nai*, *khon* and *nang yai*. Smaller ensembles typically play for *nora*, *lakon chatri* and *nang talung*. For the latter, the ensemble occasionally includes non-Thai instruments (congas, violins, guitars, etc.) alongside the piphat instruments for contemporary performances. The principal *pin peat* and piphat compositions for theatre function as overtures, transitions and closing melodies, and within the dramatic sections as 'action tunes' (called *phleng naphat* in Thai and *phleng skor* in Khmer). The latter are specific, set melodies for particular stage actions such as travelling, flying, crying, courting, meditation, monkey army assembly, and fighting. In addition to instrumental melodies, both piphat and pinn peat feature vocal music, delivered by a chorus of singers (male or female). They deliver the lyrics and text of the play. Some of the differences between piphat and pinn peat are that in the Thai ensemble the lower gong-cycle is considered to carry the basic melody, whereas in the Cambodian one it is carried by the human voice or the reed oboe. While both play cyclical patterns, piphat melodies generally have an even, steady rhythm, whereas pinn peat melodies tend to have an alternating short–long beat structure.

The standard ensemble accompanying dance, theatre and puppetry in Myanmar/Burma is the *saing waing*. Its instrumentation consists of a unique drum cycle with twenty-one tuned, upright drums suspended in a wooden frame (*patt waing*), a smaller circle of knobbed gongs in a wooden circular rack (*kyi waing*), a rectangular rack holding flat thin gongs (*maung*), a large drum (*patt ma*), a set of double-headed drums (*chauk long patt*), a multiple-reed oboe (*hne*), a small slitted block of wood (*byau*), a set of cymbals (*lingwin*) and wooden clappers (*wa let kouke*). Singers are essential to the ensemble. The lead instrument is the saing waing, whose player is the leader and conductor of the ensemble. The drummer can retune his drums by applying a special tuning paste (*patt sa*) to the drum heads, even while in the middle of a piece. The woodblock and cymbals function as time keepers within the colotomic structure of a piece; principal melodies are played by the saing waing, slight variations thereof by gong cycle, oboe and/or human voice, which creates a heterophonic texture. A basic melody can also be played by the left hand of the patt waing player, while with his right hand he plays elaboration thereof.

Melodies typically follow regular metre in 4 or 8 beats. The saing waing repertoire as accompaniment for *nat pwe*, *zat pwe* and *yokthe pwe* performances provides special, easily recognizable tunes for specific stage actions, similar to those in Thailand and Cambodia.

Vietnamese music is fundamentally different from other mainland Southeast Asian ensembles due to the strong influence of Chinese culture, music and aesthetics on its performing arts over many centuries. Music in *hat boi* opera is closest to music in Chinese opera in terms of instrumentation and function; folk *hat cheo* and *mua roi nuoc* feature ensembles with more distinctly Vietnamese instrumentation and melodies; while *cai luong* uses a combination of Vietnamese and western instruments and songs. *Hat boi* ensembles consist of Chinese-derived instruments played with considerable modification and adaptation. They include spike fiddles (*dan co/dan gao*), moon-shaped lute (*dan nguyet*), 16-string zither (*dan tranh*), oboe (*ken tieu*), flute (*ong sao*), wooden clappers, gongs, cymbals and drums. Actors sing arias that are considered Chinese in origin or Vietnamese compositions; some arias require falsetto singing. *Hat cheo* and *mua roi nuoc* both use a smaller ensemble consisting of small and large fiddle, lutes, drums and additional percussion; singers are members of the ensemble when playing for *mua roi nuoc*. The repertoire consists of set melodies for which new lyrics are created to fit the story. *Cai luong* music has its roots in ceremonial music and southern folk songs, and was further influenced in its development by Chinese and French song and music repertoire, leading to a highly syncretic and uniquely Vietnamese style. A distinguishing feature is the *vong co* ('nostalgia for the past') song. The instrumentation varies depending on the play. In a traditional genre the instruments consist of the 16-string zither, fiddles, lute, wooden clapper, drums, cymbals and gongs. In contemporary plays, western instruments such as saxophone, clarinet, trumpet, guitar and/or piano often augment or substitute for some of the traditional instruments.

Notes

1 *Ragam* or *raga* is a term that is hard to define. *Raga* in Sanskrit means colour, as well as the passion or love that one feels towards another person. *Raga*, in the specific context of Indian music, is a melodic pattern created through the combination and omission of musical notes.

2 The drawings on the floor for kalam pattu are undertaken with coloured powders made out of naturally occurring pigments. Often a whole afternoon is spent on painting such figures (*dhoolishilpam* – powder sculptures). The smallest of such figure is about forty feet in perimeter and the largest could be several times bigger than that. With the accompaniment of music and drums, the performer erases the powder sculptures later that evening through his/her performance. The scale of kalam pattu ranges from smaller, household performances to the temple performances that involve a whole village.

3 It is the highly vigorous rhythmic beats that accompany the action that makes the non-verbal image created by the actor highly powerful. For instance, in kutiyattam, when a single actor enacts *kailasodharanam*, the lifting of the mountain Himalaya, in a small space, the visual image will be lifeless without the accompaniment of the rhythm.

4 *Pappadamoru muppathu kettoru vipraneduthu bhujichu*

   1, 1 – 2, 1 – 2 – 3, 1 – 2 – 3 – 4

   Pappadamoru muppathu kettoru vipraneduthu bhujichu

   1 – 2 – 3 – 4, 1 – 2 – 3, 1 – 2, 1

5 *Vedas* are Sanskrit philosophical scriptures dated vaguely between 2000 and 1500 BCE. There are four *Vedas*, including the *Rig Veda*, *Yajur Veda*, *Sama Veda* and the *Atharva Veda*.

6 The other five consist of *wenchangluo* (*mancheungluo*, 'civil gong') a large gong 20 inches in diameter, *wuchangluo* (*mouchenglou*, 'military gong'), a smaller gong 12 inches in diameter, *wendabo* (*mandaaibat*, 'large civil cymbals') 20 inches in diameter, the slightly smaller *wudabo* (*moudaaibat*, 'large military cymbals'), and a pair of smaller gongs called *danda* (*daanda*, single stroke gong).

7 *Xipi* developed in the early Qing dynasty (1644–1911) when tunes from Xiangyang in Hubei spread to the Wuhan area and combined with local tunes. *Erhuang* was developed from huiju (Anhui opera) (Shanghai *et al.* 1981: 174).

8 For the purpose of this publication, the Uyghur Latin Yéziqi script is used rather than the more commonly used Uyghur Ereb Yéziqi (Arabic). Uyghur publications listed in both the text and bibliography utilize the standards set by the Uyghur Kompyutér Ilimi Jem'iyiti Fontliri (Uyghur Computer Language Organization) for Latin-based Uyghur language. Variations from this standard occur when referencing a past publication that used a different standardization and/or if an alternative spelling exists in established scholarship across multiple disciplines. The official governmental spelling of the Xinjiang Uygur Autonomous Region is used throughout this publication rather than the Uyghur Latin Yéziq spelling of the area.

Bibliography

Anderson, Elise (2012) 'The Construction of Āmānnisa Khan as a Uyghur Musical Culture Hero', *Asian Music*, 43 (1): 64–90.

Bellér-Hann, Ildiko (2008) *Community Matters in Xinjiang: 1880–1949: Towards a Historical Anthropology of the Uyghur*, Leiden: Brill.

Bharata (1961) *Natyasastra*, Manmohan Ghosh (trans and ed.), Volume 2, Calcutta: Asiatic Society of Bengal.

Catlin, Amy (2000) 'Karnatak Vocal and Instrumental Music', in Alison Arnold (ed.) *Garland Encyclopedia for World Music: South Asia, The Indian Subcontinent*, 209–36, New York: Garland.

Chan, Sau (1991) *Improvisation in a Ritual Context: The Music of Cantonese Opera*, Hong Kong: The Chinese University Press.

Cho, Oh Kon (Cho Okgon) (1979) *Korean Puppet Theatre: Kkoktu Kaksi*, East Lansing, MI: Michigan State University Asian Studies Center.

Cho, Oh Kon (1988) *Traditional Korean Theatre*, Berkeley: Asian Humanities Press.

Choe Ung, Yu Taesu, and Yi Daebeom (2004) *Hanguk-ui jeontonggeuk-gwa hyeondaegeuk* (Korean traditional and contemporary theatre), Seoul: Bookshill.

Crossley-Holland, Peter (1982) *Musical Instruments in Tibetan Legend and Folklore*, Los Angeles: Program in Ethnomusicology, Department of Music, UCLA.

Diehl, Keila (2002) *Echoes from Dharamsala: Music in the Life of a Tibetan Refugee Community*, Oakland: University of California Press.

Erkin, Adila (2009) 'Locally Modern, Globally Uyghur: Geography, Identity and Consumer Culture in Contemporary Xinjiang', *Central Asian Survey* 28 (4): 417–28.

Ezizi, Seypidin (1983) *Amannisaxan: Tarixi Drama* (Amannisaxan: A Historical Drama), Beyjing: Milleter neshriyati.

Gong Bohong (2004) *Yueju* (Cantonese Opera), Taishan: Guangdong renmin chubanshe.

Harris, Rachel (2008) *The Making of a Musical Canon in Chinese Central Asia: The Uyghur Twelve Muqam*, Hampshire: Ashgate.

Helffer, Mireille (1986) 'Preliminary Remarks Concerning the Use of Musical Notation in Tibet', in Jamyang Norbu (ed) *Zlos-gar: Performing Traditions of Tibet*, 69–90, Dharamsala, HP, India: Library of Tibetan Works & Archives.

Henrion-Dourcy, Isabelle (2005) 'Women in the Performing Arts: Portraits of Six Contemporary Singers', in Janet Gyatso and Hanna Havnevik (eds) *Women in Tibet*, 195–258, New York: Columbia University Press.

Hesselink, Nathan (2006) *P'ungmul: South Korean Drumming and Dance*, Chicago: University of Chicago Press.

Ilyas, Tuniyaz (2011) *Muzika: Muzika we ussul, Muzika we Tiyatr urundash* (Music: Dance Music and Theatre Music), Ürümchi: Shinjang maarip neshiryati.

Ju, Ji (2007) *Uyghur Muzikiliming Jewhiri Muqam* (Muqam: The Essence of Uyghur Music), Ürümchi: Shinjang pen-téxnika neshriyati.

Killick, Andrew (2010) *In Search of Korean Traditional Opera: Discourses of Ch'anggŭk*, Honolulu: University of Hawaii Press.

Lee Bo-hyung (Yi Bohyeong) (1978) 'Pansori saseol-ui geukjeok sanghwang-e ttareun jangdan, jo-ui guseong (The Use of Modes and Rhythmic Cycles According to the Dramatic Situation in *Pansori*)', in Cho Dong-il and Kim Heunggyu (eds) *Pansori-ui ihae* (Understanding *pansori*), Seoul: Changjak-gwa Bipyeongsa.

Light, Nathan (2008) *Intimate Heritage: Creating Uyghur Muqam Song in Xinjiang*, Berlin: LIT Verlag.

Lu Hua (1991) *Jingju dajiyue qiantan* (A Brief Discussion of Jingju Percussion), Huizhou: Renmin yinyue yinxiang chubanshe.

Mackerras, Colin (1985) 'Traditional Uygur Performing Arts', *Asian Music*, 16: 29–58.

Malm, William P. (2000) *Traditional Japanese Music and Musical Instruments*. Tokyo: Kodansha.

Mills, Simon (2007) *Healing Rhythms: The World of South Korea's East Coast Hereditary Shamans*, Aldershot: Ashgate.

Millward, James A. (2007) *Eurasian Crossroads: A History of Xinjiang*, New York: Columbia.

Möjizi, Mulla Ismatulla binni Mulla Nimatulla (1982) *Tevarixi Musiqiyun* (History of Musicians), Enver Baytur and Xamit Tömür (eds), Béyjing: milletler neshriyati.

Nambiar, Narayanan (1995) 'Rhythm and Music', *Sangeet Natak*, 111–14: 101–12.

Rajagopalan, L. S. (1995) 'Music in Kutiyattam', *Sangeet Natak*, 111–14: 113–22.

Shanghai Yishu Yanjiusuo, *et al.* (1981) *Zhongguo xiqu quyi cidian* (A Dictionary of Xiqu and Narrative Arts), Shanghai: Shanghai cishu chubanshe.

Shinjang Uyghur Aptonom Rayonluq On Ikki Muqam Tatqiqat Ilmii Jaiyiti; Shinjang Uyghur Aptonom Rayonluq Uyghur Klassik Adabiyati Tetqiqat Jemiyiti (1997) *Uyghur on ikki muqami* (The Uyghur Twelve Muqam), Ürümchi: Junggo qamus neshriyati, musical score.

Thorpe, Ashley (2007) *The Role of the Chou ('Clown') in Traditional Chinese Drama: Comedy, Criticism and Cosmology on the Chinese Stage*, Lewiston, NY: Edwin Mellen Press.

Tokita, A. M., and Hughes D. W. (eds) (2008) *The Ashgate Research Companion to Japanese Music*, Aldershot: Ashgate.

Um, Haekyung (Eom Hyegyeong) (2014) *Korean Musical Drama: P'ansori and the Making of Tradition in Modernity*, Farnham: Ashgate.

UNESCO (2003) UNESCO Culture Sector – Intangible Heritage – 2003 Convention: Uyghur Muqam of Xinjiang, available at: www.unesco.org/culture/ich/en/RL/00109, accessed 18 June 2014.

Wichmann, Elizabeth (1991) *Listening to Theatre: The Aural Dimension of Beijing Opera*, Honolulu: University of Hawai'i Press.

Xinjiang Weiwuer Zizhiqu shi er Mukamu Yanjiu Xuehui, Xinjiang Weiwuer Zizhiqu Wenhuating (1993) *Weiwuer shi er Mukamu* (Uyghur Twelve Muqam), Wulumuqi: Xinjiang renmin chubanshe.

Yao, Hai-Hsing (1990) 'The Relationship between Percussive Music and the Movement of Actors in Peking Opera', *Asian Music*, 21: 39–70.

Yung, Bell (1989) *Cantonese Opera: Performance as Creative Process*, Cambridge: Cambridge University Press.

—— (2010) *The Flower Princess: A Cantonese Opera by Tong Dik Sang*, Hong Kong: The Chinese University Press.

Zunun, Muhemmet (1995) 'Muqam Yurtining Yéngi Bahari' (Muqam Origin's New Age), in *Muqam Yurtining Yéngi Bahari*, Ürümchi: Shinjang xelq neshriyati.

7

Masks in traditional Asian theatre

*Kati Fitzgerald, CedarBough T. Saeji, Diego Pellecchia
and Margaret Coldiron*

Although not as ubiquitous as dance and music, masks are nevertheless widely used in Asian performance. Some of the best-known examples include the dance-centric genres in traditional Southeast Asian and Korean performance, Tibetan opera *lha mo* and Japanese *noh*. Focusing on a wide variety of mask performance genres in these four regions, this chapter provides an in-depth and cross-regional discussion of mask construction and performance techniques, its functions in rituals and storytelling traditions, and its role in gender performance as well as the practice of role types instead of specific characters.

I. Tibet, by Kati Fitzgerald

Tibetan masks are utilized by both clergy and lay people in the performance of Buddhist and Bön rituals, as well as in theatrical performances and folk festivals. Below are examples of how masks are utilized in two of the most well-known forms of Tibetan performance.

Lha mo

Masks play an interesting role in the modern scholarship of *lha mo* (Tibetan opera). Some Chinese folklorists credit the origins of lha mo to the purification ceremonies performed during the establishment of Tibet's first Buddhist monastery, Samye (constructed in the late 770s). This argument is based on the similarities found between masks purportedly used during the performative rituals at Samye and those used in modern performances. Although this is a dominant strain of thought in Chinese publications, it is unsupported by historical and archaeological evidence. This confluence of all performative dance into a linear narrative is certainly convenient, but unlikely to be true.

However the masks of Tibetan opera came into existence, they are now recognizable symbols of the performance tradition. The most famous and iconographic mask of lha mo is the mask of the *rngon pa* (hunters), which is dark blue in colour and made of reinforced cloth (Figure 7.1). Tibetan folklorist *sa gong dbangs 'dus* explains that the masks were made dark blue in colour because of a statement made by the renowned Kagyu Lama *'brug smyon kun dga' legs pa* (Kunga Legpa) (1455–1529) about the ferocity of the *yar 'brog mtsho* (Yamdrok Lake) fishermen:

khyed yul yar 'brog gi nya pa rnams ni
mdog sngo ba yi dam drag po phyag na rdo rje dang mtshungs

(You fishermen of Yamdrok
Share the same complexion as the ancient, wrathful Yidam Vajrapani)

(sa gong dbangs 'dus 2003: 35)

Samten Dhondup confirms that the blue colour was chosen to invoke the wrathful nature of Vajrapani (*phyag na rdo rje*) and adds that the adornment of a wish-fulfilling gem on the masks is credited to the fisherman from the opera Prince Norsang (*chos rgyal nor bzang*) (Samten Dhondup 2009: 11).

The ornamentation on the dark blue masks represents the *bkra shis rtags brgyad* (Eight Auspicious Symbols) of Tibetan iconography. Each of the eight icons is present within the mask:

1 *gter chen bum pa* (inexhaustible treasure vase) – the small mirrors covering the face of the mask;
2 *pad ma 'dab brgyad* (eight-petalled lotus flower) – entire shape of the mask;
3 *dpal be'u* (knot of eternity) – the earring;
4 *chos kyi 'khor lo* (Dharma wheel) – the moon and sun on the forehead;

Figure 7.1 A *rngon pa* of the Nepal Tibetan Lhamo Association performing the opera *Milarepa* in Ekantakuna, Kathmandu, Nepal, 7 July 2010.

(Photo by Kati Fitzgerald)

5   *dung dkar po gyas 'khyil* (white conch shell coiling to the right) – shell on the nose;

6   *gser gyi nya chung kha sprod* (pair of golden fish) – the head cover that veils the mask from the centre of the forehead to the ears;

7   *rin chen gdugs dkar* (precious white umbrella) – the topknot of hair at the top of the mask, with accompanying tassels; and

8   *chos kyi rgyal mtshan* (victory banner) – the multicoloured, silk, pillar-like brocade that flows from the back of the mask.

(Dorje 2011)

Colour plays an important role in the performance vocabulary of masks in lha mo. Samten Dhondup, opera instructor at the Tibetan Institute of Performing Arts, describes white masks as worn by trustworthy and peaceful characters. He mentions that white masks also sometimes indicate an Indian or foreign character. Likewise, the yellow masks are worn by honest and spiritually accomplished characters, made to look like the purported founder of Tibetan opera *thang stong rgyal po* himself. A green mask represents the embodiment of Green Tara (*sgrol ljang*) and is worn by a pious and loving character. A red mask symbolizes anger and may be worn by a demoness or a particularly hate-filled character. Possibly the most evocative mask of Tibetan opera is the half-white, half-black mask worn by dangerous, two-faced characters (Samten Dhondup 2009: 11). Of course, masks and costumes vary from troupe to troupe based on individual customs and available resources.

'Cham

'Cham is a form of Tibetan monastic dance ritual performed by monks on specific festival days in the Tibetan calendar. Our knowledge of 'cham performance traditions and costuming is based on modern performances. There is certainly evidence of 'cham-like dance rituals in pre-Buddhist monastic tradition, but our ability to trace a correlatory line from these ancient rituals to the present-day performances of *'cham yig* ('cham texts) is tenuous (Samten G. Karmay 1986: 58–68).

Masks play an extremely important aesthetic and spiritual role in 'cham performance. Speaking of 'cham, translator and scholar Lobsang P. Lhalungpa writes:

> The mask that each dancer wears symbolises a supernatural force which it represents both 'formally' and inwardly; in an ultimate sense, however, all these forms also signify the illusory nature of phenomena which mask (though they also reveal) the true Reality.
>
> (Lobsang P. Lhalungpa 1969: 6)

While 'cham performances may not always function as the sacred tantric ritual from which they originate, they have the potential to be a form of didactic performance as well as a spiritually beneficial practice for performers and audience alike.

'Cham masks are frequently made of wood and are more substantial than those used in lha mo performances. They can also be made of *papier-mâché* or metal. In any case, the masks are large and heavy objects. Each mask, as it contains the visage of a deity, is considered a sacred object. It is consecrated before use and kept in a safe place when not in use. Mask-making is considered a respectable art form in Tibetan society. Figure 7.2 shows one example of a 'cham mask in use today in Nepal.

There are dozens of characters in 'cham performances, among which are three ranks of skeleton dancer. The one pictured on the facing page is the highest-ranking *dur khrod bdag po* (also called *dur bdag*, *zhing skyong*) or protectors of the cemetery. The mask emulates a human skull, is crowned

Figure 7.2 dur khrod bdag po mask during the Tiji Festival in Lo Manthang, Nepal.
(Courtesy of Taylor Weidman and The Vanishing Cultures Project)

by a *khro bo rigs lnga* and the mask is flanked by two multicoloured fans (*dur bdag gi snyan brgyan*). The skeleton dancers are close kin of Yama (*gshin rje*), the god of death (De Nebesky-Wojkowitz 1976: 78–9).

Performance masks in both 'cham and lha mo are used to inform audience members of the presence of stock characters, historical figures or deities, but also serve performative or ritual purposes as performers take on the qualities of the characters they play.

II. Korea, by CedarBough T. Saeji

The mask dance-dramas, or *gamyeongeuk*, preserved under Korea's national Cultural Property Protection Law (CPPL, 1962) and related laws for preserving regional culture, are the most visible 'traditional' dramas performed in the present day. The protected mask dance-dramas are wonderfully diverse. Major differences between the colourful dramas include musical accompaniment, dance motions, costumes, mask construction and the actual stories within the dramas. The mask dance-dramas range from about an hour in length to over four hours; while one drama is entirely non-verbal and many employ colloquial language, several include complex dramatic passages situating the plays in relation to Chinese historical literature.

The mask dance-dramas hold several overarching commonalities. First, the dramas are comprised of scenes that are stand-alone stories. The scenes have a logical progression (dictated by practical details such as costume changes and performative concerns such as interspersing dialogue-heavy scenes with non-verbal or dance-focused scenes), but the major structure common to all the mask dance-dramas is the way that the dramas are presented within a shamanic

157

framework. Before the event begins, the players conduct a *gosa* opening ceremony with the masks arranged around and behind a ceremonial table, and the first scene in many dramas includes an opening and blessing of the space, such as bowing to the directions. The final act includes a ceremony that is part of the drama (performed by the players with their masks on). Full-length performances occur only about once a year; for other shows, depending on the time frame and available players, the group will choose several scenes from the drama to perform (Figure 7.3).

Second, because the dramas were originally performed mostly by illiterate peasants, slaves and itinerant performers, they use many of the same techniques found in performed oral literature from other parts of the world, such as patterns, repetition, lists, and delivering lines with excessive drama and emphasis so that the rhythm of delivery aids in recall. Realism in speaking dialogue is never a goal for the mask dance-dramas, and in modern Korea most audiences find understanding the dramas line by line to be almost impossible. Ability to understand the passages in the dramas was historically complicated by projecting to the audience from behind the mask, and in the present day it is complicated by outdated and dialectical vocabulary.

Third, the dramas do not feature specific characters. The various characters have names such as *malddugi* (horse servant), *halmi* (grandmother), *nojang* (old monk) and *yangban* (upper-class literati) rather than specific names. Therefore they represent types, not individuals. This lack of specificity helped people to identify with the characters in the dramas, and also allowed for criticism of the upper class without identifying specific families who could have taken offence. The masks are known by these same generic names. Masks are generally made of papier-mâché decorated with fur or hair, although gourd, sturdy paper, basket and wood masks also exist. Although the character may be the same in many mask dance-dramas, the masks can vary greatly, as can be seen for example in the photos of three different variations of malddugi shown in

Figure 7.3 A 2010 performance of the five-scene masked dance-drama *Goseong Ogwangdae,* here showing the literati gentlemen *yangban* using a small child from the audience to keep a mythical creature Bibi away from him.

(Photo by CedarBough T. Saeji)

158

Figure 7.4. It tends to hold true that older characters have darker faces, unless they are yangban, who have light-coloured masks (a reference to living indoors). Red masks indicate drunkenness. Scary masks may be exaggeratedly frightening, reflecting their double purpose, both in the story and frightening spirits or clearing away ghosts. Masks of female characters, reflecting Joseon ideas of beauty, have small mouths and round cheeks. Masks and costumes of mask dance-dramas that originated in the same region, unsurprisingly, tend to be more similar than those from halfway across the peninsula. Performers wear a padded headband under almost all masks. The masks are sewn to a fabric back half, almost always made of black heavyweight cotton, so that the mask is lowered over the performer's entire head, and tightened with straps tied at the nape of the neck.

Fourth, the dramas were performed by men until the very end of the Joseon dynasty (1392–1910) when occasionally a (notably beautiful) woman would be utilized, sans mask, to draw audiences to performances held in public marketplaces. Most dramas were incorporated into annual celebrations such as Dano (fifth day of the fifth lunar month), Baekjung (Buddhist All Souls' Day), Chuseok (harvest holiday) and Daeboreum (first full moon of the lunar new year). Others were performed by itinerant performers who presented multiple genres, such as the *namsadang*. At the very end of the Joseon dynasty there were also performances in markets. As such, most mask dance-drama performers were not professionals. In most areas, performers were ordinary villagers in the agricultural economy, although performers in markets (the mask dance-dramas *songpa sandae noli* and *bongsan talchum*) included labourers, small business owners, merchants and minor government functionaries.

The combination of dance, other physical actions and dialogue in the dramas varies greatly. One drama (*Gangneung Gwanno Gamyeongeuk*) is non-verbal, and all the dramas have non-verbal scenes and non-verbal characters. The dialogue – or in some cases, monologue – is interspersed with dance motions. The dance motions for key characters can be quite sophisticated, and range from extremely energetic jumping motions to stylized walking. Actions carried out with minimal props vary from spinning or weaving, to beautification (removing blackheads, washing one's face or genitalia, even applying makeup), to courtship and intercourse (the latter can be quite stylized in the modern era). The musical accompaniment for the dramas is, in all but one case, either the local style of *pungmul* drumming music, or *samyeon yukgak*, a small ensemble including a Korean fiddle (*haegeum*), transverse bamboo flute (*daegeum*) and double-reed oboe (*piri*) in addition to percussion instruments. The dramas that use the latter style are those more closely tied to the mask dance-dramas once administered by the royal performance bureau,

Figure 7.4 Malddugi masks.

(Photo by CedarBough T. Saeji)

therefore it is unsurprising that they are from Hwanghae and Gyeonggi Provinces – the closest to Seoul where the performance bureau was located. Despite these variations, there are four common themes that appear in almost every drama: ritual cleansing of the community and performance space, everyday life of the common people, releasing the pressure in a stratified society through humour, and processing the relationship of the wife and the concubine.

Finally, although the Korean government's policies to protect Korean traditional culture are based in a powerful desire to preserve a precious national patrimony, the existence of cultural policy has interrupted the natural evolution and even natural extinction of these dramas. The dramas faced huge logistical barriers during the Japanese occupation (1910–45), such as discontinuation of the festivals that had once encompassed performances, and a political climate that vacillated between suppression of Korean traditional culture (particularly during the first and final decades of occupation) and relative permissiveness. The traditional arts were sidelined when national division and war was followed by a massive effort towards modernization along a western/American model. After the CPPL was passed, some mask dance-dramas were registered based on a continual history of performance, but most were stitched together based on memories of elderly former performers, and at least one, Gangnyeong Talchum, was resurrected based on a scholar's script, a dancer from another drama, a mask maker, and a single one-time participant. The influence of scholars and government officials on the research and registration process was considerable and political. Post-certification the arts were required to remain true to the *wonhyeong* or archetypal form designated, even though determining a wonhyeong for arts that continually changed is impossible. As Korean society has continued to evolve, the dramas have become more of a re-enactment of tradition and less an expression of spontaneous Korean culture.

III. Japan, by Diego Pellecchia

Origins

Masks have been used by the inhabitants of the Japanese archipelago since the Jōmon prehistoric period (10,000–300 BC), when shell and clay masks were used for ritual purposes such as prayer and funeral rites. Most of these masks are flat objects, yet they are endowed with a refined sense of asymmetry, and with elaborate geometrical design. Some masks have holes on the sides, suggesting that a string was used to wear them, while others are small and devoid of eyes and mouth holes, and were probably meant for decoration or as part of costumes. The ritual nature of Japanese masks still characterizes their use in contemporary performance of traditional theatre and dance: masks are vessels that allow the shaman-performer to embody a deity, creating a bridge between this world and the 'other' world.

Gigaku

During the sixth and seventh centuries, Buddhism was introduced from China via Korea. The various kinds of dance and pantomime used as means of propagation of this new religion are known in Japan as *gigaku* ('skilled entertainment'), which probably originated in India or Central Asia. Though now extinct in Japan, gigaku is thought to share similarities with forms of masked procession dance skits surviving in Korea, China and Tibet. Gigaku masks are oversized, helmet-like masks covering the entire head of the performer. Extant masks are made of camphor or paulownia wood, though some were moulded with dry lacquer, a difficult technique that was also used in Buddhist sculpture. The artist first applied layers of lacquer and cloth on a clay or wooden frame, and then applied subsequent colours on the surface of the mask. Many of the extant masks were produced during the Asuka period (538–710), a time of intense import of continental culture: most of the artists and craftsmen operating in Japan at this time came from China and Korea.

The variety of gigaku mask types testifies to the cosmopolitan nature of Japan during this period: the *Chidō* mask represents a guardian spirit with a prominent nose who leads the procession; *Gokō* and *Gojo* portray a Chinese prince and princess; *Taikofu* and *Taikoji*, as well as *Suiko-ō* and *Suiko-jū*, represent Persian men, while *Baramon* is an Indian brahmin. *Konron* is a dark-skinned villain, molesting Gojo. *Kongō* and *Rikishi* are Buddhist guardian gods-wrestlers: the former is close-mouthed while the latter is open-mouthed, together forming the 'a-un' (sanskrit *aum*, or *om*) syllables that represent the beginning and end of the universe. These masks were probably modelled after the *niō* statues guarding the entrance of Buddhist temples. *Karura* represents the sacred bird *Garuda*, a character that is widely present in South and Southeast Asian mythology. *Fukusamen* ('cloth mask') are rectangular pieces of hemp cloth simply tied behind one's head, on which faces of 'western' men, characterized by facial hair, red cheeks and large eyes, were realistically painted. In addition, *Shishi*, or 'lion' masks, were super-sized objects employed in the lion dance, usually operated by two or more performers. These masks have a movable jaw that can be used to produce clapping sounds. Lion dances are still popular in countries such as China (*shiziwu*) and Indonesia (*barong*). Shishi masks were probably introduced with gigaku but survived as an independent form of performance that also appeared in some festivals.

The gigaku tradition has disappeared and one can only speculate on the way masks were used, but their extreme expression, accentuated by vivid green and red painting or realistic flesh-like skin tones, suggests that the masks were not used to produce refined effects. Their large size indicates the need to be seen clearly in open-air performances or during crowded processions. Today, gigaku masks can be admired at the Shōsōin Imperial Repository or at the Hōryūji Museum in Nara.

Processional masks

In Japan, masks have been used in Buddhist rituals such as *gyōdō*, a procession featuring characters dressed with lavish costumes and wearing Bodhisattva masks. A particular kind of these processions, called *raigō*, represents the descent on earth of Buddha Amida from the western paradise, followed by other bodhisattvas. This ritual event, still performed today, also involves a parade of characters wearing costumes and golden masks of bodhisattvas along a bridge connecting different pavilions in the Buddhist temple, symbolizing the crossing of worlds.

Bugaku

Gagaku court music and its dance counterpart, *bugaku* ('dance entertainment'), were formalized during the Heian period (794–1185). The repertoire is subdivided into 'dances of the left', originating in Southeast Asia, China and Japan, and 'dances of the right', originating in Korea and Northeast China, indicating a multicultural provenance, as in the case of gigaku. As performance became increasingly formalized and was elevated to the rank of court entertainment, masks became more refined. Unlike gigaku, bugaku still is performed today, especially during shintō rituals. Bugaku masks testify to a switch in woodcraft to the kinds of wood typical of the Japanese archipelago, such as cypress, katsura and paulownia. Masks are made by assembling multiple parts that were carved separately. They are then covered with kaolin white clay, painted with mineral pigments, and sometimes varnished with lacquer.

Smaller than gigaku masks, bugaku masks cover the face and most of the top of the head of the performer. Among the most distinctive masks are *Ryō-ō*, a dragon mask, and *Nasori*, a mask with bulging eyes and fangs, often associated with Ryō-ō. A hanging jaw, or *tsuri-ago*, is connected to the eyes, triggering a dramatic eye movement effect. *Genjōraku* and *Batō* are masks painted with intense red and used for dances that probably derived from India. Batō has long black hair made of rope attached to the back of the mask, while Genjōraku is a more complex mask made with three independent modules: the forehead, sporting bushy black eyebrows, and tsuri-ago hanging jaw. They are separated from the central part of the mask so as to provide dramatic expression during the crescendo of the dances. Other masks feature swinging noses, such as the drunkard *Kotokuraku*. *Zōmen* are hemp cloth masks, elaborations of the *fukusamen* of the gigaku tradition, used in various dances. These masks consist of a rectangular sheet of cloth on which facial features are essentialized into abstract pattern of triangles, circles and lines. Finally, *Emi-men* and *Hare-men*, together known as *Ninomai*, are a pair of grotesque masks representing a countryside man and woman.

Bugaku dances mostly consist of symmetrical choreography performed by one, two or four performers, usually wearing the same mask and costume. The beauty of masks is emphasized by the solemnity of the slow music and movements. Bugaku masks are still produced today, although the most precious, historical pieces are kept at shintō shrines such as Kasuga Taisha and Tamukeyama Hachimangu in Nara prefecture.

Kagura

For centuries, masks have been used in shintō rituals as temporary residences of gods, placed on altars along with offerings and purification items. Even today, during festivals such as the popular Gion Festival in Kyoto, masks are ritually extracted from sealed boxes and paraded with the floats. Shintō, or 'way of gods', is the contemporary collective term of various animistic cults that pre-date the coming of Buddhism from the continent. In contrast with bugaku's dignified court dances, shintō seasonal festivals in rural areas feature colourful pageants of masked characters representing supernatural creatures that visit villages, scaring the population as a way to exorcize evil. Since ancient times, the myths concerning the creation of Japan have been re-enacted in lively pantomimes known as *kagura* ('divine entertainment'), an umbrella term covering a wide variety of masked and non-masked performances associated with the shintō cult. In ancient times, masks used in kagura were carved in wood, while today those used in popular performances, such as the *iwami-kagura* from the Shimane prefecture, are made of a combination of papier-mâché and resins, cast on a clay mould. Masks are painted with vibrant colours and decorated with synthetic hair and metal parts. A large variety of masks exist, depending on the local traditions. Some masks are peculiar to a role, while others are generic and can be used to portray various characters within a certain role type. Among the most impressive kagura masks are those representing fierce deities, such as the god of sea and storms *Susanō-no-mikoto*, whose face features bulbous golden eyes, an open mouth with sharp fangs, and bushy hair. Demon masks are also fierce, for example the mask used for *Yamata-orochi*, the giant eight-headed serpent whom Susanō slays. In some cases modern special devices are used, such as the sparklers inserted in the mouth of Yamata-orochi that produce a fire-breathing effect. Kagura masks are usually donned with a white cloth covering the back of the head, neck and chin, as well as with wigs. Sharing common ritual origins with noh, many contemporary kagura masks have been subsequently influenced by noh mask-making, although the folk nature of most kagura performances puts more emphasis on stage effects that can be enjoyed by large crowds during festivals, while noh developed towards a more sophisticated aesthetic.

Noh and kyōgen masks

Noh masks were perfected in the fourteenth and fifteenth centuries. Although influenced by pre-existing traditions, they have developed distinctive features: unlike gigaku or bugaku masks, their creation and stage use are exclusive to Japan. During the fifteenth century, noh became patronized by the aristocracy, and performers adapted plays and performance techniques to the cultivated taste of a new audience. While other masked performance traditions emphasize dance or acrobatics, noh has developed a more elaborate dramaturgy, as well as complex characters that are no longer stereotypes, which require masks that allow the actor to express a wider range of expressions. Noh masks cover only the face of the actor, leaving the chin visible: unlike kagura, no cloth hides the neck and the sides of the face, as noh actors do not seek stage realism. The standard Japanese word for 'mask' is *kamen* ('temporary face'), but noh masks are normally referred to as *omote* ('face'), suggesting a quality of 'truth' of the noh mask, an object of revelation rather than concealment.

Noh mask-makers established lineages, and marked their works by signing the back of the masks. While ancient costumes are subject to wear and cannot be used in contemporary performance, masks dating back to the Muromachi period (1392–1573), when most originals (*honmen*) were created, or to the Edo period (1603–1868), when carvers focused on creating beautiful imitations (*utsushi*), are still used on stage today. Noh masks are created from blocks of *hinoki* (Japanese cypress), and carvers use *katagami* (paper templates) that reproduce the proportions of the originals to check their progress. Once the carving is complete, masks are covered with a *gofun* (shell powder) base mixed with *nikawa* (hide glue), and painted with natural colours. Some masks also feature metal golden eyes or hair inserts. Finally, masks made today are deliberately scarred to create an effect of age.

Noh masks are generally classified according to the kind of character they portray: while most masks can be used for different characters, some are unique to a specific play. For example, the famous *Hakushiki-jō* mask, used only in the ritual performance *Okina*, portrays a benevolent elderly man, and features a separate chin tied to the upper face with cords, reminiscent of the tsuri–ago hanging jaw, as well as the characteristic puffy round eyebrows. *Jō*, old men masks, are often used in plays where the main character appears in the shape of an elderly man in the first half, only to appear in its real shape of god or ghost in the second half. Some of these masks have beard, moustache and hair inserts, while in other cases hair is painted. *Onna-men*, women masks, include some of the most famous noh masks, such as *Ko-omote*, the face of a young girl (Figure 7.5). Women's masks cover a wide range of ages, from the prime of adolescence to the decrepitude of old age. Most female masks feature combed black hair, eyebrows drawn at the top of the forehead and blackened teeth, according to the aesthetics of the Heian period court women. The subtlety of women masks allows for stage effects such as *kumorasu* (clouding) or *terasu* (lighting), by which a slight tilt of the mask noticeably changes the expression from sorrow to joy. *Otoko-men*, men's masks, are used for the ghosts of the warriors of rival Genji and Taira clans. The middle-captain *Chūjō* mask is used to portray both refined Taira characters and high-ranking courtiers such as the minister Minamoto no Tōru. *Onryō* masks include those for ghosts or spirits, among which is the famous *Hannya* mask, used for women transfigured into evil spirits because of their obsessive attachment to an earthly feeling, as in the case of the jealousy of Lady Rokujō in the play *Aoi no ue*. The Hannya mask shares common features of women's masks, such as eyebrows and hair, but its extremely contorted expression, highlighted by bulging golden eyes and a huge fanged mouth, give a feeling of both rage and suffering. *Kijin*, demons and monsters, include *ō-tobide*, for roles of powerful gods, as well as supernatural beings such as *Shishiguchi* (lion), *Beshimi* (for *tengu* goblins) and *Kurohige* (for dragon gods). These

Figure 7.5 Yuki no Ko-omote, attributed to Tatsuemon. Muromachi period (1336–1573).
(Courtesy of the Kongō family)

fierce masks may be less subtle, but convey their expressive potential when the actor performs sharp left–right movements called *omote wo kiru* ('cut the mask').

While bugaku and kagura masks have big eyeholes, the small opening typical of most noh masks severely restricts the sight of the actor, who loses peripheral vision and is forced to rely on senses other than sight in order to move on the stage. The paucity of movements typical of noh performance greatly increases the expressive potential of the mask when deliberately used to create dramatic effects.

Finally, *kyogen* masks portray a range of characters, including lesser gods (*Noborihige*), capricious demons (*Buaku*) or unattractive folk women (*Oto*). Other kyogen masks are used for animal roles, such as mosquitoes, monkeys or birds. The *Kitsune* fox mask, only used in the play *Tsurigitsune* (Fox-Hunting), features a separate jaw that the actor can open and close, producing a clapping sound.

Noh and kyogen masks have been transmitted within families of actors, but after the upheavals following the Meiji Restoration, during the second half of the nineteenth century actors were forced to sell their masks to museums or to foreign collectors. Today, Japanese masks can be admired in museums in Japan and around the world, such as the National Museum and the Mitsui Memorial Museum in Tokyo, the Musée Guimet in Paris, the Metropolitan Museum of Art in New York or the Victoria & Albert Museum in London.

IV. Southeast Asia, by Margaret Coldiron

In the bewildering variety of masks and mask cultures to be found in both maritime and mainland Southeast Asia, it is possible to find some commonalities. Throughout the region, traditions of masked performance historically have been intertwined with ritual and spirituality, whether in court or village settings. In places such as Bali, even those masks that are used for secular tourist performances may be sacred or sanctified objects requiring special handling and ritual offerings and it can sometimes be difficult to distinguish between performance designed to honour deities and performance designed primarily for mortal entertainment. Most masks used for performance are made either of carved and painted wood or papier-mâché and are worn with elaborate costumes and headdresses.

Maritime Southeast Asia

Para-theatrical mask traditions

The Indonesian and Philippine chains of islands have complex indigenous cultures which have been subject to a range of influences, including traders from Turkey, Arabia, South and East Asia as well as the European colonial powers, especially Britain, Spain and the Netherlands. Some indigenous traditions of masked performance have virtually died out as a result of cultural changes associated with colonialism and globalization, and some survive only as tourist entertainment. For example, the Batak people of Sumatra created a variety of masks associated with funerary rites, either in the shape of a human face or incorporating the head of a hornbill. Evidence indicates that they were used for performance, as potent ritual tools and as grave offerings. Unfortunately, the practice of traditional Batak religion for which these masks were required has been in steep decline since the arrival of Dutch and German Christian missionaries in the mid-nineteenth century, so the performances have been lost (Hershey 1991: 25). On the other hand, in the Skala Brak area of West Lampung Sumatra an active mask tradition called *sakura* survives. Its origins may lie as far back as the third century CE in the animist practices of the Buay Tumi ethnic group, and the tradition has continued in spite of the conversion of the local population to Islam. It is a carnivalesque performance, once associated with purification and protection from negative spirits (*roh*) and now performed as part of the Idul Fitri celebrations at the end of the Muslim fasting month of Ramadan. The traditional *sakura kamak* are grotesque masks made from wood or cardboard in the shape of human or animal faces with hats, wigs or branches on their heads. They parade through the streets, loudly pounding out interlocking rhythms on hand-held frame drums, demonstrating the exorcistic roots of this practice. In recent times a modern variation, *sakura helau*, has emerged, featuring athletic choreography derived from *pencat silat*, the popular martial art of the region. These masks are rather abstract – the dancers' faces are simply wrapped in the local batik cloth, leaving just a slit for the eyes over which sunglasses are worn (Thomas 2013: 393–410).

The many cultures of the island of Borneo still produce a wide range of masks,[1] from very simple painted face coverings to complex carved wooden constructions with demonic features and glittering eyes made of shell. These continue to be used for fertility, healing and funerary rituals (Hershey 1991: 49–54). However, while these masked performances are associated with ritual and religious occasions, serving as entertainment for divinities, they also entertain the human participants and spectators. During the harvest festival, men and women of the Land Dayak (*Bidayuh*) group dance through the communal longhouse wearing demonic masks, collecting offerings and exorcizing negative spirits while entertaining their fellow villagers. Among the Iban people, simple masks with huge eyes and prominent teeth are used to 'discipline' children, warning them of dangers that lie in the forest and river. At the end of the harvest festival men and women exchange roles and clothing, and use masks to impersonate and parody the opposite sex (Heppell 1992: 25–9). Perhaps the best-known masks of this region are the spectacular *Hudoq* masks of the Dayaks, used for complex ritual performances associated with the rice harvest in which masked dancers, clad in banana leaves, dance, collect offerings and expel disease (Heppell 1992: 34–9).

Although there is some evidence of masking traditions among the diverse aboriginal cultures in the Philippine islands, the *Moriones* festival on the island of Marinduque is perhaps the most overtly theatrical, yet it is still embedded in religious ritual. As part of the events of Christian Holy Week prior to Easter, penitents don the garb of Roman soldiers, including a helmet with a visor to which a beautifully painted face mask is attached. Dozens of these costumed performers then march through the streets seeking the centurion Longinus, a Christian convert, cured of his blindness by the blood of Christ. The tradition, which began in the late nineteenth century, is part street festival and part passion play in which the masked performers enact the pursuit, capture and execution of the elusive Longinus, after which they reaffirm their Christian faith with prayers for forgiveness and absolution. The masks may be made of wood or papier-mâché and are carefully painted to depict in vivid detail a bearded, fair-skinned Roman centurion. Although the pursuit (and eventual 'execution') of Longinus involves a good deal of playful interaction between 'soldiers' and audience, the heavy burden of mask and costume and the long hours of performance constitute an act of piety on the part of the masked performers (Casurao n.d.).

Java and Bali: court, temple and village traditions

The consciously 'theatrical' mask traditions of the Indonesian islands of Java and Bali can be traced back as far as the tenth century, and have influenced many European and American theatre artists. Although long established, these are dynamic, living traditions that continue to evolve. *Topeng* is a term used for both masks and masked performance throughout Indonesia, and also refers to masked dance-dramas associated with particular regions.

Javanese topeng

In Java there are distinct topeng styles in the northwestern Cirebon region, in the central Javanese regions around Surakarta and Jogjakarta, in east Java around Malang and on the nearby island of Madura. It is generally held that the human mask performances, sometimes referred to as *wayang orang* or *wayang wong* ('human puppets'), developed from the older *wayang kulit* tradition of leather shadow puppets, because the shape of the masks and the movement of the performers mimic the shapes and movement qualities of the puppets. As in the shadow puppet shows, a *dalang*[2] usually narrates the story and may provide the voices for most of the characters, while the masked performers mime the action in time with the dalang's words. However, clown characters in half-masks may create their own physical and verbal improvisations. A full gamelan orchestra of metallophones and gongs accompanies the performance. The full-face masks, slightly smaller than the human face, are held in the performer's teeth by a short, thick leather or rubber strap. Some of the stories enacted are drawn from the *Ramayana* and *Mahabharata* epics, but the most popular and widespread dramas are based on the adventures of Prince Panji[3] (Figure 7.6) and legends of Javanese history, especially of the Hindu-Buddhist kings of the Majapahit period in the fourteenth and fifteenth centuries. The shift from Hinduism to Islam in the sixteenth century did not dislodge the tradition, but may have influenced the aesthetic qualities of masks and movements to a more stylized, refined and restrained style.

Javanese topeng masks are made of carved wood and painted with traditional motifs and colours. There are no strict templates or models, but there is a consistency in style since the

Figure 7.6 Javanese Topeng Panji, Horniman Museum.
(Photo by Margaret Coldiron)

size, shape and colours of the masks follow traditional aesthetic conventions. Character is indicated by shape and colour, from the most refined (*alus*) types, such as Prince Panji, to the strong and powerful (*gagah* or *keras*) such as Klana, to grotesque or vulgar (*kasar*) for demonic characters and clowns. The refined characters, exemplified by Panji, are white or green and female masks for Panji's beloved Candrakirana are generally painted in white, pale colours or, occasionally, gold. The oval face tapers towards the chin with finely carved, delicate features, a pointed nose and slim, almond-shaped eyes usually with a downward gaze betokening modesty and grace. In contrast, the stronger masks such as the *Patih* (king's councillor) or Klana (Panji's rival for the love of princess Candrakirana) are painted in reddish hues with strong features, bulging eyes and a prominent, upturned nose. In the masks of demons such as Cakil, these strong features are made even more prominent with the addition of sharp, jutting teeth or fangs to indicate their vulgarity and their dangerous, demonic power. The clowns (*punakawan*) from the shadow puppet repertory (Semar, Gareng, Bagong and Petruk) also turn up as topeng characters. They have endearingly coarse features and represent ordinary people, often acting as translators or interpreters of the action that goes on among the more refined characters. These are usually half-masks, held by a strap around the head, which allow the performer to speak.

There are distinct differences in style from region to region, both in the details of the masks and in aspects of the movement. For example, the masks of Cirebon are smaller and more detailed than those of Central Java, which are exquisitely refined and slightly abstract, while the masks of East Java are somewhat less refined but more dynamic.

Recounting local histories, Panji stories and Hindu epics, topeng flourished as a court art in the Sultanates of Java and continues to be popular in the villages, but today full-length performances (which might last several hours) are rare. Nonetheless, single dances of individual characters are frequently performed in mixed programmes of dances and for tourist shows. The performances are purely secular, yet certain characters maintain a powerful resonance within Javanese culture, especially the refined princes such as Panji, Rama and Arjuna whose purity and nobility make them models of right behaviour, just as the rough, lustful and greedy Klana represent the negative aspects of human character.

Balinese topeng and Bondres

Balinese topeng dance-drama also uses carved wooden masks that range in type from *halus* to *kasar* and, although the masks may seem somewhat less elegant and subtle than those in Java, they are certainly vivid and dynamic, with a powerful gaze that confronts the audience directly. Both full- and half-masks are held in place by a strong rubber strap. The stories for Balinese topeng are based on the *babad* chronicles of Balinese history and tell of spiritually pure and magically powerful kings and princes. Each performance of Balinese topeng is unique, with the story chosen for its relevance to the occasion or to the family or organization sponsoring the performance. The dialogue is improvised, not scripted, making it possible to heighten elements of the story that are significant for a particular occasion and to incorporate contemporary references and jokes that will appeal to the local audience. Each performance begins with two or three introductory, full-face masks representing the strong prime minister (*topeng keras*) and *topeng tua*, a wise but elderly courtier. Occasionally one other comic mask (*topeng lucu*) in the keras style is featured. Each full-face mask has its own headdress, special musical accompaniment and movement vocabulary appropriate to the particular character. These are followed by the *Penasar*, a high-ranking palace servant who tells the story and translates the words of the high-caste characters from the ancient Javanized Sanskrit language that the nobles speak (*Kawi*) to ordinary Balinese for the audience. The masks that follow may include the King (*Dalem*), a white, full-face mask whose words are spoken and translated by the Penasar, or the very self-important high priest (*Pedanda*, another full-face mask but with an open mouth so he can speak for himself), as well as a range of comic half-masks representing villagers and common people, who move the story along and make plenty of jokes. When the performance is part of a ritual, the final character to appear will be *Sidha Karya*, an extraordinary mask with demonic features, but whose white colour indicates his purity and sacred power. This mask, with his uncanny laughter and hopping dance, performs prayers and mantras to complete the ceremony. Balinese topeng can be performed by a single virtuoso (*topeng pajegan*) or up to five performers (*topeng panca*). There is also a composite form, *topeng prembon* ('mixed' topeng), developed in the late nineteenth century, which combines the mask characters with *arja* (Balinese 'opera') performers to create a sung dance-drama, often on romantic themes from the Panji repertoire. A gamelan orchestra of metallophones, gongs, flutes and drums accompanies this and other masked dance-dramas.

Although the character types are fixed, there is considerable latitude for innovation among masks of all types, providing the possibility for distinct characters.[4] This is especially true for the comic *Bondres* masks, which show tremendous variety and range. The costume is the same for all performers, an elaborate, multi-layered ensemble that includes white trousers and sarong, a gilded cape and highly decorated neckpiece and accessories that is based on the costume for warriors of the fourteenth-century Majapahit kingdom.

In recent years a new genre has emerged in which the comic, half-masked Bondres characters feature exclusively, outside the context of traditional topeng. It is a purely secular form, full of satire and outrageously bawdy, that is highly popular both as live performance in the villages and on television (Figure 7.7).

Rangda, Barong and Jauk

Other masked performances in Bali include the famous exorcistic *calonarang* dance-drama that tells the story of a witch or sorcerer who causes plagues and epidemics and is challenged by a powerful holy man. In the course of the drama each of these human (unmasked) characters transforms, taking on a supernatural persona embodied in a spectacular mask. The witch or sorcerer becomes Rangda, a demonic figure associated with the Hindu goddess Durga and also conflated with local protective deities. This large, whole-head mask has bulging eyes, huge fangs, and a long tongue made of decorated leather; golden flames emerge from the top of her head and her long, palm-fibre 'hair' hangs to her ankles. The costume consists of pendulous breasts and tubular appendages representing the entrails of her victims. The holy man becomes Barong, a beast with a long, shaggy body adorned with gilded leather and tiny, bright mirrors and a face (the mask) resembling an animal. There are many variations of Barong (tiger, pig, dog or lion, among others), but the most famous and popular is called Barong Ket, a mythical creature for which there is no known equivalent. This mask, too, has demonic features, including bulging eyes and fanged jaws that can be made to clack loudly. Two men dance inside this figure, balancing the huge and heavy apparatus of the body on their heads, with the man in the front also operating the mask. In tourist performances, Rangda and Barong confront one another in a battle of 'good' against 'evil' in which Rangda retreats, and the knife-wielding followers of Barong who pursue her mimic trance behaviours and engage in furious self-stabbing, before Barong reappears to bring them out of 'trance' and to bestow blessings on performers and audience. There is never a winner or loser in this confrontation, but the encounter serves as a means of balancing the forces of dark and light. In temple performances, Rangda and Barong masks (which are both held to be sacred and protective) rarely confront one another, but their sacred power when inhabited in performance often drives members of the community into trance. The iconography of the masks appears to indicate a powerful tantric influence, but might also derive from animist practices that pre-date Hindu–Buddhist beliefs, which have been the dominant feature of Balinese culture since the fourth or fifth century CE. Other masks that appear in this dance-drama are the androgynous *Telek*, who are guardians of Barong, and the playful, demonic *Jauk*. The Jauk mask can also appear as a solo performance and in dance-dramas that feature two or more Jauk, presented as entertainment at temple festivals and in tourist shows.

Wayang wong and *Parwa*

Balinese *wayang wong* is a masked dance-drama of the *Ramayana* story, and the more rarely performed *Parwa* presents stories from the *Mahabharata*. These are ceremonial performances often given for temple festivals around the time of *Kuningan*, when the deified ancestors return to heaven at the end of the Balinese New Year celebrations at *Galungan*.[5] The tradition may have come to Bali when the Javanese Hindu courts fled to Bali as Muslim Mataram Sultanate began to dominate Java in the sixteenth century. However, the Balinese hold that it began when the ruler of the Balinese kingdom of Klungkung, I. Déwa Gedé Kusumba (1775–1825), ordered the creation of a new dance-drama using 'sacred animal masks that were part of the treasury of the royal palace' (Bandem 2001: 3). Traditionally, all characters were masked, but today the monkeys, demons and narrator-servants (Twalen, Wredah, Delem and Sangut) always wear masks, while the human characters, such as Rama, Sita and Laksmana, rarely do.

Figure 7.7 Balinese topeng masks.

(Photo by Margaret Coldiron)

Mainland Southeast Asia

Among the hill tribes that inhabit the border regions of Burma, Thailand, Laos and Vietnam, there are some indigenous traditions of shamanic and ancestral masks but these are primarily associated with religious practice and are not well documented. The most prevalent and best-known masked performance forms of Cambodia, Thailand, Burma and Laos are dance-dramas based on the *Ramayana* story. The first of these may have appeared in the Khmer courts of Angkor in the ninth or tenth century and are likely to have developed under the influence of the Hindu-Buddhist culture of Sriwijaya in Sumatra and Java. The Southeast Asian versions of the *Ramayana* differ in many key ways from the better-known *Ramayana* by the Indian sage Valmiki, which has led some scholars to suggest that their source may be a Tamil or Bengali version that travelled to Southeast Asia with the traders who brought Hindu culture to the region in the third century CE (Chandavij and Pramualratana 1998: 106; Phim and Thompson 2001: 8). The similarities among these mask dance-drama traditions may be attributed to the complex history of the region. When the Siamese sacked the Khmer kingdom of Angkor in 1461, they brought the court dancers to Ayutthaya to train their own performers; Burma then sacked Ayutthaya in 1767, bringing those performers to the Burmese capital, and for most of its history, what is now Laos was under the control or influence of either the Khmer, Siamese or Burmese courts.

Thailand

In the nineteenth century the present-day states of Vietnam, Cambodia and Laos were subsumed under the French colonial mantle as French Indochina, while the British controlled Burma and Malaysia. In spite of the efforts of the European powers, however, Thailand somehow managed to avoid colonization and the arts flourished, enthusiastically supported by the courts, so that today *khon*, the traditional classical masked dance-drama of Thailand, has come to represent an important assertion of national cultural identity. In current practice, the khon presents episodes from the *Ramakien*, a version of the *Ramayana* assembled by King Rama I (reigned 1782–1809) and revised by Rama VI (reigned 1910–25). Khon was traditionally performed only by men and all characters were masked. However, today it is usually only the demonic *Yaks* and the monkey characters (*Ling*) that wear masks, while human and divine characters do not. Current practice reflects a syncretic combination of *lakon nai* (female sung dance-drama) with male *khon*; so female performers now take the roles of female characters both human and divine (Brandon 1967: 66).

The spectacular whole-head masks are made of papier-mâché shaped on a clay mould from which the mask is cut in two pieces, and then reassembled. After another layer of paper is applied, eyebrows and decorative features are painted on using natural lacquer. The masks are then sanded, painted and decorated with gilding, mirrors and polished stones. Aspects of character are indicated by head and eye shape, colour and headdress. For example, the demon Tosakanth (Ravana) has a green mask with bulging eyes; his headdress is decorated with the faces of nine of his heads (the tenth is the head of the performer, inside the mask.) His kinsman Pipek (who defects to Rama's forces) has 'crocodile-shaped' eyes and a gourd-shaped headdress. The masks are secured by thread that passes through a tiny opening in the mouth of the mask and is held in the performer's teeth. Each character type – monkey, demon, male (*phra*), female (*nang*) or divine being – has a strictly defined movement vocabulary, and some, especially the monkeys, are exceptionally athletic and acrobatic. The elaborate costumes are embroidered with glittering silver brocade and individually fitted to each performer. Performances are accompanied by a piphat orchestra of xylophones, gongs, drums, cymbals, lyre, flute and oboe. The characters do not speak, but mime as male narrators and female chorus chant and sing the story and dialogue.

Cambodia

Abundant evidence exists of dance-dramas in the Khmer courts as far back as the seventh century CE, but there have been significant gaps between the court dances that decorate the ruins of Angkor and those seen today. The traditional *robam kbach boran* and *lakhon khol* masked drama can be traced back to the nineteenth century when King Ang Duong, who had been a prisoner of the Siamese court for 27 years, returned to rule Cambodia around 1841 (Phim and Thompson 2001: 38). When the court arts flourished, from Ang Duong's succession to the overthrow of the monarchy in 1970, lakhon khol was performed by men who presented episodes from the *Reamker* (the Khmer version of the *Ramayana*), in both court and village settings. Robam kbach boran was confined to royal occasions, performed by ladies of the court enacting the *Reamker* or other stories, including *Inao* (about Prince Panji) and Jataka tales of previous incarnations of the Buddha. Support for the court arts declined after the departure of Prince Sihanouk in 1970, and dancers and teachers were actively persecuted during the Khmer Rouge period (1974–9). Since the fall of the Khmer Rouge, the classical court arts have been painstakingly reconstructed and are now regularly performed for state occasions. Lakhon khol is still performed only by men, and men now take the monkey roles in robam kbach boran. Although masks exist for all characters in the *Reamker*, today animal and demonic characters are masked while the human and divine characters usually are not. The masks are very similar to those used in Thai khon and constructed in the same manner. Performers mime the action accompanied by a *pin peat* orchestra (similar to that which accompanies Thai khon) and two or three male narrators and a female singer who provide narration and dialogue. The growing tourist industry has encouraged the development of both official and unofficial training schools so that now the performances once reserved for Khmer royalty are available in hotels and restaurants in Siem Reap as well as in the Royal University of Fine Arts in Phnom Penh.

Masks also appear in a number of ritual settings, including performances of lakhon khol at Khmer New Year celebrations (in April) to encourage rainfall, and the folkloric *Trot* dance in which dancers wearing deer headdresses are pursued by 'hunters' in papier-mâché demon masks similar to those used for the lakhon khol.

Laos

At Lao New Year (*pi maî*) in April, the masks of the sacred ancestral spirits of Pu Nheu and Na Nheu, along with their little lion, Sing Kaeo Sing Kham, emerge from their cottage and dance through the streets of Luang Prabang to bring purification and good fortune to the land. It is a ritual that relates to the origin myth of the Lao people and reflects the close kinship of Buddhism and animism in Lao religious practice.

The Phra Lak Phra Ram presents episodes from the *Ramayana* and uses papier-mâché masks for all but the female characters. This court dance-drama may have been adopted during the period of Khmer influence in the fourteenth century or may derive from the later incursions of the Siamese. The influence of Thai khon is evident in both masks and movement but the story, costumes and dance style have been adapted to local aesthetic conventions. The episodes are performed in Lao, with Lao instruments added to the *phipad* orchestra that accompanies the action.

The Lao 'Royal Ballet' was abolished, along with the monarchy, in 1975, though performances of Phra Lak Phra Lam continued in Vientiane and at New Year festivities in Luang Prabang (Figure 7.8). It was revived in 2002 and gives regular performances in the former royal palace, which is now the National Museum of the People's Democratic Republic of Laos.

Figure 7.8 Hanuman in *Phra Lak Phra Lam* at the Royal National Ballet, Luang Prabang, Laos.
(Photo by Margaret Coldiron)

Burma

The geographic location and complex history of Burma (Myanmar) have provided it with a rich theatrical culture.[6] As in other Southeast Asian countries, there are strong links between ritual and traditional performance forms. Masks are used primarily in four genres: *Kinnara* and *Kinnari* bird dances, evidence of which dates from the Pyu period (second to ninth century CE); Dance of the legendary guardian spirit (*nat*) of Mount Popa, a princess who became a Buddhist ascetic and wears a protective demon mask; the *zat pwe*, dance-drama of the Jataka stories; and *Yama Zatdaw*, the Burmese version of the *Ramayana* masked dance-drama, strongly influenced by Thai khon. Masks are made from papier-mâché, and are honoured yearly 'at the beginning and the end of the Buddhist lent, when *than-sin-pan* (orchids) are offered' (Singer 1995: 77).

Vietnam

Among the theatre cultures of Southeast Asia, Vietnam is unique in reflecting the influence of China in its performance traditions. There is no real tradition of mask theatre in Vietnam except the occasional use of a masked chorus in the indigenous folk opera known as *Hat Cheo*. Another tradition, *Tuong* (also known as *Hat Boi*), is a sung and spoken dance-drama similar to Chinese opera that features painted faces, rather than masks. While some suggest its origins might be traced to indigenous folk theatres, most scholars agree that it was imported from China when Mongol troops invaded in the thirteenth century. Until the early seventeenth century it was primarily a court entertainment but became more popular among the common people with the introduction of 'southern songs' from the waning Indo-Malay Champa kingdom (Brandon 1993: 246). There are two styles of *Tuong: chinh*, which deals in tragic/dramatic themes, and *Tuong do*, which is more akin to satirical folk theatre exposing the corruption of the wealthy and powerful. Traditional themes have to do with loyalty to the state and the king. After Vietnam gained independence from the French colonial powers, *Tuong* was regarded 'as a product of feudal society' and inconsistent with socialist values (Dình et al. 1999: 21). Gradually, however, the form was adapted to suit its new political circumstances and enjoyed increased popularity for a time, as accounts of historical events with modern patriotic themes were adapted for new or revised works performed in traditional *Tuong* style. It has been suggested that all of the characters originally wore masks, but, as the songs and dances became more complex, the use of face paints was adopted. There are four main character types: male, female, demonic and buffoon. Colours and patterns are symbolic of character and occupation, with red, for example, representing loyalty, bravery or divinity while black represents honesty, lack of culture or irascibility, and blue indicates arrogance. It is possible that one traditional mask remains in use for the character of the earth-god (Huynh 1970: 50).

A cornucopia of traditions

The mask traditions of this region reflect a rich mix of cultural influences both from outside sources, including Indian, Chinese, Middle Eastern and European traders as well as cultural exchange among and between Southeast Asian countries. So, for example, although Islamicization has discouraged mask traditions on the Malay peninsula, the *barongan* performances of southwestern Johor and Selangor states show the influence of the *reog* from north coast of Java, featuring the *Singa Barong* – a two-person tiger-like puppet-mask similar to the Balinese Barong. While there is some evidence that these *barong* traditions derive from indigenous exorcistic trance dances, they are often linked to the Chinese lion dance, a similar puppet-mask, which may be seen throughout Southeast Asia and particularly among Chinese communities in Singapore, Malaysia, Vietnam and Taiwan.

What is most exciting about the use of masks in this region is that these are living practices that form part of the spiritual and artistic lives of the people and continue to develop. The long history of cultural exchange and interaction means that these traditions are responsive to new inspirations and find new applications. Moreover, the influence of tourism and new media means that these once rare and exotic performances are now accessible to a worldwide audience.

Notes

1 Borneo is a large island to the east of Sumatra, the largest portion of which is the Indonesian province of Kalimantan; the Malay states of Sarawak and Saba and the Sultanate of Brunei areas lie along the northwest coast of the island.

2 *Dalang* or *dhalang* is the word used for the shadow puppet master of wayang kulit who narrates the story and provides the dialogue for all the characters. The dalang holds an especially high status in Indonesia because of the depth of knowledge and spiritual understanding required of those who bring to life the sacred epics.

3 Panji is a legendary prince of the East Javanese kingdom of Jenggala, who encounters many adventures in his pursuit of the beautiful princess, Candrakirana.

4 For example, among the masks used for Topeng Keras, one that is lighter in colour, with 'sweeter' features, would be used for Patih Jelantik, a nobleman who sacrifices his life to redeem his parents, who have been transformed into leeches by a curse.

5 These are events that take place at the end of the Balinese 210-day (*Pawukon*) calendar year, usually around October and April.

6 Burma borders on India, China, Thailand and Laos.

Bibliography

Bandem, I Made (2001) *Wayang Wong*, Yogya-Indonesia: Bali Mangsi Press.

Brandon, James R. (ed.) (1967) *Theatre in Southeast Asia*, London: Oxford University Press.

—— (1993) *The Cambridge Guide to Asian Theatre*, Cambridge: Cambridge University Press.

bsang rdo rje (2010) 'bod kyi lha mo'i zlos gar gyi sgyu rtsal skor gleng ba' (A Discussion about the Art of Performance of Tibetan Opera), in *bod kyi lha mo'i zlos gar gyi 'khrab gzhung phyogs bsgrigs* (Collection of the Performance Scripts of Tibetan Opera), Beijing: krung go'i bod rig pa dpe skrun khang (China Tibetology Publishing House), 1–20.

Casurao, Diosdado Granados (n.d.) 'Anthropological Reflection on Philippine Masks', in *Philippino Culture*, http://philippineculture.ph/filer/toledo-cebu/Anthropological-reflection-on-Philippine-masks.pdf, accessed 14 November 2013.

Chandavij, Natthapatra, and Promporn Pramualratana (1998) *Thai Puppets and Khon Masks*, London: Thames & Hudson.

Cho Dong-il (2006) *Talchumui Wonri Sinmyeongpuli* (Talchum's Origin in Expression of Sinmyeong), Seoul: Jishiksaneopsa.

Cho, Oh Kon (1988) *Traditional Korean Theatre*, Fremont, CA: Asian Humanities Press.

De Nebesky-Wojkowitz, René (1976) *Tibetan Religious Dances: Tibetan Text and Annotated Translation of the 'Chams Yig'*, Delhi: Pilgrims Book.

Diamond, Catherine (2012) *Communities of Imagination: Contemporary Southeast Asian Theatres*, Honolulu: University of Hawai'i Press.

Dình Quang, Lê Anh, Hà Van Câu, Nguyên Huy Hông, Trân Viêt Ngu, Tât Thâng and Hô Ngoc (1999) *Vietnamese Theater*, Hanoi: Thê Giòi Publishers.

Dorje (2011) Interview by Kati Fitzgerald Lhasa, Tibet, November.

Eisman, Fred B. Jr. (1990) *Bali: Sekala and Niskala, Volume I: Essays on Religion, Ritual and Art*. Singapore: Periplus Editions.

Emigh, John (1996) *Masked Performance: The Play of Self and Other in Ritual and Theatre*, Philadelphia: University of Pennsylvania Press.

Heppell, Michael (1992) *Masks of Kalimantan*, Melbourne: Indonesian Arts Society.

Hershey, Irwin (1991) *Indonesian Primitive Art*, Singapore: Oxford University Press.

Huynh Chieu-Duong (1985) *Le Theatre Vietnamien*, Brussels: Edition Van Tiên-D.

Huynh Khàc Dung, Tuàn-Ly (1970) *Hát Bôi: Théâtre Traditionnel du Viet-Nam*. Saigon: Kim Lai Án Quán.

Jeon, Kyungwook (2005) *Korean Mask Dance Dramas: Their History and Structural Principles*, Seoul: Youlhwadang.

—— (2008) *Traditional Performing Arts of Korea*, Seoul: Korea Foundation.

Kallayanapongsa, Angkarn (2006) *Khon: Thai Masked Dance*, Bangkok: The Crown Property Bureau.

Leiter, Samuel L. (ed.) (2007) *Encyclopedia of Asian Theatre: Volumes 1 and 2*, Westport, CT: Greenwood Press.

Lobsang P. Lhalungpa (1969) 'Tibetan Music: Sacred and Secular', *Studies in Comparative Literature*, 3 (2): www.studiesincomparativereligion.com/uploads/ArticlePDFs/92.pdf, accessed 15 July 2014.

Lucas, Heinz (1973) *Java-Masken: Der Tanz auf Einem Bein*, Kassel: Erich Röth-Verlag.

Marinduque Tourism (n.d.) *Moriones Festival* www.marinduque.gov.ph/moriones.html, accessed 14 November 2013.

Meittinen, Jukka O. (ed) (2010) *Asian Traditional Theatre and Dance* (online book), www.xip.fi/atd/Theatre Academy of Helsinki, accessed 1 December 2013.

Nishikawa, Kyotaro, and Monica Bethe (1978) *Bugaku Masks*, Tokyo: Kodansha International.

Osman, Mohammed Taib (ed.) (1974) *Traditional Drama and Music of Southeast Asia*, Kuala Lumpur: Dewan Bahasa dan Pustaka Kementerian Pelajaran Malaysia.

Phim, Toni Samantha, and Ashley Thompson (2001) *Dance in Cambodia*, Kuala Lumpur: Oxford University Press.

sa gong dbangs 'dus (2003) *bod mi'i yul srol goms gshis* (Customs of the Tibetan People), Beijing: mi rigs dpe skrun khang (Nationalities Publishing House).

Saeji, CedarBough T. (2012) 'The Bawdy, Brawling, Boisterous World of Korean Mask Dance Dramas', *Cross Currents: East Asian History and Culture Review* no. 4: 146–68.

Samten Dhondup (2009) 'On the Tibetan Traditional Theatre', in *Tibetan Arts in Transition: A Journey through Theatre, Cinema and Painting*, Rome, Italy: ASIA Onlus, 9–11.

Samten G. Karmey (1986) 'Three Sacred Bon Dances ("Cham")', in Jamyang Norbu (ed) *Zlos-gar: Performing Traditions of Tibet*, Dharamsala, HP, India: Library of Tibetan Works & Archives, 58–68.

Seo Yeonho (2002) *Han'guk Gamyeongeuk Yeongu* (Research on Korean Mask Dance Drama), Seoul: Wolin.

Singer, Noel F. (1995) *Burmese Dance and Theatre*, Kuala Lumpur: Oxford University Press.

Supriyanto, Henri, and M. Soleh Adi Pramono (1997) *Drama Tari Wayang Topeng Malang*, Malang: Padepokan Seni Mangun Dharma.

Tan, Heidi (2006) *Hidden Faces: The Art of Japanese Masks*, Singapore: Asian Civilisations Museum.

Teele, Rebecca (ed.) (1984) 'Nō/Kyōgen Masks and Performance: Essays and Interviews', *Mime Journal*, Claremont: Pomona College.

Thomas, Karen Kartomi (2013) 'Enchanting the Audience: Dramatic Devices of *Sakura* Mask Theatre in West Lampung, Sumatra', in *Asian Theatre Journal*, 30 (2, Fall).

Udaka, Michishige, and Shuichi Yamagata (2010) *The Secrets of Noh Masks*, Tokyo: Kodansha International.

Yi Duhyon (Yi Duhyeon) (1964 [1981]) *Han'gukui Talchum* (Korean Mask Dance Dramas), Seoul: Iljisa.

Yousof, Ghulam-Sarwar (1994) *Dictionary of Traditional Southeast Asian Theatre*, Kuala Lumpur: Oxford University Press.

8

Puppets in traditional Asian theatre

Kathy Foley

Traditional Asian genres often give precedence to object theatre.[1] Those learning Sundanese dance of West Java will be told to move 'more like the *wayang golek*' (rod puppet). Japanese *bunraku* traditionally held higher artistic status than its companion art of the actor's *kabuki*. Prince Damrong Rajanubhab of Thailand postulated that the *nang yai* (court large leather puppet theatre) is the antecedent of the *khon* (mask dance) and gives the dance its postures. Burmese dance emulates the *yokthe thay* string puppetry and was performed on a raised stage in the palace – puppets had higher status than actors whose feet (unlike the puppet's) could not go above the royal head (Figure 8.1).

Western theatre by contrast tends to see puppetry as a genre that reaches its perfection by becoming human. Consider the representative stories of *Pinocchio* (1883), *The Nutcracker* (1892) and *Coppelia* (1890). In each, the figure must come to life for the narrative to climax. European critics praise puppetry when it seems almost 'alive'. Realism traditionally made the marionette with its multiple jointed movement a favoured western form. Life trumps art.

This chapter will, first, explore why object theatre has often had greater status within an Asian frame than within the west and discuss why, historically, human theatre in some areas emulates puppetry. I will note that separation of object theatre into mask and puppet is not necessarily indigenous – these arts are linked. Next, core components common to various Asian puppet theatres (class differentials, religious connections, sung/narrated story, musical accompaniment, set character types and interrelation of puppetry modes, such as shadow, glove, rod, marionette, etc.) will be addressed. Finally, the historical developments will be outlined for four regions: South Asia, Central Asia, Northeast Asia and Southeast Asia.

Why object theatre?

Throughout Asia the significance of object theatre – puppet, mask and parade objects – is strong. Puppetry and mask-work are presented by a solo artist or multi-manipulator group. Frequently seen processional figures include lions and oversized human images as well as dragons performed by many manipulators who hold a pole supporting the jointed figure. Some attribute the widespread importance of figures in Asia with archaic cults of the dead, noting that in places such as China we find figures (some jointed like puppets) that accompanied notables to the

Figure 8.1 The Alchemist from the Yokthe Pwe marionette theatre of Burma.
(Photo by Brad Clark)

afterlife – the terracotta warriors of Xi'an (c. 200 BCE) are only the most elaborate example. Others see carved figures as giving a locus to the spirit of an ancestor, as with the *tau-tau*, funeral effigies of the deceased that the Toraja of Sulawesi place in galleries outside burial caves. Another figure that represents the dead is the giant *tahamaca*, a large funeral puppet of the Newars of Nepal, paraded in the annual Gaijatra (cow festival) and incinerated to free the dead soul.

Some scholars see shamanic-style exorcisms as a potential root. Throughout Asia where puppetry flourishes we often find traces of cults with shamanic specialists as intercessors between humans and spirits using performing arts to make the realities of the 'other' (positive or negative spirit of divinities, ghosts, ancestors) visible to the living. In Japan, low-caste puppeteers danced Sambaso, the old man figure bringing ritual good luck, in areas that eventually gave rise to *bunraku*: auspicious ancestors animated might bring fertility to fields and people. In *jalankung* of Java, young girls animate a figure that is used in rain making or fortune telling. In the *sanghyang deling* of Bali, two small puppets are danced to induce trance. In China, marionettes could be used in fortune telling or exorcism by Daoist masters. Additionally, plots of many of the epics for puppet narratives may link to shamanist patterns of withdrawal, tribulation (in the forest/on the mountain/beneath the sea/meeting death or the divine in struggle) and rebirth/return. The use of figures, rather than human bodies, may also facilitate otherworldly narratives: scale and body image are malleable, making non-humans (demons, gods, animals) easier to represent.

Perhaps for this reason we can find puppetry linked with ritual releases. This may include picture scroll narration (images of hell in China) and puppet shows – *Mulian jiumu* (Mulian Saves his Mother [from damnation in hell]) in China, *Bima Suwarga* (Bima in the Other World, where the hero releases his parents from purgatory) in Bali, or the *ruwatan* (where a god becomes a puppeteer to save humans from a demon Kala) in Java. The representation of the divine or demonic is displaced from the human to the object (picture, puppet or mask), deflecting sacred danger from human beings.

Beyond this pragmatic use of figure, puppet/mask may also have the function of expanding the individual performer, giving him/her the aura of power. While modern western perspective may posit the individual as unitary and defined by his/her gender, class or ethnicity, Asian puppet/mask theatres often have the idea of a solo performer/narrator telling the story using figures/masks to morph easily from one thing to another. In some genres such as bunraku or *tolpava kootho* of Kerala, India there is a single narrator (though multiple manipulators), while in Thai *nang talung* or Indonesian *wayang* one performer-puppeteer controls all the puppets and dialogue. This narrator or narrator-manipulator in object theatre is often associated – through his ability to change vocally or movement-wise from character to character – with power that is both spiritual (derived from the religious epics/stories) and artistic. Puppets and masks are a way that such a single performer can represent the cosmos. One of the reasons that we may find strong stylization of character types in voice, movement and persona in traditional Asian forms may be linked back to this idea of a unitary artist – stylization allows one performer/story holder to clearly present the different types needed in the story via masks (as with Balinese *topeng pajegan* [solo mask performer]) or with puppets (whose iconography is routinely shared with the mask and even unmasked theatre). The complete artist (narrator/masker/puppet master) is 'everything' and strict codification of voice–movement type lets the audience see the myriad potentials in the one person.

In these forms with a solo narrator, we encounter puppetry as a metaphor of microcosmic access to the macrocosm. The puppeteer is equated with the divine. These performers and their stories somehow show us the whole cosmos and the puppet master, moving in everything but never fully visible except via the mask or puppet, is highlighted. In this thinking, object theatre is a way of moving from the normal human position (i.e. individual thinking) to cosmic understanding. The human reality, the individual body, is just a 'puppet/mask', a temporary repository, for an energy that is bigger but dimly understood. For this viewpoint, which animists, Buddhists, Hindus and Sufis have variously espoused, the puppeteer better represents how the universe actually operates than the actor, who is defined by age, shape and gender. While the puppet genres that carry this object perspective may ultimately give rise to actor theatres – for example the Javanese *wayang orang* ('human puppetry'/dance-drama) or Thai *khon* (court mask dance), the ideology of the solo master who holds the story and uses 'puppets' (figures, masks or even other dancers' bodies/types) is represented in the idea of a divine puppeteer who encompasses the macrocosm.

Core components

Traditional puppetry in Asian tends to be of two kinds, 'courtly consort' or the 'big bang' (Foley 2015). Elite arts have respected performers who live in or near a palace/temple/theatre and the arts may be performed/written by aristocrats themselves; their epic stories support religious and state ideology and grow as elaborate in figures and artists as patronage will allow – this variant I term 'courtly consort' and includes, for example, Javanese shadow puppetry, Thai court shadow puppetry and Japanese bunraku. By contrast, 'big bang' arts are performed by low- class itinerants whose short open-air skits are quickly grasped by viewers lured to watch by the loud percussion, slapstick action, sexual banter and political rabble-rousing; figures and other equipment pieces are small enough to carry from place to place, manipulation is rough, the group relatively compact – since the performers are often *persona non grata*, quick exits before police sweeps are sometimes needed. Examples of big bang arts are the Rajasthani *kathaputli* and Korean *kkokdugaksi noreum*.

Within this dichotomous frame, we find some shared features. Almost all puppet genres include music, codified and appropriate to the character or action of the scene. Percussion often accents dance/movement, and songs as well as speeches are important. Performers usually train from youth under a master as they learn the style and repertoire. Stories, especially in courtly consort forms, may reference the great epics that have their base in religious or chronicle sources, and ritual openings or other religious features may inhere, even in contemporary performance. Although some forms (Japanese bunraku, Chinese shadow play) have set texts, others may generate the text in performance according to the rules of the genre. Spiritual dimensions and ritual beliefs may inhere – Indian and Southeast Asian genres traditionally started with rituals, and even the relatively secular low-class genres may borrow iconography that derives from religious ideas (snakes/dragons, monks, gods, death scenarios, phallic/fertility or god-clowns).

Although the spiritual significance in secularized forms is muted and comedy prevails, religion may still lie beneath the surface. The iconography of the characters is usually shared with mask performance and folk paintings, so the figures may be immediately recognizable as the great heroes or traditional clowns. Whether masked actor, glove or rod puppet, shadow figure or marionette, one can usually identify the character quickly. Viewers may be less focused on hearing a story that is 'new' than appreciating the artistry with which a recognized narrative is presented.

Modern urban puppetry, which has developed in the twentieth and twenty-first centuries, is a newer form that does not usually follow the pattern above. Modern companies have links with international puppetry as child and community education–entertainment or comic caricature for political critique as found in western theatre and media since at least the 1940s. Modern puppetry is an art devised by educated, urban middle-class performers who often began training in college programmes and who work in contemporary children's theatre/media companies or for educational/NGO projects. While modern performers sometimes mine traditional genres, the idea of types, rituals and traditional repertoire does not confine them. They are as apt to present, for example, Gogol's *Inspector General* as *Romance of Three Kingdoms* for a Chinese audience. These artists rarely follow traditional systems of family troupes or guru–apprentice training.

After considering these overarching features I turn to individual areas, before discussing modern work as a separate topic.

South Asia

Puppets, scroll-painting narrations and mask performances are found in many areas of India, Sri Lanka, Bangladesh, Pakistan and into the Himalaya. The earliest South Asian reference to puppetry is in the *Mahabharata* (fourth century BCE). Tamil poet Tiruvalluvar (second century BCE) wrote: 'The movements of a man who has not a sensitive conscience are like the simulation of life by marionettes moved by strings.' Some argue that the name for the director of the Sanskrit drama in the *Natyasastra* (Book of Drama, early CE), *sutradhara* or 'string puller', comes from puppetry. String, shadow and picture narration are old and German scholar Robert Pishel (1902) even posited that South Asia was the source of puppetry in the Middle East and Europe, arguing transmission via Rom (Gypsies) and other itinerant groups, but here as in other Asian countries actual historical records of practising puppeteers are scant. As an art accessible to many and often low-class/caste groups, Indian puppetry's history is not clearly documented and we may get mythical rather than factual stories of 'origin' of genres, tales that need to be critically approached. South Asia has, of course, been a locus of generating religious movements for millennia, and the various religions (Hinduism, Buddhism, Jainism and Indian Sufism) have often used puppetry in dissemination of ideas. Traditional shows often open with *puja*, mantra, and display of the elephant-headed Ganesha, god of the doorway.

String, rod, shadow and glove puppetry, masks and narration scrolls share character iconography, music/singing and story with human theatre. For examples, Karnataka's *yakshagana* theatre corresponds to *yakshagana gombeyatta* string puppetry, Kerala's *kathakali* to *pavakathakali* glove puppetry, while Assam's *bhaona*, with its Krishna tales, emulates the local *putala nach* string puppets. Painting performance links to puppetry: *patachitras* (picture scrolls) and *gopalila kundhei* puppets of Orissa share visual/performance features; *patas* (picture scrolls) and *daanger putul nach* rod puppets of West Bengal echo one other.

Though there are many stories, the Hindu epics (*Ramayana* and *Mahabharata*) and the *Puranas* ('of ancient Times'), stories of deities, are most presented in traditional puppetry. However, genres of itinerant Muslim performers are often more focused on comic scenes, trick puppets and short skits: Rajasthani *bhat* (performers of that caste) and others presented comic impersonation, puppetry and social critique from north India through Pakistan and Afghanistan to Iran. Performers of these genres use a reed (*boli*), the equivalent of the European swazzle, to create the puppet's voice.

Many traditional South Asian puppeteers are lower class, and caste prejudices plus the competition from modern media have led to diminished audiences, resulting in little recruitment of new puppeteers. Though the national arts organizations such as India's Sangeet Natak Akademi have named puppet masters as award winners, younger members of their families are usually choosing more lucrative careers than family-based puppetry, leaving the future of these arts in question. Meanwhile, in modern Pakistan and Bangladesh, Muslim *ulamas* have become more anti-theatrical than in the past, which negatively affects reception. This chapter will detail only a few of the arts, moving from south to northwest to northeast.

South

Tolu bommalattam ('leather puppet dance') is found in Andhra Pradesh (AP) and Tamil Nadu. In AP these shadow plays are usually improvised based on King Kona Reddi's Telugu *Ranganath Ramayana* (thirteenth century) or *Mahabharata* stories from *yaksagana* dance-drama texts (Figure 8.2). The translucent coloured puppets of AP are up to 1.8 m high and usually made of goatskin, while Tamil versions are smaller. Figures appear in profile, with the exception of the ten-headed demon king, Ravana. In AP Kethigadu and his sexy wife Bangarakka add low-class comedy. The 3 m white screen tilts at the top towards the audience, and about eight performers are involved. Chinna Anjannamma received a 2010 Sangeet Natak Award for work in this genre. Funded by social programmes, puppeteers may insert references to AIDs and other issues. The related *togalu gombeyatta* ('leather puppet dance') is found in Karnataka, but figures are smaller than in AP.

In Kerala *tolpava koothu* shadow theatre is traditionally performed by puppeteers called *pulavar* (scholar-poet) with stories based on palm-leaf manuscripts of the *Ramayana* by the Tamil poet Kamban (twelfth century). Performances traditionally lasted from 7 to perhaps as many as 71 nights in temples and entertained the Goddess Bhadrakali (Durga). The performance form is greatly diminished in the present era but K. K. Ramachandra Pulavar (b. 1960) of Koonathara, from a traditional puppetry lineage, besides performing in temples, has innovated plays on contemporary issues, and taught the first woman puppeteer, his daughter Rajitha Pulavar.

Bommalattam ('doll puppet dance') string-cum-rod figures of Tamil Nadu, AP and Karnataka were once patronized by the kings of Tanjavur and performed at temple festivals to bring rain. The 10 kg figures are 90 cm tall with rods attached to the hands that the manipulator operates from above. A ring with strings that hold the figure goes on the puppeteer's head. Manipulator and figure move to percussion approximating *bharatanatyam* dance. Groups such as Sri Murugan Sangeetha Bommalatta Sabha in Kumbakonam have introduced keyboard and modern lighting to attract new audiences.

Variants called *gombeyatta* ('puppet dance', wooden string puppets) are found in Karanataka and parallel *yaksagana* performance. The figures weigh 8 kg and manipulators speak for their figure, while a narrator, accompanied by musicians, guides the overall story. Bhaskar Kogga Kamath claims a 350-year family lineage.

Pava koothu (glove puppetry) is found in Tamil Nadu and *pavakathakali* ('glove puppet *kathakali*') is preserved in Irinjalakuda, Kerala. The last form is an eighteenth- century genre with face painting and costumes of *kathakali* actors replicated in the 30–60 cm wooden figures. Puppeteers are visible and their active expressions are similar to the *kathakali* performers' *abhinaya* (acting). The form was revived in 1982 by Gopal Venu (b. 1945) and a number of performers have received Sangeet Natak Akademi Awards.

In Sri Lanka in the fourth century the *Culavamsa* (royal record of the monarchs) mentions mechanical representations of gods and galloping horses. There is early mention of shadow players (*camma rupa*) as royal spies. Recent tradition, however, includes string puppetry, which follows nineteenth-century *nadagama* folk theatre. In Ambalongoda several troupes, including Sri Anura, are active. Tamil *bommalattam* groups are also active on the island. In the twentieth century, education-entertainment led to Muppet-style shows on TV and in schools. Puppetry training is given by Thidora Theatre; Dehiwala has a puppetry museum; and young artists such as Sulochana Dissanayake have created intercultural shows with Sri Lankan marionette master Premin Ganvari and Indonesian *dalang* Dede Sunarya.

Figure 8.2 A female dancer from the shadow puppet tradition of Andhara Pradesh.
(Photo by Brad Clark)

Northwest

In the northwest many puppeteers are Muslim from families called *bhats, nats* or *bhands*. Some Rajasthani puppeteers claim that *kathaputli*, one-string marionettes, began with King Vikramaditya (first century BCE) of Ujjain: supposedly *bhats* saw thirty-two (*batai pachisi*) images carved on his throne that praised royal achievements and then presented the *Simhasana Dwatrimshika* (Thirty-two Tales of the Throne) in shows. Other oral traditions claims that early repertoire was the story of the downfall of *Amar Singh Rathore*, ruler of Nagaur in the seventeenth century. However, actual performances more often represent short skits by figures (30–60 cm) of acrobats, snake and charmer, drummers, warriors and dancers. Puppets have carved wooden heads, torsos made of cloth and stuffed with rags, and (usually) skirts. Bed frames turned on their side become the booth and are decorated with the stage cloth and backdrop. A reed (*boli*) creates the high-pitched voices; bells on the puppeteer's wrist accent movements; a female drummer-interlocutor speaks with the figures. Puran Bhatt, a 2003 Sangeet Natak awardee, leads the Aakar (Shape) Toupe: his innovative play *Caravan* tells of kathputli performers' lives.

Gulabo-Sitabo of Uttar Pradesh is a seventeenth-century glove puppet street performance of Lucknow. The eponymous co-wives are the aggressive Gulabo and submissive Sitabo. Papier-mâché puppets are 60 cm, comically presented by one improvising manipulator, accompanied by musicians on drum and cymbals. Related traditions are found in Pakistan and Afghanistan. Even Iranian traditions tell that King Bharam Gur (400 CE) invited 1200 *luri* (gypsies) to his kingdom to perform. Though only a legend, travelling bhats/bhands have long been developing Indo-Iranian puppetry, satire and comedy. Though today artists are constrained by national borders, the puppetry is related. For example, Pakistani string puppetry (*putli*) corresponded to Rajasthani forms with a woman musician-interpreter accompanying her husband-manipulator.

Northeast

Vaishna themes in Oriya language form the major traditional repertory of Orissa. *Ravanachhaya* ('Ravana's shadow') is the Oriya shadow form reflecting the seventeenth- century *Ramayana* of Vishvanath Khuntia (seventeenth century). Roughly cut opaque figures that range from 20 to 60 cm are used. In 1998, Kolhacharan Sahu was honoured by Sangeet Natak Akademi. His group (Ravan Chhaya Natya Sansad) has innovated a show inspired by *pata* scroll paintings. *Gopalila kundhei* ('Cow Herder Play Puppetry') is the Oriya marionette play on Radha-Krishna and *Sakhi kundhei* ('Friend Doll') is Oriya glove puppetry done in a mix of Bengali and Oriya languages.

String, rod and glove puppetry are traditional forms found in West Bengal and Bangladesh. *Tarer putul* (string puppetry) now presents stories from *jatra* (Bengali popular theatre) or films. Puppets (60–80 cm) are made from a spongy plant. *Danger putul nach* ('rod puppet dance') uses 1 m figures (5–10 kg) which are carved wood with clay faces. Satya Narayan Putul Natya Sanstha Company is run by Nirapada Mondal, who has also studied contemporary puppetry with Kolkata artist Suresh Dutta and includes traditional stories along with innovative tales (i.e. *Arannyer Rodan* [Crying of the Forest], in which animals unite to preserve habitat). *Benir putul* (glove puppetry) is performed by one or two itinerant puppeteers with terracotta-head figures.

In both Assam and Manipur puppetry presents devotional materials. *Putul nach* ('doll dance') approximates *bhaona* (Vaishnava religious plays) using marionettes. In Manipur *laithibi jagol* ('doll dance') string puppet presents *rasleela* (Krishna plays) as an interlude to dance-dramas. This form dates from the time of Maharaja Chandrakirti Singh (1850–1886).

In Sikkim, Kashmir, Himachal Pradesh and the Himalayas (Nepal, Bhutan, including the culturally related Tibet in China), one finds historically and at present use of masks, hobbyhorses and sometimes puppets in both Tibetan-style '*cham* monks' mask dance or *Lha mo* folk dramas. These link with tantric Buddhist religion and Bon-style shamanism. Actual manipulated figures include 'butter puppets', small figures moulded for the Lamp Festival near New Year (*Losar*). Scenes might show a shaman's trance or call to prayer. Giant wood or papier-mâché figures sometimes represent Padhmasambhava, the saint culture bringer who introduced Tibetan Buddhism, as in the annual Do De Chutope Festival at Samye Monastery in Tibet before 1959. Masks are extensively employed, but puppetry can also serve as a tool of visualization in tantric practice.

Modern

Modern Indian puppetry is an urban phenomenon developed by educated, middle-class artists after the Second World War and often directed towards children or rural audiences, espousing social/educational programmes. Raghunath Goswami (1931–95) in Bombay, educator-author Devilal Samar in Udaipur, London-trained Meher Contractor (1918–92) of Darpana Academy of Performing Arts in Ahmedabad, and Suresh Dutta (1934–) of Calcutta Puppet Theatre (who studied with Russia's Sergei Obratsov) are central figures in the first generation. Ranjana Pandey of Jan Madhyam (founded in 1980, New Delhi) concentrates on the needs of women and children. Dadi Pudumjee, who trained with Swedish puppeteer Michael Meschke, has led Ishara Puppet Theatre since 1986 and assumed presidency of UNIMA-International puppetry organization in 2008. Hiren Bhattacharya of People's Puppet Theatre in Kolkata develops themes of social justice. Anarupa Roy of Katkatha Puppet Artist Trust (1997) creates innovative epic-visual productions as well as shows on AIDs and social issues. Choti Ghosh Tram Theatre in Mumbai is active in UNIMA-India. Sudip Gupta of Doll's Theatre in Calcutta presents contemporary puppetry for children. Anupama Hoskere of Dhaatu in Bangalore uses puppetry to educate children and share heritage.

In Pakistan the Lahore Arts Council led by Samina Ahmed produced puppetry in the Alhamra Arts Centre from 1986. Lok Rehas ('Folkways', Lahore) uses puppetry addressing social issues (i.e. domestic violence). Faizaan Peerzada (1958–2012) of Rafi Peer Group in Lahore created an international puppetry festival from 1992 and a puppetry museum (2004). Writer Farooq Qaiser used TV puppetry to address issues of civil society. Meanwhile, in Bangladesh Mustafa Monwar (1935–) used legends as the base for works such as *Pandit O Majhi* (The Scholar and the Boatman) and *Bahurupi* (The Clown), working on television and touring literacy and health-focused works.

China

Glove, rod, iron rod puppets (horizontal rod to the figure's back), marionettes, body/parade figures, shadow puppets, and now digital permutations exist. Early puppetry is associated with ritual, such as jointed tomb figures from Laixi district in Shandong dated to the Western Han (206 BCE–9 CE). *Yong* (grave figures) and puppets are linked and shows were given for funerals (see Rault 2009).

The Tang dynasty (618–907) included water puppets (now defunct in China but found in Vietnam) along with other genres. From the seventh century, reports of mechanical wooden monk figures that rattled begging bowls are found. Rod and string puppets played both in the streets and in the houses of the rich. The Song dynasty (960–1279) had string, shadow, water, and 'flesh puppets' (perhaps children on the shoulders of adults). 'Gunpowder' [fireworks] puppets/displays were also known. The picture 'Play of a Skeleton' by Li Song (1166–1243) shows marionette skeletons in performance; such shows may relate back to the hell scrolls that were presented by Buddhist preachers as admonishments to laymen.

In the Ming period (1368–1644), puppeteers were sometimes associated with magic, perhaps explaining why in some areas, even today, puppeteers outrank the actors in status. From this period Xianggong (Marshall Tian) was respected as the god of puppetry/acting. Puppetry was used in ritual and, even today in Taiwan, puppet performances of *Investiture of the Gods* (Fengshen yanyi) may be part of temple festivals. Southern China (Fujian, including Quanzhou and Chaozhou, and Guangdong) was important and influenced puppetry of Southeast Asia, as puppeteers travelled or emigrated from this time on to Indonesia, Malaysia, the Philippines and so forth. Marionettes from Quanzhou had sixteen to thirty strings, danced with finesse and could be used in fortune telling. Ming *budaixi* (glove puppetry) developed and continues to be strong to the present, especially in Fujian. Glove puppetry was done with multiple manipulators and full orchestra or, alternatively, by a single performer extending puppets above his head in a cloth booth hung on his body as his feet created sound effects. This shoulder pole puppetry was found all over, with different names, from 'Quilt Pole Show' in Sichuan to 'Thousand Pole Show' in Hunan. At the same time, iron rod puppetry – doll figures manipulated from behind by a main rod that attached to neck/back and two to the arms – became popular in Chaozhou, migrating to Southeast Asia too.

By the Qing dynasty (1644–1911) entertainment trumped ritual. Puppet shows became and remained an important vehicle for historical/epic narratives (*Romance of Three Kingdoms*, *Water Margin*, *Journey to the West* etc.). For each *xiqu* (opera) style, the local puppetry would correspond in its plays, singing, music, painted face/figure iconography, costumes, and so on. Smaller companies might have three or four performers who moved their bamboo pole and cloth booth from town to town. But large sedentary companies also emerged in towns with permanent built theatres – often boasting they were a 'palace theatre in the large booth' (*dagongxi*) with an imperial connection. The fall of the Qing and the political instability of the early twentieth century culminated in the founding of the People's Republic of China (1949). Puppetry was supported in Soviet-style permanent companies, providing education and indoctrination for children and the public. The Cultural Revolution of 1966–76 caused many traditional puppeteers to destroy puppets, and only urban troupes with politically acceptable presentation existed. After 1976, revival began. Modern troupes now present a wide variety of shows, primarily targeted towards families or tourist audiences. Only since 2006 has systemic work perpetuated the intangible cultural heritage aspects of puppetry.

Shadow puppetry (*yingxi*) in a Song dynasty story propagated by Gao Cheng (c. 1080) was created when Emperor Wudi (r. 141–87 BCE) mourned a dead concubine, and a Daoist master conjured her shadow onscreen. Mair (1988) sees puppetry linked to Buddhist stories (*bianwen*, 'transformation texts') narrated while showing the painted scrolls. Paper cutouts of the north (*chuanghua*, 'flowers in the window') and *jianzhi deng* (silhouettes) for Lantern Festival may also have influenced yingxi. Originally puppets were moved with strings, but eventually horizontal rods pressed the figures to the screen. The neck pivot-attachment allowed flips and turns to emulate the martial (*wu*) movements and dance of character types. Filigreed cutting and thin hides led to delicate and translucent shadows in some areas. Multiple joints facilitated movement. Shadow puppetry is found in Shaanxi, Shanxi, Luanxian Shandong, Hangzhou, Sichuan, Hubei, Hunan, Jiangxi and Chaozhou. Popular among the Manchu soldiers, the art suffered setbacks due to links with popular uprisings and was banned in the late Qing. During the People's Republic it lost audience share to film and other new media and was attacked at the time of the Cultural Revolution for association with old thought/superstition. Today, permanent professional troupes are found in Harbin, Hunan and Shaanxi. Taiwanese master Xu Funeng [Hsu Fu-neng] was a significant twentieth-century exponent of the art. Shadow puppetry in the early twentieth century was recognized as intangible cultural heritage by UNESCO and a major shadow puppetry museum opened in Chengdu (2006).

Marionettes (*kuileixi*) are most noted in Fujian where Quanzhou remains a major centre, with Huang Yique of the Quangzhou Puppet Troupe a master manipulator of these 0.85 m figures with 16–30 strings. String puppetry today is found mostly in Fujian, Guangdong, Zhejiang and Shaanxi. Figures in many areas have bodies that are made of woven bamboo. A few rural troupes maintain traces of earlier rituals. Taiwanese string puppetry, which came from Fujian in the seventeenth century, continues Daoist rituals, though few new practitioners are being trained.

Today, most marionette shows are done by government groups for secular education and entertainment. For example, at the 2012 UNIMA World Puppet Festival in Chengdu, Quangzhou Puppet Troupe, the best-known company, presented Gogol's *Inspector General*.

Rod puppetry (*zhangtou mu'ou*) has two variations: with all rods hidden under the bag costume or with visible hand rods with only the holding rod/spine hidden. While featured in Guangdong, the technique is found throughout China and is central to popular puppetry today. In Guangdong the Tang Emperor Minghuang (712–56 CE) is seen as the patron god of puppetry/theatre. Rod puppetry and the local *xiqu* style coincide. Puppeteers claim there was a repertoire of 'eighteen plays of the itinerant artists' but the legacy was largely destroyed following the Taiping Rebellion (1851–64) since artists were banned for promoting the uprising. Repertoire and traditional practices of the twentieth century are only fragments. New rod puppetry was supported by the PRC, but focused on education, presenting, for example, stories of the Long March or acceptable historical tales. Currently, groups perform a wide variety of tales that may be drawn from legends, fairy tales, ecological narratives and so on. Rod puppetry is mixed with shadows, strings, masks and digital projections in the same show – following trends in international object theatre.

Glove puppets (*budaixi*) are mostly 30 cm figures credited to Liang Binglin, a Ming scholar who failed his imperial exam but dreamt that fame was 'in the palm of the hand'. Borrowing ideas from marionette theatre, he applied his knowledge in glove puppetry, winning applause. Originally, budaixi did traditional xiqu repertoire (i.e. *White Snake* or *Tale of the Hairpin*). Now it can use any story. Budaixi went from Fujian to Taiwan, all over Southeast Asia and around the globe. It remains important in Fujian and especially in Taiwan glove puppetry is found in both old and new enlarged models. Taiwan's most innovative company was led by Huang Haidai (1901–2007), whose Pili Budaixi (Peal of Thunder Glove Puppetry), with moving scenery, modern music, and laser and digital effects, remains enormously popular for live performance, TV and film (i.e. *Legend of the Sacred Stone*, 2002). The history of Taiwanese puppetry is preserved in the Lin Liu-Hsin Puppet Theatre Museum, Taipei.

Body and parade figures, in addition to dragons, include lions, represented in the north by a two-man shaggy head/body and in the south by a more colourful and acrobatic costume. Martial arts groups perform for New Year and other events. The lion's early association with Buddhism implanted the lion throughout Asia for exorcism or good luck, where Chinese peoples have migrated. Indonesian *Barongs* found in Bali and Java and similar figures in Korea and Japan may be linked to Chinese lions.

Contemporary mainland companies today include China Puppetry Troupe (1955), Shanghai Puppetry Troupe, Puppet Theatre of Guangdong (1956), Quanzhou Puppet Troupe (1952), Theatre of Puppets and Shadows of Chengdu (1951) and Tangshan Municipal Shadow Play Company, among others. Conferences, festivals and research grow and puppet forms are inscribed as intangible cultural heritage with designated masters to train new practitioners. Meanwhile, young artists explore international and intercultural experiments, mixing virtual reality and traditional puppetry in experimental works.

Korea

Puppets are believed to have arrived in Korea by the fourth century CE and there is mention in Chinese records of puppets in Goguryeo (37 BCE–668 CE), Silla (668–918) and Goryeo (918–1342) dynasties. During the latter, puppetry was associated with nomads, perhaps related to Mongols of the Chinese Yuan dynasty (1271–1368). Sometimes puppeteers are linked to Indian origins, passing via China to Korea and on to Japan. There are references to string, glove and rod puppetry. Shadow puppetry was rare. Puppetry was presented by the Sandae Dogam (Royal Entertainment Bureau), and Joseon dynasty aristocrat Seong Hyeon (1459–1504) wrote: 'The wooden puppets are moved by strings with marvelous freedom/. . . . A variety of splendid entertainments offered to show respect/[m]ake the Chinese envoy awestruck . . .' (Jeon 2008: 61–2). Fiscal problems and puritanical Confucianism ended court support around 1634, so puppetry became pure folk art.

The traditional Korean puppet show was the *Pak Cheomji noreum* (named after the eponymous narrator, but is also called *Kkoktu Kaksi noreum* (Wife's Play) or *Doelmi* ('Concubine'). This is a part of *namsadang nori* (literally 'flower boys' performance'), a genre that presented acrobatics, masking, puppetry and drumming (*pungmul*) by an itinerant troupe of 30–40 males who also normally practised homosexual prostitution. The rough, brightly painted figures were made of wood, gourd or papier-mâché. Some puppets had moving parts, such as the red-bodied muscleman Hong Tonji with his moving penis.

Manipulators danced figures in a booth and could use a reed for the voice, while the drummer/interlocutor sat outside. Seven to ten episodes, parallel to mask dance (*talchum*) scenes, might be presented. Monks caroused; an old wife sought her husband who had taken up with a pretty concubine; a dragon might appear; someone died, and a funeral followed. Humour, sex and lampooning the elite prevailed. This show was declared Intangible Cultural Property #3 (1964).

Scholars argue that the art is related to shamanism and Buddhism. Performers often came from shaman families and music echoes shamans' drumming. Performers were attached to Buddhist shrines and sold amulets, and perhaps the skits relate to pan-Buddhist processional performances with comedy which became, for example, *gigaku* in Japan. However, the first transcriptions of plays are recent (1939), and Japanese colonialism had already caused severe deteriorations, so histories will remain unclear.

A 1960s resurgence in folk theatre research coincided with new puppetry for child audiences. Leading the 'folk'/'roots' study was Sim Usong (Shim Woo-song, b. 1934), who led Sonang Dang Theatre in developing new work on traditional themes, including *Adventures of Hong Tonji* in the 1980s. Sim founded the Gongju Folk Drama Museum with its rich puppetry holdings. Man U-ryong (d. 1978), with Sim, reconstructed *Pak Cheomji noreum* and headed a government-designated troupe in Anseong. He was recognized as a living cultural treasure for his mastery of namsadang arts. His wife Pak Kae-soon (b. 1933) inherited the troupe and by 2014 the next generation of the family was in charge. Another related namsadang-style comic art is *batal* ('masked foot'): the performer lies on his back and the puppet is mounted on the performer's legs, which extend up from the masking.

Modern puppetry in the Republic of Korea is called *inhyenng-geuk* ('doll plays' after Japanese *ningyō geki*). Cho Yong-su (1932–92) was hired by KBS-TV (Korean Broadcasting System) in 1962 to oversee children's offerings. Following American TV models, he founded Hyundai Theatre and Production Company along with his brother, Cho Yong-suk (1947–). Rod puppets, black light manipulation, marionettes and so on are used as needed. Touring shows include *Heungbu and Nolbu*, a popular *pansori* (story singing) tale contrasting the noble-hearted and greedy brothers of a *pansori* tale. This was a hit in Japan in 1982. Other important companies include Kim Hae-Kyung's Seoul Puppet Theatre, later led by Ahn Jung-ui, and Lee Kyung-hee's Orit-kwangdae group. Lee helped found UNIMA-Korea and the puppetry journal *Kkoktu-geuk*. Kang Sung Kyun founded an important modern shadow company, Yong (Shadow 1982). In 1989 Chucheon began presenting an annual puppet festival every August and supports a theatre, museum and institute of puppetry. Modern puppeteers use diverse techniques. For example, *Kkok-Du'*, by Creative Group NONI, gives the Pak Choemji story using puppets, shadows, masks and screen painting (during performance), with aesthetic visual design and references to shamanic roots.

Japan

Scholars include shamanism as an influence on Japanese puppetry, and cite late eighth-century references when a Chinese-language Buddhist text mentions *kugutsu*, a term which later became associated with puppets (see Tschudin 2009 and 2011 for more on Japan). Early manipulators were called *kugutsu mawashi* (itinerant puppeteers). The oldest figure is from the Nara period (710–84), about 15 cm, with movable arms and a rod from one leg. Similar figures could be used as a prelude to *bugaku* dances, the dance/mask/music genre associated with the imperial court. Shinto female ritual specialists (*miko*) in shrines sometimes use figures similarly in dances. *Sarugaku* (literally 'monkey music', the antecedents of *noh*) and *gigaku* (Buddhist processional dance) could include puppets, masks, and/or lion body-puppet figures. *Kairaishi-ki* (Record on Puppeteers) of Ōe no Masafusa (1041–111) described travelling low-class puppeteers whose women were prostitutes. Low-status performers were attached to Buddhist shrines. In *Shin Sarugaku ki* (Record on New Monkey Music, 10th century) there is discussion of 1 m puppet figures wrestling sumo. In 1416, in *Kanmon Goki* (Record of Things Seen and Heard), Prince Sadafu discusses puppets in court entertainments. Firework figures were known, and *matsuri* (festivals) floats, which included figures with mechanisms inside to make them move, date from this period. Today, such *karakuri ningyō*, probably inspired by Chinese mechanical figures, are still paraded; lions appear as festival figures. Rod figures in the Muromachi period (1392–1573) were sometimes presented in a box hung from the puppeteer's neck by *Ebisu kaki* (Ebisu [God of Fortune] performers). Puppets included Ebisu and the auspicious old men (Okina, Sambaso, Senzai). This genre is linked to the Sambaso rod puppeteers, whose dance of good luck is still seen in bunraku repertoire. By the seventeenth century, there were three kinds of puppetry: the puppet variant of noh (*noh ayatsuri*), Buddhist miracle play style singing (*sekkyō ayatsuri*), and what would become *ningyō jōruri* (literally 'Princess Jōruri doll'). The last would develop towards bunraku. In ningyō jōruri three elements fused: improved puppets, *gidayū* chanting and musical accompaniment (the three-stringed plucked *shamisen*). The form was named after a popular narrative: *Tale of Princess Jōruri and the Twelve Guardians*. Early plays included *Mido no munewari* (Chest Splitting of Amida Buddha), a miracle play where a girl about to be sacrificed is replaced by the Buddha, perhaps a precedent for the scenes in bunraku where retainers sacrifice their children to save the lord's child. By contrast, *Kimpira bushi* offered tales of swashbuckling heroism, which may have developed as a model for the *aragoto* (strong character) of Tokyo (Edo) kabuki and bunraku. Temples and palaces were the original sites for puppet presentations, but as cities developed the puppeteers established themselves in the entertainment quarters. In time, temporary enclosures with cloth masking and painted backdrops gave way to permanent theatres. The mechanism of the puppets advanced; Takeda Omi opened a theatre in 1662 that featured mechanical *karakuri* figures, and puppetry shared innovations – a beautiful woman could suddenly transform into a demon if desired.

In Edo, chanters such as Satsuma Jōun (1593–1669) and Sugiyama Tango-no-jō established themselves. In Osaka, the rivalry between two theatres led to further advances. Most important was the Takemoto-za where Chikamatsu Monzaemon (1653–1725) was the noted author. From a samurai family, he wrote for kabuki also, but ultimately opted for puppetry where the narrator stayed truer to the text. Chikamatsu crafted stories about epic heroes and introduced tragic tales where the lovers (usually a townsman and his geisha beloved) are caught between duty (*giri*) and human feeling (*ninjō*). A love suicide resolves the predicament. Life imitated art as more suicidal lovers imitated the shows and then shows glorified their stories. Takemoto Gidayū (1651–1714) in time developed the important chanting style that still bears his name. The Toyatake-za with writer Ki no Kainon (1663–1742) tried to keep pace with the Takemoto-za. Great scripts were developed for puppetry and then borrowed by kabuki, such as *Kanadehon Chūshingura* (1748), a story of forty-seven samurai who revenge their master's death.

The hierarchy was chanter, then musician, followed by manipulators. These stars emerged from the masking to appear visible on the stage. By the 1730s, the three-man manipulation team (head and right hand, left hand, feet) was in place. A descendant of Uemura Bunrakuken's (1751–1810) opened the Bunraku-za in Osaka in 1872. This company gave its name to bunraku.

The twentieth century brought difficulties and cuts as the company struggled with modernization and was acquired by Shikoku, the major entertainment corporation. To cut costs in the mid-nineteenth century, Nishikawa Koryu I created *kuruma* (cart) *ningyō* and the Hachiōjī Company continues this tradition today. *Otome ningyō* (young women's puppetry) was another simplification, which attached the figure to the front of the manipulator's body: a technique now maintained by Hitomi-za. At the end of the Second World War, many of the bunraku properties and puppets had been destroyed and Osaka artists were unsure of the viability of the form.

Progressive puppeteers and conservative members of the troupe split into two groups, but they were eventually reunited. Innovations in stories were tried, but usually the classics sold better and few new works became permanent repertoire. In 1963, the Bunraku Kyōkai (Society) became a non-profit organization. Bunraku was declared an Intangible Cultural Property in 1955, and by 1984 the group was the National Bunraku Theatre with a home in Osaka, but playing in Tokyo and touring. In 2003, bunraku was named a Masterpiece of Intangible Cultural Heritage by UNESCO and many of its artists have been Living National Treasures.

Other important groups include (among others) the Awaji Ningyō Kōkai and Yūki-za (founded 1635). Awaji puppetry is considered folk art and the community group performs for tourists and tours internationally. Women are often featured, while bunraku is always male. The Yuki-za has presented avant-garde works as well as traditional ones.

Meanwhile, all forms of modern puppetry are known in Japan. PUK Theatre was founded in 1929 as La Pupo Klubo by progressive and leftist artist Kawajiri Tōji, then led by his brother Taiji from 1932 to 1994. After the Second World War it emerged as PUK (1947) and became the teaching site for many other modern companies. It has a professional training programme, does TV puppetry, experiments with all puppet types and tours internationally. Its wide repertoire includes *Faustus*, Gogol plays, stories from Miyazawa Kenji, and Chinese myths. Leftist leanings mean political engagement. Much of the puppetry, however, is for child audiences or education.

Major puppet festivals are held regularly, for example at Iida where the annual festival brings national and international artists. The city is the home of a puppet museum founded by Takeda Sennosuke of the Takeda Ningyō-za (Takeda Puppet Theatre), known for television as well as theatre work. Japan is the home of both traditional and modern masters of puppetry, and some have a foot in both worlds.

Southeast Asia

Puppetry reaches an apotheosis in Southeast Asia as the major and generative art. Areas can be divided into the Sinified sphere of Vietnam and Burma, the Thai–Khmer–Lao area, outer islands including the Philippines where puppetry is more recent, and finally the Indonesia-Malay culture area where puppetry is the exemplary art.

Vietnam and Burma

These two nations have historically often shared selected techniques with south China. Vietnam's puppetry (*roi*) includes marionettes, water (*Múa roi nuoc*), rod, glove and shadow puppets, and recent object theatre techniques. *The Complete History of Dai Viet* (1021 CE) tells us that the king's birthday included a miniature mountain with moving bird and animal puppets. The first inscription (1121 CE) referencing water puppetry is from the Doi Pagoda in Nam Ha. It describes a swimming tortoise and fairy dancers – images seen in contemporary presentations. Thay Pagoda, Thay Khe Village, has a water puppet stage from the later Ly period (1533–1708) in its lake for regular performances during temple festivals. The first reference to rod puppetry comes from 1293 in Chinese officials' description of the Vietnamese king's banquet. Today, Vietnamese rod puppets are usually similar to China's wood-head 'bag' puppets with rods under the costume. As in China, we find lanterns displaying moving silhouettes called *en keo quan*. Shadow puppets, formerly in Kien Giang Province, are now extinct. Chinese-style lions and dragons, made of papier-mâché, bamboo and cloth, are danced at Chinese New Year. Firecracker puppets 'dance' and kites can be manipulated, puppet-like. Glove puppets such as Chinese budaixi play at temple festivals. String puppets are popular in Cao Bang province and have bodies, like China's, that are made of woven bamboo.

Water puppetry is associated with the Red River delta and figures are traditionally displayed on a lake or pond with manipulators in a staging house behind a bamboo screen. Puppets (some with rudders) would be attached to long bamboo poles and pushed out under the screen, emerging from murky water. Other figures were run along tracks that circled the pool just below the surface, leading to and from the booth. Figures (30 cm) are usually carved from wood with strings attached along the manipulation pole to move arms and other body parts. Teu, a clown from heaven, opened the show with village gossip (Figure 8.3) then short skits of fishing, boat racing, wrestling, and mythical animals, and then a procession of a scholar successful in his exam followed. The secret mechanisms were guarded by the all-male guilds (*phuong*) until the 1970s, when urban puppeteers from Hanoi, assisted by folklore scholar Nguyen Huy Hong (1992), began studying the art. Today, water puppetry is taught in Hanoi to both genders at Vietnamese National Puppetry Theatre (founded 1956) and Truong Dai hoc San khau – Dien anh (Institute for Performing Arts). Major Hanoi companies are Vietnam National Puppetry Theatre (Central Puppet Theatre) and Thang Long Water Puppet Theatre under Le Van Ngo.

'Land' or modern puppetry began in 1956 when Ho Chi Minh hosted the Czech troupe Radost to teach local artists Soviet-style educational puppetry. The Central Puppet Troupe began from Czech training. Now Vietnam's children's theatre companies often use puppet techniques.

Burma's characteristic puppetry is traditional *yoke thay* (marionettes), perhaps related to China's string puppetry. It dates from the fifteenth century, peaked in the nineteenth century, and is preserved via tourist presentations and instruction at the national arts academy in Rangoon today. Puppets are from 45 to 70 cm and twenty-eight characters are part of a traditional set; sex organs are always depicted, though, beneath costumes, perhaps a sign of tantric roots. A performance begins with the ritual Himantaka (Himalaya) scene. Major stories were taken from *jataka* (Buddha's previous lives) and *Wissantara*; the 'great *jataka*' is a central tale. Burmese dance, where arms hang from elbows and knees bend deep, is affected by marionette aesthetics. Manipulators are hidden behind the painted backdrop before which puppets dance. Performances traditionally

Figure 8.3 Teu is the clown character from Vietnamese water puppetry who comments on village affairs in the water puppet tradition.

(Photo by Brad Clark)

lasted all night for temple festivals and a troupe was comprised of puppeteers, singers and musicians. Significant masters of the twentieth century were U Pan Aye (Mandalay, 1931–), U Thun Gyi (Rangoon) and U Maung Hla (Pagan 1915). Mandalay Marionettes, which plays for tourists nightly, is currently the most active group. The company goes to schools and performs internationally, but local audiences are limited. Contemporary intercultural collaborations and performance art projects are also happening: Amy Trompeteer of Bread and Puppet Circus has collaborated on theatre pieces with Burmese, Thai and European puppeteers in recent years.

Thailand–Cambodia–Laos

The region shares some genres or patterns of China to the north, but court arts and shadow genres link more to Indo-Malay ideas and may be the imprint of older Southeast Asian socio-religious thinking. Fully Chinese genres are practised by Sinophone immigrants, while other genres show Thai or Lao modifications, including rod puppets, marionettes, glove puppets, Chaozhou-style iron rod puppetry and lion dance figures. Contemporary puppetry and object theatre in television and education have also developed.

Puppetry in Thailand can be divided into four major categories: central Thai court performance first recorded in the 1458 Palatine Law; popular performance of central Thailand in the nineteenth and twentieth centuries; regional genres of the Lao northeast and Malay south; and contemporary puppetry influenced by the west.

Nang yai (large opaque leather shadow puppetry) present mostly *Ramakien (Ramayana)* episodes shared with the *khon* (male mask dance) repertoire, dance stances and music. Performances, at annual ceremonies to swear fealty to the monarch, allowed the aristocrat dancers/manipulators to show loyalty to the king as representing divine power on earth. Figures of scenes or individual characters (up to 1.5–1.3 m) dance in front of and behind a 20 m × 3 m screen, as two narrators (*nai nang*) deliver the story to *piphat* orchestra accompaniment. Nang yai was probably influenced by Khmer and Javanese court models. The form is now rare, but is preserved by a number of temple groups that perform for the king's birthday and temple festivals. A ritual homage to teachers is part of Thai traditional forms.

Hun (three-dimensional rod puppetry) may have developed from Chinese influence and the court form *hun luang* (royal puppetry) of 1782 was part of the court entertainment department. The figures, preserved in the national museum in Bangkok, are 30 cm tall and were manipulated above the head in an enclosed booth with a painted backdrop. Elaborate strings along the central rod triggered movements of the arms and legs, emulating postures of mask dancers.

Popular theatre of the eighteenth and nineteenth centuries included marionettes, now infrequent, and *hun krabok*, Chinese-style 'bag' puppets, an urban genre developed by 1893 where viewers purchased tickets. Wooden or papier-mâché heads are fitted on a bamboo central rod and two rods beneath the costume move the hands. The Chinese *Three Kingdoms* and *Phra Abhamani* (based on the Thai romantic novel) were popular stories. Sakorn Yangkiosod, who took the stage name of Joe Louis in honour of the American boxer, was born in 1923 into a troupe. Though the form was outlawed from the 1940s to the 1960s, in the 1970s he revived and innovated the genre as *hun lakon lek*, with figures 70 cm tall, operated by three manipulators dancing in classical style. His grandchildren are current performers at Joe Louis Theatre, which tours internationally. An important figure in contemporary hun krabok rod puppetry is Chakrabhand Posayakrit (1943–), a major painter who restored the huang luang discussed above and innovates hun krabok performances on *Ramayana*, *Three Kingdoms* and other themes, with support from royalty and elite circles.

Marionettes, probably developed under Chinese influence, are mostly in antique shops rather than performances. The shadow puppetry of Lao speakers in northeast Thailand, *nang daloong/pramao*, is comparable to Malay south and Cambodia popular shadow forms (discussed below). Figures are usually opaque and the ubiquitous *kaen*, a reed panpipe, accompanies shows. Rod puppets are also done in Lao areas and in Luang Prabang one can see figures formerly used which correspond to Thai-style *hun krabok*. However, the most active group today does modern object theatre, affected by French Lecoq-style object theatre training.

Nang talung, performed by a solo performer (nai nang), is the translucent shadow theatre of the Malay south and was probably an offshoot of Indonesian-style wayang. Figures (30 cm) have a central 'spine' rod and one to each hand. An open-air booth has a screen about 2 m in length, raised above the ground. The percussion ensemble includes a mixture of Thai and Malay instruments and the language mixes central Thai and southern dialect. *Ramayana* stories have largely been replaced by melodramatic episodes, romantic interludes and uproarious comedy. Clowns have multiplied and are the most popular characters in this form; they remained popular to the late twentieth century. A fraught political situation and rising Islamic anti-theatrical fundamentalism, as well as modernization, threaten the form in the twenty-first century.

Professors trained in America and Europe in puppetry and children's theatre have taught modern hand, rod or string puppetry in Thailand. Graduates may launch educational TV shows, develop performances for children or perform NGO-supported works on topics of social change.

In Cambodia, *nang sbaek thom* (large leather) and *ayang* (puppet) or *nang sbaek touch* (small leather) are found. Wooden puppets (*tokkata*) are now no longer performed but were found in Siem Reap Province before the 1970s.

While the large leather puppets are believed to have been an art of the Angkor period, their current form shows influence from the nineteenth-century Thai teachers invited to the Khmer palace to help reconstruct Khmer arts. The *Reamker*, the Cambodian *Ramayana*, is the main story. The large panel puppets might include 150 in a set: Indrajit/Enthachit (a son of the Demon King of Lanka) saying his farewell to family is 1.3×1.5 m and weighs 8 kg. Presentation to *pin peat* orchestra approximates the Thai model. Indrajit fighting against Prince Ream (Rama) is a favoured scene and Punyakay, Reab's (Ravana's) niece, who disguises herself as Seda's (Sita) corpse, is another repeated scene. *Sampeah kru* (homage to the teachers) remains a feature. Vipassana Center in Siem Reap gives demonstrations and sometimes the troupe connected to the School of Fine Arts will present thi sshadow art, which has been inscribed by UNESCO as a Masterpiece of Oral and Intangible Cultural Heritage of Humanity (2005).

Sbaek touch is similar to Lao/Thai nang daloong with multiple puppet manipulators but is done with a *pin peat* orchestra. *Sang Selachey* (Conch Shell Prince) and other stories are traditional repertoire, but the genre is versatile, and NGOs have adapted the form to spread information about AIDS, sex trafficking and domestic violence. Sovanna Phum, the innovative company led by Mann Kosal, has experimented widely with puppetry on both traditional and modern themes and done international collaborations with Ong Keng Sen of TheatreWorks (Singapore) and American puppeteer Eric Bass.

Philippines

The Philippines puppet tradition dates from at least 1879 when small travelling carts (*carrillo*) presented shadow plays with cardboard figures with *moro-moro* (Christian heroes fight Muslims) repertoire. The form was modelled on European shadow theatre. Meanwhile *Higante*, giant 3 m puppets as seen in Spain, led the procession for the patron fisherman, San Clemente

(23 November), in Angono, Rizal. These *mag anak* (father, mother and child) had bodies made from bamboo and heads of papier-mâché.

Contemporary Filipino puppetry dates to the 1970s, when puppetry became theatre for young audiences. Teatrong Mulat ng Pilipinas (Aware Theatre of the Philippines) was founded in 1977 by Amelia Lapeña-Bonifacio and has garnered international acclaim. *Papet Pasyon* (Puppet Passion Play, 1985) translated the Filipino traditional recitation of Jesus' death for children. The Black Theater of Manila, Philippine Information Agency Puppet Theatre, established by Lolita Aquino in 1978, used black light and hand puppets for information dissemination. The Anino Shadowplay Collective, formed in the 1990s, is a group of multimedia artists: *Florante at Laura*, based on the 1838 metrical romance of Balthazar, represents their work.

Malaysia and Indonesia

Puppetry was not indigenous to the more distant parts of island Southeast Asia. Kalimantan's only shadow theatre seems to have been developed under Javanese influence. We find masking in many areas of Kalimantan, but not indigenous puppetry, though diasporic Chinese here, as elsewhere, presented glove puppets called *po the hi*, Southeast Asian localization of budaixi.

The major form of puppetry traditionally practised in Malaysia is shadow theatre. The *wayang kulit* (leather puppetry) had developed by the eighteenth century under Javanese and Siamese (Thai) cultural influences. As in all forms of wayang kulit, the *dalang* (puppet master) is the ritual specialist, manipulator and narrator. The silhouettes of up to 1 m are finely cut, painted, and projected on a cotton screen. The orchestra of oboe (*serunai*), drums and gongs plays a fundamental role.

Wayang kelantan (earlier called *wayang siam)* is the most important Malay genre and, like all Malaysian traditional performances, is in danger of disappearing. *Wayang gedek* has only a few performers in Kedah and Perlis: it is considered a variation on Thai nang talung, but with figures full face (rather than profile as in Thailand) and speech in Kedah dialect. *Wayang kulit purwa* and *wayang kulit melayu* are Javanese-derived leather shadow forms, which have largely vanished.

Wayang kelantan and nang talung may only have grown apart because Siam ceded Kelantan (previously part of Patani, Thailand) to the British with the Bangkok Treaty (1909). Kelantan lore claims that Mak Erak, a Siamese woman who studied wayang in Java, established the art. *Hikyat Seri Rama* (the Malay *Ramayana*) is the source and Maharaja Wana (Rawana) the featured character. Dialogue is in Kelantanese. The figures are in profile and have a movable arm. Well-known dalang of the recent period are Hamzah bin Awang Amat (1940–2001), a National Artist, who was a dalang, musician, shaman and puppet maker. Dollah Baju Merah (Dollah 'Red Shirt', 1940–2005) and Dalang Nik Mat (1951–) have been other significant artists. With the advent of modern entertainments and attacks by the PAS-led (Parti Islam Se-Malaysia) state government since 1991, it became hard to get permission to perform in Kelantan. Non-Islamic rituals and the *Ramayana* repertoire caused banning.

Modern Malay puppetry is found. For example, new multimedia artists such as Fairuz Sulaiman create experimental shows. His *Main Wayang: Hikyat Sang Kancil* (Playing Shadows: Story of Master Mouse Deer, 2014) used digital animation, V-Jing, puppetry, music and live drawing to explore environmental and social issues in contemporary Kuala Lumpur.

In Indonesia, wayang, as previously mentioned, is considered the oldest art and model for human theatre (wayang wong) (Figure 8.4). Though today we see innovations including Wayang Hip Hop (whose web page reads 'combining Javanese tradition and hip-hop beats')

Figure 8.4 Arjuna, the *Mahahbharata* hero, with his arms crossed in meditation in Wayang
Kulit Purwa of Java.

(Photo by Kathy Foley)

or performance artist Slamet Gundhono (1966–2013), a sumo-sized dalang who used woven grass puppets and dramatic acting in his stories making modern political points, puppetry in Indonesian in the twenty-first century remains largely rooted in wayang. The art has been intensely studied by international artists, from Julie Taymor and Larry Reed to western dalangs such as Mathew Cohen and Kathy Foley, author of this chapter. The art was declared a UNESCO Masterpiece of Oral and Intangible Cultural Heritage of Humanity in 2003. Wayang is a style of presenting traditional theatre in which a central puppet master/narrator or dalang is in control of both ritual and performance aspects. He, or sometimes she, delivers all the mood songs, narration and dialogue, using a wooden hammer to cue the *gamelan* orchestra and make sound effects. The dalang dances all the puppets whose movements create an aesthetic that the actor-dancer will try to follow. Shadow puppetry (wayang kulit) uses flat, perforated hide figures from 30–70 cm with three control rods: one central rod is the 'spine' and two others are attached to the hands. In some areas the dalang is also a master of the solo mask dance and both mask and puppets have ritual connections. Wayang performances are usually presented for life-cycle ceremonies (i.e. weddings or circumcisions).

The first reference to wayang comes from 907 CE when Java had already experienced Indian influence. Some feel that the art, like the stories, originated in India. Others wonder if Chinese models were involved: rod puppets (*wayang golek*), which developed on the north coast, may be Chinese influenced. Others maintain Sufi or indigenous invention, but wayang is old. *Arjuna's Meditation* (*Arjuna Wiwaha*, c. 1035) states, 'There are people who weep and are sad and aroused watching the puppets, though they know they are merely carved pieces of leather manipulated and made to speak.' The fourteenth-century *History of the Rajas of Pasai* states that shadow plays 'went on day and night in the kingdom of Majapahit'.

Some feel that Java's past is alive in Hindu–Buddhist Bali whose 300 *dalang* say they maintain the arts of pre-Islamic Java of the sixteenth century. The rituals in the *Dharma Pawayangan* (Book of the Dalang) include making holy water and old practices. Balinese figures resemble images on Majapahit temples in East Java. Noble characters speak Kawi, puppeteers' versions of old Javanese, while the clowns translate into contemporary Balinese. The normal streamlined troupe of one puppeteer and four metallophone players, the four-hour duration (9 a.m. to 1 p.m.) and the mantras probably reflect old practices. Viewers usually watch the shadow side of the screen, unlike Java where puppet side is normal. Dalang combine ritual powers, philosophy and entertainment. Specific plays such as *Bima Goes to Heaven* are required for cremations. Major dalang include I Wayan Wija (1952–), who innovated new animal puppets and new repertoire, *Tantri* stories – where a woman preserves herself by telling stories to a misogynist king – and Cenk Blonk (I Wayan Nardayana, 1966–), whose name comes from his clowns Nang Klenceng and Nang Ceblong. Cenk Blonk uses coloured lights, a greatly enlarged gamelan, female and male singers, a wider screen, and other innovations. Women have entered Balinese wayang only since 1974.

Central Javanese *wayang* was recalibrated from Hindu forms in the period of Islamization, beginning in the fifteenth century when the *wali* (Islamic saints) are believed to have converted the island by performing wayang. Sunan Kalijaga (1460–?), son of a regent of Tuban, is considered the ur-dalang. Performances were given, it is said, in the mosque and people 'paid' by saying the *sahadat*, avowing God and the Prophet.

There are myriad forms of wayang but almost all follow the rules of the *wayang kulit purwa* (*Mahabharata* and *Ramayana* tales). Most performances are not trunk (*galur*) stories, but branch (*ranting*) tales which tell of Hindu-derived heroes in stories invented in Java. Contemporary dalang see themselves as 'descendants of the wali' and say they use Hindu-derived tales to teach Islamic truths. The central Javanese puppet show has parts that correlate to three different parts of life (birth, adolescence, and our struggle ending in death), with accompanying musical shifts by the gamelan orchestra. The god-clown Semar is a high god of the universe who hides in his half-male and half-female body. Wayang history reconciles Hindu epics and Javanese history: Roden Ngabehi. Rangawarsita (1802–73), Surakarta courtier, in *Pustaka Raja* (History of Kings) traced the descent of Javanese kings from epic/purwa heroes on one side and biblical Adam and Koranic Prophets on the other. Javanese dalang continue to explore such artful interpretations of the past. K. G. Boeminata, a younger brother of the king Paku Buwana IV (1788–1820), commissioned famous sets of figures and taught B. P. K. Kusumadilaga, who wrote the *Serat Sastramiruda* to systematize music and outline plays. Great dalang of the past and present are multitudinous. Recent superstars include Nartosabdo (1925–85) who revolutionized music and was known for his clowning. Enthus Sumono (1966–), called *dalang edan* ('crazy dalang') in the 1990s, would have George Bush fighting Saddam Hussein in clown scenes with coloured lights, multiple female singers, media effects and other innovations, bringing him huge audiences.

In the early nineteenth century, Sundanese *wayang golek purwa* was born as puppet masters from Cirebon on Java's north coast migrated into the Sundanese highlands of West Java. Puppeteers who normally did stories from the Hindu epics, using leather figures and *wayang golek cepak* (rod puppets telling Amir Hamzah or Javanese tales), after migrating began doing the Hindu stories with the rod puppet figures. The figures on display at the Museum Pangeran (Prince's Museum) in Sumedang, West Java may be the oldest. The Great Sundanese puppeteers of the twentieth century came from the Sunarya clan in Jelekong, Ciparay in the Bandung area. Abah [Abeng] Sunarya, active from the 1950s, and Asep Suandar (1955–2014) were superstars. Abah might in the 1970s do a *ruwatan* (exorcistic) performance in which the high god of the universe has let his son, Demon Kala, eat people, thus providing critique of President Suharto whose offspring enriched themselves at the expense of Indonesia. Asep might portray brothers of Queen Arimbi in the *Mahabrarata* as male chauvinists blocking her rule, criticizing sexism faced by the female candidate Megawati Soekarnoputri who was elected president in 2001. Uproarious humour, musical innovation, TV appearances and multimedia were part of the family's dominance in West Java.

Lack of space prevents detailing the many other genres of wayang: anyone can take a music/language area (i.e. Java, Bali, Sunda), select the favoured medium (leather puppets, rod puppets, flat wooden puppets [*klitik*], masks, unmasked dance-actors) and repertoire (purwa [Hindu epic], *gedog* [Panji], *menak* [Amir Hamzah, chronicles], *suluh* [Indonesian independence], *Buddha* [Jataka], Shakespeare and so on), and by mixing the three elements come up with a 'new' genre, thus resulting in the dozens of 'genres' one encounters in Indonesian lists of types of wayang. Nor will I be able to discuss endangered species such as *wayang* sasak of Lombok where Islamic fundamentalism threatens continuance, or discuss *wayang beber* (scroll puppetry) and so on. But while contestations and changes take place, puppetry retains a pre-eminent role in arts and heritage discourse. Modern puppetry on TV and in modern theatre exists, but is generally less important than traditional practice and new twists on traditional wayang.

Why has Southeast Asian for over a millennium been so oriented towards puppetry? Perhaps because of a philosophical orientation that sees the different types, from demon to divine, as not really separate, but as sides of the self. As the dalang puts the 'good guy' on his right hand and the 'demon king' on his left, he is stating a human truth. The characters may be tuned by a different note on the gamelan for the puppet voice and a different walk from smooth to jerky, but everything comes from one source. Puppets are a tool to see ourselves and the universe clearly and see it whole. Demon and divine, male and female, old and young – what seems opposites is really one. Puppetry helps one think macrocosmically even as one lives out a microcosmic life, and understanding this is the dalang's and puppetry's world view.

Note

1 Material in this chapter often depends on information from the UNIMA-International, *World Encyclopedia of Puppetry Arts* edited by Karen Smith and scheduled to appear on a website sponsored by UNIMA (forthcoming). Entries began with publication in *Encyclopédie mondiale des Arts de la Marionnette* (UNIMA 2009), but most have been significantly updated or revised. As the Asia editor, compiler, contributing author, or author of most of these pieces, I worked on Asian country, company and artist entries and those give greater detail than this chapter can, especially on modern troupes. I acknowledge especially Lucie Rault (see UNIMA 2009), Tang Dayu and Fan Chen's contributions on China, Jean-Jacques Tschudin (2011, UNIMA 2009) on Japan, and Amelia Lapena-Bonifacio on the Philippines. I am indebted among many others to the writing and conversations of/with Matthew Cohen on Java and I Nyoman Sedana on Bali. The sources of this broad chapter are too many to list, but readers are directed to the bibliography in UNIMA (2009). Any mistakes are solely my own.

Bibliography

General

Baird, Bil (1965) *The Art of the Puppet*, New York: Macmillan.
Foley, Kathy (ed.) (2001) Special Issue on Puppetry, *Asian Theatre Journal* 18 (1).
Tilkasari, J. (1968) *The Puppet Theatre of Asia*, Ceylon: Department of Cultural Affairs.
UCLA Museum of Cultural History, ed. Melvin Helstien (1976) *Asian Puppets: Wall of the World*, Los Angeles: University of California.
UNIMA (2009) *Encyclopédie Mondial des Arts de la Marionnette*, Montpellier: Editions l'Entretemps.

South Asia

Awasthi, Suresh (2001) *Performance Tradition in India*, New Delhi: National Book Trust, India.
Blackburn, Stuart (1996) *Inside the Drama-House: Rama Stories and Shadow Puppets in South India*, Berkeley: University of California Press.
Chatterjee, A. (ed.) (1990) *Sangeet Natak* 98 (G. Venu, 'The Traditional Puppet Theatre of Kerala'; Jiwan Pani, 'Shadow Puppetry and Ravana Chhaya of Orissa'; K. S. Upadhayay, 'The Puppet Theatre Tradition of Karanataka'; M. Nagabhushama Sarma, 'The Shadow Puppet Tradition of Andhara Pradesh'; Venkat Swaminathan, 'Puppet Theatre in Tamil Nadu').
Contractor, Meher R. (1968) *Puppets of India*, Mumbai: Marg.
Coomaraswamy, A. K. (1929) 'Picture Showmen', *Indian Historical Quarterly*, 2.
Goldberg Belle, Jonathan (1984) 'The Performance Poetics of Tolubommalata: A South Asian Shadow Puppet Tradition', MA Thesis, University of Wisconsin-Madison.
Orenstein, Claudia (2015) 'Women in Indian Puppetry: Negotiating Traditional Roles and New Possibilities', *Asian Theatre Journal*, 33 (2).
Pani, Jiwan (1986) *Living Dolls – Story of Indian Puppets*, New Delhi: Publication Division, Govt. of India.
Pischel, Richard (1902) *The Home of the Puppet Play*, trans. Mildred Tawney. London: Luzac and Co., Publishers to the India Office.
'Puppet India.com' (2001) www.puppetindia.com/contents1.htm, accessed 15 April 2013.
Schuster, Michael (2001) 'Visible Puppets and Hidden Puppeteers: Indian *Gombeyata* Puppetry', *Asian Theatre Journal*, 18 (1), 59–68.

East Asia

China

Chen, Fan Pen (2007) *Chinese Shadow Theatre History, Popular Religion, and Women Warriors*, Montreal: McGill-Queen's University Press.
Mair, Victor (1988) *Painting and Performance: Chinese Picture Recitation and Its Indian Genesis*, Honolulu: University of Hawai'i Press.
Rault, Lucie (2009) 'China', in *Encyclopédie Mondial des Arts de la Marionnette*, Montpellier: Editions l'Entretemps.
Rault, Lucie, and Tang Dayu (Forthcoming) 'China', Fan Chen and Kathy Foley (ed. and trans), in UNIMA/Karen Smith (eds) *World Encyclopedia of Puppet Arts*, online.
Rollins, Annie (2015). 'Chinese Shadow Puppetry's Changing Apprentice System: Questions of Continuance and a Survey of Remaining Shadow Puppet Practitioners in Mainland China 2008–2013', *Asian Theatre Journal*, 32 (1): 295–318.
Ruizendaal, Robin Erik (2006) *Marionette Theatre in Quanzhou*, Leiden: Brill.
Stalberg, Roberta (1984) *China's Puppets*, San Francisco: China Books.
Wimsatt, Genevieve (1936) *Chinese Shadows Shows*, Cambridge, MA: Harvard University Press.

Korea

Anseong Municipal Namsadang Baudeogi Pungmuldan, www.namsadangnori.org/e3.htm, accessed 2 January 2012.
Cho, Oh Kon (1979) *Korean Puppet Theatre: KKoktu Kaksi*, East Lansing, MI: Asian Studies Center, Michigan State University.

Foley, Kathy (2015) 'Korean Puppets in Performance: Translating Traditions', in *The Routledge Companion to Puppetry and Material Performance*, Dassia Possner, Claudia Orenstein, and John Bell (eds), New York: Routledge.

Hyundai Puppet Theatre Presents, *Deong Deong Kung Ta Kung*, www.youtube.com/watch?v=KzAXk8 MYUyI, accessed 6 January 2013.

—— (2011?) 'The Puppet City – Hyundai Puppet Theatre', www.youtube.com/watch?v=KzAXk8 MYUyI, accessed 4 January 2013.

—— (2008) *Traditional Performing Arts of Korea*, Min Eun-young (trans), Seoul: Korea Foundation.

'Kokkdu', www.youtube.com/watch?v=yaSJuQr3Iv0, accessed 2 January 2012.

Jeon Kyung-wook (2008) *Traditional Performing Arts of Korea*, Min Eun-young (trans), Seoul: Korea Foundation.

'Namsadang Nori' (2009) [UNESCO Intangible Cultural Heritage List], www.unesco.org/culture/ich/RL/00184, Accessed 4 January 2013.

Sim Woo-Song (1997) '*Namsadang*: Wandering Folk Troupes', *Koreana: Korean Art and Culture*, 11 (2): 44–9.

Japan

Adachi, Barbara (1985) *Backstage at Bunraku*, NY: Weatherhill.

Brandon, James (ed.) (1982) *Chûshingura: Studies in Kabuki and the Puppet Theater*, Honolulu: University of Hawai'i Press.

Dunn, Charles J. (1966) *The Early Puppet Drama in Japan*, London: Luzac.

Japan Arts Council (2004) 'The Puppet Theatre Of Japan: Bunraku', www2.ntj.jac.go.jp/unesco/bunraku/en/index.html, accessed 20 June 2014.

Gerstle, Andrew (1986) *Circles of Fantasy: Convention in the Plays of Chikamatsu*, Cambridge, MA: Harvard University Press.

—— (2001) *Chikamatsu's Five Late Plays*, New York: Columbia University Press.

Jones, Stanleigh (1985) *Sugawara and the Secrets of Calligraphy*, New York: Columbia University Press.

—— (1991) *Yoshitsune and the Thousand Cherry Trees*, New York: University of Columbia Press.

Keene, Donald (trans) (1951) *The Battles of Coxinga*, London: Cambridge University Press.

—— (1961) *Major Plays of Chikamatsu*, NY: Columbia University Press.

—— (1965) *Bunraku, the Puppet Theatre of Japan*, Tokyo: Kodansha International.

Law, Jean Marie (1997) *Puppets of Nostalgia: The Life, Death, and Rebirth of the Awaji Ningyō Tradition*, Princeton: Princeton University Press.

Tschudin, Jean-Jacques (2009) 'Japan', in *Encyclopédie Mondial des Arts de la Marionnette*, Montpellier: Editions l'Entretemps.

—— (2011) *Histoire du theatre classique Japonais*, Toulouse: Anacharsis Editions.

Southeast Asia

Vietnam

Foley, Kathy (2001) 'The Metonomy of Art: Vietnamese Water Puppetry as a Representation of Modern Vietnam', *TDR* 45 (4): 129–41.

Jones, Margo (1996) 'The Art of Vietnamese Water Puppetry: A Theatrical Genre Study', PhD Dissertation, University of Hawai'i.

Nguyen Huy Hong, and Tran Trung Chinh (1996) *Vietnamese Traditional Water Puppetry*, Hanoi: Thê Giói Publishers.

Burma

Foley, Kathy (2001). 'Burmese Marionettes: *Yokthe Thay* in Transition', *Asian Theatre Journal* 18 (1): 69–81.

Ma Thanegi (1994) *The Illusion of Life: Burmese Marionnettes*, Bangkok: White Orchid Press.

Singer, Noel (1992) *Burmese Puppets*, Singapore: Oxford University Press.

Thailand

Bretton, Bonnie (2007) 'Traditional Shadow Theatre of Northeastern Thailand (*Nang Promo Thai*): Hardy Transplant or Endangered Species?', *Aseanea* (19): 113–42, www.academia.edu/6192706/Traditional_

Shadow_Theatre_of_Northeastern_Thailand_Nang_Pramo_Thai_Hardy_Transplant_or_Endangered_
Species, accessed 14 June 2014.

Broman, Sven (1996) *Shadows of Life: 'Nang Talung' Thai Popular Shadow Theatre*, Bangkok: White Orchid.

Chandavij, Natthapatra, and Pomporn Pramualratana (1998) *Thai Puppets and Khon Masks*, Bangkok: River
Books.

Dhaninivat, H.H. Prince [Kromamum Bidyalabh Brindhayakorn] (1968) *Shadow Play* (*The* 'Nang'),
Bangkok: Fine Arts Dept.

Dowsey-Magog, Paul (2002) 'Popular Workers' Shadow Theatre in Thailand', *Asian Theatre Journal*, 19
(1): 184–211.

Smithies, Michael, and Euayporn Kerdchouay (1975) 'Nang Talaung: The Shadow Theatre of Southern
Thailand', in Matini Rutnin (ed.) *The Siamese Theatre*, Bangkok: Siam Society.

Virulrak, Surapone, and Kathy Foley (2001) '*Hun*: Thai Doll Puppetry', *Asian Theatre Journal* 18 (1): 81–86

Cambodia

Kravel Pech Tum (1995) *Sbek Thom: Khmer Shadow Theater*, Ithaca, NY: Cornell University Southeast
Asia Program and UNESCO.

Phim, Toni Samantha, and Ashley Thompson (1999) *Dance in Cambodia*, New York: Oxford University
Press.

Philippines

Bonifacio, Amihan L. (1999) 'Trends and Development in Philippine Puppet Theater', *Diliman Review*,
47 (3–4): 25–31.

Fernandez, D. G. (1994) 'Puppet Theater', in *CCP Encyclopedia of Philippine Art*, Volume 7, Manila: Cultural
Center of the Philippines.

Malaysia

Ghulam-Sawar Yousef (1992) *Panggung Semar*, Selangor, Malaysia: Tempo Publishing.

Matusky, Patricia (1993) *Malaysian Shadow Play and Music: Continuity of an Oral Tradition*, Kuala Lumpur:
Oxford University Press.

Sweeny, Amin (1972) *Malay Shadow Puppets: The Wayang Siam of Kelantan*, London: British Museum.

Indonesia

Brandon, James (1970) *On Thrones of Gold, Three Javanese Shadow Plays*, Cambridge, MA: Harvard
University Press.

Cohen, Matthew Isaac (2008) 'Puppetry and the Destruction of the Object', *Performance Research* 12 (4):
123–31.

—— (2010) *Performing Otherness: Java and Bali on International Stages, 1905–1952*, Basingstoke: Palgrave
Macmillan.

—— (2014) 'Traditional and Post-Traditional *Wayang kulit* in Java Today', in John Bell, Claudia Orenstein,
and Dassia N. Posner (eds), *The Routledge Companion to Puppetry and Material Performance*, London:
Routledge.

Foley, Kathy (1993) 'Indonesia', in James R. Brandon (ed.)*Cambridge Guide to Asian Theatre*, Cambridge,
MA: Cambridge University Press.

Groenendael, Victoria M. Clara Van (1985) *The Dalang Behind the Wayang*, Dordrecht, Holland: Foris
Publications.

Herbert, Mimi (2002) *Voices of the Puppet Masters: The Wayang Golek Theatre of Indonesia*, Honolulu: University
of Hawai'i Press.

Sears, Laurie (1996) *Shadows of Empire; Colonial Discourse and Javanese Tales*, Durham, NC: Duke University
Press.

Soebardi, S. (1975) *Book of Cabolek*, La Haye: Martinus Nijhoff.

Sunarya, Abah, and Gamelan Giri Harja I (2001) 'The Origin of Kala: A Sundanese *Wayang Golek Purwa*
Play by Abah Sunarya and Gamelan Giri Harja I,' Kathy Foley (trans), *Asian Theatre Journal*, 18 (1):
1–58.

Weintraub, Andrew (2004) *Power Play, Wayang Golek Theater of West Java*, Athens: Ohio University Press.

Zurbuchen, Mary (1987) *The Language of Balinese Shadow Theatre*, Princeton: Princeton University Press.

9

Costume and makeup in traditional Asian theatre

David Mason, Alexandra Bonds, Monica Bethe,
Kirstin Pauka and Lauren Meeker

Elaborately patterned and brilliantly coloured costumes, accessories and makeup (especially painted faces) offer some of the most indelible images of Asian theatre. Using representative examples from traditional Indian, Chinese, Japanese and Southeast Asian theatre, this chapter provides a concise and technical guide to the colour mechanisms, imagery symbolisms, costume categories and makeup design patterns, as well as hair and accessories of some of the best-known genres of Asian theatre.

I. India, by David Mason

In the second century BCE, the Sanskrit grammarian Patanjali indicated incidentally that makeup has been important to traditional theatre in India for two thousand years or more. While trying to illustrate how causal forms of verbs are used, the grammarian writes: '[In] the presentation of Kamsa's killing by Vâsudeva, there are two groups of persons (actors), the followers of Kamsa are in red colour and those of Vâsudeva-Krsn---a in blue ["black" or "dark", from the Sanskrit *kala*]' (Baumer and Brandon 1993: 13). Many scholars read this passage as an indication that Patanjali's reference was a theatrical performance in which the faces of the actors were painted with colours having some conventional significance. We find a history in India of conventional colour schemes in stage makeup, and even today several important traditional theatre forms employ heavily stylized face paint with conventional colours and configurations.

The *Natyasastra*, a classical manual written in northern India by the fifth century CE, reveals that some conventions persist over long periods of time. At least, the qualities of the two colours suggested by Patanjali seem to have still been in place at the time when the *Natyasastra* was composed. In the *Natyasastra*'s crucial sixth chapter, we find that blue-ness or dark-ness (from the Sanskrit *shyama*) is associated with Vishnu and his incarnations (such as Krishna, as noted by Patanjali) and red is associated with villainy, or, at least, with the disruptive and destructive force of anger. In this chapter, the author of the shastra associates eight colours with the eight aesthetic states the author calls *rasa*. A later chapter (23 in some editions) theorizes that body paint should obscure the actor's body as much as possible, so as to strengthen the presence of the character in the performance. Indeed, the *Natyasastra* regards the painted body as the character's own body, 'concealing' the actor's body, and asserts that behind heavy, highly stylized makeup, the actor more fully becomes the character he or she plays (Rangacharya 2003: 178). This chapter also prescribes a range of colours for specific characters without much reflection on its colour scheme of chapter six. In fact, this later examination of makeup has much less interest in the ethical and emotional qualities of colours, preferring, instead, to associate colours with specific classes of characters and with what seem to be ethnic regions. Here, various shades of red are most common, suited to brahmins, kings and warriors. Blue is relatively insignificant in this chapter, and yellow seems to be more significant. Perhaps the important element of this chapter for tracing the history of makeup in Indian theatre is the *Natyasastra*'s confession that makeup schemes necessarily vary according to regional customs (Rangacharya 2003: 179). Generally, from the time of the *Natyasastra*, makeup has been extremely important to traditional theatre. In most traditional forms, makeup schemes are highly stylized, and often have some sense that colour indicates some quality of a character.

Perhaps best known among these forms is *kathakali*, in which opaque face paint entirely covers the actors' faces, and can take hours to apply. The paint colours are flat, plain and simple: green, red, black, orange and white, without intermediate shades or gradients. One colour is usually dominant, though two or three colours may be combined in bold patterns. Adopted in the seventeenth century from conventions already established by *kutiyattam* and other regional forms, the colours signify characters' qualities. Dominant colours, accordingly, indicate the dominance in a character of a particular quality, as explained below. Colours and patterns combine to identify a limited number of character classes.

In contrast with what the *Natyasastra* expects, green rather than blue, in kathakali, indicates virtue, and often appears as the face of divinity, virtue's logical extreme. The faces of exemplary heroes of sacred literature, such as Yuddhisthira and Rama, who are frequent protagonists in kathakali, will be almost exclusively green, as will the faces of gods such as Krishna. These characters will also wear the *cutti*, a wide, white trimming for the face that is one of the most distinctive makeup features of kathakali and kutiyattam. On heroic, or *pacca*, characters, the cutti is affixed to the actor's jawline with rice paste to frame the actor's face and to lend the character special dignity. In the past century, the cuṭṭi was made of rice paste and yarn that was painstakingly layered to form the facial frame (Zarrilli 1984: 171). Contemporary practice has adapted material such as styrofoam and as simple as plain printer paper, cut to the proper shape and pasted to the jaw (Figure 9.1).

Kathakali characters whose faces are red, the *cuvanna tati* characters, are the opposite of the green heroes. These evil and despicable characters also wear red beards (*tati*). Rather than framing their faces from below, white trimming obscures the upper part of their faces, flashing out from the cheekbones as though grossly exaggerated moustaches. The makeup of these villain characters also includes a white bulb, glued to the end of the actor's nose. These characters also often have fangs.

Between the green and red characters is an intermediate class of characters, the *katti* characters, who are not wholly evil nor wholly virtuous, either, and their makeup, which combines green and red patterns, swirled around each other, indicates this complexity. These characters not only wear the cutti along their jawlines, but also have white nose pieces, though these will usually be distinctly smaller than the pieces worn by red villains.

The *kari* characters, whose makeup is almost exclusively black, are also evil, like their red counterparts, but their colouring suggests a certain indeterminacy in their development. The male characters of this sort wear black beards and white nose bulbs, and are often uncivilized characters, monsters of the forest or otherwise inimical to the society of heroes and gods. Female characters of this sort are invariably demons, and are the most loathsome of the kathakali characters.

Figure 9.1 Kutiyattam makeup and costume.
(Photo by David Mason)

Some kathakali characters whose face paint may be dominated by red also wear white beards. These *vella tati* characters are not evil, but are derived to some extent from the animal world. Other animal characters, especially birds – classified as *teppu* or 'special' characters – are of another class that employs miscellaneous makeup devices, including masks. The makeup of a final class of human characters, the *minukku* – sages, messengers, servants – and virtually all non-demonic female characters is dominated by a plain, soft orange colour, without the flourishes of design found among the other classes.

One final element of kathakali makeup is worth mentioning. Just prior to performance, kathakali actors will put a tiny cantappuvu seed beneath each of their lower eyelids (Zarrilli 2000: 57). The seed, hand-rubbed for an hour prior to performance, turns the whites of the actors' eyes a fearsome red. This eye-reddening contributes to the overall otherworldly quality of kathakali characters, and in the intimate conditions in which kathakali is traditionally performed, it can have an impressive, even imposing effect on audiences.

The makeup of other performance forms of southern India – *terukkuttu, theyyam, yakshagana* and so on – show the influence of kutiyattam and kathakali. The amplified makeup in these performance forms is intended to minimize the presence of the actors and to set characters apart from everyday life, to distinguish them – whether divine or demonic, heroic or villainous – as being of another world and of another order. Theyyam, perhaps, merits special attention for pushing the transformation of the actor through makeup to a special extreme. Deliberately spanning the line between theatre and ritual, this Keralan dance-drama combines burdensome costume pieces and vivid, impenetrable makeup to erase the actor-dancer almost completely, in favour of the divinity the costume and makeup embody. The dominant colour – for theyyam's costumes and makeup – is red.

In northern India, makeup schemes tend to be less opaque and less fixed in convention, though they are still intended to announce characters' otherworldliness. In *râs lila* theatre, which dramatizes the stories of Krishna's childhood, makeup does not entirely obscure the young actors' faces (Figure 9.2). Instead, the faces of divine characters – Krishna, Radha and the girls of the village – are decorated with simple designs of plain white dots and lines, which tend to magnify the actors' own faces. Makeup in *ramlila* theatre has adopted râs lila designs. In both traditions, other, non-divine, characters mostly appear without patterned designs, although the villains are often identified using conventions that correspond with the designs of nineteenth-century melodrama – oversized, fierce, black moustaches, angled eyebrows of thick, black paint and dark circles around the eyes.

One common element between northern and southern traditions is the *tilak*. Religious characters – in conformity with the practice of religious people in India – will wear forehead markings called tilaks, the design of which is conditioned by the local style and performance form, and which indicate the religious tradition with which the wearer identifies. Tilak patterns can be complex. In general terms, tilaks distinguish between Vaishnavites and Shaivites, or devotees of Vishnu and of Shiva. Vertical lines on the forehead are most often associated with

Figure 9.2 Râs lila makeup and costume.
(Photo by David Mason)

Vishnu devotion. Horizontal lines most often suggest Shiva devotion. The makeup designs of characters in theatre performances will often incorporate a tilak to indicate characters' religious identities. For instance, the makeup designs of the râs lîlâ characters associated with Krishna – regarded as a manifestation of Vishnu – will incorporate vertical forehead lines. The makeup of a kathakali character such as Kiratha – Shiva himself in disguise – will incorporate distinctly horizontal forehead lines.

The secular forms of northern India, including *nautanki, bhavai and tamasha*, use highly conventional makeup devices in the tradition of râs lila and ramlila – fright wigs and beards, oversized crowns of glittering tinfoil, garish swathes of makeup that make the actors' eyes leap out, and so on. These devices found their way into film and television in the twentieth century, especially where these media made explicit attempts to reach the audiences which had developed their aesthetic and spiritual expectations from theatre such as râs lila or nautanki. Hence, Raj Kapoor's 1955 film *Sri 420*, one of the best-known Bollywood films, mostly strives for naturalism in its makeup design, but the villain played by Nemo nevertheless sports a grossly artificial, black moustache.

Traditional theatre makeup in India, while including very disparate regional styles, collectively eschews attempts to mimic the natural world. Makeup in these performance forms is intended to set the actors aside, and to set the characters they play apart from the world their audiences inhabit. Certainly the characters of India's many religious theatre traditions are intended to be seen as transcendent of the material world. Even the characters of the so-called secular forms of theatre are meant to be seen as entities from another time and another place, elevated by history and myth.

Very few traditional theatre forms in India rely on masks. The outstanding exceptions are the varieties of *chhau* dance-drama. There are three major types of chhau: Purulia, Mayurbhanj and Saraikela, associated with the West Bengal, Bihar and Orissa regions, respectively. Purulia and Saraikela chhau rely on masks. Historically the artistic domain of the region's farming classes, the dance-drama form developed from martial training. Chhau's characters appear in hand-made wood, muslin and papier-mâché masks, which are regarded as art objects in themselves. The Saraikela masks have a graceful simplicity, while the Purulia masks tend to be more ornate and fearsome.

II. China, by Alexandra Bonds

Over 300 forms of indigenous theatre entertainment incorporating song, dance and music have evolved in China, and these forms of music drama are commonly translated as Chinese opera. One of these forms, *jingju* (Beijing opera), established in the eighteenth century and based in the capital city, is the most widespread and influential of the theatre forms, having been nationally dominant for over one hundred years. Though each of the regional forms of music drama have their own conventions for costuming, there are shared characteristics that intersect among the varying genres. The costumes of jingju are described below as a representative example of this style.

Throughout the history of the China, clothing designated status, rank and position in society, expressed through significant colours, embroidered symbols and specific garments. Traditional theatre emerging in this rank- and clothing-conscious framework logically absorbed the language of design, emphasizing clothing details for the identification of characters. As the costumes of traditional jingju developed, they deviated from imperial dress, since actors were prohibited from wearing garments and emblems that contained references to rank and status not accorded to performers. Costumes were also exaggerated to amplify the theatrical effect through the use of colour, decoration and height to increase visibility. Early troupes were not prosperous and as their costumes were costly, a precedent arose for reusing garments for similar characters. Gradually, specific costumes became associated with certain role types, giving rise to the conventionalized style of the costumed images still in use currently. A troupe stores these costumes in trunks or cabinets and before each performance a well-trained dresser will select the costumes needed to clothe each role from the available stock. When more costumes are needed, they are ordered from and constructed in a factory based on traditional models for each garment and no designer is involved.

The costumes communicate physical characteristics and personal circumstances of the characters, though they are not used to indicate the time period, geographic location or climate. The same costumes may also be worn in a variety of genres, as the essential purpose of the garments is distinguishing the role types above all else. As each role type and its subsets have similar attributes, each also has a distinctive visual image, from their headdress and makeup, through their dress to their shoes. Apart from distinguishing the roles, the costumes also express six pairs of identifying characteristics, two of which point to their physical traits – male/female, youth/age – while the rest project their given circumstances – upper/lower status, rich/poor, military/civilian, and Han/minority. In addition to these identifiers that define the role, the costumed image may express additional details about the dramatic condition, including the event, the relationships among the characters, their state of mind and their significance to the story.

Colour symbolism

The colours for traditional jingju costumes are divided into a system of upper five and lower five colours. The upper colours are red, green, yellow, white and black, which are related to traditional Chinese beliefs of direction. The upper colours are the purest and considered more important in history; therefore they appear on garments of nobles, court officials and generals. They are commonly are worn by male and leading characters. The hues of the lower colours are variable but are usually listed as purple (resembling maroon in western terms), pink, blue, lake blue (similar to sky blue or turquoise) and bronze or olive green. The lower colours are generally present in informal scenes, though maroon and blue can be employed for court as well.

The colours onstage reflect personal attributes along with the historical traditions connected to the colours. Red stands for respect, honour and loyalty and is worn for weddings. Green has military connotations. Yellow is reserved for the emperor and his family members, as was the usage historically. White indicates loyalty as well as mourning. Brave and upright characters who enforce the law wear black. Maroon robes usually signify an older character worthy of respect. Young male ingénues can be attired in pink robes when they are romantically inclined. A blue robe denotes high status for calm, firm characters. Lake blue is utilized for youthful roles, both male and female, while olive green or bronze robes represent elderly characters.

Embroidered imagery

Hand-stitched embroidery is used to ornament and enhance the surface of the costumes, with motifs that enrich the delineation of the role types. The embroidered patterns are applied in borders, squares, circles or across the surface, and the location of the designs is standardized. Borders are used to define the edges of garments and rank badges (buzi) are square. Circles are spread evenly and symmetrically across the surface, where flowers might be scattered randomly. An integrated terrestrial pattern combining mountains, waves, clouds and dragons is reserved for the *mang* (court robe) and *nümang* (women's court robe). As the circle was believed to be the most perfect shape, it appears regularly on the clothing of royalty and higher-ranking characters. Historically, women's informal garments were frequently embellished with flowers; however, onstage, both men's and women's garments now are embroidered with floral imagery. Flowers express the harmonious existence between humans and their natural environment, and contain auspicious messages. The dragon, standing for the emperor and strength, is a composite creature appearing on the *kao* (armour) and mang worn by his warriors and officers of the court. Phoenixes, an amalgamated bird representing the empress, are embroidered on *nükao* (women's armour) and nümang. Flowers and phoenixes are embroidered in shades and tints of pretty colours, where dragons are more often embroidered in gold or silver metallic threads.

The four major costumes

In current usage, four garment types comprise the greater part of jingju dress: mang, *pi* (formal robes), kao and *xuezi* (informal robes). These four garments are worn for specific occasions by both male and female roles. *Nü* (woman) is added before each garment to indicate the woman's version of the piece. In general, the robes are ankle length for men and knee length for women, worn over a pleated skirt. Different choices in fabric, hue and decoration of each of these four main garments establish the rank of the person and the role type of the character.

The cut of the mang is similar to historical dragon robes, full-length, trapezoidal shaped, with a rounded neckline and a closing crossing to the right. The sleeves are extended at the hem with *shuixiu* (water-sleeves), lengths of white silk broadcloth to augment hand gestures. The mang is richly decorated with dragons, a symbol of the emperor, and the integrated terrestrial composition, an environment of waves, mountains and clouds. Emperors and the highest-ranking members of the court frequently wear the mang for court or official scenes. A yellow mang is reserved for the emperor, red is for close advisers and officials, and a white mang indicates loyal characters. *Sheng* (standard male roles) wear robes with the dragon in a circular configuration, while larger swirling and walking dragons appear on the robes of the *jing* (painted face roles).

The pi opens down the centre front and has a wide neckband to mid-chest. The body of the garment is slightly trapezoidal and the straight sleeves have shuixiu extensions. The pi is usually worn in daytime at non-court gatherings. *Qingyi* (younger women role type) wear pi in pastel colours while *laosheng* (mature male roles) and *laodan* (mature female roles) wear maroon or olive green pi. The embroidery on the pi usually features flowers, in sprays for young women and circular motifs for older characters.

The complex kao is constructed of thirty-one pieces, including a tabard, leg flaps, segmented sleeves, and flags (Figure 9.3). A wide padded waist piece on the front of the kao adds to the bulk of the garment. Four pennants mounted on wooden poles spreading behind the shoulders and head also increase the scale. The kao is profusely embroidered, often with metallic threads. Patterns include scales and dragons for men, and phoenixes and flowers for *daoma dan* (female generals). High-ranking generals and military officers from the roles of sheng, jing and daoma dan wear the kao/nükao when at court or engaged in battle.

The men's xuezi is a simple robe with an asymmetrical wide neckband closing to the right, with straight sleeves and shuixiu. The *nüxuezi* (women's informal robe) can be this style or with a centre front closing and a short standing band collar. This is the most common jingju garment, as it is worn for daily wear and can be seen on all of the role types and social levels. A plain xuezi/nüxuezi is also a universal inner garment worn under the other robes. *Xiaosheng* (young dignified men) often wear the xuezi in a range of pastel colours with floral embroidery. Laodan with low status and wealth appear in an off-white nüxuezi.

Figure 9.3 General Gao Chong in *Tiao huache* (Turning Aside the Iron Carts) as a wusheng (military male) wearing the kao. The four flags on his back indicate a high official in battle dress.

(Photo by Alexandra Bonds)

The remaining costumes consist of other styles of robes, short jackets, vests, trousers and skirts used to clothe the supporting roles of servants and foot soldiers. These pieces share the same geometric shapes, upper and lower colours and embroidered motifs found in the four major garments. Almost all costumes are made of silk fabrics in solid colours, though cotton is used for some garments for lower-status characters. Roles of status usually wear elevated shoes and boots with thick white soles, while servants and soldiers usually have flat shoes for ease of movement. Female characters wear flat-soled shoes, often with tassels on the toes.

Makeup

The designs of hair and makeup idealize and distinguish the role types as with the costumes. The laosheng wear natural-coloured facial makeup with faint rouge over the eyes and cheeks, accented with black liner around the eyes and on the eyebrows. The laodan wear the same facial colour, though they do not apply the rouge or as much eyeliner. The makeup for qingyi, *huadan* (lively young women) and daoma dan starts with a pale pinkish base enlivened with a blush of rouge from the arch of the brow to the cheek and heavy black eyeliner and eyebrow accents. Xiaosheng wear a similar layout of makeup, though slightly less bold. Each named jing character has a unique and identifiable facial design. The colour and overall patterns reveal their disposition, age and personality (Figure 9.4). The distinct features of the actors' faces are generally identifiable within the elaborate patterns, as the shapes heighten the eyes, brows and nose. For

Figure 9.4 Cao Cao as a jing role in *Qunying hui* (The Gathering of Heroes). The white colour of his painted face reveals his treachery.

(Photo by Alexandra Bonds)

some designs, however, the face is virtually obscured by the complexity of the pattern. The chou roles use a comical face design featuring a white patch over the nose and eyes. (The white block of makeup causes these characters to sometimes be called 'doufu [tofu] face'). The design for the face makeup of each chou character is distinct, though the differences are not as great as can be seen in the jing facial patterns.

Hair and accessories

The stage hairstyles for women's roles are constructed from numerous pieces of hair that are individually applied to the actresses' heads before each performance. The hairpieces are made of several materials, including human and artificial hair, and some of the items are interchangeable among the different roles and styles of hairdressing. Using a gel generated from shaved wood, the hairpieces are sculpted and glued to the face. The qingyi, huadan and daoma dan hairstyle features an arc of curls across the forehead and temples and sideburns shaped along the jaw. The placement of these pieces contours the face into the desired egg shape. The hair is then embellished with filigree hairpins, rhinestones, gems, pearls and flowers. The hair of laodan is grey or white and worn in a simple bun on top of the head, often encircled with a scarf.

Wrapping a piece of black silk gauze around the head at the hairline creates the hairstyle for all male roles, as the rest of the head is concealed with a headdress. Many of the male characters wear artificial beards. They are full and long for the jing characters, thinner and long for the sheng roles, and styled in comical shapes for the clowns. The men's headdresses are grouped into four loosely defined categories: ceremonial headdresses and crowns, helmets, hats and fabric hats. Crowns, helmets and some hats are made of gilded filigree with blue fabric mosaic, topped by articulated pearls and woollen balls mounted on springs. The helmets are sometimes enhanced with six-foot-long pheasant feathers gracefully arching back from either side of the head. Crowns, helmets and hats are firm constructions, generally for court and battle wear, and fabric hats are softer styles, often constructed from fabric matching the costumes, worn in less formal situations.

As actors predominantly developed the costumes, the reforms they initiated were intended to make their acting more visible to the spectators. With the actors' careful handling, the clothing becomes an expansion of the body, contributing to the refinement of the movement and projection of character. The addition of the shiuxui increases and adds elegance to the hand gestures. The pheasant feathers on the military helmets of generals are a vivid combination of beauty, power and expression, drawing attention to the wearer through the extension of line and movement. The long, voluminous robes of court demand a dignified, slow gait, while the shorter garments for clowns and servants imply a more casual bearing. The union of actor and costume creates a stage picture that is elegant and grand, while extending the actors' tools for expression.

III. Japan, by Monica Bethe

Japanese performing arts comprise a wide range of genres, from pure dance to narratives enacted with music, song and sometimes dance, to spoken theatre. Each genre reflects the period and place in which it developed: China in the seventh century (*gigaku* mimed skits), China and Korea in the seventh and eighth centuries merging with Japan in the ninth through twelfth centuries (*bugaku* court dance), Japan in the fourteenth and fifteenth centuries (*noh* danced dramas and *kyogen* comic plays) and Japan in the seventeenth to nineteenth centuries (*bunraku* puppet plays and *kabuki* theatrical dramas). Likewise, the costumes for each genre reflect the periods in which they flourished. Thus to trace the Japanese theatrical costumes over genre is to view a chronological panorama of garments based in prevalent clothing styles, but enhanced and adjusted for the stage.

Gigaku mimed skits

Although gigaku is no longer performed today, gigaku costumes and masks have been preserved in the eighth-century Shōsōin repository attached to Tōdaiji temple in Nara. Records indicate that gigaku players circumambulated a temple area and then performed a set of fourteen pieces, some musical, others mimed stories.

The masked performers wore brightly coloured costumes, patterned with broad stripes, scrolling flowers, complex floral patterns or bead rounds filled with pictorial figures such as mounted hunters or animals under a tree. Decorative techniques included both woven and dyed patterns. Complex multicoloured designs were rendered in compound weave (*nishiki*), while monochrome scroll patterns were done in twill damask (*aya*) and linked diamonds were created in open gauze weaves with crossed warps (*ra*). Dye techniques included batik (*rōkechi*), tie–dye (*kōkechi*) and clamp-resist (*kyōkechi*), where folded cloth was pressed between two boards carved with a pattern and dyes poured into the grooves.

The costumes combined upper garments, including cloaks with round collars and long funnel sleeves (*hō*), undershirts (*san*) and vests with skirt-like hems (*hanpi*) with pants (*hakama*) and leggings (*setsuyō*) or flared skirts (*mo*). While the outer garments tended to be silk, either plain or highly patterned, the undergarments were unadorned hemp. All these garments reflect Chinese clothing styles and are similar to Japanese court costumes of the Nara period (710–94).

Bugaku

Dances accompanied by orchestral music (*gagaku*) that were brought to Japan from China, Korea, Mongolia and Southeast Asia in the seventh and eighth centuries came to be known as bugaku. Systematized during the Heian period (794–1185), they were performed at official court and Buddhist ceremonies. The costumes as we know them today incorporate the broad open sleeves (*ōsode*) and long trains that add majesty and dignity to Heian court costumes.

The four main types of costume are: *kasane shōzoku* or 'layered robes' worn for quiet pieces performed by four or more dancers in unison as well as by the musicians; *ryōtō shōzoku*, a fringed vest and ankle-bound pantaloons combination worn for active solo dances; *ban-e shōzoku*, with large printed or embroidered crests worn also by imperial guards; and *bestu shōzoku*, or 'variant costumes' created for individual pieces.

When all the layers of the 'layered costumes' are worn, the inner layers are only sensed through the gauze-weave cloaks (*hō*), but when one sleeve of the hō is slipped off, a dark embroidered vest (*hanpi*) and the red-cuffed, white sleeve of the underrobe (*shitagasane*) embroidered with a large diamond pattern are revealed. The dancer kicks the train back as he swings his legs in rhythm to the music. Headgear, belts and hand-held objects help identify each piece.

The slimmer ryōtō costume gets its name from the outermost garment, a long, belted, sleeveless 'campaign jacket' consisting of a single width of brocaded cloth with a round opening for the head. Ryōtō are worn over matching pleated pantaloons tied at the ankles and a hō with bound wrists and long train. Exaggerated masks and helmets or headgear complete the figure.

The key garment in the ban-e outfit is a special style of hō decorated with large circular medallions enclosing fire-spitting bear or *shishi* lions. Early examples have woodblock-printed images in ink with hand-painted details in cinnabar and gold. Edo-period examples have embroidered pairs of beasts.

Rhythmical movement enhances these elegant costumes with an atmosphere of grace and harmony. Background stories are envisioned, rather than enacted, the costume, mask and hand-held objects providing the context

Noh and kyogen costumes

The more complex society of the fourteenth and fifteenth centuries saw the birth of narrative dramas such as noh and its sister art, kyogen, both performed by the *sarugaku* troupes. While noh brought lyrical text, instrumental and vocal music, and choreographed movement together into a multi-voiced, visually dazzling presentation of gods, ghosts, goblins and intense human emotions, kyogen focused on the man of the neighbourhood facing everyday challenges with humour and resilience. The costumes for both arts reflected everyday samurai wear, and indeed were often received straight off the backs of their patron audience.

Like the costumes that precede them, noh and kyogen costumes are ensembles of garments worn in layers with each undergarment visible somewhere. The undergarments are shaped similar to the modern kimono, their box sleeves having small openings at the wrist, and are known as 'small sleeves' or *kosode*. In the fifteenth to sixteenth centuries kosode emerged as the standard daily wear. Previously hidden undergarments were now decorated with bold designs and worn as outer robes. Typical were the pictorially patterned woven *karaori* and the *nuihaku* with stencilled gold or silver patterns combined with embroidery. Both remained basic to the noh and kyogen wardrobe, where they were worn both as underrobes and overrobes depending on the role and draping. Basically the karaori of today continue to reflect sixteenth-century aesthetics and retain Momoyama-period overall designs: broad bands (*dan*), staggered squares like a checkerboard (*dangawari*), divided patterns left and right (*katamigawari*) or shoulder and hem (*katasuso*), and open waist (*koshiaki*).

The nuihaku used in noh and kyogen reflected shifts in taste a little longer than the karaori. They remained conservative in design and technique, however, and never incorporated the highly twisted threads and gold couching popular in mid- to late Edo-period elite clothing and kabuki costumes.

Although fundamentally women's garments, both karaori and nuihaku can be worn as undergarments for male roles as well. Other kosode-cut male undergarments include the plain-weave *noshime* and the twill-weave *atsuita*. The latter can be either simple checks or incorporate pictorial patterning similar in technique to the karaori.

For many roles, a broad-sleeved garment with wide, open cuffs (*ōsode* or *hirosode*) is worn as a jacket or cloak over the kosode. Women don a gossamer dancing cloak (*chōken* or *maiginu*) when they perform an instrumental dance (Figure 9.5). Men can drape the same chōken, belting it at the waist and rolling up the right sleeve, to simulate elegant armour when enacting the memory of a battle. For a more masculine appearance, they can substitute a broad-sleeved *happi* cloak glistening with gold or silver patterns woven into a dark ground.

In this way, a single costume, draped differently in combination with different garments, gets multiple uses customized to each role. The audience, familiar with styles of garments, could read social status, gender, age (red for youth, for example) and profession from the outfits. In addition, the actor's choice of colours and patterns, their density, size, configuration and combination created an emotive image of the role suggestive of interpretation. He took care to be true to the season, but not necessarily to the poetic imagery within the text. Literal interpretation of design as meaning would appear only later, in kabuki costumes.

Most of the noh and kyogen costumes belong to the native Japanese cut of front panels overlapping to form a V-neck. Only two, the *nōshi* and the *kariginu*, follow the older style of

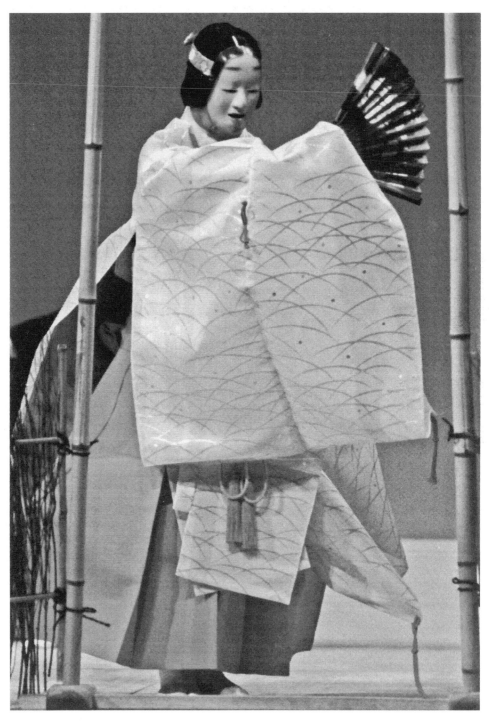

Figure 9.5 Noh *Nonomiya* performed by Yoshio Izumi wearing *chōken* dancing cloak draped
loosely over red divided skirts (*ōkuchi*).

(Courtesy of Yoshio Izumi)

round collar. Adapted for court costumes, the round collar continued to carry an image of authority and was used for roles of Heian courtiers, ministers, Chinese emperors, Shinto priests and deities.

While noh costumes evoke an image of silk, elegant patterns and gorgeous colours, hemp outer garments are the mainstay of the kyogen costumes. Samurai and servants wear the *suō*, a matched suit with broad open double sleeves, the *kamishimo*, a matched winged vest with long pantaloons (*nagabakama*), and the *kataginu* winged vest with different design pantaloons, often bound with shin guards (*kukuribakama*). These garments have dyed, rather than woven, patterns. The designs may be small repeats done in stencilled paste resist (*komon*) with the pattern showing white against a blue or brown or black background, or larger geometric or painterly patterns. Later kataginu vests tend to be bold and humorous. Freely combining stencil, hand-drawn paste resist, and painting, they might display a single large radish, a crayfish caught in a net or a medley of oversized insects.

Kabuki and bunraku puppet costumes

During the Edo period (1603–1868), the kabuki and puppet theatres provided entertainment for the merchant class in the big cities. Particularly for genre pieces about city life (*sewamono*), the costumes reflected Edo-period customs, when the kosode, in various permutations, had become the basic garment for male, female, high and low. The single robe was bound at the waist with a sash (obi), and for women's garments, the contrast of kosode and sash became the aesthetic focus. The kabuki actor Ogino Sawanojō I (1656–1704), famous for his young women's roles, set a precedent for street fashions as well as stage costume when he sported a wide obi in a 1698 performance (Shaver 1966: 50). This is but one example of the far-reaching impact of an actor's costume. Defying sumptuary laws restricting the materials, colours and styles of their clothing, the actors invented new shades and subtle changes in style that often became their personal trademark and also set fashions for the populace. Woodblock actors' prints did much to diffuse them.

By lengthening the sleeves of the kosode (*furisode*) while retaining their arm-length width and small wrist opening, young women, dancers and entertainers added festive elegance to their attire. Elite women draped long heavily decorated kosode (*uchikake*) so they were open at the front and their wadded hems brushed the floor behind.

Bunraku costumes follow styles similar to those for kabuki. The 'T' shape and box sleeves of the kosode form a perfect body for the bunraku puppets. A slit in the back allows the main puppeteer to insert his left hand, which holds the puppet head, while his right hand is slipped through the right sleeve. Another person works the left hand and a third the feet, which for women are merely his fists moving within the wadded hem of the kosode. Together, the narrator, puppeteers and shiamisen player enact a story striving for a dramatic realism that defies the woodenness of the heads. The costumes render the character as an entity in its own right.

Conversely, in kabuki, the actor is paramount and self-presentation is essential, and the costume is the vehicle to express this. The identification of actor and costume is particularly apparent in historical plays (*jidaimono*), for which exaggerated shape, grandiose size and dynamic patterning were given full play. Extra size was added to kosode for roles of lords by attaching a wide sculpted collar to the kabuki-style *omigoromo*, enhancing the impression of authoritative power. Padding might supply sculptural bulk, while gimmicks such as splints to spread boldly designed sleeves, or draping a corded curtain over the garment, added dramatic flourishes. Face paint complements the flamboyance in costume. While for genre plays relatively natural lines in black and red are drawn on a white-face ground, *aragoto* pieces came to use stereotyped, strongly emotive makeup

215

known as *kumadori*. Here, on a base colour of red (dark: anger, obstinacy; medium: passion, vigour; light: youth, gaiety) or blue (dark: gloomy, villainous; light: calm), strong shadow lines trace the muscular structure of the face. Presumably first devised by Danjūrō I, the accentuation of the lines was increased when his son added shading.

Unlike the noh and kyogen costumes that can be worn for multiple roles, the kabuki costumes are role specific, often decorated with motifs that refer to the content of the play. In *Fuwa*, for instance, the opposing personalities of two rivals in love are depicted, one with embroidery of swallows flying in slanting rain echoing words in the script, and the other with lightning and swirling clouds (Figure 9.6).

Dramatic, quick costume change lies at the core of dance-dramas (*shosagoto*), where a minimal plot strings together various dances. In *Musume Dōjōji* (Maiden at Dōjōji), nine costume changes match shifts in music and theme. Turning to the back, the actor poses with robe spread to display the gorgeous design. An attendant pulls a thread (*hikinuki*) and the red robe falls to the ground to reveal a blue kosode with cherry design. To facilitate such instant transformations, the kosode were often split in parts and the upper part shed (*hadanugi*). Cutting the sleeve seams (*bukkaeri*) of the white kosode worn by the hermit in *Kaminari* (Thunder) reveals huge flames consuming him in flames of anger.

Many of the inventive shapes, materials and techniques used in kabuki costumes were developed to overcome restrictions imposed by sumptuary laws. The prohibition of woven patterning led, for instance, to imitative embroidery incorporating gold couching, built-up

Figure 9.6 Actor's print of the kabuki *Fuwa*. From left to right: Nagoya Sanzō in a kosode with swallows and rain, and Fuya Hanzaemon in a kosode clouds and lightning.

(Courtesy of Ritsumeikan Art Research Center)

appliqué and thick cording. Economy and inventiveness led to fake garment layers and ersatz dyes for restricted colours.

In each era represented by the traditional theatre forms discussed here, the costumes reflect the garments worn by the patron class, but are adjusted in shape, pattern or material for the stage. Kabuki costumes exhibit the greatest inventiveness and exuberance in refashioning garments for theatrical effect.

IV. Southeast Asia, by Kirstin Pauka and Lauren Meeker

Costumes in Southeast Asian theatre are extremely diverse, multi-layered, highly ornate and clearly distinguished according to character types.

Vietnam

Vietnamese costumes for various folksong and folk theatrical genres, such as *quan ho* folksong, *ca Hue* and *tuong* and *cheo* theatre, are modelled after traditional everyday and/or court clothing. While such clothing is no longer worn for everyday purposes, it can still be seen in folk art, such as *dong ho* block prints. In some cases, these costumes have been updated for stage performance with brighter colours, additional sashes and, on occasion, other adornments such as sequins.

There is significant variation in *cheo* costume, depending on the character and the play. *Cheo* costumes are conventional; audience members can immediately recognize the type of character portrayed – such as the examination student, mandarin, king or queen, faithful woman, clowns, demons, fairies – based upon his or her costume style, material and colour. Both men's and women's costumes consist of one of several short shirt styles, usually for lower-status characters such as labourers and soldiers, or a long tunic, for higher-status characters. Styles and details of men's long tunics vary depending on character type. Female characters wear their hair rolled in a velvet cloth (*toc van khan*), which is then wound round the head. The ends of the hair are left free at the end in a small tuft called a 'chicken's tail' (*duoi ga*). Women with shorter hair will wear a stuffed velvet band that mimics the look of the rolled hair (Dan 2007). Men's characters will wear a turban or, for kings, warriors and mandarins on grand occasions, a lavishly decorated hat with mirrors and pom-poms.

Costumes in *tuong* theatre are also conventional and have some similarities to the Chinese jingju, though they differ in certain decorative details and in colour symbolism. Tuong uses face painting to represent different characters; different colours symbolize different character types, with red symbolizing good, loyal characters, grey for traitors, green for demons and black for honesty (Tran 1971: 74). The type of beard also signifies character type: three or five tufts in a beard indicate loyalty, a bushy beard indicates a violent character, whereas a short sparse beard signifies a traitor (Huu and Borton 2006: 19). Silk or satin tunics are embroidered with different thread colours (such as gold for kings) and different designs for kings (dragons) and queens (phoenixes). Peasants, servants and soldiers have no embroidery on their clothing (Tran 1971: 74).

Cai luong (reformed theatre), a twentieth-century theatrical form reflective of urban and modern lives, has two styles of costume. One of them is based on contemporary life and clothing (Diamond 1997: 380–1) and the other is based on *hat boi*, a southern Vietnamese form derived from court theatre, like *tuong* (a northern term), but which moved more towards folk theatre than *tuong* (Tran 1971: 70).

Cambodia

Cambodian costumes for *lakon kbach boran* follow distinctions for the four main role types: refined female, refined male, strong male/ogre, and money, with subdivision and variations according to social status or rank. High-ranking characters wear very ornate and more heavily embroidered fabrics than lower-ranking ones; these fabrics are richly textured with gems and gold or silver thread, and accessorized with more elaborate ornaments, jewellery pieces, and taller, more costly decorated headpieces. The individual costume pieces consist of fitted undergarments, a tight-fitting bodice (female) or brocaded jacket (male), and a long piece of richly decorated silk cloth (*sampot*) wrapped tightly around the lower part of the body, pleated, and secured with one or more ornate belts with gilded buckles. The wrapping style of the sampot fabric for male characters has the excess fabric pleated and tucked between the legs to the back, where it is secured with a belt, effectively creating pants. Male and female characters wear additional embroidered collars; males also have distinctive shoulder epaulettes in the shape of wings sweeping upwards, narrow gilded bands crisscrossing the chest, and ornate front and/or side panels hanging down from the belt to the knee. Female characters wear a wide, embroidered sash (*spai*) diagonally across the chest, secured on the left shoulder and hanging down the back. Monkey characters wear masks and a distinctive twisted length or fabric in the back, signifying a tail. Various combinations of delicate wristlets, anklets, ear ornaments and finger rings are worn according to role types. Royal and divine characters wear spire-shaped tiered crowns (*mkot*), while lesser characters wear smaller, less ornate headpieces or diadems. Arrangements of fresh fragrant flowers are attached to crowns and headpieces right before the start of a performance.

Thailand

Thai costumes for *khon* and *lakon* share a basic silhouette and use of similar fabrics and ornaments with Cambodian classical costumes. They are modelled on historic court dress. Male costumes consist of tight-fitting knee-length pants (*sa nap phlao*) over which highly ornate embroidered panels are draped (a single one for refined males, and three for demon and monkey characters), along with an additional cloth wrap. They are secured with a gold belt (*khem khat*). A long-sleeved tight shirt covers the upper body and is augmented with additional ornate bands crossing the chest, plus a wide ornate collar. Refined male and demon costumes also display wing-shaped shoulder epaulets (*in tha nu*), larger ones on the demon costumes. Monkey characters do not have epaulets, but like the demon characters they wear elaborate, full-face masks. Depending on the rank of the character, his crown varies in height, but generally consists of a single tipped pointy spire ornamented in gold. Additional decorative jewellery elements (*kan chiak*) hang down alongside the ears for refined males. Female dress consists of a tight-fitting bodice, a tightly wrapped silk cloth (*pha nung nang*) extending to the ankles, and secured at the waist with an elaborate gold girdle. The main upper garment (*pha hom nang*) is another piece of ornate fabric draped symmetrically over both shoulders and covering the chest. A decorated collar and chest piece along with wristlets, rings and anklets complete the body adornments. A crown similar in shape to that worn by male refined characters is used for high-status female roles. Both refined male and female characters sport a single flower ornament hanging down from the crown in front of the right ear. Folk genres such as *lakon chatri* or *nora* use simplified, less ornate versions of these garments. Demon and monkey characters in both Cambodian and Thai court performances wear elaborate masks that cover the entire head.

Indonesia

Javanese dance-drama costumes are based on versions of specific court dress modified to include elements and aesthetics of *wayang kulit* puppet design. Male performers are typically bare-chested and wear knee-length tight pants, a length of batik cloth as a hip wrap, and a second highly decorated silk wrap around the mid-section. A long dance scarf (*selendang*, *soder*) attached to a belt flows down both sides and is lifted and manipulated by the performer as part of the dance. Headdresses (*makuta*) and ornaments are reflective of similar ornaments on wayang kulit puppets and indicate specific characters. Female characters wear tightly wrapped batik cloth (*kain*) and a tight-fitting wrap around the chest. One or more long sashes are tightened around the waist and the long ends are used to accentuate dance movements. Arms and shoulders are generally bare except for decorative wristlets or gold bands around the upper arm. Small makuta for the character or golden headdresses (*siger*) and/or hair ornaments complete the design. Batik cloth sarongs and dance scarves are also the basic costume elements in many folk genres, but long-sleeved blouses or shirts are often added for modesty.

Balinese costumes show a wide variety of multi-layered wrapping styles and ornate fabrics according to role categories and performance genres (Figure 9.7). Male costumes range from fairly simple garments to highly decorated, multi-layered sets. The simplest ones are worn by the followers of the *barong* as well as by the *kecak* chorus members; these consist of two layers of fabric wrapped around the hip and thighs: a bottom layer of white (barong) or black (kecak) cloth underneath and a black-and-white (*poleng*) checked fabric on top, sometimes bordered in red. The chest remains bare. Most other male characters wear white pants or white cloth wrapped in a fashion to suggest pants as undergarment, along with a long-sleeved white or coloured shirt. Beaded leggings (*setewel*) are often strapped to the calves, and beaded wristlets are attached to the ends of the sleeves. Several layers of increasingly more ornate fabric are added. The outermost layer consists of a large piece of loose ornate fabric (*saput*) tightly strapped high on the chest. The ends of these fabrics are often manipulated as part of the dance or acting. A wide, circular, densely beaded collar (*badong*) covers the upper chest. For some characters additional front panels of printed fabric are added. In solo *topeng*, the basic costume remains the same, and the performer portrays different characters by only changing the mask and headpiece. Refined female costumes consist of several layers of cloth (kain) and sashes wrapped around the torso as tightly as the performer can tolerate. The legs are wrapped in one or more layers of fabric, reaching to the ankles, the outer layer displaying ornate silk-screened or printed gold design motifs (*prada*). For some characters, such as princesses in *gambuh*, some of the fabric is wrapped so that it forms a train at the back, which is manipulated by the feet as part of the dance. In many genres (*legong*, *sanghyang*, gambuh) a narrow, multicoloured apron-like panel hangs down in front to the mid-thigh or knee level. Like male characters, females wear a wide beaded collar around the neck extending onto the shoulders and chest. Additional gold ornaments and jewellery are worn variously on the upper arms, wrists and/or ankles. Various sizes of headpieces crafted from leather and painted in gold denote refinement level of character, social status and/or class. Fresh flowers are an important feature of the headpieces.

Besides refined and strong male and female characters, other distinct character categories with special costumes include clowns, animal characters and demonic or witch characters. While refined female (and most refined male) roles display a sleek silhouette achieved by tightly wrapping the body, clown characters display a thicker silhouette, often achieved through additional padding or hooped bamboo structures underneath the outer garments. The most prominent masked animal characters are monkeys and birds, featuring in genres that use the *Ramayana* epic as its story base (*wayang wong*, kecak). Monkey characters such as Hanuman wear white pants and a

Figure 9.7 Balinese Topeng Tua costume and mask, performed by I. Made Widana.
(Photo by Paul Gamble)

long-sleeved shirt, the latter often including sections made from a heavy fabric suggesting fur. A tail is secured at the waist and extends upwards behind the back. A hip wrap, waist sash, wide collar and curved elaborate headpiece complete the outfit. The primary bird character Jatayu sports a signature beaked mask and painted wings attached to the arms.

Demonic characters include witches (*leyak*), with Rangda foremost among them. Actors performing the Rangda character wear loose pants and a long-sleeved shirt, both with red, white and black stripes. The most striking and distinct feature is the mask with bulging eyes and large tusks, augmented with an oversized wig of thick tangled tresses, hanging down below the knees. A long, narrow red and gold fabric extends from between the large teeth to mid-torso, representing a tongue. White gloves with grotesquely long fingernails accentuate hand gestures.

Rangda's counterpart, Barong, is also a masked character which is performed by two male dancers, who share the costume and provide the fore and hind legs of the four-legged creature, with the one in front also manipulating the mask. Except for their legs which are clothed in red, white and black striped pants, both performers' bodies are completely engulfed in a large frame structure covered with light-coloured natural fibre strands to represent fur. On top of the fur, several gilded and ornate structural elements are mounted – one at the back to extend into a large arched stylized tail, one or more panels hanging over the spine of the creature, and one headpiece with extended side panels in front above the mask and extending down around the mane. A large ornately gilded and mirrored collar is loosely hung around the front part and extends down over the fur. Fresh flowers are added atop the headpiece, and woven into the beard below the mask. The overall weight of this costume is considerable, on average between 40 and 50 kg.

Bibliography

Baumer, Rachel V. M., and James Brandon (1993) *Sanskrit Drama in Performance*, New Delhi: Motilal Banarsidass.

Bethe, Monica, and Nagasaki Iwao (1992) *Patterns and Poetry: Nō Robes from the Lucy Truman Aldrich Collection at the Museum of Art, Rhode Island School of Design*, Providence: Rhode Island School of Design.

Bonds, A. B. (2008) *Beijing Opera Costumes: The Visual Communication of Character and Clothing*, Honolulu: University of Hawai'i Press.

Dan Quoc (2007) *My Thuat Cheo Truyen Thong* (The Traditional Art of Cheo), Hanoi: Nha Xuat Ban San Khau.

Diamond, Catherine (1997) 'The Pandora's Box of "Doi Moi": the Open-Door Policy and Contemporary Theatre in Vietnam', *New Theatre Quarterly* 13 (52): 372–85.

Dickenson, G. and Wrigglesworth, L. (1990) *Imperial Wardrobe*, London: Bamboo Publishing.

Eberhard, W. (1990) *Dictionary of Chinese Symbols*, Singapore: Federal Publications.

Huu Ngoc, and Lady Borton (eds) (2006) *Vietnamese Classical Opera*, Vietnamese Culture: Frequently Asked Questions, Hanoi: The Gioi.

Kasuga Taisha (ed.) (1984) *Bugaku: Treasures from the Kasuga Shrine*, Los Angeles and Nara: Olympic Arts Festival Los Angeles.

Kawakami Shigeki (1998) *Bugaku shōzoku* (Bugaku Costumes), *Nihon no bijutsu* 4, Tokyo: Shibundō.

Kirihata Ken (1993a) *Kyogen Costumes*, Kyoto Shoin Art Library of Japanese Textiles #9, Kyoto: Kyoto Shoin.

—— (1993b) *Noh Costumes*, Kyoto Shoin Art Library of Japanese Textiles #8, Kyoto: Kyoto Shoin.

—— (1994) *Kabuki Costumes*, Kyoto Shoin Art Library of Japanese Textiles #10, Kyoto: Kyoto Shoin.

Matsumoto Kaneo (ed.) (1991) *The Treasures of the Shōsōin: Musical Instruments, Dance Articles, Game Sets*, Kyoto: Shikōsha.

Matsumoto Kaneo (1993) *Shōsōin Textiles*, Kyoto Shoin Art Library of Japanese Textiles #1, Kyoto: Kyoto Shoin.

Pan X. (1995) *The Stagecraft of the Peking Opera from its Origins to the Present Day*, Beijing: New World Press.

Rangacharya, Adya (trans) (2003) *The Nâtyaśâstra: English Translation with Critical Notes*, New Delhi: Munshiram Manoharlal.

Shaver, Ruth (1966) *Kabuki Costume*, Rutland, VT: Tuttle.

Takeda, Sharon (ed.) (2002) *Miracles and Mischief: Noh and Kyôgen Theater in Japan*, Los Angeles: Los Angeles County Museum of Art.

Tanaka Yōko (2009) *Shōsōin no bugaku shōzoku* (Dance Costumes in the Shōsōin), Nihon no Bijutsu no. 520, Tokyo: Shibundō.

Tran Van Khe (1971) 'Traditional Theatre in Vietnam', in James R. Brandon (ed.) *The Performing Arts in Asia*, 70–8, Paris: UNESCO.

Vollmer, J. E. (1983) *Decoding Dragons*, Oregon: University of Oregon.

Zarrilli, Phillip (1984) *The Kathakali Complex: Actor, Performance, and Structure*, New Delhi: Abhinav.

—— (2000) *Kathakali Dance-Drama: Where Gods and Demons Come to Play*, New York: Routledge.

10

Architecture and stage of traditional Asian theatre

David Mason, Colin Mackerras, Julie A. Iezzi and Kathy Foley

Until the widespread usage of proscenium stages under western influence, theatrical performance spaces in Asia generally constituted temple, private and court stages as well as temporary and outdoor spaces. From the seventeenth century onwards, commercial urban theatres, such as Japan's *kabuki* and *bunraku* and later China's *jingju*, started to build public theatres. Some of these spaces, such as the *noh*, kabuki and bunraku stages, have maintained premodern designs until today, while others, such as China's teahouse theatres or most private and court stages throughout Asia, have yielded to the proscenium stages since the nineteenth and early twentieth centuries. This chapter discusses the history and structure of performance spaces in India, China, Japan and Southeast Asia.

I. India, by David Mason

Traditional theatre in ancient India did not commit itself to buildings that have survived. Unlike Hellenistic Greece or Imperial Rome, both of which built permanent theatres according to standardized designs, ancient theatre in India seems to have been more committed to performers than to the spaces in which they performed. The unfortunate consequence is scarce archaeological evidence across the subcontinent of the spaces that have been used for theatrical performances. Even today, India's many forms of folk theatre are less concerned with where they play than with how, so that traditional stages tend to be simple, multi-purpose and, often, temporary.

The *Natyasastra* provides a systematic description of theatre buildings that may have been used for staging classical Sanskrit dramas at the time of its own composition in the first centuries CE. With characteristic deliberation, the *Natyasastra* delineates distinct shapes and precise measurements for three kinds of theatre, each in three sizes: triangular, square and rectangular. The *Natyasastra* seems to privilege the medium size of all shapes as being best suited for humans. Most of what the text has to say concerns medium-sized, rectangular buildings, which suggests that this configuration was the most common among the spaces that may have been in use. The text measures this medium-sized, rectangular space at sixty-four *hastas* long and thirty-two hastas wide. Contemporary reasoning estimates these dimensions at nearly 30 m by 15 m. In any case, the length of the rectangle was to be twice its width, so that it could be divided neatly between performers and audience. The space given to performers was square, but was also equally divided into front and rear rectangles. The performing space, then, was a 7.5 by 15 m rectangle, spanning the width of the theatre, behind which was another such rectangle, a 'backstage' area secluded from the performance hall by a wall. The *Natyasastra* also subdivides the stage, perhaps to designate separate areas of the performing space for musicians and actors. But the *Natyasastra* draws this and other lines so cryptically that the text's smaller and smaller subdivisions of the space can be identified only speculatively.

Indeed, because no such structures survive, whether or not the *Natyasastra* describes actual spaces remains open to debate. The classical Sanskrit dramas, which consistently refer to the backstage area as the source of offstage sounds and for the entrances of characters, using the *Natyasastra*'s term '*nepathya*' (which can also refer to actors' costumes), provide anecdotal evidence that the *Natyasastra* describes some real architectural elements. And the obsessive measurements the text provides describe a space that kept audiences small and close to performers, especially considering that the length was to be equally divided, so that the audience space was merely 16 m^2. Audience members in such spaces were in close proximity to each other and to the performers. This architectural premise remains in many traditional theatre forms.

Regardless of shape and size, the *Natyasastra* prescribes ceremonial attendance to the construction of all theatres, from the selection of the building site, to the laying of the foundation, to the setting of the posts that seem to have been structurally and ritually obligatory in the case of each possible shape. According to the myth delivered by the *Natyasastra* itself, proper ceremonial construction of the space was necessary to secure the performance event against metaphysical antagonism. Spirituality aside, performers in India still commonly treat stages as sacred or hallowed spaces.

Some theatre forms that developed between 1000 and 1700 seem to have taken the *Natyasastra* as an authoritative reference, and to have developed their performance spaces accordingly. Until the twentieth century, Kerala's *kutiyattam* theatre, which can claim a continuous tradition from about 1000, took place in a handful of buildings called *kuttampalams*. These theatre buildings were located within temple complexes to which admission was highly restricted (Figure 10.1). Built in a 22 m by 15 m rectangle, the representative kuttampalam that is attached to the Vatakkunnathan temple in Thrissur approximates the measurements the *Natyasastra* prescribes for the medium-sized, rectangular theatre. Other kuttampalams in Kerala are smaller, but largely preserve the length-to-width ratio. The kuttampalams are also divided precisely in half, reserving one square for the audience and one for performers. The rear portion of the kuttampalam performing space is usually walled off as backstage space. However, the stage itself is a square centred within the rectangle prescribed by the *Natyasastra*, leaving narrow, empty space for a few audience members on either side. Elevated about a half-metre, the square stage is bounded on all four corners by pillars that support a canopy roof that matches the square stage platform (within the roofed space of the auditorium). Traditional kuttampalam theatres are generally oriented so that the performance faces in the direction of the divine image installed in the main temple of the complex.

A space that is similar in some respects is the *namghar* of the Assam region's *ankiya nat* theatre. A Hindu prayer hall, the namghar provides space for a variety of religious events, including devotional dramas that developed in the sixteenth century in monastic communities. Sizes and shapes of namghar buildings vary widely, but are traditionally rectangular. Plays that are staged in these halls are oriented towards a shrine in which a scriptural text is installed as the presiding authority over the space.

Figure 10.1 A temple theatre in Kerala.
(Photo by Farley Richmond)

In contrast to relying on such fixed buildings, most traditional theatre in India has preferred temporary, open spaces, or has been willing to adapt to available spaces that were designed for other activity. These performance forms require little or no scenery, and little in the way of architectural devices to facilitate the presentation and changing of scenery. By 1000, Hindu temples commonly included some kind of performance space, most often to facilitate dance within the view of the temple's presiding deity. In some cases, distinct, pavilion spaces were built either within a temple, or in the outdoor space before and facing a temple. In other cases, especially in the modern period, temples were designed with open space facing the shrine to make congregational worship possible and for theatrical performances intended for the deity's pleasure. Palaces, too, were often built with public halls intended for music, dance and oratory.

Some traditional forms of theatre escaped buildings altogether. *Râs lila* theatre, which developed in the sixteenth century, became popular as evening entertainment along the Braj pilgrimage route. Troupes performed with no architectural frame at all, apart from the landscape itself, which was imbued with pilgrims' devotion with a transcendental sanctity. In the twentieth century, râs lila theatre has attached itself to raised, proscenium-style stages, sometimes in buildings especially constructed for the purpose (and including modern electrical grids, lighting and audio systems). But most râs lila troupes remain mobile. The more successful troupes travel with their stages – large, elevated platforms with rigging, curtains, lighting and audio systems that can be packed up in small trucks and assembled in short order in almost any location.

Ramlila merits some special attention in this regard. Similar in style to râs lila, but dramatizing the sacred stories of the divine Ram rather than Krishna, ramlila theatre, generally, is not tied to a specific, architecturally defined space. Ramlila performances take place in open fields, in private courtyards, on city streets and in marketplaces. However, the ramlila of Ramnagar is a unique case. Each year the story of the *Ramayana* epic is dramatized in the village of Ramnagar, across the Ganges river from the spiritual metropolis of Varanasi in the village of Ramnagar. This ramlila performance uses the entire town and parts of the surrounding countryside as its 50 km^2 stage for a performance that occupies an entire month, moving its temporary platforms in order to stage different episodes from the epic in a different place each day. The principal architectural feature of this theatre is the exterior of Ramnagar Fort, an eighteenth-century Mughal castle, which provides the setting and backdrop for several days of the performance cycle.

Similar forms of traditional theatre in India have eschewed theatre buildings in order to maximize their portability. *Nautanki*, an itinerant, secular theatre form rooted in Rajasthan, became popular in the nineteenth century by playing on bare platforms set up in village and countryside locations. Nautanki venues were often theatre-in-the-round as well, which is to say that its concern for architecture was mostly in its absence. Several other similar, regional forms, such as Gujarat's *bhavai*, Maharashtra's *tamasha* and Bengal's *jatra*, have had a similar attitude towards permanent, scenic-minded stages, preferring a performance style that can go to audiences and adapt to whatever space is available.

While traditional theatre has resisted investing itself in buildings, there are a few historical anomalies in the history of theatre architecture in India. The Sitabenga Cave in the Ramgarh Hills of Chhattisgarh, for instance, seems to have been cut out of the hillside in the third century BCE for the presentation of theatrical performances. This artificial cave features terraced rows of seats carved into the cave's curved walls, and has holes on either side of the space towards which the seating is focused. Posts in these holes could have suspended a curtain, either to close off the entrance of the cave against the weather or to act as a backdrop for performances (or both). Of course, several different activities, not all of them theatrical, might be imagined in such a space. However, an inscription in the cave itself suggests that at least one of the cave's uses was the presentation of poetry and music (Varadpande 1987: 227). A curious, square amphitheatre was built during the third century CE at the base of a hill at Nagarjunakonda, near the coast east of Hyderabad. This 17 m by 14 m construction on an island colonized by Buddhist monasteries offered relatively small audiences a few rows of tiered seating on all four sides of a level playing space.

Even when theatre in India adopted the European interest in buildings designed for indoor, theatrical entertainment, it was just as likely to cling to its preference for outdoor venues. In the late eighteenth century, the British began to build indoor, proscenium theatres in Bombay (Mumbai). Members of the Parsi community began to buy these buildings in the nineteenth century to develop a professional, popular theatre by staging western and Indian plays. The Grant Road Theatre was built in Bombay in 1846 after the pattern of the Drury Lane Theatre in London. Its proscenium-style auditorium initially presented English-language plays for audiences of English colonists and Indians. At almost the same time, the Khatwadi Theatre also opened on Grant Road. The Khatwadi was an open-air theatre that staged plays in Indian languages and in nautanki style. Many of the proscenium-style theatres that were built in Bombay during the nineteenth century were converted to movie houses in the early twentieth century. In the nineteenth century, European-style proscenium theatres were built in other colonial centres, such as Madras (Chennai) and Calcutta (Kolkata). The Great National Theatre, which was designed with British opera houses in mind, opened in 1873 and burnt down during its premier production as a consequence of a fault of its gas lighting. The Minerva Theatre, which still stands, derelict, in Kolkata, opened on the same spot in 1893 (Chatterjee 2007: 215–21).

II. China, by Colin Mackerras

Ancient China lacked the vast theatres the ruins of which can still be found in Ancient Greece or Rome. Sites for performance included temporary stages set up in markets by wandering troupes, and temple stages. One authority states, aptly, that 'Since the eleventh century, the venue at which the vast majority of Chinese – rural or urban – have viewed opera has been the temple fair' (Goldman 2012: 87). From about the same time, a stage was a standard part of a temple complex, often standing apart from other buildings, and following the same or similar architectural style. Commercial playhouses existed in the cities, reaching heights of prosperity in some periods, especially eighteenth- and nineteenth-century Beijing, but were not the norm. Theatres with proscenium-arch stages did not come into existence in China until modern times. In the late imperial period, stages existed in some private mansions, especially the court.

The early period to the fourteenth century

Two forms of theatre/stage existed during the Song (960–1279) and Yuan (1279–1368) periods, namely the temple stages and the 'balustrades' (*goulan*). One writer suggests (Liu 2001: 107) that the flourishing state of structures for performance was essential for the rise of drama at that time, and vice versa, and that neither could flourish without the other. The Yuan is generally recognized as a 'golden age' for Chinese theatre.

Temples were very general throughout the country and by this time normally had stages. The less developed of these were just raised platforms of mud or brick, but there were temples with closed halls that functioned as stages in the same architectural style as the rest of the complex. The audience sat or stood in the open air in front of the stage, but the stages in the closed halls were protected from rain or snow.

The capital of China during the early Song was present-day Kaifeng. There were amusement parks there termed *wazi* (literally 'tiles') or *washi* ('tile markets'), where all kinds of entertainment were available, including song and dance, theatre, shadow theatre and puppetry. The theatres were the 'balustrades'. In Kaifeng there could be over fifty such theatres in any one 'tile market', and the largest of them might hold several thousand people. When Kaifeng was conquered by the Jurched people in 1126, the Song capital moved south to present-day Hangzhou, where the number of 'balustrades' was even greater. One scholar (Liu 2001: 109) claims that 'during the Yuan dynasty, the goulan were widely distributed, with many in every city'.

They were especially for performances, not multi-purpose structures where drama or similar shows were one of many functions. They were commercialized and formed one aspect of the highly urban society that was developing during the Song dynasty. One implication was that payment was necessary for entry. Although they had seating arrangements that could accommodate a large audience, and were designed as permanent, they were made of wood and probably not very sturdy.

This is confirmed through an incident in Songjiang, Jiangsu Province, which is described by a text of 1366 by Tao Zongyi (quoted in Mackerras 1972: 194). Tao calls the balustrade theatre a *peng* (literally 'matshed'). He says that one day there was a loud splitting sound followed shortly afterwards by the collapse of the goulan. Forty-two people were killed, but with an actor and his family escaping unharmed. The stage may have been under a different roof and does not seem to have been in the open air.

From the fourteenth to the nineteenth centuries

This incident may have contributed to the decline of the goulan. In any case, for reasons that are obscure, the goulan went out of date in the Ming dynasty (1368–1644). Urban drama performances took place not in theatres but in buildings with primary functions other than performance, such as wine-houses, guild-halls, teahouses and even brothels. The court had its own stages, and some of the educated and aristocratic elite had stages built in their own mansions. Moreover, temporary stages were very common, for it was quite possible to set them up especially for a festival or during market-time.

The most common sites for theatre performances in the late imperial era were stages built inside or just outside temples. Many temples had permanent stages, but it was always possible to put up temporary ones with within the grounds. A few points are relevant here. First, the use of temples lasted a very long time and changed comparatively little over the centuries of the late imperial era, including the architectural style. Second, a common purpose of drama was to petition the gods in the spring or to give thanks in the autumn for a good harvest, or to celebrate the god's feast-day. It did not really matter whether the temple was for Buddhism or a folk religion; it still had a stage and was a good place for drama. The stage was usually covered, though the audience sat or stood in the open air.

An extremely important general point is that throughout the country, temples were major public sites. People got together there for fairs, festivals or any other reason for public gatherings. Outside the cities, temples were by far the most important public space. They were ideal for drama performances. Whether the occasion for a drama performance was religious or not had little bearing on the content, which could be entirely secular. The audience was wide socially, including poor people and women.

The Qing dynasty and the heyday of the Beijing theatres

The grandest stages were of course those in the court. Quite a few of these still survive in the imperial palaces in Beijing, in the Summer Palace just outside the city and in the summer residence of the emperors in Jehol, where splendid drama performances were put on for the Macartney expedition in 1793. There were three kinds, varying in size. The smallest were private to one member of the court, especially the Empress Dowager Cixi (Figure 10.2); they were able to fit in a private room and had one level only. The second were the normal two-level stages that were common also outside court. Then there were the large, three-level ones on which performances could take place on more than one level at the same time. Highly complex and grand shows could take place on these large stages. However, it is notable that none of these stages were really buildings we can call theatres. The two- and three-level stages, which were designed for performance and nothing else, stood alone and apart from the audience. They were covered against the elements and, if the audience was similarly protected, they looked at the performance through a space that was itself open-air.

Another form of stage was that for invitation-only drama performances put on by private or especially hired troupes for rich men who invited guests for dinner, the latter being the host's social peers. The actors were paid by the host, although guests could contribute if they wished. The stage was either within the mansion of the host or was a public space hired especially for the occasion. These performances were occasional in the sense that they might celebrate a birthday or any other special event. They were termed *tanghui yanchu*, which one specialist translates as 'salon performances' (Goldman 2012: 97). In style, these stages were similar to normal public stages, and certainly there were none as grand as the three-level stages of the court.

Figure 10.2 The Dehe Yuan (Garden of Virtue and Harmony) stage in the Summer Palace built for the Dowager Empress Cixi in 1891.

(Photo by Alexandra Bonds)

During the Qing dynasty, private stages for the rich persisted in cities such as Yangzhou. Some of the mansions of Yangzhou's famous salt-merchants, who counted some of the richest men in the entire country among their number, included covered stages. However, the early Qing state discouraged ostentatious lifestyles, including the owning and training of private theatre troupes. It may have been partly for this reason that rich families tended towards patronizing performances in public places, such as theatres.

During the early Qing dynasty, the urban guild-halls for people from the same area or of the same calling, and other structures such as wine-houses, began to transition to buildings designed specifically for drama or similar entertainment. They were closed from the elements, in other words different from the open-air temple stages, and not free of entry, implying restrictions on who could go in. They were quite different from the open-air temple stages and, though in Beijing termed 'tea gardens' (*chayuan*), much more like what we can call 'theatres'.

Beijing during the Qing was a sharply divided city. The Inner City was for the court, as well as the major Manchu, Mongol and Han courtiers. The Outer City was for the dominantly Han ordinary people. Public theatres were banned in the Inner City, and a 'playhouse district' arose in the northern part of the Outer City, which was itself just south of the Inner City. It also happened to be right in the middle of the main commercial district of Beijing.

These playhouses were socially divided. In the best seats, termed 'official seats' (*guanzuo*), audience members sat around tables and could sip tea and eat snacks as they watched the performance, although full meals were not available. There were also 'scattered seats' (*sanzuo*) for the less wealthy, which were far less expensive. The worst place of all was termed *chizi* (pond); they were very much cheaper and less comfortable, and much rowdier and disorganized, than the 'scattered', let alone the 'official' seats. The audience sat or stood on three sides of the stage and did not necessarily give their undivided attention to the performance. The stage was a square raised platform, with a curtain at the back, but not the front. Just as with the temple or market-square stages, properties were simple and there was no possibility of complex décor.

These various forms of stages and theatres, especially the 'tea gardens', played a significant role in the rise of the *jingju* (Beijing opera). They fitted in nicely with the increasingly commercialized society, which appreciated the theatre and was willing to patronize the local drama style. The rise of the Beijing playhouse and of the jingju in the eighteenth and nineteenth centuries was part of the same social and cultural process.

Modernization and the early twentieth century

In the first decade of the twentieth century, reformers began to adopt some westernized styles of theatre, but taking their models from Japan, which had proved more willing than China to take on ideas originating in the west. In drama, one such idea was the spoken drama (*huaju*), which is discussed elsewhere. In terms of the physical structures where drama was performed, the western model introduced through Japan was the proscenium stage in a theatre. Definitely closed, and not open-air, these theatres were in modern western architectural style. The audience sat in rows facing the stage, which was not square but oblong, and were supposed to concentrate on the drama, not chat during the performance as was normal in the traditional-style theatres. Scenery could be much more complex and a curtain at the front could open and close to show the beginning and end of the show.

The first theatre open to Chinese that featured a proscenium stage of the kind found in Europe was the 'New Stage' (Xin wutai) in Shanghai, which was established in 1908 by the theatre-reformer and actor Xia Yueheng and his brothers. It had a slightly rounded downstage lip, but did not follow the traditional pattern of a square stage. The audience sat facing the proscenium, not around tables. People of any class could attend, although prices were not uniform and differed according to distance from the stage. Unlike the old-style theatres, the stage could accommodate elaborate and even machine-operated décor. Both traditional Beijing operas and contemporary spoken plays were performed there. Burnt down by fire, it was rebuilt in a different area of the city, but closed finally in 1924.

In June 1914, Beijing followed Shanghai's lead by establishing its first modern theatre, called the First Stage (Diyi wutai). During the Republican period (1912–49), more and more newly built theatre followed the westernized style. However, traditional theatres persisted, and temple stages of the old style remained the norm outside the main cities.

New theatres built since the establishment of the People's Republic of China in 1949 have almost all followed modern styles, featuring proscenium stages. Traditional theatres, including temple stages, mostly fell into disuse, especially in the main cities. The Cultural Revolution, with its attempt to suppress traditional themes and its focus on the *yangbanxi* (model plays), also saw distaste for the traditional theatre architecture.

However, the reform period has seen a major attempt to restore selected traditional theatres and even to build a few new ones (Figure 10.3). Many temple stages are again in use. A prominent example of a restored stage is the Huguang Huiguan (Huguang Native Place Association) in Beijing. Refurbished and reopened in 1997, for the tourist trade, it has a stage in very traditional style and features jingju of the old style in surroundings designed as

Figure 10.3 The restored stage at the National Kunqu Museum in Suzhou, renovated in 1986 from the Quan Jin Huiguan (All Shanxi Native Place Association).

(Photo by Colin Mackerras)

authentically traditional. Beijing's Imperial Granary, built in 1409, has recently been restored and includes a small theatre specifically designed to reproduce the kind of intimate private theatrical performances put on by the elites of the Ming and Qing dynasties in their own homes.

III. Japan, by Julie A. Iezzi

Each Japanese theatre form occupies a unique performance space. The *Kojiki* (c. 712) and *Nihongi* (720) describe a naked dance on an upturned tub to lure the Sun Goddess from the Heavenly Cave where she had hidden herself. Cited as the birth of ritual performance (*kagura*), this is also the first mention of a stage in Japan. Early stages for dance imported from China and Korea (*bugaku*) were square, utilizing open ground or hall space, or temporarily constructed on shrine or temple grounds. Records from the early Heian period (794–1185) describe square raised platforms lined on two or three sides with trees. The concept of a raised platform surrounded by trees is believed to have been imported from China, and represents, in miniature, the natural elements of a mountain and surrounding forest in which the deities dwell. There are a few occasions when bugaku is performed on the ground, as on the Grass Stage at Nara's Kasuga Shrine, but the raised stage, whether permanent or temporarily constructed, is most common. Approximately 1 m high and 7.3 m square, the stage is surrounded by a vermillion red railing, with steps at the front and back. A secondary 5.4 m square platform laid at the centre of the stage is where the dance occurs. Stages are no longer tree lined, though tall objects such as halberds are placed in the stage corners for performances, as at Itsukushima Shrine's bugaku stage.

Noh and kyogen

The first roofed stages appeared in the mid-fourteenth century with *sarugaku* (later *noh* and *kyogen*) performances. Early stages were temporary, approximately 3.6 m square raised platforms, with a *hashigakari* (bridgeway), the location of which varied depending on performance needs, placed upstage right, left, centre, or on both sides. By the late 1500s, the stage configuration had become fixed, with an approximately 5.4 m square main stage, extensions upstage for musicians and stage left for the chorus, and the hashigakari at an oblique angle from upstage right to the mirror room, a small offstage room where masks are donned.

Noh stages are built of Japanese cypress. The backboard is painted with a pine tree, a symbolic place for deities to rest, much like the real trees surrounding earlier stages. Actors enter from the mirror room, passing through the lift curtain and down the hashigakari, along which three live pines, each progressively larger, are planted on the audience side. Stage assistants and chorus enter through a small door upstage left. Corner pillars support a gabled, shingled roof over the main stage area. Each pillar is named, according to function or location, and the terms are often used in indicating stage movement. Upstage right, near the position where the *shite* (and other) characters stop upon entering the main stage, is the shite pillar. Upstage left is the flute (*fue*) pillar, near the flute player's seat. Downstage right is the eye-fixing (*metsuke*) pillar, essential for masked actors in navigating the stage. Downstage left is the *waki* pillar, near the waki position. Two hooks, overhead centre of the main stage and on the flute pillar, are today used as rope guides only for hoisting the bell in the play *Dōjōji*, though historically other plays also utilized bells. Large ceramic vessels angled beneath the stage and hashigakari floor amplify sound, principally the shite's periodic light or heavy foot stamping, critical to his dancing. Stones surrounding the stage on three sides traditionally reflected sunlight onto the roofed outdoor stage, while also bouncing sound towards the audience, who sat in manor rooms or roofed side boxes (*sajiki*) on three sides of the stage across the stone garden area.

The oldest extant stage is the Northern Noh Stage at Kyoto's Nishi Honganji temple. Built in 1581, it is thought to be a prototype for later stages. The remarkable stage at Itsukushima Shrine, built in 1680, stands in the mud at low tide and is surrounded by water at high tide, utilizing the acoustic and reflective qualities of the water. Many noh stages can be found on shrine and temple grounds, most of which date to the Meiji era during the revival of noh and kyogen after the loss of samurai patronage. After five centuries of outdoor stages, the first indoor noh theatre was built in Tokyo in 1881, bringing all the stage elements under one secondary roof, leaving a residual stone garden perimeter around the stage, and limiting audience seating to two sides: at the front, facing the pine tree, and along the hashigakari facing the chorus and waki at stage left. Some theatres have residual boxed seats in the rear of the house, or shallow balcony seating. The majority of regularly scheduled noh and kyogen performances occur in modern indoor noh theatres, such as Tokyo's National Noh theatre, equipped with a spacious lobby, coffee shop and bookstore.

Kabuki

Early kabuki stages were temporary structures very similar to noh stages, built on riverbeds and on temple and shrine grounds. As with noh, the audience watched from three sides, with wealthier patrons in roofed side boxes, and others in the unroofed orchestra pit. Though 'permanent' theatres were first licensed in 1615 and 1624 in Kyoto and Edo respectively, conceptually they remained temporary for the next century, with stage configurations easily modified by attaching additional platforms (*tsuke butai*) at various locations. A *hanamichi* (pathway leading through the audience from the back of the theatre to the stage), and small thrust stages jutting from the main stage or hanamichi into the audience, were common temporary additions in the latter part of the seventeenth century. During that time, the hashigakari grew to nearly the width of the main stage, while the main stage extended beyond the roofed area, creating a shallow thrust into the audience.

Beginning in 1724, regulations aimed at preventing the spread of fire required theatre owners to roof the entire theatre. The weight of beams needed for the expanse necessitated sturdier foundations and supporting pillars. Theatres were permitted to increase in size, using income from increased audience capacity to cover the expense of the required tile roofing (Performing Arts Network Japan 2010). From around this time the hanamichi became a permanent feature in all theatres. Candle lighting was no longer sufficient in the fully roofed theatres, so manually operated, sliding papered windows behind and above two-storey side boxes regulated light.

These sturdier, truly permanent structures laid the foundation for the development of stage machinery. Many scenic developments, pioneered in the mid-eighteenth century in Osaka theatres, were generally adopted in Edo within a few decades. Two-storey sets were used from the 1720s, large lifts for sets from 1753, the revolving stage (*mawari butai*) from 1758, and mechanisms for flying actors and pivoting large set pieces from 1761. By the end of the eighteenth century, the gabled roof over the stage had been removed in all large theatres, and three-walled interior rooms with a high degree of verisimilitude were common, preceding the box set in the west by decades. Pit-area seating was divided into boxes beginning in the 1770s, and by the end of the century Edo theatres incorporated a two-storey standing-room-only area upstage right on stage to accommodate a burgeoning population. Offstage musicians were located at the left (*kamite*) in most theatres during the Edo period, with the traveller curtain opening from stage right (*shimote*) to left. Today, musicians are offstage right, and the curtain opens from left to right. All licensed kabuki and puppet theatres had a curtained drum tower (*yagura*), bearing the crest of the theatre's licensee. Retained in contemporary and restored theatres, they no longer house drums to announce performances, so serve only a decorative function.

Western influence transformed kabuki theatres in the Meiji era (1868–1912). Tokyo's Shintomi-za (formerly Morita-za) was the first to open, in 1878, with a proscenium frame and no audience seating on stage, with Osaka's Kado-za following in 1884. During the Meiji and Taisho (1912–1925) eras, theatres grew tremendously in size, doubling stage width and audience capacity, adopting European-style facades, interior balconies and third-floor seating. Seating was gradually replaced with chairs, first in the side boxes and balcony, and finally in the floor boxes. Food and drink, once delivered to patrons inside the theatre by teahouse employees, became available in restaurants and food stalls built within the theatres.

Tokyo's Kabuki-za theatre is the main venue in the country and an icon of contemporary kabuki. Originally built in 1889, it reopened in its fifth incarnation in April 2013. Backed by a high-rise office building and including a sixth-floor kabuki museum, the 1808-seat theatre has first- and second-floor seats equipped with digital screens for supertitles, and superb sightlines through the fourth-balcony seats. Yet many features of its previous (1954) incarnation were maintained: the temple-like theatre façade, 27.27 m proscenium opening, 18.18 m long hanamichi, and 18.18 m diameter revolving stage provide continuity for audience as well as actors.

Figure 10.4 Osaka kabuki stage, c. 1840, in which the revolving stage, lift, 'empty well' and *hanamichi* (slightly more centre than in Edo theatres) are clearly visible. From the *Gakuya doku annai* (Solo Backstage Tour) series. Nishiki-e by Kano Shugen Sadanobu

(Courtesy Art Research Center Collection, Ritsumeikan University [arcUP0524])

233

Vestiges of Edo still exist, as in the 1835 Kanamaru-za, the oldest extant kabuki theatre. Renovations in 2003 restored the *budōdana*, a bamboo-latticed ceiling extending above the stage and audience. Enabling snow, cherry blossoms, even characters to descend anywhere into the theatre, it is a reminder that stage and audience were one unified space in the kabuki world. Two stage features, common in nineteenth-century theatres, today can be seen only in this theatre: a small open pit at the joint of the hanamichi and stage called the 'empty well' (*karaido*; see Figure 10.4), which when filled with mud or water is the sight of great spectacle; and a wooden railing running above the length of the hanamichi, used for flying actors, another theatrical spectacle. Other surviving Meiji, Taishō and even early Shōwa (1926–1989) era theatres (e.g. Yachiyo-za, 1911; Uchiko-za, 1916) are testaments to the extent to which the intimacy and stage machinery of Edo-period kabuki playhouses remained the standard of interior theatre design outside large urban areas well into the twentieth century. As contemporary actors seek the intimate performing experience of their ancestors, many are experiencing nostalgic revivals.

Bunraku

While puppet stages for mid-sixteenth-century itinerant performers consisted of a small box carried in front of the body, development of narrated puppet theatre (*ningyō jōruri*) in the early seventeenth century necessitated larger stages. Screen paintings of the time depict stages with two or three horizontal partitions at various heights, each of which established a ground level for the puppets, and created distinct zones in which puppets and puppeteers, hidden below, could move. Distant exterior action occurred behind the first and lowest partition, exterior action nearer to buildings behind the second partition, and interior action behind the third and highest partition. Two-partition stages established zones for exterior and interior action.

Though many advances in puppets have occurred, and puppeteers are now visible, the same basic stage principle is still apparent in Japan's two permanent theatres used for bunraku, Osaka's National Bunraku Theatre and Tokyo's National Theatre Small Hall. The space behind the first partition is for footlights and the traveller curtain. Exterior action is enacted behind the second partition on a lowered stage floor called the *funazoko* (literally 'boat bottom'), allowing better sight lines of the interior rooms, constructed behind the third partition on a higher stage level. The second and third partitions establish ground levels for puppet action, creating the illusion of a floor when viewed from the audience.

Puppeteers enter the stage from right or left into the funazoko, or into interior rooms from upstage. Side entrance curtains bear the crests of the Toyotake-za and Takemoto-za, acknowledging these important eighteenth-century Osaka bunraku theatres. The narrator and shamisen player, hidden behind the stage until the late seventeenth century, today perform in full audience view from an auxiliary stage in front of the proscenium at stage left. A small revolving stage in the floor enables quick changes of narrator and shamisen player and seamless transitions between musical divisions of a play. A screened area above the stage-left entrance is used for narrating minor scenes, while the complementary stage-right room houses musicians supplying sound effects and background music. Scenic construction is governed by the need for puppeteers to move unimpeded through space, so interior walls and doors are hung. The third partition, which forms the downstage side of the interior room, slides open so that puppeteers can easily step up into interior rooms.

Many regional puppet theatres have also seen revivals in the first decades of the twenty-first century, especially in Tokushima Prefecture, which boasts over 90 per cent of rural puppet theatres. Generally more simply constructed and without a funazoko, some of these theatres feature *fusuma karakuri*, mechanisms which enable multiple changes of perspective background scenery, painted on a series of sliding and pivoting panels. Initially developed to change backgrounds for puppet performances, *fusuma karakuri* became the main attraction in some dedicated theatres, as in the Inukai Agricultural Village Theatre.

IV. Southeast Asia, by Kathy Foley

Traditionally, Southeast Asian performance did not occur in permanent purpose-built performance spaces. Often processional performance could turn the whole area into a theatricalized environment, while sited presentations often took place in the context of religious celebrations, community festivals or family life-cycle events and performers came to the place of the celebration rather than viewers going to a theatre space.

In long houses, for example, storytelling and dances continue among the Iban and other aboriginal groups of Kalimantan, Borneo, Irian and the Philippines. Ceremonies of local healers could be outside at the river, shore or forest if spirits were the target audience.

Meanwhile, more elaborate theatricals were and are conducted in temporary spaces (sometimes the open ground of a village square or near an ancestral graves), where 'stage' was merely demarcated or structures temporarily built in front of a patron's (Java, Sumatra) or clan (Vietnam) house; a church (i.e. Philippines, East Timor, etc.), temple in Hindu (i.e. Bali) or Buddhist areas (i.e. Thailand, Cambodia, Vietnam, Burma); or the compound of a king or minor aristocrat (Java, Thailand, Cambodia, Burma, Vietnam), though some Javanese compounds have a designated space for puppet performance. Many performances were outdoors at night, lit by coconut oil lamp or, later, petromax, or electric lights. They were staged in booths or open-sided pavilions made from wood, bamboo and thatch for the event. In cities, itinerant artists often set up their instruments in an open space near a gathering place in the hope of getting an audience and tips.

Travelling or processional performances

Processional performances including dramatic elements have long been important in Southeast Asia. These might be staged for events that encompassed the whole community, such as a Javanese rice harvest festival where large puppet figures wearing red (male) and white (female) masks might be danced. Similar figures are now presented for the Independence Day parade or political rallies. In some areas, male and female figures mime copulating on the route, as with the *barong landong* (Bali). One or many lion-like figures may create processions, especially for New Year celebrations as with Balinese *barong* (leonine two-man figure); Chinese-derived lions dance for Chinese New Year in Malaysia, Singapore and Vietnam; or the 'golden lion' figure danced in Luang Prabang, Laos along with male and female ancestral figures (Po Gneu and Gna Gneu). In other areas, as among the Sundanese of West Java, a newly circumcised boy could be mounted on a lion figure carried by four martial arts (*pencak silat*) dancers with drum and gong orchestra and the community following along. Processional performances, sometimes with short dramatic interludes interspersed, can accompany a groom to the bride's house in Java.

Parades will often culminate at an important public building, the host's house or a religious establishment, with the most honoured viewers there. Processions may lead towards this site where a raised stage has been created, as for example with the Malay *hamdolok* where frame drums and dancing performers lead viewers to watch the stage drama (Ghulam-Sawar 1994: 89–90). In the Philippines, for local festivals participants may put on extravagant costumes and dance in the streets for the duration of the festival, with audiences freely joining in as the whole city is transformed into a space of communal celebration. Again in the Philippines, we may see performers representing Mary and Joseph seeking shelter in the inn (*panuluyan*). Such performances are revisited in modern 'guerrilla' theatre: Philippines Educational Theatre Association adopted *panuluyan* for street theatre attacking Marcos.

A variant parade is sometimes done on rivers. In Thailand or Cambodia royal barge festivals celebrating the monarchy had palace troupes presenting on boats for those who lined the banks. Barge performances have been re-created during the reign of Rama IX (r. 1946–) to celebrate Thailand's Chakri dynasty.

Temples, courts, homes

From a Balinese temple (*pura*) the dancer-actors may appear from the split gate of the temple and descend the steps to dance on the open space in front. In the early 1970s, prompted by tours of 'sacred' arts to Europe, Balinese redefined genres by their spaces: *wali* (inner temple and sacred), *bebali* (in front of the temple and semi-sacred) and *bali-balihan* (entertainment for secular performance space). But boundaries of the sacred can shift over time – performances introduced as entertainment are imported to temple festivals done in *bebali* spaces. Still, this idea of space as determinant of performance significance is embedded in a number of Southeast Asian forms. The particular temple should be appropriate to the performance type: for example, the semi-exorcistic *calonarang*, which features the widow-witch, Rangda, will be in a space cleared in front of a Balinese death temple (*pura dalam*). A male papaya tree that does not bear fruit and a small house on high stilts for Rangda must be placed in the open area. The audience will watch in an arena formation. Comic characters run past viewers to the graveyard, 'stealing' corpses, and Rangda emerges from her stilt house and, when temporarily subdued, exits to the graveyard. Space adds to the excitement of this witchcraft story, which appeared in its current form in the late nineteenth century. The locale facilitates trance and makes the performance eerily interesting.

In central Thailand one will find raised stages usually with a roof on pillars in or near temple compounds. Performances of *lakhon nok* (Thai mask genre outside the palace), *lakhon chatri/nora* from the south, or *likay*, a modern genre with stock characters developed since the 1880s, may take place here (or more recently near government cultural compounds). For likay, a stage about 6 m wide and 5 m deep with two entrances through the painted backdrop will serve as the acting area and to the right of the stage a smaller platform of perhaps 2.5 m square is used by the musicians. Behind the drop is the dressing area with the altar to teachers. Viewers sit or stand around the stage (Ghulam-Sawar 1994: 142). Chinese temples and clanhouses in Southeast Asia frequently have permanent open-air stages with a pillared roof for presentation of operas (*xiqu*). Smaller booths for glove, rod or other puppet traditions might be brought into or constructed in such spaces for the Hungry Ghost Festival. In Vietnam's Red River area north of Hanoi, permanent or temporary water puppet booths could be constructed in the pond facing the pagoda. Manipulators, standing in waist-high water, move puppets hidden behind a bamboo curtain descending to water level. The puppets, attached to long poles, come from beneath the murky water or enter on a track from small doors on the sides of the booth. Viewers watch from the shore (though today indoor theatres with pools also exist).

A modern use of temples is found in Indonesian *sendratari* (dance-drama). Prambanan temple complex in Central Java has a huge stage on which up to a hundred performers may dance in the *Ramayana* episodes. Other world heritage sites such as Penataran in East Java have sometimes erected temporary stages for festival performances with the ruins serving as the 'backdrop' for shows in classical dance style. Angkor Wat has sometimes been similarly deployed by the Khmer Royal Cambodian Ballet. Such presentations remind us that when these complexes were built a millennium ago, artists dedicated to these temples performed here.

Courts often had dedicated performance spaces. For example, Vietnam's Duyet Thi Duong Theatre is the oldest royal theatre in Hue, built in 1826 by Emperor Minh Mang for *tuồng* (opera). A large rectangular space houses a square stage with two doors: actors and actresses enter right and exit left. The red lacquer columns are decorated with dragon and clouds, and the blue ceiling is painted with the sun, moon and stars. Consorts watched from a screened gallery above, and the king and guests sat on chairs below. Behind the stage wall was the altar to the two theatre founders. The Khmer royal female ballet might perform in temples (Wat Phnom or Silver Pagoda) for sacred events, but their normal rehearsal and performance space was the roofed Moonlight Pavilion (Preah Thineang Chan Chhaya) of the royal palace. The original large open-walled wooden pavilion was replaced with a French-built one around 1913. Temporary seating would accommodate guests. Dancers and musicians shared the floor space with viewers. In Javanese courts, similarly, large rectangular open-sided platforms (*pendopo*) sit perhaps 1 m above the ground, with steps leading up and a roof supported by wooden pillars. Srimanganti Pendopo of the Yogyakarta Kraton (Palace) is an example. Viewers on chairs brought in for the event share the space with the dancers/puppet screen and musicians. The space might have a polished marble floor and elegant chandeliers. Such pavilions or more enclosed audience halls were sites of performance for palace women's genres, while male forms might be presented outside the palace – on the parade grounds or at religious sites. With modernization, palace spaces for elite performance became increasingly Europeanized, with electric lighting or even a European °theatre – for example Rama VI of Thailand built an European Style proscenium stage (1904) in a palace to present his plays.

Minor aristocrats or headmen would hold performances in pavilions at their own homes. Where no permanent pavilion was available, an open space would serve as a temporary site and, if needed, a raised roofed built stage. For Vietnamese *cheo*, for example, presentations were mostly held in village communal houses or their yards. The 'stage' consisted of a few mats on the ground, a screen hung behind created a 'backstage' and viewers gathered around the three open sides (Meeker 2015). Indonesian and Malay *wayang* (puppetry or dance performances) might take place on a raised booth stage with a covered roof to protect against rain (Figure 10.5). Viewers set on the ground in the open air.

Proscenium-style theatres

The move towards closed theatres with more controlled sightlines, lighting and scenic elements branched from these outdoor stages, covered with a thatch or zinc roof, with little or no scenery hung upstage and the area behind used to await the next entrance, though outdoor stages persisted in many areas through the twentieth century. European theatres, of course, were built by the colonial powers, initially reserved for western entertainments. Jakarta's Schouwburg Theatre (built in 1821, now Gedung Kesenian Jakarta) was built on the site of an 1811 theatre and Ho Chi Minh Municipal Theatre designed in 1895 by Ferret Eugene are just two examples. From around the 1890s increased use of proscenium-style theatres occurred, especially in commercial forms. Originally theatre enclosures might be made of woven bamboo with simple wooden stages about 1m high and relatively simple wing-and-drop arrangements for forms such as *wayang wong*, *kethoprak*, *sandiwara*, *bangsawan*, *komedi stambul* and so on. Walls allowed entrepreneurs to control ticketed entry. In time, full indoor theatres with proscenium stages were developed.

In both rural and urban settings today, most traditional performances take place in permanent buildings on a formal proscenium stage with its closed wings, raised platform stage and an audience oriented in one direction on permanent seats with modern lighting. A drawn curtain allows actors to do street scenes or speciality acts (as in *bangsawan*'s 'extra turn') and facilitates scene changes.

Figure 10.5 Inside a puppet booth for wayang kelantan.
(Photo by Kathy Foley)

While most popular theatres have kept song and dance highlighted, requiring a less constricted stage space than European spoken drama, the increased emphasis in Southeast Asia on realism – furniture, sets, sightlines – has had an effect. At village events the outdoor temporary stage may persist and, for formal court events, old spaces prevail; still, traditional performances today mostly take place in post-independence national theatre complexes; on proscenium stages built at performing arts schools; in purpose-built tourist performance venues, which may accommodate hundreds or even thousands; in small art and performance galleries; or in NGO or international cultural facilities in upscale districts of major cities (Alliance Française etc.). And, of course, after the Second World War or with independence, traditional theatre has been displayed in ambitious national art complexes – from Thailand's National Theatre, to Indonesian's Taman Ismail Marzuki, to Cambodia's now defunct National Theatre. Today, affluent states show their success with buildings that accomodate a thousand or more in Western modeled houses such as Singapore's Esplanade Theatres on the Bay or Kuala Lumpur's Istana Budaya ('Palace of Culture', i.e. National Theatre): there, neo-traditional performances (complete with digital projections, flying apparati, lifts, turntables and full technical possibilities) prevail. In these venues, the building itself rather than the forms displayed may be the biggest show of the evening.

Bibliography

Chatterjee, Sudipto (2007) *The Colonial Staged: Theatre in Colonial Calcutta*, New York: Seagull.
Dolby, William (1976) *A History of Chinese Drama*, London: Paul Elek.

Ernst, Earle (1974) *The Kabuki Theatre*, Honolulu: University of Hawai'i Press.

Ghulam-Sawar Yousef (1994) *Dictionary of Traditional South-East Asian Theatre*, Kuala Lumpur: Oxford University Press.

Goldman, Andrea S. (2012) *Opera and the City: The Politics of Culture in Beijing, 1770–1900*, Stanford: Stanford University Press.

Idema, Wilt L., and Stephen H. West (1982) *Chinese Theater 1100–1450: A Source Book*, Wiesbaden: Franz Verlag Steiner.

Kompira Kabuki, www.konpirakabuki.jp/index.html, accessed 15 May 2015.

Liu Yanjun (2001) *Tushuo Zhongguo xiqu shi* (Illustrated History of Traditional Chinese Drama), Hangzhou: Zhejiang Education Press.

Mackerras, Colin (1972) *The Rise of the Peking Opera, 1770–1870, Social Aspects of the Theatre in Manchu China*, Oxford: Clarendon Press.

—— (1990) *Chinese Drama: a Historical Survey*, Beijing: New World Press.

Meeker, Lauren (2015) 'Forgiving Thị Mầu, a Girl Who Dared to Defy: Performance Change and *Chèo* Theatre in Northern Vietnam', *Asian Theatre Journal*, 32 (1).

Nōson butai to wa (A country stage is. . .), www.joruri.info/butai/butai.html, accessed 23 May 2015.

Performing Arts Network Japan (2010) 'Artist Interview with Tadayoshi Kako: The unique appeal of old playhouses – Links to Edo Period theatre culture', www.performingarts.jp/E/art_interview/1005/1.html, accessed 10 June 2015.

Peterson, William (2011) 'The Ati-atihan Festival: Dancing with the Santo Niño at the "Filipino Mardi Gras"', *Asian Theatre Journal* 28 (2): 506–29.

Shadan hōjin nihon haiyū kyōkai (ed.) (2001) *Kabuki no butai gijutsu to gijutsushatachi* (Kabuki Stage Art and Artists), Tokyo: Shadan hōjin nihon haiyū kyōkai.

Shōchiku Corporation Official Website, 'History of Kabuki-za', www.shochiku.co.jp/play/kabukiza/about/history.php, accessed 22 May 2015.

Suwa Haruo, and Sugai Yukio (eds) (1992) *Nihon engeki shi no shiten* (Views on Japanese Theatre History), Volume 1, Tokyo: Benseisha.

Tokushima: The Land of Ningyo Joruri, www.kansai.gr.jp/en/art_culture/report/2010/06/vol8.html, accessed 10 May 2015.

Varadpande, Manohar Laxman (1987) *History of Indian Theatre*, New Delhi: Abhinav Publications.

Reliable websites for images and information on Japanese stages

'Japan Performing Arts Resource Center: Exploring the Noh Stage', www.glopad.org/jparc/?q=en/nohstage/explore.

'The Kabuki Stage', www2.ntj.jac.go.jp/unesco/kabuki/en/3/3_01.html.

'Traditional Theatre: Kabuki', www.japan-guide.com/e/e2090.html.

Part III
Modern theatre in Asia

11

Modern Indian theatre

Aparna Dharwadker

Anatomy of modernity

The 'modern period' in Indian theatre is said to begin with the new forms of dramatic writing and institutionalized performance that emerged under Anglo-European influences in colonial cities such as Calcutta and Bombay during the later nineteenth century, and have evolved over time to constitute an increasingly visible, multilingual field of postcolonial practice.[1] In the current critical schemes of periods and periodization in Indian theatre, however, 'modernity' functions in turn as a superfluous category, a simplistic principle of chronological demarcation without clear qualitative referents, or an essentially contested term entangled in postcolonial debates over cultural authenticity. For 200 years, scholars and critics in the west have brought the steadily expanding disciplinary orientations of Indology, philology, anthropology, history of religion, performance studies and area studies to bear on the subject of Indian theatre, but their focus has been primarily on the classical period of Sanskrit theatre, or the numerous premodern genres of religious, traditional, ritualistic, folk and intermediary performance. In India the field of criticism is dominated by studies that are concerned with theatre in a single language and region, or collections that present 'Indian theatre' as the simple sum of descriptive histories covering fourteen or sixteen major modern languages; neither approach can historicize modernity as a temporally determined aggregation of qualities that is transregional and pan-Indian in scope. A third model – that of 'nationalist' theatre histories – seeks to establish the antiquity, unity and continuity of Indian theatre and performance traditions over two millennia, but inevitably reduces the relatively recent colonial/postcolonial continuum to an inconclusive coda. In marked contrast to these strategies of omission, an overtly decolonizing strain in post-independence theory and criticism has characterized westernized conventions of representation in urban theatre (especially the proscenium stage) as damaging colonialist legacies that must be countered through a return to precolonial, indigenous traditions of performance. As I have noted elsewhere, '[w]ithin these discursive polarities, definitions of theatrical modernity are usually under- or over-determined: they denote either a hazy set of qualities with uncertain historical coordinates, or practices that must be placed under ideological erasure because of their manifest links to colonialism' (Dharwadker 2011: 426).

In this chapter I use 'modernity' as the appropriate inclusive concept for defining the key features of urban Indian theatre and charting its development over nearly two centuries, in full recognition of the attendant paradoxes and contradictions. In its broadest form, the problem is one of relating precolonial traditions appropriately to the historically unprecedented formations of the colonial and postcolonial periods. The 'long history' of representational forms on the subcontinent included the pan-Indian traditions of classical Sanskrit drama, which had begun to decline after the twelfth century CE, as well as the vast array of postclassical performance genres, which had maintained a varied presence in the lives of particular communities in specific regions for several hundred years (c. 1200–1800 CE). In relation to this history, the new western-influenced urban theatre had the qualities of a 'modern revolution' ranged against precolonial traditions at the levels of both cultural discourse and practice. After a lengthy period of erratic entrepreneurship and upper-class patronage (c. 1790–1860), during which performances took place in makeshift theatres, open-air spaces and private homes, in the 1870s theatre in both Calcutta and Bombay moved fully into the marketplace, incorporating many of the institutional features of European, especially British, theatre. Enclosed theatre buildings, darkened auditoriums, proscenium stages, painted scenery, props and mechanical stage apparatuses made their appearance in India for the first time. The borrowed practice of commercial ticket sales tapped into a growing body of educated middle-class viewers who were drawn to the new forms of commodified entertainment, and selectively accepted women on the stage as well as in the audience. The large-scale investment of capital in urban proscenium theatres and touring companies, especially by Bombay's enterprising Parsi community, also led to the first 'professional' establishments (with resident managers, playwrights, actors, musicians and technicians), which expanded their operations beyond the city to semi-urban, and even rural, areas in particular regions of the country. Over the same period of time, the cross-fertilization of Indian and western textual models produced a substantial body of literary drama, closet drama and dramatic theory in various modern Indian languages, reflecting a deep investment in the idea of theatre as cultural praxis. By the turn of the century, 'drama' had thus emerged as an institution of colonial modernity with a distinctive textual, performative and theoretical presence in urban India – differing, of course, in scale and developmental level from its Anglo-European correlates, and marking a decisive departure from *all* premodern Indian traditions of performance, classical and postclassical.

Despite the apparent dominance of western influences, however, the overwhelming creative impulse in modern Indian theatre of the later nineteenth century was to indigenize and assimilate the 'foreign' models to performative structures that would be intelligible in the linguistic and cultural registers of their immediate audiences. The subjects of representation were drawn from the repertoire of Indian myth, history, legend and folklore that was familiar and culturally resonant in itself, and could also give figurative expression to the emerging socio-political concerns of a reform-minded colonized society. While modes such as realism, naturalism and symbolism informed the text of drama, indigenous traditions of music, dance and spectacle came to dominate the styles of presentation. More ambitiously, the creative and theoretical constituents of modernity were carefully accommodated to classically derived concepts such as *natya* (aestheticized performance), *sahitya* (literature), *natak* (drama), *rangmanch* (the stage, or the theatre more broadly), *prekshan* (spectatorship) and *rasa* (aesthetic experience). Instead of English, major Indian languages such as Bengali, Marathi, Hindi, Urdu, Gujarati and Kannada emerged as the primary media of original theatrical composition for both print and performance. They also served as recipient languages for the prolific translation and adaptation of European and Indian canonical plays, and as the media of interlingual circulation within the modern *oeuvre*, thus establishing the models of intercultural and intracultural exchange that continue to mark urban performance culture prominently in India today. As the imperial language, English served as the all-important conduit through which European discourses entered the Indian languages, for effective circulation and transregional absorption. After 1870, urban theatre also took on an increasingly active and interventionist role in colonial politics, leading to the Dramatic Performances Control Act in 1876, and widespread suppression and censorship by the colonial government during the following five decades.

These colonial formations in theatre began to weaken after the arrival of talking cinema (c. 1930), and became the objects of stringent critique during the years of war, famine, progressive Left politics and militant anticolonialism in the 1940s. Since independence in 1947, still newer forms of authorship, textuality, production and reception have reshaped and transformed urban Indian theatre, in conjunction with postcolonial discourses which have thoroughly problematized the concepts of modernity, tradition and contemporaneity by creating radical connections between the past and the present. The history of modern urban theatre in India is thus a complex interplay of continuities and disjunctions, and from an early-twenty-first century vantage point, it seems to fall into four broad phases:

1   *The period of inception* (c. 1790–1870), which was marked by a strong critical interest among the urban intelligentsia, especially in the Calcutta and Bombay regions, in the potential value of Western-style theatre for Indian audiences in Indian languages. This led to limited forms of entrepreneurship, the founding of culturally conscious amateur theatre societies, and upper-class support for performances in private theatres of various kinds. In Calcutta, the capital of British India, theatre activity also oscillated for quite some time between the poles of Bengali and English, with Indian actors performing occasionally in British productions, theatre societies producing work in both languages, and major authors practising bilingual writing. These developments gave the theatre great prominence as a new urban genre, but did not create stable forms of artistic, institutional and material organization (for a discussion of key institutions and events during this period, see Chatterjee 2007: 17–68).

2   *The period of consolidation* (c. 1870–1930), when theatre became a fully-fledged commercial as well as literary form, and Indian languages came into their own as theatrical media. The Bengali public theatre in Calcutta, and two Bombay-based institutions – the Parsi theatre (using Hindi, Urdu and Gujarati) and the Marathi *natak mandalis* (theatre troupes) devoted to *sangeet nataks* (musical plays) – were the principal forms of entertainment-oriented commercial activity during this period, with primary locations in metropolitan areas but access to a wider national audience. Focusing on theatre as a business, all three organizational models gave primacy to performance over text, and depended on resident or closely associated playwrights whose work had a shifting relationship with the medium of print. However, as a literary genre, 'drama' also attracted the attention of major and minor authors who theorized its role in a national cultural renaissance, and practised it (in verse or prose) on a scale large enough to give it literary visibility in a number of languages that were *theatrically* less active than Bengali and Marathi – notably Hindi, Gujarati, Kannada, Tamil, Telugu and Malayalam. Some of these authors were successful on stage while others remained closet playwrights, but collectively they forged a lasting connection between theatre and the modern culture of print. The high colonial period in theatre was thus a complex conjuncture of art and commerce, with playwrights, impresarios, actors and artists creating a very wide range of permutations between highbrow textuality and lowbrow live entertainment.

3   *The period of revision* (c. 1940–1955), when global crises, competition with the medium of film, cultural movements on the Left and new conceptions of a 'national theatre' came together in an emphatic rejection of the forms and institutions of colonial-era theatre. The displacement of commercial theatre by cinema was a 'natural' process to some extent because films yoked capital more efficiently to mechanically reproducible mass entertainment, and had superior technological means for negotiating realism and spectacle. But colonial theatre

was also the target of an extended *ideological* critique from three distinct quarters: the Indian People's Theatre Association (IPTA), the nationwide populist movement founded in 1943; cultural theorists and bureaucrats who imagined a utopian role for theatre in the artistic life of the new nation; and theatre artists (playwrights, directors, actors) who found the profit -motive incompatible with their creative goals. These divergent arguments led to a common outcome – the delinking of serious urban theatre from commercial modes of production – which still continues to define the conditions for theatre work in India today.

4   *The period of post-independence expansion* (c. 1955 to the present), during which urban Indian theatre has emerged as a major 'new national and postcolonial' field of theory and practice, historically unprecedented in its scale and variety, and largely non-commercial in its modes of material organization. The early post-independence decades (1955–1975) were shaped by major playwrights and directors who chose to redefine theatre as a verbal and social art by distancing themselves equally from the obsolete modernity of colonial theatre, both literary and popular; from Left populism; and from the dictates of the nation-state about how 'the future Indian drama' could contribute to cultural reconstruction. This formative phase produced classic plays grounded in the narratives of myth and history or belonging to social-realist, anti-realist, existentialist, absurdist and Left-political modes, all but the last category containable under the expansive umbrella of modernism. Since the 1970s, modernist impulses have been counterbalanced by the 'theatre of roots' movement, which has critiqued Westernized conventions of representation, especially proscenium realism, as derivative and 'extrinsic', and argued for an authentically Indian modernity derived from 'intrinsic' styles of anti-realistic and environmental presentation. Hence the contest over alternative conceptions of Indianness and Indian modernity is an inherent feature of contemporary theatre discourse, creating antitheses such as realism versus anti-realism, modern versus traditional conventions of staging, urban versus rural modes of existence and cosmopolitanism versus cultural nationalism, to name some key points of contention. There are also a number of significant contemporary practices that position themselves outside the polemic of the modern/anti-modern and colonial/postcolonial debates: street theatre, protest theatre, feminist theatre, performance art by practitioners of both genders, the theatre of marginalized communities such as Dalits, or ostracized groups of transgender/transvestite performers around the country.

This synoptic view of the 'modern period' underscores the central generative paradox, that Indian theatrical modernity is at once inseparable from, and impossible to contain within, the parameters of Euro-modernity, because it represents the intersection of colonial and postcolonial processes with a much older, multilingual and multigeneric indigenous theatre and performance culture. For the same reason, Indian theatre has a nebulous relation to models of colonial and postcolonial cultural expression – for example, those dominant in the ex-colonies of sub-Saharan Africa and the Caribbean – that are predicated on the primacy of European languages as the media of original composition. As art, entertainment and social text, contemporary Indian theatre thus connects in various ways with theatre practices around the world; as a multilingual site of aesthetic and political contests in a non-western nation moving towards and beyond political independence, it constitutes a unique postcolonial field.

The remainder of this chapter takes up some key formations of the post-1850 period, and considers their constitutive role in the evolution of Indian theatrical modernity across the colonial/postcolonial divide. The sphere of modern Indian theatre is too large, heterogeneous and dispersed for a descriptive chronological survey to be feasible: I focus, instead, on discrete processes and events that have exerted a shaping influence for well over a century, and continue to inform the volatile conditions of the present. I am concerned, first, with a form of 'cultural recursivess' that finds expression in the mid-nineteenth century, and has made the 'modernity' of the new urban theatre deeply intertextual with premodern 'tradition' at the levels of theory, taxonomy and practice. Second, the emergence and phenomenal growth of print culture during the nineteenth century leads to a fundamental redefinition of authorship in urban theatre, and creates a new set of relations between playwriting, print and performance that adjust to the transformations of the post-independence period. Third, India's intracultural history of multi-lingual literacy, and the sustained intercultural encounter between major indigenous languages and the western literary-theatrical canon, have stimulated the activities of translation, trans-culturation and multilingual circulation on a scale that has gradually encompassed the nation as well as the world. Fourth, challenges to commercial modes of organization in urban theatre even during the high period of colonial-era commercialism, and the seemingly irrevocable dismantling of the theatrical marketplace in the mid-twentieth century, have destabilized the material conditions of production, and created a culture of urban performance that offers work of 'professional' quality without the concomitant support structures. Finally, an overview of the post-independence period from an early-twenty-first century standpoint indicates the presence of a 'new national' canon in urban theatre, but the plurality and increasing decentralization of theatre practices in India make it imperative for scholars and critics to postulate modernity in terms that go well beyond the nation and any one canon.

Cultural recursiveness

The secular and commercialized colonial theatre in cities such as Calcutta and Bombay was a new historical formation that could not have appeared without the direct influence of English touring companies, Victorian-style theatre architecture and European drama, especially the plays of Shakespeare. It is interesting to note, therefore, that by the mid-nineteenth century, the new modes were perceived mainly as a means of *restoring* theatre to its ancient pre-eminence as an Indian cultural form. The seminal event in this process was the European 'discovery' of classical Sanskrit theatre, which began with Sir William Jones' 1789 translation of Kalidasa's *Shakuntala*, and was continued by translators and/or scholars such as H. H. Wilson, Sylvain Lévi, Sten Konow, Ernest Horrwitz and A. B. Keith (c. 1830–1930), who established drama as the premier Sanskrit genre and Kalidasa as its pre-eminent practitioner – an iconic and precocious 'Indian Shakespeare'. This conspicuous orientalist investment in India's classical past offered Indian authors a cultural system of their 'own' that was equal in complexity and prestige to the new foreign models, and could join with them to produce an admirable new synchresis that would be both Indian and modern.

The very first full-length modern Indian prose play, Michael Madhusudan Dutt's *Sharmishtha*, is a paradigmatic example of these intersecting temporalities and cultural systems. Dutt based the play on a well-known episode in the *Mahabharata*, in which the celebrated King Yayati is cursed to premature old age, but escapes that fate by persuading his youngest son, Puru, to assume the curse. Dutt wrote it in a few weeks in 1858 because he wanted to offer a worthwhile Bengali play for performance at the Belgatchia Villa theatre in north Calcutta, which was patronized by the Rajas of Paikpara. 'The genius of the Drama,' he felt, 'ha[d] not yet received even a moderate degree of development in this country', and the objective in *Sharmishtha* was to create not merely a 'dramatic poem' but a stageable work (Dutt 1982: 571). Dutt's English translation appeared the following year under the anglicized title of *Sermista*, and in the brief advertisement he described the original play as 'the first attempt in the Bengali language to produce a classical and regular Drama' of the kind that could contribute to 'our rising national Theatre' (Dutt 1859: ix).

The *Sharmishtha/Sermista* pairing exhibits Dutt's plural cultural allegiances in that it attempts to create western-style drama in Bengali with classical myth and Sanskrit dramaturgy as the building blocks, and English as a new translational medium for disseminating the hybrid product nationally and internationally. This is the balancing act of being 'Bengali/Indian and English/western at the same stroke', of connecting to a high cultural indigenous past while 'following the modernist principles of European culture as reflected in the theories and praxis of European theatre' (Chatterjee 2007: 107). As Dutt's references to the 'genius of the drama' and the model of a 'classical and regular Drama' also make clear, his goal is nothing less than to restore this genre to the premier status it had in classical culture. The past thus emerges as the highest form of cultural capital in the nationalist project of regeneration, which becomes the Bengal, and subsequently the Indian, Renaissance.

My second example of the long reach of the past involves a range of classical Sanskrit genre-terms that resurface in the nineteenth century, and continue in the twentieth, to function as formal, theoretical and taxonomic signifiers in modern Indian theatre. The most important of these – 'natak' – appears in chapter 20 of Bharata's *Natyasastra*, at the head of a system of classification that names the ten principal *kinds* of drama and establishes qualitative differences between them. As in the Aristotelian description of tragedy, the defining features of the natak are familiarity, seriousness, unity and amplitude. It 'has for its subject-matter a well-known story, [and] for its Hero a celebrated person of exalted nature'; in an appropriate number of 'richly furnished' acts, it describes the hero's 'many superhuman powers and exploits such as, success [in different undertakings] and amorous pastimes' (Ghosh 1950: 356). Moreover, it focuses on a few main characters rather than on a large cast, and enforces social hierarchies by placing elevated characters in the regular acts and servants only in the interludes. Of the remaining dramatic kinds discussed in the *Natyasastra*, the most significant for modern practice are the *prakanran* (full-length play with an invented plot), *prahasan* (farce), *vyayog* (episode covering a single day) and *ank* (act), while the term *rupak* refers to dramatic form in general.

The influence that the Sanskrit system of classification has exerted on the Indian languages since the early nineteenth century is an accurate measure of the complex process by which 'tradition', recovered and mediated by orientalism, informs and legitimizes 'modernity' in Indian theatre. In the formative stages of modern urban dramatic writing, the old terminology establishes a genealogical and generic connection between classical and modern drama to underscore two general principles: that the modern forms have a high classical heritage, and that modern authors are conscious of this heritage and equal to the challenge of sustaining it in the present. In the modern history of the natak as both concept and artefact, for instance, three facets are worth highlighting. The first is the compulsion among modern practitioners to *name* the genre by making it an intrinsic part of the title or subtitle of a play – a practice they borrow directly from the ancients. Thus the seventh-century *Venisamhara natak* of Narayana Bhatt in Sanskrit has an exact titular counterpart in the mid-nineteenth century *Sharmishtha natak* of Michael Madhusudan Dutt in Bengali. Second, natak emerges even in the early modern decades as a versatile term for a wide range of modern dramatic practices which include new plays in the Indian languages as well as translations of western plays, such as Harchandra Ghosh's *Bhanumati chittabilas natak* (a version of *The Merchant of Venice*, Bengali, 1853), or G. B. Deval's *Jhunjharrao natak* (an adaptation of *Othello*, Marathi, 1890). Third, and most important, natak serves as the stable qualifying term in the naming of a plethora of modern dramatic genres, resulting in a versatile taxonomy that ranges from *samajik natak* (social play), *aitihasik natak* (history play) and *sangeet natak* (musical play), to *samasya natak* (problem play), *nukkad natak* (street-corner play) and *kavya natak* (verse play). Instead of representing just one of ten distinct dramatic kinds (as in the *Natyasastra*), in modern Indian usage natak comes to stand for a dramatic work of varying length, subject matter and linguistic style which the author and/or audience perceive as a work of literary and artistic merit. The recursive reference to the cultural past that began in the mid-nineteenth century has thus not only continued but proliferated in the present: the 'poetics' of Indian theatrical modernity is to a significant extent the 'history' of the formative and generative value of the classical terminology for playwrights, theatre professionals and audiences alike.

Authorship, print and performance

Authorship is a critical but constantly shifting avocation in modern Indian theatre because of the complex ways in which the categories of drama, theatre, print and performance intersect with the processes of orality and writing, both historically and in specific colonial and postcolonial contexts. The classical, postclassical and premodern 'legacies' in theatre are mainly of literary authorship dissociated from the performance event (as in the case of playwrights such as Kalidasa and Bhasa), or the performance event dissociated from proprietary authorship, literary or otherwise (as in the extensive array of ritualistic, devotional, folk-popular and balletic performance genres that constitute premodern Indian 'theatre' between the twelfth and eighteenth centuries). As a *modern* institution, therefore, authorship takes shape in India only over the course of the nineteenth century, and in the specific fields of drama and theatre it is mediated by two entirely new configurations: the culture of print, which arrives belatedly around 1800, and urban commercial theatre, which assumes its fully developed metropolitan form by the 1870s. At one end, the conjuncture of modern subjectivity, print and the burden of the (newly rediscovered) past foregrounds the figure of the author and sutures drama to literary ambition, programmes of nationalist cultural renewal and projects of social reform. At the other end, the dominance of the profit motive in new forms of commercial urban performance orients theatre towards entertainment and spectacle, and turns the author into one more kind of 'theatre worker'.

Since the mid-nineteenth century, Indian playwrights have occupied numerous positions between these polarities, creating a wide range of oppositional as well as complementary relations between the mediums of print and performance. In the commercial urban theatre of colonial cities such as Calcutta and Bombay, for example, the unstable relationships between print and theatre form along three axes that can be defined respectively as the predominantly or exclusively literary, the literary-performative and the predominantly or exclusively performative. The literary pole, definable heuristically as 'drama', implies authorial self-consciousness, writing, textuality, print, ambitious programmes of cultural enlightenment and reform, and communities of readers. The performative pole, definable as 'theatre', implies authorial abjection, orality, institutionalized performance, competitive commercial production, popular entertainment, the profit motive and communities of viewers. The middle position, representing more the exception than the norm in colonial India, implies practices that draw drama and theatre together through work that is relatively 'serious' or 'highbrow', but intended primarily for success on the stage. These distinctions, which seem quite anomalous in comparison with western practices, capture quite accurately the authorial positions of the 1860–1940 period.

The first notable cluster consists of playwrights for whom the dramatic form is an important exercise of authorship within the sphere of modern print culture, and whose work consequently has its primary, though not its only, existence in print. Michel Madhusudan Dutt (1824–73), Dinabandhu Mitra (1830–73) and Rabindranath Tagore (1861–1941) in Bengali, and Bhartendu Harishchandra (1850–86) and Jaishankar Prasad (1889–1937) in Hindi, are the principal authors in this category, covering a working time-span from the late 1850s to the 1930s. As foundational literary figures who exercise a transformative influence on the multiple genres they practise, they are acutely conscious of the classical origins of the natak form, its proximity to the western 'play' and its high cultural value in the present, but their connection to the theatre is erratic, adversarial or non-existent.

The second important type of colonial authorship involves a large body of dramatic writing that is produced specifically for performance, but also leaves a substantial, if not always 'significant', impression in print. In the Calcutta public theatre, impresarios such as Girish Chandra Ghosh (1844–1912) and Sisir Kumar Bhaduri (1889–1959) were playwright-actor-theatre managers in the tradition of David Garrick, functioning as key organizational figures at the Great National Theatre and the Star Theatre, respectively, in two different generations. Among the professional playwrights who were supported by this system, Kshirode Prasad Bidyabinode (1863–1927) and D. L. Roy (1863–1913) were the most prolific and significant, keeping up a steady supply of plays based on myth, history and social issues. In Marathi theatre, the resident/itinerant natak mandalis were founded by (and often named after) seminal figures such as Annasaheb Kirloskar (1843–85), Bal Gandharva (1888–1967) and Keshavrao Bhonsle (1890–1921), with resident playwrights who were also sometimes actors and directors. Two generations of leading Marathi playwrights – Govind Ballal Deval (1855–1916), Shripad Krishna Kolhatkar (1871–1934), Krishnaji Prabhakar Khadilkar (1872–1948) and Ram Ganesh Gadkari (1885–1919) – wrote for the natak mandalis, and collectively moulded the form of the sangeet natak as the vehicle for old and new narratives to produce the distinctive colonial culture of performance in Marathi theatre history. Other concurrent traditions in Marathi that became much stronger in the 1930s were those of the 'social problem' play, contemporary urban comedy and farce, with Mama Warerkar (1883–1964), Shridhar V. Vartak (1885–1950) and M. G. Rangnekar (b. 1907) as the leading authors, and Ibsen as the major European influence.

The third major category of colonial-era writers consists of 'playwrights' who were actually salaried employees of the Parsi theatre companies, producing scripts that had a much more erratic relation to print at the time of original composition. The textual impress that Parsi theatre created *during its most active periods* was very small in comparison with its large-scale theatrical presence over nearly a century, and its hold on the popular imagination. Among the three leading 'professional' playwrights of the Parsi theatre, Narayan Prasad Betab (1872–1945) follows the pattern of near-invisibility in print. The output of Pandit Radheshyam Kathavachak (1890–1963), in contrast, displays the print/performance complementarity typical of the literary-popular playwrights, though his plays are distinctly lowbrow, and the total output includes an autobiography (reprinted in 2004) as well as texts that the author produced as a professional 'reciter of religious/mythic tales' (*katha-vachak*). For Agha Hashra Kashmiri (1879–1935), an almost mythical figure in Parsi and Urdu theatre, the publication record is scanty until the early 1950s, but after 1954 there is an unbroken succession of individual plays in multiple editions, collections of two or three plays and one-volume 'selected works', with the multi-volume collected works appearing in 2004. Kashmiri is therefore the professional playwright chosen for the most determined effort at authorial recuperation and rehabilitation by those who wish to preserve the legacy of Parsi theatre, and the performance culture it fostered in Urdu and Hindi (see Hansen 2011).

In the post-independence period, the colonial models of authorship have undergone substantial revision. The binarism of 'literary/textual' and 'popular/performative' has ceased to exist, and the intermediary category of the literary-performative has evolved as the instrumental condition, both in itself and as a corrective to the extremes on either side. In fact, the text/performance opposition becomes unsustainable in a situation where the activity of 'authorship' has to be charted along a continuum connecting the textual and performative poles. The first group of major post-independence authors, such as Dharamvir Bharati (1926–1997), Mohan Rakesh (1925–1972), Girish Karnad (b. 1938) and Mahesh Elkunchwar (b. 1939), are literary playwrights of the same kind as Tagore and Harishchandra, but like popular playwrights such as Khadilkar and Atre (and to a much greater extent), they also belong *simultaneously* to the economies of print and performance, and produce work that is 'serious' as well as 'successful' in both modes (Figure 11.1). The second group includes figures such as Vijay Tendulkar (1928–2008), Satish Alekar (b. 1949) and Chandrashekhar Kambar (b. 1938), who maintain equally strong literary identities, but collaborate actively and over the long term with specific theatre groups as resident playwrights, actors and directors, especially of their own work. The third category involves playwrights who take on the full spectrum of theatrical roles. Utpal Dutt (1929–1993), Badal Sircar (1925–2011), Habib Tanvir (1923–2009), K. N. Panikkar (b. 1928), Ratan Thiyam (b. 1948) and Mahesh Dattani (b. 1958) are authors, actors, directors and founder-managers of their own non-commercial theatre groups. Tanvir, Panikkar and Thiyam are also the leading director–authors who have developed a range of non-realistic, non-proscenium forms by drawing upon indigenous folk, tribal, classical, ritualistic and martial arts traditions. Sircar, in contrast, was interested in creating a minimalist theatre that could provide an alternative to

Figure 11.1 Scene from Dharamvir Bharati's *Andha yug* (Blind Epoch, 1954), directed for the National School of Drama Repertory Company by Ebrahim Alkazi, New Delhi, 1974. The open-air stage is located within Purana Qila (Old Fort), a sixteenth-century fortification on an ancient archaeological site by the Yamuna river.

(Courtesy of National School of Drama)

urban realist drama as well as rural folk forms. Influenced by Jerzy Grotowski's 'poor theatre' and Richard Schechner's 'environmental theatre, his idea of a 'Third Theatre' resulted in largely non-verbal, body-centred vehicles for non-proscenium indoor and outdoor performance, in cities and villages. In addition, a growing body of authors/auteurs outside the 'mainstream' have opened up possibilities for the strategic exercise of authorship from many other political-cultural positions. Two key figures in the street theatre movement – Safdar Hashmi, a founding member of Jana Natya Manch (JANAM), and Prasanna, the founder of Samudaya – are published playwrights and theorists as well as activists. A similar balance of activism and articulation is visible in the theatre work of feminist authors, organizers, and performers (see concluding section, below).

Except for some forms of street theatre, protest theatre and feminist performance, then, the constitution of authorship through print is now a ubiquitous four-part process, regardless of the kind of theatre a playwright practises. Publication in the original language of composition, which makes a play available to its most likely readers as well as an audience larger than that of theatregoers, is followed by wider circulation through translation into multiple Indian languages, including and especially English. The process of critical recognition brings a play much wider attention than performance-related commentary, and institutionalization within the academy absorbs it into the pedagogy of literature. This cycle of print, translation, criticism and pedagogy is as relevant to the indigenized, body-centred, aurally and visually oriented total theatre of Tanvir, Panikkar *et al.* as to the text-centred theatre of Rakesh, Tendulkar and Karnad. Performance may be the primary *intended* mode of existence in many contemporary forms of theatre, but with the work of every major author available to readers, often in multiple languages, the printed text has come to represent an equally continuous parallel mode.

Multilingual literacy, translation, and transculturation

The unbroken history of multilingual literacy on the Indian subcontinent over two and a half millennia is, as Sheldon Pollock suggests, 'a story of complex creativity and textual devotion with few parallels in history' (2003: 31), with the inherent heterogeneity of indigenous formations being complicated much further by successive waves of foreign conquest and colonization. As the subcontinental equivalent of Greek and Latin, Sanskrit gave rise to more than twelve major modern Indian languages of the Indo-European family, but after 1200 CE made way for Persian, and then for English, as the pan-Indian languages of the ruling class. Beginning in the late eighteenth century, the orientalist recovery of India's classical past forged positive connections between Sanskrit and the *modern European* languages that deviated radically from the usual reductive hierarchy of colonial power relations. Contrapuntally, the institutionalization of English as the medium of education in British India after 1835 connected it on a monumental scale to the *modern Indian* languages, and made it the vital point of contact between India and the west.

This plurality and interconnectedness of languages has determined the historical conditions germane to modern Indian theatre in its various modes of existence (writing, publication and performance), and the primary vehicle of linguistic-cultural exchange is the activity of translation. From the vantage point of the present, the modes of connection can be analysed into the following chronologically overlapping strands: (i) the translation of Sanskrit plays into the modern Indian languages; (ii) the translation of Sanskrit plays into the modern European languages; (iii) the translation of Shakespeare into the modern Indian languages; (iv) the translation of other English, European, American and world theatre into the modern Indian languages; and (v) the translation of modern plays from one Indian language into another, including English, which is now both an Indian and a western language. Categories (i) and (v) are intracultural modes of exchange *between the Indian languages* that give individual works and textual clusters both transregional and national currency. Category (ii) represents the only substantial intercultural carrying across of *Indian* drama into *western* mediums, with the translated works belonging exclusively to the classical Sanskrit period. The two remaining categories – (iii) and (iv) – are intercultural or transcultural modes of colonial and postcolonial exchange in which the Indian languages serve as *recipient media* for Euro-American and world theatre from all periods.

In this network of connections, there is a fundamental theoretical distinction to be made between two forms of exchange: interlingual translation and intercultural or transcultural appropriation. The most common Indian terms for interlingual translation are *bhashantar* or *bhashantaran* (literally the 'difference' or 'movement' of *language*), and *anuvad* (repetition or emulation). From the beginning of the modern period, however, the 'translation' of western and world drama into *Indian* languages has consisted mainly in a form of transculturation for which the general Indian terms are *rupantar* or *rupantaran* (the 'difference' or 'movement' of *form*; 'changed or new form, transformation; version, rendering, adaptation'), and *anuyojan* (the remaking of ancient narratives or unfamiliar forms of expression through a new artistic consciousness). This alternative terminology denotes a search for equivalence in cultural *as well as* linguistic signs, and a meticulous 'translation of difference' so that a play embodies the cultural system as well as the language of its receiving audience. The original works as well as their 'adaptations' can therefore be conceived of as 'transcultural intertexts', bound in a relationship that postcolonial theory describes mainly as the ex-colonial periphery 'writing back' to the ex-imperial centre. In India, however, the practice began *during the colonial period itself* with the large-scale transculturation of Shakespeare, and has grown immeasurably since independence, as the canon not only of western but world drama has found its way onto the Indian stage, and into the print culture of all the major Indian languages, including English. What appears cumulatively over two centuries in urban India is an interest in translating, 'rewriting' and appropriating earlier drama and performance that is almost as compelling and pervasive as the impulse towards original composition.

All five strands of translation/transculturation have had a notable impact on modern Indian theatre, and merit brief discussion. The simultaneous translation of Sanskrit drama into the modern European as well as Indian languages by European and Indian translators (scholars, poets, playwrights, philologists, enthusiasts) was a singular event in colonial and postcolonial literary-cultural history because it involved a uniquely triangulated transhistorical exchange: it made a redemptive cultural past available to both the colonizer and the colonized (albeit for very different cultural ends), and inserted 'tradition' instrumentally into 'modernity'. The bibliographic record of this cultural interweaving is impressive in scale: for the 1800–2012 period, the Library of Congress catalogue lists almost 4,000 translations of the eight principal Sanskrit playwrights (Kalidasa, Bhasa, Shudraka, Bhavabhuti, Shri Harsha, Vishakhadutt, Krishna Mishra and Mahendra Vikram Varman) into languages such as English, French, German, Italian and Spanish, and about 1,800 translations of the same playwrights into the Indian languages, notably Hindi, Bengali, Marathi, Telugu, Kannada and Gujarati.

In post-independence India, the Sanskrit dramatic heritage has assumed a complex and multidimensional cultural role in the theatre that goes well beyond the boundaries of textual translation, both Indian and western. New scholarly editions of the principal playwrights have appeared both in the original Sanskrit and in translation in most major languages, including works of high cultural capital such as the versions of Shudraka's *Mrichchhakatika* (The Little Clay Cart, 1961) and Kalidasa's *Shakuntala* (1965) by the leading Hindi playwright Mohan Rakesh. Sanskrit plays are performed in the original (productions by K. N. Panikkar, Chandradasan), in translation (productions by Shanta Gandhi, Vijaya Mehta, Ebrahim Alkazi, Ratan Thiyam) and in inventive adaptations (Habib Tanvir's 'folk' versions of *Mrichchhakatika* as *Mitti ki gadi*, Bhasa's *Urubhangam* (The Shattered Thighs) as *Duryodhana* and Vishakhadutt's *Mudrarakshasa*). Traditionalist scholars and practitioners, especially proponents of the 'theatre of roots', have urged a return to the *Natyasastra* as the foundation for a contemporary representational aesthetic in all the performing arts, with the premodern indigenous forms restoring a cultural unity that was lost during the colonial period. In a decolonizing post-independence culture, Sanskrit drama and poetics thus represent an elite tradition that offers the richest resources for the recovery of indigeneity, cultural authenticity and Indianness, whether it is re-presented in its pristine forms or transformed in the present. At every level, the Sanskrit legacy in the original and in translation continues to inform modern theatre.

Even more pervasive and influential than the Sanskrit networks, however, is the translation and transculturation (bhashantar and rupantar) of Anglo-European-American drama. The first major phase in this process was the arrival of Shakespeare in the colonial Indian classroom and the dissemination of his works across the full spectrum of modern Indian languages (c. 1850–1920). From the beginning, the absorption of Shakespeare was dominated by trans-cultural adaptations rather than interlingual translations because of the pressing desire among theatre professionals to Indianize the playwright for the stage. The 'popular' end of this process was represented by plays such as G. B. Deval's *Jhunjharrao* (Marathi, 1890), a sensational stage musical version of *Othello*, and Urdu adaptations for the Parsi stage such as Betab's *Gorakh dhandha* (*The Comedy of Errors*, 1912) or Kashmiri's *Dilfaroza* (*The Merchant of Venice*, 1900), *Safed khoon* (*King Lear*, 1906) and *Shaheed-i-naaz* (*Measure for Measure*, 1914). At the 'literary' end, Bhartendu Harishchandra, the 'father' of modern Hindi literature, adapted *The Merchant of Venice* as *Durlabh bandhu* (Invaluable Friend), and the social reformer Gopal Ganesh Agarkar adapted *Hamlet* into Marathi under the title *Wikara vilasita* in 1882, using the play as an example of the 'malformations' caused by sensual self-indulgence among those who are socially privileged.

Since the 1940s, Shakespeare has been enmeshed in the post-independence literary-artistic renaissance in even more complex ways. Leading poets such as Harivansha Rai Bachchan and Raghuvir Sahay (Hindi), Vinda Karandikar and V. V. Shirwadkar (Marathi), Masti Venkatesha Iyengar (Kannada) and Firaq Gorakhpuri (Urdu) have translated or adapted Shakespeare's major tragedies, comedies and romances. These and other versions have been brought to the stage by leading directors such as Utpal Dutt, Ebrahim Alkazi, K. V. Subbanna, Alyque Padamsee and the East German director Fritz Bennewitz, best known for his collaborative productions of Bertolt Brecht in India. Performance acquires perhaps its greatest level of complexity when the Shakespearean adaptation incorporates a major indigenous form or presentational style, as in B. V. Karanth's yakshagana version of *Macbeth* (translated by Sahay as *Barnam vana*; see Figure 11.2), Sadanam Balakrishnan's Kathakali *King Lear* and *Othello* and Habib Tanvir's *Midsummer Night's Dream* (*Kamdeva ka apna, vasant ritu ka sapna*, 1993) in the Chhattisgarhi folk style (for a detailed discussion of Shakespeare in India, see Shormishtha Panja's chapter in this volume).

Since the 1920s, the translation of other foreign drama into Indian languages has moved well beyond Shakespeare and the exigencies of commercial theatre performance, and now represents an ever-expanding field of published texts and notable performances, although the geography of translation continues to be circumscribed. The example of Hindi, the language containing the largest body of world drama in modern translation, shows that western Europe has retained its centrality as the locus of original works, while the sphere of translation has expanded backwards to include the classical Greek playwrights, and forwards to include many early modern and middle modern authors, such as Calderón, Ben Jonson, Molière, Racine, Rostand, Beaumarchais, Goldoni, Giradoux, Sheridan, Lessing and Büchner. The core energy in translation, however,

Figure 11.2 Uttara Baokar as Lady Macbeth in *Barnam vana* (Shakespeare's *Macbeth*), translated into Hindi by Raghuvir Sahay, and directed for the National School of Drama Repertory Company by B. V. Karanth, New Delhi, 1979.

(Courtesy National School of Drama)

is focused on the major modern/ist figures of northern and western Europe – Ibsen, Chekhov, Gogol, Gorki, Strindberg, Wilde, Shaw, Maeterlinck, Pirandello, Galsworthy, Brecht, Lorca, Anouilh, Sartre, Camus, Dürenmatt, Beckett, Ionesco, Wesker and Fo, among others. The interest in American drama has remained mainly limited to Eugene O'Neill, Arthur Miller and Tennessee Williams, with an occasional play by William Saroyan varying the sequence of classics by the older trifecta.

The value placed on translation is fully reflected in the succession of major authors in various languages who have taken on the task of translating western plays. In addition to the major translations of Shakespeare mentioned earlier, in Hindi the notable translator–author pairings include Premchand and John Galsworthy (c. 1930); Rajendra Yadav and Chekhov (1958); Kamleshwar and Brecht (1970); Raghuvir Sahay and Lorca (1985); and Safdar Hashmi and Gorky (1989). In Marathi, another rich target language, Acharya Atre translated Molière; P. L. Deshpande adapted Gogol, Sophocles and Somerset Maugham; Vijay Tendulkar and Vyankatesh Madgulkar adapted Tennessee Williams; and V. V. Shirwadkar translated Maeterlinck, Oscar Wilde and Tolstoy. Brecht is the playwright with the strongest list of Indian translators, including C. T. Khanolkar, Madgulkar and P. L. Deshpande in Marathi, Badal Sircar in Bengali, Habib Tanvir in Chhattisgarhi and K. V. Subbanna in Kannada. The scale and significance of the translation activity cannot, however, obscure the issue that large regions of the world have been left virtually untouched, among them Japan, China, Canada, Australia, the Caribbean, the Middle East and Africa.

The final process – the translation of modern Indian plays into multiple Indian languages, including English – is intraculturally the most significant one. The transregional circulation of plays during the colonial period was sporadic, but the decades since independence have demonstrated that in Indian theatre the prompt recognition of new plays as contemporary classics depends not so much on publication or performance in the original language of composition as on the rapidity with which the plays are performed and (secondarily) published in *other* languages. Such proliferation keeps a play in constant circulation among readers and viewers, creating the layers of textual meaning and stage interpretation that become the measure of its significance. This method of dissemination also generates – and has already generated – a body of nationally circulating texts and performance vehicles that offers more convincing evidence of the existence of a 'national theatre' than any other institutional, linguistic or bureaucratic conception.

There are very specific mechanisms and artistic choices that have made the culture of translingual circulation possible in contemporary Indian theatre. The nationwide theatre movement of the 1960s, which began the first major transregional initiatives, gave high priority to the translation of important new plays, and succeeded in forging strong connections between the Indian languages. Leading directors such as Satyadev Dubey (Bombay), Shyamanand Jalan (Calcutta) and Rajinder Nath (Delhi) made a commitment to focus exclusively or mainly on the production of new Indian plays, rather than foreign plays from any language or period. Other prominent directors, such as Shombhu Mitra, Alkazi, Subbanna, Karanth and Arvind Deshpande were more eclectic in their choices, but made productions of new works in translation a key component of their practice. In addition, major playwrights translated each other's work so that important new plays could reach a larger audience of spectators and readers. Girish Karnad translated Badal Sircar's classic *Ebong Indrajit* (And Indrajit) into English, and Vijay Tendulkar translated Karnad's *Tughlaq* and Sircar's *Indrajit* into Marathi. A cadre of accomplished translators – among them Pratibha Agrawal, Santvana Nigam, Vasant Dev, B. R. Narayan, Shanta Gokhale and Samik Bandyopadhyay – variously forged and sustained interlingual connections between Bengali, Marathi, Kannada, Hindi and English. Oxford University Press began publishing Indian drama in English translation under its Three Crowns imprint in 1972, and has since made the plays of Badal Sircar, Girish Karnad, Vijay Tendulkar, Satish Alekar and Mahesh Elkunchwar available to national and international audiences. In 1983, the Seagull Foundation for the Arts in Calcutta also launched an ambitious programme of plays in English translation, and over three decades the list has expanded to become the largest single archive of contemporary Indian plays in a single target language.

Beyond these particularities, multilingualism and circulation in their post-independence forms have had a profound effect on dramatic authorship, theatre theory, the textual life of drama and the culture of performance: essentially, drama and theatre in each theatrically active language are enhanced by the output in every other active language. Playwrights who fashion themselves as literary authors write with the anticipation that the original text of a play will soon enter the multilingual economy of translation, performance and publication. They also construct authorship and authority as activities that must extend across languages in order to sustain a national theatre movement in a multilingual society. Significantly, although playwrights such as Tendulkar, Mahesh Elkunchwar, Chandrashekhar Kambar and G. P. Deshpande write their plays exclusively in their respective regional languages, much of their criticism appears directly in English. Collectively, playwrights and directors have constructed a framework for contemporary Indian drama and theatre in which regional theatrical traditions interact with each other, and are available for use beyond the borders of their respective provinces as well as those of the nation.

'Anti-theatricality' and the critique of commerce

Since the early modern period, the marketing of theatre as a form of commodified leisure in the west has not precluded the valuation of drama and theatre as forms of cultural capital. However powerful the theoretical attacks on 'culinary' or 'opulent' theatre, in practice commercial superstructures such as those of Broadway and the West End have continued to serve as ultimate forms of legitimation for not just popular but serious art. In India, the shift from patronal to commercial relations took place in the course of the nineteenth century and entrepreneurial energies fuelled urban theatre in the colonial metropolis for a time, making the entertainment-for-profit model more or less viable from about 1870 to 1940. But the material transaction between profit-seeking producers and paying consumers emerged as an intractable issue during the transition from colonial to postcolonial modalities, and the profit motive shifted with a vengeance from theatre to cinema during the 1940s. What we might describe as the second 'modern revolution' of the post-independence period has therefore taken place in a largely non-commercial performance culture.

There were, in fact, two forms of opposition to mainstream colonial commercial practices within the colonial period itself: the theory and practice of leading literary figures such as Harishchandra, Tagore and Prasad, who were prolific playwrights but did not participate in the culture of public performance; and the large body of more or less obscure printed drama which showed an extraordinary engagement with drama as a form, but again independent of performance contexts. The theoretical positions of Tagore *et al.* can be described as a 'proto-modernist antitheatricalism' which, like the 'constructive antitheatricalism' of high-modernist playwrights in Europe, devalues 'stage performance' precisely because of the high value placed on 'drama' (see Puchner 2002: 2). All three writers use Sanskrit theatre as a touchstone and poetry as the privileged creative medium at the heart of drama. Bharatendu persistently refers to an individual play as a *grantha* – that is, a text or tome that has its primary existence in the world of writing and print. Tagore rejects Wagner's concept of the unified art work (which brings together poetry, dance and music), western realism and even the notion that a play is realized fully only in performance, just as Prasad rejects the idea that plays should be written for the stage as a 'serious misconception about the theatre: the real effort should in fact be to provide a stage for drama' (Prasad 1936: 414). The anti-theatricalism of these judgements is both pointed and precise because all three authors have a common object of attack in the Parsi theatre, which Prasad dismisses in his 1936 essay, 'Rangmanch' ('The Stage', 1936), as a repugnant spectacle parading men in women's roles.

The two decades following Prasad's essay are singular in Indian theatre history not only because the much-maligned colonial commercial structures came to a decisive end, but because serious theatre was delinked from commercialized performance by a process that has yet to be reversed. The first serious critique of colonial practices came from the Indian People's Theatre Association (IPTA), the nationwide theatre movement that was also linked to anti-Fascist and anti-imperialist movements around the world. Its 1943 manifesto declared that art and literature could have a future only if they expressed and inspired 'the people's struggles for freedom and culture' – a test that urban drama of the previous 70 years had failed signally because of its dependence on middle-class conventionality, or its escape into 'bad history and senseless mythology' (Pradhan 1979–1985: 1: 134, 136). An important part of the IPTA's activist pro-gramme was therefore to revive the traditional, folk and intermediary performance genres from which nineteenth-century urban practitioners had distanced themselves, but which now appeared to have exactly the qualities that would dislodge bourgeois urban forms (Figure 11.3).

Figure 11.3 A scene from Bijon Bhattacharya's *Nabanna* (The New Harvest, 1944), the play produced most successfully around the nation by the Indian People's Theatre Association, under the direction of Shombhu Mitra.

(Courtesy of Sangeet Natak Akademi, New Delhi)

As this Left cultural movement declined in the 1950s, the newly independent nation-state stepped in to mediate a second phase of de-commercialization, this time in the name of a resurgent Indianness. At the landmark 5-day Drama Seminar organized by the Sangeet Natak Akademi in April 1956, the unsuitability of colonial practices to a new national theatre culture and the need to rescue theatre from the marketplace were two major topics. Influential discussants such as the Indian-English novelist Mulk Raj Anand and the actor Balraj Sahni argued that the enclosed auditorium, the proscenium stage, commercial ticket sales and naturalist staging were all imperialist impositions alien to Indian habits of performance and spectatorship. The association of drama with theatre companies was also a deterrent to serious playwriting, and had caused a serious shortage of reputable playwrights and 'good actable plays' after independence. To create a conceptual basis for their positions, the seminar participants devalued 'professional' (commercial) theatre in the same measure that they valorized 'amateur' (non-commercial theatre), and concluded that the 'future hope for the establishment of a national theatre and dramatic renaissance' lay in the 'encouragement and promotion' of amateur theatre (Kastuar 2007: 287–9, 305–6, 323).

The final strain in the rejection of commerce has proved to be the most powerful, and it consists in a *modernist* rupture from the forms of colonial modernity in the work of the first generation of post-independence playwrights. Major early-postcolonial modernists such as Bharati, Tendulkar, Sircar, Karnad and Rakesh distance themselves equally from commercialism, anti-theatrical literariness, IPTA-style populism and bureaucratic nationalism. During the 1950s and 1960s (the formative decades for modernism), serious playwriting reveals either an *unconscious* attraction to the dramatic form on the part of playwrights who have no overt concern with performance, or a *conscious* commitment to drama on the part of those who both desire and expect performance, but not with any certainty. The availability of stable institutional theatre structures is therefore not necessary to the existence of drama. But instead of producing closet plays, these conditions produce major performable works that are in fact performed in multiple languages with great success. Even at the beginning of their respective careers, the playwrights mentioned above seem to be fully formed *authors*, while being acutely aware that they are not part of any ongoing theatrical tradition. The performance culture that their work demands comes into existence gradually, as the result of strategic collaborations between like-minded theatre groups, directors, translators, actors and technical personnel. But market conditions continue to be largely absent from theatre culture in India today, mainly because film, television and video have come to stay as the dominant commercialized forms, while playwrights and theatre artists have adjusted to, or actively embraced, a non-commercial ethic.

Twenty-first-century perspectives: centre, periphery, and plurality

At the 1956 Drama Seminar, Mulk Raj Anand described post-independence theatre practitioners as 'infants with clean slates in their hands', well positioned to determine a utopian future course for Indian drama. Six decades later, a more appropriate metaphor for the field of theatre is that of a dense palimpsest in which the contours of a 'new national canon' are unmistakably, inevitably visible. Many recent commentators have justly criticized this emergent centre for its predominantly urban, middle-class, male outlook, and its separation from subaltern perspectives on gender, sexuality, nation, class and caste. However, it is both reductive and misguided to argue (as Shayoni Mitra does in a recent survey) that the accelerated processes of canon-formation after independence were legislated by some 'original proponents of postcolonial culture' who wished to institute 'hegemonies of space, gender, language, and caste' and functioned as 'caretakers of modern Indian theatre' (2014: 66, 87) Such arguments fail to distinguish between the state's propagandist rhetoric and artistic practices that were in fact counter-hegemonic, strongly critical of the nation-state and subject to impossible material conditions of survival. The energetic theatre movement of the 1955–75 period became possible mainly because theatre artists around the country grappled with the unstable conditions of writing and production, collaborated with each other and brought new work onto the stage. Certain authors and works also now appear central not because of carefully orchestrated processes of inclusion and exclusion, but because readers, viewers and theatre makers have *chosen* to engage with them repeatedly: 'canonicity' in these cases is an effect that follows, not a cause that precedes, the always-changing parameters of artistic value.

The so-called canon, moreover, does not privilege any one style or content and, beyond its obvious limitations, is inclusive in its own way. Plays such as Tanvir's *Charandas chor* (Charandas the Thief, 1974) and Thiyam's *Chakravyuha* (Battle Formation, 1984), which represent forms of total theatre inspired by regional traditions of music, dance and/or martial arts, are no less 'canonical' than Rakesh's *Ashadh ka ek din* (One Day in the Season of Rain, 1958), a modernist reimagining of the life of Kalidasa, or Elkunchwar's *Wada chirebandi* (Old Stone Mansion, 1985), a masterpiece of domestic realism. Mahesh Dattani, the playwright in English who from the beginning has challenged the status quo in relation to gender, class and sexuality in plays such as *Tara* (1990) and *On a Muggy Night in Mumbai* (1998), is no less visible than Girish Karnad, whose groundbreaking plays in Kannada (such as *Tughlaq*, 1964, *Hayavadana* [Horse-Head], 1971 and *Naga-mandala* [Play with a Cobra], 1987) demystified the premodern narratives of myth, history and folklore. As an urban practitioner of experimental-absurdist theatre in Marathi (e.g.

Mahanirvan [The Great Departure], 1974), Satish Alekar has been no less influential than the Kannada playwright Chandrashekhar Kambar, who is rooted in village culture and draws extensively on folk narratives (as in *Jokumaraswamy* [1972]). The overtly political theatre of G. P. Deshpande (*Uddhwasta dharmashala* [A Man in Dark Times], 1974) and Utpal Dutt (*Mahavidroh* [The Great Rebellion], 1985) is just as visible as the avant-garde but no less political Third Theatre of Badal Sircar (*Spartacus*, 1972; *Procession*, 1974). In the house of post-independence theatre, there have been many mansions from the beginning, and cultural prescriptions of one kind or another have had limited influence. Mitra is right, however, in arguing that the energies of the originary post-independence movement have dissipated, and the 1990s have ushered in 'a far more contingent and contestatory approach, a tactic of surviving in an increasingly neoliberal and globalizing cultural landscape' (2014: 65). My task in this concluding section is to underscore the irreducible plurality of Indian theatre in the early twenty-first century, and to focus briefly on two 'representative' sites of contestation – the 'theatre of roots' and the expanding sphere of experimental theatre activity on the part of women practitioners.

In contemporary India, theatre is written and produced in about fifteen languages that vary in their levels of activity, and exist in a hierarchical relation that adjusts to changes over a period of time. In terms of original composition, Bengali and Marathi continue to be the two leading languages, followed by Hindi, Kannada, Gujarati, Malayalam, Tamil, Telugu and Manipuri in a second cluster, and English, Assamese, Oriya, Punjabi, Sindhi and Kashmiri in a third. Languages in the first two clusters were already either prominent or visible during the colonial period; those in the last cluster have emerged mainly after independence. As mentioned earlier, the activity of translation has modified this hierarchy considerably, with Hindi and English (the national link languages) emerging as the two most important target languages for translation from the viewpoints of performance and publication, respectively. The medium of English also makes Indian plays potentially available to a worldwide audience of readers, scholars, students and theatre professionals, bridging the gap that has traditionally existed between these works and Europhone/global audiences.

The locations of theatre activity around the country correspond to the complex linguistic map outlined above. The three most active theatrical cities are the megapolises of Bombay, Calcutta and Delhi, and each hosts theatre in multiple languages: Bombay has Marathi, Gujarati, English and Hindi, Calcutta has Bengali, English and Hindi, and Delhi has Hindi, English, Punjabi and Urdu. The second tier consists of two unusually active 'regional' venues, Pune and Bangalore, and the city of Madras (Chennai), which was the capital of the Madras Presidency in British India, and is now the capital of the state of Tamil Nadu. Pune, a city of 2.5 million about 90 miles southeast of Bombay, has been home to many leading Marathi playwrights, directors, theatre groups and actors, and offers both serious and popular theatre on a scale that equals the output of the largest cities. Bangalore, the capital of the southern state of Karnataka, is an information technology hub which experienced a 50 per cent increase in its population between 2001 and 2011 (from 6.3 million to 9.6 million). Its dominant theatre language is Kannada, followed by English, and a conjunction of major creative talent, entrepreneurship and institutional support has made the city a hub on the national theatre map as well. Madras is unusual because it has a significant tradition of theatre in English as well as in Tamil, in addition to well-known experimental theatre groups and activist performance artists. It resembles Bangalore in the quality, variety and quantity of theatre activity. The third tier consists of cities such as Chandigarh, Bhopal, Heggodu, Trivandrum and Imphal, where the regional language is dominant, although English or Hindi may make an occasional appearance. The prominence of these venues in recent decades is explained at least in part by the presence of major practitioners – Neelam Mansingh Chowdhry in Chandigarh, Habib Tanvir in Bhopal, K. V.

Subbanna and his organization Ninasam in Heggodu, K. N. Panikkar in Trivandrum and Ratan Thiyam, H. Kanhailal and Lokendra Arambam in Imphal. The final tier consists of cities such as Lucknow, Jaipur, Patna, Sagar, Ahmedabad, Baroda, Nagpur, Hyderabad and Mysore, which are important regional nodes in the national network, but are not associated with the creation of important original work in theatre (Figure 11.4).

In material terms, how does this geographically dispersed and multilingual but non-commercial field manage to survive and occasionally even thrive? To understand post-independence theatre as an operative terrain we have to understand its institutional structures and patterns of interpersonal connection. In the absence of a functioning marketplace and any predictable or regular channels of production, the performance event in urban Indian theatre has come to depend on a few critical factors. The first is the founding of a theatre group by a director who remains connected with it for an extended period of time, providing artistic leadership and shepherding resources. Shombhu Mitra's Bohurupee, Utpal Dutt's People's Little Theatre and Shyamanand Jalan's Padatik in Calcutta, Vijaya Mehta's Rangayan, Satyadev Dubey's Theatre Unit and Alyque Padamsee's Theatre Group in Bombay, and Habib Tanvir's Naya Theatre, Rajinder Nath's Abhiyan and Arvind Gaur's Asmita in Delhi are metropolitan examples of a model of long-term association that is also replicated in smaller cities around the country. The groups maintain a precarious existence through private and corporate funding, ticket sales and subsidized theatre spaces; there is no regular annual season; rehearsal space is difficult to arrange and afford; actors are not always paid; and audiences are small though often stable and supportive of the work of particular directors and groups. In their turn, playwrights develop lifelong creative partnerships with one or more directors, often with very little expectation of financial return. The major exceptions to this structure are state-supported institutions of theatre training and patronage, notably the National School of Drama, which launched a Repertory Company in 1964, and the Sangeet Natak Akademi, which provides fellowships, grants, awards and production subsidies at the regional and national levels. The second factor is an active commitment on the part of key directors to *new* Indian plays, which otherwise compete in the sphere of performance with world drama in translation. The third factor is geographical dispersal, at the regional level through multiple productions in the original language of composition, and at the national level through translation.

Over six decades, other patterns of patronage and support have also had a chance to establish themselves. A great deal of production activity is enabled by private and public cultural organizations such as the Shri Ram Centre for Art and Culture in New Delhi, the National Centre for the Performing Arts and Prithvi Theatre in Bombay, Bharat Bhavan in Bhopal and the India Foundation for the Arts in Bangalore. Leading theatre organizations such as Nandikar in Calcutta, Ranga Shankara in Bangalore and Ninasam in Heggodu also organize theatre festivals that showcase old and new work. The NSD's Bharat Rang Mahotsav (India Theatre Festival) has become the largest state-supported annual forum for national and international work, and despite their smaller scale, the privately endowed Mahindra Awards for Excellence in Theatre have become a highly anticipated annual event. Multinational companies, industrial houses, large businesses and philanthropic organizations underwrite festivals and events of all shapes and sizes. A recent initiative that exemplifies the move towards autonomy among theatre professionals is Studio Safdar in New Delhi (named after Safdar Hashmi of JANAM), which advertises itself as an 'independent, non-funded arts and activism space'. Since it opened in 2012, the Studio has hosted dozens of performances, film screenings, lectures and book-launches, enabled workshops and meetings for activist groups and provided rehearsal space for theatre groups. Finally, at least in the metropolitan areas, audiences loyal to the work of particular playwrights and theatre groups have grown, despite economic hardship and distractions from the popular media.

Figure 11.4 Scene from Kalidasa's *Malavikagnimitram* (Malavika and Agnimitra), adapted by K. V. Subbanna and directed by Iqbal Ahmed for Ninasam Tirugata (Heggodu, Karnataka), 2001.

(Courtesy of K. V. Akshara)

The 'theatre of roots' movement is worth juxtaposing against this unruly backdrop because it represents a concerted effort by the state to promote a particular cultural agenda. The term was coined in a 1985 essay by the scholar, administrator and cultural critic Suresh Awasthi to describe 'the new unconventional theatre, which ha[d] been evolving as a result of its encounter with tradition for some two decades,' and was 'part of the whole process of decolonization of our lifestyle, values, social institutions, creative forms, and cultural modes' (1985: 85). Awasthi argued for an outright rejection of proscenium staging, for stylization and physicality rather than realism, for the actor's body as the primary source of a 'theatre language' and for the fluidity of the performance text over the alleged fixity of the authorial text. Among contemporary practitioners, he singled out Tanvir, Panikkar, Thiyam, Karanth and Sircar as playwrights/directors whose art was fully liberated from proscenium aesthetics, and considered their work as evidence that Indian theatre of the modern period had never been 'practiced in such diversified form, and at the same time with such unity in essential theatre values' (85). Awasthi's overall approach summed up the principal cultural-nationalist arguments of the post-independence period – westernized urban theatre was an alien imposition that did not and cannot flourish in India; the end of colonialism offers the best opportunity for correcting this aberration; and the formal, aesthetic and representational principles of indigenous performance genres offer the only possibility of an *authentic* alternative modernity in Indian theatre.

As this description indicates, the theatre of roots movement (hereafter TOR) is the clearest contemporary expression of what I have called cultural recursiveness – an appeal to the precolonial past as a redemptive cultural force in the colonial or postcolonial present. It is also the Indian equivalent of the specifically postcolonial space-clearing urge that the Kenyan writer Ngugi wa Thiong'o describes as 'decolonizing the mind'. The strength of the movement lies in the conceptual coherence it provides for the work of leading practitioners (such as those mentioned by Awasthi) who offer cutting-edge alternatives to proscenium realism, and the support it has extended to particular kinds of theatre work in a marketplace of scarce resources. For example, the Sangeet Natak Akademi's multi-year 'Scheme for Assistance to Young Theatre Workers', which organized four zonal festivals and one national festival annually from 1984 to 1991, advanced the work of many young directors who have emerged as major talents in the post-1980 period – notably Ratan Thiyam, Bansi Kaul, Prasanna, Probir Guha, Bhanu Bharati, B. Jayshree, Waman Kendre, Neelam Mansingh Chowdhry and A. Mangai. Erin Mee's recent book-length study of TOR delves systematically into theatre history, theory and contemporary practice to uncover what is most substantive about the movement: it seeks to redefine Indian modernity, 'explains' the practice of innovators such as Panikkar, Thiyam and Karnad, and continues to be a shaping influence on a new generation of theatre artists.

The polemical thrust of TOR, however, points to the self-defeating nature of positions that seek to impose uniformity on a heterogeneous field. From the beginning, proponents of the movement have adopted an exclusionary cultural rhetoric that describes *all* theatre outside the 'traditional idiom' as sterile, barren, 'western-oriented imitative work' that is fundamentally un-Indian and devoid of value. Not only is this an arrogant dismissal of the multidimensional post-independence renaissance in theatre; it also drastically simplifies the complex interchange between western and Indian systems of representation over two centuries, and the creation of syncretic cultural forms that are scrupulously Indianized (as we have noted) at the levels of form, content and experience. In another self-privileging move, TOR is presented as 'the most pervasive and influential post-Independence theatrical movement in India' and '*the* answer' to questions about the future shape of 'modern Indian theatre' (Mee 2008: 12, 263), although the state's crucial financial and organizational role in sustaining the initiative is widely known. An even more aggressive form of bureaucratic intervention is the packaging of TOR as the 'real' Indian theatre for consumption outside India, especially on the international festival circuit. The immense variety of contemporary theatre is cancelled out by these acts of cultural guardianship: India's rich precolonial theatrical legacy clearly has relevance in the present, but TOR has chosen to define that relevance in ahistorical, impossibly unitary terms.

In contrast, the growing presence of women in every sphere of theatre activity marks a multifaceted creative response to the conditions that have marginalized female practitioners in modern theatre. Both the Marathi natak mandalis and the Parsi theatre fostered the cult of the cross-dressing male actor; Binodini Dasi (1862–1941), the protégé of Girish Ghosh in the Bengali public theatre, was perhaps the only actress of the colonial period comparable in stature to the legendary Bal Gandharva (1888–1967) and Jaishankar Sundari (1889–1975). Women became much more visible as theatre actresses from the 1940s onward, and a few directors such as Shanta Gandhi, Vijaya Mehta and Joy Michael appeared in the 1950s to counterbalance the rapidly increasing roster of influential male directors. However, the persistent absence of female authors from the medium of text-based printed drama amounts to a virtual erasure of women as playwrights in the conventional sense. Mahasweta Devi's theatrical adaptations of her own Bengali short stories (*Five Plays*, 1997) make up the *only* available collection of plays in English translation by an Indian woman playwright, augmenting a handful of individual titles by Shanta Gokhale, Dina Mehta and Manjula Padmanabhan, among others. The imbalance of gender continues in recent anthologies: again, Mahasweta Devi's *The Mother of 1084* is the only play by a woman author in G. P. Deshpande's *Modern Indian Drama: An Anthology* (2000), while Chandrashekhar Kambar's *Modern Indian Plays* (also 2000) excludes women altogether. Erin Mee's *DramaContemporary: India* (2001) includes two women authors (Usha Ganguli and Tripurari Sharma) among the six playwrights featured in her selection, and *Body Blows: Women, Violence, and Survival* (2000) is the first thematically organized 'feminist' collection in English bringing together plays by Padmanabhan, Mehta and Poile Sengupta. Tutun Mukherjee's *Staging Resistance: Plays by Women in Translation* (2005) broke substantial new ground by bringing together eighteen plays from ten languages, but these numbers represented more than a century of playwriting by women (from 1855 to the 1960s). Mukherjee connects this problematic lack to 'the discourse of "gender as genre,"' which 'reveals the way [the] sex-gender system operates in the art and practice of drama and theatre and controls their cultural reproduction' (2005: 4). Unlike the autonomy and comforting privacy of print, the public, performative, collaborative and materially demanding medium of theatre seems to place women at a distinct disadvantage, especially in India, where the vast majority of them are still circumscribed within the domestic sphere.

Since the 1980s, however, the work of female professionals has indicated that instead of deploring the 'absence' of women playwrights, criticism needs to effect a conceptual shift from the category of 'author' to that of 'auteur', 'performer' or 'collaborator', and hence to recognize the distinctive and important 'texts' as well as 'works' that women artists have been producing for urban Indian theatre for three decades. There seem to be three important forms of female intervention and authorship in Indian theatre that can be juxtaposed against the concurrent male traditions. In the first, a female director takes up a play (Indian, western, or non-western) that already has an established text, and gives it her distinctive stage interpretation. This category would include Shanta Gandhi's revivals of the Sanskrit playwright Bhasa's *Madhyam Vyayog* (The Middle One) and *Urubhangam* (1965–66); Vijaya Mehta's revivals of Kalidasa's *Shakuntala* (1979) and Vishakhadutt's *Mudrarakshasa* (1975), and her productions of Karnad's *Hayavadana* and Elkunchwar's *Wada chirebandi* (1985); Amal Allana's productions of Brecht's *Mother Courage* (1993), Alekar's *Begum Barve* (1996) and Karnad's *Naga-mandala* (1999); and Usha Ganguli's productions of plays by Ibsen, Gorki, Brecht and Wesker (1978–98). Each of these examples represents the conjunction of a male playwright with a female director capable of transforming the aesthetic and cultural potential of the play in question, with the resulting product being much more than a conventional directing venture.

Second, through an individual or collective process, a female director develops a text for performance that has antecedent sources and sometimes an earlier play as a model, but no prior existence in the form in which it is brought upon the stage. The term 'auteur' is most appropriate for this form of writing, which combines elements of acting, directing and authorship. This category includes Usha Ganguli's collaboration with Mahasweta Devi to adapt her short story 'Rudali' for the stage; Tripurari Sharma's play about the 1857 rebellion, *Azizunnisa: san sattavan ka kissa* (Azizunnisa: the Tale of '57); and Anuradha Kapur's *Sundari*, a play about the cross-dressing Parsi theatre actor. Neelam Mansingh Chowdhry's acclaimed versions of Giradoux's *The Madwoman of Chaillot* ('Sheher mere di pagal aurat,' 1995), Racine's *Phaedra* ('Fida,' 1997) and Lorca's *Yerma* (1999) also belong here. In all such productions, a play comes into existence only because of the artistic leanings of a specific director, and it belongs uniquely to her.

Third, a female artist develops an original text for either solo or group performance, and 'authors' a work that tends to be non-linear, open, anti-realistic, resistant and process oriented. The works in this category are fully indigenized forms of feminist representation, variously exemplified by Saoli Mitra's *Nathabati anathabat* (Five Lords, Yet None a Protector, 2002), Usha Ganguli's *Antar-yatra* (Interior Journey, 2002; Figure 11.5), the street performances of A. Mangai and Tripurari Sharma, and the performance pieces of Maya Krishna Rao, Anamika Haksar and Kalairani, among others. The focus on performance also maximizes the potential

Figure 11.5 Usha Ganguli in *Antar-yatra* (The Interior Journey, 2002), a solo performance piece written and directed by her. This performance was in Calcutta in 2007.

(Courtesy of Usha Ganguli)

for activism. The December 2012 'Nirbhaya' rape case in Delhi, for example, has generated a nationwide feminist response in the form of performances that include '*Hai haya!*' (Shame on You) by Sohag Sen, a protest event called 'Take Back the Night', Rasika Agashe's devised piece titled 'Museum of Species in Danger', organized loitering by young women in public places in Bombay, Maya Rao's solo performance piece 'Walk' and a week-long commemoration titled *Jurrat* (Daring) in Delhi, which brought together activists and performance artists from different fields. Contained by this conflicted public sphere, Indian theatre in the present moment is not quite ready to be redefined as a subgenre of performance. But women's activism is only one sign of the broadening contexts of protest, opposition, interrogation and critique from subaltern positions which make up a field very different from the self-critical, cosmopolitan, even universalist engagements of the early-postcolonial decades.

Note

1   Since the 1990s, a number of Indian metropolises and smaller cities have officially changed their names in order to counteract British colonial orthography and history. Bombay is now Mumbai, Calcutta is Kolkata, Madras is Chennai, Bangalore is Bengaluru, Baroda is Vadodara and Trivandrum is Thiruvananthapuram. In this chapter, I have retained the older names for two reasons. First, they are intimately connected with specific phases in the history of modern theatre. For example, it would be anachronistic to state that modern urban commercial theatre first emerged in 'Mumbai' and 'Kolkata' in the mid-nineteenth century. Second, Seagull Books, a major publishing house for theatre based in Calcutta, has continued to use the older name on all its materials, and the bibliography has to reflect that choice. The use of the new city names in the chapter would therefore be inconsistent and unnecessarily confusing. For the nation's capital, I have used 'Delhi' to refer to the city as a theatrical venue, because the activities of playwrights, directors and theatre groups based in various parts of the city encompass the metropolitan area in its entirety. However, I have used 'New Delhi' to designate the location of specific institutions such as the Sangeet Natak Akademi, the National School of Drama and the Shri Ram Centre for Art and Culture, because such a designation is more precise.

Bibliography

Awasthi, Suresh (1985) 'In Defence of the Theatre of Roots', *Sangeet Natak*, 77–78: 85–99.

Chatterjee, Sudipto (2007) *The Colonial Staged: Theatre in Colonial Calcutta*, Calcutta: Seagull.

Dharwadker, Aparna (2005) *Theatres of Independence: Drama, Theory, and Urban Performance in India Since 1947*, Iowa City: University of Iowa Press.

—— (2011) 'India's Theatrical Modernity: Re-Theorizing Colonial, Postcolonial, and Diasporic Formations', *Theatre Journal*, 63 (3): 425–37.

Dutt, Michael Madhusudan (1859) *Sermista: A Drama in Five Acts*, Calcutta: C. Bose; reprinted Calcutta: A. Pine (1968).

Ghosh, Manomohan (trans and introd) (1950) *The* Natyasastra: *A Treatise on Hindu Dramaturgy and Histrionics*, Calcutta: Royal Asiatic Society of Bengal.

Gupta, Kshetra (ed.) (1982) *Madhusudan rachanabali* (The Complete Works of Michael Madhusudan Dutt), Calcutta: Sahitya Samsad.

Hansen, Kathryn (trans and ed.) (2011) *Stages of Life: Indian Theatre Autobiographies*, London: Anthem Press.

Harishchandra, Bhartendu (1883) 'Natak' (Drama), in Shivaprasad Mishra 'Rudra' (ed.) (1970) *Bhartendu granthavali* (The Works of Bhartendu), Volume 1, 743–96, Varanasi: Nagari Pracharini Sabha.

Kastuar, Jayant (introd) (2007) *Indian Drama in Retrospect*, New Delhi: Sangeet Natak Akademi.

Mee, Erin B. (2001) *DramaContemporary: India*, Baltimore: Johns Hopkins University Press.

—— (2008) *Theatre of Roots: Redirecting the Modern Indian Stage*, Calcutta: Seagull.

Mitra, Shayoni (2014) 'Dispatches from the Margins: Theatre in India Since the 1990s', in Ashis Sengupta (ed.) *Mapping South Asia Through Contemporary Theatre*, 64–102, Basingstoke: Palgrave Macmillan.

Mukherjee, Tutun (ed. and introd.) (2005) *Staging Resistance: Plays by Women in Translation*, New Delhi: Oxford University Press.

Pollock, Sheldon (ed.) (2003) *Literary Cultures in History: Reconstructions from South Asia*, Berkeley: University of California Press.

Pradhan, Sudhi (1979–1985) *Marxist Cultural Movement in India: Chronicles and Documents*, 3 vols, Calcutta: National Book Agency.

Prasad, Jai Shankar (1936) 'Rangmanch' (The Stage), in Vishnu Prabhakar and Ramchandra Shah (eds) (1991) *Prasad rachana sanchayan* (Selected Writings of Prasad), New Delhi: Sahitya Akademi.

Puchner, Martin (2002) *Stage Fright: Modernism, Anti-Theatricality, and Drama*, Baltimore, MD: Johns Hopkins Press.

Sangeet Natak Akademi Report (1958) New Delhi: Sangeet Natak Akademi.

Tagore, Rabindranath (1913) 'The Theatre', in Sisir Kumar Das and Sukanta Chaudhuri (eds) (2001) *Selected Writings on Literature and Language*, 95–9, New Delhi: Oxford University Press.

12

Modern theatre in Pakistan, Bangladesh, Nepal and Sri Lanka

*David Mason, Syed Jamil Ahmed, Carol C. Davis
and Kanchuka Dharmasiri*

This chapter focuses on modern theatre in the other South Asian nations: Pakistan, Bangladesh, Nepal and Sri Lanka.

I. Pakistan, by David Mason

The Islamic Republic of Pakistan lies in the western part of South Asia, sharing borders with Afghanistan and Iran to its west and with India on its east. To its south, Pakistan has an extensive shoreline along the Arabian sea. Karachi, Pakistan's largest city and principal port, lies on this shore, where the River Indus, which runs almost the entire north–south length of the country, joins the ocean. More than 95 per cent of Pakistan's population are Muslims, and nearly half of the population is ethnically Punjabi. The country's second-largest city is Lahore, which is the capital of Pakistan's Punjab province. The country's capital city Islamabad is much smaller – barely in the top ten largest cities in the country – though it is not only the centre of the national government, but enjoys an outsized concentration of universities, economic institutions, health-care entities and art organizations. The country's official language is Urdu, but nearly half of the country's people speak Punjabi, and significant percentages speak Pashtun, Sindhi and other regional languages. English is common. The region was part of the British Empire until 1947, when Pakistan gained its independence in the form of West Pakistan and East Pakistan, two Muslim-majority regions on opposite sides of South Asia, but comprising a single country. In 1971, East Pakistan declared its own independence and became Bangladesh. Although often on the margin of the country's culture, theatre has insisted on occupying an important place in the development of Pakistani society. Indeed, theatre nearly derailed Pakistan's very existence, as Muhammad Ali Jinnah, Pakistan's founding father, had signed a contract that would have made him a professional Shakespearean actor in 1895, had not his father insisted he become a lawyer instead (Wolpert 1984: 14).

Especially in the last half of the twentieth century, theatre in Pakistan has had to negotiate difficult terrain between government censorship, religious opposition and artistic integrity. In addition to facing a perpetually fluid political situation in Pakistan – which, in addition to East Pakistan's secession and martial law, has involved more than one military coup, as well as ongoing internal struggles between democratic processes and Islamization – artists in this putatively Islamic state have had to confront varied interpretations and implementations of Islamic proscriptions of performing arts.

Modern theatre in Pakistan might be traced to the vernacular theatre that developed in the area of Bombay (now Mumbai) in the nineteenth century. In the theatres built and managed by the Parsi community in the region, beginning, perhaps, with the Grant Road Theatre in 1846, which was built after the design of Drury Lane, popular, secular theatre developed in South Asia. The first plays on Grant Road were English-language imports or adaptations of typical, European-style melodrama. But with the opening of the Khatwadi Theatre in 1846, strong, vernacular theatre traditions appeared in Bombay. Combining the tropes of melodrama with the elements of established folk theatre forms such as tamasha, nautanki and bhaona, the plays of the Parsi Theatre industry were broad, bourgeois spectacles, whose popularity relied heavily on popular folk tunes and dancing.

The first plays in this tradition were performed in Gujarati and Marathi. But as the vernacular tradition was coming into its own in Bombay, literary drama in Urdu was developing in Lucknow. In 1853, Agha Hasan Ali, writing under the name Amanat, wrote and staged *Indar Sabha*. The play – constructed after the manner of *rás lila* and *ramlila* plays that were popular in the region of Lucknow – became the equivalent of a hit all across South Asia and beyond. The play had been translated into German by 1863 (Gupt 2005: 184–5). Under the influence of *Indar Sabha*'s popularity, new Urdu plays came into being in the Parsi theatres of Bombay by the early 1870s. In addition to several adaptations of *Indar Sabha*, Parsi theatre playwrights writing in Urdu went looking for other material. In 1871, Behramji Fardunji Marzban translated Edalji Khori's Gujarati play *Sunana Mulni Khurshed* into Urdu. The play was produced at the Victoria theatre, and its success led the Victoria's management in 1872 to commission *Benazir Badremunir*, an Urdu play that included some songs in Farsi (Gupt 2005: 115–16).

From this point, a majority of plays in the Parsi theatre industry were written and performed in Urdu. One representative playwright from among the many who emerged from this tradition was Narayan Prasad Betab, who began writing Urdu plays after encountering travelling Parsi theatre companies in Delhi in the late 1800s. The success of Betab's play *Qatl-e Nazir* reached Lahore. But when the New Alfred Theatrical Company carried Betab's popular stage adaptation of the *Mahabharata* to Lahore, audiences objected to the company's use of actresses for female roles (Brandon 1993: 211). Following Betab, Agha Hashr wrote Urdu and Hindi dramas with several companies from Calcutta to Lahore, where he died in 1935. Hashr's Urdu plays were the subject of some of the earliest university-level studies of Urdu drama in Pakistan (Gupt 2005: 85–6). Abbas Ali was born in Lahore in 1889, and attempted to stage his first play there in 1906. Ali moved to Bombay shortly thereafter to continue writing for various Parsi theatre companies. Ali's thirty plays were all published in Lahore (Gupt 2005: 94–5). While the first commercial motion picture in South Asia seems to have been based on a Marathi play, the first South Asian film with sound was Ardeshir Irani's *Alam Ara* of 1931, an adaptation of an Urdu play by Joseph David. Through the first decades of the twentieth century, many Parsi theatres in Bombay were converted to movie theatres, and many Parsi troupes became film companies. The modern Bollywood film industry emerged from the theatre buildings and theatre companies in Bombay's nineteenth-century Parsi network.

In the decades approaching the independence of South Asia from colonial rule, theatre artists who would settle in either East Pakistan or West Pakistan were active in the resistance to British occupation. Several different movements came together in the early 1940s to form the Indian People's Theatre Association (IPTA). Branches of this activist organization, which was inspired by Soviet populist theatre and European agitprop theatre, were established in Karachi and Lahore, and worked in support of the independence movement by staging short, simple, portable plays in public spaces in order to generate support for an independent South Asia. When independence arrived in the form of two separate countries, many of IPTA's members landed in India, carrying the eponymous theatre institution with them, but some new Pakistanis who had been active with IPTA carried on the tradition of socially conscious theatre through other organizations. Safdar Mir, for instance, put his IPTA experience to work leading the Government College Dramatic Club (GCDC) in Lahore, which was invested in staging the work of politically charged playwrights including Ibsen, Shaw and Gogol. Productions, including the staging of European dramas, were performed in both English and Urdu. The GCDC put many important figures – actors, directors and writers – into prominent positions in Pakistan's mainstream theatre (Ahmed *et al.* 1998: 357). Rafi Peerzada, who had worked with Max Reinhardt and Brecht in the 1920s, founded the Indian Academy of Dramatic Arts in 1930, and formed the Pakistan Drama Markaz in 1947, which, in its inception, was motivated by socialist politics and Brechtian dramaturgy. In 1974, the group was renamed the Rafi Peer Theatre Workshop. Rafi Peer is still in operation in Lahore, and sponsors international festivals for music, film and theatre.

The Pakistan Arts Council (PAC), a private endeavour formed in Lahore soon after independence, demonstrated an early commitment to promoting the artistic life of the new country. By the 1960s, PAC was sponsoring theatrical performances on a regular basis, and supporting the development of original plays. The PAC became the Lahore Arts Council, Alhamra, in 1981 (Pamment 2012: 115). To strengthen the central government's role in protecting and promoting the arts, Pakistan's parliament created the Pakistan National Council of Arts (PNCA) with legislation in 1973. The PNCA has established and sponsored commercial, repertory theatres in Pakistan. The PNCA now inhabits a custom-designed facility, meant to support several performing arts groups. A few individual provinces, following the legal precedent parliament set by establishing the PNCA, have created their own arts councils. In recent decades, the PNCA has backed an annual, multi-day, international drama festival, supporting performances in Pakistan by performing groups from around the world, and simultaneously presenting Pakistani performers to an international community. There are several national theatre festivals in Pakistan, supported by provincial governments and by private concerns.

Theatre in Pakistan has had a tougher time operating outside official government sanction. Indeed, some theatre activity in Pakistan has not only been founded on the principle of government criticism, but has been explicitly opposed to government sponsorship. What came to be known informally as 'parallel theatre' carried IPTA's tradition of using theatre as a means of political activism into the 1980s. Spurred by Muhammad Zia-ul-Haq's 1977 coup and imposition of martial law, several 'parallel theatre' groups in Pakistan's major cities pursued theatrical protest after the 'street theatre' method pioneered by IPTA. The first parallel theatre groups of note include Ajoka, Dastak and Bang. Founded by activists Madeeha Gauhar and Salman Shahid in 1983, Ajoka began by adapting regional folk theatre forms to advocate for human rights. In recent decades, Ajoka has become widely respected and well funded, forming international partnerships with, for instance, the Norwegian Agency for Development Cooperation. In 2011, Ajoka partnered with the government agency PNCA to conduct a Brecht Theatre Festival at the National Art Gallery in Islamabad. Dastak, formed in 1982 around noted communist Mansoor Saeed, asserted itself as an ideologically non–commercial theatre committed to the political education of its audiences. While Saeed himself wrote plays for Dastak, the group also favoured the work of Bertolt Brecht. Dastak's productions of *Galileo* and *St Joan* in 1985 and 1986 are regarded as pivotal productions. Another important group from this period is Tehrik-i-Niswan, formed by Sheema Kirmani in 1981 to speak for the rights of Pakistani women, the presence of whom on stage inspired violent threats. The group staged Anouilh's *Antigone*, as well as plays by Indian playwrights Safdar Hashmi and Vijay Tendulkar (Ahmed *et al.* 1998: 362). Other groups that emerged later from these primary troupes or formed on their own include Punjab Lok Rehas, Sanj, and Naya Theatre. Especially during the period of Zia's restrictions on political expression, these parallel groups made use of public, alternative spaces, and relied on public donations, to give voice to discontent and to protest repression. A type of self-consciously parallel theatre still operates in Pakistan, but largely to confront social ills rather than government oppression.

In the 1950s, a popular, private theatre movement developed some momentum with the financial support of an expanding Pakistan oil market. One consequence of this era was the establishment of the Karachi Theatre in 1956, under the cooperative direction of playwright Khwaja Moinuddin, actor Zia Mohyeddin and Sigrid Nyberg Kahle, the Swedish spouse of a German diplomat stationed in Pakistan (Brandon 1993: 212). Invested in naturalism and the broadly innocuous style of European drawing-room comedies, as opposed to the Brechtian stylization of the politically critical theatre, commercial theatre proved amenable through the country's martial law period (Pamment 2012: 115). Capitalizing on this popular theatre's durability, Tamaseel, perhaps the first Pakistani building designed and built as a commercial theatre, was constructed in Lahore in 1991 (Ahmed *et al.* 1998: 363). Several other theatres opened in other parts of the city. Contrary to the global historical trend of the twentieth century whereby theatres were systematically converted to cinema halls, some Lahore cinema halls were refitted in the 1990s to act as live theatres. In 2009, bombs exploded at the Tamaseel and three other Lahore theatres, injuring ten people, and reminding the country of its factions opposed to the performing arts and theatre, in particular.

In an effort to elevate the performing arts in Pakistan, the central government formed the National Academy of Performing Arts (NAPA) in Karachi in 2005. The school provides training programmes for music, dance, design and theatre. Zia Mohyeddin, who was involved in the founding of the Karachi Theatre and who was trained in acting at the Royal Academy of Dramatic Arts in London, was appointed as the institution's first director. NAPA is currently constructing a new theatre building intended to provide state-of-the-art facilities for its training programme.

Puppet theatre merits special consideration, since Pakistan inherited several centuries-old, South Asian puppetry traditions, including rod puppets, marionettes and shadow puppets. The PNCA established the National Puppet Theatre in 1975. In 1978, the Rafi Peer Theatre Workshop formed a puppet company and continues to operate puppetry festivals at its base in Lahore. The Lahore Arts Council founded the Alhamra Puppet Theatre in 1986. Students at the National College of Arts also maintain a puppetry society.

II. Bangladesh, by Syed Jamil Ahmed

Because any query of 'modern theatre' in Bangladesh would necessarily be underpinned by the Bengali notions of the *adhunik* ('modern') and *natak* ('theatre'), the result can only stand on unstable ground. This is because, pulled in contrary directions by discursive strands of global centres and peripheries, classical-indigenous tradition and 'western' influence, remnant feudal and bourgeois value systems, religious and cultural nationalisms, and rural and urban dichotomies, both the categories, as employed in cultural theorizing and practices of the country, are highly contentious, indeterminate and fractured. Hence, prefaced with a brief note on the mode of producing theatre in Bangladesh, this section adopts the strategy of unmasking how the effect of employing the key Bengali notions of adhunik and natak in weaving a representation of Bangladesh theatre can only reveal the interstices of a disparate narrative that invariably land us in a postcolonial act of refusing the Imperial–Oriental paradigms.

The mode of producing theatre

In Bangladesh today, 'Group Theatre' is the dominant mode of organization that is engaged in producing theatre in urban locations. Such organizations, which produce plays entirely in Bengali, and which emphasize collective egalitarianism against the dominance of celebrity performers, began to emerge in the country in 1972, immediately after a horrendous civil war fought against Pakistan in 1971. Today, it is a network of over 250 non-profit city-based groups of theatre practitioners, who are mostly middle-class students and professionals belonging to the media, advertising agencies and other private services. The groups inculcate professionalism in the work that they produce but are run by voluntary contributions of its members, box-office receipts, revenue accrued from advertisements published in souvenirs and occasional sponsorship from national and multinational industrial and trading companies. Most of the performers of the Group Theatre ensembles discussed in this section, such as Nagarik Natya Sampradaya, Aryanak Natya Dal, Theatre, Dhaka Padatik and Dhaka Theatre, are not formally trained in theatre schools.[1]

At present, five public universities in Bangladesh offer BA and MA programmes in theatre and performance studies. Most of the students who graduate from these universities are unable to sustain themselves by working full-time in theatre. Occasionally, a few directors, designers and performers are paid, but it is not enough to produce a body of full-time theatre practitioners. Consequently, there is no professional or commercial theatre in urban locations of Bangladesh.

Full-time professional theatre in Bangladesh exists in traditional/folk theatre, which is performed mostly in the rural and semi-urban areas, and bears a history of at least a thousand years. The most notable of these is the *jātrā*, which is a dying form today, and its place is being taken over by smaller bands of itinerant performers. However, the performers of most of these bands are part-time professionals, who perform only when invited to do so, and sustain themselves by a range of 'subaltern' professions such as wage labourers, rickshaw pullers, traditional doctors, petty peddlers and so on.

A lively sub-field of applied theatre, mostly produced by non-governmental organizations (NGOs), has yielded some remarkable work in theatre-for-development, theatre-in-education and psychodrama.

The adhunik as modern

Although there is very little application of the notion of adhunik in Bangladesh theatre, volumes on Bengali adhunik literature inaugurate the period from 1800, when Fort William College was founded (Huq and Rahman 2003: 440) as 'an orientalist training centre' for 'the newly recruited European civil servants' (Islam 2003: 269). However, when critical gestures, ignoring the objective of the College, hail the nineteenth century as 'the enlightened modern age' and contrast it with 'the dark middle age' of traditional literature (Azad 1992: 389), the Imperial centre slips in by the back door, in the guise of Ezra Pound's famous slogan 'Make It New' (cited in Pratt 2000: 2).

When the adhunik is thus framed, Dinabandhu Mitra (1829–74) may claim to have inaugurated modernism in Bengali theatre. Mitra's most well-known play *Nīl Darpan* (The Mirror of Indigo), actually more of a bourgeois drama in the European romanticist style, was first published from Dhaka city in 1860 and performed here in 1861. The play initiated a heated public debate all over Bengal regarding the intolerable oppression of the indigo planters, and marked the beginning of postcolonial resistance in Bengali theatre. At the same time, it lands us squarely on a postcolonial paradox: 'without modernism, postcolonial literature as we know it would perhaps not exist' (Gikandi 2006: 421). But when Guha (1993: 62–3) argues that the play is not about peasant resistance but merely an instrument 'to comfort a bhadralok[2] conscience', one is forced to concede that modernism in colonial Bengali theatre was also elitism, and, borrowing from Friedman (2001: 494), 'the supreme fiction, the master narrative, the great [bhadralok] hope'.

In this fractured terrain, which divided, on the one hand, the radicals who sought to employ science as a tool for social progress, and on the other, the traditionalists who sought to discard all that was 'western', it was Rabindranath Tagore who 'chose the difficult middle path' in reconciling the 'home' with the foreign (Dasgupta 2006: 1), as exemplified by his extensive critique of civilization and nationalism. His *Muktadhārā* (The Waterfall, 1922), most memorably performed in Bangladesh by the group named Theatre in 2011, critiques the modernity that deploys science for subjugating nature (Figure 12.1). On the other hand, his *Achalāyatan* (The Immovable, 1912), a critique of obscurant traditionalists in the guise of a moribund Brahminical society, was first performed in Comilla in Bangladesh in 1921, but perhaps most memorably by Nagorik Natya Sampraday in Dhaka in 1980.

In Nagorik's performance of *The Immovable*, Bangladesh was represented as an immovable terrain ensnared in the pettiness of religious bigotry of the Islamists. By then, religious nationalism underpinned by premodern Islamic values was already on the rise. In this context, the iconic figure who has been the silent yet pervasive touchstone of the cultural nationalists, especially in adhunik theatre, has been Tagore, although the poet himself was a stringent adversary of nationalist rhetoric and castigated the notion of nationalism as 'a cruel epidemic of evil' (Tagore 1918: 16). Nevertheless, it is to him the contemporary theatre practitioners return to rediscover the quintessence of their adhunik values of cultural nationalism.

Figure 12.1 Muktadhārā (The Waterfall) by Rabindranath Tagore, produced by Theatre and directed by Naila Azad, at the National Theatre, Dhaka, on 5 May 2011.

(Photo by Mominul Haq Dulu)

Theatre in Bangladesh became deeply entangled with cultural nationalism on the evening of 21 February 1953, when the political prisoners of a cell in Dhaka Central Jail performed Munier Chowdhury's *Kabar* (The Grave) – literally by the light of lanterns, lamps and matchsticks. An early example of 'prison theatre' undertaken entirely by the prisoners and for the prisoners, the performance of the play was held clandestinely to commemorate the crisis of 21 February 1952. On that day, thousands of students in Dhaka city had marched the streets to demand the institution of Bengali as a state language of Pakistan. Their clash with the police erupted into a conflagration in which at least nine people were killed, and the entire city of Dhaka was paralysed. If modernity signifies, within the context of social sciences, a specific set of historical conditions developing in the 'West' that includes the rise of the nation-state (Friedman 2001: 500), then the performance of *The Grave* in 1953 inaugurates that moment of modern theatre in the landmass today known as Bangladesh when the Bengali nation began to be narrated anew against Islamic signs mobilized by the postcolonial nation-state of Pakistan.

Seizing upon the birth of Bangladesh in 1971, Syed Shamsul Haq performs the notion of cultural nationalism in his verse-drama *Pāyer āwāj Pāwā Jāy* (At the Sound of Marching Feet) produced by Theatre in 1976. The performance attempted to render meaning to the Liberation War of 1971 by unmasking the deceit of a Pakistan Army officer and a Bengali-speaking Mātbar[3] who collaborates extensively with the Pakistan Army in thwarting the Liberation War, in that the officer ravished the Mātbar's daughter with his implicit consent. By mobilizing the trope of rape, the playwright demonstrates that the nation-state of Pakistan is dishonest in claiming Islamic precepts as its guiding principle, and debunks religious nationalists' claim-to-truth by desacralizing the *raison d'être* of Pakistan-predicated Islamic signs.

In the ongoing debate of national identity that continues to be fought with vehemence in the national field of politics, a theatre group named Dhaka Padatik sought a third space of enunciation, away from the dichotomous positions held by religious and linguistic nationalists, by producing a two-part adaptation of a nineteenth-century novel *Biṣād Sindhu* (The Ocean of Sorrow) by Mir Mosharraf Hossain in 1991 and 1992. The performance engaged with Islam head-on by deploying the quasi-historical legend of Karbala,[4] and challenging religious bigotry by incessant questioning of the supposed 'Islamic' values. In a critical commentary on the production, when Guhathakurta (1994: 289) observed that *The Ocean of Sorrow* was a performance that 'represents contemporary theatre in Bangladesh in every sense of the word', the use of 'contemporary' instead of 'modern' exemplifies, once again, the ambivalence regarding the adhunik theatre.

The nationalist narrations in the adhunik theatre was destabilized in 1988 when Anushilan Natya Dal based in Rajshahi University produced *Birsā Kābya* (The Song of Birsa), which showed how the Austro-Asiatic ethnic community of the Mundas waged war against British colonizers and the Bengali feudal lords in 1899–1900, to exert their right to community ownership of the forestland. In reviving the memory of the struggle, the performance delegitimized the debate of national identity by asserting that the Munda and forty-four other ethnic communities living in Bangladesh, who constitute a tiny numeral minority against the 98 per cent Bengali population, cannot be 'othered' by the cultural-religious identity debate of the Bengalis.

Natak as/and theatre

The second key notion of natak is clearly a colonial product, fashioned in imitation of what in English is known as 'drama', and in rejection of the 'traditional' ('folk' as well as Sanskrit 'classical'). Ironically, in creating the new idiom in the shadow of colonialism, the term natak was borrowed from the *Natyashātra*, where nāṭaka is one of the ten forms of Sanskrit theatre.

However, perhaps because the colonial proscenium-arch playhouse was so novel – different in all aspects from the indigenous performance space known as *āsar* – the term 'theatre' was appropriated in Bengali to denote a playhouse built in imitation of the colonizers. By extension, the act of performing or attending a performance in such a playhouse is also referred to in Bengali as 'theatre'.

As a new breed of performance known as natak, *The Mirror of Indigo* redirected European dramaturgy and performance mechanics of the proscenium-arch playhouse borrowed from the colonizers to subvert the colonial master narrative. Almost all Bengali playwrights, from the mid-nineteenth century in colonial Bengal down to the 1980s in independent Bangladesh, have composed natak by borrowing from European dramaturgy the notion of conflict as the prime driver of action. In the last quarter of the nineteenth century, Shakespeare provided the most important model to be emulated. Tagore was the first to reject the European dramaturgical model and performance code by constructing a deorientalized framework of performance code and dramaturgical vocabulary comprised of four key formulations: mode of spectatorship akin to the jātrā; privileging the written text that de-emphasized conflict; scenography shorn of an analogical mode of representation; and a presentational mode of acting that seeks to make visible the invisible 'truth' of the inner landscape.[5]

Following Tagore, but perhaps not quite along the grain of his praxis, Selim Al Deen (1949–2008) sought a new horizon in post-independence Bangladesh theatre etched in terms of distinct cultural 'roots' of the people in Bangladesh. Al Deen's plays from the middle and the late period, such as *Chākā* (*The Wheel*, 1991), *Jaibati Kanyār Man* (The Heart of the Youthful Maiden, 1992), and *Nimajjan* (The Submersion, 2004), abandon dramatic conflict, dialogue and even a linear cause-to-effect relationship in the development of the action in the plot. Instead, he embraces wholeheartedly the narrative mode of performance as seen in the indigenous theatre of Bangladesh. Not surprisingly, he refused to categorize his work as natak, and asserted that these transcend all generic parameters. Unquestionably Al Deen is a postcolonial adhunik who unmoors decisively from imperialist paradigms of dramaturgy.

A group of urban theatre practitioners with strong Marxist inclination, who called themselves Aranyak, attempted to move beyond the trajectory pursued by Rabindranath and Al Deen, by refusing the urban–rural divide that came in the wake of colonization. In 1983, they rejected their urban theatre practice, and joined the subaltern classes in rural areas as animators to produce improvised plays performed by and for the subalterns, based on their actual experience of oppression. This initiative, named *mukta nāṭak* (liberated theatre), developed into a rousing popular movement operating in isolated rural pockets of Bangladesh. Although the movement was dead by 1996, when the 'new world disorder' (Kershaw 1999: 5) commencing with the fall of the Wall had incapacitated the socialist aspirations of activists in Bangladesh, mukta natak left imprints of memorable performances in its wake that dreamt of an end to exploitation.

As for the playhouse, the proscenium-arch theatre was inaugurated in the geopolitical territory today known as Bangladesh on 18 July 1857, when the community of colonizers in Dhaka city was living in 'terror' as the native sepoys had revolted against their colonial masters. In such a context, when the English sailors of the colonial Indian navy performed two English farces (*Chaos is Come Again* and *The Original*), theatre was mobilized as a tool that sought to reclaim the threatened supremacy of the colonial master narrative.

The proscenium-arch theatre continued to be the 'universal' playhouse in the adhunik theatre from 1861, when *The Mirror of Indigo* premiered in Dhaka. A paradigm shift began to occur in the early 1980s, when scene designs inspired by Adolph Appia and Gordon Craig began to make deep encroachments into the auditorium, as in *Kittan-khola* (The Fair of Kittan-khola, Dhaka Theatre, 1981), and then to abandon the proscenium-arch stage altogether, as in

Kerāmat-mangal (Auspicious Song in Honour of a Plebeian, Dhaka Theatre, 1985). By the early 1990s, Bangladesh theatre was deeply engaged with a 'theatre of the roots' in shaping a design aesthetics that borrowed heavily from the presentational mechanics of the indigenous theatre, but at the same time, did not forget to incorporate 'western' principles of scene and light design. Today, the proscenium-arch theatre still continues to dominate Bangladesh theatre, and even the main stage of the National Theatre Complex is a proscenium-arch playhouse. Nevertheless, the fact that the complex also offers two studios with the provision of flexible staging shows that the postcolony of Bangladesh is confidently moving away from colonial-imperial heritage.

By 2004, a unique design aesthetics inspired by the indigenous theatre had contributed to the performance of *Behulār Bhāsān* (Behula Sets Her Raft Adrift, Figure 12.2) produced by the Department of Theatre, University of Dhaka. As in the indigenous theatre, the performance space was a bare platform except for a mass of straw strewn in it, and a box placed at the centre. The spectators sat all around the central platform, as they would at an indigenous *nāṭ-maṇḍap* (performance pavilion). The straw was used to create the dead body of Behula's newly wed husband who dies of snake-bite; however, the body was 'dissolved' into Behula's raft when the body was not necessary.

The structure of many performances that have sought the 'roots', such as *Behulār Bhāsān*, *Binodini* (Binodini, Dhaka Theatre, 2005) and *Chākā* (The Wheel, Department of Theatre, University of Dhaka, 2013), have followed the convention of the indigenous theatre, in which it is customary to open the performance with a *bandanā* (song of invocation) and close with a

Figure 12.2 Behulār Bhāsān (Behula Sets Her Raft Adrift), produced by Department of Theatre, University of Dhaka and directed by Syed Jamil Ahmed, at the Bharat Rang Mahotsav, New Delhi, India, 2006.

(Photo by S. Thyagarajan)

276

song of benediction. The vocabulary of these performances has also borrowed heavily from the indigenous theatre, in that dialogic as well as narrative modes of acting have been employed along with solo as well as choral songs, dance and live music.

If today there is a distinguishing feature in adhunik Bangladesh theatre, then perhaps it is the narrative mode of performance, which can be described as a multifaceted crystal sphere revolving in space, such that the performer always remains in the same 'sphere' but projects various facets of him/herself *co-present* with the characters s/he creates. In some of the best performances, this aspect has been blended uniquely with the two key questions in acting that Stanislavsky sought to resolve throughout his life, that is, 'how the actor can infuse a role with emotional and spiritual content, and how he or she can repeat a performance without it becoming tired and mechanical' (Whyman 2008: 1).

This, then, is a disparate narrative of adhunik natak in Bangladesh, where the notion of the 'modern', conceptualized 'by/as that initial moment of rupture from indigenous tradition brought about by colonialism, one that contains all subsequent disjunctions as extensions of the original breach' (Dharwadker 2008: 143), refuses the Imperial–Oriental paradigms to weave its distinct postcolonial vision of performance.

III. Nepal, by Carol C. Davis

Nepal's modern theatre began when the country opened to outside influences. For centuries, Nepal's formidable geography and fierce principalities kept it sequestered and unconquered by foreign interests. United as one country by Prithvi Narayan Shah in 1769, then governed since 1846 by the Ranas, heredity and self-serving Prime Ministers, Nepal finally began opening to western commerce, technology and thought in 1951, when King Tribhuvan Bir Bikram Shah (1906–55) wrestled power from the Ranas and established Nepal's first democratic political system.

Early modern theatre

Prolific playwright Balkrishna Sama (1902–81) is considered the father of Nepali modern drama. Sama studied in Calcutta where he was exposed to world literature, as is evident in many of his plays in which influences of Shakespeare, Hindu mythology and native Nepali history are woven together. Combining Indic and western literary traditions, themes of Sama's dramas range from adversities in love between high-*caste* leaders and lower-*caste* women, historical events that focus on virtuous heroes of the Nepali nation, and mythological subjects. Sama is credited with staging innovations, such as the first use of the proscenium theatre in Nepal and moving theatre from the court out into the city where commoners could enjoy it.

Sama's plays such as *Mutuko Vyatha* (Agony of the Heart, or Heart Ache, 1926) were written in blank verse, employed Sanskrit metre and focused on the poetics of relationship. Although actresses performed men's roles inside the court, outside it was considered inappropriate, and, in plays such as his *Mukunda Indira* (1937), Sama cast young men in women's roles. Even so, Sama was the first to initiate a tradition of writing and staging plays with relatively real human characters and relevant social themes, and *Mukunda Indira* is considered the first modern Nepali drama.

Other Nepali dramatists were stimulated by exposure to Freud and Marx, and turned from traditional, mythological and historical topics to the socially engaged and psychological themes of European romanticists, naturalists, realists and existentialists. The dramatists of early Nepali modernity were interested in predicaments of the individual character in conflict with society and also within their own psyche.

Playwright Gopal Prasad Rimal (1918–1973) was clearly struck by the realism and social engagement of Henrik Ibsen. With a theme indebted to Ibsen's *Et dukkehjem* (A Doll's House, 1879), and focusing on relations between a wife and her husband, Rimal's play *Masan* (Cremation Ground, 1945) was the first major Nepali drama to revolve around on a defiant woman. Like Ibsen's Nora, Rimal's protagonist, Helen, finds the strength to confront the husband she feels has betrayed her and to forsake him and their home.

In 1955, King Tribhuvan died and with him went royal permission for the new democratic system. His son, Mahendra Bir Bikram Shah (r. 1955–72), succeeded to the throne and assumed autocratic rule, banning political parties and instigating the party-less *panchayat*[6] system, which, while appearing to represent the people fairly, actually permitted real power to remain solely with the king.

Although he thwarted democracy, King Mahendra was a poet and patron of the arts who founded the Royal Nepal Academy in 1957 and the Rastriya Naach Ghar (National Theatre) in 1961. These theatre spaces housed Indian touring productions in the days before films came to Nepal and also supported the work of Nepali artists. Early native plays performed at these theatres include those by Sama, Rimal and brothers Govinda Bahadur Malla (b. 1922) and Vijaya Malla (1925–99), whose plays focus on the individual's need for self-expression and demonstrate interest in the human mind, especially the woman's mind. Where Govinda Bahadur Malla expresses Nepali modernity through the social realism of his plays, such as *Chiyatieko Parda* (Torn Curtain, 1959), his younger brother explores psychological realism in plays such as *Kohi kina Barbad Hos* (Why Should Someone Be Ruined, 1959). With *Pattharako Katha* (The Stones' Story, 1969), Vijaya Malla takes on a surrealistic tone, setting his play in the underworld. Initially staged with college students, the plays of Rimal and the Malla brothers were also produced in the large proscenium theatre of the Royal Nepal Academy and at the smaller proscenium Rastriya Naach Ghar, with the noteworthy actors Harihar Sharma and Shakuntala Sharma Gurung playing the leading roles.

Political theatre movement

At King Mahendra's death in 1972, his Eton- and Harvard-educated son, Birendra Bir Bikram Shah (r. 1972–2001), ascended the throne and upheld the *panchayat* political system. Members of banned opposition parties agitated for multi-party democracy, although they were persecuted, arrested, tortured and even killed for doing so. By 1979, popular resentment and simmering anger with the undemocratic and repressive character of the political system escalated into massive demonstrations.

University students used street theatre to raise awareness about the benefits of a democratic political system. Asesh Malla (b. 1955), then a student at Tribhuvan University and later considered the 'father' of Nepali *sadak naatak* (street theatre), organized the first theatre events in support of the pro-democracy movement. Malla wrote, directed and acted in plays that brought crucial political matters to light and roused people to action. In *Sadak Dekhin Sadaksamma* (From Road to Road) in 1979, Malla submerged his political ideas in covert symbolism in an effort to circumvent government censorship. Escalating his political tone and challenging repressive authoritarianism, Malla was unable to get his subsequent plays approved by the censor or staged at government-owned theatres. In 1981, he wrote *Murdabadma Utheka Haathharu* (Hands Raised in Protest) to decry government inequities and repression, only to have his production shut down and prohibited after three performances.

In April 1981, Malla formed the theatre group Sarwanam (Representing Everyone), to give expression to the will of the people through the medium of street theatre. Sarwanam actors performed on streets and in courtyards throughout the capital city, although they were harassed and arrested for doing so. Their productions of Malla's *Samapta Asamapta* (Complete Incomplete, 1981) and *Ityadi Prashnaharu* (Several Questions, 1981) condemned the *panchayat* system and governmental indifference to the will of the people. Malla's most memorable play may be the impressionistic *Hami Basanta Khojirhechou* (We Are Searching For the Spring, 1982), which uses spring as a metaphor for democracy, expresses public anger against the *panchayat* system of economic exploitation and reflects a populace looking for a better life.

By 1983 Malla discovered that throughout South Asia, people's theatre movements were forming to address issues of self-governance, national identity, postcolonial political problems and issues of human rights (women's rights, children's rights, prisoners' rights etc.). Malla decided to learn more about these movements and the techniques that might help him escape censorship while still addressing social and political issues through powerful theatre. In spite of geographical and cultural isolation, Malla initiated exchanges with other theatre troupes, principally with those in India, to share problems and concerns, techniques and solutions. During this period he connected with seminal Indian artists, including Badal Sircar, Subodh Patnaik, Probir Guha and Safdar Hashmi. From these masters, Malla learnt to make scenery using actors' bodies, to create stunning visual tableaux using only his actors, to use verbal and physical repetition to emphasize important points, to use humour to win his audiences' attention and to hold it using suspense.

With the clamour for democracy growing louder, some Sarwanam members formed additional troupes of their own. Foremost among these was Sunil Pokharel (b.1955), who founded Aarohan (To Climb Higher) in 1982. A graduate of India's National School of Drama in New Delhi, Pokharel's directorial style spans a broad range – from the agitprop style of Malla's productions to more subtle symbolism and realism, and from fully realized stage productions to those with a few iconic props and bits of costume. In 1989 Pokharel initiated Nepal's first national theatre festival, gathering in Kathmandu fledgling theatre groups from across the country and encouraging theatre activists to stand together to fight censorship and raise their united voices against the decadent, autocratic political system.

Some of the other troupes that joined Aarohan and Sarwanam in the upsurge of protest were Mithila Natyakala Parishad, founded in 1979 in Janakpur in southern Nepal, Aanam of the eastern city of Dharan, founded in 1987, and Pratibimba of the central western city, Pokhara, founded in 1990. Such theatre activism evidently unsettled the authorities and in turn brought increasingly strict curfews and stronger censorship.

Finally, on 6 April 1990, the people's movement reached its climax when the armed forces opened fire on unarmed demonstrators marching to the royal palace. With his hands now openly stained by the blood of political martyrs, King Birendra finally lifted the ban on political parties and, on 9 April 1990, Nepal won its democracy. The prevailing party-less system was replaced by a constitutional monarchy, heralding the second attempt at multi-party democracy in Nepal.

Social activist theatre

The next decade of theatre in Nepal was characterized by the turn from political to social themes as street theatre troupes collaborated with international and domestic aid organizations, such as UNICEF, Save the Children, CARE and others. Sarwanam, Aarohan and other theatre groups began to develop street dramas about social problems plaguing their society, such as child labour, alcoholism, domestic abuse, lack of education for girls, female citizenship, family planning and the growing HIV/AIDS epidemic (Figure 12.3). The street theatre they had developed during the fight for democracy was now turned towards addressing issues of equality for the deaf

Figure 12.3 The Sarwanam theatre company performing street theatre about earthquake preparedness at a school just outside Kathmandu in 2012.

(Photo by Carol Davis)

population with Aarohan's *Avaz*, witch-hunts with Sarwanam's *Baksi!* (Witch!) and misogynistic violence with Aanam's *Aaja Bholi* (These Days).

Performing world theatre

Tiring of didactic theatre, artists such as Sunil Pokharel wanted to do more aesthetic and intellectually challenging work. Pokharel initiated a series of productions of international plays aimed at developing the local intelligensia as a viable theatre audience. Plays performed included Sophocles' *Oedipus*, Moliere's *Scapan*, Jean-Paul Sartre's *The Respectable Prostitute*, Camus' *The Just*, Brecht's *The Good Women of Sichuan*, Alexandre Vampilov's *The Elder Son* and Junji Kinosita's *Yu-Juru*, as well as a number of Indian plays. These productions attracted university students excited by seeing such world dramas staged locally. Students eventually became the primary ticket purchasers for Aarohan productions and began frequenting other theatre companies as well, influencing play choices and keeping theatre youthful and vibrant.

Civil war theatre

A Maoist insurrection was fomenting, although King Birendra managed to keep it at a simmer through the last years of the twentieth century. It wasn't until his assassination on 1 June 2001 that Maoists were able to escalate their efforts by attracting popular support. With the late king's unpopular and untrusted younger brother, Gyanendra (r. 2001–2006), assuming the throne, Nepal descended into chaos, violence and full-blown civil war. Nepali plays written during this period are marked by sadness that points towards the loss of their trusted monarch, by fear brought by increasing bloodshed and by confusion about the future of their country.

Foremost among emerging Nepali playwrights of this period is Abhi Subedi, a poet, professor and scholar who created memorable portraits of a country in chaos. Subedi's plays *Aaruka Fulka Sapana* (Dreams of Peach Blossoms, 2000), *Agniko Katha* (Story of the Fire, or Fire in the Monastery, 2003; Figure 12.4) and *Thamelko Yaatra* (Journey into Thamel, 2003) are filled with images from his war-torn country. Fire, guns, explosions, disenfranchisement, despair and the loss of traditional cultural practices provide dominant motifs. Written at the same time, Asesh Malla's plays, *Ko Gardaicha Pheri Yudha ko Ghoshana* (Who is Declaring War? 2001) and *Mritu Utsav* (Death Festival, 2003), also focus on the unravelling of society, the disintegration of the family and the resulting breakdown of tradition, epitomized in the fall of the royal family.

The perdition of Nepal's multi-ethnic/multi-linguistic/multi-religious society is the focus of Pokharel's productions of Subedi's plays, which seek to capture that which is quintessentially Nepali. For *Fire in the Monastery*, Subedi locates his feelings of destruction, loss and despair in a Buddhist milieu, borrowing from traditions not his own, yet undeniably those of other peoples living in Nepal. Pokharel and his actors visited Gelugpa Buddhist monasteries and sat in on ceremonies that are foreign to their Hindu experience, yet immediately available in the Kathmandu valley they call home. *Fire in the Monastery* opens with the blowing of *dungdkar* (conch shell bugle) and the low drone of *dungchen* (long brass trumpets), typical of Gelug practice.

Figure 12.4 Actors of the Aarohan Gurukul theatre company performing in *Agniko Katha* (Story of the Fire) by Abhi Subedi in 2012.

(Photo by Carol Davis)

Actors in robes borrowed from Gelugpa monks chant and meditate, while others in masks perform ritually inspired dance. Subedi and Pokharel borrow theatrically rich traditions from outside their own ethnicity and religion, but from within their national boundaries, demonstrating that all in Nepali society are adversely affected by the depredations of war.

Postwar theatre

In 2006, a coalition of parties abolished the Nepali monarchy and King Gyanendra was forced to relinquish his throne as Nepal shifted from a kingdom to a parliamentary republic. Fighting ceased in an uneasy truce as party officials worked on a new constitution. With peace achieved, Nepali theatre artists began to develop permanent homes for their nomadic or fledging theatre troupes. In 2003 Aarohan inaugurated Gurukul, a theatre with a training school on a centrally located hill in Kathmandu. Over time they added another theatre space, rehearsal hall, library, café and residences for their students in training. The Aarohan Gurukul complex became the artistic heart of the theatre community until 2012, when it was demolished by the landowner for more lucrative ventures.

The large industrial southern city of Biratnagar was the first city outside the capital to gain a substantial theatre complex when Aarohan Gurukul received land ceded to them by the government. Built in 2011, the theatre, studio and training complex is perhaps the most sophisticated in Nepal. Continuing the trend, Sarwanam also moved off the street in 2012 when it opened its doors to a theatre, rehearsal hall, art gallery and café, offering space not only to its artists, but to other theatre companies as well. In 2012, Mandala Theatre, a group formed in 2009, inaugurated their theatre building in Kathmandu. All of these theatre troupes had felt their efforts thwarted by the high price of staging plays in the cavernous Rastriya Naach Ghar (refurbished at great expense in 2009), where musty plays are performed to nearly empty houses, so all of these theatre companies share their spaces with other troupes. The government-sponsored theatre is the only one that gives the impression that theatre has taken a step backwards in the past few years. The independent theatre troupes have the same kind of energy and drive they had when they were fighting for democracy, channelling their energy into artistic expression. Whether they are working in their new theatre spaces or conducting Kachahari (Forum) theatre in rural areas for the betterment of women, children and the disenfranchised, Nepali theatre artists are driven to use their talents to improve their society.

One recent trend is the production of Nepali adaptations of masterpieces from the world theatre. Beginning with Sunil Pokharel's revision of Henrik Ibsen's *A Doll's House* as *Putaliko Ghar* (2003), the trend has continued with adaptations of other non-Nepali dramas. The most memorable of these include The Actors Studio's adaptation of Lu Xun's *The True Story of Ah Q* (1921) as *Talak Jung vs Tulke* (2008), directed by Anup Bharal, Shailee Theatre's adaptation of Nikolai Gogol's *The Government Inspector* (as *Sarkari Nirichyek*, 2010), directed by Nabaraj Budhathoki, and Freelancing Group's adaptation of Arthur Miller's *A View From the Bridge* (as *Poolbata Herda*, 2011), directed by Eelum Dixit.

Such re-visionings of world drama re-focus these plays onto situations in present-day Nepal. While Ibsen's Nora slams the door to find a new life, Pokharel's Nora slams the door but takes a seat just outside the theatre's exit to be passed by audience members as they leave. This blocking suggests that in Nepal today it is nearly impossible for a woman to leave her family and home. Similarly, with the re-imagined *A View From the Bridge*, director Dixit addresses the currently relevant issue of Nepali expats who seek better lives outside their country.

On 25 April 2015, a 7.8 magnitude earthquake devastated Nepal, followed by large aftershock and a 7.3 quake on 12 May. Over 9,000 people died, and more than 8 million were directly affected. Nepal's poor infrastructure and dysfunctional government produced little repair. Theatre artists and citizens suspended normal activities to get food and supplies to those most affected. In August 2015, politicians finally crafted a new constitution, though it diluted the political voice of Madhesis in southern Nepal and clashes claimed lives and closed borders with India, resulting in shortages and a national standstill. In spite of political and natural disasters, theatre resumed, attesting to the resilience and vitality of Nepali theatre.

IV. Sri Lanka, by Kanchuka Dharmasiri

The notion of a modern theatre is mired in complexity in postcolonial settings because although performances are a familiar art form in many of these cultures, the enclosed proscenium theatre structure and the commercially based theatre model is an import during the colonial era. When one unravels the landmarks of modern theatre in Sri Lanka, a myriad of questions arise: Did the modern theatre begin with the introduction of Indian musicals in 1867 or did the moment of change come about after the production of Ediriweera Sarachchandra's *Maname* in 1956? What exactly do we categorize under the term modern? Another question arises as a result of the locations of performance. Where is the modern theatre located? It is often the theatre in the metropolis that gets designated as a modern theatre, while scarce attention is paid to performances that take place in non-urban settings. When one speaks about theatre in Sri Lanka, the issue of language also enters the debate because performances are done in Sinhala, Tamil and English. With an awareness of such issues, this section attempts to provide several important milestones that mark Sri Lankan theatre in the postcolonial era. It will look at theatres in Sinhala, Tamil and English, respectively, to examine a few pivotal moments in these theatres. While it focuses on certain events and specific playwrights, it inevitably leaves out many names and incidents, which are beyond the scope of the essay.

Sinhala theatre

In the early to mid-nineteenth century, performances in Sri Lanka occurred in multiple spaces and were manifold. Though less frequent, traditional performances such as *kolam* and *sokari* – stylized pieces using dance, music and masks – and *nadagam*, performances with music and dance, continued in rural areas; they were enacted on village threshing floors, in front yards of houses and in common fields. With the introduction of Indian Parsi musicals to the island, a new mode of performance, *Nurti*, plays with spectacular scenery and music, developed in Colombo, the urban centre. Nurti were staged inside buildings with an entrance fee and diverged from the traditional performances, which took place in villages free of charge. C. Don Bastian (1852–1921) and John de Silva (1857–1922) were at the forefront of using Nurti to enact historical legends and religious stories. At the same time, the early nineteenth century saw the development of dialogue plays influenced by European theatre traditions. The staging of European and Russian plays, mostly comedies, and their translations became popular in universities and urban theatre spaces. In the 1940s, Ediriweera Sarachchandra (1914–96), Professor of Sinhala at the University of Peradeniya (then the University of Ceylon) and a versatile figure in theatre, literature and criticism, translated plays by Gogol, Molière and Chekhov.

During the cultural resurgence that took place in 1940s, after more than four centuries of colonial rule, dramatists felt the need to find a distinct mode of theatre that addressed the identity of postcolonial Sri Lanka. Sarachchandra, who had thus far been mainly involved in productions of translated plays in the university, realized that such works were not adequate to capture the sentiments of the times. In 1956 he created *Maname*, a play that brought together diverse theatrical traditions such as Japanese *noh* and nadagama. The play was adapted to fit the proscenium stage and revolves around the themes of chastity, power and kingship. His next play, *Sinhabahu* (1961), based on the myth of the origin of the Sinhala race, grapples with issues related to filial piety, civilization and identity.

Sarachchandra's work was instrumental in creating a renewed interest in theatre and the 1960s was a time when dramatists explored and experimented with a variety of modes. Some artists embraced Sarachchandra's style: Gunesana Galapaththy's *Sanda Kinduru* (The Moon Mermaid, 1957) and Dayananda Gunawardena's *Nari Bena* (The Fox Son-in-Law, 1961) were such productions. Some attempts to produce plays using Sarachchandra's notions were marred by the superficial embracing of the formal aspects (Abeypala 1998: 53). At the same time, dramatists such as Sugathapala de Silva (1928–2002) and groups such as Apey Kattiya (Our Folk) diverged from Sarachchandra's aesthetics, claiming that the classical language and the stylist mode were not adequate to address contemporary socio-economic and political issues. Apey Kattiya focused on the lives of young men and women who had moved to the city, speaking about the plight of the workers and the dilemmas of marriage and family while boldly addressing issues related to sexuality in plays such as *Boding Karayo* (The Tenants, 1962) and *Tattu Gewal* (Apartments, 1964). Apart from these two trends, dramatists such as Henry Jayasena (1931–2009) experimented with combining techniques from stylistic and dialogue plays. In *Janelaya* (Window, 1962) he focused on urban workers who were trapped in an office and captured the monotony of their existence.

In the 1960s and 70s translations became prolific as the works of Bertolt Brecht, Samuel Beckett, Luigi Pirandello, Tennessee Williams and many others were translated into Sinhala. Among these, Henry Jayasena's translation of Brecht's *The Caucasian Chalk Circle* in 1967 gained wide popularity and has been running continuously for more than forty years. Sugathapala de Silva's translations of Luigi Pirandello's *Six Characters in Search of an Author* in 1965 and Tennessee Williams' *A Cat on a Hot Tin Roof* in 1966 introduced novel forms and themes to the Sinhala theatre. Translations were mostly done from European and American plays and Indian Sanskrit plays; there was no such interchange between Sinhala and Tamil theatres, though ethnic antagonism had been evolving as a central issue within the country's political landscape since 1950s. Unlike the 1940s, where the focus was on light satires, dramatists tuned to more serious works in the 1960s and 70s.

The 1971 youth uprising marked the onset of the 70s. Frustrated by the increasing economic inequality and lack of employment, Janatha Vimukthi Peramuna (JVP, People's Liberation Front) rebelled against the state with an armed insurrection. They had a strong youth following in the rural areas in the south. Their attempt was discovered and the state took repressive measures to curb the movement. Thousands of youth were tortured and killed as a result. Dhamma Jagoda's 1973 play, *Malavun Nagithiy* (The Dead Awaken), was influenced by the youth uprisings and the subsequent violence that was inflicted on them.[7] The socio-economic changes in the 70s culminated with the introduction of economic liberalization in 1977 with the United National Party coming into power. Many dramatists captured the changing socio-economic ethos from earlier on in the decade. Sugathapala de Silva's *Dunna Dunugamuwe* (1972) depicts a man's struggle to negotiate his political aspirations to gain workers' rights and his personal dilemma as he battles to procure medical aid for his sick child. Parakrama Niriella's 1976 stylistic play *Sekkuwa* focuses on the common man/worker who is exploited ruthlessly by the local landowners, politicians and international capitalist forces. R. R. Samarakoon's realist plays *Ahasin Wetunu Minissu* (Folk Who Fell from the Sky, 1971) captures the misery of poor men and women inhabiting an urban landscape, and *Kelani Palama* (The Kelani Bridge, 1978) portrays day-to-day struggles of the men and women living near the premises of the Kelani River Bridge.

With the economic changes, the landscape of theatre was also shifting. Though there were plays such as Niriealla's *Sekkuwa* and Simon Nawagaththegama's *Suba saha Yasa* (1974), which travelled to different parts of the island, theatre was in fact getting centralized in Colombo.[8] It is to challenge such a trajectory that Vivurtha Veedi Natya Kandayama (The Wayside and Open Theatre), the first political street theatre group in Sri Lanka, was formed in 1974. The pioneering members of the group, G. K. Haththotuwegama (1939–2009), Parakrama Niriealla (1949), H. A. Perera (1952–2010) and others collaborated to create plays that probed the changing socio-economic and political fabric of the country. Through their plays performed in the streets, on village threshing floors and in factories, they drew attention to the way in which commodity fetishism was making us puppets in the global market. They were ardent critics of capitalism and the commercialization of the arts. The group collaborated with farmers and workers and sought audiences who were excluded by the modern theatre spaces. The Wayside was instrumental in developing an alternative theatrical movement in southern Sri Lanka as several other street theatre groups such as Janatha Wedikawa (People's Stage), Dharana Street Theatre Group and Galu Nade burgeoned in different parts of the island.

The deregulation of the economy and its effects on society and individuals became much-discussed issues in the 1980s. While Ranjith Dharmakeerthi captures the change of the feudal system to a capitalist system via the story of two generations of factory owners in *Modara Mola* (Modara Mill, 1982), Jayalath Manorathna explores the place of the traditional artist in the changing economic landscape in *Tala Mala Pipila* (The Talipod Flower has Blossomed, 1988). The 1980s, which saw another uprising by the JVP-led youth movement, also witnessed its violent suppression in 1989. Thousands of youth were killed and many disappeared in this 'time of terror'.[9] Ashoka Handagama's *Magatha* (1989) addressed this issue with a symbolic story of a cow that had lost its calf. K. B. Herath's *Naga Gurula* (1991), a play set in a Cuban context, spoke of

Figure 12.5 The Wayside and Open Theatre performed Rookadayo (puppets) in a school playground in Pathegama, Kuruwita, Sri Lanka, 2010

(Photo by Kanchucka Dharmasiri)

disappearing children. Dharmasiri Bandaranayaka, who had already discussed the issue of totalitarianism in 1976 with his play *Ekadipathi* (The Dictator), continued to explore the theme through his translation of *The Dragon* by Yevgeny Schwartz in 1985.

In the 1990s and the beginning of the twenty-first century, within a context of rampant commercialization of media and culture, dramatists have moved to grapple with a variety of themes using different techniques. We see the proliferation of dialogue plays in Sinhala, especially via the works of playwrights such as Rajitha Dissanayake and Dhnanjaya Karunarathne. Dissanayaka focuses on issues related to the disillusions of the contemporary individual, media culture, postmodern angst and the search for meaning and the lack of it in his plays such as *Weeraya Merila* (The Hero is Dead, 2002) and *Apasu Herenna Bae* (No Turning Back, 2008). Karunarathna's dramatics, with plays such as *Chandrawathi samaga Rathriyak* (A Night with Chandrawathi, 1995) and *Acid Wessa* (Acid Rain, 2014), probes sexual and personal topics with which Sri Lankan audiences are not completely at ease. Priyankara Rathnayaka, a choreographer and director, re-creates Greek classics that are relevant to the current political context. Kapila Kumara Kalinga, who began his theatrical career in the 1980s, experiments with performing spaces with productions such as *Untitled*, and site-specific plays such as *An Incident in 2020* (2010). Furthermore, a range of children's plays have been developed through the works of Somalatha Subasinghe and Kaushalya Fernando. One should also note that a wave of light comedies have taken audiences by storm in the beginning of the twenty-first century, with plays such as Ravindra Ariyarathna's *Balloth Ekka Bae* (It's not Possible with Dogs) breaking box-office records.

Tamil theatre

In the early nineteenth century, *kooththu*, traditional performances with dance and music, continued to take place in the north, east, and in the upcountry areas. Kooththu were enacted in open spaces. The arrival of Parsi troupes on the island affected Tamil performances in the north and east in a manner similar to the way they influenced Sinhala theatre. V. V. Veiramuththu is one among several dramatists who successfully incorporated the musical and dramatic qualities of Parsi pieces to his plays. On the other hand, the impact of European dramatic forms, especially dialogue plays, was visible in Tamil theatre in the 1940s. Kandaswami Kanapathipillai, a professor of Tamil at the University of Peradeniya, focused on issues related to the Tamil middle class in his social satires. He critiqued cultural practices based on class and caste. Kanapathipillai wrote *Thurokokilal* (The Traitors) in 1956, in which he portrayed a separatist group's battle against the state. His plays were performed outside the university as well. While kooththu took place in open-air spaces, with the arrival of Parsi musicals and the production of dialogue plays, the proscenium became a dominant space where plays were performed.

The energy created by Sarachchandra's *Maname* sparked interest in the Tamil theatre communities as well. As stated earlier, nadagama was one of the sources for *Maname*, and nadagama in turn was influenced by kooththu. This connection motivated S. Vidyanandan, another professor in the Department of Tamil, to explore the roots of traditional kooththu further. His research and subsequent experiments led to the creation of *Nondi Nadagama* in 1961. Experiments of traditional kooththu culminated in 1972 with the creation of *Ravanesan*, a script based on *Ramayana* that Vidyanandan and Sinniah Maunaguru created together. The play captures the epic fight between Rama and Ravana, the rulers of India and Lanka, focusing on issues related to war, justice and chastity. The play also focuses on the plight of ordinary men and women in times of violent strife.

Tamil theatre in the latter part of the twentieth century developed along two lines: plays influenced by traditional kooththu and western dramatic forms. Sinniah Maunaguru took forward the experiments with the kooththu form in his efforts to use the traditional dramatic style to address contemporary issues related to class and caste in plays such as *Sangaram* (Destruction) produced in the late 1960s. Dramatists such as Tarcisius and Sundaralingam continued to experiment with modern and traditional forms. Balendran translated works by Bertolt Brecht and Tennessee Williams while writing his own plays based on middle-class issues. In Jaffna, the College for Dramaturgy was established in 1978 under the aegis of Kulanthei Shanmugalingam. Therefore, Tamil theatre in the 1970s developed in a variety of directions.

Yet, a rupture in Tamil theatre occurred in 1983 with the anti-Tamil riots, which broke out in the south of the country. Some groups associated with the government allegedly initiated the violence against the Tamil community, killing and displacing many. Thousands of houses of Tamils were burnt and their belongings looted. As a result, Tamil dramatists in Colombo and Kandy dispersed; many left the country and some went to the north and the east. That same year, the three-decade-long war between the LTTE (Liberation Tigers of Tamil Eelam) and the Sri Lankan government broke out. Hence, Tamil theatre faced obstacles from all directions and was not able to continue smoothly with their work. The spaces of performance were one of the main concerns and artists were forced to seek alternative avenues as a result of the security situation. Thus, the theatre that continued in the north and east resorted to the streets, common fields and the backyards of houses. A foremost playwright and director who worked in Jaffna during the war was Kulanthei Shanmugalingam, who focused on themes related to violence, war and migration as well as class, gender and caste oppression in his work. One of his best-known plays, *Man Sumantha Meniyar* (With Sweat and Dust and on their Shoulders, 1985), depicts the plight of ordinary men and women as they deal with the violence and terror caused by the war. In *Velvithee* (The Sacrificial Fire, 1993), he examines the double oppression directed at women in times of violence.

Theatre Action Group (1990), led by Sithamparanathan, was initiated by a group of artists and lecturers in the University of Jaffna. Their participatory theatre practice was carried out with the intention of helping victims of war grapple with emotional traumas. Sivagnanam Jeyasankar has been continuingly experimenting with koothhu in Batticaloa, a city in the Eastern Province, but his approach has been different from previous ones. In his desire to 'formulate an organic form of community theatre based on koothhu', Jeyasankar works with traditional koothhu performers in their own communities and uses the traditional form to address contemporary issues (Jeyasankar 2008: 27). Another aim of the reformulation process is to give valance to indigenous performance traditions in the face of increasing globalization.

There are also theatre groups that cannot be divided along language lines, especially Janakaraliya, a mobile theatre, which started their work in 2003, founded by Parakrama Niriella and H. A. Perera. Janakaraliya produces plays in Sinhala and Tamil and translates their work between these two languages. Janakaraliya also travels to diverse locations in the island, especially to rural areas where many theatre groups do not reach, in order to make theatre accessible to a wide audience.

A brief note on English theatre

English theatre in Sri Lanka mainly developed in the universities, especially through the works of E. F. C. Ludowyk (1906–1985). He directed numerous plays, including Molière's *The Imaginary Invalid* in 1935 and Jean Anouilh's *Antigone* in 1950. These plays were staged in the University of Peradeniya and also in venues in Colombo. The plays appealed to an English-speaking middle class and 'English theatre was subjected to a potent and rapid development in Colombo after 1950' (Kariyawasam 1982: 37). Stage and Set, a group based in Colombo which started their work in the 1960s, brought together English theatre practitioners such as Ernest McIntyre, Karen Breckenridge, Iranganie Serasinghe and Haig Karunaratne and practitioners of Sinhala theatre such as Henry Jayasena. Stage and Set produced plays by Shakespeare, Brecht, Pirandello and Arthur Miller. They staged MacIntyre's *Education of Miss Asia* in 1971, a social satire that portrays the attempt to instill intellectual values in Miss Asia who is about to contest for Miss World. The follies of the English-speaking middle class in Sri Lanka have been a common theme in English theatre, especially in Indu Dharmasena's plays. We see playwrights such as Ruwanthie de Chickera moving towards different themes through her plays: *Kalumali* (2012), a play that was performed in English and Sinhala, captures the complexities that middle-class women face in contemporary society, while *Grease Yaka* (2014) explores the breeding of unfounded fears in society. Most English plays are staged only in Colombo, often in the Lionel Wendt Theatre.

Notes

1 An exception to this rule of thumb is a few graduates who studied theatre abroad, mostly at the National School of Drama in India.
2 The term *bhadralok* (literally 'well-mannered person') is derived from Bengali. It denotes the new class of refined, educated people who were the product of the colonial reign in Bengal, and who successfully harnessed economic and class privilege to caste ascendancy. Today, the *bhadralok* identity is considerably eroded.
3 A *mātbar* is a traditional village elder who exerts considerable influence by means of his economic leverage.
4 The quasi-historic legend recounts 'the martyrdom of the Prophet's grandsons Hasan and Hussein as a result of the rivalry between them and Yezid, the son of Muawiya, over the succession to the Caliphate' (Awwal 2003: 228).
5 Rabindranath's performance code and dramaturgical vocabulary is most clearly enunciated in two essays, Raṅgamañcha and Antar Bāhir, supplemented by the preamble of the play *Phālgunī* and a few verbal observations.
6 *Panchayat* means, 'rule by five'. Panchayat is an authoritarian one-party system, although the word means rule by five elders. Local *panchayats* were councils of landowners that chose representatives to district *panchayats*, which, in turn, sent representatives to the National Panchayat. However, King Mahendra retained executive power, appointing nearly half of the members of the National Panchayat as well as the prime minister and cabinet, and banning all political parties. For more on *panchayat*, see Brown (1996).
7 It was the same year that Jagoda started the Ranga Shilpa Shalika in Colombo, the first theatre and actor training institute in Sri Lanka.
8 G. K. Haththotuwegama claims that 'the audiences for the plays in the modernist Sinhala theatre were easily definable as the urbanized, predominately bilingual and Sinhala-only speaking bourgeoisie' (Haththotuwegama 2012: 210).
9 Ranjini Obeyesekere uses the term 'time of terror' to designate this violent period in Sri Lankan history in *Sri Lankan Theatre in a Time of Terror*.

Bibliography

Abeypala, Roland (1998) 'The Development of Theatre in Post-Independence Sri Lanka (1948–98),' in *Abhinaya*, Baththaramulla: Department of Cultural Affairs, 12–85.
—— (ed.) (2000) *Abhinaya*, Volume 7, Battaramulla: Department of Cultural Affairs.
Afzal-Khan, Fawzia (2005) *A Critical Stage: the Role of Secular Alternative Theatre in Pakistan*, New Delhi: Seagull.
Ahmed, Samina, Zain Ahmed, and Salman Peerzada (1998) 'Pakistan', in Don Rubin (ed.) *The World Encyclopedia of Contemporary Theatre*, Volume 5, 443–57, New York: Routledge.
Awwal, Mohammad Abdul (2003) 'Biṣād-Sindhu', in Sirajul Islam (ed.) *Banglapedia: National Encyclopedia of Bangladesh*, Volume 2, 227–28, Dhaka: Asiatic Society of Bangladesh.
Azad, Humayun (1992) 'Bangla Literature in the Nineteenth Century', in Sirajul Islam (ed.) *History of Bangladesh 1704–1971, Volume Three: Social and Cultural History*, 389–408, Dhaka: Asiatic Society of Bangladesh.

Bogamuwa, Chandrasiri (ed.) (2003) *Abhinaya*, Volume 9, Battaramulla: Department of cultural Affairs.

Brandon, James R. (ed.) (1993) *The Cambridge Guide to Asian Theatre*, Cambridge: Cambridge University Press.

Brown, T. Louise (1996) *The Challenge to Democracy in Nepal: A Political History*, London: Routledge.

Chakraborti, Dipendu (2006) 'Tagore's Drama: A Critique of Western Modernity', in Krishna Sen and Tapati Gupta (eds) *Tagore and Modernity*, Kolkata: Das Gupta & Co.

Chowdhury, Kabir (1985) 'Sahitya Samalochana Paribhasha', in Kabir Chowdhury and Syed Manzurul Islam (eds)*Sahitya Samalochana O Nandantattva Paribhasha*, Dhaka: Bangla Academy.

Dasgupta, Uma (2006) 'Rabindranath Tagore and Modernity', in Krishna Sen and Tapati Gupta (eds) *Tagore and Modernity*, Kolkata: Das Gupta & Co.

Dharwadker, Aparna (2008) 'Mohan Rakesh, Modernism, and the Postcolonial Present', *South Central Review*, 25 (1): 136–62.

Friedman, Susan Stanford (2001) 'Definitional Excursions: The Meanings of Modern/Modernity/ Modernism', *Modernism/Modernity*, 8 (3): 493–513.

Gikandi, Simon (2006) 'Preface: Modernism in the World', *Modernism/Modernity*, 13 (3): 419–24.

Guha, Ranajit (1993) 'Neel-Darpan: The Image of a Peasant Revolt in a Liberal Mirror', in David Hardiman (ed.) *Peasant Resistance in India 1858–1914*, Delhi: Oxford University Press.

Guhathakurta, Meghna (1994) 'The Representation and Characterization of Women in Contemporary Theatre: The Case of Bishad Shindhu', in Firdous Azim and Niaz Zaman (eds), *Infinite Variety: Women in Society and Literature*, 283–93, Dhaka: University Press.

Gupt, Somnath (2005) *The Parsi Theatre: Its Origins and Development*, Kathryn Hansen (trans), Calcutta: Seagull.

Haththotuwegama. G. K. (2012) 'Unresolved Contradictions, Paradoxical Discourses and Alternative Strategies in Post-Colonial Sinhala Theatre', in Kanchuka Dharmasiri, Lohan Gunaweera, and Nicole Calandra (eds) *Streets Ahead with Haththotuwegama*, Maharagama: Ravaya.

Huq, Mohammad Daniul, and Aminur Rahman (2003) 'Bangla Literature', in S. Islam (ed.) *Banglapedia: National Encyclopedia of Bangladesh*, Volume 1, 437–54, Dhaka: Asiatic Society of Bangladesh.

Islam, Sirajul (2003) 'Fort William College', in Sirajul Islam (ed.) *Banglapedia: National Encyclopedia of Bangladesh*, Volume 4, 269–70, Dhaka: Asiatic Society of Bangladesh.

Jeyasankar, Sivagnanam (20°08) *Drum of a Herald*, Batticaloa: Third Eye Publications.

Kariyawasam, Tissa (1979) *Sinhala Natyaye Vikashanaya* (The Development of Sinhala Theatre 1867–1911), Colombo: Pradeepa Publishers.

—— (1982) *Vishva Vidyaleeya Natya Vansaya* (The University Drama Era), Colombo: Godage Publishers.

Kershaw, Baz (1999) *The Radical in Performance: Between Brecht and Baudrillard*, London: Routledge.

Mamun, Muntasir (2006) *Unish Shatake Purbabange Theatre O Natak*, Dhaka: Sahitya Bilas.

Obeyesekere, Ranjini (1999) *Sri Lankan Theatre in a Time of Terror*, California: Sage.

Pamment, Claire (2012) 'A Split Discourse: Body Politics in Pakistan's Popular Punjabi Theatre', *TDR* 56 (1): 114–27.

Pratt, William (2000) '"To Have Gathered From The Air A Live Tradition": Pound's Poetic Legacy', in Helen M. Dennis (ed.) *Ezra Pound and Poetic Influence: The Official Proceedings of the 17th International Ezra Pound Conference*, 1–10, Amsterdam: Rodopi B.V.

Rathnayaka, L. D. (1963) *Neethigna John de Silva Nataka Ithihasaya* (The History of Proctor John de Silva Dramatic Literature), Colombo: An Author Publication.

Sarachchandra, Ediriweera (1966) *The Folk Drama of Ceylon*, Colombo: Department of Cultural Affairs.

Sengupta, Ashis (ed.) (2014) *Mapping South Asia through Contemporary Theatre*, New York: Palgrave Macmillan.

Shanmugalingam, Kuzhanthai (2007) *Shanmugalingam: Three Plays*, S. Pathmanathan (trans), Colombo: Kumaran Book House.

Sithamparanathan, K. (2003) 'Interventions and Methods of the Theatre Action Group', *International Journal of Mental Health, Psychological Work and Counseling in Areas of Armed Conflict*, 1 (1): 44–7.

Sivathamby, Kartigesu, and Wijerathna Pathiraja (2000) 'Sri Lankawe Demala Natya Kalawa' (Tamil Theatre in Sri Lanka), in Roland Abeypala (ed) *Abhinaya*, Volume 7, Battaramulla: Department of Cultural Affairs.

Tagore, Rabindranath (1918) *Nationalism*, London: Macmillan.

Whyman, Rose (2008) *The Stanislavsky System of Acting: Legacy and Influence In Modern Performance*, Cambridge: Cambridge University Press.

Wolpert, Stanley (1984) *Jinnah of Pakistan*, New York: Oxford University Press.

13

Modern Japanese theatre

John K. Gillespie

The Meiji years and the challenge of change

Japan's Edo period (1603–1868), marked by autocratic rule, regimented neo-Confucian social stratification and official isolation, yielded an increasingly stable, mostly peaceful land. Any change was evolutionary, as demonstrated by the rise of a basically secular society, vigorous middle class and money-based economy. Revolutionary change was unthinkable. Yet, that is exactly what Commodore Matthew C. Perry and his fleet of Black Ships heralded with their trips to Japan in 1853 and 1854. While Perry fulfilled his specific assignment, prising Japan open after centuries-long isolation, the ensuing social, political and cultural changes jolted the country to its existential core, hastening the demise of the Tokugawa Shōgunate and the onset of the Meiji period (1868–1912). Intimidated by Perry's gun-laden frigates and chafing under a spate of unequal treaties foisted on them by the United States. and other western nations, the Japanese were at loose ends: whether to aggressively confront the arrogance of western countries and fight to gain the respect that Japan deserved or obsequiously submit to western dominance.

The ensuing socio-political questions engendered widespread confusion and ambivalence, symbolized by the nationalistic rallying cry *sonnō-jōi* (revere the emperor, expel the barbarian), even while many Japanese were convinced that the country's lengthy stasis had outlived its usefulness and needed change. If Japan became a modern nation, could it retain Japanese qualities? Did becoming modern mean becoming less Japanese or, worse, western? What did it mean to be Japanese in the modern world? And what of Japanese identity? While a vague consensus among intellectuals gradually coalesced around the notion of *bunmei kaika* (civilization and enlightenment), all manner of cultural developments, serious intellectual pursuits and ludicrous fads alike – including blind embrace of things western and disdain for aspects of their own culture – vied for attention under that catch-all rubric and catalysed an already unstable mix. Some liberal thinkers, for example, actually advocated English over Japanese as the national language and even intermarriage with westerners to improve the Japanese racial stock, while thousands of woodblock prints and traditional art objects, acquired for the equivalent of pennies from Japanese apparently oblivious to their worth, left Japan in droves with enterprising western speculators.

Japanese theatre after Perry perfectly reflected that turn of events. My purpose here is to consider the principal phases and issues critical to developing modern theatre in Japan from the late nineteenth century to the early twenty-first: reforming traditional Japanese theatre practices; adapting western approaches to playwriting and performance; escaping increasingly pervasive translated western plays and their Japanese derivative, *shingeki* (new theatre); and, finally, evolving a vibrant, creative, indigenous Japanese modern theatre.

Traditional Japanese theatre's deeply entrenched practices made any innovation hugely challenging. With ingrained, centuries-old attitudes, themes, plots and histrionic styles, how even to get started? Japan's ambivalence to its post-Perry status exactly foreshadowed the key issues facing Japanese theatre. How to make it modern? Did modernized mean westernized? Indeed, the early consensus of those powerful enough to influence theatre's transformation was axiomatic: if the old is to cede ground, a new reality can emerge only if a new voice is developed to express it. Yet, in that historical context, Japan had little to go on. It should hardly be surprising, therefore, that the phenomenon of a modern theatre would gain traction only incrementally, its initial efforts tentative and uncertain within the amorphous giddiness of massive cultural change in the Meiji years. Although theatre was then held in low regard by Japan's officialdom and aristocrats, a coterie of reform-minded intellectuals helped establish a fundamental context for change, developing the first utterances of the requisite new voice that would reflect the new era.[1]

Consider these pivotal steps occurring in a two-decade period bookended by two Japanese government actions: one, in 1871, announcing that theatre should become respectable entertainment and acting a respectable profession; two, in 1891, officially rescinding the centuries-old stricture against women on stage. Such thinking gained momentum when members of the Iwakura Mission, sent abroad in 1871–73 to study western values and institutions, were stunned to see western leaders entertaining dignitaries with plays, which would have been inconceivable in Japan. Yet, in 1876, Mission leader Iwakura Tomomi (1825–83) arranged a *noh* performance for the imperial family. In 1878, Mission member (later Japan's first prime minister) Itō Hirobumi (1841–1909) organized a meeting with prominent kabuki figures Ichikawa Danjūrō IX (1838–1903), Onoe Kikugorō V (1844–1904) and Morita Kan'ya XII (1846–97), urging creation of a high-class theatre culture with actors recognized as artists 'held in high esteem' (Powell 2002: 9). In 1879, Iwakura invited visiting American ex-president Ulysses S. Grant to a noh play. Asked his impressions afterwards, though he apparently slept throughout, the rough-hewn old soldier uttered words that became famous. 'You must preserve this', he said, giving noh theatre, then barely subsisting, unlikely encouragement. In 1886, *Engeki kairyōkai* (Theatre Reform Society) was established to elevate theatre's – that is, kabuki's – reputation. The very next year, foreign minister Inoue Kaoru (1836–1915) arranged a kabuki performance for the imperial family, a first for them.

Those events were critical in further strengthening the rationale to pursue theatre reform. Early results, however, were predictably unfortunate, mainly because focus was not on developing a truly new voice but reforming the old one. A play in 1881 featured, for example, a character sporting such western accessories as a straw hat, leather boots, umbrella, valise and large pocket watch. Another production used western actors, untrained in kabuki techniques (the producer, swept up by the latest fads, even proclaimed his preference for beer over sake and cooked over raw fish). That sort of extreme pendulum swing, rather than reforming kabuki, only made it less stylized, even more realistic, thereby lessening its charm and keeping it for a time in the realm of low-class entertainment for the uneducated masses. Traditional plays, thus 'reformed', were never as popular as the old, unreformed favourites.

Loosening the grip of traditional theatre: shinpa and other kabuki avatars

Perhaps, however, the reform attempt was necessary to pave the way for other initiatives. A more concerted effort, *shinpageki* (new school drama), popularly known as *shinpa* (also spelt *shimpa)*, materialized with the activist Sudō Sadanori (1867–1907) around 1888 in reaction to perceptions of political repression. Sudō rounded up fellow activists as actors – amateurs all – appropriately termed *sōshi*, meaning simultaneously 'hooligan' but also 'courageous young man'. Their action-packed performances, called *sōshi shibai* (agitprop plays), drew spectators with politically based plots and raw action appealing to many ordinary Japanese not necessarily attracted to theatre.

Building on Sudō's efforts to create drama beyond kabuki's stentorian grip, the multi-talented actor-impresario Kawakami Otojirō (1864–1911) also produced successful anti-government shinpa plays reflecting his commoner status – for example, how to succeed in life, even if not born to wealth. He created action-oriented spectacles based on current events and featuring a frenetic mix of movement, dance, music and comedic, satirical scenes.[2] Not missing an opportunistic beat for financial gain, he abruptly changed from anti-government activist to government supporter, to leverage Japan's victories in the Sino-Japanese (1894–95) and Russo-Japanese (1904–05) wars with characteristically sensational performances, extolling war heroes in fight scenes so realistic that actors often drew blood. Snaring huge popularity among disaffected kabuki fans, his successes enabled shinpa nearly to eclipse kabuki in popularity during the 1890s.

Kawakami's work was stimulated in substantial part by his knowledge of western theatre. Studying in France in 1893, Kawakami was among the first Japanese theatre figures to see plays in Europe. Returning to Japan, he distanced himself further from kabuki with western music, actors in contemporary attire and, in perhaps shinpa's most radical departure, using actresses. By the early twentieth century, performances of adapted western plays began to occur with increasing frequency. It is unfortunate that no film of Kawakami's or other such pioneering performances exists, for they must have been curious indeed; invariably done within the directors' and actors' limited experience, physical movement and declamation were hardly different from kabuki or shinpa. Yet, western influence was ubiquitous. Partly because of his brief experience in France and later interaction with Japan's pre-eminent modernizer Fukuzawa Yukichi (1835–1901) at Keio University, Kawakami decided to take his wife Sadayakko (1881–1946) and his troupe abroad, not just to glean more from western theatre but, impresario that he was, he also envisioned opportunities to perform. They made two trips, 1899–1901 and 1901–02, witnessing performances in America, England, France, Germany and Russia, and staged several performances of their own, including appearances by Sadayakko who, though a trained geisha distinguished in Tokyo for her prominent patrons, had no experience with shinpa, much less kabuki. Kawakami, however, aware of the importance of actresses in the west, had his wife rehearse certain roles prior to leaving Japan; once in San Francisco, with her image on posters everywhere, her appearance on stage became inevitable. Although their performances on the tour were advertised as kabuki and they indeed employed some kabuki titles, most of their titles and all their plays were adapted, with scenarios pared down, since the actors' lines, spoken in Japanese, would be incomprehensible to the audiences, and they embellished the stage action with visual elements. That approach yielded a sort of 'bastardised' or 'pseudo-kabuki' (Kano 2001: 91–5), especially as regarded by Japanese officials and some Japanese citizens, who, steeped in traditional notions – for example, actors were lower-class denizens and women should not be on stage – censured the troupe for allowing Sadayakko to perform and for misrepresenting traditional kabuki, even though Kawakami's troupe was adapting kabuki, not actually trying to perform it. Nevertheless, Japanese officials were well aware that western audiences, with the extremely rare exceptions of the odd critic or citizen who had seen kabuki in Japan, would not be able to distinguish between kabuki, pseudo or otherwise, and shinpa. Kawakami, of course, was hardly concerned with maintaining Japanese traditions; he and his band of actors were adept, even renowned, in Japan for their characteristic style of shinpa. Above all, he was about making money and gaining recognition for his new brand of theatre.

With their freewheeling entrepreneurial ways, the Kawakamis learnt much on their travels and were buoyed by the stunningly positive reactions they received from American and European audiences. Sadayakko quickly became the main attraction, often eliciting enthralling responses; she far outstripped Kawakami who had always been the troupe's principal newsmaker in Japan. She was even compared favourably to the reigning divas of the western stage, Sarah Bernhardt in France, Ellen Terry in Britain and Eleonora Duse in Italy.[3] Back in Japan after their second tour, the couple proceeded to stage plays with unkabuki-like contemporary themes, which they did through their shinpa productions but also by adapting western plays in shinpa style, initially, in 1903, with *Othello*, the court scene in *The Merchant of Venice*, and *Hamlet*. Theirs were not the first such adaptations. The acclaimed shinpa actor Ii Yōhō (1871–1932) had already staged Shakespeare's *Julius Caesar* in 1901, and in 1902 Hanafusa Ryūgai (1872–1906) had mounted a shinpa version of Ibsen's *An Enemy of the People*, with a Japanese setting. There were, in fact, quite a number of shinpa adaptations of western drama, including other plays by Shakespeare, Goethe and Alphonse Daudet. While little in these efforts to adapt western drama to the shinpa stage would pass muster as good theatre, with their novel approach, Kawakami and his contemporaries effectively gave Japanese spectators an alternative to traditional kabuki.

Shinpa achieved that and more. Its golden age was from about 1895 through the end of the Meiji period in 1912, marked especially by the plays of Izumi Kyōka (1873–1939) and adaptations from his novels.[4] The form gradually took on a more romantic ethos and grew into melodrama, perhaps analogous to soap operas with an elegant veneer (Poulton 2001: 23–4). Kyōka adapted his novel *Giketsu kyōketsu* (Loyal Blood, Valiant Blood, 1894) to create *Taki no shiraito* (The Water Magician, 1895), his most successful play. His fiction was often appraised as dramatic, this novel especially so. The main character Taki no Shiraito, stage name of a female entertainer, is in love with a law student and supports him by paying his tuition. When her final instalment, money gained from a patron, is stolen, she breaks into her patron's home to find more and, panicked, kills him. At her trial, the prosecuting attorney is, quite predictably, her true love performing his first official assignment. She makes a dramatic confession and, as a consequence, the prosecutor, knowing she killed for his sake, commits suicide. (In the play's first production, none other than Kawakami himself played the attorney role.) Today, we would likely find this play somewhat cloying, but it was well within the ethos of the day, one Japanese critic terming it 'a tour de force'. Such plays were so successful in the waning days of the Meiji period that shinpa continued to challenge kabuki as the most popular form of Japanese drama, attracting such luminaries as Mori Ōgai (1862–1922) and Mayama Seika (1878–1948) to write for it (Poulton 2001: 17–40).

What role did shinpa play in modern Japanese theatre's development? It has been characterized as an offshoot of kabuki, an early modern form, and a bridge between the traditional and the modern. Perhaps all three possibilities are applicable. It certainly arose from kabuki, keeping the *onnagata* (female impersonator) and using similar stylized movements, gestures, language and diction. It was certainly an early modern form, in that it was not kabuki, used actresses and incorporated current attire, use of music, lighting and stories. It was also a bridge of sorts linking the traditional with the modern or maybe just a stepping stone between them. While most spectators expected nothing more than a good melodramatic story, some observers saw contradictions. One critic noted his negative reaction to the disparity between the traditional language of Kyōka's characters and their up-to-date situation and attire, a disjunction causing other critics to feel 'an inherent resistance' to Kyōka's style of dramatization (Poulton 2001: 39–40).

In addition, traditional Japanese theatre, including shinpa, is often characterized by a unifying harmony among the aspects of performance: music, spoken or chanted utterance, and physical movement. Without such harmony, Kitamura Tōkoku (1868–1894) observes in 1893, 'no beauty would emerge'. Yet, he immediately asserts that this very feature represents an unavoidable contradiction: 'I have come to realize that there is no way to eliminate the defective convention of symmetrical harmony in Japanese drama', which, he continues, will pose future 'difficulty' (quoted in Rimer *et al.* 2014: 11). Of course, Kitamura, though writing about poetic drama, has identified a key challenge facing the attempts to reform and modernize kabuki.[5] With respect to shinpa, therefore, while most observers acknowledge its worthiness for study and appreciation, its mixed vision failed to move it forward; rather, it soon came to be seen as 'anachronistic' and 'old-fashioned' (Poulton 2001: 39), even 'disregarded' (Rimer 1974: 54). What, therefore, shinpa provided in terms of steps towards a modern Japanese theatre, beyond the relatively superficial aspects of contemporary dress, hairstyles and music, was, above all, the realization that no amount of reform of kabuki nor even further reform of shinpa would produce a legitimate Japanese modern theatre.

The shinpa phenomenon faded by 1915, but other kabuki avatars cropped up, including *shinkokugeki* (new national theatre) and *shin-kabuki* (new kabuki). Both were clearly bound to traditional kabuki in stage action and diction, despite some western-inspired techniques. Shinkokugeki, for example, brainchild of the swashbuckling Sawada Shōjirō (1892–1929), while maintaining kabuki-like stylization, departed from it in what became Sawada's dramatic signature: sword-fighting scenes so vigorous and popular in the 1920s that sell-outs were common. The term shin-kabuki, coined in 1919, referred to plays written under western influence, having both literary and dramatic merit, by playwrights unattached to kabuki companies. Performed with the look and feel of kabuki, shin-kabuki productions avoided certain standard techniques, such as *mie* (climactic poses), attempting greater verisimilitude. Even the accompanying music was different, less pervasive, as in western drama, than in traditional kabuki. Still, the key difference was using contemporary themes and psychological realism. The influential Tsubouchi Shōyō (1859–1935) wrote *Kiri hitoha* (A Paulownia Leaf, 1894), considered the first shin-kabuki play. Its structure, partly influenced by *Hamlet*, demonstrated that kabuki could be enjoyed not only for its action and moral undergirding but also for its literary and intellectual value. The play went unperformed for 10 years, conservatives feeling it went too far, reformists not far enough. Finally staged in 1904, it stimulated positive reactions among intellectuals and playwrights, inspiring other kabuki outsiders to write shin-kabuki plays. The phenomenon received a huge boost when Ichikawa Sadanji II (1880–1940) inherited his father's (Ichikawa Sadanji I, 1842–1904) kabuki company and its stage, Meiji-za (Meiji Theatre), and focused on such plays. Shin-kabuki was for a few years during the Taishō period (1912–26), before shingeki gathered momentum, Japan's most advanced form of modern theatre.

In short, whatever emerged as 'new' in Japanese theatre through the 1890s, kabuki and its ethos were so deeply ingrained that it remained 'the only yardstick by which audiences and critics could judge theatre' (Powell 2002: 12). That assessment remained more or less intact, as can be gleaned from descriptions of acting and diction, in spite of wider exposure of Japanese theatre modernizers to western theatre, even into the early stages of shingeki in the 1920s. Acting and directing through the Meiji period were thoroughly redolent of kabuki, including stylized movement, declamatory style and using onnagata. As a result, many forward-looking theatre figures found themselves in the ungainly position of finally realizing that reforming their traditional theatre was a cul-de-sac, that they actually needed to break from it and merge with the (western) present.

Western drama and the emergence of shingeki

That challenge provided the stimulus for two groundbreaking organizations ostensibly more progressive than attempts at reforming kabuki. The first was Bungei Kyōkai (Literary Arts Society), founded by Shōyō in 1906. A Waseda University professor influential in reforming Japanese literature and theatre, Shōyō made this organization into Japan's first educational theatre workshop. He purveyed his theories in two critical works: *Shōsetsu shinzui* (The Essence of the Novel, 1885) and an essay 'Wagakuni no shigeki' (Japan's Historical Drama, 1893–94). Shōyō unambiguously rejected neo-Confucian didacticism – that is, that artistic endeavours should include morally uplifting lessons – and fixed character types then prevailing in fiction and theatre. With many intellectuals, he regarded kabuki as low-class, even risqué – in short, a corrupt form. Yet, he wanted to reform not abandon it. He wanted a serious theatre for adults, featuring intellectually stimulating ideas, a theatre worthy of respect beyond Japan, as Shakespeare, Ibsen and Chekhov were respected outside their countries. To that end, Shōyō advocated an idea-centred, plot-focused theatre, as opposed to Japan's centuries-long actor-centred tradition. He envisioned transforming kabuki's presentational style to one that was, as in the west, representational. A key to his strategy: he refused to accept former kabuki actors into the Literary Arts Society, preferring young people without acting experience, trainable from scratch. In addition, his work on Ibsen and Shakespeare was less to grasp their plays' moral underpinnings than to apply their exemplary playwriting techniques to reforming kabuki. By staging such plays as *Hamlet* (1907 and 1911), Ibsen's *A Doll's House* (1911) and *Julius Caesar* (1913), the Literary Arts Society presented not only an idea of western theatre to the Japanese public but also an inkling of what reformed kabuki might be.

Perhaps more promising was the second organization, Jiyū Gekijō (Free Theatre*)*, founded in 1909 by Osanai Kaoru (1881–1928), inspired by André Antoine's Théâtre Libre (est. 1887) in Paris and Otto Brahms' Freie Bühne (est. 1889) in Berlin. Osanai, a Tokyo University graduate who for a time took a position at Keio University where he encountered the influence of Fukuzawa, staunchly advocated naturalism and grew impatient with the plodding reform efforts of Shōyō and the Literary Arts Society. Osanai bonded with Sadanji II, who, while continuing with shin-kabuki, nonetheless agreed that kabuki was unredeemable. Sharing an activist passion to forge a new theatre, the two became the first shingeki pioneers to see plays in Europe. That experience gave Osanai the means to achieve his goal – that is, in Ibsen's social implications, particularly exposing bourgeois hypocrisies, he encountered the ideal modern theatre, prototypically naturalistic and psychological, precisely what he sought for Japan. He and his young troupe so revered Ibsen, for example, that they denigrated not only kabuki and shinpa but also Shakespeare, and virtually sneered at Shōyō's more staid Literary Arts Society. Osanai and Sadanji II were convinced that a completely new brand of theatre was realizable only by breaking completely with traditional Japanese forms and importing western plays.

Free Theatre's first production was Ibsen's *John Gabriel Borkman* (1909), generally considered the first shingeki play. Still, while Osanai felt he was breaking through traditional barriers, he shared common ground with earlier reform efforts; his performances, like those of Kawakami and Sadayakko, remained firmly within kabuki's grip. Even shorn of certain traditional conventions, Osanai's *Borkman*, using some retrained kabuki actors, featured stylized movements, gestures and declamation, onnagata and Sadanji II himself as Borkman speaking in a high-pitched, undeniably kabuki-style voice. The production had the rather odd occurrence of a woman in a female role interacting with an onnagata. Similar such scenes had already occurred in shinpa and in Shōyō's first production of *Hamlet*, and might well stand as symbolic of the tortuous transition from tradition to modern on the Japanese stage. Yet, the production was enthusiastically received, giving Japanese audiences a memorable taste of what a more modern theatre could be. Osanai, in fact, invented the word 'shingeki' to categorize what he was trying to do. He ultimately had incalculable influence in establishing at least the awareness of appropriate techniques for enacting western plays, and hence, for a new kind of theatre to emerge.

His approach, however, contained an insidious glitch, ultimately retarding the development of an indigenous modern theatre. The widespread preference among reform-minded Japanese for performing translated western plays eventually led Osanai to openly recognize the so-called *honyaku jidai* (age of translation), proclaiming his intention to perform only translated plays in his new venue, Tsukiji Shōgekijō (Tsukiji Little Theatre), established in 1924 with left-leaning, Meyerhold-influenced Hijikata Yoshi (1898–1959). Osanai and Hijikata embraced the latest European plays by, among others, Frank Wedekind, Maxim Gorki, Gerhart Hauptmann, Anton Chekhov and Maurice Maeterlinck. The legacy, therefore, of the Free Theatre, as of the Theatre Reform Society and Shōyō's Literary Arts Society, had more to do with transplanting western plays than with fostering a new kind of Japanese theatre. In addition, although both Shōyō and Osanai encouraged Japanese playwrights to write new plays – Osanai's *Borkman* staging inspired such figures as Kyōka, Kikuchi Kan (1888–1948) and Yamamoto Yūzō (1887–1974) to do so (Rimer *et al.* 2014: 19) – it was largely lip service. Shōyō made his own attempt, *En no gyōja* (En the Ascetic, 1916), a psychological re-examination of a Buddhist saint's life, written with influences from Ibsen and *The Tempest*. It is generally considered the first shingeki play by a Japanese playwright. Yet, Osanai only consented to stage it a decade later, in 1926. Moreover, its stage action, despite western influences, was undeniably derivative of kabuki and hardly compelling theatre. Shōyō had stature enough within the theatre community to have his play staged, albeit *en retard* – not the case with most other Japanese playwrights, at pains to find directors or venues. In legitimating translated plays as Japan's modern theatre, Shōyō and Osanai may have satisfied Japanese curiosity about western life, culture and, more narrowly, theatre, but, paradoxically, both because of and despite their influence, they inadvertently obfuscated their intended goal, ultimately hindering the development of new plays by Japanese playwrights. A few such plays are worthy of critical note and some managed to have performances in the 1910s and 1920s – work by Kyōka, Kikuchi, Kubota Mantarō 1889–1963) and Tanaka Chikao (1905–95), among others – and are an important ingredient rounding out the transition from the traditional to the truly modern.[6] Still, the paucity of such performances is a principal reason why a truly new Japanese theatre had such a long gestation period. Indeed, most new Japanese plays, until about 1960, can properly be considered derivative of western forms.

The grand effort to realize a new, modern, indigenous theatre in Japan might well be regarded, therefore, an exercise in frustration. Whatever the Japanese did, the west would pop up. How to adapt western playwriting techniques? How to adapt western stagecraft? Were these even possible? Could Japanese theatre be modern and not western? It is appropriate here to cite Donald Keene's sweeping assessment in 1955: 'In the past seventy years or more Japanese literature has been intimately affected by all European trends and, in fact, may be regarded in effect as forming a part of the modern movement in western literature' (Keene 1955: 18–19). Keene's provocative assessment, though referring to modern Japanese literature, easily applies to modern Japanese theatre (slower than fiction to develop). That it would take such a long time to find its native voice and that it could be considered part of the modern movement in western theatre became fully apparent when a figure such as Osanai's associate, Sadanji II, asserted that nothing new could come from kabuki or shinpa but only from first completely absorbing western values. Osanai reinforced that view by aligning himself with the iconic Fukuzawa and his famous suggestion that Japanese, to join the modern world, should figuratively 'leave Asia' (to learn from the west), which Osanai updated with his slogan, 'ignore tradition'.

Shingeki takes hold

For shingeki to be viable as its own brand, the issue of kabuki stagecraft had to be resolved. Many reformers, like Shōyō, persistently maintained the position, while regarding kabuki as anachronistic and corrupt, that they were justly proud of its rich tradition; reform, therefore, was all it needed. Other figures, like Osanai, wanted nothing more to do with kabuki. Yet, neither camp appeared capable of stagecraft totally bereft of kabuki approaches. What was preventing the modernization that virtually everyone claimed to want?

Stagecraft is distinctive depending on the cultural values of those developing it. Kabuki actors, masters of an extensive vocabulary of gestures, often improvised; having virtually nothing in common with western values, however, they were unable to improvise when performing western plays. In addition, despite the years of discipline necessary to master traditional Japanese acting techniques, Shōyō and Osanai appear to have put little effort into instilling similarly extensive western disciplines in their actors, and almost none into training them in western values. In a classic case of cultural jet lag, what they envisioned doing far exceeded their skill set to do. The lack of specifically targeted training can be seen particularly in the two principal culprits of kabuki stagecraft: stylized declamation and physical movement, so Japanese actors in translated western plays were often inadvertently awkward, even comical.

Resolution of these pesky issues finally came from three sources during the Taishō period (1912–26). The first was Shimamura Hōgetsu (1871–1918), Shōyō's principal Literary Arts Society protégé, who broke with the morally conservative Shōyō in 1913, after the eminent man fired his star actress, Matsui Sumako – shingeki's first marquee name – over her illicit affair with the married Shimamura. Following Matsui out, Shimamura, freed from Shōyō's ponderous leadership, quickly founded his own group, Geijutsuh-za (Art Theatre). Having seen plays in Europe, he preferred, like Shōyō and Osanai, to stage translated western plays but added a new ploy to prise declamation and acting from kabuki's grip. He positioned himself as a western-style director, a striking departure from kabuki's actor-centred tradition, and insisted that his actors stick to the text, exactly memorizing their lines with prescribed movements and gestures, and not devolve into kabuki-like fanciful diction and stylization. In the 1920s, Hijikata, primarily with proletarian plays, reinforced the director-centred approach.

The second source was proletarian theatre. As Japanese tasted democratic freedoms and Christian and socialist tenets during Taishō, proletarian theatre gradually rose to compete with translated western plays. Although few proletarian plays, laden with socio-political baggage, can sustain aesthetic consideration, they still created a context encouraging departures from traditional stagecraft, including action demanding thoroughgoing realism, and, for the first time, Japanese playwrights felt encouraged by seeing their plays reach the stage.

The final key to releasing theatre from kabuki's grip was supplied by Kishida Kunio (1890–1954), following his European sojourn in the early 1920s working with the reform-minded Jacques Copeau in Paris. Returning to Japan in 1923, armed with contemporary European ideas of stagecraft, Kishida required realism (though opposing the generally didactic proletarian plays) to better render his vision for modern Japanese theatre: non-political, realistic portrayals of contemporary society, with lines spoken conversationally, not declaimed, and informed by psychological motivations – in short, plays that could be read as well as enacted and enjoyed for their conceptual insights into the human condition. His influence was ubiquitous as fledgling shingeki gradually gained traction and it continues today; the company he founded in 1937, Bungaku-za (Literary Theatre), became the most important shingeki company and remains active. Moreover, the principal recognition for Japanese playwrights – Kishida Kunio gikyoku-shō (Kishida Kunio Drama Prize) – bears his name (Rimer 1974: 1–122).

Yet, even with kabuki's grip slackened, it should hardly surprise that shingeki, epigonic of western drama, would continue to develop tentatively. Consider two examples. Perhaps the most noteworthy proletarian play is Kubo Sakae's (1900–58) *Kazanbaichi* (Land of Volcanic Ash, 1937–38), a fascinating, densely epic play – performances lasted six hours, with a cast of sixty

– his attempt to corroborate Marxist social theory systematically and aesthetically. The main characters are subordinate to the action: farmers, ordinary citizens, opposing official government policies. The play may have warmed the hearts of activists but was less ideal for aspiring actors. Perhaps Kishida's best play, *Sawa-shi no futari musume* (The Two Daughters of Mr. Sawa, 1935), reveals his characteristic themes: family deterioration, absent fathers, life's daily complexities. The dialogue shows his penchant for psychological realism and drama as literature. His plays were exemplars of word-centred, fourth-wall realism, quite performable, if not masterpieces (Rimer 1974: 123–41).

Featuring real-life stories of contemporary Japanese, Kishida's approach gradually dominated modern Japanese theatre. What had been launched with early-Meiji efforts to reform kabuki had now evolved and become orthodoxy. Beyond plays on uniquely Japanese subjects, there was little discernible difference between shingeki and the western drama from which it had descended. Probably the best early example – certainly, the most popular – was Morimoto Kaoru's (1912–46) *Onna no isshō* (The Life of a Woman, 1945). Originally a leftist, Morimoto joined the Literary Theatre, honed his skills and became more accomplished as playwright and director than his mentor Kishida. Morimoto's play was written during Second World War hardships, its first performance coming in April 1945 amid the relentless strafing of Tokyo by Allied planes. It somehow ran for ten performances to near sell-out audiences. The action centres on Nunobiki Kei, an orphan adopted by a well-to-do family. She shows gratitude by rendering unflagging service to the family for many years, then marries the eldest son and heir. He lacks business sense, but Kei also shines in that arena and works vigilantly for the family's ongoing prosperity. Yet, in the measure that she is successful, she gradually loses the ready warmth and sensitivity that the family had grown to expect of her. One by one, the family members move out – including her husband, who eventually dies – and she is left alone in the large home. The play ends with Kei, now 56 but looking considerably older, sitting alone in the ruins of the firebombed house.

Why was this play so successful? It was, first, written by a Japanese playwright for Japanese audiences, quite rare until the rise of proletarian theatre. Second, it was well written and performed, featuring fully developed characters, not mere types, with whom the audience could identify. Third, the renowned Sugimura Haruko (1909–1997), icon of stage and screen, played Kei. Finally, whether their theatre is old or new, the Japanese appear to prefer characters not, as often in western drama, self-assertive and resisting destiny, like Ibsen's Nora, but those silently submitting to it, like Kei.

Postwar culture and the rise of angura: rejecting western drama and shingeki

Despite Japan's inevitable postwar preoccupation with the raw exigencies of quotidian survival and rebuilding devastated lives, by the early 1950s a cultural renaissance was already under way. The stimulus came from awareness of the pressing need for psychological survival, centred on the critical question, first broached in the Meiji years though now with greater urgency, of personal and national identity. What did it mean to be Japanese? What kind of country was Japan to be? And what of the relationship with the west? Could one be Japanese and also a citizen of the world? Although shingeki was increasingly dominant, many theatre figures were becoming disaffected with its limitations in framing Japan's particular postwar situation. So what was to be done? While answers were hardly clearer than half a century earlier, consider those offered by one playwright and two influential groups heralding the coming era of radical change and experimentation.

The playwright, Kinoshita Junji (1914–2006), wrote *Yūzuru* (Twilight Crane, 1949), a folk drama recalling Bertolt Brecht's *Lehrstücke*: a rustic rescues a crane with injured wing; reborn, the crane becomes a beautiful woman who visits the sincere, though plodding, rustic and becomes his wife. Yet when he sells some of her weaving for a profit, he loses his innocence and the woman, saddened, becomes once again a crane and flies away. Staged essentially as orthodox shingeki, the play appealed less for the characters' psychological motivations than for its evocation of Japan's mythical past, eliciting a keenly felt nostalgia for a state of ur-Japaneseness, a kind of mythic homeland, now lost, rendering powerful comment on the issue of Japanese identity. It enjoyed instant fame and has been among the most performed postwar Japanese plays.

The group Jikken Kōbō (Experimental Workshop), founded in 1951 by fourteen artists of diverse disciplines, ventured a different answer. Its mission: to retrieve their arts from war's rubble – a daunting challenge, given the war-induced pessimism among many Japanese towards manifestations of an older, even discredited, Japan. Indeed, many artists strongly felt that official efforts to sustain traditional Japanese arts had become so pro forma as to render them anachronistic. One group member mused that if traditional concepts and practices could not find relevant expression in contemporary reality, they could not be considered valid. Noh actor Kanze Hisao (1925–78) was concerned enough to doubt the authenticity of his own tradition: to restore its vitality, Japan must, he declared, 'learn and absorb' western plays. Experimental Workshop collaborated on several stage productions with prominent theatre figures. Their best work, *Pierrot Lunaire* (1955), created with playwright-director Takechi Tetsuji (1912–88), combined music by Arnold Schönberg with aspects of noh. There were only three characters, Columbine, played by shingeki actress Hamada Yōko (n.d.); Pierrot, by *kyogen* actor Nomura Mansaku (1931–2004); and Harlequin, by Kanze Hisao. Takechi found common ground combining Schönberg's *Sprechstimme* (spoken melody) and the vastly different noh *utai* (recitative), both regarded simultaneously as musical instruments and speech channels. In addition, Takechi was able to facilitate a harmonic convergence – using noh-inspired masks, costumes recalling surrealism, chiaroscuro lighting and scripted gestures – of western psychological reality and the dream-like aura of noh performances. The collaborative atmosphere – mixing several mutually influencing Japanese and western arts – yielded a fascinating piece of intercultural theatre, termed 'transgressive' art (Tezuka 2011: 68–73), pointing beyond shingeki.

The other group responding to questions of identity included Hijikata Tatsumi (1928–86) and Ōno Kazuo (1906–2010), whose collaboration, from 1954, developed *butō* (also known as *ankoku butō*, dance of utter darkness). Their aesthetic imperative was formulated in overt opposition to western influence in modern Japanese dance and to distance themselves from traditional Japanese dance. Paradoxically influenced by Antonin Artaud and Jean Genet, key figures in avant-garde French theatre, and by the German Mary Wigman's *Neue Tanz*, they fashioned a dance style emerging sui generis, they felt, from the Japanese body, capable of retrieving memories and gestures enshrouded in Japan's distant past. Their butō is less conceptual than revivifyingly existential. Nothing, therefore, is fixed, though dancers are often nearly naked, bodies painted white, moving with contorted gestures, and evincing grotesque, erotic imagery.

Angura: the first generation

The conceptual and histrionic strains underlying such aesthetic endeavours surely signalled modern Japanese theatre's breakout phase. Many 1960s theatre figures were already bluntly opposed, like Hijikata and ōno, to ubiquitous western influences, as in shingeki, and to traditional Japanese performing arts; they envisioned a uniquely Japanese modern theatre. The pent-up mix of aesthetic disaffection with activist politics reached explosive proportions during the troubled renewal of the U.S.–Japan Security Treaty (Anpo) in 1960, marked by nationwide mobilization of unions and students, regarded even then as the symbolic launch pad for Japan's postwar counterculture, including *angura* (Japanese pronunciation of the first syllables of 'under' and 'ground') and *shōgekijō* (little theatre) playwrights and directors. Their political efforts failed (Anpo was duly renewed), but their aesthetic fervour fuelled a powerful resistance to shingeki's then dominant, western-influenced, text-centred, fourth-wall realism and catalysed a revolution in Japanese theatre, ultimately creating plays that were iconoclastic and rife with experimentation.[7]

What characterizes the performances of this revolutionary group? Seven figures are generally considered the prime movers: playwrights Terayama Shūji (1935–83), Shimizu Kunio (1936–), Betsuyaku Minoru (1937–), Kara Jūrō (1940–) and Satō Makoto (1943–); and directors Ninagawa Yukio (1935–) and Suzuki Tadashi (1939–). While diverse in their respective approaches to writing and staging plays, they held many issues in common: socio-political activism; anti-westernism; personal and national identity; nostalgia for a mythic Japanese homeland or lost vitality by reconnecting with Japanese myths to explore what it meant to be Japanese; personal and collective memory, the (im)possibility of cultural reproduction; metatheatre and redefining the meaning of theatre, theatre space, and the relationship between performance and theatregoer; often absurdist dialogue; and, reflecting their generation's pessimism, plays were often dark and brooding (Rolf and Gillespie 1992: 1–9).

Consider four representative plays. Betsuyaku's watershed work *Zō* (Elephant, 1962) features a survivor of the Hiroshima bomb and his nephew. The survivor struggles to crystallize the irreversible reality of his life's overwhelming experience, hard and unchanging, by baring the large keloid scar on his back in public. As he incrementally succumbs to atomic disease, however, his experience inexorably recedes from public view. His nephew urges him to cease his ineffectual struggle and simply accept his fate. As the play ends, the nephew too has contracted atomic disease; his plight surely will be even less noticeable than his uncle's. Betsuyaku here renders trenchant commentary, figuratively comparing contemporary Japanese to blind persons describing an elephant; unable to embrace the whole, each can offer only a partial, highly subjective description, like the bomb survivor. Not only has the Second World War's impact faded, Betsuyaku suggests, but also Japan's vast – elephant-like – vital cultural traditions are slowly eroding. The impoverishment of experience portrayed here signals the growing impotence of Japanese to appreciate and sustain those traditions; the very means once used to grasp their identity are gradually vanishing.

In Kara's play *Jon Shirubā – Shinjuku koishiya yonaki-hen* (John Silver: Tears of Nostalgia in Shinjuku, 1967; Figure 13.1), the wandering pirate interacts with characters desiring meaningful lives, including physical love. They seek to recover their vital Japanese past, now veiled in war's aftermath, including, following the demise – that is, humanising – of the emperor, what we might appropriately term a messianic replacement, and of their identities. The play's poster reinforced this. Angura posters were not merely designed to convey information but themselves were meta-suggestions to be vivified in performance, tantamount to being another character. This one, by Yokoo Tadanori (1936–), evokes the play's unsettled atmosphere by featuring the black silhouette of a naked woman with traditional Japanese coiffure, his style recalling, not imitating, traditional Japanese art (Goodman 1999: 61). Directly experiencing the play, Yokoo suggests, could move spectators to fill in the black silhouettes of their lost identities – an expectation of audience reaction foreign to shingeki. The play simultaneously provides compelling analogy: linking the lowly, disenfranchised actors, called *kawara kojiki* (also *kawara-mono*, riverbed beggars), from kabuki's nascent period with rootless postwar Japanese youth.

Figure 13.1 Poster of *John Silver: Tears of Nostalgia in Shinjuku*, designed by Yokoo Tadanori.

(Courtesy of Yokoo Tadanori)

Play and poster, therefore, were inseparably melded, constituting a visual, concrete attempt to transcend a modernism shaped by universalist notions that playwright and artist saw as denying or trivializing cultural differences and an existential attempt to escape from the morass that contemporary Japan had become.

Using John Silver, a western persona, is curiously ironic, because angura figures generally denigrated any western influence as a manifestation of the very modernism and orthodox shingeki that they were struggling to overcome. It further signals a fundamental about-face, taking hold in the early 1970s, in the first angura generation's disaffection with traditional Japanese theatre, sparked only on realizing that western figures whose work they actually revered – Paul Claudel, Bertolt Brecht, Jean-Louis Barrault, Jerzy Grotowski, Tadeuz Kantor and Peter Brook – deeply appreciated traditional Japanese theatre, even appropriating some aspects in their work. The young Japanese activists thereupon felt obligated to reconsider those traditions to fulfil their respective experimental visions. Kara, ahead of his angura peers in appreciating the historical link to tradition, perceived solidarity between his troupe's efforts and those lowly actors – that is, riverbed beggars – regarding his performances as updated kabuki (Rolf and Gillespie 1992: 252–7; Ōzasa 1980: 33–5).

The third play, Terayama's *Jashūmon* (Heretics, 1972), aligns with Betsuyaku and Kara in expressing a similar anti-shingeki theme but Terayama was programmed to shock – an overt purpose of his company Tenjō Sajiki (Peanut Gallery, est. 1967); indeed, he revelled being a 'cultural outlaw', a 'bad-boy trickster' (Sorgenfrei 2005: 17–50). In *Heretics*, a young man obsessed with marrying a sadistic prostitute must, she insists, abandon his aged mother to die on a mountain. Inept at fulfilling this sordid task, the youth finally claims success. The prostitute marries him but refuses sex until he can show proof. Meanwhile, she has sex with other men, driving her husband mad with frustration. Terayama's performance beguiles with a musical mixture of jazz, rock and Buddhist incantation. He shocks, however, with grotesque, erotic makeup and costumes and by inverting or perverting traditional Japanese myths and forcefully manipulating spectators to make them aware of and angry at their placid, manipulated existences. The play ends with the mad young protagonist attempting to murder the prostitute and her lovers, his manipulators. He is indeed visibly manipulated by *kuroko* (traditional Japanese theatre stagehands dressed in black, implying invisibility) by strings attached to his appendages. The actors then, manifesting metatheatre, remove masks, makeup and costumes, and further destroy the set as it opens onto the street. The protagonist's situation stands as a metaphor for Japan's new generation. The play ends only when all spectators leave, their heads presumably resonating with aphoristic slogans having existentialist implications: Who is manipulating whom? Terayama challenges every social norm, questions everything, what is real, whom can one trust, what is theatre, who are the actors and who the audience? He wrote the play – that is, manipulated the words – but who manipulates the playwright (Sorgenfrei 2005: 83–7)?

The fourth play to consider here is Shimizu's *Gakuya* (The Dressing Room, 1977), presenting the plight of four actresses, two ghosts and two alive (one soon becomes a ghost), desperately seeking the eternally elusive roles that will properly place them in the dressing room, the womb-like space that is their figurative homeland. Shimizu employs a modified noh structure, including a lengthy play-within-a-play, updating it with the contemporary angura ethos. He also evokes Chekhov – the play being rehearsed is *The Seagull* and, once there are three dead actresses, they are analogous to Masha, Olga and Irina in *The Three Sisters*. They desperately had aspired to become lead actresses, but, in fact, they merely attained the level of prompter or lowly supporting roles. The dressing room stands as a powerful symbol of the ambiguity of modern life in Japan. Rather than warm and welcoming, it represents a stark disconnect with the actresses' memories, aspirations and expectations, proving instead to be a place of betrayal – a bleak rendering of the contemporary Japanese quest for identity (Rolf and Gillespie 1992: 119–24).

The first angura generation shared at least four other fundamental characteristics. First, they had to cadge performance space wherever possible, in storefronts, factories, warehouses, tents, recycled cafés, even on city streets. It was fly-by-night, with, for example, the movie house Art Theatre Shinjuku Bunka, where, after the evening's last screening, a troupe would quickly prepare the impossibly cramped stage to perform for an avid, late-night crowd. Shimizu's early efforts, directed by Ninagawa, were there. Terayama questioned actor, audience and performance space, often performing on sidewalks; startled pedestrians became part of the show. In 1967, Kara, founder of Jōkyō Gekijō (Situation Theatre, est. 1963), set up his signature Red Tent at Shinjuku's Hanazono Shrine, later in vacant lots, a practice he still follows.

Second, energy was often valued over discipline. There was hardly any formalized training in angura troupes. Traditional Japanese acting was built on rigorous, lifelong training; actors, having internalized standard vocabularies of movements and gestures, would hardly rehearse. Such discipline in angura was unlikely, because there was no tradition and, therefore, no financial support; new plays and directors with diverse approaches demanded not a single, ossified repertoire of skills but flexibility and willingness to learn a wide range of them; and, until angura emerged and Ninagawa and Suzuki developed their actor disciplines, Japanese theatre was largely actor, not director, centred; so, for angura, where the director held sway, actor training took a back seat to performance. Kara, for example, has never trained his actors, instead barking orders during rehearsals. Many angura plays resembled non-stop yelling fests, as though screaming in untold decibels were a suitable stand-in for actor discipline.

Third, performance was mostly ascendant over text, liberating what Kara famously called the 'privileged' body of the actor to utilize anti-realist, stylized movement, even ironically, by appropriating certain aspects of traditional noh and kabuki totally disregarded by shingeki. Kara, with his 'riverbed beggar' lineage, has enabled a space of unfettered physical creativity, without orthodox shingeki's restrictions. Suzuki, who, like many of his contemporaries, had originally eschewed the Japanese classics, gradually evolved his own theory of movement – his term: 'the grammar of the feet' (Suzuki 1986: 3–24) – stylized, rhythmic, fundamental, clearly related in certain ways to traditional Japanese histrionics. Suzuki's plays are often pastiches of well-known Greek or Shakespearean tragedies; what happens on stage is less significant than how.[8]

Fourth, there was often an eclectic mix, heralded by Experimental Workshop and utilized by Terayama, Kara and Satō, of various interdependent arts. Stage design was not a backdrop but integral to the performance, posters and lighting design often tacitly configured as separate dramatis personae. Music, like characters' movements and utterances, was sometimes integrally interwoven, as generally in Japanese traditional forms, with the action.

The post-1960 evolution of Japanese theatre reflected the nation's socio-economic changes: Japan emerged from postwar deprivations to a trebling of income during the decade and, in hosting the Olympics and launching the Shinkansen 'bullet train' (both in 1964), a growing sense of national confidence, signalling a gradual relaxation of anti-government, anti-western intensity. While socio-political activism may have been incipient angura's common currency, those playwrights rarely delved into raw political rhetoric. They were influenced as much by the zeitgeist as by their ideas; Shimizu has said, for example, that he joined the 1960 demonstrations simply because everybody else did (Rolf and Gillespie 1992: 115). Any didactic tendency was subsumed in the fervour of their drive to create new, compelling plays and theatregoing experiences. The inarticulateness of their public policy ideas convincingly bears this out; probably not a single one was ever implemented.

The second angura generation

Angura's second generation emerged around 1970, including, among others, Ōta Shōgo (1939–2007), Takeuchi Jūichirō (1947–), Yamazaki Tetsu (1947–), Tsuka Kōhei (1948–2010) and Okabe Kōdai (1945–), so proximate in age and work to the first generation as to be a subset. Yamazaki actually started in Kara's company, and ōta is often even included with the first but, despite his age, he, like other second-generation figures, took longer to develop. Their era runs from about 1970 into the1990s, just as the first generation's ran from 1960 into the early 1980s. They share many inclinations with the first: the ubiquitous identity issue, metatheatre, social criticism, absurdist dialogue. Their distinctiveness emerges in responding to 1970s youth whose increasing affluence was inversely proportional to their sense of self or embrace of any compelling ideology. Conspicuous, therefore, is their non-ideological approach, blending reality and fantasy, often bitter or satirical humour, plots based on actual crimes and, for some, filmic playwriting.

Tsuka was the first to achieve recognition, his *Atami satsujin-jiken* (Atami Murder Mystery, 1973) gaining immense popularity on stage and screen. Betsuyaku's influence is strongly evident in, for example, *Yūbinya-san chotto* (Excuse Me, Mr Postman, 1970), including the absurdist dialogue tinged with Beckettian and Pirandellian tones and the profound riff on identity. Postal workers fill empty moments by role-playing as students, gangsters, lovers. Suddenly, a young man enters and discovers that the workers were reading his love letters, but, in a compelling twist, he is inexorably drawn into their game, as they respond to him by exchanging identities to become him and his lover to act out his affairs. Tsuka, a Korean-Japanese well experienced in bias and identity issues, draws a vivid image of the complex, shifting nature of identity in contemporary Japan.

Another second-generation example, Takeuchi's *Ano ōgarasu saemo* (That Large Crow, Even, 1980), features dialogue recalling Beckett and Ionesco and a surrealist aura from Takeuchi's admiration for André Breton; his troupe's name, Hihō reibankan (Arcanum 0), honoured André Breton's poetic, dream-like work *Arcanum 17*. The title can also mean 'that large glass, even', the Japanese for Marcel Duchamp's work, 'The Bride Stripped Bare by Her Bachelors, Even', a quizzical installation sandwiched between two large panes of glass.[9] Takeuchi's play has three bachelors, carrying a large, invisible pane of glass, who get lost but finally stumble on the possible destination, a porn actress's home. Peeping through a keyhole they become overwrought with wild imagination about her. They finally enter her house's wide-open backdoor carrying the invisible glass and, swallowed up by their erotic fantasies, stage action that constitutes a meta-rendering of at least one of those fantasies. Takeuchi examines not only the 'peeping Tom' instinct but also the relationship of stage and spectator. What are playgoers seeing? Are they any different from the three men peeping through the keyhole? Does the pane of glass separating spectators from stage somehow refract what they are seeing? Perhaps the glass is a metaphorical mirror reflecting reality – that is, the action on stage. Or is everything they see, reflection or otherwise, merely fantasy? Making little explicit, Takeuchi overlays reality and fantasy. Critic Shichiji Eisuke notes, 'there's not even a razor's edge separating reality and illusion' in Takeuchi's plays (Japan Playwrights Association 2003 V: 331–32). Takeuchi leverages Duchamp's well-known piece to achieve a remarkable metatheatrical experience; parodying his play and himself, he nudges playgoers to abandon any divide between reality and illusion and move beyond conventional interpretation.

The third generation

The milestone document 'Manifesto 1979', issued by Satō Makoto's Kokushoku tento 68/71 (Black Tent 68/71), famously stated, 'There is no theatre here', thereby pronouncing ageing angura dead (Japan Playwrights Association 2002 IV: 2). The year 1980, therefore, marked a new direction. In Japanese, 'third', beyond enumeration, implies 'new and different'. While the second generation sought distinctive ways of leveraging the first's pioneering achievements, the third, intent on their own approach, left both behind. Amid growing 1970s affluence, culminating in the late-1980s 'bubble economy', few theatre figures had weighty social experiences. Activism was hardly an afterthought; playwrights and audiences preferred frivolous entertainment and ready laughter. While not totally lacking socio-political awareness, their plays initially resembled fad-of-the-moment slapstick with crowd-pleasing spectacles, tiered stages, pop music, puns, sight gags and rafts of shouting characters moving frenetically about. Performances cloned universally popular *manga* (comics). Themes included alienation, identity, conformity, reality and fantasy (often effected through science fiction), theatre itself and, for some, social oppression. Noteworthy figures, including Kitamura Sō (1952–), Noda Hideki (1955–), Watanabe Eriko (1955–), Kōkami Shōji (1958–) and Kawamura Takeshi (1959–), among others, contributed their share of such lightness before developing more mature voices. Noda and Kōkami were hugely popular, constantly selling out.

None of them claimed the 'third generation' designation, seeing little connection with preceding generations, instead framing their work as 'new and different'; Kawamura called his troupe Daisan Erochika (Third Erotica, est. 1980), Watanabe's was Sanjū-Maru (Three Circles, est. 1980) and Kōkami's Daisan Butai (Third Stage, est. 1981). Still, despite their avowed purpose to distinguish themselves from earlier angura generations, some links with the past existed. Kitamura, Noda and Watanabe evince palpable influence from Kara; the troupe Shinjuku Ryōzanpaku was founded in 1986 by younger members of Kara's and Satō's companies. Moreover, while the third generation were distancing themselves from first and second, just as those generations had done from shingeki and western influence, their experience, seen in historical perspective, though somewhat different – they were considerably younger – was probably not altogether as new or different as they imagined; the same existential concerns remained, though with fascinating twists. Uchida Yōichi observes, for example, that they 'radicalised' the quest for identity, by linking, consciously or not, their 'third' efforts with the incongruous, simultaneous growth of Japan's 'bubble economy', emergence of third-world countries and decline of Marxist ideology (Japan Playwrights Association 2001 III: 4–5).

Consider three third-generation plays. Kitamura's *Hogi uta* (Ode to Joy, 1979), an apocalyptic fable, features husband-and-wife itinerant performers, Gesaku and Kyōko, whose dialogue suggests that ongoing nuclear destruction is their way of life. Bumbling through a devastated city, they encounter a mysterious man, Yasuo, who joins them and realizes that they have no set destination. Performing, Gesaku misplays a trick, catching a speeding bullet; he dies but almost immediately regains life. Was it the mysterious Yasuo's work? Who is he? Their names carry clues, Gesaku sounding like the Japanese *gikyoku* (play), Kyōko like *kyokō* (fiction) and Yasuo like *yasu* (Jesus). Once Gesaku calls him Yeshua (Jehovah). This creates a metatheatrical implication, since, in fact, *Ode to Joy* may well reference playwriting itself or its very performance. The constant humour, quick repartee, evocation of directionless lives, questioning identity, merging reality and fantasy are common ground here and for many third-generation figures.

With little substantial socio-political experience, this generation often articulated their identity quest by turning inward and using science-fiction fantasy. Watanabe's *Gegege no ge* (Kitarō the Ghost Buster, 1982), another fable, explores the interrelationship of three apparently unconnected characters. The complicated plot, without demarcation between past and present or reality and fantasy, features two characters doubled – are they the same? – fostering an otherworldly aura. And who is the old woman in bed as the play opens? Is the action real or just what she has dreamt? Watanabe, her title lifted from a popular manga *Gegege no Kitarō*, infuses humour at every turn and personifies the disconcerting confusions of memory. The play's various implications, poignantly reflecting contemporary Japan's mnemonic confusion and unsettled grasp of reality, resonate in one's head long after it is over.

With her emergence as an accomplished playwright/director, Watanabe represents a wave of women finally gaining recognition in what had been a fairly exclusive male club. Of course, Sadayakko, Matsui Sumako and Sugimura Haruko had already achieved success as performers. A few others, like Okada Yachiyo (1883–1962), Osanai's elder sister, with her one-act *Tsuge no kushi* (The Boxwood Comb, 1912), and Akimoto Matsuyo (1911–2001) with her masterpiece *Hitachibō Kaison* (Kaison the Priest of Hitachi, 1964), a restructured Japanese legend, gained recognition as playwrights. Still, women as playwrights, directors and leaders of their own troupes were exceedingly rare until the 1980s. In addition to Watanabe, Kishida Rio (1950–2003) joined Terayama's troupe in 1973, became his primary playwriting collaborator, wrote his groundbreaking piece *Nokku* (Knock, 1975) and, after Terayama's untimely death in 1983, formed her own company Kishida Jimusho + Rakuten-dan (Kishida Office + Optimist Company). And Kisaragi Koharu (1956–2000) formed her company NOISE in 1983, taking up signature 1980s issues such as women's changing social roles and the impact of urban environments and ubiquitous machines on human beings. She is often compared to her contemporaries Watanabe and Noda. Female-directed troupes are now no longer exceptions.[10]

In his overt physicality, Kawamura reveals influence from Terayama, Kara and Suzuki, but he opposes their desire to reconcile present with past history and their inclination to social activism. His fascinating *Nippon uōzu* (Nippon Wars, 1984) creates a plausible dystopian Japan where government authorities, convinced war is inevitable, develop androids to fight it. They undergo comprehensive training in human emotions but lack memory, a human necessity, so they are each programmed with different memories. The crux comes when the now-humanoid androids question the war, as humans might, and, deciding it is not their war, plot to destroy their controller. Then they learn that their decision was merely another programmed reaction. Having 'rehearsed' the gamut of their human capacities, they are pronounced ready for war. Kawamura constructs a riveting image of the less-than-subtle manipulation and entrapment of contemporary Japanese, even questioning his role as playwright – that is, image manipulator.

Quiet theatre: the 1990s and beyond

Three trends distinguish Japanese theatre in the 1990s and early twenty-first century: *shizukana engeki* (quiet theatre), contrasted to the preceding decade's often rafter-raising hilarity; historical grounding, allowing concrete connections between the past and Japanese attitudes today; and metatheatre, particularly an existential consideration of theatre itself – that is, some plays are about themselves – drawing on notions of existence, identity and memory to provoke questions about the very phenomenon of theatre. Metatheatre has indeed been prominent in the angura era. Senda Akihiko observes that over half the plays he reviewed in the 1970s and 80s manifested metapatterns (Senda 1997: 10). Topics include ethnic (in)tolerance, social sensitivity, the clash between old and new ways, introspection and, of course, identity. In addition, there is widespread use of diverse arts, including dance, complex stage design, mirrors, DVD projection and other digital equipment.

Perhaps the best-known quiet-theatre practitioner, Hirata Oriza (1962–), founder of Seinendan (Young People's Group, est. 1983), has characters speaking quite naturally, backs often to the audience, exactly like friends meeting by chance or chatting over drinks. While Noda's early characters appear to compete in shouting, Hirata's often speak so softly that one strains to hear them. His play *Sōru shimin* (Citizens of Seoul, 1989) features a Japanese family in 1909 Korea (a year before annexation by Japan), showing profound differences between the two cultures, including Japan's unconscious prejudice towards Koreans. For example, a Japanese woman, barely conversant in Korean, muses off-handedly that the sound of Korean is not 'suited for literature' (Japan Playwrights Association 1999 I: 67–8). A single utterance may seem unremarkable, but, in its very ordinary quietness, Hirata would make us conscious of its subconscious depth, reflecting his sense of Japan's current confusion; people don't confront obvious prejudice, assuming it is natural, reflected here interpersonally. Lacking empathy, Japanese are hardly able, he suggests, to share deep feelings with others; thus diminished, they are, not surprisingly, confused over identity.

The second trend distinguishing Japanese theatre in the 1990s and early in this century, historical grounding, anchors action in events recognized by all Japanese. The playwright can then focus on stimulating the spectator's historically prepared antennae to provoke greater awareness of what it means to be human, to connect with others. Consider Sakate Yōji's (1962–) *Kujira no bohyō* (Epitaph for the Whales, 1993), portraying Japan's relationship to whales, following the whaling ban in 1988. The resulting social confusion, even desperation, takes on political overtones in a strong critique of Japan. The play features tension between older Japanese, who find eating whales traditional and natural, and younger Japanese, who find killing whales wrong. Sakate gives voice to the plight of the oppressed – whether whales or whalers who lost their livelihood with the ban – realizing his vision through wonderfully inventive stagecraft. He is clearly heir to the first generation of playwrights, such as Terayama and Kara, in his *Gesamtkunstwerk*-like approach, drawing on butō, music, film, painting. He even borrows from noh, as with Shimizu's *The Dressing Room*, rendering the featured whaling family's secret past within the central character's dream, thereby magnifying and intensifying the emotions expressed. Finally, distinctions between right and wrong for the central character are no clearer than between reality and dream.

The third trend explores the nature of theatre itself. Certainly, 'quiet theatre' implicitly counters prevailing notions of what theatre is or should be; some plays would explicitly overturn those notions. In addition to Sakate's play, moving seamlessly between reality and dream, past and present, Miyazawa Akio's (1956–) *Hinemi* (1992) moves us to question what exactly is being staged, what its purpose is, and why we are there watching it. The main character Satake takes on the Sisyphean task of drawing a map of Hinemi, his hometown, which no longer exists, to anchor his life and identity. Working from memory, selective and faulty, and unsatisfied with his accuracy, he throws each drawing away, continually redoing his work. Just as past, present and future blend fluidly, so the contours of his map are indistinct. Miyazawa suggests that just as drawing the map reforms how Satake regards his world, so the theatre shapes how we look at life; the playwright, like Satake, alters the map (of theatre).

Conclusions

After a 90-year gestation period involving many incipient murmurs, a distinctively new Japanese theatre voice finally became audible around 1960. Once the struggle to escape kabuki's grip on performance style succeeded, once the obeisance paid to translated western plays subsided, once activists surged past orthodox shingeki to realize a truly indigenous Japanese drama, the new voice gained timbre, though only amid the din of competing voices.[11] Traditional Japanese theatre has continued, kabuki popular, above all. Shinpa performances, charmingly nostalgic, occasionally still occur. Takarazuka, with its melodramatic, formulaic, all-female, musical romances, still sells out. The appeal of *taishū engeki* (popular drama), with conventional plots and dramaturgy, remains strong. Established shingeki companies still command large audiences and the best theatre venues. Translated western plays, adeptly directed and acted, also continue to flourish. So indigenous, new, cutting-edge Japanese theatre became and remains simply one form among others.

Moreover, western influence has been and remains unavoidable: Ibsen, Chekhov, Shakespeare, Realism, Expressionism, Surrealism; Artaud on Terayama and Kara, Beckett and Ionesco on Betsuyaku, Tennessee Williams on Shimizu. Angura and its subsequent generations were all aware of postwar theatre's vibrant experimental atmosphere in North America and Europe: Julian Beck, Judith Malina and The Living Theatre; Joseph Chaikin and The Open Theatre; Ellen Stewart and LaMama (where Terayama and his troupe performed in 1970). Many angura figures saw plays overseas and read European philosophers such as Walter Benjamin and theatre theorists such as Jan Kott. They knew and respected the iconoclastic work of, among others, Bertolt Brecht, Jean-Louis Barrault, Peter Brook, Jerzy Grotowski, Tadeusz Kantor, Ariane Mnouchkine and Robert Wilson. Western influence also filtered indirectly through the poly-math Terayama: theorist, director, dramatist, cinema auteur, photographer, poet, socio-political provocateur, he became perhaps the one true giant of experimental performance among angura figures, his shadow far-reaching. Kara and Satō, also with strains of western influence, inspired other playwrights and companies. Conspicuously different from pre-angura figures, however, playwrights now internalized those influences – owned them – no longer simply deriving their work from them but freely adapting what they found applicable to their own autochthonous theatre visions. They gradually shed, therefore, the ambivalence towards western influences so deeply felt by many pre-angura and early angura playwrights.

That process continues today. Asari Keita (1933–), founder of Gekidan Shiki (Four Seasons Company, 1953), famous for musicals and shingeki, suggested 50 years ago that it would be mid-twenty-first century before 'a Japanese synthesis' develops from the head-on confrontation with western culture (Powell 2002: 192). That may be happening ahead of schedule, but what truly matters is the genuine appeal and compelling vision of Japan's vibrant cutting-edge theatre. New playwrights and directors continue to establish styles reminiscent of, or distinctive from, their precursors, most still active. While new topics can emerge, many original reactions to Japan's opening in the nineteenth century remain in the conversation, even if rendered in a different idiom: the unending question of identity and the metatheatrical means, including blending phases of time, merging reality and illusion, plumbing the deep reaches of the human psyche or memory, that might somehow respond to it more tellingly, more authentically than earlier generations had done. Moreover, all kinds of performance formats and all kinds of approaches appear to be current, existing side by side, sometimes even within the same production.

Finally, since the advent of Terayama's early overseas performances in the 1960s and 70s, followed by the vast appeal engendered by Suzuki's distinctive emphasis on acting's corporeal disciplines – thousands of actors around the world have undergone his training – then by Ningawa and his hugely popular, large-scale stagings of Greek and Shakespearean tragedies, invitations to work overseas have increased exponentially, including more recently other cutting-edge Japanese figures such as Hirata, Sakate and Matsuda Masataka (1968–), among others, whose work has garnered attention beyond Japan. Shimizu Shinjin's (1956–) Kaitaisha (Theatre of Deconstruction, est. 1985), perhaps the most experimental group since Terayama's Peanut Gallery, has non-Japanese members and might be considered a global company. Noda, through his company NODA MAP (est. 1993), invites western actors for joint play development and per-formance in and out of Japan. Kawamura, with his current company T Factory (est. 2002), is jointly creating a production, 'Tokyo/New York Correspondence Chapter 1, On The Street', with the American multimedia artist and director John Jesurun. Okada Toshiki (1974–), founder of chelfitsch (a variation on 'selfish', est. 1998), captures the current Japanese youth lifestyle with wit and hyper-colloquial language; he too occasionally uses non-Japanese actors and has performed successfully in the UNITED STATES and Europe. The original western influence on realizing modern, indigenous Japanese theatre has come full circle, the best such drama now tendering its own influence – purveying its own styles – in the west. That, too, will be an ongoing story.

Notes

1 For more on the historical context and development of modern Japanese theatre in the late nineteenth and early twentieth centuries, see Ibaraki (1980: 1–45), Ortolani (1990: 233–78), Powell (2002: 1–134), Rimer *et al.* (2014: 1–26), 73–85; and Poulton (2010: 1–25).

2 Many attended Kawakami's productions to see him perform a popular satirical ballad, *Oppekepe bushi* (the title is onomatopoeic), in the *rakugo* (storytelling) tradition. That is what most Japanese likely remember him for today, if they actually know his name.

3 For a fuller accounting of Kawakami's insurgent theatre work, the Kawakamis' trips abroad and an insightful discussion of the cultural underpinnings of the quite divergent reactions in the west and in Japan to Sadayakko's appearances on stage, see Kano (2001: 57–119).

4 For more on Izumi Kyōka as dramatist and the theatre and cultural context of his era, see Poulton (2001: 1–79). Many Japanese writers who become famous are often referred to by their given or pen names. Izumi is one such person, so he is referred to here, after first mention, as Kyōka. Two other writers with that distinction who are mentioned here more than once are Kitamura Tōkoku and Tsubouchi Shōyō.

5 Ironically, the 'symmetrical harmony' that Tōkoku regards as problematic for modernizing the Japanese stage was often the aspect of traditional Japanese performance that most appealed to twentieth-century western theatre figures, when they first encountered it. For more on that influence, see Gillespie, 137–48.

6 For a fuller accounting of such plays with their historical and aesthetic context, see Poulton (2010: 29–45).

7 For more on the emergence of angura and development of a Japanese modern theatre, see Ōzasa (1980: 6–51), Senda (1995: 1–156), Rolf and Gillespie (1992: 1–9), and Rimer *et al.* (2014: 177–87, 315–25, 501–09).

8 Suzuki, who directed Betsuyaku's early plays in the 1960s, insisted on the primacy of the director and performance, while Betsuyaku staunchly held to the primacy of text. So he broke with Suzuki and became independent. Among the first angura generation, the directors Suzuki and Ninagawa, and the playwright-directors Terayama, Kara and Satō, prioritized performance, while Betsuyaku and Shimizu prioritized text.

9 The original work is in the permanent collection in the Philadelphia Museum of Art, but a replica is in the Komaba Museum, University of Tokyo.

10 For further information on contemporary female Japanese playwrights and directors, see the introductory essays in Japan Playwrights Association (1999–2008), especially 2004 VII 1960s Pt. 2; 2001 III 1980s Pt. 1; 2002 IV 1980s Pt. 2; 1999 I 1990s Pt. 1; 2000 II 1990s Pt. 2; 2006 IX 1990s Pt. 3; and 2007 X 1990s Pt. 4.

11 A brief comment on three playwrights not included here. Abe Kōbō (1924–1993) wrote well-received plays, notably *Tomodachi* (Friends, 1967). Yet, his influences and work show greater connection with the west than with the ethos linking angura playwrights. While Mishima Yukio (1925–70) was connected with traditional theatre, even writing shin-kabuki plays, his *kindai nōgaku* (modern noh plays), though borrowing seeds from noh, flowered into fine pieces hardly characterized by noh but by contemporary anomie and disjunctive human interactions. Text-centred and without cutting-edge stagecraft or mythic undergirding, such work is less angura than orthodox shingeki. Inoue Hisashi (1934–2010) is possibly Japan's most beloved contemporary playwright. While centred on profound issues, his work invariably appeals, with laughter, word-play, plot twists, and music, always with humanism, a specifically Japanese spiritual sensitivity, and a deep affection for the Japanese people. His dramaturgy, however, is mostly consonant with shingeki.

Bibliography

Gillespie, John K. (1992) 'L'Oeil Écoute: The Impact of Traditional Japanese Theatre on Postwar Western Performance', *Modern Drama* 35 (1): 137–48.

Goodman, David G. (1999) *Angura: Posters of the Japanese Avant-Garde*, New York: Princeton Architectural Press.

Ibaraki Tadashi (1980) *Nihon shingeki shōshi* (Japanese Shingeki: A Brief History), Tokyo: Mirai-sha.

Japan Playwrights Association (ed.) (1999–2008) *Half a Century of Japanese Theatre*, 10 vols, Tokyo: Kinokuniya shoten.

Kano, Ayako (2001) *Acting Like a Woman in Modern Japan: Theatre, Gender, and Nationalism*, New York: Palgrave.

Keene, Donald (1955) *Japanese Literature: An Introduction for Western Readers*, New York: Grove Press.

Ortolani, Benito (1990) *The Japanese Theatre: From Shamanistic Ritual to Contemporary Pluralism*, Princeton: Princeton University Press.

Ōzasa Yoshio (1980) *Dōjidai engeki to gekisakkatachi* (Contemporary Plays and Playwrights), Tokyo: Geki shobō.

Poulton, M. Cody (2001) *Spirits of Another Sort: The Plays of Izumi Kyōka*, Ann Arbor, MI: Center for Japanese Studies.

—— (2010) *A Beggar's Art: Scripting Modernity in Japanese Drama, 1900–1930*, Honolulu: University of Hawai'i Press.

Powell, Brian (2002) *Japan's Modern Theatre: A Century of Continuity and Change*, London: Japan Library.

Rimer, J. Thomas (1974) *Toward a Modern Japanese Theatre: Kishida Kunio*, Princeton: Princeton University Press.

Rimer, J. Thomas, Mitsuya Mori, and M. Cody Poulton (eds) (2014) *The Columbia Anthology of Modern Japanese Drama*, New York: Columbia University Press.

Rolf, Robert, and John K. Gillespie (eds) (1992) *Alternative Japanese Drama: Ten Plays*, Honolulu: University of Hawai'i Press.

Senda Akihiko (1995) *Nihon no gendai engeki* (Japan's Modern Theatre), Tokyo: Iwanami shoten.

—— (1997) *The Voyage of Contemporary Japanese Theatre*, J. Thomas Rimer (trans), Honolulu: University of Hawai'i Press.

Sorgenfrei, Carol Fisher (2005) *Unspeakable Acts: The Avant-Garde Theatre of Terayama Shūji and Postwar Japan*, Honolulu: University of Hawai'i Press.

Suzuki Tadashi (1986) *The Way of Acting: The Theatre Writings of Tadashi Suzuki*, J. Thomas Rimer (trans), New York: Theatre Communications Group.

Tezuka Miwako (2011) 'Experimentation and Tradition: The Avant-Garde Play *Pierrot Lunaire* by Jikken Kōbō and Takechi Tetsuji', *Art Journal*, 70 (3): 64–85.

14

Modern Chinese theatre

Siyuan Liu

Like many other Asian cultures, China has a long theatrical tradition that involves speech, songs, dance, conventionalized movement and acrobatic combat.[1] Its modern theatre, known as *huaju* (spoken drama), started in the first decade of the twentieth century as China was forced to open up to the world as a result of global colonialism. Huaju's evolution over the past century has many similarities with other Asian countries, including a hybrid beginning of indigenous and western theatre, a long period of commitment to realism in mid-century, a rediscovery of indigenous performance combined with avant-garde experiment since the late 1970s, and an inclination towards globalization in the new millennium. As the same time, China's modern history has uniquely impacted its huaju, including a colonial-modern beginning that benefited from western church school dramatics in its major port cities and modern Japanese theatre, an 8-year War of Resistance against Japan (1937–45) that disrupted the trend of theatrical professionalism and paradoxically provided neutral space for theatre from ideological concerns, and the control of the Chinese Communist Party (CCP) since 1949 which often made theatre part of the state ideological apparatus.

This chapter will provide a historical survey of huaju through the past century, with focus on historical and theatrical backgrounds and major trends, as well as significant plays, artists and organizations, with balance between description and analysis. In terms of historical periods, it will be roughly equally divided before and after 1949.

Emergence of the spoken theatre (1900s–1910s)

In the second half of the nineteenth century, China suffered a series of military defeats at the hands of western powers and Japan, which led to a series of attempts at technical, constitutional and cultural reforms. After the failed constitutional reform in 1898, a group of leading intellectuals were exiled in Japan where they witnessed, among other issues, Japan's success in reforming kabuki into respectable theatre and utilizing a new hybrid spoken theatre *shinpa* (new school drama) to actively propagate Meiji reform ideals and nationalism. As a result, they advocated for using theatre to propagate nationalist conscience while denouncing Chinese theatre as indulging in obscenity, trivializing historical heroes and being incapable of inspiring nationalism.

One of the origins of spoken theatre came from student productions in China's port cities that were forced to open up to international settlement after the Opium War (1839–1942).

This was especially true in Shanghai, where amateur theatre flourished in the international communities and in church and Chinese schools, fostering the first generation of new drama artists. At the same time, some Chinese students in Tokyo formed the Chunliu She (Spring Willow Society) at the end of 1906 and staged several plays in the following years, starting from an act of *La Dame aux Camélias* in February 1907 and, in June, a five-act adaptation of *Uncle Tom's Cabin* renamed as *Heinu yutian lu* (Black Slave's Cry to Heaven). This production is generally considered the beginning of modern Chinese theatre because of its nationalist message, predominant reliance on speech rather than singing and dance, five-act structure, complete script and ensemble acting, as well as (semi-)realistic costumes, set design and makeup. Before repatriating to Shanghai after the 1911 Revolution, the group staged several other productions in Tokyo, including Victorien Sardou's *La Tosca*, by conscientiously imitating shinpa performance styles. In time, their shinpa-based style contested and hybridized with locally trained artists in Shanghai to establish China's first form of spoken theatre, known as *wenmingxi* (civilized drama).

The first large-scale new theatre production in Shanghai was another *Black Slave's Cry to Heaven* performance staged by Wang Zhongsheng (1884?–1911) in October 1907, which used a different script. This production also introduced modern lighting and the proscenium stage to the Chinese theatre community, as it was staged in the western-style Lanxin (Lyceum) Theatre, leading to a building boom of proscenium-stage theatres. In spring 1908, Wang staged his second and last new play in Shanghai, *Jiayin xiaozhuan* (Joan Haste), with the help of Ren Tianzhi (dates unknown), who had lived in Japan and was familiar with shinpa. Ren returned to Shanghai in 1911 before the Revolution to form the Jinhua Tuan (Evolutionary Troupe), which staged shinpa-style nationalist plays along the River Yangtze. Its performance style relied heavily on scenarios and improvisation and a role category system following the *jingju* (Beijing opera) model. In time, Ren's style became the dominant force in wenmingxi performance.

However, neither Ren's group nor the repatriated Spring Willow were able to survive commercially in Shanghai until Zheng Zhengqiu (1888–1935), a former jingju critic and pioneer film writer and director, created a sensational melodramatic hit titled *E jiating* (An Evil Family) in 1913 with his Xinmin She (New People Society). Zheng's success ushered in a brief commercial boom for wenmingxi in the mid-1910s that focused on audience accessibility and acceptance. Most shinpa and European (mostly through shinpa) plays were localized, with Chinese names and environment. The performance style was a hybrid of speech and singing from jingju arias and popular tunes, improvisation based on scenarios, and co-existence of female impersonators and emerging actresses, who often endured social bias in a still conservative society.

By the late 1910s, this hybrid style received heavy criticism for abandoning modern theatre's nationalist and enlightenment roots in pursuit of popular entertainment. As a result, the following decade became an antithesis to wenmingxi, with amateur theatres, vehement anti-feudal spirit and dazzling formal experimentations.

Amateur theatres, social criticism, and formal experiments (1920s)

One of the most important events in modern Chinese cultural history is the *Xin wenhua yundong* (New Cultural Movement) of the late 1910s, which sought to upend traditional Chinese culture, including its theatre. For the 2 years between March 1917 and March 1919, the bastion of the movement, the *Xin qingnian* (New Youth) magazine, published articles on the future of theatre in almost every issue, culminating in two special issues: the Ibsen issue in June 1918 and the dramatic reform issue in October of the same year.

One direct effect of the attention on theatre's social efficacy was the focus on young people's individual freedom against feudal ethics of patriarchal tyranny. One of the earliest plays of this genre is Hu Shi's *Zhongshen dashi* (The Main Event in Life, 1919), a one-act play about a young woman leaving home for her lover against the objections of her parents. Another example was the play *Zhuo Wenjun* (1923) by Guo Moruo (1892–1978) on a West Han dynasty (206 BCE–9 CE) woman who, as a widow living in her father's home, elopes with the famous writer Sima Xiangru (179–127 BCE) when they fall in love through music. Still another important play was a one-act by Tian Han (1898–1968) titled *Huohu zhiye* (The Night the Tiger Was Caught, 1922), which takes place in a village at night when the wealthy hunter Wei Fusheng and his helpers set up a trap to catch a tiger as dowry for his daughter Liangu's upcoming wedding to an important family. When a creature is trapped and mortally wounded, everyone is surprised to find the assumed tiger to be a young man called Huang Dasha, Liangu's childhood lover who has fallen out of her father's favour because of family misfortunes. At the end of the play, the father drags Liangu away to flog her while Dasha kills himself with a hunting knife. The play injected the theme of class division into the clash of generations as well as a rural perspective on top of the mostly urban plays.

This rural emphasis was further delineated in the full-length three-act *Dachu youlingta* (Breaking Out of Ghost Pagoda, 1928; Figure 14.1) by the female playwright Bai Wei (1894–1987), herself a victim of arranged marriage before escaping to Japan. Written at the height of the anti-warlord Northern Expedition campaign in 1928 that would reunite China, the play depicts three women in varying stages of 'breaking out' of the 'ghost pagoda', the house of a rural tyrant, Hu Rongsheng. It is a hauntingly powerful play that points towards viable paths of self-fulfilment for independent women as well as the still dominant feudal power that ruthlessly smothers two young lives.

While the theme of individual freedom was popular among plays of the 1920s, they were written in diverse styles that were far from being restricted to realism. In fact, this was a decade that witnessed a flourishing of modernist styles (known at the time as neo-romanticism), especially aestheticism, symbolism and expressionism. One important expressionist play of this decade is Hong Shen's *Zhao Yanwang* (Yama Zhao, 1922), which borrowed the bewildering dark forest from Eugene O'Neill's *The Emperor Jones* to stage the miserable life of soldiers caught in the endless civil wars. Similarly, aestheticism's dogged pursuit of beauty and sensual pleasure against rigid moral codes, as embodied by Oscar Wilde, provided another outlet for the irresistible creative energy of the decade. The productions of his *Lady Windermere's Fan* (1924) and *Salomé* (1929) were important events in modern Chinese theatre.

Among plays influenced by *Salomé*, *Pan Jinlian* (1928) by the former Spring Willow actor Ouyang Yuqian (1889–1962) transformed the play's eponymous heroine from a historically notorious woman of lust, who kills her husband out of love for his brother Wu Song, into an individualistic and modern woman created in Salomé's spirit as an individual willing to pursue her love interest regardless of death. While in Japan, Bai Wei, the author of *Breaking Out of Ghost Pagoda*, was especially fascinated by the symbolist plays *The Blue Bird* and *The Sunken Bell*. Her 1926 poetic and symbolic play *Linli* is a wildly imaginative piece about the triangular love between a poet and two sisters. Two of the play's three acts take place within Linli's dreams in which her passion and her sister's youthfulness are so potent as to bring about the demise of Death himself.

Another dramatic form that flourished in the 1920s was comedy, largely propelled by those returning from Britain, especially Ding Xilin (1893–1974) and Yuan Changying (1894–1973). Yuan studied literature at the University of Edinburgh and the Sorbonne. Her *Jiehun qian de yiwen* (A Kiss before the Wedding, 1930) is in the same vein as *The Importance of Being Earnest*.

Figure 14.1 Book cover of the 1936 edition of *Dachu youlingta* (Breaking Out of Ghost
Pagoda) by Bai Wei (Shanghai: Chunguang shudian).

Ding's one-act comedies represent some of the genre's highest achievements by dramatizing
the same vexing social issues of the decade with humour, wit and verbal elegance. His *Yizhi
mafeng* (A Wasp, 1923), for example, is another play on the choice between love and arranged
marriage, but was written as a stylistic union of Ibsen and Wilde. Instead of shooting or storming
out of the home, the play conveys an urbane elegance for the educated youth even as they
struggle with the same issues as their rural counterparts.

In tandem with the theoretical and dramatic achievements of the decade was the theatrical
rejection of wenmingxi's commercialism through the amateur theatre movement, known in
Chinese as *aimeiju* (a transliteration of amateur which literally means 'aesthetic drama'). Chen
Dabei (1887–1944), a wenmingxi veteran, wrote *Aimei de xiju* (Amateur Theatre, 1922) on the
history and characteristics of amateur theatre, as well as instructive chapters on playwriting,
directing, performance and design. One of the best-known groups in the north was the Nankai
Xinju Tuan (Nankai School New Drama Troupe) in Tianjin under the direction of Columbia-
educated Zhang Pengchun (1892–1957), which trained a number of important practitioners,
including Cao Yu (1910–96), huaju's best playwright.

Figure 14.2 The 1924 production of *Lady Windermere's Fan* retitled *Shao nainai de shanzhi* (The Young Mistress's Fan) by Shanghai Xiju Xieshe (Shanghai Stage Society), directed by Hong Shen.

(From *Shibao tuhua zhoukan*, 1924)

Back in Shanghai, after wenmingxi's decline, a group of male actors, led by the star Wang Youyou (1888–1937), staged George Bernard Shaw's *Mrs. Warren's Profession* in 1920, which was met with strong resistance from the audience against its alien content, made worse by the fact that none of the practitioners in Shanghai or elsewhere at the time had first-hand knowledge of professional theatre in the west. This situation was changed in 1922 when Hong Shen, who had studied theatre at Harvard under George Pierce Baker, returned to Shanghai and became China's first professional director in his works with the Shanghai Xiju Xieshe (Shanghai Stage Society). Hong gradually built up a director-centred rehearsal system and cemented gender-appropriate casting. In 1924, he directed Oscar Wilde's *Lady Windermere's Fan*, which is generally considered the first 'authentic' huaju production that adhered to the modern western production conventions of strict rehearsal under a coherent directorial vision, although it still presented a localized, Chinese mise-en-scène (Figure 14.2).

Another important theatre group of the 1920s was the Nanguo She (Southern China Society) led by Tian Han. Through several public performances and tours in the late 1920s that staged *Pan Jinlian*, *Salomé* and Tian Han's own plays, the society became a rallying point that brought together discrete huaju forces, especially Hong Shen and Ouyang Yuqian, as they prepared for the maturing of huaju in the following decade.

Maturity of Huaju (1930–7)

After wenmingxi and the amateur theatre movement – after ideological and formal experiments in dramaturgy of the 1920s – huaju came of age in the 1930s and turned to realistic observation and depiction of social realities. In addition, the looming national crisis and international leftist theatre movement pushed many theatre practitioners to seek serving the masses and venture into agitprop theatre. Tian Han, for example, publicly 'turned left' and rejected his works of the 1920s as self-focused. In 1931, the Zuoyi Xijujia Lianmeng (Left-wing Dramatists League) was formed in Shanghai with Tian Han as its nominal head.

Another backdrop to this popular theatre movement was the natural progression of huaju's dramatic proficiency and theatrical professionalism. Dramatically, multi-act plays replaced one-acts and a number of outstanding works brought huaju dramaturgy to a new height, culminating in Cao Yu's four masterpieces between 1934 and 1941, which elevated modern Chinese dramatic literature into a peak rarely surpassed in the subsequent decades. Theatrically, the decade witnessed the return of professional theatres, as evidenced by the success of Zhongguo Lüxing Jutuan (China Travelling Theatre Company, 1933–1947) and the rise of quality productions together with maturing actors and directors.

Cao Yu published his first play *Leiyu* (Thunderstorm) in 1934 before graduating from Tsinghua University in Beijing, quickly followed by *Richu* (Sunrise, 1936), *Yuanye* (The Savage Lang, 1937) and *Beijing ren* (Peking Man, 1941). *Thunderstorm* is a story of two families, the capitalist Zhous and the servant Lus, which are deeply intertwined through love, incest and class clashes over two generations, eventually leaving the young dead and the old shattered. Taking place within a suffocating summer day, the play skilfully appropriates western dramatic masterpieces – from fate and retribution in Greek tragedy to neoclassic unities to Ibsen's *Ghosts* to John Galsworthy's *Strife* – to expand the popular theme of young individuals versus the feudal family with much more complicated characters. In terms of structure, *Thunderstorm* follows the unity of time, place and action with an unbearably tight and inescapable rhythm that leads to the physical and emotional destruction of its major characters (Figure 14.3).

In 1936, Cao Yu published *Sunrise*, a story about the traps facing Chinese Noras after leaving home for independence. Set primarily in a hotel room in a big city in northern China (presumably Tianjin), the play portrays a kaleidoscope of characters around Chen Bailu, an

Figure 14.3 A scene from a 2007 production of *Leiya* (Thunderstorm, 1934) directed by Wang Yansong.

(Courtesy of Wang Yansong)

educated young woman who once married a poet in the countryside, only to leave him and the boredom of the country for a life supported by bank manager Pan Yueting and surrounded by other high-society figures, such as a foreign educated bureaucrat who complains about his wife and a rich widow in pursuit of a young gigolo. Bailu also tries but fails to rescue from the claws of gangsters a girl, Xiao Dongxi (Pipsqueak) who is sold to a low-class brothel and eventually hangs herself. The play also includes characters from other social strata, including Bailu's former friend Fang Dasheng who attempts but fails to lead her to a new life, the miserable but kind-hearted prostitute Cuixi, the hotel steward Wang Fusheng who peppers Bailu with bills and betrays Pipsqueak to the gangsters, Pan's secretary Li Shiqing who pays for his social-climbing scheme with the life of his son, and the dismissed bank clerk Huang Xingsan driven to kill his own children. Compared to *Thunderstorm*'s airtight structure, *Sunrise*'s concentric feature allows character development in their own circles in parallel subplots.

Comedy also matured in the 1930s and 40s, as plot-driven well-made plays, as English-style comedy of manners following Ding Xilin, and as satires. As it happens, critics generally agree that it was Li Jianwu (1906–1982)'s *Zhe buguo shi chuntian* (It's Only Spring), published in 1934 (the same year as Cao Yu's *Thunderstorm*), that signified a milestone for huaju comedy as it successfully combined plot construction with characterization. The play takes place in Beijing during the Northern Expedition (1926–1928) when the Kuomintang army in southern China battled with warlords in the north in order to unify the country. It is set in the living room of the Beijing Police Chief where his wife is visited by her former lover Feng Yunping, who turns out to be a revolutionary from the south being pursued by the police as soon as he arrived in Beijing. A detective comes to the Chief's home to deliver the letter that ends up in the hands of his wife who, through a series of intrigues, eventually ensures Feng's safe departure from her and Beijing. As a literary scholar who had studied in France and was well versed in Moliere, Victorien Sardou and Eugene Scribe, Li Jianwu was a master of witty dialogue, intriguing plot twists and intricate character delineation.

The maturity of dramatic literature contributed to the re-emergence of professional huaju theatre, most prominently represented by the China Travelling Theatre Company (CTTC) founded by Tang Huaiqiu (1898–1953), who had studied aviation engineering in France before forming with Tian Han Southern China Society in Shanghai in 1926. In 1933, he founded CTTC, which debuted in Nanjing in February of the following year with a localized version of Eugene Walter's *The Easiest Way* titled *Mei Luoxiang* (after the play's heroine Laura Murdock). From the beginning, the company refused support from the government or other institutions and relied on box-office receipts and private support. For the following 2 years, it moved up to Beijing and toured neighbouring cities while accumulating a solid repertoire. By the time the company returned to Shanghai in 1936, it shocked the city's entertainment world with *Thunderstorm* and *La Dame aux Camélias*, finally winning long-term contracts for huaju in large-scale theatres. During the war, the company went through a number of ups and downs but ultimately survived. It eventually disbanded in 1947. Over its 13-year history, it premiered a considerable number of plays with its quality actors and production standard, proving the viability of professional spoken theatre.

Parallel to CTTC were Shanghai's leftist spoken theatre artists who formed the Leftist Dramatists Association in 1930 and staged several contemporary European plays. A seminal event of the movement was Shanghai Stage Society's 1933 production of *Roar, China!* by Soviet playwright Sergei Tretyakov (1892–1937), a favourite of international leftist theatre since its 1926 premiere at the Meyerhold Theatre. Based on a true 1924 incident in Sichuan Province where the captain of the British gunboat *HMS Cockchafer* demanded the hanging of two Chinese coolies for the accidental death of an American merchant, the play used spectacular stagecraft

– including onstage canons from the warship aimed at the audience – to create powerful anti-imperial sentiment featuring a group of defiant coolies and their wives.

Apart from leftist plays, Shanghai also witnessed several productions of European realistic classics that attempted to create 'authentic' western mise-en-scène with realistic acting, including *Uncle Vanya* (1930) by Xinyou Jutuan (Xinyou Theatre); *A Doll's House* (1935), *The Inspector General* (1935) and *The Storm* (by Russian playwright Alexander Ostrovsky, 1937) by Shanghai Yeyu Juren Xiehui (Shanghai Amateur Dramatists Association); and *Romeo and Juliet* (1937) by Shanghai Yeyu Shiyan Jutuan (Shanghai Amateur Experimental Company). These productions were part of a conscientious effort to elevate the actors' performance skills through challenging plays; they strove for realistic set, costumes and makeup, together with wigs and artificial noses and chins. The actors studied their characters in part by watching Hollywood and Soviet movies and observing white Russian émigrés in local Russian restaurants.

One of the best-known plays depicting life in pre-war Shanghai is *Shanghai wuyan xia* (Under Shaghai Eaves), written by Xia Yan (1900–1995) in 1937 right before the war but debuted in 1940. Set in an alley, it uses a cross-section of a two-storey building to portray the lives of its five tenant families. With a set design that reveals a cross-section of the building capable of showing each room, the play maintains a remarkable mixture of tragic and comic elements.

One notable theatrical experiment that stood out during this period was the success of Xiong Foxi, a Columbia graduate (with an MA) and former head of the Theatre Department of National Arts School (Guoli Yizhuan) in Beijing, in leading the theatre division of a high-profile rural literacy campaign in Ding Xian County in northern China between 1932 and 1937. There, he and his colleagues staged outdoor peasant productions that utilized traditional, folk and western theatrical techniques and incorporated mass audience participation. Radically different from realistic proscenium plays, their productions were seen as a new model for bringing huaju to China's 85 per cent rural population, as the Ding Xian peasants not only enjoyed huaju but also put on their own productions. Unfortunately, the experiment was abruptly halted by Japanese invasion in northern China in July 1937.

Huaju during and after the War of Resistance against Japan (1937–1949)

When the war broke out in July, huaju practitioners quickly mobilized to collectively stage a three-act play *Baowei Lugou qiao* (Defend the Marco Polo Bridge) in Shanghai. Soon, they formed thirteen performance troupes that moved to the front and the interior, performing agitprop theatre such as the living-newspaper piece *Fangxia nide bianzi* (Put Down Your Whip). Eventually, two huaju centres emerged during the 8 years of war, one around the temporary capital of Chongqing in the southwest interior and the other remained in Shanghai. Most well-known huaju practitioners moved to the interior with the wartime government, together with the Guoli Xiju Xuexiao (National Theatre School), which eventually settled in the small town of Jiang'an about 150 miles from Chongqing.

Despite the war, this period is often regarded as huaju's golden era, in part as a result of the natural progress of spoken theatre's decades of experimentation in dramaturgy and production. Cao Yu, for example, finished his third play *The Savage Land* right before the war and his fourth – arguably his last quality original – play *Peking Man* in 1940. At the same time, the war also created opportunities for the development of spoken theatre in certain directions. One of them is the proliferation of historical plays, extolling historical heroes against foreign invasions or those making patriotic choices during similarly taxing times. Two such periods drew special attention: the Southern Ming dynasty (1644–62), when the issue of resistance or cooperation with the

Manchu Qing (1644–1911) by the ethnic Chinese in the south mirrored the choices facing every Chinese under Japanese occupation, and the Warring States period (475–221 BCE), with its many stories of patriotic heroes. This period was the focus of several of Guo Moruo's plays, including *Qu Yuan* (1942) on a patriotic poet and official. The Southern Ming plays include two adaptations of the famous *kunqu* play *Taohua shan* (The Peach Blossom Fan) on the love story between a high-class courtesan and a famous scholar before and after the fall of Ming.

These new versions of *The Peach Blossom Fan* also point to a re-evaluation of the role of traditional theatre in spoken drama. This was in part a practical question during the war as theatres sought popular recognition both with the working masses for the purpose of agitation and as a survival strategy in urban theatre, especially in Shanghai. For example, one of the most popular huaju plays of this time, *Qiu Haitang*, enjoyed an unprecedented 5-month run after its premiere in Shanghai in December 1942, thanks to a meandering and sentimental plot based on a popular novel and the extensive infusion of jingju performance by the actor Shi Hui (1915–57). During the span of the five-act play, he performed three arias that became the emotional highlights of the play. Another aspect of huaju popularization was localization of western plays, a reversal of the pre-war emphasis on 'authentic' translation and production which proved to be less accessible to the average Shanghai audience. When wartime professional theatres relied solely on the box-office, they reverted to the practice of localizing western plays to ensure favourable reception. For example, Li Jianwu localized Sardou's *La Tosca* to the Chinese civil war era of the 1920s with the title *Jin Xiaoyu* and recast *Macbeth* to China's Five Dynasties (907–60) era in an adaptation titled *Luanshi yingxiong* (The Hero of the Turmoil).

However, this trend of huaju popularization did not survive the end of the war in August 1945 because professional huaju lost ground to the flood of Hollywood movies banned during Japanese occupation, and mainstream huaju practitioners returning from the interior rejected such attempts as artistically inferior. The most notable play written and produced after the war was *Shengguan tu* (Promotion Scheme, 1945) by Chen Baichen (1908–94). Inspired by Nikolai Gogol's *The Inspector General*, the play, as a divergence from the previous social comedies exemplified by Ding Xilin and Li Jianwu, was a biting political satire of official corruption and was enthusiastically embraced by the audience immediately after the war when corruption was rampant and civil war between the nationalists and communists was imminent.

Early years of the People's Republic of China (1949–66)

On 1 October 1949, the People's Republic of China was established under the leadership of the Chinese Communist Party. Over the following half-century, arts in China, including its modern theatre, were heavily influenced by the shifting domestic and international political environment. At the same time, while there is no doubt that strong ideological demand on theatre restricted dramatic and theatrical creation, the dynamic between theatre and the state was often complicated – a relationship that periodically produced fascinating pieces.

Unlike traditional theatre, which was the target of reform after 1949, huaju flourished in the 1950s as part of the state-sponsored theatre system. Most major cities established their own theatres and important figures of the pre-1949 leftist huaju movement such as Tian Han were entrusted with the task of overseeing both modern and traditional theatre. At the same time, unlike traditional theatres where private companies occupied the majority of theatres for at least a decade, private huaju companies essentially disappeared. As the political and cultural centre, Beijing saw the establishment of three huaju theatres: Beijing Renmin Yishu Juyuan (Beijing People's Art Theatre, BPAT), Zhongyang Shiyan Huajuyuan (Central Experimental Theatre) and Zhongguo Qingnian Yishu Juyuan (China Youth Art Theatre).

During these 17 years, several forces were at work that shaped the political environment for huaju. To start with, the dominating theory governing literature and the arts was Mao Zedong's thoughts on the subject developed in the 1940s, which defined the arts as a cog in the revolutionary machine. It should represent workers, peasants and soldiers as the driving force of history and expose their class enemies as reactionaries against social progress. From time to time, this official policy was affected by domestic and international politics that allowed closer scrutiny of social problems and official corruption, although such 'thawing' periods were inevitably short-lived and followed by ideological tightening and persecution of the artists who had spoken their mind.

In terms of practitioners, many established playwrights, directors and actors occupied influential positions, although most of them, especially playwrights, struggled to create new works that fitted official ideology. The only established author who thrived in this period was Lao She (1899–1966), who turned his talent as a novelist into writing several notable plays, especially *Longxu gou* (The Dragon Beard Ditch, 1951), which celebrated an urban reconstruction project in Beijing, and *Chaguan* (Teahouse, 1958), which used a fictional Beijing teahouse to depict the lives of ordinary Chinese from late Qing (1898), the Republican warlord era (1920s) and the late 1940s.

The Dragon Beard Ditch was representative of early 1950s optimism of the new republic as well as huaju's embrace of its role in expressing such feelings, both genuine and with official prodding. Tasked by Premiere Zhou Enlai to eulogize a reconstruction project in Beijing, Lao She wrote the play about the fate of several low-class families who live in a compound near the Dragon Beard Ditch before and after 1949. Staged by BPAT under the direction of the French-educated Jiao Juyin (1905–75), it became a smashing success that solidified the reputation of the artists and the theatre. In 1958, many of the same artists, again led by Lao She, Jiao and the leader actor Yu Shizhi (1927–2013), created *Teahouse* in which Yu played the manager of a Beijing teahouse that was the canvas to the fate of various social classes in the first half-century. It is a brilliant panorama of Beijing society filled with witty dialogue, trenchant commentary and unforgettable characters that could only be (and has been) with the local colour and ensemble talent of BPAT.

In a way, though, Lao She's characters in these two contemporary classics were atypical of the representatives of 'new China' – workers, peasants and soldiers – who populated a proliferation of one-act plays under the active support of cultural authorities in Beijing. While typically focused on bolstering heroes of the new society and criticizing backward thinking and habits, some of the best plays did stand out, with realistic characters, well-constructed plots and lively dialogue filled with local colour. The best known of the group include Jin Jian's *Zhao Xiaolan* (1952) and Sun Yu's *Funü daibiao* (The Women's Representative, 1953), which focus on new rural women, and Cui Dezhi's *Liu Lianying* (1955), which portrays textile workers.

At the same time, these plays also represent the era's stale dramatic formula of only three types of dramatic conflict: between advanced and backward ideology for factory workers, whether to join the people's commune for peasants, and fighting between communists and enemy armies. This criticism is from a newspaper article in June 1957 titled 'Disizhong juben' (The Fourth Type of Script), in which the author praised what he saw as the fourth type of play that strove to break out of this formula. Specifically, he discussed the Shanghai production of *Buguniao you jiaole* (The Cuckoo Sings Again) by Yang Lüfang and an earlier play *Tonggan gongku* (Through Thick and Thin). Indeed, while still focused on the life of peasants in a commune, *The Cuckoo Sings Again* was a breath of fresh air by pitting a pair of vibrant youths – the female Tong Yanan (the 'cuckoo') and male Shen Xiaoya – as both model workers and lead singers among the young villagers against two leaders of their work unit: Wang Bihao, a member of the Communist

Youth League local committee and Tong's boyfriend at the beginning of the play, and Kong Yucheng, a party member and head of the Youth League committee and youth production brigade. The play was a smashing success thanks to its criticism of local leaders of the CCP and the Youth League, its uplifting message of youthful vibrancy and a brilliant production filled with songs under the direction of Huang Zuolin (1906–94), one of the directors of the 1942 *Qiu Haitan* and now Associate Artistic Director of Shanghai Renmin Yishu Juyuan (Shanghai People's Art Theatre).

While still a minority, social critical plays, especially those directed towards bureaucratic officials, were on the rise in the mid-1950s right until the summer of 1957, when it was abruptly halted by the Anti-Rightist Movement, which first invited open criticism of the Party and then persecuted half a million people nationwide for speaking their minds. Until then, both one-act and multi-act plays were written and staged to expose emerging conflicts of the new society. One of them, *Dongxiao hengchui* (The Vertical Flute is Played Horizontally, by Hai Mo, 1956), is similar to *The Cuckoo Sings Again* by pitting a retired soldier against bureaucratic and corrupt rural officials during the process of forming communes, only with much darker and realistic depictions of life in rural China. The other multi-act piece praised as 'the fourth type of play', *Through Thick and Thin* (by Yue Ye, 1956), discusses the phenomenon of communist officials leaving their wives in the countryside to marry young and educated women since entering the cities as high-ranking officials after 1949.

Apart from multi-act plays, several one-acts also focused on exposing contemporary concerns. A slight variation of the theme of high-ranking officials forgetting rural folks who helped them during wartimes is the focus of *Bei yiwangle de shiqing* (Something Forgotten, by Duan Chengbin, 1957). Another prominent achievement in social criticism came from several satires on bureaucratic attraction to meetings, central planning and selfish flattery of higher-ups while ignoring urgent needs of ordinary people. The earliest piece of this genre was Xing Ye's *Kaihui* (The Meeting, 1953), in which a district official insists on holding a meeting of villagers for him to lecture about drought alleviation methods. A prominent playwright of the genre was Wang Shaoyan, who wrote several plays around the corrupt, bureaucratic and incompetent Director Chen of a city's supply and sales system, including *Putao lanle* (The Grapes Are Rotten) which satirizes his disastrous decision to buy half a kilogram of grapes for everyone in the city. The best-known satire of this period was He Qiu's *Xin juzhang laidao zhiqian* (Before the New Director Arrives, 1955), which depicts the head of a general services department who orders elaborate remodelling of a new office for the arriving bureau director while assigning the existing director's office to himself, ignores leaks in the workers' dormitories and leaves bags of cement in the rain only to be rescued by the workers under the direction of the new director who has arrived without ceremony.

However, these plays and their authors became the target of the Anti-Rightist Movement and some of them were condemned and exiled to the countryside. With social critical plays off limits and propaganda drama too formulaic, history plays again became a hot topic in the late 1950s, especially for veteran playwrights. Some of the best-known include Tian Han's *Guan Hanqing* (1958) on a Yuan dynasty (1279–1368) dramatist, Cao Yu's *Dan jian pian* (Courage and the Sword, 1961) on an ancient king's bitter experience of national revival, and Guo Moruo's *Cai Wenji* (1959) and *Wu Zetian* (1960) on two famous women in Chinese history, all staged by Beijing People's Art Theatre.

The early 1960s was a period of tug of war in policies towards the arts, with visible consequences for huaju plays. On the one hand, the policies of the late 1950s, including the Anti-Rightist Movement and the 1958 Great Leap Forward, had severely harmed the national economy and constrained artistic creation. As a result, CCP leadership was forced to adopt more pragmatic economic measures and arts policies between 1960 and 1962. On the other hand, CCP chair Mao Zedong, while temporary sidelined from state administration, was never happy with such pragmatic and liberal policies and admonished the party to 'never forget class struggle' in 1962, followed by two directives condemning cultural authorities for ignoring contemporary class struggle in 1963 and 1964. As a result of such conflicting messages, huaju experienced another mini-boom that nevertheless focused mostly on the theme of class struggle.

Some of the most representative plays of this period focused on sacrificing individual or small-group gains for collective advancement in factories or villages, including *Nianqing de yidai* (The Young Generation) by Chen Yun, *Qianwan buyao wangji* (Never Forget) by Cong Shen and *Fengshou zhihou* (After the Harvest) by Lan Cheng, all premiered in 1963. *The Young Generation* focuses on two young geologists in Shanghai, one determined to return to his team despite crippling leg problems and the other having faked a sickness report in order to stay in the city. *Never Forget* is about Ding Shaochun, a motor factory worker married to the daughter of a former grocery shop owner, whose selfish little bourgeois actions almost causes Ding costly mistakes at work. The third play, *After Harvest*, takes place in a village where a good harvest results in the ideological clash between the party secretary Aunt Zhao, who wants to sell extra grain to the country, and her husband, who insists on selling it on the market to buy horses, which allows a former pedlar and donkey seller to embezzle from the village treasury. The lesson of these plays served as warnings to the audience who should remain vigilant against impure ideological deviations and guard against individualism, which would cause serious harm to socialist construction.

One remarkable exception from such ideological propaganda is a play based on a wildly popular movie with the same title, *Li Shuangshuang* (1963) by Li Zhun, and starring the award-winning actress Zhang Ruifang, who masterfully portrayed a new peasant woman capable of laughter and cries, a loving mother and wife who, despite her timid husband's misgivings and threats, remains outspoken for the welfare of the village and its female members. Some of the most memorable sequences of the film and play are around the relations between the couple, during cooking a meal, when the husband threatens to work outside the village, or when he returns. In her down-to-earth optimism and frustration, Li Shuangshuang resembles the heroine in *Cuckoo Sings Again*.

Huaju's near disappearance during the Cultural Revolution (1966–1976)

The most notable achievement in Chinese theatre during the Cultural Revolution is the two rounds of revolutionary model plays, which included jingju, ballet and the symphony version of one of the jingju plays. Huaju productions ranged from non-existence to mere propaganda. At the beginning of the Cultural Revolution, regular theatrical performance ground to a halt, as was the case of all other normal social activities. However, Red Guards of various theatres, universities and schools, including the two theatre academies in Beijing and Shanghai, did put on revolutionary plays appropriate for the occasion. In the summer of 1967, different factions of the Red Guards from Central Theatre Academy staged several such plays and even toured throughout the country. By autumn of 1968, as workers and soldier moved into universities and schools to curtail absolute anarchy, these activities came to an end, as did huaju performance for the next several years.

The return of huaju, as well as most other performance forms, occurred after an unsuccessful coup by Mao's heir apparent Lin Biao in September 1971. Starting from 1973, some new plays were written on the topical issue of the 'two lines' between radicals that were in power and pragmatists before the Cultural Revolution led by Liu Shaoqi, the National President persecuted to death in 1969. One such play, *Fenghua zhengmao* (In Their Prime, 1974) by Tianjin Renmin Yishu Juyuan (Tianjin People's Art Theatre), pitted a middle-school teacher in the early 1960s, who takes her students to learn from fishermen in the docks, against the school principal who insists on traditional classroom education, which the play denounces as following bourgeois ideology.

Post-Mao introspection, experiments, and censorship (1977–1989)

The Cultural Revolution ended in October 1976 after the death of Mao Zedong and the arrest of his wife Jiang Qing and her clique, known as the Gang of Four. In the following years, China went through tremendous political, economic and cultural changes, all of which had a profound effect on huaju.

The first – and to a certain extent last – wave of huaju's post-1976 glory was manifest in several plays that depicted the last days of the Cultural Revolution by staging a national revulsion of the Gang of Four and amplifying an ecstatic mood of liberation. The most famous plays of this group include *Yu wu sheng chu* (In the Land of Silence, 1978) by Zong Fuxian and the satire *Fengye hongle de shihou* (When the Maple Leaves Turned Red, 1977) by Jin Zhenjia and Wang Jingyu. Soon, this euphoria turned to daunting social issues of economic and ideological reconstruction, or what was known as 'setting wrong things right' (*boluan fanzheng*), a policy adopted at the 1978 Third Plenum of the Eleventh CCP Congress which turned the party's focus from class struggle to economic development. One such play was *Baochunhua* (Winter Jasmine, 1979) by Cui Dezhi, the author of the 1955 one-act *Liu Lianying*. Like his earlier play, *Winter Jasmine* is also about life in a textile factory where the manager and party secretary Li Jian, returning from years of persecution during the Cultural Revolution, is determined to focus on quality control of the product by promoting a model worker with an ideologically questionable – a rightist – mother.

Throughout the first half of the 1980s, dramatic depictions of social problems remained a politically sensitive balancing act for the government. On the one hand, the authorities studiously avoided high-handed political persecutions reminiscent of the 1950s and 60s. On the other hand, it censored, altered or delayed a number of productions because of their realistic content, starting from *Jiaru woshi zhende* (If I Were Real, 1979) by the Shanghai playwright Sha Yexin. Based on a real criminal trial Sha witnessed, the play focuses on Li Xiaozhang, a young man desperate to return to Shanghai from the countryside (where millions of 'educated youths' were sent during the Cultural Revolution) by pretending to be the son of a high-ranking official in Beijing and successfully tricking a slew of fawning and corrupt officials. The play's sympathetic treatment of Li and exposure of official corruption triggered a national symposium on play-writing in Beijing in February 1980, which ended with a long speech by Hu Yaobang, head of the CCP Propaganda Department, who would soon become the Party Secretary General. He praised Sha's talent but insisted on script revision, which Sha refused and the play was never staged. The censorship of *If I Were Real* set up a precedent for dealing with other contemporary plays, including *Xiaojing hutong* (Small Well Lane, 1981) by Li Longyun, a Lao She-style depiction of the tumultuous lives of residents in a Beijing lane after 1949. A straightforward depiction of the dark moments in PRC history and characters who are by turns upright, selfish, victimized, farcical, scheming and villainous, its production by Beijing People's Art Theatre was delayed for 4 years, until 1985.

Huaju's formal experiments started in the late 1970s as part of the excitement in (re)discovering world theatre in the twentieth century after three decades of fossilized knowledge that froze on Ibsen and Stanislavski. All of a sudden, translations of modern theatre, from symbolism to expressionism to Bertolt Brecht to theatre of the absurd, became talk of the town. The first glimpse of these techniques on stage came in a 1979 production of Brecht's *Life of Galileo* at the Central Youth Theatre under the direction of Chen Yong, which shocked the Chinese theatre circle with its distancing devices, forcing the audience to ponder the relations between power and individual choice.

One of the most innovative and controversial playwrights who combined formal experiments and ideological provocation – and consequently received more scrutiny and censorship – was the future Nobel Prize winner Gao Xingjian, who wrote *Juedui xinhao* (Absolute Signal, 1982, with Liu Huiyuan), *Chenzhan* (Bus Stop, 1983), *Yeren* (Wild Man, 1985) and *Bi'an* (The Other Shore, 1986) before emigrating to France. Gao studied French literature in college in the early 1960s and was a translator before becoming a resident playwright for BPAT. His French background, extremely rare for his generation of playwrights, gave him special insight into the works of Jean-Paul Sartre and Samuel Beckett. His *Absolute Signal* is generally regarded as the first little theatre production in China, which was staged in a banquet room in Capital Theatre, BPAT's home theatre. Directed by Lin Zhaohua, Gao's partner in all his plays at BPAT, with simple platforms, railings, chairs and a few lights, the play tells the story of a thwarted robbery of a night freight train. The immediacy and unpretentiousness of presentation supported a non-linear structure with multiple flashbacks and out-of-sequence monologues and dialogues that were from time to time lit only with flashlights. While the play ran 159 performances and was widely copied throughout the nation, Gao's next play *Bus Stop* was summarily banned after a few performances because of its content, reminiscent of *Waiting for Godot*, about a group of characters waiting at a suburban bus stop where buses passing by never stop until they eventually discover, after 10 years, that the stop has been cancelled.

Among other experimental plays that challenged realist orthodoxy, *Wuwai you reliu* (Hot Currents Outside the House, 1980), by Ma Zhongjun *et al.*, brings a ghost on stage. *Guazai qiangshang de Lao B* (Old B on the Wall, 1984) by Sun Huizhu lets an eternal understudy in a theatre walk off a wall where he has been hanging as a cardboard cutout. In *Yige sizhe dui shengzhe de fangwen* (The Dead Visiting the Living, 1985) by Liu Shugang a man, who was stabbed to death on a bus when he tried to stop a robbery and was allowed to bleed to death by indifferent onlookers returns to interrogate the witnesses. *Mofang* (Rubik's Cube, 1985), by Tao Jun *et al.*, uses nine episodes of different performance formats to portray a kaleidoscope of contemporary life. In the same year, *WM*, another innovative play with creative movement of the chorus on a bare stage, an onstage synthesizer and drum set, and bold lighting and costume design, was censored after several dress rehearsals because of its frank depiction of the educated youth after the Cultural Revolution.

Despite the *WM* episode, more formally innovative and thematically provocative plays emerged in Beijing and Shanghai. Of these plays, BPAT's *Gou'erye niepan* (Uncle Doggie's Nirvana, 1986) by Jinyun focuses on the plight of a peasant from 1949 to the early 1980s through his cycles of possessing and losing land and other properties, an experience enhanced by the play's imaginative manipulation of temporal and spatial planes. Written by Sha Yexin, author of *If I Were Real*, and staged by Shanghai People's Art Theatre, *Kongzi, Yesu, Pitoushi Lienong* (Confucius, Jesus Christ and John Lennon, 1987) is a satire in which Confucius, Jesus Christ and John Lennon are sent by God from a chaotic heaven to the human world on an investigative mission, only to encounter a ruthlessly materialist state and a 1984-style authoritarian regime. Written by Chen Zidu, Yang Jian and Zhu Xiaoping, *Sangshuping jishi* (Sangshuping Chronicles, 1988) takes place in 1968–9 in the yellow earth plateau of Shaanxi Province where greed and savage customs lead to the oppression and persecution of outsiders and women. Performed by a graduating class at the Central Theatre Academy and directed by its president Xu Xiaozhong, the production blended dialogue with dance and singing to tell a despairing story that deeply resonated with the mood of cultural introspection of the late 1980s. This was also the theme of *Tianxia diyi lou* (The World's Top Restaurant, 1988) by He Jiping, which, while set in a duck restaurant in early twentieth-century Beijing, is ultimately a piece of cultural self-interrogation as it focuses on the sabotages of its reformed-minded manager by the restaurant's owners and employees.

Avant-garde and main-melody plays of the 1990s

This sense of urgency for a cultural self-examination was abruptly truncated the following year after the Tiananmen Incident and the ensuing government control for ideological and political stability. For huaju, such measures resulted in a split between 'main-melody' plays by state-owned companies aimed at winning government awards vital for the theatres' financial survival and the rise of avant-garde productions by auteur-style directors that represented huaju's true creative energy. Among the outstanding main-melody productions, *Shang Yang* (1996, by Shanghai People's Art Theatre, written by Yao Yuan, directed by Chen Xinyi) dramatized the life and death of a reformer during the Warring States era (476–221 BC). Another play, *Shengsi chang* (The Field of Life and Death, 1999), was adapted and directed by Tian Qinxin for the Central Experimental Theatre from a 1934 novella by Xiao Hong about a group of peasants in a remote Manchurian village under Japanese occupation. Both were powerful and melodramatic productions directed by two of the most active contemporary female directors.

The directors that garnered most attention during this decade were Lin Zhaohua, Mou Sen and Meng Jinghui, all of whom directed translated and original plays that pushed formal and content boundaries. All three also worked outside the state-owned theatre system for their provocative productions, even though only Mou was an independent director. Lin created his own studio, which allowed him to stage bold experiments impossible for BPAT where he served as deputy artistic director and directed such hit proscenium productions as Guo Shixing's *Niaoren* (Bird Men, 1993), a stimulating and farcical study of cultural misunderstandings between China and the west. In his own studio, Lin staged his interpretations of *Hamlet* (1990), Friedrich Dürrenmat's *Romulus the Great* (1994), *Faust* (1994), *Three Sisters Waiting for Godot* (1998, a postmodern combination of the two plays) and several other Chinese and European plays.

In the early 1990s, subversive adaptation of European plays became a notable strategy that challenged official ideological hegemony. Lin's 1990 *Hamlet* contested the dichotomy of good and evil by having 'To Be or Not To Be' delivered by the three actors who play Hamlet, Claudius and Polonius and, at the end of the play, letting the actor who played Hamlet fall as Claudius was stabbed by Hamlet and then the actor who mainly played Claudius deliver Hamlet's final lines to Horatio. His choice of *Romulus the Great* went even further to challenge the concept of patriotism, since Dürrenmat's pseudo-historical play depicts the last Roman emperor as intentionally sabotaging the imperialist empire by focusing exclusively on hen-rearing during German invasion. Lin's subversive choice was enhanced by doubling Romulus, his wife, daughter and courtiers with marionettes that appeared on stage with or without the actor playing the same role, while Romulus remained the only character who was never substituted by a puppet, the only voice of reason on stage.

In 1991, Meng Jinghui, in his last year as an MFA directing student at the Central Theatre Academy, directed two theatre of the absurd plays, *The Bald Soprano* and *Waiting for Godot*, the latter after failing to receive permission to stage it on a coal pile on campus. These two plays resonated with the audience with their absurdity and desperation, as the former ended with three minutes of pause that confused the audience and the latter taking place in a white-washed hospital-like room and ending with Vladimir breaking the windows with his umbrella. Meng's 1998 adaptation of Dario Fo's *Accidental Death of an Anarchist* (adapted by Huang Jisu) layered the original play's farcical denunciation of police brutality with intertextual allusion to Chinese realities and theatrical classics such as famous scenes from *Teahouse*, which made the play both politically poignant and culturally relatable to the Chinese audience.

Meng's signature blend of provocation and entertainment started soon after he joined the Central Experimental Theatre, although many of his productions were independently produced, including the 1992 *Sifan* (Worldly Pleasures), which combines scenes from a Ming dynasty *kunqu* play about a nun escaping from the nunnery and falling in love with a monk with two stories of tasting forbidden love from Boccaccio's *Decameron*. The production stood out for its fluid staging and cheeky irreverence, which included no set and plenty of physical and verbal jokes and allusions, all wrapped up in anti-authoritarian defiance in the pursuit of love and sexual libertarianism. This defiance is further demonstrated in his 1994 'anti-play' *Wo ai XXX* (I Love XXX), which has no plot or characters and is exclusively composed of declarative lines, each of which starts with 'I love. . .'. On a bare stage lined with TV sets and folding chairs in the background, he used various combinations of the chorus to comment on world and Chinese events of the twentieth century and the life experience of his generation, born in the 1960s. Meng's ingenious combination of youthful passion, irreverent mockery and imaginative staging combining the farcical and the dramatic with creative usage of music – sometimes with a live band onstage – has largely contributed to the revived interest in huaju among young urban audiences.

At the other end of the spectrum was Mou Sen, whose three productions in the early 1990s went further than his peers in separating performance from the dramatic text. Mou, who studied literature at Beijing Normal University and was a devotee of Jerzy Grotowski's poor theatre, directed Ionesco's *Rhinoceros*, Stravinsky's *A Soldier's Story* and Eugene O'Neill's *Great God Brown* between 1987 and 1989 with his independent Wa Shiyan Jutuan (Frog Experimental Theatre). In 1993, Mou trained a group of students who had failed to enter professional performance programmes to stage a movement-centric production based on Gao Xingjian's *The Other Shore* that shocked Beijing's arts circle as a deeply spiritual piece on the meaning of self-doubt, physical labour, and awakening. In May of the following year, he created *Ling dang'an* (File Zero) for Kunsten Festival des Arts in Brussels, which subsequently toured Europe and North America but did not perform in China. The three-person performance broadcasts a long poem about personnel files as a looped audio recording that is stopped and restarted repeatedly by an actor and actress. Layered on top of this is the recollection by the third actor about growing up in the remote interior on account of his father's history. At the same time, the other actor welded steel bars onto a metal scaffold to which the actress affixed apples and tomatoes, which were eventually fed to a blower that spat out the bloody liquid.

In December of the same year, Mou Sen created *Yu aizi youguan* (Related to AIDS), which was closer to a happening than theatrical performance. For three nights, Mou had thirteen amateur performers chitchat on stage while frying meatballs and making stuffed steamed buns for thirteen labourers building a brick wall at the sides of and behind the audience. In the end, the labourers were invited to a long table on stage to have supper and, during one night, dance with the dancer Jin Xing, who was about to undergo transgender surgery. This combination of mundane daily routine of cooking and suggestive building of an enclosing wall made the production an important piece of provocation, albeit understandably within a highly selective group of the cultural elite.

The mid and late 1990s also witnessed the re-emergence of Chinese nationalism, as evident in such anti-American books as *Zhongguo keyi shuo bu* (China Can Say No, 1996, by Song Qiang *et al.*). The most prominent theatrical manifestation of this phenomenon is the 2000 production of *Qie Gewala* (*Che Guevara*, by Huang Jisu *et al.*), which glorified the Argentinian revolutionary as an anti-imperialist hero.

Globalization and commercial huaju in the new millennium

At the beginning of the twenty-first century, globalization and a state policy to turn theatre into part of the cultural industry have added a great deal of ideological, organizational and performance diversity to huaju. The new National Theatre, established in 2001 by combining the National Youth Art Theatre and the National Experimental Theatre, instituted a producer system. Its most successful director, Tian Qinxin, has collaborated with her producer Li Dong to orchestrate savvy promotional campaigns for all her productions. Similarly, Shanghai Dramatic Art Centre, formed in 1995 by merging the Shanghai People's Art Theatre and Shanghai Qingnian Huaju Tuan (Shanghai Youth Huaju Company), has a strong department of publicity, marketing and programming under Yu Rongjun, a prolific playwright who has combined popular elements of 'white-collar theatre' for Shanghai's middle-class audience and serious observations of contemporary life.

The other side of the effort to push huaju into the cultural industry was the privatization of most state-owned companies and the emergence of private theatres. An example of the latter category is the Penghao Juchang (Penghao Theatre) in Beijing, which was founded by Wang Xiang, a dentist, in 2008. Located right outside the Central Theatre Academy, it has leveraged talents from the academy to stage independent plays, including a self-reflective piece on the relationship between the theatre and local cultural history titled *Luoguxiang de gushi* (The Story of Gong and Drum Lane, 2009). Another notable phenomenon is the rise of campus theatres as universities have begun to establish theatre programmes, often together with media studies. One recent production by the Department of Theatre, Film, and Television Art of Nanjing University, entitled *Jianggong de mianzi* (Face for Mr. Chiang Kai-shek, 2012), became the talk of the nation. Written by an undergraduate student, Wen Fangyi, and directed by the department head Lü Xiaoping, the play depicts three professors debating in 1943 whether to honour a dinner invitation by President Chiang Kai-shek, pitting the independence of pre-PRC intellectuals against their persecution during the Cultural Revolution.

In a way, the rise of student productions is reminiscent of the early days of huaju from student dramatics in Shanghai and Tokyo, as well as their contribution to wenmingxi and the maturity of huaju. Indeed, modern Chinese theatre has come a long way through the hybridity of wenmingxi at the beginning of the twentieth century, the youthful exuberance and formal experiments of the 1920s, the leftist turn as well as dramatic and theatrical maturity of the 1930s, rediscovery of history plays and traditional elements during occupation, and the multiple waves of ideological ebb and flow in the PRC years that nevertheless created memorable plays and productions in the past half-century.

Note

1 This chapter is condensed from the author's two chapters in *Modern Asian Theatre and Performance 1900–2000* (Methuen, 2014): 'Modern Chinese Theatre before 1949' (Chapter 3) and ' Modern Chinese Theatre after 1949' (Chapter 4).

15

Modern theatre in Hong Kong, Taiwan, Korea and North Korea

Gilbert C. F. Fong, Shelby Kar-yan Chan,
Katherine Hui-ling Chou, Yun-Cheol Kim
and Ji Hyon (Kayla) Yuh

I. Hong Kong, by Gilbert C. F. Fong and Shelby Kar-yan Chan

Hong Kong, an ex-colony imbued with British and Chinese influences, is the vortex of competing discourses that juxtaposes culture with politics, language and identity. With few or nearly non-existent 'natural', 'authentic' or 'historical' identity discourses, this mega-city evinces a hybridized permeability, contesting and consolidating the terms and territories of all hovering influences, yet pledging exclusive loyalty to none. The problematic of Hong Kong theatre relates to (de)colonization and contributes, through the prioritization of Cantonese performance, to the complexity of the ongoing identity debate in the territory.

In Hong Kong the theatre has frequently been used, consciously or subconsciously, as an identity laboratory, a site for articulation, formulation, contestation and legitimatization of a Hong Kong identity. As a public form of cultural expression, the theatre is also part of a polyvocal community, and its interaction with the public offers a forum for negotiation and scrutiny of commonly held values and perceptions. The local theatre tends to project an idealized image of a Hongkonger. In terms of intellectual orientation and points of interest, it leans towards romanticism rather than realism. Unlike cinema and television in Hong Kong, with their penchant to respond actively to current affairs, the theatre seldom concerns itself with reflections or interpretations of socio-political events. Instead, local theatre artists often go on inward quests to find and express higher and better visions than the reality that confronts their society.

The transformational value of change should be emphasized when one examines the translationality of Hong Kong theatre. The persistent learning process does not necessarily entail indiscriminate copy-and-paste. With translation, which involves filtering, adapting and transfiguring, imported artistic and cultural discourses are converted into bricks and mortar for a growing theatre and self-identity. The insistence on using the Cantonese dialect on stage is pertinent to the need to translate, since even borrowing stories from plays written for Mandarin performance would involve intralingual translation. The southern dialect (especially the Hong Kong variety, which is different from those used in other parts of Guangdong Province), plays a pivotal role in shaping Hong Kong theatre. Its particular syntax, vocabulary and openness have possibly formulated a distinctive Hong Kong mentality and world view reflected on the stage. The acceptance of the legitimacy of Cantonese in written form in the 1970s has not only provided impetus for writing a Hong Kong culture and identity, but also promoted the reading of its own indigeneity (its history and origins) and otherness through a self-made reading glass which is Hong Kong Cantonese. At times during the onset of mainland Chinese politics and culture, Cantonese has taken on the role of a defence-mechanism, a firewall of sorts, blocking the influx of Mandarin talents and theatrical works. In this manner the development of Hong Kong theatre, in content and acting as well as production, contributes, at times unwittingly, to the evolution of an individual Hong Kong theatrical style.

Beginning of Hong Kong theatre (1911–36)

At the turn of the twentieth century, Hong Kong, though under British colonial rule, still maintained a close tie with mainland China, its culture regarded as a branch of the broader Chinese tradition. Hong Kong theatre, following its mainland counterpart, mainly put on plays that were operatic in style. The earliest record of 'spoken drama' (known as *baihuaxi*, meaning plain language plays) performed in Hong Kong was reported in *Huazi ribao* (Chinese Characters Daily) on 29 October 1908, in an advertisement for the performances by Xianshen Shuofa She (Show and Tell Society) on 30 and 31 October of the same year. Baihuaxi, consisting mainly of dialogues but interspersed with operatic scenes, marked the beginning of modern Hong Kong theatre as we know it today. At the time, many drama troupes were closely associated with anti-Manchu revolutionaries, and they put on baihuaxi performances to secretly raise funds for the revolution and to promote its causes, such as republicanism, anti-feudalism, social equality and modernization of China. There were more than fifty performances in 1911 and up to eighty in 1912. By the early 1920s, baihuaxi burgeoned in schools and in public theatres. With the rise of urban culture, baihuaxi was soon commercialized and became known as *wenmingxi* (civilized drama), which had no written scripts and the actors performed according to a synopsis and improvised the dialogues. Recent studies, however, have pointed out that wenmingxi was important to the development of Hong Kong theatre, as it succeeded in introducing new and foreign elements while retaining traditional elements to accommodate local culture.

Rise of anti-Japanese drama (1937–45)

Soon after the Japanese invasion of China in 1937, a host of mainland Chinese dramatists, such as Hong Shen (1894–1955), Ouyang Yuqian (1889–1962) and Jin Shan (1911–82), fled south and sought temporary refuge in the British colony. Well-established drama troupes, such as the Zhongguo Lüxing Jutuan (China Travelling Theatre Company), Zhonghua Yishu Jutuan (Chinese Art Theatre Company) and Zhongguo Jiuwang Jutuan (China Rescue Theatre Company), gave large-scale war-themed charity performances and hosted seminars at schools and in the community. They expanded the repertoire, introduced sophisticated production techniques and set the standard for the discipline and operation modes of professional troupes. More importantly, their patriotic fervour attracted a huge number of spectators into the theatre, arousing not only resistance sentiments but also interest in spoken drama in Hong Kong. By 1938, more than twenty amateur and professional theatre companies came into existence, putting on more than two hundred shows under the banner of the War of Resistance. From the second half of 1939 to the first half of 1940, the territory was the home base for around eighty amateur troupes and school drama societies.

The development of Hong Kong theatre in this period was mainly determined by the war effort. Consequently, plays became highly didactic, with lofty and patriotic ideals, and socio-political concerns overrode artistic and commercial discourses. On the other hand, the dearth of resources locally available, in terms of talent, play scripts and production techniques, meant that Hong Kong theatre, though becoming more mature, relied heavily on the support and guidance of more experienced practitioners from the mainland.

Emergence of translated drama (1946–76)

The Japanese occupation of Hong Kong ended on 15 August 1945. Despite the postwar destitution, Hong Kong theatre recovered swiftly. After 1949, many Chinese dramatists, such as Yao Ke (1905–91) and Hu Chunbing (1906–60), stayed and resided in Hong Kong, laying the groundwork for Hong Kong theatre. Some joined Zhongying Xuehui (Sino-British Club) and conducted seminars, published books and journals about drama, and offered support to many budding drama societies at schools and in the community.

The mid-1950s saw the beginning of governmental support for performing arts. The first Hong Kong Arts Festival came into being in 1955 and continued for 5 more years until 1960. Zhongwen Xiju Zu (Chinese Drama Group) of the Sino-British Club staged one or two Chinese historical plays during the festival, including *Qinggong yuan* (Sorrows of the Qing Court, 1955), *Honglou meng* (Dream of the Red Chamber, 1955) and *Xixiang ji* (Romance of the West Chamber, 1956). Historical drama became a popular genre, as it was able to bypass political censorship, and the lavish productions and elaborate period costumes, made possible with government subsidies, provided attractive visual excitement which appealed to the audience.

The dearth of original play scripts had been a hindrance to the development of Hong Kong theatre. In the 1960s, reliance on Chinese spoken drama canons (such as the plays by Cao Yu) as well as adaptations from historical stories, classical literature and Cantonese opera solved only part of the problem, but these traditional Chinese themes were not enough to capture and hold the attention of a younger and more westernized generation of audiences. Translated plays from the west thus rose to the occasion and occupied centre stage. One of the pioneers of drama translation was Chung King-fai (1937–), who was the first Chinese to receive a Master of Fine Art degree from Yale University. Upon returning to Hong Kong in 1962, he introduced contemporary American plays (e.g. plays by Arthur Miller, Thornton Wilder and Tennessee Williams) and theatre of the absurd, as well as Broadway musicals, to the Hong Kong stage. Although translated drama was not a novelty in the local theatre, Chung's advocacy revolutionized its image, practice and public reception. He insisted on a foreignization approach to staging western plays, so as to retain their 'original flavour' (Chung's words, in Fong 2009: 184) to rejuvenate local theatre and to raise the standard of both the practitioners and the audience. He also initiated a break with 'the shackles of realism' (Fong 2009: 184), which had been dominating local productions, and galvanized the theatre artists into taking a more abstract and minimalistic approach. He was bent on breaking 'the fourth wall' and set examples by directing plays such as Miller's *Death of a Salesman* and Wilder's *Our Town*. The popularization of translated plays substantially expanded the repertoire of Hong Kong theatre and enriched its range of performance styles. Since Chung, translated drama has become a staple in Hong Kong theatre.

Professionalization (1977–97)

The 1980s saw the Hong Kong theatre in full swing. With governmental support, the first two professional theatre companies were established: the Xianggang Huaju Tuan (Hong Kong Repertory Theatre, HKREP) in 1977 and Zhongying Jutuan (Chung Ying Theatre Company) in 1979. Since its establishment, HKREP has been the flagship theatre company in Hong Kong.

With relatively comfortable financial resources and a stable artistic and production team, HKREP built up a repertoire of considerable scale and diversity. More than three decades of regular and variegated performances of reasonable quality have accumulated a substantial audience base for the troupe and the theatre scene in general.

Chung Ying (literal translation is 'Sino-British') was first started as an auxiliary of the British Council in 1979 with the aim of promoting English through drama performances. In 1982 Chung Ying became an independent not-for-profit organization. Predominantly a British troupe in terms of staff and repertoire, it launched its first Cantonese production in the third season in 1981, but almost all its plays were translated plays until the early 1990s. Under the artistic directorship of Bernard Goss (?–1988) from 1984 to 1988, Chung Ying began to connect with the local Chinese community through highly localized translations. In 1986, Goss directed a Sinified version *The Twelfth Night* and moved the setting from Illyria in the fifteenth century to Guangzhou in the Tang dynasty; he was then able to render the dialogues, songs, actors' movement and costumes in a Sinified style. This popular Shakespearean adaptation blazed a trail in the localization of translated drama.

Jinnian Ershimianti (Zuni Icosahedron) was founded in 1982 by artistic director Danny Yung (Rong Nianzeng). It has since become the representative of the avant-garde in Hong Kong theatre, known for introducing multimedia and installation art onto the Hong Kong stage. In many of its productions, dialogue was a dispensable element, rendering the presentation zen-like and relying on directness rather than mediation through words. Zuni is also prone to deconstructing classical texts and re-presenting them in images, sound, colour and form. The company has had great impact on the theatrical style and content of Hong Kong theatre. It has also been the breeding ground for many theatrical talents with an experimental bent. For example, Edward Lam (Lin Yihua), an early member of the group, has formed his own company, famous for combining the experimental with popular culture; his company Feichang Lin Yihua (Edward Lam Dance Theatre), self-styled to be cultured and fashionable, has been a favourite of the younger audience in Hong Kong.

In 1985, the School of Drama of the Xianggang Yanyi Xueyuan (Hong Kong Academy of Performing Arts) was established, and for the first time professional courses in acting, directing, playwriting and technical arts were made available in the territory. Over the years, the Academy has produced excellent talents for the stage (and for the movies and television), thus contributing to the professionalization and institutionalization of Hong Kong theatre.

Assimilation with popular culture (late 1970s to the present)

For the postwar generation that grew up in the glory of Hong Kong's popular music, film and television, which dominated the entertainment scene in Southeast Asia from the 1970s to the 1990s, the boundary between 'high art' and 'low art' became blurred. These young people formulated a new breed of theatregoers, and they engaged drama in a way that called for interaction with their everyday life in the city.

Popular culture thus began to permeate the theatre scene, and an increasing degree of intertextuality developed between the two. Frequent references were made on the stage to films, comics, Cantopop, advertisements and television shows. In particular, translated plays by Rupert Chan (*Twelfth Night*, 1995; *Spring Fever Hotel*, 1996) and Szeto Wai-kin (Situ Weijian) (*Move Over, Mrs. Markham*, 1995) adopted an abundance of witty but nonsensical one-liners which characterized the films by Michael Hui (Xu Guanwen) and Stephen Chow (Zhou Xingchi). The prevalence of Cantopop and karaoke has probably inspired a new dramatic genre, which might be termed 'semi-musical'. Newer troupes such as W Chuangzuo She (W Theatre) and

Chuntian Wutai (Spring-Time Group) often incorporate pop songs into their productions. Deployment of pop singers in the cast proved convenient and profitable, enlarging the audience base with pop music fans who are not among the usual theatregoers. Other stage productions, however, appeared to be less tame, developing a love–hate relationship with popular culture. The 'Hong Kong Collective Memory Trilogy' by Juchang Zuhe (Theatre Ensemble) and Edward Lam Dance Theatre, including *Da yulejia* (The Big Entertainer, 2004, 2005), *Wanshi gewang* (The King of Pop Songs, 2006) and *Wanqian shinai he taiqing* (My Life as a TV, 2007), parodied and satirized television shows and pop concerts in Hong Kong. These pop drama shows, albeit highly commericalized, help forge a sense of identity. While affirming the local, the contemporary and the vernacular, they also allow the heterogeneous audience to define themselves and to identify collectively.

The plays in this period, with their emphasis on translations from western countries, represented the move away from a China-centric theatrical tradition, and the willingness and insistence for Hong Kong theatre to develop on its own terms and take inspiration from all sources in an increasingly globalized theatrical community.

Root-searching (mid-1980s to present)

The return of sovereignty to the PRC had been looming over Hong Kong and its theatre since the early 1980s. A few questions were often asked: What is Hong Kong? Where is home? Who am I? On stage, the quest for answers was at times metaphysical, political and personal, with an increasing number of original plays in the years running up to the handover in 1997. In 1984, Chung Ying wrestled with the most compelling issue of the time by staging a topical play aptly called *Woshi Xianggang ren* (I am a Hongkonger), written by Raymond To (Du Guowei) and Hardy Tsoi (Cai Xichang). The play inquires into what is essential Hongkongness and laments the identity crisis of the Hong Kong people during the transition period. Gerald Tsang (Zeng Zhuzhao) and Yuen Lup-fun's (Yuan Lixun) *Shi hai* (Gone with the Sea, 1984) and Joanna Chen's (Chen Yinying) *Hua jin gaolou* (Crown Ourselves with Roses, 1998) suggest that a kind of primeval home for Hong Kong and its people can be found in indigenous rural villages and in Hong Kong's history.

The turn of the century witnessed the emergence of socio-political lampoons, which consist of a dozen loosely related pop pastiches with the purpose of castigating the establishment. The *Donggong xigong* (East Wing West Wing) series by Zuni Icosahedron (eleven productions in the series as of 2014) and the *Xiaoren guo* (Little Hong Kong) series by W Theatre (four productions as of 2014; Figure 15.1), both box-office successes, came across as a kind of political participation which is accessible and hilarious to ordinary Hongkongers.

By the mid-2000s a generation of young independent theatre artists had come into the limelight with their one-man shows, which invariably examine their own situations in Hong Kong society. In *Luan dao bao* (The Queer Show, 2006), Joey Leung Cho-yiu (Liang Zuyao) made a confession about being a homosexual in town. With a series of chick-flick shows, such as *29+1* (2005), *Zaijian bu zaijian* (Goodbye But Goodbye, 2007) and *Tiffany* (2012), Kearan Pang (Peng Xiuhui) became a self-styled spokesperson for eligible bachelorettes. Wong Wing-sze (Huang Yongshi), in her *Po diyu yu bai juhua* (My Grandmother's Funeral, 2008), reconstructed Hong Kong-styled Daoist funeral rituals and recounted her life as an outlier in her own family and in society. Each with several re-runs, these stylized and personalized shows are candid and pertinent representations of the beliefs, attitude and lifestyle of young Hongkongers. They provide opportunities for both individual expression and communal bonding.

Figure 15.1 Poster of *Little Hong Kong* Season 4.
(Courtesy of W Theatre)

A century ago the theatre of Hong Kong started with borrowing and shadowing; it still thrives on adaptations from various sources today. As time goes by, it evinces greater confidence, autonomy and versatility to convert imported discourses into its own, gradually developing immunity to the predominance of any single source. With increasing accents on local language and culture, Hong Kong theatre is maturing into a robust arena reflective of contemporary life and sentiments in the territory. The happenings on the stage may not have determined the identity of Hongkongers, but they give the people a voice and a site to determine its writing and shaping for themselves.

II. Taiwan, by Katherine Hui-ling Chou[1]

Shingeki (new drama), *huaju* (spoken drama) and *xiandai xiju* (modern and contemporary theatre) represent the three phases of Taiwan's modern theatre, and are generally seen as reflecting the shifting power structures of the island. Japan's rule of Taiwan following the Qing dynasty's 1895 cession introduced shingeki as the official model style for theatre under the *Kōminka* (Japanization) movement. After the Second World War, Mandarin-speaking Chinese huaju troupes flocked to this reclaimed territory of the Republic of China, making 'huaju' the preferred term for all non-musical theatrical performances. The same term was used by the Kuomin Tang (Nationalist Party, KMT) after they fled the mainland in 1949; the party used huaju to propagate anti-communist and re-sinicization messages. Following the rapid economic growth of the 'Taiwan Miracle', the KMT lifted its 38-year martial law in 1987, paving the way for the current flourishing of modern and contemporary theatre.

Recent research has explored the interplay of modern theatre, politics, and cultural and educational policies. Taiwan's constant state of conflict, negation and convergence along the path of modernization has played out on stage in a long battle over modernity and how to represent the shifting political and cultural status quo.

Launching modern theatre in the early colonial rule, 1897–1937

The earliest attempts to establish modern theatre in Taiwan occurred in several playhouses built in Taipei in the first years of Japanese colonial rule (1895–1945). These include the *Naniwa-za* (Naniwa Theatre, established 1897), the first professional theatre to present traditional *naniwa-bushi* (a story-singing form) exclusively for Japanese audiences (Chiu, 1997); and *Damshui xiguan* (Damshui Theatre), built a year later to present Chinese *xiqu* (traditional musical theatre) for locals. Takamatsu Toyozirou (1872–1952), who helped bring cinema to Taiwan, renovated the Naniwa-za into the *Asahi-za* (Asahi Theatre) in 1906 to accommodate film screenings; built eight more theatres between 1908 and 1911; and established the *Taiwan seigeki renshuju* (Taiwan Orthodox Drama Company) in 1909, recruiting local students to study *shinpa* (new-style drama) and kabuki and perform in realistic settings on kabuki-style revolving stages (Shih, 2010). Because none of the xiqu genres in Taiwan used Hokkien Chinese,[1] then spoken by over 80 per cent of residents, Takamatsu created new Hokkien adaptations of current events and folk legends; these plays featured social issues such as child brides and Chinese settlers fighting against Manchurian Qing's feudalist rule.

Taiwan seigeki lasted for 7 years until the eventual loss of local interest, an ironic result of Takamatsu's contributions to Taiwan's theatrical infrastructure. New theatres built by Takamatsu attracted so many mainland troupes performing *jingju* (Beijing opera), *huidiao* (Anhui opera), *sipingdiao* (flower drum song) and *wenmingxi* (civilized drama) that locals much preferred these to what one critic dismissed as Takamatsu's 'awkward imitations of Japanese' (Shih 2010: 43).

The 1920s brought two attempts at local shingeki. Members of the Taiwan Bunka Kyokai (Taiwan Culture Association), who initiated the New Cultural Movement in 1921 to resist colonial rule in part by writing and performing in vernacular Chinese, founded several shingeki troupes. Political divisions and a lack of professional-level theatrical skills, however, hampered their efforts. More successful was Xingguang Yanju Yanjiuhui (Starlight Drama Research Association), led by Chang Wei-hsian (or Zhang Weixian, 1905–72). As self-proclaimed anarchists who loathed the theatrical conventions of Taiwanese opera, Starlight drew inspiration from wenmingxi performed in Amoy (Xiamen), a harbour city in Southern Fujian province where a dialect phonetically similar to Hokkien is spoken. In 1924, Starlight presented Hu Shi's *The Greatest Event in Life* together with three other pieces at Taipei's Novel Hall.[2] Their use of a local tongue won Starlight overnight success, but Chang disbanded the group in 1928 to study theatrical production and Dalcroze Eurhythmics in Tokyo. In 1930, Chang founded Minfeng Theatre Troupe, applying his new skills to plays such as Ibsen's *An Enemy of the People*. Four years later, he became the first to present Hokkien shingeki alongside Japanese shingeki.

Wartime struggle and the sound of resistance, 1936–49

From 1936 to 1949, Taiwan underwent the second Sino-Japanese War (1937–1945), the transferral of sovereignty to the Republic of China in 1945, the Chinese Civil War (1946–1949) and the KMT's retreat to Taiwan in 1949.

During the Kōminka movement, theatrical permits were granted only to those who performed in Japanese. Students were mobilized into youth shingeki troupes; local performers forced to 'cleanse' their work of music turned to these troupes for inspiration, resulting in a hybrid genre called *gailiang xi* (reformed shingeki).

Meanwhile, some Japanese-educated Taiwanese returned home and, alarmed by the restrictive assimilation policies, formed private shingeki troupes that looked like the youth troupes but gave voice to resistance. Futaba Kai (Double Leaf Troupe), established by Chien Kuo-hsian (Jian Guoxian, 1913–54), debuted with the 1943 premiere of Chien's *Mount Ali*, which re-imagined a Taiwanese aboriginal folktale as a drama of resistance against assimilation. Also in 1943, Lin Tuan-chiu (Lin Tuanqiu, 1920–98), former playwright for Tokyo Takarazuka Theatre Company (later to become Toho Co., Ltd.), co-founded the Kosei Theatre Society with former Starlight/Minfeng members. Lin's *Yanji* (Castrated Chicken), *Gaosha guan* (Takasago Hotel) and *Yide* (The Good Doctor) all won critical acclaim. In *Castrated Chicken*, Lin 'uses a traditional Chinese medicine shop as a metaphor for the tragic fate of the Taiwanese people' (Shih 2014: 24), cunningly utilizing Taiwanese folk songs and local Hokkien tunes to skirt the prohibition of Chinese languages on stage (25). Lin's works won the hearts of his Taiwanese audience and laid claim to a genuinely Taiwanese shingeki, subverting the colonial policy of assimilation. However short-lived the productions, Lin's plays are considered the dawn of the New Drama Movement.

The 1945 transfer of sovereignty to the Republic of China (ROC) brought a 're-sinicization' policy, provoking ambivalent response. Cultural endeavours interrupted by the Kōminka Movement resumed: former shingeki actors performed in Hokkien, folk artists developed a hybrid of shingeki and Taiwanese opera and Mandarin-speaking huaju troupes from China flocked to Taiwan, all contributing to a vibrant modern theatre. And yet, Mandarin became the national language, used not only in civil services but in film, modern theatre, radio and television. Hokkien was considered a 'dialect' and 'backward', and was prohibited in schools, though allowed in local traditional theatre. A split between Hokkien shingeki and the mainland's Mandarin huaju became inevitable.

Futaba founder Chien Kuo-hsien attacked KMT corruption in *Bi* (Wall, 1946). Chien wrote *Wall* first in Japanese, then in Chinese, and finally entrusted director Song Fei-wo (Song Feiwo, 1916–92) to translate into vernacular Hokkien. Produced by the new Sheng-feng Yanju Yanjiuhui (Holy Beacon Theatre Troupe), *Wall* features a stage literally split in two by a wall: on one side, 'wines and foods gone rotten are scattered behind the crimson doors'; on the other, 'corpses and skeleton are found frozen dead at the wayside' (Wu 1987: 190). *Wall* was a critical and popular hit, but was soon banned for 'provoking class struggle' (Ou 2013: 187). Holy Beacon scheduled another new work to premiere on 27 February 1947, but the run was cut short by the notorious 2/28 military crackdown.[3] Chien spent 6 years as a fugitive before being arrested and sentenced to death as a Chinese Communist spy in 1954. The script of *Wall* was unpublished until his widow released it after martial law was lifted in 1987, eventually publishing it in 1994. In 2013, Beijing authorities surprisingly acknowledged that Chien Kuo-hsien, long considered wrongly persecuted in Taiwan, had been among 'eight hundred anonymous communist comrades working undercover in Taiwan in the 1940s and 1950s' (Zhan 2013).

Transition and rehabilitation under repression, 1950–65

The 2/28 incident and ensuing martial law undoubtedly impeded cultural production. Wartime destruction of theatres, high rental prices for new and surviving venues, a heavy tax on public performances and the rise of film and television all presented formidable challenges. Amid all this, the so-called *fangong kang'e ju* (oppose communism, resist Russia drama) took centre stage.

In 1950, the KMT launched the Chinese Literature and Arts Award Committee (CLAAC) to 'encourage new creations that contribute to the development of nationalism and bestow the policy of opposing communism and resisting Russia' (Li 2003: 45). Generous awards attracted numerous scripts conveying designated political messages. The thematically monotonous huaju created from 1951 to 1959 attracted little attention, but the CLAAC was indicative of the KMT's new awareness of the political potential of cultural output; Taiwan's first higher education programmes in spoken drama were also established in the 1950s.

Just as audiences were tiring of propagandistic huaju, Li Man-kui (Li Mangui, 1907–75), congresswoman, western-educated scholar, playwright and CLAAC committee member, returned from overseas in 1960 and introduced Taiwan to western 'little theatre'. Li co-founded Zhongguo Huaju Xinshang Weiyuanhui (Chinese Association for Appreciation of Spoken Drama) to promote non-profit theatre productions by private troupes. She proposed replacing 'huaju', then synonymous with anti-communist drama, with *wutaiju* (staged drama). The enthusiastic response catalysed the emergence of not-for-profit little theatre and an art subsidy policy that would characterize Taiwan's modern theatre for decades.

The institutionalization of modern theatre, together with cultural policies and new technologies, impelled shingeki from the stage. Hong Kong's Amoy film industry inspired the production of Hokkien films in Taiwan, and many whose careers had begun in Taiwanese opera but had later been forced to perform reformed shingeki now worked in low-budget films marketed to locals. Other elite shingeki artists such as Chang Wei-hsian and Lin Tuan-chiu, who had created resistant drama during the Japanese rule, now sought to produce higher-quality projects. At Yufeng Film Co. and Hushan Studio, both established in 1958, Lin directed and produced five highly praised films before the companies closed down in 1965. Former shingeki actors and technicians who had transitioned from theatre to film had to shift again, this time to television. Mandarin has been Taiwan's primary onstage language ever since.

Tide of modernism, 1965–1979

Two festivals were established by Li Man-kui and CLAAC to nurture modern theatre in an age of television and film: the Shijie Juzhan (World Drama Festival [WDF], 1967–84) and the Qingnian Juzhan (Young Artists Festival [YAF], 1968–84). The WDF featured productions by college students majoring in foreign languages, while YAF productions were mainly by campus huaju clubs. Self-taught dramatist Yao Yi-wei (1922–97), also co-editor of *Modern Literature*, the advent of Taiwan's own modernist literature, published *Laizi fenghuangzhen de ren* (The Person from Phoenix Town) in 1963 and *Sun Feihu qiangqin* (Sun Feihu Kidnaps His Bride) in 1965. A contemporary adaptation of the thirteenth-century Chinese classic *Xixiang ji* (Romance of the West Chamber), *Sun Feihu* blends western classical drama with a story from dynastic China, tackling contemporary themes of identity and existentialism along the way.

Experiments in theatrical modernism were doubtless inspired partly by a broader quest for formal and thematic innovation, marked by the introduction of western modernist literature by *Literature* magazine in 1955, the establishment of *Modern Literature* magazine in 1960 and the *Wuyue Huahui* (Fifth Moon Group, after the Parisian Salon de Mai) in 1957, the import of American modern dance via José Limón in 1961 and Martha Graham in 1967, the relocation from Hong Kong to Taiwan of Mandarin-language filmmakers such as Richard Li Han-hsiang (Li Hanxiang, 1926–96) and King Hu (Hu Jinquan, 1932–97) starting in 1963, and the arrival of *Juchang* (Theatre) and *Ouzhou* (Europe) magazines in 1965, which introduced locals to absurdism, European surrealism and American 'happenings'.

In the 1970s, several notable artists returned from the United States, injecting Taiwanese performing arts with a renewed vigour. Lin Huai-min (1946–), who had trained with the Martha Graham Dance School and the Cunningham Dance Company, established Yunmen Wuji (Cloud Gate Dance Theatre), Taiwan's most renowned modern dance troupe, in 1973. In 1980, Gate's Yunmen Shiyan Juchang (Cloud Gate Experimental Theatre) began to foster Taiwan's first postwar generation of theatre technicians. Because of his brief experience with LaMama theatre in New York, psychology scholar Wu Jing-jyi (Wu Jingji, 1935–) was invited by Jin Shijie (1951–), Chuo Ming, Huang Cheng-huan and Hugh Kuo-Shiu Lee (Li Guoxiu, 1955–2013) to host Cardinal Tien's Experimental Theatre in 1976; they went on to found the Lan Ling Theatre Workshop in 1980, with a focus on physical theatre. In 1978, musician Hsu Po-yun (Xu Boyun, 1944–) established the now-legendary Xinxiang Wenhua Tuiguang Gongsi (New Aspect Promotion Cooperation), which hosted international artists and groups, including Shriram Bharatiyaka Kala Kendra (1979), Pinok and Matho Mime (1979), Zuini Icosahedron Theatre (1982), Merce Cunningham Dance Company and John Cage (1984), and the *butoh* troupe Byakko-Sha (1986) (Fan 2008: 20–35).

The 1970s also brought gradually relaxed political control and greater state expenditures on arts and culture. The transfer of the National Foundation for Arts and Literature from the Nationalist Party to the Ministry of Education in 1974, the inclusion of Cultural Construction in the Ten-Part National Development Plan in 1978 and the first government-sponsored International Festival of Arts in 1979 all contributed significantly to the development of arts in Taiwan.

Miracles and mystifications: the little theatre movement, 1980–94

The Experimental Theatre Festival launched in 1980, linking to Li Man-kui's little theatre (though this hardly reflects the diversity of modern theatre before and after the abolishment of martial law). The Festival produced xiqu adaptations such as *Hezhu xinpei* (Hezhu's Marriage, New Version, 1980), a modernized jingju comedy; a Yuan dynasty drama called *Jiu fengchen* (Rescue of Fallen Beauty); and innovative work such as *Women doshi zheyang zhangda de* (The Way We Grew Up, 1984), collectively created by Stan Lai (Lai Sheng-chuan, 1956–) and his students; and *Ziji de fangjian* (Closet in the Room, 1984), a self-reflective piece by the Malaysian-born Tsai Ming-liang (who would go on to become an acclaimed film director).[4]

With the 1983 establishment of the Committee for Cultural Construction and Development (CCCD), private troupes began working in larger, more commercial venues, seemingly at odds with the ethos of not-for-profit little theatre. Lan Ling Theatre Workshop collaborated with television actors on their large-scale *Daimian* (Masquerade) in 1983, and the Performance Workshop (under the direction of Stan Lai) went even further in marrying innovation to commercial success with *Nayiye women shuo xiangsheng* (One Evening, We Performed Crosstalks, 1984)[5] and *Anlian taohuayuan* (Secret Love in Peach Blossom Land, 1986). While the former adopted the form of a Beijing-based folk comic performance (a common approach at ETF), the latter exemplified modern theatre in Taiwan just before martial law was lifted in 1987. In the play, a melodrama huaju, 'Secret Love', has to rehearse on stage alongside period farce 'Peach Blossom Land' due to limited space and incompetent management, a farcical snapshot of Taiwan in transition.

A boom in small-scale, experimental-leaning troupes ensued.[6] The 'martial law generation' produced works that were daring in both content and form. Li Huan-hsiun (Li Huanxiong, 1962–) co-founded the Hezuo'an Jutuan (Rive-Gauche Theatre Group) in 1986 to produce aesthetically poetic theatre of images. Visual artist Tian Chi-yuan (Tian Qiyuan, 1964–96) established Linjiedian Juxianglu (Critical Point Theatre) in 1988, premiering with *Mao shi* (Homosexual Love in China, 1988), which posited that Confucius may have been gay and criticized ruling authorities who denied and concealed the presence of homosexuality through-out history.[7] Several members of Lan Ling left to form new troupes, each with its own style. Prominent actress Liu Ching-min (Liu Ruoyu, 1956–) returned from studying with Grotowski in California to establish U Juchang (U Theatre Troupe) in 1988. Hugh K. S. Lee (1955–2013) and his Pingfeng Biaoyanban (Ping-fong Acting Troupe), founded in 1986, produced probably the island's best comedies until Lee's death in 2013; touring to Shanghai in 1994, Ping-fong was also the first modern theatre troupe from Taiwan to tour in China since 1949. Such innovative artistic energy often leads critics and scholars to over-interpretation. Li Huan-hsiung once mentioned in the 2003 interview conducted by the author that critics had called his early work derivative of Pina Bausch, but that he 'hadn't even heard of the name back then'.

Much as Taiwan's democratic reform peaked in the 1990s, theatre practitioners stopped seeing theatrical reform as their primary goal. Art management and professionalism became the new focus. Guotuo Jutuan (Godot Theatre Troupe, established 1988) and Lüguang Jutuan (Greenray Theatre Troupe, established 1993) turned commercial and began producing Mandarin musical theatre in 1995 and 1994, respectively, and Greenary went on to collaborate with screenwriter Wu Nianzhen on productions of *guomin xiju* (drama for the ordinary people) beginning in 2001. By then, four former little theatre groups, including Performance Workshop, Ping-fong, Godot and Greenray, had become self-sustainable. Art subsidies in Taiwan evolved to promote independent management in the arts, discouraging political interference, but not commercialism.

Marching towards industrialization?

Cuts to subsidies were offset by talk of upgrading the creative industry and a value-added economy as the Law for the Development of the Cultural and Creative Industries (CCI) took effect in 2010. The number of new modern stage productions grew from 700 in 2004 to 900 in 2009. Though the growing modern theatre community seemed to have responded to the policy shift with apparent fervour, the professionalization of performing arts in Taiwan is ongoing, and it is unrealistic to expect near-term industrialization. Whatever its promise, CCI represents a crisis for many: a reduction in the subsidies that have been so vital to the evolution of modern theatre in Taiwan.

At least two troupes established in the 1990s have thrived. Jinzhi Yanshe (Golden Bough Theatre) was established in 1993 by Wang Rong-yu, former member of Lan Ling, guest dancer of Cloud Gate's *Songs of Wanderer* and erstwhile student of the Grotowski method. Wang revived the hybrid form of *gezaixi* (Taiwanese opera) and shingeki passed down by his actress mother; the company is now the only modern theatre troupe that regularly performs in Hokkien. Chuangzuoshe Jutuan (Creative Society Theatre Ensemble), co-founded in 1997 by seven artists, is among the few troupes to focus on original works about Taiwan. To defy the misconception that 'experimental' theatre must also mean poorly made little theatre, Creative Society mounts polished productions of original work by founding members Chi Wei-ran (Ji Weiran), Li Huang-hsiung, Katherine Hui-ling Chou (Zhou Huiling) and Wei Ying-chuan (Wei Yingjuan), as well as emerging playwrights such as Zan Jae (Zhan Jie).[8] Golden Bough and Creative Society have brought to a tentative détente the long struggle for decolonization fought by Taiwan's theatre practitioners as they have sought to develop voices of their own. The former brings into new life the hybrid cultural product of the Japanese colonization, which dwindled in the 1960s pro-mainland KMT rule. The latter endeavoured to foster more theatrical imaginations about Taiwan onstage, enriching the foreign-imported genre with the island's diverse socio-cultural heritages (Figure 15.2).

Figure 15.2 A scene from *Shaonian jinchai nan Meng Mu* (He is My Wife, He is My Mother, 2009), produced by Creative Society, written and directed by Katherine Hui-ling Chou.

III. Korea, by Yun-Cheol Kim

Modern Korean theatre began with the introduction of western theatre and indoor theatre buildings around the time when Korea was annexed to Japan in 1910. Before that, Korean theatre was represented by *pansori* (narrative and dramatic singing) and *talchum* (mask dance-drama). These traditional forms were very flexible depending on the interaction they had with the audience: their dramatic structure and style of performance were frequently adjusted to the demand, expectation and response from the audience (Seo and Lee 2000: 22). They were quite proto-theatrical.

It is a widely accepted notion that *singeuk* (literally 'new theatre', meaning modern Korean theatre) began with the performance of *Eunsegye* (The Silver World) in 1908 at Korea's first indoor theatre Hyeomnyulsa. Adapted from Lee In-jik's novel, this play was done in the pansori style, but with stark modifications: its narrative was realistic rather than folkloric; its roles were not performed and sung by a single performer as before but assigned to several singers; and it employed an indoor set. Before delving into the development of singeuk, a term borrowed from the Japanese *shingeki* (new theatre), we need to pay attention to *sinpageuk*, which was also borrowed from the Japanese *shinpa* (new school theatre) in the same period, a hybrid of *kabuki* and western spoken drama. Later, shinpa was followed by the shingeki theatre movement as the Japanese society moved towards modernization by westernization. Japan had covertly attempted to suppress traditional Korean culture and transplant Japanese shinpa theatre even before its annexation of Korea (Kim 2013: 15). Throughout the 1910s sinpageuk dominated Korea, led by the Japan-educated Lim Seong-gu (1887–1921), Yun Baek-nam (1888–1954) and Lee Ki-sae (dates unknown). They adapted shinpa plays, discussed real social matters and dramatized serialized novels in daily newspapers. They also created actor-centred popular theatres. Murder, revenge, love scandals and domestic tragedy became frequent themes of this trend, usually culminating in rewarding the good and punishing the evil. Sensationalism and excessive emotionalism were its predominant production aesthetics.

Against this banal sinpageuk, the singeuk movement was initiated by intellectuals, mostly those who were studying in Japan in the 1910s and after. They introduced western dramatists, mostly Irish, such as William Butler Yeats, Lady Gregory, John Millington Synge and others. Just like the Irish playwrights who tried to awaken the national spirit under colonization, the singeuk activists wanted to achieve the same educational goals for the colonized Koreans with realistic plays. Between the 1920s and the liberation from the Japanese rule in 1945, the majority of the plays introduced were realistic and naturalistic dramas by modern European dramatists such as Henrik Ibsen, August Strindberg, Anton Chekhov, Leo Tolstoy and Ivan Turgenev, romantic plays by Victor Hugo and modernist plays by Gerhart Hauptmann and Eugene O'Neill. Korean intellectuals used the theatre to enlighten the public about modern western ideas of democracy and the rights of individuals, and to encourage national consciousness. This helped Korean theatre to shift from staging in the style of sinpageuk, a sensationalist, exaggerated emotional approach, to staging in the style of singeuk, a more natural, true-to-life one. Stanislavsky was also introduced at this time and facilitated the movement. This new realistic approach to staging was perpetrated most importantly by director Hong Hae-seong (1894–1957) in the 1930s. He was a member of the Japanese Tsukiji Little Theatre in Tokyo under the leadership of Osanai Kaoru (1881–1928), where he learnt and practised realistic staging and acting by the Stanislavsky system for 5 years from 1924 to 1929 (Seo 2000: 183). By far the most important singeuk playwright was Kim Woo-jin (1897–1926). He created a theatre company called Geukyesulhyeophoe (Theatrical Art society) in 1920 with Hong Hae-seong and others who were studying in Japan. Kim Woo-jin was the leader of the singeuk movement, with multiple talents: he translated and wrote about European plays, invested money for his company productions, directed his own translations and wrote five experimental plays, including *Lee Yeong-nyeo* (1925), which deals with prostitution in the manner of Shaw's *Mrs. Warren's Profession*, *Nanpa* (Shipwreck, 1926) in expressionist style and *Sandoeji* (The Wild Boar, 1926), which employs all styles from realism, naturalism and symbolism to expressionism to express the life-force of a young Korean man.

Hong Hae-seong was the first full-fledged stage director in Korea with rich and long experience as a staff member at the Tsukiji Little theatre, which was known as the best shingeki theatre of Japan. With Kim Woo-jin, he advocated for director-centred play production, the little theatre movement, theatre education for the public, training professional set designers, the Stanislavsky system and faithful interpretation and production of the dramatist's spirit (Seo and Lee 2000: 96–99).

The most important group in this vein, however, was Geukyesulyeonguhoe (The Theatre Arts Study Group, hereinafter The Group). It was formed in 1931 and served as a driving force of the modern theatre movement until it was forcibly closed down by the Japanese government in 1938. The Group staged thirty-two plays, including twelve Korean plays. It was particularly successful in the realistic staging of western dramas, most of which were directed by afore-mentioned Hong Hae-seong. The Group launched the little theatre movement in the 1930s and attempted to create some good examples of the naturalistic staging of European drama. Its greatest achievement, however, was the discovery of director-playwright Yu Chi-jin (1905–74). After Hong left the Group, Yu directed most of its repertories, but his major achievement is found in his own plays. He was not happy with the dominance of European plays over Korean ones, nor with Japanese censorship separating Koreans from their cultural tradition (Yang, 1996: 145). He wrote realistic plays beginning with *Tomak* (A Shabby House, 1931), a tragedy of two poor families that shocked people with its realistic portrait of characters; *Binminga* (The Slum, 1933), a tragedy of poor labourers; *So* (The Oxen, 1935), a well-made play about struggling farmers; *Chunhyangjeon* (The Story of Chunhyang, 1936), his first history play; *Maeuitaeja* (Prince Maeui, 1937), the first of his major history plays, and many others. He continued to write plays until the late 1950s. Near the end of his career, his dominant style was melodrama, as shown in *Nadoinganidoeryeonda* (I, too, Want to Be a Man, 1953) and *Jamae* (Sisters, 1955).

In the 1930s, another outstanding playwright, Ham Se-deok, emerged with his *Sanheoguri* (Mountainside, 1936), which is very similar both thematically and structurally to Synge's *Riders to the Sea*. He extended the theme further 5 years later with *Mueuidogihaeng* (Journey to Mueui Island). *Dongseung* (Child Buddhist, 1939) is known as his best realist play by far, which links human love with the Buddha's enlightenment. With Yu Chi-jin and Ham Se-deok flourishing in the 1930s, the realist tradition of modern Korean theatre was partially established (Kim 1985: 203–4).

Between liberation in 1945 and the end of the Korean War in 1953, theatre productions were minimal, although there were some ideological agitprop theatre productions. It is remark-able, however, that Korea's most talented comic dramatist, Oh Yeong-jin, debuted in this theatrically dormant period with *Maengjinsadaekgyeongsa* (The Wedding Day of Maengjinsa's Family, 1943), which is a social satire in the form of slapstick on the traditional arrangement of marriage. Another of his plays, *Saraitnunleejungsaenggaka* (His Excellency Lee Jungsaeng Is Alive, 1946), is performed relatively frequently even today, with a darker theme but sharper characterization of the principal who collaborates with the Japanese government during its rule and continues anti-Korean activities even after liberation.

It was only after the U.S.-led UN forces succeeded in preserving the political system of South Korea after the Korean War that theatre became revived significantly. The war left a huge trauma in the conscious and subconscious of Koreans and it has been one of the permanent subject matters of Korean theatre ever since. Two plays among so many deserve our special attention: Cha Beom-seok's *Sanbul* (Mountain Fire, 1962) and Noh Gyeong-sik's *Daljib* (House of the Moon, 1971). *Mountain Fire* is widely recognized as the best realist play since liberation. Surprisingly, it does not deal with ideological conflicts between North and South, but with basic human desires between a woman of the South and a soldier from the North in an extremely difficult and dangerous situation of war. *House of the Moon* is more epic in structure, dealing with the tragedies of three generations of women in a family between Japanese rule and the Korean War.

The period between the beginning of the 1960s and the mid-1980s coincides with the 25 years of de facto military governance under three generals-turned-president, initiated by Park Jeong-hee in 1961. The military dictatorship limited freedom of speech through rigid censorship, and the theatre was no exception. A striking fact of this time was that absurdist dramatists Ionesco, Beckett and Albee were the three most frequently produced western dramatists. The theatre of the absurd was a big leap for a Korean audience that had been exposed almost exclusively to realistic western drama.

Based on the fact that so many young college graduates founded community theatres, many scholars agree that contemporary Korean theatre began in the early 1960s. Groups such as Shilheomgeukjang (The Experimental Theatre), Gwangjang (The Plaza), Dari (The Bridge), Jayu (Liberty) and Minjung (The People) all began to produce non-realist western drama, including modified realism, epic and avant-garde theatre. Among these diverse styles, theatre of the absurd exerted the greatest influence on contemporary Korean theatre. There were more productions of absurd drama in the 1960s than in any other decade. Its influence on Korean theatre was first seen in the plays of Park Jo-yeol (1930–), Lee Hyun-hwa (1943–), and O Tae-seok (1940–).

The 1960s is very remarkable in Korean theatre history, because people first began to recognize as a common goal the importance of establishing a national identity in their works. Playwright Yun Dae-seong (1939–) was the first to use traditional masks in his play *Mangnani* (The Executioner, 1969), a social satire on the corruption of the ruling class. This is considered the first attempt to combine a western tragic narrative and elements of Korean traditional performing arts. O Tae-seok followed suit, but to better effect, helped by two outstanding directors, Yoo Deok-hyeong (1938–) and Ahn Min-soo (1940–). He became Korea's foremost playwright with *Chobun* (Grass Tombs, 1973) and *Tae* (Lifecord, 1974), which were directed by Yoo and Ahn, respectively. For *Grass Toms* Yoo employed western experimental theatre styles and the choreographed movements of Asian martial arts to create an impressive non-verbal theatre. Ahn applied an Artaudian style to *Lifecord*, a historical drama of the most tragic and destructive father–son relationship in the Yi dynasty's (1392–1909) royal families.

Under the severe censorship of the time, Korean theatre artists developed a theatrical form called *madanggeuk* (yard theatre), a kind of guerrilla theatre, based on the principles of the traditional mask dance-drama. The mask dance-drama has long sympathized with the struggling and abused common people, and criticized the corrupt ruling class. Madangeuk is a postmodern political theatre, performed in the form of site-specific theatre. The place and time for the show were communicated secretly, and the performers fled the site after each performance to avoid arrest by the police. Later, it was developed into the form of musical theatre by director Sohn Jin-chaek, who created the genre called *madangnori*.

From the 1970s on, intercultural theatre has become a prominent phenomenon of contemporary Korean theatre. One of its first examples of this vein is O Tae-seok's *Soetuggi nori* (Servant Soetuggi's Play, 1972), which adapted Moliere's *The Tricks of Scapin* to Korean traditional mask dance-drama. Ahn Min-soo also adapted and directed Shakespeare's *Hamlet* based on Buddhist perspective in his *Hamyoltaeja* (Prince Hamyeol, 1976). Kim Jeong-ok (1932–) reinterpreted Garcia Lorca's *Blood Wedding* (1982), using traditional Korean clowning, shamanistic dance, music and chanting. The most distinguishing characteristic of contemporary Korean intercultural theatre from the 1990s on is the rereading of those classics only as excuses or devices to develop Korean issues. O Tae-seok staged his adaptation of *Romeo and Juliet* (2001), which uses the background of Korean history under Japanese control. He stunned the audience, both foreign and domestic, by reversing the ending with a holocaust, with even much stronger hostility between the two family factions. He also adapted Shakespeare's *The Tempest* (2011) in the setting of tenth-century Korea. Other well-known artists include Yang Jeong-woong (1968–), the most internationalist director in Korea who has adapted Shakespeare's *A Midsummer Night's Dream* (2002) into *Hanyeorumbameuikum*, a Korean folk play of goblins; Lee Yun-taek (1952–), who put *Hamlet* (1996) in the frame of a Korean shamanic ritual; and Lee Zaram, who wrote the music and performed in her own adaptations of Bertolt Brecht's *A Good Woman of Setzuan* and *Mother Courage and Her Children*, which she transformed into Korean pansori – or 'one-person opera' – performances, *Sacheon-ga* (Song of Szechwan, 2008) and *Ukchuk-ga* (Song of Mother Courage, 2012), respectively. She plays more than fifteen characters in each show. She writes and sings her own pansori music, transforming the form of pansori from theatrical music into musical theatre.

Recently, a new approach to intercultural theatre has been adopted by a young director named Kim Hyun-tak (1970–), who frequently adapts classical western texts, but without 'Koreanizing' them. His theatre has no obsession with the 'Koreanness' that has long preoccupied his predecessors. *Medea on Media* (2011), which Kim Hyun-tak has adapted from Euripides' play, for example, is not approached psychologically at all. As the title implies, Kim puts *Medea*

Figure 15.3 A scene from Kim Hyun-tak's production of Kim Hyun-tak's *Death of a Salesman*.
(Courtesy Kim Hyun-tak)

in today's culture, dominated by the political power of the media. Medea is neither the usual character of a woman full of homicidal hysteria, nor a warrior of feminist fights. She is deconstructed both psychologically *and* ideologically. Likewise, he even puts Willy Loman on a treadmill and makes him run throughout the 80-minute show of *Death of a Salesman* (2010, Figure 15.3).

Starting in the 1990s, it was feminist theatre that made up the most popular stream in Korean theatre. Feminist ideas had long been suppressed in Korea's Confucian, patriarchal society – but once unleashed, they exploded all at once. The most successful achievement in this vein, in terms of aesthetic and thematic approach, is *Lady Macbeth* (1998), restructured and directed by Han Tae-sook (1950–). She remains faithful to Shakespeare's narrative frame, but refocuses it on Lady Macbeth's reactions, resulting in a form of hypnotic or therapeutic theatre. She reinforces Lady Macbeth's subconscious with the performance art of Lee Young-ran's object theatre, and accompanies these with a live band, Gong-myeoung, which plays traditional Korean music, so as to make a hybrid theatre.

Writings and performances related to gay love used to be as marginalized as feminist theatre was, but it has also become a theme of contemporary Korean theatre. There have been several Korean plays dealing very cautiously with this subject matter. Among them, *Seo-an yolcha* (The Train for Seo-An, 2003), again written and directed by Han Tae-sook, is by far the most successful. The play is set against the story of Emperor Qingshi Huang of China's Qin dynasty (221–206 BCE), who filled his tomb with clay soldiers and horses to protect himself from ageing and death, and highlights a man's desire to possess another man by confiscating all his documents and memory. Director Han invited artist Lim Ok-sang (1949–) to sculpt contemporary versions of the clay figures and, as with her *Lady Macbeth*, employed Gong-myeong, the traditional percussion band, confirming once again the identity of her theatre.

At the same time, 'history theatre' stands exceptionally at the centre of contemporary Korean theatre. It does not approach history with facts, but looks back with a revisionist's eye on errors in history and calls for a new history, or history as it should have been. For example, Lee Yun-taek consistently questions the social responsibility of intellectuals in his dealings with history. His first history play, *Munjejeokinganyeonsan* (Problematic Person, King Yeon-san, 1995), looks into this question. In the play, intellectuals easily change sides according to where power lies. The ruling aristocracy's orientation towards power is skilfully woven into the story of King Yeon-san, who was arguably the most vengeful and womanizing king in the history of the Yi dynasty (1392–1897).

The most distinguishable and important dramatic form in Korea since 2000 is the theatre of everydayness. Park Keun-hyeong (1963–), another dramatist who directs his own plays, has been the main catalyst in this vein. Beginning with *Cheongchunyechan* (Homage to Youth, 1999), he has been writing a couple of plays every year, that are mostly centred on disintegrating families: fathers have lost their power; mothers are either dead or deadly aloof from their children; and children miss their families even before they disintegrate. *Amudomulsogeseo sumshijiannunda* (Nobody Breathes in the Water), 2000), *Jib* (The Hous, 2002) and *Kyeong-Sook, Kyeong-Soogiabeoji* (Kyeongsook, Kyeongsoogi's Dad, 2006) are good examples of this track. *Neomunolagimara* (Don't Panic Too Much, 2009) is by far the best in terms of dramatic form and its thematic contemporaneity. With the situation and characters similar to those of Sam Shepard's *Buried Child*, or Harold Pinter's *The Homecoming*, Park continues his portraits of the absurd world. With Father as present absence, Mother as absent presence, an irresponsible first son, his wife flirting extra-maritally and in front of her brother-in-law, the second son suffering from constipation and missing Mother who has deserted the family – the composition of the family itself foregrounds the disintegration of the family. Park is epitomizing familial disintegration through the minutely detailed everydayness of the dramatic actions; he also transcends the limits of realism and moves towards absurdism or modified realism by employing highly expressive devices. Choi Jin-a (1968–) has recently joined this group with her *1dong28Beonjichasookine* (1–28, Cha-Sook's House, 2010), in which she lectures about house construction by way of her characters, who are trying to build a new house on the site of their old house. No particular dramatic purpose is revealed. They just recollect their memories of the old house and their late father who built it, and try to realize their concept of how a house should be designed. The dramatic action flows from the discussion to the completion of the house's construction. One common feature of these writers is that they write these everyday plays in order to highlight the absurdity of our daily lives, which have already become absurd enough.

Modern Korean theatre began in the early 1920s, when the country was under Japanese rule, by those students who studied in Tokyo and were heavily influenced by Japanese theatre productions. Realism was their preoccupation. As Korea went through big social changes caused by liberation from Japan in 1945, the Korean War (1950–3) and coup d'état (1961), however, the themes and styles of theatre have changed accordingly. National traumas, from Japanese colonization, ideological division to brutal war, were predominantly dealt with. For a quite long while after the military coup, Korean theatre turned to the theatre of the absurd in order to avoid censorship, while delivering social dissatisfaction with the then dictatorship. Aesthetically, people began to seek 'Koreanness' in their styles by adopting those principles of the Korean traditional performing arts for their contemporary subject matters. Ever since Korea became really democratic in 1986, intercultural theatre that mingles the aesthetics of Korean traditional performing arts and western classic texts has prevailed. Recently, however, young theatre artists are trying to transcend this nationalist approach and go global with their concentration on the everydayness of life in their theatre productions.

IV. North Korea, by Ji Hyon (Kayla) Yuh

What we now consider as 'North Korean' theatre has roots in colonial Korea, where there were complicated yet vibrant theatrical activities despite the growing oppression and censorship from imperial Japanese forces in Korea. Along with Korean productions of western classics such as Chekhov's *Three Sisters* and Maurice Maeterlinck's *The Blue Bird*, there were plays by homegrown playwrights about the lives of Koreans in colonial Korea (Jang 2005: 295, 328–9). Among them were Song Young (1903–77) and Ham Se-deok (1915–50), who later became the first generation of theatre artists in North Korea. When Korea was divided in the wake of the nation's independence from Japan in 1945, the North was under the trusteeship of the Soviet Union, and many theatre artists who were predisposed to socialist ideals relocated themselves to the North. Therefore, the earliest stage of North Korean theatre, especially when it came to the spoken drama, exhibited socialist and pro-proletariat dispositions with close ties to literary and theatrical traditions of Soviet Union and East European theatre.

However, this tradition faced an abrupt break after the Korean War, as Kim Il-sung consolidated his military dictatorship and established *juche* (self-reliance) ideology to be the governing principle of the nation.[9] Theatre, along with other art forms, soon became a crucial instrument to idolize Kim Il-sung as the legitimate and almost omnipotent leader of the nation. To that end, the contributions and legacies of the first generation of theatre artists in the North were erased from official records in favour of the alleged theatrical achievements of Kim Il-sung created during the years when he battled against the Japanese army in the 1920s.

Through an extensive campaign entitled *Munye hyeongmyeong* (Revolution of Literature and Art), Kim Il-sung's legacy was reinvented and established as the single root of North Korean theatre. In assisting his father Kim Il-sung, Kim Jong-il, as the future successor of the leadership, firmly believed in the utilitarian merits of art and literature, especially film, as a way to further education and propaganda for the government. Accordingly, he devised campaigns in the fields of film, *gageuk* (music drama) and theatre to modernize North Korean art and literature, and make them more readily applicable and accessible to contemporary audiences, with close and relatable role models for them to emulate and learn from. Furthermore, it was through this campaign that a set of detailed ground rules for creating and promoting art and literature were established in order to propagate the theories and mandates of juche ideology.

Kim Jong-il launched *Gageuk hyeongmyeong* (Revolution of Music Drama) at the end of the 1960s and chose *Pibada* (Sea of Blood, 1971) as the first work of *hyeongmyeong gageuk* (revolutionary gageuk). Initially written by Kim Il-sung under the title of *Hyeolhae*, a transliteration of the Chinese title of the same meaning, *Sea of Blood* was allegedly produced as a play during his anti-Japanese battles in Manchuria in 1936. As a story of an ordinary mother who becomes a revolutionary fighter against the oppressive Japanese army, it provides a portrayal of North Korean society under Japanese occupation through the challenges that the mother endured. The mother figure is used to instil in the audience the value of choosing to serve the state at the expense of one's personal comfort, by showing how she rose above the oppression of the Japanese colonial forces under the guidance and encouragement of the Dear Leader, Kim Il-sung.

Premiered in 1971, *Sea of Blood* proved to be successful to the extent that it gave birth to a few social movements which showed that people empathized with the characters they saw on stage, and wanted to emulate them in obeying Kim Il-sung's commands both at work and at home. Moreover, the songs from the production soon became popular songs, and were sung and enjoyed outside the theatre. In fact, music was one of Kim Jong-il's main innovations during the campaign (Chun 2013: 218–19). The music of *Sea of Blood* was mostly tonal with many instances of leaps and disjunctions in melody, which was intended to magnify the robust and strong sentiment of the show. Most of the songs followed a simple structure of *jeolga* (stanzaic song) so that the audience could easily sing along and empathize with the struggles of the characters on stage. Another significant element was *pangchang* (song-aside), which often served as a third-person commentary that embodied the agenda of the state, as it was the voice of the offstage reality. Following the success of *Sea of Blood*, other Pibada-style revolutionary gageuk pieces were produced in the 1970s, including *A True Daughter of the Party* (1971); *The Flower Girl* (1972); *Tell O' the Forest!* (1972); and *The Song of Mount Geumgang* (1973). They all shared very similar anti-Japanese sentiment in their theme.

Yeongeuk hyeongmyeong (Revolution of Drama), the third instalment of the campaign, began in the early 1970s, coinciding with successful gageuk productions. The main purpose of the campaign was similar to that of the Revolution of Gageuk, in that the government wanted to modernize outmoded traditional plays that did not embody the ideological values of the nation. It was also during this phase that Kim Jong-il officially recognized *hangil hyeongmyeong yeongeuk* (anti-Japanese revolutionary drama), a body of plays by a group of young guerrilla soldiers who fought against the Japanese colonial army during the 1920s and 30s, as the true origin of North Korean drama. From the repertoire that had been available, Kim Jong-il chose *Seonghwangdang* (*The Shrine*) to be the first North Korean revolutionary drama to be produced by the state-run Gungnip Yeongeukdan (National Theatre Company), the one and only producer of staged plays in North Korea (Min 2001: 34, 2002: 367). What was particularly significant about this decision was that proclaiming the tradition of anti-Japanese revolutionary drama to be the only legitimate root of contemporary North Korean theatre essentially placed Kim Il-sung as its sole root, as Kim Il-sung is supposed to have taken a central role in the creation of the genre (Park 2007: 139).

As with the case of *Sea of Blood*, the original script for *The Shrine* was also attributed to none other than Kim Il-sung himself, supposedly written in 1928 when he battled against the Japanese colonial army in Manchuria. The original text of the play is said to have been lost, and it could be argued that *The Shrine*, which was adapted and produced in 1978, is a new creation and an outcome of the ideas set forth through the Revolution of Drama. Kim Jong-il, however, placed great value on the core message of the new adaptation, which allegedly shared that of the original creation by Kim Il-sung. Consequently, possessing the right kind of message remained essential in the tradition of Revolutionary Drama that followed *The Shrine*.

The play revolves around the scheme of a wise male servant, Dolsoe, who enlightens people about the importance and possibility of being one's own master. Dolsoe employs a series of plans that reveal the foolishness of the negative characters, who are represented by a landlord, a magistrate of the town and various types of religious people such as a Christian lady and a well-known shaman of the town. *The Shrine* works as a satire, but unlike previous examples of satire that featured one-dimensional characters and conflicts, it tells a story of the complex and realistic struggles of more lifelike characters to which the contemporary North Korean audience could relate, and more importantly, learn from (Park 2007: 151).

The Shrine's significance does not only lie in its narrative and message, which were in line with juche ideology. Kim Jong-il implemented renovations in stage technology and playwriting strategies that would maximize and enhance juche realism, a form of social realism that is more specific to juche ideology. One of them was a dramaturgical convention that was named *dajangmyeon guseonghyeongsik* (multi-scenic compositi_became distant from the lives of ordinary North Korean men and women. This was the impetus behind the changes that came about in the 1980s for gageuk and in the 1990s for plays.

For gageuk, there emerged a new genre called *hyeongmyeongjeok minjok gageuk* (revolutionary national gageuk), or *Pibada*-style minjok gageuk (*Pibada*-style national gageuk). The first production of this new genre was *Chunhyangjeon* (The Story of Chunhyang), a gageuk based on one of the most widely known folk tales about a love story between Chunhyang, the daughter of a prostitute, and Mongryong, the son of an aristocrat. One of the most significant thematic differences between the play's earlier forms and its revolutionary national gageuk version can be found in the portrayal of Wolmae, Chunhyang's mother, and Bangja, Mongryong's servant. Originally, Wolmae was a retired prostitute who provided comic relief along with Bangja. However, in the new version, Wolmae and Bangja were portrayed as more serious characters, which added more weight to them and reinforced the revolutionary attitude of these two proletariat characters.

As a *Pibada*-style national gageuk, the similarity between *Sea of Blood* and *The Story of Chunhyang* could be found in their uses of jeolga and pangchang, as well as the importance placed on juche socialism. However, the new production of *The Story of Chunhyang* took into consideration the critiques against *Pibada*-style revolutionary gageuk, which were that the form was too westernized and that it seemed to have lost touch with tradition, especially in terms of its music and content. It was to remedy such criticism that *The Story of Chunhyang* was revisited, because it was, and remains, one of the best-known folktales in Korea. Moreover, the details of the musical conventions had changed in *Pibada*-style national gageuk compared to *Pibada*-style revolutionary gageuk. For example, *The Story of Chunhyang*'s score pursued traditional Korean sound and melody by using more modern adaptations of traditional musical instruments (Chun 2013: 404–7).

When it came to plays, revolutionary drama continued to be written and produced, but since the 1990s only a few new works have been added to the repertoire. In fact, the 1990s proved to be one of the most difficult decades faced by the North Koreans, with Kim Il-sung's death, economic hardship, and famine that crippled the nation. Given this situation, Kim Jong-il sought to strengthen his new leadership by prioritizing the North Korean army, and carried out a campaign called *Seongun Hyeongmyong* (Military-First Revolution). During this time, *gyeonghuigeuk* (light comedy), a genre of plays that had existed since the 1950s, was updated to *hyeongmyeongjeok gyeonghuigeuk* (revolutionary light comedy) to embody the legacies of revolutionary drama yet reflect the changed time. Following the conventions found in revolutionary drama, revolutionary light comedy sought to teach the manners and perspective of North Koreans to support the government agenda during the period of Military-First Revolution. Therefore, the plays of this tradition focused on the greatness of Kim Jong-il as their new leader, and also the solidarity that people should establish with the soldiers who were to be the backbone of society. For example, in *Cheollyeong* (The Hill of Cheollyeong), which is often quoted as the representative work for revolutionary light comedy, the people of a town join forces with the soldiers in climbing up a hill known for its rugged and dangerous trails. Kim Jong-il's presence figures heavily in encouraging the soldiers and townspeople to finish the task. *The Hill of Cheollyeong* is also notable in that it hints at the possible new direction for playwriting, as the play features a poet who serves as a narrator at times.

Another performance genre that is more widely known to those who live outside North Korea is the Grand Mass Games and Artistic Performance, which began in 1999 under Kim Jong-il's guidance. As the name indicates, it is a hybrid genre that merges mass games with performances of dance, music, acrobatics and storytelling, staged at a large stadium with more than 100,000 performers and spectators. Instituted in 2000 through a production titled *Baekjeon baekseung Chosun nodongdang* (Invincible Workers Party of Korea), the production of *Arirang* in 2002 firmly instituted the form as a new performance genre for the new century that is capable of further cultivating the participants' allegiance to the leadership and the government (Park 2007: 217).[10]

It is clear that the history of North Korean theatre has been very closely related to the political circumstances, the agenda of the government and the specific leadership. One of the changes that Kim Jong-un has implemented since he took office in 2012 was to expand the role of Chosun Jungang Yesul Bogeupsa (The Office of Chosun Central Art Distribution), a government body that was established in 1972 by Kim Jong-il to ensure centralized control over the marketing, sales and distribution of all theatrical productions. In 2012, Kim Jong-un renamed it Gukga Gongyeon Yesul Unyeongguk (National Theatrical Art Management Agency), and added programming and archiving responsibilities to the organization's main function, thus further strengthening government control in theatre productions across the nation. Also, Moranbong Akdan (Moranbong Band), an all-female band, has been gaining popularity since Kim Jong-un took office, which further contributed to the proliferation and dissemination of the popular music that often comes out of gageuk pieces.

Technology has also given North Koreans greater access to South Korean popular culture, but they remain underground, as people would be penalized for the possession and distribution of such materials. For now, theatrical productions remain under the strict control of the government, and we must wait and see how Kim Jong-un and his governments utilize theatre for the new leadership in what is turning out to be a more volatile political and social environment.

Notes

1 Part of this section was derived from research projects sponsored by Ministry of Science and Technology, ROC. My gratitude to their generous support.
2 *Gezaixi* (Taiwanese Opera), the only xiqu genre to originate in Taiwan, was not created until the 1920s.
3 The other three works were *Furong Jie* (Calamity of Beauty), *Bamu xi* (Eight-Acts Play) and *Huoli lianhua* (Lotus in Ashes).
4 The 2/28 Incident is an anti-government uprising that resulted in the massacre of over ten thousand civilians starting on 28 February 1947.

5 Video of the 1992 revival of *Closet in the Room* can be viewed at eti-tw.com, an electronic archive hosted by the author.
6 The English title of this play was provided and confirmed in a 2014 email from Stan Lai.
7 By 1992, about fifty-four troupes had been established in Taiwan (Hwang, 1996: 199–222).
8 Video of both works is available at eti-tw.com.
9 Works by Golden Bough and Creative Society are available at eti-tw.com.
10 Although based on classic Marxist/Leninist thought, juche is unique in that it emphasizes self-reliance, and demands that North Korean proletariats should be masters of their own fate. As observed by Johannes Schönherr, it was juche ideology that allowed North Korea to keep a certain distance from the Soviet Union and China and protect the country's autonomy against two powerful countries that used to be North Korea's allies (Schönherr 2012: 35). Juche ideology was possible in North Korea because it was preceded and accompanied by a thorough idolization and indoctrination of the superiority of the country's infallible and all-powerful leader, Kim Il-sung, who protected the helpless North Koreans from all enemies with his wisdom and strength which often seem almost superhuman (McEachern 2010: 51–82). By the 1960s, Kim Il-sung's charismatic and totalitarian leadership as well as the tenets of juche ideology, which are self-reliance, self-sustenance and self-defence, had become the pillars that would sustain North Korean society for many years to come.
11 Since its last production in 2013, *Arirang* mass games have been cancelled for 2 consecutive years for reasons unclear to the public.

Bibliography

Chang Wei-hsian (1954) 'Wo de yanju huiyi' (My Life on Stage), Taipei Wenwu (Taipei Cultural Relic), 2 (3): 104–113; reprinted in Zeng Xianzhang (2003) Chang Wei-hsian, Taipei: TNUA Press: 154–64.

Chen Pei-feng (2006) Tonghua de tongchuang yimeng: rizhi shiqi Taiwan de yuyan zhengce , jindaihua yu rentong (The Different Intentions behind the Semblance of 'Duoka:' The Language Policy, Modernization and Identity in Taiwan During the Japanese-Ruling Period). Taipei: Rye Field Publishing Co.

Chiu Kun-liang (1997) Xinju yu jiuju: rizhi shiqi Taiwan xiju bianqian, 1985-1945 (New Drama and Old Drama: The Changing Course of Theatre in Taiwan under the Japanese Rule, 1895-1945). Taipei: Independent News Press.

Choi Yoo-joon (2003) 'Bukhan minjok gageuk chunhyangjeon' (North Korean Ethnic Opera Chunhyangjeon), in Korean National University Of Arts (ed.) Nambukhan gongyeonyesului daehwa: chunhyangjeongwa chogi kyoryu Ggongyeon (A Conversation between South and North Korean Performing Arts: Through Early Stages of Exchange Performances), Seoul: Sigongsa. 275–322.

Chou, Katherine Hui-ling (2003) Interview with Li Huang-hsiong. Chungli, Taiwan, 13 March 2003.
——— (2014a) Electronic Intermix in Taiwan. Available at www.eti-tw.com/, accessed 8 September 2014.
——— (2014b) Private email with Stan Lai, 10 October 2014.
——— (2014c) 'Taiwan xiandai juchang de chanye xiangxiang: yige "canyu guanchazhe" de juchang minzuzhi chubu shuxie' (Art as Industry? A Participant-Observer's Account of the Changing Course of Modern Theatre in Taiwan), Xiju yanjou (Journal of Theatre Studies), 13: 145–74.

Chun Hyun-sik (2013) Bukhanui gageuk yeongu: Pibadawa chunhyanggjeoneul chungshimeuro (A Study on North Korean Opera: Focusing on Pibada and Chunhyangjeon), Seoul: Seonin.

Fan Man-nong (2008) Xinxiang sanshi nian, 1978-2008 (The Thirtieth Anniversary of New Aspect, 1978-2008), Taipei: International New Aspect Cultural and Educational Foundation.

Fong, Gilbert C. F. (2009) 'Xianggang dangdai xiju de dianjizhe – Zhong Jinghui' (The Foundation-Builder of Hong Kong Drama – Chung King Fai), in Tian Benxiang and Gilbert C. F. Fong (eds.) Xianggang huaju shigao (Preliminary History of Hong Kong Drama), Shenyang: Liaoning jiaoyu chubanshe.

Hwang Mei-shu (1996) 'Taiwan xiao juchang yanbian chutan' (A Tentative Study of the Development of the Little Theatre in Taiwan), Shijie xinwen chuanbo xueyuan renwen xuebao (Journal of Humanities and Social Science), 5: 199–222.

Jeon Yeong-seon (2006) 'Bukhanui chulpanbodochegewa naeyong bunseok' (North Korean Publication and Broadcasting System and Contents Analyses), in Bukhan Yeongu Hakhoe (ed.) Bukhanui eonrongwa yesul (North Korean Broadcasting and Arts), Seoul: Kyeong-in Munhwasa.

Bibliography

Kang Dong-wan and Park Jeong-ran (2011) Hallyu Bukhaneul Heundeulda: Namhan Yeongsangmaecheui Bukhan Yutonggyeongrowa Jumin Uisik Byeonhwa (Hallyu Shakes North Korea: Channels for the Imports of South Korean Media and the Changes in North Koreans' Thoughts), Seoul: Neulpoom Plus.

Kim Bang-ock (1985) 'Aspects of Modernity Shown in the Early Korean Plays', in Korean Theatre Studies, vol 2, Seoul: Saemunsa.

Kim Miy-he (2013) Acts and Scenes: Western Drama in Korean Theatre, Seoul: Hollym.

Kim Suk-young (2010) Illusive Utopia: Theatre, Film, and Everyday Performance in North Korea, Ann Arbor: University of Michigan Press.

Li Huang-liang (2003) Taiwan zishen xijujia congshu: Li Man-kui (Taiwan Master Thespians Series: Li Man-kui). Taipei, Taiwan: Guoli Taibei Yishu Xueyuan (National Taipei Institute of Arts).

McEachern, Patrick (2010) Inside the Red Box: North Korea's Post-Totalitarian Politics, New York: Columbia University Press.

Min Byeong-wook (2001) Bukan Yeongeukui Ihae (Understanding North Korean Theatre), Seoul: Samyeongsa.

Min Byeong-wook and Koo myeong-ok (2002) Bukhan Kyeongheegeuk (North Korean Light Comedy), Seoul: Yeongeukgwa Ingan.

Ou Su-ying (2013) 'Yanju yu zhengzhi: Jian Guoxian de ximeng rensheng' (Drama and Politics: Jian Guoxian's Puppetmaster), Taiwanxue yanjiu (Research in Taiwan Studies), 16: 181–206.

Park Yeong-jeong (2007) Bukhan Yeongeuk/Heegokui Bunseokgwa Jeonmang (Analyses and Prospect on North Korean Theatre/Plays), Seoul: Yeongeukgwa Ingan.

Schönherr, J. (2012) North Korean Cinema: A History, Jefferson, NC: McFarland.

Seo Yeon-ho and Lee Sang-woo (2000) Korean Theatre 100 Years, Seoul: Hyeonamsa.

Shih Wan-shun (2010) 'Zhimindi xinpaiju de chuangcheng: Taiwan zhengju de meixue yu zhengzhi' (Creating the Colonial-Versioned Shinpa Drama – The Aesthetics and Politics of Taiwan Seigeki), Xiju xuekan (Theatre Journal), 12: 35–71.

—— (2014) 'Daoyan: erzhan qijian zhimindi Taiwan de xiju jiezuo – Lin Tuan-chiu de Yanji, Gaosha guan, yu Yide' (Introduction: Theatrical Masterpieces in Colonial Taiwan during the Second World War – Tuan-chiu Lin's Castrated Chicken, Takasago Hotel, and The Good Doctor," in Katherine Hui-ling Chou and Yi-hsiu Lee (eds.) Lin Tuan-chiu juzuo xuan: Yanji (Selected Plays of Tuan-chiu Lin: Castrated Chicken), Biaoyan Taiwan huibian: juben, sheji, jishu, 1943–, Xiju juben guan (Performing Taiwan: Script, Design and Stagecraft, 1943–, Drama Script Series), Taiwan: Guoli zhongyang daxue biaoyan yishu zhongxin. 16–28.

Wang, David Der-Wei (2013) 'Post-Loyalism,' trans. Brian Bernards, in Shu-mei Shih, Chien-Hsin Tsai, and Brian Bernards (eds.) Sinophone Studies: A Critical Reader, New York: Columbia Press.

Wu, Zhuoliu (1987) Taiwan lianqiao (Taiwan Golden Dewdrop). Taipei: Taiwan wenyi chubanshe.

Xu Yaxiang (2006) Shishi yu quanshi: rizhi shiqi Taiwan baokan xiqu ziliao xuan du (History and Historiography: Selections of News Stories about Xiqu in Taiwan under the Japan Rule), Yilan, Taiwan: Guoli chuantong yishu zhongxin.

Yang Seung-guk (1996) A Study on the History of Criticism on Modern Korean Theatre, Seoul: Taehaksa.

Zan Jae (2013) Ni lü (Self Re-Quest), in Katherine Hui-ling Chou and Yi-hsiu Lee (eds.) Biaoyan aiwan huibian: juben, sheji, jishu, 1943- xiju juben guan (Performing Taiwan: Script, Design and Stagecraft, 1943–, Drama Script Series). Taiwan: Guoli zhongyang daxue biaoyan yishu zhongxin.

Zen Xianzhang (2003) Taiwan zishen xijujia congshu: Chang Wei-hsian (Taiwan Master Thespians Series: Chang Wei-hsian). Taipei: Guoli taibei yishuxueyuan.

Zhan Jiabao (2013) 'Beijing wuming yingxiong guangchang luocheng, jinian Taiwan xunnan yinbi zhanxian lieshi' (Beijing Memorial for Anonymous Communist Comrades Working Undercover in Taiwan Inaugurated), iFeng Military News, 3 December 2013. Available at http://news.ifeng.com/mil/bigpicture/detail_2013_12/03/31762771_0.shtml#p=1, accessed 31 July 2014.

16

Modern theatre in mainland Southeast Asia

Thailand, Burma (Myanmar), Laos, Cambodia and Vietnam

Pawit Mahasarinand, Ty Bamla, Jennifer Goodlander, Khuon Chanreaksmey, Siyuan Liu and Trinh Nguyen

I. Thailand, by Pawit Mahasarinand

Geographically, it is impossible for Thailand – right in the middle of the Indochina peninsula and between the Indian and Pacific Oceans – to close herself off from foreign relations and their influences. Like the way several genres of its traditional theatre had been influenced by Indian, Chinese and Southeast Asian counterparts, the development of modern theatre owes a great deal to the translation and adaptation of European and American drama as well as the adjustment of their theatrical presentation styles to fit the local Thai audience's taste.

At the height of western imperialism, Thai openness and adaptability were most seriously tested, and Thailand, or Siam at that time, survived by turning 'semi-colonial' (Tungtang 2011: 40). Apart from negotiating with and giving a considerable amount of land and resources to the western powers, both King Mongkut (Rama IV, r. 1851–68) and his son King Chulalongkorn (Rama V, r. 1868–1910) sponsored their royal children and noblemen to study abroad at major European universities in various fields. Upon their return, these princes and noblemen spearheaded the country's rapid modernization and thus the country, unlike many other Asian countries, was able to maintain its independence. However, this does not mean that the development of modern theatre in Thailand was slower than its counterpart in the colonized countries.

Early modern theatre

In the reign of King Chulalongkorn, Thai theatre arts began to open its arms to western counterparts. Similar to the method of westernization in many other fields, Thai royal family members and noblemen set forth the development of theatre arts. Three hybrid theatrical forms emerged: *lakhon phanthang* (dance theatre set in historical periods and featuring characters of various nationalities), *lakhon duekdamban* (stylistic and textual modification of classical court dance theatre or *lakhon nai*) and *lakhon rong* (western-styled musical theatre). The leaders were two princes – the king's brothers Prince Naris and Prince Narathip – and two noblemen – Chao Phraya Mahin and Chao Phraya Deves – all of whom had previously lived in Europe.

At the country's first commercial theatre, an indoor proscenium playhouse named The Prince Theatre, Chao Phraya Mahin's troupe experimented in lakhon phanthang by using western ballet movements to choreograph scenes involving foreign characters. In lakhon duekdamban, Prince Naris collaborated with Chao Phraya Deves as they adapted the text and performance of lakhon nai, cutting, rearranging and rewriting the script in addition to up-pacing the classical dance routines and ending the show with an elaborate finale. Shortly afterwards, Prince Narathip adapted traditional Malay musical theatre *bangsawan* into lakhon rong. His first play was *Sao Khruea Fa* (his adaptation of Puccini's *Madama Butterfly*), in which a military officer from Bangkok won and broke the heart of a northern woman, and the acting showcased a progression towards the representational style of western theatre (Rutnin 2008: 92–4).

The popularity of these three hybrid forms proves that by carefully adopting and ingeniously adapting western forms, these directors' and producers' practices successfully integrated these innovations into the repertory of Thai theatre. These three dramatic genres were highly influenced by European theatre, yet they were Thai creations. Like their counterparts in science and technology, these noble playmakers showed that the modernization of the country was better executed by local people who knew both sides of the coin. More importantly, this modernization process was sensitively carried out without ignoring the country's classical roots, or clearly segregating the differing cultures into 'modern' and 'traditional', or 'civilized' and 'barbaric', but by finding their middle ground.

The modernization continued in the subsequent reign of King Vajiravudh (Rama VI, r. 1910–25). Acclaimed as the 'father of modern Thai theatre', King Vajiravudh wrote scripts for traditional theatre performances, and also acted in, produced and directed his Thai translations and adaptations of European plays. In addition, he penned original English-language plays, employing such modern ideological themes as democracy.

King Vajiravudh penned fifty Thai-language *lakhon phut* (spoken plays) in a period of 21 years (Duangpatra 2001: 52–3). Twenty-four of these lakhon phut were original Thai plays 'written from His Majesty's imagination' (ibid. 52), meaning he was inspired by some of the European plays he had either watched or read. The other twenty-six plays were either translated or adapted from English and French plays. Among these, three are literal translations – Shakespeare's *As You Like It*, *The Merchant of Venice* and *Romeo and Juliet*, the first two of which have been in the secondary school curriculum of, interestingly, Thai literature classes (Rutnin 2008: 101). Not only did he translate them precisely, from the title to the last line, but he also transformed Shakespearean blank verses into *klon bot lakhon* (dramatic poems), despite the fact that they were to be spoken, not sung and danced to as in traditional theatre productions. In other words, although these three plays were translated line by line, they were not carbon copies of the English originals. This was perhaps to make sure that Thai audiences would be partly accustomed to a new genre from the beginning.

Another evidence of the rising popularity of lakon phut is the fact that in this reign four new playhouses were built at four palaces in Bangkok, an additional three at summer palaces upcountry, exclusively for the socially elite audiences, and several commercial playhouses outside the palace for the general public (Rutnin 2008: 139).

Apart from being a new dramatic genre, lakhon phut introduced western theatre practices. For example, traditionally in Thailand, male and female performers were prevented from acting in the same production and traditional genres were specifically divided as such. In King Rama VI's reign, gender-appropriate casting became common practice for lakhon phut (Malakul

1996: 39). In such a male-dominated society, this can probably be regarded as a social revolution, again influenced by western civilization but without being a colony.

In this golden age of Thai theatre, while new and western-influenced forms were practised, traditional forms also enjoyed their own prominence. While there were hybrid forms, the traditional ones retained their strict standards of practice. This was the time when the country enjoyed its widest variety of theatrical activities. Later on, Thailand would elect to adopt some and ignore others.

The Royal Household, the most significant patron of Thai performing arts, suffered a major financial crisis in the reign of King Prachatipok (Rama VII, r. 1925–35). As a result of the country changing its government system from absolute monarchy to democracy in 1932 and the subsequent aftermaths of the Second World War, many theatre troupes dispersed and cinemas were substituted for playhouses. The new government's Department of Fine Arts chose to support only traditional performing arts, and the National Theatre, opened in 1965, has mostly produced and presented traditional works. Elsewhere, the public enjoyed productions of lakhon rong much more than lakhon phut, which they still considered 'foreign' and less entertaining. This is probably because Thai people, like many Asian counterparts, were more accustomed to stylized presentation than closer-to-life representation.

Development of contemporary theatre

In the late 1960s, the development of contemporary Thai theatre, particularly the re-emergence of lakhon phut as *lakhon phut samai mai* (modern spoken drama), owes a great deal to the translation and adaptation of modern European and American drama. The pioneers were two female university professors, Chulalongkorn University's Sodsai Pantoomkomol (b. 1934) and Thammasat University's Mattani Mojdara Rutnin (b. 1937), who founded the country's first two theatre departments where students can study acting, directing, design, management, dramatic literature and criticism and earn their bachelor's degrees in western theatre. A few generations of theatre-major students have followed their professors' paths – returning to teach in their home departments after completing their graduate studies in the UK or the United States.

Mainstage productions by both schools as well as subsequently founded drama departments in other universities in the following decades have presented the Thai theatregoing public, who seek an alternative to traditional theatre, movies and television dramas, with a wide variety of modern European and American plays in translation and adaptation – from realism to theatre of the absurd. Notable examples are: *Khwamtai Khong Salesman* (Miller's *Death of a Salesman*) and *Raeng Loki* (O'Neill's *Desire Under the Elms*) in the 1970s; *Nimit Maya* (Strindberg's *A Dream Play*) and *Maekha Songkhram* (Brecht's *Mother Courage and Her Children*) in the 1980s; *Achan Kha* (Mamet's *Oleanna*) and *Khothot Thi Kuen Prasat* (Handke's *Offending the Audience*) in the 1990s; and *Khoi Godot* (Beckett's *Waiting for Godot*) and *Wai Fai* (Wedekind's *Spring Awakening*) in the 2000s.

It is noteworthy that in contemporary Thai theatre, adaptations, in which translators make some changes in the context to better communicate with the local Thai audience, outnumber translations. Only translations, however, were published. While there are two Thai stage versions of *Death of a Salesman* – the translation in 1971 and the adaptation in 1986 – only the translation was published. While *Desire Under the Elms* was adapted – and the setting relocated to northeastern Thailand – when it was staged in 1976, the Cabot family moved back to New England when the translation was published in 1990.

Thai theatre students' interest in translation and adaptation of European and American plays as well as writing original Thai lakhon phut samai mai in the European and American dramatic

Figure 16.1 Television actors perform in *Onlaman Lang Ban Sai Thong* (Mayhem in the Sai Thong Mansion).

(Courtesy of Dreambox)

Figure 16.2 Patravadi Theatre's *Lo Rak Lo Lilit Lilit Phra Lo* (The Tragic Romance of Phra Lo).

(Courtesy of Patravadi Theatre)

paradigm, which has outnumbered the former since the turn of the century, has been, accordingly, high. For example, they made use of this medium of free expression – neither controlled nor censored like newspaper, radio and television – in their political demonstrations against military governments from the late 1960s to the mid-1970s.

Apart from staging many translations and adaptations of existentialist and absurdist plays by Beckett, Pinter, Albee and Ionesco as a reaction against the rise of American imperialism and capitalism as well as the Thai military government, university students in this period wrote and performed a lot of political plays to voice their comments on politics and society, oftentimes not in conventional theatre spaces. Professional theatre companies such as Makhampom Theatre Group, Maya and Crescent Moon Theatre also emerged from these political theatre activities and have remained active up to the present day, although their works have been less political and more social in this century. Apparently, this new political role of lakhon phut samai mai, a dramatic genre highly influenced by European and American theatre, differs significantly from those of other genres in traditional Thai theatre.

While it is a fact that one cannot work professionally and solely as a modern theatre artist in Thailand, most drama school graduates have applied their theatrical skills to the television, advertising and movie industries. Nonetheless, some of them have taken time off from their regular work to form theatre troupes and from time to time staged productions.

In 1985, a group of Thammasat and Chulalongkorn University alumni formed Theatre 28. Aiming to present sophisticated western plays that ask the audience to think about human existence and the social values imposed on each person, the company has staged, for example, translations of Brecht's *Galileo*, Frisch's *Biography: A Game*, Durrenmatt's *The Visit* and Ionesco's *Rhinoceros* at various venues. In 1987, their *Su Fan An Yingyai* (Wasserman's *Man of La Mancha*) at the National Theatre was the most acclaimed Thai theatre production of the decade.

The rise of commercial theatre was evident in the 1980s and 90s. Monthienthong Theatre, a professional theatre in the 150-seat cocktail lounge of a four-star hotel, was a place to be for well-to-do theatre aficionados to watch television and movie actors in original modern Thai plays as well as translations and adaptations of, among others, Coward's *Blithe Spirit* and Shaw's *Arms and the Man*. Their most popular production, *Chan Phuchai Na Ya* (Crowley's *The Boys in the Band*), ran for more than a year.

When Monthienthong Theatre closed in 1992, another commercial theatre company, DASS Entertainment (later known as Dream Box), had already been in business since 1990. At their regular venue, the 600-seat proscenium theatre Bangkok Playhouse built in 1993 (now known as M Theatre), middle- and upper-class audiences watched lakhon phut samai mai and *lakhon phleng* (Broadway-styled Thai musical theatre) penned by the company's resident playwright Daraka Wongsiri (b. 1954), in addition to translations and adaptations of, for example, Christie's *The Mousetrap*, Shaffer's *Amadeus* and Reza's *Art*. Their most popular play, with four revivals and more than a hundred performances, a record for lakhon phut samai mai, was *Onlaman Lang Ban Sai Thong*, Wongsiri's hybridization of *Noises Off* and a popular Thai novel *Ban Sai Thong* (Figure 16.1). Thailand's most prolific playwright's other representative works include such dramas as *Kulap Si Lueat* (Crimson Roses) and *Phinaikam Khong Ying Wikoncharit* (A Madwoman's Will) as well as satirical comedies such as *Thuen Thuek* (Old Maids) and *Sam Sao Sam Sam* (Three Misbehaving Ladies).

Another major company is Patravadi Theatre, which was active from 1992 until 2011, when their riverside 300-seat open-air playhouse and 80-seat studio were heavily damaged by flood. Internationally renowned actress, playwright and director Patravadi Mejudhon (b. 1948) has reinterpreted traditional dramas in modern contexts and experimental styles drawn from both traditional and modern performing arts. Examples of what scholars refer to as *lakhon khanop niyom mai* (theatre of new tradition) are *Chalawan: The Likay Musical*, an adaptation of *lakhon nok* titled *Kraithong*, and *Lo Rak Lo Lilit Lilit Phra Lo*, from classical literature *Lilit Phra Lo* (Figure 16.2).

In 2002, smaller companies formed the Bangkok Theatre Network (BTN) and have since organized the Bangkok Theatre Festival (BTF) in a park, cafés and bars in the historic neighbourhood of Bang Lamphu as well as the Bangkok Art and Culture Centre (BACC) in the city centre, attracting more than 50,000 local and foreign spectators every November.

Theatre in Thailand today

In one of the world's favourite tourist and expatriate destinations, foreign audiences are drawn more towards such 'tourist shows' as a lady-boy cabaret *Calypso Bangkok* (since 1988), cultural performance extravaganzas *Phuket Fantasea* (since 1998) and *Siam Niramit* (since 2005), a Korean non-verbal comedy whose context has been adapted into Thai *Cookin' Nanta* (since 2013), and a martial arts show *Muay Thai Live: The Legend Lives* (since 2014). However, these differ greatly from the contemporary theatre works that are being staged almost every week.

The two current hubs are Muangthai Rachadalai Theatre and Democrazy Theatre Studio, two representatives of commercial and independent theatres The former is a 1,495-seat proscenium playhouse atop a shopping mall where the resident company Scenario has been staging *lakhon phleng* since 2007. Most of its works are adapted from popular Thai novels and television dramas, such as *Banlang Mek* (The Throne of Cloud), *Khanglang Phap* (Behind the Painting) and *Si Phaendin* (Four Reigns). The latter is a blackbox studio reconfigured from a two-unit shophouse, with a maximum capacity of eighty spectators, where BTN members have been presenting a wide variety of works since 2009. Scenario, which is also a television production company and whose stage and screen works are regarded as middle- to lowbrow, is successful in expanding the spectatorship of contemporary Thai theatre by simple and familiar plots, spectacular production design and superstar casts as well as lucrative marketing plans. Democrazy has a higher number of productions, a wider variety of dramatic content and theatrical styles, high to middle brow, with shorter runs and a marketing scheme that relies heavily on social media. As the Ministry of Culture allocates much more of its budget to the preservation of traditional theatre, Scenario relies solely on ticket sales and sponsorship, while Democrazy relies on the former only (Mahasarinand 2014: 5–6).

While the only two modern theatre artists to have been consecrated as National Artists are Pantoomkomol and Mejudhon, in 2011 and 2014 respectively, theatre artists have been honoured with the Office of Contemporary Art and Culture's Silpathorn Awards since 2004 – respectively Anatta Theatre Group's Pradit Prasartthong, Patravadi Theatre's Manop Meejamrat, Pichet Klunchun Dance Company's Pichet Klunchun, Sema Thai Puppet Theatre's Nimit Pipitkul, Crescent Moon Theatre's Sineenadh Keitprapai, Moradok Mai's Janaprakal Chandruang, 8X8 Theatre's Nikorn Sae Tang and B-Floor Theatre's Jarunan Phantachat.

Critics formed the Thailand centre of the International Association of Theatre Critics (IATC) in 2011, and have been recognizing exemplary theatre works and artists with the annual IATC-Thailand Awards since 2013, when Mejudhon was honoured with the first lifetime achievement award.

As Bangkok is a primate city – in other words, there is no second city in Thailand – theatre productions rarely tour to other provinces where various forms of traditional theatre gain more popularity.

In conclusion, modern theatre activities in Thailand, which continues to project its exotic images in tourism campaigns, have been significantly overlooked by foreign scholars, critics and audiences, most of whom are only exposed to or interested in traditional theatre. Nevertheless, the outside world is gradually getting an overview of the thriving scene, thanks in part to the significantly rising number of modern Thai theatre productions invited to overseas festivals.

II. Burma (Myanmar), by Ty Bamla

During the late eighteenth and early nineteenth centuries, the so-called golden age of Burmese theatre, new drama forms evolved, including marionette theatre and the Thai *khon*, a form of mask dance theatre enacting the story of *Ramayana* (some dances are labelled *Yodayar* in reference to the city of *Ayutthaya*). Marionette theatre (*yothe thay thabin*) is the inspiration for many movements in traditional Burmese dance, whose movements are reminiscent of puppets.

After the First Anglo-Burmese War (1824–6), the city of Moulmein (now Mawlamyine) in lower Burma had a substantial Anglo-Burmese population (also known as Little England). After the Third Anglo-Burmese War in 1885, Upper Burma was annexed. Sometimes, Burma is referred to as 'the Scottish Colony' owing to the heavy role played by the Scots in colonizing and running the country. *Anyeint pwe* (also know as *a-nyeint*), a variety performance form featuring female dancers and male performers, started during this period. The first known anyeint troupe was formed in Mandalay around 1900, by comedian U Chit Phwe and his wife, the dancer Ma Sein Thone. The form was especially appealing to the growing merchant class in British Burma who patronized and sponsored these performances. Another modern form that started in the mid-nineteenth century is *pya zat* (or *khat pau pya zat*, 'contemporary play'), the spoken drama, which can be both serious and comic. Famous playwrights include Thakin Kodaw Hming (1875–1964), whose prolific plays and satires earned him the name of the Burmese George Bernard Show, and former prime minister U Nu (1907–95), whose *Pyi thu aung than* (The People Win Through, 1951), a critique of communism, made him internationally known because of its first English performance at the Pasadena Playhouse in 1957. While pya zat thrived during the socialist period (1962–88), it has lost its appeal as an independent form since then, although it remains popular as part of the traditional all-night variety show *zat pwe* (Diamond 2012: 200–11).

The Junta era and beyond

Anyeint reached its apogee in the 1970s, during a period of socialist rule. One of the most influential troupes was Manadalay's Lamin Taya (The Hundred Moon Troupe). In 1973, the troupe's scriptwriter, Maung Myat Hmaing, wrote *Dancer of Ganges*, which was one of the first Burmese plays to include the concept of democracy. The comedian Zarganar ('Tweezers', b. 1961) is widely considered to be the most popular comedian and satirist under the Burmese Military Junta. Moe Nat Thuza (Heavenly Fairies) was his first theatre group and its performance was broadcast on national television. In 1986, he formed the group Mya Ponnama (Emerald Tales); he was immensely popular with the audience because of his willingness to use farcical routines to highlight government failures. In 1989, just before the general election in 1990, he wrote and directed the satiric pya zat play titled *Da thung sar nyi lar khan* (Beggars' National Convention), which he and his ensemble performed in front of an overcrowded audience in Yangon City Hall (YCH) at Rangoon. After the play ended, the troupe were escorted from the stage and driven directly to Insein Prison. Another anyeint group, the Thee Lay Thee, is known in Burma for cracking jokes and performing satirical skits about the Junta under the mentorship of Zarganar. In 2009, Zarganar won the International Writer of Courage Award of the inaugural PEN Pinter Prize.

Two of the most influential theatre performers in anyeint are Myit Tha (Metta) and Khun Thee (Areca Nut). They started their theatre company, called Ta Khaing Lone Shwe (Golden Branches), in 1986. In 1988, they broke through in their career with two pya zat-like comedies, *Wa zi yar* and *A May Chwey Ma Hla Hla Lay* (A Fabulous Daughter-in-Law for Mom), directed by Bo Ka Lay Tint Aung and Gi Ta Lu Lin Maung ko Ko, which premiered in the National Theatre of Yangon. These contemporary plays offered prominent discussions of the social, economic and current situation of the country. Decades later, most comedian and theatre performers were influenced by Khun Thee's and Myit Tha's acting techniques. Under the Military Junta, one of Myit Tha's crack jokes was a hit throughout the country, for which he has been banned from performance indefinitely on stage or in the any media in Burma. That prominent joke is: 'After graduating from high school, you've already finished education for life.' At that time, universities and colleges were closed indefinitely and most high school graduates had nowhere to go to study.

Two influential comedians and actors are Moe Dee and Moss (d. 2013). They both came from zat pwe, travelling all over the country, and then broke into the film industry in the early 1990s. Moss and Moe Dee were the first theatre artists to receive the best supporting Academy Award in Burmese theatre and film history. Because of their unconventional path, many actors from theatre crossed over to film and TV in Burma, including Kyaw Kyaw Bo, a theatre artist who became a film star, and Min Mun Khun, a film star who occasionally performs on the stage.

Blend of contemporary theatre and performances

In the age of globalization, one notable phenomenon in contemporary Burmese theatre is the mix of theatre and performance arts that often involves international artists. For example, Rey Buono, a director well respected in Southeast Asia, co-directed with American director Ruth Pongstaphone a play based on Samuel Beckett's *Act Without Word I* in the Yangon-based iUi #1 International Performance and Theatre festival in 2008, which was supported by the Institut Français de Birmaie. In 2013, Robert Woodruff, who is on the faculty of Yale School of Drama, joined Pongstaphone in co-directing an original documentary theatrical performance created with the poet Nyein Way, titled *No Longer/Not Yet*. It highlighted the political situation of Burma, which was just out of the Military Junta but still far from democracy.

Under pressure from the oppressive Junta before 2011, underground theatre and activist organizations such as Hands Held High and Generation Waves were blacklisted. Hands Held High created the pya zat called *Youngsters' Dreams* at Alice Baldwin Auditorium at the American Center, Rangoon, in late 2006. Both government agents and the opposition party National League for Democracy were invited and all performers were monitored by government officials. Nevertheless, Hands Held High organized a workshop for activists, theatre artists and journalists in Rangoon and Chiang Mai, Thailand. While the group Thukhuma Khayeethe cancelled a performance due to 'permission withheld' from Burma's Junta, they have partnered with the New York-based Bond Street Theatre since 2009 (BWW News Desk 2014).

The country has been opening up and the most significant change occurred in 2013 when media organizations no longer needed to submit their content to a censorship board before publication. One prominent performance form that has thrived after severe censorship by the Junta is *thangyat*, a folk art form that combines rhyming couplet with music and is sung to the beat of a traditional *hsaing waing* ensemble. The performers focus on providing topical information to the audience in a way that satires politics, current events and social mores. It accompanies the Burmese New Year's Thingyan Water Festival, which is now celebrated on 13–16 April (see Panoramic Journeys). While its history is unknown, thangyat is a cornerstone in the country's New Year celebrations, where performers dance and recite humorous lyrics that respond to the country's situations. Similar to slam poetry, which is associated with the vocal delivery style found in hip-hop music, thangyat draws heavily on the tradition of rhythmically poetic or unrhymed narrative formula. The lead performer uses traditional theatrical devices, including shifting voices and tones, while the followers may recite an entire script in ironic melody. Some scripts are in a question and answer format while stretching the boundaries of the traditional *ka-byar loot* dance, beatboxing, or using highly choreographed repetitive movement. The questioner is called Ah-Tain (the call) and the followers are known as Ah-Puak (the crack-jokers).

Thangyat showcases had been officially banned for over three decades by civil laws that were aimed at preventing citizens from assembling and chanting slogans. In 2012, Mandalay-based Pa Pa Lay of the Moustache Brothers performed thangyat on a float during the parades in Mandalay, home to about forty thangyat troupes in the past (Roper 2013). In 2013, Burma held the first thangyat contest for three decades, offering a rare glimpse into an extraordinary performance form, which remains little known outside its native land.

In Burma, theatre, dances and performances have been critical about politics, religions, economics and national reconciliation since British Burma. The next parliament is expected to choose the country's next president in early 2016. This will be Burma's second general election since the country began to emerge from decades of military rule in 2011. Today, most performing artists are concerned about the election in 2016. What is unique about contemporary theatre is its ambiguous way of making performances and educating the public under any circumstances. The contemporary aesthetic of theatre is highly hybrid; the epic performances coming out under dictatorship and the spirit of making contemporary theatre are geared towards the next generation. This is the most exciting time in Burmese performance history and artists are willing to move forward with high momentum to connect with national and international theatre forms and create new ones. In a way, Burmese theatre artists have the voice of Burma.

III. Laos, by Jennifer Goodlander

The main challenge facing performance in Laos is defining a particular Lao aesthetic that can speak to a developing national identity; Laos gained independence from France in 1975. This effort is complicated by Laos' close cultural and political ties to its more powerful neighbours, Thailand, Cambodia and Vietnam, and by a diverse population consisting of forty-nine different ethnic minorities (Lao, Khmou and Hmong are the largest three). Many of the performance genres and theatrical trends in Laos can be understood as a history of its relationships with its neighbours and shifting political and cultural favouritisms over time. Lao historiography reflects this complex search for identity, but 'Lao writers, however, wherever they might be living, have gone back to the past in search of symbols and founding myths on which to root and legitimate the modern Lao nation-state' (Goscha and Ivarsson 2003: xii). Artists, likewise, join this discourse of using the past as material from which to fashion a contemporary theatre.

Fā Ngoum founded the *mandala*, or imperial kingdom, of Lan Xang in the middle of the fourteenth century and strove to unite Lao into one great kingdom.[1] His rule has become the stuff of myth and legend, demonstrated today as he is credited with the origins of many contemporary 'traditional' performance forms. For example, the Central Lao Opera Troupe was established in 1972 to perform *lam* (or *mawlam*) *leung* (Lao opera). This genre is similar to Thai *likay* and borrows heavily from Malay *bangsawan* as well – but members of the troupe 'insist on its antiquity, saying that its material originated during Fa Ngoum's reign' (Diamond

2012: 252). Without entering into the debate about the form's true origins, this historical insistence demonstrates the importance of the 'first Laos king' to the formation of contemporary identity that is played out today through the performing arts.

The Ministry of Information and Culture in Laos divides theatre into four genres: lam leung, *lakhon tukata* (puppetry), *lakhon vao* (spoken drama) and *Phralak Phraram* (the Lao version of the *Ramayana*). Each of these differs as to the level of official and popular approval it enjoys. Lam leung is not only the most traditional of Laos performance, but remains the most popular, especially in rural areas. There are two kinds of puppetry, *ipok*, or rod puppets, are the oldest, but are surpassed in popularity by several European-influenced styles. Lakhon vao and Phralak Phraram both lack widespread support from Lao audiences – but for different reasons. Each genre must negotiate funding and censorship, and strive to appeal to local youth audiences.

Foreign NGOs often use theatre as a means to teach audiences about different important social issues. The Lao National Puppet Theatre troupe, based in Vientiane, was formed in 1978 by twenty Lao students who had studied puppet making and performance in Bulgaria. They use rod puppets, glove puppets and a newly created style called *hun kabong*, which combines hand puppets made from recycled materials with human actors. This new style has proven very popular and the troupe is often hired to use the puppets to tell stories that teach about HIV/AIDS awareness and prevention, issues regarding hygiene and sanitation, and other topics. UNICEF sponsored the troupe to tour to remote areas of Laos to teach villagers about the dangers of avian bird flu. In one scene a rooster crows about the threats of the deadly disease, both startling and delighting the audiences of adults and children (UNICEF 2007). The group is dependent on NGO funding, which according to their director Souvandy Chanthavong limits their ability to innovate or create other stories based on traditional Lao tales (Diamond 2012: 260). For example, in 1990 a foreign sponsor commissioned an entire set of ipok puppets to be made so the troupe could present Lao stories in the traditional style. But the puppets are rarely used because they do not have the same appeal as the newer hun kabong style (ASEAN Puppetry Association 2013).

Many theatre groups receive much of their funding directly from the government, which carefully controls the style and content of the plays. Lao opera troupes, lam leung, perform both traditional Lao stories and socialist propaganda plays – many of which were written in the 1970s. Today, the government requires the Central Lam Leung Troupe to add two new plays to its repertoire each year, based on political or socialist themes. Plays go through a long process to be approved by the censors. The repertoire of both old and new has proved difficult for the genre because young people are not interested in the 'old stories' and do not find the socialist plays to be relevant to their current situation. Lam leung enjoys its greatest popularity in rural villages and holds little appeal in urban centres (Diamond 2012: 251–63).

Spoken drama, lakhon vao, did not develop as a strong genre during the French colonial period as it did in Cambodia and Vietnam. In 1980 the government established the Central Spoken Drama Troupe by sponsoring dramatists from Vietnam and Uzbekistan to come and train artists. Their first major production, *Hom kin bouadeng* (Fragrant Red Lotus), was commissioned to celebrate the tenth anniversary of Lao independence. The final script was a difficult balancing act between the artists and government, but played to audiences numbering in the thousands who found 'realistic' theatre to be an interesting novelty. The troupe prospers, but does not thrive. Commissioned to produce two new plays a year by the Lao government, the actors still struggle to find work or to produce theatre that might please the main funding source in Laos, the NGOs (Diamond 2012: 263–67).

The town of Luang Prabang, known for its temples, mix of unique traditional and colonial architecture, and vibrant night market, serves as a showcase of heritage and tradition for the national government. The city was declared a UNESCO World Heritage Site in 1995, stating that it was a place of 'universal value' for humanity both in history and in the present day (UNESCO 1995). The heritage designation makes Luang Prabang an important tourist destination, and this is reflected in the types of performing arts located there. The Royal Ballet Theatre performs the Lao version of the *Ramayana*, called *Phralak Phraram*, three times a week for audiences of tourists at the National Museum. The museum is at the site of the Royal Palace, and the former living quarters of the king are displayed, but there is no mention of the last king or how he was overthrown. 'In the Lao present, without king or royal lineage, the Marxist State has sought legitimation through the invocation of a Lao past, albeit one where certain elements have been obscured' (Dearborn and Stallmeyer 2010: 119). The written history of the troupe states that in 1975, after fifteen centuries of annual performances for the king, the socialist government banned the genre. In 1993 the Institution of Cultural Research and the Provincial Government Office in Luang Prabang revived the troupe and in 2002 it was established as a regular feature (Luangprabang-Laos.com 2014). Historically a court drama, this form never had popular appeal to a Lao audience, who still rarely attend. Like the palace, the performance demonstrates the complex ways the Lao government simultaneously invokes and rewrites the past to form a national culture for the present. A similar kind of performance was attempted in the capital city of Vientiane, but as a location it did not have the cultural appeal of Luang Prabang for foreign audiences (Diamond 2012: 271).

Popular theatre struggles to find an audience, as many young people prefer to listen to Thai pop music or watch Thai soap operas on television. These young people see Lao culture and traditions as backward and are drawn to the modern entertainments of nearby Bangkok and the global culture they represent (Diamond 2012: 272–3). Foreign NGOs hold much of the Lao arts scene in a stranglehold because it provides the main funding source. In order for theatre to thrive in Laos, it must continue to find a way to reach a local audience through creativity, modernization and relevance for local audiences.

IV. Cambodia, by Khuon Chanreaksmey and Siyuan Liu

Theatre is known as *lakhon* in the Khmer language. In Cambodia, there are many forms of theatre, which are generally considered in three main categories: classical, folk and modern theatre. Most Cambodian theatre incorporates dance movement, especially in classical and folk forms such as *robam boran (or robam kback boran*, classical dance-drama), *lakhon khol* (masculine masked dance theatre), classical court dance (Royal ballet) and large shadow puppet theatre (*sbek thom*). They have existed since ancient times, while the modern theatre, including spoken drama, was influenced by the western style.

Cambodia was a French protectorate for almost a century (1863–1953), after the protectorate agreement was signed by King Norodom (r. 1860–1904). The French brought many elements to Cambodia, including religion and the arts.

Between the nineteenth and twentieth centuries, many modern popular forms emerged by borrowing from foreign genres – both western and neighbouring cultures – for Khmer audiences, including *yike*, *lakhon bassac* and spoken drama. Yike is a form of dance-drama that ostensibly traces its root to the country's Islamic Cham minorities, although its present form also includes native response in the late nineteenth century to tours by Malay *bangsawan* ('Malay opera') troupes and modern staging technology. It gained wide popularity through the mixture of traditional and western performance – hand gestures similar to classical dance and myth and historical events and court figures which are mixed with modern scenery and new plots that were enhanced by witty improvisation and humorous burlesques. The performers include both genders, unlike court dance. It largely remained a performance of farmers until the 1960s when they were encouraged by King Norodom Sihanouk's government to turn professional. After the fall of the Khmer Rouge, it enjoyed a 'golden age' in 1980, with as many as '250 theatrical troupes . . . functioning in the country' (Diamond 2012: 134). In recent decades it has also adopted contemporary social issues, which had been restricted to spoken drama. One such example is a 2005 adaptation of a 1964 novel titled *Phoum Derachham* (A Miserable Village), which depicts the oppression of the French colonial authority in the 1920s over local vendors who kill a tax policeman.

Lakhon bassac is Cambodian operatic drama developed in the early twentieth century in the River Bassac region of southern Vietnam by the ethnic Khmer. Lakhon bassac's origin can be traced to Chinese theatre, most evidently in its musical instrumentation (drums, gongs, chimes and wood blocks) and opera-style sung dialogue, but also in its costumes, modified face painting, martial art movements (*kabat*) and acrobatics (*hun*). Its 'repertoire of 155 plays from Chinese, Vietnamese, and French sources were adapted to local tastes, such as altering the villains in Vietnamese hat boi from Chinese to Vietnamese!' (Diamond 2012: 137). The genre has maintained its popularity with audiences throughout the century. Before the rule of the Khmer Rouge in the mid-1970s, professional companies performed in Phnom Penh, Battambang, Siem Reap and other cities, while amateur performers, with the occasional addition of urban troupes, entertained the audience in the countryside and performed at religious festivals, taking days to enact one story. In contrast to the fate suffered by traditional dance and other arts, bassac was embraced by the Khmer Rouge between 1975 and 1979 for propaganda purposes, depicting anti-American heroes and disseminating 'party policy on everything from the need to improve rice production and dike and railway repair to warning the masses of the implacable threat posed by the Vietnamese' (Post Staff 2001).

The Cambodia spoken drama *lakhon niyeay*, aka. *lakhon ciet* (literally 'national drama'), started in the late 1930s after the French Protectorate invited spoken drama theatres from neighbouring countries – Thailand, Indonesia and Vietnam – to visit Cambodia, which inspired the first Cambodian modern theatre troupe Lakhon Vatana Phirum (Phirum Theatre of Progress). 'This troupe performed for a long time and became well known, leading to the birth of other similar smaller troupes who took the form of this "new" theater and performed it frequently' (Ly 2001: 97). After a hiatus during the Second World War, spoken theatre resumed under the guidance of Guy Porée, the French cultural attaché. He assembled a group of his servants and their friends to form the Theatre Nouveau, which performed farcical skits based on western classics and contemporary plays, including a 'half-hour version of *The Merchant of Venice* [that] was an especial favorite, because the problem of money lending is familiar to Cambodians who saw Shylock as a Chinese usurer' (Bowers 1956: 181). In 1946, it became the Ecole du théâtre nouveau (School of New Theatre), with a mandate to train artists for 'a modern theater worthy of the Cambodian artistic traditions' (quoted in Ly and Muan 2001: 67). It turned into the Ecole nationale du théâtre (National School of Theatre) in 1957–8, with its associated company becoming the Lakhon Cheat (National Theatre), a term used interchangeably with lakhon niyeay at the time.

The most important figure in the development of lakhon niyeay is the playwright and director Hang Thun Hak (1924–75), who had studied theatre in France and was active with anti-colonial guerrillas in the early 1950s. After independence in 1955, he wrote edgy social critical plays and taught a group of students to perform them, often under severe scrutiny from censors, but managed to survive under the protection of Queen Kossamak. Huang's *Thma Raom* (The Dancing Stone) attacked the complicity of government officials in the illegal marketing of Khmer antiquities on the international art market. His *Kanya Chareya* (The Ethical Girl) depicts an upper-class girl who confronts the culture of bribery through which her father, a high-placed Cambodian, enriches himself. In the early 1960s, the government sent six students abroad – to France (two), the United States (one) and China (three) – to study theatre. Their return helped to establish the Royal University of Fine Arts in 1965, with Hang Thun Hak as the Dean of its Department of Dramatic and Choreographic Arts. While starting with lakhon niyeay, the department later taught lakhon yike and lakhon bassac, and, after the 1970 coup, incorporated the former royal classical ballet troupe (Ly and Muan 2001: 65–73, 103–10).

As the 'national theatre', lakhon niyeay was also used for educational and entertainment purposes in the late 1960s by taking advantage of National Radio of Cambodia, broadcast throughout the country, bringing it to many who never saw it on stage. Unfortunately, lakhon niyeay suffered significant damage during the politically tumultuous years of the 1970s, first during the Khmer Republic era (1970–5) when a military coup overthrew Prince Norodom Sihanouk, who subsequently cooperated with the Khmer Rouge in a war to retake the government, and then during the rule of the Khmer Rouge (1975–9), which massacred most lakhon niyeay artists during the Cambodian genocide. Hang Thun Hak served in top posts in the Khmer Republic government, including as its prime minister, and was executed in 1975 soon after the Khmer Rouge entered the capital. Most lakhon niyeay scripts stored at the Royal University of Fine Arts 'were destroyed by the Khmer Rouge or insects in the intervening years of disuse, and *lakhon niyeay*'s roots have not been sufficiently deep enough to be revived in the current environment' (Diamond 2012: 141).

Once surviving artists regrouped after the genocide of the late 1970s, they quickly established lakhon niyeay troupes in the capital, at the School of Fine Arts (which became a university again in 1989), and at the Department of Arts, both under the Ministry of Information and Culture. Spoken drama was popular for a while with contemporary audiences. But the National Theatre building, which opened in 1968 with an ambitious production of *A Midsummer Night's Dream*, suffered a fatal fire in 1994 near the end of refurbishment and was eventually torn down in 2008, leaving no permanent house for lakhon niyeay (Diamond 2012: 122). Nowadays, spoken drama is not so active due to the difficulty of attracting local audience members when the other forms of theatre, such as dance theatre, yiké and lakhon bassac, are active and broadcast on national and private TV channels. But spoken drama is still practised and taught at schools of fine arts, arts institutions and organizations. The two nominal troupes, the National Theatre Company of Cambodia Lakhon Niyeay Troupe and the Royal University of Fine Art's Lakhon Niyeay Troupe, only perform by commission from foreign NGOs, as evidenced by the 2001 *Chivit dor propey* (A Wounded Life) written by three teachers at the University and 'based on real stories of trafficked women' (Diamond 2012: 141).

V. Vietnam, by Trinh Nguyen

There are five principal forms of theatre that are performed today in modern Vietnam: (1) *cheo*, popular folk theatre; (2) *mua roi nuoc*, water puppetry; (3) *hat boi* (commonly referred to as *tuong* in north Vietnam), Chinese-based classical theatre; (4) *cai luong*, modern folk opera; and (5) *kich noi*, spoken drama. The first three genres are generally not considered to be 'modern' because of their dates of origin and performance characteristics. Cai luong and kich noi, on the other hand, came about in the twentieth century, with strong influences in style and content from the west.

Although cheo, mua roi nuoc and hat boi emerged between the eleventh and twelve centuries, they continue to hold a significant role in the world of performance art in Vietnam to this day. For this reason, this section will first briefly review these forms before presenting cai luong and kich noi.

The birth and aesthetic of each form is linked to a particular region of Vietnam, with cheo and mua roi nuoc from the north, cai luong in the south, and hat boi and kich noi found throughout the country. Cheo theatre has its roots in village festivals in northern Vietnam along the Red River Delta. It is a form of popular traditional musical theatre with stories taken from Vietnamese legends, poetry, history and daily life that have been passed down orally by anonymous authors. These stories are basically satirical in intent, often commenting on the peasant classes, farmers, monks, rich people, intellectuals, students, monks and so on. Standard stock characters such as a hero, heroine, clown and maiden are the soul of the play, offering romance, tragedy and comedy with poetry, song, dance and pantomime. Cheo uses vernacular language and for every situation or character, there is a specific song or declamatory style. It does not employ elaborate scenery, costume, makeup or gesture. Cheo is generally performed outdoors on one or two bed mats spread in the middle of a communal house. Today, it can be seen performed inside a theatre setting.

Hat boi is a form of Vietnamese classical theatre that also emerged in the eleventh century when a Mongolian actor, Ly Nguyen Cat, was captured by the Tran Emperor of Vietnam. In return for his life, Ly Nguyen Cat was ordered by the imperial court to teach the young elites of Vietnam the art of acting. By the eighteenth century hat boi had also become popular among commoners. Hat boi stories derived from Chinese and Vietnamese history, featuring loyal generals or ministers, filial piety and patriotism, often with the imperial family struggling against traitors, who invariably lose out in the end. As a result of its origin, hat boi's costumes, makeup, gestures and music are heavily influenced by Chinese theatre. Hat boi does not attempt to depict physical realities and is mainly portrayed through symbolic, conventional gestures and minimal scenic pieces. The acting area is bare and rectangular in shape, with minimal stage properties such as a table and a few chairs that can be rearranged to depict different sceneries.

Cheo continues to be mainly performed in north Vietnam while hat boi can be seen throughout the country. However, the popularity of both forms has declined in recent decades. The government seems especially to favour cheo and mua roi nuoc as a distinctively indigenous mass-based theatre.

Similar to cheo, mua roi nuoc also originated around the Red River Delta in north Vietnam, and dates back to the eleventh century. At first, many towns and villages in Vietnam had communal ponds that were used for mua roi nuoc performances. Presently, water puppetry is performed in a pool of water, with the water surface being the stage. During performance, watertight and durable wood and lacquered puppets are controlled by a pole and string apparatus hidden under the water surface by puppeteers standing in waist-deep water behind the stage. While puppets play their roles according to the direction of puppeteers, performers of cheo theatre sing songs to tell the story in words. The play generally focuses on the daily life of rural people, with folklores, Vietnamese legends and history that are passed down through many generations. Traditionally, the shows were thought to keep the spirits entertained enough so that they would not cause mischief. Today, water puppetry is a popular form of entertainment for local children and foreigners, who mainly rely on the visual impact of ten to twenty vignettes, typically performed in puppet theatres in Hanoi and Ho Chi Minh City, to understand the show.

While cheo and mua roi nuoc are strictly associated as dramatic genres from northern Vietnam, cai luong is classified as a southern theatrical form. Cai luong came into being at the turn of the twentieth century when Vietnamese people and customs encountered aspects of western culture introduced by the French. The French occupation of Vietnam, starting in 1858, led to rapid westernization of certain sections of society, and particularly the educated urban elite who attended French schools. In this new political reality, they were taught to read and write in a new Vietnamese script created by the French, called *quoc ngu* (national language), based on the Roman alphabet, and they were introduced to French literature, music and theatre. This new generation of Vietnamese became well versed in French culture. They were the first to experiment with mixing Vietnamese traditions and modern French influence. Out of such curiosity, playfulness and political intentions emerged a modern musical theatre form called cai luong.

Cai luong developed as a modernized form of hat boi mixed with modern Vietnamese vernacular and naturalistic acting style. Stylization and conventions borrowed from hat boi theatre, combined with French influence, created a hybridized form between spoken drama, mainly French realism, and classical Vietnamese theatre. It first appeared in the rural areas of the Mekong Delta in approximately 1910, with musicians performing spoken declamations and stylized gestures known as *ca ra bo* (singing with gesture) with musical accompaniment. As it developed, the cai luong repertoire slowly expanded, adopting stories, musical influences and performance styles from the court and folk genres of different regions of the country. Music, instruments, themes, plots, forms and costumes were also borrowed, primarily from the Chinese and French. It flourished in the urban centres under the management of producers who made cai luong a component of vaudeville and circus shows as they introduced many innovations in content, form and technology.

Cai luong is described as a kind of musical theatre or operetta. Approximately 60 per cent of a cai luong play contains music and songs. The backbone of cai luong is a melody called *vong co* ('nostalgia for the past'), which came from the Mekong Delta in the south of Vietnam around the same time that ca ra bo also emerged. It is typically associated with approximately twenty songs, each of which can be sung with different emotional tempos to make up various versions. Vong co is sung in a first-person narrative with spoken words often interspersed between singing melodies of vong co to allow the character to express his/her deep inner feelings of joy, anger, love and happiness. The vong co song is usually performed in a duet with the practice of placing spoken dialogue between the sung phrases, with attention to maintaining the flow of the melody established by the previous singer. Improvisation is allowed in the middle of a phrase but the performer must maintain the rhythm within the sung phrase.

The first note, however, is the most important in the phrase and is held. The ability to capture the sentiment of this first note is the crucial test of an aspiring cai luong singer. No performer can become a cai luong star without being able to handle this note successfully. If the performer enters the song from his/her line of dialogue, he/she may begin singing on any word he/she chooses, since the performer usually sings a number of words before the musicians start to accompany him/her. The soul of the performer and the character is expressed by the actor's ability to manipulate the sound of the word. Thus, the success of a cai luong play depends on the sweet voices of the cast. It is said that the spectators go to a cai luong show mainly to see how their favourite performers deliver the songs in a play. After the delivery of the first word by the performer, the audience typically gasps in recognition, followed by clapping, which is expected from the audience.

The orchestra consists of wind, stringed and percussion instruments such as the *tranh* (16-stringed zither), *nguyet kim* (two-string moon lute), *dan ty ba* (pear-shaped lute), *dan nhi* (two-string spike fiddle), *dan bau* (monochord), *tieu* (the straight flute) or *sao* (transverse flute). The 'modern and western' instruments of violin and guitar were added to the orchestra sometime at the start of the 1930s.

Cai luong normally highlights Vietnamese moral values through mainly two types of play, categorized as ancient and modern. Modern cai luong plays consist of stories about modern Vietnamese society that often deal with a romantic love story blended with family and social relationships. Ancient cai luong plays include plots based on Chinese and Vietnamese legends and history from feudal times, with performers dressed as kings, queens and warriors in old-fashioned costumes. An ancient cai luong play can be identified by its elaborate and colourful costumes and dress pieces with large and beautiful glittery hairpieces (Figure 16.3). Although cai luong remained extremely popular as late as the 1980s, nowadays its popularity has dwindled, especially among the younger generation.

As cai luong was being developed in the early twentieth century, another important modern form of theatre, kich noi, was also introduced to Vietnam. While cai luong is mainly a musical form, kich noi is primarily spoken dialogue. Stylized acting, elaborate costume and makeup, songs and conventionalized scenes found in cai luong plays were removed and replaced by western realistic theatre.

Similar to cai luong, kich noi also gained popularity among the same group of local intellectuals who were French-educated and required not only to study but create performances based on plays written by Corneille, Racine and Molière. For instance, Molière's comedy *The Miser* (L'Avare) became the first French drama to be produced in Vietnam. Plays on contemporary life make up the majority of the repertory of kich noi and it quickly became a vehicle used for social and political criticism. *Ong Tay An-nam* (The French Annamite), published in 1931 by Nam Xuong (1905–58), was the first play to have dealt directly with the value of westernization and the nationalism of Europeanized Vietnamese.

Adapting the Russian art style of socialist realism, kich noi quickly became a form of theatrical resistance for Vietnamese nationalists as tension escalated first with the French during the

Figure 16.3 Cai luong play *Thuy Kieu* performed at the Pan Asian Repertory Theatre, New York, 2011, directed by Nguyen Thi Minh Ngoc, with Ngoc Dang as Thuy Kieu and Leon Quang Le as Ho Ton Hien.

(Photo by Nguyen Minh Ngoc)

Indochina War (1945–54) and then later with the Americans during the Vietnam War (1954–75). After the Vietnam War ended, kich noi remained rooted in socialist realism until the 1980s when a new generation of artists began to produce plays critiquing the failure of socialism, growing corruption and extreme consumption affecting the country at the time. Luu Quang Vu (1948–88) was one of the most prolific playwrights of this new generation. His most famous play, *Hon Truong Ba, da hang thit* (Truong Ba's Soul in the Butcher's Skin, 1988), confronted the ineffectiveness of the Vietnamese establishment and the clash between traditional and modern values.

Kich noi in Vietnam today is an assortment of dramas, including those dealing with contemporary Vietnamese society, plays based on Vietnamese children's folktales, and foreign adapted plays such as Shakespeare's *A Midsummer Night's Dream* and *Miss Saigon*, many of which are showcased at two popular kich noi theatres, including Nha Hat Tuoi Tre Viet Nam (Youth Theatre of Vietnam) in Ho Chi Minh City and Nha Hat Kich (Spoken Drama Theatre) in Hanoi.

For the past few decades, experimental theatres have appeared in smaller theatres in Ho Chi Minh City, such as the Nha Hat Kich San khh Nhh 5B (5B Little Theatre) and Nha Hat Tuoi Tre ViYP Nam (Youth Theatre of Vietnam). In 2006 the Vietnam Association of Theatre Artists organized the first national experimental theatre festival to allow artists throughout the country to meet one another and to exchange ideas in the hope of creating new artistic methods to attract the audience. Interest in experimental theatres in Vietnam is slowly growing because young Vietnamese artists are more willing to test out new approaches to scriptwriting, directing, acting and staging. In the process they are introducing innovative theatrical genres that will hopefully appeal to contemporary audiences.

Theatres in Vietnam have always evolved with the social-political reality of Vietnam. By the early 1980s, it had become evident that the Communist Party was struggling to maintain its ideology in the face of pressing, especially economic, realities. In order to save Vietnam from gradual degeneration, the party decided to introduce new reform known as *doi moi* ('change anew') in 1986. As a part of doi moi reform, the government enacted a policy known as *xa hoi hoa* (literal translation, 'socialization', also known as 'privatization' in western terms). Xa hoi hoa directly impacted Vietnamese theatres, as the Ministry of Culture and Information has now decided that society and not the government has the responsibility to support the arts financially. However, the government did not propose a socialization plan, causing theatre companies to struggle in an effort to transition from total reliance on state subsidies to greater financial independency. While the government decided to let go of its financial responsibilities for the arts, it was unwilling to release its grip on state ideological control and censorship, which further exasperated the existing problem by discouraging new creative works that the government deemed as acceptable.

As the theatres in Vietnam struggle to stay afloat, performers face many associated difficulties. The small amount of subsidy provided to the theatres by the government is not enough for performers to earn a living wage. Many performers today do not consider acting as their main profession. Those who have a harder time letting go of performing find themselves resorting to *chay* shows ('running to shows'), performing at many restaurants and nightclubs in one night to supplement their income.

Despite the gloomy prospects discussed above, my research in 2010 revealed some promising changes. Since the 1990s the Vietnamese government at large has made some efforts to help identify challenges and propose solutions. Their efforts to revitalize theatre through television shows, performance competitions, festivals and conferences are evidence of these efforts.

Further, many informants I interviewed in Vietnam in 2010 consistently defined Vietnamese theatres in relationship to the nation's culture and people. They believe that theatre will not disappear because it is a key gateway into the 'heart and mind' of the Vietnamese. Such sentiments also hold true today among the Vietnamese diaspora communities. Skits from well-known hat boi, cai luong and kich noi plays are most commonly viewed through extremely popular live recordings of Vietnamese music concerts produced in the United States, known as 'Paris By Night' or 'Asia'. It is through such cultural media that these stage forms remains popular and beloved among Vietnamese emigrants living overseas. It allows the older generations to hang on to their distant homeland and to pass on a piece of themselves to their foreign-born children and grandchildren. In this sense, Vietnamese theatre both in Vietnam and overseas will continue to endure, as its people have done through many historical periods of conflict and transformation.

Note

1 For more on Fā Ngoum and the roles his story plays in the creation of contemporary Laos identity, see Goscha and Ivarsson (2003).

Bibliography

Addiss, Stephen (1971) 'Theater Music of Vietnam', *Southeast Asia: An International Quarterly*, 1 (1–2): 129–52.

ASEAN Puppetry Association (2013) 'Laos', www.aseanpuppetry.org/country-members/laos/, accessed 10 September 2014.

Bawi, Nuam (2013) 'Banned for Years, Satirical Shows Return for Thingyan', *Myammar Times*, www.mmtimes.com/index.php/lifestyle/6487-banned-for-years-satirical-shows-return-for-thingyan.html, accessed 10 April 2015.

Bowers, Faubian (1956) *Theatre in the East: A Survey of Asian Dance and Drama*, New York: Ayer Company Publication.

Brandon, James R. (1967) *Theatre in Southeast Asia*, Cambridge, MA: Harvard University Press.

BWW News Desk (2014) 'Bond Street Theatre Joins Burmese Troupe Thukhuma Khayeethe to Spread Conflict Resolution', *Broadway World*, www.broadwayworld.com/article/Bond-Street-Theatre-Joins-Burmese-Troupe-Thukhuma-Khayeethe-to-Spread-Conflict-Resolution-20140623, accessed 10 April 2015.

Dac Nhan (1987) *Tim hieu am nhac cai luong* (Understanding the Music of Cai Luong), Ho Chi Minh: Nha xuat ban.

Dearborn, Lynne M., and John C. Stallmeyer (2010) *Inconvenient Heritage: Erasure and Global Tourism in Luang Prabang*, Walnut Creek, CA: Left Coast Press.

Diamond, Catherine (1997) 'The Pandora's Box of "Doi Moi": The Open-Door Policy and Contemporary Theatre in Vietnam', *New Theatre Quarterly*, 13.

—— (2012) *Communities of Imagination: Contemporary Southeast Asian Theatres*, Honolulu: University of Hawai'i Press.

Duangpatra, Jukkrit (2001) *Plae, Plaeng Lae Prae Rup Bot Lakhon* (Translation, Adaptation and Transmutation of Play Scripts), Bangkok: Samnak Phim Siam.

Garfias, Robert, 'Burmese Hsaing and Anyein', Asian Society, http://asiasociety.org/burmese-hsaing-and-anyein?page=0,0, accessed 10 April 2015.

Goscha, Christopher E., and Soren Ivarsson (2003) 'Introduction', in Christopher E. Goscha and Soren Ivarsson (eds) *Contesting Visions of the Laos Past: Lao Historiography at the Crossroads*, xi–xxix, Copenhagen: Nordic Institute of Asian Studies.

Ha Van Cau (1994) *Phong cach va thi phap trong nghe thuat cai luong* (Styles and Laws in the Art of Cai luong), Hanoi: Vien San Khau.

Hauch, Duane Ernie (1972) 'The Cai Luong Theatre of Vietnam, 1915–1970', unpublished dissertation, Southern Illinois University.

Le Long Van (1989) *Ke chuyen cai luonng* (Telling Stories about Cai Luong), Thanh Pho Ho Chi Minh: Nha Xuat Ban Thanh Pho Ho Chi Minh.

Luangprabang-Laos.com (2014) 'Royal Ballet Theatre', www.luangprabang-laos.com/Royal-Ballet-Theatre, accessed 9 September 2014.Luong Tu (1987) 'Cai luong, a Theatre in Rapid Development', *Vietnam Social Sciences*, Thanh Pho Ho Chi Minh: Committee for Social Sciences, 56–60.

Ly Daravuth and Ingrid Muan (2001) *Cultures of Independence: An Introduction to Cambodian Arts and Culture in the 1950's and 1960's*. Phnom Penh: Reyum.

Ly Theam Teng (2001) 'Research on Lakhaoun Khmer', in Ly Daravuth and Ingrid Muan (eds) *Cultures of Independence: An Introduction to Cambodian Arts and Culture in the 1950's and 1960's*, 90–9, Phnom Penh: Reyum.

Mackerras, Colin (1987) 'Theatre in Vietnam', *Asian Theatre Journal* 4 (1): 1–28.

Mahasarinand, Pawit (2014) 'Contemporary Theatre in a City of Contrasts: Muangthai Rachadalai Theatre and Democrazy Theatre Studio,' paper presented at International Federation of Theatre Research conference, University of Warwick.

Malakul, Pin (1996) *Ngan Lakhon Khong Phrabat Somdet Phra Ramathibodi Srisintara Mahavajiravudh Phra Mongkutklao Chao Phaendin Siam* (Introduction to the Theatrical Works of His Majesty King Vajiravudh of Siam), Bangkok: Thai Watthana Phanit.

Nguyen Dinh Nghi (1995), *Tuyen tap cheo cai luong* (A Journal of Cheo Cai luong), Hanoi: Van Hoa Thong Tin.

Nguyen, Khai Thu (2010) 'Sensing Vietnam: Melodramas of Nation from Colonialism to Market Reform', unpublished dissertation, University of California, Berkeley.

Nguyen, Phong T. (ed.) (1991) *New Perspective on Vietnamese Theatre*, Yale University: Southeast Asia Studies.

Panoramic Journeys, 'South East Asian Festival', www.panoramicjourneys.com/thingyan-festival.php, accessed 10 April 2015.

Pham Duy (1975) *Music of Vietnam*, Dale R. Whitesid (ed.), Carbondale and Edwardsville: Southern Illinois University Press.

Post Staff (2001) 'Last Act for Khmer Bassac Opera', *The Phnom Penh Post*, 11 May, www.phnompenhpost.com/national/last-act-khmer-bassac-opera, accessed 3 December 2014.

Roper, Matt (2013) 'Freedom From Fear: Remembering Comedian U Pa Pa Lay', *Huffington Post*, www.huffingtonpost.co.uk/matt-roper/u-pa-pa-lay-burma_b_3713271.html, accessed 10 April 2015.

Rutnin, M. M. (2008) 'Phatthanakan khong nattasin lae kanlakhon samai mai' (Development of Modern Dance and Theatre), in K. Pramoj and N. Sanitwong Na Ayutthaya (eds) *Laksana Thai III: Sinlapa Kan Sadaeng* (Thainess III: Performing Arts), Bangkok: Thai Watthana Phanit.

Song, Ban (1960) *The Vietnamese Theatre*, Hanoi: Foreign Language Publication.

Song, Kim (1983) *Cuoc doi san khau cua chung toi* (The Theatre Lives of Ours), Hanoi: Nha Xuat Ban Van Hoa.

Tran Van Khai (1970) *Nghe thuat san khau Viet Nam* (The Art of Vietnamese Theatre), Saigon: Nha Sach Khai Tri.

Truong Binh Tong (1983) *Nghe thuat cai luong* (The Art of Cai Luong), Hanoi: Vien San Khau.

Tungtang, Paradee (2011) 'Shakespeare in Thailand', unpublished thesis, University of Warwick.

UNESCO (1995) 'Town of Luang Prabang', http://whc.unesco.org/en/list/479, 4 September 2014.

UNICEF (2007) 'Puppets Tour for Bird Flu Prevention in Lao PDR', www.unicef.org/eapro/media_6157.html, accessed 16 September, 2014.

Vien San Khau (1987) *Lich su san khau Viet Nam* (A Theatre of Vietnam), Hanoi: Vien San Khau.

Vuong Hong Sen (1968) *Nam muoi nam me hat* (Fifty Years of Addiction to Singing), Saigon: Pham Quant Khai.

17

Modern theatre in maritime Southeast Asia

Indonesia, Malaysia, the Philippines and Singapore

Michael Bodden

In July 1975, Indonesian playwright/director W. S. Rendra's Bengkel Teater (Theatre Workshop) performed Rendra's own play, *Kisah perjuangan suku Naga* (The Struggle of the Naga Tribe, 1975) in Jakarta's Taman Ismail Marzuki performing arts complex to large, appreciative audiences (Lane 1979: xxv). This play was interesting not only because it offered a thinly veiled critique of some of the then New Order government elite's development policies and attitudes, but also because, through the presence in the dramatis personae of a *'dalang'* (puppeteer) who incorporated aspects of the *wayang kulit* (shadow theatre) puppeteer and clown figures, as well as a dramatic structure that paralleled that of a traditional wayang play, Rendra's work embodied a growing trend in modern Indonesian theatre to 'indigenize' contemporary theatre performances. In fact, Rendra (1935–2009) had been leading the way in incorporating elements of Indonesia's traditional theatres into modern, western-style theatrical performance for several years prior to *The Struggle of the Naga Tribe*, including *Oedipus Rex* (1969), influenced by traditional Balinese dance-dramas and rituals, *Waiting for Godot* (1970), using the sense of humour found in traditional folk drama, and *Macbeth* (1970), in which the actors performed in Javanese surjan shirts (Gillitt 2001: 159).

This fusion of western, or western-inspired, dramatic texts with elements of local culture and performance traditions points to one central dynamic of much modern theatre in the maritime countries of Southeast Asia. This dynamic involved both a desire to participate in and perform a global culture dominated by the western countries that had once colonized much of Southeast Asia, and at the same time an urgent need to create novel ways of performing modern theatre that highlighted the cultural identity of these newly independent nations as something distinctive and 'local'. In what follows, I will describe the historical trajectory of the modern theatres of Indonesia, Malaysia, the Philippines and Singapore from the late nineteenth century to the present moment, examining the productive tensions of this twofold desire, as well as mapping the ways in which theatre practitioners in each country tried to resolve the dilemma. In doing so, it will become clear that in each country, the progression from a series of hybrid forms to a more strict adherence to western-style naturalism or psychological realism, followed by a newer hybrid fusion of western-style theatre with local traditions, was also accompanied by ongoing negotiations between the fledgling national states and theatre makers over the shape of national culture. This negotiation sometimes involved a convergence of interests, at other times the domination of one party over the other, and at still other times a struggle between theatre practitioners and the governments of their countries to control the use and interpretation of both western and local traditional cultures. Though there are similarities in the general pattern, both theatre and state in each country faced specific social landscapes and challenges that determined the exact ways in which the negotiations or conflicts between theatre makers and the state apparatus play out.

Traditional theatres and early hybrid forms

Indonesia boasts of a rich array of traditional performance arts, including puppet theatres, dance-dramas, trance ritual dances, masked performances and many others. The Malaysia/Singapore areas can similarly point to a number of unique traditions, quite a few of which are related to those in Indonesia. In the Philippines, there seem to be relatively few pre-Spanish dramatic forms save the rituals and dances of various local tribes (Tiongson 1989: 27–8). Hispanization of the Philippines saw the development of Christian-themed folk theatre genres such as the *sinakulo* (passion play) and the *komedya*, which dramatized localized versions of European courtly romances in which Christian knights fought against their rivals, the Moors (ibid.: 29–30).

Many of the earlier forms of theatre in maritime Southeast Asia were epic in nature, their plots ranging widely over time and space, and combined drama with music and clowning. In these genres, actors played types rather than complex and developing individualized characters. In many instances, these performing arts were linked to spirituality and religious observance. They often presented well-known stories in highly stylized forms with set patterns of scenes and events, generally valuing continuity with traditional form and content over innovation and creativity, although these kinds of performance may have changed substantially over time to complement social changes, as has been shown with the case of Javanese wayang kulit (leather puppet performance) shadow puppet theatre (Ras 1976; Sears 1996).

Towards the end of the nineteenth century (roughly the 1880s–1890s), new forms were brought to Southeast Asia both from Europe and via mediators, such as the Parsi theatre of India, which drew heavily on European theatrical conventions. The overall effect of these influences was to lay the groundwork for more modern styles of western-inspired theatre in the coming century. From the European musical theatre, emergent popular theatre in the Malay peninsula, Singapore and the archipelago, such as the Malaya-Singaporean *bangsawan* ('of the nobility') and Surabaya's *Komedie Stamboel* (Istanbul-style theatre), may have borrowed the 'proscenium stage, wing-and-drop set, focused stage lighting, emotive character-based acting, musical accompaniment, division of the plays into scenes and acts, makeup and costumes, and many of the plots of plays.' From the Parsi theatre they may have got some of the same elements, as well as South Asian and Middle Eastern stories, concepts of modern commercially oriented management and the combination of melodrama, song and dance, and spectacle. Finally, the religious function of much earlier performance was replaced in the performance of these genres by an emphasis on commercialism and entertainment (Cohen 2006: 41–2; Tan 1993: 18–25). These theatre genres, in turn, strongly influenced the development of a great variety of folk theatre forms in the Dutch Indies and British Malaya, such as *lenong*, *ludruk*, *ketoprak*, *abdulmuluk*, *sandiwara* ('secret news' or spoken drama), the Sino-Malay *opera derma* (charity opera) and *jikey*

(Cohen 2001: 320; 2006: 3–4; 2010: xi; Sumardjo 1992: 110–12). Furthermore, there was a lively cross-border traffic of bangsawan troupes between North Sumatra in the Dutch Indies and British Malaya (and especially Penang and Singapore). As the Second World War ended and these performers found film a more lucrative arena, Malayo-Indonesian bangsawan performers helped establish Singapore as a centre of film production in the Malay world (Plomp 2012: 382–3).

In the Philippines, a similar phenomenon was occurring with the introduction of the Spanish musical form, the *zarzuela*, beginning in 1878 or 1879. Ensuing Filipino-created productions from the early twentieth century onwards featured romantic and social melodrama, western-style musical ensembles, painted drop curtains, makeup, songs in the intervals between acts, and were performed on proscenium stages (Fernandez 1978: 32, 99–140; Lapeña-Bonifacio 1972: 14). In contrast to the Spanish-derived religious pageants, however, Filipino zarzuela plays began to incorporate a greater sense of realism in story, plots, costumes and the presentation of contemporary issues, including some anti-colonial pieces (Tiongson 1989: 31–2). Most stories focused on love among the elites, incorporating many comic episodes and attacks on perceived social ills such as usury, addiction to cockfighting, corrupt politicians and facile Americanization (Tiongson n.d.: 17).

Original spoken dramas began to be written and staged as early as 1878 in the Philippines (Fernandez 1978: 28) and the late 1880s or 1893 in the Dutch Indies, while being pioneered much later in British Malaya (1940s). In the Indies these were chiefly published to meet the need of amateur groups wishing to stage komedi stambul[1] plays (Sumardjo 1992: 373; Cohen 2010: ix–xi). However, more consistent and numerous productions of original Southeast Asian dramas only began in the twentieth century. Responding to American occupation of the Philippines, local writers such as Aurelio Tolentino (1867–1915) and Juan Abad (1872–1932) composed allegories of Filipino servitude, rebellion and liberation whose productions, *Kahapon, Ngayon at Bukas* (Yesterday, Today and Tomorrow, 1903) and *Tanikalang Guinto* (The Golden Bracelet, 1902) led to the arrest of both playwrights by American colonial authorities (Lapeña-Bonifacio 1972; Lumbera 1984: 36–40). Many original zarzuelas were also composed in a variety of local languages by playwrights such as the Tagalog Severino Reyes (1861–1942) from around the turn of the century until the early 1930s (Lumbera 1984: 40–2). By the 1930s and 40s, English-language drama in a realist vein was being written, though performances seemed confined mainly to the universities where they were staged by university drama clubs (Fernandez 1983: 7).

As Matthew Cohen has written, Indies writers began to pen original plays from at least the beginning of the twentieth century, while a more substantial corpus of dramatic texts began to be produced and performed from the mid-1920s on (see Cohen, this volume). Plays were written both for the Sino-Malay amateur stage and for commercial troupes. In addition, nationalist allegories inspired partly by traditional theatre forms – Rustam Effendi's (1903–79) *Bebasari* (Essential Liberty, 1926) and Sanusi Pané's (1905–68) *Sandhykala Ning Majapahit* (Twilight over Majapahit, 1932) are two examples – were also created and performed by nationalist youth groups, showing as they do early attempts to create modern, western-realist inspired new dramas drawing influence from sources as diverse as Shakespeare and Tagore, but that also exhibit the persistence of traditional models. *Essential Liberty*, for instance, though offering significant characterization and politico-ethical debates, also echoes the plot of the *wayang Ramayana* story and employs Sumatran *pantun* poetic metre to structure its language (Winet 2010: 25). Sanusi Pané's play, similarly, though adding considerable realism in the depiction of its major character's internal spiritual and ethical debates, as well as its construction of a plot of political intrigue, still features several elements that tie it to wayang representations such as evocations of the ideal kingdom, a meditating hero, clown servants and ogre-like enemies (Bodden 2010a: 27–8).

The rise of psychological realism

However, psychological realism or naturalism, seen in the region as the definitive, current form of modern, western theatre, and partially realized in some of the work by Sino-Indonesian writers and commercial theatre groups such as Miss Riboet's Orion and Dardanella, was increasingly viewed as the style to emulate in order to participate in a global artistic modernity. This becomes especially evident in a number of the plays written in the Philippines in the 1940s, and in the Dutch Indies, after a series of 1930s debates about whether 'Asian' or 'western' cultures were the best basis for a future Indonesian national culture, from the mid–late 1930s (Bodden 2010a: 27–8). Indonesian Armin Pané's (1908–70) *Lukisan Masa* (A Portrait of the Times, 1937) is a good example. This play portrays the ways in which the economic depression affected the gendered dynamics of employment in the Indies. Lack of available employment creates an existential crisis for the hero, Suparman, who betrays a promise to his fiancée, Harsini. Currently unemployed, his pride will not allow him to be supported by Harsini's schoolteacher's salary. An array of supporting characters all begin to be fleshed out as people with individualized psychological profiles, behaviours and tag lines that identify them and allow the audience or reader to catch a glimpse of their underlying personae. Similarly, the issues of concern in the characters' milieu – gender relations, changing times, the ties between parents and children, economic opportunities – all highlight the shift towards an ever more 'realist' or 'naturalist' style of drama. Wilfrido Ma. Guerrero's English-language *Wanted: A Chaperon* (1940) is a Philippine example of this trend. Guerrero (1911–95) constructs a domestic comedy of manners in which a father and mother must cope with the changing dating habits of their children, which raise the spectre of gossip and result in social misunderstandings. In addition, Guerrero's 'parents' are also beset by unscrupulous and dull-witted servants, suggesting class dimensions of colonial Philippine society. *Wanted: A Chaperon* demonstrates Guerrero's keen capacity for fleshing out types – the family patriarch, the indulgent mother, the pampered son and daughter, the seemingly dull-witted but stubbornly resistant servant – into more complex characters while carefully observing domestic issues of the day.

During the Japanese occupation, Indonesian theatre was fashioned into a propaganda instrument for the new colonial power, with itinerant troupes performing in regions such as North Sumatra (Bodden 2010b: 55), or popular commercial theatre troupes mounting plays on converted cinema stages, all of which had to submit their scripts for approval to Japanese censors (Winet 2010: 126–7). The Japanese occupation was also a time when an amateur group, seen by Indonesian theatre historians as seminal in ushering in an age of modern, western-style theatre, Sandiwara Penggemar Maya (the Illusion Amateur Theatre), was formed. In its short existence (May 1944–late 1945) Maya mainly staged original plays by Usmar Ismail (1921–71) and his brother, Abu Hanifah (1906–81, writing under the name of El Hakim) asserting a strong sense of nationalism and, in Hanifah's case, the required pan-Asian and anti-western sentiments. Most interesting is Ismail's *Liburan Seniman* (Artists' Holiday, 1944), in which young nationalist theatre makers argue that the new theatre has to articulate profound ideas and contribute to the spiritual uplift of the nation. As though engaged in a polemic with the commercial theatre of the Dutch colonial era, Usmar's heroes argue against an older style of theatre which they see as lurid, overly sentimental and offering only empty dreams. This subplot of *Artists' Holiday* marks the growing sense of serious purpose, and at the same time a suspicion, if not always outright rejection, of theatre as a commercialized, popular form of entertainment. This mistrust of commercial theatre remained a strong presence in modern Indonesian drama theatre from the 1950s to well into the 1980s.

Independence and the dominance of western-style realism

The end of the Second World War also brought the era of colonialism closer to conclusion, with the Philippines gaining independence in 1946, Indonesia in 1949 after a 4-year struggle, Malaysia in 1957 and Singapore in 1963. During these years, fledgling national cultures sought to position themselves as equals on a global stage, though in the 1950s and early 1960s, as noted above for the immediate pre-war era, that often meant attempting to imitate western or socialist cultures, frequently perceived as the global cultural standards. Only in the late 1960s did postcolonial states begin to consolidate their existence, summoning public debates about new patterns of national culture. As a result of this process, new and more complicated relations between modern theatre movements and nation-states gradually began to become evident.

For a decade or more after the Second World War, psychological realism dominated the modern stage in the Philippines and Indonesia. Professional actors from the commercial theatres frequently moved to the more lucrative arena of film. Others, like Wilfrido Guerrero, continued to write English-language domestic dramas like his 1948 play, *Three Rats*. In *Three Rats*, a husband murders his wife and her lover after a series of scenes suggesting that superficially Americanized Filipinos tend to fall back upon traditional rules and means of settling conflicts in situations of moral confusion. Nick Joaquin's (1917–2004) *Portrait of the Artist as a Filipino* (1952) showed a similar cultural clash as ageing Hispanized Filipinos struggle to adapt their genteel manners to the more mercenary, commercial ways of the younger generation, and a resentful, formerly impoverished youth. Tragic social circumstances were highlighted by other playwrights as well. Severino Montano (1915–80) authored plays such as *Sabina* (1953), in which a young girl languishing in the gloomy and limited life of a small farming village tragically falls in love with and becomes pregnant by an American businessman who loves her in return, but cannot marry her. Alberto Florentino's (1931–) *The World is an Apple* (1960) raised class issues by showing the lack of choices confronting the poor.

Indonesia's outstanding dramatist of the late 1940s and early 1950s, Utuy Tatang Sontani (1920–79), created tense works in which a variety of characters search for genuine humanity amid the storm of social revolution and the aftermath of independence. His most famous play, *Awal dan Mira* (Awal and Mira, 1949) is the story of an outsider critical of what he sees as the many defects of contemporary society, but who nonetheless places all his faith in his love for a coffee-shop attendant whose social background is radically different from his and whose true circumstances he does not really understand. As the play progresses, the audience realizes that this anti-hero, Awal, may be mentally unbalanced, unable to see his own weaknesses even as he brutally dismisses all others as 'clowns' (Aveling 1979: 19–25). Sontani's pessimistic reading of post-independence Indonesian society was one response to changing social conditions and the chaos following the war of independence. However, other Indonesian 'realist' plays of the period, such as Muhammad Ali's (1927–) radio play, *Lapar* (Hungry, 1952), Motinggo Busye's (1937–99) *Malam Jahanam* (Night of the Accursed, 1958) or Misbah Yusa Biran's (1933–2012) *Bung Besar* (Big Comrade, 1958), exhibit similar pessimism on topics such as the difficult economic times for the urban poor following independence, individual narcissism and morality, and political cynicism and hypocrisy.

The Malaysian pattern is similar to that of Indonesia and the Philippines, though it began later and its development was more compressed. Much Malaysian literary activity, including the writing and staging of plays, took place in Singapore, which was then a part of British Malaya, with writers such as Usman Awang (1929–2001) and Kalam Hamidi (1936–) residing there until after independence in 1957 (Jit 1989b: 211–13). On Malaysia's peninsula, the Malayan Theatre Arts Group (MATG) staged English-language plays, while Malay-language playwrights such as Shahrom Husain (1919–2008) penned bangsawan-style *purbawara* ('old stories') dramas glorifying the Malay sultanates, the mythological and legendary heroes of the past, and the Malay warrior spirit. However, beginning in the early 1960s, a few years after independence, the leadership of the MATG was claimed by local Malaysians, and Husain and others began to create more tightly scripted Malay-language dramas still focused on the past, but more critical of what were deemed feudal values. The results were to be seen in Husain's *Si Bongkok Tanjung Puteri* (The Hunchback of Tanjung Puteri, 1961), which featured an ugly, rude and aggressive anti-hero who rebels against establishment forces of late nineteenth-century Johore as they are reconciling themselves to British involvement in their affairs. Similarly, Usman Awang's *Matinya Seorang Pahlawan* (Death of a Hero, 1961) reversed traditional values of the Hang Tuah/Hang Jebat legend in presenting the rebel, Hang Jebat, as a hero rather than a traitor, because he rebels against the arbitrary rule of his sultan, becoming an exemplar struggling for truth and justice (Jit 1989a: 179–80).

During the 1960s, as had happened earlier in the Philippines and Indonesia, more realist-style plays with contemporary themes, characters and sets became dominant among Malaysian amateur theatre groups. Many of these dramas took current social issues as their core, and were set in the sitting rooms of the main character's household (Nanney 2007: 861). Mustapha Kamil Yassin (1925–) became the foremost advocate of the new style, arguing that the poetic purbawara dramas clung too tightly to the past. Yassin wrote mostly comic plays, the most famous of which is *Atap Gending Atap Rembia* (Tiled Roof, Thatched Roof, 1963), suggesting reconciliation between rural and urban, young and old, ethnic Chinese and Malays. Despite its realist attempt to represent modern situations, the play still features two clown servants reminiscent of the shadow theatre (Jit 1989a: 180). Usman Awang's *Tamu di Bukit Kenny* (Visitors at Kenny Hill, 1967) is another good example of this realist trend. It portrays the travails of a government official to whom everyone brings their complaints. Amid the stress of his position, he must also face the fact that in the spirit of Malaysia's modern development, his children have acquired foreign bad habits such as dancing to rock and roll and reading pornographic materials. *Visitors at Kenny Hill* thus shows the perceived contradictions of modernization for Malay intellectuals such as Awang (Nanney, 2007: 861).

Singapore's modern theatre culture is characterized by several distinctive language streams, a phenomenon tied to the island nation's multi-ethnic makeup as constructed by colonial immigration policies. Though beginning as separate streams, they would partially cross-pollinate, especially from the 1980s on, to create distinctively multicultural initiatives that could characterize the modern local identity of Singaporean culture. In 1955, the durable Malay-language Sriwana group was formed, and under Kalam Hamidi's leadership a 4PM (association of Malay Youths) theatre group also began to stage both purbawara style dramas as well as *drama moden*, the Malay name for realist-style modern plays. Modern Chinese-language theatre also dates its genesis to 1955 with the establishment of the Singapore Amateur Players (also known as the Singapore Arts Theatre, SAP). This group, mainly alumni of Chung Cheng high school, had been trained in western dramaturgy and Stanislavskian acting methods and wished to promulgate progressive social messages in their dramas. SAP staged works by Cao Yu, Ibsen, Chekhov and Gorky, among others, though during the era of the Chinese Cultural Revolution, it did create theatre similar to the militant non-naturalistic theatre common then in China. Kuo Pao Kun (1939–2002), a key figure in much later Singaporean theatre, became active in the late 1960s, staging 'epic' naturalist plays with the Arts Ensemble of the Practice Performing Arts School where he taught. Many of Kuo's plays were based on real-life stories of economic and social dislocation in a rapidly developing and corporatizing Singapore. English-language theatre also flowered briefly in the early 1960s, centred on the activities of the Experimental Theatre Club

(ETC) and two playwrights whose work the ETC staged, Lim Chor Phee and Goh Poh Seng (1936–2010). The plays of the former focused on the hedonistic and materialistic aspects of Singapore society, while the latter wrote sympathetic portrayals of Singapore's teochew working class (Jit 1989b).

Such work in Singapore highlights the political and ideological struggles engulfing much of independence- and post-independence-era Southeast Asia. These conflicts were clearly expressed in modern Indonesian theatre as well, where the last decade of President Sukarno's rule (1955–65) witnessed the creation of left-aligned cultural groups such as Lekra (Lembaga Kebudayaan Rakyat or the Institute of People's Culture) and rival Islamic cultural groups such as Lesbumi (Lembaga Seni Budaya Islam – The Institute of Islamic Art and Culture). Most political parties eventually sponsored their own cultural organization, and the period saw a remarkable output of a wide range of dramas and performances. There was some experimentation with the use of traditional forms for modern dramas in this period, though different modes of realism still dominated, and there were increasing demands for plays to conform to leftist ideas of appropriate revolutionary nationalist content. Leftist groups such as Lekra created revolutionary realist plays that decried regional rebellions, agitated for the implementation of legislated land reform and condemned what they saw as greedy, unpatriotic capitalist-bureaucrats. The most famous of these is Bachtiar Siagian's (1923–2002) *Batu Merah Lemabah Merapi* (The Red Rock of Merapi Valley, 1959), which portrays a coalition of loyal nationalist prisoners, led by an heroic and ultimately, self-sacrificing communist cadre, attempting to escape from certain death in a concentration camp run by a regional separatist group. Lekra members also formed agitprop groups in some locations, as well as larger mobile song and dance ensembles. Islamic groups presented plays based on Islamic scriptural stories, on the exploits of legendary and historical Islamic figures or on Islam's role in the national revolution. A well-crafted example is Mohammed Diponegoro's (1928–82) *Iblis* (Devil, 1961). *Devil* retells the story of Ibrahim's temptation to abandon his vow to sacrifice his son for God. Nationalist groups developed their own works as well, the best known of which was an S. M. Ardan (1932–2006) version of the Jakarta area tale of *Nyai Dasima*. In Ardan's retelling of the tale, Dasima, the native mistress of a European colonial, desires to leave her European master and live with her own people once again. Feeling spurned and vengeful, her master hires a thug to murder her. A number of these groups, across the political spectrum, also experimented with creating colossal dance-dramas or *sendratari* celebrating their parties, or themes and events which illustrated their political slant on key social issues (Bodden 2012). The destruction of the communist party and the subsequent fall from power of President Sukarno after 30 September 1965, however, also ended the era of party-affiliated cultural organizations and the polarized atmosphere that had increasingly prevailed from 1962 on.

National consolidation and new explorations of traditional heritage

The late 1960s marked a pivotal period in many ways. It was a time in which social dynamics increasingly began to determine the relations of modern theatre to local nation-states. In the Philippines, a crisis in both government (perceptions of corrupt candidates in the 1969 presidential election) and economy (U.S. pressure to open the Philippines more freely to U.S. exports, undermining local production) led to large-scale militantly nationalist protest movements. In the radical nationalist upsurge of the period, young playwrights such as Paul Dumol had already begun to write critical dramas. His *Ang Paglilitis ni Mang Serapio* (The Trial of Mang Serapio, 1968) was written for an absurdist-style performance replete with a circus atmosphere and all the actors, except the one portraying Serapio, wearing white face paint, like clowns. The plot follows a beggars' syndicate trial of one of its members who dared to possess hope and dreams of happiness. The rhetoric of the beggars' syndicate judge and court echo elements of Catholicism, capitalism and the Philippine state at the time. More realist was Bonifacio Ilagan's *Welga!* (*Strike!*, 1972), which shows the education and radicalization of a group of workers leading up to their strike action. At the same time, activist theatre groups performed at mass rallies, presenting short, well-constructed agitprop pieces that borrowed ideas from sources as varied as Brecht, Piscator and the model opera plays of the Chinese Cultural Revolution. These groups strove to create an anti-illusionistic theatre that, eschewing the sentimentalism of most Philippine traditional popular theatre, attempted to instruct the audience and urge them to think critically about what they were viewing (Bodden 1993).

The declaration of martial law on 22 September 1972 temporarily forced this movement underground, but in the world of Philippine culture and theatrical production, strongly nationalist writers and practitioners found ways of voicing their concerns again within a few years. Thus, nationalism and a strong opposition to U.S. neo-imperialism led much of the Philippines modern theatre to experiment with rediscovered traditional theatre forms, and to create a trenchant vein of social criticism critical of Marcos' 'New Society' even during the years of the Marcos dictatorship (Stauffer 1974: 168; Stauffer 1979: 192–3; Wurfel 1988:16–21, 60–1; Hawes 1987: 35–8; Fernandez 1983: 11–12). The ongoing existence of U.S. military bases and trade relationships also ensured such nationalism's existence as a force that heavily coloured much modern Philippine theatre well into the 1990s and beyond (Goodno 1991: 70–2).

Philippine playwrights used a range of techniques to get around Marcos-era censorship: looking sympathetically at the life of the poor, focusing on past events to signal present-day shortcomings, expressionistic dramatizations of folklore or history, and absurdism (Tiongson, n.d., 26–9). Malou Jacob's (1948–) *Juan Tamban* (1979), one of the best-known dramas of the 1970s, combines expressionist anti-illusionistic devices with a realist plot. Jacob uses a chorus as narrator and commentator to stitch together a story in which a middle-class social worker is radicalized by her relations with a young boy living on the streets of Manila (Tiongson 1989: 36; Bodden 1996: 30–5).

During the same period some activist practitioners and scholars, such as Nicanor Tiongson and Doreen Fernandez (1934–2002), undertook research into older theatrical forms such as the Hispanicized religious pageants and courtly romances, as well as the zarzuelas. Some of this research was channelled into the creation of contemporary versions of these traditional genres, such as Babaylan Theater's 'modern sinakulos' (1970s) or Nicanor Tiongson's updated zarzuela, *Pilipinas Circa 1907* (1982), which parallels a romance subplot with the struggle for control of a local cigar factory. In each case, Filipinos and Americans compete, allowing Tiongson's work to deliver an emotional charge to nationalist aspirations for control of the Philippines' political economy (Tiongson n.d.: 29; Bodden 1996: 36–40). Others drafted elements of local, regional cultures to tell stories of embattled cultural minorities (Tiongson 1989: 35–6).

In Indonesia, with the radical left eliminated and leftist ideas dangerously stigmatized, theatre practitioners felt less immediate compulsion to voice social criticism in the early years of General Suharto's New Order regime. However, a trend that had begun in the waning years of Sukarno's rule, an exploration of traditional forms undertaken both by leftists who wanted to connect with larger numbers of people and by their liberal opponents who sought new possibilities outside western-style realism, now began to flourish fully. Indonesian modern theatre makers' impulse to explore possible traditional roots for modern theatrical work was similar to aspects of what was occurring at roughly the same time in the Philippines, but the context and conditions forming it ensured that one of the key factors was a desire for creative freedom, while hopes to engage with wider local audiences and to highlight Indonesian theatre's unique identity on an international stage may also have played a role (Goenawan, 1980: 91–142; Gillitt 2001: 109).

While staging many classics of western theatre, director/playwrights such as Teguh Karya (1937–2001), W. S. Rendra and Arifin C. Noer (1941–95) also began to adapt their works to local traditions using costumes drawn from local culture and history, and modifying the language and plots to fit more closely with local concerns. These practitioners also started to perceive ways in which traditional dramatic structures and other cultural elements might be incorporated into staging modern plays (Gillitt 2001: 103–4). At the same time that this neo-traditionalist impulse was growing, Indonesian playwrights and directors also discovered and began to experiment with the absurd, inspired largely by Rendra's staging of Beckett's *Waiting for Godot* (*Menuggu Godot*, 1970) (Bodden 2009: 917). During these years, too, Rendra, Noer, Putu Wijaya (1944–) and many others began writing original plays for the stage, while the Jakarta Arts Council sponsored yearly playwriting competitions. The result was an exceedingly productive period for modern Indonesian theatre and drama.

Knowledge of traditional forms greatly influenced playwriting. Arifin C. Noer made use of the Jakarta popular theatre lenong as well as structuring many of his plays around folk tales and beliefs. Rendra's most famous plays, *Mastodon dan Burung Kondor* (Mastodon and the Condors, 1973) and *The Struggle of the Naga Tribe* (1975), took inspiration and some structural elements from ketoprak and wayang kulit. And Putu Wijaya, perhaps the most productive of all these playwrights, created absurdist dramas such as his famous *Aduh!* (Ouch!, 1973), with circular structures that drew heavily on Balinese philosophy and painting concepts (Rafferty 1989; Gillitt 2001). In the late 1970s and early 1980s, N. Riantiarno (1949–), another prolific playwright, rose to prominence with a series of plays featuring transvestite characters, musical numbers, and broad humour and clowning that echoed both the *ludruk* theatre of East Java and the commercial theatre troupes of the colonial era, such as Komedie Stamboel or Miss Riboet's Orion.

All of these playwright-directors worked by forming their own troupe of amateur or semi-professional actors and mounted short runs (from a few days to two/three weeks) of each new production. Most depended on subsidies from Jakarta's Taman Ismail Marzuki performing arts centre and the Jakarta Arts Council, but also developed their own audiences, though Teguh Karya's Teater Populer's early residence at the Hotel Indonesia (1968–72) and Riantiarno's Teater Koma were able to operate with relatively more commercial success (Karya 1993: 16; Janarto 1997).

The New Order, especially in Mayor Ali Sadikin's Jakarta (1966–77) and at the Taman Ismail Marzuki performing arts complex, initially offered relative freedom to create for modern theatre groups, and given the polarization of the late Sukarno years, playwrights were leery of creating works that were too directly political. But after Suharto's government handily won the engineered elections of 1971 and began to consolidate its power, popular protest against the government's economic development policies and corruption also began to increase (McDonald 1980: 125–41; Schwarz 2000: 29–37). Concerned, modern theatre workers, too, had begun to voice criticism of prevailing conditions. This was evident in Arifin C. Noer's plays about the urban poor and migrants to the city scrambling to survive and find a place for themselves, Rendra's political allegories about tyrants and the temptations of power using plays by Sophocles, Shakespeare and Schiller, and Putu Wijaya's meditations on urban alienation. Yet as the New Order consolidated its power, and began to censor and ban, avoiding direct political statements while offering oblique social criticism became a necessity for Indonesian playwrights and their groups (Bodden 2010a: 32–9). Rendra's 1978 arrest and subsequent muzzling for several years after plays such as *Mastadon and the Condors* and *Struggle of the Naga Tribe*, and in light of his sharply critical protest poetry, underscored this point. In fact, this tension also highlighted the fact that modern theatrical neo-traditionalists and the New Order government, though both claimed to base their legitimacy and ideas on local traditions, had very different conceptions of what those traditions meant and how they should function in art and society.

In Malaysia, 1969 was a watershed year. The communal riots of 13 May shattered the post-independence stability the country had enjoyed since 1957 and led to policies designed to increase ethnic Malay participation in the economy and education, perceived to have been dominated up to that point by ethnic Chinese Malaysians (Sardesai 1989: 252–4). In the realm of modern theatre, this meant a turn away from the western realism of the drama moden and an attempt to explore Malay identity by incorporating Malay cultural elements more assertively into modern drama and performance. It also meant that some practitioners, such as Syed Alwi (1930–2008) and the Indo-Malaysian director, Krishen Jit (1940–2005), formerly active with the English-language MATG (Malayan Arts Theatre Group), made a conscious decision to switch from English-language theatre, now perceived as alien and exclusive, to Malay in order to explore the ways in which ethnic and communal identity could be rendered less exclusive (Rajendran 2013; Ishak 1986: 18–23). This paradigm change was also accompanied by a tendency to explore dreams, fantasy and the absurd. Dinsman (Che' Shamsudin Othman, 1947–), one of the younger, emerging playwrights of this period, argued that after the 13 May 1969 riots, life could no longer be seen from the perspective of realism or naturalism as Malays entering urban modernity confronted traditional beliefs and values. Pioneers of the new style, *teater kontemporari*, such as Bidin Subari (1937–), Noordin Hassan (1929–) and Syed Alwi, wrote and staged their major works in the early to mid-1970s, working, at first, with little financial support and facing obstacles in the form of permits, taxes and high stage rental fees (Ishak 1986: 24–30).

Bidin Subari's plays of the late 1960s were similar to the 'sitting room'-centred *drama moden* of Usman Awang and others, often showing the travails of the emerging Malay official class whose children were cut off from traditional moral values and floundering in the midst of modern sexual relations. By the mid-1970s, responding to the new trend, Subari relocated his plays to the urban slums and prostitution complexes and fashioned them into absurdist farces (Jit 1981: 66–7; Jit 1989a: 184–5). Noordin Hassan's most famous work, *Bukan Lalang Ditiup Angin* (It's Not the Tall Grass that is Blown by the Wind, 1970), was a non-linear piece that made use of a variety of elements from traditional Malay culture – poetry, music, comic scenes, and chorus – some of which were drawn from the Indo-Malaysian hybrid form, *boria*. The play placed folk theatre characters and images in a contemporary environment and included oblique references to the events of 13 May 1969 (Jit 1981: 69–70; 1989a: 182). Syed Alwi's Malay-language plays of the mid-1970s such as *Tok Perak* (1975), directed by Krishen Jit, juxtaposed modern multimedia with elements of wayang kulit, Malay poetry and martial arts in telling the stories of outsiders coping with difficult relations to settled communities (Jit 1989a: 183–4).

A younger generation was emerging at the same time, including playwrights such as Dinsman, Johan Jaaffar (1953–), and Hatta Azad Khan (1952–). These younger writers, encouraged by tours of the Indonesian theatre group, Teater Keliling, from 1973 to 1975, which featured the works of Putu Wijaya and Arifin C, Noer, turned towards an absurdist style to portray the experience of urban life (Jit 1989a: 184). They also further developed the Hang Tuah/Jebat story, continuing to fashion the traditionally vilified Jebat, who rebels against what he sees as his Sultan's injustice, into a modern hero promoting social action to overcome the establishment's rigid bureaucracy (Nanney 1988: 170–3).

The 1970s, then, were one of the most interesting and innovative periods in maritime Southeast Asian modern theatre history, a time when practitioners in Indonesia, Malaysia and the Philippines were all concerned, for a variety of reasons, to uncover local and national roots for their modern theatre productions. The decade was also a time in which grassroots theatre practices were being developed in the Philippines. During the rise of militant nationalism in the late 1960s, Filipino Cecilia Guidote (1943–) had founded the Philippines Educational Theatre Association (PETA) in order to promote a national theatre of the Philippines that was to include a professional company, the Kalinangan Ensemble, and branches reaching out to a variety of popular communities. Though soon after the Declaration of Martial Law Guidote herself went into exile in the United States, her vision was pursued by her successors at PETA. Along with developing a reputation for high-quality stage productions and nurturing a young generation of playwrights, PETA also expanded a training programme of grassroots theatre. In PETA's workshops (influenced by liberation theology and based initially on Paolo Friere's *Pedagogy of the Oppressed*, Viola Spolin's *Improvisation for the Theater* and Jearnine Wagner and Kitty Baker's work on creative dramatics for children) and those of other groups building the network of Philippines grassroots theatre, such as the Mindanao Sulu Pastoral Conference Secretariat's Creative Dramatics Program, participants from peasant, worker, slum or other social groups would be encouraged to map out the social dynamics of their community, then to build a play based on that map and their own personal experiences. This served to raise the consciousness of the participating group, provide for its members a more critical framework for analysing the conditions of their lives, and in many cases give birth to a new community cultural group. As a result, a large community theatre network took shape in the Philippines from the late 1970s to the mid-1980s. This network participated in many events leading up to the ousting of President Marcos in 1986, but by the late 1980s, its method of grassroots theatre had also been spread to the other countries of island Southeast Asia through training programmes that brought theatre activists from Indonesia, Malaysia and Singapore to the Philippines for short periods (Fernandez 1995: 104–5; van Erven 1992; Bodden 1993). PETA's workshop methods, as practised by the Yogyakrata-based Arena Teater and others, took root in Indonesian NGO circles, but were fiercely condemned and banned in Malaysia and Singapore as subversive (Bodden 2010a; van Erven 1992: 233–4; Peterson 2001: 39–42).

Modern theatre in Singapore has in general, since at least the 1970s, had to operate under the watchful eyes of government censors. In 1976, Kuo Pao Kun, whose work in Singaporean-Chinese theatre in the 1960s has been mentioned above, was detained for 4 years in a government crackdown on dissent as a result of his involvement in 'go into life' activities which saw theatre workers living among ordinary workers, peasants and fishermen, then returning to create theatre based on their observations (Peterson 2001: 35–9). Robert Yeo's (1940–) play, *One Year Back Home*, which contains some mild criticism of the ruling People's Action Party, experienced trouble gaining a performance permit in 1979 (it was eventually performed in 1980), even though it portrays the opposition as ineffectual (Diamond 2012: 159–60). Under a government policy issued in September 1992, plays were prohibited if they had the potential to erode core moral values of society, subvert the nation's stability and security, or create misunderstanding or conflict in Singapore's multicultural society (Peterson 2001: 28–30). The Necessary Stage's main writer, Haresh Sharma (1965–), and its key director, Alvin Tan, became embroiled in controversy in 1994 after attending a Forum Theatre workshop given by Augusto Boal in New York, then returning and attempting to practise forum theatre in Singaporean high schools. After an incendiary newspaper report, the government voiced support for The Necessary Stage group, but banned the use of forum theatre as potentially subversive (ibid.: 44–50). In a similar vein, performance art protests of the anti-gay policing in 1993 resulted in a ban on further performances by the artists involved and a tighter set of regulations on performance art itself (ibid: 153–8).

Despite such government pressures to conform to its preferred political and moral scripts for national culture, Singaporean theatre experienced a spectacular boom from the mid-1980s on, much of it in a specifically Singaporean English peppered with words and phrases from other locally used languages that constituted one way of indigenizing local stage productions. This English-language theatre blossomed with the work of Stella Kon (1944–) and Kuo Pao Kun. Kon's monodrama, *Emily of Emerald Hill* (1985), follows the life of a young woman who marries into a well-to-do Chinese family, gradually becoming the controlling matriarch of the clan. The play suggests the sacrifices necessary to achieve such power as, at the same time against the backdrop of changing times, it shows the decline of the way of life the family enjoyed. Kuo's works included the monologues critical of excessive Singaporean bureaucracy, *The Coffin is Too Big for the Hole* (1984) and *No Parking on Odd Days* (1985), as well as *Mama Looking for Her Cat* (1988), a multilingual play that switched between English and various dialects of Chinese prevalent in Singapore.

Globalization, musicals and new themes

The TheaterWorks company of Singapore was instrumental in encouraging and staging new works by younger, developing writers such as Ovidia Yu (1961–), Eleanor Wong (1962–), Russell Heng and Tan Tarn How (1960–). A number of these, such as Yu's *Three Fat Virgins* (1992) and Heng's *Lest the Demons Get to Me* (1992), broached gay and lesbian issues, a theme that submerged again after the clampdown of the mid-1990s, then re-emerged in the 2000s as Singapore tried to rebrand itself as a centre for cosmopolitan, global culture (Peterson 2001: 142–60; Lim 2005). TheatreWorks also produced works mildly critical of the Singaporean government, such as Tan Tarn How's plays *The Lady of Soul and Her Ultimate 'S' Machine* (1993) and *Undercover* (1994), which contained comic criticisms of Singaporean censorship and security apparatuses, respectively. Further, the group participated in the production of a number of musicals, such as Michael Chiang's (1955–) *Beauty World* (1998), but the company probably gained its widest international exposure for its intercultural theatre efforts, most notably Ong Keng Sen's (1963–) direction of a pan-Asian reworking of Shakespeare, *Lear* (1997–99). Many viewed this production as visually stunning and, given that it featured artists from a number of Asian countries, each acting in a traditional idiom from their point of origin, as a way for Asia to take pride in an international-calibre show. Critics, however, saw no integration of the various Asian forms and suggested that the play was just a set of juxtaposed Asian theatrical elements divorced from their local contexts and issues (Peterson 2001: 214–18; Diamond 2012: 178–9, 313–14). Intercultural theatre productions were also undertaken by William Teo's (1957–2001) Asia in Theatre Research Centre with its 1993 staging of *Macbeth* (Peterson 2001: 203–13).

Another of Singapore's major theatre companies, The Necessary Stage, as David Birch has argued, has committed itself to a theatre in which writer, director, actors and the community are engaged in a collaborative process. In over 25 years of theatre TNS has staged numerous productions representing the lives of Singapore's ordinary people, but also its marginalized. Works such as *Still Building* (1992), about members of Singapore's underclasses trapped in a collapsed building, and *Off Centre* (1993), about the difficulties of ex-psychiatric patients finding acceptance, are but two examples (Birch 2004).

As Singapore has attempted to position itself as an international centre for the arts comparable to New York or London, some critics have argued that its festivals display an aversion to works with local content. Instead, they assert, Singapore's festivals have shown a growing predilection to invite and encourage performances that are slick and beautiful, but increasingly devoid of 'the particulars of culture, politics, and place', catering to an international elite whom Singapore hopes to attract (Peterson 2009: 114; Wong 2012). Similarly, Lim asserts that recent representations of gays in Singapore theatre that might be viewed as legitimizing Singapore's image as a global arts mecca are depoliticized, cut off from a grassroots base even as they appear to embody a radical kind of sexual politics. His analysis includes a production of Haresh Sharma's *Mardi Gras* (2003), performed by The Necessary Stage, that struts gay sexuality but, he argues, provides no critical examination of the problems of gay life in Singapore (Lim 2005).

Indonesian theatre entered the 1980s engaged in over a decade of exploration of the possibilities of traditional performance for modern theatre. Many younger groups in Central Java performed plays about the power struggles in mythical or historical kingdoms as ways of voicing criticism of the contemporary state, often replicating aspects of wayang kulit or the Central Javanese folk theatre, ketoprak, whose main material consisted of retellings of past historical legends (Hatley 1993). Also, in the Yogyakarta area of Central Java, a new genre, *sampakan*, presented modern dynamic comedies sympathetically portraying the lives of ordinary people. These plays, in which actors played music while not acting their roles, and engaged in folk-theatre-style joking, became very popular on Java in the mid- to late 1980s. Most prominent was the group, Gandrik, which, like its competitors, mixed Javanese with contemporary Indonesian to achieve its distinctively local flavour (Figures 17.1 and 17.3). At the same time, in Jakarta, N. Riantiarno's Teater Koma was attracting record audiences with its plays about the urban poor, transvestites, and the inequities of national economic development, including *Bom Waktu* (Time Bomb, 1982) and *Opera Kecoa* (Cockroach Opera, 1985). These plays mixed elements of colonial-era commercial theatres with the Broadway-style musical and relevant social commentary (Figure 17.2).

Figure 17.1 Teater Koma's Gandrik's Sampakan-style *Dhermit* (Evil Wood spirits, 1987) performed in Yogyakarta.

(Photo by Michael Bodden)

Figure 17.2 Teater Koma's *Sandiwara Para Binatang* (Animal Farm, 1987).
(Photo by Michael Bodden)

As the 1980s came to a close, avant-garde groups in Jakarta took a different tack, representing their sense of urban alienation and political unease in highly physical performances in which texts were either minimal, or cobbled together from fragments of other plays and texts. These groups, Teater Sae, Teater Kubur and others, initiated a new wave of experimental theatre, highly abstract but emotionally powerful, that radically transformed elements of traditional theatre or avoided them altogether. Another group, the Bandung-based Teater Payung Hitam, turned even further away from using traditional elements in their performances, deploying the actors' bodies and abstract sets to create multi-interpretable and striking political allegories (Figure 17.4). Its experiments with Peter Handke's play, *Kaspar* (1994–2003), about the way language moulds us into compliant subjects, led the group to a rejection of the national language in many of their productions, since the group's director, Rahman Sabur (1957–), felt that Indonesian had been manipulated too heavily by 30 years of New Order rule (Bodden 2010a).

In Indonesia, as in Singapore, theatre practitioners needed to be adept to avoid censorship. Some of the experimental work of the early to mid-1990s was one way to avoid direct, verbal statements of political critique, while others, long frustrated with government muzzling and the perceived lack of freedom under Suharto's government, began to take a more direct approach. Riantiarno and Koma's 1990 play, *Suksesi* (Succession), touched on the politically sensitive issue

Figure 17.3 Teater Koma's *Sandiwara Para Binatang* (Animal Farm, 1987).
(Photo by Michael Bodden)

of presidential succession and mimicked the idiosyncratic speech of the president while allegorizing the rapacious business behaviour of his family. The eventual ban of the play began a long struggle with the New Order's censorship apparatus, which included a play by noted Islamic writer and thinker Emha Ainun Nadjib (1953–) about peasant land rights issues, several plays by a vibrant worker's theatre movement centred on the greater Jakarta region, and a monologue written and performed by Ratna Sarumpaet (1949–), *Marsinah Menggugat* (Marsinah Accuses, 1997) about a labour activist whose rape and murder raised a huge public outcry. As each case of banning occurred, public debate forced the government into backpedalling, denials and changing justifications. Such theatrical works, and the debates about their banning, contributed in a modest way to the pro-democracy reform movement and the ousting of Suharto in May 1998 (Bodden 2010a: 273–309).

Several new trends emerged in the post-Suharto era. Aside from a few 'documentary'-style plays that took up the traumatic issues of the end of the Suharto era, many playwrights felt the loss of theatre's vital role as a forum for social protest. Some, such as Yogyakarta's Teater Garasi in its series, *Waktu Batu* (Stone Time, 2002–4), took up issues of trauma and identity formation in the context of the colonial experience and local cultural history and legends. Gender issues, with a particular focus on women, have also been taken up by theatre workers, occasionally collaborating with local non-government women's advocacy organizations. Most memorable, perhaps, was Makassar-based Shinta Febriany's (1979–) *namaku adam Tanpa Huruf Kapital* (My Name is adam With a Small 'a,' 2003), in which both male and female domestic roles, and women's fantasies and fears about men, are physically embodied and articulated (Bodden 2007; Hatley 2007: 193–5). Another trend emerging in the 2000s was the tendency of many theatre groups in the Central Javanese areas of Yogyakarta and Solo to engage with local communities in a variety of ways, both to help foster a sense of community and to represent the involved communities on stage (Hatley 2008). Finally, in a fascinating example of intercultural theatre, world-renowned director Robert Wilson (1941–), in collaboration with Bali-based practitioners Restu Imansari (1966–) and Rhoda Grauer, mounted a stage version of a massive South Sulawesi Bugis epic entitled *I La Galigo*. This major production made use of an all-Indonesian cast and included a *bissu* transvestite ritual priest, Puang Matoa Saidi (1958–2011), and a master of the South Sulawesi *pakarena* dance, Coppong Daeng Rannu (1920–), touring to Singapore in 2004, then Europe and North America, before being successfully performed in Jakarta (2005) and Makassar (2011) (Cohen 2005; Bianpoen 2011).

By the end of the 1970s, a resurgence of conservative Islam in Malaysia caused Malay theatre to turn away from formal experimentation and representation of alternative belief systems. This led practitioners such as Krishen Jit to return to English-language theatre and reinforced

Figure 17.4 Teater Payung Hitam's *Tiang Setemngah Tiang* (Flag at Half Mast, 1999).
(Photo by Michael Bodden)

the split between English-language and Malay theatres. The Malay-language theatre has tended to focus on nationalist allegories featuring anti-colonial struggles and the exploits of mythical/ historical figures, religious allegories and criticisms of the materialism of nouveaux-riche Malays. (Rajendran 2013: 152; Diamond 2012: 276–308; Zulkifli 2012). In particular, in the past 15 years since the dedication of the Istana Budaya as the premiere national venue for theatre, there has been a marked tendency to stage colossal musical productions valorizing historical figures such as the first prime minister Tunku Abdul Rahman, or re-presenting legendary stories of the Malays' glorious past. Often, such productions follow successful films, such as the hit *Puteri Gunung Ledang* (The Princess of Mt Ledang, 2005). A number of these big production musicals have tried to make use of modernized elements of bangsawan as though conforming to the urging of a former minister of culture and tourism (Zulkifli 2012).[2] Other theatre groups have tried to experiment with use of traditional *mak yong* in modern performance, or mounted performances ruminating on the decline of traditional forms (Diamond 2012: 292–3). This type of theatre is mainly focused on Malays and defining Malaysian culture as an ethnic Malay domain, despite large Chinese- and Indo-Malaysian populations.

English-language theatre, on the other hand, though limited to a smaller audience, attempts to present works that see Malaysia as a project inclusive of all – Malays, Chinese, Indians and Eurasians. Founded by Krishen Jit, K. S. Maniam (1942–), Marion D'Cruz (1953–) and others in 1984, the Five Arts Centre at times questioned the boundaries of racial separation through plays such as Maniam's *The Cord* (1984) and Leow Puay Tin's *Family* (1998), both directed by Krishen Jit. Jit was also instrumental in a production of Kee Thuan Chye's (1954–) *1984 Here and Now* (1985), which played to packed houses with its passionate condemnation of race politics and final call to the audience to take action, all while under the watchful eyes of the Special Police Branch (Lo 2004: 56, 83; Diamond 2012: 302–3). Other groups have since continued to produce relevant modern theatre in English, notably the Actor's Studio, founded in 1989, including *Tunku the Musical* (2007), which emphasized Malaysia's first prime minister's multicultural ideals. In 1994, Malaysia's first all-women's company, Kuali, was formed and mounted works such as *Kuala Lumpur Knockout* (1996) and *Hang Li Po* (1998), which challenged government representations of women. Other groups have also criticized various aspects of Malaysian government policy through satire or more serious drama since the 1997 Asian economic crisis and the government's harassment of opposition politician Anwar Ibrahim (Diamond 2012: 280–2, 302–4).

Though not as well researched as Malay or English-language production, many Chinese-language productions are staged, including developments in the Chinese musical by the Dama Orchestra company. Under the leadership of Khor Seng Chew, the group scored a huge success with its rendition of *Butterfly Lovers* (2006), in which the lyrics and dialogue were delivered in Mandarin with accompanying surtitles, and narration in English (Loo and Loo 2012). Young Chinese Martial artist Lee Swee Seng did a stunning adaptation of *Farewell My Concubine* (2011), collaborating with wushu-trained artists. His performances combine narrative, wushu, dance and digital projection and have been performed in Malaysia before touring internationally. Young Chinese-language artists create experimental theatre and avant-garde shadow pieces. Writers such as Mark Beau de Silva work regularly with a group of primarily Chinese-language actors to lampoon Chinese, Malay and Indian culture in equal measures. The One Malaysia ideal of the current government may be best represented in comedy where all communities are equal targets in the eyes of young Malaysians (Kathy Foley, personal communication, 2014).

Modern Philippine theatre since the fall of Marcos continued to produce protest plays such as *Panata Sa Kalayaan* (Oath to Freedom, 1986), which PETA took on an international tour at the same time as the Peryante and UP Repertory companies toured it around the Philippines.

The play used several folk legends to represent the rise of people's power and continuing problems. Social-realist playwrights such as the prolific Rene Villanueva (1954–2007) took up issues such as the killing of journalists during martial law, Philippine workers abroad, the U.S. military bases and women's social position (Fernandez 1995; van Erven 1992: 56–9). Equally productive playwright Tony Perez also deepened a trend, begun in the late Marcos years, to turn inward to investigate Filipino psyches as in Perez's *Sa North Diversion Road* (1988), which portrays a number of unfaithful husbands to explore marriage and gender relations, or Bienvenido Noriega's (1952–94) *Bongbong at Kris* (1987), a comedic fantasy about a kidnapping turned love relationship between children of the Marcos and Aquino families.

Modern Philippine theatre also deepened its exploration of folk forms, motifs and cultural elements. One example is PETA's 1993 staging of a Philippine version of the *Ramayana* whose mis-en-scène was derived from ethnic Maranao costuming, dance and games. At the National Theatre Festival of 1992, an Iloilo City high school troupe, Dagyaw Theatre and Dance Company, staged the Western Visayas epic poem, *Hinilawod* (Tales from the Mouth of the Halawod River), using elements of traditional dance, music, costumes and chants (Fernandez 1995: 109–13). Other groups created updated versions of zarzuelas or komedyas.

But Philippine nationalism has embarked on other theatrical adventures as well. Responding to stubbornly persistent corruption and economic inequality, the Cultural Centre of the Philippines' resident theatre company, Tanghalang Pilipino, staged Malou Jacob's *Anatomiya ng Korupsiyon* (Anatomy of Corruption) in 1998. In the same year, the centennial of the Philippines' declaration of independence sparked the staging of several works that examined the life and works of the great Philippine patriot, novelist and martyr, Jose Rizal (1861–96) (Diamond 2012: 228–35). Given the deep influence of western naturalism in the Philippines, and the comparative lack of formalized gesture available from local genres, Philippine theatre seems to have tried to inculcate a sense of national identity through local thematic content and details of staging (Diamond 2012: 223). But they have also sought to realize this identity through connections with other Asian and Southeast Asian countries and cultures. Al Santos' Cry of Asia project (1989–97), in which artists from ten Asian countries participated in a cultural caravan tour across Europe, was one effort towards this latter end. PETA's production of a Philippine version of the *Ramayana* was another hint of this strategy, as was the similarly themed pan-Asian *Realizing Rama* (1998) production sponsored by ASEAN, with the creative leadership of Nicanor Tiongson and Denisa Reyes. PETA, itself, also organized an annual Mekong Arts Festival in different Southeast Asian cities after 2005 and established a branch in Thailand in collaboration with local Thai groups (van Erven 1992: 235–8; Diamond 2012: 223–4). As has also been the case in Indonesia, even many Philippine groups producing foreign plays choose their productions based on the relevance of the particular play to local history or conditions (Diamond 2012: 224; Bodden 2009).

Finally, as elsewhere in island Southeast Asia, the past 20 years have also seen an interest in women's and gender issues come to the fore in modern Philippine theatre. The New Voice Company (NVC) has been one of the most visible practitioners of this trend, staging works such as *Oleanna*, *Top Girls*, *I Am a Woman* and *Vagina Monologues*. The latter play encountered difficulty finding sponsors and NVC was not allowed to advertise the production on television or radio, but through word of mouth the play still became a popular success. Even more popular was Tanghalang Pilipino's production of a musical based on Carlo Vergara's (1971–) comic book character, Zsazsa Zaturnnah (2005–7), a gay hairdresser who swallows a pink stone that has fallen from the heavens and is thereby transformed into a voluptuous and campy super-heroine. The play served as a comic enactment of gay pride and social acceptance, becoming a smash hit in the process (Diamond 2012: 238).

Conclusion

In conclusion, modern theatre in maritime Southeast Asia has taken a trajectory from early hybrid genres and plays to emulating western realism (albeit with remnants of tradition persisting in such productions) to conscious new experimentation with hybrid productions merging modern and traditional elements, and finally, into pan-Asian and intercultural collaborations. As both modern theatre and the newly independent nation-states of the region coalesced, debates and confrontations took place about what national cultures should look like and what kinds of public criticism were appropriate for the arts. Struggles over censorship and strategies to avoid it became commonplace throughout the region, and new issues, such as gender identities and conflicts, have mounted a variety of local stages. Yet, whether framed by strong anti-imperialist and nationalist sentiments, the humanist desire for free experimentation and resistance to a neo-feudal authoritarianism, ethnic and linguistic divides and exclusionary visions of national culture, or attempts to create mutli-ethnic performance languages and become a global arts centre, the modern theatres of maritime Southeast Asia have undertaken dynamic explorations in order to find fitting idioms for their ongoing work.

Notes

1 I use 'Komedie Stamboel' to signify the original Surabaya-based company which created this particular hybrid genre of theatre, and 'komedi stambul' to represent the genre itself as performed by both the Komedie Stamboel company and its many imitators.
2 Kathy Foley (personal communication, 2014) disputes Zulkifli's account. She suggests that the musicals have little to do with bangsawan, also arguing that 'Puteri Gunung Ledang in most Malay's inter-pretation was not about the glorious past but a feminist revisioning of a women who the legendary past had given a "bad rap"'.

Bibliography

Aveling, Harry (1979) *Man and Society in the Works of the Indonesian Playwright Utuy Tatang Sontani*, Honolulu: University of Hawai'i Southeast Asian Studies Program Southeast Asia paper No. 13.

Bianpoen, Carla (2011) '"I La Galigo" Returns Home', *The Jakarta Post*, 21 April, www.thejakartapost.com/news/2011/04/21/%E2%80%98i-la-galigo%E2%80%99-returns-home.html, accessed 14 May 2014.

Birch, David (2004) 'Celebrating the Ordinary in Singapore in Extraordinary Ways: The Cultural Politics of The Necessary Stage's Collaborative Theatre', in Taan Chong Kee and Tisa Ng (eds) *Ask Not: The Necessary Stage in Singapore Theatre*, 43–70, Singapore: Times Editions-Marshall Cavendish.

Bodden, Michael H. (1993) 'Imagining the Audience as Agent of its Own History: Brecht, Grassroots Theater and Representations of Inter-Class Alliance in the Philippines and Indonesia', unpublished dissertation, University of Wisconsin-Madison.

—— (1996) 'Class, Gender, and the Contours of Nationalism in the Culture of Philippine Radical Theater', *Frontiers* XVI (2/3): 24–50.

—— (2007) 'Languages of Trauma, Bodies, and Myths: Learning to Speak Again in Post-1998 Indonesian Theatre', in Michael Leaf and Abidin Kusno (eds) *Arts, Popular Culture, and Social Change in the New Indonesia*, 119–51, Vancouver: UBC Institute of Asian Research, Centre for Southeast Asian Research, www.iar.ubc.ca/centres/csear/webpage/content.html. Website name: Arts, Popular Culture and Social Change in the New Indonesia: Seminar Proceedings.

—— (2009) 'Membuat drama asing berbicara kepada penonton Indonesia: universalisme dan identitas pasca-colonial dalam teater-seni Indonesia modern', in Henri Chambert-Loir (ed.) *Sadur: sejarah terjemahan di Indonesia dan Malaysia*, Jakarta: Kepustakaan Populer Gramedia (KPG).

—— (2010a) *Resistance on the National Stage: Theater and Politics in late New Order Indonesia*, Athens: Ohio University Press.

—— (2010b) 'Modern Drama, Politics, and the Postcolonial Aesthetics of Left-Nationalism in North Sumatra: the Forgotten Theater of Indonesia's Lekra, 1955–65', in Tony Day and Maya H. T. Liem (eds) *Cultures at War: the Cold War And Cultural Expression in Southeast Asia*, Ithaca, NY: Cornell University Southeast Asia Program.

—— (2012) 'Dynamics and Tensions of Lekra's Modern National Theatre, 1959–1965', in Jennifer Lindsay and Maya H. T. Liem (eds) *Heirs to World Culture: Being Indonesian 1950–1965*, Leiden: KITLV Press.

Cohen, Matthew I. (2001) 'On the Origin of the Komedie Stamboel: Popular Culture, Colonial Society, and the Parsi Theatre Movement', Bijdragen tot de Tall', Land- en Volkekunde, 157 (2): 313–57.

—— (2005) 'I La Galigo by Robert Wilson; Rhoda Grauer; Rahayu Supanggah: Review', *Asian Theatre Journal*, 22 (1): 138–49.

—— (2006) *The Komedie Stamboel: Popular Theatre in Colonial Indonesia, 1981–1903*, Athens: Ohio University Press.

—— (ed.) (2010) *The Lontar Anthology of Indonesian Drama, Volume 1: Plays for the Popular Stage*, Jakarta: The Lontar Foundation.

Diamond, Catherine (2012) *Communities of Imagination: Contemporary Southeast Asian Theatres*, Honolulu: University of Hawai'i Press.

Fernandez, Doreen G. (1978) *The Iloilo Zarzuela: 1903–1930*, Quezon City: Ateneo de Manila Press.

—— (1983) 'Contemporary Philippine Drama: The Liveliest Voice', *Philippine Studies* 31: 5–36.

—— (1995) 'The Playbill after 1983: Philippine Theatre after Martial Law', *Asian Theatre Journal* 12 (1): 104–18.

Gillitt, Cobina (2001) 'Challenging Conventions and Crossing Boundaries: A New Tradition of Indonesian Theatre from 1968–1978', unpublished dissertation, New York University.

Goenawan Mohamad (1980) *Sex, Sastra, Kita* (Sex, Literature, Us), Jakarta: Sinar Harapan.

Goodno, James B. (1991) *The Philippines, Land of Broken Promises*, London: Zed Books.

Hatley, Barbara (1993) 'Constructions of "Tradition" in New Order Indonesian Theatre', in Virginia Mattheson Hooker (ed.) *Culture and Society in New Order Indonesia*, 48–69, Kuala Lumpur: Oxford University Press.

—— (2007) 'Subverting the Stereotypes: Women Performers Contest Gender Stereotypes, Old and New', *Review of Indonesian and Malaysian Affairs*, 41 (2): 173–204.

—— (2008) 'Indonesian Theatre Ten Years After Reformasi', *Journal of Indonesian Social Sciences and Humanities*, 1: 53–72.

Hawes, Gary (1987) *The Philippine State and the Marcos Regime: The Politics of Export*, Ithaca: Cornell University Press.

Ishak, Solehah (1986) 'The Emergence of Contemporary Malay Theatre', *Tenggara*, 19: 17–42.

Janarto, Herry G. (1997) *Tetaer Koma: Potret Tragedi & Komedi Manusia (Indonesia)*, Jakarta: Grasindo.

Jit, Krishen (1981) 'Teater Moden Malaysia – satu esei retrospektif', in Zakaria Ariffin (ed.) *Drama Melayu Moden dalam Esei*, 52–79, Kuala Lumpur: Dewan Bahasa dan Pustaka Kementerian Pelajaran.

—— (1989a) 'Contemporary Malaysian theatre', *Tenggara*, 23: 179–87.

—— (1989b) 'Modern Theatre in Singapore: A Preliminary Survey', *Tenggara*, 23: 210–26.

Karya, Teguh (1993) 'Teguh Karya tentang Teguh Karya', in N. Riantiarno (ed) *Teguh Karya & Teater Populer 1968–1993*, Jakarta: Sinar Harapan.

Lane, Max (1979) 'Translator's Introduction', in W. S. Rendra, *The Struggle of the Naga Tribe*, New York: St. Martin's Press.

Lapeña-Bonifacio, Amelia (1972) *The 'Seditious' Tagalog Playwrights: Early American Occupation*, Manila: Zarzuela Foundation of the Philippines.

Lim, Eng-Beng (2005) 'The Mardi Gras Boys of Singapore's English Language Theatre', *Asian Theatre Journal*, 22 (2): 293–309.

Lo, Jacqueline (2004) *Staging Nation: English Language Theatre in Malaysia and Singapore*, Hong Kong: Hong Kong University Press.

Loo F.-Y. and Loo, F.-C. (2012) 'Innovation for Survival? Dama Orchestra's Butterfly Lovers – The Musical on a Contemporary Multiracial Malaysian Stage', *Asian Theatre Journal*, 29 (2): 339–56.

Lumbera, Bienvenido (1984) *Revaluation: Essays on Philippine Literature, Cinema, and Popular Culture*, Manila: Index.

McDonald, Hamish (1980) *Suharto's Indonesia*, Victoria, Australia: Fontana.

Nanney, Nancy (1988) 'Evolution of a Hero: the Hang Tuah/Hang Jebat Tale in Malay Drama', *Asian Theatre Journal*, 5 (2): 164–74.

—— (2007) 'Malaysia', in Gabrielle H. Cody and Evert Sprinchorn (eds) *The Columbia Encyclopedia of Modern Drama*, New York: Columbia University Press.

Peterson, William (2001) *Theater and the Politics of Culture in Contemporary Singapore*, Middletown, CT: Wesleyan University Press.

—— (2009) 'The Singapore Arts Festival at Thirty: Going Global, Glocal, Grobal', *Asian Theatre Journal*, 26 (1): 111–34.

Plomp, Marije (2012) 'The Capital of Pulp Fiction and Other Capitals: Cultural Life in Medan, 1950–1958', in Jennifer Lindsay and Maya H. T. Liem (eds) *Heirs to World Culture: Being Indonesian 1950–1965*, Leiden: KITLV Press.

Rafferty, Ellen (1989) 'The Tontonan Theatre of Putu Wijaya', in Ellen Rafferty (ed.) *Putu Wijaya in Performance*, Madison: University of Wisconsin Center for Southeast Asian Studies.

Rajendran, Charlene (2013) 'The Politics of Difference in Krishen Jit's Theatre in the 1970s: "A Time of Intense Questioning" in Malaysian Culture', *Asian Theatre Journal*, 30 (1): 145–71.

Ras, J. J. (1976) 'The Historical Development of the Javanese Shadow Theatre', *Review of Indonesian and Malaysian Studies*, 10: 50–76.

Rendra, Willibrordus S. (1979) *The Struggle of the Naga Tribe*, New York: St. Martin's Press.

Sardesai, Damodar R. (1989) *Southeast Asia Past and Present*, Boulder, CO: Westview Press.

Schwarz, Adam (2000) *A Nation in Waiting: Indonesia's Search for Stability*, Boulder, CO: Westview Press.

Sears, Laurie J. (1996) *Shadows of Empire: Colonial Discourse and Javanese Tales*, Durham, NC: Duke University Press.

Stauffer, Robert (1974) 'The Political Economy of a Coup: Transnational Linkages and Philippine Response', *Journal of Peace Research*, 11 (3): 161–79.

—— (1979) 'The Political Economy of Refeudalization', in David Rosenberg (ed.) *Marcos and Martial Law in the Philippines*, Ithaca, NY: Cornell University Press.

Sumardjo, Jakob (1992) *Perkembangan Teater Modern dan Sastra Drama Indonesia*, Bandung: Citra Aditya Bakti.

Tan Sooi Beng (1993) *Bangsawan: A Social and Stylistic History of Popular Malay Opera*, Singapore: Oxford University Press.

Tiongson, Nicanor G. (1989) 'Theatre in the Philippines Today', *Tenggara*, 23: 27–37.

—— (n.d.) *What is Philippine drama?* Quezon City: the Philippine Educational Theater Association.

van Erven, Eugène (1992) *The Playful Revolution: Theater and Liberation in Asia*, Bloomington: Indiana University Press.

Winet, Evan D. (2010) *Indonesian Postcolonial Theatre: Spectral Genealogies and Absent Faces*, New York: Palgrave Macmillan.

Wong, Melissa W. (2012) 'Negotiating Class, Taste, and Culture via the Arts Scene in Singapore: Postcolonial or Cosmopolitan Global?', *Asian Theatre Journal*, 29 (1): 233–54.

Wurfel, David (1988) *Filipino Politics: Development and Decay*, Ithaca, NY: Cornell University Press.

Zulkifli Mohamad (2012) 'The Secret Life of Nora: Review', *Asian Theatre Journal*, 29 (2): 461–65.

Part IV

Perspectives of modern and contemporary Asian theatre

18

The beginning of spoken theatre in Asia

Colonialism and colonial modernity

Anita Singh, Matthew Isaac Cohen, Maki Isaka and Siyuan Liu

This chapter focuses on the beginning of modern theatre in Asia by comparing two paths that led to theatrical modernity: (1) India and Indonesia as examples of nations under western colonization and (2) Japan and China, which modernized under the threat of global colonialism, a situation known as colonial modernity. Within the latter pair, China also differed from Japan in the sense that while it was never colonized, it was forced to open concessions in port cities with large western settlements. A comparison of the two models yields drastic differences, as spoken theatre in colonies started with settler theatres, colonial education and local commercial ventures, whereas the colonial modernity model witnessed local elites seizing on western-style spoken drama as a tool of enlightenment for the mostly illiterate populace. Within this group, Japan's new theatre received full blessing from the ruling class to stage the rising empire, while China's port cities such as Shanghai also witnessed limited theatrical productions by western settlers and in church schools. China also learnt western theatre through Japan.

I. India, by Anita Singh

India's encounter with the west between the late eighteenth and early twentieth centuries had wide-ranging political, economic, social and cultural consequences. In the field of theatre this encounter changed almost everything – its form, direction and pace (Jain 1992: 61). Established in the British settlements in Calcutta and subsequently in Bombay, the colonial experience unquestionably caused the beginning of modern theatre in India. Colonial encounter occasioned the influence of western and European models on local theatrical traditions. The development of modern theatre through European contact also saw the reinvigoration of Sanskrit theatre, which came to be reappraised and recuperated because of nationalist objectives and orientalist admiration. The modern theatre birthed out of this colonial presence was fashioned simultaneously by imperatives of empire, nationalism and nativism; this was a metropolitan genre created by a bilingual high-caste bourgeois, who strategically adapted elements from an array of models that included the Sanskrit theatre, traditional theatre and European theatre (Solomon 2009: 3–30).

The early English settlers started a theatre for their own recreation and amusement, called the Play House (1753–6), in Lalbazar Street. This theatre was set up with the support of David Garrick (1717–79), a renowned London actor. However, it was destroyed during the siege of Calcutta in 1756 by Siraj-ud-Daulah (Nawab of Bengal 1733–57). Almost 19 years later, the New Play House or the Calcutta Theatre was built (1775–1808); it was called the New Play House to distinguish it from the 'old play house' of Lalbazar. The Calcutta theatre, patronized by Warren Hastings, staged exclusively British repertoires such as *The School for Scandal*, *Richard III* and *Hamlet*, among others. It was so exclusive that even the ushers and doorkeepers were English (Bharucha 1983: 8). For this theatre David Garrick sent a large number of painted scenes from London and an artist named Bernard Messink. *The Merchant of Venice* was reviewed in *Selections Calcutta Gazettes 29* (one of the earliest English-language newspapers in India, founded in 1784) as: 'On Monday evening the Comedy of the "Merchant of Venice" was performed here to a very full theatre. Shylock never appeared to greater advantage, and the other characters were in general, well supported' (Seton-Karr 1864: 29). On 11 November 1784, a production of *Hamlet* was advertised as follows:

> We hear the tragedy of 'Hamlet' will be performed in the course of next week; but the managers have thought proper to omit the farce of the 'Mock Doctor.' For the better accommodation of the Ladies and Gentlemen of the Settlement, the Gallery is to be converted into Boxes.
>
> (Seton-Karr 1864: 30)

The appearance of women on stage was a great innovation of Calcutta Theatre. Mrs Bristow's appearance on stage was reviewed as:

> The assembly was attracted by the novel appearance of a lady whose condescension to grace the Calcutta stage would alone entitle her to lasting remembrance and whose representation of the most ingenious captivating character of Celia will assure for her the perpetual admiration of all who had the happiness to observe it.
>
> (Dasgupta 1934: 207–17)

In 1808 the Calcutta Theatre closed due to financial pressures.

Mrs Bristow founded a private theatre (1789–90) in her Chowringhee house where she entertained her wide circle of friends. She was so popular that it was said that when she left India in 1790, 'for long Calcutta refused to be comforted' (Busteed 1897: 107–44). The Chowringhee Theatre (1813–39), or the private subscription theatre as it was first called, was built on a commodious structure in the year 1813. Horace Hayman Wilson (1786–1864), the renowned Sanskrit scholar, D. L. Richardson (1801–65), the educationist, and Dwarkanath Tagore (1794–1846), who was associated with the Bengal renaissance, all contributed to this theatre. It was inaugurated on 25 November 1813 with a tragic drama, *Castle Spectre*. It received the patronage of Warren Hasting and his wife, among others, who graced the performance of Goldsmith's *She Stoops to Conquer* on 13 May 1814.

Mrs Leach opened a theatre named Sans Souci Theatre (1839–49) at Waterloo Street. It formally opened on 8 March 1841 with Sheridan Knowless' *The Wife* under the benefaction and immediate presence of Governor General Auckland. In August 1848, a performance of *Othello* directed by James Barry had Mrs Leach's daughter in the role of Desdemona, with a Bengali, Basihnav Charan, 'Addy', playing the role of Othello. This performance became significant in the chronicles of Indian theatre because a native played the lead role for the first time in an otherwise all-English cast. This performance was reported as 'Real unpainted nigger Othello' who set 'the whole world of Calcutta agog' (Raha 1978: 13). In hindsight, the racist implications of such a casting are not lost on us. During a performance of *The Merchant of Venice*, Mrs Leach was fatally burnt when her costume caught fire. Financial constraints eventually led to the closure of the theatre. Chowringhee and Sans Souci were specially known for their Shakespeare performances, such as *Henry IV, Richard III, The Merry Wives of Windsor, The Merchant of Venice* and *Othello*. In the meantime, several other playhouses were founded, including the Wheeler Place Theatre (1797–98), Atheneum Theatre (1812–14), Dum Dum Theatre (1817–24) and Baitaconah Theatre (1824).

The success of these theatres inspired a Russian adventurer to open a Bengali theatre on 27 November 1795. Herasim Lebedeff (1749–1817), with the help of his tutor Golaknath Das, staged a Bengali version, called *Kalpanik Sangbadal*, of the English play *The Disguise* by Jodrell (Bharucha 1983: 8). Lebedeff made the translations and the performers were all Bengalis. For Adya Rangacharya, author of *The Indian Theatre*, this performance heralded the birth of the modern theatre (1975: 94). Lebedeff's theatre was, however, abruptly shut down. But the playhouse exercised a great influence upon educated Bengalis and inspired them to possess a theatre of their own.

The first native who gained admittance to an English theatre was Dwarkanath Tagore (1794–1846), an enlightened aristocrat who was one of the founding members of a private subscription theatre formed in 1813. His membership was a development that revealed the gradual lessening of tensions between the British and the affluent members of Indian society, and can be seen as a strategic move to expose the natives to western culture and values and to create 'a class of persons Indian in blood and colour, but English in tastes, opinions, in morals, and in intellect' (Macaulay 1920: 107–17).

The English theatre entertained officers, merchants, scholars and clerks of the East India Company. All these theatres were intended exclusively for the amusement of the English. Besides employing local actors, the playhouses also brought actors from London. Mrs Chester, for example, came from London's Royal Theatre and Mrs Atkinson from Drury Lane Theatre; and James and Mrs Barry, Mrs Deacle, Miss Cowley and James Vining came from the Covent Garden and Drury Lane Theatres (Singh 2012: 195). The touring companies performed and popularized Shakespeare's plays. Teachers as eminent as Henry Derozio (1809–31) and D. L. Richardson helped create an appreciation of Shakespeare in the students and taught them not just to memorize and recite his lines but also to perform his plays. Macaulay remarked of Richardson: 'I may forget everything else about India, but your reading of Shakespeare never' (Presidency College, *Centenary Volume* 1956: 4). Hindu College and Sanskrit College became proficient in performance and recitations of Shakespeare. In 1837, the students performed *The Merchant of Venice* at the Government White House under the guidance of Dr Wilson. David Hare Academy students staged it twice in 1853. Hemendra Nath Dasgupta reported that some six to seven hundred Indians and Englishmen attended the play and were quite pleased with the performance (1988: 299). The promotion of Shakespeare's works in colonial Calcutta was, in effect, 'reproducing the metropolitan culture as a part of the civilizing mission of the British Raj' (Singh 1996: 122) and 'Shakespeare kept alive the myth of English cultural refinement and superiority – a myth that was crucial to the rulers' political interests in India' (Singh 1989: 446).

Subsequently, the English colonial authorities encouraged the natives to start their own theatres. The desire to have theatres of their own found expression both by the English-educated Indian elite and from orthodox nationalists. Prasanna Kumar Tagore (1801–86) picked up the thread. In 1832, he built a makeshift auditorium in his garden-house at Narkeldanga. Although this theatre was set up for a Bengali audience and was established in a predominantly Bengali quarter, the plays performed were either in English or English translations of Sanskrit plays. The theatre was inaugurated with the performances of Act V of Shakespeare's *Julius Caesar* and Act I of Bhavabhuti's *Uttarramcharit* (The Story of Rama's Later Life), translated into English by H. H. Wilson. Although only a few English plays were staged there, it was a new beginning that was followed up by others, including Nabin Chandra Basu (Shyam Bazar Theatre 1833) and Parry Mohan Bose (Jorasanko Natyasala 1854).

Vidya Sundar (Vidya and Sundar: Escapades of a Pair of Lovers, 1836) was among the first of the private performances. Staged in various parts of the residence of Nabin Chandra Basu, including the garden and the drawing room (Bharucha 1983: 9), the production relied heavily on sophisticated equipment imported from England. It was in a proscenium form but retained the *Jatra* (folk form of West Bengal) style. The play was a hybrid of occident and oriental features and this hybrid character remained the hallmark of Bengal theatre as well as the Indian theatre scene in most parts of the next centuries. The play was a dramatization of the life of the Bengali poem *Annada Mangal* (Happiness and Well-being, 1752–3) by Bharatchandra Ray (1712–60). As a play it was clumsy but its historical importance was immense. It inspired aristocrats such as Jyotindranath Tagore (1849–1925) to patronize theatre by privately sponsoring performances of Bengali plays.

By 1840 there was a demand among theatregoers in Bengal to see plays that would address the changing attitudes in society as well as being entertaining. The first original play in Bengali was Ram Narayan Tarkaratna's (1822–86) *Kulin Kulasarvasa* (All About a Kulin Clan, 1853) and later *Naba-Natak* (New Drama, 1867); both were social plays on the evils of *kulin* (upper class) polygamy. Michael Madhusudhan Dutt (1824–73) wrote *Sarmistha* (1858) based on a romantic episode from *Mahabharata*, which questioned Hindu norms. His other play, titled *Ekei Ki Bale Sabhyata?* (Is this Called Civilization?, 1860) satirizes an anglicized babu Naba Kumar and discusses female emancipation and widow remarriage.

Productions with nationalist tendencies soon employed theatre as a forum for social and political ideas designed to shape opinions and raise social and political consciousness. On 7 December 1872, Girish Chandra Ghosh's The National Theatre in Calcutta – Calcutta's first public theatre house – opened with the production of Dinabandhu Mitra's (1858–9) *Nildarpan* (The Mirror of Indigo). With vivid realism and melodrama, the play detailed the devastation of an Indian landowner and depicted the ruthless exploitation of the Bengali *ryots* (hired cultivators) by the British indigo planters. The play ends tragically, with Golokchandra Basu, the Indian landowner, hanging himself and his wife Savitri dying in a fit of madness. There is also the scene where a planter, Mr Rogue, attempts to rape a peasant girl, Kshetromoni. Violation of woman became symptomatic of the violation of Mother India. Thus rape was used as a political strategy to show the heinous crime a sahib could inflict on the native.

The production of *The Mirror of Indigo* in Lucknow in 1875 erupted in violence, which led to the interruption of the play, and the political developments soon led to strict enforcement of censorship rules. The British instituted the Dramatic Performances Control Act in 1876 under the administration of Viceroy Northbrook. The Act sought to empower the British administration to control the theatre scene in India. Subsequently, political and social protests were forced underground and Indian playwrights had to write their plays under the thinly veiled guise of historical and mythological subjects. Many playwrights turned their attention to corruptions in Hindu society and addressed a host of social injustices; common among them were child marriage, sati and the dowry system.

Girish Chandra Ghosh (1844–1912) was one of the most renowned figures of Bengali commercial theatre, who had established the Star, the Emerald and the Minerva Theatre and wrote around seventy plays, which are loosely structured, episodic, and full of coincidence, supernatural intervention and songs. He claimed Shakespeare as his model and had a production of *Macbeth* in 1893 in the Minerva Theatre. His *Balidan* (Sacrifice, 1905) deals with the evils of the dowry system, and *Sasti ki Santi?* (Punishment or Peace?, 1908) was a social drama based on the suffering of widows, arguing for their right to remarry. His historical plays were *Siraj ud-Daulah* (1906) and *Mir Kasim* (1907); the first play was based on Siraj ud-Daulah, the nawab of Bengal, who resisted the military aggression and the duplicity of Robert Clive, the English army officer who founded the East India Company. It was daring of Ghosh to idealize Siraj ud-Daulah's actions, since he was inextricably linked in the minds of the British with the infamous Black Hole of Calcutta episode where 146 Englishmen were incarcerated. Not surprisingly, the Dramatic Performance Act was imposed on the play. *Mir Kasim* was a play based on another nawab of Bengal who opposed the British; the play was structured as a tale of bravery, conspiracy and love.

In the northern scene the nationalistic passion was reflected in Bharattendu Harishchandra's (1850–85) political satire *Bharat Durdasha* (India's Wretched Condition, 1875) and *Andheri Nagri* (The Lawless State, 1881). He wrote eighteen plays with nationalist and reformatory views and rendered them realistic in form. He revised the form of Sanskrit plays to create new genres for Hindi drama, historical, satirical and lyrical plays.

In south India in the late nineteenth century, plays based on the new western model were written in languages such as Tamil, Telugu, Kannada and Malayalam. Some names associated with the theatre were: Pammal Sambandha Mudaliar (1873–1964), described as the founding father of Tamil theatre; Gubbi Veeranna (1890–1974), a pioneer in Kannada theatre; and Dharamavaram Krishnamchari (1853–1912), a renowned Telugu dramatist. Their plays contained stories drawn from mythological, historical or social events, but their form and structure were based on superficial imitation of Shakespeare's plays.

Krushnaji Prabhakar Khadilkar (1872–1948), an activist and theatre worker from Maharashtra, had accepted the English model in his plays. His *Kichak Vadh* (The Assassination of Kichak, 1907) is a play based on an episode in the *Mahabharata*, where Kichak, a minister at the court of Virat, tries to molest Draupadi, and is slain by her husband. The play symbolically represented the resistance to British rule and the molestation stood as a metaphor for the colonial government in India.

Another dramatist to assume a political stance in the 1930s by defying the Dramatic Performance Act was Manmatha Roy (1899–1988); his allegorical intention in *Karagar* (Prison, 1930) was too blatant to be ignored. At that time, prisons were crowded with Indian political prisoners who were jailed because of their association with Gandhi's civil disobedience movement. The message the play projected was that just as Lord Krishna ultimately vanquished the tyrant Kamsa, the Indian political prisoners would finally overthrow the British. *Karagar* was promptly proscribed.

The effects of English education, the influence of western civilization and the rise of political consciousness created the foundation for plays that attacked orthodoxies and addressed social evils on the one hand and, on the other, a set of plays that provided entertainment for the increasing population of big cities consequent upon industrialization. By the late nineteenth century, with the emergence of a stream of urban drama, the rise of commercial theatres, the Parsi theatre and the formation of the socially, politically and culturally conscious Indian People's Theatre Association (IPTA), there was a shift in the thematic convention and performative tradition which resulted in theatre practices that were essentially a paradigm of hybridism fashioned out of multiple strains of westernization, Sanskrit-based revivalism and indigenous genres, and melodramatic performance conventions.

II. Indonesia, by Matthew Isaac Cohen

Spoken theatre, referred to in Indonesia today alternately as *sandiwara* or *teater*, emerged in the first decades of the twentieth century as the result of multiple streams of influence – the European modern theatre known from both playtexts and performances, cinema, Chinese drama, nineteenth-century popular musical theatres of Indonesia, including the *komedi stambul*, and Indonesia's diverse premodern heritages. James Brandon (1967: 39) has famously described spoken theatre as Southeast Asia's 'non-popular theatre', and it has certainly been true that Indonesian drama's audiences have been limited to educated elites for most of its history. Spoken theatre, since its early twentieth-century beginning, has been a nexus of social activity for students, a vehicle for self-expression and the righting of personal injuries, a form of social and political commentary and critique, a means to raise funds for charitable causes, and a mode for exploring exogenous ideas and forms. Spoken theatre took on particular political import in a set of canonical plays, dating from 1926 to 1938, by authors from the island of Sumatra, performed at youth congresses and political gatherings in Java and elsewhere.

The islands of Indonesia, particularly Java and Bali, are justly famous for a stupefying variety of traditional forms of theatre, including rod and shadow puppetry, masquerade, trance dance, courtly dance-drama, raucous folk comedy and mask play. In these classical, folk and popular theatres, improvised spoken dialogue is typically mixed with song and chanting. Spoken drama was introduced to the Indonesian archipelago with imperialism and colonialism. The daily records of the Castle of Batavia, the epicentre of Dutch imperialism in the seventeenth-century East Indies, note a theatrical performance by a group of soldiers when this military fortress in Batavia (present-day Jakarta) was under siege in 1619. The records mention a play about 'the King of Denmark and the King of Sweden'. Some scholars (i.e. Winet 2010: 20–4) have assumed that this was William Shakespeare's *Hamlet*, but more likely it was the Dutch play *Historiaal spel van Koningh Reynier van Norwegen ende de schoone Langerta* (Historical play of King Reynier of Norway and the Beautiful Langerta) by I. I. van Wassenburgh, published in Rotterdam earlier that decade. Similar sorts of ad hoc dramatic performances were enacted in spaces found by European military and civilian personnel stationed in Indonesia throughout the seventeenth and eighteenth centuries.

One of the most active amateur dramatic societies was the Bataviaschen Schouwburg (Batavia Theatre), which entertained the public with Dutch-language plays in a Batavia hotel between 1757 and 1770. The first dedicated theatre space for the performance of spoken drama was the Bachelor's Theatre, known also as the Military Theatre, a 250-seat bamboo theatre funded by subscription, which opened in Batavia in 1814 with a performance of *The Heir at Law* (1808), a five-act comedy by George Colman the Younger. Java at this time was under British rule due to the Napoleonic wars in Europe, and English-language theatre operated as a mode of inculcating European social niceties and reforming the 'degraded' mestizo culture of urban Java. While the British left Java in 1816, an enthusiasm for drama persisted under Dutch colonialism. In the course of the nineteenth century, each of the major cities of Java – Batavia, Semarang and Surabaya – erected a public theatre with a proscenium stage, known as a *schouwburg* in Dutch or *gedung komedi* in the lingua franca of Malay, which hosted visiting theatre and opera troupes. Local dramatic societies, such as the Spectacle-Français sous la Direction de Messieurs les Amateurs du Théâtre Hollandois, established in Batavia in 1837 by the *directeur* F. Minard, also trod *schouwburg* boards (Berg 1881; Diehl 1990: 345–61).

Europeans were, of course, a small minority in colonial Indonesia, never amounting to more than 0.5 per cent of the population, clustered in the administrative and commercial centres and military barracks. Few non-Europeans had the privilege of attending the spoken dramas performed on the stages in the municipal theatres, nor amateur companies' enactments of drawing-room dramas and farces on the smaller stages of exclusive European clubs in towns and cities around the archipelago. European theatre was experienced and consumed by non-Europeans only indirectly, through a variety of popular musical theatres that sprang into existence in the last decades of the nineteenth century in the islands of Java and Sumatra, all of which hybridized the performance aesthetics of European theatre, Chinese opera, Parsi theatre (which toured to Southeast Asia starting in the 1870s) and indigenous Southeast Asian theatrical arts.

The most famous and influential of the hybrid-popular theatres was komedi stambul, or 'Istanbul-style commercial theatre', a commercial form of Malay-language operetta that originated in Surabaya in 1891 (Cohen 2006). The flagship Komedie Stamboel (using the old-style Dutch orthography), the company which gave the genre its name, had nothing to do with Istanbul other than the use of the *Arabian Nights* as a source for plays and the fez as a principal costume item worn by the actors, impoverished mixed-race 'Eurasian' or 'Indo' actors of Javanese-Dutch descent. Initially the resident theatre company of a Chinese-owned public theatre that also hosted Chinese opera, acrobatic troupes, *topeng* (mask dance) and European magicians, the Komedie Stamboel began to tour Java and Madura within its first year of operation and quickly diversified its dramatic repertoire to include European fairy tales, operatic adaptations, true-crime dramas and even musical versions of Shakespeare. Unlike its European predecessors, komedi stambul and other Indonesian hybrid-popular theatres of its ilk were rarely scripted in full. Some actor-managers wrote out brief scenarios and drilled novice actors in their lines, but it was expected that old saws could improvise dialogue from the most meagre of outlines. There are scattered references to soldiers performing Malay-language farces in army barracks and garrisons, but there are no reliable accounts of spoken theatre being written or performed in Malay or other languages of the archipelago before the twentieth century.

The emergence of purely spoken theatre in Malay coincides with the flowering of the so-called *Indische toneel*, Dutch-language colonial drama about the Indies performed on *schouwburg* stages and elite social clubs in colonial Indonesia as well as in the Netherlands. The early Indo and Chinese playwrights who wrote in Malay all express familiarity with the Indische toneel plays of Victor Ido (aka Hans van de Wall), Jan Fabricius and Henri van Wermeskerken. In fact, the first published Malay-language spoken drama, *Lelakon Raden Beij Soerio Retno* (The Tale of Sir Surio Retno, 1901), by the Indo journalist Ferdinand Wiggers, was based loosely on W. G. van Nouhuys' three-act play *Eerloos* (Infamy), which Ido had produced to commercial and critical success at Batavia's *schouwburg* in 1900. It is difficult to ascertain if Wiggers' play, which concerns the profligate son of a district tax collector who returns home from his medical studies in the colonial capital of Batavia to bring disgrace on his family, was crafted for literary consumption or commissioned for performance. Some scholars believe that it was written for students at the School tot Opleiding van Inlandsche Artsen (School for Training Native Doctors or STOVIA), but to date no references to contemporary performances have been located. The fact that the ending of the two-act play is written only in outline form would militate against amateur enactment, and it is too dialogue based to be performed on the komedi stambul stage.

Wiggers did not go on to publish another play and it was not until 1919 that another Malay-language spoken drama was published: *Allah jang Palsoe* (1919; The False Gods), a six-act spoken drama by the Bogor-born writer and businessman Kwee Tek Hoay, loosely adapted from a short story by the popular English novelist E. Phillips Oppenheim. In the decade leading up to this play, Chinese playwrights occasionally penned scripts for *opera derma* ('charity' opera), also known in Hokkien as *cu te hi*. This was a form of amateur musical theatre hybridizing Chinese opera and komedi stambul aesthetics, performed, as the name suggests, mostly to benefit Chinese philan-thropic causes. A number of Malay-language opera derma scripts were published in souvenir editions or for the purpose of future enactments, in editions known as *buku rol opera* (opera roll books). In his introduction to *Allah jang Palsoe*, Kwee looks back at this dramatic repertoire and criticizes it for its melodrama excesses. According to Kwee, *opera derma* plays typically showed the:

> exploits of a profligate, evil, or brutal tycoon who uses trickery to obtain a pretty virgin, the daughter or fiancée of a pauper. You could be sure that when the tycoon puts his evil plan into effect you will see evildoers prepared to rob or deceive with illegal opium; a Chinese or indigenous medicine man intent on trickery; a bordello with sex workers who drain money from misguided young men.
>
> (Kwee 1919: 5)

Kwee was aware of the development of Chinese spoken drama, known as *wenmingxi* or 'civilized drama', and its political significance in modernizing China, and saw a need to break away from *opera derma* to forge realistic problem drama under the stamp of Norwegian playwright Henrik Ibsen, generating plays that were 'more modern, more fitting with current thinking, which can be seen by people from other ethnic groups without embarrassment' (vi).

Kwee's first published play, which included as an appendix his translation of an article about the development of wenmingxi, was well received, and led to two decades of flowering of Sino-Malay spoken drama and a fast decline of *opera derma*. Chinese youths avidly consumed published European plays (typically in English translation), magazines promoted the latest developments in Chinese theatre, playwriting contests were organized, drama societies were established and drama was taught and performed in schools. Spoken drama was touted as enhancing confidence in public speaking, reforming society and redressing social ills such as gambling, avarice and alcohol abuse. Chinese practitioners referred to their Malay-language spoken-language dramas as *toneel*, the Dutch word for theatre, as an assertion of equality with the European stage. In the 1920s, toneel (also spelt *tonil* and *tunil*) plays along the same lines were authored in Malay as well as Javanese, Sundanese and other local languages by indigenous authors. The realistic problem drama achieved particular purchase in Sumatra, where it was known vernacularly as *komedi bicara* (spoken theatre).

Toneel began to be performed for mass audiences with the establishment in 1925 of the Orion theatre company under the management and ownership of Chinese newspaperman Tio Tik Djien, known professionally at T. D. Tio, Jr. Orion, later known as Miss Riboet's Orion or just Miss Riboet after Tio's wife and leading lady, instituted some radical changes in the existing komedi stambul system, dispensing with all non-diegetic singing and dancing (except as cabaret acts referred to as extra turns, performed between acts of plays), dimming auditorium lights 'to enthral the audience in a stage illusion' (Jedamski 2008: 499), adapting Westerns and swashbuckling adventures from the cinema into character-driven potboilers, reducing the number of scenes from twenty or more to eight or nine, and polishing performances through rehearsal and rigorous planning. Orion's huge popularity made Miss Riboet a national celebrity, with a lucrative recording contract and her own cosmetics line, and stimulated many imitators, most notably Dardanella, owned and managed by Russian variety artists Willy Klimanoff, known professionally as Adolf Piëdro, and his mother Ivera. While plays for both Dardanella and Orion were mostly based on Hollywood films in the 1920s, the success of Tio's 1930 play *Gagak Solo* (Crow of Solo), an original drama about a succession struggle in the central Javanese royal court of Surakarta, prompted toneel makers to mine indigenous subjects. Both Orion and Dardanella toured widely in the 1930s, not only in Indonesia but also around the Asian region, picking up new performers and stories for dramatization in the course of their travels. Plays expressed a sense of national pride that was also percolating in the anti-colonial movement, and showed awareness of

Indonesian cultures and societies as part of the Asian region (Cohen 2010b: 179–87). Plays still often had western sources – Kwee Tek Hoay's *Mait Idoep* (The Living Corpse; translated in Cohen 2010b: 57–94) and Andjar Asmara's *Dr Samsi* (in Cohen 2010a: 101–29), both written for Dardanella, were inspired respectively by Ibsen's *Ghosts* and the Hollywood film *Madame X*.

The nationalist movement also produced spoken drama for performances at political gatherings – mostly historical pageants and symbolic dramas under the stamp of Rabindranath Tagore – intended to inculcate a sense of national belonging, imagine precedents for the nation-in-formation, critique feudalist and colonialist ideologies, propagate national symbols and provide outlets for collaboration and building networks (Bodden 1997; Bodden and McGlynn 2010: 1–72). Many of these plays drew on published Dutch-language scholarship and translations of ancient Javanese texts, but the most important nationalist playwrights – Roestam Effendi, Muhammad Yamin and the brothers Sanoesi Pané and Armijn Pané – were all Dutch-educated intellectuals of Sumatran origin (Figure 18.1). Their plays, written in both Dutch and Indonesian

Figure 18.1 Njai Lenggang Kantjana by Armijn Pané (1938). Nationalist costume dramas of this sort, often based on Dutch scholarly editions of classical Javanese and Sundanese texts, were popular at youth congresses and nationalist meetings in the 1920s and 30s, allowing for the embodiment of nationalist sentiments and the visualizing of a glorious ancient past that might lead to an even more glorious future after the end of colonialism. Pané's script was published in full in the literary journal *Poedjangga Baroe* in 1939. An earlier dramatization of this same Sundanese tale by Dutch school teacher Johannes Scholte had been performed to some acclaim at Batavia's *schouwburg* in 1916.

(From *Pandji Poestaka*, 4 March 1939: 334)

(as Malay was renamed in 1928), proposed ancient Java's mighty kingdoms, committed heroes and stirring symbols as models for action and points of reference in the anti-colonial struggle. Not surprisingly, there is a tendency in these plays to emphasize political discourse over stage action, and while often reprinted and studied as literature, they are rarely performed.

The Indonesian islands fell under Japanese control between 1942 and 1945, and theatre practitioners and companies were enlisted into the Japanese wartime propaganda machine (Hutari 2009). With a ban on Dutch vocabulary, toneel was renamed *sandiwara*, a Sanskritic coinage attributed to the Javanese potentate Mangkunegara VII, meaning 'secret news'. A theatre training academy was set up in the capital city of Batavia, renamed Jakarta; a sandiwara union under the direction of filmmaker and playwright Hinatsu Eitarō, a Korean national born Heo Yeong, established to oversee propaganda plays; script competitions held at regional levels; plays and photographs of productions published in magazines and books. German and Japanese theatrical models received approbation, and Ibsen remained in vogue as Norway was a neutral country, but cultural authorities militated against American, British and Dutch influences. Professional sandiwara companies under Japanese patronage benefited from free public transport, and the spoken theatre, which had declined in the 1930s due to competition from cinema and the worldwide depression, surged in popularity. A spoken drama such as Kotot Sukardi's *Bende Mataram* (The Mataram Signal Gong; in Cohen 2010a: 131–46) could be premiered simultaneously by six sandiwara companies operating across Java, with rigid standards of production enforced.

After independence, the Japanese occupation was nostalgically recollected by theatre people as sandiwara's high point. The film industry, which nearly ceased production under wartime austerities, resumed activity and most of the large-scale popular theatre companies disbanded. Sandiwara plays continued to be written and performed after independence, but mostly at the local level by students and amateurs. The dominant political parties in the 1950s paid greater attention to folk theatres performed in local languages than Indonesian-language spoken drama, and it was not until the 1968 opening of the national art centre Taman Ismail Marzuki in Jakarta and the establishment of theatre departments in the conservatoires of Yogyakarta, Bandung, Jakarta and Padang Panjang starting in the 1970s that spoken drama reached the level of accomplishment and public recognition of the past.

III. Japan, by Maki Isaka

Modern times saw simultaneous births of modernized and traditionalized cultures in many realms, including Japanese theatre. 'Traditional Japanese theatre' is a modern, blanket and bracketed concept subsuming *noh*, *kyogen*, *bunraku* and *kabuki*. Each of these, however, had previously started as a 'crazy', 'low-class' and more often than not 'queer' performing art and ended up traditionalized at a particular moment in history and for a particular reason. The earlier part of modern times in Japan (the Meiji period [1868–1912] onward) witnessed the latest case of such transition, namely that of kabuki. Not only did it 'complete'[1] the transformation process and establish traditional Japanese theatre as a category thus defined, but it simultaneously helped delineate *shin-engeki*. Theatrical enterprises emerged anew at that time, by presenting themselves as the antitheses of 'tradition', which was at that precise moment in the middle of dynamic, unstable, self-defining procedures itself. Simply put, the new and the old were concurrently defining themselves by claiming a specific positionality vis-à-vis each other.

Shin-engeki is a generic term signifying 'new' (*shin*) 'theatre' (*engeki*). Among many kinds of shin-engeki, *shinpa* and *shingeki* are now two surviving words, distinguished as proper nouns (i.e. specific genres). Literally shinpa means 'new' 'faction/school' and shingeki 'new' 'drama'.

The nomenclature indicates that the attribute of 'new' was of foremost importance to this theatrical trend. Shin-engeki, however, did not come into being in a vacuum. Kabuki had long been a popular, contemporary theatre of the populace, identifying itself as that which *kabuku* (literally being strange, queer, tilted, crazy and so on). Should there be any new/old faction, kabuki had always belonged to a new party. In line with this history, kabuki tried to become a new theatre itself in modern times, but in vain. In the late nineteenth century, when shin-engeki enterprises emerged, the then tercentennial kabuki theatre, for the first time in its history, came to be termed as *kyūgeki* (old theatre) and *kyūha* (old faction/school), reflecting (1) its new identity to represent the 'old' and (2) the formation of a specific, modern new/old dichotomy. This illustrates the singularity of newness at the beginning of modern times, a singular kind of newness that shin-engeki reified, but kabuki could not.

The newness in question was called for in an extremely rapid and political manner. The new Meiji government's state policy of modernization and westernization was urgent and comprehensive, and theatre even became 'one of the most conspicuous sites for the new government to display Japan's legitimacy as an advanced nation' (Kano 2001: 6). Among the existing theatres, none was ready to fulfil this mission. Having lost its samurai patrons due to the change from samurai shogunate to a new government, *noh* was in too dire a situation. Kabuki was in effect the only existing theatre capable of trying, but no matter how novel and innovative, kabuki's previous idea of something exciting and fresh (namely, 'that which kabuku') was far from appropriate for the politically charged assignment. Until then, kabuki had been a vulgar, hedonistic theatre of the people, subject to surveillance by the shogunate which equated it to prostitution. Figuratively, playhouses were categorized as 'evil places' (*akusho*), along with brothels. Kabuki came to face a crisis in this context and needed to redefine itself to survive the cultural upheaval and meet the expectation that it represented the culture of a legitimate and advanced nation. Simplifying to the extreme, three methods to legitimize kabuki were by modernizing, westernizing or traditionalizing it. Some attempts at the first two options were made (e.g. *Hyōryū kidan seiyō kabuki* [Western Kabuki: Strange Drifting Tale, 1879] by Kawatake Mokuami and *Kairiku renshō asahi no mihata* [The Rising-Sun Flag's Consecutive Victories on the Seas and Land, 1894] by Fukuchi Ōchi). The ensuing box-office failures, however, made kabuki resort to the third option: kabuki 'hurried to make itself classical' (Ōzasa 1985: 53). It was instead of this kabuki – and noh, for that matter – that newly emerging shin-engeki became synonymous with newness.

Around 1890 began what were called *sōshi-shibai* and *shosei-shibai*. It is suggestive that these were named using the attributes of people engaged in them: 'theatre' (shibai) of 'students' (shosei) and 'courageous-political-youngsters' (sōshi). Among them were events marking the onset of shin-engeki: an 1888 production of the troupe of Sudō Sadanori (1867–1907) and an 1891 production of Kawakami Otojirō's (1864–1911) *Itagaki-jun Sōnan Jikki* (Disaster Strikes Itagaki: A True Story). The Sudō-troupe's performance is considered to be the birth of shin-engeki in general; it is contingent whether it was the inception of shinpa (Ortolani 1995: 233–5)[2] or, alternatively, the prototype of shingeki differentiated from shinpa (ōzasa 1985: 479). As for shingeki proper, the following two events are said to signify its origins: the foundation of Bungei Kyōkai (The Literary Society) in 1906 by Tsubouchi Shōyō (1859–1935) and of Jiyū Gekijō (The Free Theatre) in 1909 by Osanai Kaoru (1881–1928). Other troupes important for shingeki include Geijutsuza (The Art Theatre, est. 1913) by Shimamura Hōgetsu (1871–1918) and Osanai's Tsukiji Shōgekijō (The Tsukiji Little Theatre, est. 1924). Major productions in its early history include Ibsen's *John Gabriel Borkman* (The Free Theatre, November 1909), *A Doll's House* (The Literary Society, September and November 1911), *Hamlet* (The Literary Society, May 1911), Tolstoy's *Resurrection* (The Art Theatre, March 1914) and *The Power of Darkness* (The Art Theatre, July 1916).

The brief history above hints at two elements of shin-engeki's newness: (1) enunciation (the act of production) and, by extension, *who* did the act and *how* and (2) the enunciated (a product thus generated), that is, *what* was staged. Earlier types of shin-engeki were called 'student theatre' and 'theatre of courageous, political youngsters', emphasizing the issue of *who*, and shingeki's repertoire was clearly heavily western-centric, at least in its early days.

In terms of the *who* question, shin-engeki pioneers – 'courageous, political youngsters' and 'students' – were amateur actors, the emergence of whom was a new phenomenon. Occupations prior to the Meiji era had not belonged to the realm of 'doing' (individual job) but that of 'being' (family status). Theatre was, thus, not so much individual activities as family businesses in which qualified members of households were engaged.[3] Accordingly, professional kabuki acting on a substantial scale (i.e. except for personal amusement etc.) was monopolized by insiders already situated in kabuki circles. The two pioneering productions mentioned above were thus unprecedented, because, if 'Sudō was the first to show the possibility of survival outside the *kabuki* world, Kawakami . . . [proved] that stardom and financial reward independent from *kabuki* were possible even for a man of obscure origins without any family connections with the professional theatre world' (Ortolani 1995: 235).

'Financial reward' in the excerpt above deserves our attention. The advent of 'courageous, political youngsters' and 'students' as theatre practitioners was deeply related to drastic social transformation. Owing to rapid changes in governments, there emerged both unemployed populations as well as the Freedom and People's Rights Movement in the 1870s and 1880s, and shin-engeki functioned for them both as a means of propaganda and as an income source. For example, Sudō was a journalist working for the Liberal Party newspaper (Shinonome Shinbun) published by Nakae Chōmin (1847–1901). In turn, Kawakami dubbed himself Jiyū Dōji ('Liberty Kid') after Jiyūtō, that is, the Liberal Party pivotal to the people's rights movement. Husband of the famous former geisha and pioneering actress Kawakami Sadayakko, he was initially a Liberal Party member himself.

Importantly, not only societal status and finances but also the 'west' helped define the amateurs in question. (Differently put, the 'west' characterized not only shin-engeki's repertoire but also its actors.) It is most explicit in shingeki, which was modelled after contemporary modern western theatre. At that time, a new movement started in Europe with the foundation of the Théâtre Libre in Paris in 1887 by André Antoine (1858–1943), followed by many little free theatres,[4] which denied existing theatre traditions (the star system, well-made plays, and commercialism) and hence necessitated amateurs who did not belong to the establishment.

These multi-layered significances of the new amateur actors can also be classified into two aspects: (1) the physical and (2) the epistemological. First, basic training for kabuki acting consists of kabuki dance and a certain chanting called *gidayū*.[5] Based on a performative premise (i.e. repetitive doing creates a being), such training implants kabuki grammar into an actor's body, the vocal cords included. While not limited to kabuki, or traditional Japanese theatre for that matter,[6] the weight kabuki placed on dancing and chanting/singing was perceived by shin-engeki practitioners as the signifier of the 'retarded' past; these practitioners thus avoided the long-lasting theatrical grammar of song and dance (Kamiyama 2009: 272; Kano 2001: 67–9). If we take this claim by shin-engeki at face value, amateur actors with no traditional theatrical grammar seemed to have won an advantage over professionals in the physical aspect.

Shin-engeki necessitated a new body differentiated from a kabuki body, and this new body is usually described as a body that does not dance and sing. Germane to this physical element are a few critical footnotes. First, shinpa turned out to be an exception to this 'body that neither dances nor sings', as it ended up congenial to kabuki (see below for more). Second, the denial of traditional grammar does not mean the absence of any grammar. For example, the Tsukiji

Little Theatre's actors were trained in the Dalcroze method of eurhythmics: an educational system of harmonious bodily movements originated by Émile Jaques-Dalcroze, a Swiss music teacher approximately contemporary to Osanai (Yamamoto 1994: 29, 39). This new theatre body might well be just another kind of *dancing* body, and yet this possibility was apparently invisible to those associating shingeki with a body that neither dances nor sings – shingeki practitioners, its audiences and those who shared their epistemological conditions. We see here another familiar example of the assumed superiority of the unmarked (invisible) as universal and natural. If this new body appeared natural, without foregrounding singing and dancing, it means that the form in question was *made naturalized* to the eyes of specific viewers, themselves historical products in their own right (i.e. westernized, modernized etc.).

Nevertheless, it was certainly true that shin-engeki necessitated a new type of body differentiated from a body dancing and singing in the kabuki manner. This change in requirements for the physical is understandable considering the backdrop of the aforementioned new theatrical movement, which resulted in the spread of little free theatres cross-culturally, shingeki ones included: naturalism. Depending on temporal, geographic and epistemological locations, naturalism can mean many things; what is vital to the present case is as follows. The enunciated (a product) was made valorized over enunciation (the act of production) and its process. Eventually, it reached the extreme, and such an illusionary idea as the objective truth (i.e. an ultimately superior enunciated independent of enunciation) became a master concept. Theatre too was in line with this trend, and across the fourth wall, audiences would peep at a slice of life faithfully 'reconstructed' *as is* onstage. Actors' re/construction process is epistemologically made invisible here. Theatre (enunciated) demanded that actors (the subject of enunciation) be totally loyal to itself (enunciated).[7] While theatre that does not sing in and of itself – or spoken drama for short – had already existed in traditional Japanese theatre (i.e. kyogen), premodern and modern spoken drama must be differentiated in terms of this *as is* quality.

Importantly, shin-engeki thus defined (amateurs' new theatre as the antithesis of traditional theatre) still retained its ties to the traditions, and this aspect posits an intriguing issue more visibly in shingeki than it does in shinpa. Figuratively, the two founders of shingeki demonstrated such associations. In 1884, Shōyō published the first unabridged Japanese translation of a Shakespearean play: *Shīzaru kidan: Jiyū no tachi nagori no kireaji* (Strange Tale of Caesar: Blade of Freedom, Wistful Sharpness) (Tsubouchi 1927: 293–439). From its title to its text in its entirety, this translation of *Julius Caesar* is an authentic bunraku text, which no gidayū chanters and kabuki actors would find difficult to chant. Shōyō later regretted having done such work, and in 1911 produced a very literal translation of *Hamlet*. It is also noteworthy that Shōyō wished to create *kokugeki* (national theatre) by combining 'the blood and flesh of kabuki and the bones of Shakespeare' (Ōzasa 1985: 38–9). As for the case of Osanai, his involvement in the traditions was materialized as his cooperation with kabuki actors, including kabuki's male *onnagata* (actors in charge of women's roles). Unlike Shōyō, Osanai himself did not convert throughout his life, although the kabuki actor with whom he had worked for the Free Theatre later declined his invitation to join the Tsukiji Little Theatre. In short, Osanai's enterprise was to change kabuki professional actors into amateur, docile actors as far as shingeki was concerned, revealing its association with the past in a dramatic manner.

Osanai's idea regarding the target of such 'docility' is noteworthy. While the concrete target of loyalty was shifting from scriptwriter to director, the priority of the enunciated (theatre) over enunciation (actors, process etc.) was consistent. Furthermore, the 'west', whatever the definition is, towers persistently behind the theatre as what Osanai calls the *hongoku* (home country) of the new theatre (1964b: 37).[8] To be exact, he does mention non-European countries, but references remain mostly rhetorical. In one quite telling example from an essay published in

1915, Osanai 'commends' China as a better student of the west and Chinese theatre as a handy model for the depraved shingeki (Osanai 1964a: 29). In this image, it is the west, which is behind the good student, that truly matters. Given this, it is clear that Osanai's 'compliment' to Javanese masque, Chinese opera and Korean dance-drama is unmistakably based on, or in line with, the Eurocentric mindset of *datsua nyūō* (escaping from Asia and entering Europe). These two issues – the superiority of the enunciated and that of the west – together demonstrate how deeply shingeki was fated to be entwined with, if not synchronized in a temporal sense, the state policy of modernization and westernization.

In the end, shinpa's tie to the past appeared less 'contradictory' than that of shingeki. If shingeki found its 'home country' in its perception of the 'west', that of shinpa turned out to be kabuki. Considering the issue of 'to whom one renders homage', it seems rather effective to read early shin-engeki (e.g. 'courageous-political-youngsters theatre') as the prototype of shingeki and not as the inception of shinpa. Figuratively, shinpa also functioned as a new venue for actors who wished to do kabuki but could not have much hope in kabuki proper (e.g. minor kabuki actors and their relatives, female offspring of kabuki actors etc.). It is thus no wonder that shinpa's acting style was congruous with kabuki's, based on a dancing and singing kabuki-ish body, and that some shinpa actors openly imitated kabuki actors.[9] In other words, shinpa's physical grammar remained, in effect, that of kabuki (and not, for example, that of shingeki based on the Dalcroze method). This also emphasized how precarious the new/old dichotomy was, both in theory and in practice.

IV. China, by Siyuan Liu

Without doubt, global colonialism was a significant reason for the emergence of western-style spoken theatre in Asia. This is true not only for colonized nations such as India and Indonesia, but a handful of countries, such as Japan and China, that escaped colonization but nevertheless were motivated by its threat to embark on modernization and westernization, including that of their theatre. Within the latter group, China, as a semi-colonial nation, also differed from Japan, with large sections of its port cities being forced to open up for international settlement under western jurisdiction. These so-called concession areas provided a chance for the Chinese population, especially students in Christian schools, to witness some limited western plays and to perform in school productions. At the same time, these concessions served as a reminder of national humiliation and the need for modernization, prompting calls for reforming traditional theatre and the creation of a new spoken theatre so as to enlighten a largely illiterate populace.

This enlightenment and nationalist mission for spoken theatre was also influenced by Japan's faster theatrical modernization and active participation in the nation's empire-building, beginning with the influx of Chinese students to Japan after the 1894–5 Sino-Japanese War and of a group of political exiles after the failed constitutional reform in 1898. For over a decade afterwards, Japan served both as the group's inspiration and as its base of operations in their advocacy for political and cultural, including theatrical, reform. In particular, Japan's use of popular literature and entertainment for nation-building and mass education inspired one of the group's leaders, Liang Qichao, who in 1902 identified the powers of popular literature (primarily vernacular novels and drama) to permeate, immerse, shock and transcend (*xun, jin, ci, ti*) (Liang 1999). Another member of the group, Ou Jujia, demonstrated the enormous power of Japan's new theatre in an article of the same year titled 'Guanju ji' (Watching Plays). In it, he described watching the Japanese being deeply moved by theatrical performance depicting the Meiji Restoration. In contrast to the Japanese example, he denounced his native Cantonese opera as trivializing historical heroics and dwelling on 'affairs of obscenity and sounds of a lost nation' (*shangfeng zhishi, wangguo zhiyin*). In what would soon become a frequent refrain from similar essays following Ou's lead, the article ends with the call for reforming Chinese theatre so that it will be endowed with the power to reflect and change the world. In a way, the article became the opening shot of a sustained campaign for calls to reform Chinese theatre and to borrow western spoken theatre as a tool of social and political reform.

His call was followed by many in the next few years, which witnessed a proliferation of new newspapers and magazines. One incomplete report found roughly forty reformed jingju scripts published between 1902 and 1912 (Ma 1999: vol. 1, 331). In addition, there were many contemporary costume plays (*shizhuang jingju*) that did not have or publish full scripts. These plays included more speech than singing compared to traditional plays, less conventionalized performance and contemporary clothes, and were more focused on contemporary issues such as world colonialism (*Guazhong lanyin* [Seeds of the Melon, Cause of the Orchid], 1904, on Turkey's occupation of Poland), political and constitutional reform (*Weixin meng* [Dream of Reform], 1903) and social reform (*Heiji yuanhun* [Victim of Opium], 1911). Some of these plays, such as *Victim of Opium*, were adapted by the emerging spoken theatre *wenmingxi* (civilized drama) as well as silent film.

Indeed, spoken theatre emerged in China largely as a response to the need for social and political reform, as a performance genre that could better respond to the call of the time than traditional theatre. For example, *Heinu yutian lu* (Black Slave's Cry to Heaven, adapted from *Uncle Tom's Cabin*), the first recognized Chinese spoken drama play which was staged in Tokyo by Chinese students in June 1907, transformed the original novel's anti-slavery message to a call of arms against the mistreatment of Chinese labourers in the United States and the danger of imminent national demise (Figure 18.2). Before and during the 1911 Revolution that overthrew the Qing dynasty (1644–1911), the new drama troupe Jinhua Tuan (Evolutionary Troupe) actively spread revolutionary messages through such plays as *Dongya fengyun* (Storms of East Asia, 1911), a cautionary tale of Korean resistance to Japanese occupation, and *Gonghe wansui* (Long Live the Republic, 1912) which chronicled the revolution. In 1915, during the height of wenmingxi's commercial success in Shanghai, its major companies actively responded to territorial and constitutional crises, such as the Japanese demand for Chinese territories in the so-called Twenty-One Demand and President Yuan Shikai's imperial restoration attempt, by staging anti-colonial and anti-despotic plays such as Victorien Sardou's *Tosca* and *Patrie* (Fatherland) as well as those about the misery of Korean annexation.

In terms of new theatre's genealogy, China also shared some characteristics with colonial India and Indonesia in the sense that while China was never colonized by western powers, its major port cities, especially Shanghai, had large numbers of westerners stemming from international settlement in concession areas who staged amateur performances, built at least one proscenium theatre (Lanxin [Lyceum]) and Japanese-style theatre (Dongjin xi [Tokyo Theatre]), invited touring companies from abroad and taught Chinese students to perform Shakespeare and topical plays. While the Chinese and westerners' theatrical activities were largely segregated and western performance rare crossed over into the Chinese sphere, some interactions between the two communities proved crucial to local new theatre. For example, the performance of the local version of *Black Slave's Cry to Heaven* in October 1907 (independent from the Tokyo version) in the Lyceum Theatre made its modern architecture and stage technology available to most Chinese audience for the first time, thus prompting a building boom of proscenium theatres – starting from the 1908 Xin Wutai (New Stage) – which replaced old teahouse-style theatres for both traditional and new spoken theatre in the city in the next decade.

Another significant impact of the international community was school dramatics, which provided initial exposure to spoken theatre to Chinese students in church schools by the turn

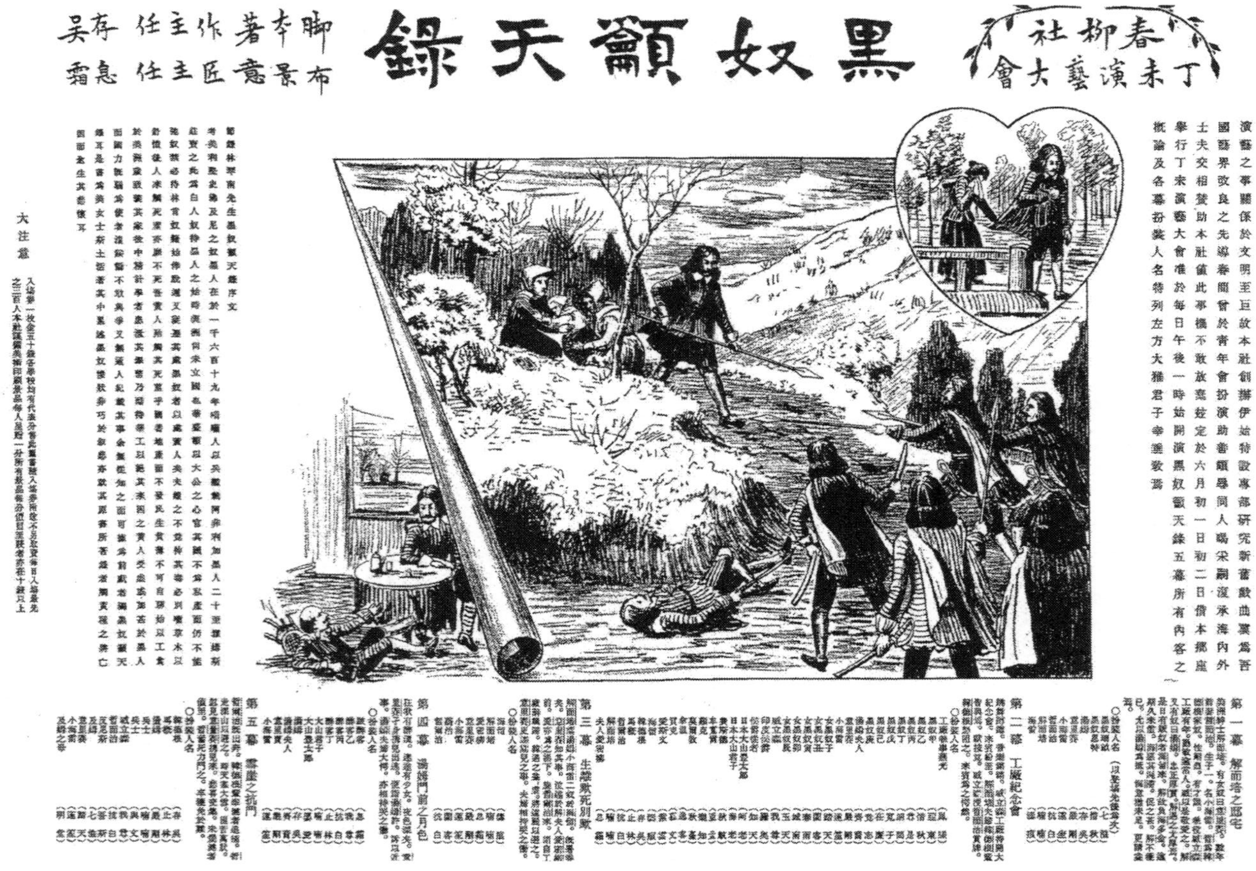

Figure 18.2 Poster of *Heinu yutian lu* (Black Slave's Cry to Heaven) by *Chunliu she* (Spring Willow Society), 1 and 2 June 1907, Tokyo's Hongō-za theatre.

(Courtesy of Waseda University's Tsubouchi Shōyō Theatre Museum) of the twentieth century. The 1914 *Xinju shi* (History of New Drama) started its chronicle of new theatre in Shanghai by crediting St. John's University's dramatic productions in the winter of 1899, which was quickly followed by other local schools (Zhu 1914: 1). Such widespread student dramatics paved the way to spoken theatre in Shanghai and elsewhere in two significant ways. The first was removing the stigma of acting as a socially outcast profession unfit for the educated. The other was lowering the bar of entry for amateur actors unable to perform in traditional theatre without long and arduous training in singing, movement, acrobatics and conventionalized performance. On the other hand, this misconception of new theatre's low requirement on skill sets would ultimately become wenmingxi's Achilles' heel, leading to its demise by the end of the 1910s when it had become a casualty of overdevelopment. In other words, while Shanghai's international settlement inspired amateur Chinese dramatic activists, the lack of wider interaction between the two communities meant that the Chinese students had to look elsewhere for the right model of theatrical and dramatic inspiration.

That inspiration came from Japanese *shinpa*. Like many other areas in late Qing China, the learning of western theatre's dramatic and performance techniques came through the prism of Japan, which had westernized much faster than the rest of East Asia to the point of defeating China in the 1894–5 Sino-Japanese War. Soon afterwards, Chinese students flooded into Japan in the hope of studying western technology and arts. While none of them specifically studied theatre, they watched shinpa plays for language training. Soon, three students at the Tokyo Bijutsu Gakkou (Tokyo School of Fine Arts) – Li Shutong (1880–1942), Zeng Xiaogu (1873–1936) and Huang Ernan (1883–1971) – started the Chunliu She (Spring Willow Society) which staged the landmark production of *Black Slave's Cry to Heaven* in 1907. It is considered China's first modern theatre production because of its nationalist message as well as its reliance on speech, five-act structure, a complete script, ensemble acting and (semi)realistic costume, set and makeup. In 1909, the society, now under the leadership of Lu Jingruo (1885–1915), who had studied shinpa more than any other Chinese student, staged a Chinese version of Victorien Sardou's *La Tosca* (retitled *Relei* [Hot Tears]) in wholesale imitation of a shinpa production. This method of direct emulation earned the Spring Willow high praise from their fellow wenmingxi practitioners as the genre's most artistic group when they returned to Shanghai after the 1911 Revolution, although they, like the Evolutionary Troupe before them, were not able to make a sustained commercial run in Shanghai with their brand of new theatre.

What eventually made new spoken theatre viable was a hybrid approach that combined foreign inspiration with local entertainment elements familiar to the Shanghai audience, as Zheng Zhengqiu (1888–1935) did in 1913 with a serialized domestic melodrama titled *E jiating* (An Evil Family) which ran for five cliff-hanger-filled nights in ten episodes. Zheng's success allowed wenmingxi to mushroom for the rest of the decade in Shanghai as the hybridization of western, Japanese and indigenous theatrical modes in several aspects. Ideologically, it mixed nationalist and political plays with commercial entertainment. Dramatically, wenmingxi performance relied mostly on scenarios and improvisation, with a small portion of full scripts, mostly by the Spring Willow Society. Its staging of foreign plays – European and shinpa melodrama – mostly localized their place, characters and cultural elements, although some small percentage of plays was performed with European or Japanese mise-en-scène. In terms of performance, it mixed spoken theatre with singing and female impersonation with emerging actresses.

By the early 1920s, wenmingxi's hybridity was no longer compatible with the ethos of the *Xin wenhua yundong* (New Cultural Movement), which called for, among others, an embrace of Ibsen-based social critical realism and a complete rejection of traditional theatre, resulting in the coinage of the term *huaju* (spoken drama) to denote this new and pure form. This was also the era that benefited from direct contact with western theatre, as the first group of artists returned from studying theatre in the U.S, starting with Hong Shen (1894–1955), who returned to Shanghai in 1922 after studying playwriting at George Pierce Baker's 47 Workshop at Harvard. Working with the amateur group Xiju Xieshe (Shanghai Stage Society), Hong established gender-appropriate casting and a director-centred rehearsal system. In 1924, he successfully staged his localization of Oscar Wilde's *Lady Windermere's Fan*, which became a model for staging modern western plays, making it culturally and logistically possible for other amateur and school/college groups to perform such plays. This localization strategy turned out to have significant effect on the growth of huaju because a number of playwrights and actors started from such student dramatics, including huaju's greatest playwright Cao Yu (1910–96) and one of its best directors Jiao Juyin (1905–75).

Meanwhile, professional huaju education also started in 1925 when Yu Shangyuan (1897–1970) and Zhao Taimou (1889–1968), who had studied theatre at Carnegie Institute of Technology and Columbia, returned to Beijing to establish a theatre department at the Guoli Yizhuan (National Arts School). In 1926, Xiong Foxi (1900–65) took over the department after receiving an MA in drama from Columbia University and served as its head until it disbanded in 1932. Through 7 eventful years, the department produced the first generation of huaju professionals in China.

Other sources of inspiration for huaju's emergence in the 1920s came from Europe and Japan (through *shingeki*'s foreignizing approach to modern European theatre). One of the leaders of the huaju movement, Tian Han (1898–1968), returned from Japan in 1922 after 6 years and started the Nanguo She (Southern China Society) in Shanghai, which mainly staged his one-act modernist and realistic plays such as *Huohu zhiye* (The Night the Tiger was Caught, 1924) but also two European plays with western mise-en-scène: *Salomé* (1929) and *Carmen* (1930). European influence in the decade was mainly manifested through one-act comedy playwrights who had studied in Britain and France, especially Ding Xilin (1893–1974), whose *Yizhi mafeng* (A Wasp, 1923) and *Yapo* (Oppression, 1925) represent some of the best achievements of modern Chinese comedy and were widely staged by amateur groups.

By the mid -1930s, huaju had reached its maturity, as evident from Cao Yu's four-act play *Leiyu* (Thunderstorm, 1934), which is still considered one of the most representative huaju plays, and the first professional company Zhongguo Lüxing Jutuan (China Travelling Theatre Company), which was established in 1933 by Tang Huaiqiu (1898–1953), who had been a major actor in Tian Han's Southern China Society. Thus, it took more than three decades for modern Chinese theatre to reach dramatic and theatrical maturity as a result of the combined influence of Euro-American, Japanese and indigenous Chinese theatre.

Notes

1 I bracketed the word 'complete', as kabuki repeated a similar transition (from 'contemporary' to 'traditional' theatre) after the Second World War (Brandon 2006: 1–110). The repetition does not nullify the significance of each transition, be it one in Meiji or in the post-Second World War era.

2 The only surviving shinpa troupe today, Gekidan Shinpa [Troupe Shinpa], takes this theory http://shochiku.co.jp/shinpa/about/birth/ (accessed 26 May 2014).

3 Household membership was not exclusively defined by blood relations in premodern Japan. Adoption was a frequently used method to secure the lineage and business of a household; it also concerns a performative premise of cultivation (*shugyō*): a training system for acting (and beyond) in premodern Japan, in which repeated and devoted training (doing) will create body and mind (being) (Isaka 2005b: 29–30, 65–8).

4 Examples include, but are not limited to, the Freie Bühne in 1889 by Otto Brahm (1856–1912), the Independent Theatre in 1891 by Jacob Thomas Grein (1862–1935) and the Moskovskii

khudozhestvennyi akademicheskii teatr imeni M. Gor'kogo in 1898 by Konstantin Sergeevich Stanislavskii (1863–1938).

5 *Gidayū* is a musical genre, named after Takemoto Gidayū (1651–1714), a famous chanter in the puppet theatre (present-day bunraku). Sometimes also called *jōruri*, gidayū-chanting is considered indispensable not only for bunraku but also for kabuki elocution.

6 Song and dance were conceptualized by noh dramatist and theorist Zeami (1363–1443) as the two fundamental aspects of noh (Zeami 1974: 112). See also Liu (2013: 2–3).

7 'Loyalty to the enunciated' was a significant concept, as it was associated with amateur actors. Osanai states that actors must be 'docile' (1965: 112–13). In terms of theoretical elements, he was by far the most acute thinker, by separating actual amateurs and what I call 'amateurity', but such theoretical achievement was made possible by its practical incompetence (Isaka 2005a, 2005b). For example, working with professional kabuki actors, Osanai accused Hōgetsu's the Art Theatre of pursuing 'depraved dualism' to seek artistic and pecuniary success simultaneously (1964b: 35–65).

8 The aforementioned lineup of early-shingeki repertoire matches this sentiment. Naoki Sakai lucidly defines the west as a modern, culturally imagined unity with no immanent substance (1996: 22–3).

9 For example, a shinpa major onnagata, Kitamura Rokurō (1871–1961), explicitly admitted his admiration for such kabuki actors as Ichikawa Danjūrō IX (1838–1903) and Ichikawa Kumehachi I (c. 1846–1913), whom he openly imitated. Considering this, the nomenclature of shinpa – 'new *faction/ school*' – could not have been more accurate and incisive.

Bibliography

Berg, N. P. van den. 1881. 'Het toneel te Batavia in vroegeren tijd' (Batavia's Theatre in Former Times), *Tijdschrift voor Indische Taal-, Land- en Volkenkunde* (Journal of Indonesian Linguistics, Geography, and Ethnography), 26: 313–411.

Bharucha, Rustom (1983) *Rehearsals of Revolution*, Honolulu: University of Hawai'i Press.

Bodden, Michael H. (1997) 'Utopia and the shadow of nationalism: The plays of Sanusi Pane, 1928–1940', *Bijdragen tot de Taal-, Land- en Volkenkunde* (Journal of the Humanities and Social Sciences of Southeast Asia), 153: 332–55.

Bodden, Michael, and John H. McGlynn (eds) (2010) *The Lontar Anthology of Indonesian Drama, Volume 2: Building a National Theatre*, Jakarta: Lontar.

Brandon, James R. (1967) *Theatre in Southeast Asia*, Cambridge, MA: Harvard University Press.

—— (2006) 'Myth and Reality: A Story of Kabuki during American Censorship, 1945–1949', *Asian Theatre Journal*, 23 (1): 1–110.

Busteed, H. E. (1897) *Echoes From Old Calcutta: Being Chiefly Reminiscences of the Days of Warren Hastings, Francis and Impey*, London: Richardson Printer.

Cohen, Matthew I. (2006) *The Komedie Stamboel: Popular Theater in Colonial Indonesia*, Athens: Ohio University Press.

—— (ed.) (2010a) *The Lontar Anthology of Indonesian Drama, Volume 1: Plays for the Popular Stage*, Jakarta: Lontar.

—— (2010b) *Performing Otherness: Java and Bali on International Stages, 1905–1952*, Basingstoke: Palgrave Macmillan.

Dasgupta, Hemendranath (1934) *The Indian Stage*, Volume 1, Calcutta: Metropolitan Printing & Publishing House.

—— (1988) *The Indian Theatre*, Delhi: Gian Publishing House.

Diehl, Katherine Smith (1990) *Printers and Printing in the East Indies to 1850, Volume 1: Batavia*, New Rochelle, NY: Aristide D. Caratzas.

Gekidan Shinpa (Troupe Shinpa) www.shochiku.co.jp/shinpa/about/birth/, accessed 26 May 2014.

Hutari, Fandy (2009) *Sandiwara dan Perang: Politisasi terhadap Aktivitas Sandiwara Modern Masa Jepang di Jakarta, 1942–1945* (Sandiwara and War: The Politicization of Modern Theatre Activity during the Japanese Period in Jakarta, 1942–1945), Jakarta: Ombak.

Isaka, Maki (2005a) 'Osanai Kaoru's Dilemma: "Amateurism by Professionals" in Modern Japanese Theatre', *TDR*, 49 (1): 119–33.

—— (2005b) *Secrecy in Japanese Arts: 'Secret Transmission' as a Mode of Knowledge*, New York: Palgrave.

Jain, Nemi Chandra (1992) *Indian Theatre: Tradition, Continuity and Change*, New Delhi: National School of Drama.

Bibliography

Jedamski, Doris (2008) '"... and then the Lights Went Out and It was Pitch-Dark": From Stamboel to Tonil – Theatre and the Transformation of Perceptions', *South East Asia Research*, 16: 481–511.

Kamiyama Akira (2009) *Kindai engeki no suimyaku: Kabuki to shingeki no aida* (Water Vein of Modern Theatre: Between *Kabuki* and *Shingeki*), Tokyo: Shinwasha.

Kano, Ayako (2001) *Acting Like a Woman in Modern Japan: Theater, Gender, and Nationalism*, New York: Palgrave.

Kwee Tek Hoay (1919) *Allah jang Palsoe: Satoe Lelakon Komedi dalem Anem Bagian* (The False Gods: A Play in Six Parts), Batavia: Tjiong Koen Nie/Electr. Druk.

Liang, Qichao (1999) 'Popular Literature in Relation to the Masses', Faye Chunfang Fei (trans), in Faye Chunfang Fei (ed) *Chinese Theories of Theater and Performance from Confucius to the Present*, 109–11, Ann Arbor: University of Michigan Press.

Liu, Siyuan (2013) *Performing Hybridity in Colonial-Modern China*, New York: Palgrave Macmillan.

Ma Shaobo (ed.) (1999) *Zhongguo jingju shi* (A History of Chinese Beijing Opera), Beijing: Zhongguo xiju chubanshe.

Macaulay, Thomas Babington (1920) 'Minute by the Hon'ble T. B. Macaulay, dated the 2nd February 1835', in H. Sharp (ed.) *Bureau of Education. Selections from Educational Records*, Part I (1781–1839), Calcutta: Superintendent, Government Printing; reprint, Delhi: National Archives of India, 1965, 107–17.

Ortolani, Benito (1995) *The Japanese Theatre: From Shamanistic Ritual to Contemporary Pluralism*, rev. edn, Princeton: Princeton University Press.

Osanai Kaoru (1964a) 'Mokei butai no maede' (Being in Front of a Stage Model), in Sugai Yukio (ed.) *Osanai Kaoru engekiron zenshū* (The Complete Writings on Theatrical Theory of Osanai Kaoru), Volume 1, 26–9, Tokyo: Miraisha.

—— (1964b) 'Shingeki fukkō no tameni' (In the Interest of the Renaissance of *Shingeki*), in *Osanai Kaoru engekiron zenshū*, Volume 1, 35–65, Tokyo: Miraisha.

—— (1965) 'Engeki no jissaika to shite' (In My Capacity as a Theater Practitioner), in *Osanai Kaoru engekiron zenshū*, Volume 2, 111–15, Tokyo: Miraisha.

Ōzasa Yoshio (1985) *Nihon gendai engekishi: Meiji Taishō hen* (History of Japanese Contemporary Theatre: The Meiji and Taishō Eras), Tokyo: Hakusuisha.

Presidency College Calcutta (1956) *Centenary Volume*, Calcutta: W.B.G. Press.

Raha, Kironmoy (1978) *Bengali Theatre*, New Delhi: National Book Trust.

Rangacharya, Adya (1975) *The Indian Theatre*, New Delhi: National Book Trust.

Sakai Naoki. (1996) 'Joron: Nashonaritī to bo/koku/go no seiji' (Introduction: Nationality and the Politics of Mother/Nation's/Tongue), in Sakai Naoki, Brett de Bary, and Iyotani Toshio (eds) *Nashonaritī no datsukōchiku* (Deconstruction of Nationality), 9–53, Tokyo: Kashiwa Shobō.

Seton-Karr, W. S. (1864) *Selections Calcutta Gazettes, of the Years 1784, 1785, 1787, 1787, and 1788, Showing the Political and Social Condition of the English in India*, Calcutta: Military Orphan Press.

Singh, Jyostna (1989) 'Different Shakespeares: the Bard in Colonial/Postcolonial India,' *Theatre Journal*, 41 (4): 445–58.

—— (1996) *Colonial Narratives/Cultural Dialogues: 'Discoveries' of India in the Language of Colonialism*, London: Routledge.

Singh Thakur, Vikram (2012) 'From "Imitation" to "Indigenization": A Study of Shakespeare Performances in Colonial Calcutta', *Alicante Journal of English Studies*, 25: 193–208.

Solomon, Rakesh H. (2009) 'Towards a Genealogy of Indian Historiography', in Nandi Bhatia (ed.) *Modern Indian Theatre: A Reader*, New Delhi: Oxford University Press.

Thakurta, Guha P. (1930) *The Bengali Drama*, London: Kegan Paul, Trench, Trubner & Co.

Tsubouchi Shōyō (1927) *Shīzaru kidan: Jiyū no tachi nagori no kireaji* (Strange Tale of Caesar: Blade of Freedom, Wistful Sharpness), in *Shōyō senshū* (Selected Works of Shōyō), supplement 2, 293–439, Tokyo: Shun'yōdō.

Wiggers, F. (1901) *Lelakon Raden Beij Soerio Retno* (The Tale of Sir Surio Retno), Batavia: Oeij Tjaij Hin.

Winet, Evan Darwin (2010) *Indonesian Postcolonial Theatre: Spectral Genealogies and Absent Faces*, Basingstoke: Palgrave Macmillan.

Yamamoto Yasue (1994) *Aruite kita michi* (The Path I Have Walked), Tokyo: Chūōkōronsha.

Zeami Motokiyo (1974) *Shikadō* (The Path to the Flower), in Omote Akira and Katō Shūichi (eds) *Zeami Zenchiku* (Zeami and Zenchiku), *Nihon shisō taikei* (Collected Japanese Thought), Volume 24, 111–19, Tokyo: Iwanami Shoten.

Zhu Shuangyun (1914) *Xinju shi* (History of New Drama), Shanghai: Xinju xiaoshuo she.

19

Gender performance and the rise of actresses in traditional Asian theatre

*Anita Singh, Maki Isaka, Siyuan Liu, Kathy Foley,
Jennifer Goodlander and Ashley Robertson*

Modernity significantly complicated gender performance in Asia. While women usually performed together with men in ancient times, as evident in Indian *kutiyattam* or the Chinese Yuan dynasty (1271–1368) *zaju*, actresses were often banned from the stage just as popular theatrical forms such as *kathakali*, *kabuki* and *jingju* emerged in the seventeenth and eighteenth centuries. Thus, the modern passages that opened to actresses (as in Chinese theatre) or largely remain blocked (kathakali and Japanese theatre) on the professional stage together with actors offer fascinating insights into the changes and resistance in gender performance. This ideology of gender performance is further complicated by issues of impersonation and cross-gender representation as well as class, narrative and genres, as demonstrated in the following sections on India, China, Japan and Southeast Asia (with a case study on female dalang [puppet master] in Java and Bali).

I. India, by Anita Singh

Female artists in Sanskrit theatre

The account of the female performer as encoded in Bharata's *Natyasastra*, written between 200 BC and 200 AD, is indicative, and even reflective, of the social status of women. The image of an actress that materializes from *Natyasastra* is of an accomplished theatre artiste with natural and acquired qualities. They functioned not just as artists but also had supplementary value as far as the king was concerned. Bharata writes: 'Women well versed in all kinds of dance and in the use of different limbs in dance and acting should be placed in the royal theatre' (34.70). *Natyasastra* illustrates the function of female artists that made them not only significant but also indispensable to theatre (Figure 19.1).

Figure 19.1 Aurangabad cave no. 7 showing dancing women and all-female musicians (seventh century AD).

(Courtesy of American Institute of Indian Studies, Varanasi)

Decline of Sanskrit theatre

The ninth and tenth centuries marked the decline in the Sanskrit theatre. The Sanskrit language accessible to the upper caste underwent *apabhramsas* (non-Sanskrit linguistic forms) and this led to the popularity of performances in regional dialects. Concurrently Kautilya in the chapter 'Ganikadhyaksha Prakarana' in *Arthashastra* states that women spectators who came without their husband's permission to see plays by *streepreksha* (all-female theatre) were fined six *panas* and twice as much if caught watching plays by *purushpreksha* (male theatre) (Varadpande 1979: 35–41). Society's concern about spectator-women reflected the asphyxiating atmosphere within which female artists performed. The custom of women actors completely disappeared over a period of time.

Devadasis

In medieval India, the temple became a pronounced centre of the cultural activities of a community. Theatre institutions thrived under its patronage. Diverse female communes, which gradually became devoted to temples, were known by their local names: *Jogin* or *Bhogam-Vandhi* (Andhra Pradesh), *Penkettu* (Kerala), *Theveardiyar* (Tamil Nadu), *Kudikar* (West Coast), *Murali*, *Jogateen* and *Aradhini* (Maharastra), *Maharis* (Orissa). Roughly they existed from the tenth to the nineteenth century. The generic term devadasi literally translates as servants of god. The devadasis followed a *murai* (organized way of life) (Srinivasan1985: 1869–76). Rituals were performed at various points of time: at dedication, a *muttu* (sacred necklace) was tied round her neck to signify her as a *nityasumangali* (a woman of ever-auspicious married status) (Kersenboom 1987). Devadasis performed the *sadir*, a form of solo dance, which fuses abstract pure dance with emotional and devotional components. It was performed in temples and kings' courts and to select audiences in private spaces. Sadir is believed to be the precursor of Bharatanatyam.

One of the most illustrious devadasi attached to the court of Nayaka King of Tanjore, Partapsimha (1739–63) was Muddupalani (fl. c. 1750). She was well versed in both Telugu and Sanskrit literature, and came from a devadasi family; her mother and grandmother were also both devadasis and poets. She became well known for her controversial erotic narrative poem *Radhika Santwanam* (*Appeasing Radhika*). Another renowned devadasi was Bangalore Nagarathnamma (1878–1952), an Indian Carnatic singer and cultural activist who began the Tyagaraja Aradhana festival in commemoration of the Carnatic singer Tyagaraja at Thiruvaiyaru. She translated and promoted Muddupalani's *Radhika Santwanam*. The mid-nineteenth century witnessed a series of social reforms that dislodged the devadasis from their traditional socio-cultural roles. Likened to prostitutes, they did not fit into the new woman image that was being fashioned by colonialism and by an upsurge of homegrown patriarchies that prized women's domestic roles. At this point, devadasis such as T. Balasaraswathi and Nagarathnamma fervently opposed the abolition of the devadasi system. In 1947, the Madras Devadasi (Prevention of Dedication) Act outlawed dedication in the southern Madras Presidency and in 1988 it was finally outlawed in all of India.

Traditional folk theatre

In the surviving Sanskrit theatre, *kutiyattam* (combined acting) is believed to have existed 2,000 years ago. Male actors from the *chakyar* (a brahmin group) caste enacted female roles, and actresses belonging to the *nangyar* caste (in the Malayali social system) also enacted female roles, played the cymbals and sang Sanskrit *slokas* (two-line verses). Being a ritual theatre, it was performed inside the *kuttampalam* (temple theatre). From the sixteenth century, with the emergence of the *bhakti* (devotional religion) movement, actresses from the nangyar caste developed the *nangyar kuttu* (a solo performance by women) from Sri Krishna's life (Moser 2011). In the 1970s, Paninkulan Rama Cakyar discarded caste restrictions regarding the induction of performers. In *Kalamandalam* (Centre for Arts), he taught three women from outside the Nangyar caste: P. N. Girija (in 1971), C. K. Shailaja (in 1973) and P. S. Sathi (in 1976). Three women, Kalamandalam Girija, Margi Sathi and Usha Nangiar, revived this form by reinterpreting traditional stories. In 1986, Kalamandalam Girija, the first female student of Painkulam Rama Cakyar, presented the rewritten narratives of mythological heroines Kunti, Gandhari and Madhavi in the nangyar kuttu format and actively promoted kutiyattam through training students and organizing workshops.

Usha Nangiar from the traditional nangyar caste learnt nangyar kuttu under Ammannur Kuttan Chakyar and Guru Ammanur Madhava Cakyar. She teaches kutiyattam at Sri Sankara Sanskrit University of Kerala. In 1990, she performed inside the temple kuttampalam as a ritual service, and introduced innovations in dress and *abhinaya* (expressions). She has performed the complete nangyar kuttu repertoire at Vṭaakkunathan Shiva Temple of Thrissur. After her marriage she was not invited to perform at this temple. Orthodoxy still impacts the lives of female artistes: she can retain her rights as a nangyar only if she marries within her community, while chakyar can preserve his performing rights even if he was not married to a an Illodamma (female member of the chakyar community). Usha's performance manual *Abhinetri* (Actress) documents the dramaturgical need for reinventing female characters, and in her performances she has re-created the classical characters of Subhadra, Mandodari, Menaka, Draupadi and Sakuntala.

Margi Sathi studied in Kutiyattam Kendra Centre (Trivandrum) and then joined the group Margi and adopted its name. Through her compositions, she has reclaimed the character of Sita in *Sitayanam* (The Journey of Sita) and the story of chaste Kaṇṇagi from the Tamil epic *Cilapadikaram* (Story of the Anklet). Apart from teaching, Margi Sathi has used mass media to promote kutiyattam (Casassas 2012: 1–30).

Younger actresses, including Margi Usha, Kalamandalam Sindhu and Kapila Venu, among others, are re-energizing the form through their compositions and keeping the tradition of nangyar kuttu alive.

Kathakali (story play), as a stylized classical dance-drama on the life of Shri Krishna, originated in the seventeenth century in Kerala. It is a male stronghold, however, even though there have been women Kathakali performers in recent decades.[1] P. Geetha's book, *Kaliyammamar*, depicts the lives of over a hundred women dancers and portrays in part the struggles of Chavara Parukutty, a Dalit Kathakali dancer, who has performed for 50 years. Kottarakkara Bhadra, Ranjini K. P. and Haripriya Namboodiri are veteran Kathakali artistes. There are several reasons why this form has not been conducive for women performers. To start with, it could be because of its physical nature and martial arts training. Also, troupes largely comprise male artists and the actress is considered a hindrance. The art requires years of arduous preparation that is denied to women, and the stigma of being an *aattakari* (dancer) is always there. The female artiste is prohibited from performing during menstruation. There is an entrenched belief in Kerala society in upholding female sexual decorum and antique notions of ritual purity still persist. The conservatism within the male hegemony of Kathakali remains unopposed to this day (Pitkow 1998: 48–105).

Yakshagana (song of the Demi-Gods), the folk tradition of Karnataka, culled episodes involving the exposition of valour, strength, courage and manly prowess from the *Mahabharata*, *Ramayana* and the *Bhagavata*. These heroic themes were suitable to the vigorous style of *Tandava* dance for which a female character was unsuitable. The absence of women is also recorded in other forms of folk tradition, namely *raslila*, *ramlila*, *jatra*, *nautanki*, *tamasha* and many more. Young boys who had good looks, good voices and good memories were recruited around the age of 8 to 10 years to impersonate women. In *nautanki*, a secular semi-operatic folk theatrical form of northern India (Uttar Pradesh, Punjab and Rajasthan), men impersonated women, as they did in other traditional theatres. Around the 1920s, women became performers in nautanki troupes. According to Katherine Hansen, nautanki theatre as well as myth, epic and popular cinema do not reflect actual social relations, gender differences and power alignments but rather produce and perpetuate them (1992: 7).

Gulab Bai (1926–96) was the first established woman performer in nautanki who performed at the age of 12 in the 1930s (Mehrotra 2006). Soon she started playing the heroine roles – Laila in *Laila Majnu*, Farida in *Bahadur Ladki* (Brave Girl), Shireen in *Shireen Farhad*, Taramati in *Raja Harishchandra* and so on. In the mid-1950s, she set up her own company – the Gulab Theatrical Company. Her daughters Madhu and Asha continue to run the Gulab Theatrical Company.

Jyotsna Dutta (1940–2002) was the first female artiste in the professional *jatra* (procession or journey), a folk theatrical form from Bengal (Figure 19.2). The early actresses of the jatra came from the red-light area of Kolkata, as acting on stage was taboo for women (Ghosh 2013: 77–85). Before them, *ranis* (drag queens) enjoyed the status of the most popular figures of the jatra.

Women performers have perpetually remained on the margins of mainstream middle-class discourse. The middle class imagined the nation as a highly 'idealized' and 'respectable' version

Figure 19.2 Jyotsna Dutta as Sonai in Brajendra Kumar Dey's *Sonai Dighi* (1959).
(Courtesy of Tarun Kumar Dey)

of its own image; in the nation's search for a sovereign identity, the question of 'respectability' became crucial, assuming its sharpest form where the issues concerned women (Singh 2004: 1–24). Gender identities are environmentally conditioned and the increasing contribution of women in theatre can play a substantial role in challenging cultural stereotypes.

II. Japan, by Maki Isaka

All major genres in traditional Japanese theatre (*noh, kyogen, bunraku* and *kabuki*) are all-male theatre. This statement nearly amounts to common sense today but necessitates critical, multi-fold annotation. For hidden behind such 'common sense' is the overlooked impact *from* females, whether compatibility between women in general and male performers of women's roles, or the contribution of female theatre practitioners (who existed, albeit quasi-secretly). What was happening in Japan at the beginning of modern times – the Meiji period (1868–1912) onwards – helped nullify the necessity for such annotation, muted its critical implications and thereby naturalized the seemingly straightforward statement above. The 'common sense' was thus established at that time. By focusing on kabuki, what follows debunks the 'naturalizing' process in question and thereby expounds gender issues in traditional Japanese theatre in modern times. Among the abovementioned theatrical genres, kabuki is the optimum example to examine gender issues owing to the existence of *onnagata* (actors in charge of women's roles).[2]

Onnagata have existed ever since the early seventeenth century, that is, the early days of kabuki, yet they have changed greatly throughout the four centuries since. In particular, the distinction between premodern and modern onnagata was categorical; thus 'onnagata-as-we-know-them-today' only came into being in the Meiji era. Kabuki playwright Takeshiba Kisui (1847–1923) recollected in 1920 that kabuki 'totally changed within the past forty or fifty years, . . . and onnagata changed most drastically' (1920: 36).

One of the immediate changes in kabuki was directly related to the collapse of the samurai class, because it also resulted in the extirpation of artistic patronage by samurai, leaving their *protégés* – some kabuki actors included – unemployed.[3] Kabuki actors who had performed at their patrons' residences ended up facing the alternatives of retirement or 'relocation', with some of them shifting the venue of their performance from private mansions to playhouses. Because these kabuki actors were women at that time,[4] it meant that female kabuki actors moved from relatively invisible and closed circles to a more visible theatre market. For example, Ichikawa Kumehachi I (c. 1846–1913) started her kabuki career at samurai residences as an apprentice to a famous kabuki actor under the patronage of several powerful samurai households. After the master lost her patrons around 1863, indicative of the approaching fall of the samurai class, Kumehachi performed in theatres in new Meiji Japan. Well trained in kabuki basics in a traditional manner, she was renowned particularly for such established onnagata roles as Princess Yaegaki of *Honchō nijūshikō* (The Twenty-Four Paragons of Filial Piety in This Country) and dancer Hanako of *Dōjōji* (Dōjōji Temple), and was praised for being indistinguishable from male onnagata (Isaka 2006, 2016).

Female kabuki actors were thus made possible specifically in modern times by societal and economic changes. Kumehachi recollects her days after her master lost the performance venue and the source of their allowance:

> I was doing nothing in particular [for a while]. . . . And then I heard of a small troupe led by one Danzaburō, a disciple of Danjūrō VIII. . . . I badly wanted to become an actor, so I cut off my hair and made it into [a male hairstyle] and joined the troupe.
>
> (Ichikawa 1907: 82–3)

After the emergence of those women with kabuki training willing to perform, the Metropolitan Police Department gave permission in 1891 for theatrical productions with male and female performers, although the likes of Kumehachi did not wait until 1891.

However, female kabuki actors were never outsiders to kabuki circles. Kumehachi's aforementioned reputation for being authentic in performance – not only attractive but also true to the mainstream tradition of kabuki – suggests that female kabuki actors were not considered newcomers differentiated from the male actors who had preceded and coexisted with them. Master–disciple relationships and family ties illustrate the connection. After her female master, Kumehachi also studied with two major male kabuki actors: first, the renowned onnagata Iwai Hanshirō VIII (1829–82), and after he passed away, Ichikawa Danjūrō IX (1838–1903), who dominated the kabuki world. Others like her also had similar backgrounds. For example, Matsumoto Kinshi was Matsumoto Kinshō's disciple; Bandō Noshio was the daughter of Bandō Shūchō II (and the wife of Shūchō III); Ichikawa Rikinosuke was Ichikawa Gonjūrō's disciple; and Bandō Tamasaburō III was the daughter of Morita Kan'ya XII, the great grandfather of the present Tamasaburō (Bandō Tamasaburō V: b. 1950). Tamasaburō III passed away in the United States in 1905, where she had been dispatched for an international exposition the year before.

Meiji Japan also saw the birth of another kind of female actor, namely modern spoken theatre actresses whose definition relied on the new idea of natural femininity grounded in women's bodies (Kano 2001: 17, 22). Unlike these modern actresses, and despite the fact that they were brought to the public stage by social conditions in Meiji, modern female kabuki actors were paradoxically bound by premodern concepts. Meiji transformations thus simultaneously resulted in the advent of modern female kabuki actors economically and yet destined their wane epistemologically. Their era was indeed short-lived – through about 1910 – at least in an overt manner.[5]

Their decline was due to the same reason behind the downfall of male premodern onnagata – such as one of Kumehachi's masters, Hanshirō – the versatility suited to a porous labyrinth of gendering. It was performative versatility obtained through repetitious, devoted and lifelong training that created a being with an appropriate and internalized second nature. If his disciple was commended for being indistinguishable from men onstage, Hanshirō was complimented for being capable of passing as a woman in society 'even when wearing just lingerie' (Takeshiba 1920: 36). He was famous for performing in plays by Kawatake Mokuami (1816–93), one of the most famed and 'authentic' kabuki playwrights. Hanshirō was hence a good old-fashioned onnagata representing premodern traditions, whom Mokuami's disciple Kisui praised as 'the most impressive' onnagata who 'surely looked like none other than a woman' (ibid.: 36). But his way of doing onnagata could not survive the premodern/modern juncture; it was impossible to find the same kind of onnagata 'after he passed away' (ibid.: 36).

Instead of female onnagata being indistinguishable from men and male onnagata being able to pass as women, modern onnagata were defined in the same manner as modern actresses in the sense that they were 'scientifically' controlled by their 'natural' sex. They are first and foremost male and only perform artistic/artificial femininity onstage. A telling anecdote illustrative of the premodern/modern shift can be found in how Nakamura Utaemon V (1865–1940) became a kabuki actor. The prime onnagata of his time, instrumental in a new definition of onnagata and their modern artistry, Utaemon was not born into a kabuki family. Upon his father's death in 1874, he was introduced to Hanshirō for possible adoption. The match did not materialize, however. Utaemon recollected, 'I thought, no way can I go to that "Big Forehead" who looks like a woman. . . . So I ended up being adopted by Shikan' (Ihara 1935: 17–18). Because of Hanshirō's forte in passing as a woman (and *not* despite it), the renowned premodern onnagata was intuitively and categorically rejected by the *enfant terrible*, who later became his counterpart in modern times.

Utaemon's career was filled with elements unprecedented for onnagata, which became explicitly visible after the death of Danjūrō IX. This is when Utaemon reached the apex of kabuki circles as a whole, a significant accomplishment for onnagata in the masculinity-centric kabuki world. His supremacy was symbolized by his ascendance to the positions of Kanbu Gigei Iinchō (Executive Chairperson of Technique) at the Kabuki-za theatre and President of Dai Nihon Haiyū Kyōkai (Great Japan Association for Actors). In addition, Utaemon took on the challenge of a series of title roles of *shin-kabuki* (new kabuki) plays that had been written by Tsubouchi Shōyō (1859–1935) but were hardly produced until then, for example Lady Yodo of *Kiri hitoha* (One Leaf of a Paulownia, 1894–5) in March 1904. A founder of *shingeki* (new theatre), Shōyō was an outsider for kabuki, and his shin-kabuki should be seen in the context of the modern survival of kabuki. Having been regarded as vulgar entertainment akin to prostitution, kabuki struggled to legitimize itself in a modern nation, which in turn was trying to legitimize itself as an advanced nation amid worldwide colonialism. Creating rational and historically accurate kabuki plays, such as *One Leaf of a Paulownia*, was one attempt at modernizing kabuki.

If compatibility between the femininity of women in society and onnagata on stage was required for premodern onnagata, then the denial of such interchangeability was indispensable to modern onnagata's survival, which was intricately connected to the aforementioned kabuki's survival strategy. The changing relationships between women and onnagata were concomitant with the reorganization of dichotomized maps of gender. Modern onnagata survived such reconfiguration by being successfully deployed in a newly established dichotomy of 'natural femininity of actresses' versus 'artistic/artificial femininity of male *onnagata*.'[6] Along with the premodern mode of onnagata such as Hanshirō, female 'traditional' onnagata, such as Kumehachi, were also unable to secure their lot in these modern categories.

As we have seen, the changes in the multi-layered phenomenon related to 'gender' – including identities, perception, its underlying logic and so on – in kabuki at the outset of modern Japan were drastic. The present-day understanding of the onnagata's gender performance as artistry exclusive to male onnagata is a direct result of this transformation, and that definition seems as firm as rock. Appearances can be deceptive here.

For one thing, contemporary onnagata's involvement in international collaborative projects helps re-emphasize the relativity of the weight of gender. For example, Bandō Tamasaburō V has worked with female actors (e.g. former Takarazuka Revue actors Asami Rei and Minami Yoshie); participated in *kunqu* productions with Chinese actors in which he spoke and sang in Chinese (Kyoto, Japan: 2008; Beijing and Suzhou, China: 2008 and 2009); and appeared in stage and film productions directed by the Polish director Andrzej Wajda (Tokyo, Japan: 1989; Warsaw, Poland: 1993; film: 1994), in some of which he worked with Polish supernumeraries. These collaborations inevitably entail many acts of crossing (language, ethnicity, not to mention performance grammar), thus reminding us of the very *relativity* of the weight of gender.

For another, even though the 1910s witnessed the wane of female kabuki actors in modern times, Japanese theatre saw their resurrection in internationally recognized Yamada Isuzu (1917–2012). Just as Kumehachi's contribution to mainstream kabuki was erased in kabuki historiography, Yamada's stage career in kabuki is being eradicated. Despite her own identity as a stage actor as well as her pride in her kabuki career (Tsuda 1997: 126, 143), she is now primarily, or exclusively even, remembered as a film star, as became bluntly obvious in many of her obituaries. This is despite the fact that Yamada joined kabuki troupes numerous times, performing alongside such major male onnagata as Onoe Baikō VII (1915–95) and Nakamura Utaemon VI (1917–2001), the second son and heir of Utaemon V. Theatre critics regarded Yamada as reminiscent of the historical female kabuki actors, and indeed her acting was acclaimed as that of a *tate-oyama* (kabuki 'leading-onnagata') when she played, along with male kabuki actors, *Yaji Kita Tōkaidōchū hiza-kurige* (Yaji and Kita's Walking Tour on the Tōkaidō Highway) by Jippensha Ikku (1765–1831) in July 1968.

Together, these two examples[7] help us recognize how dynamically the current artistry of onnagata is still related to its history, albeit under its seemingly secure present definition as artistry exclusive to male onnagata. Before being valorized in modern times, gender was not *the* ultimate index for bisecting people; the male/female distinction had merely been one of multiple criteria that categorized humans. At the beginning of modern times, though, the rigid two-sex binary system became a certain meta-imperative, surpassing distinctions based on these other markers such as class and age, and modern *onnagata* ended up performing femininity in this context. Japanese theatre had long been cognizant of the relativity of the weight of gender (see, for example, Zeami 1974: 21), of which these recent international collaborations remind us. Furthermore, the example of Yamada helps underline the 'common sense' that, on the levels of both praxis and discourse, kabuki remains an all-male art despite the existence of female practitioners; behind this phenomenon is the constant rewriting in historiography.

III. China, by Siyuan Liu

Both male and female performers graced the Chinese stage before actresses were banned in the early Qing dynasty (1644–1911), although they never completely disappeared from the stage in remote and rural areas. This embargo of actresses largely corresponded with the rise of *jingju* (Beijing opera) as the most dominant form of traditional Chinese theatre, which blended southern (from Anhui and Hubei provinces) and northern (especially *bangzi* [clapper opera]) genres, as well as the previous national form, *kunqu*, from the Ming dynasty (1368–1944). By the end of the Qing in the late 1800s, actresses started to reappear on stage in major cities, first in Shanghai's international concession areas in all-female troupes known as *mao'erban* (Mao'er troupe, possibly named after Li Mao'er, the owner of the first such company). The first permanent theatre solely for actresses, the Meixian Chayuan (Beautiful Fairies Teahouse) opened in 1894. By the turn of the twentieth century, mixed-gender performances in jingju and Hebei bangzi appeared in Tianjin, China's second-largest concession city about 90 miles south of Beijing, which was followed in the French Concession in Shanghai around 1910. By contrast, Beijing only allowed actresses after the fall of the Qing dynasty in 1912; mixed-gender performance was initially included but was quickly banned in 1913 and not reinstated until 1931. For the two decades in between, actresses in Beijing performed in female-only theatres, the most famous of which was a stage in Chengnan Youyiyuan (South of the City Amusement Park), which attracted almost all the female stars of both male and female roles in Beijing.

Several ramifications are obvious as a result of the two-century-long history of gender performance, starting from the fact that male actors, who performed female roles exclusively during jingju's emergence, created the performance conventions for these roles and continued to dominate in terms of perceived artistic attainment and star power well into the twentieth century. Known as *nandan* ('male' [*nan*] experts of 'female roles' [*dan*]), they were best known through the 'sida mingdan' (four major dan) actors – Mei Lanfang (1894–1961), Cheng Yanqiu (1904–58), Shang Xiaoyun (1900–76) and Xun Huisheng (1900–68). Together, they created some of the most memorable plays in the 1920s and 1930s, which promoted dan stars over the previously dominant *sheng* (male role) stars in popularity and further solidified the models of performing femininity in jingju for both male and female performers. Even today, all styles, or *pai* (school), of dan performance are named after these and other male stars. One of their most significant contributions was the new role category *huashan* (flower robe) as a combination of the traditional female types of *qingyi* (black clothing), which depicts virtuous women with emphasis on singing skills, *huadan* (flower dan), which performs livelier characters with a focus on gestures and movement, and the acrobatic-centric *daomadan* (sword and horse dan) of female generals. First created by Wang Yaoqing (1881–1954), who had taught all four major dan, and glorified in their new core repertoire, the huashan type became the perfect new carrier of strong heroines infused with modern sensitivities.

For the emerging actresses, their appearance was greeted with both ecstatic enthusiasm and societal prejudice. The first generation came from eclectic backgrounds that included former prostitutes as well as daughters of poor families seeking a change of fortune, of merchants and bureaucrats in love with the theatre, and of actors born to the profession. Like their male counterparts, the actresses also performed both male and female roles, initially as a necessity of female-only troupes, although some continued to thrive in sheng roles even after the wide acceptance of mixed-gender performance. The most famous example was Meng Xiaodong (1908–77), one of the best successors of the highly popular *laosheng* (older male) star Yu Shuyan (1890–1943). In this sense, the role categories in jingju and Chinese theatre in general were considered performance categories defined by the conventions of the four essential skills – *chang* (singing), *nian* (speech delivery), *zuo* (dance-acting) and *da* (stage combat) – which were not necessarily linked to the performer's biological sex.

Nevertheless, the emergence of actresses was generally greeted with enthusiasm from the audience, which prompted them, at times, to rival the brightest male stars. For example, the dan actress Liu Xikui (1894–1964), who was among the first group of actresses who moved from Tianjin to Beijing after 1912, became so popular that she made the 'king of theatre' Tan Xinpei (1847–1917) lament after one invited performance that he was inferior to the male Mei Lanfang and female Liu Xikui. Furthermore, she was asked by the top male star Yang Xiaolou (1878–1938) to fill his 3,000-seat theatre Diyi Wutai (Number One Stage), and collected more votes in a 1918 popularity contest for the best actress than Mei did for the top actor. Despite such popularity, Liu's personal life nevertheless served as a reminder of the tremendous obstacles faced by actresses during this period. She had to rebuff repeated harassments from powerful fans, including Yuan Shikai (1859–1916), the President of the Republic of China, and the warlords who took quick turns to control the capital after Yuan's death. Such unwanted attention eventually drove her to marry a lower-level army officer in 1920 at the age of 26 and leave the stage permanently.

By the 1930s, jingju actresses had gained much more societal acceptance, amid persisting prejudice. In 1930, Tianjin's *Beiyang huabao* (Peiyang Pictorial) held a competition for 'sidan kundan' (four major dan actresses) to rival the four major male dan; the winners were Hu Bilan (1909–53), Meng Lijun (1911–91, later replaced by Xin Yanqiu [1910–2008]), Xue Yanqin (1906–86) and Zhang Eyun (1911–2003). In the same year, the first mixed-gender jingju school, Zhonghua Xiqu Zhuanke Xuexiao (Chinese Theatre School), opened in Beijing, and ultimately trained over 200 students before its closure in 1941 during the Japanese occupation. By the end of the 1930s and the beginning of the 1940s, strong graduates of the school and other emerging jingju actresses born around 1920 pushed female dan performers to sustained new heights that often rivalled nandan actors, in part as a result of the hiatus from stage by Mei Lanfang and Cheng Yanqiu in protest against the Japanese invasion (1937–45).

Some of the best known among them were Yan Huizhu (1919–66), Wu Suqiu (b. 1922), Tong Zhiling (1922–95) and Li Yuru (1923–2008). Yan was the daughter of Yan Jupeng (1890–1942), one of the so-called four major laosheng, a lineage that allowed her to study with some of the best performers of female roles, including Mei Lanfang. Yan also inherited Mei's company actors, musicians and dresser during the latter's absence from the stage. These factors made Yan a pre-eminent second-generation performer of the Mei school. The other three actresses all enrolled in the Chinese Theatre School, although only Li finished the 8 years of training between 1932 and 1940. She first formed her own troupe with fellow graduates, then collaborated with some of the top laosheng stars and eventually became one of the best actresses of her generation, with a wide range of repertoire. Wu was expelled from the school for dating a male student and Tong was pulled from it by her father after only 2 months, although both continued to study with well-known stars. In 1939 and 1940, Wu's and then Tong's fame rocketed during their successive tours to Shanghai, where they became synonymous with two plays that became the trump cards for jingju actresses as well as the symbol of their supposed corrupting power. The plays were *Da piguan* (Cleaving Open the Coffin, a.k.a. *Hudie meng* [The Butterfly Dream]) and *Fang mianhua* (Spinning Cotton). The former is among a group of plays about astray and murderous wives and the latter a contemporary-clothed medley of songs, a star vehicle for demonstrating mimetic capabilities. The actresses' performance of the wife's desire and vehemence in the former play and their refreshingly modern clothing and imitational abilities in the latter signified the shifting of star power in the battle of the sexes but also led to the plays' censorship in Shanghai and Beijing in 1944.

After the establishment of the People's Republic of China in 1949, cross-gender performance were no longer taught in theatre schools, including the newly established Zhongguo Xiqu Xuexiao (Chinese School of Traditional Theatre), although existing nandan continued to perform. The combined result of female-only training for dan roles and the gradual diminishing of nandan led to the drastically shifted landscape of femininity performance in jingju and other forms of traditional Chinese theatre, deeming no longer operable the old division between the performers' biological sex and their assumed role category. Since the 1980s, however, nandan training has seen some revival through private apprenticeship since it is still not officially taught in theatre schools. One of the earliest and best-known new nandan actors is Hu Wenge (b. 1967), the only male student of Mei Lanfang's son Mei Baojiu (b. 1934), who is widely considered one of the best existing interpreters of Mei's style. Still, Hu and others like him are exceptions to the overwhelming dominance of actresses in virtually all female role categories, including qingyi, huadan, daomadan, huashan and *laodan* (older women) which still keep some of their masculine singing styles. The only exception is the *choupozi*, mostly old (with some young) comical women who are still performed by *chou* (clown) actors.

IV. Southeast Asia, by Kathy Foley

This section will briefly explore the ideology of gender in traditional Southeast Asian forms, noting the patterns of both impersonation and cross-gender representation (females playing males and men playing women) as well as the differences in classes (elite vs. village), narratives (female melodramas vs. male power struggles) and tools (dance, poetry and humour for females vs. puppets and masks for men). While gender is defined by role type/movement and separable from the biological sex of the actor, today we may see more tendency towards a gender-straight theatre in which the performer's birth sex will match the character danced. Though the emphasis will be on Indonesian forms, selected genres from mainland Southeast Asia will be referenced.

Ideology of gender

Perhaps to a greater extent than in other parts of the world, women held significant roles in Southeast Asian village rituals. We see patterns of women (or transvestite males) as shamans, especially in areas such as Kalimantan, the early Philippines and Burma. To the present, women (or transvestite men) may remain associated with village rice harvest celebrations, courtship events and proto-theatrical events that link light sexual banter, poetry, singing games, dancing and fun. Group dancing by males and females in gender-separated groups (as in Rancakalong, Sumedang, Indonesia) was possible. There are many popular theatres that grew from village roots and they may be attributed to a foundress (i.e. Thai *nora*) or have women in starring roles (i.e. Indonesian *ronggeng* [courtesan]-style theatres such as *topeng betawi* in Jakarta). All of these may come from village roots where we see that women could perform before marriage (as in the play/dance *nini towok* and *jalangkung* [girls' puppeteering to make rain] and *sintren* [trance performance where girls foretell the future]), and in old age when older women dance as *kaul* (vow) at grandchildren's weddings or circumcisions. In Hindu-Buddhist Bali we see that women can perform throughout their lives in group dances at temple festivals (i.e. *gabor*). In most areas, however, we see that 'good women' (wives/mothers), if not part of a palace troupe, stopped dancing with adolescence/marriage. Only certain women who specialized as courtesans (i.e. ronggeng) or shamans (i.e. Burmese *nat kadaw*) generally danced in their prime (Figure 19.3). Ronggengs were either married to other performers, unmarried, or men dressed as women – indeed, it is even said that the Islamic male saint Sunan Kalijaga was the first ronggeng who converted viewers with his songs of divine love.

Men traditionally were prominent in directing ceremonies associated with death or dealing with dangers that beset the village. Men predominate in Southeast Asia in puppet, mask and dance-theatre genres (i.e. *wayang, topeng, wayang wong*), and they often created all-male popular theatre troupes that developed performances based on martial (*pencak silat*) dance styles such as Jakarta's *lenong* or Sumatra's *randai*. In male genres, men played women, and in a number of mask and puppet genres one male (though, on Java, sometimes a woman) played all the roles. Battles, which needed martial arts techniques, power struggles over a kingdom, kidnapped princess and other issues predominated in male genres.

Though most areas long ago converted to Buddhism, Islam or Christianity, these early indigenous patterns may make it easier for women to perform here than in other areas of Asia, at least in village celebrations or in the ruler's palace. Pure dance and joking genres often featured women or female impersonators in combination with one or more clowns, while puppetry and mask dances are more routinely aligned with male performers.

The androgyne is also represented. (The major clown of the island region (i.e. Semar, god-clown of Java in puppetry and mask dance) is a hermaphrodite and wears a body wrap of black-and-white checked material (*poleng*). This androgynous clown may have some relation to the *bissu* (transgender priests of traditional Sulawesi [Celebes]) and the *abdi dalam badut* (court clown) of Solo in Java who accompanied the female *srimpi* court dance, making accents with an archaic bone instrument. These Solonese badut, who joked about sex but are never a locus of male sexuality, wore *poleng* body wraps and were involved with palace *tayub* (dance parties featuring ronggeng/*tledhek*/*lengger* courtesan singer-dancers). They traditionally oversaw and shared in the earnings of these female entertainers of the capital city (Sutterheim 1935). This puppet clown and court position of a rather androgynous figure may have an analogue in the male clown performer of popular ronggeng forms previously mentioned, who acts as the *centeng* [gate-keeper/troupe head], doing shaman-like opening rituals, providing comic repartee and overseeing earnings from the group (including, in times past, payments for sleeping with the singer-dancers).

The court clown that aligns with the androgyne, Sutterheim proposed, had links to tantric Indian religious sects of the Indian middle ages (*kalamukas* and *pasupata*), who used performance as part of a left-handed path to enlightenment. They associated with dancing girls, and exhibited odd behaviours (comedy, ashes/white on body, bones, phallus–vulva imagery): they tried to smash gender, death and other limitations to reach the eternal. Links are speculative, but we find references to such groups in medieval Java. The presence of one or two clown-like but rather asexual males with female performance genres (i.e. court dance in Java, *mak yong* in Malaysia, ronggeng theatres) raises the possibility that an obscure tantric legacy is dimly remembered in the mythos of the god-clown Semar and the structural role of clown-shaman in courtesan traditions. Ideologically the hermaphroditic Semar, encompassing both genders, is a fuller representation of cosmic reality than either the iconic female (dancer-singer) or the core male (either the puppeteer-mask dancer or the strong male dancer – who partners with the ronggeng for prestige, see Spiller 2010). This 'ideal' of androgyny may partly explain the widespread phenomena of men dancing as women, storied links to an Islamic saint performing as woman and (though less frequent) women dancing as men. Even children's Javanese trance games, boys' *lais* and girls' *sintren*, involves the trancer at some point wearing clothes of the opposite sex.

Performers, by learning all the role types both male and female, can 'know everything', and such performers are associated with power. Thus the ultimate performers tend to be the narrators/puppetmasters, the clown and the solo mask dancer: he (and sometimes she), through performance, can represent all genders, classes and ages. While theoretically a woman can

Figure 19.3 Tayuban is a traditional dance genre of West Java where a professional female dancer called a ronggeng dances with male partners for tips.

(Photo: Kathy Foley)

Figure 19.4 Transgender performer Didik Nini Towong does a Yogyakarta, Central Javanese
  style female palace choreography.

(Courtesy of Didik Nini Towong)

do all roles, in practice men predominated, and, aside from selected palace genres, it was usually easier for a man to play women without losing status than for a woman to perform after puberty (Figure 19.4).

Patterns of impersonation

Set body stances and patterns of movement; voices highlighting different resonators and rhythms; masks and puppets – all these features let viewers know what the gender, status and personality of the character is. Even in classical theatres there are usually four pre-eminent roles (refined prince, princess, warrior/monkey, ogre), with the additional but differentiated clowns who operate under slightly different rules (the clown is not a 'type' but generally a specific, named character). Thus viewers read the figure's gender off the movement, voice and costume of the performer. In some forms such as Indonesian *topeng* (mask dance), a single performer may do all the character types in a virtuoso presentation that accelerates from refined to demonic. In Bali, topeng will be presented by the male mask dancer (as in *topeng pajegan*), but in forms found along the north coast of Java (*topeng Cirebon*) it may be a female.

This stylization, of course, extends to multi-person troupes, such as those that arose in or near the courts. In these court groups the mixing of males and females in a single group was traditionally not sanctioned, since these females were the minor wives or relatives of the lord. Hence, inside courts all-female troupes were sometimes developed and supplemented with one or two male clowns. Examples might be the Javanese bedhaya and *srimpi* – refined female dances (where no strong characters are presented) – and the *langendriyan* (a female dance-drama where women play all the roles, including the ogre-like villains of *Damar Wulan* [about an eponymous prince set to work in the stables]); the female *mak yong* of Malaysia, which told local tales, likewise had two *peran* (clowns); the Thai court's *lakhon nai* (female abstract dance and dance-drama doing *Ramakien* [*Ramayana*] and other stories); the Khmer court's all-female *lakhon kbach boran* on the Rama story (*Ramker*); and Bali's female *legong*. In these all-female palace forms, the more dance-like numbers are believed to be hundreds of years old. Dramas may have developed somewhat later, with *mak yong* and *langendriyan*, for example, early twentieth-century developments. Women (or sometimes the monarch) often took the lead in training, selecting dancers and so on. Many of these court genres favoured delicate singing and sometimes the dancers (Thailand and Cambodia) only danced the movements while singers presented the narrative. Texts for presentations in the Thai court, for example, were written by the king. For the female performers, the scenes of pathos (kidnapped Lady Sida longing to return to her beloved husband) or the melodrama of Anjasmara sneaking past her father to marry the 'stableboy', a princely Damar Wulan, were emphasized more than the battle scenes. Women dancers were not as 'rough' as the males in the ogre roles and, in forms such as *langendiryan*, they used makeup that made them look beautiful rather than redden their faces to play an ogre as a man might. But females could still dance with strength that could contrast ogre and the prince.

Meanwhile, outside the palace all-male troupes might do the same stories (as in Thai *lakhon nok* and Khmer *lakhaon khol* [mask dance]), with slight men taking the female roles. In other instances, all-male troupes might do the same stories as in *khon* (Thai court mask dance), Lao *khon* or Balinese *wayang wong* – all of which presented the *Ramayana* stories. Men were more likely to wear masks and do energetic feats. Acrobatic monkeys or leaping demons might be emphasized in the male genres, though the epic sources of both male and female theatre were the same. The techniques of dance for the male playing the female were analogous to the woman playing the same role. In some palaces (i.e. Yogyakarta), young men even did the bedhaya, the most refined and abstract of female dances, exquisitely coiffed and dressed to embody the royal female. One might argue that these configurations of the female as the strong male (the woman dancing Menak Jingga, antagonist of the *Damar Wulan* story), or the male as the refined female (*bedhaya*), were the ultimate arts: representing the androgyne, the person who contains their opposite.

By the twentieth century we see performances of theatres such as *wayang wong* moving outside the palace and playing for a paying audience (i.e. the Sriwedari troupe of Surakarta) with a mixed troupe, but women tended still to play refined male roles – perhaps to exemplify the ideal. In areas such as Bali we often see genres where women play both the refined male and female roles, while the men may play the female clowns. Genres exist such as *arja* (operatic dance-drama), which started as all-male in the nineteenth century, became all-female in the twentieth, and sometimes at present are all-male. Gender performance remains just that: gender performance.

Courtesan performance

Meanwhile there was, as previously noted, popular traditional theatre outside the palaces in Indonesia that featured females or transvestite males as stars. These were ronggeng arts. Ronggeng dancers might be trained in the palaces, but they were also travelling the roads of colonial Java, playing on market squares or hired for celebrations in the homes of local aristocrats or for community celebrations.

Ronggeng is said to have come from village rice harvest celebrations. Indeed, portions of the song repertoire of these singer-dancers are often in the *pantun* metres – songs improvised while women worked at the *lesung* (rice pounding block). The interlocking pounding of the wooden sticks that separated the rice from the husk might be thought of as a kind of protogamelan and girls could take turns singing. Males might hang out nearby and sing back, teasing with similarly rhymed responses. Male clowning was also a feature. These village games, at rice harvest time, could expand into fuller entertainments, with sexual banter, and, so people say, ronggeng was born. These singing games between the sexes are, of course, part of a wider Southeast Asian courting pattern that includes forms such as *ayay* in Cambodia and singing that developed into the professional *mohlam* singers of Laos. But ronggeng is different from courtship singing – the singer-dancer becomes a professional. The Indonesian female professional performers of more recent arts, whether they be singer, dancer or actress, must trace roots back to this courtesan artist who combined all three arts in her repertoire.

Ronggeng arts often opened (after some mantra by the troupe head/clown) with solo or group dances by the featured female/s. The movements might be from the solo mask dance, showing the different types from refined to coarse, or be drawn from the martial arts dance repertoire (*pencak silat*). The clown would improvise patter, the women would sing, and the group might then perform a melodramatic play in which clown and ronggeng were featured. The play, like commedia dell' arte, has an outline (usually a love story) agreed upon, but dialogue was and is improvised. The performance would end with couple dances between the actresses and male audience members. Courtesans, in times past, might be sexually available. Men might take them as wives, but many ronggeng did not 'settle down' for long and, after divorce, returned to the stage (Figure 19.5).

Figure 19.5 Courtesan dancer–actresses were found in various genres in Sunda, West Java. The performance often started with a solo mask dance and then the dancer would act in an improvised melodramatic story of young love temporarily threatened. Today the links with sexual availability are no longer active and genres are seen as 'heritage' arts.

(Photo: Dept. Kebudayaan Jabar)

428

Female impersonators could take the same roles. *Lengger* dancers in east Java and *gandrung* performers in Bali might be males. The *ludruk* theatre of Surabaya had men playing the female roles. *Joget* in areas of Kalimantan and Malaysia is another of these ronggeng arts with female impersonators. As with women, while dancing or singing, female impersonators might share racy rhymes or field the groping hands of tipsy partners (making sure, however, they got the tip). Transvestite performers might be available as homosexual prostitutes.

In mask dance by solo performers or in larger troupes, men could routinely play female roles, but mask dance *dalang* were unlike ronggeng, not perceived as courtesans per se. They labelled themselves as the descendants of the *wali* (saints) and came from professional dance/ puppetry families. These women, too, usually gave up performing when they married non-performers, but might, like Ibu Rasinah (1930–2010) or Ibu Sawitri (1923?–99), return to dancing in their fifties or sixties, or, like Ibu Suji (1937–82), dance whenever she divorced in a long life of serial monogamy with multiple marriages.

Present situation

In modern performance of traditional genres, women in the period 1950–90 broke many barriers. Women in court genres continued to have important voices in places such as Cambodia and Central Java. In Indonesia, dancers, singers and actresses, in the post-independence period, were elevated through the class status of newer dancers who came from the elite. Such new women were promoted first by the Sukarno and then by the Suharto Government in national cultural displays. Newly educated, modern women emerged from dance academies or government dance associations. Social dance with audience members was no longer the norm. Major figures such as Balinese Bulantrisna Jelantik (1947–), Sundanese Irawati Durban Arjo (1943–), Javanese Retno Maruti (1947–) and others became nationally recognized. Tatih Saleh (1944–2006) helped introduce *jaipongan* for a middle-class, modern woman, reclaiming the ronggeng dance with a new high-performance status by modern elite women.

In contemporary Indonesia it became harder for a male to dance the female roles – impossible in the elite 'classical' tradition. Men continue to play females in mask dance genres (i.e. Balinese *topeng*). But most forms, such as Thai *khon*, have incorporated women in female roles (and sometimes also refined male roles), but these beautiful women usually dance unmasked. Khmer dance in the 1960s went from an all-female group to males dancing monkey roles under the leadership of Queen Kossamak (1904–75). In 2013, Princess Buppha Devi (1943–) began to choreograph males in the *yak* (ogre) role. In martial-arts-based forms such as Sumatran *randai*, women have advanced (Pauka 1998). Rosnan Rahman in Malaysia is breaking the gender line by dancing the prince (*pak yong*) – formerly almost always done by a woman – in contemporary *mak yong*, but traditionalists complain that the flavour is, thus, lost.

Mask and puppet work is now more open to women who have performed Balinese *topeng* (1997), puppetry (1975, see next section) and, of course, Javanese forms. But parts of the repertoire remain 'off limits' (Balinese *topeng's* Sidha Karya mask and wayang's *ruwatan* ['Making Safe']). Only time will tell if women will be able to play these tales requiring macrocosmic under-standings of power.

Meanwhile, some talented cross-gender contemporary performers are found: Javanese dancer Didik Nini Towok (born Kwee Tjoen Lian, 1954–), whose image was seen in Figure 19.4, is one of the few major Indonesian male artists who dances primarily female roles, mostly in innovative art-theatre pieces, in his search to renew transgender performance and explore what he calls 'mystical gender'. In Southeast Asia gender performance, the lines remain somewhat permeable. In the popular 'Panji Semirang' dance of Bali, the heroine, Sekar Taji, disguised as a male, may be danced by either a male or a female – boundaries blur.

V. Case study: Indonesian *dalang*, by Jennifer Goodlander and Ashley Robertson

Wayang kulit (shadow puppetry) in Bali and Java is considered one of the oldest and most important genres of Indonesian performance. The *dalang* (puppet master) is the central figure in a wayang performance, and is revered for his knowledge of history, myth and religion, as well as his skills in performance. Typically a dalang is male – but women also perform as dalang in both Java and Bali. Though some Javanese feel that women who come from dalang families have always been able to perform, women who perform frequently are an innovation in Bali and still relatively rare in Java, so this somewhat recent phenomenon demonstrates some of the differences between Javanese and Balinese wayang kulit and their respective social and historical context. Women dalang must be understood as a reflection of national ideologies of gender equality and local values surrounding wayang performances.

Wayang kulit in Bali is most often performed as an inextricable part of a ritual or religious celebration. The dalang is regarded as a kind of priest in Balinese society because he can make holy water and the puppets are considered sacred objects endowed with powerful spiritual properties of their own. In the past, women had little or no opportunity to study wayang kulit because the skills of a dalang were typically passed down from father to son. A dalang would probably never teach a daughter, and women rarely watch the performances (Hobart 1987: 185).[8] Therefore, until recently, the idea of a woman dalang, although difficult to confirm historically, was not even a possibility in Bali.

Ni Ketut Trijata is credited as the first Balinese woman dalang and her story demonstrates the role that state and international influences play within local arts. In the 1970s, opportunities to study *pedalangan* (art of wayang kulit) opened up, with state sponsorship of national schools and universities dedicated to the study and teaching of traditional arts – giving any student, both men and women, the opportunity to study wayang kulit. But no female students enrolled. I Nyoman Sumandhi, then head of the Performing Arts High School, decided, after his experience of teaching American women wayang in the United States, that women in Bali should study and perform wayang kulit as well. Sumandhi hoped to demonstrate that women in Indonesian arts have the same opportunities and abilities to perform male genres (Foley and Sumandhi 1994: 285).[9] Trijata was reluctant to study at first – 'women were not even allowed to touch the wayang puppets', she explained to me in an interview – but finally she decided to give it a try. In 1977, Trijata performed in front of an audience for the first time – and soon performed all over Bali for festivals and government-sponsored competitions (Interview 2009). Other women soon followed, such as Ni Wayan Rasiani, Ni Nyoman Tjandri and Ni Wayan Surtatni. Some of these women make their living teaching wayang at schools or universities, while others use their pedalangan skills to excel in other performance genres, such as arja or drama gong – contemporary genres that provide more female-friendly roles[10] – but few university-educated women actually perform as dalang. One reason is the enormous cost to acquire the puppets, box and other items necessary for a performance, which limited the success of both male and female graduates who did not come from dalang families because they did not have easy access to puppets and other materials (Sedana 1993: 26). The other reason is that the university provides training for performance only, but not the necessary ritual initiation in order for a dalang to perform at religious ceremonies. It is likely, however, that women dalang, just like their male student counterparts, underwent ritual initiation on their own. Even so, it has not increased the frequency of their performances and speaks to how separate the opportunity provided by the university was from the actual conditions of performance.

The experience of one woman dalang, Ni Wayan Nondri, demonstrates how any significant dalang, man or woman, often comes from a family of dalang and receives his or her education through a lifetime of exposure and teaching. Nondri was the daughter and wife of two very well-known dalang, which provided her with an early and, for a woman, unusual exposure to the art. When her husband I Ketut Madra died in a car crash in 1979, leaving her with three children to support, she decided to become a dalang. With the help of her brother, she was able to start performing 3 months later. She explained:

> After my husband died, I felt I must study how to do wayang. I felt what else could I do? Since I was little, the stories and the puppets made me happy. It was like I was married to all things wayang.
>
> (Nondri 2009)

It was not easy; as a woman she still had a family to take care of during the day before going out and performing at night. Also, she had to adjust her performance schedule around menstruation, because a woman is considered polluted during that time and cannot enter the temple or touch sacred objects. Nondri explained to me that she retired a few years ago and does not perform any more, allowing her sons to take the opportunities that might have been given to her. Men of her generation still perform, and Nondri's actions indicate that in spite of her success, it is still more 'appropriate' for a man to perform wayang kulit – even successful women dalang are hindered by the late nights, often risqué comedy and religious restrictions.

From a Javanese perspective, while lacking a comprehensive historic record for reference, female dalang may have always existed – or at least women of dalang lineage have always had the opportunity to study *pedalangan*. Unlike the Balinese form, Javanese shadow practice is not primarily linked to ritual performance and is often staged as a form of public entertainment. As a result of this religious disassociation, Javanese dalang are often regarded as *dukun*-like, or shamanistic spiritual advisers, rather than priest-like. Much like the Balinese account, however, wayang's dependency on oral transmission and apprenticeship limited wayang training almost exclusively to members of legacy lineage.[11] This all changed in the 1920s when Dutch influence over education reform began to affect dalang training methods[12] (see Brandon 1967; Clara van Groenendael 1985; Sears 1996; Schechner 1990, 1993). Through the establishment of pedalangan schools, a system of unified instruction in the art of shadow play was implemented – providing opportunities for all dalang hopefuls. At the same time, despite the absence of a dalang legacy prerequisite, the pedalangan programmes did and continue to attract students from dalang families – with the vast majority being male members. Popularity trends still very much favour dalang lineage, as very few non-lineage dalangs (if any) find success in the wayang world.

According to Javanese oral tradition, the earliest mention of a female dalang dates back as far as the mid-eighteenth century, during the time of the Mataram kingdom. Structured much like an origin myth, the tale is also believed to offer an explanation for the marked differences between East Javanese and Central Javanese wayang styles and aesthetic forms. In 1740, two dalang – a husband (Kyi Panjang Mas) and his wife (Nyi Panjang Mas) – were forced out of the capital of Kartasura by the Chinese rebellion. Their paths then diverged, with Kyi Panjang Mas travelling towards the west whereas Nyi Panjang Mas headed east. Following their

431

separation, it is believed that Nyi Panjang Mas' performative techniques deviated slightly from her husband's traditional methods – choosing to implement smaller wayang puppets, featuring fewer *Punakawan* (clown-servant characters) and highlighting the struggles of women within her interpretations of the *lakon*, or wayang stories (Pausacker 1981, 1986). While this record may provide intriguing insight into the history of women within Javanese shadow performance, it seems that some members of the wayang community remain divided on the actual existence of Nyi Panjang Mas as a dalang, occasionally referring to her as a pseudo-historical character.[13]

The twentieth century proved a significant turning point concerning shadow theatre participation and membership in Java – ushering a number of women into the puppeteering arena (Figure 19.6). A woman by the name of Kenjatjarita[14] (or Kenyocarito, 1909–?) entered the wayang scene in the early 1900s – serving as one of the first Javanese female performers of pedalangan. The daughter of a puppeteer, Kenjatjarita began practising at the age of 8. By the age of 13, she was considered a popular dalang in the Klaten and Boyolali regions, having studied under the tutelage of six *gurus* (teachers) by the time of her first commissioned performance (Suratno 1993). Although women such as Kenjatjarita have existed within the Javanese dalang community for at least a century, their exact numbers still remain a mystery. It is safe to say, however, that the majority of female dalang resides in Central Java, especially around the region of Surakarta. Of the Central Javanese demographic, Nyi Kenik Asmorowati (Sragen, Central Java) and Wulan Sri Panjangmas (Wonogiri, Central Java), both in their early thirties, are two examples of today's more popular female dalang – often performing across Java and other islands of the Indonesian archipelago, attracting hundreds of viewers. Additionally, Woro Mustiko Siwi, a 12-year-old dalang from Semarang, is a representative and prime example of the burgeoning

Figure 19.6 Woman dalang Sarwianti ('Antik') performing at the Surakarta Kraton, 2014.
(Photo by Ashley Robertson)

community of female dalang youth – having performed for the governor of Central Java at the age of 11. Often studying within local performing arts studios (or *sanggar*), such young girls serve to push the next generation of dalang forward – promoting continued female participation and advancing the status of women within wayang:

> [Women dalang] are incredible! Not everyone can become a dalang, let alone a woman. . . . For a woman who is taking care of her family during the afternoon, she still can handle the puppets at night. [Female dalang are] just as interesting as male dalang. That's emancipation of women![15]

Women dalang in both Balinese and Javanese contexts are often criticized for having higher voices, weaker bodies, or said to be lacking the spiritual power necessary for performance. The future of women dalang in Java and Bali both present different possibilities. Women dalang in Bali remain a rare thing, and at present most of the women studying wayang kulit at the university continue on to careers in radio, television or other kinds of performance. As long as wayang kulit in Bali retains its status as a primarily ritual performance, there will probably always be doubt about the efficacy or appropriateness of women dalang. In Java, women dalang have perhaps a more sustainable future. Even though they are not as popular as male dalang, there are women performing on a regular basis. Despite these stable performance frequencies, however, the sometimes ritual context of Javanese wayang remains a strong barrier for full participation.[16] The phenomenon of women dalang is but one way to understand how both the arts and society are changing in Indonesia – and who knows what the future will bring?

Notes

1 Daugherty and Pitkow studied and documented the presence of the all-female Kathakali troupe, the Tripunithura Kathakali Kendram Ladies Troupe. For an account of this troupe, which still performs to this day, see their article (Daugherty and Pitkow 1991).
2 In contrast to onnagata as specialists, noh actors playing women and bunraku chanters projecting the lines of women characters are generalists, performing not only women's but also men's roles (and even entities other than humans).
3 This was a common fate for all who depended on the patronage of the samurai class. A more famous example than less-talked-about kabuki actors who had performed at their patrons' residences is the fate of noh and kyogen actors.
4 Initially, some male kabuki actors performing at playhouses had moonlighted in this area, but considering the shogunate's surveillance, possible cross-class interactions between the samurai-class members and male actors were too risky for both parties, as was explicitly proven by a certain incident in 1714. When the affair of a male kabuki actor with a high-ranking female official was exposed, it resulted in blanket punishment for all the parties concerned, even including capital punishment and a total shutdown of the theatres. Accordingly, these kabuki actors performing at the samurai's residences eventually became all-female actors who did not perform at playhouses.
5 See Edelson (2009) for the Ichikawa Girls' Kabuki Troupe as a typical venue of their survival. See Isaka (2016) for analysis of female onnagata in 'mainstream' kabuki – including a rare but substantial case of re-emergence in the late twentieth century – and how they have been erased from historiography.
6 For the 'natural femininity' of actresses, see Kano (2001); for the artistic/artificial femininity of male onnagata, see Isaka (2006); and for dichotomy and deployment, see Isaka (2016).
7 For more details and analysis of Tamasaburō V's activities, see Isaka (2016); for more details on Yamada, see Isaka (2013 and 2016).
8 In my own experience (2008–14) I rarely, if ever, saw women watching a wayang kulit performance at night for a ceremony. Sometimes performances around Ubud or of very well-known dalang such as CengBlonk would have more women in the audience. Women would have exposure to wayang

lemah, or day wayang, but few people, if any, stop and watch a wayang lemah performance because it is done for the gods as a necessary part of a ceremony. Women at ceremonies are often busy preparing offerings and food, setting offerings, and praying.

9 Wayang kulit was not the only artistic genre being used as a platform to demonstrate women's equality through the arts by the state (Susilo 2003: 7).

10 For an excellent overview of women performing arja, see Natalie Kellar (2004).

11 Apprenticeships were extended to women of lineage, as well; however, the more popular positions for females within wayang were typically *pesinden* (singer) or *gender* player (if their husband was a dalang).

12 Printed versions of *lakon* (palm leaf) manuscripts came into existence in the 1840s as a result of colonial influence, but were very unpopular with dalang and were rarely used in practice until the establishment of pedalangan schools.

13 Based on personal conversations between Robertson and several Central Javanese dalang.

14 Kenyocarito experienced a number of name changes from birth, but she was best known as a dalang under this name (see Suratno 1993).

15 Quote from an audience member after a female *dalang* performance in Yogyakarta, Java. Dewijayanti, email message to Robertson, 10 August 2013 (translated from Indonesian).

16 Women dalang in Java have performed and continue to perform ritual wayang, such as *ruwatan* (an exorcism ritual); however, they are performed infrequently and by only a very select few who feel prepared and well equipped to do so.

Bibliography

Arjo, Irawati Durban (1989) 'Women's Dance among the Sundanese of West Java', *Asian Theatre Journal*, 6 (2): 168–78.

Bharata (1951) *The Natyasastra*, Manmohan Ghosh (trans), Calcutta: The Asiatic Society.

Brandon, James R. (1967) *Theatre in Southeast Asia*, Cambridge, MA: Harvard University Press.

Casassas, Coralie (2012) 'Female Roles and Engagement of Women in the Classical Sanskrit Theatre *Kutiyattam*: A Contemporary Theatre Tradition', *Asian Theatre Journal*, 29 (1): 1–30.

Clara van Groenendael, Victoria M. (1985) *The Dalang Behind the Wayang: The Role of the Surakarta and the Yogyakarta Dalang in Indonesian-Javanese Society*, Dordrecht: Foris Publications.

Cohen, Mathew Isaac (2006) *The Komedie Stamboel: Popular Theater in Colonial Indonesia, 1891–1903*, Athens: Ohio University Press.

—— (2010) *Performing Otherness: Java and Bali on International Stages, 1905–1952*, Basingstoke: Palgrave Macmillan.

Cooper, Nancy (2004) 'Tohari's Trilogy: Passages of Power and Time in Java', *Journal of Southeast Asian Studies*, 35 (3): 531–56.

Daugherty, Diane, and Marlene Pitkow (1991) 'Who Wears the Skirts in Kathakali?' *TDR*, 35 (2): 138–56.

Diamond, Catherine (2012) *Communities of the Imagination: Contemporary Southeast Asian Theatres*, Honolulu: University of Hawai'i.

Edelson, Loren (2009) *Danjūrō's Girls: Women on the Kabuki Stage*, New York: Palgrave.

Foley, Kathy, and I. Nyoman Sumandhi (1994) 'The Bali Arts Festival: An Interview with I. Nyoman Sumandhi', *Asian Theatre Journal*, 11 (2): 275–89.

Geetha (2011) *Kaliyammamar*, Chengannur: Rainbow Books.

Ghosh, Gourab (2013) 'Jyotsna Dutta, and After', in Anita Singh and Tarun Mukherjee (eds) *Gender, Space and Resistance: Women and Theatre in India*, New Delhi: D.K. Printworld.

Goodlander, Jennifer (2012) 'Gender, Power, and Puppets: Two Early Women Dalang in Bali', *Asian Theatre Journal*, 29 (1): 54–77.

Hansen, Katherine (1992) *Grounds For Play: The Nautanki Theatre of North India*, Delhi: Manohar Publications.

Hatley, Barbara (1995) 'Women in Contemporary Indonesian Theatre: Issues of Representation and Participation', *Bijdragen tot de Taal-, Land- en Volkenkunde*, 151 (4): 570–601

—— (2008) *Javanese Performances on an Indonesian Stage: Contesting Culture, Embracing Change*, Honolulu: University of Hawai'i Press and Asian Studies Association of Australia.

Hobart, Angela (1987) *Dancing Shadows of Bali*, London: Routledge & Kegan Paul.

Hughes-Freeland, Felicia (2008) 'Gender, Representation, Experience: The Case of Village Performers in Java', *Dance Research: The Journal of the Society for Dance Research*, 26 (2): 140–67.

Ichikawa Kumehachi (1907) 'Gigei no hanashi' (On Artistic Technique), *Engei Gahō*, 1 (4): 79–86.

Ihara Toshirō (ed.) (1935) *Utaemon jiden* (Autobiography of Utaemon), Tokyo: Shūhōen Shuppanbu.

Isaka, Maki (2006) 'Women *Onnagata* in the Porous Labyrinth of Femininity: On Ichikawa Kumehachi I', *U.S.-Japan Women's Journal*, 30–31: 105–31.

—— (2013) 'What Could Have Happened to "Femininity" in Japanese Stagecraft: A Memorial Address to Yamada Isuzu (1917–2012) ', *positions: asia critique*, 21 (3): 755–59.

—— (2016) *Onnagata: A Labyrinth of Gendering in Kabuki Theater*, Seattle: University of Washington Press.

Kano, Ayako (2001) *Acting Like a Woman in Modern Japan: Theater, Gender, and Nationalism*, New York: Palgrave.

Kellar, Natalie (2004) 'Beyond New Order Gender Politics: Case Studies of Female Performers of the Classical Balinese Dance-Drama *Arja*', in *Intersections: Gender, History, and Culture in the Asian Context* 10, http://intersections.anu.edu.au/issue10/kellar.html, accessed 20 October 2014.

Kersenboom, Saskia C. (1987) *Nityasumangali*, Delhi: Motilal Banarsidass.

Lim, Eng-Beng (2005) 'Glocalqueering in New Asia: The Politics of Performing Gay in Singapore', *Theatre Journal*, 57 (3), 383–405.

Lysloff, René T. A. (2001) 'Rural Javanese "Tradition" and Erotic Subversion: Female Dance Performance in Banyumas (Central Java)', *Asian Music*, 33 (1): 1–24.

Ma Shaobo (ed.) (1999) *Zhongguo jingju shi* (A History of Chinese Beijing Opera), Beijing: Zhongguo xiju chubanshe.

Mehrotra, Deepti Priya (2006) *Gulab Bai: The Queen of Nautanki Theatre*, India: Penguin.

Moser, Heike (2011) 'How Kutiyattam Became Kuti-attam, "Acting Together," or: The Changing Role of Female Performers in the Nannyar-Kuttu-Tradition of Kerala', in Heidrun Bruckner, Hanne M. de Bruin, and Heike Moser (eds) *Between Fame and Shame: Performing Women – Women Performers in India*, 169–89, Wiesbaden: Harrassowitz.

Muddapalani (2012) *Radhika Santawanam* (The Appeasement of Radhika), Sandhya Mulchandani (trans), India: Penguin.

Nondri, Ni Wayan (2009) Interview with the Author, 16 April.

Palermo, C. (2005) 'Confidence Crisis for Bali's Women Mask Dancers', *Inside Indonesia*, www.insideindonesia.org/feature-editions/crossing-male-boundaries, accessed 13 May 2014.

Pauka, Kirstin (1998) 'The Daughters Take Over? Female Performers in Randai Theatre', *TDR*, 42 (1): 113–21.

Pausacker, Helen (1981) 'Women and Wayang Kulit in Central Java', *Restant*, 9: 75–80.

—— (1986) 'Limbuk Wants to be a Dalang: the Role of Women in Wayang Kulit in Central Java', *Inside Indonesia*, 9: 30–1.

Pitkow, Marlene Beth (1998) *Representations of the Feminine in Kathakali: Dance-drama of Kerala State, South India*, PhD dissertation, New York University.

Schechner, Richard (1990) 'Wayang Kulit in the Colonial Margin', *TDR*, 34: 25–61.

—— (1993) *The Future of Ritual: Writings on Culture and Performance*, London: Routledge.

Sears, Laurie (1996) *Shadows of Empire: Colonial Discourse and Javanese Tales*, London: Duke University Press.

Sedana, I. Nyoman (1993) *The Training, Education, and the Expanding Role of the Balinese Dalang*, unpublished MA thesis, Brown University.

Singh, Lata (2004) 'Women Performers as Subjects in Popular Theatres: Tamasha and Nautanki', *History and Sociology of South Asia*, 4 (1): 1–24.

Spiller, H. (2010) *Erotic Triangles: Sundanese Dance and Masculinity*, Chicago: University of Chicago.

Srinivasan, Amrit (1985) 'Reform and Revival: The Devadasi and Her Dance', *Economic and Political Weekly*, XX (44): 1869–76.

Suratno. (1993) 'Penulisan Biografi Nyi Njatatjarita', unpublished thesis, Sekolah ISI Surakarta.

Susilo, Emiko Saraswati (2003) *Gamelan Wanita: A Study of Women's Gamelan in Bali*, Honolulu, Hawai'i: Center for SE Asian Studies, Southeast Asia Paper, no. 43.

Sutterheim, W. F. (1935) 'A Thousand Years Old: Profession in the Princely Courts on Java', *BKI*, 92:186–96.

Takeshiba Kisui (1920) 'Meiji shonen no onnagata' (*Onnagata* in the Early Meiji Era), *Engei Gahō*, 7 (10): 36–44.

Tan Sooi Beng (1995) 'Breaking Tradition: Women Stars of Bangsawan Theatre,' *Bijdragen tot de Taal-, Land- en Volkenkunde*, 151 (4): 602–16.

Bibliography

Thowok, Didik Nini, and Laurie Margot Ross (2005) 'Mask, Gender, and Performance in Indonesia: An Interview with Didik Nini Thowok', *Asian Theatre Journal*, 22 (2): 214–26.

Tsuda Rui (1997) *Kikigaki joyū Yamada Isuzu* (Verbatim Account, Actress Yamada Isuzu), Tokyo: Heibonsha.

Varadpande, Manohar Laxman (1979) *History of Indian Theatre: Classical Theatre*, New Delhi: Abhinav.

Zeami, Motokiyo (1974) *Fūshikaden* (Transmission of Teachings on Style and the Flower), in Omote Akira and Katō Shūichi (eds) *Zeami Zenchiku* (Zeami and Zenchiku), *Nihon shisō taikei* (Collected Japanese Thought), Volume 24, 13–65, Tokyo: Iwanami Shoten

Gender performance and the rise of actresses in modern Asian theatre

*Anita Singh, Ayako Kano, Siyuan Liu, Jan Creutzenberg
and Kathy Foley*

This chapter continues the examination, from the previous one, of the relationship between modernity, gender performance and the rise of actresses in Asian theatre from the point of view of modern spoken theatre. It focuses on the battles between female impersonation that reflected traditional concepts of gender fluidity and gender-specific casting based on modern realistic representation, as well as the roles of nationalism, women's liberation movements and commercial forces. The following sections provide examples from India, Japan, China, Korea and Southeast Asia.

I. India, by Anita Singh

Female impersonators

Women's visibility in the performance space in India in the last century or so has been the outcome of, as Kathryn Hansen states, 'a lengthy process of negotiation, wherein the performer's status and image have been reworked to incorporate the signs of Indian womanhood' (1999: 127–47). Colonial India and the independent state after it had a dual and paradoxical attitude towards the woman question. The domestic sphere became a repository of India's spirituality; the *devadasi* (temple dancer), the *tawaif* (courtesan) and even the actress fell beyond the pale of this good woman, chaste wife and mother empowered by spiritual strength and posited as an iconic symbol of the nation.

Parsi theatre (prevalent between the 1850s and 1930s) was the most intriguing for its use of gender and cross-dressing. According to Pande:

> Master Champalal, an erstwhile player of female roles in various travelling Parsi theatre companies for nearly a decade. He recounted in great detail the intense *sadhana* (Discipline) that was required of young thespians to become the perfect woman on the stage, whose *chal dhal* (gait and graces) even women from good families secretly emulated.
>
> (2006: 1647)

Through the autobiographies of female impersonators Jayshankar Sundari (1889–1975) and Fida Husain (1899–2001) we know the particular experience of female impersonation. Speaking of his role-playing, Jayshankar describes how he was changed into a woman with female sensibility:

> A beautiful young female revealed herself inside me. Her shapely intoxicating youth sparkled. Her feminine charm radiated fragrance. She had an easy grace in her eyes, and in her gait was the glory of Gujarat. She was not a man, she was a woman. An image such as this was the one I saw in the mirror.
>
> (Hansen 2011: 210)

The exclusion of the female body from the theatrical space, which was supplanted by men posturing as women, was partly on religious grounds as women on stage would function as a bodily conduit of sin and it also went against social precepts regarding correct womanly conduct and the new national imaginary which placed a high premium on female chastity, domesticity, purity and spirituality. Men took over and created a sanitized image of Indian women by fashioning her according to the precepts of appropriate femininity. The female image enabled patriarchal power not only the materiality of the female self but also its symbolic projection.

Rise of the professional theatre and the real women

Colonial India saw a steady rise of women in the public domain, a figure fashioned by new needs and structures of professionalism in theatre, by the new urban topography and the emergence of the 'New Women' as an ideological and ideal construct. However, the lived experiences of actresses reveal the proliferation in discourses of respectability, which considered them as dubious social subjects.[1]

Binodini Dasi (1862–1941) was the fifth professional actress in Bengal in the nineteenth century.[2] Born to prostitution, her career started as a courtesan and from the ages of 12 to 23 Binodini became a popular actress. Her autobiographies *Aamar Katha* (My Story) and *Aamar Abhinetri Jeebon* (My Life as an Actress) are about her private fears and aspirations and also how she negotiated the requirements of respectability in nuanced ways.

Indian People's Theatre Association

During India's freedom movement in the 1940s, the India People's Theatre Association (IPTA) emerged as a cultural platform where for the first time the involvement of women as stage performers became socially reputable. They largely came from respectable families and were adequately educated, as opposed to the actresses in the early colonial period. Their presence prompted a fundamental departure from the nationalist colonial theatre and its fixation with domestic conjugality, which was sanctioned for the mainstream theatre actress in the name of the nationalist cause that fetishized Hindu women: 'IPTA created actresses whose new social and ideological commitments would create ultimately a new perception of the actress persona, a break with the domesticated personification' (Dutt and Munsi 2010: 117). The inhibited presence of the actresses and 'the demure hidden gazes could be replaced with strong expressions and direct audience contact' (ibid.: 118). Most of the women were involved with the Central Squad of IPTA as a result of their association with student politics. Dina Pathak (1923–2002), Shanta Gandhi (1917–2002) and Gul Bardhan (1928–) were part of the students' movement at Bombay. Shanta Gandhi founded the central ballet troupe of IPTA and performed extensively through the 1950s. As a theatre director, dancer and playwright, she re-energized the classical and traditional theatre. Among her most noted plays was *Jasma Odan* (Tale of Jasma of Odh community of Gujarat, 1967), which was based on a Gujarati legend in *bhavai* style (a folk theatre form from Gujarat), on the custom of *sati* (the practice of widow immolation). She served as the Chairperson of National School of Drama (1982–1984) and was awarded the Padmashree (India's fourth highest civilian award) in 1984 and the Sangeet Natak Akademi Award (the highest national recognition for practising artists) in 2001. Dina Pathak was known for her student activism in the pre-independence era when folk theatre was used extensively as an anti-colonial tool. Her play *Mena Gurjari* (Tale of A Woman, Mena from Gurjar Community, 1953) in Bhavai folk style was a popular theatre production.

Tripti Mitra (1925–89), an IPTA member, later went on to form Bohurupee theatre group with her husband Shombhu Mitra. Sova Sen (1923–), wife of Utpal Dutt, was the lead performer in the play *Nabanna* (1944), an important IPTA production about Bengal famine. Reba Roychoudhury (1925–) and Preeti Banerjee (1922–), members of the *Mahila Atma Raksha Samiti* (formed in the wake of the Bengal Famine), and Rekha Jain (1924–2010), wife of Nemi Chandra Jain (who was a theatre activist of the Friends of Soviet Union), were other important actresses of the IPTA.

Actresses and the contemporary stage

'Towards Equality: Report of the Committee on the Status of Women in India' (1974) by the Ministry of Education and Social Welfare revealed total invisibility and neglect of women's economic roles. It raised alarm as to the status of women in India, leading to large-scale research and the institutionalization of women's studies. All this stimulated a new spate of theatrical activities and innovations and encouraged the visibility of women in public spaces. The actress, already an accepted figure since the formation of the IPTA, was now widely seen performing on the stage and the streets.

The genre of self-written solo performances by women flourished and became popular proscenium presentations in the cities in the 1980s. For example, Mallika Sarabhai (*In Search Of Goddess*, 2000; *Sita's Daughters*, 1990; *Shakti – The Power of Women*, 1989) subverts the mythical women and rewrites the icons as powers of Shakti for modern women through the use of dance and Brechtian dialogue with the audience and narration (Figures 20.1 and 20.2). Saoli Mitra's 1983 solo performance on Draupadi was titled *Nathvati Anathvat* (Five Lords, Yet None a Protector).[3] In the play she is the *sutradhara* (story teller), the *kathak* (dancer) and the performer, and effectively conveys Draupadi's version of the tale. Mita Vashista's solo performance *Lal Ded* (2004) is based on her research on the life of the medieval Kashmiri mystic poetess Lal Ded. Mita enacts the play as a theatrical collage of poems, songs, thoughts and philosophies of Lal Ded.

Street plays by women have become popular since the 1970s. *Mulgi Zali Ho!* (A Girl Is Born!, 1983), written by Jyoti Mhapsekar and performed by the cultural troupe Stree Mukti Sanghatana (Women's Liberation Organization), is a musical play with an all-female cast, which discusses reactions within a family when a girl is born. Maya Rao from the Theatre Union (a street play group formed in 1979) was involved in the making and performance of two widely performed street plays, *Om Swaha* (tribute to the gods and goddess for their benediction, 1979) on the issue of dowry and *Dafa no.180* (Indian Penal code no. 180, 1981) on the Indian law of conviction for rape.

Writers/performers from the northeast of India have contributed significantly to making strong political statement through their performance. Sabitri Heisnam (1946), an actress from Manipur, has received various honours for her contributions to theatre; she was granted the Sangeet Natak

Figure 20.1 Mallika Sarabhai in *In Search Of Goddess.*
(Courtesy of Mallika Sarabhai)

Figure 20.2 Mallika Sarabhai in *In Search Of Goddess.*
(Courtesy of Mallika Sarabhai)

Akademi Award in 1991 for acting and Padmashree in 2007. She played the eponymous Draupadi (in a play based on Mahasweta Devi's story 'Draupadi') in 2000 in a Kalakshetra Manipur production directed by her husband Kanhailal Heisnam. It was an unusual performance by Sabitri who completely disrobes on the proscenium stage, but the act of disrobing undercuts any trace of sensuality. Sabitri as Draupadi challenges the rape script of a suffering and shamed victim by standing stark naked in front of her rapists, terrorizing them with her naked state. Sabitri's performance transmutes the proscenium space into a space of revolt against the violation of human rights.

It is evident that the ideological position of society directly reveals the changing conceptions of women artists. The ongoing innovations and experiments carried out by women performers underscore the impossibility of subsuming contemporary women's involvement in theatre under a uniform frame. Artists through their performance are examining questions about what the stage space could and should stand for today and often these interrogations are an open celebration of feminism.

II. Japan, by Ayako Kano

Actresses emerged in modern Japan amid modernization and westernization, nation-building and empire-building. The central government had banned women from performing in public since 1629, although a small number of women had continued to perform privately in the mansions of wealthy patrons of the warrior class. For example, Ichikawa Kumehachi (c. 1846–1913) had been training to become such a performer, but the regime change of 1868 led to the disappearance of this kind of patronage (Isaka 2006). When the women's public performance ban was lifted in 1890, the first generation of actresses appeared from the ranks of these performers, including Ichikawa Kumehachi, as well as from the ranks of entertainers associated with the pleasure quarters.

The appearance of actresses coincided with a number of social, cultural, and political changes: in the status of women in society, in the status of theatre in the nation and in the status of Japan in the world. Women's lives were increasingly shaped by the new government's ideology of turning them into 'good wives and wise mothers' for the next generation of modern citizens. Theatre was increasingly promoted as a cultural showcase and pedagogical institution for the modern state. And Japan was beginning to assert itself as a colonial and imperial power, especially after winning the Sino-Japanese War in 1895 and the Russo-Japanese War in 1905.

In premodern kabuki and dance, femininity was achieved in and through performance via the careful positioning of shoulder muscles, the manipulation of the long sleeves of the kimono, and the graceful curves delineated in dance. In modern theatre, the definition of femininity was eventually understood to reside directly and naturally in the body of the performer. The actresses' rise to artistic and social prominence in late nineteenth- to early twentieth-century Japan therefore signalled two seemingly contradictory moves at once: on the one hand it represented a progressive step forward, as women entered into arenas previously reserved for men and garnered public attention. But on the other hand, it represented a problematic tightening of a definition of gender grounded in the physical body rather than in performative achievement. This narrower definition of gender constrained women into roles and behaviours on stage and off that were regarded as deriving from their biological nature. Arguably, it also made possible the kind of feminism we know today, but it came at a cost (Kano 2001).

The double-edged nature of the rise of the actress is also observable in China in the early twentieth century (Cheng 1996, 2002), or in Restoration England (Howe 1992), where women claiming a place on stage also made them vulnerable to voyeurism and exploitation. What complicates the Japanese case is that the introduction of actresses was intimately tied to the process of modern nation-building and empire-building, a process in which Japan was emulating the West in many respects, and also beginning to impose its values on the rest of the East. Whether one portrays this process as a belated Japan imitating Western imperialism, or more as a simultaneous unfolding of Japanese and Western imperial ambition in global competition, what remains undeniable is that Japan became an imperial power in the context of Western imperialism, and that this process is imbricated with the development of modern Japanese theatre, including modern actresses.

For example, one could say that the beginning of modern Japanese theatre coincided with the Sino-Japanese War of 1894–1895, when the stylized portrayal of battle in the traditional kabuki theatre appeared hopelessly old-fashioned. It was the realism of fistfights and fireworks, brought to the stage by upstart modern theatre troupes, eventually labelled 'new school' (*shinpa*), that was accepted as more faithfully representing modern warfare. This was the beginning of a kind of modern, masculine and 'straight theatre' (*seigeki*) (Hyōdō 2005). In contrast to it, the kabuki theatre, whose name was derived from the word 'to slant' (*kabuki*), was often regarded as outdated and effeminate (Kano 1997, 2001).

The Theatre Reform Society (Engeki Kairyōkai), established by members of the political elite in 1886, advanced several goals to showcase Japan to the West. This included eliminating what it saw as the old-fashioned and embarrassing practice of using male actors impersonating female roles (*onnagata*). The first 'male and female joint performance' occurred in 1891, with six women participating. Many initial performers were either *geisha*, daughters of *kabuki* performers, or female performers trained in kabuki, such as Ichikawa Kumehachi. The social status of these women was traditionally regarded as low, presenting a problem to the reformers.

The first professional actress in modern Japan is considered to be Kawakami Sadayakko (1871–1946), a former geisha who started performing while touring abroad with her husband Otojirō (1864–1911). While travelling in the United States and in Europe, Sadayakko performed in orientalist pastiches with titles such as *The Geisha and the Samurai*, but upon returning to Japan, she performed the role of a modern and Western-trained woman both on stage and off (Downer 2003). She also appeared in plays that orientalized Japan's Asian neighbours, thus symbolizing the formation of the Japanese empire. She established the Imperial Actress School (Teikoku Joyū Yōseijo) in 1908, which later became affiliated with the Imperial Theatre (Teikoku Gekijō), and trained the next generation of actresses in both traditional and modern performance arts. Given the traditionally low status and loose reputation of kabuki actors as well as geisha, many prospective actresses from bourgeois backgrounds faced considerable opposition from their families and schools against entering the acting profession.

The Kawakami troupe is considered to be one of the originators of the 'new school' (*shinpa*) genre. Although it initially set itself in opposition to the 'old school' of kabuki, shinpa eventually became a hybrid genre, focusing on staging melodrama from the early twentieth century, deploying both actresses and onnagata. With the exception of actress Mizutani Yaeko (1905–79) who became a well-known star in this genre, shinpa continued to be dominated by men. Yet many of the most memorable roles in the genre were those of melodramatic heroines, such as those based on the novels of Izumi Kyōka (1873–1939).

Among the first group of students to be trained in modern European-style theatre, called 'new theatre' (*shingeki*), was the actress Matsui Sumako (1886–1919). She was a student of the Theatre Institute (Engeki Kenkyūjo) of the Literary Art Society (Bungei Kyōkai), established in 1909 as one of the first attempts to school men and women in the techniques of modern theatre. Matsui Sumako became a star of the Literary Art Society, and later formed her own troupe, the Art Theatre (Geijutsuza), together with director Shimamura Hōgetsu (1871–1918).

Because Shimamura was a married man and a university professor, their professional and sexual liaison created a scandal. Before her suicide in 1919, Matsui Sumako premiered plays with memorable female characters. Her Japanese premiere of Henrik Ibsen's *A Doll's House* in 1911 coincided with the founding of the first feminist literary journal, *The Blue Stockings (Seitō)*. Thus actresses and the roles of 'new women' performed by them came to be identified with the beginnings of the feminist movement in Japan. And yet, women on stage continued to be regarded as sexual commodities, and this perception dogged the first modern actresses such as Yamakawa Uraji (1885–1947), Izawa Ranja (1889–1928) and Hanayagi Harumi (1896–1962). The top shingeki theatre troupes pointedly focused on translations of European plays. In performing the heroines from dramas by Ibsen, Shakespeare and Tolstoy, Japanese actresses embodied the ambition of Japan to become fully modern and to fully identify with the West.

The two actresses, Kawakami Sadayakko and Matsui Sumako, can be seen as representing two different stages in the complex process that forged modern Japanese actresses. Eventually, Matsui Sumako's sensual, physical and natural appeal based on 'Westernesque' (Levy 2006) aesthetics was seen to have triumphed over Kawakami Sadayakko's classically trained geisha style. The rivalry and the victory of Matsui Sumako signalled the dawn of a new regime of gender and theatrical performance (Kano 2008).

The years following the first generation of actresses saw women take on a variety of roles on stage and off. The all-female Takarazuka theatre was founded in 1913 by entrepreneur Kobayashi Ichizō (1873–1957) to attract families to his hotspring resort. By the 1930s it had become a fully fledged troupe known for French-style revues. Its female performers of male roles (*otokoyaku*) attracted the adoration of generations of female fans (Robertson 1998; Stickland 2007; Yamanashi 2012). To compete with Takarazuka, the production company Shōchiku created its own all-female troupe. The 1920s and 1930s saw other venues emerge, such as the Casino Folies (1929) and Moulin Rouge (1931), capitalizing on the sexual appeal of the 'modern girl' (*moga*).

Meanwhile, serious actresses, especially those in shingeki troupes, diligently worked to establish their professional credentials. Tamura Akiko (1905–83), Yamamoto Yasue (1902?–93) and Sugimura Haruko (1906? –97) were among them (Powell 2002). While some actresses distinguished themselves in proletarian theatre, Okada Yoshiko (1902–92) created a sensation in 1938 by eloping with a lover to Soviet Russia. Many stage actresses also began appearing in cinema and later on television, including Mizutani Yaeko and Kishida Kyōko (1930–2006).

After the end of the Asia-Pacific War, a new generation of remarkable stage actresses such as Shiraishi Kayoko (1941–) and Ri Reisen (1942–) emerged from the underground and small theatre movements in the 1960s and 70s. The portrayal of women during this time tended to focus on the darker side, such as sexually exploited women and mad women. These theatre groups were also often dominated by charismatic, even authoritarian male directors (Eckersall 2006). But this was also the era of 'women's lib'. Female playwrights had been rare during the pre-war period, with a few exceptions such as Hasegawa Shigure (1879–1941) and Okada Yachiyo (1883–1962). But women's questioning of male representation began to be heard on stage as well as on the streets.

The 1980s and 90s saw the emergence of many female playwrights, some with specifically feminist sensibilities, including Kisaragi Koharu (1956–2000), Kishida Rio (1946?–2003) and Nagai Ai (1951–). The staging of female characters created by female playwrights became no longer a rare occurrence. Some women such as Kisaragi and Watanabe Eriko (1955–) led their own theatre troupes. Meanwhile, some actresses became celebrated for repeated performance of particular plays. Sugimura Haruko performed Morimoto Kaoru's *A Woman's Life (Onna no isshō)*, portraying a woman whose long life spanned the Meiji (1868–1912), Taishō (1912–26) and Shōwa (1926–89) eras. Kinoshita Junji's *Twilight Crane* (*Yūzuru* 1949) was performed over a thousand times by Yamamoto Yasue. The record-holder, *Diary of a Vagabond* (*Hōrōki*) based on Hayashi Fumiko's autobiographical work depicting bohemian life, has been performed over two thousand times by Mori Mitsuko (1920–2012) since its 1961 premiere.

Acting like a woman in modernizing Japan meant several contradictory things at once. It meant entering an arena previously dominated by men and thus widening the scope of acceptable behaviour for women. But it also meant becoming part of a discourse that defined femininity as something grounded in the physical body. It meant the possibility of acting out roles that embodied feminist ideals, but it also meant accepting the risk of being objectified and sexually exploited. It meant being at the vanguard of introducing Western dramas and their potentially liberating influences, but it also meant performing a role in modern theatre's representation and reproduction of nationalist and imperialist ambitions. The Japanese actresses in the early part of the twentieth century embodied these contradictions, and elucidated the intertwining of nationalism, theatrical reform and the modern formation of gender.

III. China, by Siyuan Liu

As a result of the censorship of actresses in the Qing dynasty (1644–1911, see Chinese section in the previous chapter), the earliest actors in modern Chinese theatre *huaju* (spoken drama) were all men. Such performance started from students in church schools at the turn of the twentieth century in Shanghai, China's largest port city with a large international settlement population. The first generally acknowledged huaju production, the 1907 adaptation of *Uncle Tom's Cabin* titled *Heinu yutian lu* (Black Slave's Cry to Heaven), was staged by the all-male Chunliu She (Spring Willow Society) in Tokyo. In the early 1910s, the Spring Willow became one of the core groups of *wenmingxi* (civilized drama) that thrived in Shanghai during the decade, a hybrid commercial theatre based on European melodrama, Japan's hybrid modern theatre *shinpa* (new school drama) and Chinese theatre. Virtually all early wenmingxi actors were men, including those performing female roles. Known as *nandan* (male experts of female roles), a term borrowed from traditional theatre, these actors followed one of two roots in their performance of femininity. The first was through emulation of Japanese shinpa's *onnagata* (male experts of female roles in Japanese theatre) by members of the Spring Willow Society, especially Ouyang Yuqian (1889–1962) and Ma Jiangshi (dates unknown). They closely studied the performance of two top shinpa onnagata, Kawai Takeo (1878–1942) and Kitamura Rokurō (1871–1961), respectively. Ouyang started imitating Kawai in 1909 when the Spring Willow staged an adaptation of Victorien Sardou's *La Tosca* that was based on a 1907 shinpa production with Kawai performing Tosca. Ma was considered wenmingxi's pre-eminent actor of tragic heroines because of his portrayal of the protagonist in the shinpa classic *Burugui* (*Hototogisu* in Japanese, The Cuckoo) starring Kitamura, which Ma adapted from Japanese. The other route of wenmingxi's female impersonation was through a *jingju* (Beijing opera)-style role category system that allowed actors to concentrate on specialized subcategories of female characters, including plaintive (*aiyan*), girlish (*jiaohan*), maidenly (*guige*), coquettish (*huasao*), gallant (*haoshuang*) and shrewish (*pola*). Almost all other wenmingxi companies apart from the Spring Willow followed this system.

With wenmingxi's success in Shanghai, new drama performance by all-female troupes started in 1912, initially provoking considerable public interest. One of these performances was given by the Nüzi Xinjutuan (Women's New Drama Troupe) at the Lanxin (Lyceum) Theatre. For three nights, it played to full houses of audiences eager to see women performing in contemporary clothes. Although the Education Department of Jiangsu Province petitioned the

Shanghai Magistrate to 'swiftly ban' the performance on the ground of morality, all-female wenmingxi performances thrived in Shanghai. The first mixed-gender company was the Minxing She (Prosperity Society) established by the actor Su Shichi in 1914, in part as a result of Su's inability to lure established nandan actors from other companies. The success of its first actress, Shen Nongying, opened the door to other actresses in some mixed-gender companies. While the Prosperity had its ups and downs and mixed-gender performance provoked fierce debate, the company outlasted most other wenmingxi groups. It eventually disbanded in the summer of 1917.

However, the company's popularity failed to introduce mixed-gender performance to the three major wenmingxi companies: the Spring Willow, the Xinmin She (New People Society) and the Minming She (People's Voice Society). The reasons behind their objection are personal, performative and ideological. To begin with, Su earned the enmity of all three companies in the process of forming the Prosperity, as he departed from the New People and poached actors from the three companies. Second, the star power of nandan actors in these companies made it commercially unnecessary for the companies to hire actresses. Finally, many of the most influential wenmingxi voices expressed strong antipathy to this first adventure in mixed-gender performance on the wenmingxi stage, denouncing the Prosperity and other mixed-gender companies as no more than a novelty act and commercial adventure.

Such denunciation also revealed the class division in wenmingxi's gender performance, because virtually all of the prominent wenmingxi practitioners, those who could afford to study in Japan or in prominent Shanghai schools, were from upper- and upper-middle-class backgrounds. By contrast, many of the first actresses were from fallen middle-class families, war refugees or prostitutes. Therefore, while the charge against the Prosperity's owners' commercial intentions might very well be true, class consciousness was obviously behind the prominent practitioners' contempt of the mixed-gender companies' audience and moral standard. Indeed, the emerging actresses often endured misogynist resentment from fellow actors, critics and the press, which intruded into their private lives and assumed their moral corruption and corruptive power. In the typically short biographies of wenmingxi actresses, their origins and current lives – especially their affairs with fellow actors or wealthy benefactors – occupy just as much space as comments of their talent on stage. However, some contemporary critics did defend the actresses and their contribution to wenmingxi by pointing out the hypocrisy and hyperbole of such moralist scrutiny, as well as the artistic advantage of realistic mixed-gender performance, while arguing the irrelevance of focusing on the impact of the actresses' social life to societal morality.

Ultimately, it was the suggestion of realism in the new and less conventionalized wenmingxi that made the moralists cringe at the prospect of direct and naturalistic depiction of love on stage. In fact, wenmingxi's debate over the appropriateness of having actresses assuming female roles essentially focused on the issue of citationality, with its supporters arguing that the practice was more natural than female impersonation and its opponents resorting to moralistic arguments asserting that mixed-gender casting resulted in obscenity. To them, while the performance conventions of both traditional theatre and wenmingxi's female impersonation refrained from straightforward depiction of romantic or erotic scenes, realistic depictions of love on stage by performers of the opposite sex was simply too naturalistic to bear.

This prejudice remained in the early 1920s when wenmingxi largely lost its popularity and was overtaken by the *aimeiju* (amateur theatre) movement, which also used female impersonation. This practice was finally broken in 1923 when Hong Shen (1894–1955), who had studied playwriting in George Pierce Baker's 47 Workshop at Harvard, installed mixed-gender casting at the Shanghai Xiju Xieshe (Shanghai Stage Society). Influenced by Freudian aversion to cross-dressing, Hong, after returning to Shanghai in 1922, first tried to skirt the dominant practice by writing and starring in an all-male play, *Zhao Yanwang* (Yama Zhao), which borrowed Eugene O'Neill's expressionistic *The Emperor Jones* to protest against China's endless civil wars. After the production failed, he joined the all-male Stage Society in July 1923 as its Paiyan Zhuren (Director of Rehearsal and Performance). For its September performance of two one-act plays, *Zhongshen dashi* (The Main Event in Life) and *Pofu* (The Shrew), he cast three female students, Qian Jianqiu, Wang Yuqing and Wang Yujing, in the former and allowed the still-preferred (by others) all-male cast in the latter. The audience first watched the natural performance of the actresses and went on to laugh at the mannerism of the female impersonation in the second play, thus ending the practice at the Stage Society. Hong consolidated his reputation as the foremost huaju director with up-to-date knowledge of western theatrical practice, including gender-appropriate casting, the following year with his localized production with Oscar Wilde's *Lady Windermere's Fan* – renamed *Shao nainai de shanzi* (The Young Mistress's Fan) – with Qian Jianqiu as Mrs Erlynne and Wang Yuqing as Lady Windermere.

However, gender-appropriate casting often remained elusive in most school and university productions, which during this time was a fertile ground for huaju's emerging talents, as exemplified by its greatest playwright, Cao Yu (1910–96). He started his theatre experience in 1925 with *The Young Mistress's Fan* at Tianjin's Nankai School, a bastion of huaju in northern China that nevertheless had separate theatre productions for male and female students in divided campuses until 1929, when the school allowed a mixed-gender production of Cao Yu's adaptation of John Galsworthy's *Strife*. A more dramatic version of gender politics in school productions took place in Beijing's Yenching University, a Christian institute with separate male and female campuses, where in November 1926 the faculty halted a decision by the Yenching Weekly Society to stage their next play – an adaptation of Goldoni's *The Mistress of the Inn* by the future huaju director Jiao Juyin – by the male campus with a mixed-gender cast. In their reaction to the decision, the faculty, while announcing fund-raising for the production, decided to poll the female students, who had to sign their answers, with four questions: '1) Is China ready for mixed-cast performance? 2) Is mixed-cast performance at the present time a detriment to our university's interest and reputation? 3) Are you willing to join this play's cast? 4) Do your parents approve of your performance?' (Anon. 1926). Unsurprisingly, the answer to such loaded questions without the protection of anonymity resulted in the decision, sourced to the result of the female students' votes, that mixed-gender performance was unfortunately impossible. For its planned performance at the New Year party on 30 December, while the female campus performed a one-act play *Yipian aiguo xing* (A Patriotic Heart), the male campus cancelled the *Mistress of the Inn* performance with the excuse that the female lead was sick and instead showed a film.

Other educational institutions were more tolerant of actresses. Hong Shen directed three plays at Shanghai's Fudan University between 1928 and 1930 with mixed-gender casts. Furthermore, China's first professional huaju programme, the theatre department of the Guoli Yizhuan (National Arts School), installed mixed-gender practice from its beginning in 1925. It was established in Beijing by Yu Shangyuan (1897–1970), Zhao Taimou (1889–1968) and Wen Yiduo (1899–1946), who had returned from the United States after studying theatre and fine art. The Columbia-educated Xiong Foxi (1900–65) took over the department in 1926. Together, they trained the first generation of college-level male and female huaju practitioners.

As a result of the training in school performance, several actresses performed in well-known western plays in Shanghai by the late 1920s and early 1930s, most notably Chen Ying as the Mirandolina in *Mistress of the Inn* (1928), Yu Shan as Salomé (1929) and Carmen (1930), and Jiang Qing as Nora in *A Doll's House* (1935) and Katerina in Aleksandr Ostrovsky's *The Storm* (1937). Chen Ying (1907–88) was a student at Fudan University and the first female member of its dramatic club when she was chosen by Hong Shen, who selected the play largely because

Figure 20.3 Yu Shan as Salomé holding John the Baptist's head at the end of Southern China Society's 1929 production of *Salomé*.

(Photo from *Zhongguo daguan tuhua nianjian* [Chinese Illustrated Yearbook], 1930: 76)

of her, as the heroine of Goldini's action-packed comedy. Yu Shan (1908–68) was educated at Nankai Girls School and Jinling Daxue (University of Nanking), where she was recruited by the playwright Tian Han to lead his Nanguo She (Southern China Society)'s production of *Salomé* in 1929 (Figure 20.3). Her bold performance caused a sensation and prompted the follow-up production of *Carmen* which featured a similarly strong-willed heroine. Her uninhibited performance, however, prompted rumours of her affairs that forced her to leave the stage after these two roles. Jiang Qing (1914–91), the future Madam Mao known at the time as Lan Ping, came from Shandong Province to Shanghai where she shone brightly as Nora in the Shanghai Yeyu Juren Xiehui (Amateur Dramatists Association) production of *A Doll's House* in 1935, which led to Katerina in *The Storm* in 1937 by the same company.

While single-sex performance in gender-segregated schools persisted into the 1940s, these and other performances helped to firmly establish the legitimacy of actresses on the huaju stage, which corresponded with the maturity of huaju in terms of dramaturgy and production by the mid-1930s.

IV. Korea, by Jan Creutzenberg

Traditional performing arts in premodern Korea were a male domain, as social customs prevented women from performing in public. Female entertainers (*gisaeng*) were an exception, as they catered to the upper class in semi-private settings. Trained in various arts, gisaeng had a unique status, existing 'between male and female' (Mueller 2013: 67), and their services traditionally included music and lyrical song, but not acting. As the only professional female performers, gisaeng would become important protagonists in the modernization and urbanization of theatre in the early twentieth century.

Male performers of traditional arts (*gwangdae*)[4] routinely manipulated and voice-acted 'female' puppets in *kkokdugaksi noreum* (puppetry) and enacted female stock characters such as the grandmother, the old wife or the concubine in *talnori* (mask dance-play). On rare occasions, gisaeng or female shamans would be cast for specific roles in talnori, such as 'the winsome beauty Somu', but these cases were clearly marked as exceptions, because the female dancers 'would perform with the mask worn like a hat atop their heads, and the audience would increase in size as locals seized an opportunity to stare at the young woman' (Saeji 2012: 153–4).

In the solo art *pansori* (epic singing-storytelling), an unusually wide pitch range allows the singer to embody men, women, animals and supernatural creatures and switch between these various roles with ease. This vocal flexibility and the fact that each performance is 'pitched to fit the range of the performer rather than choosing the performer that fits the range of the composition' (Mueller 2013: 135–6) make these cross-gender performances possible and plausible.

In the mid-nineteenth century, pansori advocate and scholar Sin Jae-hyo (1812–84) edited various hitherto orally transmitted pieces according to the tastes of emerging aristocratic audiences and paved the way for women performing pansori. His student and protégée Jin Chae-seon (1842–?), considered the first female singer, gave her debut at a court banquet in 1867 – cross-dressed, according to an eyewitness (Park 2003: 71, 228). Besides the novelty factor and the gender non-specificity of the pansori voice, the association of gisaeng with 'the atmosphere of elegance and temperance preferred by the upper classes' (Mueller 2013: 104) contributed to the subsequent acceptance of female performers in this new environment.

Today, the majority of pansori practitioners are female (Mueller 2013: 235) and the preservation associations of talnori include many women who, like men earlier, are not restricted to female roles (Saeji 2012: 154).[5] Gender roles remain flexible in the traditional arts, which throughout the early twentieth century continued to be performed in 'separate ways' by male kwangdae and female gisaeng (Killick 2010: 51). In contrast, emerging new theatre genres such as melodramatic *sinpageuk* and realist *singeuk* relied more and more on mixed casts, leading to the birth of the actress.

Shinpa (jap. 'new school'), a hybrid version of traditional *kabuki* and European spoken theatre, was introduced to colonial Korea by Japanese ensembles who at first performed for fellow Japanese audiences. Soon, beginning in 1911 with the company Hyeoksindan ('Innovative Ensemble'), Korean artists adapted this new kind of theatre for nationalist and commercial causes, creating a genre called *sinpageuk*. Like kabuki, early Korean sinpageuk featured *onnagata* impersonators, male actors specializing in women's roles (kor. '*yeohyeong baeu*'; Kim 2006: 12). The first mentions of women acting on stage coincide with the introduction of cinematic intermezzos, so-called *yeonswaegeuk* ('kino-drama'), representing tendencies towards the spectacular on the one hand and more lifelike depictions in theatre on the other hand (U 2007: 183).[6]

The *singeuk* ('new drama') movement was initiated by the ensemble Towolhoe in the early 1920s and stressed realism and political impetus over the melodramatic nostalgia now associated with popular sinpageuk. While sinpageuk and its improvisatory acting style shared many aspects with the performer-centred traditional arts, singeuk introduced scripts – new pieces or translations of Western works – and pre-defined stage directions.[7] Like the *shingeki* performances that the members of Toweolhoe had witnessed when studying in Japan, singeuk featured female performers from the beginning.

As it proved difficult to find women who were capable and willing to perform, most of the early theatre actresses were former gisaeng, a profession whose reputation had suffered from Japanese work policies (see Kim 2007: 2).[8] Some of them, after first steps in theatre, found a career in the emerging movie industry, recorded songs and became popular stars. Newspaper advertisements highlighting female performers attest to the fact that women on stage were still considered a special, marketable event and expected to act as crowd-pullers for presumably mostly male audiences. On the other hand, the unconventional lifestyle and the modern characters they embodied made early actresses important role models for the emancipatory 'new woman' (*sinyeoseong*) movement.[9]

The lives of these early actresses are clouded by fragmentary, inconsistent or biased records and existing testimonies often focus on their dramatic lives offstage and the personal scandals surrounding them. In his series of biographical essays on early actresses, Kim Nam-seok suggests that Ma Ho-jeong (1876–?), a former palace entertainer, was the first actress that we know by name. Ma joined the sinpageuk ensemble Chwiseongjwa in 1920 at the age of 45 and took mostly supporting roles (Kim 2006: 9–18). She generally stood in the shadow of later – and younger – actresses such as Yi Wolhwa (1905–33) or Bok Hye-suk (1904–82), who made their stage debut around the age of 20.

The precarious life between unstable stage career and social demands put much pressure on these early actresses. Many stars suffered personal crises and died early, such as Yi Wolhwa (1905–33) and Yi Gyeong-seol (1912–34); others, such as actress-singer Yi Aerisu (1910–2009), had to leave behind public life after failed marriages or other 'scandals' (see Kim 2006: 337–44). One of the few actresses who managed to sustain her career by making the switch from popular sinpageuk to progressive singeuk was Kim Seon-yeong (1914–95). As shingeuk-realism, the non-profitable avant-garde in the colonial era, became the mainstream in post-Liberation South Korea, Kim performed in the opening production of the newly founded National Theatre (*Weonsullang* [Master Wonsul], 1950) and other popular pieces. Later, she went to North Korea where she continued to work as a 'people's actress' (Kim 2006: 281–336).

From gisaeng entertainers to theatre actresses, women on stage have shaped the world of theatre – and Korean society in general – in many ways that remain yet to be explored in full. With the rise of singeuk-realism to the dominant theatre style after 1945, gendered casting remains the de facto standard on South Korean theatre stages. Even the originally all-female ensemble Yeoin Geukjang ('Women Theatre'), which had served as a stepping stone for many famous actresses, women dramatists and directors, began to hire male actors soon after its foundation in 1966.

Apart from traditional arts where the gender of performer and role are independent from each other, the only form of theatre that features consistent cross-gender casting up until now is *yeoseong gukgeuk* ('female national theatre').[10] Performed exclusively by women, this genre experienced a huge boom in the 1950s, but is nowadays performed by the few remaining ensembles on rare occasions only. Like *changgeuk*, yeoseong gukgeuk incorporates traditional pansori singing and dance, but tends to 'emphasize sumptuous settings, gorgeous costumes, dashing heroes, and dainty heroines' (Killick 2010: 110).[11] Like the productions of Yeoin Geukjang, yeoseong gukgeuk does not deal with explicitly feminist subjects but provides its mostly female audiences 'a site of contestation over gender relations' (ibid.: 123).

V. Southeast Asia, by Kathy Foley

In Southeast Asia, women appearing as actresses were generally not controversial: women always performed, but the social status of non-elite performers remained in question until the second half of the twentieth century and, in some areas with rising religious fundamentalism, may remain a problem. The rise of the actress is bound up with the development of urban popular genres, spoken drama and links with film and television. With modernization, the male playing the female has been, except in rural areas, largely abandoned. But with the rise of gender studies, some (usually male) artists are either questioning 'gender straight' casting or exploring gay/lesbian/transexual sexualities or constructedness of gender (see, for example, Lim 2005; Thowok and Ross 2005; Diamond 2012: 163–6). This section will only scratch the surface of complex histories, urging much more research to build on the efforts of scholars such as Cohen (2006, 2010), Tan (1995), Diamond (2012), Hatley (1995, 2008) and so on, who have begun to historicize the work of important women in popular and modern drama.

Commercial forces, modernity and local feminisms have widened the female sphere throughout Southeast Asia. Beginning around 1880, a range of new transnational urban hybrid theatres appeared, originally modelled on the Parsi Theatre of Bombay in which European-inspired inclusion of actresses had elevated commercial appeal. *Bangsawan*, first seen in Penang, quickly indigenized and toured throughout maritime Southeast Asia. Tan (1995) found that female performers who entered the theatre in the early twentieth century noted economics as their prime motivator. They often entered a troupe when parental divorce or deaths left them bereft. They trained in dance and singing during the day and performed at night. Some, as adults, would develop as central figures (*seri panggung*, female stars) of this highly popular theatre. Bangsawan was soon replicated in other modern forms and women were recruited. Komedie Stamboel and *sandiwara* developed in Java, where female performers usually came from the lower-class, Chinese (rare) and Indo (Eurasian) groups. In Burma, Po Sein (1882–1954) revolutionized theatre by having the 'prince' touch the 'princess' (a female dancer) and incorporating Eurasian women in the chorus numbers between the acts. *Likey* in Thailand and *cai luong* in Vietnam, likewise, were genres that showed their modernity by incorporating actresses among their other innovative features. Filipino theatre was more fully attuned to Western cultural features than performance of other countries, including accepting women onstage: Atang de la Rama (1902–91) began in *sasuela*s and went on to *bodabil* (vaudeville) and film as well as producing and writing her own plays. Actress Daisy Avellana (1917–2013) not only starred in her husband's plays and films but also helped write them. Katy de la Cruz (1907–2004) was the 'Queen of bodabil'.

Noted Indonesian performers include Miss Tjitjih (1908–36) of Sundanese language *sandiwara* and Miss Ribut in Tio Dek Djin's company – Miss Ribut Orion (Orient) Opera. Dewi Dja (born Misri, 1914–89), 'discovered' as a singing–dancing street performer of East Java, became the star of Dardanella and eventually ended up in Hollywood performing in Bob Hope and Bing Crosby's *Road* movies. Another Dardanella star was Ratna Asmara (c. 1930–c.1981), who would found with her husband Andjar Asmara (Abisin Abbas 1902–61) a new company, Bolero, and in time became one of the first Indonesian woman film directors. These 'stars' were actor-singer-dancers of great charisma and were often the wives of the group leader, who might be producer-director-writer and/or actor. Malay bangsawan women also noted their transnational influences: Mina Alias was trained in Java at Miss Ribut's while Menak Yem, known as queen of dance, learnt her Samba and Rumba steps from the Filipino artists in Malaysia who had developed their expertise in bodabil in their homeland.

As the twentieth century progressed, women coming from the educated elite began to enter the arts, especially in the period after independence. Some artists had classical dance training as children, but others merely encountered spoken drama while in college. Many of the actresses in these new troupes, generally led by dynamic male author-directors, did not rely on income from acting: they worked in education, or advertising/event management or film and television for livelihood. Modern theatre pieces generally had a limited run and the costs were often paid by the group's leader or via grant subventions. Intellectual stimulation and work with like-minded activists on local scripts or explorations of international dramatic literature were often the attractions for these women. Many actresses would perform until marriage and motherhood, then cease. But those named here persisted. Jakarta's Teater Popular (Popular Theatre) of film and stage director Teguh Karya became a training ground for important Indonesian actresses, including university literature lecturer Tuti Indra Malon (1939–89) and film luminary Christine Hakim (1956–). Teater Bengkel (Workshop Theatre) of W. S. Rendra was a more politically charged training ground: playwright Arifin C. Noer trained with Rendra before founding his Teater Kecil (Little theatre) with actress Yayang Noer (born Lidia Djunita Pamontjak, 1952–), daughter of a major figure in the independence struggle and the featured female in Arifin's poetic but politically charged stage work and film. Rata Riantiarno (1952–), who trained with Arifin's Teater Kecil, married Teater Popular actor–playwright–director Nano Riantiarno, and together they founded Indonesia's most economically viable company, Teater Koma. She is both a powerful actress and an astute producer–fundraiser. Talented women were crucial in the success of modern theatre, but normally were featured in groups led by men.

It has only been since the 1980s that women more regularly emerged as directors, conceptualizers and playwrights. These university-educated women may have begun as actresses/dancers, but go on to develop their own work and/or found companies. Thai Patravadi Medjudhon, trained in traditional Thai dance and spoken drama, runs an intimate theatre in Bangkok and seeks to link aspects of traditional culture, Buddhist philosophy and new work. Malaysia's Faridah Merican (1942–) was exposed to theatre in school: she has, in addition to acting and directing, become the major producer of English-language and new work theatre in Kuala Lumpur Performing Arts Centre. Jo Kukathas (1962–) is director and leader of Instant Café Theatre, which addresses silences and inequalities in Malaysian national policies. Tiara Jacquelina [Eu Effendi] (1967–) runs Enfiniti Productions, which furthers the development of Malaysia's new musical comedy: she is best known for *Puteri Gunung Ledang* (2006), retelling a local legend from a female perspective.

Major playwrights include Filipina Malou Levista-Jacob (1948–), who developed important work (i.e. *Juan Tamban*, 1979) opposing the Marcos dictatorship. Singapore's Stella Kon (1944–) is best known for the monodrama *Emily of Emerald Hill*, which chronicles social changes in local Chinese society from a female perspective. Thai playwright Daraka Wongsiri, a drama graduate of Chulalongkorn University, co-founded Dreambox (1990), which presents her plays and adaptations of western scripts for the upscale Bangkok audience. Indonesian playwright Ratna Sarumpaet (1959–) founded Satu Merah Panggung (One Red Stage): a 1993 play on the death of Marsinah, a woman labour organizer, brought her to prominence and her work addresses political and social injustice. Balinese Cok Sawitri (1968–) is a poet–activist whose 1990 *Pembelaan Dirah* (Dirah's Defence) developed into a cycle rethinking the tale of Rangda, the widow-witch featured in the *calongarang-barong* dance-drama, envisioning her as a female divine purifier and saviour. Another emerging Indonesian theatre maker is Maria Tri Sulistyani (1981–) of Papermoon, leading a contemporary puppet theatre for adults: her *Mwathirikam* (2011) examined the history of the 1965 Indonesian mass killings.

These are only a few of the growing number of women from the educated elite directing, writing, producing and devising their own works. Their education and status have largely stilled the moral criticisms that plagued the pre-Second World War female performer, but females, in Muslim areas, sometimes face societies that are growing more religiously conservative and calling for bans on males mixing with females onstage and urging women to cover arms, shoulders and heads and retreat towards the private sphere. These women mentioned promise continued growth in female presence on urban Southeast Asian stages and expansion of the repertoire to include more female voices, but they may also be meeting areas of cultural resistance.

Notes

1 Sarkar in *Hindu Wife, Hindu Nation* analyses how the actress became the key figure around whose public presence raged debates of new social ideology and nationalist agenda.
2 Golap, Shyama, Jagattarini and Elokeshi from Bengal were the first four professional actresses also drawn from *abhadra* (disreputable) quarters.
3 Draupadi is a character from the epic *Mahabharata*; married to five husbands, she is sold in a game of dice.
4 When the term 'gwangdae' ('performer', 'entertainer', 'clown') is used today, it can refer to both men and women.
5 Some reservations seem to remain until today, though, as pansori scholar and performer Chan E. Park notes: 'Men are sometimes discouraged form learning from women for fear their voices may be emasculated. On a psychological level, a woman singer may have a fear of losing her femininity' (2003: 228).
6 This slight turn towards realism seems to have contributed to the acceptance of actresses, as a 'fourth wall' between stage and audience results in an 'objectification of the performer [which] might more closely reflect the traditional relationship of *kisaeng* [. . .] within an aristocratic space in service of the elite audience' (Mueller 2013: 22).
7 On 'Korea's first director' Hong Hae-seong, see Oh (2007).
8 The colonial government had reformed the classification system for gisaeng from three separate categories to a unified group that included professional performers as well as prostitutes (Mueller 2013: 66).
9 Bok Hye-suk (1904–82), a former gisaeng, had studied at the Joseon Baeu Hakgyo ('Joseon Actors School') and performed the role of Nora in the Korean premiere of Ibsen's *A Doll's House*, a graduation performance of the acting school. On Nora in Korea and the 'new woman' movement, see Choi 2012; on gisaeng as role models, see Kim (2007): iii–iv.
10 *Gukgeuk*, literally 'national drama', is a contemporary term for what today is called changgeuk, a music drama performed by an ensemble of pansori singers (on changgeuk, see Killick 2010; see also Killick's chapter in this book).
11 The focus on visual appeal and dance, rather than refined pansori technique, leads some scholars to retrospectively dismiss yeoseong gukgeuk as a degenerate derivative of changgeuk (see Killick 2010: 114). Killick argues, however, that both genres in fact shared many aspects, including repertory, style and personnel, and attributes the generally negative assessment of yeoseong gukgeuk to gender-biased views on women performing a 'national' art (ibid.: 115–17).

Bibliography

Anonymous (1926) 'Xiaowen: heyan wenti' (University News: The Issue of Mixed-Gender Performance), *Yanda zhoukan*, (104): 19.

Arjo, Irawati Durban (1989) 'Women's Dance among the Sundanese of West Java', *Asian Theatre Journal*, 6 (2):168–78.

Cheng, Weikun (1996) 'The Challenge of the Actress: Female Performers and Cultural Alternatives in Early Twentieth Century Beijing and Tianjin', *Modern China*, 22 (2): 197–233.

—— (2002) *The Use of 'Public' Women: Commercialized Performance, Nation-Building, and Actresses' Strategies in Early Twentieth-Century Beijing*, Women & International Development Working Paper, East Lansing: Michigan State University.

Choi Hyaeweol (2012) 'Debating the Korean New Woman: Imagining Henrik Ibsen's "Nora" in Colonial Era Korea', *Asian Studies Review*, 36 (1): 59–77.

Cohen, Mathew Isaac (2006) *The Komedie Stamboel: Popular Theater in Colonial Indonesia, 1891–1903*, Athens: Ohio University Press.

—— (2010) *Performing Otherness: Java and Bali on International Stages, 1905–1952*, Basingstoke: Palgrave Macmillan.

Cooper, Nancy (2004) 'Tohari's Trilogy: Passages of Power and Time in Java', *Journal of Southeast Asian Studies*, 35 (3): 531–56.

Dasi, Binodini (1998) *My Story* and *My Life as an Actress*, Rimli Bhattacharya (ed. and trans), New Delhi: Kali for Women.

Diamond, Catherine (2012) *Communities of the Imagination: Contemporary Southeast Asian Theatres*, Honolulu: University of Hawai'i.

Downer, Lesley (2003) *Madame Sadayakko: The Geisha Who Bewitched the West*, New York: Gotham.

Dutt, Bishnupriya, and Urmimala Sarkar Munsi (2010) *Engendering Performance: Indian Women Performers in Search of an Identity*, India: Sage.

Eckersall, Peter (2006) *Theorizing the Angura Space: Avant-garde Performance and Politics in Japan, 1960–2000*, Leiden: Brill.

Hansen, Kathryn (1998) '*Stri Bhumika*: Female Impersonators and Actresses on the Parsi Stage,' *Economic and Political Weekly*, 33 (35): 2291–300.

—— (1999) 'Making Women Visible: Gender and Race Cross-Dressing in the Parsi Theatre', *Theatre Journal*, 51 (2): 127–47.

—— (2011). *Stages of Life: Indian Theatre Autobiographies*, London: Anthem Press.

Hatley, Barbara (1995) 'Women in Contemporary Indonesian Theatre: Issues of Representation and Participation', *Bijdragen tot de Taal-, Land- en Volkenkunde*, 151 (4): 570–601.

—— (2008) *Javanese Performances on an Indonesian Stage: Contesting Culture, Embracing Change*, Honolulu: University of Hawai'i Press and Asian Studies Association of Australia.

Howe, Elizabeth (1992) *The First English Actress: Women and Drama, 1660–1700*, Cambridge: Cambridge University Press.

Hughes-Freeland, Felicia (2008) 'Gender, Representation, Experience: The Case of Village Performers in Java', *Dance Research: The Journal of the Society for Dance Research*, 26 (2): 140–67.

Hyōdō, Hiromi (2005) *Enjirareta Kindai: 'Kokumin' no Shintai to Pafōmansu*, Tokyo: Iwanami shoten.

Isaka, Maki (2006) 'Women Onnagata in the Porous Labyrinth of Femininity: On Ichikawa Kumehachi I', *U.S.-Japan Women's Journal*, 30–31: 105–31.

Jang, Yeonok (2014) *Korean P'ansori Singing Tradition: Development, Authenticity, and Performance History*, Plymouth: Scarecrow Press.

Kano, Ayako (1997) 'Japanese Theater and Imperialism: Romance and Resistance', *U.S.-Japan Women's Journal*, 12: 17–47.

—— (2001) *Acting Like a Woman in Modern Japan: Theater, Gender, and Nationalism*, New York: Palgrave.

—— (2008) 'Two Actresses in Three Acts: Theater, Gender, and Nationalism in Modern Japan', in D. Croissant, C. V. Yeh and J. S. Mostow (eds) *Performing 'Nation': Gender Politics in Literature, Theater, and the Visual Arts of China and Japan, 1880–1940*, Leiden: Brill.

Killick, Andrew (2010) *In Search of Korean Traditional Opera: Discourses of Ch'anggŭk*, Honolulu: University of Hawai'i Press.

Kim Jeong-eun (2007) *Ilje Sidae Gisaeng-gwa Yeobaeu-wa-ui Gwangye: Daepyo-jeok-in Yeobaeu-reul Jungsim-euro* (The Relationship between Gisaeng and Actresses under Japanese Occupation: Focusing on the Representative Actresses), unpublished MA thesis, Sookmyung Women's University.

Kim Nam-seok (2006) *Joseon-ui Yeobaeu-deul* (Actresses of Joseon), Seoul: Saemi.

Levy, Indra A. (2006) *Sirens of the Western Shore: The Westernesque Femme Fatale, Translation, and Vernacular Style in Modern Japanese Literature*, New York: Columbia University Press.

Liang, Qichao (1999) 'Popular Literature in Relation to the Masses', Faye Chunfang Fei (trans), in Faye Chunfang Fei (ed) *Chinese Theories of Theater and Performance from Confucius to the Present*, 109–11, Ann Arbor: University of Michigan Press.

Lim, Eng-Beng (2005) 'Glocalqueering in New Asia: The Politics of Performing Gay in Singapore', *Theatre Journal*, 57 (3): 383–405.

Liu, Siyuan (2013) *Performing Hybridity in Colonial-Modern China*, New York: Palgrave Macmillan.

Lysloff, René T. A. (2001) 'Rural Javanese 'Tradition' and Erotic Subversion: Female Dance Performance in Banyumas (Central Java),' *Asian Music*, 33 (1): 1–24.

Ma Shaobo (ed.) (1999) *Zhongguo jingju shi* (A History of Chinese Beijing Opera), Beijing: Zhongguo xiju chubanshe.

Mitra, Saoli (2006) *Five Lords, Yet None A Protector and Timeless Tales*, Kolkata: Stree.

Mueller, Ruth H. (2013) *Female Participation in South Korean Traditional Music: Late Chosŏn to the Present Day*, unpublished PhD thesis, University of Sheffield.

Oh, Saejoon (2007) *The Implantation of Western Theatre in Korea: Hong Hae-sng (1894–1957), Korea's First Director*, unpublished PhD thesis, Louisiana State University.

Palermo, Carmecita (2005) 'Confidence Crisis for Bali's Women Mask Dancers', *Inside Indonesia*, www.insideindonesia.org/feature-editions/crossing-male-boundaries, accessed 13 May 2014.Pande, Mrinal (2006) 'Moving beyond Themselves: Women in Hindustani Parsi Theatre and Early Hindi Films', *Economic and Political Weekly*, 29 April, 1646–53.

Park, Chan E. (2003) *Voices from the Straw Mat: Toward an Ethnography of Korean Story Singing*, Honolulu: University of Hawai'i Press.

Pauka, Kirstin (1998) 'The Daughters Take Over? Female Performers in Randai Theatre', *TDR*, 42 (1): 113–21.

Powell, Brian (2002) *Japan's Modern Theatre: A Century of Change and Continuity*, London: Routledge.

Robertson, Jennifer Ellen (1998) *Takarazuka: Sexual Politics and Popular Culture in Modern Japan*, Berkeley: University of California Press.

Saeji, CedarBough (2012) 'The Bawdy, Brawling, Boisterous World of Korean Mask Dance Dramas: A Brief Essay to Accompany Photographs', *Cross-Currents: East Asian History and Culture Review*, 4: 146–68, available from http://cross-currents.berkeley.edu/e-journal/issue-4, accessed 1 June 2014.

Sarkar, Tanika (2003) *Hindu Wife, Hindu Nation: Community Religion and Cultural Nationalism*, Delhi: Permanent Black.

Spiller, Henry (2010) *Erotic Triangles: Sundanese Dance and Masculinity*, Chicago: University of Chicago.

Stickland, Leonie R. (2007) *Gender Gymnastics: Performing and Consuming Japan's Takarazuka Revue*, Melbourne: Trans Pacific Press.

Sutterheim, W. F. (1935) 'A Thousand Years Old: Profession in the Princely Courts on Java', *BKI*, 92: 186–96.

Tan Sooi Beng (1995) 'Breaking Tradition: Women Stars of Bangsawan Theatre,' *Bijdragen tot de Taal-, Land- en Volkenkunde*, 151 (4): 602–16.

Thowok, Didik Nini, and Laurie Margot Ross (2005) 'Mask, Gender, and Performance in Indonesia: An Interview with Didik Nini Thowok', *Asian Theatre Journal*, 22 (2): 214–26.

U Su-jin (2007) 'Yeonswaegeuk-ui Geundae Yeongeuksa-jeok Uiui: Tekeunolloji-wa Sasil-jok Mijangsen, Yeobaeu-ui Deungjang' (The Relevance of Kino-Drama in Modern Theatre: Technology and Realist Mise-en-Scène, the Entrance of the Actress), *Sangheo Hakbo*, 20: 167–96.

Yamanashi, M. (2012) *A History of the Takarazuka Revue Since 1914: Modernity, Girls' Culture, Japan Pop*, Boston: Global Oriental.

Yu Hyeon-ju (2004) *1920nyeondae Yeongeuk Munhwa-wa Sinyeoseong-ui Hyeongseong* (Theatre Culture of the Nineteen-Twenties and the Rise of the New Woman), unpublished MA thesis, Dongguk University.

Zhu Shuangyun (1914) *Xinju shi* (History of New Drama), Shanghai: Xinju xiaoshuo she.

21

Modern Asian theatre and indigenous performance

Anita Singh, Carol Fisher Sorgenfrei, Siyuan Liu,
Jan Creutzenberg and Kathy Foley

This chapter examines modern spoken Asian theatre's complex relationship with traditional and folk performance in the past century. Examples from India, Japan, China, Korea and Southeast Asia all point to a pattern of initial mixture of western and traditional forms in the development of a new form of theatre. It was then followed by an almost complete rejection of indigenous modes of total theatre and entertainment in pursuit of social critical and illusionist realism in the mode of Ibsen and Stanislavski, which limited modern theatre to the urban elite or, in the words of James Brandon, 'unpopular theatre' (1967: 39).[1] By the second half of the century, influenced by western absurdist theatre and internal changes – independence (India and Southeast Asia), anti-American movement (Japan), liberation from authoritarianism (Korea) or awakening from cultural nihilism (China) – spoken theatre re-embraced indigenous performance.

I. India, by Anita Singh

Traditional performance and the spoken word

In the classical period (200 BCE–200 CE), theatre in India was referred to as *drishkavya* (visual poetry), the spectator was *prekshaka* (one who sees) and the theatre house *prekshagriha* (seeing place). The theatrical space along with the spoken words relied on the non-verbal communication where the actors conveyed *bhavas* (states of mind) using *abhinaya* (acting). Abhinaya was four-fold: *sattvika* (temperamental), *angika* (physical), *vachika* (verbal) and *aharya* (dress, makeup). We cannot think of Sanskrit theatre without the works of Bhasa, Kalidas, Shudraka, Vishakhadatta, Bhavabhuti and Shriharsha, whose works afforded such performance. In subsequent ages, the *natya* (drama) was not based on any dramatic work, as scripts were prepared with the materials from oral narratives that were rendered through narrative singing, miming and dramatic dance. The most important feature of the regional theatres from 1000 CE to 1700 CE was the decreasing importance of the written dramatic text. There was such an overwhelming emphasis on music and dance that written and spoken words could not acquire substantial prominence. Colonial rulers (1858–1947) labelled the prevalent folk performances, which lacked standard text, relied on improvisation and were largely sung or recited, as vulgar and obscene and the classical form as esoteric and obsolete. Thus in colonial view, theatre practice in India was almost non-existent, with the possible exception of ancient Sanskrit drama such as *Shakuntala*. The colonial presence saw the rise of modern urban productions on the proscenium stage with scripted texts as drama.

Post-independence search for a new theatre idiom

The demolition of local forms that was induced by western theatre and its text-based phenomenon disavowed the aesthetic tradition of the *Natyasastra* and the folk performing traditions. It was inevitable that in the course of decolonization and as a part of cultural renaissance to return to that root, an indigenous, non-realistic style of production incorporating dance, music and rhythmic movement became the new Indian theatre language (Mee 2008: 3–5). The three decades between the 1960s and 1980s were a period of intense search and experimentation. There were many reasons for this change, including a growing awareness of the imitative nature of native works of the previous century and the international theatre world's disillusionment with naturalistic and realistic styles and methods. These trends led to a search for an imaginative, intimate and socially relevant theatre (Jain 1992: 84–6).

Institutionalizing theatre

A new theatre idiom outside the proscenium theatre that stimulated a move away from the spoken form to a rich theatrical tradition was formulated and encouraged with the formation of the National School of Drama in New Delhi (1959), an autonomous institution funded by the state. Another significant institution was Sangeet Natak Akademi (The National Academy for Music, Dance and Drama), which was instituted in 1952 to support and cultivate the advance of the arts. It played a vital role in sculpting Indian theatre through its scheme of financial assistance to directors who worked for the revival of classical and folk forms on modern stage. A roundtable conference on the contemporary relevance of traditional theatre organized by the Academy in 1971 will always be remembered as a locus for contemporary Indian theatre because of its rejection of the proscenium theatre aesthetics by most directors and appeal to incorporating traditional performance as an important ingredient of national theatre that restores an indigenous Indian tradition, interrupted by colonialism, in the nationalistic postcolonial imagination (Bhatia 2009: xxi).

Theatre of roots

In her *The Theatre of Roots: Redirecting the Modern Indian Stage*, Erin Mee has largely divided contemporary Indian theatre into two conspicuous categories: modern theatre inspired by the western stage (with an emphasis on text and an exclusion of dance, music and spectacle) and roots theatre inspired by the Sanskritic tradition. She maintains that the roots movement has represented the single most significant attempt that 'challenged colonial culture by reclaiming the aesthetics of performance and by addressing the politics of aesthetics' (Mee 2008: 2–5). It was the first deliberate attempt at fashioning a body of work for urban audiences that combined modern European theatre with traditional Indian performance while maintaining its distinction from both. For this reason, the emphasis was shifted more to performance, while text-based western dramaturgy took a back seat. Suresh Awasthi (1918–2004), the general secretary of the National Academy for Music, Dance and Drama, coined the term 'Theatre of Roots' and declared it to be 'the whole process of decolonization of lifestyles', with the purpose of positioning modern theatre 'back on the track of the great *Natyasastra* tradition' (Awasthi and Schechner 1989: 48–69). The incorporation of dance, music and songs operates from an oral rather than a literary base (Crow and Banfield 1996: 12). The flexible use of time and space, mingling of the human with the non-human, opened up new dramaturgical and performance strategies, which began to enlarge the expressive possibilities of a new modern style.

Modern practitioners

Significant directors and dramatists such as Habib Tanvir (1923–2009), Shanta Gandhi (1917–2002), B. V. Karanth (1929–2002), Neelam Mansingh Chowdhry (b. 1951), Sombhu Mitra (1915–97), K. N. Panikkar (1928–2009), Shiela Bhatia (1916–2008), Satyadev Dubey (1936–2011), Ratan Thiyam (1928–2009), Badal Sircar (1925–2011), Utpal Dutt (1929–93) and Girish Karnad (b. 1938) subverted the patriarchal authority of the playwright and creatively linked the classical theatrical tradition and the folk performance with modern urban theatre. They refashioned the folk content, form, orientation and stylization to develop a self-conscious critique of the colonial past on the one hand and to make a vibrant vocabulary of the common people on the other.

Dramatists such as Panikkar, Thiyam, Karnad and Karanth harked back to the traditional folk theatrics and reinvented myths and legends to adapt to contemporary interests, while dramatists such as Tanvir and Sircar were sculpting a new theatre idiom out of the western and Indian folk theatre elements. The crux of these experiments was to privilege a semiotics of sight, sound, movements and gesture as against the primacy of the spoken word theatre.

Reinventing the classical and the folk forms

Kavalam Narayana Panikkar sourced his theatre from the classical tradition by following the heritage of *kathakali*, *kuttiyattam* and *kalaripayattu* martial art of Kerala. The high discipline of *Natyasastra* tradition remained the foundation and forte of Panikkar's theatre. As a Sanskrit scholar, Panikkar modernized, restructured and reorganized the productions of *Sakuntalam* (Shakuntala, 1982), *Urubhangam* (The Breaking of the Thighs, 1988), *Madhyam Vyayog* (The Middle One, 1979), *Swapnavasavadattam* (The Dream of Vasavadatta, 1996) and *Dootavakyam* (Messenger's Speech, 1996). His plays interweave patterns of music and dance with dramatic action.

Babukodi Venkataramana Karanth appropriated the ritualistic and conventional *natyadharmi* tradition and the flexible improvisational convention of the *lokadharmi* (realistic) tradition. He was trained in the *yakshagana* and *harikatha* traditions of Karnataka and employed conventional practices in the crafting of modern theatre. His theatre group in Bangalore was called BeNaKa, an acronym for *Bengalooru Nagara Kalavidaru* (Bangalore City Theatre). He directed *Macbeth* (1982) in Hindi using yakshagana form and *King Lear* (1990) using kathakali style. His other popular production, *Jokumaraswamy* (Fertility God, 1972), was based on a folk myth of fertility in north Karnataka to satirize the entrenched institution of feudalism. His plays draw strength from folklore and mythology interwoven with contemporaneity, and resonate with a lyrical quality. As a director his plays are characterized by ingenuity and improvisation; he gave prominence to movement on the stage, polysemic images and the semiotics of overall ambience.

For Girish Karnad, the Natak Company and the folk tradition of yakshagana were early influences. His oeuvre is a fertilization of classical, folk forms and western theatre, especially Brechtian epic theatre. His plays are premised on myths, *puranas*, epics, history, folk tales and his uncanny sensibility to devise them for contemporary conditions. Karnad's engagement with myth begins with *Yayati* (1961), a tale from the *Mahabharata*. He psychoanalytically reinterpreted the myth (the story of the mythological king Yayati, cursed to old age, demanding that his son Puru lend him his youth). The play was written against the background of Karnad's departure for Oxford as a Rhodes scholar, contrary to the wishes of his parents. Hence, the play became a rejection of parents anticipating sacrifice on the part of their children for their own selfish motives.

His historical play *Tuglaq* (1964) critiques the post-Nehruvian era in Indian politics. Well-known directors such as Ebrahim Alkazi, Satyadev Dubey and Amal Allana have staged plays written by him. In his plays he keeps space for improvising the acting and dialogue whenever the occasion necessitates, this built-in participatory tactic making his plays anti-realistic and non-cathartic in nature.

Playwright-director Ratan Thiyam and his group Chorus Repertory Theatre (formed in Imphal, Manipur in 1976) attempted to revive in his productions, such as *Chakravyuh* (Army Formation, 1984), *Uttara Priyadarshika* (The Final Beatitude, 1996) and *Karnabharam* (Karna's Burden, 1979), age-old Manipuri history as well as folk and traditional Manipuri martial arts of *thang ta*. Thiyam makes his theatre with the distinctive quality deriving from Manipuri folklore, aural and visual aesthetics, and thematic explorations of the Hindu epic tradition along with an influence of *Natyasastra*.

Naya Theatre

Habib Tanvir's association with the Indian People's Theatre Association since its inception in 1943 and the Progressive Writers Association founded in 1946 stimulated his interest in folk culture. His interaction in 1958 with unprofessional *nacha* (folk form of Chhattisgarh, with dance usually done by *yadavas*, a caste which is considered to be descendant of Lord Krishna) performers such as Thakur Ram, Madan Lal, Bulwa, Lalu Ram, Brij Lal, Devi Lal and Fida Bai Markham helped him to initiate the troupe Naya Theatre in 1959. It included the different modes of dance-drama of Chhattisgarh, such as *pandavani* (folk ballad depicting stories of Pandavas from the epic *Mahabharata*), *chandaini gonda* (dance form) and *panthi* (ritual dance of the Satnami community), and used *matrubhasa* (the actor's tongue). There was also a conscious use of improvisation techniques. In 1958, he produced the Sanskrit play *Mricchakatika* (The Little Clay Cart) in Chhattisgarhi, with Naya Theatre actors, in folk style. He also broke away from realistic theatre in *Agra Bazar* (Agra Market, 1954), which was performed under the aegis of Qudsia Zaide's (1914–60) amateur group called the Hindustani Theatre (1954–8). It was a brief and simple story that valorizes the poetry of Nazir Akbarabadi (1735–1830) and takes ordinary people's lives and struggles as its inspiration and subject. The play is rendered in *nautanki* (operatic folk drama from Uttar Pradesh) style following the pattern of operatic narration with cloaked *fakirs* singing the songs. The play introduced a totally new theatrical sensibility that is full of songs and music.

Third Theatre

In the hands of Badal Sircar, non-verbal kinetic, tactile and paralinguistic components became the essential part of theatrical communication. In 1967, he started the theatre group Satabdi. He devised a new non-proscenium free theatre, called Third Theatre, by assimilating different performative techniques of other alternative theatre practitioners such as Jerzy Grotowski, Richard Schechner and Julian Beck. As a result, he created an inexpensive, flexible, portable and poor theatre. He amalgamated the ritualistic creed of the first theatre (folk theatre) with the socio-political purpose of the second theatre (proscenium) to fit the socio-political and cultural consciousness of India. Inspired by the techniques of *Jatra* (folk form of Bengal), the Third Theatre had two modes of production, the *anganmanch* (enclosed space/intimate theatre) and the *muktamanch* (free/outdoor production), or performing at parks, playgrounds and streets before huge audiences. In 1986, he started *gramparikrama* (village tour) to reach to people in the remotest villages. In his Europe tour (1968), he came across Yuri Petrovich Lyubimov's production of Gorky's *The Mother*, John Reed's *Ten Days that Shocked the World* and Brecht's *Galileo*, and read Jerzy Grotowski's concept of poor theatre. He was amazed by their powerful body language, gestures and ensemble performance, with minimized usage of sets, costumes, backdrops, music and lights. As a result, he began to utilize body language, gestures and the chorus to replace props. He presented *Sagina Mahato* (1970) as an experimental production of non-proscenium performance. *Bhooma* (1975) is one of his most powerful plays. It has no story, no character and no plot and presents its content with the sensations created by the body, gestures, sounds and movements. Although *Evam Indrajit* (And Indrajit, 1963), *Baki Itihas* (Remaining History, 1965) and *Shesh Noi* (There's No End, 1969) were composed in the proscenium, his style for a minimalist theatre was well reflected in these productions. He later produced them in anganmanch format. In his plays *Michhil* (Procession, 1974), *Basi Khabar* (Stale News, 1978) and *Sukhapathya bharoter itihash* (Indian History Made Easy, 1965), the semiotics of the Third Theatre is related to the stage behaviour, which combines linguistic and non-linguistic, visual and auditory, textual and meta-textual elements together to create a system of sign.

Modern theatre saw the rise of these practitioners, among others, as creative craftsmen. The directors' creativity changed the entire dynamics of the text's relationship with the audience. For the first time, theatrical textuality became a fluid concept arising out of multiple reading and readers. Folk forms appropriated by the dramatists from the 1960s to the 1980s became a tool of dramaturgy to subvert not only the proscenium theatre but the very canonical notion of text and dramaturgy, as their plays often followed the techniques of improvisational acting, which depended on the actors' skill and the situation.

II. Japan, by Carol Fisher Sorgenfrei

In considering the use of traditional performance in modern and contemporary Japanese theatre, the first thing that strikes one is how completely *shingeki*, appearing in the early twentieth century, turned its back on Japanese tradition. Shingeki was (and remains) primarily interested in making theatre reminiscent of the psychological realism that is generally considered the norm in text-based, Euro-American drama. This emphasis dovetails neatly with the general cultural and political tendencies of Japan in the first half of the twentieth century: a desire to reject tradition and to learn from and surpass the West. With the end of Japan's imperial dreams and the devastating defeat of the Second World War, modern theatre (like the rest of society) found itself adrift, without a clear direction. To the disillusioned youth of the day, Western models felt imposed, while Japanese traditional models stank of the nation's discredited past. One impetus for a new direction in theatre and the arts was the widespread unrest over the 1960 (and later, the 1970) renewal of AMPO (the security treaty with the United States, which essentially made permanent Japan's military dependency on the United States). A related impetus was the participation of Japanese youth in the international anti-Vietnam war, anti-establishment, pro-psychedelic drug movement.

Thus, the second thing one notices about the use of 'tradition' is how completely the little theatre movement (*shōgekijō undō*, also called *angura* – the Japanese pronunciation of 'underground'), which emerged in the 1960s and was closely aligned with the anti-establishment mood of the times, turned its back on shingeki, the new 'tradition' associated with modernity. In so doing, it opened the door to the rediscovery, redeployment and reinterpretation of aspects of traditional Japanese theatre and culture in a contemporary context. In a third variation of this ongoing pattern of rejection and reinvention, many twenty-first-century theatre artists (in line with both globalization and a renewed call for Japan's military independence) have turned their own backs not only on traditional Japanese theatre, but on shingeki and angura as well. This most recent group aligns itself with globally consumed Japanese cultural products such as robotics, Hello Kitty and anime. At the same time, these artists reject the psychological realism of shingeki, the theatricality of traditional theatre and the avant-garde experiments of angura. Many also insist that Japanese language and culture are unique yet globally valid, a paradoxical perspective that I call Japan-centrism. Japan-centrism (or J-centrism) is a subtle suspicion (or validation) of Japanese exceptionalism and superiority that has existed for centuries, going hand-in-hand, or alternating with, an equally powerful suspicion of Japanese inferiority. J-centrism is not confined to the far right, but permeates much of contemporary Japanese discourse (Sorgenfrei, 2014a). Among the younger generation of theatre artists, Hirata Oriza's (1962–) theoretical writings on language offer examples of J-centrism (Sorgenfrei, 2013: 192–4). Among older artists, we see this perspective in Suzuki Tadashi's (1939–) emphasis on the 'universality' of the Japanese body.

Mishima Yukio's (1925–70) so-called 'modern *noh* plays' are probably the most famous works purporting to use traditional theatre, but such a perspective is misleading. They are in fact shingeki dramas that re-imagine the stories of noh plays without using traditional techniques. The strategy of referencing and revising pre-existing material has been employed by Japanese poets and playwrights in all periods. For example, many kabuki plays are reworkings of noh stories, just as many noh plays are reworkings of even earlier literary antecedents such as *Genji monogatari* (The Tale of Genji) or *Heike monogatari* (The Tale of the Heike). In contrast, the theatre artists discussed below embrace traditional performance techniques, regardless of the origin of their scripts. As suggested above, most such artists began their careers in the ferment of the angura movement of 1960s–1970s.

Playwright-director Kara Jūrō (1940–) founded Jōkyō Gekijō (Situation Theatre) in 1962 or 1963, terming his actors '*kawara kojiki*' (riverbed beggars), one of the pejorative terms applied to the earliest kabuki actors. For him, the disruptive, anti-establishment nature of early kabuki defined the purpose of theatre. Kara rejects all aspects of shingeki realism, foregrounding the actors' bodies rather than their psychology. His works, like traditional Japanese theatre genres, are 'total theatre' pieces that inextricably entwine music, spectacle, language and the body. Early plays focused on the otherness of characters such as pirates, beggars, outlaws or non-Japanese minorities. Like the wandering outcasts of early kabuki, his troupe performed in makeshift venues, including ruined buildings. In 1967, he first used what has become his trademark: a large red tent which he set up in shrines, public parks and other locations. In the Red Tent, audiences were denied the luxuries of western-style theatres, such as comfortable seating. They might be squeezed together in close physical proximity to the actors, occasionally even stepped on by them. Like the rapidly shifting society in which they were created, the early plays seemed to lack a coherent narrative. Time, space and characters metamorphosed without rationale; nevertheless, audiences were spellbound and deeply moved. Staging often included a modification of kabuki's *hanamichi* (runway); actors wore ragged costumes and variations of kabuki-like, white makeup. However, it is Kara's return to the spirit of kabuki, rather than his use of specific techniques, that defines his indebtedness to traditional performance. In 1988, he founded Kara-gumi (the Kara Company), which continues to perform both in Japan and in locales such as Korea, Palestine and Bangladesh. Kara, who was born in Japanese-occupied

Manchuria, often writes of the dispossessed or victims of prejudice, with a special emphasis on the marginalization of resident Koreans in Japan (*zainichi* Koreans). His chief actress is zainichi Korean Ri Reisen (1942–). Unlike the artists discussed below, Kara has rejected the Western festival circuit and its attendant international acclaim.

Terayama Shūji (1935–83) formed his Tenjō Sajiki (Peanut Gallery) theatre company in 1967. Like Kara, his goal was to break the boundaries of shingeki realism and to defy all aspects of the establishment, but unlike Kara, he also craved the admiration of international festival organizers and arts pundits. In the 16 years of its existence, Tenjō Sajiki performed abroad over 300 times, often at major arts festivals. Critics singled out Terayama as one of the stars of the international avant-garde theatre, along with artists such as John Cage, Merce Cunningham and Jerzy Grotowski. Although Terayama used many contemporary staging elements that clearly aligned him with the Western avant-garde (such as his multi-locale 'city theatre' and apparently random actions that were similar to 'happenings' or 'guerrilla theatre'), he also borrowed freely from traditional Japanese performance: not only noh, *kyogen*, kabuki and *bunraku*, but also the lowbrow entertainments of his rural youth, including wandering circuses, side-shows, magicians and musician-storytellers. His works often feature rural superstitions, elements of folk religion, and characters or legends remembered from his childhood. An award-winning poet, Terayama's theatrical language is filled with complex word-play and song lyrics. Kabuki-like white makeup, transvestite performers, a preference for dark candle-lit spaces (typical of indoor kabuki prior to electricity), the use of masks, storyteller-musicians, the occasional use of one or more hanamichi, and the incorporation of dance, song, Buddhist rituals, dwarfs, fire-eaters, side-show 'freaks,' magic, and the evocation of a lost, mythical 'Japan' typified many of his works. Terayama creatively employed the *kurogo* (black-robed stage assistant sometimes seen in kabuki). Traditionally, the kurogo is 'invisible,' someone who conveniently removes props or helps an actor with an unwieldy costume. In bunraku, the puppet manipulators (although not called kurogo) are often dressed and hooded in black, to signal their non-existence. Bunraku puppets are 3 to 4 feet tall, controlled by one to three men who hold and manipulate them via sticks or invisible, internal mechanisms. The puppets are not marionettes. In Terayama's iteration, however, the kurogo (including black-robed puppet masters) became avatars of fate. Unlike traditional kurogo, they sometimes spoke and had desires of their own. For example, in *Jashūmon* (Heretics, first performed 1971), they literally controlled characters by pulling puppet-strings attached to the actors, and they stalked through the audience brandishing naked samurai swords, kidnapping audience members who were forced to join the onstage action. In European productions of *Jashūmon*, the aggressiveness of the kurogo caused hysteria, anger and even violence (Sorgenfrei, 2005: 147, 270–3).

Director Ninagawa Yukio's (1935–) Japanese-flavoured Shakespeare and Greek tragedies, which generally include his 'trademark' of falling cherry blossoms, have been presented at prestigious venues and international festivals throughout the world. His direction often borrows freely from all aspects of traditional Japanese theatre and culture, often mingling well-known Western classical or Japanese pop music with traditional flute music as well as visual and verbal imagery evocative of kabuki, noh, Buddhism or Shinto. His most famous productions (including those that tour abroad) are fully readable only to an older, more traditional Japanese audience or to others well versed in Japanese culture. Looking at his Japanese-inflected productions, Western critics unfamiliar with the subtleties of Japanese culture and history sometimes see only exotic spectacle. Consequently, he has unfairly been accused of fostering the Orientalist view of an unchanging Japan. A closer look reveals meaning that often critiques Japan's infamous 'historical amnesia' in regard to its imperialist past, or that references current social problems. In addition, his works clearly demonstrate appreciation for the sheer theatricality and beauty embedded in traditional performance. Ninagawa does not deconstruct Western classics. Rather, he presents the original script (sometimes cut), translated into contemporary Japanese and imbued, via both language and visual elements, with powerful political/social implications. For example, in *Medea* (first performed 1978; translation by Takahashi Mutsuo), references to specific aspects of ancient Greek religion were rendered in Japanese, using Shinto terminology, in a production that reflects both the abject position of women in traditional Japanese culture and their potential power (Smethurst 2002). His *Macbeth* (first performed 1980; translation by Odashima Yushi) is set inside a gigantic *butsudan*, a household Buddhist altar in which the spirits of ancestors reside, clearly suggesting the dangers of venerating the militaristic past. Subtle variations exist in the same play when performed in Japan or the West. For example, in Japanese productions of *Medea*, the male actor playing Medea shifted between the typical female voice of the *onnagata* (male expert of female roles) and a more masculine voice; when performed in Athens to an audience assumed to be less familiar with kabuki, the actor used a more consistently male voice (Smethurst 2002: 8–9). Both choices emphasized the social constructedness of 'woman', and both performances read as 'kabuki-like' without being precise imitations of kabuki. Similarly, the viewer attuned to Japanese traditional performance can see how Ninagawa transforms kabuki *kata* (forms or gestures) to signify something entirely different from the original. For example, when Medea declares her intention to murder her children, she and the chorus pull long red ribbons from their mouths, a powerful image that looks as if they are draining their own life-blood. This inverts (perhaps even subverts) a kabuki and bunraku technique in which a lovelorn woman sucks red ribbons into her mouth (Smethurst 2002: 12–13). Unlike these more famous works, many of his Shakespeare productions in Japan, where he is in the process of presenting every Shakespeare play in order to fully introduce the Bard to his audience, are indistinguishable from standard shingeki.

In contrast to Ninagawa's desire to interpret the classics, Suzuki Tadashi is intent on deconstructing them. A prime example is *Toroia no Onna* (The Trojan Women), which premiered in 1974 (translation by Matsudaira Chiaki, additional poetry by Ōoka Makoto) and toured internationally through 1989. Set in the smouldering ruins of postwar Tokyo among starving women and marauding soldiers, observed by Jizō (a Buddhist bodhisattva traditionally seen as compassionate but here depicted as detached and uncaring), the work strives for universality by invoking and conflating classical Greek tragedy, recent Japanese memory, disillusion with religion, and the horrors of war. Suzuki creates scripts using '*honkadori*' (allusive variation), the technique of intertextual mélange typical of kabuki and classical Japanese literature. Performed in his signature style, which reflects and re-envisions aspects of noh and kabuki, *The Trojan Women* starred the charismatic angura actress Shiraishi Kayoko (1941–), whose powerful, gravelly voiced acting has been described as 'neo-kabuki' (Carruthers 2004: 126), and also featured well-known professional noh and shingeki actors working in their own, distinctive styles. The chorus's and soldiers' acting typified Suzuki's training method, emphasizing the lower half of the body, in contrast to western performance, which focuses on the upper body. The Suzuki Method's exercises derive from once common Japanese movements (such as squatting to use the traditional toilet or to plant rice) as well as from various traditional Japanese performance and martial arts. The resulting style is mesmerizing, slow and intense, punctuated by shocking moments of violence. While the language and content of works such as *The Trojan Women* clearly condemn Japan's militaristic past and rightist-leaning current government, the rhetoric of performance and Suzuki's written commentaries offer a different view: a fervent belief that great acting can only be achieved by unlearning modern, Western ways and retraining the body in traditional Japanese practices, which then become the one true, universal theatrical language. Suzuki maintains that actors of all ethnicities can benefit from this training. The Suzuki Method of

Acting is taught throughout the world, including major acting schools and universities in Europe and North America. As suggested above, Suzuki's ideology epitomizes J-centrism (Sorgenfrei, 2014b: 349–51).

Miyagi Satoshi (1959–), a generation younger than those discussed earlier, is a disciple of Suzuki. Miyagi is known for his innovative use of bunraku and kabuki techniques. Like Suzuki, he emphasizes physicality as a key to interpretation of text. Unlike Suzuki, he seldom deconstructs or creates scripts, preferring (like Ninagawa) to interpret Japanese and Western classics. His signature style separates the voice and the body, referencing bunraku, which has a narrator (*jōruri* or *gidayu*) who voices all roles and puppeteers who never speak. A related tradition in kabuki is termed *ningyō-buri*, in which the actor/dancer performs as though he is a bunraku puppet, allowing himself to be manipulated by onstage puppeteers. Miyagi's most famous work is *Medea*, a script that seems to resonate with many Japanese directors. In Miyagi's interpretation, all lines are voiced by a male chorus, dressed as Japanese academics or jurists from the early twentieth century. The play has a newly written prologue to justify its setting, which is a restaurant/brothel in which Korean women serve as geisha/prostitutes for this distinguished clientele. The men desire to see a production of *Medea*. In the prologue, each woman has a brown paper bag covering her head, and she holds a picture of her face (reminiscent of a photo of the dead) over her genitals. The clients remove the paper bags as they cast the show based on the photos. During the course of the play, which is a shortened but otherwise intact version of Euripides' script, the actress who plays Medea pulls off her Japanese kimono to reveal her native Korean dress underneath. She performs a Korean shamanic ritual in preparation for murdering her son, whose father Jason is costumed as a Japanese military man. At the play's conclusion, the walls and ceiling, as well as thousands of books, come tumbling down onto the heads of the confused chorus. In this way, Miyagi demonstrates the rebellion of voiceless sexual slaves (so-called 'comfort women') and other victims of Japanese imperialism, militarism and prejudice.

This discussion has necessarily focused primarily on the innovators of the 1960s, several of whom remain cultural and artistic powerhouses today. For many Japanese and non-Japanese theatre artists, festival presenters and scholars, their work exemplifies the best of postwar Japanese theatre; for others, especially younger artists and scholars who focus on whatever is currently in vogue, their work may seem outdated or even Orientalist. Whether one applauds or condemns their creations, no one can deny these artists' profound impact. Their influence has also resulted in the use of Japanese (and to a lesser extent, other Asian) performance traditions outside Asia. Modifications of such traditions are increasingly visible on the international festival circuit among artists such as Robert Wilson, Robert LaPage, Arianne Mnouchkine or Simon McBurney, as well as in blockbuster musical extravaganzas such as Julie Taymor's *The Lion King*.

III. China, by Siyuan Liu

The role of traditional Chinese theatre, collectively known as *xiqu* (song drama), in modern spoken theatre *huaju* (spoken drama) has been a point of contention since the latter's inception at the turn of the twentieth century. The first form of modern theatre *wenmingxi* (civilized drama), which thrived in Shanghai in the 1910s, borrowed performance conventions from *jingju* (Beijing opera), including singing and female impersonation. Such hybridity, however, became a source of its notoriety as an impure form in the following decades. In the late 1910s, the New Cultural Movement launched a full-throated attack on indigenous theatre as part of its effort to denounce traditional culture. As a result, huaju was generally averse to traditional theatre in major parts of the twentieth century in its attempt to establish dramaturgical and performance fidelity to modern western theatre. Nevertheless, it also experienced intermittent attempts by some of its most forward-looking practitioners to absorb indigenous elements. Time and again, these practitioners proved to be more in tune with world theatre, while their local detractors remained trapped in Ibsenian social critical realism and Stanislavskian illusionist representation.

Such orthodoxy was, however, absent from wenmingxi at the turn of the twentieth century, which was a hybrid of European melodrama, traditional Chinese theatre and Japan's first modern theatre *shinpa* (new school drama). The shinpa connection through Chinese students studying in Tokyo proved to be significant for wenmingxi's hybrid approach because it borrowed much of kabuki convention such as female impersonation, stylized movement and speech delivery, and some singing and dancing. Famous for their 1907 adaptation of *Uncle Tom's Cabin* in Tokyo, these students, under the aegis of the Chunliu She (Spring Willow Society), returned to Shanghai after the end of the Qing dynasty in 1911. There, their shinpa-based performance style hybridized with local practitioners' preference for including a jingju-style role category system, singing with musical accompaniment of jingju and folk songs, and using mostly plot scenarios and improvisation (instead of full scripts), as was the case of popular jingju instalment plays and contemporary costume plays of the time.

While there was an active contemporary debate about such hybrid conventions as female impersonation (see China section in the previous chapter) and singing, hybridity of Chinese and Western theatrical elements was an accepted practice, a consensus that drastically change by the end of the decade. In October 1918, the Beijing-based *Xin qingnian* (New Youth) magazine, the mouthpiece of the anti-traditional New Cultural Movement, published a dramatic reform special issue. While it included one essay that defended indigenous theatre's theatricality, conventionality and musicality, the majority of the articles denounced old theatre, especially jingju, as 'toys' and 'tricks' with no social efficacy or literary value, and claimed that it could not be utilized for the sake of social enlightenment. For them, the only path to achieving this function was by removing the 'vestiges' of the old society and adopting new concepts, methodologies, forms and stage technologies from the West, particularly realistic theatre, as embodied by Henrik Ibsen. To this end, the magazine's only other special issue, published in June of the same year, was dedicated to Ibsen, with three translated plays and two introductory articles.

As a result of such fierce attack on traditional theatre and wenmingxi's perceived deficiency in dramaturgical and performative hybridity, the *aimeiju* (amateur theatre) movement of the following decade shunned jingju in pursuit of formal and ideological purity, even though most productions of Western plays were still localized in mise-en-scène. To this end, the term huaju ('spoken drama') appeared in 1922 as an equivalent of 'drama', in contrast to *geju* (opera), as an attempt to purge modern theatre of hybrid and indigenous elements supposedly detrimental to huaju's social critical message. Nevertheless, theoretical and practical attempts to include Chinese theatre in huaju persisted and can be found in every decade since then.

In 1926, a group of scholars who had recently studied theatre and fine art in the United States and Britain openly questioned huaju's social critical message and aversion to traditional theatre in their Guoju Yundong (National Theatre Movement) in Beijing. Led by Yu Shangyuan (1897–1970) and Zhao Taimou (1889–1968), professors at the Guoli Yizhuan (National Arts School) who had studied theatre at Carnegie Institute of Technology and Columbia, the movement sought to channel contemporary Euro-American fascination with Asian performance in their revolt against realism. Calling Ibsen's introduction to China 'the wrong track of theatre', the movement published a weekly theatre supplement in Beijing's most prominent *Chenbao* (The Morning Post) newspaper that summer and called for the re-evaluation of 'old theatre', especially the formal beauty of its conventionality, in order to enhance huaju's aesthetic appeal. Specifically, it borrowed the presentational *xieyi* (literally 'writing meaning') metaphor from Chinese painting, where it is used to contrast the realistic and representational *xieshi* ('writing reality'), as a way to understand the essence of Chinese theatre that could ideally complement realistic theatre. While their arguments were well aligned with contemporary Euro-American theatrical movements, they received fierce pushback from Yu and Zhao's students at the National Arts School and others like them, deeply indoctrinated with social critical theatre. Consquently, the *Chenbao Theatre Supplement* folded in September after only fifteen weekly issues. Zhao and Yu left Beijing at the end of the summer and entrusted the department to Xiong Foxi (1900–65), fresh with a master's degree in theatre from Columbia.

Faced with the students' fierce resistance to Yu's previous attempt to introduce jingju training, Xiong allowed several jingju enthusiasts to transfer to the music department and led the rest down a speech-only path with his training and productions. However, when the department was closed in 1933, he and several others in the department moved to Ding Xian County in the nearby Hebei Province where, until the Japanese invasion in 1937, he achieved great success in hybridizing huaju with traditional and folk performance as the director of the drama division of a high-profile literacy campaign. There, he and his colleagues staged outdoor spoken theatre productions that utilized traditional (jingju and local *bangzi* [clapper opera]) conventions as well as street theatre performance forms, such as stilts, land boats and dragon lanterns, and incorporated mass participation of the peasant audience. Most of his productions, especially his two signature plays *Guodu* (Cross the River, 1935) and *Longwang qu* (Dragon King Canal, 1937), were based on events familiar to the peasants. They were staged in outdoor theatres specially built for such purposes, cast local peasants as group characters, incorporated musical and dance sequences, utilized bold colours and symbolic design and movements, and included happy endings to suit the expectations of peasant audiences who were also encouraged to participate during the performance.

Meanwhile, mainstream huaju in Shanghai in the 1930s took a turn to the ideological left in the face of imminent Japanese invasion. Aesthetically, there was also an initial attempt at introducing Stanislavski through authentic Western-looking productions. During the Japanese invasion (1937–45), however, when most mainstream huaju practitioners moved to the southwest interior with the nationalist government, commercial huaju theatre in Shanghai reinstated some of wenmingxi's hybrid techniques for popular appeal, including adaptations of traditional plays and inserting jingju singing, speech patterns, gestures and movement in huaju performance. For example, the theatre historian Zhou Yibai (1900–77) adapted a number of classical Chinese plays with well-structured plot lines and topical themes, choreographing some of the movement patterns based on the classical genre *kunqu*. One of the most popular huaju plays of this time, *Qiu Haitang*, largely benefited from its lead actor Shi Hui's (1915–57) brilliant jingju singing and performance of the protagonist's melodramatic life as a jingju actor of female roles.

After the war, however, such theatrically and ideologically hybrid performance quickly ended with the return of the huaju establishment to the major cities. This trend of speech purity intensified after the establishment of the People's Republic of China in 1949. Furthermore, as a result of China's close relationship with the Soviet Union, its theatre experts came to China to teach the Stanislavski system, making it the dominant method of huaju performance. However, after many languid productions in the 1956 National Huaju Festival, calls for a Chinese system of huaju performance began to emerge, which was soon put into practice by Jiao Juyin (1905–75), a director at the Beijing Renmin Yishu Juyuan (Beijing People's Art Theatre). Jiao had been the principal of a jingju school in Beijing in the 1930s before earning a PhD in theatre at the University of Paris. In 1956, he chose *Hufu* (The Tiger Tally, 1942), a historical play of palace intrigue during the Warring States period (476–221 BCE), for his huaju sinicization experiment (Figure 21.1). Debuted in January 1957 after 8 months of rehearsal, the production used extensive jingju role-type-specific speech patterns and eye, hand and body movement techniques as its essential performance vocabulary. It was aided by an open (not box) set design with strategic set pieces, a jingju percussion orchestra and traditional costumes with water-sleeves, which the actors used for a wide range of expressions. At first, Jiao's experiment met stiff resistance from the actors, who had just staged Maxim Gorky's *Egor Bulychev and Others* under a soviet director and therefore viewed xiqu's emphasis on stylized performance as formalist – an ideological taboo of the time. It was only because of the intervention by the theatre's Party Secretary Zhao Qiyang that Jiao could continue his experiment.

Eventually, the actors became Jiao's willing followers and the production was widely acclaimed as the right direction of huaju localization. Jiao continued his experiment with three more productions of classical-costumed plays with convincing success. The continued immersion in indigenous theatre even allowed Jiao and his actors to adopt xiqu principles – such as well-controlled tempo changes, the externalization of inner thoughts through movement and gestures, and facing the audience during speech – in his modern plays, especially the 1958 *Chaguan* (Teahouse), widely hailed as a huaju classic production. Unfortunately, Jiao was not allowed to direct – and continue his effort to build a uniquely Chinese style of spoken theatre – after 1963, during a heightened ideological atmosphere that led to the Cultural Revolution, during which he died in 1975.

Figure 21.1 A scene in *Hufu* (The Tiger Tally, 1957) directed by Jiao Juyin at Beijing People's Art Theatre. From left to right: Zheng Rong (as Hou Ying), Yu Shizhi (Lord Xinling), Zhu Lin (Lady Ruji) and Dai Ya (King of Wei).

(Courtesy of Beijing People's Art Theatre)

After the Cultural Revolution, the idea of xieyi, originally proposed in the National Theatre Movement of 1926, was revived in the 1980s, particularly by the Shanghai director Huang Zuolin (1906–94). Huang had studied theatre in England in the 1930s and was one of the directors of the 1942 hit play *Qiu Haitang*. Having directed Brecht's *Mother Courage and Her Children* in 1959, he proposed in 1962 to appropriate Brecht and Chinese theatre to break Stanislavsky's monopoly. His 1987 *Zhongguo meng* (China Dream) used only an actor and an actress to tell the love story of a Chinese dancer and her American boyfriend, using a combination of Chinese and western acting techniques on a bare stage that turns into over 20 different locales. His 1991 production of *Naozhong* (Alarm Clock) incorporated extensive jingju techniques, especially during a scene when the protagonist has to stand still, as if dead, behind his portrait for two and half minutes. Huang told the actor to learn the technique of performing this scene from the famous jingju *chou* (clown) actor Liu Binkun, well known for a similar performance before 1949 as a paper puppet in the jingju play *Da piguan* (Cleaving Open the Coffin).

In recent years, while most huaju productions have remained in the speech-centric realm, the division between huaju and xiqu has been less rigid. For example, the Beijing People's Art Theatre director Li Liuyi (b. 1961), who grew up in a *chuanju* (Sichuan opera) family, used xiqu actors in his trilogy of historical heroines in 2000s – *Mu Guiying*, *Hua Mulan* and *Liang Hongyu*. While primarily a huaju director, he has also directed xiqu plays. A similar case is the director Chen Xinyi (b. 1938), who originally trained as a xiqu actress before becoming a huaju director. In other words, while the division between huaju and xiqu is still clear, the border has become more porous.

IV. Korea, by Jan Creutzenberg

The adaptation of traditional stories in spoken theatre goes back to the early twentieth century when western-style drama was introduced in Korea. During the colonial period the progressive *singeuk* ('new theatre') movement dramatized several popular pieces of *pansori* (epic storytelling) to foster a nationalist spirit when Japanese censorship prohibited overtly political theatre. In 1938, a Japanese-language version of the classic *Chunhyang-jeon* (Story of Chunhyang), which featured elements from *kabuki*, sparked a heated debate about modern Korean identity. The power and potential danger of tradition clearly came to the fore between 'the colonizer's affirmation of the play as an exemplary cultural exchange . . . [and] the colonized's protest against it as an "inaccurate" or "unfaithful" translation' (Suh 2010: 171; see also Kwon 2014).

When a new generation of South Korean directors and playwrights began to use traditional aesthetics and techniques on a larger scale in the 1970s, they were likewise concerned with a new identity for Korean theatre, this time in opposition to the dominance of western-style singeuk-realism. In contrast to the cultural policies of the Park Chung-hee regime, which since 1964 had designated a number of Important Intangible Cultural Properties (*Jungyo muhyeong munhwajae*) for preservation in their 'original' form, thus rendering them 'immutable, unchangeable and unchallengeable' (Howard 2006: 28), these experimental productions took much more liberties in creating theatre relevant to contemporary audiences.

Directors such as Yu Deok-hyeong, An Min-su and O Tae-seok at the Drama Centre as well as Kim Jeong-ok and his ensemble Jayu had become acquainted with western avant-garde such as epic theatre, absurdist theatre or Artaud's theatre of cruelty while studying abroad. In their plays, which were based on myths, legends, historical events or folk practices, they confronted these non-realist styles with traditional arts. Initially sparked by an interest in western theatre, these experimental approaches also reached back to the west – the pan-Asian *Hamlet*-adaptation *Hamyeol Taeja* (Prince Hamyeol, 1976, directed by An Min-su) was the first Korean play that extensively toured Europe and the United States.[2]

Heo Gyu and his ensemble Minye Geukjang (Folk Arts Theatre), on the other hand, searched within the Korean folk traditions for contemporary meaning. Minye's efforts to revive so-called *minjokgeuk* (literally 'ethnic theatre'), an 'autonomous ethnic culture' independent from foreign influences (Baek 2009: 299) that emphasizes 'the expressive aspects of traditional performance as uniquely characteristic of the nation's cultural heritage' (Lee GI 2008: 12), were paralleled by the emerging *madang-geuk* ('village square-theatre') movement.[3]

Whether experimentalist or revivalist, these directors and playwrights shared an interest in the open, episodic structure of traditional arts characterized by a 'principle of gaps' (*teum-ui weolli*) and their flexible use of space – often in the form of an empty stage reminiscent of the *madang* ('village square') – that enables audience participation. Both concepts are fundamental to most traditional folk arts and, at the same time, proved highly relatable to international avant-garde practices of the time (Kim 2012: 211–21).

In the 1980s, the number of small, experimental ensembles greatly expanded, including O Tae-seok's Mokhwa Repertory and the ensemble Yeonwoo Stage (Park 2013). Heo Gyu, in turn, dedicated his efforts to *changgeuk* ('singing drama', a hybrid genre of staged pansori) and its 'madang-ization' at the National Theater (Killick 2010: 131–4).[4] Son Jin-chaek and his ensemble Michu filled stadiums with their TV-broadcast productions of *madang nori*, an eclectic mixture of well-known folk tales, humour and traditional dance and song that was inspired by madanggeuk but stripped of its critical intentions and ideology (Kim 2012: 116–18).

Shamanist rituals, whose dramatic potential had been used in the theatre since the 1970s, made a comeback in the theatre of the 1990s, often as a dramatic device to reflect on past events.[5] Son Jin-chaek, for example, in his 1992 production of Bak Jo-yeol's anti-war-piece *O Janggun-ui Baltop* (O Chang-Gun's Toenail, translated in Nichols 2009), framed the absurdist plot with a shaman whose 'invocation' calls the spirits of the characters on stage to perform the play (Shim 2004: 222). In Lee Yun-taek's 1989 piece *Ogu: Jugeum-ui Hyeongsik* (O-gu: A Ceremony of Death, translated in Lee 2007), which depicts a family conducting a ritual for the ageing mother, the proceedings of the ceremony are part of the plot. The play caused a major debate between theatre critics and directors about whether shamanist rituals can be considered theatre and if they should be put on stage (Kim 2012: 151).[6]

Segyehwa ('globalization' or 'internationalization') was introduced as a new national policy by the Kim Young-sam administration (1993–8), the first democratically elected government since Park Chung-hee, and has shaped Korean cultural politics until today. International festivals, workshops and conferences in Korea as well as guest performances abroad allowed for more bilateral 'foreign relations' than ever before. 'Transnational theatre works' such as the Broadway-style musical *The Last Empress* (1995) or the non-verbal performance *Cookin' Nanta* (1997–), where rhythmic patterns drawn from traditional drumming are performed on kitchen equipment, 'visualize and embody the intricate ways that the concept of Western cultural hegemony, as an epitome of the global, has wrestled both with demands for globalization and efforts to reclaim and justify the value of tradition and national identity' (Lee 2015: 3). In the case of spoken theatre, staging western classics with traditional methods proved a successful strategy to attract and foster foreign audiences.

Localized productions of Shakespeare in particular, which offer both new interpretations of the acknowledged plays and impressions of Korean tradition, have received considerable international attention. While the use of Shakespeare as an 'entrance ticket' to the worldwide festival circuit has been a contentious subject,[7] the concrete approaches differ largely. In O Tae-seok's *Romeo and Juliet* (2002), the actors employ different kinds of traditional body techniques to produce a dynamic performance flow. Yang Jeong-ung, in his adaptation of *A Midsummer Night's Dream* (2002), populates the Athenian forest with traditional characters and mythical creatures from Korean folklore, such as the goblin-like *dokkaebi*, to evoke the supernatural atmosphere of the play in a distinctively Korean way. Lee Yun-taek creates a Korean *Hamlet* (1996) by organizing the scenes from the original play according to the proceedings of a shamanist ritual, recasting Hamlet's story as a spiritual re-animation.[8]

Two major trends characterize intercultural theatre practice today: international co-productions and a further blurring of genre boundaries.

In 2008, Lee Yun-taek was invited by the Japanese ensemble Ku Na'uka to restage their existing production of *Othello*, an interpretation of the piece in *mugen* ('dream') *noh* style. Lee added a further layer of localization by using a shaman-like character who communicates with the spirit of Desdemona, represented by a noh actor. The resulting piece, *Monghwan-ui Osello* (Dream Othello), 'a creative betrayal' both of Shakespeare's original play and the conventions of noh, sheds new light on the links between both Asian traditions (Hamana 2009: 351).

Bereullin Gaettongi (The Berlin Gaettong, 2008) is a German–Korean remake of a Korean play, now set in re-unified Germany (Figure 21.2).[9] A cast of rubber foam creatures, built by the German puppet maker Florian Loycke and controlled by members of the Yeonhuidan Georipae (Theater Troupe 'Georipae'), plays a series of short sketches about post-unification phenomena such as economic exploitation or stereotypes about east–west marriages and relates them to the situation in divided Korea. Gaettong, an anarchic character from Korean folklore whose name literally means 'dog shit', saves the day when the economic and emotional crises seem to take the upper hand. Juxtaposed with references to Korean and German history and pop culture quotes, the traditional characters, dances and songs serve the greater cause: a humorous encounter between two countries that share the experience of national division (Creutzenberg 2008).

Lee Ja-ram, a former child star, trained pansori performer, lead singer of a folk band and occasional theatre or musical actor, is emblematic of a new wave of professional traditional artists whose works blur genre boundaries. Her ongoing series of Brecht-adaptations, for example, presents a dialogue between epic theatre and pansori. In *Sacheon-ga* ('Song of Sichuan', 2007), she transfers the parabolic plot of *The Good Person of Szechwan* to contemporary Korea in order to address social injustice, political corruption and gender stereotypes.[10] She tells and enacts the story of the good person in a capitalist world as a solo performer, in accordance with pansori conventions. In addition to the traditional single-drum accompaniment, she is backed up by several musicians and a multi-religious trio of singing and dancing gods. The wide scale of voices, sounds and moods that pansori offers serves as an effective means to stage the heroine's double identity and the resulting moral dilemma (Creutzenberg 2011).

More and more young performers trained in the traditional arts (*yeonhui*) are entering the world of theatre instead of – or in addition to – pursuing a career within the state-sponsored system of Important Intangible Cultural Properties. Gugak Musical Collective Taroo employs different styles of traditional music (gugak) to stage performances for contemporary audiences and works in a variety of genres, including musical (*Unhyeongung Romaenseu* [Unhyeon Palace Romance], 2012) and children's theatre (*Hayan Nunsseop-ui Horangi* [The Tiger with the White Eyebrows], 2011). For the 'Pansori Hamlet Project' (2011), Taroo collaborated with the theatre ensemble Peullei Wideu (Play With). Together they retold and staged various key scenes, integrating pansori-style singing and conventional stage acting into a metadramatic experiment.

Although some directors have developed their own acting methods,[11] the future of distinctively 'Korean' theatre seems to lie in artistic collaborations. The growing number of highly skilled *yeonhui* professionals who leave the restrictions of government-sponsored preservation policies behind will certainly contribute to the dialogue between traditional music, performing arts and the world of theatre.[12] While the search for a modern identity of

Figure 21.2 Dream Othello by Theater Troupe 'Georipae', directed by Lee Yun-taek.

(Courtesy of Theater Troupe 'Georipae')

Korean theatre continues, the genre-bending, border-crossing results show viable ways for the productive combination of traditional and modern elements, live on stage.

V. Southeast Asia, by Kathy Foley

Though the word is important in Southeast Asian traditional theatres, text was most often improvised except in select palace traditions: hence movement, music and visual elements were co-equal with word in generating performance. Generally, set text was for priests/elites who could read, while the oral–aural–improvised was for the people. It therefore makes sense that modern text-based drama was and is embraced by elites. The upper class's exposure to western models often came via colonial education systems where Molière, Shakespeare or Realists with social significance were in late nineteenth- and early twentieth-century curricula. Exposure to European forms inspired drama that used tools of the colonial oppressor in local modernization and independence agitations implemented through plays that were innovative, serious and modern. Meanwhile, traditional theatre was often considered heritage, which some would jettison as not 'real' (i.e. 'written') literature while others wanted it to be preserved 'without change'. Hence in the Southeast Asian colonial period[13] only limited elements from traditional theatre were used in the emerging elite modern urban drama.

This section will discuss selected developments after the Second World War, using two major periods. The first is the 'roots' period of the 1960s–1980s, when dramatists of the now fully independent nations sought to reconcile colonial textual theatre with local performance, resulting in hybrids as performers sought local roots to cement national pride and decolonization of the mind. Artists borrowed selectively from indigenous materials to create text-focused performances and stagings that began to reference traditional theatres. However, few of the urban writer-directors had deep understanding of indigenous traditions they emulated. Like Peter Brook or Robert Wilson, the urban director/author might borrow images or cast a traditionally trained master, but work still lacked a deep synthesis. The second period, from the mid-1980s to the present, has more artists who may actually be trained in traditional practices but who have begun to innovate within modern drama/performance, but the forms themselves are involving and the divides between tradition and modernity collapse. Is this modern theatre with traditional elements or modern traditional theatre?

Additionally, artists (who often see themselves as international post-modernists working in a post-dramatic mediated world) use tradition with different intentions. Grassroots people's theatre workers with NGO funding may disseminate health education or counter religious fundamentalisms with elements of Javanese *ketoprak*; local Chinese artists may insert *xiqu* references to resist the anti-Chinese pushes in countries that have discriminated against that diaspora; local governments may blandish grants to highlight the heritage of a particular group to win elections. The manifestations are many, but the intents are diverse.

Maritime Southeast Asia

In both Indonesia and the Philippines the move to incorporate traditional theatre in modern scripted drama was part of a post-independence push against the perceived western hegemony that manifested in part, it was felt, in the pro-capital dictatorial governments led by Presidents Suharto (1967–98) and Marcos (1965–81). The 'development' ideology was countered with a sort of protest in a 'roots' movement in the arts.

In Indonesia, W. S. Rendra (1935–2009) is often credited with the first introduction of local elements in *Kisah Perjuangan Suku Naga* (Struggle of the Naga Tribe, 1975). In actuality there were earlier efforts, but still Rendra made it a movement. The beginning was reminiscent of opening *wayang* shadow play and the end was like a *perang agung* (climatic battle); *gamelan* instruments were used; and *Mahabharata* villainy was referenced to attack contemporary corruption.

The trend began. Putu Wijaya (1944–) of Teater Mandiri (Independent Theatre) used Balinese music. Arifin C. Noer (1941–95) put in comics comparable to *wayang punakawan* clowns. Ikranegara (1943–) incorporated Balinese *topeng* masks in monodramas. Sardono Kusumo (1945–) created *Cak Tari Rina*, using 'monkey chant' chorus with Balinese villagers. Perhaps the best-received melding was by author-director Nano Riantiarno (1949–), a Chinese-Indonesian, whose Teater Koma (Comma Theatre) did *Sampek Engtay* (Butterfly Lovers, 1988) and *Opera Ular Putih* (White Snake, 1994) during the Suharto era when Chinese culture was censored. While not *xiqu*, he offered musical comedy versions of traditional narratives, with costume and movement referencing traditions. Riantarno's *Opera Prima Donna* (1993) combined nostalgia for popular early twentieth-century *bangsawan* with political impact: the fading bangsawan diva refuses to make way for a younger replacement (lampooning Suharto desperately hanging on to power). Riantiarno's *Republik Bagong* (Republic of Bagong, 2001) used wayang clowns to satirize the chaos of multiple political parties fighting after Suharto's fall.

Companies such as Dinasti, Garasi and Gandrik use models of *ketoprak* (Javanese popular theatre) but address politico-social issues. For example, Garasi explored traditional ritual exorcistic narratives in their 2006 *Waktu Batu* (Stone Time) series probing Javanese identity (Hatley 2008: 202–11). Borrowing from traditional comic forms to make politico-social comment has been mined frequently. For example, Yogjakarta-based Gedag-Gedig successfully uses Javanese *dagelan* comedy (Hatley 2008: 238–40).

In the Philippines, traditional forms were tapped to attack Marcos from the 1970s to the 1980s. For example, Behn Cervantes (1938–2013) directed Bonifacio Ilagan's (1951–) *Pagsambang Bayan* (Nation's Worship, 1977), modelled on the Mass, to resist martial law. *Sinakulo ning Balen* (Maundy Thursday Play of the Nation, 1983) by Virgilio Vitug (1951–) used the traditional Easter play to upbraid corruption. Amelia Lapeña-Bonifacio (1930–) taped pan-Asian materials, from Japanese *noh* to Filipino *pasyon* (passion play), using puppets or actors. In the 1970–80s, new *sasuwela* (Spanish-influenced twentieth-century popular theatre) plays were frequent in the 'roots' push: Lapeña-Bonifacio's *Ang Bundok* (Mountain 1977) and Nicanor Tiongson's *Filipinas circa 1907* (1985) based on *Filipinas para los Filipinos* (Philippines for the Filipinos, loosely adapted from Serverino Reyes' 1905 work) evoked national identity.

Since the 2000s, companies have revived older genres in contemporary works (see Tiatco 2009; Tiatco and Bonifacio-Ramolete 2010). Felicidad Mendoza's *Perlita ng Silangan*, a contemporary *komedya*, was staged in Paranaque in 2006 by noted director Soxi Topacio, who mixed traditional performers with modern theatre actors. In 2008, the University of the Philippines Dulaang UP put on *Orosman and Zafira* by Sir Anril Tiatco, which combined keyboard and *kulingtan* gongs and borrowed dances of diverse indigenous groups (skipping Christian–Moor stereotypes for a pre-Christian Philippines). Musicals are a site for reworking; Dulaang University of the Philippines's *Atang* (2009) was a bio-drama of sarsuwela singer-actress Honorata 'Atang' de la Rama (1905–91) by Floy Quintos with dance by Dexter Santos, who updated the sarsuwela *Ang Kiri* (The Flirt) by inserting contemporary music and issues (sex, drugs and gangs) so as to create controversy as to whether real sarsuwela can be so 'hip' (Tiatco and Bonifacio-Ramolete 2010; Figure 21.3).

In the Philippines, many Catholic social justice groups practise Boal-influenced techniques. PETA, the Philippines Educational Theatre Association, has taught this method throughout Southeast Asia. While such groups are more devoted to social betterment than theatre per se,

Figure 21.3 Dulaang University of the Philippines ensemble in *Ang Kiri* (The Flirt).
(Courtesy of University of Philippines, Diliman)

artist-trainers often use local genres. For example, Malou Jacob's *Macli-ing* (1988) used Cordillera people's dance in a piece exploring the rights of mountain peoples. Father Rudolf M. Galenzoga in Mindano has been bringing Christians, Muslims and indigenous groups together through theatre since 1987. In Illigan City he staged *Mindanao People's Conference* (2009), using theatre/dance to end religious/ethnic strife.

Timorese people's theatre groups use local dance and other localism in NGO theatre-of-the-oppressed projects. Brunei, by contrast, has currently limited projects, as the move towards fundamentalist Islam curbs performance.

Mainland Southeast Asia

Malaysians' relationship with heritage theatre is complexified by ethnic divides. The early 'roots' efforts in the 1970s were embraced by artists of diverse backgrounds as nation-building. Relationships with Indonesian auteurs such as Rendra and Arifin C. Noor were part of transnational work. Government/universities-funded projects to develop new Malay scripts and the National Culture Policy (1970) made Malay culture central to national culture. Krishan Jit (1939–2005) directed works such as Noordin Hassan's *Bukan Lalang Ditiup Angin* (Not The Tall Grass Blown By the Wind, 1970) with elements from *boria* Islamic theatre. Syed Alwi's 1974 *Tok Perak* used multimedia to tell of a healer, starring a local healer. Government funds flowed for new *bangsawan*, but rather than the multi-ethnic mix of that early twentieth-century popular theatre, Chinese and Indian elements were edited out and Malay features over-emphasized (Tan 1993).

This primacy of Malay culture, in a nation where Chinese- and Indian-Malaysians comprise about 40 per cent, helped stall the Malay 'roots' movement in modern theatre. Minority communities have responded with private support to build their own arts in new works; the Temple of Fine Arts' *Midsummer's Night Dream* or *Butterfly Lovers* used Indian, Chinese and modern dance in new combinations. Leow Puay Tin's (1957–) *Family* (1992) adapted the Chinese Yang Family woman warrior tale and her *Three Children: A Play* (1992) used Hokkien street opera (musicians on stage) to show growing up in Malacca. Dama Orchestra did *Butterfly Dream* (2006) as a modern musical with bel canto voices and mixed traditional and western instruments.

Separate and unequal support for Malay genres/themes continues. The government sponsors modern fully funded bangsawan programmes monthly, beginning in 2007, and the National Theatre (Istana Budaya) creates new musicals with a traditional flavour, such as the lavish *Dibawah Lindungan Kabah* (Under the Protection of the Ka'ba, 2014, directed by Rosminah Tahir). With chorus dancing in Minangkabau *silat* martial style, it mixed modern singing with Sufi swirling in a moralistic tale of young love blocked. Full merging of cultures is usually confined to modern dance, though artists such as Odissi-trained ethnic Malay dancer-director Ramli Ibrahim (1953–) cross boundaries comfortably. Children's theatre is another space where divides vanish, as in the work of groups such as Rhythm in Bronze.

In Singapore, Kuo Kao Pun (1939–2002) and Ong Keng Seng (1963–) have been forces in melding modernity and tradition, especially through training programmes or intercultural productions. Kuo created his Theatre Practice training course, which exposes students to Chinese, Japanese, Indonesian and Indian as well as Western theories of acting and staging. Ong Keng Sen in his 'Flying Circus' project brought together traditional Southeast Asian artists and modern practitioners to develop productions such as his *Lear* (1997) and *Desdemona* (2000), often mixing genres (i.e. *noh, jingju, khon* in modern scripted theatre). He has also done culture-specific work (i.e. *The Continuum: Beyond he Killing Fields*, 2000, a collaboration of Khmer dance and puppet artists).

The situation in Thailand and Cambodia has been different, in that traditional dance theatre has remained twined with class and is an important political-social force. In the early years, a king, prince or queen might be in charge, and if the ruler wanted change, innovation was easy – Rama VI (King Vajravudh, 1880–1925), for example, wrote over 100 plays, moving between Wilde-like drawing-room satires and innovative dance-drama forms. But, to the present, lower-status innovators can find their use of traditional dance in non-traditional ways controversial. Traditional dance continues unabated and royal involvement as patron or even choreographer (Princess Bhuppa Devi, Cambodia) continues. Here, melding of traditional dance in a spoken drama is not about finding roots – everyone knows where their roots are. Innovation, however, has happened: Patravadi Menujhon's Buddhist plays mix Thai dance, Buddha's teachings and modern performance art. Her 2010 *Phra Lor* told a traditional tale as a play-within-a-play about a spoilt actress and her director as khon dance mixed with projections, and western violin melded with Thai music (Diamond 2010). The Bangkok Theatre Festival, which began in 2002, can have many students from theatre programmes at Thammasat or Chulalongkorn University doing their new works with wild *likay* costumes or presenting other old/new works.

Surapone Virulak (2015) notes current experiments in the successful *Pan Tai Norasing: The Musical* (funded by National Research Institute) in which Niwet Waew Samana, a traditional puppeteer, used traditional figures with new manipulation, modern lighting and new stage design. Pradit Prasatthong presented the traditional *Khun Chang, Khun Paen* (names of two men who vie for one woman) in spoken drama. In the original story, the heroine is blamed for having 'two hearts' and not being true to her nobler suitor. This was a new reading, sympathetic to the female position. *Hom Rong: The Musical* (2015) was the biography of an important Thai musician of the early twentieth century, Sorn Silapabanleng (Figure 21.4). It was directed by Teerawat Anuvatudom and based on Ittisoonthorn Vichailuck's film *Overture* (2004): Surapone

Figure 21.4 A scene from *Hom Rong: The Musical.*
(Courtesy of Surapone Virulak)

Virulrak in an email (29 June 2015) notes, 'The play used Thai traditional music as the key element throughout the performance. All actors could play Thai music professionally.' Virulrak himself did a new *jataka Kaki* about a woman who has three husbands: the group began from the King Rama I script but let the heroine defend herself, again showing greater sympathy for the female roles than traditional interpretations give. Social work via traditional theatre also employs mixes: for example, Chalermchai Piromrak, a khon teacher from Angthong Province, is developing a project on sex and violence among teenagers using khon dance elements.

In Cambodia, Laos, Vietnam and Burma, the advances in modern drama in fusions with tradition have sometimes been limited by the economic and political situations. Government support can leverage events. For example, in Cambodia, Hang Thun Hak (1926–75), as head of the Royal Academy of Fine Arts in Phnom Penh, developed *lakon niyeay* (spoken drama) with the support of the crown and directed large-scale government pageants that used dance along with text to promote nation-building via performances prior to the Southeast Asian War. Proeung Chhieng, vice-rector of the Academy of Fine Arts, in the twenty-first century has done some of the same work and often with the support of Princess Bhuppa Devi, creating neo-modern work.

Small projects are funded by NGOs or cultural organizations such as Alliance Français, Goethe Haus or Japanese foundations, such as projects addressing health or social issues (trafficking, AIDS). Sometimes pure intercultural collaborations are mounted by artists of different nationalities. One sees such projects in Cambodia, Laos, Vietnam and Burma, but the efforts are often transitory. Of these countries, only Vietnam has a fully developed modern spoken drama programme. There has been mixing of modern drama and traditional *hat boi* in modern intercultural work such as *A Midsummer's Night's Dream* (2000) under the auspices of the Vietnam

America Theater Exchange (VATE), which used some local elements for the comedy. Nguyen (2011) reports on a series of workshop performances that she and Cliff Moustache from Norway did exploring Shakespeare or devising new work, and included elements of *hat boi* and *cai luong* to allow traditionally trained artists to explore modern scripts that were collaboratively created. Other explorations take place. For the twenty-fifth anniversary of the death of noted *kich noi* spoken drama playwright Luu Quang Vu in 2013, there were many manifestations of his work, including a version of *Hon Truong ba da hang thit* (Truong Ba's Spirit in a Butcher's Body, 1985) with Cheo-style costumes and other traditional features. Works directed towards child audiences may also often tap tradition in terms of story, sound or dance elements.

The traditional arts are alive and infusing modern Southeast Asian spoken drama.

Notes

1 Brandon was referring specifically to the situation in Southeast Asia; it holds true for the rest of the continent.
2 On the revival of tradition in the 1970s, see Kim (1995) and, more recently but in Korean, Kim (2006) and Kim (2012); on discourses about tradition that relate to theatre, see Baek (2009).
3 On madanggeuk, see Lee (2003).
4 On changgeuk, see also Killick's chapter in this volume.
5 On interpretations of *Hamlet* inspired by shamanism, see Lee (2011).
6 On theatre and shamanist ritual from an ethnographic perspective, see Kendall (2009: 67–70).
7 Debates focused in particular on Lee Yun-taek's production of *Hamlet*. While Lee Hyon-u argues that staging Shakespeare served as 'one of the best methodologies to satisfy the ambivalent desire of Korean people in the 1990s to acquire something global as well as something traditional' (Lee 2009: 42), Im Yeeyeon concludes that Lee's 'aspiration to reach universality through Shakespeare' (Im 2008: 263) is symptomatic of the postcolonial predicament in Korean society and destined to prove futile. For a more positive evaluation of the 'semiotic ambiguity' of Lee's *Hamlet*, see Creutzenberg (2009). On Lee's *Hamlet* and other 'globalized' Shakespeare productions, see also Lee HJ 2015: chapter 5.
8 Full-length videos of these three productions, including multilingual subtitles, are available (after free registration) at the Asian Shakespeare Intercultural Archive (http://a-s-i-a-web.org/).
9 The original play *San neomeo Gaettong-a* (Beyond the Mountains: Gaettong) by Kim Gyeong-hwa was adapted by Marcus Braun and directed by Alexis Bug.
10 *Sacheon-ga* (2007) and the second Brecht-pansori *Eokcheok-ga* ('Song of Courage', based on *Mother Courage and her Children*, 2011) are written and performed by Lee Ja-ram, directed by Nam In-u and produced by the ensemble Pansori Mandeulgi Ja.
11 Kim Bang-ok (2006) discusses various cases, including Lee Yun-taek's breath-based 'Korean' acting method.
12 The flexibility of pansori, 'an amalgamation of the poetic, the dramatic, the narrative, the vocal, and the musical' (Park 2003: 12), might make it the most obvious candidate for experimental cross-over theatre. But other genres, such as mask dance-drama (Saeji 2012) or puppetry (Foley 2014), are likewise used as material for new kinds of theatre.
13 Thailand was never officially colonized, but still had to balance French and British to maintain sovereignty.

Bibliography

Awasthi, Suresh, and Richard Schechner (1989) 'Theatre of Roots: Encounter with Tradition', *TDR*, 33 (4): 48–69.
Baek Hyeon-mi (2009) *Hanguk Yeongeuksa-wa Jeontong Damnon* (The History of Korean Theatre and Discourses on Tradition), Seoul: Yeongeuk-gwa Ingan.
Bhatia, Nandi (2009) *Modern Indian Theatre: A Reader*, New Delhi: Oxford University Press.
Brandon, James R. (1967) *Theatre in Southeast Asia*, Cambridge, MA: Harvard University Press.
Carruthers, Ian (2004) 'Suzuki's Euripides (I): *The Trojan Women*', in Ian Carruthers and Takahashi Yasunari (eds) *The Theatre of Suzuki Tadashi*, 124–53, Cambridge: Cambridge University Press.

Creutzenberg, Jan (2008) Review of *Berlin Gaettong*, *OhmyNews International*, 12 November 2008, available from http://english.ohmynews.com/articleview/article_view.asp?no=384129&rel_no=1, accessed 1 June 2014.

—— (2009) 'To Be or Not to Be (Korean): Lee Youn-taek's *Hamlet* and the Reception of Shakespeare in Korea', *Shakespeare Seminar*, 7: 21–38, available from www.shakespeare-gesellschaft.de/fileadmin/media/wso_7_2009_creutzenberg.pdf, accessed 1 June 2014.

—— (2011) 'The Good Person of Korea: Lee Jaram's *Sacheon-ga* as a Dialogue between Brecht and *Pansori*', *Brecht Yearbook*, 36: 225–240.

Crow, Brian, and Chris Banfield (1996) *An Introduction to Post-Colonial Theatre*, Cambridge: Cambridge University Press.

Diamond, Catherine (2010) '*Phra Lor*, by Patravadi Medjudhon, directed by Patravadi Medjuhon and Manop Meejamrat', *Asian Theatre Journal*, 27 (2): 366–70.

Fernandez, Doreen (1996) *Palabras: Essays on Philippine Theatre*, Quezon: Ateneo De Manila Press.

Foley, Kathy (2014), 'Korean Puppetry and Heritage: Hyundai Puppet Theatre and Creative Group NONI Translating Tradition', in D. N. Posner, C. Orenstein and J. Bell (eds), *The Routledge Companion to Puppetry and Material Performance*, New York: Routledge.

Gillit Cobina (1995) '*Tradisi Baru*; A New Tradition of Indonesian Theatre', *Asian Theatre Journal*, 12 (1): 164–74.

Hamana, Emi (2009) '*Othello* in Japanese Dream *Noh* Style with Elements of Korean Shamanism: The World is a Festival', in Lee Yun-taek (ed.) *Facing Hamlet/Haemlit-gwa Majuboda* (bilingual edition), Gimhae: Doyo.

Hatley, Barbara (2008) *Javanese Performances on an Indonesian Stage: Contesting Culture, Embracing Change*, Honolulu: University of Hawai'i Press and Asian Studies Association of Australia.

Howard, Keith (2006) *Preserving Korean Music: Intangible Cultural Properties as Icons of Identity* (Perspectives on Korean Music 1), Aldershot: Ashgate.

Im, Yeeyon (2008) 'The Location of Shakespeare in Korea: Lee Yountaek's *Hamlet* and the Mirage of Interculturality', *Theatre Journal*, 60 (2): 257–76.

Jain, Nemi Chandra (1992) *Indian Theatre: Tradition, Continuity and Change*, New Delhi: National School of Drama.

Kendall, Laurel (2009) *Shamans, Nostalgias, and the IMF: South Korean Popular Religion in Motion*, Honolulu: University of Hawai'i Press.

Killick, Andrew (2010) *In Search of Korean Traditional Opera: Discourses of Ch'anggŭk*, Honolulu: University of Hawai'i Press.

Kim, Ah-Jeong (1995) *The Modern Uses of Tradition in Contemporary Korean Theatre: A Critical Analysis from an Intercultural Perspective*, unpublished PhD thesis, University of Illinois at Urbana–Champaign.

Kim Bang-ok (2006) 'Hanguk Hyeondae Yeongi-e isseoseo Jeontong-jeok Yoso-ui Suyong-gwa Mosaek: Talchum Sawi-ui Doip-buteo "Hanguk-jeok Yeongi-ui Weolli-kkaji" (The Search and Incorporation of Traditional Elements in Contemporary Korean Acting: From Mask Dance to a 'Korean Principle of Acting')', *Hanguk Yeongeukhak*, 28: 53–126.

Kim Mi-do (2006) *Hanguk Hyeondaegeuk-ui Jeontong Suyong* (The Reception of Tradition in Contemporary Korean Theatre), Seoul: Yeongeuk-gwa Ingan.

Kim Suk-gyeong (2012) *Jeontong-ui Hyeondaehwa-wa: 5 In-ui Yeonchulga-deul* (The Modernization of Tradition: Five Directors), Seoul: Yeongeuk-gwa Ingan.

Kwon, Nayoung Aimee (2014) 'Conflicting Nostalgia: Performing *The Tale of Ch'unhyang* in the Japanese Empire', *Journal of Asian Studies*, 73: 113–41.

Lee, Gang-Im (2008) *Directing Koreanness: Directors and Playwrights under the National Flag, 1970–2000*, unpublished thesis, University of Pittsburgh.

Lee Hyon-u (2009) 'Populist Shakespeare in Democratized South Korea', in Hyon-u Lee (ed) *Glocalizing Shakespeare in Korea and Beyond*, Seoul: Dongin Publishing.

—— (2011) 'Shamanism in Korean *Hamlets* since 1990: Exorcising *Han*', *Asian Theatre Journal*, 28 (1): 104–28.

Lee, Hyunjung (2015) *Performing the Nation in Global Korea: Transnational Theatre*, Basingstoke: Palgrave Macmillan.

Lee, Namhee Lee (2003) 'Between Indeterminacy and Radical Critique: *Madang-gŭk*, Ritual, and Protest', *positions*, 11 (3): 555–84.

Lee Yun-Taek (2007) *Four Contemporary Plays by Lee Yun-Taek*, Dongwook Kim and Richard Nichols (trans), Lanham, MD: University Press of America.

Mee, Erin B. (2008) *The Theatre of Roots: Redirecting the Modern Indian Stage*, Kolkata: Seagull.

Nguyen, Khai Thu (2011) Another *Midsummer Night's Dream* in Ho Chi Min City', *Asian Theatre Journal*, 28 (1): 199–221.

Nichols, Richard (ed) (2009) *Modern Korean Drama: An Anthology*, New York: Columbia University Press.

Nur Nina Zuhra [Nancy Nanney] (1992) *An Analysis of Modern Malay Drama*, Shah Alam: Biroteks MARA Institute of Technology.

Oh, Saejoon (2007) *The Implantation of Western Theatre in Korea: Hong Hae-Sŏng (1894–1957), Korea's First Director*, unpublished thesis, Louisiana State University.

Park, Chan E. (2003) *Voices from the Straw Mat: Toward an Ethnography of Korean Story Singing*, Honolulu: University of Hawai'i Press.

Park, Jungman (2013) 'Yeonwoo Mudae and the Korean Theatre Movement in the 1980s', *Asian Theatre Journal*, 30 (1): 67–89.

Peterson, William (2001) *Theatre and the Politics of Culture in Contemporary Singapore*, Middletown. CT: Wesleyan University Press.

Rutnin, Mattaini (1996) *Dance, Drama, and Theatre in Thailand: The Process of Development and Modernization*, Chiang Mai: Silkworm.

Saeji, CedarBough T. (2012), 'Review of *Chushyeoyo* and *Good Pan*', *Asian Theatre Journal*, 29 (1): 291–301.

Shim, Jung-Soon (2004) 'The Shaman and the Epic Theatre: The Nature of Han in the Korean Theatre', *New Theatre Quarterly*, 20 (3): 216–24.

Smethurst, Mae (2002) 'Ninagawa's Production of Euripides' *Medea*', *American Journal of Philology*, 23 (1), 1–34.

Sorgenfrei, Carol Fisher (2005) *Unspeakable Acts: The Avant-Garde Theatre of Terayama Shūji and Postwar Japan*, Honolulu: University of Hawai'i Press.

—— (2013) 'Guilt, Nostalgia and Victimhood: Korea in the Japanese Theatrical Imagination', *New Theatre Quarterly*, 29 (2): 185–200.

—— (2014a) 'Strategic Unweaving: Itō Michio and the Diasporic Dancing Body', in Erika Fischer-Lichte, Torsten Jost and Saskya Iris Jain (eds) *The Politics of Interweaving Performance Cultures*, 201–22, New York: Routledge.

—— (2014b) 'Alluring Ambiguity: Gender and Cultural Politics in Modern Japanese Performance', *New Theatre Quarterly*, 30 (4): 341–51.

Suh, Serk-Bae (2010) 'Treacherous Translation: the 1938 Japanese-Language Theatrical Version of the Korean Tale *Ch'unhyangjŏn*', *positions*, 18 (1): 171–98.

Tan Sooi Beng (1993) *Bangsawan: A Social and Stylistic History of Popular Malay Opera*, Singapore: Oxford University Press.

Tiatco, Sir Anril Pineda (2009) 'Postscript to University of the Philippines Komedya Fiesta 2008: Prelude to a Discourse on National Theatre', *Asian Theatre Journal*, 26 (2): 281–302.

Tiatco, Sir Anril Pineda, and Amihan Bonifacio-Ramolete (2010) 'Performing the Nation Onstage: An Afterthought on the University of the Philippines Sarsuwela Festival 2009', *Asian Theatre Journal*, 27 (2): 307–32.

Tiongson, Nicanor (1989) *Dulaan: An Essay on Philippine Theatre*, Manila: Cultural Center of the Philippines.

Virulrak, Surapone (1990) 'Theatre in Thailand Today', *Asian Theatre Journal*, 7 (1): 95–104.

—— (2015) Personal email, 29 June.

22

Traditional Asian performance in modern and contemporary times

Arya Madhavan, Jonah Salz, Min Tian, CedarBough T. Saeji
and Jennifer Goodlander

This chapter examines the evolution and continuation strategies of traditional Asian performance forms in modern and contemporary times, through colonialism, modernity, nationalism, independence and globalization, with a focus on India, Japan, China, Korea and Southeast Asia. Some of the common issues examined include preservation, reform and innovation; governmental, institutional and market forces behind such changes; and the interaction between local artists and international institutions and markets.

I. India, by Arya Madhavan

Traditional theatrical performances from India exert undeniable influence in creating its cultural identity and self. The broad spectrum of Indian traditional theatres range from structurally complex and heavily stylized, 2,000-year-old Sanskrit theatre, *kutiyattam*, to the relatively 'new' and marginally stylized, eighteenth-century *tamasha* theatre. According to *Natyasastra*, performance is a site where multiple artistic and literary agencies such as music, dance, visual arts, poetry, literature, drama, percussion and architecture claim simultaneous existence (Pisharodi 1987: 102). Such an all-encompassing nature of performance also makes a strict definition of Indian theatre in line with western dramatic practice highly improbable. Moreover, a comprehensive survey of the contemporary status of traditional theatrical performances from India calls for much larger scope, since its spectrum is too broad for the scale of this section. Therefore, in the interest of focus, this section will critically analyse the evolution, endurance and existence tactics of two of the major traditional theatrical performances from India, namely kutiyattam and *kathakali*.

Performances, for the people in India, form a fundamental part of their cultural, religious and social lives. Some are performed during religious festivals or on social occasions, while others now exert a status independent of social or religious practices. Originating from the south Indian state of Kerala, kutiyattam and kathakali have their own individual histories in terms of their survival in twenty-first-century India. Kathakali has always been a highly popular theatre, due particularly to the spectacular concoction of music, dance, costumes and rhythm (something which drew me to kathakali from the age of 3; my earliest childhood memories contain vivid impressions of kathakali). It was never a temple theatre, was usually performed outside the temple walls and was never attached to any particular caste rites. Its wider audience reach, along with royal patronage and the active support of the high-caste landlords, through extending financial aid to maintain kathakali training centres (*kalari*) and companies, has ensured its continued existence since the 1600s. However, what really influenced the sustenance of this performance was its institutionalization under the initiative of Kerala Kalamandalam, the internationally reputed performance training centre in Kerala in 1930, which also saved kathakali from the danger of disappearance owing to the waning of royal patronage in the 1900s. The brand name of Kalamandalam assured quality and uniformity in training, as well as career openings for its disciples. Paradoxically, the extreme popularity of kathakali has been considered as one of the major factors behind the decline of kutiyattam from the 1950s through to the 1990s.

In *Indian Theatre: Traditions and Performance*, Farley Richmond states this:

> *Kutiyattam* appeals to the taste of intellectuals and rarely to those of the untutored . . . with the declining fortunes of the Kerala temples in the recent years, patronage has waned. Performances are rarely commissioned. . . How long *kutiyattam* will withstand the severe pressures to make more radical changes in its formal style of presentation, or even if it will survive to the end of the century, is uncertain.
>
> (1993: 88)

The concerns raised by Richmond in the above passage is completely justified considering the number of kutiyattam performers in in the 1980s and 90s, which amounted to a modest twenty or fewer. The fate of kutiyattam would have been entirely different without its institutionalization in 1965 under Kalamandalam and internationalization, following the UNESCO proclamation in 2001, which recognized it as the 'oral and intangible heritage of humanity'. The post-UNESCO phase of kutiyattam is highly productive, one that ensures hopes for its survival.

What brought kutiyattam so close to extinction from the 1960s through to the 1990s? Does it share the same history of kathakali's waning royal patronage? Kutiyattam is a 2,000-year-old temple theatre form, performed exclusively by higher-caste *chakyar* (actors) and *nambyar* (men are percussionists and women – *nangyar* – actresses) communities (see Richmond *et al.* 1993; Madhavan 2010), with an unbroken record of performance history since the ninth century at the very least (Heike Moser traces the actress in kutiyattam to as early as 898; Moser 2011). The performance was principally understood and appreciated by high-class Brahmins inside the temple structure[1] and the audience were required to have substantial knowledge of Sanskrit and the ability to follow the gestural communication patterns. Its unique performance structure[2] also added to the complexity of the theatre. Such social inaccessibility, combined with the intellectual and aesthetic demands exerted on the audience, added to the exclusivity of the performance. Additionally, kutiyattam was not as 'colourful' and flamboyant as kathakali. Lack of performances and waning temple patronage equally contributed to its decline; members of the actor and percussion families increasingly started leaving their family trade in search of better economic prospects and students outside the castes were not permitted to take up the lessons. The disintegration of feudal economic support in the independent democratic India nearly doomed kutiyattam. It is in this context that institutionalization and internationalization become significant in the history of contemporary kutiyattam.

It is also worth enquiring whether Kalamandalam was effective in reversing the decline of kutiyattam in the 1980s and 90s. Interestingly, the existing studies on kutiyattam do not enquire into and analyse the success/failure of institutionalization in saving kutiyattam in the 1970s through to the 1990s, a worry reflected in Richmond's writing. Kalamandalam, in the 1980s and 90s, failed to recruit talented students capable of carrying the institutional name. According to Margi Sathi, educated in Kalamandalam in the 1980s and a leading exponent of kutiyattam, students turned away from taking up its studies largely for economic reasons (Sathi: 2014). A kutiyattam performance involving five or six artists was often paid only a fraction of what a *bharatanatyam* dance performer or a kathakali performer was paid. About fifteen years ago, I was invited to perform a kutiyattam piece for a fee of mere Rs. 1500 (equivalent to £16), which hardly met the basic expenses involved in a kutiyattam performance. Paradoxically, an experienced and senior kutiyattam performer at that time also struggled to earn a fee far higher than Rs. 1500. Sathi recollects having to turn down several performance venues due to the lack of respectable pay during the late 1990s and early 2000s (Sathi: 2014). In comparison, during the same time period, a bharatanatyam performance by a senior dancer was easily paid between Rs. 50,000 and 60,000 for a single performance. As a business venture, a kutiyattam school did not present a healthy financial future for a new student, and this was one of the main reasons why Kalamandalam, despite being the only institution open to members of all castes, failed to reverse the decline of kutiyattam.

In many ways, kutiyattam and kathakali took divergent trajectories in reaching the space that they currently occupy in the cultural sphere of Indian performances. But I argue that three major distinctive aspects which designed and defined the success and 'fate' of these two performances are: (a) institutionalization, (b) internationalization and (c) the emergence of female roles and actresses.

Institutionalization

Thirty-five years after it opened in 1930, Kalamandalam opened a kutiyattam department in 1965 and admitted, for the first time, non-*chakyar/nambyar* students into its course, in the face of firm opposition from the caste performers. This was the most significant development in the history of kutiyattam, with far-reaching impacts. Primarily, it opened the gates for members outside the traditional actor/percussionist families to undertake kutiyattam tutelage. Three out of four students at Kalamandalam in 1965 were non-chakyar/nambyar, a trend that continues even today.

Although kutiyattam was primarily a temple theatre form, restricted to the performance and enjoyment of higher-caste members of the Kerala social strata, the efforts of master teacher Mani Madhava Chakyar (1899–1990), who started performing outside temples in the 1940s, deserves mention (Poulose 2005: 14). Although these performances amounted to not even a handful in number, they opened up the path for future secular stages for a strictly conventional theatre. In the twenty-first century, kutiyattam is performed mostly by non-chakyar/nambyar performers and the caste exclusivity of this theatre is no longer a barrier to its public reach and secular outlook. Under the leadership of Guru Painkulam Rama Chakyar (1910–80), the first department head of kutiyattam, Kalamandalam also introduced major changes to the kutiyattam pedagogy and performance practice through the systematization of actor training, restructuring of the performance and remodelling of the costumes. Systematization of the pedagogy to suit the requirements of an institutional syllabus was a key contribution of Rama Chakyar to the training method of kutiyattam. Rama Chakyar also revised several long kutiyattam plays to four- or five-hour performances, suitable for modern audiences, without sacrificing the quality and the complexity of its acting style (Poulose 2005: 35; Namboothiri 2005: 44). For instance, the comical Sanskrit play critiquing Buddhist doctrines, *Bhagavadajjukam* (The Saint and the Courtesan), written by Bodhayana in the seventh century CE, was performed in kutiyattam style over 35 days. Rama Chakyar edited the elaborate performance text (*attaprakaram*) to produce a 5-hour staging of the same play. Such editing by Rama Chakyar did not sacrifice either the comic nature of the play or the quality of its acting.

According to Sivan Namboothiri, a senior kutiyattam performer, Chakyar collaborated with the master costume maker Govinda Warrier and thoroughly remodelled the costumes to increase their aesthetic appeal (2005: 44). The headgear of the female characters, for example, was remodelled in its current shape and the sleeve length of the male costume was increased to cover the entire arm. Most crucially, Rama Chakyar also systematized the actor training pattern, especially the facial acting of kutiyattam, during his time at Kalamandalam. The *navarasa* training, the elaborate facial expression of the nine rasa (love, valour, melancholy, mockery, wonder, fearful, odious, terrible, peacefulness), was not a training element before its introduction by Rama Chakyar into kutiyattam actor training. All these supplemented the aesthetic appeal of kutiyattam on modern stages. It was these key changes to kutiyattam that prepared it to survive against the odds in twentieth-century India.

On the other hand, the major contribution of Kalamandalam to twentieth-century kathakali is a deeper understanding of characterization that was introduced by the kathakali master Pattikkanthodi Ramunni Menon. His in-depth understanding of *Natyasastra* and his training with scholars of the Kodungallur royal family of Kerala contributed to the refinement of characterization that we see in kathakali today.[3] According to M. P. Sankaran Namboothiri, what we see today as 'Kalamandalam style' was introduced and developed by Ramunni Menon in the 1930s (Namboothiri 2014). The complex, yet deliciously subtle histrionics of kathakali, developed by Ramunni Menon at Kalamandalam, is the fundamental reason for its popular appeal and wider reach in contemporary India. Menon reconsidered the character structures of protagonists in fourteen kathakali plays and elaborately recorded his innovations. More importantly, his newly developed approach to characterization was transferred through generations of popular kathakali maestros and Menon's students such as Keezhpadam Kumaran Nair, Vazhenkada Kunju Nair and Kalamandalam Krishnan Nair (Namboothirippad and Namboothiri 2013: 104–16). In effect, what we see in kathakali today in terms of character exploration is the legacy of Ramunni Menon. Zarrilli writes that 'Menon's interpretation exemplifies the increasing focus in *kathakali* on virtuosic elaboration of the complexities of the "internal" state of being of its major characters' (2000: 28). Institutional restructuring of kathakali performance also introduced the editing of all-night performances into shorter three-hour pieces so that they are performed in an evening programme between 6:30 and 9:30. Also initiated during this time were such practices as writing, devising and staging new plays, restaging and restoring the non-performed 'original' scenes of the plays, and expanding existing scenes to suit the connoisseur audience (ibid. 2000: 9). The result of these changes was the unprecedented popularity of kathakali and the celebrity status of kathakali performers such as Kalamandalam Krishnan Nair, Kalamandalam Ramankutti Nair, Kalamandalam Gopi and Kottakkal Sivaraman.

Internationalization

Kathakali and kutiyattam have attracted international scholars and been staged on several non-Indian stages for the last five decades at the very least. These two theatres are among the most internationally travelled traditional theatres from India. In 1980, Painkulam Rama Chakyar and his students performed kutiyattam at its first international venue in France under the auspices of the Mandapa Centre in Paris (in 1967, Mandapa Centre took kathakali to Paris). However, the key event, which raised the international profile of kutiyattam, was the 2001 UNESCO declaration of kutiyattam as the 'Oral and Intangible Heritage of Humanity'.

Margi School, a centre for kathakali and kutiyattam, submitted the proposal to UNESCO, collaborating with leading performers and kutiyattam schools, and the venture was a bold initiative to bring more international support to kutiyattam and save this dying theatre. Consequently, new kutiyattam schools were established and the existing ones received monetary grants to expand their pedagogical activities. The UNESCO declaration opened a series of funding avenues, both national and international, including a funding scheme set up by the Indian government in 2008 to protect and propagate kutiyattam. Such efforts supported the revival of old performance texts preserved, or sometimes discarded, by the chakyar and nambyar families and encouraged young students to study kutiyattam. Margi now extends weekend classes to school children and provides a small stipend to support their travel costs. Public interest in kutiyattam has subsequently increased in recent years and there are frequent kutiyattam performances in and out of Kerala.

As a direct impact of international associations, some intercultural experiments have taken place in kathakali and marginally in kutiyattam. Kathakali *King Lear*, conceived by the French choreographer Annette LeDay and the Australian playwright/director David McRuvie, first performed in 1989 by leading kathakali maestros such as Kumaran Nair, Padmanabhan Nair and Kalamandalam Gopi, is a landmark in the history of contemporary kathakali (see Daugherty 2005; Zarrilli 2000). Smaller in scale, kutiyattam *Macbeth* was adapted and performed as a single-act play by Margi Madhu, using the acting method of *nirvahanam*,[4] a single person performing a story in retrospect. In this mono-act performance, Madhu enacts the recollections of Macbeth and the events leading up to his coronation as king, including the killing of Duncan and the death of Lady Macbeth. As Madhu himself admits, this project was in response to the questions posed to him with regard to the feasibility of performing a western play in kutiyattam style (Madhu 2012).

Emergence of female roles and actresses

Another significant development in the history of contemporary kutiyattam and kathakali is the increasing importance placed on enhancing female roles and creatively empowering actresses to experiment within these forms. In this section, I will be looking at the contributions of Kottakkal Sivaraman, a highly innovative female impersonator in kathakali, and kutiyattam actress Margi Sathi.

Kottakkal Sivaraman (1936–2010) represents a turning point in the history of female characters on kathakali stages. Traditionally, kathakali has always been men's theatre – men performing, singing, teaching and undertaking all backstage activities. The patriarchal characteristic of kathakali is well reflected in the nature and representation of female characters on stage. Only a handful of female characters are taught to students and most of them lack depth as a character. Damayanthi, the heroine of the kathakali play *Nalacharitham* (Story of Nala), rich in characterization and challenging to any actor, is never taught in the studio. It is in this context that Sivaraman's contributions to kathakali become highly significant. Sivaraman gave 'life' to female characters on stage, adding multi-tonality to the female characters in katha-kali plays. His contributions are so significant that the history of the female characters in kathakali can easily be divided into two – before and after Sivaraman. As the disciple of Vazhenkada Kunju Nair, who trained with Ramunni Menon, Sivaraman applied Menon's methods of character analysis, transferred through Kunju Nair, to the female characters of kathakali. The effect of this is most visible in Sivaraman's characterization of Damayanthi, who becomes a strategic, strong and intelligent queen in his hands. Before Sivaraman, the character lacked depth and purpose, even though the playwright of *Nalacharitham* created a strong female character in Damayanthi. According to connoisseurs, Sivaraman has famously re-authored *Nalacharitham* as

Damayanthi-charitham (Story of Damayanthi). Furthermore, Sivaraman's artistic interference into the devising of female characters and their characterization is aesthetically and conceptually comparable to Ramunni Menon's approach to and experiments with characterization in kathakali in the 1930s. In a personal conversation in 2001, he mentioned that female characters were serving only a decorative purpose on stage and no serious attention was paid either to female characterization or emotive training in performing female roles on stage. Sivaraman's Damayanthi was a major shift in the treatment of female roles in kathakali. Unfortunately, Sivaraman did not receive the international recognition bestowed on Mei Lanfang for his female impersonation in *jingju* (Beijing opera), although he is highly popular among kathakali connoisseurs in India.

There had been attempts by a handful of women to perform women's roles in kathakali since the 1960s. Chavara Parukkutti, a pioneering female kathakali performer, has successfully replaced men in performing female roles for the past four decades. An all-female kathakali troupe, Thrippunithura Kathakali Kendram (Thrippunithura Kathakali Centre) at Kerala, has now been regularly performing both female and male roles in kathakali since 1975 and it is now increasingly popular in and outside Kerala.

Kutiyattam, unlike many other Asian theatre forms, allows the participation of both female and male performers. However, female presence on stage has been strictly limited for the past several centuries. There was a separate acting manual for female performers telling the stories of the Hindu God Krishna, which was performed over 41 nights of performance. This performance is known as *nangyarkuthu*,[5] and the acting manual for nangyarkuthu is thought to have been written about a thousand years ago by King Kulasekhara. This acting manual was published in 1984 and it paved way for the revival of nangyarkuthu. Bridging the gap of 1,000 years, in 1998 Margi Sathi wrote *Sreerama Charitam Nangyaramma Kuthu* (Rama's Story Nangyarkuthu), which was the first female text in the history of kutiyattam and nangyarkuthu. Sathi's pioneering text inaugurated a series of new nangyarkuthu productions in Kerala, championing the increasing significance of, and the need to acknowledge, the female voice in a largely male-dominated kutiyattam theatre. Kutiyattam has a large repertory of Rama plays, all focusing on the male characters of *Ramayana*, but Sita is often presented as a lighted lamp, with her lines rendered by the female percussionist on the stage. A strong female presence is hardly seen in most of the Rama plays in kutiyattam, perhaps with the exception of the lustful demoness Surpanakha whose breasts and nose are mutilated as a punishment for expressing her passion. Sathi's text, on the contrary, provides ample opportunities for performing Sita, the heroine of the epic *Ramayana*, on stage and the attempt is well received by the kutiyattam actors and the audience.

To conclude, I would argue that traditional theatre in India has a bright future, one that will flourish in changing times by accommodating the changing demands of contemporary society. Kathakali and kutiyattam have taken an ambitious path of aesthetic and cultural evolution over the past 50 years, thanks to national and international funding grants as well as institutionalization, which brought new vigour and energy to the theatre forms. Their survival in contemporary India is ensured by the Indian and international cultural and bureaucratic agencies as well as the continuing viewership of various audiences in secular settings.

II. Japan, by Jonah Salz

Japanese traditional theatre maintained the vigour of its main classical theatre forms – noh, kyogen, kabuki and bunraku – via accommodation to changing audience tastes, state support, technological innovation and actor (and spectator) education. Here I would like to sketch the major approaches, ranging from the conservative transferring of old wine into new bottles (familiar plots newly interpreted) to new brews, blends and brands (revivals, new text generation, inter-genre collaborations, international experiments, and strategies for accessibility).

Traditional forms had always been syncretic; the abrupt change to the modern era necessitated by foreign pressure and domestic rebellion resulted not in radical transformation but in adding yet another layer to the palimpsest of traditional forms. The Meiji Restoration of 1868 totally upended the theatrical establishment. Instantly, crucial aspects of their entire repertoire were made obsolete. Confucian ideology and Buddhist philosophy were officially disdained, as feudal hierarchies were abandoned for the all-important imperial mission of building a modern state. Noh and kyogen actors found themselves immediately impoverished, without samurai status or patronage; bunraku and kabuki playwrights discovered that the worlds they depicted were now passé. But then the genres' paths diverged, as noh haltingly regained its position among the new elites of society, kyogen nurtured its popular appeal and bunraku stumbled along, while kabuki exploded in size and popularity, released from restrictions on both form and content.

Noh repositions itself as an elite hobby

The art of noh had been maintained over five centuries by institutions for preservation and patronage that suddenly lost all authority and wealth. Actors in regional cities, where part-time teaching of commoners or nobility had continued as a profession throughout the Edo period, were less affected. These secondary branches helped revive noh and kyogen in Edo (Tokyo).

Noh returned to prominence through sponsorship by those returning from study missions to America and Europe, where they had investigated western institutions for Japan's modern state to emulate. Inevitably, their European and American hosts had invited them to the theatre or the opera, enjoying elegant entertainments as emblems of modern Western civilizations. These returning diplomats determined to provide a similar cultural experience for their own rising elite. Along with the Rokumeikan (Deer-cry Pavilion), a western-style building hosting dance receptions, and department stores, the theatre was encouraged as an instrument for the inculcation of modern ideas in contemporary society. Progressive politicians began tinkering with kabuki but soon discovered that its popular anti-authoritarianism and complicated traditions could never be properly tamed, so they turned to noh as a proper representative of national values and beauty. Nōgaku, a newly coined term that included both noh and kyogen, replacing the less dignified *sarugaku* noh (monkey music), aligned itself to the new political powers. Eventually noh became a pastime of the middle classes, repositioned from a ceremonial art to a precious hobby with social, spiritual and physical benefits. Moreover, with the discovery of Zeami's writings and the establishment of a noh theatre journal from 1910, nōgaku was given newfound respect by scholars of poetry, literature and comparative theatre.

Postwar renaissance: restoration, adaptation, collaboration

One might have expected noh's anachronistic, slow and feudal forms to have faded away after Japan's disastrous loss and occupation after the Second World War. Remarkably, along with Japan's phoenix-like economic revival, noh-kyogen experienced a late twentieth-century revival, deemed its Golden Age.

Noh's renaissance was due to both conservative and experimental currents. Even while reverently retaining the transmitted traditions, nōgaku performers experimented at the edges of these traditions. They revived extant plays, resuscitating those that might only exist as fragments of texts or summaries. Performing rare variants was another way of gaining attention and expanding the scope of interpretation. In the postwar years, kyogen was esteemed for its forceful, anti-authoritarian spirit. Kyogen actors produced all-kyogen recitals, taught at culture centres, universities and acting academies, and experimented with other genres, drawing the attention of modern theatre performers and gaining new cross-over fans.

Meanwhile, attempts were made to restore nōgaku as popular theatre. Takechi Tetsuji, son of a rich industrialist, sought to revive medieval Japanese festive creativity through inter-genre collaborations. Three pairs of brothers – Kanze Hisao and Hideo, Nomura Mannojō and Mansaku, Shigeyama Sensaku and Sennojō – collaborated with Takechi, then continued his approach to gaining a better understanding of noh and kyogen's contemporary appeal in productions of new and revived plays, adaptations of folktales, W. B. Yeats' *At the Hawk's Well* (*Takahime*, The Hawk Princess) and Samuel Beckett. Outdoor, torchlit noh performances aimed to restore noh-kyogen's mystery and popular appeal; over a hundred were performed annually in their 1990s heyday.

Today, a handful of individual performers perform the lion's share of *shinsaku noh* (new noh) and collaborative experiments. Umewaka Genso has performed noh adaptations of the ballet *Giselle*, *Shiranui* (Phosphorescence), concerning the chemical pollution causing Minamata disease, and an adaptation of the popular manga *Garasu no kamen* (Glass Mask). Matsui Akira has toured widely teaching noh and performing collaborative experiments, appearing in Eugenio Barba's multicultural *Ur-Hamlet*, Chen Shi-zheng's tri-national *Forgiveness* and in new and English-language noh as well as Greek, Shakespeare, Yeats and Beckett adaptations. Kyogen actor Nomura Mansai is active as an actor in films and television, director and producer, reinterpreting the Japanese writer Akutagawa Ryūnosuke and Shakespeare with kyogen techniques.

Although Mishima Yukio's 1950s series of *kindai nōgaku* (modern noh) were written for the Bungaku-za modern theatre company, other playwrights wrote for noh's particular structure and mise-en-scène. Physician Tada Tomio wrote a series of plays on contemporary themes: the ethics of organ transplantation, the tragedy of nuclear war and the cruel fate of Korean comfort women. Umehara Takeshi followed his successful super-kabuki with 'super-kyogen' concerning cloning, ecological disaster and nuclear bombs. Whether such new works gain traction in the regular repertoire remains doubtful; only a few, such as noh-style adaptations of Yeats' *At the Hawk's Well* (*Taka no ii*; *Takahime*) and Cludel's *Woman and Shadow*, are regularly revived.

Bunraku

With only a single bunraku troupe, the dolls and properties owned by the government and performers essentially civil servants, bunraku is inevitably the most conservative of classical traditions.

Even before the Meiji Restoration, bunraku had become a lesser art form, yet continued producing at a diminishing number of specialist theatres, competing against the resurgent kabuki as well as new forms of entertainment, including the cinema and variety shows. By 1913 the Bunraku-za was the only troupe in existence. However, in 1909, the title of the Osaka theatre passed from the Uemura family who had promoted the puppet theatre for three generations to the Shōchiku entertainment corporation, which also owned contracts for kabuki actors and most theatres in the country. They re-established postwar bunraku at Osaka's Yotsubashi Bunraku-za in 1946, but as spectator interest declined, and fewer youth chose to enter the arduous training, the future was precarious. The troupe split when a relatively younger group formed the Mitsuwakai in 1946 to free itself from Shōchiku's feudalistic control; those who remained were known as Chinamikai.

Shōchiku continued to encourage young audiences by adapting kabuki dance-plays such as *Musume Dōjōji* (Dōjōji Maiden), as well as folk stories and newly written plays such as those by novelists Tanizaki Jun'ichirō and Mishima. Even foreign works were attempted, including *Madame Butterfly* and *Hamlet* (1956), *Romance of the Three Kingdoms* and *La Traviata* (1957). Yet such measures were insufficient: performances by the Chinamikai reduced from 166 at the new theatre in 1956 to just 31 in 1962, with similar decreases in other cities, and with the rival Mitsuwakai.

In 1963, Shōchiku ceded control to the Bunraku Association, comprised of a merged single troupe, supported by the Osaka prefecture and city, and the public broadcaster NHK. In 1966, National Theatre in Tokyo was built for both kabuki and bunraku sponsorship and training programmes; The National Bunraku Theatre in Osaka was built in 1984. It features an exhibitions hall, a small hall for showing archival films, and a research library. In 1990, bunraku was declared a UNESCO Intangible Cultural Asset. However, the puppet theatre's subsidized stability masks an economic fragility that is still being tested.

Kabuki adapts

Kabuki thrived as the people's entertainment. Kabuki had always been at the forefront of adapting new machinery and spectacle. Western imports such as the Christian cross, telescope, pocket watch and steam engine quickly made their way onto the kabuki stage. With the Meiji Restoration and dissolution of the shogunate, the feudal system that had existed for nearly three hundred years was destroyed, symbolized by the banning of samurai topknots and public display of swords. Suddenly kabuki's contemporary settings for everyday plays, much less its historic plays, had irrevocably become period pieces. Yet at the same time, restrictions on theatre construction, stories and costuming were removed, as were legal distinctions between large and small theatres. Kabuki almost instantly became more popular and widespread.

Even while producing familiar classics, new kabuki approaches were attempted. Onōe Kikugoro V briefly experimented with *zangirimono*, set in Meiji with the close-cropped hair of contemporary hairstyles, and featuring modern elements such as trains, photographs and streetlamps. Answering calls for the elimination of the nonsensical fantasies of many plots were *katsureki*, period plays featuring more realistic acting and staging verisimilitude, championed by Ichikawa Danjurō IX. Yet both these types were soon abandoned when they proved unpopular. Without protection by the shogunate, formerly sacrosanct noh plays were kabukified. These *matsubamemono* (pine-tree backdrop) plays not only borrowed the plots, as in previous adaptations, but used a specially raised dance floor, side-curtain and noh instrumentation (with shamisen added). Tsubouchi Shōyō, Shakespeare translator and playwright, advocated a more literary approach, and pioneered plays still set in the Edo period but featuring greater psychological realism. These were often based on novels written or adapted by journalists from outside the kabuki world, such as Okamoto Kidō. These *shin-kabuki* (neo-kabuki), which used lighting for atmospheric effect and less *keren* spectacle, eventually became a substantial portion of the current repertoire.

For a time it was not certain whether kabuki would remain a vibrant traditional genre or blend into the eclectic modern theatre scene. As the only professional actors of the time, kabuki actors were enlisted in Japan's budding *shingeki* (new theatre) movement from the 1910s, to interpret both Japanese plays and translated western dialogue in plays by Ibsen and Gorky. The socialist influence that swept Japanese letters in the 1920s critiqued the inherent feudal nature of kabuki's plots, caste-like hierarchy of family monopolies on acting styles and roles, and lack of gender equality. The egalitarian Zenshin-za theatre troupe championed shin-kabuki, such as plays by Mayama Seika, which attempted to depict the social conditions and psychological undergirding in quasi-kabuki style. They adjusted to both the nationalist demands of the 1930s and the anti-communist purges of the 1950s.

Shooting stars and guiding lights

Actors and managers from within kabuki have always been at the forefront of attempting vanguard experiments. Late twentieth-century kabuki has been blessed with a dynamic group of leading actors who have pioneered personal projects to gain massive new followings for kabuki, still profitable as commercial entertainment.

Kabuki supported the Second World War (as it had previous wars) with patriotic new plays and 'comfort performances' for the troops. However, when American occupation censors (GHQ) threatened the traditional plots concerning loyalty, vengeance and suicide, Shōchiku successfully argued that kabuki was classical entertainment for the masses, so continued the classics along with new adaptations while repositioning itself once again as 'classical theatre'. In the postwar years, Danjurō XII emulated early modern kabuki experiments pioneered by Kikugorō V and Danjurō IX, who made novel interpretations of classic plays, not merely repeating inherited *kata* of famous previous performers. He has revived plays that had fallen out of the repertoire such as *Kagekiyo*, collaborating with a team of scholars to revive a mise-en-scène similar to that in the seventeenth century. Nakamura Kanzaburō's Heisei-za re-popularized kabuki by appealing to the nostalgic past, holding performances at temporary, outdoor stages or centuries-old regional theatres to re-create the festive fun of Edo townsperson's entertainment.

Sakata Tōjūrō (1931–) has long carried the flag for *kamigata* (Kyoto/Osaka) kabuki tradition, starring in 'Takechi kabuki', a series of productions from 1953 to 1968 that brought a new dynamism and realism to authentic texts. His passionate interpretation of the courtesan Ohatsu in *Love Suicides at Sonezaki*, performed over 1300 times, displayed *kamigata* kabuki's special warm humanism and opportunities for individual acting choices, as opposed to the fixed, stylized kata of Edo-style kabuki. Chikamatsu-za was founded to reinterpret the great playwright in faithful productions. Ichikawa Ennosuke employs stage technology to enhance psychologically realist portraits of conflicted heroes. Revivals of dozens of Edo-period plays required substantial cutting, rewriting, and splicing scenes for shows along with flashy 'super-kabuki' that emphasize 'speed, spectacle, and story'. They borrow from old *keren* devices and quick changes of costume (Ichikawa Ennosuke has 'flown' through the audience over five thousand times), but also employ modern technology such as pre-recorded music, atmospheric lighting, film projection and dry-ice fog.

International ventures and access strategies

Tours overseas provided important opportunities for traditional actors to interact with artists and students, to have their art taken seriously as contemporary performance by international critics and theatre professionals (Figure 22.1). Many tours have proved milestones for spreading Japanese culture, and reinvigorating the traditions at home. A troupe led by Ichikawa Sadanji II visited Moscow and St Petersburg in 1928 to great acclaim, even influencing Sergei Eisenstein's film theories. Kabuki was produced on Broadway in the 1950s, and rising star Ennosuke toured Broadway in the 1970s. Onnagata Bandō Tamasaburō became a hot ticket at the Metropolitan Opera in 1985, a landmark for kabuki's recognition as aesthetically refined stage spectacle on a grand scale. According to *Variety* magazine, kabuki's commercial showmanship was on display amid the desert pyramids and fountains, among the revues and postmodern circuses of Las Vegas

Figure 22.1 Ichikawa Somegorō VII starred in *Koi-Tsukami* (Fight with a Carp), a 30-minute kabuki play featuring projected 3D animations at the Bellagio Casino, Las Vegas in August 2015. This is part of a series of forthcoming 'Kabuki spectacles' Shōchiku is planning to produce. The portable kabuki stage was set inside the lake at the casino, with traditional scenery shifted with vertical back-panels, and projected animations in the mists of the dancing fountains.
(Courtesy of Shōchiku)

in the summer of 2015. Bunraku's month-long tour to the U.S. west coast in 1962 healed a rift between rival troupes, just prior to their amalgamation under the Bunraku Association.

Since Meiji, nōgaku has sought to be recognized as a world-class art. In addition to performing regularly, Umewaka Minoru taught many illustrious amateurs, including the first western disciples of the art, Edward Morse and Ernest Fenollosa. The latter's notes were introduced to the west by Ezra Pound in the influential *Noh: or Accomplishment* (1916). Noh has been received as emblematic of Japanese high culture, with frequent tours since 1954, even giving outdoor, torchlit performances at New York's Central Park in 1995. Noh troupes now tour frequently overseas. Kyogen made its inaugural overseas tour with Nomura Manzō in 1963 on a long national tour that included teaching workshops. Regular overseas performances in Europe and the United States by the Nomura, Shigeyama and Izumi families, sometimes with adaptations of Shakespeare and Beckett, have helped kyogen gain international recognition as a powerful form of actorly expression, independent from noh.

Yet critics, performers, and producers agree that the future for traditional forms other than kabuki is not bright. Distance between performer and spectator has grown physically and psychologically. Theatre structures have become larger and stages wider, increasing spectator/actor separation by lighting and raked seating. Performances have become precious, indoor entertainments brilliantly lit, without shadows, acoustically perfect. Classical plots depending on archaic notions of beauty and feudal ideology, and obscure everyday customs have grown further removed from life in rapidly changing modern Japan. Audiences have become increasingly older, with fewer students supporting the necessary pyramid of amateur disciples and connoisseur spectators.

The four classical genres have attempted various strategies for accessibility as art and entertainment. Guidebooks with concise summaries, photographs and, later, manga cartoons have been published. Copious programme notes and summaries, pre-show workshops and lectures, and titles – projected on LED-light panels on the backs of seats (noh-kyogen), above the stage (bunraku) or on hand-held devices (kabuki) – have been supplemented by rentable earphone guides, sometimes also in English. Contemporary playwrights have been commissioned – philosopher Umehara Takeshi for noh and kyogen; director-playwright Noda Hideki for kabuki; light-comedy playwright Mitani Kōki for bunraku – yet these are often one-time-only causes célèbres with little effect on either traditional or modern theatres.

If spectators cannot be lured to traditional stages, actors will make 'deliveries'. Performers tour regional civic centres and commercial theatres, performing bowdlerized forms at schools nationwide. Websites, both official and fan-managed, include schedules, summaries of plays, interviews, photos, news items and video clips. Some argue that such accessibility for forms that were *never* easily understood distracts spectators from direct contemplation of the live, unmediated performance.

While some view these as healthy outreach activities by long-sheltered genres, others see them as the desperate attempt to maintain relevance in an entertainment industry that is hyperactive, digitized and globalized. Such efforts at accessibility may be contrary to the very aspect that might sustain Japanese traditional arts as creative, popular and influential forms: their very anachronism. By developing an empathic understanding of the aesthetics, social conditions and belief systems depicted in traditional forms' classical repertoire, spectators can experience the spirit of ritual enlightenment or festive joy found in few other places in modern Japan.

III. China, by Min Tian

At the turn of the twentieth century, with the introduction of Western culture into China, Chinese *xiqu* (traditional Chinese theatre) was influenced by the ideas of western theatre. The necessity of political and economic reform in the late Qing dynasty brought about a movement of cultural reform in China, which culminated in the 1919 May Fourth Movement. As traditional Chinese culture was reassessed from the perspective of Western culture, Chinese xiqu was re-evaluated according to the paradigms of Western realistic theatre. Thus some of the most radical intellectuals of the time such as Chen Duxiu (1879–1942), Hu Shi (1891–1962) and Fu Sinian (1896–1950) either called for a total reform of Chinese xiqu from the perspective of Western realistic theatre or simply decided that it should be eradicated altogether. Even some of the noted xiqu practitioners spoke against Chinese xiqu. For instance, Ouyang Yuqian (1889–1962), who began his career in the new theatre, argued against the old practices of xiqu. Qi Rushan (1875–1962), who travelled to Europe and studied European theatre and later became an adviser to the famous *jingju* (Beijing opera) actor Mei Lanfang (1894–1961), advocated reform in Chinese xiqu on the basis of Western theatre. Qi recalled that in his lectures he spoke against the simplicity of Chinese xiqu and in favour of Western realistic costume, scenery, lighting and makeup. Qi's lectures left a deep impression on some leading xiqu performers such as Tan Xinpei (1847–1917) and Mei Lanfang. Tan, then the most accomplished and renowned jingju actor who specialized in *laosheng* (old man), acknowledged that he felt ashamed of Chinese xiqu in contrast to Western theatre as introduced by Qi Rushan. Thus, during the first decade of the twentieth century, the dominance of the traditional theatre was challenged by ideas of Western realistic theatre as understood by those radical Chinese intellectuals.

In 1908, Shanghai saw the establishment of the New Stage (Xin Wutai) – the first theatre in China with a proscenium arch, a revolving stage, and new light and scenery equipment. The plays staged at the New Stage were mostly so-called *gailiang xinxi* (reformed new plays) and *shizhuang xinxi* (new plays in modern costumes). They were adaptations of Chinese and foreign histories, stories and plays, and were staged either in imitation of Western realism or in a radically altered performance style of Chinese xiqu. The new style significantly reduced singing in the service of lifelike speech and melodramatic action, and resorted to realistic scenery and lighting devices. Under the influence of these new trends, jingju actors such as Mei Lanfang and Ouyang Yuqian competed to perform in gailiang xinxi or shizhuang xinxi. In the 1920s and 1930s, other jingju actors such as Cheng Yanqiu (1904–58), Shang Xiaoyun (1900–76) and Xun Huisheng (1900–68) who, together with Mei Lanfang, were hailed as four leading *nandan* (man playing a woman's role), made great efforts to experiment with realism in their performances, incorporating quasi-realistic scenery and realistic-psychological acting techniques. Meanwhile, during those years, one of the major developments in the Chinese theatre was the phenomenal rise and flourishing of *haipai jingju* (Beijing opera in Shanghai style), which exerted a major impact and lasting influence on the modern development of jingju. Originating in Shanghai and quickly spreading to Beijing and Tianjin, two strongholds of traditional jingju, haipai jingju drew on new social and cultural ideas, dramatized sensational contemporary and historical events, and relied on powerful visual and illusionistic effects from scenic spectacles and realistic as well as melodramatic acting. Because of its unconventional or sometimes outright anti-traditional approaches, haipai jingju was vilified and attacked by traditionalists for its disregard of the rules of traditional jingju and for its violent infringement of the traditional integrity of Chinese xiqu, but was praised by reformers for its daring innovations, which were deemed necessary to revitalize the decadent tradition of jingju. Zhou Xinfang (1895–1975), who incorporated and experimented with realistic scenery and acting techniques from *huaju* (spoken drama) and American films, was one of haipai's most outstanding and accomplished proponents and practitioners.

The first reaction against the radical assault on Chinese xiqu by intellectuals of the May Fourth Movement came from the National Theatre Movement (Guoju Yundong), launched in the second half of the 1920s by a group of writers, critics and theatre educators led by Yu Shangyuan (1897–1970), one of the most prominent theorists and practitioners of modern Chinese theatre, who committed themselves to the cause of creating a new Chinese national theatre. Here it should be noted that, in contrast to the idea of a national theatre as proposed primarily by Qi Rushan, this nationalist-oriented theatre movement did not represent a reassertion of the dominance of Chinese xiqu, nor a total rejection of Western realism, but rather a negotiation between these two theatrical forces for a genuine alternative. However, in strong opposition to the radical reformers, the proponents of the National Theatre Movement argued that, in contrast to realism, Chinese xiqu was a pure art – conventionalized, presentational and symbolic, and thereby objected to the adoption of the western-style proscenium stage and realistic scenery because of their incompatibility with the presentational nature of Chinese xiqu.

In spite of its ambitious goal, the dream of the National Theatre Movement never materialized. New efforts to elevate jingju as China's national theatre in the 1930s, however, would have a major impact on the destiny of jingju and Chinese xiqu as a whole. Qi Rushan, who had reversed his early stance against Chinese xiqu and was then serving as a literary adviser to Mei Lanfang, became one of the most vocal and dedicated proponents of jingju as China's national theatre. He advocated and attempted a systematic and 'scientific' study of jingju and, in particular, Mei Lanfang's art. On the strength of Mei Lanfang's popularity on China's national stage and the success of his international tours of Japan and the United States, Qi Rushan, with the support of Mei Lanfang and some other jingju actors and conservative critics, made a forceful and persistent campaign for the establishment of jingju as China's national theatre.

The idea of elevating jingju as China's national theatre was challenged and ultimately rejected by writers and critics of the Left-Wing Theatre Movement. For these writers and critics, Chinese xiqu as the product of China's feudal society was saturated with feudal ideology and had long become too ossified to represent contemporary social life. Consequently, it must be radically reformed or simply replaced by a proletarian revolutionary theatre. During the years of Chinese national resistance against Japanese aggression and occupation, a radical reform of Chinese xiqu both in content and in form became an even greater necessity for mass education, propagation and agitation. While the content centred on contemporary or historical subjects that could reflect and respond to the needs of the national struggle against the Japanese, the form was subject to modernization and popularization in order for a mass audience to understand the content better and to be educated and inspired more effectively.

With the founding of the People's Republic of China in 1949, the new regime launched a nationwide campaign for the reform of xiqu. The politically and ideologically oriented campaign focused not only on the content of the plays but also on their forms of performance and production, and as a result, the vast majority of the plays that were perceived to be not in complete conformity with the official ideology and political needs were banned from the stage outright or suffered irrevocably from revisions that radically altered their traditional artistic integrity and identity.

During the 1950s when the Stanislavsky System was formally accepted as the orthodoxy in Chinese theatre circles, primarily thanks to the political and ideological ties between the Soviet Union and newly established communist China, it had a profound and pervasive influence on Chinese xiqu. Many xiqu performers, directors and theorists not only studied and used Stanislavsky's theory in their theoretical construction of the traditional theatre, but also applied his ideas to their performances and productions. Great efforts were made to align Chinese xiqu with Stanislavsky's 'scientific' system, either by finding in xiqu a confirmation of Stanislavsky's ideas or by reforming it from the 'scientific' perspective of Stanislavsky's system.

During the decade of the Cultural Revolution (1966–76), the Chinese theatrical scene was dominated by a number of modern and revolutionary jingju 'model plays' (yangbanxi). In sharp contrast to traditional xiqu plays, these 'modernized' and 'revolutionized' plays were based on realistic and melodramatic stories from the Chinese revolution and contemporary life and were formulated for ideological propaganda and political agitation. The staging of these plays made effective use of the conventional forms and techniques of jingju acting to theatricalize the melodramatic actions and to portray and glorify larger-than-life and consummate characters of revolutionary spirit and heroism. The political and ideological monopoly of these plays on the Chinese stage greatly popularized this radically altered form of jingju, but it also brought irrevocable losses to the tradition and artistic integrity of jingju and Chinese xiqu as a whole.

In the 1980s, under the influence of Western anti-realist avant-garde theatre, in particular its interpretations and uses of Chinese xiqu, Chinese theatre witnessed a revived interest in xiqu among Chinese theatre artists. It is of particular importance that many artists in huaju broke away from the Ibsenite naturalism and from Stanislavsky's psychological realism and purported to return to the tradition of Chinese xiqu. Vsevolod Meyerhold's idea of conventional theatre and Bertolt Brecht's idea of the 'Alienation-effect', which drew on Chinese xiqu, significantly affected the Chinese modern theatre's concept of theatre in general and, in particular, its under-standing and use of Chinese xiqu. The essence of Chinese xiqu and its core ideas such as *chengshihua* (conventionalization) and *xuni* (suppositional) were redefined from the anti-realist and anti-illusionist perspectives of Western avant-garde theatre, in particular Meyerhold's idea of conventional theatre and Brecht's idea of the 'Alienation-effect'. Heavily influenced by Brecht's and Meyerhold's ideas, the interpretations and uses of Chinese xiqu by huaju directors and playwrights such as Huang Zuolin (1906–94), Gao Xingjian (1940–), Hu Weimin (1932–89), Xu Xiaozhong (1928–), and others, were greatly instrumental in redefining the essence of Chinese xiqu. Thus the identity of Chinese xiqu was once again renewed and reinvented in its negotiations with the new ideological, political and cultural as well as theatrical realities.

While jingju remained the dominant form of Chinese xiqu, various regional theatrical forms also gained a new life in the 1980s. New efforts were made to enhance the techniques of acting, the composition of music and the method of staging; to renew and expand the repertoire; and to reform the organization and management system of theatre companies. Theatre schools and professional programmes trained new generations of actors; state-sponsored television programmes introduced different forms of xiqu to a national audience; and national theatre festivals provided opportunities for young xiqu actors to shine and gain recognition before a national audience. In contemporary China, with the rise of China's international status and of renewed Chinese nationalism, Chinese xiqu has been protected as a national treasure and has been used as valuable cultural capital to project the image of China as a newly rising political and economic power on the global stage with a time-honoured history and cultural tradition.

Internationally, in the first decades of the twentieth century, the Orientalist and Eurocentric approaches to Chinese xiqu appeared to have been reversed with the rise of the anti-realist avant-garde theatre. The Eurocentric view of Chinese xiqu was redefined and reconfigured in the productions of a number of Chinese or pseudo-Chinese plays in the first half of the twentieth century, such as *The Yellow Jacket*, *Turandot* and *The Chalk Circle*. These productions were more or less tied to the newly rising anti-realist avant-garde movement in the European and American theatre. In these productions, Chinese materials and elements of the Chinese theatre were no longer treated from the outdated neo-classical and realist perspectives but from the new aesthetic of the anti-realist avant-garde theatre.

Mei Lanfang's 1919 tour of Japan marked not only Mei's first international triumph but also the first time the world outside China saw the finest representation of Chinese xiqu by China's best artist, the newly crowned 'Great King of Actors'. Mei's stated goal to introduce and propagate Chinese theatre to an international audience was accomplished with unquestionable success. The impact of Mei's success and the influence of Chinese xiqu, however, remained confined to Japan, a country that had maintained a historical and cultural relation to China for more than two thousand years. In contrast, Mei Lanfang's 1930 tour of the United States was geographically and culturally a truly international adventure as the Chinese actor performed for the first time in the West for an ethnically and culturally diversified audience. For the first time, American audiences saw the Chinese theatre with a venerable history and tradition as performed and interpreted by its finest exponent. American theatre artists and critics received Mei Lanfang's performance of Chinese xiqu with enthusiasm and admiration. Aside from the effect of Orientalism and exoticism, the opportune conditions of contemporary American theatre made local artists and audiences more receptive to Mei's art and the conventionalized and non-realistic Chinese theatre. Pregnant with new ideas of anti-realism developed from the influence of European continental and Russian theatres, the American theatre saw the Chinese theatre as a welcome relief from the dominance of its nineteenth-century photographic realism. America's critical responses to Chinese theatre were intrinsic to America's self-examination of its theatrical conditions and to the new ideas and practices being developed on the contemporary stage.

Mei Lanfang's 1935 Soviet tour attracted a host of internationally respected theatre artists. The Soviet responses to Mei's performances were tied to the political and ideological conditions of contemporary Soviet theatre. The Soviet theatre artists, such as Meyerhold, Sergei Eisenstein and Alexander Tairov, saw Mei's art in the interests of their continuing struggles to define and defend their different and competing theories and practices as the model for the future of the Soviet theatre. Likewise, Brecht's response to Mei's performance was ideologically oriented and his critical interpretation of Chinese acting served to further validate and legitimate his theory and practice. Such intercultural interpretations and appropriations of Chinese xiqu as practised by these most influential theatre artists of the twentieth century represented an increasing impact and influence of Chinese xiqu on the international stage; they contributed to the modern renewal and reinvention of the tradition and 'modernity' of Chinese xiqu, but at the same time they also added, with new potency, to the modern erosion of xiqu's historical, cultural and artistic integrity and identity as Chinese xiqu was inevitably displaced and misinterpreted out of its historical, cultural and aesthetic contexts.

In the second half of the twentieth century, European and American theatre artists such as Jerzy Grotowsky, Eugenio Barba, Richard Schechner and Peter Sellars all demonstrated a keen interest in Chinese xiqu. Grotowsky, Barba and Schechner had extensive investigation into xiqu by directly engaging Chinese xiqu actors and artists with a view to incorporating its ideas into their theories and practices. Sellars staged his postmodern adaptation of Tang Xianzu's late sixteenth-century kunqu *Mudan ting* (The Peony Pavilion); a 'complete' and 'authentic' version of the same play and, most recently, a new version of *Farewell My Concubine* (Bawang bie ji) were produced by Chen Shizheng, a Chinese-born actor and director now based in New York; at Stratford-upon-Avon, the Royal Shakespeare Company staged *The Orphan of Zhao* (Zhaoshi guer); and in mainland China and Taiwan, various xiqu forms have been used in the performances of Shakespeare and Greek tragedies. These were just a few of the many intercultural experiments on Chinese xiqu that took place in the world during the second half of the twentieth century and the first two decades of the twenty-first. With the impact of globalization and with an ever-growing number of Chinese actors performing on the international stage, Chinese xiqu will continue to be renewed and reinvented, to contribute to the development of world theatre, and to play an increasingly important role in identifying and strengthening not only the theatrical but also the cultural presence of China and Chinese communities and diaspora across the globe.

IV. Korea, by CedarBough T. Saeji

Three main primary reincarnations of traditional theatre in modern Korea have re-imagined tradition in new ways: *madanggeuk*, *yeonhuigeuk* and *changgeuk*.

During the Korean pro-democracy movement (1970s and 1980s), activists became interested in re-appropriating Korean tradition from government control (as registered items of protected traditional culture), and to that end learnt mask dance-dramas and *pungmul* drumming. Motivated youth staged what appeared to be a traditional performance, but after a crowd had amassed and the show was under way, the traditional would often give way to a more explicit political message. Over time these young people realized that they no longer needed to clothe their politics within tradition, and the genre madanggeuk (outdoor theatre) was born. Through their connection with the democratization movement, these plays by and large focused on spoken and mimed messages. Owing to the performers' background training in mask dance-drama and pungmul, and a desire to remain allied with Korean folk culture, their plays often incorporated traditional music and movement, with the players clad in Korean traditional clothing. In the present day, many madanggeuk are performed without these elements, on a variety of themes limited only by the imagination of those involved. New members of madang-geuk troupes may never have learnt pungmul or mask dance-dramas, and although some troupes explicitly continue to incorporate tradition and train their members in these skills, others do not.

Although madanggeuk originally appeared to be the naturally evolving future of Korean traditional theatre, today *yeonhui* groups, or groups performing yeonhuigeuk (yeonhui is a loose term for traditional folk theatre), have emerged. One reason for the resurgence of this term is the opening of a department in yeonhui at the Korean National University of the Arts. The department trains students in mask dance-drama (Figure 22.2), pungmul, shamanic performance and the skills of the traditional itinerant Korean performers, the *namsadang*. Yeonhui groups, often including graduates of the university, have thorough traditional training and reassemble various traditions into full-length shows. Many yeonhui groups create new stories as a framework for presenting traditions they have learnt. Instead of limiting themselves to one art or one genre (such as a single village's pungmul style or one traditional folk dance), they combine styles and genres in a single show. This may include the lion dance from Bongsan's mask dance-drama, the spinning disks from Namsadang, drumming in a pan-regional style and newly coined humorous dialogue delivered in a traditional style.

Figure 22.2 After the modern masked dance company Cheonha Jeil Tal's co-founder Son Byeongman passed away just days before a performance, the performance became a tribute and ritual. Here fellow co-founder Heo Changyeol dances the part of the piteous leper from the dance *Goseong ogwangdae* before a paper cutout representing Son.

(Photo by CedarBough T. Saeji)

Finally, changgeuk is the restaging of the epic *pansori* tales that were originally sung by a solo singer accompanied by a drummer. In changgeuk, similar to an opera or a musical, each character is voiced by a different singer on an often elaborate set with props. *Changgeuk* was first staged in the early twentieth century and contributed to the ongoing success of the pansori genre by providing an alternative setting in which to hear the distinctive singing style. When staging pansori as changgeuk, the music expands from a single drummer to include multiple Korean traditional instruments, and other traditional arts such as dance may be presented in a scene only briefly described in the original tale. Newly composed changgeuk that are not based on the traditional pansori epics have been less successful.

V. Southeast Asia, by Jennifer Goodlander

Traditional performances such as dance, puppets and masked dramas taking place as part of religious rituals or royal ceremony are often the first kind of performance that people imagine when they think of theatre in Southeast Asia. In reality, traditional performance in contemporary society is just as likely to be Balinese *wayang kulit* (shadow puppetry) on a jumbotron with a rock band, a Cambodian dance presented as part of a Christmas dinner at a hotel in Siem Reap, or dancers moving in hypnotic unison past skyscrapers for the king's birthday celebration in Thailand.

In order to describe the fate of traditional theatre in Southeast Asia today, it is necessary to investigate what is meant by 'traditional performance'. Catherine Diamond defines traditional theatre in Southeast Asia as 'the theatre considered authentic to the peoples of Southeast Asia before European intervention' (2012: 2). Even though many of the performances considered 'traditional' might date back for several generations, it is important to note that traditional performance is always changing in response to historical and cultural influences – and not all 'traditions' existed before or without European influence within the region.[6] For example, the performance form known as *sarsuwela* (comic operetta) in the Philippines is a local derivative of the Spanish operetta form called *zarzuela* and developed in the late nineteenth century (ibid.: 271). Even the process of naming some performances 'tradition' while excluding others demonstrates how tradition as a designation carries contemporary meaning and value. Tradition is not a static entity that carries forward from the past unchanging into the present, rather it is better to focus on what a nation considers traditional and how that tradition continues to function in the present. I focus on how the dynamic processes of nationalism, tourism and globalization are both strengthening and changing traditional performance throughout the region. Because of space limitations, this section is not attempting a comprehensive description of traditional theatre around Southeast Asia. Rather, I offer a variety of examples in different countries throughout the region in order to pinpoint general trends and contexts in order to provide a framework for thinking about how traditional theatre reflects and changes along with Southeast Asian identities.

Traditional performance is often understood within a narrative of loss or extinction. Early descriptions of traditional performance in Southeast Asia were often accompanied by laments that surely these performances would disappear – that they could not compete with modern advances for a modern society (see Kartomi 1995). Government and local organizations have combined in order to focus efforts on preserving traditional performances for a new generation. State-sponsored schools and universities that focus on artistic training have been a large part of this effort – the scope and locations of such programmes vary around the region. Indonesia has one of the largest and most diverse networks of arts institutions. There are high schools, colleges and universities dedicated to the arts, some of which, such as Institut Seni Indonesia Yogyakarta, teach western-style orchestra and modern dance together with classical Javanese dance, music, theatre and *wayang* (see Hough 1999). Students learn traditional performance, experiment with intercultural forms and technology, and produce scholarship about the history and practice of performance. Other countries such as Thailand teach traditional arts as part of the curriculum of general universities; for example, Chulalongkorn University in Bangkok, Thailand offers an MA in Thai classical dance that combines practice and scholarship, and a PhD in traditional Thai performing arts. Cambodian Living Arts, an organization based in Phnom Penh, works to preserve, teach and advocate for traditional dance, puppetry and theatre in Cambodia and abroad (Figure 22.3). In the spring of 2013, the organization sponsored a festival of Cambodian arts in New York City to celebrate 'the extraordinary resilience of the Cambodian nation and its artists' (Season of Cambodia 2013). These efforts demonstrate concern that if something is not done, traditional performances might be lost, but that is not the only reason that many of these programmes and organizations exist.

Television, movies and other media are often blamed for a declining interest in traditional performance, especially among a country's youth, but these technologies have also inspired artistic innovation and adaptation. Jogya Hip Hop Foundation is a group in Jogjakarta, Indonesia that combines hip-hop music, Javanese language, *wayang* and gamelan in order to 'paint a portrait of daily life in Jogjakarta where tradition and modernity grow together' (Intel Visibly Smart 2011). They use computers not only to mix and make their music, but in order for them to reach an international audience. Rather than simply competing with theatre, technology helps previously

Figure 22.3 Groups such as Sovana Phum in Cambodia work to revive traditional performances such as *sbeik thom* (large shadow puppet).

(Photo by Jennifer Goodlander

isolated forms find new audiences. *Nang talung* (ritual Thai shadow puppetry), initially a primarily rural form of entertainment in small villages, was the subject of a hit song in 1995 by the group Chaamaa and has reached urban centres through performances on television and subsequently at festivals. Technology, used now in both presentation and dissemination, 'creates a mingling of tradition with modernity [that] is greatly enjoyed by local audiences situated in a world that utilizes both ancient traditional practices and modern technology in daily life' (Dowsey-Magog 2002: 201). Many performance genres all over the region now use electric lights and sound systems. Although this often makes it easier for audiences to see and hear performances, it has also changed the aesthetics. For example, for *randai* in Sumatra, audiences are now often configured proscenium style to accommodate a stage and lights rather than in a circle in the village, and microphones limit or change the movement of the actors (Latrell 1999: 256). VCDs, DVDs, cassette tapes, and more recently YouTube and Facebook are popular ways to preserve, promote and share performance with a larger audience. Even as technology changes the performance genres, some complain that the original intent of the performance is lost. Jan Mrázek writes that many Javanese *dalang* complain that television is 'destroying *wayang*' because it fails to 'transmit essential aspects – the total experience, the story and its crucial moments, the feelings' because the producers do not care to take the time to 'understand *wayang*' (2007: 299). I have witnessed videotapes of *wayang kulit* performances and recorded *gamelan* at Balinese temple festivals because they are cheaper and sometimes more convenient. Traditional performance has survived in many cases because it has remained relevant to the societies producing it – negotiating modernity and technology will continue to be an important part of that relevance moving into the future.

Traditional performing arts have been utilized as a means to articulate 'national identity' in many ways as Southeast Asian nations gained independence in the latter half of the twentieth century. In Indonesia *dalang* (puppeteers) and other artists were employed as cultural officers by the early Indonesian government, while their work was disseminated through television and cassettes (Weintraub 2004: 7). Sometimes, situating traditional performance as national culture has focused on performances of 'the people', or from the village. *Mua roi nuoc* (Vietnamese water puppetry) dates from the seventeenth century and was performed in remote villages as part of temple festivals, and the practice was a closely guarded local secret. In 1986, initiatives to expand puppetry into urban centres were started by the government to bring water puppetry to international audiences and venues, to 'serve as a beginning point for helping the world understand significant aspects of [Vietnam's] rich culture'. Today, water puppetry can be studied at the university and both Vietnamese and international audiences enjoy watching the art form as a kind of nostalgia for an idealized past (Foley 2001: 132–9). At other times, court forms have been preferred over folk forms. For example, in Thailand, the court forms of *khon* (masked dance theatre) and *lakhon nai* (inner court theatre) have been idealized by the government over folk forms and favoured in terms of description ('high' art versus 'low' art), funding and place in society. These choices reflect the hierarchy of Thai society, which places the king at the centre of Thai politics and identity (Jungwiwattanaporn 2010: 69–70). In each case, traditional performing arts change in accordance with contemporary values and needs.

As part of a larger effort to preserve culture as natural treasures, UNESCO passed the Convention for the Safeguarding of Intangible Cultural Heritage in 2003, which provided a system to document, preserve and nurture the performing arts as one of several kinds of heritage.[7] There is concern that the UNESCO convention's efforts to record and document the performances designated within will make those works available for exploitation by outsiders. Although some scholars worry about intellectual property rights, and misuse might result in greater secrecy rather than access (Brown 2012: 94–5),[8] Southeast Asia remains woefully behind in protecting intellectual property, and currently the violation of intellectual property is a bigger concern than overprotection to the point of secrecy. For example, Ron Jenkins describes how in Bali a painter, a puppeteer and a priest used shadow puppetry to protest corruption in I Nyoman Gunarsa's 8-year legal battle over the forgery of his paintings (2010). The UNESCO designation has also fuelled disagreements as to 'whose' culture a particular art form or genre belongs. Chong traces the heated debates between Indonesia and Malaysia over different genres of dance, puppetry and textiles that have resulted in large, sometimes violent, protests at the civic and government levels (2012: 2–3). Not all of the countries in Southeast Asia have participated in the UNESCO programme to the same extent. For example, Thailand only recently began the process of registering performance genres such a *khon* (masked dance-drama) and *fawn lep* (fingernail dance); Malaysia includes only one, *mak young* theatre, a type of dance-drama; and Singapore, the Philippines and Laos have none. As tangible benefits manifest – such as a 2010 grant to the Museum Wayang in Jakarta, Indonesia – perhaps more Southeast Asian nations will participate in the UNESCO programme.

I have given many examples of traditional performance that are thriving, but some traditional performance genres around Southeast Asia are struggling to continue. In Malaysia, Beth Osnes describes how recent deaths of leading artists have left wayang and mak yong (dance-drama) without a clear lineage (2010: 157). *Saman* (dance of a thousand hands), a dance from Aceh, Indonesia, is listed by UNESCO as 'in Urgent Need of Safeguarding', because it is being replaced by other, more modern entertainments, elderly teachers are passing away without successors, and much of the youth population is emigrating to other parts of Indonesia for better opportunities (UNESCO 2011). Only time will tell how and why some genres continue and others fall out of practice.

Globalization and increased access to travel have provided opportunities for artistic exchange. Performers in Bali have had many opportunities to see and work with international artists and this has influenced their own creative work. I Made Bandem and Fredrik Eugene deBoer describe, at the end of their seminal work on traditional Balinese dance, how artists are incorporating movements from modern dance and musical instruments such as violins and guitars into their compositions based on traditional themes, such as the *Barong* (sacred animal mask danced by one or two people) (1995: 141–2). Sometimes new creations become traditions, such as *kecak*, or the monkey chant dance, which is often credited for its invention to the German musician-painter Walter Spies in the 1930s, but today is often performed both for tourists and for temple ceremonies. These kinds of global exchange are not new – *tuong* (dramatic opera) in Vietnam shares many similarities with Chinese operatic forms, including music, story, gestures and character types, indicating a likely shared history. Yet, tuong is considered 'a most original and outstanding form of national music drama' within the Vietnamese press (Mackerras 1987: 5). Perhaps in another generation other globally inspired performance forms will also become 'traditional' markers of cultural identity.

Tourism has changed the context of many performances in both positive and negative ways. Michel Picard argues that in Bali, tourism, together with Balinese cultural resilience, has strengthened Balinese performing arts through increasing the arts' economic viability and visibility. Tourism, in Bali and beyond, must be understood 'not as an external force striking Bali from outside, like a missile hitting a target, but it is a process transforming Balinese society from inside – today, tourism has become an integral part of Bali's culture' (Picard 1990: 74). Likewise, tourism has helped foster the continuation of many traditional performing arts around Southeast Asia. Tourism does, however, change the performance landscape because of the types of performance that are viable for a foreign audience and the need for the performances to happen at a set time in an accessible context. All-night performances are shortened to an hour, costumes and story are selected to appeal to an audience who know little about the form or culture, and sometimes performing night after night for money instead of the gods drains the energy from the performance. Yet, tourism has saved some genres from inevitable demise. Kathy Foley describes how tourism revitalized the *yokthe thay* (marionette theatre) in Burma (Myanmar), with the precaution that the art form risks being turned into a troupe of global nostalgia without local value or meaning (2001: 69–70).

Traditional performance often not only means a certain type of performance, but also refers to a method of passing a performance form down from teacher to student together with cultural values (Diamond 2012: 3). In the modern era, the methods of training artists and performers have greatly changed. Systems that often kept performance as a 'sacred' knowledge only taught within family lines have been complemented by, and sometimes replaced by, national schools teaching the arts to any student with the desire and talent to learn. Anthropologist Brett Hough analyses the arts university in Bali and recognizes the tension between state ideals and local norms that often split culture into two domains: the official domain, which informs policy decisions, and the autonomous domain, which constitutes local identity, language and values (1999: 236–7). Schools such as Institut Seni Indonesia (Indonesian Arts University, ISI) are sites of tension between these two cultural domains. On the one hand, the schools are run by the state (for example, the *rektor*, or university president, is ultimately appointed by a committee in Jakarta) and adhere to state ideologies. On the other, these same schools teach local arts and traditions to a mostly local population of students. Hough notes that the primary goal of the education system is to develop a national culture, because it forms the basis of a culture that will foster modernity and development (1999: 237–9). Nevertheless, there is often a practical difference between students trained in a national school versus one educated more traditionally; and the reasons for seeking a formal education vary from place to place. Professor I Nyoman Sedana in the puppetry programme at ISI-Denpasar argues that a Balinese puppeteer or dalang trained only at the university would not have sufficient knowledge to be successful; but also, as a trend, most artists desire the official recognition that a degree provides, no matter their skill or experience before going to school (1993: 21, 32–4).

Traditional performance continues to play a crucial role in the formation of a Southeast Asian subject position. It changes with and in response to fluctuations happening both within and outside each society. Tourism, global and local conservation projects, changing technological capabilities, artistic innovations, nationalism, politics and public education at all levels will continue to influence traditional performing arts in many ways as theatre continues to be a reflection and comment on society and culture. These variations, however, are not new – but rather must be understood as part of a larger continuum of dynamism and change that has always been a part of these performances marked 'traditional'.

Notes

1 According to the caste practice of Kerala, members of lower castes were restricted from any access to the inside of the temple complex. Their entry to the temples was granted through the landmark Temple Entry Proclamation in 1936.

2 The performance structure of Kudiyattam is also unique. Plays are never completed in one single night. The norm is to complete an act of a play taking at least eleven nights, which means that a normal two- to three-hour-long play is elaborated and extended to some forty or more nights. The focus is on the elaborate enactment of verses or lines of characters by drawing stories from Indian folk traditions, myths and even local beliefs and practices. The actors write their own performance texts, known as *Attaprakaram*, based on the play and directorial notes, known as *kramadeepika*, which include detailed descriptions of scene blocking, entrances and exits of all the characters and their costume and makeup.

3 M. P. Sankaran Namboothiri believes that the history of kathakali can be divided into two phases: before Ramunni Menon's training at Kodungallur and after his training. In a personal conversation

[2014], Namboothiri explained to me that Ramunni Menon's contribution to the nature of characterization in kathakali is very large indeed. Read Zarrilli (2000: 28) for an example of how he changed a 'one-dimensional' character into a highly complex one.

4 *Nirvahanam* is a performance technique used in kudiyattam when the events of the past are recapitulated by the protagonist of any particular act.

5 Nangyarkuthu, an offshoot of kutiyattam, is the mono-act performance of the kutiyattam actress, extending its acting method of nirvahanam, the enactment of the story in the previous act by the leading character of the current act. This may take up to forty-one nights, and nangyarkuthu adopts nirvahanam style for the performance. The acting and singing styles of kutiyattam and nangyarkuthu are the same. The use of the term *nanga*, relating to *nangyar*, meaning the actress of kudiyattam, is traced back to 898 CE.

6 In a recent book, Denise Varney and her co-authors suggest that the theatre or 'cultural practice' that owes 'little or nothing to European culture offers a regional modernity based in the continuing specificity of the Asia-Pacific in the present' (2013: 2). I argue that because of dynamic flows of globalization, that a notion of a cultural form that has resisted influence is romantic and perhaps naive. As I argue in this section, what is considered 'tradition' has undergone great change in response to many influences – some are local and others are not.

7 The complete list of heritage identified in 2006 is: (a) oral traditions including language; (b) performing arts; (c) social practices, rituals and festive events; (d) knowledge and practices concerning nature and the universe; and (e) traditional craftsmanship. The convention was expanded in 2006 to cover multiple submissions from each country.

8 It should be noted that Brown is writing primarily about indigenous peoples in the Americas or Australia – but the point he makes about cultural appropriation has resonances in Southeast Asia as people there attempt to balance preservation and accessibility with the rights of the artists.

Bibliography

Bandem, I Made, and Fredirik deBoer (1995) *Balinese Dance in Transition: Kaja and Kelod*, Kuala Lumpur: Oxford University Press.

Brown, Michael F. (2012) 'From the Archive: Safeguarding the Intangible', *Museum Anthropology Review*, 16 (2): 93–7.

Bruckner, Heidrun, de Bruin, Hanne M., and Moser, Heike (eds) (2011) *Between Fame and Shame: Performing Women – Women Performers in India*, Wiesbaden: Harrassowitz.

Chen, Xiaomei (2002) *Acting the Right Part: Political Theater and Popular Drama in Contemporary China*, Honolulu: University of Hawai'i Press.

Chong, Jing Winn (2012) '"Mine, Yours, or Ours?": The Indonesia-Malay Disputes over Shared Cultural Heritage', *Sojourn: Journal of Social Issues in Southeast Asia*, 27(1): 1–53.

Daugherty, Diane (2005) 'The Pendulum of Intercultural Performance: "Kathakali King Lear at Shakespeare's Globe"', *Asian Theatre Journal*, 22(1): 52–72.

Diamond, Catherine (2012) *Communities of Imagination: Contemporary Southeast Asian Theatres*, Honolulu: University of Hawai'i Press.

Dowsey-Magog, Paul (2002) 'Popular Workers' Shadow Theatre in Thailand', *Asian Theatre Journal*, 19 (1): 184–211.

Foley, Kathy (2001) 'The Metonymy of Art: Vietnamese Water Puppetry as Representative of Modern Vietnam', *TDR*, 45 (4): 129–41.

Goldstein, Joshua (2007) *Drama Kings: Players and Publics in the Re-creation of Peking Opera, 1870–1937*, Berkeley: University of California Press.

Hough, Brett (1999) 'Education for the Performing Arts: Contesting and Mediating Identity in Bali', in Raechelle Rubinstein and Linda H. Connor (eds) *Staying Local in the Global Village: Bali in the Twentieth Century*, 231–63. Honolulu: University of Hawai'i Press.

Intel Visibly Smart (2011) 'Jogja Hip Hop Foundation', www.youtube.com/watch?v=bR66rXGnegU, accessed 13 October 2013.

Jenkins, Ron (2010) *Rua Benida In Bali: Counterfeit Justice in the Trail of Nyoman Gunarsa*, Yogyakarta: Indonesia Institute of Arts.

Jungwiwattanaporn, Parichat (2010) 'Kamron Gunatilaka and the Crescent Moon Theatre: Contemporary Thai Theatre as Political Dissent', Dissertation, University of Hawai'i at Manoa.

Kartomi, Margaret J. (1995) '"Traditional Music Weeps" and Other Themes in the Discourse on Music, Dance and Theatre of Indonesia, Malaysia and Thailand', *Journal of Southeast Asian Studies*, 26 (2): 366–400.

Latrell, Craig (1999) 'Widening the Circle: The Refiguring of West Sumatran Randai', *Asian Theatre Journal*, 16 (2): 248–59.

Lei, Daphne P. (2006) *Operatic China: Staging Chinese Identity Across the Pacific*, New York: Palgrave Macmillan.

Li Ruru (2010) *The Soul of Beijing Opera: Theatrical Creativity and Continuity in the Changing World*, Hong Kong: Hong Kong University Press.

Liu, Siyuan (2009) 'Theatre Reform as Censorship: Censoring Traditional Theatre in China in the Early 1950s', *Theatre Journal*, 61 (3): 387–406.

Mackerras, Colin (1975) *The Chinese Theatre in Modern Times, from 1840 to the Present Day*, London: Thames & Hudson.

—— (1987) 'Theatre in Vietnam', *Asian Theatre Journal*, 4 (1): 1–28.

Madhavan, Arya (2010) *Kudiyattam Theatre and the Actor's Consciousness*, Amsterdam: Rodopi.

Madhu, Margi (2012) Interview with the Author, 20 October.

Moser, Heike (2011) 'How Kutiyattam Became Kuti-attam, "Acting Together," or: The Changing Role of Female Performers in the Nannyar-Kuttu-Tradition of Kerala', in Heidrun Bruckner, Hanne M. de Bruin, and Heike Moser (eds) *Between Fame and Shame: Performing Women – Women Performers in India*, 169–89, Wiesbaden: Harrassowitz.

Mrázek, Jan (2007) 'Conclusion: Ways of Experiencing Art: Art History, Television, and Javanese Wayang', in Jan Mrázek and Morgan Pitelka (eds) *What's the Use of Art: Asian Visual and Material Culture in Context*, 272–304, Honolulu: University of Hawai'i Press.

Namboothiri, M.P.S (2014) Interview with the Author, 18 April.

Namboothiri, Sivan (2005) 'My Guru', in K. G. Poulose (ed.) *Kudiyattathinte Puthiya Mukham*, 43–6, Tripunithura: International Centre for Kutiyattam.

Namboothirippad, Killimangalam Vasudevan and Namboothiri, M. P. S. (2013) *Kathakaliyude Rangapatha Charithram*, Kozhikode: Mathrubhumi Printing and Publishing.

Osnes, Beth (2010) *The Shadow Puppet Theatre of Malaysia: A Study of Wayang Kulit with Performance Scripts and Puppet Designs*, Jefferson, NC: McFarland.

Picard, Michel (1990) '"Cultural Tourism" in Bali: Cultural Performances as Tourist Attraction', *Indonesia*, 49: 37–74.

Pisharodi, K. P. Narayana (1987) *Bharata Muniyude Natyasastram, Volume I*, Trichur: Kerala Kalamandalam.

Poulose, K. G. (ed.) (2005) *Kudiyattathinte Puthiya Mukham*, Tripunithura: International Centre for Kutiyattam.

Richmond, Farley P., Swann, Darius L., and Zarrilli, Phillip B. (1993) *Indian Theatre: Traditions of Performance*, Delhi: Motilal Banarsidass.

Sathi, Margi (2014) Interview with the Author, 14 August.

Season of Cambodia (2013) 'About SOC', at http://seasonofcambodia.org/about-soc/, accessed 15 September 2013.

Sedana, I. Nyoman (1993) *The Training, Education, and the Expanding Role of the Balinese Dalang*, MA thesis, Brown University.

Tian, Min (2008) *The Poetics of Difference and Displacement: Twentieth-Century Chinese-Western Intercultural Theatre*, Hong Kong: Hong Kong University Press.

—— (ed.) (2010) *China's Greatest Operatic Male Actor of Female Roles: Documenting the Life and Art of Mei Lanfang, 1894–1961*, Lewiston, NY: Edwin Mellen Press.

—— (2012) *Mei Lanfang and the Twentieth-Century International Stage: Chinese Theatre Placed and Displaced*, New York: Palgrave Macmillan.

UNESCO (2011) 'Saman Dance', available at www.unesco.org/culture/ich/index.php?lg=en&pg=00011& USL=00509, accessed 15 December 2013.

Varney, Denise, *et al.* (2013) *Theatre and Performance in the Asia-Pacific*, London: Palgrave Macmillan.

Weintraub, Andrew (2004) *Power Play, Wayang Golek Theater of West Java*, Athens: Ohio University Press.

Wichmann, Elizabeth (1990) 'Tradition and Innovation in Contemporary Beijing Opera Performance', *TDR*, 34 (1): 146–78.

Zarrilli, Phillip B. (2000) *Kathakali Dance-Drama: Where Gods and Demons Come to Play*, London: Routledge.

23

Intercultural theatre and Shakespeare productions in Asia

Shormishtha Panja, Suematsu Michiko, Alexa Huang
and Yong Li Lan

This chapter examines intercultural theatre in Asia through the lens of Shakespearean productions in India, Japan, the Sinophere theatres of China, Hong Kong and Taiwan, and Southeast Asia. As the quintessential western dramatist, Shakespeare has captured the imagination of Asian theatre artists from the beginning of modern Asian theatre, as localized adaptations, as foreignizing translations and productions, and as intercultural hybridization that is performed through the many traditional and folk forms of contemporary Asia.

I. India, by Shormishtha Panja

One of the first things one notes about intercultural theatre is the disappearance of the idea of universal principles and the rescuing of local cultures from the hegemonic homogeneity of globalization. Intercultural theatre cannot avoid discussion of plurality and difference, of socio-economic bases, of transformations brought about by globalization. Intercultural theatre challenges the idea that cultural traditions and artefacts are national property, state or nation specific, that cultures are 'secured by their origins' (Kennedy and Yong 2010: 10) or that borrowings and appropriations cannot but be rampant. Intercultural theatre is often a hybrid of theatre rooted in a specific geographical location with very specific cultural markers, for example *Kathakali*, and one transported from another different culture, such as Shakespeare. The resulting hybrid performance challenges givens of cultural dominance, that is, that the west is dominant and the Asian material feminized (ibid.: 11). Bodies and gestures, and not just words, are crucial here, exploding the myth that performing bodies are pure and authentic cultural essences; the demon of interculturalism is universalism (U. Chaudhuri 2002: 36).

Intercultural theatre also raises the important question of whether cultural identity is fixed or volatile. No one in the audience can completely own an intercultural performance; part of it usually remains unintelligible to all. Intercultural performance underlines the importance of location: disparate responses to the same production depending on one's location are a hallmark of intercultural performance (Phillips 2010: 243; Kennedy and Yong 2010: 12–14). Intercultural theatre reflects 'provisionality, partiality of belonging' that characterizes many spectators in Asia (Kennedy and Yong 2010: 16). It inevitably raises questions of identity.

Just as intercultural performance foregrounds the mobility and circulation of cultures, it also puts the spotlight on the spectator as global tourist. There is, necessarily, a fragmentation of audiences and genres, a fragmentation of univocal national theatre. However, in India, a country that never had a national theatre, this is not a concern.

Intercultural theatre raises questions of the commodification of cultures and of cultural piracy. There are dangers of irresponsible interculturalism. Daryl Chin observes that deploying 'elements from the symbol system of another culture is a very delicate enterprise' and one has to be on guard against 'cultural imperialism' (Chin 2003: 403). The borrowed material should be allowed to speak in its own language; rather than imposing a meaning on it, one should allow meaning to rise naturally from it. The perils are manifold: 'Colonial legacies frame it, economic imbalances complicate it, and orientalist accusations are barbs that Western artists who go this route will encounter' (Daugherty 2005: 67). Similarly, Asian artists face the criticism of pandering to the west. However, through all this disparateness, dangers and difference, the important issue in intercultural theatre remains the human encounter (Pavis 2010: 13).

A vital thing to be kept in mind while discussing intercultural theatre in India is that Shakespeare came to India through a different route from the one taken in Japan, China and Korea. Indians read Shakespeare in English and in translation. His texts are part of the curriculum. He has been used as an educational tool by colonial rulers, often as a means of intellectual manipulation as Jyotsna Singh argues. In India there is not much talk of Asian theatre. Debates in India revolve around caste, community, religion and gender and not about an imaginary Asian community, as Bharucha points out (Bharucha 2010: 255).

Pre-independence Shakespeare on the Indian stage

Indigenous theatrical performance could challenge, consciously or unconsciously and through adaptation, the status of Shakespeare as a marker of universal cultural value; on stage, Shakespeare is not an 'accommodating ideal' (Singh 1989: 458) erasing or eliding all traces of cultural difference. Phillips writes of the political economies of the new Asias challenging the 'bland universality of the Shakespeare institution' (Phillips 2010: 242), but this was happening more than a century ago in colonial India.

Since India is a collection of enormously diverse regional cultures, I shall discuss some of the major regional Shakespeare productions and translations. After a Christmas 1780 performance of *Othello* at the Calcutta Theatre, there were twenty-three productions of Shakespeare, mostly tragedies and romances, in Bengali between 1852 and 1899. Boishnob Choron Addy created quite a stir as the first Indian Othello in 1848 at the Sans Souci theatre. Two famed actor-directors staging Shakespeare in Calcutta in Bengali were Girish Chandra Ghosh (1844–1912) and Amarendrananth Dutta (1876–1916). While Ghosh preferred remaining true to the original and lost the audience's interest quite speedily, Amarendranath preferred adaptations. His *Horiraj* (c. 1896), an adaptation of *Hamlet*, proved quite popular, while Ghosh's expensive *Macbeth* (1893), 'in the European style', bombed.

Durlabh bandhu (Rare Friend, 1880), a translation of *The Merchant of Venice* by Bhartendu Harish Chandra, the father of modern Hindi theatre, was the earliest example of Shakespeare in Hindi. Harivanshrai Bachchan translated *Macbeth* (1956) and *Othello* (1958) into Hindi verse (Awasthi 1964: 51–62). In Urdu, the earliest translation was in 1884. Those of Syed Mehdi Hasan Ahsan Lucknowi were of better quality than others. There was a Shakespeare Theatre Company (1912–13) which staged the so-called 'Indian Shakespeare' Agha Hashr's melodramatic poetic-prose translation of *Hamlet* titled *Safed Khoon* (White Blood), which even had Hamlet singing (Hasan 1964: 132–9).

On the Marathi stage, between 1867 and 1915 there were sixty-five productions of Shakespeare, mostly free adaptations, but in the next thirty-nine years there were only two. The increasing decadence of the Marathi stage and its fondness for song and dance have been offered as partial explanation. There were musical versions of *The Winter's Tale* and *Measure for Measure*. *Zunzarrao* (1890) was the most successful *Othello* production, revived as late as 1950 (Rajadhyaksha 1964: 83–94).

In Parsi theatre, Shakespeare held a place second to none. The languages were Hindi, Urdu, Gujarati, even English. The playwrights were Hindu and Muslim. At least a dozen Shakespeare plays were adapted and staged. It was popular, rambunctious fare, freely adapted, replete with songs and dances. New situations and characters were added. The motives and situations were changed to suit Indian mores. There were prose, verse and rhyming couplets. The famed Victoria Natak Mandali company had thirty-five plays as part of its repertoire. It toured throughout the Far East, Mandalay, Rangoon, Bangkok, Java and then London (Mehta 1964: 41–50). On the Gujarati stage between 1865 and 1915, many plays were staged in different locations: Surat, Ahmedabad, Saurashtra and Bombay. In the 1860s in Bombay there were twenty dramatic clubs, including the Shakespeare Natak Mandali. The bulk of the unprinted scripts are lost (Mehta 1964: 41–50).

There are four major south Indian languages, Tamil, Kannad, Telegu and Malayalam. In Tamil, there were thirty Shakespeare productions in English and Tamil by 1900, which were presented as entertainment, not for edification or as exemplars of literary value (Subramanyam 1964: 120–6). In Kannad, *Othello, The Merchant of Venice* and *Romeo and Juliet* were translated in prose and in *Kanda Vritta* stanzas (traditional Puranic plays popular in Kannada), and enacted by the Palace Company around 1881 under the patronage of the Maharaja of Mysore (Rao 1964: 63–72). In Telegu, V. Vasudeva Shastri wrote a verse adaptation of *Julius Caesar* in 1876, with its metre akin to iambic pentameter. In the preface he said he had done his best to introduce 'Hindu customs and manners where I could'. This was followed in 1880 with a prose and verse adaptation of *The Merchant of Venice* by Guruzada Shriramamurti. The names, locations and incidents were Indianized. Dukes of Ephesus became Princes of the Chola Kingdom and even Shakespeare became Sulapani (Rajamannar 1964: 127–31). In Malayalam, while prose translations of Shakespeare appeared as early as 1893 (*The Taming of the Shrew* by Kandathil Varghese Mapilai), performances were rare. Interestingly, the radio station All India Radio (AIR) Trivandrum-Kozhikode broadcast adaptations of all four major tragedies, *Romeo and Juliet, Merchant, Julius Caesar* and *The Tempest*, specially written for AIR (Pillai 1964: 73–82).

In the northeastern state of Assam, the first Shakespeare translation, *The Comedy of Errors*, was published in 1888. *The Merchant of Venice* or *Banij Kunwar* (Merchant Prince, 1946), by Atul Chandra Hazarika, was a popular production. P. Talukdar and Narayan Bezbarua were well-known playwrights who adapted and translated Shakespeare. Radio adaptations were also prevalent (Barua 1964: 12–15).

Between 1919 and 1953 there was a lull in Shakespeare performances on the Indian stage. One of the reasons could be that the national movement against the British colonial rulers was gaining momentum. By 1942, Gandhi's Quit India movement was in full swing. In the light of this, performing an English playwright's works on the Indian stage would probably be considered unpatriotic.

Indian Shakespeare post-independence

Shakespeare performance post Indian independence in 1947 falls into two major categories: productions in English and adaptations of Shakespeare in the Indian languages. The latter may be further subdivided into performances that follow Shakespeare's text faithfully with literary translations, as in Ebrahim Alkazi's production of *King Lear* (1964) in Hindi and *Othello* (1969) in Urdu, and productions that adapt the Shakespearean text radically. The latter may Indianize the characters and situations and perform the play in an indigenous theatre form such as *kathakali* (from Kerala), *nautanki* (a form from Uttar Pradesh with emphasis on music), *yakshagana* (from Karnataka) and *jatra* (from Bengal, with emphasis on dialogue). There may also be a combination of one or more of these forms within a single performance, for example Tanvir's adaptation of *A Midsummer Night's Dream* fuses *Rabindranritya*, a form of dance used in Rabindranath Tagore's dance-dramas, with folk theatre. These adaptations, with the addition of music, dance, colourful costumes and makeup, can make the original play unrecognizable to an uninitiated viewer. Some outstanding productions are *Barnam Vana* (Birnam Forest, 1979) based on *Macbeth*, *Othello* (1996 onwards) and *King Lear* in kathakali (1989), and *Kamdeo ka Apna Basant Ritu ka Sapna* (The Love God's Own, a Spring Reverie, 1993) based on *A Midsummer Night's Dream*. *Barnam Vana* is an adaptation directed by B. V. Karanth for the National School of Drama Repertory in the yakshagana style. Yakshagana is a folk theatre form from Karnataka in south India that originated in the sixteenth century. The term literally means 'songs of the demi-gods'. A minimum of fifteen performers and as many musicians are needed for this lively, fast-paced form filled with songs, dances and improvised dialogue. Of particular note are the poetic songs or *prasangas* sung by the chief vocalist or *bhagvata*. Karanth says that the yakshagana form appealed to him because the characters in Shakespeare's play seem to have the same larger-than-life quality as the yakshagana characters, and the emotional tensions of the play can be captured through the rhythms of the actors' body movements. Also, *Macbeth* abounds in battle scenes, another hallmark of yakshagana. Karanth preferred the 'fluid rhythm and strong dramatic style' of yakshagana to kathakali, whose *mudra*s (movements), he felt, 'defy understanding'. In his Director's Note in the performance programme, Karanth says that yakshagana is especially developed in the 'presentation of characters' entries and exits, battle scenes and the expression of emotional tensions through the rhythm of body movements'. Karanth also seems to have in mind Bharata's *Natyasastra*. Karanth says that the *rasas* of valour (*vira rasa*), wrath (*krodha rasa*) and terror (*bhayanaka rasa*) abound in *Macbeth*, making it particularly suited to an Indian adaptation.

Kathakali, a highly stylized blend of dance, music and theatre originated in seventeenth-century Kerala, is performed outdoors in family compounds or near temples; lately proscenium stage productions have become common. There was a 1989 kathakali production of *Lear* by the Kerala State Arts Academy and the Paris-based theatre group Keli. Sadanam Balakrishnan's International Centre for Kathakali in New Delhi has produced *Othello* in the kathakali style since 1996. Only five scenes were enacted in the two-hour-plus performance. Not only is there no fresh interpretation of the play, but also there is a worrying erasure of the racial conflict: what Loomba terms Othello's difference in terms of colour or religion is unfortunately elided (Loomba 1998: 160). Apart from this, there is a *Julius Caesar* adaptation titled *Charudattam*, which was scripted, directed and sung by Sadanam Harikumar and presented by Satwikam of Kalasadanam (north Kerala). The play reduced the original to ten scenes. It was innovative in the portrayal of an ambivalent Cassius, who is neither *pacca* (green), the traditional heroic and upright character type, nor *karutta tati* (black beard), the conventional evil plotter. Instead, this Cassius has specially designed makeup, costume, choreography and songs. In addition to these complete plays, scenes from *A Midsummer Night's Dream* and *Macbeth* have also been staged in kathakali style. However, these productions were not without controversies. *Lear*, for example, satisfied neither uninitiated western audiences and critics, who were left perplexed, nor Malayalam critics, who felt that kathakali codes had been violated with a woman performing

Cordelia (the French actor–dancer Annette Leday; traditional kathakali is an all-male perform-ance) and with Lear appearing without the customary headdress in the storm scene (Daugherty 2005: 56–72). What is crucial to understand is that both Shakespeare and kathakali are altered in this encounter, and purists must accept this. Something goes and something stays. The betrayal of the laws of intercultural performance is the condition of its existence (Phillips 2010: 249–50). As Zarrilli puts it, 'the arena of performance is a site of constant renegotiation of the experiences and meanings that constitute culture' (Zarrilli 1992: 16).

Kamdeo ka Apna Basant Ritu ka Sapna (The Love God's Own, a Spring Reverie, 1993) is an adaptation of *A Midsummer Night's Dream* directed by Habib Tanvir (1925?–2009), who was trained at the Royal Academy of Dramatic Art and the Old Vic and was the founder of the Naya Theatre. It deals only with the rude mechanicals, for which Tanvir enlisted tribal performers speaking in the Bastar dialect. Tanvir was a pioneer in the combination of folk theatre and politics. The language used is a hybrid of Hindi and the Bastar dialect of the tribals. Tanvir's art abolishes the hierarchies between folk and classic forms. At no point was his trained consciousness valorized over that of the unschooled tribal performers. Tanvir did not romanticize folk and neither was he an artist who produced authentic folk pieces. Influenced by Brecht, he was a thoughtful and highly sophisticated urban artist who made an ideological choice of choosing the folk improvisational techniques and music and combining it with his own socialist but humorous look at the socio-political situation. For example, the tribal performers, particularly the actor playing Bottom, were not discouraged from occupying centre stage each time they delivered their lines. The musicians were visible on stage and did not hide in the wings. A number of contemporary English words appeared in the script, and one of the rude mechanicals was told to 'xerox' his part, hinting at the omnipresence of globalization. As one critic put it, he was a 'Midas turned upside down' – whatever he touches 'loses its sheen: it becomes rough and turns to Chattisgarhi' (Deshpande 2003) – Chattisgarh was the tribal performers' home state.

In Bengal, Utpal Dutt's (1929–93) Calcutta-based Little Theatre Group produced a variety of Shakespeare's plays, including *The Merchant of Venice* (1953), *Macbeth* (1954), *Julius Caesar* (1957), *Romeo and Juliet* (1964) and *A Midsummer Night's Dream* (*Choitali Rater Shopno* in Bengali, 1964). However, in light of the violence that had gripped Bengal politics in the 1960s and 1970s, to 'stick to Shakespeare or Bernard Shaw was unbearable', writes Dutt (1977: 48–72). When he returned to Shakespeare, he did ninety-eight performances of *Macbeth* for Bengal's villagers in the jatra style, an overblown, melodramatic style with an emphasis on dialogue that is performed all night, out in the open, very different from his earlier restrained proscenium productions.

Royston Abel's *Othello: A Study in Black and White* (1999–2000) is a thought-provoking production of the United Players' Guild that embeds *Othello* in a contemporary English play about a group of Indian actors rehearsing Shakespeare's play and foregrounds tensions, other than racial, in contemporary Indian society: class, urban versus rural, metro versus small town, and the anglicized versus *desi* (indigenous). One of the most popular and dynamic recent Hindi adaptations of Shakespeare in the nautanki style is *Piya Behrupiya* (Chameleon Lover, *Twelfth Night*) by Atul Kumar and The Company Theatre, which was performed at the London Globe in April 2012 and then all across India to full houses. It is a riot of colour, music (folk and quawali), dance and hilarity in the nautanki style, with English words liberally thrown in for comic effect, and metatheatrical effects, as when Sebastian, who is also the translator of the play, bemoans the fact that the translator gets no credit and that he himself has been sidelined as an actor. Kumar has also staged *Nothing like Lear*, a one-man show, and *Hamlet the Clown Prince*. One could challenge his statement that Shakespeare 'is always a super hit' in India 'because Shakespeare's tales and human conditions are quite timeless, space-less and cultureless – they are simply human' (Vincent 2012), because there is so little Shakespeare staged in India today.

Kumar's attitude to the Bard is, however, far from reverential: '[T]he comedy works very well when you disrespect it and shakes hands readily with the audience' (Gupta 2012).

The study of Shakespeare on the Indian stage has served to highlight the differences between the situation in India and other parts of Asia with regard to Shakespeare performance, the colonial heritage of the literary icon and the resulting familiarity and ease with which the Indians regard Shakespeare, and the ways in which intercultural performance brings to the forefront the dangers and hurdles of meshing the two cultures together, indeed the near-impossibility of intercultural theatre itself.

II. Japan, by Suematsu Michiko

When performing Shakespeare outside the English-speaking world, Shakespeare must undergo linguistic and 'cultural' translation within a local context. Through this process of cultural adaptation, the aesthetics and staging strategies of each culture distinguish the production. Eclectic use of Asian aesthetics in Shakespeare performances in the west has long been criticized as orientalist appropriation; however, borrowing and appropriating either foreign or domestic aesthetics is an intercultural strategy adopted also by Asian Shakespeare. In terms of authenticity, borrowing and appropriating aesthetics in any performance is problematic, but the choice in this process mirrors the intercultural subtext of the performance and defines its unique interaction with Shakespeare. For instance, in the case of Japanese Shakespeare, the complex negotiation of disciplinary boundaries among the local, traditional performance forms *noh*, *kabuki* and *bunraku* had been going on for centuries, and this intracultural interaction, or a 'meeting and exposure of differences of cultures within seemingly homogenized groups' (Bharucha 1996: 128), was replicated in their engagement with Shakespeare.

The discussion of the intercultural strategy of Japanese performances of Shakespeare should begin by identifying what these performances share with their counterparts in other Asian cultures. First, in Asian Shakespeare performances, realistic and formal modes – or representational and non-representational modes – of acting often coexist and they can be switched smoothly and flexibly within one production, or even within one scene. This duality is a great advantage in presenting the multiple layers of reality that make Shakespearean drama exceedingly rich in meaning. The second characteristic, the subordinate position of language within the performance, mainly concerns Asian Shakespeare performances that draw on traditional theatre forms. As Dennis Kennedy and Yong Li Lan (2010: 17) point out, these performances tend to foreground 'the embodied' or 'the corporeal' over verbal expression. Shakespeare's language, which prevails in English performances, loses its absolute dominance when translated, and other 'corporeal' elements such as sets, costumes, gestures, singing and dancing fill the gap. These scenographic and physical elements create a spectacle that leaves an exceedingly sensory impression and have helped some Asian Shakespeare productions travel beyond linguistic boundaries. This spectacle has often been recognized in the west as a fascinating addition to Shakespeare's language; however, it is far from a decorative addition, as it vitally concerns the cultural attitudes towards the text and the intercultural strategy of some Asian performances of Shakespeare.

What distinguishes Japanese performances of Shakespeare from those of other Asian cultures is their reception process through 'a kind of inverse colonialism' (Sasayama *et al.* 1998: 4). In the tide of westernization, 'reform' of premodern or traditional theatre practices was implemented through dedication to modern European realism. One of the earliest examples of Japanese performances of Shakespeare that tried to 'reform' kabuki with Shakespearean plots was soon followed by productions of full-text translations that strove to edify audiences with Shakespeare's dramatic ingenuity, among which was the 1911 Bungei Kyokai (the Literary

Society) production of *Hamlet*, translated and directed by Tsubouchi Shōyō. With his emphasis on language in a performance, Tsubouchi paved the way for the *shingeki* (new theatre) movement (see Chapter 18).

A naturalistic shingeki approach that was initially applied to the productions of European writers such as Ibsen and Chekhov soon became the standard for Japanese performances of Shakespeare, which sought an 'authentic' western mise-en-scène. For instance, the 1955 production of *Hamlet* by Bungaku-za (The Literary Theatre), one of the leading shingeki companies, was famously an almost exact copy of the Old Vic production of *Hamlet* (1954) with Richard Burton. The fact that this Bungaku-za production was hailed with enthusiasm because of its 'authenticity' and became legendary in the stage history of Shakespeare in Japan epitomizes shingeki's absolute deference to the west as a place of authority at that time. Following shingeki's submission to the cultural hegemony of the west, each subsequent Japanese performance of Shakespeare has had to determine its cultural position, either by challenging or accepting western cultural supremacy.

A vehement reaction against this shingeki orthodoxy was started in the 1960s by the underground *shogekijo* (Little Theatre) movement led by avant-garde stage directors such as Kara Juro, Suzuki Tadashi and Ninagawa Yukio. One of the examples of Shakespearean performance that challenged that of shingeki was the legendary *Ninagawa Macbeth* (1980). With its blatant departure from the shingeki dramaturgy that had dominated Shakespeare performances on the Japanese stage, the Japanese framework and aesthetics of this production surprised Japanese audiences as greatly as it did the British audiences who saw it later in Edinburgh (1985) and London (1987).

In *Ninagawa Macbeth*, Ninagawa relocated the setting to a feudalistic Japan of medieval warlords and incorporated characteristically Japanese visual rhetorical devices. The stage was framed by a huge structure similar to a *butsudan*, a Buddhist home altar that enshrines the spirits of ancestors. When the sliding doors of the butsudan frame opened and the world of *Macbeth* in sixteenth-century Japan unfolded onstage, audiences felt as if they were witnessing the hurly-burly of their distant ancestors (Ninagawa 2001: 212–13). This framework at once worked as a tunnel through time and as a bridge across cultures. Other Japanese stage pictures used lavishly in this production – cherry blossoms, kimonos and Buddhist statues – also visibly connected the play to the Japanese audience. Ninagawa's successive productions through the early 1990s, including *The Tempest* (1987) and *A Midsummer Night's Dream* (1994), repeatedly employed similar Japanese aesthetics and established the definitive Ninagawa style: an emphasis on visuals and an entirely eclectic hybridization of eastern and western cultures. In short, Ninagawa's formula of cultural translation to local idiom in this period, which was to undergo a degree of transformation in subsequent years, remained rather straightforward: he would find non-verbal images ingrained in the text and visualize them with typical Japanese aesthetics and stage pictures. This characteristic use of stage pictures, which originally aimed to evoke 'the collective Japanese memory', reshaped the Japanese image of Shakespeare once and for all; however, it also subjected Ninagawa to criticism for directing orientalist Shakespeare – first because his choice was too arbitrary and eclectic, and second because the chosen stage pictures were stereotypical exotic commonplaces. And yet, his 'eclectic' choice was at least true to the intercultural subtext of Japanese culture, where antithetical aesthetics of the east and west and the premodern and modern coexisted in a mishmash.

In terms of an intercultural context, the 1990s were a watershed decade. For one thing, the Japanese had begun to find it increasingly difficult to share 'the collective Japanese memory' to which Ninagawa had resorted. For instance, directors from the younger generation, such as Noda Hideki and Kawamura Takeshi, sought a Japanese identity not in traditional Japanese aesthetics but in modern subcultures and countercultures, such as the worlds of comics and sci-fi. Furthermore, the opening of the Tokyo Globe Theatre, which exclusively mounted Shakespeare plays from 1988 to 2002 until it was closed down after the collapse of the 'bubble economy' and reopened as a theatre for pop idols, spurred diversification and decanonization of Japanese Shakespeare, and consequently diminished the domineering influence of shingeki.

Regularly inviting companies around the world while offering Japanese companies of any genre an opportunity to experiment with Shakespeare, Tokyo Globe, through its privileged space, sanctioned an unprecedentedly wide range of cultural exchange through Shakespeare for theatre practitioners and audiences alike. A variety of Shakespeare productions from the UK and other European and Asian countries revealed each culture's sense of ownership of Shakespeare, avowing their freedom to find new ways to reflect the current intercultural reading of Shakespeare. This encouraged diverse genres of Japanese performing arts, including traditional theatre forms, dance, ballet and opera, to explore their theatrical identity through Shakespeare. The rediscovery of Shakespeare at this site also took the form of intercultural collaboration, such as the 1997 ITI (International Theatre Institute) production of *King Lear* directed by Kim Jeong-ok, the former president of ITI, with a cast from six countries: Japan, Korea, the United States, Germany, Bulgaria and Mexico. While the production's objective to enlighten audiences with onstage international collaboration evolved into nothing more than a multicultural theatre 'event' or 'showcase' of cultures, to the Japanese audiences who were only accustomed to the practice of inviting (mostly non-Asian) directors from overseas to direct Japanese performances, the collaboration of a multinational cast with Asian leadership at least offered a new experience. Intercultural collaborations in the 1990s include Ong Keng Sen's *Lear* (1997), the PETA (Philippine Educational Theater Association)/Kuro Tento production of *Comedy of Romeo and Juliet* (1997) and Nonon Padilla's *Romeo and Juliet* (1998), all of which had a mixed cast from different Asian regions and attempted, with varying degrees of success, to dramatize Asian traditions and realities from Asian perspectives. They proved that Shakespeare performance in Japan was ready to go beyond an east–west dichotomy and redefine its cultural situation in relationship to other Asian cultures.

In this changing climate, Ninagawa has shifted his intercultural strategy, increasingly staging Shakespeare performances without apparent Japanese frameworks or visuals since the late 1990s. For instance, Japanese aesthetics are hardly recognizable in his 2001 production of *Macbeth* and his 2004 production of *Titus Andronicus*, which was restaged in 2006 as a part of the Complete Works Festival (RSC) in Stratford-upon-Avon. His All Male Shakespeare Series, which started in 2004 with *As You Like It*, is again devoid of an overt Japanese framework or visual cues. What distinguishes most of these all-male productions from his earlier attempts, for instance *Media* (1978), is his exploitation of a young male cast in an unabashedly populist manner. At a glance, period costumes and classical sets remind us of the traditional shingeki Shakespeare performances, which Ninagawa long rebelled against. However, beneath this seeming resemblance lies Ninagawa's characteristic drive to further liberate and popularize Shakespeare by introducing the theme of boys' love. The theme and conventions of boys' love are widespread in Japanese cultural forms, from kabuki to manga, and it seems that in this series – Ninagawa's version of manga Shakespeare, in a sense – he sought a new strategy to stage localized Shakespeare that resonates with a younger audience.

His search for a new intercultural strategy also resulted in *Shochiku Grand Kabuki Twelfth Night*, which was performed in Tokyo (2005, 2009) and in London (2009). This was Ninagawa's only attempt to stage Shakespeare within the single performative mode of traditional theatre, kabuki. Unlike Shakespearean performances in indigenous theatre forms since the 1980s, which had straightforwardly applied their non-realistic dramaturgy, Ninagawa challenged the numerous and rigorous stage conventions of kabuki by adding naturalism in his customary mix-and-match style.

The most complex intraculturalism, or interactions of different cultures within Japanese culture, can be seen in the 2007 production of *Hamlet* directed by Kurita Yoshihiro, the fifth production of the Ryutopia Noh Theatre Shakespeare Series (Figure 23.1).[1] All productions in this series are staged in traditional noh theatres, although none of them have been staged in an authentic noh style with noh performers. Rather, by exploiting the possibilities of the noh stage and borrowing from various traditional Japanese theatre forms, Kurita tries to 'produce a new mixed breed of original Shakespeare' (Kurita and Tanaka 2006). The most striking feature of this production was Kurita's decision to let Hamlet remain seated and immobile during the entire performance. When stage lights revealed Hamlet sitting downstage centre of the noh stage, cross-legged in *zazen* (a posture for Zen meditation) style, the audience knew that he was meditating on his past and about to narrate his history. Kurita took advantage of the noh stage and its aesthetics in various ways, one of them being this use of the *Mugen* noh (the noh of dream vision) framework in which the dead or a visitor from another world appears before a stranger and narrates his or her past. Far from diminishing his stage presence, the immobility of Hamlet established his dominance on the stage. He was given a privileged stance from which he could control everything happening and exist in multiple levels of reality within the play. Hamlet, as a meditator on his past, acted as creator of his own story, and while he played a character in the play himself, he could also make everyone act at will. Following Zeami's notion that noh theatre is basically a space where audiences witness an 'epiphany', or an advent of the invisible, Kurita decided that everything on the bare noh stage should be seen through Hamlet's eyes.

To compensate for his lack of movement, Hamlet appointed three *tsukaima* (familiar spirits) and a *joruri* narrator (narrator with *shamisen*, a three-stringed musical instrument) as his surrogates. The contribution of the tsukaima was physical, while the joruri's was verbal, as he narrated the action on a different level of reality. The tsukaima and joruri served as more than dramatic

Figure 23.1 Hamlet, Ryutopia Noh Theatre Shakespeare Series (2007).
(Courtesy of Ryutopia Series)

necessities tasked with materializing Hamlet's vision on stage. This division of movement and speech between them best exemplifies the complex interaction of multiple indigenous theatrical forms in Kurita's production. First, the division is loosely based on noh, in which the audience is supposed to follow the narrative, irrespective of the non-realistic division of movement and speech between actors and chorus, by appreciating what is happening onstage as a whole. Furthermore, the movement of tsukaima to the accompaniment of the joruri's narration brings to mind another traditional theatre, bunraku, in which puppets act out a play to joruri accompaniment. The way the tsukaima figures were actually presented on the stage also complicated the use of indigenous theatrical forms here. To convey their inhuman identity, the three tsukaima figures always moved like dolls. This personification of dolls by actors is a kabuki practice called *ningyoburi* (acting that imitates the exaggerated motions of puppets). Thus, Kurita's exploitation of the non-realist environment of the noh stage resulted in an intricate combination, rather than a simple juxtaposition, of multiple theatrical forms in this production.

In a different mode of interculturalism, a shift in the representation of characters from the realistic to the formal not only outlined their emotional journey within the play but also critically reassessed the history of Shakespeare's assimilation in Japan, starting from shingeki monopoly. All characters, apart from Hamlet, the tsukaima and the joruri, gradually outgrew their realistic acting mode to adopt a more formal and ritualistic one before finally becoming completely motionless and speechless like Hamlet himself. By the beginning of the final duel scene, the realistic mode of speech and movement had been abandoned. The duel was performed symbolically by a row of characters who walked on the stage vertically to the joruri narration of a sword fight from the First Player's 'Pyrrhus speech'. Finally, the characters slowed their walking and knelt at the front of the stage, becoming completely motionless with their eyes closed.

The symbolic dimension to the final duel scene clearly makes visible the conflict between the two antithetical modes of acting: realism and formalism. The latter's victory in this performance was consummated in Hamlet's final line: 'The rest is silence.' In silence, everything disappears into Hamlet's consciousness and then into nothingness. The production thus ended with a celebration of the silence underlying traditional Japanese aesthetics. In Zen meditation, silence offers rich possibilities for comprehending what is beyond verbal expression and logical analysis. It is also the essence of formalism. The final silence that consumed everything promised triumph to the dying Hamlet, who would probably find the ultimate truth and peace of mind once he finished relating his story.

With an intricate mixture of traditional theatre forms and a shift from realistic to formal modes of acting, the Ryutopia *Hamlet* fully dramatizes the intracultural style of Japanese Shakespeare performance as well as the historical context that has shaped that style. The gradual disengagement with realistic modes of acting in this production of *Hamlet* epitomizes the history of Shakespearean performance in Japan, which can be largely understood as a struggle against the standard imposed by shingeki. What Kurita aimed to do in this complex performance was to provide a statement of Japan's current relationship to what Shakespeare and shingeki represent. In witnessing the onstage negotiation with the realist shingeki presentation of Shakespeare, a Japanese audience renews its awareness of Japan's cultural position.

III. Sinophone theatres: China, Hong Kong and Taiwan, by Alexa Huang

Along with a number of Japanese and Western canonical poets and writers, Shakespeare and his works have played a significant role in the development of Chinese and Sinophone theatres in China, Hong Kong and Taiwan. Hundreds of works have emerged in Mandarin and a wide range of Chinese dialects, performing styles and genres. The encounters between 'Shakespeare' and genres and values represented by the icon of 'China' have enriched Chinese-language theatrical traditions as well as global Shakespearean performance history. In the following pages, I shall focus on the challenges and changes to Chinese-language theatres.

The transmission of Renaissance culture in China began with the arrival of the first Jesuit missionaries in 1582, followed by the Dominicans and Franciscans in the 1630s. Illustrated British travel narratives record British emissaries' experience of attending theatrical productions in Tianjin and Beijing during the reign of the Qianlong emperor (1736–1795), including the mission of Lord George Macartney. One of the emissaries' diary entries briefly comments on the similarity between an unnamed Chinese play and Shakespeare's *Richard III*. With the decline of the Qing empire in the nineteenth century, Chinese interests in Western modes of thinking and political systems intensified. Both Shakespeare and China were 'translated' – to use the word to mean transformed or metamorphosed, as Peter Quince does in *A Midsummer Night's Dream* – in the late nineteenth century according to clashing ideologies of modernization, westernization and revalidation of traditional Chinese values. Along with John Milton and other 'national' poets, Shakespeare's name entered the discourse of nationalism. Shakespeare was first mentioned in passing in 1839 in a compendium of world cultures translated by Lin Zexu, a key figure in the first Opium War (1839–1842). By the time Chinese translations became available and substantive critical engagements with Shakespeare were initiated, there was already over half a century of reception history in which Shakespeare was frequently evoked to support or suppress specific agendas.

There are several recurrent themes in Chinese-language adaptations of Shakespeare. Universalization, as opposed to localization, has been a popular strategy among Chinese directors and translators. This strategy has produced plays performed 'straight', with visual and textual citations of what was perceived to be authoritative classical performances (such as Laurence Olivier's versions). Some early 1920s performances, especially those involving students or drama societies, in Shanghai followed this pattern. If the play seems foreign, according to advocates of this approach, that only guarantees its aesthetics have been preserved in a way that benefits the audience. Adaptations that localise the plays are another popular approach.

A second strategy is to localize the plot and setting of a play, and assimilate Shakespeare into the local worldviews. It folds Shakespeare into local performance genres. An example is Huang Zuolin's *Xieshou ji* (The Story of Bloody Hands, 1986), a *kunqu* opera adaptation of *Macbeth*. The complex idioms of Chinese theatrical forms were increasingly seen by the performers and their sponsors not as an obstacle but as an asset in creating an international demand for the traditional theatre form.

The third strategy involves pastiche, dramaturgical collage and extensive, deconstructive rewritings. It sometimes changes the genre of a play by accessing dormant themes that have been marginalized by centuries of Anglocentric criticism and performance traditions. The emergence of parody is a sign that Shakespeare's global afterlife has reached a new stage. The stories have become so familiar to the 'cross-border' audiences that the plays can be used as a platform for artistic exploration of new genres. For instance, in writing a *huaju* play called *Shamuleite*, or *Shamlet* (1992), Lee Kuo-hsiu, one of the most innovative Taiwanese playwrights and directors to emerge in the 1980s, turned high tragedy, or what was known to Renaissance readers as 'tragic history', into comic parody. He suggests in the programme that *Shamlet* is a revenge comedy that 'has nothing to do with *Hamlet* but something to do with Shakespeare'. This strategy has been used to counter stereotypical construction of local and foreign cultures. It has also been used as the artists' personal branding in international markets for intercultural theatre works, such as Wu Hsing-kuo and his solo Beijing opera *Li'er zaici* (Lear Is Here, 2000) in which the performer inserts his own life story. Playing ten characters from Shakespeare's tragedy, Wu extrapolates the themes of domestic conflict, construction of selves and others, and notions of duty to family and duty to the state and mingles these themes with his autobiography.

These three themes coexist throughout the history of Chinese and Sinophone Shakespeares. As in almost all instances of transnational borrowing, a select, locally resonant group of 'privileged' plays has held continuous sway in the Chinese-speaking world. *The Merchant of Venice* is the first Shakespearean play known to be staged, and it continues to fascinate Chinese audiences today. The reception of the play exemplifies the complex processes of reading between, with, and against the genres of comedy and tragedy. Early modern printers and readers were uncertain about the play's genre. The 1623 folio placed it under 'comedies' as simply *The Merchant of Venice* (rendering the titular character ambiguous), but the entry in the Stationers' Register on 22 July 1598 – the first mention of the play – focuses attention on Shylock by calling it 'A Book of the Merchant of Venice, or Otherwise Called the Jew of Venice'. The later generic ambiguity carried over when the play came to China, where it has often been staged and received as a romantic comedy rather than a tragedy fuelled by religious tensions (as has mostly been the case since the twentieth century in the democratic West). The play has also been parodied on stage. A travesty by Francis Talfourd entitled *Shylock, or, The Merchant of Venice Preserved*, was staged in Hong Kong in 1867 for British expatriates. The Hong Kong Amateur Dramatic Club revived the production in 1871, as the mercantile-themed play proved relevant to the social milieu of a trade colony. The trial scene from *The Merchant of Venice* was performed in 1896 by the graduating class of St. John's University, a missionary college in Shanghai, followed by another student performance in 1902. In time, Mandarin-language performances began to dominate the stage, and today, the play remains a staple of high school and college curricula and is often chosen for the graduation *huaju* (spoken drama) productions of Chinese and Taiwanese universities.

In terms of performance style, Shakespeare has figured prominently in the shaping of contemporary Chinese theatre, where the genres of *xiqu* (stylized theatre with more than 360 regional variations) and huaju (post-1907 Western-influenced spoken drama theatre, including obsolete subgenres) coexist. The earliest-documented xiqu Shakespeare was based on *Hamlet* and titled *Shaxiong duosao* (Killing the Elder Brother and Snatching the Sister-in-Law) and performed in *chuanju* (Sichuan opera) style. Other artists followed suit. The Yisu She (Custom Renewal Society) staged *Yibang rou* (A Pound of Flesh) in the *qinqiang* opera style in 1925 in Shaanxi Province in northern China. Although stylized performances of Shakespeare in different genres of Chinese opera have existed since the early twentieth century, the 1980s were a turning point, when Shakespeare became more regularly performed in different forms of stylization in China, Taiwan, Hong Kong and elsewhere, and entered the collective cultural memory of Chinese opera performers and audiences. The revived interest in Chinese-opera Shakespeare was encouraged by increased exchanges among performers based in mainland China and in the Chinese diaspora.

Beyond Chinese opera, performances of Shakespeare that involve China at their centre of imagination frequently highlight linguistic differences. Languages served as markers of ethnic differences in *Yumei and Tianlai*, a bilingual Taiwanese–Mandarin *Romeo and Juliet* at the Shakespeare in Taipei festival in 2003. The Montagues and the Capulets are each assigned a different language, complicating the experience of artists in the Chinese diaspora and the play's capacity as a national allegory. Key scenes from *Romeo and Juliet* were staged in two plays-within-a-play in Ning Caishen's *Romeo and Zhu Yingtai*, directed by He Nian and produced by the Shanghai Dramatic Arts Center (May 2008), in which French, Japanese, English and Mandarin Chinese were spoken. In what Ning called 'a tragedy told in comic manners', the star-crossed lovers traversed 1937 Shanghai and present-day New York in search of new personal and cultural identities.

The differing situations in other parts of the Chinese-speaking world led to varied histories of reception. Kawakami Otojirō's (1864–1911) *Othello* (a *shinpa* production in Japanese) in 1903 recast Taiwan as the outpost of the colonial Japanese empire, moving Venice to Japan and Cyprus to the Penghu Archipelago west of Taiwan. When Muro Washiro (the Othello figure), a dark-faced Japanese colonial general in Taiwan, commits suicide at the end of the play, he compares himself to an 'uncivilized' Taiwanese aboriginal inhabitant (*seiban* [raw savage]). An island off the southeast coast of mainland China, Taiwan has had complex relationships with the dominant 'fatherland' (*zuguo*) across the strait and with Japan to the north. While not directly responsible for the scarcity of western dramas from the early to the mid-twentieth century, the island's intense focus upon the essentialized aspects of Japan and China prevented the growth of translated dramas from European languages. In the first half of the twentieth century, tours of Japan's all-female Takarazuka performances to Taiwan occasionally included Shakespeare. The earliest-documented Chinese-language performance of Shakespeare in Taiwan was *Yi yun* (Clouds of Doubt) staged by the Shiyan Xiao Juchang (Experimental Theatre of Taipei) in February 1949 and based on *Othello*. A few other performances followed, but until martial law was lifted in 1987, Taiwan's theatre remained shaped by political censorship in significant ways, first by the Japanese colonial cultural policy and then by the anticommunist cultural policy of the KMT regime.

The presence of Shakespeare at theatre festivals in Taiwan in the 1980s and 1990s took a different form from mainland China's post-revolutionary Shakespeare boom, which was initiated by state-endorsed and government-sponsored Shakespeare festivals in 1986 and 1994. The month-long 'Shakespeare in Taipei' festival (May 2003), for instance, focused more on providing a platform for artistically innovative and commercially viable experimental works. As a multilingual society (Mandarin, Taiwanese, Hakka and aboriginal languages), Taiwan has produced a signifi-cant number of mainstream performances either entirely in a dialect or with a mixture of Mandarin and a local dialect or English. Some of these works reflect Taiwan's multiply determined history, while others question that history and the much-contested 'Chineseness' of the island's identity. These tendencies provide interesting contrasts to the ways in which mainland Chinese artists imagine China. By the same token, while mainland China is certainly multilingual, it is Taiwan and Hong Kong that have established strong traditions of Shakespeare performances in one or more dialects. The few mainland Chinese performances of Shakespeare in local dialects were commissioned and sponsored by the government for festivals or produced by ethnic minority students in actor training programmes. The linguistic diversity of Taiwan and Hong Kong theatres fosters distinctive views of 'Shakespeare' and what counts as 'Chinese'.

With strong dual traditions of English and Cantonese Shakespearean performances in huaju and *yueju* (Cantonese opera), Hong Kong theatre reflects the tension between southern Chinese culture and the British legacy. After Hong Kong was ceded to Britain for 150 years in the 1842 Treaty of Nanjing, Englishness became an important element throughout the social structure. Under the British government, theatre was supported and encouraged as 'a wholesome diversion from the tedium of military life'. English literature was established as a subject of study in Hong Kong's school system and in 1882 students began studying Shakespeare for exams, initiating a form of 'domination by consent'. Shakespearean drama became part of the repertoire of the Hong Kong Amateur Dramatic Club that was active in the 1860s and 1870s. The so-called amateur theatre was in fact noncommercial theatre rather than nonprofessional. Such performances entertained British expatriates and brought 'a touch of the British culture' to Hong Kong residents. As in Japan, nineteenth-century China and Hong Kong saw sporadic perform-ances of 'authentic' Shakespeare in English that exposed local residents to the contemporary

English culture. What was meant by authentic Shakespeare was a performance style that purported to present Shakespeare as he was conceived to have been played in his lifetime. Shakespeare festivals (23 April 1954; April 1964; 24–29 January 1984) and experimental Shakespearean performances emerged in the mid-twentieth century. Since the 1980s, a considerable amount of energy has been directed not toward the postcolonial question but toward Hong Kong's global status and its Chinese heritage, as evidenced by the productions of the Hong Kong Repertory Theatre (founded in 1977), the largest professional theatre in Hong Kong, and performances by students of the Hong Kong Academy for Performing Arts and other universities.

Despite the association of Shakespeare and Englishness, Shakespeare was not resisted as an image of colonization. Political changes have hardly affected him. Some contemporary Hong Kong scholars are surprised to find that 'local experimentations with Shakespeare in post-modernist and Chinese styles have continued to flourish [in Hong Kong]' (Tam *et al.* 2002: ix). This continued prominence, they argue, shows that 'Shakespeare has transcended his British heritage and become part of the Hong Kong Chinese tradition' (Tam *et al.*). While partly true, this view blurs the historical conditions surrounding early performances. One crucial reason why Shakespeare seems to transcend his British heritage is that Britain never colonized Hong Kong the way it did with India. This special historical condition – an indirect colonial structure that Mao Zedong later called semi-colonialism – informed Hong Kong's performance culture in the late nineteenth and early twentieth centuries. If the practitioners of the new theatre were resisting anything, it was the Chinese past. The same is true of other treaty ports, such as Shanghai, that were home to a host of European concessions but had no overarching colonial institution.

The uses of Shakespeare's plays in spoken drama and Chinese opera are informed by a paradigm shift from seeking authenticity to foregrounding artistic subjectivity. Shakespearean themes and characterization have enriched, challenged and changed Chinese-language theatres and genres. Chinese and Sinophone Shakespeares have become strangers at home.

IV. Southeast Asia, by Yong Li Lan

Southeast Asia is a relatively new region, whose individual histories of Shakespeare performance in disparate languages, theatre cultures and socio-political contexts pre-date their collocation as 'Southeast Asian' by about fifty years. Prior to the Second World War, the region was generally referred to as the Indies, or by names denoting colonial governance, such as Nederlands-Oost-Indië (modern Indonesia) or the Straits Settlements (Penang, Dinding, Malacca and Singapore). Its coherence as a region originated in efforts by the world powers to exert influence over how these countries de-colonized (with the exception of Thailand, which has never been subject to external government). Conversely, people and likewise theatre practices in the region continue to identify themselves by country or by part of a country, not as 'Southeast Asian'. Southeast Asia was therefore from the first a region after colonialism. Its diverse contemporary theatre practices have in common a backdrop of contentions over a national culture made up of layers of historical alliances and hostilities between different points of cultural reference.

Given these conditions for intercultural practice, a binary opposition between colonial western culture and indigenous traditions is rarely seen, where we could say that Shakespeare, coming from the former, is re-created by the latter. Or if a binary formula seems to apply, it must be recognized as an effect designed to perform national culture for a specific agenda; for example, as the national entry in a festival of world Shakespeare, or to stake a claim to the 'national' within an *intracultural* conflict. Rather, Shakespeare's work, perceived as classic in the sense of an enduring, high model of western realism, allows the engagement of the notion of the traditional

– although the tradition referenced is not always, or only, a tradition directly associated with his plays. Two common approaches can be distinguished: (a) a radical re-scripting of the play; and (b) an upholding of the received standard (western) Shakespeare performance, through the use of the original English text or an authoritative translation, but often differentiating the production's cultural character from that standard by several striking changes.

Traditional Macbeths

The style of Shakespeare performance thought of as 'traditional' in Southeast Asia is perhaps so regarded in many other places. Disseminated through Asia by English touring companies, early films and theatre practitioners and scholars who travelled and studied in the West in the early twentieth century, the style centres upon naturalist acting by star actors which, by twenty-first century norms, appears somewhat grandiloquent and mannered. Importantly for this essay, it is also a period costume style. In the British colonies of Malaya, Burma and Singapore, this style was imported into local theatre culture through amateur theatricals put on by British expatriates, servicemen and school-based groups (such as The Stage Club and Changi Theatre Club in Singapore). Examples in this tradition are now uncommon in English,[2] but it is still produced in translation in countries that were not British colonies. In translation, the traditional values with which this performance style is aligned are not only those represented by the original western classic (poetry, grand vision, dramatic characters), but also the literary values and cultural history embodied in the translated canon. In other words, performing Shakespeare in translation carries cultural pride in the unique qualities and character of one's own language, at a high point of its achievement that equals and rivals Shakespeare, by re-creating him.

The historical point to which the translated classic refers is the project of modernization through westernization, which occurred in different countries over slightly different periods of the late nineteenth and early twentieth centuries. In Vietnam between 1917 and 1926, French-trained translators and intellectuals such as Nguyen Van Vinh (1882–1936) translated western (mostly French) plays and novels into the romanized Vietnamese alphabet, quoc ngu (literally 'national language', made compulsory by the French administration in 1910). Their project was to refine and promote quoc ngu, and at the same time introduce western genres and modern ideas into Vietnamese society (Nguyen 2011; Goscha 2003). In the postcolonial era, state-sponsored histories have foregrounded the western-style Vietnamese literature written in quoc ngu that emerged from this period of westernization.[3] However, the translated western classic is the counterpart of these original works, in that the translation itself becomes a classic of national literature, carrying the resonance of a seminal text of the modern nation's cultural identity as an *international* identity. Translations from a later period share this lineage. In Thailand, Shakespeare was first translated into Thai by King Vajiravudh (1881–1925), who is credited with stimulating the golden age of modern Siamese drama through his original plays as well as translations of classics from several languages, and who introduced major educational and administrative reforms along western lines. In Paradee Tungtang's account:

> The King's works are famous and widely read so that, to some extent, the King's name overshadows that of the original playwright; his translated works ostensibly become 'original' in their own right and are studied nowadays as classic pieces of Thai literature.
>
> (Tungtang 2011: xxiii)

The intercultural value of the translated text is thus in its duality: it presents at once as an extension of the authority of the world classic, and as national literary heritage.

As opposed to original plays dating from this founding period of nationalism, in the early twenty-first century Shakespeare in translation, produced in the conventional naturalist style, has the advantages of an indeterminate notion of the traditional, which can be flexibly purposed. Two recent productions of *Macbeth* provide examples.[4] The Vietnam Youth Theatre, one of the foremost theatre companies in Vietnam with fast-growing international engagements, has a flagship production first staged in Hanoi and Ho Chí Minh City in 2002. This *Macbeth* toured to China (Beijing, 2003 and Shanghai, 2005), was revived in 2008 as Vietnam's contribution to the global Shakespeare Schools Festival, and invited to the World Shakespeare Festival (Liverpool, 2012). The highly respected, scholarly translation by Bùi Phụng is matched by a very expensive production relative to the company's meagre funding, with elaborate western-styled costumes for a large cast and a set of marble columns; this grand staging was regarded as necessary in order to uphold the cultural status of Shakespeare.[5] While the scenography employs a local rendition of western traditional staging, it also includes prominent elements drawn from *tuong* (Vietnamese classical opera): three large drums placed at centre stage are beaten by the witches throughout the performance, and Lady Macbeth's death is depicted by an intense dance sequence where she is tied to a long swathe of red silk, representing blood, in which she is gradually wrapped by the witches. Its long international stage history and combination of Shakespearean and Vietnamese stage traditions have mutually reinforced the Vietnam Youth Theatre's creation of a classic national production in its *Macbeth*.

In this position, the production installs several familiar nationalist signifiers as traditional. First, while otherwise following Bùi's translation, the production inserts two scenes not in Shakespeare's play. The first opens the play, before the witches appear, with the triumphal return from civil war by Macbeth with his troops, flanked by Banquo and Macduff, and set to Bruckner's Eighth Symphony. This scene is treated with a grand ceremonial display of troops in formation and is clearly emblematic of national victory in war. So, too, the sentimental farewell between Macduff, his wife and his son while his men kneel in the background is a scene of the national hero's family in wartime: 'Son, come here and embrace your father, he might never return this time' (A|S|I|A, 1:40:46). These two scenes do not attempt to adapt Shakespeare's *Macbeth* as an analogy of Vietnam's national history; rather, they appear almost as a logical necessity for a production in Vietnam in the early twenty-first century whose subject is civil war, lifting out of Shakespeare's fiction in paradigmatic Vietnamese moments. A second major change is to the dramatis personae: Lady Macbeth and Lady Macduff are here Mrs Macbeth and Mrs Macduff. In the publicity flyer, the reduction of Shakespeare's aristocratic characters to commoner status is placed alongside the elevation of the performers by their communist state titles. All press reviews specify that Mrs Macbeth is played by People's Artist Nguyen Lan Huong, Macbeth by Merited Artist Anh Tu and the play directed by People's Artist Le Hung. Through these scenes and titles, Shakespeare functions as a cipher for the traditional that extends its status of a world classic to the achievements of the communist nation-state, and conversely, becomes contemporary Vietnamese. Comparing this production to the thinly attended performances of *Macbeth* in English by the British company TNT on tour in Ho Chi Minh City (Anon. 2011), a blogger, Heo, felt that the emotional content of the play wasn't as stirring as the Vietnamese version. 'I was not as emotionally fulfilled as I was when I saw the Vietnamese hit, which tells the story of modern life', and is set in modern-day Hanoi (quoted in *Thanh Nien* 2011).

In a different context but with a performative similarity, a traditional production of Shakespeare in translation staged a tradition of international modernity in Thai theatre education. Chulalongkorn University's Drama Department produced *Macbeth* in 2011 in Bangkok to mark the department's 40th anniversary, and invited its alumni to participate in it. This sold-out production generated much excitement; roles were so over-subscribed that Macbeth and

Lady Macbeth were played by alternate pairs of actors, and additional non-speaking parts included thirteen witches among a cast of forty-eight. Reviews listed the cast and design team of prominent figures in television, media and industry, who all participated without fee (Soosip 2011; Musiket 2011). The production also inaugurated the university's new black box theatre, the Sodsai Pantoomkomol Centre for Dramatic Art, named after the theatre teacher who pioneered theatrical arts studies at university level in Thailand and is regarded by many to have been the driving force in the development of Thai modern theatre through her teaching of Stanislavskian naturalism (Tungtang 2011: 186–90). Chulalongkorn University's *Macbeth* thus brought together a new site, a living lineage of performance stars, and their mentor. The production gathered its community together in the celebratory creation of a local tradition of theatre education, and because this was the performative value of the occasion, the production values and style were exemplary. The translation by the director, Nopamat Veohong, employed a literary, old-fashioned idiom that, according to reviews, 'captures the emotion and the poetic beauty of the original. Once you adjust your ear to the stylisation, you can appreciate the same linguistic beauty for which Shakespeare is esteemed' (Nantapon 2011).[6] The acting, costumes and staging were modelled upon a high tradition of naturalist western productions, incorporating no elements of Thai traditional performance.

In contemporary Southeast Asian theatres, traditional productions of Shakespeare in translation perform a sign of the modernity of a national culture that shares a world heritage. Their enactment of the traditional, in both literary and theatrical respects, accommodates the treatment of local histories, performance elements and idioms as traditions to be equally taken for granted and uncontested as Shakespeare. Naturally, then, traditional-styled Shakespeare in translation is often produced as an educational enterprise, and thus an exercise in modelling. Instead of staging difference, these productions harmonize or even altogether avoid indigenous theatrical elements, to place the weight of the intercultural transaction on the performative production of national traditions.

Shakespeare and intracultural pasts

The alternative to traditional productions of Shakespeare in translation is an overtly intercultural practice of adaptation. Bold re-scriptings of Shakespeare's plays retain his plot outline as a reference point for a past world with which Shakespeare's story and its values are in some way compared. Frequently, this past is pre-national, and differentiating the adaptation from Shakespeare's play and from local performance alike functions as a means of resisting a hegemonic national narrative – not of claiming national identity, as is often assumed in intercultural theory. Instead, dissonances between languages, registers, theatrical vocabularies and dramatic modes, such as the realist and the symbolic, stage contending influences and narratives of the past.

Mak Yong Titis Sakti (Mak Yong Drops of Magic) by The Actors' Studio in Kuala Lumpur adapted *A Midsummer Night's Dream* to the ancient Malay form of mak yong in 2009 (Figure 23.2). This production co-opted Shakespeare's status as a world author to support mak yong in the religious controversy concerning its animist basis, particularly its invocation of spirits. Public performances of mak yong were banned in 1991 in its home state of Kelantan by the Pan-Malaysian Islamic Party (PAS) which rules Kelantan. *Mak Yong Titis Sakti* participated in the lobbying in the Malaysian capital to legitimate mak yong by re-situating it as an international performance form, and as national heritage, following its classification by UNESCO as a Masterpiece of the Oral and Intangible Heritage of Humanity in 2005. Instead of myths of royal personages (the mak yong repertoire), Shakespeare's lovers provided broad comedy. The performance did not observe the prescribed arrangement of musical instruments, actors and audience in alignment with compass directions (Sarwar 1976: 76–81). Here, a decorative and faintly mysterious air was created by set panels painted in pastels and glittering, intricate costumes, overlaid by coloured lighting and overhung with a lamp of red roses trailing garlands. The original Malay magic was transposed onto the *Dream*'s foreign, thus non-potent, magic, while its style preserved a kind of animism. The king's solution to the lovers' problems was to invoke a spirit: a beautiful girl with magical properties who does not speak, called Flower (*Bunga*). The mak yong formulae of fixed dramatic sequences, speech and songs were sufficiently followed, if abbreviated, for the director Norzizi Zulkifli to assert, 'the staging itself stays true to the style of mak yong which fuses together singing, dance, drama, romance and comedy' (Chua 2009).

The contention over mak yong's legitimacy in an Islamic society is understood to be driven by the political conflict between PAS and UMNO, the largest Malaysian party which dominates the coalition ruling party (Hardwick 2013), a conflict symbolically mapped between Kelantan and Kuala Lumpur respectively. This spatial figuration of the intracultural, however, occludes its temporality. Elder Peran and Younger Peran, the divine clowns of mak yong, respectively represented the older culture of Kelantan, which once ruled the Patani sultanate extending over south Thailand, and the newer cosmopolitan capital of Kuala Lumpur established by the British colonial government. Elder Peran spoke Kelantanese and Younger Peran mixed colloquial Malay and English. Their comic improvisation stole the show, with the Younger often puncturing the formality of the Elder by an incongruous register, word-play and topical references. Younger Peran introduced the performance by joking with the audience about their mobile phones and Facebook, before Elder Peran performed the rite to consecrate the stage with prayers followed

Figure 23.2 Mak Yong Titis Sakti (Mak Yong Drops of Magic), Kuala Lumpur, 2009.
(Courtesy of Kuala Lumpur Performing Arts Centre)

by flinging of fistfuls of rice towards the four corners. Thus Kelantan and Kuala Lumpur are not only political loci but also time periods for differing visions of Malay culture. The humour generated by juxtaposing the two Perans' incongruous frames of cultural reference dramatized the disparities, but also the cooperation, between the slow, ceremonial world of mak yong and the urban wit of contemporary Malay life.

The recuperation of heritage emphasized material culture in a play for children, *The Nonya Nightingale* by Paper Monkey Theatre in Singapore in 2010. This production combined the storylines of *King Lear* and *The Emperor's Nightingale* to teach children about Peranakan culture two generations ago. The Peranakans are a migrant Chinese community who arrived in the Malay archipelago from the sixteenth century onwards, becoming a wealthy merchant class with distinctive cultural practices. In British Malaya, Peranakans were educated in English schools (unlike Malays), and formed a bridge community between the British and the Malays; hence they were also called 'the King's Chinese'. Linking Peranakan heritage to Shakespeare therefore taps the root of the English language in the region as it branches into non-standard vernacular Englishes. In *The Nonya Nightingale*, the actors' speech patterns changed with the era in which a scene was set, from the 'Singlish' (Singaporean English) spoken today to the inflections and idioms of Malay-accented English that marked the Peranakan voice. The treatment of the story through object puppetry gave a voice and character to everyday Peranakan objects used as puppets: a miniature grandfather clock, a thermos flask, a china tiffin-carrier and an old-fashioned metal candle-holder respectively represented the matriarch Mrs Neo and her three daughters, Abigail, Barbara and Cordelia. Cordelia spoke standard international English, transcending time frames and cultures, whereas Mrs Neo used typical Peranakan expressions that are now seldom heard. 'Mouth got diamond cannot talk,' she muttered of her cousins, the Bibi twins, a pair of bright red Peranakan shoes who giggled and squealed when spoken to. Against nostalgia for a vanishing way of life were set the Peranakan culture's materialism and aspirations for a western-style affluence that caused Mrs Neo to disown Cordelia. Whereas Chulalongkorn University's *Macbeth* celebrated its tradition of international theatre education, *The Nonya Nightingale* staged its education in heritage with the ambivalent feelings of a family history.

Mak Yong Titis Sakti and *The Nonya Nightingale* were both productions in former British colonies, intended for local audiences, not international touring. They used Shakespeare to bring into view intracultural relationships to the past in cultural practices and speech idioms. International collaborations span the range from formal, theatrical interculturality to socio-cultural interactions dramatized without contrasting theatrical styles. An example of the latter type of performance was *Romeo at Julieta: Isang Komedi* (2008). This production resulted from a decade's collaboration between Black Tent Theatre in Japan and the Philippine Educational Theatre Association (PETA), and toured Japan and the Philippines. Its Filipino Juliet went to Japan to make a living as a karaoke bargirl and its Romeo was a Japanese farmer named Tamio. The production's social realism presented an ordinary nightclub, Verona Bar, and costumes by turns flashy and everyday. The social degradation of the characters' lives was satirized by implied comparison with the poetry and noble characters of Shakespeare's play. Nevertheless, the depiction of a problematic trade between the two countries in the 1990s to early 2000s (Parrenas 2011) accommodated the protagonists' aspiration to Romeo and Juliet's ideal romance through comic exchanges across the language barrier, and ensemble musical numbers delivered with infectious spiritedness. That fugitive idealism supported a dream-like moment at the heart of the production, when past and present momentarily recognized each other. Tamio's grandfather, who had been a soldier in the Japanese occupation of the Philippines during the Second World War, and was now suffering from senile dementia, mistook Julieta for the Filipino comfort girl Maria with whom he had fallen in love during the occupation and who was killed. Tamio's grandfather and Julieta joined in singing an old Tagalog folk song, 'Babalik ka rin' (I believe you will return), which the grandfather had learnt from Maria, and Julieta had sung in her childhood. The multilingual script in Tagalog, Japanese and English by Rody Vera and Yamamoto Kiyokazu, as well as the rehearsal process documented by the companies, testify to the symbolic value of this collaboration across the antagonism of the two countries' historical and present economic relationships.[7]

At the opposite end of the spectrum of intercultural strategies from *Romeo at Julieta* is the work of the Singaporean director Ong Keng Sen, where each performer employed his or her own performance form and language. Ong's practice for Shakespeare brought performers together from the whole Asian region as well as Europe and the United States in four productions: *Lear* by the Japan Foundation (1997), *Desdemona* by TheatreWorks (2000), *Search: Hamlet* by TheatreWorks and Face to Face (2002) and *Lear Dreaming* by TheatreWorks (2012). These productions increasingly tested the premises of intercultural performance, a dominant and controversial strand of which has been the interaction of premodern Asian theatres with western canonical texts. *Lear* broke new ground by employing multiple Asian traditions, matched to the characters of *King Lear*: the Old Man was played by a *noh* actor, the Older Daughter by a *jingju* actor and the Younger Daughter by a Thai dancer. As a challenge to orientalist expectations of Asian traditions (Ong 2001), *Desdemona* juxtaposed contemporary practices such as video installation with ancient forms such as *kutiyattam*, and treated the plot of *Othello* as an occasion to explore the intercultural process, introducing the performers' thoughts and training into a many-layered performance. *Search: Hamlet* put greater pressure on notions of the intercultural as the theatrical presentation of two or more cultures, by individuating the traditional 'cultural performance'. Set at the originary site of Kronborg castle, the production brought together performers known for their individual styles of working in different genres, who devised their own music and dialogue in workshops. The result, which omitted the title character of Hamlet himself, was a refraction of the original play into the supporting characters and surrounding performance cultures around the canonical centrality of Hamlet and Shakespeare. Ong's productions increasingly foregrounded musical interculturality, combining *gamelan* with western strings, saxophone and the vocals of the Danish rock star Dicte in *Search: Hamlet. Lear Dreaming* was a piece of music theatre, with a series of soundscapes set against vivid colour washes that contrasted the principal characters' music: the Older Daughter Wu Man's pipa, the noh actor Umewaka Naohiko's sonorous delivery, the *jeongga* (Korean traditional song) of the Mother Kang Kwon Soon and the choric gamelan troupe.

Ong's productions draw upon artistic forms in diverse mediums from across the Asian region, and combine them in striking, unexpected contrasts that at once showcase the range and expressive power of Asian performances and problematize an audience's reaction to them by self-conscious framing. They depart from other Shakespeare productions in the Southeast Asian region by not engaging a local history. In general, in the early twenty-first century, traditionally styled productions of Shakespeare in translation employ Shakespeare to project or create national traditions, and adaptations of his plays use Shakespeare to bring into view the tensions adhering to the presence of pre-national pasts in contemporary society. At the same time, Ong's work enlarges an inter- and intracultural approach that is characteristic of Shakespeare adaptation in the region, where the plurality of artistic modes and sources, the fissures between different pasts, and the multiple languages or regional varieties of a language manifest the movement of political boundaries, and of peoples across them, in recent history. While atypical in their grand scope, their orientation towards international presentation and their lack of specific social context, Ong's productions nevertheless display an aesthetic of disjunctiveness between disparate elements that the stable tradition of Shakespeare enables in Southeast Asian adapatation. The choice of adapting Shakespeare could be described as an occasion for the intersection between the place of cultures and their time.

Notes

1   The full production of the Ryutopia *Hamlet* can be seen online in the Asian Shakespeare Intercultural Archive (A|S|I|A) at http://a-s-i-a-web.org.
2   In Hong Kong, this tradition continued until its reunification with China in 1997. For more information, see Ingham (2002).
3   For instance, the plays of Vu Trong Phung and realist novels by Nhất Linh from the 1930s. See Pelley (2002) and; Tran Huy Lieu *et al.* (1971, 1985).
4   This chapter's research materials derive from two successive research projects supported by the Singapore Ministry of Education (Relocating Intercultural Theatre, MOE2008-T2-1-110; and Digital Archiving and Intercultural Performance, MOE2013-T2-1-011).
5   Personal interview with Truong Nhuan, deputy director of Vietnam Youth Theatre, translation by Nguyen Ha Nguyen, 20 June 2011, Hanoi. Nhuan stressed that the company rarely produces Shakespeare because 'Shakespeare is too expensive'.
6   Nopamat Veohong had previously translated and directed three other Shakespeare plays for the department; see Veohong.
7   A counterpart to *Romeo at Julieta* was the *Pikaresuku Iago* (Picaresque Iago) by Ryuzanji Jimusho in 1992, which adapted *Othello* to a post-apocalyptic setting in which Othello was the captain of a band of migrant workers collecting rubbish, and fell in love with a Filipino bar hostess named Desdemona.

Bibliography

Anonymous (2011) 'Macbeth in Vietnam: Toil and Trouble for Naught', *Thanh Nien*, 4 November, www.thanhniennews.com/entertainment/macbeth-in-vietnam-toil-and-trouble-for-naught-21789.html, accessed 22 June 2014.
Asian Shakespeare Intercultural Archive (A|S|I|A), video-recordings and scripts, http://a-s-i-a-web.org: Vietnam Youth Theatre's *Macbeth*, Chulalongkorn University's *Macbeth*, The Actors Studio's *Mak Yong Titis Sakti*, Paper Monkey's *The Nonya Nightingale*, Black Tent Theatre and PETA's *Romeo at Julieta*, Japan Foundation's *Lear*, TheatreWorks' *Desdemona*, TheatreWorks and Face to Face's *Search: Hamlet*, and TheatreWorks' *Lear Dreaming*, accessed 22 June 2014.
Awasthi, Suresh (1964) 'Shakespeare in Hindi', *Indian Literature*, 7 (1): 51–62.
Banham, Martin (ed.) (1988) *Cambridge Guide to World Theatre*, Cambridge: Cambridge University Press.
Barua, Navakanta (1964) 'Shakespeare in Assamese', *Indian Literature*, 7 (1):12–15.
Bharucha, Rustom. (1996) 'Under the Sign of the Onion: Intracultural Negotiations in Theatre', *New Theatre Quarterly*, 12(46): 116–29.
—— (2010) 'Foreign Asia/Foreign Shakespeare: Dissenting Notes on New Asian Interculturality, Post-Coloniality and Re-Colonization,' in Dennis Kennedy and Yong Li Lan (eds) *Shakespeare in Asia: Contemporary Performance*, 253–81, Cambridge: Cambridge University Press.
Chaudhuri, Sukanta (n.d.) 'Shakespeare in India', Shakespeare Internet Editions, http://internetshakespeare.uvic.ca/Library/Criticism/shakespearein/india1/, accessed 1 December 2014.
Chaudhuri, Una (2002) 'Beyond a "Taxonomic Theater": Interculturalism after Postcolonialism and Globalization', *Theater*, 32 (1): 33–47.
Chin, Daryl (2003) 'Interculturalism, Postmodernism, Pluralism', in Philip Auslander (ed) *Performance: Critical Concepts in Literary and Cultural Studies*, Volume 2, 395–404, London: Routledge.
Chua, Dennis (2009) 'Shakespeare Goes Mak Yong', *NST Online*, 1 June.
Das Gupta, Hemendra Nath (1944–46) *The Indian Stage*, Volume 2, Calcutta; Rpt. Delhi: Munshiram Manoharlal, 2002.
Daugherty, Diane (2005) 'The Pendulum of Intercultural Performance: "Kathakali King Lear" at Shakespeare's Globe', *Asian Theatre Journal*, 22 (1): 52–72.
Deshpande, Sudhanva (2003) 'Habib Tanvir: Upside-down Midas', *IMC India*, http://india.indymedia.org/en/2003/09/7941.shtml, accessed 5 December 2014.
Dutt, Utpal (1977) 'Little Theatre *o Ami*' (Little Theatre and I), *Epic Theatre*: 48–72.

Goscha, Christopher E. (2003) '"The Modern Barbarian": Nguyen Van Vinh and the Complexity of Colonial Modernity in Vietnam', *European Journal of East Asian Studies*, 3 (1): 135–69.

Gupta, Nidhi (2012) 'A Masala-tinged Poem, Sung to Perfection', *Sunday Guardian*, 2 September.

Hardwick, Patricia (2013) 'Embodying the Divine and the Body Politic: Mak Yong Performance in Rural Kelantan, Malaysia', in Timothy P. Daniels (ed.) *Performance, Popular Culture, and Piety in Muslim Southeast Asia*, 77–104, Houndmills: Palgrave Macmillan.

Hasan, Mohammad (1964) 'Shakespeare in Urdu', *Indian Literature*, 7 (1): 132–39.

Indian Literature (1964) Shakespeare Issue, 7 (1).

Ingham, Mike (2002) 'Shakespeare in Asian English-Language Productions', in Kwok-Kan Tam, Andrew Parkin, and Terry Siu-han Yip (eds) *Shakespeare Global/Local: The Hong Kong Imaginary in Transcultural Production*, 29–42, Frankfurt: Peter Lang.

Jain, Nemi Chand (1992) *Indian Theatre: Tradition, Continuity and Change*, New Delhi: Vikas.

Karanth, K. Shivaram (1997) *Yakshagana*, New Delhi: Abhinav.

Kaushal, J. N. (ed.) (1992) *Rang Yatra: Twenty-five Years of the NSD Repertory Company*, Delhi: National School of Drama.

Kennedy, Dennis, and Yong Li Lan (eds) (2010) *Shakespeare in Asia: Contemporary Performance*, Cambridge: Cambridge University Press.

Kurita, Yoshihiro, and Nobuko Tanaka (2006) 'Filtering Shakespeare with Noh', *The Japan Times*, 17 August.

Lal, Ananda (ed.) (2004) *The Oxford Companion to Indian Theatre*, New Delhi: Oxford University Press.

Lal, Ananda, and Sukanta Chaudhuri (eds) (2001) *Shakespeare on the Calcutta Stage*, Calcutta: Papyrus.

Loomba, Ania (1998) 'Local Manufacture Made-in-India Othello Fellows: Issues of Race, Hybridity and Location in Post-colonial Shakespeares', in Ania Loomba and Martin Orkin (eds) *Post-colonial Shakespeares*, 143–163, London: Routledge.

Mehta, Chandravan C. (1964) 'Shakespeare and the Gujarati Stage', *Indian Literature*, 7 (1): 41–50.

Minami, Ryuta, Ian Carruthers, and John Gillies (eds) (2001) *Performing Shakespeare in Japan*, Cambridge: Cambridge University Press.

Mitra, Ipshita (2012) 'I wish I could do *Hamlet* all my life: Atul Kumar', *The Times of India*, 17 August, http://timesofindia.indiatimes.com/life-style/people/I-wish-I-could-do-Hamlet-all-my-life-Atul-Kumar/articleshow/15530848.cms, accessed 5 December 2014.

Musiket, Yanapon (2011) 'Play Marks Four Decades of Drama', *Bangkok Post*, 7 June.

Nantapon (2011) 'Behold the Thai Macbeth', *The Nation*, 9 June.

Nguyen, Cindy (2011) 'Beyond Betrayal: Collaborators in Early 20th Century French Colonial Vietnam', *Columbia East Asia Review*, 4: 43–58.

Ninagawa, Yukio (2001) 'Interview with Ninagawa Yukio', in Ryuta Minami, Ian Carruthers, and John Gillies (eds) *Performing Shakespeare in Japan*, Cambridge: Cambridge University Press.

Ong Keng Sen (2001) 'Encounters', *TDR*, 45 (3): 126–33.

Panja, Shormishtha (2006) 'Not Black and White but Shades of Grey: Shakespeare in India', in Sukanta Chaudhuri and Chee Seng Lim (eds) *Shakespeare without English: the Reception of Shakespeare in Non-Anglophone Countries*, 102–16, New Delhi: Pearson Longman.

—— (2008) 'Shakespeare on the Indian Stage: Resistance, Recalcitrance, Recuperation', in Robert Henke and Eric Nicholson (eds) *Transnational Exchange in Early Modern Theater*, 215–24, Aldershot: Ashgate.

—— (2014) 'Lebedeff, Kendal, Dutt: Three Travellers on the Indian Stage', in Robert Henke and Eric Nicholson (eds) *Transnational Mobilities in Early Modern Theater*, 245–64, Aldershot: Ashgate.

Parrenas, R. S. (2011) *Illicit Flirtations: Labor, Migration and Sex Trafficking in Tokyo*, Stanford, CA: Stanford University Press.

Pavis, Patrice (2010) 'Intercultural Theater Today', *Forum Modernes Theater*, 25 (1): 5–15.

Pelley, Patricia M. (2002) *Postcolonial Vietnam: New Histories of the National Past*, Durham, NC: Duke University Press.

Phillips, John W. P. (2010) 'Shakespeare and the Question of Intercultural Performance', in Dennis Kennedy and Yong Li Lan (eds) *Shakespeare in Asia: Contemporary Performance*, 234–52, Cambridge: Cambridge University Press.

Pillai, Kainikkara M. Kumara (1964) 'Shakespeare in Malayalam', *Indian Literature*, 7 (1): 73–82.

Prasher, Kalyani (2014) 'Why Atul Kumar is House Full', *Yahoo News*, 5 March, https://in.news.yahoo.com/why-atul-kumar-is-house-full-100141409.html, accessed 5 December 2014.

Raha, Kironmoy (1978) *Bengali Theatre*, New Delhi: National Book Trust, 1980.

Rajadhyaksha, M. V. (1964) 'Shakespeare in Marathi', *Indian Literature*, 7 (1): 83–94.

Rajamannar, P. V. (1964) 'Shakespeare in Telegu', *Indian Literature*, 7 (1): 127–31.

Rao, A. N. Moorthy (1964) 'Shakespeare in Kannada', *Indian Literature*, 7 (1): 63–72.

Sarwar, Ghulam (1976) 'The Kelantan Mak Yong Dance Theatre: A Study of Performance Structure', PhD thesis, University of Hawai'i.

Sasayama, Takashi, J. R. Mulryne and Margaret Shewring (1998) *Shakespeare and the Japanese Stage*, Cambridge: Cambridge University Press.

Singh, Jyotsna (1989) 'Different Shakespeares: the Bard in Colonial/Postcolonial India', *Theatre Journal*, 41 (4): 445–58.

Soosip (2011) 'Chula's Macbeth all out of "spots"', *The Nation*, 7 June.

Subramanyam, Ka Naa (1964) 'Shakespeare in Tamil', *Indian Literature*, 7 (1): 120–6.

Suematsu, Michiko (2009) 'The Tokyo Globe Years 1988–2002', in Alexa Huang and Charles S. Ross (eds) *Shakespeare in Hollywood, Asia, and Cyberspace*, Indianapolis: Purdue University Press.

—— (2010) 'Import/export: Japanizing Shakespeare', in Dennis Kennedy and Yong Li Lan (eds) *Shakespeare in Asia*, Cambridge: Cambridge University Press.

Tam, Kwok-kan, Andrew Parkin, and Terry Siu-Han Yip (eds) (2002) *Shakespeare Global/Local: The Hong Kong Imaginary in Transcultural Production*, New York: Peter Lang.

Tran Huy Lieu *et al.* (1971, 1985) *Lich su Viet Nam* (History of Vietnam), 2 vols, Hanoi: Social Sciences.

Tungtang, Paradee (2011) 'Shakespeare in Thailand', PhD dissertation, Warwick University.

Veohong, Nopamat (n.d.) 'Transporting the Bard through Time: A Look into Thailand's Productions of Three Shakespearean Comedies', unpublished paper.

Vincent, Pheroze L. (2012) 'Piya Behrupiya is up Delhi's Alley', *The Hindu*, 12 August, www.thehindu.com/features/.../piya-behrupiya-is.../article3754223.ece, accessed 1 December 2014.

Yong Li Lan (2011) 'Of Spirits and Sundry Other Phenomena in Intercultural Shakespeare: Text and Performance', *Anglistica*, 15 (2), *Shakespeare in the Media: Old and New*, http://anglistica.unior.it/node/378/cover, accessed 22 June 2014.

Zarrilli, Phillip B. (1990) 'Kathakali', in Farley P. Richmond, Darius L. Swann and Phillip B. Zarrilli (eds) *Indian Theatre: Traditions of Performance*, 315–57, Honolulu: University of Hawai'i Press.

—— (1992) 'For Whom is the King a King? Issues of Intercultural Production, Perception, and Reception in a *Kathakali King Lear*' in Janelle G. Reinelt and Joseph R. Roach (eds) *Critical Theory and Performance*, 16–40, Ann Arbor: University of Michigan Press.

24

Modern musicals in Asia

*Makiko Yamanashi, Sissi Liu, Gilbert C. F. Fong,
Shelby Kar-yan Chan, Fan-Ting Cheng,
Ji Hyon (Kayla) Yuh and Caleb Goh*

This chapter examines American-style musicals in Japan, China, Hong Kong, Taiwan, Korea and Southeast Asia. Inspired by vaudeville, jazz and Broadway musical tunes, the genre started in the early twentieth century in Japan, where the all-female Takarazuka Revue started in 1914, and China, where the composer Li Jinhui started highly popular *gewuju* (song and dance theatre) in the 1920s. In recent decades, Asian musicals have experienced another boom, thanks to the influence of mega-musicals from Broadway and their Asian tours, which have inspired highly energetic pieces that validate popular culture, celebrate nationalism, deconstruct historical narratives or restage literary and cultural classics.

I. Japan, by Makiko Yamanashi

If challenged terminologically, musical theatre in Japan harks back to ancient times. Music has always played a significant role in Japanese traditional performing arts. Whether folk or ritual performance, 'theatre' in Japan has been basically *ongaku-geki* (musical theatre). Transliterated from the English 'musical', *myūjikaru* today often refers to American-style musicals, emphasizing dramatic narrative using microphones targeting mass audiences in a highly commercial market.[1]

To understand western-style myūjikaru productions in a Japanese context, however, it is important to look at Japanese musical theatre in a broader historical scope. Until the Meiji Restoration in the late nineteenth century (c.1867–89), besides various regional festive spectacles, *kabuki*, *noh* and *kyogen* had formed the mainstream of common people's entertainment.[2] In these genres, music not only functioned to highlight atmosphere for the drama, but also played an effective narrative role accompanied by oral presentation. This domestic convention of music theatres was the foundation for the development of Japanese musicals in terms of foreign importation, native appropriation and the interaction between different theatrical techniques that inspired the powerful industry and popular market of today's myūjikaru.

Influenced by foreign productions and through the Meiji regulation to educate students and children in western music, increasing numbers of Japanese people began to enjoy western melodies and even to perform western plays. The first western-style opera done by the Japanese was Gluck's *Orfeo ed. Euridice* in 1903. It was performed by the students of Tokyo College of Music, including the future internationally known soprano Miura Tamaki (1884–46) (Hasegawa 2008).[3]

Thus, in Japan, eager reception of western music theatres at an early stage was largely dependent on student endeavours. More professional establishments such as the Imperial Theatre employed the Italian performer Giovanni Vittorio Rossi (1867–?) in 1912 to present opera productions such as Offenbach's *Orpheé aux Enfers*, Puccini's *Madame Butterfly* and Mozart's *Die Zauberflöte*, but saw an unsuccessful end to these attempts in 1916. Highbrow operas and operatic productions were staged at the theatre but mostly failed to win audience appreciation and applause (Kobayashi 1980:7).[4] To sing western melody in Japanese was no easy matter due to different vowels, phrasings and intonations, unless lyrical translations were appropriately done. Japanese texts for the Imperial Theatre productions were translated by Kobayashi Aiyū (1881–1945), who made a considerable contribution to popularizing western music with Japanese lyrics.

After the dissolution of the Imperial Theatre's opera team in 1916, Kobayashi and others gathered in Tokyo's Asakusa district and fostered the boom of so-called 'Asakusa opera'. Asakusa opera was a type of music theatre by a group of Japanese stage performers based in the district who popularized highbrow western operatic productions for the wider Japanese public. Takagi Tokuko (1891–1919), who had studied in America, brought back American-style revue shows blending ballet, variety show and vaudeville, which triggered the boom of Asakusa opera culture in the 1910s. Distinguished singers in Asakusa included Taya Rikiizō (1899–1988), Fujiwara Yoshie (1898–1976) and Kishida Tatsuya (1892–1944), who later led the Japanese music theatre scenes.[5] Situated on the east side of the capital since the Edo period, Asakusa, known as the long-established downtown area encompassing the pleasure-quarter of Yoshiwara, remained a centre of Japanese music theatre until 1923, when the Great Kantō Earthquake dealt a fatal blow to its cultural epoch.

Given this background, it can be said that modern Japanese musical theatres have their roots in the 1910s and 1920s when a number of new musical theatre movements combined western influence with Japanese conventions. One of the most important persons who saw potential in these modern theatrical currents was Kobayashi Ichizō (1873–1957), the Kansai-based railroad entrepreneur and founder of Takarazuka Kageki-dan (in official English, Takarazuka Girls' Opera until 1940, and Takarazuka Revue Company afterwards) (Figure 24.1). He started the all-young-female music theatre in 1914 with its motto to employ western music for Japanese dramas and dance numbers, to create a new type of kabuki as a counterpoint to the all-male Japanese theatre (Yamanashi 2012: chapter 3). Kishida from Asakusa opera joined Takarazuka in 1919 and became one of the most prominent playwright-directors in Takarazuka's formative years. It was Kishida's *Mon Paris* (1927) and *Parisette* (1930) by his junior choreographer Shirai Tetsuzō (1900–83) that defined the 'Takarazuka revue style': the usage of a grand staircase and the apron bridge around the orchestra pit became the inevitable attributes of this mega music theatre. Takarazuka boosted a trend of so-called shōjo-kageki (girls' opera) across the country: Shōchiku, which owns the biggest official kabuki company, created OSK (Osaka Shōchiku Kageki-dan, known also as Nippon Kageki-dan) in 1922 and its Tokyo-based SKD (Shōchiku Kageki-dan) in 1928. Moreover, numerous other small girls' musical troupes also thrived (Kurahashi and Tsuji 2005). Influenced by Parisian revues and American shows, the 1930s Japan saw a nationwide enthusiasm in the 'revue' as a new music theatre genre. In a tribute to the Parisian original, there was even a revue house named Moulin Rouge Shinjuku-za, which opened in 1931. NDT (Nichigeki Dancing Team) was another successful company that was created in 1936 and based at Nihon Theatre, where a team of men and women rivalling the all-girls troupes performed until 1977.

Takarazuka continued producing non-stop hits at the time when the company acquired its own theatre in central Tokyo, just around the corner of Hibiya Park in 1936. Kobayashi himself wrote scenarios and encouraged young writers to experiment with bolder adaptations of foreign music, lyrics and performance techniques to stimulate changes in Japanese audience's taste and

Figure 24.1 Takarazuka Revue's *La Romance* (1936), with male-impersonators Kuniko Ashihara and Hisami Fujihana.

(Photo by Hiroshi Fujioka)

interest. Given the various repertories, from Shakespeare to Japanese folk tales, all done with singing and dancing at the microphone-equipped grand theatre, there is no doubt that Takarazuka laid the foundation for Japanese myūjikaru consumption. Just as Fred Astaire, Ginger Rogers and the Ziegfeld Follies helped spread American musicals through Hollywood musical films, Takarazuka girls also contributed to Japanese musicals in the pre-war film industry. They were hired in a number of myūjikaru films by PCL (Photo Chemical Laboratory), which started in 1932 and merged, in 1937, into Toho (Tokyo Takarazuka Ltd), which continued to feature Takarazuka performers in its early films. For Takarazuka stage productions, Utsu Hideo (1902–88) was especially known for taking in American musical elements characterized by jazz and tap dancing, whereas his senior choreographers Kishida and Shirai borrowed more from Parisian revues.

Japanese theatrical activities were severely restricted after 1940 during the Second World War, especially those with western themes. It was not until the mid-1950s, after the American occupation, that the Imperial Theatre reopened as a centre of so-called 'Toho-myūjikarusu' (Toho musicals). Its in-house production team included Kikuta Kazuo (1908–73), one of the most prominent playwrights for postwar Japanese musicals (Inoue 2011).[6] Today, the Imperial Theatre hosts mostly foreign musical adaptations, such as *My Fair Lady* and *Fiddler on the Roof*, and fan-based spectacles by Janiizu, a group of popular teenage idols.

Tokyo Takarazuka Theatre, as one of the significant centres for Japanese musical productions, was taken over by the American Occupation Force from 1946 to 1955 and renamed as the Ernie Pyle Theatre after the American journalist Ernie Pyle (1900–45). Ever since the reopening, all-female Takarazuka has continued to lead the Japanese musical scene by successfully staging

American musicals such as *Oklahoma!* (1967) and *West Side Story* (1968) as well as manipulative adaptations of European hit musicals such as Austrian *Elisabeth* and French *Romeo et Juliette*. As a result, the Hibiya district re-emerged as a hub for new musical entertainment after the second half of the 1950s. In 1963, Nissei Theatre opened with Japan's first hosting of a grand opera company, Deutsche Oper Berlin, followed by an increasing number of foreign musical theatres, which in turn affected domestic productions. In the field of traditional theatre, the kabuki actor Ichikawa Ennosuke III (1939–) reinvented kabuki as a new type of musical theatre with a faster, western-style pace known as *super-kabuki*, which is carried on by his successors.

Now, the musical has achieved full recognition in Japan. People use the English word myūjikaru in a broad sense to mean music theatre in general. There are an increasing number of other companies representing Japanese musical scenes. Transcultural or mixed-media productions are increasing in the twentieth-first century. An independent musical company, Gekidan Shiki (Four Seasons Theatre Company, est. 1953), specializes in direct adaptations of Broadway and West End musicals such as *Phantom of the Opera*, *Lion King*, and *Wicked* while regularly staging original productions. On a smaller scale, there are a number of innovative musical companies, including Ongakuza Musical Company (est. 1977) and Myūjikaru-za (est. 1995). Representative original works by the former include *Ai tabu Bottchan* (I Love Bottchan), which is based on the classical novel *Bottchan* by Soseki Natsume. Well-known works by the latter include *Swing Jazz*, a story of jazz players during the Second World War. More unique to the field, yet with a considerable fan base, is Muscle Musical (2001–11), which made acrobatic shows using its performers' athletic talents; it also performed several times in Las Vegas. However, Gekidan Shinkansen is another popular company, which produces original rock musicals in innovative kabuki style.

A recent phenomenon worth noting is the musicals based on *manga* (Japanese comics), *anime* (Japanese animation) or computer games. They are those cultural media that have gained considerable international fandom. To name a few successful examples, Takarazuka adopted the popular manga by Riyoko Ikeda (1947–), *Berusaiyu-no-bara* (The Rose of Versailles), in 1974 and has frequently restaged it. It has also adapted *Black Jack* (1994 and 2012) and *Phoenix* (1994) by Osamu Tezuka (1928–89). In the new millennium, a new sport manga *Teni-myu* (Tenisu no Ojisama: The Prince of Tennis Musical) by Takeshi Konomi (1970–) has turned into an all-male musical series since 2003 and is still gaining tremendous popularity. Another hit manga-based musical, *Kuroshitsuji* (Black Butler), based on the internationally popular Gothic comic by Yana Toboso (1984–), has been continuing since 2010. As media technology develops, video games are becoming a common source for the contemporary Japanese musical scene. Again, all-female Takarazuka took the initiative to stage the popular games *Gyakuten-saiban* (Phoenix Right, 2009, 2013) and *Sengoku Basara* (Devil Kings, 2013) by adding adequate singing and dancing. By adapting manga and video games for the stage, these experiments with mixed media in subject matters and techniques have resulted in increasing audience numbers, expanding not only the diversity of Japanese musical theatre but also the horizon of musical goers.

It can be said that new Japanese musicals are strongly being inspired by young popular cultures. In the Japanese theatre scene today, therefore, myūjikaru represents a hybrid genre. Throughout the past century, reception and consumption of western music theatres such as opera, operettas, revues and shows have stimulated Japanese music theatre conventions, resulting in complex yet dynamic productions.

II. China, by Sissi Liu

'Musical theatre' (*yinyueju*) as an imported term has been unstable and much contested through-out the history of its development as a theatrical genre in China. Along with yinyueju, *gewuju* (song and dance theatre), *yueju* (music drama) and *qinggeju* (light opera) have all been used to describe a similar concept. In the first complete Chinese musical theatre history published in 2012 – *Zhongguo yinyue jushi, jindai juan* (A History of Chinese Musicals, Modern Volume) by Wen Shuo – the term is used loosely to include most, if not all, performance genres that encompass music/singing, including *xiqu* (traditional Chinese theatre), *minjian xiaoqu* (folk tunes), film musicals, revolutionary model operas and ballet. In this chapter, my definition of Chinese musical theatre is limited to staged works that are influenced by western (especially Broadway) musical theatre, which are distinct from the Chinese forms mentioned above: traditional theatre, folk tunes, modern operas and ballet created in the mode of classical western styles.

However, there are also problems with this definition. First of all, as a highly sophisticated genre, the Broadway musical theatre is not a singular form. Some of its classics, such as *Porgy and Bess*, *Sweeney Todd* and *A Little Night Music*, have blurred boundaries with opera. Furthermore, since the late 1960s, it has grown into different shapes and forms that comprise the concept musical, the rock musical, the jukebox musical and the imported megamusical. Consequently, its influence could be ambiguous. The second problem is that it seems to exclude the contribution of the traditional theatre and folk tunes to the Chinese musical theatre, confining its music style to exclusively western-influenced popular tunes. However, this assessment ignores the fact that many popular modern and contemporary tunes are clearly imprinted with xiqu and folk tunes and a great number of these forms feature popular songs.

To draw clearer parameters for this term, I propose two additional concepts. One, the Broadway book musical from the Golden Age and the megamusical should be the two loci of comparison. Works from the early Chinese musical theatre era (1920s–1970s) were inspired by Broadway book musicals, whereas Chinese musical theatre since the 1980s displays substantial megamusical influence. Two, Chinese musical theatre is highly hybrid from its very genesis. The Broadway musical theatre, developed out of nineteenth-century European light opera, opera comique and operetta, and matured in the 1920s under the influence of vaudeville, burlesque, minstrelsy and early jazz, is itself innately hybrid and has little in common with highly conventionalized xiqu forms such as *jingju* and *kunqu*. From the 1920s onwards, modern theatre practitioners tried to revolutionize the 'outdated' xiqu and sought a new and more 'advanced' form of musical theatre. They did not simply take the existent Broadway musical theatre and infuse it with Chinese content. Instead, they made innovations in the form to cater to the constantly changing political climate, Chinese aesthetics and native palates.

The genre began with Li Jinhui (1891–1967) and his gewuju (song and dance theatre). Endorsing the popularization of Mandarin, moral values and aesthetic education on a national level, Li created highly successful children's gewuju pieces that highlighted the anti-feudalist and nationalist ideology and love of beauty, with works such as *Putao xianzi* (The Grape Fairy, 1923; Figure 24.2), *San hudie* (Three Butterflies, 1924) and *Xiao xiao huajia* (The Little Painter, 1926). Inspired by American jazz records, popular tunes from Broadway musicals and Hollywood movies as well as Chinese folk music, Li composed such love songs as *Maomao yu* (The Drizzle) and *Taohua jiang* (Peach Blossom River). As sheet music and gramophone records became popular, Li's music was played to a wider circulation in venues such as nightclubs and cabarets, which later led to controversy in the perceived content and context of his music.

His musical theatre successfully integrated popular songs, dances and well-made (love) stories, all of which were key features of the Broadway book musical. He also established the first music school – Zhonghua gewu xuexiao (The Chinese Song and Dance School) – in 1927 to train professional musical theatre actors without charge. From this school graduated several of the brightest stars of the 1930s and 1940s, including 'golden voice' Zhou Xuan (1920–57) and the legendary actress Wang Renmei (1914–87). However, Li encountered severe attacks

Figure 24.2 Li Jinhui's daughter Li Minghui (1909–2003) posing for *Putao Xianzi* (The Grape Fairy) in 1927 as a student of The Chinese Song and Dance School.

(From *Shibao huatu* [The Eastern Times Photo Supplement], 24 July 1927)

from leftist composers such as He Luting and Nie Er in the wake of Japan's annexation of Manchuria in 1931, who criticized Li's music as 'decadent', 'opium in disguise' and 'completely inappropriate' by encouraging people to indulge in demeaning pleasure in times of war (Sun 2007).

To confront Li's 'decadent' inventions, leftist composers and theatre practitioners created notable works such as *Wang Zhaojun* (1930, Zhang Shu), *Yangzijiang shang de fengbao* (Thunderstorm over the Yangtze River, 1934, Tian Han and Nie Er), *Mulan congjun* (Mulan Joins the Army, 1945, Xu Ruhui) and *Meng Jiang Nü* (Lady Meng Jiang, or The Great Wall, 1946, lyrics by Jiang Chunfang). Integrating western operatic structure into the songs, dances and a story well known to the Chinese, *Meng Jiang Nü* is the first production on the Chinese stage that is officially termed 'yinyueju' (musical). Re-enacting the myth that Meng Jiang Nü wept so sadly for her husband who had died building the Great Wall that a part of the wall collapsed, it was composed and directed by the Jewish composer Aaron Avashalomov (1894–1965), who was well versed in Chinese musical vocabulary as he grew up in a Russian–Chinese border town and moved to China in 1914. Presented once as the ceremony to celebrate Chiang Kai-Shek's sixtieth birthday, the show was highly claimed and arranged to tour the United States, which for various reasons failed to materialize. However, it also received stringent criticism. Hong Shen, a pioneer of modern Chinese theatre, calls the show 'neither fish nor fowl' but a hodge-podge of all sorts of confused elements – traditional Chinese opera, western opera, tap dance, ballet, a mixture of 'stylized' and realistic set and mise-en-scène – which do not make very good sense as a whole. He points out that the songs fail to communicate Chinese sentiments and the whole production is a 'westerner's interpretation of a Chinese myth' (Hong 1959). While there is truth in Hong's assessment, he unfortunately missed the play's formal significance. Indeed, *Meng Jiang Nü* is less comparable to a book musical than the form of 'music drama' as Richard Wagner intended it – a multidimensional form of expression, resembling Greek drama that uses music and poetry as the primary elements for the full expression of dramatic action. The mix of music, poetry and drama, along with Wagner's conception of *Gesamtkunstwerk* (total art work), revolutionized the world of opera and inspired Chinese theatre practitioners in the early twentieth century, as evidenced in *Meng Jiang Nü*.

The quasi-music-drama form that emphasizes the function of music can be found in many stage productions in the early People's Republic of China from 1949 to 1966, during which state-commissioned works dominated the stage. Particularly noticeable are folk-tune-based operas telling nationalist stories or honouring communist heroism that celebrate the founding of a new nation. These works include *Baimao nü* (White Haired Girl, 1945, later adapted into ballet and revolutionary model opera), *Liu Hulan* (1948), *Xiao Erhei jiehun* (Xiao Erhei's Marriage, 1952), *Honghu chiweidui* (The Red Guards on Honghu Lake, 1959), *Jiang Jie* (Sister Jiang, 1964) and *Ayiguli* (1966).

The 1980s witnessed, for the first time, Broadway muicals on the Chinese stage. Beyond importing Broadway-style film musicals such as *Singing in the Rain* and *The Sound of Music*, theatre makers started translating and staging Broadway musicals. In 1986, students from Shanghai Theatre Academy staged *My Fair Lady*. In 1987, in collaboration with The Eugene O'Neill Theater Center, Zhongguo Geju Yuan (Chinese National Opera House) translated and staged *The Music Man* and *The Fantasticks*. Since then, *West Side Story*, *The Sound of Music*, *Cats*, *Phantom of the Opera*, *Beauty and Beast* and *Les Miserables* were successively introduced to China (Liao 2002). The direct importation of musicals took place in 2003. As a result of the collaboration between Andrew Lloyd Weber and Zhongguo Duiwai Jituan Gongsi (China Arts and Entertainment Group, CAEG), *Cats* with its original West End cast landed in Shanghai Grand Theatre and became a smashing hit. In the following years CAEG imported *Rent*, *West Side Story*, *The King and I*, *42nd Street*, *The Lion King* and *Aida*, all of which turned out to be less successful. In 2011, the Chinese version of *Mamma Mia*, performed in Chinese with an all-Chinese cast, premiered in Shanghai, and had a run of over 300 performances in nineteen Chinese cities to a total of 500,000 viewers within two years.

The 1980s also marked the birth of contemporary Chinese musical theatre. *Women xianzai de nianqingren* (We the Young People Today, 1982) by Xiangtan Opera Company and National Opera is recognized by many theatre historians as the 'first original musical' of the contemporary era. Notable works include *Da cuo che* (Wrong Act; a.k.a. Papa, Can you Hear me?, 1985) by Shenyang Theatre Company, *Richu* (Sunrise, 1988) by Musical Theatre Centre of the National

Opera, and *Yuniao bingzhan* (Canary Military Depot, 1999) by the Opera Troupe of the General Political Department of the People's Liberation Army. These operas reflected the zeitgeist of a thriving post-Mao China, and Chinese theatre practitioners' arduous efforts in finding their own voices as they slowly felt their way to creating an 'original Chinese musical theatre' that looks to the Broadway musical theatre as the most successful model. In the 1990s, motivated by the incentives to compete with Korea and Japan and to emerge in the global musical theatre scene, China finally established schools to train musical theatre talents, starting in 1995 in the Central Academy of Drama with the help of the Japanese musical theatre director Keita Asari. This act of making musical theatre a formal discipline in higher education marked the legitimization of Broadway-influenced Chinese musical theatre – which had been scorned by serious scholars since the 1920s – and provided fertile soil for the saplings of Chinese musical theatre to grow in the new century.

Many contemporary productions reflect the nostalgia of a lost empire. For instance, in 2005, state-sponsored *Dianying zhige* (Song of Light and Shadow), a musical to celebrate the centennial anniversary of Chinese cinema, presented Chinese film history through a character who was born in the same year as the Chinese cinema, employing nostalgic songs of various historical periods to remind the audience of 'the good old days'. The award-winning *Die* (Butterflies, 2007), produced by Li Dun and toured internationally, tells the classic Chinese story of the Butterfly Lovers. Taking place in a lost kingdom, it employs grandiose spectacles clearly influenced by the Broadway megamusical. Another form of spectacle musical combines cultural heritage and tourist production. Examples of this new form include *Songcheng qiangu qing* (The Romance of the Song Dynasty) at the Songcheng Theme Park in Hangzhou and *Jiuzhai qiangu qing* (The Romance of Jiuzhai), an outdoor tourist production that showcases the natural scenery and native cultures of Jiuzhaigou.

Transnational collaboration is another prominent characteristic of contemporary musical theatre, as China strives for global success. *Butterflies* (2007), directed by Canadian director Gilles Maheau, was a collaborative effort by artists from six countries. Historical musical *Dahong denglong* (The Red Lantern, 2013) was co-directed by American director Copeland Woodruff. Chinese musical theatre practitioners also look for transnational recognition to guarantee domestic commercial success. In 2014, after the success of *Butterflies*, Songlei Diezhiwu Yinyueju Jutuan (Songlei Musical Theatre Ensemble) produced *Mama, zai aiwo yici* (Mama, Love Me Once Again) and exported it to South Korea, winning the First Prize of the Daegu International Musical Festival. Megamusical-styled *Wangpai youxi* (The Joker's Game), also produced by Songlei, has been aiming for its premiere on Broadway. Advertised as 'the world's first magic musical,' it was workshopped in 2014 in Beijing and is under the direction of musical theatre veteran Tony Stimac.

Chinese musical theatre, since Li Jinhui's inauguration of gewuju in the 1920s, has come a long way. Chinese musical theatre practitioners have continued to explore new ways to incorporate western (especially Broadway) style into a form that accommodates Chinese taste, reflects Chinese cultural values and, more recently, embraces the international musical theatre market and resonates with the current practice and philosophy of transnational collaboration. Contemporary Chinese musical theatre, with a short history of a barely over 30 years, is growing at a relatively rapid rate, despite major challenges such as competition from other forms of media, a shortage of theatres to stage Broadway-level productions and a limited number of musical theatre programmes in higher education. However, as the self-important reverie of a lost ancient empire gives way to a humble dream of a worthy competitor in the global arena of musical theatre, the possibilities for a thriving Chinese musical theatre are unbounded.

III. Hong Kong, by Gilbert C. F. Fong and Shelby Kar-yan Chan

Hong Kong people are no strangers to singing and dancing on the stage. There are plenty of songs and dances in Cantonese opera, and Chinese film musicals, first started in the 1930s in Shanghai, soon spread to Hong Kong. During the 1940s and 50s, local cinema frequently mixed Cantonese opera tunes with Cantonese cover versions of western pop compositions, which were inserted in between dialogues. The lyrics were printed as subtitles for the audience to follow and sing along. The 1960s was a period of westernization, and Hollywood film musicals, such as *West Side Story* (1961), *My Fair Lady* (1964) and *The Sound of Music* (1965), played to favourable audiences in Hong Kong. Big studios such as Shaw Brothers and Motion Pictures & General Investment (Dianying Maoye or Dianmao) produced blockbuster *gewupian* (song and dance film) with the help of Japanese choreographers and cameramen. Cantonese film musicals, starring pop idols such as Connie Chan (Chen Baozhu) and Josephine Siao (Xiao Fangfang), afforded happy and tuneful moments to factory girls and the lower middle class. Notable examples include *Qianjiao baimei* (Les Belles, 1961), *Caise qingchun* (Colourful Youth, 1966) and *Xianggang huayueye* (Hong Kong Nocturne, 1967). The wave of big-budget film musicals subsided only in the 1970s with the rise of the macho kung fu films.

Musical theatre in the modern western style began to emerge in the 1970s and became more popular from the late 1980s. There are new musical productions almost every year, taking up, however, less than a tenth of total theatre productions. The ongoing evolution sees a western form fused with modernized Chinese literary classics and popular culture that accentuates urban life and the local dialect Cantonese. There are three main types of musical productions in Hong Kong.

Original book musicals

Cantonese book musicals first came onto the stage by adopting ready-made stories – either written by local playwrights or adapted from famous literary works – which were then incorporated with songs and dances crafted to suit the characters and their situations in the stories. In 1972, the first western-styled stage musical *Bai Niangniang* (Madame White) appeared in Hong Kong. Actress and singer Rebecca Pan (Pan Dihua) adopted the western form of musicals to tell the Chinese folk story 'Legend of the White Snake'. Pan also played the titular role. The dialogues and songs were rendered in Mandarin.

Starting from the 1980s, upon the imminent return of sovereignty to mainland China in 1997, local theatre artists were keen to carve out a way for the so-called 'Hong Kong musicals'. In 1987, the first original Cantonese musical took to the stage. Eric Pun's (Pan Guangpei) *Huangjin wu* (Dream of the Golden Mansion) was a trailblazer, lamenting the materialistic escapism of university graduates in the face of the uncertainty over Hong Kong's future. Raymond To (Du Guowei) wrote *Chengzhai fengqing* (Tales of the Walled City, 1994, 1999), a historical romance about the Kowloon Walled City, which was turned into a musical by the Hong Kong Repertory Theatre Company (HKREP) with the participation of the Hong Kong Chinese Orchestra and Hong Kong Dance Company.

By the late 1990s, some drama troupes aspired to produce original musicals. Among them two were particularly significant: while Yanxi Jiazu (Actors' Family) staked stronger artistic claims, Chuntian Wutai (Spring-Time Group) was unabashed about its commercial bent. In 1993, Actors' Family presented its first musical *Yushang 1941 de nühai* (1941 Girl!), which was set during the fall of Hong Kong into Japanese hands in the Sino-Japanese War. Its musical adaptations of the modern Chinese writer Shen Congwen's *Biancheng* (The Border Town, 2001) and Bertolt

Brecht's *The Good Person of Szechwan* (2003) were made to highlight the versatility and expressiveness of the kind of Cantonese spoken by Hong Kong people. The show's lyricist Chris Shum (Shen Weizong) wanted to exploit the 'elegance, wit, fun, vernacular and vulgarity' of the local dialect, while composer Leon Ko's (Gao Shizhang) scores were often of neat and orderly phrasing suitable for Cantonese lyrics (Choi 2010: n.p.). Spring-Time, despite its profit-making and crowd-pleasing intentions, also appeals to the so-called 'collective memories' of Hong Kong people. Its inaugural production *Wo he chuntian youge yuehui* (I Have a Date With Spring) in 1995 (originally a HKREP production in 1992) was a tribute to the nightclub singers in the 1960s, which became an instant hit and was adapted into a namesake television drama series in 1996.

The 1997 box-office smash *Xue lang hu* (Snow Wolf Lake) was the quintessence of Cantopop music whose prominence spilt over into the theatre. Based on Chung Wai Man's (Zhong Weimin) novel, the concert-like musical was created by Jacky Cheung (Zhang Xueyou), who was one of the 'Four Heavenly Kings' of Cantopop, and starred mostly pop singers. The lyrics were first written in Cantonese and then rewritten in Mandarin, which helped its popularity during its tour of Singapore, Malaysia and many parts of China. The tour ran from 1997 to 2006 and boasted 102 performances, breaking records for audience and performance numbers in the history of Hong Kong.

After the disastrous SARS epidemic in 2003, which devastated businesses, property prices and people's confidence, the Hong Kong government wanted to perk up its citizens and approached HKREP to stage a comforting and reassuring production for the populace. *Suansuan tiantian Xianggang di* (Sweet & Sour Hong Kong, 2003, 2004) was the musical version of a stage play entitled *Mingyue heceng shi liangxiang* (We are One Family, 2001), written by the mainland Chinese playwright He Jiping. The songs and musical score were done by Joseph Koo (Gu Jiahui) and James Wong (Huang Zhan; 1941–2004); they both wrote many catchy tunes for television shows and Cantopop singers. The embodiment of a didactic and positive message – the reconciliation between mainland immigrants and the local population – was characteristic of government propaganda. The form 'spoken drama', spruced up with song and dance, could represent a new model to attract audiences into the theatre.

Translation and adaptation of western musicals

Like spoken drama, the musical theatre in Hong Kong has been relying on translation and adaptation of western titles, especially in the 1980s when musicals were still a western art transplant to be learnt, taught and explored. Borrowing from Broadway and West End musicals, local theatre artists acquired orchestral scores, dance routines, lyrics and scripts to translate from, as well as cultural credence and marketing appeal to the audience. The first Cantonese musical in Hong Kong was a translation of *West Side Story* (1980), which was a HKREP production directed by Chung King-fai (Zhong Jinghui). As dean of the School of Drama of the Hong Kong Academy of Performing Art, Chung rendered a Broadway title into Cantonese every 2 years from 1989 to 2003 to train students in the drama, music and dance schools.

Towards the millennium, the trend of faithful translations veered towards adaptations which, with the rise of the local entertainment industry, highlighted the language and culture of the territory. In 1997, Spring-Time moved the setting of *My Fair Lady* to Hong Kong in the 1920s and produced a romantic comedy with overtones of Sino-Hong Kong integration. In 2004, Zhong Jutuan (TNT Theatre) staged a Cantonese adaptation of *Man of La Mancha*. In 2005, Fengche Cao Jutuan (Windmill Grass Theatre) rendered *I Love You, You're Perfect, Now Change* on stage, which became a hit among the younger generation. The Cantonese lyrics of these

Figure 24.3 Poster of W Theatre's *Liangzhu xiashi chuangi* (Butterfly Lovers, 2005).
(Courtesy of W Theatre)

three musicals are invariably highly colloquial, with sprinkles of local slangs, jokes and references to popular culture. This insistence on localism is in tandem with the surging interest in Hong Kong identity starting in the mid-1980s.

Semi-musicals

The new millennium witnessed an introspective turn of Hong Kong drama, precipitated by the gloomy political and economic climate and the more youthful and self-centred audience demographics. If the pre-millennium theatre tended towards exploring identity issues vis-à-vis nation, history and language, the new generation of young urbanites is more interested in their personal concerns, such as friendship, sexuality and office politics. Equally, young theatre artists often draw attention to the strength and ubiquity of popular culture and play around with the tropes of mainstream cinema and television, comics and advertisements, resulting in a new dramatic genre that can be termed 'semi-musical'. Semi-musicals are similar to jukebox musicals, where pop music is contextualized and incorporated into a dramatic plot, but often sidestepping linear stories in favour of skits which revolve around a common theme and a few central characters but not necessarily related to the main storyline. Dialogues are also interlaced with Cantopop songs, as a slick means for amplification of sentiments, rather than character development or plot exposition. W Chuangzuo She (W Theatre) and its sister company Windmill Grass Theatre are known for producing star-studded semi-musicals with a focus on romantic relationships. Their productions, such as *Liangzhu xiashi chuanqi* (Butterfly Lovers, 2005; Figure 24.3), *Yiqi yihui* (Once in a Lifetime, 2007) and *Kai guanxi* (Open Relationship, 2011), were box-office hits.

In the West, musicals are on the decline as a cultural force and are now mostly relegated to tourist fare, but in Hong Kong they are a rising star in the theatre, probably due to the populace's bent towards entertainment and escapism. Musicals in Hong Kong are essentially utilitarian, in the sense that they are marketable box-office hits (especially if they feature film or television stars), and the song and dance routines mainly serve amusement purposes. There are also suggestions of staging musicals in the upcoming West Kowloon Cultural District as tourist attractions, making the area into another Broadway or West End. Musicals are also used to train acting students or even as tools for English-language education. The form of Hong Kong musicals, like Hong Kong culture itself, is a hodge-podge of modern and classical choreography and Broadway and Cantopop music. Even though the genre is getting more popular, a unique style of Hong Kong musical is yet to emerge.

IV. Taiwan, by Fan-Ting Cheng

The genre of the Taiwanese musical emerged in the 1980s, known as 'the time of liberation' when martial law ended, numerous social movements occurred and the economy took off. This social atmosphere deeply influenced the development of the artistic and cultural industries in Taiwan, triggering the birth of the Taiwanese musical. *Qi Wang* (King of Chess), which premiered in 1987 in Taipei, is commonly recognized as the first locally produced musical. A product of collaboration among many celebrated local theatre practitioners, including Hsu Bo-Yun (Xu Boyun), Wu Jing-Jyi (Wu Jingji) and Li Tai-Hsiang (Li Taixiang), the piece uses modern dance, orchestra and local popular rhymes to theatrically reinterpret Chang Hsi-Guo (Zhang Xiguo)'s novel of the same name. The story features the journey of a chess child prodigy being exploited by a capitalist society, which mirrors Taiwan's experience of rapid social transformations during the 1970s. While financial issues caused the production to close quickly, *King of Chess* paved a possible path for future musical productions.

In the 1990s, with the return of many theatre practitioners who had studied abroad, the development of the Taiwanese musical was mobilized by various western theatrical and cinematic methods and popular cultures (Lin 2010). Productions such as Lüguang Jutuan's (Greenray Theatre Company) *Lingdai yu gaogenxie* (Neckties and High-heeled Shoes, 1994) and Guotuo Juchang's (Godot Theatre Company) *Dabizi qingsheng* (Cyrano de Bergerac, 1995) demonstrated the growth of the Taiwanese musical, and laid a solid foundation for the genre's future blossoming. The former describes the complex ecology of a local business office, emphasizing the struggles towards a capitalist environment. The latter adapts Edmond Rostand's *Cyrano de Bergerac*, importing celebrated western literature and trendy theatre methods, including Stanislavski acting and stage combat, jazz choreography and Broadway-style composing and arranging, to Taiwan. Both musicals, either by content or method, reflect the economic and cultural pressure Taiwan shares when confronting the global development of capitalism.

After 2000, identity conflicts among different groups on the island, as well as political and economic tensions between the island and other countries, urged musical practitioners to search for novel artistic approaches that effectively worked on these issues. The first episode of Dafeng Yinyue Juchang's (Dafeng Musical Company) Taiwanese musical trilogy, *Siyue wangyu* (April Rain, 2007), adopted Minnan, Hakka and Japanese to delineate the historical context of the legendary composer Teng Yu-Hsien (Deng Yuxian), denoting a postcolonial awareness that turns to local cultures. Not as heavy and sentimental as *April Rain*, Li Huan-Hsiung (Li Huanxiong)'s comedic musical adaptations of Jimmy Liao (Liao Fubin)'s illustrations, *Dixiatie* (Sound of Colors, 2003), *Xingyun'er* (Mr Wing, 2005) and *Xiangzuo xiangyou zou* (Turn Left, Turn Right, 2008) attempt to create a local brand that delineates the postmodern scenario of urban Taiwan as penetrated by Western media and culture. These musicals effectively cooperate with the entertainment industry, using a great amount of pop-cultural symbols to attract younger audiences.

Although growing rapidly, the Taiwanese musical does not yet function as a reflexive, performative genre that targets the urgent issues of political violence and gender normativity that have haunted the island within its postcolonial particularities. As a popular type of performance that usually consists of entertaining elements of music and dance, musicals sometimes become an effective weapon for promoting a certain political ideology. The (in)famous national centennial musical *Mengxiangjia* (Dreamers, 2011) manifests the Kuomintang's construction of the Republic of China (ROC) identity which erases the diversity of national interpretation through its problematic juxtaposition of two stories of 'dreaming' across different generations: one is the youth's dream of contributing to the ROC centennial celebration through artistic creation in 2011 and another the martyrs' dream of establishing the ROC in 1912 (Chi 2011). With its controversial seven million dollars' worth of funding and the rough integration of traditional *jingju* (Beijing opera) and contemporary melodrama, the musical ignited the fury of many local theatre practitioners, which led to fights among island citizens with different political standpoints. Nevertheless, the debate resulting from the musical emphasizes a valuable reconsideration of the alliance between politics and aesthetics, urging both local practitioners and audiences to recognize the national myth and political violence that may be constructed and enhanced by government-sponsored performances.

Musicals that oppose the official identity do exist. Jinzhi Yanshe's (Golden Bough Theatre) *Huangjin haizeiwang* (Pirates and Formosa, 2011) aims to trouble the 'descendants of dragon' identity by humorously fleshing out the multiracial and multicultural components of the island (Figure 24.4). A cross-cultural comedic musical, the piece combines the minority rituals with *opela gezaixi*, a performing technique that mixes and matches *xiqu* (traditional theatre) and various local subcultures, to emphasize the postcolonial networking of diverse groups on the island.

Figure 24.4 Golden Bough Theatre's *Huangjui haizeiwang* (Pirates and Formosa, 2011).
(Courtesy of Golden Bough Theatre)

While also challenging the official history, Jade Y. Chen (Chen Yuhui)'s stage adaptation *Haishen jiazu* (Mazu's Bodyguard, 2009) resorts to a solemn, realistic tone of gezaixi acting and expressionist modern dance to 'allegorize' the unmarked traumas of local women (Chen 2009). While appealing, these musicals still risk reinforcing the patriarchal gender norms that have disciplined how local women move and perceive their bodies. Similar characterizations of female roles exist in both de-colonial musicals – that is, women who function either as sexy stunners that copy masculine behaviour, or 'ideal' angels of the house that unconditionally support their male partners to achieve national grand projects. The democratic and liberal surfaces of these resistant musicals obscure their gender issues, making them seem only slightly or not at all important.

Beside the gender operations, racial complexity seems to be another issue raised by the musicals. Taipei Aiyueju Gongchang's (Philharmonic Theatre) recent musical *Chongfan Relanzhe* (Zeelandia: Return to Formosa, 2014) exemplifies the attempt of visioning the island's future through the optimistic lens of hybridity (Wang 2014). The musical describes the romance between a Dutch colonizer and a Siraya woman, emphasizing the utopic sense of love and dream among the different racial groups on the island. The multimedia projections of the island landscape as well as the Broadway-style musical used indeed help generate a fantasy towards the Zeelandia (seventeenth-century Dutch fortress in Taiwan) relic. However, the positive trope of hybridity risks hiding the actual horror and violence produced by colonization.

In contrast to the practitioners devoted to the cross-cultural musicals mentioned above, many young practitioners started producing musicals that critique present social issues within the current Taiwanese context rather than collective traumas from the past. Tianzuo Zhihe Juchang's (Perfect Match Theatre) *Tiantang bianyuan* (The Edge of Heaven, 2013) probes the effects of alienation in local urban life through a story that describes the poetic interaction between the living and the dead. *Mulan Shaonü* (Mulan, 2011), a collaboration by Tainanren Jutuan (Tainaner Ensemble) and Fengxiyue Gongzuoshi (Studio M), reinterprets the folktale of Mulan by adopting various local slangs and insider jokes to approach the issues of LGBTQ identification that challenge local gender norms. Not only have these musicals integrated issues and themes that directly resonate with the collective memories and feelings of contemporary life on the island, they have also adopted diverse performing methods on stage and included multimedia and internet installations. These musicals have broadened and enriched the genre of the Taiwanese musical, mobilizing further critical discussions on this specific type of performance.

V. Korea, by Ji Hyon (Kayla) Yuh

The first time Koreans saw American musicals was during the 1920s and 30s, but by the 1940s, Koreans began to see cabaret-style revues as well as prototypes of musicals based on folk tales such as *Gyeonwoo Jingnyeo*, a love story between Gyeonwoo, an earth-bound man, and Jingnyeo, a fairy from the heavenly realm. However, many argue that the conventions of American musical theatre, especially those of musical comedy, are not found in the works that were created before 1966.

Indeed, 1966 was an important year in Korean musical theatre history, with the emergence of a Korean language production of *Porgy and Bess*, the first commercial production of an American musical in Seoul.[7] The producers for the Korean production cut some scenes and simplified the music from the original, while keeping about twenty songs from the original score. Although the cast could have better emphasized the 'pathos of African Americans', most of the reviewers seemed to agree that the 1966 production of *Porgy and Bess* confirmed the potential of a fully fledged musical production in Korea (Yoo 2009: 85).

In the same year, Koreans saw the premiere of *Saljjagi obseoye* (Sweet, Come to Me Stealthily), which is considered to be the first homegrown musical created in the tradition of American musical theatre. This was conceived and produced as an inauguration piece for the second phase of Yegrin Theatre Company (Yegrin Akdan, whose name changed to Yegrin in the later years), a private company that was re-established with the support of the government, which saw Yegrin as a means to outdo North Korea's large-scale performances (KNAA 2014: 419).

Based on *Baebijang-jeon* (Tale of Chief Aide Bae), a folktale about the love between a prudish aristocrat and a high-level courtesan who looks down on all aristocrats for their hypocrisy, *Sweet, Come to Me Stealthily* starred Patty Kim, a top female singer at the time, as the courtesan Aerang. To maximize the benefit of having a star in the show, the producers recorded Aerang's theme song and had it played on radio and television before the production officially opened, which helped the show's publicity. Musically speaking, it followed the conventions of American popular music and movie musicals, while maintaining the melodic familiarity of Korean folk songs. The choreography was also more advanced than previous works, thanks to the use of wireless microphones which allowed more creative staging. Most importantly, the creators of the show had carefully studied the conventions of American musical comedy, and tried to apply elements such as satire, choreography of the mundane gestures, and syncopated rhythm in music (KNAA 2014: 261). *Sweet, Come to Me Stealthily* proved to be an instant success, and was followed by a few revivals in the 1970s (Yoo 2009: 187).

Throughout the 1980s and 90s, Koreans saw a number of homegrown musicals as well as Korean language productions of well-known foreign titles such as *Jesus Christ Superstar*, *The Sound of Music* and *Guys and Dolls*. Until then, Korean language productions of American musicals were adaptations freely done without properly securing the rights for a local language production. However, this changed in 1987 when Korea joined the Universal Copyright Convention (UCC), which discouraged producers from borrowing the existing works from the United States without securing proper copyrights, and encouraged artists to create their own works.

Jihacheol ilhoseon (Line 1), a small-sized adaptation of a German musical titled *Linie 1*, was one outcome of these changes in the early 1990s (Figure 24.5). Although an adaptation, it borrowed only the setting of the original German piece, and filled it with the stories of people who lived in Seoul and rode the subway line 1. With strong characters and timely updates that appropriately reflected Korean society, it ran for 15 years, receiving a total of 4,000 performances until it closed in 2008.[8]

In 1996, ACOM International's *The Last Empress* premiered to the Korean audience. Based on the historical story about Queen Min who was killed by Japanese assassins in the midst of political turmoil at the turn of the century, the production was meticulously planned, with a view towards encouraging nationalistic sentiment among Koreans and propagating Korea's culture to audiences outside Korea (Park 2011: 670). The successive overseas performances of *The Last Empress* in New York, London and Vancouver, which performed to mostly unimpressed audiences, were widely celebrated in Korea as a great feat of Korean musical theatre as well as Yoon Ho Jin, the main producer of the company.

Following in the footsteps of *The Last Empress* was *Nanta* (1997), a non-verbal performance that was created in the fashion of *Stomp*, but with a different setting: a restaurant kitchen on a wedding day. Much like *The Last Empress*, *Nanta* was produced with hopes of touring outside Korea. In 2003, in collaboration with New York's Broadway Asia Company, *Nanta* performed

Figure 24.5 Hakchon's *Jihacheol ilhoseon* (Line 1).
(Courtesy of Hakchon)

in New York's New Victory Theater under the different title of *Cookin'* for about a month. After this, the show moved to Minetta Lane Theater for a long-term production for 2004–5 season in New York. Regardless of the mixed reviews, *Nanta* was celebrated as the first Korean show staged in New York for a long-term engagement.

However, the current popularity of musical theatre in Korea owes much to the 2001 local production of *The Phantom of the Opera* (Opera-ui Yuryeong), which was the first sit-down production that ran for more than a month. Behind the success was also the marketing plan that Seol and Company, the main producer, employed, utilizing the play's established brand value on Broadway and overseas. The unprecedented success of *The Phantom* gave rise to a new generation of producers, local talent and audience as well as investors who witnessed the potential of musicals in Korea. It was followed by another successful enterprise, *Jekyll and Hyde* in 2004. Thanks to Frank Wildhorn's music, its intense drama and Cho Seung Woo, a relatively rookie actor who perfectly delivered the intensity of the drama, *Jekyll and Hyde* quickly became one of the repertoires that received frequent revivals in the past decade. Despite the criticism that they set the precedence for disproportionate investment in foreign musicals over homegrown works, both *The Phantom* and *Jekyll and Hyde* contributed a great deal to Korean musical theatre, as they found new audiences and expanded the market exponentially.

Throughout the 2000s, American and European musicals remained more popular, but Korean audiences saw a great number of Korean original musicals, which were often smaller and more intimate in nature. *Finding Mr. Kim*, which started as a college thesis project by Kim Hye Sung (Music) and Jang Yu Jeong (Book and Lyrics) in 2004, was developed into a commercial piece in 2006. A story of a woman who falls in love with a guy who is a private investigator hired to find her first love from 10 years ago, it became one of the most popular original musicals and ran for the next 8 years, until 2014, at various small venues in Daehangno, the theatrical centre of Seoul.[9]

The government was also interested in the process, as the rise of musical theatre coincided with the rise of Hallyu (Korean Wave), and the musical was one of the forms that was thought to be able to capitalize on the popularity of Korean culture, especially that of celebrities.[10] Believing that the musical could promote the nation's cultural development, Daegu, a city about two hours from Seoul by train, launched Daegu International Musical Festival (DIMF) in 2006. It was designed for new musicals to win a grant for development, for college productions to win a contest and for international exchanges. For the first few years, DIMF also had a partnership with the New York Musical Festival (NYMF), and exchanged productions that were well received during the festival.

Recently, the successful 2009 revival of *Dreamgirls* started with a tryout production in Seoul. While an idiosyncratic example of an individual producer's own interests and business strategy, this production also reflects a larger trend in the Korean musical theatre industry's turn to overseas markets. Korea continues to build international connections, especially with Japan and China, to compensate for the saturated domestic market. There also are a greater number of examples where American and European creators were hired for a development of a new work for Korean audiences, as well as examples of larger productions created by local artists who came out of the legacies of the 2000s.

As of 2014, Korean musical theatre is faced with a number of challenges, such as a saturated domestic market, rising production costs and a lagging economy in general. Considering the commercial nature of the musical theatre, the impact of these challenges cannot be avoided. However, considering the vibrant local talents who are motivated to create Korean musicals, it seems to signal a new phase of the musical's development in Korea.

VI. Southeast Asia, by Caleb Goh

The musical theatre in Southeast Asia is considered a contemporary form of entertainment based heavily on a western construct. It did not exist in its western form until the end of the twentieth century with the exposure to touring productions of Broadway and West End musicals, such as *Les Misérables*, *The Phantom of the Opera* and *Cats*, predominantly by Australian companies. The Southeast Asian musicals began by imitating the western form, but their evolution has earned them the term 'hybrid musical theatre'. These hybrid productions are most successful when they blend authentic ethnic elements with the spectacle of the Broadway-style musical, thus creating a strong bond with the audience through the familiarity of the material alongside commercial western pizazz. While the ultimate goal, at least for some of the Southeast Asian countries, is for a homegrown musical to hit Broadway or the West End, none has had sufficient financial backing or support to see that dream come to fruition yet. Culturally, much of the material would need to be altered in order to be appealing and accessible to a wider audience. In countries such as Singapore and the Philippines, which have greater government interest in making this goal a reality, the possibility of success might be looming in the near future.

As such, only Singapore, Malaysia, Thailand and the Philippines have had significant development in this genre. Indonesia has enjoyed several successful productions, particularly with two local hit productions, *Laskar Pelangi* (The Rainbow Troops) and *Keong Mas* (The Golden Snail), which followed the western format. The other countries, such as Laos, Myanmar and Cambodia, have little or no development in the way of musical theatre.

In 2008, the Cambodian 'rock opera' *Where Elephants Weep* was mounted. The story was based on a famous Cambodian legend but was additionally contemporized to include the after-effects of the Khmer Rouge genocide. Composer Him Sophy combined traditional Cambodian music with western opera as well as contemporary pop. Unfortunately, this production, by John Burt of the Cambodian Living Arts, alongside western collaborators, ended up featuring Cambodians in only minor roles and as puppeteers and musicians. Owing to the extent of foreign input and lack of local expertise or interest, this musical theatre venture has remained the only production of its kind.

Brunei's modern theatricals emerged only after independence in 1984 and its musical theatre still lags behind other art forms. Furthermore, productions must receive official endorsement before being staged, and the threat of interrogation and prosecution is ever present. In spite of these limitations, however, the International School of Brunei (ISB) set the stage for musicals in 2006 by mounting *Oliver!* at the Empire Theatre. The cast received a standing ovation on the opening night, prompting the subsequent mounting of *West Side Story* later in the year. That same year, Bakat Arts Production staged Brunei's first Broadway-style musical, *Asli!* (Original!). Written and composed by Rachel Malai Ali, the founder of Instant Café Theatre in Kuala Lumpur, *Asli!* was an exciting musical of song, dance and theatre that combined the ethnic sounds of gongs, flutes, gamelan and hadrah with modern-day electric guitars, drums and keyboards.

Malaysia

Malaysia is a country that has seen its musical theatre industry flourish in recent years. Before its independence in 1957, most shows were helmed by expatriates, through the Malayan Arts Theatre Group (MATG). Although locals were given opportunities to perform, they were rarely offered lead roles. It was only after independence that there was a 'rise in national consciousness, and this greatly encouraged local theatre practitioners to participate more actively in decolonising the theatre industry' (Lo 2004: 51). The MATG constitution was actively altered in 1965 to encourage full participation for locals in the theatre arts.

By the late 1980s, numerous new theatre companies had sprouted. Among them were Krishen Jit's Five Arts Centre, The Actors Studio and Instant Café Theatre. The Actors Studio in particular, established in 1989 by Joe Hasham and Faridah Merican, was known for bringing mainstream American, Australian and British theatre to Kuala Lumpur, including many musical theatre productions, thus paving the way for native musical theatre.

Since the new millennium, musicals have garnered a strong following and an increase in musical theatre offerings in the country, especially in Kuala Lumpur. Although the up-and-coming musical theatre company PAN Productions, under the leadership of Nell Ng, is a company that focuses on mounting musical theatre classics, the hope is eventually to produce an original English-language musical that is indicative of Malaysia, its culture and its people (Ng, personal communication, 23 February 2014; Figure 24.6).

The trend to create more original musicals has already begun. Chin San Sooi, a founding member of Five Arts Centre, has staged musicals based on Chinese Malaysian history and Chinese legendary tales, including *Morning in Night, Yap Ah Loy – The Play* and *Reunion*. Starting in 2002, Dama Orchestra, which is among the more significant Chinese orchestras in Malaysia, began staging full-length music dramas by combining various songs in a themed sung-through musical format, using popular songs from the likes of *Cats* and *Jesus Christ Superstar*. With this natural progression, in 2006 they mounted *Butterfly Lovers*, which marked their first serious theatrical musical work. The show played at the Kuala Lumpur Performing Arts Centre (KLPAC) to packed houses. Audience members who initially had reservations about the production praised its quality. It went on tour at Genting Highlands, Pahang and Perth, Australia in 2007.

Figure 24.6 The Kit Kat Girls in *Cabaret* by PAN Productions, Malaysia.
(Courtesy of PAN Productions)

Original musicals in Malaysia currently have great emphasis on history, Muslim quests and folklore. Owing to the fragmentation in languages and communities, there is little cross-pollination among the language groups. Malay-language groups would often stick to performing and mounting original Malay musicals, while their English-language counterparts would do the same. On the fiftieth anniversary of Malaysia's independence in 2007, two large-scale musicals shed light on this linguistic divide. The Actors Studio presented the original English-language musical, *Tunku the Musical*. It was the second musical theatre venture for new composers Lim Chuang Yik and Teng Ky-Gan, and focused on Tunku Abdul Rahman's rule as Malaysia's first prime minister, the events leading up to Malaysia's independence, the secession of Singapore and the racial riots. This was a revolutionary production considering that the controversy of politics was rarely exposed in Malaysian musicals. The Malay-language offering was produced by the Istana Budaya (The Palace of Culture), titled *Teater Muzikal Putra* (Musical Theatre Son). It dealt similarly with the persona of Tunku but focused more on the battle for independence from the British. Written by Rahimidin Zahari, it charted the life and times of Tunku from his youth to his ascent to power as the first prime minister of Malaysia.

In 2006, the Istana Budaya engaged iconic Singaporean composer, Dick Lee, to write the music for *Puteri Gunung Ledang, the Musical* (The Princess of Mt Ledang, the Musical). Based on a film of the same title, the musical was a large spectacle drawing over 20,000 people during its first of three runs. Many have credited *The Princess of Mt Ledang* with changing Malaysians' view of local musicals. Its success led to the commissioning of Lee for a subsequent spectacle, *P. Ramlee – the Musical*. Chronicling the life and achievement of the entertainment icon Tan Sri P. Ramlee, the musical even paid homage to the traditional Malay theatrical form *bangsawan* by bringing it 'up to date as a modern musical so that it was once again reinterpreting a western genre for the local audience and gaining popularity by incorporating contemporary song and dance' (Diamond 2012: 288).

In 2011, Istana Budaya produced a musical titled *Lat Kampung Boy Sebuah Muzikal* (Lat Village Boy The Musical), based on a comic of the same title by Malaysia's most famous cartoonist, Lat, which depicted his childhood in Perak. Initially conceived by the Malaysian National Institute of Translation in 2009, the musical was produced and directed by Hans Isaac, in consultation with Lat (Wee 2011). In 2013, a government-supported musical titled *Asmara Songsang* (Abnormal Desire) toured schools and universities to spread the message of the supposed 'perils' of being lesbian, gay, bisexual and transgender (LGBT) in Malaysia. It sparked controversy over its 'state-sponsored bigotry' (Hodal 2013: 31). Written and directed by Rahman Adam, 73, the musical presented a one-sided view of the issue and displayed an arguably narrow-minded and bigoted government stance on social policy. Steeped in religion and politics, Malaysia was not new to seeing current issues being highlighted in musicals. Just a few years earlier, in 2010, *Mahathir, the Musical*, a megamusical in Kuala Lumpur, focused on Malaysia's former strong-arm leader, Mahathir Mohamad.

Musical theatre in Malaysia is still a burgeoning industry and its growth has been significant in the past decade, gradually placing greater emphasis on historical topics, cultural icons and socio-political slants in its theatrical voice.

The Philippines

The musical theatre began to flourish in 1986 when the Cultural Center of the Philippines (CCP) was revamped. Artistically led by theatre scholar and playwright Nicanor Tiongson, this shining emblem of elite Manila culture, built at the behest of First Lady Imelda Marcos, was restructured into a mini ministry of the arts, 'leading the way toward the Filipinization, democratization and decentralization of the arts. The emphasis was on forming a cultural identity that the nation's people could be proud of' (Brandon 1993: 221). Broadway's influence has been prevalent in this particular venue, as tours of mega-musicals such as *Miss Saigon*, *Mamma Mia* and *The Phantom of the Opera* make regular appearances here.

The exposure to Broadway musicals as well as rock and pop music has led Filipinos to create original modern musicals, which commonly use Filipino folklore and ethnic music motifs, such as Rio Alma-Tito Climaco's *Bernardo Carpio* in 1976 and Bienvenido Lumbera-Jim Paredes' *Bayani* (Hero) in 1977. Other musicals are inspired by contemporary life, personalities and social or political issues, such as Gines Tan's *Magsimula Ka* (Begin, 1983) and Ryan Cayabyab's *Katy* (1988). In 1998, the resident company of the CCP, Tanghalang Pilipino, staged an original musical production, *Ilustrado* (Cultured), based on the life of the Filipino nationalist, Jose Rizal. Playwright Chris Millado, who is the head of the CCP's performing arts department, directed a musicalized version of an award-winning comic by Carlo Vergara titled *Ang Kagila-gilalas na Pakikipagsapalaran ni Zsazsa Zaturnnah* (The Amazing Adventures of Zsazsa Zaturnnah). *Zsazsa Zaturnnah: Ze Muzikal* was such a phenomenal hit that it has since toured around Manila and has become the company's longest-running musical. In 2006, it was adapted into a film, *Zsazsa Zaturnnah: Za Moveeh*. In the past few decades, producers, writers and directors of musicals have also selected elements from *sarsuela* (a Spanish traditional form of musical comedy) and *bodabil* (an indigenized form of Filipino vaudeville) to structure original musicals.

Filipinos have a natural proclivity towards musical theatre owing to their embrace of American culture. This embrace has led to a western sensibility with regard to performance. 'Filipino acting is imbued with a kind of naturalism more familiar to western spectators and less inclined to the formalized gesture seen in other Asian theatres' (Diamond 2012: 223). This western performance style has helped to put Filipino actors in the forefront of musical theatre casting, with producers finding them more similarly suited to the sensibilities of the musicals currently being produced on the Great White Way. *Miss Saigon*, in particular, was the pivotal musical that sparked the interest of producers and directors, making Filipinos, to this day, the default Asian ethnic group when Asian-specific roles are required in American musicals.

Singapore

Singapore is a multicultural society – a 'melting pot' of major Asian cultures comprised predominantly of Chinese, Indian and Malay. This diversity has led to great exposure to different forms of artistic and theatrical expression from the varied ethnic communities, from Chinese operas to Mandarin plays, Malay folk dances, Bollywood-style extravaganzas, street acrobatic acts and contemporary dance performances. Further enriching the cultural diversity coexisting in the country was the Anglo influence, which played a significant part in defining the amalgamation of cultures within the society. As Singapore progressed towards independent statehood, the hybrid nature of the theatre was solidified, with English as the primary medium for performance. The English language proved to be a dynamic medium of cultural expression, projecting a vibrant and 'hip' image, which accounted for the relatively young theatre clientele (Peterson 2001: 58).

Along with Singapore's emergence as a global economic power in the 1980s, there was a steady and meteoric rise in affluence in the society. This sparked a unique quest in a young and modern Southeast Asian country – the endeavour to develop a Singaporean or Asian-themed musical that could meet with financial and artistic success abroad:

Because of the potential for huge financial rewards and the prestige associated with 'making it' on the West End or Broadway, no cultural terrain in Singapore has received more conscious engineering on the part of the government or prominent individuals in the arts community than the Singaporean musical.

(Peterson 2001: 196)

Significant support from private corporations and the National Arts Council has resulted in numerous Asian-themed musicals, including several that have had long runs locally and in overseas tours.

Singapore's first original musical theatre production, *Beauty World*, was mounted in 1988 and marked the changing status of the Singaporean performing arts. Constructed by playwright Michael Chiang and composer Dick Lee, the musical shed light on Singapore in the 1960s through a working-class setting of a Chinese cabaret. Since its premiere, the musical has been revived no fewer than five times, and paved the way for a plethora of original musical theatre productions, most commonly in English, Mandarin and Malay. One of the leading theatre companies, the Singapore Repertory Theatre (SRT), stages original musicals on a regular basis. Their production choices 'point to the presence of a "taste" for cultural consumption of productions originating from or influenced by the west among Singapore's well-heeled elites' (Wong 2012: 235). Original musicals by this illustrious company include *Sing to the Dawn* (1996), *A Twist of Fate* (1997) and *Forbidden City* (2002). All these productions have the common factor of Singapore's pioneering and definitive musical theatre composer, Dick Lee, writing the music for each of these commercially and critically successful musicals. Since *Beauty World*, Lee has continued to fuse Broadway-style music with Singaporean content in an attempt to create a

Figure 24.7 Caleb Goh (Jack) in *Jack & the Bean-Sprout!* by W!ld Rice, Singapore.
(Courtesy of W!ld Rice)

definitive Singaporean identity within and outside the country. His prolific body of work has expanded to collaborations and composition contributions to large-scale musicals in Malaysia, Japan and Hong Kong.

Musical theatre exploration in Singapore has also extended beyond the western-style Broadway vernacular. In the late 1990s, Mandarin plays and musicals began to slowly gain popularity. While roughly only 300 tickets would be a guaranteed sell for a Mandarin musical previously, now audiences flock in droves. The 2010 revival of Toy Factory's hit 1996 musical, *December Rains*, played to about 20,000 people. For the past decade, another leading theatre company, W!ld Rice, has been producing sophisticated musical theatre comedies in the vein of the British pantomime (Figure 24.7). These musicals are localized and acted as political and social satire under the guise of humour, with original music in each offering. Artistic Director Ivan Heng researched the most popular British pantomimes and created in 2003 the very first family-friendly and localized pantomime musical, *Cinderel-lah!*, a local take on the fairytale classic *Cinderella*. Since then, W!ld Rice's pantomime musicals have amassed a solid fan base, and plan to continue well into the future (Heng).

Broadway musicals have had a huge impact on the burgeoning Singapore theatre scene and numerous productions from professional tours have been presented on a regular basis. Even local theatre companies such as W!ld Rice, SRT, Toy Factory and Pangdemonium! mount localized or faithfully interpreted versions of these musicals. Many theatres have been constructed to house these mega-musicals; the most common venues are the Esplanade Theatre and the MasterCard Theatres at Marina Bay Sands.

Thailand

Theatre in Thailand today offers the audience a range of experiences, from the most traditional dance-dramas to Broadway-style productions. Mainstream productions are most prevalent in the country's capital Bangkok, the site for most of the theatre companies and performers. Many big musical spectacles are staged, especially since there is a growing interest in musical theatre among students. These include original Thai productions such as *Prisana the Musical* (2012) as well as adaptations and localizations from Broadway musicals, such as a Thai version of Jerry Herman's *La Cage Aux Folles* in 2010. One of the major theatre companies, Dass Entertainment, has provided quality professional entertainment since its inception in 1986, with five or six productions a year. They even built the first privately owned theatre in Thailand, the Bangkok Playhouse, in 1993.

Presently, one of the most prolific musical theatre personalities currently in Thailand is Takonkiet 'Boy' Viravan. A *lakorn* (TV soap opera) and musical theatre director, he was exposed to American theatre when he studied in Boston. Setting up his own company back in Thailand, he specializes in creating and mounting new musicals with Thai themes. In 2013, he debuted his new musical based on the Thai novel, *Luerd Kattiya* (The Royal Blood), and has announced that he has plans eventually to bring one of his musicals to Broadway.

Although theatre is well established in Thailand, it also faces many continuing problems: a lack of quality directors and playwrights, a less than enthusiastic response from mass audiences to spoken drama, and an almost total lack of government support for innovative ventures from the state. Thailand's musical theatre industry is a burgeoning one, which mounts productions almost solely in the Thai language. The development of an English-language musical to cater to an international audience became a reality in 2015 when Viravan's extremely successful Thai musical *Khang Lang Phab* (Behind the Painting) caught the attention of American composing team, Richard Maltby Jr. and David Shire. The musical was subsequently adapted and translated to English to cater to an American audience, renamed Waterfall, and has since enjoyed two tryout runs at the Pasadena Playhouse (California), and Seattle's 5th Avenue Theatre (Washington), in the hopes of transferring to Broadway in the near future.

In today's flourishing musical theatre climate, the large-scale Southeast Asian productions are often discussed on the internet, in magazine articles, in blogs and in person. They have attracted not only the regular theatregoer but also those who might not have experienced a musical event of such proportion before. With greater exposure and musical theatre education come greater interest and desired investment. If the goal is to have a Broadway or West End musical come from this part of the world one day, many Southeast Asian countries are on the right developmental track in making that theatrical dream a reality.

Notes

1   The first American musical to be fully adapted in Japanese was *Oklahoma!* (1967) by Takarazuka Revue Company, but prior to that, the first original Japanese myūjikaru is said to be *Fanny* (1950) or *Morgan Oyuki* (1951) produced at the Imperial Theatre.

2   The Meiji government promoted kabuki, noh and kyogen as traditional Japanese theatre genres, especially identifying kabuki as a counterpoint to Grand Opera in Europe. This coincided with the time when a number of new musical theatres began to serve the Japanese public through adopting western-style music, dance and acting. With the aim of establishing an emblematic home for western-style productions, the Imperial Theatre was built in 1911 facing the Imperial Palace. Until then, except for a few foreign establishments such as the Gaiety Theatre in Yokohama where travelling troupes from abroad would occasionally perform, there was no proper theatre in Japan to accommodate western-style productions on a large scale.

3   Tokyo College of Music was founded in 1887. The national education of western music for schools began in 1910.

4   For instance, the founder of the Takarazuka Revue, Kobayashi Ichizō, recalls seeing their first Japanese opera, *Yuya*, in 1912.

5   Taya made his entire career as a lead singer for operas and operettas. Fujiwara organized his own theatre group, Fujiwara Kageki-dan (Fujiwara Opera Company), and staged mainly Italian repertoires regularly at Hibiya Kokaidw (Tokyo Metropolitan Hibiya Public Hall), which had functioned as one of the modern centres for western music concerts and theatre productions since 1929.

6   Before the war, Kikuta also wrote for Asakusa Casino Follies in musical comedy style.

7   In fact, there had been other productions of *Porgy and Bess* prior to the 1966 production, one in 1948 and the other in 1962. However, the 1948 production was a play without music, while the 1962 production was considered to be a play with music, as there was little choreography and many songs had been cut from the original script.

8   Kim Min Ki, a folk singer and activist who was the mastermind of the Korean adaptation, is still recognized both in Korea and Germany for his re-creation of *Line 1*. Kim won multiple awards in Korea for his work on *Line 1*, including the Special Achievement Award from the sixth Korean Musical Awards in 2000. He was also awarded a Goethe-Medaille from the Goethe Institute in 2007. Additionally, the original creators of the show, honouring Kim Min Ki's work, have refused royalties from the Korean production since its 1,000th performance in 2001.

9   Daehangno literally means college street in Korean, and is a neighbourhood that is of approximately 450,000 m². It serves as home to many theatrical festivals, as well as other cultural activities. More significantly, there are about two hundred small to medium-sized theatres in this neighbourhood alone. This means that there will be more than a hundred theatrical offerings of varying degrees of production quality on any given night.

10 Hallyu, which literally means Korean wave, refers to the rise of popularity of Korean popular products such as Korean popular music (K-pop) and Korean drama (K-drama).

Bibliography

Ang, Jimmy (2011) *Cabaret* (Photograph), Malaysia: PAN Productions.

Brandon, James R. (1993) *The Cambridge Guide to Asian Theatre*, Cambridge: Cambridge University Press.

Chang, Lavender (2013) *Jack & the Bean-Sprout!* (Photograph), Singapore: W!ld Rice.

Chen, Jade Y. (2009) *Haishen jiazu* (Mazu's Bodyguards), Taipei: Ink Publishing.

Chi Wei-Jan (2011) 'Mengxiang huanmie de guojia (The Country without Dreams)', *China Times*, 17 October, A14.

Choi Chang Ju (1999) *Hanguk gamyeongeukgwa myujikeol* (Korean Mask Drama and Musical), Seoul: Em Aed.

Choi Min Woo (2014) *Myujikeol sahwehak* (Musical Sociology), Seoul: Ikon.

Choi, Joyce Ying Ying (2010) 'Musicals with Hong Kong Characteristics', *Muse*, 41, available at www.musemag.hk/MuseTheatre/2010/Muse%20Jun%202010_41_F.htm, accessed 2 September 2014.

Diamond, Catherine (2012) *Communities of Imagination*, Honolulu: University of Hawai'i Press.

Hasegawa Yumiko (2008) 'Meiji-ki no shōka-wo irodotta seiyōkyoku (The Influence of Western Music on Songs during the Meiji)', exhibition catalogue of Kunitachi College of Music Library.

He Luting (1999) 'Yinyue de xiandaixing' (The Modernity of Music), in *He Luting quanji* (Complete Works of He Luting), Shanghai: Shanghai yinyue chubanshe.

Hodal, Kate (2013) 'Malaysia musical spreads anti-gay message', *The Guardian*, 29 March, www.theguardian.com/world/2013/mar/28/anti-gay-lgbt-musical-malaysia, accessed 28 January, 2014.

Hong Shen (1959) 'Meng Jjiangnü gei women de jiaoxun' (Lessons from *Meng Jiangnü*), in *Hong Shen wenji* (Collected Works of Hong Shen), Beijing: Zhongguo xiju chubanshe.

Hsieh Hsiao-Mei (2002) 'Hupiezai jiqi lishi yuanyou ("*Opela*": Its Definition and Historical Development)', *Zhongwai wenxue* (Chung Wai Literary Monthly), 31 (1): 157–74.

Inoue Yoshie (2011) *Kikuta Kazuo no Shigoto* (Works by Kikuta Kazuo): *Asakusa, Hibiya Takarazuka*, Tokyo: Shakaihyōron-sha.

Kakita Hajime (2012) 'Amerika-he-no omoi: Sho-sakka, Utsu Hideo (Towards America: Show-maker Utsu Hideo)', paper presented at Takarazuka History and Culture symposium at BB Museum Kobe.

Kim Deok Ho, and Won Yong Jin (eds) (2008) *Amelikanaijeisyeon: Haebang ihu hangukeseoui migukwa* (Americanization: Americanization in Post-Independence Korea), Seoul: Pureun Yeoksa.

Kim Ui Kyung, and Yoo In Kyung (eds) (2008) *Park No-hong'ui daejung yeonyesa 1: Hanguk akgeuksa, Hanguk geukjangsa* (Park No Hong's History of Popular Entertainment Part I: Histories of Korean Akgeuk and Theatre Venues), Seoul: Yeongeukgwa Ingan.

KNAA (ed.) (2014) *Yesulsa gusul chongseo 1: Park Yong-gu, hanbando leunesangseu'ui gihwoekja* (Oral Interviews on the History Arts 1: Park Yong Gu, the Producer of Renaissance in Korean Peninsula), Seoul: Korean National Arts Archive.

Kobayashi Ichizō (1980) *Takarazuka Manpitsu* (Notes on Takarazuka), Osaka: Hankyū Dentetsu.

Kurahashi Sigeru and Tsuji Norihiko (2005) *Shōjo-kageki no Kōbo* (The Rise and Fall of Girls' Opera), Tokyo: Seikyu-sha.

Lee Su Geun, and Go Hee Un (eds) (2010) *Myujikeol baewoo isibinaege mudda* (Asked 20 Musical Theatre Actors/Actresses), Seoul: Su Film

Liao Xianghong (2002) 'Zhongguo yinyueju de chansheng fazhan yu xianzhuang' (The Birth, Development, and Current Situation of Chinese Musical Theatre), www.musicalchina.com/read.php?nid=106&id=690, accessed 10 December 2014.

Lim, Albert K. (2014) *Monkey Goes West* (Photograph), Singapore: W!ld Rice.

Lin Tsai-Yun (2010) *Taiwan yinyueju fazhanshi* (The History of Taiwanese Musical), available at http://paper.wenweipo.com/2010/01/10/YC1001100006.htm, accessed 24 February 2014.

Lo, Jacqueline (2004) *Staging Nation: English Language Theatre in Malaysia and Singapore*, Hong Kong: Hong Kong University Press.

Marumoto Takashi, Itō Naoko and Hasegawa Etsurō (eds) (2009) *Opera-gaku no chihei: Sōgōbutaigeijyutsu eno gakusaiteki apurōhi* (The Horizon of Opera Studies: An Inter-disciplinary Approach to Stage Arts), Tokyo: Sairyu-sha.

Nakano Masaaki (2011) *Mūran Rūgu Shinjuku-za* (Moulin Rouge Shinjuku Theatre), Tokyo: Shinwa-sha.

Ongaku no Tomo-sha (ed.) (2003) *Grand Opera* spring issue, Tokyo: Ongaku no Tomo-sha.

Park Man Kyu (2011) *Hanguk mujikeolsa* (The History of Korean Musicals Since 1941), Seoul: Hanul Academy.

Peterson, William (2001) *Theater and the Politics of Culture in Contemporary Singapore*, Middletown, CT: Wesleyan University Press.

Seol Do Yoon (2005) *Opelaui yulyeong, gamyeoneul beodda: Myujikeol opelaui yulyeong'e gwanhan modeungeot* (The Phantom of the Opera Unmasked: Everything about the Musical *The Phantom of the Opera*), Seoul: Sup.

Sun Ji'nan (2007) *Li Jinhui yu Lipai yinyue* (Li Jinhui and Li-Style Music), Shanghai: Shanghai Yinyue Xueyuan chubanshe.

Wang, Chun-Yen (2014) *Yi diguo zhiyan ruhe xunyuan* (How to Trace the Root through the Lens of Empire), available at http://pareviews.ncafroc.org.tw/?p=10940, accessed 30 June 2014.

Wee, Teo C. (2011) 'From Kampung Boy to Musical Theatre', *The Straits Times*, 15 January.

Wen Shuo (2012) *Zhongguo yinyueju shi jindai juan* (A History of Chinese Musicals, Modern Volume), Beijing: Xiyuan chubanshe.

Wong, Melissa W. (2012) 'Negotiating Class, Taste, and Culture via the Arts Scene in Singapore: Postcolonial or Cosmopolitan Global?', *Asian Theatre Journal*, 29: 233–254.

Yamanashi Makiko (2012) *A History of the Takarazuka Revue Since 1914: Modernity, Girls' Cuture, Japan Pop*, Leiden: Global Oriental & Brill.

Yoo In Kyung (2009) *Hanguk myujikeolui segye: Jeontonggwa hyeonksin* (The World of Korean Musicals: Tradition and Innovation), Seoul: Yeongeukgwa Ingan.

Glossary

The use of **bold** in glossary entries indicates the type of dance/theatre to which they apply, which are listed elsewhere in the glossary.

adhunik: the most common word for 'modern' in several Indian languages

agemaku: 1) five-coloured lift curtain at the end of the **noh hashigakari**, opened via two poles connected to the bottom corners, which pull the curtain up and back; 2) **kabuki** theatre curtain leading from the rear of the hall to **hamanachi**

ai-kyogen: interlude narratives or narrator preceding or between acts of **noh** play

aimeiju: amateur theatre movement in China in the 1920s

akarimado: 'light window', paper-covered shutters in pre-Meiji era **kabuki** theatres, opened and closed by window guards to regulate the amount of light in the theatre

akgeuk: 'music theatre', a type of variety show that became popular in Korea during the 1930s and 40s

angura: 'underground', from the Japanese pronunciation of the first syllables of 'under' and 'ground', a modern Japanese theatre movement of the 1960s

anka: an individual act in a play (Sanskrit), India

ankiya nat: 'one-act play', a major genre of performance in the state of Assam, India

anuvad: repetition or emulation; the most common Indian term for translation

anuyojan: remaking of older narratives through a new artistic consciousness, India

anyeint pure: Barmese variety performance featuring female dancers and male clowns. Its contemporary form usually opens with a short poem or song and followed by a mixture of dance, short plays, **thangyat**, and physical or satirical comedy

apabhrama: general term for a number of transitional languages that emerged after Sanskrit and Prakrit, and developed subsequent into early forms of the modern Indian languages.

apsara: a celestial dancing nymph (Hindu mythology)

aragoto: 'rough style' acting in **kabuki** featuring bellows, stamps and cross-eyed poses

asar: a gathering/sitting/party or a performance space, Bangladesh and India

ato-za: 'rear seat', rear area of the **noh** stage, where musicians and stagehands sit

attakatha: 'acted story', text of a **kathakali** play written in verse and song

ayang: small leather shadow puppet show, Cambodia

ayay: sung poetry featuring a male and female couple, Cambodia

baihuaxi: 'plain language plays', early form of spoken theatre in Hong Kong

baixi: hundred games circus in Han dynasty China

bangsawan: popular late nineteenth-century and early twentieth- century touring theatre, Malaysia and Southeast Asia *bangzi*: clapper opera, China

banqiangti: 'beat-tune form', one of the two principal music systems in **xiqu**

barachum: monk's cymbal dance, Korea

barong: animal-like body puppet, often leonine, Bali and Java, Indonesia

barong landong/landung: giant male and female body figures used in parades, Bali, Indonesia

bazi gong: 'techniques with weapons', movement sequences used for combat scenes with stage properties such as swords and spears in Chinese indigenous theatre

bedhaya: female court dancer or dance, Java, Indonesia

benir putul: glove puppetry, Bengal, India

beopgochum: monk's large barrel drum dance, Korea

bhagavata: chief singer, director, and/or producer of **yakshagana**, as well as other genres of performance in south India

Bhagavata Purana: Sanskrit narrative text, dating from early in the Common Era, devoted to the worship and mythology of the god Vishnu, specifically in his incarnation as Krishna

Bharata: the sage to whom the composition of the **Natyasastra** is attributed (c. 300 CE)

bharatanatyam: modern development of dasiattam (dance of temple courtesans), Tamil Nadu, India

Bhasa: the earliest extant Sanskrit playwright (c. 2nd century CE), and author of thirteen plays, parts of which are incorporated in the **kutiyattam** form of Kerala. Three of the plays have also had major revivals in the post-independence period

bhashantar: interlingual translation, India

bhat: also *nat*, professional entertainer, puppeteer, storyteller in Rajasthan and north India

bhava: human emotion or state of being conveyed by performers through their acting

bhavai: folk theatre in rural areas of western India, especially in the state of Gujarat

binli: protocol rites in ancient China

bkra shis rtags brgyad: 'eight auspicious symbols', symbols used in Tibetan art and architecture to illustrate positive attributes, actions and outcomes

bodabil: 'vaudeville' of the early twentieth century, the Philippines

boli: reed instrument used to alter puppet voice, India

bommalattam: 'doll puppet dance' string and rod figures of Tamil Nadu, Andhara Pradesh and Karnataka, India

bon: a religious tradition of Tibet that has distinct characteristics separating it from Buddhism, yet shares many common rituals and practices

bongsan talchum: a mask dance-drama from Hwanghae Province, Korea

bongwong: aria types in **yuet kahk**

boria: Islamic popular sung theatre of Penang, Malaysia

Brahma: the creator god attributed with creating drama and theatre, India

budaixi: hand puppets in China

bugaku: imperial court dance, Japan

bugaku-men: masks used in **bugaku**

bunmei kaika: 'civilization and enlightenment', Japan

bunraku: puppet theatre with three manipulators per figure, Japan

buong song: female court dance to bring rain, Cambodia

butō: also *ankoku butō*, 'dance of utter darkness', Japan

buzi: rank badge on official's robe in **xiqu**

'cham: a monastic performance ritual of Tibet that incorporates the use of masks, costumes and dance to enact purification and offering rituals

cai luong: reformed theatre of the twentieth century, Vietnam *calonarang*: dance-drama telling of the widow-witch, Rangda, Bali, Indonesia

canjunxi: Chinese adjutant plays

carnatic music: the style of classical music practised in southern India

cham: an Islamic ethnic minority in Cambodia

chandaini gonda: dance form of Chhattisgarh, India

chang: singing in **jingju**

changgeuk: 'singing theatre', Korean **pansori** modernized with multiple performers and operatic staging

cheo: popular musical theatre with origins in the Red River Delta of northern Vietnam, today performed in classical and modernised forms

Cheoyongmu: the Dance of Cheoyong is a court dance by five masked performers, Korea

chirikara: rhythmic patterns played by **kabuki** hayashi ensemble

chizi: 'pond', the worst seats in Qing period playhouses

chou: 'ugly', clown role type in **xiqu**

choupuozi: comical old women in **xiqu**

cutti: an ornament appearing as part of the faces of some characters in **kutiyattam** and **kathakali** theatre that runs along the jawline to form a starkly white, inch-wide frame for an actor's face

da: stage combat in **jingju**

Daehangno: 'college street', a theatre district located in Seoul, South Korea that serves as a home to about 200 small to medium-sized theatres and dozens of festivals

dagelan: comic repartee in Central Java, Indonesia

dajangmyeon guseonghyeongsik: 'multi-scene plot structure', a dramaturgical strategy in North Korea's revolutionary drama in which more flexible division called jang substitutes for the traditional divisions of act and scene

dalang: puppet master, Indonesia and Malaysia

dan: standard female role type in **xiqu**

dangak: Korean court music originally imported from China

daoma dan: 'sword and horse women', female-general role type in **xiqu**

Dasarupa: a treatise on Sanskrit dramatyrgy attributed to Dhananjay (10th centry CE). It focuses on the ten major kinds of classical plays, and the principles of their construction.

dengaku: field entertainment, Japan

Devata: a deity, a divine being (Hindu mythology)

dikir: Islamic song chant performance form, Malaysia and Indonesia

dizi: Chinese side-blown flute

dou: semantic and musical unit of a line in **jingju**

Dramatic Performances Control Act (1876): the act of censorship passed by the British colonial government to control urban Indian theatre. The act continues to be enforced in post-independence India

ebisu kaki: puppeteer performers associated with Ebisu, god of good luck, Japan

erhuang: a musical mode in **jingju**

fukusamen: cloth masks used in **gigaku**

funazoko: 'boat bottom', the lowered stage floor area between the second and third partition of the **bunraku** stage

furi: dance characterized by mimetic gestures, Japan

furyū: flashy costumes and noisy masked processional performance

gabor: women's temple dance, Bali, Indonesia

gagaku: Chinese imported musical ensemble accompanying **bugaku** dance performance *gageuk*: 'song theatre', a term used for western opera as well as indigenous music theatre that was created in the fashion of western opera in North Korea

gailiang xinxi: reformed new theatre in early twentieth-century China

gamelan: bronze percussion orchestra, Indonesia

gamugeuk: 'song and dance theatre', a term for 'musical' usually used to downplay western influences in the genre, Korea

gamyeongeuk: mask dance-dramas, Korea

gandogaeshi: **kabuki** scenery changing technique in which a large set piece is pivoted on its side, revealing another set

ganggangsullae: a women's performance combining song, circle dance and play elements, from the southwestern coastal region, Korea

gar: a kind of court performance of the Dalai Lamas performed by young men

geommu: sword dance, Korea

gewuju: Chinese song and dance theatre*geza*: offstage ensemble in **kabuki**

gezaixi: a form of sung-drama performed in Minnan, the dialect of the major Han ethnic group in current Taiwan

gidayū-bushi: music and chant in **bunraku**

gigaku: masked dance-drama imported from Chinese court in the seventh century, Japan

gisaeng: female Korean entertainers catering to the elite with music and song, often compared to Japanese geisha; members of a sub-group of **gisaeng** were also involved in prostitution

gling rje ge sar rgyal po'i sgrung: 'Epic of King Gesar', an epic cycle comprised of hundreds of exploits of King Gesar of Ling

gofun: shell powder used as base for the painting of a **noh** or **kyogen** mask

gombeyatta: wooden string puppets of south India

gopalila kundhei: marionette play on Radha-Krishna themes, Orissa, India

gosa: opening ceremony held before a performance with an altar and ritual offerings, Korea

goulan: 'balustrade', large urban Chinese theatres of the Song and Yuan periods

guanzuo: 'official seats', the best searts in Qing period playhouses

gugak: Korean traditional music

Gulabo-Sitabo: glove puppetry named after main characters, northwest India and Pakistan

Guoju Yundong: National Theatre Movement, China

gwangdae: performers of folk arts, historically mostly male, often used in reference to **pansori** singers

Hadrah: one of Brunei's Malay traditional musical instruments, which is made from hard wood and its surface is covered using stingray leather

halmi: Korean mask dance-drama character of the grandmother

hamdolok: frame drumming, dancing and drama, Malaysia

hamton: the opening dance sequence of **yike**, an offering to the spirits and ancestors of the art form

hana: 'flower', the ultimate aim of **noh** expression

hanamichi: 'flower path', a walkway extending from a **kabuki** stage through the audience, used for special entrances and exits

hannya: a type of **noh** mask representing the living spirit of a resentful woman, dead woman, or an ogress

hansam: long sleeve extensions that are part of the costumes in several Korean dances and some mask dance-dramas

hashigakari: long passageway from offstage right to the main **noh** stage, used for entrances and acting

hat boi: also *tuong* classical opera, Vietnam

hayashi: instrumental ensemble of drums and flutes in **noh**

hengemono: 'transformation pieces', **kabuki** dance-plays featuring several costume changes

heureumsik ipche mudaemisul: 'three-dimensional running stage art', set design principle that was to accompany **dajangmyeon guseonghyeongsik** in North Korean revolutionary drama

higante: giant festival puppets, the Philippines

hiraki: a dance movement in **noh** where the feet move backwards while the arms open, often follows the **shikake**

hō: a round-collar outer garment with open sleeves

hon butai: main stage area, in **noh** and early **kabuki**

honyaku jidai: 'age of translation'

hsaing waing: traditional Burmese folk musical ensemble

huadan: 'flower woman', lively young women role type in **xiqu**

huaju: Chinese spoken drama

huashan: 'flower robe', a twentieth-century **jingju** combination of the traditional female types of **qingyi**, **huadan** and **daomadan**

hun krabok: sack rod puppets, Thailand

hun lakhon lek: rod puppetry with three manipulators, Thailand

hun luang: court rod puppets, Thailand

huqin: Chinese two-string fiddle

hyangak: Korean court music

hyeongmyeong yeongeuk: 'revolutionary play', a genre of spoken drama in North Korea that developed in the 1970s under the guidance of Kim Jong-il

hyōbanki: popular actor critiques assessing appearance and talents, Japan

iemoto: head of stylistic school, top of hierarchical pyramid of licensed professionals, Japan

ilmu: Confucian ritual line dance, Korea

Indian People's Theatre Association (IPTA): the cultural organization founded by the Communist Party of India in 1943, which launched the first nationwide populist theatre movement in the country

ingan munhwajae: human cultural property, colloquially used for officially acknowledged and sponsored practitioners of a specific **Jungyo Muhyeong Munhwajae**, Korea

inhyeong-geuk: modern puppetry, Korea

iro: half-spoken/half-sung vocal style in **gidayū-bushi**, Japan

jalangkung: girls' rainmaking trance game with doll made out of a water dipper, Java, Indonesia

janggu: Korean hourglass drum

japsaek: dancing and clowning players part of some Korean percussion bands

jatra: a genre of indigenous performance prevalent in Bangladesh and India

jeolga: a stanzaic song in Korean

ji: sung melodic text in **gidayū-bushi**, Japan

jidaimono: **bunraku** and **kabuki** plots on historical subject matter

jiju: **xiqu** form originated and popular in northeastern China

jili: 'auspicious rites' in ancient China

jing: also *hualian*, painted face role type in **xiqu**

jingju: 'capital drama', Beijing opera

jinju: **xiqu** form originated in Shanxi Province and popular in mid-north and northwestern China

jiuta-mai: dances of the Kansai area geisha, created to be performed in private settings, which is performed to jiuta music played on a **shamisen**, Japan

jiutai: supporting chorus in **noh**

jo-ha-kyū: 'slow-breaking-fast', a rhythmic structure found in all levels of **noh** performance from a phrase of music or movement to the build of an entire play

joget: social dance, Indonesia and Malaysia

Jongmyo jerye: a Confucian ritual, Korea

Jongmyo Muhyeong Munhwajae: Important Intangible Cultural Property, an official designation for performing arts and crafts deemed worthwhile for official preservation and sponsorship on a national level, Korea

junli: martial rites in ancient China

ka byar loot: basic form and repetitive movement of traditional Burmese dance

kabuki: traditional Japanese theatrical form featuring performer who 'sing, dance, and act' in spectacular melodramas originating four hundred years ago

kabuki odori: 'kabuki dance', dances from or in the **kabuki** theatre that are created by **kabuki** artists and choreographers

kachahari: the Nepali variation of Augusto Boal's Forum theatre

kagami no ma: 'mirror room', a room just off the **hashigakari** blocked from the audiences view by a curtain where **noh** actors put on their masks before entering the stage

kagura: a genre of Japanese folk performing arts for the gods, with shrine maiden (miko), village (sato) and court (mikagura) varieties

kakegoe: 1) in Kabuki, shouts of praise from audience during a performance; 2) non-melodic vocal utterances by instrumentalists, Japan

kalaripayattu: martial arts practised in Kerala

Kalidasa: iconic Sanskrit playwright (5th century CE) and author of three **natakas**, the most famous of which is *Abhijnanashakuntalam* (The Recognition of Shakuntala)

kamen: 'temporary face', general word for 'mask' in Japanese

kami-mai: 'god dance', an instrumental dance in **noh** used in some plays where the main character is a deity

Kamigata: referring to Kyoto, Osaka, Nara performance styles

kamite: 'upper hand', stage left, in **kabuki**, **bunraku** and contemporary Japanese theatre

kancha: a wooden pole top with hollowed-out seeds or metal balls, used to keep the rhythm in **robam trot**

kanjin noh: subscription **noh** performances held on temporary stages to raise funds

kao: stage armour in **xiqu**

karaori: a kosode-cut garment with multicoloured pictorial patterning, which became the iconic **noh** costume for women in the sixteenth century

kari: the 'black' class of characters in **kathakali** theatre. Black dominates the colour scheme of these characters, who are, generally, monstrous and villainous

kata: 'pattern', set forms in all aspects of Japanese traditional art

katagami: paper templates for **noh** and **kyogen** masks

katari: dramatic storytelling, employed in almost all traditional genres, Japan

katarimono: narrative style **shamisen** genres, Japan

kathak: from *Katha* story; form of north Indian classical dance also practiced in other parts of the country, often under royal patronage

kathakali: a highly popular dance-drama form from the southwestern state of Kerala, India

katōbushi: a narrative **shamisen** style, Japan

katsurekigeki: **kabuki** plays, accurate in period and mise-en-scène, promulgated by Danjurō IX

katti: villainous **kathakali** characters, marked, usually, by an excess of red makeup, and also by a facial ornament that resembles a grotesquely oversized, starkly white moustache

kawara kojiki: also *kawara-mono*, 'riverbed beggars', originally referring to kabuki actors, held in low esteem during that form's nascent period

kbach: gesture, often hand gestures, used in dances, Cambodia

kbach baat: the basic series of gestures and movements that one learned across nearly all theatre and dance genres in Cambodia. Similar to the western ballet barre work, these gestures make up the basis of **robam boram**

keren: **kabuki** spectacle employing acrobatics or mechanical devices

khon: mask court dance-drama telling Rama story, Thailand

kimari: a brief pause/pose in **kabuki**, or nihon buyo, similar to **kabuki** mie

Kimpira bushi: early puppetry with heroic tales named after the hero Kimpura, Japan

kirido: small upstage left door on a **noh** stage

kiyomotobushi: a narrative **shamisen** style, Japan

kizewamono: **kabuki** plays featuring low-life characters written in the early nineteenth century

kkokdugaksi noreum: traditional Korean puppet theatre

ko-omote: **noh** mask representing a young girl

kogaki: variant **noh** texts or choreography

kolam: stylized performance using dance and masks, Sri Lanka

komai: short comic dances and songs in **kyogen**

komedya (also *moro-moro*): heroic performances of Christian–Muslim conflicts, the Philippines

Kōminka: Japanization movement in Taiwan, 1936–45

kōshaku: narrative performance describing origins of deities or temple founders

koshi wo ireru: 'putting in the koshi', grounding the body to the earth while also lifting the top of the spine and crown of the head; also refers to the proper use of the koshi in all dance and performance movement, Japan

kosode: 'small sleeve', T-shaped kimono that began as a white undergarment but in the sixteenth century emerged as the main garment for all classes, ages and sexes, being decorated with tie-dye, embroidery, painting and printing, and woven with patterns

kotoba: 1) spoken non-melodic text in **noh**; 2) spoken mode in **gidayu-bushi**, situated in relation to **ji** and **iro**

kotsuzumi: small hourglass hand drum played in noh and **kabuki**

kouta: 'short songs', popular as party or love songs, sung in **kyogen**

kru: Khmer word for a teacher of any kind, also learned village elders

kuileixi: marionettes, China

kumadori: stylized **kabuki** makeup for strong characters

kunqu: Chinese Kunshan Opera

kurogo: **kabuki** and **bunraku** stagehands dressed in black, implying invisibility

kuromisu: 'black screen', offstage right area behind a blind in **kabuki**, where atmospheric music and sound effects are played

kusemai: rhythmic dance to drum and flute, incorporated into noh by Kan'ami

kutiyattam: a genre of temple theatre in Kerala

kuttampalam: temple theatre

kuurchak oyun: glove puppet plays behind a folding screen, Kyrgyzstan

kyogen: comic plays performed alongside **noh**

lakhon: all genres of theatre and dance drama, Cambodia

lakhon bassac: Cambodian operatic drama, developed in the early twentieth century in the Bassac River region of southern Vietnam by the ethnic Khmer

lakhon khol: all-male mask dance-drama, Cambodia

lakhon kbach boran: same as **robam boran**

lakhon nai: court lady performance, Thailand

lakhon niyeay: Cambodian spoken drama, a.k.a lakhon ciet (lit. 'national drama')

lakhon nok: traditional drama outside the courts, previously an all-male form, Thailand

lakhon phut: Thai spoken drama

lakhon yike: a Cambodian operatic theatre that incorporates song, dance, acting and gestural sequences choreographed to the rhythms of **skor yike**

langendriyan: all-female palace dance opera, Central Java, Indonesia

lanhua zhi: 'orchid-fingers', a basic finger gesture for young and middle-aged female role types in **xiqu**

laodan: mature women role type in **xiqu**

laosheng: mature male role type in **xiqu**

legong: female prepubescent court dance/dancer, Bali, Indonesia

lenong: popular improvised theatre of Jakarta area in the early twentieth century, Indonesia

lha mo or *a lce lha mo*: lhamo, a form of secular Tibetan performance often translated as opera

li: 'reason' in Chinese

lianquti: joined song form, one of the two principal music systems in **xiqu**

likay: popular theatre, Thailand

lingzi gong: 'techniques of feathers', techniques of holding and dancing with feathers attached to hats in **xiqu**, usually performed by the young dignified male role type

ludruk: popular theatre of Surabaya area, Indonesia

madanggeuk: a form of Korean outdoor political theatre that employs traditional means to articulate dissenting opinions, developed in the 1970s and 80s

madang nori: a Korean musical version of **madang-geuk**, stripped of its ideological implications

Mahabharata: Sanskrit epic that is also the longest poem in the world; a major narrative source for modern Indian literature in numerous genres

mai: dance characterized by slow, circular movements that are kept low to the ground, Japan

main peteri: a healing trance genre with a female clientele, Kelantan, Malaysia

mak yong: female dance-drama form of Kelatan (Malaysia), Patani (Thailand), and the Riau islands (Indonesia)

malddugi: Korean mask dance-drama character of the horse servant

mang: court robe in **xiqu**

masu: seats divided into a square grid, on the house floor area of traditional **kabuki** theatres

mawari butai: revolving stage in kabuki, first developed by playwright Namiki Shoza and used in the play *Sanjikkoku Yobune noh Hajimari* at Osakas Kado **noh** shibai theatre in the twelfth lunar month of 1758

meriyasu: melodic patterns and solo melodies played on **shamisen** in **bunraku**

meshrep: celebratory communal Uyghur gatherings that incorporate various traditional performing art forms

metsuke: 'eye-fixing', downstage right pillar of the **noh** stage

mie: 'freeze frame', frozen pose of dynamic tension in **kabuki**

minjok geuk: a form of theatre that strives to use exclusively traditional techniques, independent from foreign influences, Korea

minukku: the class of **kathakali** characters that is most 'human', and hence has the least stylized costumes and makeup

mohiniyattam: a classical dance form from the southwestern state of Kerala, India

mohlum: sung theatre to pan pipe music, Laos

monomane: imitative, realistic expression in **noh**

moro-moro: also *komedya*, heroic performances of Christian–Muslim conflicts, the Philippines

mua roi nuoc: water puppetry, Vietnam

mudra: Sanskrit term for hand gestures, in the performance, India

mugen noh: two-act plots in which a seemingly living character appears in the first act, then returns as a ghost in the second act to re-enact a scene of suffering

mumu: a generic term for all types of Korean shamanic ritual dance

munye hyeongmyeong: 'literature and art revolution', a series of campaigns that North Korea implemented from the 1960s through to the 1990s as a means to revolutionize the realm of culture in order to establish cultural tools for propaganda

muqam: predominant Uyghur melody type possibly derived from the Arabic maqam modal system

myūjikaru: American-style musical in Japan

nabichum: monk's butterfly dance, Korea

nacha: folk form of Chhattisgarh, India

Nadagam: performances with music and dance, Sri Lanka

nagauta: a lyric **shamisen** style, Japan

nambyar: caste of male temple servants in Kerala who play a pot-shaped drum in **kutiyattam**

namghar: a 'name house' used for congregational worship and for devotional theatre in Assam

namsadang: itinerant variety show performance by groups of men, Korea

nandan: male female impersonator role type in **xiqu**

nang ma: nangma, a form of musical performance popular in Tibet that involves singing, dancing and a small orchestra

nang sbaek thom: large court leather puppets telling Rama tales, Cambodia

nang sbaek touch: also *ayang*, small leather shadow puppets, Cambodia

nang talung: small leather puppet show, south Thailand

nang yai: large court leather puppets telling Rama tales, Thailand

nangyar kuttu: solo performance of women related to **kutiyattam**

nangyar: caste of female temple servants who perform **kutiyattam** and a separate genre of performance called **nangyar kuttu**

nanxi: Chinese southern drama

natak: the term for 'drama' as well as an individual 'play' in the modern Indian languages, derived from Sanskrit **nataka**

natak mandalis: touring theatre troupes that performed musical plays in Marathi during the colonial period, India

nataka: the most important of ten major dramatic genres in Sanskrit, it is between five and ten acts in length, follow a mythic or historical narrative with a noble hero, and focuses on the erotic (srngara) or the heroic (vira)

natasin: classical dance theatre, Thailand

natya: aesthetic performance, especially with reference to theatre and dance, India

Natyasastra: ancient Sanskrit treatise on the arts of performance attributed to the sage Bharat Muni and conjecturally dated between 200 BCE and 200 CE

nautanki: a secular semi-operatic folk, urban-rural form of musical theatre, northern India

Neak Ta: local spirits that offer protection and wealth and bring rains in Cambodia

Neang Seda: Sita, Rama's wife from the *Ramayana*, Cambodia

nepathya: a 'backstage' area identified by the Natyasastra's description of theatre buildings, and noted by most Sanskrit dramas

nian: speech delivery in **jingju**

nihon buyo: 'Japanese dance', styles or genres of Japanese classical dance *nikawa*: hide glue used in **noh** and **kyogen** mask-making

ningyō buri: a special movement technique used in **kabuki** where an actor mimics the movement of a **bunraku** puppet while being manipulated by a second actor who acts as puppet operator

ningyō jōruri: all narrated puppet forms, Japan

nōgaku: a nineteenth-century term for both **noh** and **kyogen**

noh: lyric, masked Japanese dance theatre performed continuously for over half a millennium

nojang: Korean mask dance-drama character of the old monk

nōkan: seven-hole transverse flute used in **noh** and **kabuki**

nōmai: a genre of Japanese folk performing arts

nōmen: **noh** mask (also omote)

nrityam: 'dance movement'; term for dance as a component of drama and performance

nükao: women's armour in **xiqu**

nümang: women's court robe in **xiqu**

nüpi: women's formal robe in **xiqu**

Nurti: plays with spectacular scenery and influenced by Indian Parsi musicals, Sri Lanka

nüxuezi: women's informal robe in **xiqu**

obi: waist sashes and cords that secure garments in place, which can be from 1 to 40 cm wide and tied with any number of knots either at the front or at the back, Japan

odori: dance characterized by lively movements, used extensively in **kabuki**

omote: '**noh** mask' (literally 'face')

onnagata: **kabuki** specialists in female role types

opela gezaixi: a specific style of **gezaixi** using integrated Japanese popular songs and a western orchestra during the Japanese colonial period in Taiwan to survive the censorship of the colonial government

orteke: goat dance puppet show, Uzbekistan

ōsode: 'broad sleeve', garments, generally outer cloaks. Often the open-cuff sleeves are double width and sometimes they have cords at the cuff for tying them at the wrist, Japan

otoko-mai: 'male dance', an instrumental dance in **noh** used in some plays where the main character is a historical male or male warrior

otokoyaku: female performer of male roles, Japan

otome ningyō: women's puppetry, Japan

otsuzumi: hourglass drum played at the hip in **noh**

pacca: the most divine class of **kathakali** characters, whose makeup scheme is mostly green

pandavani: folk ballad from Chhattisgarh, India, depicting stories of Pandavas from the epic Mahabharata

pangchang: 'song-aside'; a dramaturgical device in North Korean revolutionary play and **gageuk** that is used to emphasize the propagandistic message of the story

pansori: Korean singing-storytelling performed by a solo vocalist with drum accompaniment

panthi: ritual dance of the Satnami community of Chhattisgarh, India

panuluyan: Christmas play about Jesus' birth, the Philippines

pasyon: recitation or performance of Jesus' crucifixion and death, the Philippines

pata, patachitras: picture scrolls and narration, India

pava koothu: puppet theatre, Tamil Nadu, India

pavakathakali: glove puppetry doing **kathakali** repertoire, Kerala, India

pencak silat: martial arts dance, Indonesia and Malaysia

pi: formal robe in **xiqu**

pihuang: music system used in **jingju**

pin peat: classical orchestra, Cambodia

prahasana: 'farce' in Sanskrit

prakarana: full-length play with an invented rather than mythic or historical plot; otherwise similar to the **nataka**

prasanga: the story of a play in **yakshagana** of Karnataka state, India. Composed in verses to be sung and limited spoken dialogue

Preah Ream: Prince Rama, the character from Ramayana, Cambodia

prekshan: spectatorship, India

puju: **xiqu** form originated in the Shanxi Province and popular in mid-north and northwestern China

pungmul: drumming music played while dancing to accompany group activities and employed in village celebrations and rituals in farming and fishing communities throughout Korea, which uses two gongs and two drums as the primary instruments

pungmulpae: Korean percussion band

purana: 'ancient text' in Sanskrit, often narrative in form, with religious, philosophical, and mythological content

purushpreksha: male theatre, India

purwa: repertoire of *Ramayana* and *Mahabharata* stories, Indonesia

putala nach: string puppetry of Assam and Manipur in northeastern India

qinggeju: Chinese light opera

qing: 'feeling' in Chinese

qingyi: 'black clothing', young demure woman role type in **xiqu**

qoshaq: an improvised section of many Uyghur *meshrep* performances consisting of recitation of spontaneous folk songs and poems by the audience

raga: melodic pattern used to organize classical Indian music

rakandai: upstage right first-floor standing-room-only audience section in **kabuki**, from the late nineteenth century to the early Meiji period

Ramlila: devotional theatre tradition of northern India that stages the story of the epic hero Rama

Ramayana: one of two major Sanskrit epics. Source of many plays and genres of performance in India

randai: martial arts dance-drama of Minangkabau, Sumatra, Indonesia

rangmanch: stage, or the broader field of theatre, India

rankou gong: 'techniques of beards', dance-acting techniques of performing with beards in **xiqu**, usually performed by older dignified male role type

Râs lila: devotional theatre of the Braj region of India that dramatizes the scriptural narratives of Krishna's childhood

rasa: 'juice', 'essence' or 'flavour', pleasurable aesthetic experience created through art and 'consumed' by the audience, India

Reamker: Cambodian version of the Hindu epic the *Ramayana*

reog ponorogo: performance with large mask of lion-tiger figure, Java, Indonesia

robam: dance genres, and specific dances

robam boran: or robam kbach boran, classical dance-drama, Cambodia

robam prapreiney: folk dance, Cambodia

robam trot: a ceremonial folk dance to bring rain and prosperity for the New Year, also inspiration for a theatrical folk dance developed by the Ministry of Culture in Phnom Penh

roi: puppetry, Vietnam

ronggeng: female Singer-dancer-courtesan who appears in many genres of Indonesia and Malaysia

rupak: dramatic form, India

ruwatan: ritual 'making safe' performance, Java and Sunda, Indonesia

sadak naatak: street theatre, Nepal

sageuk: Korean historical drama

sajiki: covered box seat areas on house right and left, in **noh** and **kabuki**

sakhi kundhei: glove puppetry of Orissa, India

sakura: mask dance of Sumatra, Indonesia

salpuri: an artistic professionalized folk dance inspired by shamanic dance, Korea

samhyeon yukgak: a small Korean ensemble including a haegeum, daegeum, two piri and a janggu, often used to accompany performances

sampeah kru: a ceremony practiced by Cambodian artists to honour the spirits and ancestors of the arts

sandiwara: popular improvised theatre of the early twentieth century, Java; historical scripted dramas of the twentieth century, Malaysia

sangeet natak: musical drama in Marathi; the principal theatrical form in this language during the colonial period, India

sanghyang deling: trance puppet genre of Bali, Indonesia

sanzuo: 'scattered' seats, seats in Qing period playhouses that were less expensive and not as good as the 'official seats'

sarsuwela: popular late nineteenth–early twentieth-century music theatre influenced by the Spanish zarzuela, the Philippines

sarugaku: one group of medieval performance troupes doing proto-plays and dance-dramas that formed the basis for **noh** and **kyogen**

sayū: a dance movement in **noh** that makes a left–right zigzag pattern

sendratari: dance-drama without dialogue innovated in 1960s, Indonesia

sensu: a kind of folding fan made of paper and bamboo used in Japanese classical dance or **kabuki** dance, which is weighted at the base to enable certain flourishes

seri: stage lift in **kabuki**, used for actors or sets

seungmu: an artistic professionalized folk dance inspired by the monk's dance, Korea

sewamono: **bunraku** and **kabuki** plots depicting the everyday life of commoners

shamisen: Japanese three-string skin-covered plucked lute that forms the core of music in **kabuki** and **bunraku**

shanzi gong: 'techniques of fans', techniques of performing with fans in **xiqu**

sheng: standard male role type in **xiqu**

shikake: a dance movement in **noh** where the hands and feet are drawn forwards

shimedaiko: stick-struck barrel-shaped drum in **kabuki**

shimote: stage right, in **kabuki**, **bunraku** and contemporary Japanese theatre

shin buyō: 'new dance', dances created in Japanese classical dance or **kabuki** dance style, but set to popular recorded music

shingeki: 'new theatre', referring to translated western plays and Japanese plays derived from western influence

shinjumono: **bunraku** and **kabuki** plots resolved in double suicide

shin-kabuki: 'new **kabuki**', referring to kabuki written under western influence

shinkokugeki: 'new national theatre', Japan

shinobue: transverse bamboo flute in **kabuki**

shinpa: 'new school', popular name for **shinpageki**, devised to distinguish the form from 'old school drama', mainly **kabuki**

shinpageki: 'new school drama', Japan

shirabyoshi: medieval dancers to rhythmic drum and flute, Japan *shishi*: 'lion dance', generic term for lion mask used in processional performances such as shishi-mai

shite: the 'doer', the lead role category in a **noh** play, also the category of noh actors who perform lead and companion roles, sing in the chorus and act as stage attendants

shizhuang xinxi: new plays in modern costumes, popular in early twentieth-century **xiqu**

shizukana engeki: quiet theatre, a phenomenon of modern Japanese theatre in the 1990s and early twenty-first century

shōgekijō: 'little theatre', sometimes used interchangeably with **angura**, referring to post-1960 experimental theatre, often performed in small, cramped spaces

shosagoto: dance-plays in **kabuki**

shoujuan gong: 'techniques of handkerchiefs', techniques of manoeuvring handkerchiefs in **xiqu**, usually performed by young lively female role type

shuaifa gong: 'techniques of hair', techniques of manoeuvring hair, part of the headdress, in **xiqu**, usually performed by martial dignified and young dignified male role types

shuixiu: water sleeves in **xiqu**

shuixiu gong: 'techniques of water-sleeves', techniques of skilful manoeuvring the silk pieces that extend from each sleeve in **xiqu**, usually performed by young and middle-aged female and young dignified male role types

shushi: dramatic exorcism rites performed by **yamabushi**

sida nvingolan: the four great famous male **dan** in **jingju**

singeuk: theatre based on Western realism, introduced by Korean exchange students in the 1920s

sinmyeong: ecstatic release achieved through successful high-energy group performances, Korea

sinpa-geuk: a genre that was derived from Japanese **shinpa**, a reformed version of **kabuki** in colonial Korea

sintren: female trance dance play, Java, Indonesia

skor yike: a large framed drum used for Cambodia's **lakhon yike**, also used as an accompaniment for Chum poetic narratives

sloka: a verse form divided into quarters, commonly used in Vedic scripture and Sanskrit poetry

sokari: stylised performance using dance, music, and masks, Sri Lanka

songpa sandae noli: a Korean mask dance-drama from Gyeonggi Province, the region surrounding Seoul

sōshi: 'hooligan' and/or 'courageous young man', referring to actors in early **shinpa** plays by Sudo Sadanori

sōshi shibai: agitprop drama

srimpi: female court dance genre, Java, Indonesia

stamboel: popular twentieth-century urban theatre inspired by **bangsawan**, Java, Indonesia

streepreksha: all-female theatre, India

suriashi: 'sliding step', a walk in which the whole foot glides along the floor then lifts from the toes as the step is completed, Japan

sutradhara: literally, string holder. The director or stage manager in Sanskrit drama

tachimawari: stylized, choreographed fight scenes in **kabuki**

taepyeongmu: an artistic professionalized folk dance with shamanic elements, Korea

tahamaca: large funerary puppet for parade, Nepal

taishū engeki: popular drama, Japan

Takemoto-za: puppet theatre in Osaka from 1684 to 1767, established by Takemoto Gidayū

talchum: Korean mask dance-drama variant from Hwanghae Province, often used colloquially to describe all Korean mask dance-dramas

talnori: mask play, see **gamyeongeuk**

tamasha: itinerant, popular entertainment theatre of Maharashtra, India

tanghui yanchu: 'salon performances', China

tanzi gong: 'techniques on carpets', basic techniques involving basic flips, multiple flips, rolling and twisting, one-on-one fighting, leaping with a spring board, and other assorted techniques in **xiqu**

tarer putul: string puppetry of Bengal, India

tati: the 'beard' characters of **kathakali**, including heroic and villainous types, inferior or secondary to **kathakali**'s paragons of virtue

tayū: vocalist in **gidayū–bushi**, honorific form also use in other genres such as **kabuki**

tayub: social dance genre of courtesan dancers, Java, Indonesia

tenugui: a long strip of cotton or silk fabric used as a prop in **kabuki** and **kabuki** dance

teppu: a grouping of miscellaneous **kathakali** characters, including kathakali's few bird characters – the only kathakali characters to use masks

terukkuttu: devotional folk theatre of Tamil Nadu, India

teyyam: ritualistic dance-drama of northern Kerala, India

thang stong rgyal po (Thangtong Gyalpo): important Tibetan saint of the fourteenth century known for building iron bridges and founding Tibetan opera

thangyat: Burmese folk art form combining rhythmic couplets with music sung to the beat of a hsaing waing

Theatre of Roots: the name coined in 1985 for a movement that rejects the legacies of western theatre in India, and seeks to return urban theatre to its aesthetic roots in indigenous languages, forms and traditions

tilak: a marking on the forehead that indicates a person's religious affiliation, India

tishen: 'holding the attention', a basic eye technique in **xiqu**

togalu gombeyatta: leather shadow puppet theatre of Karnataka, India

tokiwazubushi: a narrative **shamisen** style, Japan

tolpava koothu/kothoo: leather shadow puppet theatre of Kerala, India

tolu bommalattam: leather shadow puppet theatre of Andhra Pradesh, India

topeng betawi: improvised colonial-era dance theatre of the Jakarta area, Indonesia

topeng pajegan: solo mask dance performance, Bali, Indonesia

topeng: mask, Indonesia

Toyotake-za: puppet theatre in Osaka from 1703 to 1765, established by Takemoto Gidayū's apprentice, Toyotake Wakadayu

tsuke butai: 'attached stage', temporarily constructed additional sections of the **kabuki** stage, common in the seventeenth and early eighteenth centuries

tsure: the companion role in a **noh** play

tsuri-ago: hanging jaw tied to the body of the **bugaku** mask with ropes or thread

tsuyogin: **noh** 'strong style' chant

Twelve Uyghur Muqam: twelve suites of music based on Turdi Axun's version of the Uyghur muqam, sometimes considered the Kashgar-Yarkend variant of Uyghur muqam music

utai: 'recitative' in **noh** theatre

utamono: lyric style **shamisen** genres, Japan

vaisnavism: one of the major branches of Hinduism focused on the incarnation of the god Vishnu

vella tati: **kathakali**'s 'white' tati sub-group, consisting of valorous but subordinate characters

vesa: dress or costume, India

vyayoga: a dramatic episode covering the events of a single day, India

wagoto: gentle-style **kabuki** acting, popularized in **Kamigata** *waki*: the secondary or 'listener' role category in a **noh** play, also the category of **noh** actors who perform these roles

wayang: shadow, puppet or dance theatre, Indonesia and Malaysia

wayang beber: scroll puppetry, Java, Indonesia

wayang gedek, gedog: shadow puppetry telling stories of the heroic Prince Panji, Java, Indonesia and Malaysia

wayang golek: rod puppetry in Java and Sunda, Indonesia

wayang golek purwa: rod puppetry telling Mahabharata- and Ramayana-based tales, Sunda, Indonesia

wayang kelantan: leather shadow puppetry telling *Ramayana* tales, Kelantan, Malaysia

wayang klitik: flat wooden puppetry, Java, Indonesia

wayang kulit: leather shadow puppetry, Indonesia and Malaysia

wayang kulit purwa: leather shadow puppet theatre telling Mahabharata- and Ramayana-based tales, Indonesia (especially Java) and Malaysia

wayang melayu: Kelantanese puppetry telling Panji stories, Malaysia

wayang wong: human dance –drama in Java and Sunda, Indonesia; masked dance-drama telling *Ramayana* tales, Bali, Indonesia

wazi: also washi, 'tiles' or 'tiles markets', amusement parks of the Song period in China

wen: 'civil' in **xiqu**

wenmingxi: civilized drama, the earliest form of modern Chinese theatre

wonhyeong: the archetypal form of a performing art designated by the Korean government for protection, a key concept of the **Jungyo Muhyeong Munhwajae** system

woyu: 'crouching fish', a basic movement convention in **xiqu** requiring combined use of legs and the area between the rib cage and the top of the pelvis

wu: 'military' in **xiqu**

wudan: military female role type in **xiqu**

wusheng: military male role type in **xiqu**

xiaosheng: young dignified male role type in **xiqu**

xiezi: 'wedge', introductory act in **zaju**

Xin Wutai: New Stage, first proscenium stage in China built in 1908

xinbian lishi ju: newly written historical drama

xipi: a musical mode in **jingju**

xiqu: 'song' theatre, generic term for over 300 genres for indigenous, traditional Chinese theatre

xuezi: informal robe in **xiqu**

yagura: drum tower, found in **kabuki** and **ningyō jōruri** theatres, traditionally a sign of a sanctioned licence, as well as a tool for announcing shows

yakshagana: folk theatre form from the southern state of Kerala, India

yamabushi: mountain ascetics appearing in widely traditional Japanese performing arts

yangban: Korean upper-class literati

yangbanxi: revolutionary model plays created before and during China's Cultural Revolution (1966–1976)

yeonhui: a Korean term for traditional 'folk theatre' performing arts such as mask dance-drama, shamanic ritual, **pungmul** and anything else performed by itinerant troupes

yeonhuigeuk: newly created performances in Korea based on traditional arts

yeonswae-geuk: a form of 'kino-drama', theatre with intermissions of movie projections that was popular in the early colonial period, Korea

yeoseong gukgeuk: Korean all-female opera with **pansori**-style singing, except for the gendered casting, in many ways similar to **changgeuk**, Korea

yike: see **lakhan yike**

yinyueju: Chinese musical theatre

yoshino: upstage right second-floor standing-room-only audience section in **kabuki**, from the late nineteenth century to the early Meiji period

yothe thay: marionette theatre, Burma

yowagin: **noh** 'weak style' chant

yuanchang: 'round circles', a basic step technique in **xiqu**

yueju: depending on the two Chinese characters, (1) **yuet kahk**, Cantonese Opera in Mandarin pronunciation; (2) Shaoxing Opera; (3) music drama

yuet kahk: Cantonese drama or opera in romanticized Cantonese pronunciation

yugen: dark, mysterious beauty exalted by **Zeami** as the peak of **noh** performance

yuka: stage for the narrator(s) and **shamisen** player(s) in **ningyō –jōruri**

yunshou: 'cloud hands', a basic movement convention in **xiqu** requiring combined use of the hands, arms, neck, eyes, shoulders and torso

zaju: 'variety drama', Yuan dynasty Chinese theatre

zangirimono: 'cropped-hair pieces', **kabuki** plays depicting contemporary life in the nineteenth century

zat pwe: Burmese all night variety show, including musical theatre, dance, **pya zat**, and **anyeint**

Zeami: founder of **noh** and author of many secret treatises concerning **hana** (the flower)

zho ston: Shoton Festival that celebrates the end of the spring retreat; the time during which Tibetan operas are traditionally performed

zikir: also *dikir*, Islamic song-movement performance, Indonesia and Malaysia

zōmen: cloth masks with abstract patterns used in **bugaku** performance

zuo: dance-acting in **jingju**

Index

Index

Made in the USA
San Bernardino, CA
20 January 2020